ADMIRALTY AND MARITIME LAW

ABRIDGED EDITION

ADMIRALTY AND MARITIME LAW

ABRIDGED EDITION

ROBERT FORCE
A.N. YIANNOPOULOS
MARTIN DAVIES

Beard Books
Washington, D.C.

ISBN 1-58798-296-X

Printed in the United States of America

CONTENTS

CHAPTER 5 — CHARTER PARTIES

CHAPTER 6 — PERSONAL INJURY AND DEATH CLAIMS

Chapter 1

ADMIRALTY JURISDICTION AND PROCEDURE

A. Introduction

1. The Constitution of the United States

Article I

Section 1. All legislative Powers herein granted shall be vested in a Congress of the United States... .

* * *

Section 8. The Congress shall have the Power...

To regulate Commerce with foreign Nations, and among the several States, and with the Indian Tribes;

* * *

To constitute Tribunals inferior to the Supreme Court;

To define and punish Piracies and Felonies committed on the high Seas, and Offenses against the Law of Nations;

To declare War, grant Letters of Marque and Reprisal, and make Rules concerning Captures on Land and Water;

* * *

To make all Laws which shall be necessary and proper for carrying into Execution the foregoing Powers, and all other Powers vested by this Constitution in the Government of the Untied States, or in any Department or Officer thereof.

* * *

Article III

Section 1. The judicial Power of the United States, shall be vested in one Supreme Court, and in such inferior Courts as the Congress may from time to time ordain and establish.

Section 2. The judicial Power shall extend to ... all Cases of admiralty and maritime Jurisdiction.

Note: Implementation of Article III

The admiralty law of the United States has grown out of the statement in Article III, Section 2 of the Constitution. Article III, however, is not self-executing. It does not establish an admiralty judicial system; it just confers the judicial power. Congress had to implement Article III, which it did in the Judiciary Act of 1789, *infra.* The Supreme Court has interpreted this constitutional provision to contain three separate grants of power: (1) it empowered Congress to confer admiralty and maritime jurisdiction on the "Tribunals inferior to the Supreme Court" which were authorized by Art. I., Sect. 8, Cl. 9; (2) it empowered the federal courts in their exercise of admiralty and maritime jurisdiction which had been conferred to them, to draw on the substantive law "inherent in the admiralty and maritime jurisdiction and to continue the development of this law within constitutional limits; and (3) it empowered Congress to revise and supplement the maritime law within the limits of the Constitution.

---

2. The Judiciary Act of 1789

Chapter XX. An Act to Establish the Judicial Courts of the United States

1st Cong., 1st Sess., Sept. 24, 1789

1 Stat. 76

§ 9 ... [T]he district courts shall have, exclusively of the courts of the several States, cognizance of all crimes and offenses that shall be cognizable under the authority of the United States, committed within their respective districts, or upon the high seas;... and shall also have exclusive original cognizance of all civil causes of admiralty and Maritime jurisdiction, including all seizures under laws of impost, navigation or trade of the United States, where the seizures are made, on waters which are navigable from the sea by vessels of ten or more tons burthen, within their respective districts as well as upon the high seas; saving to suitors, in all cases, the right of a common law remedy, where the common law is competent to give it; and shall also have exclusive original cognizance of all seizures on land, or other waters than as aforesaid, made, and of all suits for penalties and forfeitures incurred, under the laws of the United States.

* * *

And the trial of issues in fact, in the district courts, in all causes except civil cases of admiralty and maritime jurisdiction, shall be by jury.

---

3. U.S.C. Title 28: Judiciary and Judicial Procedure

§ 1333. Admiralty, maritime and prize cases

The district courts shall have original jurisdiction, exclusive of the courts of the States, of:

(1) Any civil case of admiralty or maritime jurisdiction, saving to suitors in all cases all other remedies to which they are otherwise entitled.

(2) Any prize brought into the United States and all proceedings for the condemnation of property taken as prize.

B. Navigable Waters: Evolution of the Requirement

1. The Basic Standard

Note: The Common Law Tradition

There are no comprehensive statutory criteria which can be used for determining when a case is within the admiralty and maritime jurisdiction of the federal courts, although there are some statutes such as the Admiralty Extension Act and the Death on the High Seas Act (DOHSA), which confer admiralty jurisdiction in specified circumstances. Unlike some countries, the United States does not have a comprehensive maritime code. There are numerous statutes that contain the substantive maritime law to be applied to certain transactions and events such as the Carriage of Goods by Sea Act (COGSA). However, these statutes are limited in scope. Therefore, much of the maritime law of the United States has been made by the courts in the tradition of the common law. This has occurred not only in regard to substantive rules but also with respect to the rules for determining jurisdiction. While, in 28 U.S.C. § 1333, Congress has declared in general terms that the federal courts may exercise jurisdiction in "admiralty" and "maritime" cases, it has, for the most part, been left to the courts to define the scope and meaning of those terms. In other words, the courts have had to formulate their own criteria for determining when a case comes within their admiralty and maritime jurisdiction.

The English courts give a rather narrow scope to their "admiralty" jurisdiction. The federal courts of the United States have, after a somewhat restrained beginning, interpreted the scope of admiralty and maritime jurisdiction in a much broader vein. In several cases decided in the mid-nineteenth century, the United States Supreme Court rejected the "tidal waters" and "within the county" rules which were applied in England and began to equate the scope of admiralty jurisdiction with "navigable waters."

It is also important to note that the early decisions on the scope of admiralty jurisdiction often were bound up with a consideration of the scope of another constitutional provision: the power of Congress to regulate commerce under Article I, section 8 of the United States Constitution. The exercise of admiralty jurisdiction by federal courts was seen as going hand-in-hand with efforts by Congress to make the United States a national economic unit and to break down the barriers of State parochialism and protectionism. Water transportation was the major mode of interstate and foreign commerce, and played a crucial part in opening up and linking together the western territories and the Atlantic seaboard states.

JACKSON *et al.* v. THE STEAMBOAT MAGNOLIA

61 U.S. (20 How.) 296, 15 L. Ed. 909 (1857)

Mr. Justice GRIER delivered the opinion of the court

The only question presented for our consideration on this appeal is, whether the court below had jurisdiction.

The libel purports to be in a cause of collision, civil and maritime. It alleges that the steamboat Wetumpka, a vessel of three hundred tons burden, was on a voyage from New Orleans to the city of Montgomery, in Alabama; that while ascending the Alabama river, she was run into and sunk by the steamboat Magnolia, which was descending the same.

The answer of the respondents, among other things, alleges "that the collision took place far above tide-water, on the Alabama river, in the county of Wilcox, in the State of Alabama, and therefore not within the jurisdiction of the District Court sitting in admiralty."

This plea was sustained by the court, and the libel dismissed. The record does not disclose the reasons on which this judgment was based. It is presumed, therefore, to be founded on the facts stated in the plea, viz:

1. That the collision was within the body of a county.
2. That it was above tide-water.

1. The Alabama River flows through the State of Alabama. It is a great public river, navigable from the sea for many miles above the ebb and flow of the tide. Vessels licensed for the coasting trade, and those engaged in foreign commerce, pass on its waters to ports of entry within the State. It is not, like the Mississippi, a boundary between coterminous States. Neither is it, like the Penobscot, (*see Veazie v. Moore*, 14 How., 568,) made subservient to the internal trade of the State by artificial means and dams constructed at its mouth, rendering it inaccessible to sea-going vessels. It differs from the Hudson, which rises in and passes through the State of New York, in the fact that it is navigable for ships and vessels of the largest class far above where its waters are affected by the tide.

Before the adoption of the present Constitution, each State, in the exercise of its sovereign power, had its own court of admiralty, having jurisdiction over the harbors, creeks, inlets, and public navigable waters, connected with the sea. This jurisdiction was exercised not only over rivers, creeks, and inlets, which were boundaries to or passed through other States, but also where they were wholly within the State. Such a distinction was unknown, nor (as it appears from the decision of this court in the case of *Waring v. Clark*, 5 How., 441) had these courts been driven from the exercise of jurisdiction over torts committed on navigable water within the body of a county, by the jealousy of the common-law courts.

When, therefore, the exercise, of admiralty and maritime jurisdiction over its public rivers, ports, and havens, was surrendered by each State to the Government of the United States, without an exception as to subjects or places, this court cannot interpolate one into the Constitution, or introduce an arbitrary distinction which has no foundation in reason or precedent.

The objection to jurisdiction stated in the plea, "that the collision was within the county of Wilcox, in the State of Alabama," can therefore have no greater force or effect from the fact alleged in the argument, that the Alabama river, so far as it is navigable, is wholly within the boundary of the State. It amounts only to a renewal of the old contest between courts of common law and courts of admiralty, as to their jurisdiction within the body of a county. This question has been finally adjudicated in this court, and the argument exhausted, in the case of *Waring v. Clark*. After an experience of ten years, we have not been called on by the bar to review its principles as founded in error, nor have we heard of any complaints by the people of wrongs suffered on account of its supposed infringement of the right of trial by jury. So far, therefore, as the solution of the question now before us is affected by the fact that the tort was committed within the body of a county, it must be considered as finally settled by the decision in that case.

2. The second ground of objection to the jurisdiction of the court is founded on the fact, that though the collision complained of occurred in a great navigable river, it was on a part of that river not affected by the flux and reflux of the tide, but "far above it."

This objection, also, is one which has heretofore been considered and decided by this court, after full argument and much deliberation. In the case of the *Genesee Chief*, (12 How., 444,) we have decided, that though in England the flux and reflux of the tide was a sound and reasonable test of a navigable river, because on that island tide-water and navigable water were synonymous terms, yet that "there is certainly nothing in the ebb and flow of the tide that makes the waters peculiarly suitable for admiralty jurisdiction, nor anything in the absence of a tide that renders it unfit. If it is a public navigable water on which commerce is carried on between different States or nations, the reason for the jurisdiction is precisely the same. And if a distinction is made on that account, it is merely arbitrary, without any foundation in reason—and, indeed, contrary to it." The case of the Thomas Jefferson (10 Wheaton) and others, which had hastily adopted this arbitrary and (in this country) false test of navigable waters, were necessarily overruled.

Since the decision of these cases, the several district courts have taken jurisdiction of cases of collision on the great public navigable rivers. Some of these cases have been brought to this court by appeal, and in no instance has any objection been taken, either by the counsel or the court, to the jurisdiction, because the collision was within the body of a county, or above the tide. (*See Fritz v. Bull*, 12 How., 466; *Walsh v. Rogers*, 13 How., 283; *The Steamboat New World*, 16 How., 469; *Ure v. Kauffman*, 19 How., 56; *New York and Virginia S.B. Co. v. Calderwood*, 19 How., 245.)

In our opinion, therefore, neither of the facts alleged in the answer, nor both of them taken together, will constitute a sufficient exception to the jurisdiction of the District Court.

It is due however, to the learned counsel who has presented the argument for respondent in this case, to say, that he has not attempted to impugn the decision of this court in the case of *Waring v. Clark*, nor to question the sufficiency of the reasons given in the case of the *Genesee Chief* for overruling the case of the *Thomas Jefferson*; but he contends that the case of the *Genesee Chief* decided that the act of Congress of 1845, "extending the jurisdiction of the District Court to certain cases upon the lakes," &c., was not only constitutional, but also that it conferred a new jurisdiction, which the court did not possess before; and consequently, as that act was confined to the lakes, and "to vessels of twenty or more tons burden, licensed and employed in the business of commerce and navigation between ports and places in different States and Territories," it cannot authorize the District Courts in assuming jurisdiction over waters and subjects not included in the act, and more especially where the navigable portion of the river is wholly within the boundary of a single State. It is contended also that the case of *Fritz v. Bull*, and those which follow it, sustaining the jurisdiction of the court of admiralty over torts on the Mississippi river, cannot be reconciled with the points decided in the former case, as just stated, unless on the hypothesis that the act of 1845 be construed to include the Mississippi and other great rivers of the West; which it manifestly does not.

But it never has been asserted by this court, either in the case of *Fritz v. Bull*, or in any other case, that the admiralty jurisdiction exercised over the great navigable rivers of the West was claimed under the act of 1845, or by virtue of anything therein contained.

The Constitution, in defining the powers of the courts of the United States, extends them to "all cases of admiralty and maritime jurisdiction." It defines how much of the judicial power shall be exercised by the Supreme Court only; and it was left to Congress to ordain and establish other courts, and to fix the boundary and extent of their respective jurisdictions. Congress might give any of these courts the whole or so much of the admiralty jurisdiction as it saw fit. It might extend their jurisdiction over all navigable waters, and all ships and vessels thereon, or over some navigable waters, and vessels of a certain description only. Consequently, as Congress had never before 1845 conferred admiralty jurisdiction over the Northern fresh-water lakes *not* "navigable from the sea," the District Courts could not assume it by virtue of this clause in the Constitution. An act of Congress was therefore necessary to confer this jurisdiction on those waters, and was completely within the constitutional powers of Congress; unless, by some unbending law of nature, fresh-water lakes and rivers are necessarily within the category of those that are not "navigable," and which, consequently, could not be subjected to "admiralty jurisdiction," any more than canals or railroads.

When these States were colonies, and for a long time after the adoption of the Constitution of the United States, the shores of the great lakes of the North, above and beyond the ocean tides, were as yet almost uninhabited, except by savages. The necessities of commerce and the progress of steam navigation had not as yet called for the exercise of admiralty jurisdiction, except on the ocean border of the Atlantic States.

The judiciary act of 1789, in defining the several powers of the courts established by it, gives to the District Courts of the United States "exclusive original cognizance of all civil cases of admiralty and maritime jurisdiction, including all seizures. &c., when they are made on waters which are *navigable from the sea* by vessels of ten or more tons burden, &c., as well as upon the high seas."

So long as the commerce of the country was centered chiefly on the Eastern Atlantic ports, where the fresh-water rivers were seldom navigable above tide-water, no inconvenience arose from the adoption of the English insular test of "navigable waters." Hence it was followed by the courts without objection or inquiry.

But this act does not confine admiralty jurisdiction to tide-waters; and if the flux and reflux of the tide be abandoned, as an arbitrary and false test of a "navigable river," it required no further legislation of Congress to extend it to the Mississippi, Alabama, and other great rivers, "navigable from the sea." If the waters over which this jurisdiction is claimed by within this category, the act makes no distinction between them. It is not confined to rivers or waters which bound coterminous States, such as the Mississippi and Ohio, or to rivers passing through more than one State; nor does the act distinguish between them and rivers which rise in and pass through one State only, and are consequently "*infra corpus comitatus.*" The admiralty jurisdiction surrendered by the States to the Union had no such bounds as exercised by themselves, and is clogged with no such conditions in its surrender. The interpolation of such conditions by the courts would exclude many of the ports, harbors, creeks, and inlets, most frequented by ships and commerce, but which are wholly included within the boundaries of a State or the body of a county.

It seems to have been assumed, in the argument of this case, that because the District Courts had not exercised their admiralty jurisdiction above tide-water before the decision of this court of the case of the *Genesee Chief*, that such jurisdiction had been exercised by them as conferred by the act of 1845. It is upon this mistaken hypothesis that any difficulty is found in reconciling that case with the case of *Fritz v. Bull*, which immediately followed it.

The act of 1845 was the occasion and created the necessity for this court to review their former decisions.

It might be considered in fact as a declaratory act reversing the decision in the case of the Thomas Jefferson. We could no longer evade the question by a judicial notice of an occult tide without ebb or flow, as in the case of *Peyroux v. Howard*, (7 Pet., 343.) The court were placed in the position, that they must either declare the act of Congress void, and shock the common sense of the people by declaring the lakes not to be "navigable waters," or overrule previous decisions which had established an arbitrary distinction, which, when applied to our continent, had no foundation in reason.

In conclusion, we repeat what we then said, that "courts of admiralty have been found necessary in all commercial countries, not only for the safety and convenience of commerce, and a speedy decision of controversies where delay would be ruin, but also to administer the laws of nations in a season of war, and to determine the validity of captures and questions of prize or no prize in a judicial proceeding. And it would be contrary to the first principles on which this Union was formed, to confine these rights to the States bordering on the Atlantic, and to the tide-water rivers connected with it, and to deny them to the citizens who border on the lakes, and the great navigable streams of the Western States. Certainly, such was not the intent of the framers of the Constitution; and if such be the construction finally given to it by this court, it must necessarily produce great public inconvenience, and at the same time fail to accomplish one of the great objects of the framers of the Constitution; that is, perfect equality in the rights and privileges of the citizens of the different States, not only in the laws of the General Government, but in the mode of administering them."

The decree of the court below, dismissing the libel for want of jurisdiction, is therefore reversed, and it is ordered that the record be remitted, with directions to further proceed in the case as to law and justice may appertain.

Mr. Justice McLEAN delivered a separate opinion, and Mr. Justice CATRON, Mr. Justice DANIEL, and Mr. Justice CAMPBELL, dissented. Mr. Justice CATRON concurred with Mr. Justice CAMPBELL in the opinion delivered by him.

---

2. *The Modern Standards*

Note: Interpretations of "Navigable Waters"

The admiralty jurisdiction of the federal courts extends not only to events on the high seas and territorial seas but to the inland waters of the United States so long as they satisfy the requirement of being "navigable waters". The interpretation of the term "navigable waters of the United States" has, itself, been the subject of a number of differing federal decisions. It refers to bodies of water that are navigable in fact, which means waters that are used or capable of being used as waterborne highways for commerce, *i.e.*, those presently sustaining or those capable of sustaining the transportation of goods or passengers by watercraft. Furthermore, in order to qualify as navigable waters of the Untied States, bodies of water must "form in their ordinary condition by themselves, or by uniting with other waters, a continued highway over which commerce is or may be carried on with other States or foreign countries in the customary modes in which such commerce is conducted by water." *The Daniel Ball*, 77 U.S. (10 Wall.) 557, 563, 19 L. Ed. 999 (1871).

Generally, inland water of the United States is "navigable" if: (1) it is capable of supporting maritime commerce; (2) it runs through two states or empties into the sea; and, (3) it is presently sustaining maritime commerce. Note that it is sufficient that the body of water be a *link* in the highway of interstate commerce. In other words, if a body of water (sustaining maritime commerce) runs into another body of water (sustaining maritime commerce) which runs between two states, admiralty jurisdiction applies.

---

a. "Contemporary Navigability in Fact" Test

LeBLANC v. CLEVELAND

198 F.3d 353, 2000 AMC 609, (2d Cir. 1999)

PARKER, Circuit Judge:

Etoile LeBlanc and Stephen Ossen appeal from an order of the United States District Court for the Northern District of New York (Lawrence E. Kahn, Judge), entered October 1, 1997, dismissing their claims for lack of subject matter jurisdiction. The district court based the dismissal on its conclusion that the portion of the Hudson River in which the accident giving rise to appellants' claims took place was not a navigable waterway for purposes of establishing federal admiralty jurisdiction.

We affirm.

I. Background

On July 4, 1994, Etoile LeBlanc and Stephen Ossen suffered personal injuries when the kayak they were paddling on the Hudson River was struck by a recreational motor boat operated by Terry Cleveland and owned by Robert Grant. LeBlanc and Ossen had rented their kayak from JRD Retailers, Ltd., d/b/a Syd & Dusty's Outfitters ("JRD"). The collision occurred approximately 29 miles upstream of Fort Edward, near Lake Luzerne.

On March 29, 1995, LeBlanc and Ossen sued Grant and Cleveland in the Southern District of New York, invoking federal admiralty jurisdiction. They alleged that Grant and Cleveland negligently caused the collision and their resulting injuries. On September 22, 1995, the action was transferred to the Northern District of New York. Cleveland and Grant then brought third-party complaints against JRD. Pursuant to Rule 14(c) of the FEDERAL RULES OF CIVIL PROCEDURE, these third-party complaints allowed the case to proceed as if LeBlanc and Ossen had sued JRD as well as Cleveland and Grant. FED. R. CIV. P. 14(c).

On July 22, 1997, JRD moved to dismiss the complaint filed by LeBlanc and Ossen for lack of subject matter jurisdiction. *See* FED. R. CIV. P. 12(b)(1). On October 1, 1997, the district court granted the motion, finding that the Hudson River is not "navigable in fact" at the location at which the accident took place and that, consequently, the court lacked admiralty jurisdiction over the lawsuit. The court acknowledged that the Hudson River below Fort Edward is a navigable waterway because it permits passage to the open sea. Nonetheless, the court found that the "part of the Hudson [where the accident took place] cannot ... be accessed from Fort Edward due to the presence of numerous areas of rapids, ... [nine] dams, and at least three major waterfalls of 30 feet or more in height." As a result, the court concluded that "[n]othing in the records suggests that the Hudson north of Fort Edward is now, or has ever been, an artery of maritime commerce" sufficient to support a finding of navigability necessary to the exercise of federal admiralty jurisdiction. LeBlanc and Ossen timely appealed.

II. Discussion

On appeal, LeBlanc and Ossen argue that the district court erred in finding that the Hudson River is unnavigable north of Fort Edward for purposes of establishing federal admiralty jurisdiction. In support of this argument, they contend, first, that the district court applied an incorrect standard when it found that navigability was precluded in part due to the existence of artificial dams. Appellants urge this Court to adopt a standard that focuses on the historic navigability of the river in its natural, unimproved state, rather than its present, improved state. Second, they assert that, whether the test focuses on historic or contemporary navigability, the Hudson is sufficiently navigable at the site of the accident to support federal admiralty jurisdiction over their claims. After setting forth the applicable standard of review, we address each argument in turn.

* * *

B. The Proper Standard for Determining Navigability

Appellants first contend that the district court applied an incorrect legal standard in finding admiralty jurisdiction lacking. Specifically, they argue for a jurisdictional test that focuses on the historic navigability of the waterway in question, without reference to present-day artificial obstructions, rather than on its contemporary navigability, including artificial dams. Under an historic navigability test, the argument continues, the district court erred in refusing to take into account the fact that, prior to 1951 and before the construction of several impassable dams, the logging industry regularly used the Hudson River upstream of Fort Edward to float logs to timber mills. For the reasons discussed below, appellants' argument fails.

* * *

The district court, like virtually every other court to consider the question of navigability for admiralty jurisdiction purposes, applied the definition of navigable waters first articulated in *The Daniel Ball*, 77 U.S. (10 Wall.) 557, 19 L. Ed. 999 (1870):

> Those rivers must be regarded as public navigable rivers in law which are navigable in fact. And they are navigable in fact when they are used, or are susceptible of being used, in their ordinary condition, as highways for commerce, over which trade and travel are or may be conducted in the customary modes of trade and travel on water. And they constitute navigable waters of the United States within the meaning of the acts of Congress, in contradistinction from the navigable waters of the States, when they form in their ordinary condition by themselves, or by uniting with other waters, a continued highway over which commerce is or may be carried on with other States or foreign countries in the customary modes in which such commerce is conducted by water.

Id. at 563; *see also Grubart*, 513 U.S. at 529-30, 115 S.Ct. 1043 (applying *The Daniel Ball* for purposes of determining admiralty jurisdiction); *In re Petition of Boyer*, 109 U.S. 629, 631-32, 3 S.Ct. 434, 27 L.Ed. 1056 (1884) (same). The district court found, and the parties did not dispute, that the Hudson River downstream of Fort Edward can be and is used as a continuous highway for interstate commerce because it permits passage beyond New York both to the south, where it empties into the Atlantic, and to the north, via the Champlain Canal (which begins near Fort Edward) and the St. Lawrence. However, the court found that the accident site is separated from Fort Edward, and therefore from any interstate or international waterway, by numerous impassable rapids, falls, and artificial dams.

Appellants do not dispute that *The Daniel Ball* sets forth the basic navigability test for purposes of admiralty jurisdiction. Instead, they first contend that by focusing on whether rivers are navigable "in their ordinary condition," the *Daniel Ball* test required the district court to measure navigability by reference to the river's historic, unimproved state, rather than its present, improved state.

This argument is foreclosed by subsequent Supreme Court caselaw. In *United States v. Appalachian Electric Power Co.*, 311 U.S. 377, 407, 61 S.Ct. 291, 85 L.Ed. 243 (1940), the Court found that "ordinary condition" as used in *The Daniel Ball* refers not to the absence of human interference with the course of the river, but "to volume of water, the gradients and the regularity of the flow" of the waterway. *Id.* at 407, 61 S.Ct. 291. Thus, under the *Daniel Ball* test, an otherwise unnavigable river may not be rendered navigable simply because, in extraordinary conditions, its waters rise high enough to support forms of transportation normally impossible. 1 STEVEN F. FRIEDELL, BENEDICT ON ADMIRALTY § 142, at 9-6 (7th ed. 1998) ("It is not enough that a fishing skiff or gunning canoe can be made to float at high water ... or that logs, poles and rafts are floated down in high waters."). But nothing in *The Daniel Ball* indicates that an historically navigable river remains navigable for admiralty jurisdiction purposes when it is made impassable by an artificial obstruction.

Perhaps recognizing that their interpretation of *The Daniel Ball* lacks legal support, appellants next rely on *The Montello*, 87 U.S. (20 Wall.) 430, 22 L.Ed. 391 (1874), claiming that it "refined" the *Daniel Ball* test discussed above. In *The Montello*, the Supreme Court was called upon to determine whether Congress had the authority under the Commerce Clause to regulate steamships plying the waters of Wisconsin's Fox River. Congress's power to regulate activity on the Fox River turned on whether the river was navigable. Setting forth the standard of navigability applicable in this context, the Court wrote:

> The capability of use by the public for purposes of transportation and commerce affords the true criterion of the navigability of a river, rather than the extent and manner of that use. If it be capable in its natural state of being used for purposes of commerce, no matter in what mode the commerce may be conducted, it is navigable in fact, and becomes in law a public river or highway.

Id. at 441-42. Appellants contend that by referencing the "natural state" of the river in question, the *Montello* Court made clear that navigability should be judged without reference to artificial obstructions. Indeed, the Supreme Court has since specifically held that, for purposes of defining Congress's power to regulate under the Commerce Clause, an otherwise navigable river cannot be rendered unnavigable by the construction of artificial dams. *See, e.g., Economy Light & Power Co. v. United States,* 256 U.S. 113, 123, 41 S.Ct. 409, 65 L.Ed. 847 (1921).

Nonetheless, appellants' reliance on *The Montello* and its progeny is misplaced. As noted above, *The Montello* did not define navigable waters for purposes of establishing the limits of admiralty jurisdiction; instead, it defined navigable waters for the purpose of delimiting Congress's power to regulate under the Commerce Clause. The Supreme Court has recognized that the definition of navigable waters used in one context does not necessarily apply in another. *See Kaiser Aetna v. United States*, 444 U.S. 164, 170-72, 100 S.Ct. 383, 62 L.Ed.2d 332 (1979). Rather, "any reliance upon judicial precedent must be predicated upon careful appraisal of the purpose for which the concept of 'navigability' was invoked in a particular case." *Id.* at 171, 100 S.Ct. 383 (internal quotations omitted).

Careful appraisal of the purposes for which the *Montello* Court invoked the concept of navigability reveals that the same definition should not be used to determine the limits of the federal judicial power under Article III or 28 U.S.C. § 1331(1). As the Ninth Circuit put it:

> The definitions of navigability may vary because, as in the present case, the purposes served by the commerce clause and admiralty jurisdiction may vary. Congress' commerce power is designed in part to preserve and protect the nation's waterways which, in their natural condition, are navigable in interstate commerce. By virtue of this power, Congress may prevent or regulate obstruction of these waterways by the states through which they pass. The damming of a previously navigable waterway by a state cannot divest Congress of its control over a potentially useful artery of commerce, since such obstructions may always be removed. Hence the courts have reasonably held that a navigable river is not rendered non-navigable by artificial obstruction.
>
> However, if the damming of a waterway has the practical effect of eliminating commercial maritime activity, no federal interest is served by the exercise of admiralty jurisdiction over the events transpiring on that body of water, whether or not it was originally navigable. No purpose is served by application of a uniform body of federal law, on waters devoid of trade and commerce, to regulate the activities and resolve the disputes of pleasure boaters. Only the burdening of federal courts and the frustrating of the purposes of state tort law would be thereby served.

Adams v. Montana Power Co., 528 F.2d 437, 440-41 (9th Cir. 1975) (citations omitted); *see also Chapman v. United States*, 575 F.2d 147, 149-50 (7th Cir. 1978) (*en banc*) (quoting *Adams*).

Recognizing the distinction between legislative authority under the Commerce Clause and admiralty jurisdiction, every circuit court to confront the question has rejected the historic navigability jurisdictional test when determining admiralty jurisdiction. In *Adams*, the Ninth Circuit held that a dam that prevented a waterway from being used as an artery of interstate commerce also prevented federal courts from exercising admiralty jurisdiction over a recreational boating accident that occurred on the waterway. *Adams*, 528 F.2d at 440-41. Similarly, *in Livingston v. United States*, 627 F.2d 165 (8th Cir. 1980), the Eighth Circuit rejected a plaintiff's claim that because a river was navigable before the construction of an impassable dam, it remained navigable for all time:

> [T]he closing of waters to commercial shipping should likewise have the effect of eliminating admiralty jurisdiction over them. In other words, the concept of "naviga-

> bility" in admiralty is properly limited to describing a present capability of the waters to sustain commercial shipping.

Id. at 169-70 (footnote omitted); *see also Three Buoys Houseboat Vacations USA Ltd. v. Morts,* 921 F.2d 775, 778 (8th Cir. 1990) ("the standard is one of 'contemporary navigability in fact' "). And in *Chapman*, the Seventh Circuit held that, even if a dammed river was navigable for purposes of the Commerce Clause, it was not navigable for admiralty jurisdiction purposes where it was not susceptible of commercial navigation "in [its] present [dammed] state." *Chapman,* 575 F.2d at 151. Those cases in which circuit courts have found dammed waterways navigable for jurisdictional purposes are easily distinguished by the fact that the waterway in question formed the border between two states, thereby rendering it capable of supporting interstate commerce despite the existence of artificial dams blocking downstream flow. *See, e.g., Mullenix v. United States*, 984 F.2d 101, 103-04 & n. 3 (4th Cir. 1993) (Potomac River navigable at point at which it forms the border of Maryland and West Virginia and supports ferry traffic between the two states); *Finneseth v. Carter,* 712 F.2d 1041, 1044 (6th Cir. 1983) (lake navigable where it straddled the border of Tennessee and Kentucky).

As their final argument in favor of an historic navigability standard, appellants point us to *Adirondack League Club, Inc. v. Sierra Club*, 92 N.Y.2d 591, 684 N.Y.S.2d 168, 706 N.E.2d 1192 (1998). In *Adirondack League*, the New York Court of Appeals used an historic navigability standard for the purpose of identifying those "waterways [that] are of such practical utility that private ownership from the time of the original grant from the State or sovereign is subject to an easement for public travel." *Adirondack League,* 92 N.Y.2d at 601, 684 N.Y.S.2d at 170, 706 N.E.2d at 1194 (citation omitted). *Adirondack League,* of course, had nothing whatsoever to do with admiralty jurisdiction in the federal courts. Moreover, to state the purpose for which *Adirondack League* utilized the historic navigability standard is to distinguish it from the purpose admiralty jurisdiction serves. By its very nature, the process of determining which waterways are subject to public easements dating from a land grant by the State requires an historic navigability standard; under a contemporary navigability standard, the present-day owner of riparian rights could defeat a public easement merely by erecting an impassable obstacle in the waterway. This, of course, would defeat the purpose of the public easement doctrine. In contrast, and as discussed above, the purpose of federal admiralty jurisdiction is best served if the test for navigability is determined with reference to present-day artificial obstructions.

Thus, in light of the policies served by federal admiralty jurisdiction, we hold that a waterway at the situs in issue is navigable for jurisdictional purposes if it is presently used, or is presently capable of being used, as an interstate highway for commercial trade or travel in the customary modes of travel on water. Natural and artificial obstructions that effectively prohibit such commerce defeat admiralty jurisdiction.

C. The District Court's Application of the Legal Standard

Of course, under the contemporary navigability standard for purposes of determining admiralty jurisdiction, that we adopt today, it is immaterial that, prior to 1951 and before the construction of many of the nine dams, logs were floated down the Hudson near the accident site. Nonetheless, appellants contend that even under the contemporary navigability standard, the district court had before it sufficient evidence of present-day navigability to support a finding of jurisdiction. But in the face of the district court's unchallenged factual findings, this argument necessarily fails.

As noted at the outset, the district court found that the Hudson River downstream of Fort Edward is capable of supporting interstate commerce. The court also found that "the presence of natural obstructions such as white water and falls as well as the presence of more recent man-made dams absolutely prevent continuous travel by any type of boat from the place of the accident to the waters below Fort Edward." Finally, the district court determined that the presence of dams between Fort Edward and the accident site would now impede any attempt to float timber on this stretch of the Hudson absent extraordinary river conditions. Appellants do not take issue with any of these findings on appeal. Nor could they: Each enjoys substantial support in the record and is not clearly erroneous.

Instead, appellants contend only that the Hudson is navigable at the accident site because kayakers can portage around the dams separating the site from Fort Edward. But this argument lacks any legal support. Appellants cite, and we have found, no published decision holding that the possibility of recreational use assisted by multiple portages is, by itself, sufficient to render a waterway navigable for admiralty jurisdiction purposes. Navigability requires that the body of water be capable of supporting commercial maritime activity. It is irrelevant that the body of water is capable of supporting non-commercial maritime activity. "A waterway is navigable provided that it is used or susceptible of being used as an artery of commerce. Neither non-commercial fishing nor pleasure boating ... constitutes commerce. Commerce for the purpose of admiralty jurisdiction means activities related to shipping." *Adams,* 528 F.2d at 437; *see also Foremost,* 457 U.S. at 675, 102 S.Ct. 2654 (pleasure boating is "noncommercial maritime activity"). The possibility that the waterway is capable of supporting non-commercial maritime activity of the type suggested by appellants does not render the waterway capable of supporting "commercial trade or travel in the customary modes of travel on water," as our holding today requires. As a result, the court did not err in finding that it lacked jurisdiction over appellants' claims.

III. Conclusion

For the foregoing reasons, the judgment of the district court is affirmed.

Note

Compare the principle case, *LeBlanc v. Cleveland* with *Complaint of Paradise Holdings, Inc.*, 795 F.2d 756, 1987 AMC 104 (9th Cir. 1986), indicating that the test for determining the navigability of inland waters was not applied to tidal water.

Note: Different Definitions of "Navigability"

> The Supreme Court has recently observed that precedent in this area must be evaluated carefully in light of "'the *purpose* for which the concept of "navigability" was invoked in a particular case.'" *Kaiser Aetna v. United States*, 444 U.S. 164, 171, 100 S.Ct. 383, 388, 62 L.Ed.2d 332 (1979) (quoting with approval from the district court opinion, 408 F. Supp. 42, 49 (emphasis in original)). The Court in that case identified four separate purposes underlying definitions of "navigability": to delimit the boundaries of the navigational servitude; to define the scope of Congress' regulatory authority under the commerce clause; to determine the extent of the authority of the Corps of Engineers under the Rivers and Harbors Act of 1899; and to establish the limits of federal admiralty jurisdiction. Each of these areas of the law might well require a different definition of "navigability."

Livingston v. United States, 627 F.2d 165, 169, 1982 AMC 1065 (8th Cir. 1980), *cert. denied*, 450 U.S. 914, 101 S. Ct. 1354, 67 L. Ed. 2d 338 (1981).

---

b. Seasonal Navigability

Note

Does the fact that a body of water is not navigable in fact during part of the year defeat admiralty jurisdiction? In *Wilder v. Placid Oil Company*, 611 F. Supp. 841 (W.D. La. 1985), *aff'd sub nom. Sanders v. Placid Oil Co.*, 861 F.2d 1374, 1989 AMC 912 (5th Cir. 1988) the court had to decide whether Catahoula Lake, a low lying portion of the Little River in the State of Louisiana, is navigable for purposes of admiralty jurisdiction.

> Defendant finally argues that the seasonal navigability over the weir renders the Little River above the weir and Catahoula Lake non-navigable. This argument also has no merit. Many rivers have portions of their waters which are impassable at certain times of the year. The upper Mississippi and the Saint Lawrence Seaway are examples of rivers that freeze during the winter months. Does this make those waters any less "navigable waters" for purposes of admiralty jurisdiction? We think not.

611 F. Supp. 841, 847 (W.D. La. 1985).

---

c. Artificial Bodies of Water

Note

Does the fact that the body of water is man-made preclude it from being "navigable"?

> The Illinois and Michigan Canal is an artificial navigable waterway connecting Lake Michigan and the Chicago river with the Illinois river and the Mississippi river.
>
> * * *
>
> We take judicial notice of this historical fact that the canal... is capable of being navigated by vessels, which a canal of such size will accommodate, and which can pass from Mississippi river to Lake Michigan and carry on interstate commerce, although the canal is wholly within the territorial bounds of the state of Illinois.
>
> * * *
>
> Navigable water situated as this [Erie] canal is used for the purposes for which it is used, a highway for commerce between ports and places in different states, carried on by vessels such as those in question here (horse drawn barges), is public water of the United States, and within the legitimate scope of the admiralty jurisdiction conferred by the Constitution and statutes of the United States, even though the canal is wholly artificial, and is wholly within the body of a state, and subject to its ownership and control; and it makes no difference as to the jurisdiction of the district court that one or the other of the vessels was at the time of the collision on a voyage from one place in the state .to another place in that state.

Ex Parte Boyer, 109 U.S. 629,631-632, 3 S. Ct. 434, 27 L. Ed. 105 (1884).

---

d. The Commerce Clause: "Historical" Navigability Requirement

For purposes of regulatory jurisdiction under the Commerce Clause, U.S. Const. art. I, § 8, cl. 3, it is sufficient to show historical navigability (i.e., that the waters in question were once navigable) rather than "contemporary navigability in fact", which is the requirement for adjudicatory jurisdiction (i.e. the jurisdiction of admiralty courts to hear and decide disputes). *Land and Lake Tours, Inc. v. Lewis*, 738 F.2d 961 (8th Cir.), *cert. denied*, 469 U.S. 1038, 105 S. Ct. 517, 83 L. Ed. 2d 406 (1984). In that case, the U.S. Court of Appeals for the Eighth Circuit held that the U.S. Coast Guard had jurisdiction to conduct safety inspections of amphibious vehicles operating on Lake Hamilton, Arkansas, a lake that was not "presently navigable in fact". The court said:

> The case at bar did not involve the district court's article III admiralty jurisdiction, but instead Congress' article I power to regulate interstate commerce. As noted in *Kaiser Aetna v. United States*, 444 U.S. at 173-74, 100 S. Ct. at 389-90, Congress' article I power to regulate interstate commerce does not depend upon "navigability." Here, the federal government has an intense interest in the safety of passenger vessels, and the safety of passenger vessels has a substantial effect on interstate commerce. Undoubtedly Congress may require the inspection of passenger vessels, impose safety requirements, and "exercise its authority for such other reason as may seem to it in the interest of furthering navigation or commerce." *Id.* at 174, 100 S. Ct. at 390.
>
> * * *

Thus, the vessel safety specifications and periodic safety inspection requirements represent an exercise of Congressional power under the commerce clause, which has been delegated to the Coast Guard.

C. Maritime Torts

Note: Jurisdiction in Tort — Locus & Nexus

It is now established that in tort cases, a party seeking admiralty jurisdiction must satisfy two requirements. The first requirement is referred to as the maritime location criterion (locus) and the second requirement is referred to as the maritime nexus criterion. Maritime location is satisfied by showing either that the tort occurred on navigable waters or that injury or damage which was sustained on land was caused by a vessel in navigable waters. Until the Supreme Court's decision in *Executive Jet Aviation, Inc. v. City of Cleveland*, 409 U.S. 249, 93 S. Ct. 493, 34 L. Ed. 2d 454, 193 AMC 1 (1972) *infra*, locality was the sole criterion for admiralty tort jurisdiction. The maritime nexus criterion is of relatively recent origin and was created by the Supreme Court to restrict the scope of admiralty tort jurisdiction for various policy reasons including considerations of federalism and a desire to confine the exercise of admiralty jurisdiction to situations which implicate national interests. Maritime nexus is satisfied by showing that the tort bore some relationship to traditional maritime activity as will be more fully developed, *infra*.

---

1. Torts Occurring on Navigable Waters: The Maritime Location Criterion

Notes

1. The locality requirement for admiralty tort jurisdiction was enunciated in *The Plymouth*, 70 U.S. (3 Wall.) 20, 18 L. Ed. 125 (1865), a case involving a fire aboard ship which had spread to and damaged a nearby wharf. There the Court stated:

> [T]he wrong and injury complained of must have been committed wholly upon the high seas or navigable waters, or, at least, the substance and consummation of the same must have taken place upon these waters to be within the admiralty jurisdiction.
>
> * * *
>
> ... The jurisdiction of the admiralty over maritime torts does not depend upon the wrong having been committed on board the vessel, but upon its having been committed upon the high seas or other navigable waters.
>
> ... Every species of tort, however occurring, and whether on board a vessel or not, if upon the high seas or navigable waters, is of admiralty cognizance.

The locality test was strictly applied as the Court stated further that:

> [T]he simple fact that [the fire originated] on navigable waters, but, the whole damage done upon the land, the cause of action not being complete on navigable waters, affords no ground for the exercise of the admiralty jurisdiction.

In most run of the mill maritime tort suits jurisdiction is beyond challenge. In typical situations involving collisions, or injury to persons or damage to property aboard a vessel in navigable waters, admiralty jurisdiction is evident.

This locality test, of course, was established and grew up in an era when it was difficult to conceive of a tortious occurrence on navigable waters other than in connection with a waterborne vessel. Indeed, for the traditional types of maritime torts, the traditional test has worked quite satisfactorily. As a leading admiralty text has put the matter:

> It should be stressed that the important cases in admiralty are not the borderline cases on jurisdiction; these may exercise a perverse fascination in the occasion they afford for elaborate casuistry, but the main business of the [admiralty] court involves claims for cargo damage, collision, seamen's injuries and the like—all well and comfortably within the circle, and far from the penumbra. G. GILMORE & C. BLACK, THE LAW OF ADMIRALTY 24 n. 88 (1957).

Executive Jet Aviation, Inc. v. City of Cleveland, 409 U.S. 249, 93 S. Ct. 493, 34 L. Ed. 2d 454, 1973 AMC 1 (1972).

But as the *The Plymouth, supra*, shows, events which have their origin on the water may effect interests on land. Conversely, events which begin on land may impact on vessels in navigable waters. Thus, the strict locality rule has been modified both by Congress and the courts. In *The Blackheath*, 195 U.S. 361, 25 S. Ct. 46, 49 L. Ed. 236 (1904), the Supreme Court held that damage done by a vessel to fixed navigational aids, in this cases, a channel light, was within admiralty jurisdiction, despite the fact that the light was built on pilings and was not truly on "navigable waters. The Court continued to relax the rule in "borderline cases. *See*, *The Admiral Peoples*, 295 U.S. 649, 55 S. Ct. 885, 79 L. Ed. 1633 (1935), *infra*. In 1948, Congress extended tort jurisdiction to injuries and damage sustained on land with the enactment of the Admiralty Extension Act. *See*, Section 2, *infra*.

2. In *The Admiral Peoples*, 295 U.S. 649, 55 S. Ct. 885, 79 L. Ed. 1633 (1935), a passenger fell to the dock from a gangplank leading from the dock to the ship. The Supreme Court held that the passenger's action against the ship *in rem* did fall within the court's admiralty jurisdiction. The Court said:

> The basic fact in the instant case is that the gangplank was a part of the vessel. It was a part of the vessel's equipment which was placed in position to enable its passengers to reach the shore. It was no less a part of the vessel because in its extension to the dock it projected over the land... Neither the short distance that she fell nor the fact that she fell on the dock and not in the water, alters the nature of the cause of action which arose from the breach of duty owing to her while she was still on the ship and using its facility for disembarking. 295 U.S. 649, 651-52 (1935).

3. Under the locality test, a tort occurs ordinarily where plaintiff sustained injury. In most cases, plaintiff sustains injury either on navigable waters (admiralty jurisdiction) or on land (no admiralty jurisdiction). As *The Admiral Peoples, supra*, shows there are cases at the outer margin. If a vessel in navigable waters allides with a wharf and a person standing on the wharf in knocked from the wharf into the water and drowns and at the same time a person standing on the deck of the vessel is thrown from the vessel onto the wharf where she sustains a fatal injury, where did "the tort" occur? *The Admiral Peoples* may be read as suggesting that it is the exact place where defendant's wrongful conduct first impacted the plaintiff, rather than where plaintiffs sustained their ultimate injuries. In *Thompson v. Chesapeake Yacht Club*, 255 F. Supp. 555, 558 (D. Md. 1966) the court held that a person who, because of defendants negligence, fell through a hole in a pier into navigable water had no action in admiralty because his cause of action originated on land. In posing the question of where the tort occurred the court said that "it might be more accurate to determine where the negligent act or omission becomes operative or effective upon he plaintiff, so as to cause him injury." This approach created some anomalies in the law as the Court observed in *Executive Jet Aviation, Inc. v. City of Cleveland*, 409 U.S. 249, 93 S. Ct. 493, 34 L. Ed. 2d 454, 1973 AMC 1 (1972).

[I]t is the perverse and casuistic borderline situations that have demonstrated some of the problems with the locality test of maritime tort jurisdiction. In *Smith & Son v. Taylor*, 276 U.S. 179 (1928), for instance, a longshoreman unloading a vessel was standing on the pier when he was struck by a cargo-laden sling from the ship and knocked into the water where he was later found dead. This Court held that there was no admiralty jurisdiction in that case, despite the fact that the longshoreman was knocked into the water, because the blow by the sling was what gave rise to the cause of action, and it took effect on the land. Hence, the Court concluded, "the substance and consummation of the occurrence which gave rise to the cause of action took place on land." 276 U.S., at 182. In the converse factual setting, however, where a longshoreman working on the deck of a vessel was struck by a hoist and knocked onto the pier, the Court upheld admiralty jurisdiction because the cause of action arose on the vessel. *Minnie v. Port Huron Terminal Co.*, 295 U.S. 647 (1935). *See also The Admiral Peoples*, 295 U.S. 649 (1935).

---

2. *Injury or Damage Sustained on Land: The Admiralty Extension Act*

46 U.S.C.A. § 30101

§ 30101. Extension of jurisdiction to cases of damage or injury to land

(a) In General—The admiralty and maritime jurisdiction of the United States extends to and includes cases of injury or damage, to person or property, caused by a vessel on navigable waters, even though the injury or damage is done or consummated on land.

(b) Procedure—A civil action in a case under subsection (a) may be brought *in rem* or *in personam* according to the principles of law and the rules of practice applicable in cases where the injury or damage has been done and consummated on navigable waters.

46 U.S.C. § 740 (1948)

(Superseded Version)

a. Text

The admiralty and maritime jurisdiction of the United States shall extend to and include all cases of damage or injury, to person or property, caused by a vessel on navigable water, notwithstanding that such damage or injury be done or consummated on land.

In any such case suit may be brought *in rem* or *in personam* according to the principles of law and the rules of practice obtaining in cases where the injury or damage has been done and consummated on navigable water....

Note: The Purpose of the Admiralty Extension Act

The legislative history of the Admiralty Extension Act describes its purposes, and the inequities which it was designed to correct:

> As a result of the denial of admiralty jurisdiction in cases where injury is done on land, when a vessel collides with a bridge through mutual fault and both are damaged, under existing law the owner of the bridge, being denied a remedy in admiralty, is barred by contributory negligence from any recovery in an action at law. But the owner of the vessel may bring a suit in admiralty recover half damages from the bridge, contributory negligence operating merely to reduce the recovery. Further, where a collision between a vessel and a land structure is caused by the fault of a compulsory pilot, the owner of the land structure is without remedies for his injuries since at law a compulsory pilot is not deemed the servant of the vessel's master or owner... . But if the vessel sheers off the land structure to collide with another vessel in the vicinity, the owner of the second vessel, by an in rem proceeding in admiralty, may recover full damages, for the wrong is viewed as that of the vessel itself and compulsory pilotage is no defense... . [The Admiralty Extension Act] would correct these inequities as a result of providing that the admiralty courts shall take cognizance of all of them.
>
> * * *
>
> Adoption of the bill will not crate new causes of action. It merely specifically directs the courts to exercise the admiralty and maritime jurisdiction of the United States already conferred by article III, section 2 of the Constitution and already authorized by the Judiciary acts.

U.S. Code Cong. Serv. 1898, 1899-1900 (1948).

This interpretation was confirmed in the Fifth Circuit in *Louisville & N.R. Co. v. M/V Bayou Lacombe*, 597 F.2d 469, 1980 AMC 2914 (5th Cir. 1979), in which a railroad company sought relief at admiralty for damage done by a vessel to the company's railroad bridge:

> The [Admiralty extension Act] does not create new causes of action; it merely expands the locality rule of ... torts. As a result of the Act, a plaintiff is no longer precluded from suing in admiralty when a vessel collides with a land structure, such as a bridge.

597 F.2d 469, 472 (1979) (citations omitted).

---

b. Application of the Admiralty Extension Act: Cases and Notes

DULUTH SUPERIOR EXCURSIONS, INC. v. MAKELA

623 F.2d 1251, 1980 AMC 2518 (8th Cir. 1980)

BRIGHT, Circuit Judge

Duluth Superior Excursions, Inc. and Flamingo Excursions, Inc. (collectively, Excursions) brought this action in federal court seeking to limit their potential liability to Joseph Makela under the Shipowner's Limitation of Liability Act, 46 U.S.C. §§ 181-189 (1976). The district court dismissed the action, holding that Excursions had failed to establish federal admiralty jurisdiction under 28 U.S.C. § 1333(1) (1976). For the reasons set forth below, we conclude that this determination was erroneous. Accordingly, we reverse.

I. Background

On the night of August 12, 1977, Joseph Makela was struck and seriously injured by a car while crossing Harbor Drive in Duluth, Minnesota. The driver of the car was allegedly intoxicated. Both Makela and the car's driver had just disembarked from the S.S.

Flamingo after a three-hour privately chartered cruise around the Duluth-Superior harbor. The organizers of the charter cruise, having advertised it as a "booze cruise," had brought several kegs of beer on board. The Flamingo was owned by appellant Flamingo Excursions, Inc., and operated by appellant Duluth Superior Excursions, Inc.

In September 1977, Makela's attorney notified Excursions that a tort claim would be filed against them. Excursions responded by filing the present action in federal court on February 10, 1978, seeking to limit their potential liability to the value of the S.S. Flamingo, her equipment, and any pending freight as of August 12, 1977. *See* 46 U.S.C. § 183(a) (1976).[1] Excursions offered an ad interim stipulation for value in the sum of $51,000, alleging that this sum exceeded the aggregate value of their interest in the vessel.

In October 1978, Makela filed a tort action in Minnesota state court, naming as defendants the driver of the car that struck him, the driver's father, the cruise organizers, and Excursions.[2] Makela's claim against Excursions was that Excursions inadequately supervised the passengers aboard the Flamingo, who consequently became illegally intoxicated, and that Excursions failed to provide a safe means of exit for these passengers. The federal action brought by Excursions against Makela was dismissed for want of jurisdiction on November 8, 1979.

II. Analysis

In *Executive Jet Aviation v. City of Cleveland*, 409 U.S. 249, 93 S. Ct. 493, 34 L. Ed. 2d 454 (1972), the Supreme Court recounted the history of maritime tort jurisdiction. Traditionally, the test of jurisdiction was whether the tort was "located" on navigable waters. *E.g., The Plymouth*, 70 U.S. (3 Wall.) 20, 18 L. Ed. 125 (1866). Because this test has proven unsatisfactory in many cases, the Court in *Executive Jet* placed its imprimatur on the more modern test of whether the alleged wrong is related to traditional maritime activity. *See id.* at 261, 93 S. Ct. at 501.[3]

In the case at hand, there is little question that the wrongs allegedly committed by Excursions took place on navigable waters.[4] The district court held, however, that Excursions failed to show the requisite relationship between these wrongs and traditional maritime activities. The district court based this holding upon its conclusion that inadequate supervision, illegal intoxication, and failure to provide a safe exit are not traditional maritime acts.

---

[1] 46 U.S.C. § 183(a) provides in pertinent part as follows:

> (a) The liability of the owner of any vessel, whether American or foreign, for any ... act, matter, or thing, loss, damage, or forfeiture, done, occasioned, or incurred, without the privity or knowledge of such owner or owners, shall not, except in the cases provided for in subsection (b) of this section, exceed the amount or value of the interest of such owner in such vessel, and her freight then pending. The district court did not reach the issue of whether this statute applies here; neither do we.

[2] The parties have informed us that this lawsuit has not yet gone to trial.

[3] At issue in *Executive Jet* was a claim for property damage to an airplane that crashed and sank in Lake Erie. The Court in that case held specifically that, absent either a showing of a significant relationship between the wrong and traditional maritime activity or legislation to the contrary, claims arising from airplane accidents over navigable waters are not cognizable in admiralty. *Id.* at 268, 93 S. Ct. at 504.

[4] It is true, as Makela notes, that the injury he suffered was consummated on dry land. That fact, however, does not change the locale of appellants' alleged rongs, nor does it destroy admiralty jurisdiction in this case. *See* text at note 5 *infra*.

The district court may well have been correct in this surmise. The question before the court, however, was whether these alleged acts were related to (*i.e.*, occurred in connection with) traditional maritime activities. Carrying passengers for hire is undoubtedly a traditional maritime activity, and suits in tort for personal injuries to passengers are clearly included in admiralty jurisdiction. *E.g.*, *St. Hilaire Moye v. Henderson*, 496 F.2d 973 (8th Cir.), *cert. denied*, 419 U.S. 884, 95 S. Ct. 151, 42 L. Ed. 2d 125 (1974). *See* G. GILMORE AND C. BLACK, THE LAW OF ADMIRALTY 23 & 23 n.77 (2d ed. 1975). The nature of the allegedly negligent acts underlying Makela's claims against appellants is largely irrelevant. It is sufficient for purposes of admiralty jurisdiction in this case that a passenger is suing for personal injuries allegedly due to the negligence of the vessel's owners and crew on navigable waters. *See Kermarec v. Compagnie Generale*, 358 U.S. 625, 79 S. Ct. 406, 3 L. Ed. 2d 550 (1959); *Gibboney v. Wright*, 517 F.2d 1054, 1059 (5th Cir. 1975).

To be sure, the accident that injured Makela occurred on dry land. Under the terms of the Admiralty Extension Act, 46 U.S.C. § 740 (1976), however, this circumstance does not destroy admiralty jurisdiction over Makela's claims against the appellants. The Admiralty Extension Act provides in pertinent part:

> The admiralty and maritime jurisdiction of the United States shall extent to and include all cases of damage or injury, to person or property, caused by a vessel on navigable water, notwithstanding that such damage or injury be done or consummated on land.

In *Gutierrez v. Waterman S.S. Corp.*, 373 U.S. 206, 210, 83 S. Ct. 1185, 1188, 10 L. Ed. 2d 297 (1963), the Supreme Court held that the Admiralty Extension Act applies not only to injuries caused by the impact of a vessel itself, but also to those due to alleged acts of negligence by a vessel's crew. In that case, a longshoreman was injured when he slipped on loose beans that had been spilled on the dock from defective bags in the course of unloading. The defendant argued that the federal courts lacked jurisdiction to hear the longshoreman's claims. The Court held, however, that admiralty jurisdiction is established when it is alleged that the shipowner commits a tort while or before the ship is being unloaded, and the impact of which is felt ashore at a time and place not remote from the wrongful act. [*Id.* at 210, 83 S. Ct. at 1188 (footnote omitted).] These conditions for admiralty jurisdiction are fully satisfied in the present case.[5] *Cf. Tullis v. Fidelity and Casualty Co. of New York*, 397 F.2d 22, 23-24 (5th Cir. 1968) (admiralty jurisdiction established by a crew boat passenger's allegation that defendant boat owner failed to provide a reasonably safe means of debarking).[6]

* * *

[5] Although it might be argued that Makela's injury is remote from the wrongful act, the accident occurred some six minutes after the S. S. Flamingo docked on a street that adjoins the dock. In our view, this is not sufficiently remote in time and space to destroy admiralty jurisdiction. We intimate no view as to whether Makela's injury was remote in the sense of not having been proximately caused by the appellants' alleged acts of negligence. That issue remains for the trier of fact to decide. *But cf. Pryor v. American President Lines*, 520 F.2d 974 (4th Cir. 1975), *cert. denied*, 423 U.S. 1055, 96 S. Ct. 787, 46 L. Ed. 644 (1976), and cases there cited (requiring proximate cause to invoke the Admiralty Extension Act in cases where the only permissible inference

Here, Mr. Makela, like the plaintiff in *Byrd*, was a passenger aboard a commercial vessel and the defendants are its owners and operators. Their alleged negligence, unlike that of the defendant driver in *Peytavin*, involves their performance of maritime duties in caring for their passengers. *Cf. St. Hilaire Moye v. Henderson, supra* (admiralty defendants found negligent in their operation of a pleasure boat).[7] Finally, we note that the sequence of causal events alleged in this case started on board the vessel and ended on land, calling into play the Admiralty Extension Act. None of the cases cited by Makela shares this last critical feature. Nor do they address the duties of vessel owners or operators to their passengers, a traditional maritime concern.

We conclude, then, that Makela's claim against Excursions comes within the admiralty jurisdiction of the federal courts. We reverse the decision of the district court dismissing the appellants' action, and remand the case for further proceedings consistent with this opinion.

Question

Plaintiff is injured on land by bombs dropped during a training exercise by U.S. Navy aircraft from a U.S. Navy aircraft carrier. Does the case fall within admiralty jurisdiction by operation of the Admiralty Extension Act? See *Anderson v. U.S.*, 317 F.3d 1235, 2003 AMC 94 (11th Cir. 2003).

Note

Whittington v. Sewer Construction Co., Inc., 541 F.2d 427, 1976 AMC 967 (4th Cir. 1976) provides an example of the opposite situation from cases like *The Admiral Peoples, supra* and *Duluth Superior Excursions, supra.* The plaintiff fell into a barge from a cable suspended from a winch mounted on a bridge. The court held that his claim did not fall within the admiralty jurisdiction. The negligence of which he complained took place on the land, where the winch was. The fact that he sustained his injuries on navigable waters was immaterial.

---

is that the vessel did not proximately cause the injury).

[6] In *Gutierrez v. Waterman S.S. Corp., supra,* the Supreme Court not only found admiralty jurisdiction, but also held that the defendant shipowner was negligent towards the plaintiff longshoreman and strictly liable for breach of its warranty of seaworthiness. The Court restricted the scope of this latter holding in *Victory Carriers, Inc. v. Law*, 404 U.S. 202, 92 S. Ct. 418, 30 L. Ed. 2d 383 (1971), another longshoreman suit for dockside injuries, this time caused by equipment owned and operated by the stevedore. After observing that "in *Gutierrez, supra,* federal admiralty jurisdiction was clearly present since the Admiralty Extension Act on its face reached the injury there involved[,]" the Court stated:

> The decision in *Gutierrez* turned, not on the "function" the stevedore was performing at the time of his injury, but, rather, upon the fact that his injury was caused by an appurtenance of a ship, the defective cargo containers, which the Court held to be an "injury, to person ... caused by a vessel on navigable water" which was consummated ashore under 46 U.S.C. § 740. The Court has never approved an unseaworthiness recovery for an injury sustained on land merely because the injured longshoreman was engaged in the process of "loading" or "unloading." [*Id.* at 210-11, 92 S. Ct. at 424 (footnote omitted).]

[7] Makela points out that his injuries, like those of the whiplash victim in *Peytavin*, show no particular maritime character. The same thing is true, however, of the fall on spilled beans suffered by the plaintiff longshoreman in *Gutierrez, supra. Cf. The Admiral Peoples*, 295 U.S. 649, 55 S. Ct. 885, 79 L. Ed. 1633 (1935) (admiralty plaintiff who fell off a step at the end of a gangplank onto the dock recovered damages). We do not consider the nature of the plaintiff's injury to be critical in determining the scope of admiralty jurisdiction.

Notes

1. *Application of the Admiralty Extension Act by the Supreme Court: Proximate Cause*

In order for a plaintiff to invoke maritime jurisdiction under the Admiralty Extension Act, it must be alleged that the proximate cause of the plaintiff's injury on shore was negligence by the vessel or its defective appurtenances. This rule may be gleaned from two seminal Supreme Court decisions.

In *Gutierrez v. Waterman Steamship Corp.*, 373 U.S. 206, 83 S. Ct. 1185, 10 L. Ed. 2d 297 (1963), a longshoreman sued for injuries sustained when he slipped on beans that had become scattered about a dock during their unloading due to defective cargo containers.* The court found that:

> The shipowner knew or should have known that injury was likely to result to persons who would have to work around the beans spilled from the defective bags, and it was negligent in allowing cargo so poorly stowed or laden to be unloaded. Petitioner fell on the beans and injured himself, and such injuries were proximately caused by the respondent's negligence and the unseaworthiness of its cargo or cargo containers. *Id.* at 207.

In determining that a claim had been properly raised under the Admiralty Extension Act, the Supreme Court stated:

> I
>
> Respondent contends that it is not liable, at least in admiralty, because the impact of its alleged lack of care or unseaworthiness was felt on the pier rather than aboard ship. Whatever validity this proposition may have had until 1948, the passage of the Extension of Admiralty Jurisdiction Act, 62 Stat. 496, 46 U.S.C. § 740, swept it away when it made vessels on navigable water liable for damage or injury "notwithstanding that such damage or injury be done or consummated on land." Respondent and the carrier *amici curiae* would have the statute limited to injuries actually caused by the physical agency of the vessel or a particular part of it—such as when the ship rams a bridge or when its defective winch drops some cargo onto a longshoreman. *Cf. Strika v. Netherlands Ministry of Traffic*, 185 F.2d 555 (C.A. 2d Cir.); *Hagans v. Farrell Lines*, 237 F.2d 477 (C.A. 3d Cir.). Nothing in the legislative history supports so restrictive an interpretation of the statutory language. There is no distinction in admiralty between torts committed by the ship itself and by the ship's personnel while operating it, any more than there is between torts "committed" by a corporation and by its employees. And ships are libeled as readily for an unduly bellicose mate's assault on a crewman, *see Boudoin v. Lykes Bros. Co.*, 348 U.S. 336, 339-340; *The Rolph*, 299 F. 52 (C.A. 9th Cir.), or for having an incompetent crew or master, *see Keen v. Overseas Tankship Corp.*, 194 F.2d 515, 517 (C.A. 2d Cir.), as for a collision. Various far-fetched hypotheticals are raised, such as a suit in admiralty for an ordinary automobile accident involving a ship's officer on ship business in port, or for someone's slipping on beans that continue to leak from these bags in a warehouse in Denver. We think it sufficient for the needs of this occasion to hold that the case is within the maritime jurisdiction under 46 U.S.C. § 740 when, as here, it is alleged that the shipowner commits a tort while or before the ship is being unloaded, and the impact of which is felt ashore at a time and place not remote from the wrongful act. *Id.* at 209-10.

However, in *Victory Carriers, Inc. v. Law*, 404 U.S. 202, 92 S. Ct. 418, 30 L. Ed. 2d 383, 1972 AMC 1 (1971), the Court found that the Act did not encompass the injuries of a longshoreman which occurred during the loading process when the overhead protection rack of his fork lift, owned by the stevedoring company, came loose and fell on him. Confronted with the argument that the Act extended to the injury because the longshoreman had been engaged in the service of a vessel on navigable waters, the Court held:

---

* At one time, the Supreme Court recognized an action for unseaworthiness on behalf of longshoremen who qualified as "Sieracki seamen". This action was legislatively overruled by the 1972 Amendments to the Longshore Harbor Workers' Compensation Act. 33 U.S.C. § 905(b) (1982). (Eds.)

The decision in *Guitars* turned, not on the "function" the stevedore was performing at the time of his injury, but, rather, upon the fact that his injury was caused by an appurtenance of a ship, the defective cargo containers, which the Court held to be an "injury, to person... caused by a vessel on navigable water" which was consummated ashore under 46 U.S.C. § 740. The Court has never approved an unseaworthiness recovery for an injury sustained on land merely because the injured longshoreman was engaged in the process of "loading" or "unloading."[11] *Nacirema Operating Co. v. Johnson*, 396 U.S., at 223, a case decided several years after *Gutierrez*, makes this quite clear:

> There is much to be said for uniform treatment of longshoremen injured while loading or unloading a ship. But even construing the Extension Act to amend the Longshoremen's Act would not effect this result, since longshoremen injured on a pier by pier-based equipment would still remain outside the Act. *Id.* at 210-11, 92 S. Ct. at 424.
>
> * * *
>
> Consequently, the Supreme Court declined to "extend the reach" of the Act "to pier-side accidents caused by a stevedore's pier-based equipment." *Id.* at 204, 92 S. Ct. at 421.

In *Margin v. Sea-Land Services, Inc.*, 812 F.2d 973, 1988 AMC 1213 (5th Cir. 1987), the plaintiff a welder, suffered an injury dockside. Stevedores using a crane on the dock were lowering a hatch cover from an adjacent vessel over the plaintiff's worksite. Plaintiff feared that it might be dropped on him and when he tried to escape, he fell and injured his shoulder. The plaintiff claimed admiralty jurisdiction under the Admiralty Extension Act arguing the Act extends admiralty jurisdiction to this case because the vessel being unloaded was in navigable waters. The court dismissed the case for lack of subject matter jurisdiction as the Act only confers maritime jurisdiction when a plaintiff on shore can allege an injury proximately caused by a vessel on navigable waters or by its defective appurtenances. Here, land based equipment was operated negligently; there was no vessel negligence.

2. *Liability of Shipbuilders Under the Act*

In *Nissan Motor Corp. v. Maryland Shipbuilding, etc.*, 544 F. Supp. 1104, 1983 AMC 663 (D. Md. 1982), *aff'd*, 742 F.2d 1449 (4th Cir. 1984), the court applied the Admiralty Extension Act to a case involving a car manufacturer whose storage lot was located adjacent to a shipbuilding company. Nissan alleged its cars had been damaged as a result of the smoke and paint that emanated from the shipbuilder's activities. The court noted that the preliminary question was whether the case would be heard under Admiralty or Diversity jurisdiction. Finding that jurisdiction was properly invoked under the Admiralty Extension Act, the court held that the paint damage to Nissan's cars was caused by spray painting operations conducted from a barge or from the painting of vessels located on navigable waters. Further, the court ruled that the smoke damage was caused by emissions of soot and ash by vessels located on navigable waters or berthed at the defendant's piers.

---

[11] In *Gutierrez*, the Court concluded that "things about a ship, whether the hull, the decks, the machinery, the tools furnished, the stowage, or the cargo containers, must be reasonably fit for the purpose for which they are to be used." 373 U.S., at 213. In *Alaska S.S. Co. v. Petterson*, 347 U.S. 396 (1954), *aff'g* 205 F.2d 478 (CA9 1953), and *Rogers v. United States Lines*, 347 U.S. 984 (1954), rev'g 205 F.2d 57 (CA3 1954), the Court decided without opinion that an unseaworthiness recovery would be possible to a longshoreman injured by equipment brought aboard ship by the stevedore company. In both these cases, the accident occurred on navigable water: both longshoremen were injured while in the hold of a ship by defective apparatus attached to the ship's gear.

3. The Modern Criteria for Jurisdiction in Tort: Locality Plus Nexus

a. The Nexus Criterion

JEROME B. GRUBART, INC. v. GREAT LAKES DREDGE & DOCK COMPANY

513 U.S. 527, 115 S. Ct. 1043, 130 L. Ed. 2d 1024, 1995 AMC 913 (1995)

Justice SOUTER delivered the opinion of the Court.

On April 13, 1992, water from the Chicago River poured into a freight tunnel running under the river and thence into the basements of buildings in the downtown Chicago Loop. Allegedly, the flooding resulted from events several months earlier, when the respondent Great Lakes Dredge and Dock Company had used a crane, sitting on a barge in the river next to a bridge, to drive piles into the river bed above the tunnel. The issue before us is whether a court of the United States has admiralty jurisdiction to determine and limit the extent of Great Lakes's tort liability. We hold the case to be within federal admiralty jurisdiction.

I

The complaint, together with affidavits subject to no objection, alleges the following facts. In 1990, Great Lakes bid on a contract with the petitioner city of Chicago to replace wooden pilings clustered around the piers of several bridges spanning the Chicago River, a navigable waterway within the meaning of *The Daniel Ball*, 10 Wall. 557, 563, 19 L. Ed. 999 (1871). *See Escanaba Co. v. Chicago*, 107 U.S. 678, 683, 2 S. Ct. 185, 188-189, 27 L. Ed. 442 (1883). The pilings (called dolphins) keep ships from bumping into the piers and so protect both. After winning the contract, Great Lakes carried out the work with two barges towed by a tug. One barge carried pilings; the other carried a crane that pulled out old pilings and helped drive in new ones.

In August and September 1991, Great Lakes replaced the pilings around the piers projecting into the river and supporting the Kinzie Street Bridge. After towing the crane-carrying barge into position near one of the piers, Great Lakes's employees secured the barge to the river bed with spuds, or long metal legs that project down from the barge and anchor it. The workers then used the crane on the barge to pull up old pilings, stow them on the other barge, and drive new pilings into the river bed around the piers. About seven months later, an eddy formed in the river near the bridge as the collapsing walls or ceiling of a freight tunnel running under the river opened the tunnel to river water, which flowed through to flood buildings in the Loop.

After the flood, many of the victims brought actions in state court against Great Lakes and the city of Chicago, claiming that in the course of replacing the pilings Great Lakes had negligently weakened the tunnel structure, which Chicago (its owner) had not properly maintained. Great Lakes then brought this lawsuit in the United States District Court, invoking federal admiralty jurisdiction. Count I of the complaint seeks the protection of the Limitation of Vessel Owner's Liability Act (Limitation Act), 46 U.S.C.App. § 181 *et seq.*, a statute that would, in effect, permit the admiralty court to decide whether Great

Lakes committed a tort and, if so, to limit Great Lakes's liability to the value of the vessels (the tug and two barges) involved if the tort was committed "without the privity or knowledge" of the vessels' owner, 46 U.S.C.App. § 183(a). Counts II and III of Great Lakes's complaint ask for indemnity and contribution from the city for any resulting loss to Great Lakes.

The city, joined by petitioner Jerome B. Grubart, Inc., one of the state-court plaintiffs, filed a motion to dismiss this suit for lack of admiralty jurisdiction. FED. R. CIV. P. 12(b)(1). The District Court granted the motion, the Seventh Circuit reversed, *Great Lakes Dredge & Dock Co. v. Chicago*, 3 F.3d 225 (1993), and we granted certiorari, 510 U.S. ___, 114 S. Ct. 1047, 127 L. Ed. 2d 370 (1994). We now affirm.

II

* * *

A

A federal court's authority to hear cases in admiralty flows initially from the Constitution, which "extend[s]" federal judicial power "to all Cases of admiralty and maritime Jurisdiction." U.S. CONST., Art. III, § 2. Congress has embodied that power in a statute giving federal district courts "original jurisdiction ... of ... [a]ny civil case of admiralty or maritime jurisdiction...." 28 U.S.C. § 1333(1).

The traditional test for admiralty tort jurisdiction asked only whether the tort occurred on navigable waters. If it did, admiralty jurisdiction followed; if it did not, admiralty jurisdiction did not exist. *See, e.g.*, *Thomas v. Lane*, 23 F.Cas. 957, 960 (No. 13902) (CC Me. 1813) (Story, J., on Circuit). This ostensibly simple locality test was complicated by the rule that the injury had to be "wholly" sustained on navigable waters for the tort to be within admiralty. *The Plymouth*, 3 Wall. 20, 34, 18 L. Ed. 125 (1866) (no jurisdiction over tort action brought by the owner of warehouse destroyed in a fire that started on board a ship docked nearby). Thus, admiralty courts lacked jurisdiction over, say, a claim following a ship's collision with a pier insofar as it injured the pier, for admiralty law treated the pier as an extension of the land. *Martin v. West*, 222 U.S. 191, 197, 32 S. Ct. 42, 43, 56 L. Ed. 159 (1911); *Cleveland T. & V.R. Co. v. Cleveland S.S. Co.*, 208 U.S. 316, 319, 28 S. Ct. 414, 415, 52 L. Ed. 508 (1908).

This latter rule was changed in 1948, however, when Congress enacted the Extension of Admiralty Jurisdiction Act, 62 Stat. 496. The Act provided that "[t]he admiralty and maritime jurisdiction of the United States shall extend to and include all cases of damage or injury, to person or property, caused by a vessel on navigable water, notwithstanding that such damage or injury be done or consummated on land." 46 U.S.C.App. § 740. The purpose of the Act was to end concern over the sometimes confusing line between land and water, by investing admiralty with jurisdiction over "all cases" where the injury was caused by a ship or other vessel on navigable water, even if such injury occurred on land. *See, e.g.*, *Gutierrez v. Waterman S.S. Corp.*, 373 U.S. 206, 209-210, 83 S. Ct. 1185, 1187-1188, 10

L. Ed. 2d 297 (1963); *Executive Jet Aviation, Inc. v. City of Cleveland*, 409 U.S. 249, 260, 93 S. Ct. 493, 500-501, 34 L. Ed. 2d 454 (1972).

After this congressional modification to gather the odd case into admiralty, the jurisdictional rule was qualified again in three decisions of this Court aimed at keeping a different class of odd cases out. In the first case, *Executive Jet, supra*, tort claims arose out of the wreck of an airplane that collided with a flock of birds just after take-off on a domestic flight and fell into the navigable waters of Lake Erie. We held that admiralty lacked jurisdiction to consider the claims. We wrote that "a purely mechanical application of the locality test" was not always "sensible" or "consonant with the purposes of maritime law," *id.*, at 261, 93 S. Ct., at 501, as when (for example) the literal and universal application of the locality rule would require admiralty courts to adjudicate tort disputes between colliding swimmers, *id.*, at 255, 93 S. Ct., at 498. We held that "claims arising from airplane accidents are not cognizable in admiralty" despite the location of the harm, unless "the wrong bear[s] a significant relationship to traditional maritime activity." *Id.*, at 268, 93 S. Ct., at 504.

The second decision, *Foremost Ins. Co. v. Richardson*, 457 U.S. 668, 102 S. Ct. 2654, 73 L. Ed. 2d 300 (1982), dealt with tort claims arising out of the collision of two pleasure boats in a navigable river estuary. We held that admiralty courts had jurisdiction, *id.*, at 677, 102 S. Ct., at 2659, even though jurisdiction existed only if "the wrong" had "a significant connection with traditional maritime activity," *id.*, at 674, 102 S. Ct., at 2658. We conceded that pleasure boats themselves had little to do with the maritime commerce lying at the heart of the admiralty court's basic work, *id.*, at 674-675, 102 S. Ct., at 2658-2659, but we nonetheless found the necessary relationship in "[t]he potential disruptive impact [upon maritime commerce] of a collision between boats on navigable waters, when coupled with the traditional concern that admiralty law holds for navigation...." *Id.*, at 675, 102 S. Ct., at 2658.

In the most recent of the trilogy, *Sisson v. Ruby*, 497 U.S. 358, 110 S. Ct. 2892, 111 L. Ed. 2d 292 (1990), we held that a federal admiralty court had jurisdiction over tort claims arising when a fire, caused by a defective washer/dryer aboard a pleasure boat docked at a marina, burned the boat, other boats docked nearby, and the marina itself. *Id.*, at 367, 110 S. Ct., at 2898. We elaborated on the enquiry exemplified in *Executive Jet* and *Foremost* by focusing on two points to determine the relationship of a claim to the objectives of admiralty jurisdiction. We noted, first, that the incident causing the harm, the burning of docked boats at a marina on navigable waters, was of a sort "likely to disrupt [maritime] commercial activity." *Id.*, 497 U.S., at 363, 110 S. Ct., at 2896. Second, we found a "substantial relationship" with "traditional maritime activity" in the kind of activity from which the incident arose, "the storage and maintenance of a vessel ... on navigable waters." *Id.*, at 365-367, 110 S. Ct., at 2897-2898.

After *Sisson*, then, a party seeking to invoke federal admiralty jurisdiction pursuant to 28 U.S.C. § 1333(1) over a tort claim must satisfy conditions both of location and of connection with maritime activity. A court applying the location test must determine whether the tort occurred on navigable water or whether injury suffered on land was caused by a vessel on navigable water. 46 U.S.C.App. § 740. The connection test raises two issues. A court, first, must "assess the general features of the type of incident involved," 497 U.S., at 363, 110 S. Ct., at 2896, to determine whether the incident has "a potentially disruptive impact on maritime commerce," *id.*, at 364, n. 2, 110 S. Ct., at 2896, n. 2. Second, a court must determine whether "the general character" of the "activity giving rise to the incident" shows a "substantial relationship to traditional maritime activity." *Id.*, at 365, 364, and n. 2, 110 S. Ct., at 2897, 2896, and n. 2. We now apply the tests to the facts of this case.

B

The location test is, of course, readily satisfied. If Great Lakes caused the flood, it must have done so by weakening the structure of the tunnel while it drove in new pilings or removed old ones around the bridge piers. The weakening presumably took place as Great Lakes's workers lifted and replaced the pilings with a crane that sat on a barge stationed in the Chicago River. The place in the river where the barge sat, and from which workers directed the crane, is in the "navigable waters of the United States." *Escanaba Co.*, 107 U.S., at 683, 2 S. Ct., at 188-189. Thus, if Great Lakes committed a tort, it must have done it while on navigable waters.

It must also have done it "by a vessel." Even though the barge was fastened to the river bottom and was in use as a work platform at the times in question, at other times it was used for transportation. *See* 3 F.3d, at 229. Petitioners do not here seriously dispute the conclusion of each court below that the Great Lakes barge is, for admiralty tort purposes, a "vessel." The fact that the pile-driving was done with a crane makes no difference under the location test, given the maritime law that ordinarily treats an "appurtenance" attached to a vessel in navigable waters as part of the vessel itself. *See, e.g., Victory Carriers, Inc. v. Law,* 404 U.S. 202, 210-211, 92 S. Ct. 418, 424-425, 30 L. Ed. 2d 383 (1971); *Gutierrez,* 373 U.S., at 209-210, 83 S. Ct., at 1187-1188.[1]

Because the injuries suffered by Grubart and the other flood victims were caused by a vessel on navigable water, the location enquiry would seem to be at an end, "notwithstanding that such damage or injury [have been] done or consummated on land." 46 U.S.C.App. § 740. Both Grubart and Chicago nonetheless ask us to subject the Extension Act to limitations not apparent from its text. While they concede that the Act refers to "all cases of damage or injury," they argue that "all" must not mean literally every such case, no matter how great the distance between the vessel's tortious activity and the resulting harm. They contend that, to be within the Act, the damage must be close in time and space to the activity that caused it: that it must occur "reasonably contemporaneously" with the negligent conduct and no "farther from navigable waters than the reach of the vessel, its appur-

[1] Grubart argues, based on *Margin v. Sea-Land Services, Inc.*, 812 F.2d 973, 975 (CA5 1987), that an appurtenance is considered part of the vessel only when it is defective. *See Brief for Petitioner* in No. 93-762, pp. 34-35 (Grubart Brief). *Margin*, however, does not so hold. It dealt with a land-based crane that lowered a ship's hatch cover dangerously close to a welder working on a dock, and its result turned not on the condition of the hatch cover, the putative appurtenance, but on the fact that the plaintiff did not allege that "vessel negligence proximately caused his injury." 812 F.2d, at 977. Indeed, the argument that Congress intended admiralty jurisdiction to extend to injuries caused by defective appurtenances, but not to appurtenances in good condition when operated negligently, makes no sense. *See Gutierrez,* 373 U.S., at 210, 83 S. Ct., at 1188 ("There is no distinction in admiralty between torts committed by the ship itself and by the ship's personnel while operating it ...").

tenances and cargo." For authority, they point to this Court's statement in Gutierrez, *supra*, that jurisdiction is present when the "impact" of the tortious activity "is felt ashore at a time and place not remote from the wrongful act." *Id.*, at 210, 83 S. Ct., at 1188.[2]

The demerits of this argument lie not only in its want of textual support for its nonremoteness rule, but in its disregard of a less stringent but familiar proximity condition tied to the language of the statute. The Act uses the phrase "caused by," which more than one Court of Appeals has read as requiring what tort law has traditionally called "proximate causation." *See, e.g., Pryor v. American President Lines*, 520 F.2d 974, 979 (CA4 1975), *cert. denied*, 423 U.S. 1055, 96 S. Ct. 787, 46 L. Ed. 2d 644 (1976); *Adams v. Harris County*, 452 F.2d 994, 996-997 (CA5 1971), *cert. denied*, 406 U.S. 968, 92 S. Ct. 2414, 32 L. Ed. 2d 667 (1972). This classic tort notion normally eliminates the bizarre, *cf. Palsgraf v. Long Island R. Co.*, 248 N.Y. 339, 162 N.E. 99 (1928), and its use should obviate not only the complication but even the need for further temporal or spatial limitations. Nor is reliance on familiar proximate causation inconsistent with *Gutierrez*, which used its nonremote language, not to announce a special test, but simply to distinguish its own facts (the victim having slipped on beans spilling from cargo containers being unloaded from a ship) from what the Court called "[v]arious far-fetched hypotheticals," such as injury to someone slipping on beans that continue to leak from the containers after they had been shipped from Puerto Rico to a warehouse in Denver. 373 U.S., at 210, 83 S. Ct., at 1188. *See also Victory Carriers, supra*, 404 U.S., at 210-211, 92 S. Ct., at 424-425.

* * *

C

We now turn to the maritime connection enquiries, the first being whether the incident involved was of a sort with the potential to disrupt maritime commerce. In *Sisson*, we described the features of the incident in general terms as "a fire on a vessel docked at a marina on navigable waters," *id.*, at 363, 110 S. Ct., at 2896, and determined that such an incident "plainly satisf[ied]" the first maritime connection requirement, *ibid.*, because the fire could have "spread to nearby commercial vessels or ma[d]e the marina inaccessible to such vessels" and therefore "[c]ertainly" had a "potentially disruptive impact on maritime commerce." *Id.*, at 362, 110 S. Ct., at 2896. We noted that this first prong went to potential effects, not to the "particular facts of the incident," noting that in both *Executive Jet* and *Foremost* we had focused not on the specific facts at hand but on whether the "general features" of the incident were "likely to disrupt commercial activity." 497 U.S., at 363, 110 S. Ct., at 2896.

The first *Sisson* test turns, then, on a description of the incident at an intermediate level of possible generality. To speak of the incident as "fire" would have been too general to differentiate cases; at the other extreme, to have described the fire as damaging nothing but pleasure boats and their tie-up facilities would have ignored, among other things, the

[2] At oral argument, counsel for the city undercut this argument by conceding that admiralty jurisdiction would govern claims arising from an incident in which a ship on navigable waters slipped its moorings, drifted into a dam, and caused a breach in the dam that resulted in flooding of surrounding territory. Tr. of Oral Arg. 17.

capacity of pleasure boats to endanger commercial shipping that happened to be nearby. We rejected both extremes and instead asked whether the incident could be seen within a class of incidents that posed more than a fanciful risk to commercial shipping.

Following *Sisson,* the "general features" of the incident at issue here may be described as damage by a vessel in navigable water to an underwater structure. So characterized, there is little question that this is the kind of incident that has a "potentially disruptive impact on maritime commerce." As it actually turned out in this case, damaging a structure beneath the river bed could lead to a disruption in the water course itself, App. 33 (eddy formed above the leak); and, again as it actually happened, damaging a structure so situated could lead to restrictions on the navigational use of the waterway during required repairs. *See Pet. for Cert.* in No. 93-1094, p. 22a (District Court found that after the flood "[t]he river remained closed for over a month," "[r]iver traffic ceased, several commuter ferries were stranded, and many barges could not enter the river system ... because the river level was lowered to aid repair efforts"). *Cf. Pennzoil Producing Co. v. Offshore Express, Inc.*, 943 F.2d 1465 (CA5 1991) (admiralty suit when vessel struck and ruptured gas pipeline and gas exploded); *Marathon Pipe Line Co. v. Drilling Rig Rowan/Odessa,* 761 F.2d 229, 233 (CA5 1985) (admiralty jurisdiction when vessel struck pipeline, "a fixed structure on the seabed"); *Orange Beach Water, Sewer, and Fire Protection Authority v. M/V Alva,* 680 F.2d 1374 (CA11 1982) (admiralty suit when vessel struck underwater pipeline).

In the second *Sisson* enquiry, we look to whether the general character of the activity giving rise to the incident shows a substantial relationship to traditional maritime activity. We ask whether a tortfeasor's activity, commercial or noncommercial, on navigable waters is so closely related to activity traditionally subject to admiralty law that the reasons for applying special admiralty rules would apply in the case at hand. Navigation of boats in navigable waters clearly falls within the substantial relationship, *Foremost,* 457 U.S., at 675, 102 S. Ct., at 2658-2659; storing them at a marina on navigable waters is close enough, *Sisson, supra,* 497 U.S., at 367, 110 S. Ct., at 2898; whereas in flying an airplane over the water, *Executive Jet,* 409 U.S., at 270-271, 93 S. Ct., at 505-506, as in swimming, *id.*, at 255-256, 93 S. Ct., at 498-499, the relationship is too attenuated.

On like reasoning, the "activity giving rise to the incident" in this case, *Sisson, supra,* 497 U.S., at 364, 110 S. Ct., at 2897, should be characterized as repair or maintenance work on a navigable waterway performed from a vessel. Described in this way, there is no question that the activity is substantially related to traditional maritime activity, for barges and similar vessels have traditionally been engaged in repair work similar to what Great Lakes contracted to perform here. *See, e.g., Shea v. Rev-Lyn Contracting Co.*, 868 F.2d 515, 518 (CA1 1989) (bridge repair by crane-carrying barge); *Nelson v. United States,* 639 F.2d 469, 472 (CA9 1980) (Kennedy, J.) (repair of wave suppressor from a barge); *In re New York Dock Co.*, 61 F.2d 777 (CA2 1932) (pile driving from crane-carrying barge in connection with the building of a dock); *In re P. Sanford* Ross, Inc., 196 F. 921, 923-924 (EDNY 1912) (pile driving from crane-carrying barge close to water's edge), *rev'd on other grounds,* 204 F. 248 (CA2 1913); *cf. In re The V-14813,* 65 F.2d 789, 790 (CA5 1933) ("[t]here are many cases holding that a dredge, or a barge with a pile driver, employed on navigable waters, is subject to maritime jurisdiction"); *Lawrence v. Flatboat*, 84 F. 200 (SD Ala.1897) (pile driving from crane-carrying barge in connection with the erection of bulkheads), aff'd sub nom. *Southern Log Cart & Supply Co. v. Lawrence*, 86 F. 907 (CA5 1898).

The city argues, to the contrary, that a proper application of the activity prong of *Sisson* would consider the city's own alleged failure at properly maintaining and operating the tunnel system that runs under the river. City Brief 48-49. If this asserted proximate cause of the flood victims' injuries were considered, the city submits, its failure to resemble any traditional maritime activity would take this case out of admiralty.

The city misreads *Sisson*, however, which did not consider the activities of the washer/dryer manufacturer, who was possibly an additional tortfeasor, and whose activities were hardly maritime; the activities of *Sisson*, the boat owner, supplied the necessary substantial relationship to traditional maritime activity. Likewise, in *Foremost*, we said that "[b]ecause the 'wrong' here involves the negligent operation of a vessel on navigable waters, we believe that it has a sufficient nexus to traditional maritime activity to sustain admiralty jurisdiction...." 457 U.S., at 674, 102 S. Ct. at 2658. By using the word "involves," we made it clear that we need to look only to whether one of the arguably proximate causes of the incident originated in the maritime activity of a tortfeasor: as long as one of the putative tortfeasors was engaged in traditional maritime activity the allegedly wrongful activity will "involve" such traditional maritime activity and will meet the second nexus prong. Thus, even if we were to identify the "activity giving rise to the incident" as including the acts of the city as well as Great Lakes, admiralty jurisdiction would nevertheless attach. That result would be true to *Sisson*'s requirement of a "substantial relationship" between the "activity giving rise to the incident" and traditional maritime activity. *Sisson* did not require, as the city in effect asserts, that there be a complete identity between the two. The substantial relationship test is satisfied when at least one alleged tortfeasor was engaging in activity substantially related to traditional maritime activity and such activity is claimed to have been a proximate cause of the incident.

Petitioners also argue that we might get a different result simply by characterizing the "activity" in question at a different level of generality, perhaps as "repair and maintenance," or, as "pile driving near a bridge." The city is, of course, correct that a tortfeasor's activity can be described at a sufficiently high level of generality to eliminate any hint of maritime connection, and if that were properly done *Sisson* would bar assertion of admiralty jurisdiction. But to suggest that such hyper-generalization ought to be the rule would convert *Sisson* into a vehicle for eliminating admiralty jurisdiction. Although there is inevitably some play in the joints in selecting the right level of generality when applying the *Sisson* test, the inevitable imprecision is not an excuse for whimsy. The test turns on the comparison of traditional maritime activity to the arguably maritime character of the tortfeasor's activity in a given case; the comparison would merely be frustrated by eliminating the maritime aspect of the tortfeasor's activity from consideration.[4]

---

[4] The city also proposes that we define the activity as "the operation of an underground tunnel connected to Loop buildings." City Brief 49-50. But doing this would eliminate the maritime tortfeasor's activity from consideration entirely. This (like the choice of a supreme level of generality, described in the text) would turn *Sisson v. Ruby*, 497 U.S. 358, 110 S. Ct. 2892, 111 L. Ed. 2d 292 (1990), on its head, from a test to weed out torts without a maritime connection into an arbitrary exercise for eliminating jurisdiction over even vessel-related torts connected to traditional maritime commerce.

Grubart makes an additional claim that *Sisson* is being given too expansive a reading. If the activity at issue here is considered maritime-related, it argues, then virtually "every activity involving a vessel on navigable waters" would be "a traditional maritime activity sufficient to invoke maritime jurisdiction." Grubart Brief 6. But this is not fatal criticism. This Court has not proposed any radical alteration of the traditional criteria for invoking admiralty jurisdiction in tort cases, but has simply followed the lead of the lower federal courts in rejecting a location rule so rigid as to extend admiralty to a case involving an airplane, not a vessel, engaged in an activity far removed from anything traditionally maritime. *See Executive Jet*, 409 U.S., at 268-274, 93 S. Ct., at 504-506; *see also Peytavin v. Government Employees Ins. Co.*, 453 F.2d 1121, 1127 (CA5 1972) (no jurisdiction over claim for personal injury by motorist who was rear-ended while waiting for a ferry on a floating pontoon serving as the ferry's landing); *Chapman v. Grosse Pointe Farms*, 385 F.2d 962 (CA6 1967) (no admiralty jurisdiction over claim of swimmer who injured himself when diving off pier into shallow but navigable water). In the cases after *Executive Jet*, the Court stressed the need for a maritime connection, but found one in the navigation or berthing of pleasure boats, despite the facts that the pleasure boat activity took place near shore, where States have a strong interest in applying their own tort law, or was not on all fours with the maritime shipping and commerce that has traditionally made up the business of most maritime courts. *Sisson*, 497 U.S., at 367, 110 S. Ct., at 2898; *Foremost*, 457 U.S., at 675, 102 S. Ct., at 2658-2659. Although we agree with petitioners that these cases do not say that every tort involving a vessel on navigable waters falls within the scope of admiralty jurisdiction no matter what, they do show that ordinarily that will be so.[5]

III

Perhaps recognizing the difficulty of escaping the case law, petitioners ask us to change it. In cases "involving land based parties and injuries," the city would have us adopt a condition of jurisdiction that "the totality of the circumstances reflects a federal interest in protecting maritime commerce sufficiently weighty to justify shifting what would otherwise be state-court litigation into federal court under the federal law of admiralty." City Brief 32. Grubart and the city say that the Fifth Circuit has applied a somewhat similar "four-factor test" looking to "the functions and roles of the parties; the types of vehicles and instrumentalities involved; the causation and the type of injury; and traditional concepts of the role of admiralty law." *Kelly v. Smith*, 485 F.2d 520, 525 (CA5 1973); *see also Molett v. Penrod Drilling Co.*, 826 F.2d 1419, 1426 (CA5 1987) (adding three more factors: the "impact of the event on maritime shipping and commerce"; "the desirability of a uniform national rule to apply to such matters"; and "the need for admiralty 'expertise' in the trial and decision of the case"), *cert. denied* sub nom. *Columbus-McKinnon, Inc. v. Gearench, Inc.*, 493 U.S. 1003, 110 S. Ct. 563, 107 L. Ed. 2d 558 (1989). Although they point out that *Sisson* disapproved the use of four-factor or seven-factor tests "where all the relevant

---

[5] Because we conclude that the tort alleged in Count I of Great Lakes's complaint satisfies both the location and connection tests necessary for admiralty jurisdiction under 28 U.S.C. § 1333(1), we need not consider respondent's alternative argument that the Extension of Admiralty Jurisdiction Act, 46 U.S.C.App. § 740, provides an independent basis of federal jurisdiction over the complaint.

entities are engaged in similar types of activity," this rule implicitly left the matter open for cases like this one, where most of the victims, and one of the tortfeasors, are based on land. *See* 497 U.S., at 365, n. 3, 110 S. Ct. at 2897 ("Different issues may be raised by a case in which one of the instrumentalities is engaged in a traditional maritime activity, but the other is not"). The city argues that there is a good reason why cases like this one should get different treatment. Since the basic rationale for federal admiralty jurisdiction is "protection of maritime commerce through uniform rules of decision," the proposed jurisdictional test would improve on *Sisson* in limiting the scope of admiralty jurisdiction more exactly to its rationale. A multiple factor test would minimize, if not eliminate, the awkward possibility that federal admiralty rules or procedures will govern a case, to the disadvantage of state law, when admiralty's purpose does not require it. *Cf. Foremost, supra,* at 677-686, 102 S. Ct., at 2659-2664 (Powell, J., dissenting).

Although the arguments are not frivolous, they do not persuade. It is worth recalling that the *Sisson* tests are aimed at the same objectives invoked to support a new multifactor test, the elimination of admiralty jurisdiction where the rationale for the jurisdiction does not support it. If the tort produces no potential threat to maritime commerce or occurs during activity lacking a substantial relationship to traditional maritime activity, *Sisson* assumes that the objectives of admiralty jurisdiction probably do not require its exercise, even if the location test is satisfied. If, however, the *Sisson* tests are also satisfied, it is not apparent why the need for admiralty jurisdiction in aid of maritime commerce somehow becomes less acute merely because land-based parties happen to be involved. Certainly Congress did not think a land-based party necessarily diluted the need for admiralty jurisdiction or it would have kept its hands off the primitive location test.

Of course one could claim it to be odd that under *Sisson* a land-based party (or more than one) may be subject to admiralty jurisdiction, but it would appear no less odd under the city's test that a maritime tortfeasor in the most traditional mould might be subject to state common-law jurisdiction. Other things being equal, it is not evident why the first supposed anomaly is worse than the second. But other things are not even equal. As noted just above, Congress has already made the judgment, in the Extension Act, that a land-based victim may properly be subject to admiralty jurisdiction. Surely a land-based joint tortfeasor has no claim to supposedly more favorable treatment.

Nor are these the only objections to the city's position. Contrary to what the city suggests, City Brief 10, 14-15, 25-26, 30, exercise of federal admiralty jurisdiction does not result in automatic displacement of state law. It is true that, "[w]ith admiralty jurisdiction comes the application of substantive admiralty law." *East River S.S. Corp. v. Transamerica DeLaval Inc.*, 476 U.S. 858, 864, 106 S. Ct. 2295, 2298-2299, 90 L. Ed. 2d 865 (1986). But, to characterize that law, as the city apparently does, as "federal rules of decision," City Brief 15, is "a destructive oversimplification of the highly intricate interplay of the States and the National Government in their regulation of maritime commerce. It is true that state law must yield to the needs of a uniform federal maritime law when this Court finds inroads on a harmonious system. But this limitation still leaves the States a wide scope." *Romero v. International Terminal Operating Co.*, 358 U.S. 354, 373, 79 S. Ct. 468, 480-

481, 3 L. Ed. 2d 368 (1959) (footnote omitted). *See East River, supra*, at 864-865, 106 S. Ct., at 2298-2299 ("Drawn from state and federal sources, the general maritime law is an amalgam of traditional common-law rules, modifications of those rules, and newly created rules" (footnote omitted)). Thus, the city's proposal to synchronize the jurisdictional enquiry with the test for determining the applicable substantive law would discard a fundamental feature of admiralty law, that federal admiralty courts sometimes do apply state law. *See, e.g., American Dredging Co. v. Miller*, 510 U.S. ___, ___, 114 S. Ct. 981, 987, 127 L. Ed. 2d 285 (1994); *see also* 1 S. FRIEDELL, BENEDICT ON ADMIRALTY § 112 p. 7-49 (7th ed. 1994).[6]

Finally, on top of these objections going to the city's premises there is added a most powerful one based on the practical consequences of adopting a multifactor test. Although the existing case law tempers the locality test with the added requirements looking to potential harm and traditional activity, it reflects customary practice in seeing jurisdiction as the norm when the tort originates with a vessel in navigable waters, and in treating departure from the locality principle as the exception. For better or worse, the case law has thus carved out the approximate shape of admiralty jurisdiction in a way that admiralty lawyers understand reasonably well. As against this approach, so familiar and relatively easy, the proposed four- or seven-factor test would be hard to apply, jettisoning relative predictability for the open-ended rough-and-tumble of factors, inviting complex argument in a trial court and a virtually inevitable appeal.

Consider, for example, just one of the factors under the city's test, requiring a district court at the beginning of every purported admiralty case to determine the source (state or federal) of the applicable substantive law. The difficulty of doing that was an important reason why this Court in Romero, *supra*, was unable to hold that maritime claims fell within the scope of the federal-question-jurisdiction statute, 28 U.S.C. § 1331. 358 U.S., at 375-376, 79 S. Ct., at 481-482 ("sound judicial policy does not encourage a situation which necessitates constant adjudication of the boundaries of state and federal competence"). That concern applies just as strongly to cases invoking a district court's admiralty jurisdiction under 28 U.S.C. § 1333, under which the jurisdictional enquiry for maritime torts has traditionally been quite uncomplicated.

Reasons of practice, then, are as weighty as reasons of theory for rejecting the city's call to adopt a multifactor test for admiralty jurisdiction for the benefit of land-based parties to a tort action.

---

[6] We will content ourselves simply with raising a question about another of the city's assumptions, which does not go to anything dispositive for us. It is true that this Court has said that "the primary focus of admiralty jurisdiction is unquestionably the protection of maritime commerce," *Foremost Ins. Co. v. Richardson*, 457 U.S. 668, 674, 102 S. Ct. 2654, 2658, 73 L. Ed. 2d 300 (1982); *see Sisson*, 497 U.S., at 367, 110 S. Ct., at 2898; *see id.*, at 364, n.2, 110 S. Ct., at 2896- 2897, n.2, a premise that recently has been questioned, *see* Casto, *The Origins of Federal Admiralty Jurisdiction in an Age of Privateers, Smugglers, and Pirates*, 37 AM.J.LEGAL HIST. 117 (1993). However that may be, this Court has never limited the interest in question to the "protection of maritime commerce through uniform rules of decision," as the city would have it. City Brief 19. Granted, whatever its precise purpose, it is likely that Congress thought of uniformity of substantive law as a subsidiary goal conducive to furthering that purpose. *See* Currie, *Federalism and the Admiralty: "The Devil's Own Mess,"* 1960 S. CT. REV. 158, 163 ("[A] uniform law was apparently one reason for the establishment of the admiralty jurisdiction in 1789" (footnote omitted)). But we are unwilling to rule out that the first Congress saw a value in federal admiralty courts beyond fostering uniformity of substantive law, stemming, say, from a concern with local bias similar to the presupposition for diversity jurisdiction. *See* THE FEDERALIST No. 80, p. 538 (J. Cooke ed. 1961) (A. Hamilton) ("maritime causes ... so commonly affect the rights of foreigners"); 1 M. FARRAND, RECORDS OF THE FEDERAL CONVENTION OF 1787, p. 124 (1911); 2 *id.*, at 46; *see generally* D. ROBERTSON, ADMIRALTY AND FEDERALISM 95-103 (1970). After all, if uniformity of substantive law had been Congress's only concern, it could have left admiralty jurisdiction in the state courts subject to an appeal to a national tribunal (as it did with federal-question jurisdiction until 1875, and as the Articles of Federation had done with cases of prize and capture).

Accordingly, we conclude that the Court of Appeals correctly held that the District Court had admiralty jurisdiction over the respondent's Limitation Act suit. The judgment of the Court of Appeals is

Affirmed.

Justice O'CONNOR, concurring.

I concur in the Court's judgment and opinion. The Court properly holds that, when a court is faced with a case involving multiple tortfeasors, some of whom may not be maritime actors, if one of the putative tortfeasors was engaged in traditional maritime activity alleged to have proximately caused the incident, then the supposedly wrongful activity "involves" traditional maritime activity. The possible involvement of other, nonmaritime parties does not affect the jurisdictional inquiry as to the maritime party. Ante, at 1051-1052. I do not, however, understand the Court's opinion to suggest that, having found admiralty jurisdiction over a particular claim against a particular party, a court must then exercise admiralty jurisdiction over all the claims and parties involved in the case. Rather, the court should engage in the usual supplemental jurisdiction and impleader inquiries. *See* 28 U.S.C. § 1367 (1988 ed., Supp. V); FED. R. CIV. P. 14; *see also* ante, at 1047. I find nothing in the Court's opinion to the contrary.

Justice THOMAS, with whom Justice SCALIA joins, concurring in the judgment.

I agree with the majority's conclusion that 28 U.S.C. § 1333(1) grants the District Court jurisdiction over the great Chicago flood of 1992. But I write separately because I cannot agree with the test the Court applies to determine the boundaries of admiralty and maritime jurisdiction. Instead of continuing our unquestioning allegiance to the multi-factor approach of *Sisson v. Ruby*, 497 U.S. 358, 110 S. Ct. 2892, 111 L. Ed. 2d 292 (1990), I would restore the jurisdictional inquiry to the simple question whether the tort occurred on a vessel on the navigable waters of the United States. If so, then admiralty jurisdiction exists. This clear, bright-line rule, which the Court applied until recently, ensures that judges and litigants will not waste their resources in determining the extent of federal subject-matter jurisdiction.

I

* * *

As recently as 1972, courts and parties experienced little difficulty in determining whether a case triggered admiralty jurisdiction, thanks to the simple "situs rule." *In The Plymouth*, 3 Wall. 20, 36, 18 L. Ed. 125 (1866), this Court articulated the situs rule thus: "[e]very species of tort, however occurring, and whether on board a vessel or not, if upon the high seas or navigable waters, is of admiralty cognizance." This simple, clear test, which Justice Story pronounced while riding circuit, *see Thomas v. Lane*, 23 F.Cas. 957, 960 (CC Me.1813), did not require alteration until 1948, when Congress included within the admiralty jurisdiction torts caused on water, but whose effects were felt on land. *See Extension of Admiralty Jurisdiction Act*, 62 Stat. 496, 46 U.S.C.App. § 740.

The simplicity of this test was marred by modern cases that tested the boundaries of admiralty jurisdiction with ever more unusual facts. In *Executive Jet Aviation, Inc. v. City of*

Cleveland, 409 U.S. 249, 93 S. Ct. 493, 34 L. Ed. 2d 454 (1972), we held that a plane crash in Lake Erie was not an admiralty case within the meaning of § 1333(1) because the tort did not "bear a significant relationship to traditional maritime activity." *Id.*, at 268, 93 S. Ct., at 504. What subsequent cases have failed to respect, however, is *Executive Jet's* clear limitation to torts involving aircraft. As we said: "One area in which locality as the exclusive test of admiralty tort jurisdiction has given rise to serious problems in application is that of aviation.... [W]e have concluded that maritime locality alone is not a sufficient predicate for admiralty jurisdiction in aviation tort cases." *Id.*, at 261, 93 S. Ct., at 501 (emphasis added). Our identification of the "significant relationship" factor occurred wholly in the context of a discussion of the difficulties that aircraft posed for maritime law. In fact, while we recognized the extensive criticism of the strict locality rule, we noted that "for the traditional types of maritime torts, the traditional test has worked quite satisfactorily." *Id.*, at 254, 93 S. Ct., at 497. Thus, *Executive Jet*, properly read, holds that if a tort occurred on board a vessel on the navigable waters, the situs test applies, but if the tort involved an airplane, then the "significant relationship" requirement is added.

Although it modified the strict locality test, *Executive Jet* still retained a clear rule that I could apply comfortably to the main business of the admiralty court. Nonetheless, the simplicity and clarity of this approach met its demise in *Foremost Ins. Co. v. Richardson*, 457 U.S. 668, 102 S. Ct. 2654, 73 L. Ed. 2d 300 (1982). That case involved the collision of two pleasure boats on the navigable waters, a tort that some commentators had argued did not fall within the admiralty jurisdiction because it did not implicate maritime commerce. *See, e.g.*, Stolz, *Pleasure Boating and Admiralty: Erie at Sea*, 51 CALIF.L.REV. 661 (1963). The Court could have resolved the case and found jurisdiction simply by applying the situs test. Instead, responding to the arguments that admiralty jurisdiction was limited to commercial maritime activity, the Court found that the tort's "significant connection with traditional maritime activity" and the accident's "potential disruptive impact" on maritime commerce prompted an exercise of federal jurisdiction. 457 U.S., at 674-675, 102 S. Ct., at 2658-2659.

It is clear that *Foremost* overextended *Executive Jet*, which had reserved the significant relationship inquiry for aviation torts. As Justice SCALIA noted in *Sisson*, *Executive Jet* is better "understood as resting on the quite simple ground that the tort did not involve a vessel, which had traditionally been thought required by the leading scholars in the field." 497 U.S., at 369-370, 110 S. Ct., at 2899 (opinion concurring in judgment). *Executive Jet* did not in the least seek to alter the strict locality test for torts involving waterborne vessels. *Foremost*, however, converted *Executive Jet* 's exception into the rule. In addition to examining situs, *Foremost* required federal courts to ask whether the tort bore a significant relationship to maritime commerce, and whether the accident had a potential disruptive impact on maritime commerce. 457 U.S., at 673-675, 102 S. Ct., at 2657-2659. The lower courts adopted different approaches as they sought to apply *Foremost's* alteration of the *Executive Jet* test. *See Sisson, supra*, 497 U.S., at 365, n. 4, 110 S. Ct., at 2897, n. 4 (citing cases).

Sisson then affirmed the inherent vagueness of the *Foremost* test. *Sisson* involved a marina fire that was caused by a faulty washer-dryer unit on a pleasure yacht. The fire destroyed the yacht and damaged several vessels in addition to the marina. In finding admiralty jurisdiction, the Court held that the federal judicial power would extend to such cases only if: (1) in addition to situs, (2) the "incident" poses a potential hazard to maritime commerce, and (3) the "activity" giving rise to the incident bears a substantial relationship to traditional maritime activity. 497 U.S., at 362-364, 110 S. Ct., at 2895-2897. The traditional situs test also would have sustained a finding of jurisdiction because the fire started on board a vessel on the waterways. Thus, what was once a simple question—did the tort occur on the navigable waters—had become a complicated, multifactor analysis.

The disruption and confusion created by the *Foremost-Sisson* approach is evident from the post-*Sisson* decisions of the lower courts and from the majority opinion itself. Faced with the task of determining what is an "incident" or "activity" for *Sisson* purposes, the Fourth, Fifth, and Ninth Circuits simply reverted to the multi-factor test they had employed before *Sisson. See Price v. Price*, 929 F.2d 131, 135-136 (CA4 1991); *Coats v. Penrod Drilling Corp.*, 5 F.3d 877, 885-886 (CA5 1993); *Delta Country Ventures, Inc. v. Magana*, 986 F.2d 1260, 1263 (CA9 1993). The District Court's opinion in this case is typical: while nodding to *Sisson*, the court focused its entire attention on a totality-of-the-circumstances test, which includes factors such as "the functions and roles of the parties" and "[t]he traditional concepts of the role of admiralty law." Pet. for Cert. of Chicago 32a. Such considerations have no place in the Sisson test and should have no role in any jurisdictional inquiry. The dangers of a totality-of-the-circumstances approach to jurisdiction should be obvious. An undefined test requires courts and litigants to devote substantial resources to determine whether a federal court may hear a specific case. Such a test also introduces undesirable uncertainty into the affairs of private actors—even those involved in common maritime activities—who cannot predict whether or not their conduct may justify the exercise of admiralty jurisdiction.

Although the majority makes an admirable attempt to clarify what *Sisson* obscures, I am afraid that its analysis cannot mitigate the confusion of the *Sisson* test. Thus, faced with the "potential to disrupt maritime commerce" prong ante, at 1050, the majority must resort to "an intermediate level of possible generality" to determine the "'general features'" of the incident here, *id.*, at 1051. The majority does not explain the origins of "levels of generality," nor, to my knowledge, do we employ such a concept in other areas of jurisdiction. We do not use "levels of generality" to characterize residency or amount in controversy for diversity purposes, or to determine the presence of a federal question. Nor does the majority explain why an "intermediate" level of generality is appropriate. It is even unclear what an intermediate level of generality is, and we cannot expect that district courts will apply such a concept uniformly in similar cases. It is far from obvious how the undefined intermediate level of generality indicates that the "incident" for *Sisson* purposes is that of a vessel damaging an underwater structure.

The majority also applies levels of generality to the next prong of *Sisson*—whether the tortfeasor is engaged in "activity" that shows a "substantial relationship to traditional maritime activity." The majority decides that the activity is repair work by a vessel on a navigable waterway. But, as the petitioners rightly argue, the "activity" very well could be bridge repair or pile driving. One simply cannot tell due to the ambiguities intrinsic to *Sisson* and to the uncertainty as to the meaning of levels of generality. The majority's response implicitly acknowledges the vagueness inherent in *Sisson*: "Although there is inevitably some play in the joints in selecting the right level of generality when applying the *Sisson* test, the inevitable imprecision is not an excuse for whimsy." *Ante*, at 1052. The Court cannot provide much guidance to district courts as to the correct level of generality; instead, it can only say that any level is probably sufficient so long as it does not lead to "whimsy." When it comes to these issues, I prefer a clearer rule, which this Court has demanded with respect to federal question or diversity jurisdiction. Indeed, the "play in the joints" and "imprecision" that the Court finds "inevitable" easily could be avoided by returning to the test that prevailed before *Foremost*. In its effort to create an elegant, general test that could include all maritime torts, *Sisson* has only disrupted what was once a simple inquiry.

II

* * *

In place of *Sisson* I would follow the test described at the outset. When determining whether maritime jurisdiction exists under § 1333(1), a federal district court should ask if the tort occurred on a vessel on the navigable waters. This approach won the approval of two Justices in *Sisson*, *see* 497 U.S., at 373, 110 S. Ct., at 2901 (SCALIA, J., joined by White, J., concurring in judgment). Although Justice SCALIA's *Sisson* concurrence retained a "normal maritime activities" component, it recognized that anything a vessel does in the navigable waters would meet that requirement, and that "[i]t would be more straightforward to jettison the 'traditional maritime activity' analysis entirely." *Id.*, at 374, 110 S. Ct., at 2902. I wholly agree and have chosen the straightforward approach, which, for all of its simplicity, would have produced the same results the Court arrived at in *Executive Jet*, *Foremost*, *Sisson*, and this case. Although this approach "might leave within admiralty jurisdiction a few unusual actions," *ibid.*, such freakish cases will occur rarely. In any event, the resources needed to resolve them "will be saved many times over by a clear jurisdictional rule that makes it unnecessary to decide" what is a traditional maritime activity and what poses a threat to maritime commerce. *Id.*, at 374-375, 110 S. Ct., at 2901-2902.

* * *

Note: Limits on Grubart

The Court in *Grubart* suggests that practically any tort involving a vessel in navigation will satisfy the criteria for admiralty tort jurisdiction. Is that a fair reading of *Grubart*? If so, do you agree. Consider the following. Plaintiffs were injured by carbon monoxide fumes in a houseboat they rented from the appellant H_2O Houseboat Vacations (H_2O) at Lake Havasu in Arizona. At the time of the incident, the houseboat was tied to the shore of Lake Havasu which was a navigable waterway. Plaintiffs slept on the houseboat the night before they were to take it out on the lake the next day. As it was summertime they closed all of the windows in the sleeping area of the houseboat, turned on the air conditioning, and went to sleep. During the night, plaintiffs were seriously injured by carbon monoxide fumes within the houseboat which were probably the result of faulty equipment aboard the houseboat. H_2O filed its own action in the federal district court seeking to limit its liability under the Vessel Owner's Liability Act.

The Ninth Circuit in *H_2O Houseboat Vacations, Inc. v. Hernandez*, 103 F.3d 914, 1997 AMC 390 (9th Cir. 1996) used the following approach:

> The "connection" prong of the Grubart test has two subparts. The first subpart asks whether the general features of the incident causing the injury indicate the incident had a "potentially disruptive impact on maritime commerce." *Id.* To decide this question, we must first determine what was the incident that caused the injury. *See id.* at __, 115 S. Ct. at 1050-51.
>
> The Court told us how to do this in *Sisson v. Ruby*, 497 U.S. 358, 110 S. Ct. 2892, 111 L. Ed. 2d 292 (1990). There, a fire was caused by a defective washer/dryer aboard a pleasure boat docked at a marina on a navigable body of water. *Id.* at 360, 110 S. Ct. at 2894-95. The fire burned not only the boat itself but the marina and other boats docked nearby. *Id.* The Court did not describe the incident broadly as a "fire," nor narrowly as a "fire ... damaging nothing but pleasure boats." *Grubart*, 513 U.S. at —, 115 S. Ct. at 1051. Rather, in *Sisson*, the Court described the incident at "an intermediate level of possible generality" as " 'a fire on a vessel docked at a marina on navigable waters.'" *Grubart*, 513 U.S. at —, —, 115 S. Ct. at 1051, 1050 (quoting *Sisson*, 497 U.S. at 363, 110 S. Ct. at 2896). The question was whether that incident, so described, had a potential to disrupt maritime commerce. The court held it did.
>
> Here, the incident that caused the injury was the emission of carbon monoxide fumes inside a contained space within a houseboat tied to the shore. This incident had no potential to disrupt maritime commerce. The carbon monoxide was dangerous only because it was contained in the sleeping area of the houseboat. The fumes would not be dangerous if they escaped. This is far different from the fire on the boat in *Sisson*. There, the fire had the potential of spreading to other boats and to the marina. Indeed, it did.
>
> It is possible to speculate that the houseboat would have posed a hazard to maritime commerce if it had slipped its tie to the shore and had drifted onto Lake Havasu with the Hernandez family inside unconscious from carbon monoxide, or if the Hernandez family had taken the boat out on the lake and whoever was steering the boat had been overcome with carbon monoxide fumes and lost consciousness.
>
> Such speculation, however, would require us to ignore the actual "incident" that caused injury to the Hernandez family. That incident was the emission of carbon monoxide fumes encapsulated within the houseboat tied to the shore. That incident, defined as required by *Sisson* and *Grubart*, did not have the potential to disrupt maritime commerce.

Is this a proper application of the *Grubart* criteria?

Note: Application of Executive Jet in the Lower Federal Courts

The *Executive Jet* decision did not make clear whether the nexus requirement was applicable only in aircraft cases or whether it supplemented the locality test in maritime tort cases generally. It also did not set forth the elements of the nexus criterion. Lower federal courts tried to fill this vacuum by adopting the nexus test as a supplement to the locality test. Some courts also tried to elaborate the elements of nexus. Prominent among these courts was the Court of Appeals for the Fifth Circuit. Prior to the Supreme Court decisions in *Foremost* and *Sisson*, the Fifth Circuit decided *Kelly v. Smith*, 485 F.2d 520, 1973 AMC 2478 (5th Cir. 1973), *cert. denied sub nom. Chicot Land Company, Inc. v. Kelly*, 416 U.S. 969, 94 S. Ct. 1991, 40 L. Ed. 2d 558 (1974). In the *Kelly* case, deer poachers surreptitiously slipped across the Mississippi River and landed on an island. Upon their discovery they fled the scene in their boat. While navigating in the Mississippi River they were fired upon by some people on the island and one of the poachers was wounded. The injured person brought suit. In determining whether the action was within admiralty jurisdiction, the court enumerated four factors which it deemed relevant to determine if the nexus requirement had been met, to wit: "the function and roles of the parties; the types of vehicles and instrumentalities involved; the causation and the type of injury; and traditional concepts of the role of admiralty law." Subsequent to the *Foremost*, but before *Sisson*, the Fifth Circuit in *Molett v. Penrod Drilling Co.*, 826 F.2d 1419, 1988 AMC 2112 (5th Cir. 1987), *cert. denied sub nom. Columbus McKinnon, Inc. v. Gearench*, 493 U.S. 1003, 110 S. Ct. 563, 107 L. Ed. 2d 558 (1989) added several factors namely, "(1) the impact of an event on maritime shipping and commerce (2) the desirability of a uniform rule to apply to such matters and (3) the need for admiralty expertise." Even after Sisson some courts continued to apply the *Kelly* factors, although *Sisson* cast some doubt on their continued viability. After the Supreme Court's decision in *Jerome B. Grubart, Inc. v. Great Lakes Dredge & Dock Company*, *infra*, it has become clear that the application of the *Kelly* factors was expressly rejected by the Supreme Court in *Grubart*. *Coats v. Penrod Drilling Corp.*, 61 F.3d 1113, 1996 AMC 1 (5th Cir. 1995).

Notes

1. *Jurisdiction Over Aviation Torts*

The Supreme Court in *Executive Jet* held that a crash into the navigable waters of the United States by a plane on a flight between places within the continental U.S. lacks a sufficient maritime nexus to support admiralty jurisdiction. 409 U.S. 249, 274 (1974). The Court, however, did not foreclose admiralty jurisdiction in all air crashes. To the contrary, it opined that admiralty jurisdiction *might* be appropriate where a plane engaged in an intercontinental flight crashes in navigable waters, inasmuch as such flights typically require the plane to fly over broad stretches of international waters and transportation over these bodies of water traditionally has been performed by vessels. 409 U.S. at 271. Subsequently, the Supreme Court in a case brought under the Death on the High Seas Act, (DOHSA) 46 U.S.C.A. § 30302 (formerly 46 U.S.C. § 761), stemming from the crash of a helicopter in the Gulf of Mexico, held that DOHSA, in and of itself, is sufficient to confer admiralty jurisdiction. *Offshore Logistics, Inc. v. Tallentire*, 477 U.S. 207, 221, 106 S. Ct. 2485, 91 L. Ed. 2d 174, 1986 AMC 2113 (1986). Despite its conclusion that DOHSA confers admiralty jurisdiction, the Court also stated that:

> [notwithstanding] this statutory provision, admiralty jurisdiction is appropriately invoked here under traditional principles because the accident occurred on the high seas and in furtherance of an activity bearing a significant relationship to a traditional maritime activity. Although the decedents were killed while riding in a helicopter and not a more traditional maritime conveyance, that helicopter was engaged in a function traditionally performed by waterborne vessels: the ferrying of passengers from an "island" albeit an artificial one to the shore. *Id.* 218 (citations omitted).

See also Miller v. U.S., 725 F.2d 1311, 1984 AMC 1169 (11th Cir.), *cert. denied*, 469 U.S. 821, 105 S. Ct. 94, 83 L. Ed. 2d 40 (1984); *Roberts v. United States*, 498 F.2d 520, 524 (9th Cir.), *cert denied*, 419 U.S. 1070, 95 S. Ct. 656, 42 L. Ed. 2d 665, (1974); *Icelandic Coast Guard v. United Technologies Corp.*, 722 F. Supp. 942 (D. Conn. 1989) (products liability). As a general proposition, aircraft have not been deemed to be vessels. *See Smith v. Pan Air Corp.*, 684 F.2d 1102, 1112, 1983 AMC 2836 (5th Cir. 1982) (a seaplane) and *Barger v. Petroleum Helicopters, Inc.*, 692 F.2d 337, 339, 1993 AMC 2854 (5th Cir. 1983) (a helicopter). That fact is not necessarily fatal to admiralty jurisdiction and depending on the circumstances does not preclude a finding of "nexus", as the *Tallentire* decision demonstrates. Suppose a helicopter is ferrying personnel from Louisiana to a fixed platform in the Gulf of Mexico, two miles off the Louisiana coast. Does the Court's finding of nexus in *Tallentire* independent of DOHSA, compel the conclusion that a crash in territorial waters likewise supports admiralty jurisdiction. If so, what law applies in a wrongful death action? *See Yamaha Motor Corp. v. Calhoun,* 516 U.S 199, 116 S. Ct. 619, 133 L. Ed. 2d 578, 1996 AMC 305 (1996).

If an intercontinental flight, *e.g.*, London to New York, has crossed the Atlantic Ocean and crashes on land immediately after having crossed the U.S. coast, is there admiralty jurisdiction? Would such a situation fail the locality test. *Cf. Smith v. Pan Air Corp.*, 684 F.2d 1102, 1983 AMC 2836 (5th Cir. 1982). Suppose the pilot of a plane is negligent while the plane is over the high seas and this negligence results in a crash on land. Would there be admiralty jurisdiction? If a flight from one point in the continental United States to another point in the continental United States, *e.g.*, New Orleans to Miami, crashes in the Gulf of Mexico, which analysis prevails *Executive Jet* or *Tallentire*? *See Sullivan v. 43rd Aviation Flying Club, Inc.*, 16 Av. Cas. (CCH) ¶18, 260 (D. Conn. 1981).

2. ***Nexus v. Locus: Can Nexus Without Locus Ever Be Sufficient?***

Some commentators have suggested that the locality requirement be subsumed into the nexus requirement and not stand as an independent criterion. There are instances where the maritime interests are so strong that adherence to a strict locality rule would impede the fundamental purposes of admiralty jurisdiction:

> Whether a tort occurs on the water should be one factor to be considered in determining whether the tort meets the nexus requirement. The admiralty extension Act has helped by including damage done on land by vessels in navigable waters, and the courts have made an exception for seamen's claims arising out of their maritime status. As the courts are becoming accustomed to requiring a maritime nexus for tort claims as they have for contract claims, there seems to be no principled reason for excluding tort claims merely because they lack a maritime local.

1 Benedict on Admiralty § 171, p. 11-30 - 11-31 (7th ed. rev. by S. Friedel 1988) (citations omitted). *See also* Robert Force, *Determining Admiralty Tort Jurisdiction: An Alternative Analytical Framework*, 21 J. Mar. L. & Com. 1, 78-80 (1990).

The requirement of locality for admiralty jurisdiction has sometimes been dispensed with in torts involving seamen. For example, in a "blacklisting" case involving seamen suing marine protection and indemnity insurers for tortious interference with employment, the court found that the case was "so interwoven with present and potential maritime contractual relationships... as to fall within that jurisdiction." *Carroll v. Protection Maritime Ins. Co.*, 512 F.2d 4, 8-9, 1975 AMC 1633 (1st Cir. 1975). The court found admiralty jurisdiction despite the fact that there was no direct connection to navigable waters, holding that the indirect connection, to employees on vessels in navigable waters, together with the potential impact on maritime contractual relationships, was sufficient.

However, in *LaMontagne v. Craig*, 817 F.2d 556, 1987 AMC 2477 (9th Cir. 1987), the Ninth Circuit denied jurisdiction in a case of alleged defamation of an officer on a merchant vessel by the vessel's chief engineer, through a letter sent to the shipping company. The alleged tort occurred on land and not navigable waters, and admiralty jurisdiction was therefore denied. But, in another case involving defamation, the same court reached the opposite conclusion where the tortious activity occurred aboard ship. In *Guidry v. Durkin*, 834 F.2d 1465, 1988 AMC 1979 (9th Cir. 1987), the Ninth Circuit found admiralty jurisdiction where the defendant-crew member wrote the alleged defamatory statement while on board his vessel, and gave it to the telex operator for transmission to shore. According to the court, the locality requirement was met because "all prima facie requirements for tortious libel were met at sea." (834 F.2d at 1470).

Torts committed against personnel engaged in oil or gas exploration or removal activities on fixed platforms satisfy neither the location nor nexus criteria. *Rodrigue v. Aetna Casualty & Surety Co.*, 395 U.S. 352, 89 S. Ct. 1835, 23 L. Ed. 2d 360 (1969). The Supreme Court there held that, generally, oil rigs are artificial islands, not vessels in navigation, and therefore "the accidents [in question] had no more connection with the ordinary stuff of admiralty than do accidents on piers." *Id.* at 360. The same reasoning was applied to an oil and gas worker who was *fortuitously* present on a vessel at the time of the accident. *In re Dearborn Marine Services, Inc.* 499 F.2d 263, 1975 AMC 1850 (5th Cir. 1974), *cert. dismissed*, 423 U.S. 886, 96 S. Ct. 163, 46 L. Ed. 2d 118 (1975).

The locality question is also raised where damages arise from torts occurring on a vessel during repairs. In *Sea Vessel, Inc. v. Reyes*, 23 F.3d 345, 1994 AMC 2736 (11th Cir. 1994), the court found that the locality test was satisfied where injuries resulted from a fire aboard a dry-docked vessel. Although the "water [had been] removed from about her," the vessel was not on "land," according to the court, any more "than would be such a vessel if fastened to a wharf in a dry harbor where, by the natural recession of the water by the ebbing tide, she for a time might be upon dry land." (23 F.3d at 348-49) "[T]he proposition that such repairs are made on land would practically deprive the admiralty courts of their largest and most important jurisdiction in connection with such repairs." (*Id.* at 348.)

3. *Products Liability*

The Supreme Court has held that the tort of products liability is part of the general maritime law. Products liability claims, thus, must satisfy the locus and nexus criteria. *East River Steamship Corp. v. Transamerica Delaval,* 476 U.S. 858, 106 S. Ct. 2295, 90 L. Ed. 2d 865, 1986 AMC 2027 (1986). It has been held generally that shipyard construction and repair workers cannot invoke admiralty jurisdiction in their asbestosis suits against asbestos manufacturers because maritime nexus is lacking. *Oman v. Johns-Manville Corp.*, 764 F.2d. 224, 1985 AMC 2317 (4th Cir.), *cert. denied sub nom, Oman v. H.K. Porter Co.*, 474 U.S. 970, 106 S. Ct. 351, 88 L. Ed. 2d 319 (1985) (using the *Kelly* four factor nexus test now rejected in *Grubart).* Should the same result be reached in a similar suit brought by a seaman? Compare, *Swogger v. Waterman Steamship Corp.*, 518 N.Y.S.2d 715, 1987 AMC 2679 (1987), *aff'd,* 546 N.Y.S.2d 80 (N.Y.A.D. 1989) with *Lingo v. Great Lakes Dredge & Dock*, 638 F. Supp. 30 (E.D.N.Y. 1986).

D. Maritime Contracts

Note: The Nature of a Maritime Contract

> In general, a contract relating to a ship in its use as such, or to commerce or navigation on navigable waters, or to transportation by sea or to maritime employment is subject to maritime law and the case is one of admiralty jurisdiction, whether the contract is to be performed on land or water.
>
> * * *
>
> A contract is not considered maritime merely because the services to be performed under the contract have reference to a ship or to its business, or because the ship is the object of such services or that it has reference to navigable waters. In order to be considered maritime, there must be a direct and substantial link between the contract and the operation of the ship, its navigation, or its management afloat, taking into account the needs of the shipping industry, for the very basis of the constitutional grant of admiralty jurisdiction was to ensure a national uniformity of approach to world shipping.

1 BENEDICT ON ADMIRALTY 182, p. 12-4, 5, 6 (7th ed. rev. by S. Friedell 1988).

---

1. Types of Contracts Within the Cognizance of Admiralty

a. Marine Insurance Policies

INSURANCE COMPANY v. DUNHAM

78 U.S. (11 Wall.) 1, 20 L. Ed. 90 (1870)

Mr. Justice BRADLEY delivered the opinion of the court

* * *

The case, as thus brought before us, presents the question, whether the District Court for the District of Massachusetts, sitting in admiralty, has jurisdiction to entertain a libel *in personam* on a policy of marine insurance to recover for a loss.

This precise question has never been decided by this court. But, in our view, several decisions have been made which determine the principle on which the case depends. The general jurisdiction of the District Courts in admiralty and maritime cases has been heretofore so fully discussed that it is only necessary to refer to them very briefly on this occasion.

The Constitution declares that the judicial power of the United States shall extend "to all cases of admiralty and maritime jurisdiction," without defining the limits of that jurisdiction. Congress, by the Judiciary Act passed at its first session, 24th of September, 1789, established the District Courts, and conferred upon them, among other things, "exclusive original cognizance of all civil cases of admiralty and maritime jurisdiction."

As far as regards civil cases, therefore, the jurisdiction of these courts was thus made coextensive with the constitutional gift of judicial power on this subject.

* * *

The admiralty courts were originally established in that and other maritime countries of Europe for the protection of commerce and the administration of that venerable law of the sea which reaches back to sources long anterior even to those of the civil law itself; which Lord Mansfield says is not the law of any particular country, but the general law of nations; and which is founded on the broadest principles of equity and justice, deriving, however, much of its completeness and symmetry, as well as its modes of proceeding, from the civil law, and embracing, altogether, a system of regulations embodied and matured by the combined efforts of the most enlightened commercial nations of the world. Its system of procedure has been established for ages, and is essentially founded, as we have said, on the civil law; and this is probably one reason why so much hostility was exhibited against the admiralty by the courts of common law, and why its jurisdiction was so much more crippled and restricted in England than in any other state. In all other countries bordering on the Mediterranean or the Atlantic the marine courts, whether under the name of admiralty courts or otherwise, are generally invested with jurisdiction of all matters arising in marine commerce, as well as other marine matters of public concern, such as crimes committed on the sea, captures, and even naval affairs. But in England, partly under strained constructions of parliamentary enactments and partly from assumptions of public policy, the common law courts succeeded in establishing the general rule that the jurisdiction of the admiralty was confined to the *high* seas and entirely excluded from transactions arising on waters within the body of a county, such as rivers, inlets, and arms of the sea as far out as the naked eye could discern objects from shore to shore, as well as from transactions arising on the land, though relating to marine affairs.

With respect to contracts, this criterion of locality was carried so far that, with the exception of the cases of seamen's wages and bottomry bonds, no contract was allowed to be prosecuted in the admiralty unless it was made upon the sea, and was to be executed upon the sea; and even then it must not be under seal.

Of course, under such a construction of the admiralty jurisdiction, a policy of insurance executed on land would be excluded from it.

But this narrow view has not prevailed here. This court has frequently declared and decided that the admiralty and maritime jurisdiction of the United States is not limited either by the restraining statutes or the judicial prohibitions of England, but is to be interpreted by a more enlarged view of its essential nature and objects, and with reference to analogous jurisdictions in other countries constituting the maritime commercial world, as well as to that of England. "Its boundary," says Chief Justice Taney,[1] "is to be ascertained by a reasonable and just construction of the words used in the Constitution, taken in connection with the whole instrument, and the purposes for which admiralty and maritime jurisdiction was granted to the Federal government." "Courts of admiralty," says the same judge in another case,[2] "have been found necessary in all commercial countries, not only for the safety and convenience of commerce, and the speedy decision of controversies where delay would often be ruin, but also to administer the laws of nations in a season of war, and to determine the validity of captures and questions of prize or no prize in a judicial proceeding. And it would be contrary to the first principles on which the Union was formed to confine these rights to the States bordering on the Atlantic, and to the tide-water rivers connected with it, and to deny them to the citizens who border on the lakes and the great navigable streams which flow through the Western States."

In accordance with this more enlarged view of the subject, several results have been arrived at widely differing from the long-established rules of the English courts.

* * *

Secondly, as to *contracts*, it has been equally well settled that the English rule which concedes jurisdiction, with a few exceptions, only to contracts made upon the sea and to be executed thereon (making *locality* the test) is entirely inadmissible, and that the true criterion is the nature and subject-matter of the contract, as whether it was a maritime contract, having reference to maritime service or maritime transactions.

* * *

The subject could be very copiously illustrated by reference to the decisions of the various District and Circuit Courts. But it is unnecessary. The authoritative decisions of this court have settled the general rule, and all that remains to be done is to apply the law to each case as it arises.

It only remains, then, to inquire whether the contract of marine insurance, as set forth in the present case, is or is not a maritime contract.

It is objected that it is not a maritime contract because it is made on the land and is to be performed (by payment of the loss) on the land, and is, therefore, entirely a common law transaction. This objection would equally apply to bottomry and respondentia loans, which are also usually made on the land and are to be paid on the land. But in both cases

---

[1] *The Steamer St. Lawrence*, 1 Black, 527.

[2] *The Genesee Chief*, 12 Howard, 454.

payment is made to depend on a maritime risk; in the one case upon the loss of the ship or goods, and in the other upon their safe arrival at their destination. So the contract of affreightment is also made on land, and is to be performed on the land by the delivery of the goods and payment of the freight. It is true that in the latter case a maritime service is to be performed in the transportation of the goods. But if we carefully analyze the contract of insurance we shall find that, in effect, it is a contract, or guaranty, on the part of the insurer, that the ship or goods shall pass safely over the sea, and through its storms and its many casualties, to the port of its destination; and if they do not pass safely, but meet with disaster from any of the misadventures insured against, the insurer will pay the loss sustained. So in the contract of affreightment, the master guarantees that the goods shall be safely transported (dangers of the seas excepted) from the port of shipment to the port of delivery, and there delivered. The contract of the one guarantees against loss from the dangers of the sea, the contract of the other against loss from all other dangers. Of course these contracts do not always run precisely parallel to each other, as now stated; special terms are inserted in each at the option of the parties. But this statement shows the general nature of the two contracts. And how a fair mind can discern any substantial distinction between them on the question whether they are or are not, maritime contracts, is difficult to imagine. The object of the two contracts is, in the one case, maritime service, and in the other maritime casualties.

And then the contract of insurance, and the rights of the parties arising therefrom, are affected by and mixed up with all the questions that can arise in maritime commerce,—jettison, abandonment, average, salvage, capture, prize, bottomry, &c.

Perhaps the best criterion of the maritime character of a contract is the system of law from which it arises and by which it is governed. And it is well known that the contract of insurance sprang from the law maritime, and derives all its material rules and incidents therefrom. It was unknown to the common law; and the common law remedies, when applied to it, were so inadequate and clumsy that disputes arising out of the contract were generally left to arbitration, until the year A.D. 1601, when the statute of 43 Elizabeth was passed creating a special court, or commission, for hearing and determining causes arising on policies of insurance.

* * *

These facts go to show, demonstrably, that the contract of marine insurance is an exotic in the common law. And we know the fact, historically, that its first appearance in any code or system of laws was in the law maritime as promulgated by the various maritime states and cities of Europe. It undoubtedly grew out of the doctrine of contribution and general average, which is found in the maritime laws of the ancient Rhodians. By this law, if either ship, freight, or cargo was sacrificed to save the others, all had to contribute their proportionate share of the loss. This division of loss naturally suggested a previsional division of risk; first, amongst those engaged in the same enterprise; and, next, amongst associations of ship-owners and shipping merchants. Hence it is found that the earliest form of the contract of insurance was that of mutual insurance, which, according to Pardessus, dates back to the tenth century, if not earlier, and in Italy and Portugal was made obligatory. By a regulation of the latter kingdom, made in the fourteenth century, every ship-owner and merchant in Lisbon and Oporto was bound to contribute two per cent. of the profits of each voyage to a common fund from which to pay losses whenever they should occur.[12] The next step in the system was that of insurance upon premium. Capitalists, familiar with the risks of navigation, were found willing to guaranty against them for a small consideration or premium paid. This, the final form of the contract, was in use as early as the beginning of the fourteenth century,[13] and the tradition is, that it was introduced into England in that century by the Lombard merchants who settled in London and brought with them the maritime usages of Venice and other Italian cities. Express regulations respecting the contract, however, do not appear in any code or compilation of laws earlier than the commencement of the fifteenth century. The earliest which Pardessus was able to find were those contained in the Ordinances of Barcelona, A.D. 1435; of Venice, A.D. 1468; of Florence, A.D. 1523; of Antwerp, A.D. 1537, &c.[14] Distinct traces of earlier regulations are found, but the ordinances themselves are not extant. In the more elaborate monuments of maritime law which appeared in the sixteenth and seventeenth centuries, the contract of insurance occupies a large space. *The Guidon de la Mer*, which appeared at Rouen at the close of the sixteenth century, was an elaborate treatise on the subject; but, in its discussion, the principles of every other maritime contract were explained. In the celebrated marine ordinance of Louis XIV, issued in 1681, it forms the subject of one of the principal titles.[15] As is well known, it has always formed a part of the Scotch maritime law.

Suffice it to say, that in every maritime code of Europe, unless England is excepted, marine insurance constitutes one of the principal heads. It is treated in nearly every one of those collected by Pardessus, except the more ancient ones, which were compiled before the contract had assumed its place in written law. It is, in fact, a part of the general maritime law of the world; slightly modified, it is true, in each country, according to the circumstances or genius of the people. Can stronger proof be presented that the contract is a maritime contract?

But an additional argument is found in the fact that in all other countries, except England, even in Scotland, suits and controversies arising upon the contract of marine insurance are within the jurisdiction of the admiralty or other marine courts.[16]

* * *

The answer of the court, therefore, to the question propounded by the Circuit Court will be, that the District Court for the District of Massachusetts, sitting in admiralty, HAS JURISDICTION to entertain the libel in this case. Answer accordingly.

---

[12] 2 Pardessus, Lois Maritimes, 369; 6 *Id.* 303.

[13] *Id.* vol. 2, pp. 369, 370; vol. 4, p. 566; vol. 5, pp. 331, 493.

[14] *Id.* vol 5, pp. 493, 65; vol. 4, pp. 598, 37.

[15] Lib. 3, title 6.

[16] *See* Benedict's Admiralty, § 294, ed. 1870.

b. Contract for Repairs

NORTH PACIFIC STEAMSHIP CO. v. HALL BROTHERS CO.

249 U.S. 119, 39 S. Ct. 221, 63 L. Ed. 510 (1919)

Mr. Justice PITNEY delivered the opinion of the court

This is a direct appeal under § 238, Judicial Code (Act of March , 1911, c. 31, 36 Stat. 1087, 1157), involving only the question whether the cause was within the admiralty jurisdiction of a District Court of the United States.

Both parties are corporations of the State of California. Appellee, which for convenience may be referred to as the "Shipbuilding Company," filed its libel *in personam* against appellant, which we may call the "Steamship Company," to recover a balance claimed to be due for certain work and labor done, services rendered, and materials furnished in and about the repairing of the steamship *Yucatan*. The Steamship Company filed an answer denying material averments of the libel, and a cross-libel setting up a claim for damages for delay in the making of the repairs. The cause having been heard upon the pleadings and proofs, there was a decree for a recovery in favor of the Shipbuilding Company and a dismissal of the cross-libel. After this the Steamship Company filed a motion to arrest and vacate the decree and to dismiss the cause for want of jurisdiction. The motion was submitted to the court upon the pleadings, the proofs taken upon the hearings of the merits, and some slight additional proof. It was denied, and the present appeal followed.

The facts were these: In the month of May, 1911, the Steamship Company was the owner of the American steamer *Yucatan*, which then lay moored or tied up at dock upon the waters of Puget Sound at Seattle, in the State of Washington. The vessel, which was of steel construction, was in need of extensive repairs. She had been wrecked, and had remained submerged for a long time; ice floes had torn away the upper decks, and some of her bottom plates also needed to be replaced. She was under charter for an Alaskan voyage, to be commenced as soon as the repairs could be completed. The Shipbuilding Company was the owner of a shipyard, marine railway, machine shops, and other equipment for building and repairing ships, situate upon and adjacent to the navigable waters of Puget Sound at Winslow, in the same State, and had in its employ numerous mechanics and laborers. Under these circumstances it was agreed between the parties that the Shipbuilding Company should tow the vessel from where she lay to the shipyard, haul her out as required upon the marine railway to a position on dry land adjacent to the machine shop—the place being known as the "dry dock," and the hauling out being described as "docking"—and should furnish mechanics, laborers, and foremen as needed, who were to work with other men already in the employ of the Steamship Company, and under its superintendence; and the Shipbuilding Company was also to furnish plates and other materials needed in the repairs, and the use of air compressors, steam hammers, riveters, boring machines, lathes, blacksmith forge, and the usual and necessary tools for the use of such machines. At the time the contract was made, another vessel (the *Archer*) was upon the dry dock, and it was uncertain how soon she could be returned to the water. It was understood that the *Yucatan* should be hauled out as soon as the *Archer* came off, should remain upon the dry dock only during such part of the work as required her to be in that position, and at other times should lie in the water alongside the plant. For the services to be performed and the materials and equipment to be furnished the Shipbuilding Company was to receive stated prices, thus: for labor of all classes, the actual rate of wages paid to the men plus 15 per cent.; for use of tug and scow, a stated sum per hour; for hauling out the vessel and the use of the marine railway, a stated sum for the first 24 hours, and a specified rate per day for 6 "lay days" immediately following the hauling out; for each working day thereafter, another rate; for vessel lying alongside the dock for repairs, no charge; for the running of air compressors, a certain charge per hour; for the use and operation of other machines, certain rates specified; and for materials supplied, invoice prices and cost of freight to plant, with 10 per cent. additional.

The vessel was docked and repaired in the manner contemplated by the agreement; she was brought to the shipyard on the 27th of May, and lay in the water alongside of the dock there until the 17th of June, during which time upper decks and beams were put in and other work of a character that could be done as well while she was afloat as in the dry dock. On June 17 she was hauled out and remained in dry dock for about two weeks while her bottom plates were renewed. During the same period the propeller was removed to permit of an examination of the tail shaft, and as the shaft showed deterioration a new one was ordered to be supplied by a concern in San Francisco. Upon completion of the work upon the bottom plates, and on the 5th of July, the vessel was returned to the water and lay there for about two weeks awaiting arrival of the new tail shaft. When this arrived the vessel was again hauled out, the tail shaft and propeller were fitted, and the remaining repairs completed. Libelant's claim was for work and labor performed, services rendered, and materials furnished under the circumstances mentioned, and was based upon the agreed scale of compensation.

The question in dispute is whether a claim thus grounded is the subject of admiralty jurisdiction; appellant's contention being that the contract, or at least an essential part of it, was for the use by appellant of libelant's marine railway, shipyard, equipment, and laborers in such manner as appellant might choose to employ them, and that it called for the performance of no maritime service by libelant.

* * *

It must be taken to be the settled law of this court that while the civil jurisdiction of the admiralty in matters of tort depends upon locality—whether the act was committed upon navigable waters—in matter of contract it depends upon the subject-matter—the nature and character of the contract; and that the English rule, which conceded jurisdiction, with a few exceptions, only to contracts made and to be executed upon the navigable waters, is inadmissible, the true criterion being the nature of the contract, as to whether it have reference to maritime service or maritime transactions. *People's Ferry Co. v. Beers*, 20 How. 393, 401; *Philadelphia, Wilmington & Baltimore R.R. Co. v. Philadelphia, &c. Steam*

Towboat Co., 23 How. 209, 215; *Insurance Co. v. Dunham*, 11 Wall. 1, 26; *The Eclipse*, 135 U.S. 599, 608.

* * *

Neither in jurisdiction nor in the method of procedure are our admiralty courts dependent alone upon the theory of implied hypothecation; it being established that in a civil cause of maritime origin involving a personal responsibility the libelant may proceed *in personam* if the respondent is within reach of process.

* * *

That a materialman furnishing supplies or repairs may proceed in admiralty either against the ship *in rem* or against the master or owner *in personam* is recognized by the 12th Rule in Admiralty, adopted in its present form in the year 1872 (13 Wall. xiv) after a long controversy that began with *The General Smith*, 4 Wheat. 438, and ended with *The Lottawanna*, 21 Wall. 558, 579, 581. *See The Glide*, 167 U.S. 606.

It is settled that a contract for building a ship or supplying materials for her construction is not a maritime contract. *People's Ferry Co. v. Beers*, 20 How. 393; *Roach v. Chapman*, 22 How. 129; *Edwards v. Elliott*, 21 Wall. 532, 553, 557; *The Winnebago*, 205 U.S. 354, 363. In the case in 20 Howard the court said (p. 402): "So far from the contract being purely maritime, and touching rights and duties appertaining to navigation (on the ocean or elsewhere), it was a contract made on land, to be performed on land." But the true basis for the distinction between the construction and the repair of a ship, for purposes of the admiralty jurisdiction, is to be found in the fact that the structure does not become a ship, in the legal sense, until it is completed and launched. "A ship is born when she is launched, and lives so long as her identity is preserved. Prior to her launching she is a mere congeries of wood and iron—an ordinary piece of personal property—as distinctly a land structure as a house, and subject to mechanics' liens created by state law enforcible in the state courts. In the baptism of launching she receives her name, and from the moment her keel touches the water she is transformed, and becomes a subject of admiralty jurisdiction." *Tucker v. Alexandroff*, 183 U.S. 424, 438.

In *The Robert W. Parsons*, 191 U.S. 17, 33, 34, it was held that the admiralty jurisdiction extended to an action for repairs put upon a vessel while in dry dock; but the question whether this would apply to a vessel hauled up on land for repairs was reserved, the language of the court, by Mr. Justice Brown, being: "Had the vessel been hauled up by ways upon the land and there repaired, a different question might have been presented, as to which we express no opinion; but as all serious repairs upon the hulls of vessels are made in dry dock, the proposition that such repairs are made on land would practically deprive the admiralty courts of their largest and most important jurisdiction in connection with repairs."

In *The Steamship Jefferson*, 215 U.S. 130, it was held that the admiralty jurisdiction extends to a claim for salvage service rendered to a vessel while undergoing repairs in a dry dock.

What we have said sufficiently indicates the decision that should be reached in the case at bar. The contract as made contemplated the performance of services and the furnishing of the necessary materials for the repairs of the steamship *Yucatan*. It was an entire contract, intended to take the ship as she was and to discharge her only when completely repaired and fit for the Alaskan voyage. It did not contemplate, as is contended by appellant, either a lease, or a contract for use in the nature of a lease, of the libelant's marine railway and machine shop. The use of these was but incidental; the vessel being hauled out, when consistent with the progress of other work of the Shipbuilding Company, for the purpose of exposing the ship's bottom to permit of the removal and replacement of the broken plates and the examination of the propeller and tail shaft. In *The Planter* (*Peyroux v. Howard*), 7 Pet. 324, 327, 341, the vessel, requiring repairs below the water line as well as above, was to be and in fact was hauled up out of the water; and it was held that the contract for materials furnished and work performed in repairing her under these circumstances was a maritime contract. We think the same rule must be applied to the case before us; that the doubt intimated in *The Robert W. Parsons*, 191 U.S. 17, 33, 34, must be laid aside; and that there is no difference in character as to repairs made upon the hull of a vessel dependent upon whether they are made while she is afloat, while in dry dock, or while hauled up by ways upon land. The nature of the service is identical in the several cases, and the admiralty jurisdiction extends to all.

This is recognized by the Act of Congress of June 23, 1910, c. 373, 36 Stat. 604, which declares that "Any person furnishing repairs, supplies, or other necessaries, including the use of dry dock or marine railway, to a vessel, whether foreign or domestic," upon the order of a proper person, shall have a maritime lien upon the vessel.

* * *

The principle was recognized long ago by Mr. Justice Nelson in a case decided at the circuit, *Wortman v. Griffith* (1856), 3 Blatchf. 528, 30 Fed. Cas. No. 18,057, which was a libel *in personam* to recover compensation for services rendered in repairing a steamboat. Libelant was the owner of a shipyard with apparatus consisting of a railway cradle and other fixtures and implements used for the purpose of hauling vessels out of the water and sustaining them while being repaired. Certain rates of compensation were charged for hauling the vessel upon the ways, and a per diem charge for the time occupied while she was under repair, in cases where the owner of the yard and apparatus was not employed to do the work but the repairs were made by other shipmasters, as was done in that case. The owner of the yard and apparatus, together with his employees, superintended and conducted the operation of raising and lowering the vessel and also of fixing her upon the ways preparatory to the repairs, a service requiring skill and experience and essential to the process of repair. Mr. Justice Nelson held there was no substantial distinction between such a case and the case where the shipmaster was employed to make the repairs; and that the admiralty jurisdiction must be sustained.

Nor is the present case to be distinguished upon the ground that the repairs in which libelant was to furnish work and materials and the use of a marine railway and other equipment were to be done under the superintendence of the Steamship Company. This affected the quantum of the services and the extent of the responsibility, but not the essential character of the services or the nature of the contract, which, in our opinion, were maritime.

Decree affirmed.

---

c. Enforceability of Oral Contracts

In *Kossick v. United Fruit Co.*, 365 U.S. 731, 81 S. Ct. 886, 6 L. Ed. 2d 56 (1961), the Supreme Court held that an oral contract was enforceable under general maritime law. General maritime law governed because the contract was a maritime one. The contract was enforceable even though it would have been struck down by the New York Statute of Frauds if state law had been applicable.

---

2. Preliminary, Collateral and Mixed Contracts

Note: Overview of Agreements

Agreements preliminary to maritime contracts, even though directly relevant to them, are not within the cognizance of admiralty. One example of such agreements is an agreement to make or procure a particular maritime insurance policy, although the policy itself is a maritime contract. *Angelina Casualty Co. v. Exxon Corp., U.S.A., Inc.*, 876 F.2d 40, 1989 AMC 2677 (5th Cir. 1989).

Agreements merely collateral to a maritime contract are not ordinarily cognizable in admiralty, either. For example, a bond securing the performance of a charter party. *Rhederi Actien Gesellschaft Oceana v. Clutha Shipping Co.*, 226 F. 339 (D. Md. 1915).

Contracts may contain maritime as well as non-maritime obligations. With respect to such contracts, the general rule is that a contract will not be within the admiralty jurisdiction unless it is wholly maritime. However, there are exceptions. On one hand, if the non-maritime element is separable from the maritime element, and may be litigated separately without prejudice to either party, the maritime element will be within the admiralty jurisdiction. On the other hand, if the non-maritime element is inseparable, the question then will be whether it is incidental or significant. If it is inseparable and incidental, maritime jurisdiction will encompass the entire claim. If it is inseparable and significant, admiralty will not have jurisdiction over the claim. *Kuehne & Nagel v. Geosource, Inc.*, 874 F.2d 283 (5th Cir. 1989).

---

a. Executory Contracts

TERMINAL SHIPPING CO. v. HAMBERG

222 F. 1020 (D. Maryland, 1915)

ROSE, District Judge

This is a libel *in personam* with a clause of foreign attachment. It sets up a contract between the respondents and the libelant, by which the latter until December 31, 1915, was to do all stevedoring work required by the respondents' vessels at the port of Baltimore, except when some charter otherwise provided. It alleges that the Bertha arrived at this port, but that its master declined to permit the libelant to do the stevedoring work, although it tendered its services and had rigged up its gears and was ready and willing to perform. It is asserted that by such refusal the libelant lost $75, that being the amount of profit which it says it would have made, had it done the work under the contract and been paid the contract price.

To this libel the respondents have excepted, and on two grounds: First, that the cause of action is not within the jurisdiction of a court of admiralty; and, secondly, that the damages sought to be recovered are purely speculative.

There are cases in which recovery may be had for loss of profits. *Pennsylvania Steel Co. v. New York City Ry. Co.*, 198 Fed. 745, 117 C.C.A. 503. Under other circumstances they cannot be. *De Ford v. Maryland Steel Co.*, 113 Fed. 72, 51 C.C.A. 59. Whether in this case they can be will depend upon the facts as they may be shown in evidence. The question should not be determined on the face of the pleadings alone.

The second exception will therefore be overruled.

The breach of an executory contract does not, ordinarily, at least, give the injured party a maritime lien upon the ship, and therefore a libel filed *in rem* may not be filed to recover therefor. *Schooner Freeman v. Buckingham*, 18 How. 182, 15 L. Ed. 341; *Scott v. Ira Chaffee* (D.C.) 2 Fed. 401. It has also been decided that executory contracts to furnish all provisions that certain ships may require at a particular port, or all coal that they will need at that place, are not maritime contracts, and that admiralty has no jurisdiction, even *in personam*, to award damages for their breach. *Diefenthal v. Hamburg-Amerikanische Packetfahrt Actien-Gesellschaft* (D.C.) 46 Fed. 397; *Steamship Overdale Co., Ltd., v. Turner* (D.C.) 206 Fed. 339. In the case last cited it was pointed out that a contract to buy coal or provisions is not in its nature maritime, and does not become so until the coal or the stores are furnished to the ship.

The libelant in this case says that a contract to do stevedoring work on a ship calls for a service which can never be otherwise than maritime. Whatever may have been the original difference of opinion on the subject, it is now clearly settled that stevedoring services are maritime. *Atlantic Transport Co. of West Virginia v. Imbrovek*, 234 U.S. 52, 34 Sup. Ct. 733, 58 L. Ed. 1208, 51 L.R.A. (N.S.) 1157. Respondent replies that the contract is executory, and that for a breach of such a contract there is no remedy in the admiralty.

The reasoning, if not the express language, of Justice Story on circuit in *Andrews v. Essex Fire & Marine Ins. Co.*, 1 Fed. Cas. 889, goes far to justify this contention. In a number of cases in which a right of action *in rem* has been denied, doubt has been expressed as to whether there was any jurisdiction even *in personam*. *The Seven Sons* (D.C.) 69 Fed. 271. On the other hand, the jurisdiction *in personam* has been expressly sustained in a case on all fours with this. *The Allerton* (D.C.) 93 Fed. 219. The Circuit Court of Appeals for the Seventh Circuit has upheld such jurisdiction where the breach complained of was that of an executory contract for towing. *Boutin v. Rudd*, 82 Fed. 685, 27 C.C.A. 526.

The question seems to have been foreclosed in this circuit by the decision of the Circuit Court of Appeals in *Baltimore Steam Packet Co. v. Patterson*, 106 Fed. 736, 45 C.C.A. 575, 66 L.R.A. 193. It was there distinctly held that for the failure of a shipper to furnish cargo which he had bargained to ship recovery may be had in the admiralty upon a libel *in personam*.

It follows that the first exception must also be overruled.

---

b. General Agency Contracts

EXXON CORPORATION v. CENTRAL GULF LINES, INC.

500 U.S. 603, 111 S. Ct. 2071, 114 L. Ed. 2d 649, 1991 AMC 1817 (1991)

Justice MARSHALL, delivered the opinion of the Court

This case raises the question whether admiralty jurisdiction extends to claims arising from agency contracts. In *Minturn v. Maynard*, 17 How. 477 (1855), this Court held that an agent who had advanced funds for repairs and supplies necessary for a vessel could not bring a claim in admiralty against the vessel's owners. *Minturn* has been interpreted by some lower courts as establishing a *per se* rule excluding agency contracts from admiralty. We now consider whether *Minturn* should be overruled.

I

This case arose over an unpaid bill for fuels acquired for the vessel, *Green Harbour ex William Hooper* (*Hooper*). The *Hooper* is owned by respondent Central Gulf Lines, Inc. (Central Gulf) and was chartered by the Waterman Steamship Corporation (Waterman) for use in maritime commerce. Petitioner Exxon Corporation (Exxon) was Waterman's exclusive worldwide supplier of gas and bunker fuel oil for some 40 years.

In 1983, Waterman and Exxon negotiated a marine fuel requirements contract. Under the terms of the contract, upon request, Exxon would supply Waterman's vessels with marine fuels when the vessels called at ports where Exxon could supply the fuels directly. Alternatively, in ports where Exxon had to rely on local suppliers, Exxon would arrange for the local supplier to provide Waterman vessels with fuel. In such cases, Exxon would pay the local supplier for the fuel and then invoice Waterman. Thus, while Exxon's contractual obligation was to provide Waterman's vessels with fuel when Waterman placed an order, it met that obligation sometimes in the capacity of "seller" and other times in the capacity of "agent."

In the transaction at issue here, Exxon acted as Waterman's agent, procuring bunker fuel for the *Hooper* from Arabian Marine Operating Co. (Arabian Marine) of Jeddah, Saudi Arabia. In October 1983, Arabian Marine delivered over 4,000 tons of fuel to the *Hooper* in Jeddah and invoiced Exxon for the cost of the fuel. Exxon paid for the fuel and invoiced Waterman, in turn, for $763,644. Shortly thereafter, Waterman sought reorganization under Chapter 11 of the Bankruptcy Code; Waterman never paid the full amount of the fuel bill. During the reorganization proceedings, Central Gulf agreed to assume personal liability for the unpaid bill if a court were to hold the *Hooper* liable *in rem* for that cost.

Subsequently, Exxon commenced this litigation in federal district court against Central Gulf *in personam* and against the *Hooper in rem*. Exxon claimed to have a maritime lien on the *Hooper* under the Federal Maritime Lien Act, 46 U.S.C. § 971 (1982 ed.).[1] The District Court noted that "[a] prerequisite to the existence of a maritime lien based on a breach of contract is that the subject matter of the contract must fall within the admiralty jurisdiction." 707 F. Supp. 155, 158 (SDNY 1989). Relying on the Second Circuit's decision in *Peralta Shipping Corp. v. Smith & Johnson (Shipping) Corp.*, 739 F.2d 798 (CA2 1984), *cert. denied*, 470 U.S. 1031, 105 S. Ct. 1405, 84 L. Ed. 2d 791 (1985), the District Court concluded that it did not have admiralty jurisdiction over the claim. *See* 707 F. Supp, at 159-161. In *Peralta*, the Second Circuit held that it was constrained by this Court's decision in *Minturn v. Maynard*, *supra*, and by those Second Circuit cases faithfully adhering to *Minturn*, to follow a *per se* rule excluding agency contracts from admiralty jurisdiction. *See Peralta*, *supra*, at 802-804. The District Court also rejected the argument that Exxon should be excepted from the *Minturn* rule because it had provided credit necessary for the Hooper to purchase the fuel and thus was more than a mere agent. To create such an exception, the District Court reasoned, "'would blur, if not obliterate, a rather clear admiralty distinction.'" 707 F. Supp., at 161, *quoting Peralta*, *supra*, at 804.[2]

The District Court denied Exxon's motion for reconsideration. The court first rejected Exxon's claim that in procuring fuel for Waterman it was acting as a seller rather than an agent. Additionally, the District Court declined Exxon's invitation to limit the *Minturn* rule to either general agency or preliminary service contracts.[3] Finally, the District Court determined that even if it were to limit *Minturn*, Exxon's contract with Waterman was both a general agency contract and a preliminary services contract and thus was excluded from admiralty jurisdiction under either exception. *See* 717 F. Supp. 1029, 1031-1037 (SDNY 1989).

The Court of Appeals for the Second Circuit summarily affirmed the judgment of the District Court "substantially for the reasons given" in the District Court's two opinions. App. to Pet. for Cert. A2, judgt. order reported at 904 F.2d 33 (1990). We granted certiorari to resolve a conflict among the Circuits as to the scope of the *Minturn* decision[4] and to consider whether *Minturn* should be overruled. 498 U.S. ___, 111 S. Ct. 750, 112 L. Ed.

---

[1] The relevant provision of the Federal Maritime Lien Act has been amended and recodified at 46 U.S.C. § 31342.

[2] In the same action, Exxon also claimed a maritime lien on the *Hooper* for a separate unpaid fuel bill for approximately 42 tons of gas oil Exxon had supplied directly to the Hooper in New York. The District Court held that because Exxon was the "supplier" rather than an agent with respect to the New York delivery, the claim for $13,242 fell within the court's admiralty jurisdiction. The court granted summary judgment in Exxon's favor on this claim. 707 F. Supp., at 161-162. This ruling is not at issue here.

[3] The preliminary contract rule, which excludes "preliminary services" from admiralty, was enunciated in the Second Circuit as early as 1881. *See The Thames*, 10 F. 848 (SDNY 1881) ("The distinction between preliminary services leading to a maritime contract and such contracts themselves have [*sic*] been affirmed in this country from the first, and not yet departed from"). In the Second Circuit, the agency exception to admiralty jurisdiction—the *Minturn* rule— has been fused with the preliminary contract rule. *See Cory Bros. & Co. v. United States*, 51 F.2d 1010, 1012 (CA2 1931) (explaining *Minturn* as involving a preliminary services contract). In denying Exxon's motion for reconsideration, the District Court declined to "disentangle" the two rules, asserting that Circuit precedent had established the rule of *Minturn* "as a subset of the preliminary contract rule." 717 F. Supp. 1029, 1036 (SDNY 1989).

[4] *Compare E. S. Binnings, Inc. v. M/V Saudi Riyadh*, 815 F.2d 660, 662-665, and n. 4 (CA11 1987) (general agency contracts for performance of preliminary services excluded from admiralty jurisdiction); and *Peralta Shipping Corp. v. Smith & Johnson (Shipping) Corp.*, 739 F.2d 798 (CA2 1984) (all general agency contracts excluded), *cert. denied*, 470 U.S. 1031, 105 S. Ct. 1405, 84 L. Ed. 2d 791 (1985) with *Hinkins Steamship Agency, Inc. v. Freighters, Inc.*, 498 F.2d 411, 411-412 (CA9 1974) (*per curiam*) (looking to the character of the work performed by a "husbanding agent" and concluding that the contract was maritime because the services performed were "necessary for the continuing voyage"); and *id.*, at 412 (arguably limiting *Minturn* to general agency as opposed to special agency contracts); and *Hadjipateras v. Pacifica, S.A.*, 290 F.2d 697, 703-704, and n.15 (CA5 1961)

2d 770 (1991). Today we are constrained to overrule *Minturn* and hold that there is no *per se* exception of agency contracts from admiralty jurisdiction.

II

Section 1333(1) of Title 28 U.S.C. grants federal district courts jurisdiction over "any civil case of admiralty or maritime jurisdiction." In determining the boundaries of admiralty jurisdiction, we look to the purpose of the grant. *See Insurance Co. v. Dunham*, 11 Wall. 1, 24 (1871). As we recently reiterated, the "fundamental interest giving rise to maritime jurisdiction is 'the protection of maritime commerce.'" *Sisson v. Ruby*, 497 U.S. ___, ___, 110 S. Ct. 2892, 2897, 111 L. Ed. 2d 292 (1990), *quoting Foremost Ins. Co. v. Richardson*, 457 U.S. 668, 674, 102 S. Ct. 2654, 2658, 73 L. Ed. 2d 300 (1982). This case requires us to determine whether the limits set upon admiralty jurisdiction in *Minturn* are consistent with that interest.

The decision in *Minturn* has confounded many, and we think the character of that three-paragraph opinion is best appreciated when viewed in its entirety:

> The respondents were sued in admiralty, by process *in personam*. The libel charges that they are owners of the steamboat Gold Hunter; that they had appointed the libellant their general agent or broker; and exhibits a bill, showing a balance of accounts due libellant for money paid, laid out, and expended for the use of respondents, in paying for supplies, repairs, and advertising of the steamboat, and numerous other charges, together with commissions on the disbursements, &c.
>
> The court below very properly dismissed the libel, for want of jurisdiction. There is nothing in the nature of a maritime contract in the case. The libel shows nothing but a demand for a balance of accounts between agent and principal, for which an action of *assumpsit*, in a common law court, is the proper remedy. That the money advanced and paid for respondents was, in whole or in part, to pay bills due by a steamboat for repairs or supplies, will not make the transaction maritime, or give the libellant a remedy in admiralty. Nor does the local law of California, which authorizes an attachment of vessels for supplies or repairs, extend to the balance of accounts between agent and principal, who have never dealt on the credit, pledge, or security of the vessel.
>
> The case is too plain for argument.

17 How. 477. While disagreeing over what sorts of agency contracts fall within *Minturn's* ambit, lower courts have uniformly agreed that *Minturn* states a *per se* rule barring at least some classes of agency contracts from admiralty. *See* n.4, *supra.*[5]

(holding an agency contract for management and operation of a vessel within admiralty jurisdiction and limiting *Minturn* to actions for "an accounting as such"). *See also Ameejee Valleejee & Sons v. M/V Victoria U.*, 661 F.2d 310, 312 (CA4 1981) (espousing a "general proposition of law" that a general agent may not invoke admiralty jurisdiction while a special agent can).

[5] As early as 1869, however, this Court narrowed the reach of *Minturn* and cast doubt on its validity. *See The Kalorama*, 10 Wall. 204, 217 (1869) (distinguishing *Minturn* and allowing agents who had advanced funds for repairs and supplies for a vessel to sue in admiralty where it was "expressly agreed that the advances should be furnished on the credit of the steamer").

Minturn appears to have rested on two rationales: (1) that the agent's claim was nothing more than a "demand for a balance of accounts" which could be remedied at common law through an action of *assumpsit*; and (2) that the agent had no contractual or legal right to advance monies "on the credit, pledge, or security of the vessel." The first rationale appears to be an application of the then-accepted rule that "the admiralty has no jurisdiction at all in matters of account between part owners," The *Steamboat Orleans v. Phoebus*, 11 Pet. 175, 182 (1837), or in actions in *assumpsit* for the wrongful withholding of money, *see Archawski v. Hanioti*, 350 U.S. 532, 534, 76 S. Ct. 617, 620, 100 L. Ed. 676 (1956) ("A line of authorities emerged to the effect that admiralty had no jurisdiction to grant relief in such cases"). The second rationale appears to be premised on the then-accepted rule that a contract would not be deemed maritime absent a "hypothecation" or a pledge by the vessel's owner of the vessel as security for debts created pursuant to the contract. In other words, to sue in admiralty on a contract, the claimant had to have some form of a lien interest in the vessel, even if the action was one *in personam*. *See e.g.*, *Gardner v. The New Jersey*, 9 F. Cas. 1192, 1195 (No. 5233) (D. Pa. 1806); *see generally*, Note, 17 CONN. L. REV. 595, 597-598 (1985).

Both of these rationales have since been discredited. In *Archawski*, *supra*, the Court held that an action cognizable as *assumpsit* would no longer be automatically excluded from admiralty. Rather, "admiralty has jurisdiction, even where the libel reads like *indebitatus assumpsit* at common law, provided the unjust enrichment arose as a result of the breach of a maritime contract." 350 U.S., at 536, 76 S. Ct., at 621. Only 15 years after *Minturn* was decided, the Court also cast considerable doubt on the "hypothecation requirement." In *Insurance Co. v. Dunham*, 11 Wall. 1 (1871), the Court explained that, in determining whether a contract falls within admiralty, "the true criterion is the nature and subject-matter of the contract, as whether it was a maritime contract, having reference to maritime service or maritime transactions." *Id.*, at 26. Several subsequent cases followed this edict of *Dunham* and rejected the relevance of the hypothecation requirement to establishing admiralty jurisdiction. *See North Pacific S.S. Co. v. Hall Bros. Marine Railway & Shipbuilding Co.*, 249 U.S. 119, 126, 39 S. Ct. 221, 223, 63 L. Ed. 510 (1919); *Detroit Trust Co. v. The Thomas Barlum*, 293 U.S. 21, 47-48, 55 S. Ct. 31, 40, 79 L. Ed. 176 (1934).[6]

Thus, to the extent that *Minturn's* theoretical underpinnings can be discerned, those foundations are no longer the law of this Court. *Minturn's* approach to determining admiralty jurisdiction, moreover, is inconsistent with the principle that the "nature and subject-matter" of the contract at issue should be the crucial consideration in assessing admiralty jurisdiction. *Insurance Co. v. Dunham*, *supra*, at 26. While the *Minturn* Court viewed it as irrelevant "that the money advanced and paid for respondents was, in whole or in part, to pay bills due by a steamboat for repairs or supplies," the trend in modern admiralty case

[6] These decisions were part of a larger trend started in the 19th century of eschewing the restrictive prohibitions on admiralty jurisdiction that prevailed in England. *See e.g.*, *Waring v. Clarke*, 5 How. 441, 454-459 (1847) (holding that the constitutional grant of admiralty jurisdiction did not adopt the statutory and judicial rules limiting admiralty jurisdiction in England); *The Propeller Genesee Chief v. Fitzhugh*, 12 How. 443, 456-457 (1852) (rejecting the English tide-water doctrine that "measure[d] the jurisdiction of the admiralty by the tide"); *Insurance Co. v. Dunham*, 11 Wall., at 26 (rejecting the English locality rule on maritime contracts "which concedes [admiralty] jurisdiction, with a few exceptions, only to contracts made upon the sea and to be executed thereon").

law, by contrast, is to focus the jurisdictional inquiry upon whether the nature of the transaction was maritime. *See e.g., Kossick v. United Fruit Co.*, 365 U.S. 731, 735-738, 81 S. Ct. 886, 890-92, 6 L. Ed. 2d 56 (1961). *See also Krauss Bros. Lumber Co. v. Dimon S.S. Corp.*, 290 U.S. 117, 124, 54 S. Ct. 105, 107, 78 L. Ed. 216 (1933) ("Admiralty is not concerned with the form of the action, but with its substance").

Finally, the proposition for which *Minturn* stands—a *per se* bar of agency contracts from admiralty—ill serves the purpose of the grant of admiralty jurisdiction. As noted, the admiralty jurisdiction is designed to protect maritime commerce. *See supra*, at ___. There is nothing in the nature of an agency relationship that necessarily excludes such relationships from the realm of maritime commerce. Rubrics such as "general agent" and "special agent" reveal nothing about whether the services actually performed pursuant to a contract are maritime in nature. It is inappropriate, therefore, to focus on the status of a claimant to determine whether admiralty jurisdiction exists. *Cf. Sisson*, 497 U.S., at ___, n.2, 110 S. Ct., at 2896, n.2 ("the demand for tidy rules can go too far, and when that demand entirely divorces the jurisdictional inquiry from the purposes that support the exercise of jurisdiction, it *has* gone too far").

We conclude that *Minturn* is incompatible with current principles of admiralty jurisdiction over contracts and therefore should be overruled. We emphasize that our ruling is a narrow one. We remove only the precedent of *Minturn* from the body of rules that have developed over what types of contracts are maritime. Rather than apply a rule excluding all or certain agency contracts from the realm of admiralty, lower courts should look to the subject matter of the agency contract and determine whether the services performed under the contract are maritime in nature. *See generally Kossick, supra*, at 735-738 (analogizing the substance of the contract at issue to established types of "maritime" obligations and finding the contract within admiralty jurisdiction).

III

There remains the question whether admiralty jurisdiction extends to Exxon's claim regarding the delivery of fuel in Jeddah. We conclude that it does. Like the District Court, we believe it is clear that when Exxon directly supplies marine fuels to Waterman's ships, the arrangement is maritime in nature. *See* 707 F. Supp., at 161. *Cf. The Golden Gate*, 52 F.2d 397 (CA9 1931) (entertaining an action in admiralty for the value of fuel oil furnished to a vessel), *cert. denied sub nom. Knutsen v. Associated Oil Co.*, 284 U.S. 682, 52 S. Ct. 199, 76 L. Ed. 576 (1932). In this case, the only difference between the New York delivery over which the District Court asserted jurisdiction, *see* n. 2, *supra*, and the Jeddah delivery was that, in Jeddah, Exxon bought the fuels from a third party and had the third party deliver them to the *Hooper*. The subject matter of the Jeddah claim, like the New York claim, is the value of the fuel received by the ship. Because the nature and subject matter of the two transactions are the same as they relate to maritime commerce, if admiralty jurisdiction extends to one, it must extend to the other. *Cf. North Pacific, supra*, at 128 ("There is no difference in character as to repairs made upon... a vessel... whether they are made while she is afloat, while in dry dock, or while hauled up [on] land. The nature of the service is identical in the several cases, and the admiralty jurisdiction extends to all").[7] We express no view on whether Exxon is entitled to a maritime lien under the Federal Maritime Lien Act. That issue is not before us, and we leave it to be decided on remand.

The judgment of the Court of Appeals is reversed, and the case is remanded for further proceedings consistent with this opinion.

It is so ordered.

---

c. **Note: Contracts to Lease Containers**

In *CTI-Container Leasing Corporation v. Oceanic Operations Corporation*, 682 F.2d 377, 380-81, 1982 AMC 2541 (2d Cir. 1982) the court considered the issue of whether or not a contract to lease container was a maritime contract.

> The question whether a contract for acquisition of cargo shipping containers is a maritime contract has apparently provoked little comment. The use of such containers, which are portable receptacles in which large numbers of smaller packages may be transported, is a relatively recent development that "enables the use of two or more modes of transportation, marine, motor, rail, or air, to transport goods on a door-to-door basis." Tombari, *Trends in Oceanborne Containerization and Its Implications for the U.S. Liner Industry*, 10 J. MAR. L. & COM. 311, 311 (1979). Characterized by one commentator as "[o]ne of the most important technological developments in the transportation of goods by sea since steam replaced sail," Simon, *The Law of Shipping Containers*, 5 J. MAR. L. & COM. 507, 507 (1974), containerization has revolutionized maritime cargo-handling techniques. As the Supreme Court has described it,
>
> > containerization permits the time-consuming work of stowage and unstowage to be performed on land in the absence of the vessel. The use of containerized ships has reduced the costly time the vessel must be in port and the amount of manpower required to get the cargo onto the vessel.
>
> *Northeast Marine Terminal Co. v. Caputo*, 432 U.S. 249, 270 (1977) (footnote omitted). Consequently, in a variety of contexts, the container has been characterized as "a modern substitute for the hold of the vessel," *id.*, and as "'functionally a part of the ship,'" *Japan Line, Ltd. v. County of Los Angeles*, 441 U.S. 434, 443 (1979) (*quoting Leather's Best, Inc. v. S.S. Mormaclynx*, 451 F.2d 800, 815 (2d Cir. 1971).[5]

Given the function of the container and the growing dependence on the maritime industry on containerization, a shipowner's lease of containers has been held a maritime contract, *Integrated Container Service, Inc. v. Starlines Container Shipping, Ltd.*, 476 F. Supp. 119 (S.D.N.Y. 1979), much as other agreements for the acquisition of ship equipment have been viewed as maritime contracts, *e.g.*, *Radiomarine Corp. v. Gulf Northern Co.*, 394 F. Supp. 381 (E.D. Mo. 1975) (radio and radar systems); *Houston-New Orleans, Inc. v.*

---

[7] As noted, the District Court regarded the services performed by Exxon in the Jeddah transaction as "preliminary" and characterized the rule excluding agency contracts from admiralty as "a subset" of the preliminary contract doctrine. *See supra*, at 607, and n.3. This Court has never ruled on the validity of the preliminary contract doctrine, nor do we reach that question here. However, we emphasize that *Minturn* has been overruled and that courts should focus on the nature of the services performed by the agent in determining whether an agency contract is a maritime contract.

[5] None of these cases dealt with the maritime nature of a lease of containers, and each clearly arose in a maritime context. See *Japan Line, Ltd. v. County of Los Angeles, supra* (local tax on containers used on Japanese ships in commerce with United States); *Northeast Marine Terminal Co. v. Caputo, supra* (applicability of Longshoremen's and Harbor Workers' Compensation Act, 33 U.S.C. § 901 *et seq.* (1976), to longshoremen injured while unloading containers that had been removed from ships); *Leather's Best, Inc. v. S.S. Mormaclynx, supra* (applicability of $500 package limitation in Carriage of Goods by Sea Act, 46 U.S.C. § 1304(5) (1970) to the container as a whole rather than to packages within.)

Page Engineering Co., 353 F. Supp. 890 (E.D. La. 1972) (control panel for crane mounted on ship). We concur in the view that a lease of cargo containers for use on a ship is a maritime contract.

The case before us focuses principally on the antecedent question of whether the agreement between CTI and Oceanic leased containers for use on a ship. Since containers may be used not only in ocean transport, but also in overland transport by truck or train or in overseas transport by freighter airplane, *see e.g.*, Schmeltzer & Peavy, *Prospects and Problems of the Container Revolution*, 1 J. MAR. L. & COM. 203, 204-06 (1970); Tombari, *Trends in Oceanborne Containerization and Its Implications for the U.S. Liner Industry, supra*, Oceanic argues that the containers leased here could have been used for purposes other than ocean transport, and that the lease has no necessarily maritime flavor.[6] Our review of the record persuades us that the district court properly viewed the lease between CTI and Oceanic as indicating that the containers would be transported by ship.

---

d. Mixed Contract Relating to Maritime and Non-Maritime Matters

NORFOLK SOUTHERN RAILWAY CO. v. KIRBY

543 U.S. 14, 125 S. Ct. 385, 2004 AMC 2705 (2004)

Justice O'CONNOR delivered the opinion of the Court

This is a maritime case about a train wreck. A shipment of machinery from Australia was destined for Huntsville, Alabama. The intercontinental journey was uneventful, and the machinery reached the United States unharmed. But the train carrying the machinery on its final, inland leg derailed, causing extensive damage. The machinery's owner sued the railroad. The railroad seeks shelter in two liability limitations contained in contracts that upstream carriers negotiated for the machinery's delivery.

I

This controversy arises from two bills of lading (essentially, contracts) for the transportation of goods from Australia to Alabama. A bill of lading records that a carrier has received goods from the party that wishes to ship them, states the terms of carriage, and serves as evidence of the contract for carriage. *See* 2 T. Schoenbaum, Admiralty and Maritime Law 58-60 (3d ed.2001) (hereinafter Schoenbaum); Carriage of Goods by Sea Act (COGSA), 49 Stat. 1208, 46 U.S.C. App. § 1303. Respondent James N. Kirby, Pty Ltd. (Kirby), an Australian manufacturing company, sold 10 containers of machinery to the General Motors plant located outside Huntsville, Alabama. Kirby hired International Cargo Control (ICC), an Australian freight forwarding company, to arrange for delivery by "through" (i.e., end-to-end) transportation. (A freight forwarding company arranges for, coordinates, and facilitates cargo transport, but does not itself transport cargo.) To formalize their contract

---

6 Oceanic also argues that the lease was partially nonmaritime because after the containers were seized by the Philippine government they were held on land. We find no merit in this or any of Oceanic's other arguments.

for carriage, ICC issued a bill of lading to Kirby (ICC bill). The bill designates Sydney, Australia, as the port of loading, Savannah, Georgia, as the port of discharge, and Huntsville as the ultimate destination for delivery.

In negotiating the ICC bill, Kirby had the opportunity to declare the full value of the machinery and to have ICC assume liability for that value. Cf. New York, N.H. & H.R. Co. v. Nothnagle, 346 U.S. 128, 135, 73 S.Ct. 986, 97 L.Ed. 1500 (1953) (a carrier must provide a shipper with a fair opportunity to declare value). Instead, and as is common in the industry, see Sturley, Carriage of Goods by Sea, 31 J. Mar. L. & Com. 241, 244 (2000), Kirby accepted a contractual liability limitation for ICC below the machinery's true value, resulting, presumably, in lower shipping rates. The ICC bill sets various liability limitations for the journey from Sydney to Huntsville. For the sea leg, the ICC bill invokes the default liability rule set forth in the Carriage of Goods by Sea Act. The COGSA "package limitation" provides:

"Neither the carrier nor the ship shall in any event be or become liable for any loss or damage to or in connection with the transportation of goods in an amount exceeding $500 per package lawful money of the United States ... unless the nature and value of such goods have been declared by the shipper before shipment and inserted into the bill of lading." 46 U.S.C. App. § 1304(5).

For the land leg, in turn, the bill limits the carrier's liability to a higher amount. So that other downstream parties expected to take part in the contract's execution could benefit from the liability limitations, the bill also contains a so-called "Himalaya Clause." It provides:

"These conditions [for limitations on liability] apply whenever claims relating to the performance of the contract evidenced by this [bill of lading] are made against any servant, agent or other person (including any independent contractor) whose services have been used in order to perform the contract."

Meanwhile, Kirby separately insured the cargo for its true value with its co-respondent in this case, Allianz Australia Insurance Ltd. (formerly MMI General Insurance, Ltd.).

Having been hired by Kirby, and because it does not itself actually transport cargo, ICC then hired Hamburg Südamerikanische Dampfschiflahrts-Gesellschafft Eggert & Amsinck (Hamburg Süd), a German ocean shipping company, to transport the containers. To formalize their contract for carriage, Hamburg Süd issued its own bill of lading to ICC (Hamburg Süd bill). That bill designates Sydney as the port of loading, Savannah as the port of discharge, and Huntsville as the ultimate destination for delivery. It adopts COGSA's default rule in limiting the liability of Hamburg Süd, the bill's designated carrier, to $500 per package. See 46 U.S.C. App. § 1304(5). It also contains a clause extending that liability limitation beyond the "tackles"—that is, to potential damage on land as well as on sea. Finally, it too contains a Himalaya Clause extending the benefit of its liability limitation to "all agents ... (including inland) carriers ... and all independent contractors whatsoever."

Acting through a subsidiary, Hamburg Süd hired Petitioner Norfolk Southern Railroad (Norfolk) to transport the machinery from the Savannah port to Huntsville. Delivery failed. The Norfolk train carrying the machinery derailed en route, causing an alleged $1.5

million in damages. Kirby's insurance company reimbursed Kirby for the loss. Kirby and its insurer then sued Norfolk in the United States District Court for the Northern District of Georgia, asserting diversity jurisdiction and alleging tort and contract claims. In its answer, Norfolk argued, among other things, that Kirby's potential recovery could not exceed the amounts set forth in the liability limitations contained in the bills of lading for the machinery's carriage.

The District Court granted Norfolk's motion for partial summary judgment, holding that Norfolk's liability was limited to $500 per container. Upon a joint motion from Norfolk and Kirby, the District Court certified its decision for interlocutory review pursuant to 28 U.S.C. § 1292(b).

A divided panel of the Eleventh Circuit reversed. It held that Norfolk could not claim protection under the Himalaya Clause in the first contract, the ICC bill. It construed the language of the clause to exclude parties, like Norfolk, that had not been in privity with ICC when ICC issued the bill. 300 F.3d 1300, 1308-1309 (2002). The majority also suggested that "a special degree of linguistic specificity is required to extend the benefits of a Himalaya clause to an inland carrier." Id., at 1310. As for the Hamburg Süd bill, the court held that Kirby could be bound by the bill's liability limitation "only if ICC was acting as Kirby's agent when it received Hamburg Süd's bill." Id., at 1305. And, applying basic agency law principles, the Court of Appeals concluded that ICC had not been acting as Kirby's agent when it received the bill. Ibid. Based on its opinion that Norfolk was not entitled to benefit from the liability limitation in either bill of lading, the Eleventh Circuit reversed the District Court's grant of summary judgment for the railroad. We granted certiorari to decide whether Norfolk could take shelter in the liability limitations of either bill, 540 U.S. 1099, 124 S.Ct. 981, 157 L.Ed.2d 811 (2004), and now reverse.

II

The courts below appear to have decided this case on an assumption, shared by the parties, that federal rather than state law governs the interpretation of the two bills of lading. Respondents now object. They emphasize that, at bottom, this is a diversity case involving tort and contract claims arising out of a rail accident somewhere between Savannah and Huntsville. We think, however, borrowing from Justice Harlan, that "the situation presented here has a more genuinely salty flavor than that." *Kossick v. United Fruit Co.,* 365 U.S. 731, 742, 81 S.Ct. 886, 6 L.Ed.2d 56 (1961). When a contract is a maritime one, and the dispute is not inherently local, federal law controls the contract interpretation. *Id.*, at 735, 81 S.Ct. 886.

Our authority to make decisional law for the interpretation of maritime contracts stems from the Constitution's grant of admiralty jurisdiction to federal courts. *See* Art. III, § 2, cl. 1 (providing that the federal judicial power shall extend to "all Cases of admiralty and maritime Jurisdiction"). See 28 U.S.C. § 1333(1) (granting federal district courts original jurisdiction over "[a]ny civil case of admiralty or maritime jurisdiction"); R. Fallon, D. Meltzer, & D. Shapiro, Hart and Wechsler's The Federal Courts and the Federal System 733-738 (5th ed.2003). This suit was properly brought in diversity, but it could also be sustained under the admiralty jurisdiction by virtue of the maritime contracts involved. *See*

Pope & Talbot, Inc. v. Hawn, 346 U.S. 406, 411, 74 S.Ct. 202, 98 L.Ed. 143 (1953) ("[S]ubstantial rights ... are not to be determined differently whether [a] case is labelled 'law side' or 'admiralty side' on a district court's docket"). Indeed, for federal common law to apply in these circumstances, this suit must also be sustainable under the admiralty jurisdiction. *See Stewart Organization, Inc. v. Ricoh Corp.*, 487 U.S. 22, 28, 108 S.Ct. 2239, 101 L.Ed.2d 22 (1988). Because the grant of admiralty jurisdiction and the power to make admiralty law are mutually dependent, the two are often intertwined in our cases.

Applying the two-step analysis from *Kossick*, we find that federal law governs this contract dispute. Our cases do not draw clean lines between maritime and non-maritime contracts. We have recognized that "[t]he boundaries of admiralty jurisdiction over contracts—as opposed to torts or crimes—being conceptual rather than spatial, have always been difficult to draw." 365 U.S., at 735, 81 S.Ct. 886. To ascertain whether a contract is a maritime one, we cannot look to whether a ship or other vessel was involved in the dispute, as we would in a putative maritime tort case. *Cf.* Admiralty Extension Act, 46 U.S.C.App. § 740 ("The admiralty and maritime jurisdiction of the United States shall extend to and include all cases of damage or injury ... caused by a vessel on navigable water, notwithstanding that such damage or injury be done or consummated on land"); R. Force & M. Norris, 1 The Law of Seamen § 1:15 (5th ed.2003). Nor can we simply look to the place of the contract's formation or performance. Instead, the answer "depends upon ... the nature and character of the contract," and the true criterion is whether it has "reference to maritime service or maritime transactions." *North Pacific S.S. Co. v. Hall Brothers Marine Railway & Shipbuilding Co.*, 249 U.S. 119, 125, 39 S.Ct. 221, 63 L.Ed. 510 (1919) (citing Insurance Co. v. Dunham, 11 Wall. 1, 26, 20 L.Ed. 90 (1871)). *See also Exxon Corp. v. Central Gulf Lines, Inc.*, 500 U.S. 603, 611, 111 S.Ct. 2071, 114 L.Ed.2d 649 (1991) ("[T]he trend in modern admiralty case law ... is to focus the jurisdictional inquiry upon whether the nature of the transaction was maritime").

The ICC and Hamburg Süd bills are maritime contracts because their primary objective is to accomplish the transportation of goods by sea from Australia to the eastern coast of the United States. See G. Gilmore & C. Black, Law of Admiralty 31 (2d ed.1975) ("Ideally, the [admiralty] jurisdiction [over contracts ought] to include those and only those things principally connected with maritime transportation" (emphasis deleted)). To be sure, the two bills call for some performance on land; the final leg of the machinery's journey to Huntsville was by rail. But under a conceptual rather than spatial approach, this fact does not alter the essentially maritime nature of the contracts.

In Kossick, for example, we held that a shipowner's promise to assume responsibility for any improper treatment his seaman might receive at a New York hospital was a maritime contract. The seaman had asked the shipowner to pay for treatment by a private physician, but the shipowner, preferring the cheaper public hospital, offered to cover the costs of any complications that might arise from treatment there. We characterized his promise as a "fringe benefit" to a shipowner's duty in maritime law to provide "'maintenance and cure.'" 365 U.S., at 736-737, 81 S.Ct. 886. Because the promise was in furtherance of a "peculiarly maritime concer[n]," *id.*, at 738, 81 S.Ct. 886, it folded into federal maritime law. It did not matter that the site of the inadequate treatment—which gave rise to the contract dispute—was in a hospital on land. Likewise, Norfolk's rail journey from Savannah to Huntsville was a "fringe" portion of the intercontinental journey promised in the ICC and Hamburg Süd bills.

We have reiterated that the "'fundamental interest giving rise to maritime jurisdiction is "the protection of maritime commerce."'" *Exxon, supra*, at 608, 111 S.Ct. 2071 (emphasis added) (quoting *Sisson v. Ruby*, 497 U.S. 358, 367, 110 S.Ct. 2892, 111 L.Ed.2d 292 (1990), in turn quoting *Foremost Ins. Co. v. Richardson*, 457 U.S. 668, 674, 102 S.Ct. 2654, 73 L.Ed.2d 300 (1982)). The conceptual approach vindicates that interest by focusing our inquiry on whether the principal objective of a contract is maritime commerce. While it may once have seemed natural to think that only contracts embodying commercial obligations between the "tackles" (*i.e.,* from port to port) have maritime objectives, the shore is now an artificial place to draw a line. Maritime commerce has evolved along with the nature of transportation and is often inseparable from some land-based obligations. The international transportation industry "clearly has moved into a new era—the age of multimodalism, door-to-door transport based on efficient use of all available modes of transportation by air, water, and land." 1 Schoenbaum 589 (4th ed.2004). The cause is technological change: Because goods can now be packaged in standardized containers, cargo can move easily from one mode of transport to another. *Ibid. See also NLRB v. Longshoremen*, 447 U.S. 490, 494, 100 S.Ct. 2305, 65 L.Ed.2d 289 (1980) ("'[C]ontainerization may be said to constitute the single most important innovation in ocean transport since the steamship displaced the schooner'" (citation omitted)); G. Muller, Intermodal Freight Transportation 15-24 (3d ed.1995).

Contracts reflect the new technology, hence the popularity of "through" bills of lading, in which cargo owners can contract for transportation across oceans and to inland destinations in a single transaction. See 1 Schoenbaum 595. Put simply, it is to Kirby's advantage to arrange for transport from Sydney to Huntsville in one bill of lading, rather than to negotiate a separate contract—and to find an American railroad itself—for the land leg. The popularity of that efficient choice, to assimilate land legs into international ocean bills of lading, should not render bills for ocean carriage nonmaritime contracts.

Some lower federal courts appear to have taken a spatial approach when deciding whether intermodal transportation contracts for intercontinental shipping are maritime in nature. They have held that admiralty jurisdiction does not extend to contracts which require maritime and nonmaritime transportation, unless the nonmaritime transportation is merely incidental—and that long-distance land travel is not incidental. *See, e.g., Hartford Fire Ins. Co. v. Orient Overseas Containers Lines*, 230 F.3d 549, 555-556 (C.A. 2 2000) ("[T]ransport by land under a bill of lading is not 'incidental' to transport by sea if the land segment involves great and substantial distances," and land transport of over 850 miles across four countries is more than incidental); Sea-Land Serv., Inc. v. Danzig, 211 F.3d 1373, 1378 (C.A. Fed.2000) (holding that intermodal transport contracts were not maritime contracts because they called for "substantial transportation between inland locations and ports both in this country and the Middle East" that was not incidental to the transportation by sea);

Kuehne & Nagel (AG & Co.) v. Geosource, Inc., 874 F.2d 283, 290 (C.A.5 1989) (holding that a through bill of lading calling for land transportation up to 1,000 miles was not a traditional maritime contract because such "extensive land-based operations cannot be viewed as merely incidental to the maritime operations"). As a preliminary matter, it seems to us imprecise to describe the land carriage required by an intermodal transportation contract as "incidental"; realistically, each leg of the journey is essential to accomplishing the contract's purpose. In this case, for example, the bills of lading required delivery to Huntsville; the Savannah port would not do.

Furthermore, to the extent that these lower court decisions fashion a rule for identifying maritime contracts that depends solely on geography, they are inconsistent with the conceptual approach our precedent requires. *See Kossick*, 365 U.S., at 735, 81 S.Ct. 886. Conceptually, so long as a bill of lading requires substantial carriage of goods by sea, its purpose is to effectuate maritime commerce—and thus it is a maritime contract. Its character as a maritime contract is not defeated simply because it also provides for some land carriage. Geography, then, is useful in a conceptual inquiry only in a limited sense: If a bill's sea components are insubstantial, then the bill is not a maritime contract.

Having established that the ICC and Hamburg Süd bills are maritime contracts, then, we must clear a second hurdle before applying federal law in their interpretation. Is this case inherently local? For not "every term in every maritime contract can only be controlled by some federally defined admiralty rule." *Wilburn Boat Co. v. Fireman's Fund Ins. Co.*, 348 U.S. 310, 313, 75 S.Ct. 368, 99 L.Ed. 337 (1955) (applying state law to maritime contract for marine insurance because of state regulatory power over insurance industry). A maritime contract's interpretation may so implicate local interests as to beckon interpretation by state law. See Kossick, supra, at 735, 81 S.Ct. 886. Respondents have not articulated any specific Australian or state interest at stake, though some are surely implicated. But when state interests cannot be accommodated without defeating a federal interest, as is the case here, then federal substantive law should govern. *See Kossick, supra*, at 739, 81 S.Ct. 886 (the process of deciding whether federal law applies "is surely ... one of accommodation, entirely familiar in many areas of overlapping state and federal concern, or a process somewhat analogous to the normal conflict of laws situation where two sovereignties assert divergent interests in a transaction"); 2 Schoenbaum 61 ("Bills of lading issued outside the United States are governed by the general maritime law, considering relevant choice of law rules").

Here, our touchstone is a concern for the uniform meaning of maritime contracts like the ICC and Hamburg Süd bills. We have explained that Article III's grant of admiralty jurisdiction " 'must have referred to a system of law coextensive with, and operating uniformly in, the whole country. It certainly could not have been the intention to place the rules and limits of maritime law under the disposal and regulation of the several States, as that would have defeated the uniformity and consistency at which the Constitution aimed on all subjects of a commercial character affecting the intercourse of the States with each other or with foreign states.'" *American Dredging Co. v. Miller*, 510 U.S. 443, 451, 114 S.Ct. 981, 127 L.Ed.2d 285 (1994) (quoting *The Lottawanna*, 21 Wall. 558, 575, 22

L.Ed. 654 (1875)). *See also Yamaha Motor Corp., U.S.A. v. Calhoun,* 516 U.S. 199, 210, 116 S.Ct. 619, 133 L.Ed.2d 578 (1996) ("[I]n several contexts, we have recognized that vindication of maritime policies demanded uniform adherence to a federal rule of decision" (citing *Kossick, supra,* at 742, 81 S.Ct. 886; *Pope & Talbot,* 346 U.S., at 409, 74 S.Ct. 202; *Garrett v. Moore-McCormack Co.,* 317 U.S. 239, 248-249, 63 S.Ct. 246, 87 L.Ed. 239 (1942))); *Romero v. International Terminal Operating Co.,* 358 U.S. 354, 373, 79 S.Ct. 468, 3 L.Ed.2d 368 (1959) ("[S]tate law must yield to the needs of a uniform federal maritime law when this Court finds inroads on a harmonious system[,] [b]ut this limitation still leaves the States a wide scope").

Applying state law to cases like this one would undermine the uniformity of general maritime law. The same liability limitation in a single bill of lading for international intermodal transportation often applies both to sea and to land, as is true of the Hamburg Süd bill. Such liability clauses are regularly executed around the world. See 1 Schoenbaum 595; Wood, Multimodal Transportation: An American Perspective on Carrier Liability and Bill of Lading Issues, 46 Am. J. Comp. L. 403, 407 (Supp.1998). *See also* 46 U.S.C.App. § 1307 (permitting parties to extend the COGSA default liability limit to damage done "prior to the loading on and subsequent to the discharge from the ship"). Likewise, a single Himalaya Clause can cover both sea and land carriers downstream, as is true of the ICC bill. *See* Part III-A, infra. Confusion and inefficiency will inevitably result if more than one body of law governs a given contract's meaning. As we said in Kossick, when "a [maritime] contract ... may well have been made anywhere in the world," it "should be judged by one law wherever it was made." 365 U.S., at 741, 81 S.Ct. 886. Here, that one law is federal.

In protecting the uniformity of federal maritime law, we also reinforce the liability regime Congress established in COGSA. By its terms, COGSA governs bills of lading for the carriage of goods "from the time when the goods are loaded on to the time when they are discharged from the ship." 46 U.S.C.App. § 1301(e). For that period, COGSA's "package limitation" operates as a default rule. § 1304(5). But COGSA also gives the option of extending its rule by contract. See § 1307 ("Nothing contained in this chapter shall prevent a carrier or a shipper from entering into any agreement, stipulation, condition, reservation, or exemption as to the responsibility and liability of the carrier or the ship for the loss or damage to or in connection with the custody and care and handling of goods prior to the loading on and subsequent to the discharge from the ship on which the goods are carried by sea"). As COGSA permits, Hamburg Süd in its bill of lading chose to extend the default rule to the entire period in which the machinery would be under its responsibility, including the period of the inland transport. Hamburg Süd would not enjoy the efficiencies of the default rule if the liability limitation it chose did not apply equally to all legs of the journey for which it undertook responsibility. And the apparent purpose of COGSA, to facilitate efficient contracting in contracts for carriage by sea, would be defeated.

III

[On the merits of the case, the Court held that that Norfolk was entitled to rely on the COGSA limitation of liability, which was extended to it both by the Himalaya clause in the Hamburg Süd bill of lading and by the Himalaya clause in the ICC bill of lading. So far as the Himalaya clause in the ICC bill of lading was concerned, the Court held that there was no reason to read it restrictively so as to require some privity of contract between the carrier (ICC) and the person seeking protection under the clause (Norfolk). So far as the Hamburg Süd bill of lading was concerned, the Court held that Kirby was bound by its terms (including the Himalaya clause) because ICC was to be regarded as Kirby's agent "for a single, limited purpose: when ICC contracts with subsequent carriers for limitation on liability". These aspects of the case are considered in more detail in Vol. 1. Eds.]

IV

We hold that Norfolk is entitled to the protection of the liability limitations in the two bills of lading. Having undertaken this analysis, we recognize that our decision does no more than provide a legal backdrop against which future bills of lading will be negotiated. It is not, of course, this Court's task to structure the international shipping industry. Future parties remain free to adapt their contracts to the rules set forth here, only now with the benefit of greater predictability concerning the rules for which their contracts might compensate.

The judgment of the United States Court of Appeals for the Eleventh Circuit is reversed, and the case is remanded for further proceedings consistent with this opinion.

It is so ordered.

Notes:

1. *Commercial Union Ins. Co. v. Sea Harvest Seafood Co.*, 251 F.3d 1294, 2001 AMC 1990 (10th Cir. 2001) involved the issue as to whether suit on a Marine Open Cargo Policy for a warehouse to warehouse shipment came within the court admiralty jurisdiction. A shipment of frozen shrimp was transported from Bangkok, Thailand to Philadelphia, Pa. The cargo was unloaded from the vessel in California and sent by rail to Chicago and from there by rail to Philadelphia. In transferring the cargo from one train terminal to another, someone forgot to hook up the electrical generator that controlled the refrigeration system. Consequently, when the shipment arrived in Philadelphia the shrimp had spoiled. Notwithstanding the loss occurred on the land portion of the journey, the court characterized the land portion of the transport portion as "incidental to the overall maritime nature of the policy." *Compare Hartford Fire Ins. Co. v. Orient Overseas Container Lines (UK) Ltd.*, 230 F.3d 549, 2001 AMC 25 (2d Cir. 2000).

2. Short term storage in a land based facility after cargo has been discharged from a vessel does not preclude the exercise of admiralty jurisdiction. Long term storage, however, is not incident to the carriage of goods by sea. It is an end in and of itself. *Brosonic Co., Ltd. v. M/V "Mathilde Maersk"*, 120 F. Supp. 2d 372, 2001 AMC 506, (S.D.N.Y. 2000), *aff'd*, 270 F.3d 106 (2d Cir. 2001).

Chapter 2

FEDERALISM AND ADMIRALTY JURISDICTION

A. Introduction: Concurrent Jurisdiction: "Saving to Suitors"

Admiralty jurisdiction in the United States is further complicated because, under the federal system, it is possible to have concurrent state and federal jurisdiction over a claim. 28 U.S.C. § 1333 purports to give exclusive jurisdiction in admiralty and maritime cases to the federal courts, "*saving to suitors in all cases all other remedies to which they are entitled.*" The "saving to suitors" clause is interpreted to reserve to suitors the right of a non-admiralty remedy in all cases where the law is competent to give such a remedy. If a state court that entertains a case of a particular class as to which federal admiralty jurisdiction extends, that suit may be brought in state court, notwithstanding the fact that the case may also have been brought as an admiralty action in federal court. For example, ordinary maritime tort and contract cases may be brought in state court. Saving to suitors will also support bringing suit in federal court under diversity jurisdiction on a claim that is controlled by substantive maritime law.

B. Proceedings *In Rem*

THE HINE v. TREVOR

71 U.S. 555, 18 L. Ed. 451, 4 Wall. 555 (1866)

Mr. Justice MILLER delivered the opinion of the court

The record distinctly raises the question, how far the jurisdiction of the District Courts of the United States in admiralty causes, arising on the navigable inland waters of this country, is exclusive, and to what extent the State courts can exercise a concurrent jurisdiction?

Nearly all the States—perhaps all whose territories are penetrated or bounded by rivers capable of floating a steamboat—have statutes authorizing their courts, by proceedings *in rem*, to enforce contracts or redress torts, which, if they had the same relation to the sea that they have to the waters of those rivers, would be conceded to be the subjects of admiralty jurisdiction. These statutes have been acted upon for many years, and are the sources of powers exercised largely by the State courts at the present time. The question of their conflict with the constitutional legislation of Congress, on the same subject, is now for the first time presented to this court.

* * *

[T]he State courts have been in the habit of adjudicating causes, which in the nature of their subject-matter, are identical in every sense with causes which are acknowledged to be of admiralty and maritime cognizance; and they have in these causes administered remedies which differ in no essential respect from the remedies which have heretofore been considered as peculiar to admiralty courts. This authority has been exercised under State statutes, and not under any claim of a general common-law power in these courts to such a jurisdiction.*

It is a little singular that, at this term of the court, we should, for the first time, have the question of the right of the State courts to exercise this jurisdiction, raised by two writs of error to State courts, remote from each other, the one relating to a contract to be performed on the Pacific Ocean, and the other to a collision on the Mississippi River. The first of these cases, *The Moses Taylor*, had been decided before the present case was submitted to our consideration.

The main point ruled in that case is, that the jurisdiction conferred by the act of 1789, on the District Courts, in civil causes of admiralty and maritime jurisdiction, is exclusive by its express terms, and that this exclusion extends to the State courts. The language of the ninth section of the act admits of no other interpretation. It says, after describing the criminal jurisdiction conferred on the District Courts, that they "shall also have exclusive original cognizance of all civil causes of admiralty and maritime jurisdiction, including all seizures under laws of impost, navigation, or trade of the United States, when the seizures are made on waters which are navigable from the sea by vessels of ten or more tons burden." If the Congress of the United States has the right, in providing for the exercise of the admiralty powers, to which the Constitution declares the authority of the Federal judiciary shall extend, to make that jurisdiction exclusive, then, undoubtedly, it has done so by this act. This branch of the subject has been so fully discussed in the opinion of the court, in the case just referred to, that it is unnecessary to consider it further in this place.

It must be taken, therefore, as the settled law of this court, that wherever the District Courts of the United States have original cognizance of admiralty causes, by virtue of the act of 1789, that cognizance is exclusive, and no other court, state or national, can exercise it, with the exception always of such concurrent remedy as is given by the common law.

* * *

If the facts of the case before us in this record constitute a cause of admiralty cognizance, then the remedy, by a direct proceeding against the vessel, belonged to the Federal courts alone, and was excluded from the State tribunals.

---

* Prior to the repudiation of the "tidal waters" and "within the county" restrictions on federal admiralty jurisdiction, litigation arising out of events and transactions involving inland waterways, in the absence of diversity jurisdiction, were often tried in state courts. As to matters cognizable in admiralty, state courts also exercised jurisdiction under the savings to suitors clause. (Eds).

It was a case of collision between two steamboats. The case of *The Magnolia*,* to which we have before referred, was a case of this character; and many others have been decided in this court since that time. That they were admiralty causes has never been doubted.

* * *

It is said that the statute of Iowa may be fairly construed as coming within the clause of the ninth section of the act of 1789, which "saves to suitors, in all cases, the right of a common-law remedy where the common law is competent to give it."

But the remedy pursued in the Iowa courts, in the case before us, is in no sense a common-law remedy. It is a remedy partaking of all the essential features of an admiralty proceeding *in rem*. The statute provides that the vessel may be sued and made defendant without any proceeding against the owners, or even mentioning their names. That a writ may be issued and the vessel seized, on filing a petition similar in substance to a libel. That after a notice in the nature of a monition, the vessel may be condemned and an order made for her sale, if the liability is established for which she was sued. Such is the general character of the steamboat laws of the Western States.

While the proceeding differs thus from a common-law remedy, it is also essentially different from what are in the West called suits by attachment, and in some of the older States foreign attachments. In these cases there is a suit against a personal defendant by name, and because of inability to serve process on him on account of non-residence, or for some other reason mentioned in the various statutes allowing attachments to issue, the suit is commenced by a writ directing the proper officer to attach sufficient property of the defendant to answer any judgment which may be rendered against him. This proceeding may be had against an owner or part owner of a vessel, and his interest thus subjected to sale in a common-law court of the State.

Such actions may, also, be maintained *in personam* against a defendant in the common-law courts, as the common law gives; all in consistence with the grant of admiralty powers in the ninth section of the Judiciary Act.

But it could not have been the intention of Congress, by the exception in that section, to give the suitor all such remedies as might afterwards be enacted by State statutes, for this would have enabled the States to make the jurisdiction of their courts concurrent in all cases, by simply providing a statutory remedy for all cases. Thus the exclusive jurisdiction of the Federal courts would be defeated. In the act of 1845, where Congress does mean this, the language expresses it clearly; for after saving to the parties, in cases arising under that act, a right of trial by jury, and the right to a concurrent remedy at common law, where it is competent to give it, there is added, "any concurrent remedy which may be given by the State laws where such steamer or other vessel is employed."

THE JUDGMENT IS REVERSED, and the case is remanded to the Supreme Court of Iowa, with directions that it be

DISMISSED FOR WANT OF JURISDICTION.

---

* 20 Howard, 296.

C. Suits In Personam: Attachment

ROUNDS v. CLOVERPORT FOUNDRY AND MACHINE COMPANY

237 U.S. 303, 35 S. Ct. 596, 59 L. Ed. 966 (1915)

Mr. Justice HUGHES delivered the opinion of the court

The Cloverport Foundry and Machine Company, the defendant in error, brought this suit against F.T. Rounds and S.A. Jesse, of Owensboro, Kentucky, in the Breckinridge Circuit Court of that State, to recover the sum of $5,668.65 for work and materials furnished under a contract to repair and rebuild a steamboat formerly known as the 'R. D. Kendall' and renamed the 'Golden Girl.' The defendants were the owners of the vessel. A specific attachment was issued under §§ 2480 to 2486 of the Kentucky Statutes which provided for a lien upon watercraft for work and supplies, etc., and the defendants procured a release of the boat by executing a forthcoming bond. By special demurrer, the defendants challenged the jurisdiction of the court to entertain the action upon the ground that the subject-matter was exclusively cognizable in the admiralty. The demurrer was overruled, and the defendants, reasserting the absence of authority in the court, answered denying the allegations of the petition and setting up a counter-claim for damages alleged to have been caused by defective work and by delay in completion. Upon the trial, the counter-claim was dismissed and the Company had judgment against the defendants for the amount demanded in its petition; it was further adjudged that, by virtue of the attachment and the applicable law, the plaintiff had a lien upon the vessel for the payment of the judgment and the vessel was ordered to be sold and the proceeds applied to the debt. The Court of Appeals of the State affirmed the judgment. 159 Kentucky, 414.

The question presented on this writ of error relates solely to the jurisdiction of the state court. It is contended by the plaintiff in error that the contract in suit was for repairs on the vessel and therefore was maritime in character; that the proceeding was *in rem* and beyond the competency of the local tribunal.

* * *

On the other hand, the defendant in error denies that the contract was maritime, contending that the old boat was dismantled, its identity destroyed, and a new boat built, and that the case in this aspect falls within the decisions relating to contracts for the original construction of a vessel.

* * *

Further, it is urged in support of the judgment that the proceeding was *in personam*, and not *in rem*; that the attachment and direction for sale were incidental to the suit against the owners and for the purpose of securing satisfaction of the personal judgment. Accordingly, it is said, the proceeding was within the scope of the 'common law remedy' saved to suitors by the Judiciary Act. 1 Stat. 77; Rev. Stat., § 563; Judicial Code, § 24.

As the last point is plainly well taken, it is unnecessary to go further. It is well settled that in an action *in personam* the state court has jurisdiction to issue an auxiliary attachment against the vessel; and, whether or not the contract in suit be deemed to be of a maritime nature, it cannot be said that the state court transcended its authority. The proceeding *in rem* which is within the exclusive jurisdiction of admiralty is one essentially against the vessel itself as the debtor or offending thing,—in which the vessel is itself 'seized and imploded as the defendant, and is judged and sentenced accordingly.' By virtue of dominion over the thing all persons interested in it are deemed to be parties to the suit; the decree binds all the world and under it the property itself passes and not merely the title or interest of a personal defendant.

* * *

Actions *in personam* with a concurrent attachment to afford security for the payment of a personal judgment are in a different category.

* * *

And this is so not only in the case of an attachment against the property of the defendant generally, but also where it runs specifically against the vessel under a state statute providing for a lien, if it be found that the attachment was auxiliary to the remedy *in personam*.

* * *

In the case of *Leon v. Galceran,** *supra*, the suit was *in personam*, in a court of the State of Louisiana, to recover mariner's wages. Under a statute of the State the vessel was subject to a lien or privilege in favor of the mariner; and accordingly at the beginning of the suit, on the application of the plaintiff who asserted his lien, a writ of sequestration was issued and levied upon the vessel which was afterwards released upon the execution by the owner, the defendant in the suit, of a forthcoming bond, with surety. Judgment was recovered by the plaintiff for the amount claimed, and the vessel not being returned, suit was brought in the state court against the surety. Upon writ of error from this court to review the judgment in the latter action, it was contended, with respect to the issue and levy of the writ of sequestration, that the vessel had been seized under admiralty process in a proceeding *in rem* over which the state court had no jurisdiction *ratione materioe* and hence that the bond was void. The contention was overruled and the jurisdiction of the state court maintained. As this court said in *Johnson v. Chicago &c. Elevator Co.*, *supra*, in reviewing *Leon v. Galceran*, *supra*, it was held that 'the action *in personam* in the state court was a proper one, because it was a common law remedy, which the common law was competent to give, although the state law gave a lien on the vessel in the case, similar to a lien under the maritime law, and it was made enforceable by a writ of sequestration in advance, to hold the vessel as a security to respond to a judgment, if recovered against her owner, as a defendant; that the suit was not a proceeding *in rem*, nor was the writ of sequestration; that the bond given on the release of the vessel became the substitute for her; that the common law is as competent as the admiralty to give a remedy in all cases where the suit is *in personam* against the owner

---

* 78 U.S. 185 (1870)] (Eds.).

of the property; and that these views were not inconsistent with any expressed in *The Moses Taylor*, in *The Hine v. Trevor*, or in *The Belfast*.'

The result of the decisions is thus stated in *Knapp, Stout & Co. v. McCaffrey*, 177 U.S. 638, 646, 648. 'The true distinction between such proceedings as are and such as are not invasions of the exclusive admiralty jurisdiction is this: If the cause of action be one cognizable in admiralty, and the suit be *in rem* against the thing itself, though a monition be also issued to the owner, the proceeding is essentially one in admiralty. If, upon the other hand, the cause of action be not one of which a court of admiralty has jurisdiction, or if the suit be *in personam* against an individual defendant, with an auxiliary attachment against a particular thing, or against the property of the defendant in general, it is essentially a proceeding according to the course of the common law, and within the saving clause of the statute (§ 563) of a common law remedy.'

In the present case, as we have said, the suit was *in personam* and the attachment was in that suit. It had no other effect than to provide security for the payment of the personal judgment which was recovered, and it was for the purpose of satisfying this judgment that, in the same proceeding and by the terms of the judgment, the vessel was directed to be sold. It was within the scope of the common law remedy to sell the property of the judgment debtors to pay their debt. We are not able to find any encroachment upon the exclusive jurisdiction vested in the Federal court in admiralty. *Judgment affirmed.*

Notes

1. *State Court Jurisdiction in Maritime Cases*

Consider carefully the reasoning of the court in *The Hine*. Is the holding on exclusive jurisdiction based on the constitution or on statute? Is there not a logical flaw in the court's interpretation of the saving to suitors clause in the sense that the court assumes that saving common-law *remedies* is the same as saving concurrent state *jurisdiction*? Why didn't the court interpret the saving to suitors clause as preserving common-law remedies in federal (not state) court? Given the court's interpretation of the saving to suitors clause, can't almost all admiralty actions (except *in rem* actions) be brought in state court? Is this proper? Isn't the policy of the saving to suitors clause to preserve trial by jury rather than to preserve state court jurisdiction? This could be done by providing for a jury trial in federal court.

What is the essential difference between admiralty *in rem* actions and state law attachment proceedings? Is there really any distinction between the two? Suppose a state penal statute specifically allows sale and forfeiture—good against the world—of illegally used fishnets. Can such a forfeiture proceeding be brought in state court? *See C.J. Hendry v. Moore*, 318 U.S. 133, 63 S.Ct. 499, 87 L.Ed. 663 (1943) [forfeiture proceeding allowed in state courts because, as a matter of history, forfeiture proceedings could be brought at common law].

In 1948, the saving to suitors clause was revised to read as follows: "saving to suitors in all cases all other remedies to which they are otherwise entitled." 28 U.S.C. § 1333.

Is this 1948 formulation broader than its predecessor in that the limitation "common law remedies" is now gone? Robertson, after reviewing the cases, states as follows: "Thus, it appears that the '48 language has neither narrowed nor broadened the scope of common law jurisdiction saved, despite the fact that cases like *The Moses Taylor* and *Hendry* were based squarely and solely on the notion that the saving clause inquiry requires only that it be ascertained whether the state proceeding in question amounts to a common law remedy, and despite the fact that

that language is altogether missing from the new saving clause." D. ROBERTSON, ADMIRALTY AND FEDERALISM 134 (1970).

2. *Statutory Proceedings*

Practically any case which could be brought under 28 U.S.C. § 1333 may be brought in state court at the plaintiff's discretion. There are exceptions, such as where a statute expressly or impliedly confers exclusive jurisdiction in federal admiralty courts. Congress has provided by statute for exclusive federal jurisdiction for several types of maritime actions. Notable examples are the Limitation of Liability Act [46 U.S.C.A. §§ 30501-30512, formerly 46 U.S.C. § 183 *et seq.*], the Ship Mortgage Act [46 U.S.C.A. §§ 31301-31343, formerly 46 U.S.C. § 911 *et seq.*], the Death on the High Seas Act [46 U.S.C.A. §§ 30301-30308, formerly 46 U.S.C. § 761 *et seq.*], the Suits in Admiralty Act [46 U.S.C.A. §§ 30901-30918, formerly 46 U.S.C. § 741 *et seq.*], and the Public Vessels Act [46 U.S.C.A. §§ 31101-31113, formerly 46 U.S.C. § 781 *et seq.*]. However, the court may "read out" the term "exclusive" as the courts have done with the Death on the High Seas Act. *See Offshore Logistics, Inc. v. Tallentire*, 477 U.S. 207, 207, 106 S.Ct. 2485, 91 L.Ed.2d 174, 1986 AMC 2113 (1986). Limitation of liability proceedings can only be brought in federal court under admiralty jurisdiction. However, there is concurrent jurisdiction of the state and federal courts over proceedings to determine liability on the underlying claims and to apportion the fund. The federal courts have exclusive jurisdiction over *in rem* proceedings to foreclose a preferred ship mortgage under the Ship Mortgage Act of 1920, 46 U.S.C.A. §§ 911-984 (recodified as 46 U.S.C.A. §§ 31301-31343).

Is federal court jurisdiction exclusive on the outer continental shelf, where the OCS Lands Act specifies "exclusive federal jurisdiction?" In *Gulf Offshore Oil Co. v. Mobil Oil Co.*, 453 U.S. 473, 101 S.Ct. 2870, 69 L.Ed.2d 784, 1981 AMC 2033 (1981), the court, in an action involving personal injuries to a worker on a fixed-platform drilling rig, held that "[n]othing inherent in exclusive federal sovereignty over a territory precludes a state court from entertaining a personal injury suit concerning events occurring in the territory and governed by federal law." 453 U.S. at 481. Are there sound reasons for this holding?

---

3. *Sources of Law*

SOUTHERN PACIFIC COMPANY v. JENSEN

244 U.S. 205, 37 S. Ct. 524, 61 L. Ed. 1086, 1996 AMC 2076 (1917)

Mr. Justice McREYNOLDS delivered the opinion of the court

Upon a claim regularly presented, the Workmen's Compensation Commission of New York made the following findings of fact, rulings and award, October 9, 1914:

> 1. Christen Jensen, the deceased workman, was, on August 15, 1914, an employee of the Southern Pacific Company, a corporation of the State of Kentucky, where it has its principal office. It also has an office at Pier 49, North River, New York City. The Southern Pacific Company at said time was, and still is, a common carrier by railroad. It also owned and operated a steamship El Oriente, plying between the ports of New York and Galveston, Texas.
> 2. On August 15, 1914, said steamship was breathed for discharging and loading at Pier 49, North River, lying in navigable waters of the United States.
> 3. On said date Christen Jensen was operating a small electric freight truck. His work consisted in driving the truck into the steamship El Oriente where it was loaded with cargo, then driving the truck out of the vessel upon a gangway connecting the vessel

with Pier 49, North River, and thence upon the pier, where the lumber was unloaded from the truck. The ship was about 10 feet distant from the pier. At about 10:15 A.M., after Jensen had been doing such work for about three hours that morning, he started out of the ship with his truck loaded with lumber, a part of the cargo of the steamship El Oriente, which was being transported from Galveston, Texas, to New York City. Jensen stood on the rear of the truck, the lumber coming about to his shoulder. In driving out of the port in the side of the vessel and upon the gangway, the truck became jammed against the guide pieces on the gangway. Jensen then reversed the direction of the truck and proceeded at third or full speed backward into the hatchway. He failed to lower his head and his head struck the ship at the top line, throwing his head forward and causing his chin to hit the lumber in front of him. His neck was broken and in this manner he met his death.

* * *

7. The injury was an accidental injury and arose out of and in the course of Jensen's employment by the Southern Pacific Company and his death was due to such injury. The injury did not result solely from the intoxication of the injured employee while on duty, and was not occasioned by the wilful intention of the injured employee to bring about the injury or death of himself or another.

This claim comes within the meaning of Chapter 67 of the Consolidated Laws as re-enacted and amended by Chapter 41 of the Laws of 1914, and as amended by Chapter 316 of the Laws of 1914.

Award of compensation is hereby made to Marie Jensen, widow of the deceased, at the rate of $5.87 weekly during her widowhood with two years' compensation in one sum in case of her remarriage; to Harold Jensen, son of the deceased, at the rate of $1.96 per week and to Evelyn Jensen, daughter of the deceased, at the rate of $1.96 per week until the said Harold Jensen and Evelyn Jensen respectively shall arrive at the age of eighteen years, and there is further allowed the sum of One Hundred ($100) Dollars for funeral expenses.

In due time the Southern Pacific Company objected to the award "upon the grounds that the Act does not apply because the workman was engaged in interstate commerce on board a vessel of a foreign corporation of the State of Kentucky which was engaged solely in interstate commerce; that the injury was one with respect to which Congress may establish, and has established, a rule of liability, and under the language of Section 114,[1] the Act has no application; on the ground that the Act includes only those engaged in the

[1] Section 114.

The provisions of this chapter shall apply to employers and employees engaged in intrastate, and also in interstate or foreign commerce, for whom a rule of liability or method of compensation has been or may be established by the Congress of the United States, only to the extent that their mutual connection with intrastate work may and shall be clearly separable and distinguishable from interstate or foreign commerce, except that such employer and his employees working only in this state may, subject to the approval and in the manner provided by the commission and so far as not forbidden by any act of Congress, accept and become bound by the provisions of this chapter in like manner and with the same effect in all respects as provided herein for other employers and their employees.

operation of vessels other than those of other states and countries in foreign and interstate commerce, while the work upon which the deceased workman was engaged at the time of his death was part of the operation of a vessel of another state engaged in interstate commerce, and hence does not come within the provisions of the Act; further, that the Act is unconstitutional, as it constitutes a regulation of and burden upon commerce among the several States in violation of Article I, Section 8, of the Constitution of the United States; in that it takes property without due process of law in violation of the 14th Amendment of the Constitution; in that it denies the Southern Pacific Company the equal protection of the laws in violation of the 14th Amendment of the Constitution because the Act does not afford an exclusive remedy, but leaves the employer and its vessels subject to suit in admiralty; also that the Act is unconstitutional in that it violates Article III, Section 2, of the Constitution conferring admiralty jurisdiction upon the courts of the United States."

Without opinion, the Appellate Division approved the award and the Court of Appeals affirmed this action (215 N.Y. 514, 519), holding that the Workmen's Compensation Act applied to the employment in question and was not obnoxious to the Federal Constitution.

* * *

In *New York Central R.R. Co. v. White*, 243 U.S. 188, we held the statute valid in certain respects; and, considering what was there said, only two of the grounds relied on for reversal now demand special consideration. First. Plaintiff in error being an interstate common carrier by railroad is responsible for injuries received by employees while engaged therein under the Federal Employers' Liability Act of April 22, 1908, c. 149, 35 Stat. 65, and no state statute can impose any other or different liability. Second. As here applied, the Workmen's Compensation Act conflicts with the general maritime law, which constitutes an integral part of the federal law under Art. III, § 2, of the Constitution, and to that extent is invalid.

* * *

Article III, § 2, of the Constitution, extends the judicial power of the United States "To all cases of admiralty and maritime jurisdiction;" and Article I, § 8, confers upon the Congress power "To make all laws which may be necessary and proper for carrying into execution the foregoing powers and all other powers vested by this Constitution in the government of the United States or in any department or officer thereof." Considering our former opinions, it must now be accepted as settled doctrine that in consequence of these provisions Congress has paramount power to fix and determine the maritime law which shall prevail throughout the country. *Butler v. Boston & Savannah Steamship Co.*, 130 U.S. 527; *In re Garnett*, 141 U.S. 1, 14. And further, that in the absence of some controlling statute the general maritime law as accepted by the federal courts constitutes part of our national law applicable to matters within the admiralty and maritime jurisdiction. *The Lottawanna*, 21 Wall. 558; *Butler v. Boston & Savannah Steamship Co.*, 130 U.S. 527, 557; *Workman v. New York City*, 179 U.S. 552.

In *The Lottawanna*, Mr. Justice Bradley speaking for the court said: "That we have a maritime law of our own, operative throughout the United States, cannot be doubted. The general system of maritime law which was familiar to the lawyers and statesmen of the country when the Constitution was adopted, was most certainly intended and referred to when it was declared in that instrument that the judicial power of the United States shall extend 'to all cases of admiralty and maritime jurisdiction.'... One thing, however, is unquestionable; the Constitution must have referred to a system of law coextensive with, and operating uniformly in, the whole country. It certainly could not have been intended to place the rules and limits of maritime law under the disposal and regulation of the several States, as that would have defeated the uniformity and consistency at which the Constitution aimed on all subjects of a commercial character affecting the intercourse of the States with each other or with foreign states."

By § 9, Judiciary Act of 1789, 1 Stat. 76, 77, the District Courts of the United States were given "exclusive original cognizance of all civil causes of admiralty and maritime jurisdiction;... saving to suitors, in all cases, the right of a common law remedy, where the common law is competent to give it." And this grant has been continued. Judicial Code, §§ 24 and 256.

In view of these constitutional provisions and the federal act it would be difficult, if not impossible, to define with exactness just how far the general maritime law may be changed, modified, or affected by state legislation. That this may be done to some extent cannot be denied. A lien upon a vessel for repairs in her own port may be given by state statute, *The Lottawanna*, 21 Wall. 558, 579, 580; *The J. E. Rumbell*, 148 U.S. 1; pilotage fees fixed, *Cooley v. Board of Wardens*, 12 How. 299; *Ex parte McNiel, 13 Wall.* 236, 242; and the right given to recover in death cases, *The Hamilton*, 207 U.S. 398; *La Bourgogne*, 210 U.S. 95, 138. *See The City of Norwalk*, 55 Fed. Rep. 98, 106. Equally well established is the rule that state statutes may not contravene an applicable act of Congress or affect the general maritime law beyond certain limits. They cannot authorize proceedings *in rem* according to the course in admiralty, *The Moses Taylor*, 4 Wall. 411; *Steamboat Co. v. Chase*, 16 Wall. 522, 534; *The Glide*, 167 U.S. 606; nor create liens for materials used in repairing a foreign ship, *The Roanoke*, 189 U.S. 185. *See Workman v. New York City*, 179 U.S. 552. And plainly, we think, no such legislation is valid if it contravenes the essential purpose expressed by an act of Congress or works material prejudice to the characteristic features of the general maritime law or interferes with the proper harmony and uniformity of that law in its international and interstate relations. This limitation, at the least, is essential to the effective operation of the fundamental purpose for which such law was incorporated into our national laws by the Constitution itself. These purposes are forcefully indicated in the foregoing quotations from *The Lottawanna.*

A similar rule in respect to interstate commerce deduced from the grant to Congress of power to regulate it is now firmly established. "Where the subject is national in its character, and admits and requires uniformity of regulation, affecting alike all the States, such as transportation between the States, including the importation of goods from one State into another, Congress can alone act upon it and provide the needed regulations. The absence of any law of Congress on the subject is equivalent to its declaration that commerce in that matter shall be free." *Bowman v. Chicago & Northwestern Ry. Co.*, 125 U.S. 465, 507, 508;

Vance v. Vandercook Co., 170 U.S. 438, 444; *Clark Distilling Co. v. Western Maryland Ry. Co.*, 242 U.S. 311. And the same character of reasoning which supports this rule, we think, makes imperative the stated limitation upon the power of the States to interpose where maritime matters are involved.

The work of a stevedore in which the deceased was engaging is maritime in its nature; his employment was a maritime contract; the injuries which he received were likewise maritime; and the rights and liabilities of the parties in connection therewith were matters clearly within the admiralty jurisdiction. *Atlantic Transport Co. v. Imbrovek*, 234 U.S. 52, 59, 60.

If New York can subject foreign ships coming into her ports to such obligations as those imposed by her Compensation Statute, other States may do likewise. The necessary consequence would be destruction of the very uniformity in respect to maritime matters which the Constitution was designed to establish; and freedom of navigation between the States and with foreign countries would be seriously hampered and impeded. A far more serious injury would result to commerce than could have been inflicted by the Washington statute authorizing a materialman's lien condemned in *The Roanoke*. The legislature exceeded its authority in attempting to extend the statute under consideration to conditions like those here disclosed. So applied, it conflicts with the Constitution and to that extent is invalid.

Exclusive jurisdiction of all civil cases of admiralty and maritime jurisdiction is vested in the Federal District Courts, "saving to suitors, in all cases, the right of a common law remedy, where the common law is competent to give it." The remedy which the Compensation Statute attempts to give is of a character wholly unknown to the common law, incapable of enforcement by the ordinary processes of any court and is not saved to suitors from the grant of exclusive jurisdiction. *The Hine v. Trevor*, 4 Wall. 555, 571, 572; the *Belfast*, 7 Wall. 624, 644; *Steamboat Co. v. Chase*, 16 Wall. 522, 531, 533; *The Glide*, 167 U.S. 606, 623. And finally this remedy is not consistent with the policy of Congress to encourage investments in ships manifested in the Acts of 1851 and 1884 (Rev. Stats., §§ 4283-4285; § 18, Act of June 26, 1884, c. 121, 23 Stat. 57) which declare a limitation upon the liability of their owners. *Richardson v. Harmon*, 222 U.S. 96, 104.

The judgment of the court below must be reversed and the cause remanded for further proceedings not inconsistent with this opinion.

Reversed.

Dissent: MR. JUSTICE HOLMES, dissenting

* * *

There is no doubt that the saving to suitors of the right of a common-law remedy leaves open the common-law jurisdiction of the state courts, and leaves some power of legislation at least, to the States. For the latter I need do no more than refer to state pilotage statutes, and to liens created by state laws in aid of maritime contracts. Nearer to the point, it is decided that a statutory remedy for causing death may be enforced by the state courts, although the death was due to a collision upon the high seas. *Steamboat Co. v. Chase*, 16

Wall. 522. *Sherlock v. Alling*, 93 U.S. 99, 104. Knapp, *Stout & Co. v. McCaffrey*, 177 U.S. 638, 646. *Minnesota Rate Cases*, 230 U.S. 352, 409. The misgivings of Mr. Justice Bradley were adverted to in *The Hamilton*, 207 U.S. 398, and held at least insufficient to prevent the admiralty from recognizing such a state-created right in a proper case, if indeed they went to any such extent. *La Bourgogne*, 210 U.S. 95, 138.

The statute having been upheld in other respects, *New York Central R.R. Co. v. White*, 243 U.S. 188, I should have thought these authorities conclusive. The liability created by the New York act ends in a money judgment, and the mode in which the amount is ascertained, or is to be paid, being one that the State constitutionally might adopt, cannot matter to the question before us if any liability can be imposed that was not known to the maritime law. And as such a liability can be imposed where it was unknown not only to the maritime but to the common law, I can see no difference between one otherwise constitutionally created for death caused by accident and one for death due to fault. Neither can the statutes limiting the liability of owners affect the case. Those statutes extend to non-maritime torts, which of course are the creation of state law. *Richardson v. Harmon*, 222 U.S. 96, 104. They are paramount to but not inconsistent with the new cause of action. However, as my opinion stands on grounds that equally would support a judgment for a maritime tort not ending in death, with which admiralty courts have begun to deal, I will state the reasons that satisfy my mind.

No doubt there sometimes has been an air of benevolent gratuity in the admiralty's attitude about enforcing state laws. But of course there is no gratuity about it. Courts cannot give or withhold at pleasure. If the claim is enforced or recognized it is because the claim is a right, and if a claim depending upon a state statute is enforced it is because the State had constitutional power to pass the law. Taking it as established that a State has constitutional power to pass laws giving rights and imposing liabilities for acts done upon the high seas when there were no such rights or liabilities before, what is there to hinder its doing so in the case of a maritime tort? Not the existence of an inconsistent law emanating from a superior source, that is, from the United States. There is no such law. The maritime law is not a *corpus juris*—it is a very limited body of customs and ordinances of the sea. The nearest to anything of the sort in question was the rule that a seaman was entitled to recover the expenses necessary for his cure when the master's negligence caused his hurt. The maritime law gave him no more. *The Osceola*, 189 U.S. 158, 175. One may affirm with the sanction of that case that it is an innovation to allow suits in the admiralty by seamen to recover damages for personal injuries caused by the negligence of the master and to apply the common-law principles of tort.

Now, however, common-law principles have been applied to sustain a libel by a stevedore *in personam* against the master for personal injuries suffered while loading a ship, *Atlantic Transport Co. v. Imbrovek*, 234 U.S. 52; and *The Osceola* recognizes that in some cases at least seamen may have similar relief. From what source do these new rights come? The earliest case relies upon "the analogies of the municipal law," *The Edith Godden*, 23 Fed. Rep. 43, 46,—sufficient evidence of the obvious pattern, but inadequate for the specific origin. I recognize without hesitation that judges do and must legislate, but they can do so only interstitially; they are confined from molar to molecular motions. A common-law judge could not say I think the doctrine of consideration a bit of historical nonsense and shall not enforce it in my court. No more could a judge exercising the limited jurisdiction of admiralty say I think well of the common-law rules of master and servant and propose to introduce them here *en bloc*. Certainly he could not in that way enlarge the exclusive jurisdiction of the District Courts and cut down the power of the States. If admiralty adopts common-law rules without an act of Congress it cannot extend the maritime law as understood by the Constitution. It must take the rights of the parties from a different authority, just as it does when it enforces a lien created by a State. The only authority available is the common law or statutes of a State. For from the often repeated statement that there is no common law of the United States, *Wheaton v. Peters*, 8 Pet. 591, 658; *Western Union Telegraph Co. v. Call Publishing Co.*, 181 U.S. 92, 101, and from the principles recognized in *Atlantic Transport Co. v. Imbrovek* having been unknown to the maritime law, the natural inference is that in the silence of Congress this court has believed the very limited law of the sea to be supplemented here as in England by the common law, and that here that means, by the common law of the State. *Sherlock v. Alling*, 93 U.S. 99, 104. *Taylor v. Carryl*, 20 How. 583, 598. So far as I know, the state courts have made this assumption without criticism or attempt at revision from the beginning to this day; *e.g. Wilson v. MacKenzie*, 7 Hill (N.Y.), 95. *Gabrielson v. Waydell*, 135 N.Y. 1, 11. *Kalleck v. Deering*, 161 Massachusetts, 469. *See Ogle v. Barnes*, 8 T.R. 188. *Nicholson v. Mounsey*, 15 East, 384. Even where the admiralty has unquestioned jurisdiction the common law may have concurrent authority and the state courts concurrent power. *Schoonmaker v. Gilmore*, 102 U.S. 118. The invalidity of state attempts to create a remedy for maritime contracts or torts, parallel to that in the admiralty, that was established in such cases as *The Moses Taylor*, 4 Wall. 411, and *The Hine v. Trevor*, 4 Wall. 555, is immaterial to the present point.

The common law is not a brooding omnipresence in the sky but the articulate voice of some sovereign or quasi sovereign that can be identified; although some decisions with which I have disagreed seem to me to have forgotten the fact. It always is the law of some State, and if the District Courts adopt the common law of torts, as they have shown a tendency to do, they thereby assume that a law not of maritime origin and deriving its authority in that territory only from some particular State of this Union also governs maritime torts in that territory—and if the common law, the statute law has at least equal force, as the discussion in *The Osceola* assumes. On the other hand the refusal of the District Courts to give remedies coextensive with the common law would prove no more than that they regarded their jurisdiction as limited by the ancient lines—not that they doubted that the common law might and would be enforced in the courts of the States as it always has been. This court has recognized that in some cases different principles of liability would be applied as the suit should happen to be brought in a common-law or admiralty court. *Compare The Max Morris*, 137 U.S. 1, with *Belden v. Chase*, 150 U.S. 674, 691. But hitherto it has not been doubted authoritatively, so far as I know, that even when the admiralty had a rule of its own to which it adhered, as in *Workman v. New York City*, 179

U.S. 552, the state law, common or statute, would prevail in the courts of the State. Happily such conflicts are few.

It might be asked why, if the grant of jurisdiction to the courts of the United States imports a power in Congress to legislate, the saving of a common-law remedy, *i.e.*, in the state courts, did not import a like if subordinate power in the State. But leaving that question on one side, such cases as *Steamboat Co. v. Chase*, 16 Wall. 522, *The Hamilton*, 207 U.S. 398, and *Atlantic Transport Co. v. Imbrovek*, 234 U.S. 52, show that it is too late to say that the mere silence of Congress excludes the statute or common law of a State from supplementing the wholly inadequate maritime law of the time of the Constitution, in the regulation of personal rights, and I venture to say that it never has been supposed to do so, or had any such effect.

* * *

Mr. Justice PITNEY dissented, in a separate opinion. Mr. Justice BRANDEIS and Mr. Justice CLARKE concurred in the dissent, both upon the grounds stated by Mr. Justice HOLMES and upon those stated by Mr. Justice PITNEY.

* * *

D. Problems of Federalism

1. Choice of Law

The maritime law of the United States is *federal* law derived either from court decisions or from statute. The federal judiciary also enjoys the power to fashion substantive admiralty law rules and does so freely especially in cases of general maritime tort and contract. In *Southern Pacific v. Jensen* 244 US. 205, 214, 37 S. Ct. 524, 61 L. Ed. 1086, 1996 AMC 2076 (1917), the Supreme Court articulated the source of this federal power:

> Article III. sec. 2, of the Constitution, extends the judicial power of the United States "To all cases of admiralty and maritime jurisdiction;" and Article I. sec. 8, confers upon the Congress power "To make all laws which may be necessary and proper for carrying into execution the foregoing powers and all other powers vested by this Constitution in the government of the United State or in any department or officer thereof." Considering our former opinions, it must now be accepted as settled doctrine that in consequence of these provisions Congress has paramount power to fix an determine the maritime law which shall prevail throughout the country. *Butler v. Boston & Savannah Steamship Co.*, 130 U.S. 527 (1889); *In re Garnett*, 141 U.S. 1, 14). And further, that in the absence of some controlling statute the general maritime law as accepted by the federal courts constitutes part of our national law applicable to matters within the admiralty and maritime jurisdiction... .

Note that this means that the power of Congress to enact legislation pertaining to maritime matters is independent of the Commerce Clause. Doesn't this also mean that the *federal* maritime law is applicable in state court actions under the saving clause as well as in federal court on grounds of diversity? In theory the choice of the forum is not supposed to influence the legal principles that are applicable. *See* D. ROBERTSON, ADMIRALTY AND FEDERALISM 242-46 (1970). Where federal maritime law is applied in state saving to suitor clause actions or in diversity cases, isn't it the reverse of the rule in *Erie v. Tompkins*, 304 U.S. 64, 58 S.Ct. 817, 82 L.Ed. 1188 (1938)?

Both admiralty tort and contract cases present situations which are within the federal judicial power and are also within state judicial power. However, as discussed above, an admiralty case is an admiralty case wherever it is brought. It must be governed generally by the same principles and rules of substantive maritime law regardless of whether it is brought in a state or federal court. When a case meets the criteria for admiralty jurisdiction, such as those that apply in tort cases, then the substantive rules of federal maritime tort law must be applied regardless of whether suit is brought in a federal court or in a state court. On the other hand, state law may be used to supplement federal law where it is not considered to be incompatible with federal law or where the state interest outweighs the national interest of uniformity. In the absence of a federal statute or clearly established maritime law precedent, state law should be applied.

In *Dean v. Maritime Overseas Corp.*, 770 F. Supp. 309, 1993 AMC 2112 (E.D.La. 1991), *aff'd*, 981 F.2d 1256 (5th Cir. 1992), the court stated:

1. The "Savings to Suitors" Clause

The United States Constitution provides that the judicial power of the federal courts extends to "all Cases of admiralty and maritime Jurisdiction." U.S. CONST. art. III, § 2. Congress has codified this grant of federal jurisdiction in Title 28, United States Code, Section 1333, which provides in part:

> The district courts shall have original jurisdiction, exclusive of the courts of the States, of:
>
> (1) Any civil case of admiralty or maritime jurisdiction, saving to suitors in all cases all other remedies to which they are otherwise entitled.

28 U.S.C. § 1333 (Supp. 1989); *see* 14 C. WRIGHT, A. MILLER & E. COOPER, FEDERAL PRACTICE AND PROCEDURE § 3672 (1985 & Supp. 1991). The federal courts, therefore, have exclusive jurisdiction over all cases involving purely maritime matters. The "savings to suitors" clause, however, reserves the right of a plaintiff to pursue nonmaritime remedies in all other cases.

This clause, in general, provides for the application of common law remedies in all cases where such law is competent. One commentator has noted that,

> Since the common law is competent in all cases where the suit is *in personam*, a plaintiff in such causes may elect either to proceed in admiralty or to bring an ordinary civil action, either at law in state court or in a federal district court under federal diversity jurisdiction (or some other basis of federal jurisdiction). This rule is subject to two qualifications. There is exclusive admiralty jurisdiction over proceedings *in rem*, because the *in rem* action was not known to the common law... .

T. SCHOENBAUM, ADMIRALTY AND MARITIME LAW § 3-13 (Prac. ed. 1987) (footnotes omitted); *see* G. GILMORE & C. BLACK, THE LAW OF ADMIRALTY § 1-13 (1975). The *in personam* suit, therefore, provides plaintiffs with a choice of forum either in state court or federal court, unless preempted by a federal statute. Moreover, the "savings to suitors" clause prohibits a defendant from removing a case from state court solely on the basis of maritime jurisdiction unless the suit falls under the federal courts' exclusive maritime jurisdiction.

> The "savings to suitors" clause, however, does not preempt the application of federal maritime law where the claim arises under admiralty law—no matter whether the suit has been brought in federal court or state court. *See Atlantic & Gulf Stevedores, Inc. v. Ellerman Lines, Ltd.*, 369 U.S. 355, 359-60, 7 L. Ed. 2d 798, 82 S. Ct. 780 (1962); *Pope & Talbot, Inc. v. Hawn*, 346 U.S. 406, 409-11, 98 L. Ed. 143, 74 S. Ct. 202 (1953); *McCraine v. Hondo Boats, Inc.*, 399 So.2d 163, 165 (La. 1981), *cert. denied*, 458 U.S. 1105, 73 L. Ed. 2d 1366, 102 S. Ct. 3483 (1982). In fact, the United States Supreme Court in *Pope & Talbot* noted that, while state law may supplement federal maritime policies, federal maritime law controls rights of recovery rooted in admiralty. 346 U.S. at 409; *see Askew v. American Waterways Operators, Inc.*, 411 U.S.

325, 338, 36 L. Ed. 2d 280, 93 S. Ct. 1590 (1973). Further, the Supreme Court rejected the contention that a suit brought in diversity must be heard under state law. *Pope & Talbot, Inc.*, 346 U.S. at 411.

---

2. Application of State Law

Introductory Note

As indicated in the preceding Note, "Maritime Law Preemption of State Law", "despite the fact that maritime law is federal law regardless of the forum in which the case is heard, there are several theories under which state decisional law or legislation may be applied in maritime cases. First, the state or common-law rule may be "borrowed" and applied as the federal maritime law. For example, the law of general maritime torts applies common-law negligence, causation, and other state law tort rules. *See Watz v. Zapata Offshore Co.*, 431 F.2d 100, 1970 AMC 7307 (5th Cir. 1970); *Petition of Kinsman Transit Co.*, 338 F.2d 708 (2d Cir. 1964), *cert. denied sub nom Continental Grain Co. v. City of Buffalo*, 380 U.S. 944, 85 S. Ct. 1026, 13 L. Ed. 2d 963 (1965). Second, sometimes state law may be applied despite the existence of a rule formulated under the general maritime law where local interests outweigh any competing federal interest in uniformity. (Application of state wrongful death statute to death of a "non-seafarer" in state territorial waters. *Yamaha Motor Corp., U.S.A. v. Calhoun*, 516 U.S. 199, 116 S. Ct. 619, 1996 AMC 305 (1996). Third, state statutory law that touches upon maritime matters may be upheld and followed if it is a valid exercise of the state's authority and does not interfere with the essential uniformity of maritime law. *See Askew v. American Waterways*, 411 U.S. 325, 1973 AMC 811 (1973).

AMERICAN DREDGING COMPANY v. MILLER

510 U.S. 443, 114 S. Ct. 981, 127 L. Ed. 2d 285, 1994 AMC 913 (1994)

Justice SCALIA delivered the opinion of the Court

This case presents the question whether, in admiralty cases filed in a state court under the Jones Act, 46 U.S.C. App. § 688, and the "saving to suitors clause," 28 U.S.C. § 1333(1), federal law pre-empts state law regarding the doctrine of *forum non conveniens*.

I

Respondent William Robert Miller, a resident of Mississippi, moved to Pennsylvania to seek employment in 1987. He was hired by petitioner American Dredging Company, a Pennsylvania corporation with its principal place of business in New Jersey, to work as a seaman aboard the M/V John R., a tug operating on the Delaware River. In the course of that employment respondent was injured. After receiving medical treatment in Pennsylvania and New York, he returned to Mississippi where he continued to be treated by local physicians.

On December 1, 1989, respondent filed this action in the Civil District Court for the Parish of Orleans, Louisiana. He sought relief under the Jones Act, which authorizes a seaman who suffers personal injury "in the course of his employment" to bring "an action for damages at law," 46 U.S.C. App. § 688(a), and over which state and federal courts have concurrent jurisdiction. *See Engel v. Davenport*, 271 U.S. 33, 37, 46 S. Ct. 410, 412, 70 L. Ed. 813 (1926). Respondent also requested relief under general maritime law for unseaworthiness, for wages, and for maintenance and cure. *See McAllister v. Magnolia Petroleum Co.*, 357 U.S. 221, 224, 78 S. Ct. 1201, 1203, 2 L. Ed. 2d 1272 (1958) (setting forth means of recovery available to injured seaman).

The trial court granted petitioner's motion to dismiss the action under the doctrine of *forum non conveniens*, holding that it was bound to apply that doctrine by federal maritime law. The Louisiana Court of Appeal for the Fourth District affirmed. 580 So.2d 1091 (1991). The Supreme Court of Louisiana reversed, holding that Article 123(C) of the Louisiana Code of Civil Procedure, which renders the doctrine of *forum non conveniens* unavailable in Jones Act and maritime law cases brought in Louisiana state courts, is not preempted by federal maritime law. 595 So.2d 615 (1992). American Dredging Company filed a petition for a writ of certiorari, which we granted. 507 U.S.—, 113 S. Ct. 1840, 123 L. Ed. 2d 466 (1993).

II

The Constitution provides that the federal judicial power "shall extend ... to all Cases of admiralty and maritime Jurisdiction." U.S. CONST. Art. III, § 2, cl. 1. Federal-court jurisdiction over such cases, however, has never been entirely exclusive. The Judiciary Act of 1789 provided:

> That the district courts shall have, exclusively of the courts of the several States... exclusive original cognizance of all civil causes of admiralty and maritime jurisdiction... within their respective districts as well as upon the high seas; *saving to suitors, in all cases, the right of a common-law remedy, where the common law is competent to give it.*

§ 9, 1 Stat. 76-77 (emphasis added). The emphasized language is known as the "saving to suitors clause." This provision has its modern expression at 28 U.S.C. § 1333(1), which reads (with emphasis added):

> The district courts shall have original jurisdiction, exclusive of the courts of the States, of:
>
> > (1) Any civil case of admiralty or maritime jurisdiction, *saving to suitors in all cases all other remedies to which they are otherwise entitled.*

We have held it to be the consequence of exclusive federal jurisdiction that state courts "may not provide a remedy in rem for any cause of action within the admiralty jurisdiction." *Red Cross Line v. Atlantic Fruit Co.*, 264 U.S. 109, 124, 44 S. Ct. 274, 277, 68 L. Ed. 582 (1924). An *in rem* suit against a vessel is, we have said, distinctively an admiralty proceeding, and is hence within the exclusive province of the federal courts. *The Moses Taylor*, 4 Wall. 411, 431, 18 L. Ed. 397 (1867). In exercising *in personam* jurisdiction, however, a state court may "'adopt such remedies, and... attach to them such incidents, as it sees fit' so long as it does not attempt to make changes in the 'substantive maritime law.'"

Madruga v. Superior Court of California, 346 U.S. 556, 561, 74 S. Ct. 298, 301, 98 L. Ed. 290 (1954) (quoting *Red Cross Line, supra*, 264 U.S., at 124, 44 S. Ct., at 277). That proviso is violated when the state remedy "works material prejudice to the characteristic features of the general maritime law or interferes with the proper harmony and uniformity of that law in its international and interstate relations." *Southern Pacific Co. v. Jensen*, 244 U.S. 205, 216, 37 S. Ct. 524, 529, 61 L. Ed. 1086 (1917). The issue before us here is whether the doctrine of *forum non conveniens* is either a "characteristic feature" of admiralty or a doctrine whose uniform application is necessary to maintain the "proper harmony" of maritime law. We think it is neither.[1]

A

Under the federal doctrine of *forum non conveniens*, "when an alternative forum has jurisdiction to hear [a] case, and when trial in the chosen forum would 'establish ... oppressiveness and vexation to a defendant.... out of all proportion to plaintiff's convenience,' or when the 'chosen forum [is] inappropriate because of considerations affecting the court's own administrative and legal problems,' the court may, in the exercise of its sound discretion, dismiss the case," even if jurisdiction and proper venue are established. *Piper Aircraft Co. v. Reyno*, 454 U.S. 235, 241, 102 S. Ct. 252, 258, 70 L. Ed. 2d 419 (1981) (quoting *Koster v. (American) Lumbermens Mut. Casualty Co.*, 330 U.S. 518, 524, 67 S. Ct. 828, 831, 91 L. Ed. 1067 (1947)). In *Gulf Oil Corp. v. Gilbert*, 330 U.S. 501, 67 S. Ct. 839, 91 L. Ed. 1055 (1947), Justice Jackson described some of the multifarious factors relevant to the *forum non conveniens* determination:

> An interest to be considered, and the one likely to be most pressed, is the private interest of the litigant. Important considerations are the relative ease of access to sources of proof; availability of compulsory process for attendance of unwilling, and the cost of obtaining attendance of willing, witnesses; possibility of view of premises, if view would be appropriate to the action; and all other practical problems that make trial of a case easy, expeditious and inexpensive. There may also be questions as to the enforcibility [sic] of a judgment if one is obtained....
>
> Factors of public interest also have [a] place in applying the doctrine. Administrative difficulties follow for courts when litigation is piled up in congested centers instead of being handled at its origin. Jury duty is a burden that ought not to be imposed upon the people of a community which has no relation to the litigation. In cases which touch the affairs of many persons, there is reason for holding the trial in their view and reach rather than in remote parts of the country where they can learn of it by report

[1] Justice STEVENS asserts that we should not test the Louisiana law against the standards of *Jensen*, a case which, though never explicitly overruled, is in his view as discredited as *Lochner v. New York*, 198 U.S. 45, 25 S. Ct. 539, 49 L. Ed. 937 (1905). *See post*, at 990-991. Petitioner's pre-emption argument was primarily based upon the principles established in *Jensen*, as repeated in the later cases (which Justice STEVENS also disparages, *see post*, at 991) of *Knickerbocker Ice Co. v. Stewart*, 253 U.S. 149, 40 S. Ct. 438, 64 L. Ed. 834 (1920), and *Washington v. W.C. Dawson & Co.*, 264 U.S. 219, 44 S. Ct. 302, 68 L. Ed. 646 (1924), *see* Brief for Petitioner 12-13. Respondent did not assert that those principles had been repudiated; nor did the Solicitor General, who, in support of respondent, discussed *Jensen* at length, *see* Brief for the United States as Amicus Curiae 5, 11-13, and n. 12. Since we ultimately find that the Louisiana law meets the standards of *Jensen* anyway, we think it inappropriate to overrule *Jensen* in dictum, and without argument or even invitation.

> only. There is a local interest in having localized controversies decided at home. There is an appropriateness, too, in having the trial of a diversity case in a forum that is at home with the state law that must govern the case, rather than having a court in some other forum untangle problems in conflict of laws, and in law foreign to itself.

Id., at 508- 509, 67 S. Ct., at 843.[2]

Although the origins of the doctrine in Anglo-American law are murky, most authorities agree that *forum non conveniens* had its earliest expression not in admiralty but in Scottish estate cases. *See Macmaster v. Macmaster*, 11 Sess.Cas. 685, 687 (No. 280) (2d Div.Scot.) (1833); *McMorine v. Cowie*, 7 Sess.Cas. (2d ser.) 270, 272 (No. 48) (1st Div.Scot.) (1845); *La Société du Gaz de Paris v. La Société Anonyme de Navigation "Les Armateurs Français,"* [1926] Sess.Cas. (H.L.) 13 (1925). *See generally* Speck, *Forum Non Conveniens and Choice of Law in Admiralty: Time for an Overhaul*, 18 J. MAR. LAW & COM. 185, 187 (1987); Barrett, The Doctrine of Forum Non Conveniens, 35 Cal.L.Rev. 380, 386-387 (1947); Braucher, The Inconvenient Federal Forum, 60 Harv.L.Rev. 908, 909 (1947); *but see* Dainow, *The Inappropriate Forum*, 29 ILL. L. REV. 867, 881, n. 58 (1935) (doctrine in Scotland was "borrowed" from elsewhere before middle of 19th century).

Even within the United States alone, there is no basis for regarding *forum non conveniens* as a doctrine that originated in admiralty. To be sure, within federal courts it may have been given its earliest and most frequent expression in admiralty cases. *See The Maggie Hammond*, 9 Wall. 435, 457, 19 L. Ed. 772 (1870); *The Belgenland*, 114 U.S. 355, 365-366, 5 S. Ct. 860, 864-865, 29 L. Ed. 152 (1885). But the doctrine's application has not been unique to admiralty. When the Court held, in *Gilbert, supra*, that *forum non conveniens* applied to all federal diversity cases, Justice Black's dissent argued that the doctrine had been applied in maritime cases "[f]or reasons peculiar to the special problems of admiralty." *Id.*, 330 U.S., at 513, 67 S. Ct., at 845. The Court disagreed, reciting a long history of valid application of the doctrine by state courts, both at law and in equity. *Id.*, at 504-505, and n. 4, 67 S. Ct., at 840-842, and n. 4. It observed that the problem of plaintiffs' misusing venue to the inconvenience of defendants "is a very old one affecting the administration of the courts as well as the rights of litigants, and both in England and in this country the common law worked out techniques and criteria for dealing with it." *Id.*, at 507, 67 S. Ct., at 842. Our most recent opinion dealing with *forum non conveniens*, *Piper Aircraft Co. v. Reyno*, 454 U.S. 235, 102 S. Ct. 252, 70 L. Ed. 2d 419 (1981), recognized that the doctrine "originated in Scotland, and became part of the common law of many States," *id.*, at 248, n. 13, 102 S. Ct., at 262, n. 13 (citation omitted), and treated the *forum non conveniens* analysis of *Canada Malting Co. v. Paterson S. S., Ltd.*, 285 U.S. 413,

---

[2] *Gilbert* held that it was permissible to dismiss an action brought in a District Court in New York by a Virginia plaintiff against a defendant doing business in Virginia for a fire that occurred in Virginia. Such a dismissal would be improper today because of the federal venue transfer statute, 28 U.S.C. § 1404(a): "For the convenience of parties and witnesses, in the interest of justice, a district court may transfer any civil action to any other district or division where it might have been brought." By this statute, "[d]istrict courts were given more discretion to transfer ... than they had to dismiss on grounds of *forum non conveniens*." *Piper Aircraft Co. v. Reyno*, 454 U.S. 235, 253, 102 S. Ct. 252, 264, 70 L. Ed. 2d 419 (1981). As a consequence, the federal doctrine of *forum non conveniens* has continuing application only in cases where the alternative forum is abroad.

52 S. Ct. 413, 76 L. Ed. 837 (1932), an admiralty case, as binding precedent in the nonadmiralty context.

In sum, the doctrine of *forum non conveniens* neither originated in admiralty nor has exclusive application there. To the contrary, it is and has long been a doctrine of general application. Louisiana's refusal to apply *forum non conveniens* does not, therefore, work "material prejudice to [a] characteristic featur[e] of the general maritime law." *Southern Pacific Co. v. Jensen*, 244 U.S., at 216, 37 S. Ct., at 529.

B

Petitioner correctly points out that the decision here under review produces disuniformity. As the Fifth Circuit noted in *Ikospentakis v. Thalassic S. S. Agency*, 915 F.2d 176, 179 (1990), maritime defendants "have access to a *forum non conveniens* defense in federal court that is not presently recognized in Louisiana state courts." We must therefore consider whether Louisiana's rule "interferes with the proper harmony and uniformity" of maritime law, *Southern Pacific Co. v. Jensen, supra*, 244 U.S., at 216, 37 S. Ct., at 529.

In *The Lottawanna*, 21 Wall. 558, 575, 22 L. Ed. 654 (1875), Justice Bradley, writing for the Court, said of the Article III provision extending federal judicial power "to all Cases of admiralty and maritime Jurisdiction":

> One thing... is unquestionable; the Constitution must have referred to a system of law coextensive with, and operating uniformly in, the whole country. It certainly could not have been the intention to place the rules and limits of maritime law under the disposal and regulation of the several States, as that would have defeated the uniformity and consistency at which the Constitution aimed on all subjects of a commercial character affecting the intercourse of the States with each other or with foreign states.

By reason of this principle, we disallowed in *Jensen* the application of state workers' compensation statutes to injuries covered by the admiralty jurisdiction. Later, in *Knickerbocker Ice Co. v. Stewart*, 253 U.S. 149, 163-164, 40 S. Ct. 438, 441, 64 L. Ed. 834 (1920), we held that not even Congress itself could permit such application and thereby sanction destruction of the constitutionally prescribed uniformity. We have also relied on the uniformity principle to hold that a State may not require that a maritime contract be in writing where admiralty law regards oral contracts as valid, *Kossick v. United Fruit Co.*, 365 U.S. 731, 81 S. Ct. 886, 6 L. Ed. 2d 56 (1961).

The requirement of uniformity is not, however, absolute. As *Jensen* itself recognized: "[I]t would be difficult, if not impossible, to define with exactness just how far the general maritime law may be changed, modified, or affected by state legislation. That this may be done to some extent cannot be denied." 244 U.S., at 216, 37 S. Ct., at 529. A later case describes to what breadth this "some extent" extends:

> It is true that state law must yield to the needs of a uniform federal maritime law when this Court finds inroads on a harmonious system[,] [b]ut this limitation still leaves the States a wide scope. State-created liens are enforced in admiralty. State remedies for wrongful death and state statutes providing for the survival of actions... have been upheld when applied to maritime causes of action.... State rules for the partition and sale of ships, state laws governing the specific performance of arbitration agreements, state laws regulating the effect of a breach of warranty under contracts of maritime insurance—all these laws and others have been accepted as rules of decision in admiralty cases, even, at times, when they conflicted with a rule of maritime law which did not require uniformity.

Romero v. International Terminal Operating Co., 358 U.S. 354, 373-374, 79 S. Ct. 468, 480-481, 3 L. Ed. 2d 368 (1959) (footnotes omitted).

It would be idle to pretend that the line separating permissible from impermissible state regulation is readily discernible in our admiralty jurisprudence, or indeed is even entirely consistent within our admiralty jurisprudence. Compare *Kossick, supra* (state law cannot require provision of maritime contract to be in writing), with *Wilburn Boat Co. v. Fireman's Fund Ins. Co.*, 348 U.S. 310, 75 S. Ct. 368, 99 L. Ed. 337 (1955) (state law can determine effect of breach of warranty in marine insurance policy).[3] Happily, it is unnecessary to wrestle with that difficulty today. Wherever the boundaries of permissible state regulation may lie, they do not invalidate state rejection of *forum non conveniens*, which is in two respects quite dissimilar from any other matter that our opinions have held to be governed by federal admiralty law: it is procedural rather than substantive, and it is most unlikely to produce uniform results.

As to the former point: At bottom, the doctrine of *forum non conveniens* is nothing more or less than a supervening venue provision, permitting displacement of the ordinary rules of venue when, in light of certain conditions, the trial court thinks that jurisdiction ought to be declined. But venue is a matter that goes to process rather than substantive rights—determining which among various competent courts will decide the case. Uniformity of process (beyond the rudimentary elements of procedural fairness) is assuredly not what the law of admiralty seeks to achieve, since it is supposed to apply in all the courts of the world. Just as state courts, in deciding admiralty cases, are not bound by the venue requirements set forth for federal courts in the United States Code, so also they are not

---

[3] Whatever might be the unifying theme of this aspect of our admiralty jurisprudence, it assuredly is not what the dissent takes it to be, namely, the principle that the States may not impair maritime commerce, *see post*, at 994, 995. In *Fireman's Fund*, for example, we did not inquire whether the breach-of-warranty rule Oklahoma imposed would help or harm maritime commerce, but simply whether the State had power to regulate the matter. The no-harm-to- commerce theme that the dissent plays is of course familiar to the ear—not from our admiralty repertoire, however, but from our "negative Commerce Clause" jurisprudence, *see Bendix Autolite Corp. v. Midwesco Enterprises, Inc.*, 486 U.S. 888, 891, 108 S. Ct. 2218, 2220, 100 L. Ed. 2d 896 (1988). No Commerce Clause challenge is presented in this case.

Similarly misdirected is the dissent's complaint that Article 123 of the Louisiana Code of Civil Procedure unfairly discriminates against maritime defendants because it permits application of *forum non conveniens* in nonmaritime cases, *see post*, at 993. The only issue raised and argued in this appeal, and the only issue we decide, is whether state courts must apply the federal rule of *forum non conveniens* in maritime actions. Whether they may accord discriminatory treatment to maritime actions by applying a state *forum non conveniens* rule in all except maritime cases is a question not remotely before us.

bound by the federal common-law venue rule (so to speak) of *forum non conveniens*. Because the doctrine is one of procedure rather than substance, petitioner is wrong to claim support from our decision in *Pope & Talbot, Inc. v. Hawn*, 346 U.S. 406, 74 S. Ct. 202, 98 L. Ed. 143 (1953), which held that Pennsylvania courts must apply the admiralty rule that contributory negligence is no bar to recovery. The other case petitioner relies on, *Garrett v. Moore-McCormack Co.*, 317 U.S. 239, 248-249, 63 S. Ct. 246, 252-253, 87 L. Ed. 239 (1942), held that the traditional maritime rule placing the burden of proving the validity of a release upon the defendant pre-empts state law placing the burden of proving invalidity upon the plaintiff. In earlier times, burden of proof was regarded as "procedural" for choice-of-law purposes such as the one before us here, *see, e.g., Levy v. Steiger*, 233 Mass. 600, 124 N.E. 477 (1919); Restatement of Conflict of Laws s 595 (1934). For many years, however, it has been viewed as a matter of substance, *see Cities Service Oil Co. v. Dunlap*, 308 U.S. 208, 212, 60 S. Ct. 201, 203, 84 L. Ed. 196 (1939)—which is unquestionably the view that the Court took in *Garrett*, stating that the right of the plaintiff to be free of the burden of proof "inhered in his cause of action," "was a part of the very substance of his claim and cannot be considered a mere incident of a form of procedure." 317 U.S., at 249, 63 S. Ct., at 253. Unlike burden of proof (which is a sort of default rule of liability) and affirmative defenses such as contributory negligence (which eliminate liability), *forum non conveniens* does not bear upon the substantive right to recover, and is not a rule upon which maritime actors rely in making decisions about primary conduct—how to manage their business and what precautions to take.

* * *

C

* * *

Accordingly, we have held that the Jones Act adopts "the entire judicially developed doctrine of liability" under the Federal Employers' Liability Act (FELA), 35 Stat. 65, as amended, 45 U.S.C. § 51 *et seq. Kernan v. American Dredging Co.*, 355 U.S. 426, 439, 78 S. Ct. 394, 401, 2 L. Ed. 2d 382 (1958). More particularly, we have held that the Jones Act adopts the "uniformity requirement" of the FELA, requiring state courts to apply a uniform federal law. *Garrett, supra*, 317 U.S., at 244, 63 S. Ct., at 250. And—to come to the point of this excursus—despite that uniformity requirement we held in *Missouri ex rel. Southern R. Co. v. Mayfield*, 340 U.S. 1, 5, 71 S. Ct. 1, 3, 95 L. Ed. 3 (1950), that a state court presiding over an action pursuant to the FELA "should be freed to decide the availability of the principle of *forum non conveniens* in these suits according to its own local law." We declared *forum non conveniens* to be a matter of "local policy," *id.*, at 4, 71 S. Ct., at 2, a proposition well substantiated by the local nature of the "public factors" relevant to the *forum non conveniens* determination. *See Reyno, supra*, 454 U.S., at 241, and n. 6, 102 S. Ct., at 25 and n. 6 (quoting *Gilbert*, 330 U.S., at 509, 67 S. Ct., at 843).

* * *

Amicus the Solicitor General has urged that we limit our holding, that *forum non conveniens* is not part of the uniform law of admiralty, to cases involving domestic entities. We think it unnecessary to do that. Since the parties to this suit are domestic entities it is quite impossible for our holding to be any broader.

The judgment of the Supreme Court of Louisiana is *Affirmed.*

* * *

Justice STEVENS, concurring in part and concurring in the judgment

It is common ground in the debate between the Court and Justice KENNEDY that language from the majority opinion in *Southern Pacific Co. v. Jensen*, 244 U.S. 205, 37 S. Ct. 524, 61 L. Ed. 1086 (1917), correctly defines this Court's power to forbid state tribunals from applying state laws in admiralty cases. *See ante*, at 985, *post*, at 993. In my view, Jensen is just as untrustworthy a guide in an admiralty case today as *Lochner v. New York*, 198 U.S. 45, 25 S. Ct. 539, 49 L. Ed. 937 (1905), would be in a case under the Due Process Clause.

In the *Jensen* case, five Members of this Court concluded that the State of New York did not have the authority to award compensation to an injured longshoreman because application of the state remedy would interfere with the "proper harmony and uniformity" of admiralty law. 244 U.S., at 216, 37 S. Ct., at 529. Justice Holmes' dissenting opinion in *Jensen*, no less eloquent than his famous dissent in *Lochner*, scarcely needs embellishment. *See id.*, at 218-223, 37 S. Ct., at 529-532.[1] Nonetheless, like *Lochner* itself, *Jensen* has never been formally overruled. Indeed, in *Knickerbocker Ice Co. v. Stewart*, 253 U.S. 149, 40 S. Ct. 438, 64 L. Ed. 834 (1920), the same majority that decided *Jensen* reached the truly remarkable conclusion that even Congress could not authorize the States to apply their workmen's compensation laws in accidents subject to admiralty jurisdiction. *See also Washington v. W.C. Dawson & Co.*, 264 U.S. 219, 44 S. Ct. 302, 68 L. Ed. 646 (1924).

As Justice Brandeis stated in dissent in *Washington*, it takes an extraordinarily long and tenuous "process of deduction" to find in a constitutional grant of judicial jurisdiction a strong federal pre-emption doctrine unwaivable even by Congress. *See id.*, at 230-231, 44 S. Ct., at 306-307. *Jensen* and its progeny represent an unwarranted assertion of judicial authority to strike down or confine state legislation—even state legislation approved by Act of Congress—without any firm grounding in constitutional text or principle. In my view, we should not rely upon and thereby breathe life into this dubious line of cases.

Jensen asks courts to determine whether the state law would materially impair "characteristic features" of federal maritime law. 244 U.S., at 216, 37 S. Ct., at 529. The unhelpful abstractness of those words leaves us without a reliable compass for navigating maritime pre-emption problems. As Justice KENNEDY demonstrates, the *forum non conveniens* doctrine may be classified as a "characteristic feature" of federal admiralty jurisprudence

[1] The central theme of Holmes' dissent was that nothing in the Constitution or in the Judiciary Act's grant of jurisdiction over admiralty cases to the district courts prevented New York from supplementing the "very limited body of customs and ordinances of the sea" with its statutory workers' compensation remedy. *Southern Pacific Co. v. Jensen*, 244 U.S. 205, 220, 37 S. Ct. 524, 531 (1917). Holmes' *Jensen* dissent was the source of his famous observations that "judges do and must legislate, but they can do so only interstitially[,]" *id.*, at 221, 37 S. Ct., at 531, and that "[t]he common law is not a brooding omnipresence in the sky but the articulate voice of some sovereign or quasi-sovereign that can be identified[,]" *id.*, at 222, 37 S. Ct., at 531.

even though it did not *originate in*, nor is it *exclusive to*, the law of admiralty. Compare *ante*, at 985-987 with *post*, at 993-995. There is, however, no respectable judicial authority for the proposition that every "characteristic feature" of federal maritime law must prevail over state law.

As JUSTICE KENNEDY observes, *post*, at 993, it is not easy to discern a substantial policy justification for Louisiana's selective "open forum" statute, which exempts only federal maritime and Jones Act claims from the State's general *forum non conveniens* policy. The statute arguably implicates concerns about disruptive local restrictions on maritime commerce that help explain why admiralty has been a federal subject. I am not persuaded, however, that the answer to those concerns lies in an extension of the patchwork maritime pre-emption doctrine. If this Court's maritime pre-emption rulings can be arranged into any pattern, it is a most haphazard one. *See generally* Currie, *Federalism and the Admiralty: "The Devil's Own Mess,"* 1960 S. CT.REV. 158. Such a capricious doctrine is unlikely to aid the free flow of commerce, and threatens to have the opposite effect.

In order to decide this case, it is enough to observe that maritime pre- emption doctrine allows state courts to use their own procedures in Savings Clause and Jones Act cases, *see Offshore Logistics, Inc. v. Tallentine*, 477 U.S. 207, 222-223, 106 S. Ct. 2485, 2494-2495, 91 L. Ed. 2d 174 (1986), and that *forum non conveniens* is, as the Court observes, best classified as a kind of secondary venue rule. Equally significant is the fact that Congress, which has unquestioned power to decree uniformity in maritime matters, has declined to set forth a federal forum convenience standard for admiralty cases. *Ante*, at 989-990. It also appears to have withheld from Jones Act defendants the right of removal generally applicable to claims based on federal law. *See* 28 U.S.C. § 1445(a); 46 U.S.C.App. § 688(a); *In re Dutile*, 935 F.2d 61, 62 (CA5 1991). Congress may "determine whether uniformity of regulation is required or diversity is permissible," *Washington*, 264 U.S., at 234, 44 S. Ct., at 307 (Brandeis, J., dissenting). When relevant federal legislation indicates that Congress has opted to permit state "diversity" in admiralty matters, a finding of federal pre-emption is inappropriate. Just as in cases involving non-maritime subjects, *see, e.g.*, *Cipollone v. Liggett Group, Inc.*, 505 U.S. —, —, 112 S. Ct. 2608, 2617, 120 L. Ed. 2d 407 (1992), we should not lightly conclude that the federal law of the sea trumps a duly enacted state statute. Instead, we should focus on whether the state provision in question conflicts with some particular substantive rule of federal statutory or common law, or, perhaps, whether federal maritime rules, while not directly inconsistent, so pervade the subject as to preclude application of state law. We should jettison *Jensen's* special maritime pre-emption doctrine and its abstract standards of "proper harmony" and "characteristic features."

The *Jensen* decision and its progeny all rested upon the view that a strong pre-emption doctrine was necessary to vindicate the purpose of the Admiralty Clause to protect maritime commerce from the "unnecessary burdens and disadvantages incident to discordant legislation[.]" *Knickerbocker Ice Co.*, 253 U.S., at 164, 40 S. Ct., at 441. *See also Washington*, 264 U.S., at 228, 44 S. Ct., at 305; *Jensen*, 244 U.S., at 217, 37 S. Ct., at 529. Whether or not this view of the Clause is accurate as a historical matter, *see* Castro, *The*

Origins of Federal Admiralty Jurisdiction in an Age of Privateers, Smugglers and Pirates, 37 AM. J. LEGAL HIST. 117, 154 (1993) (original purpose of Clause was to ensure federal jurisdiction over prize, criminal and revenue cases; private maritime disputes were viewed as matters for state courts), protection of maritime commerce has been a central theme in our admiralty jurisprudence. While I do not propose that we abandon commerce as a guiding concern, we should recognize that, today, the federal interests in free trade and uniformity are amply protected by other means. Most importantly, we now recognize Congress' broad authority under the Commerce Clause to supplant state law with uniform federal statutes. Moreover, state laws that affect maritime commerce, interstate and foreign, are subject to judicial scrutiny under the Commerce Clause. And to the extent that the mere assertion of state judicial power may threaten maritime commerce, the Due Process Clause provides an important measure of protection for out-of-state defendants, especially foreigners. *See Asahi Metal Industry Co. v. Superior Court of California, Solano County.*, 480 U.S. 102, 107 S. Ct. 1026, 94 L. Ed. 2d 92 (1987); *Helicopteros Nacionales de Colombia v. Hall*, 466 U.S. 408, 104 S. Ct. 1868, 80 L. Ed. 2d 404 (1984). [FN3] Extension of the ill-advised doctrine of *Jensen* is not the appropriate remedy for unreasonable state venue rules.

Accordingly, I concur in the judgment and in Part II-C of the opinion of the Court.

Justice KENNEDY, with whom Justice THOMAS joins, dissenting.

The Court gives a careful and comprehensive history of the *forum non conveniens* doctrine but, in my respectful view, draws the wrong conclusions from this account and from our precedents. Today's holding contradicts two just and well-accepted principles of admiralty law: uniformity and the elimination of unfair forum selection rules. When hearing cases governed by the federal admiralty and maritime law, the state courts, to be sure, have broad discretion to reject a *forum non conveniens* motion. They should not be permitted, however, to disregard the objection altogether. With due respect, I dissent.

Neither the Court nor respondent is well positioned in this case to contend that the State has some convincing reason to outlaw the *forum non conveniens* objection. For the fact is, though the Court seems unimpressed by the irony, the State of Louisiana commands its courts to entertain the *forum non conveniens* objection in all federal civil cases except for admiralty, the very context in which the rule is most prominent and makes most sense.... Louisiana's expressed interest is to reach out to keep maritime defendants, but not other types of defendants, within its borders, no matter how inconvenient the forum. This state interest is not the sort that should justify any disuniformity in our national admiralty law.

In all events, the Court misapprehends the question it should confront. The issue here is not whether *forum non conveniens* originated in admiralty law, or even whether it is unique to that subject, but instead whether it is an important feature of the uniformity and harmony to which admiralty aspires. *See Southern Pacific Co. v. Jensen*, 244 U.S. 205, 216, 37 S. Ct. 524, 529, 61 L. Ed. 1086 (1917). From the historical evidence, there seems little doubt to me that *forum non conveniens* is an essential and salutary feature of admiralty law. It gives ship owners and operators a way to avoid vexatious litigation on a distant and unfamiliar shore. By denying this defense in all maritime cases, Louisiana upsets international and interstate comity and obstructs maritime trade. And by sanctioning Louisiana's law, a rule explicable only by some desire to disfavor maritime defendants, the Court condones the forum shopping and disuniformity that the admiralty jurisdiction is supposed to prevent.

In committing their ships to the general maritime trade, owners and operators run an unusual risk of being sued in venues with little or no connection to the subject matter of the suit. A wage dispute between crewman and captain or an accident on board the vessel may erupt into litigation when the ship docks in a faraway port. Taking jurisdiction in these cases, instead of allowing them to be resolved when the ship returns home, disrupts the schedule of the ship and may aggravate relations with the state from which it hales. *See* Bickel, *The Doctrine of Forum Non Conveniens As Applied in the Federal Courts in Matters of Admiralty*, 35 CORNELL L.Q. 12, 20-21 (1949) ("holding a ship and its crew in an American port, to which they may have come to do no more than refuel, may, in the eyes of the nation of the flag be deemed an undue interference with her commerce, and a violation of that 'comity and delicacy' which in the more courtly days of some of the earlier cases were considered normal among the nations" (footnote omitted)).

From the beginning, American admiralty courts have confronted this problem through the *forum non conveniens* doctrine. As early as 1801, a Pennsylvania District Court declined to take jurisdiction over a wage dispute between a captain and crewman of a Danish ship. *Willendson v. Forsoket*, 29 F. Cas. 1283 (No. 17,682) (Pa.1801). "It has been my general rule," explained the court, "not to take cognizance of disputes between the masters and crews of foreign ships." *Id.*, at 1284. "Reciprocal policy, and the justice due from one friendly nation to another, calls for such conduct in the courts of either country." *Ibid.*

Dismissals for reasons of comity and *forum non conveniens* were commonplace in the 19th century. *See, e.g., The Infanta*, 13 F. Cas. 37, 39 (No. 7,030) (SDNY 1848) (dismissing claims for wages by two seamen from a British ship; "This court has repeatedly discountenanced actions by foreign seamen against foreign vessels not terminating their voyages at this port, as being calculated to embarrass commercial transactions and relations between this country and others in friendly relations with it");....

Long-time foreign trading partners also recognize the *forum non conveniens* doctrine. The Court notes the doctrine's roots in Scotland. *See La Société du Gaz de Paris v. La Société Anonyme de Navigation "Les Armateurs Français,"* [1926] Sess.Cas. 13 (H.L.1925) (affirming dismissal of breach of contract claim brought by French manufacturer against French ship owner who had lost the manufacturer's cargo at sea). English courts have followed Scotland, although most often they stay the case rather than dismiss it. *See The Atlantic Star*, [1974] App.Cas. 436 (H.L.1973) (staying action between a Dutch barge owner and a Dutch ship owner whose vessels had collided in Belgian waters, pending the outcome of litigation in Antwerp); *The Po*, [1990] 1 Lloyd's Rep. 418 (Q.B.Adm.1990) (refusing to stay action between Italian ship owner and American ship owner whose vessels had collided in Brazilian waters); *The Lakhta*, [1992] 2 Lloyd's Rep. 269 (Q.B.Adm.1992) (staying title dispute between Latvian plaintiffs and Russian defendant, so that plaintiffs could sue in Russian court). The Canadian Supreme Court has followed England and Scotland. *See*

Antares Shipping Corp. v. Delmar Shipping Ltd. (The Capricorn), [1977] 1 Lloyd's Rep. 180, 185 (1976) (citing *Atlantic Star and Société du Gaz*).

From all of the above it should be clear that *forum non conveniens* is an established feature of the general maritime law. To the main point, it serves objectives that go to the vital center of the admiralty pre-emption doctrine. Comity with other nations and among the States was a primary aim of the Constitution. At the time of the framing, it was essential that our prospective foreign trading partners know that the United States would uphold its treaties, respect the general maritime law, and refrain from erecting barriers to commerce. The individual States needed similar assurances from each other. *See* THE FEDERALIST No. 22, pp. 143-145 (C. Rossiter ed. 1961) (Hamilton); Madison, *Vices of the Political System of the United States*, 2 WRITINGS OF JAMES MADISON 362-363 (G. Hunt ed. 1901). Federal admiralty and maritime jurisdiction was the solution. *See* 2 J. Story, COMMENTARIES ON THE CONSTITUTION OF THE UNITED STATES § 1672 (5th ed. 1833); The Federalist No. 80, *supra*, at 478 (Hamilton). And so, when the States were allowed to provide common law remedies for *in personam* maritime disputes through the saving to suitors clause, it did not follow that they were at liberty to set aside the fundamental features of admiralty law. "The confusion and difficulty, if vessels were compelled to comply with the local statutes at every port, are not difficult to see.... [T]he Union was formed with the very definite design of freeing maritime commerce from intolerable restrictions incident to such control." *Washington v. W.C. Dawson & Co.*, 264 U.S. 219, 228, 44 S. Ct. 302, 305, 68 L. Ed. 646 (1924). Accord, *The Lottawanna*, 21 Wall. 558, 575, 22 L. Ed. 558 (1875); *Jensen*, 244 U.S., at 215-217, 37 S. Ct., at 528-529.

Louisiana's open forum policy obstructs maritime commerce and runs the additional risk of impairing relations among the states and with our foreign trading partners. These realities cannot be obscured by characterizing the defense as procedural. *See ante*, at 988-989; *but see* Bickel, 35 CORNELL L.Q., at 17 ("[T]he *forum non conveniens* problem... is inescapably connected with the substantive rights of the parties in any given type of suit, rather than... 'merely' an 'administrative' problem"). The reverse-*Erie* metaphor, while perhaps of use in other contexts, *see Offshore Logistics, Inc. v. Tallentire*, 477 U.S. 207, 222-223, 106 S. Ct. 2485, 2494-2495, 91 L. Ed. 2d 174 (1986), is not a sure guide for determining when a specific state law has displaced an essential feature of the general maritime law. *See Exxon Corp. v. Chick Kam Choo*, 817 F.2d 307, 319 (CA5 1987) ("drawing conclusions from metaphors is dangerous"). Procedural or substantive, the *forum non conveniens* defense promotes comity and trade. The States are not free to undermine these goals.

It is true that in *Missouri ex rel. Southern R. Co. v. Mayfield*, 340 U.S. 1, 71 S. Ct. 1, 95 L. Ed. 3 (1950), we held the state courts free to ignore *forum non conveniens* in FELA cases. But we did not consider the maritime context. Unlike FELA, a domestic statute controlling domestic markets, the admiralty law is international in its concern. A state court adjudicating a FELA dispute interposes no obstacle to our foreign relations. And while the Jones Act in turn makes FELA available to maritime claimants, that Act says nothing about *forum non conveniens*. *See* 46 U.S.C.App. § 688.

In any event, the Court's ruling extends well beyond the Jones Act; it covers the whole spectrum of maritime litigation. Courts have recognized the *forum non conveniens* defense in a broad range of admiralty disputes: breach of marine insurance contract, *Calavo Growers of Cal. v. Generali Belgium*, 632 F.2d 963 (CA2 1980); collision, *Ocean Shelf Trading, Inc. v. Flota Mercante Grancolumbiana S.A.*, 638 F.Supp. 249 (SDNY 1986); products liability, *Matson Navigation Co. v. Stal-Laval Turbin AB*, 609 F.Supp. 579 (ND Cal.1985); cargo loss, *The Red Sea Ins. Co. v. S.S. Lucia Del Mar*, 1983 A.M.C. 1630 (SDNY 1982), *aff'd*, 729 F.2d 1443, 1983 A.M.C. 1631 (CA2 1983); and breach of contract for carriage, *Galban Lobo Trading Co. v. Canadian Leader Ltd.*, 1963 A.M.C. 988 (SDNY 1958), to name a few. *See Brief for Maritime Law Association of the United States* as *Amicus Curiae* 12. In all of these cases, federal district courts will now hear *forum non conveniens* motions in the shadow of state courts that refuse to consider it. Knowing that upon dismissal a maritime plaintiff may turn around and sue in one of these state courts, *see Chick Kam Choo v. Exxon Corp.*, 486 U.S. 140, 108 S. Ct. 1684, 100 L. Ed. 2d 127 (1988), a federal court is now in a most difficult position. May it overrule a *forum non conveniens* motion it otherwise would have granted, because the state forum is open? *See Ikospentakis v. Thalassic S.S. Agency*, 915 F.2d 176, 180 (CA5 1990) (reversing the grant of plaintiff's voluntary dismissal motion, because the *forum non conveniens* defense was not available to defendants in the Louisiana court where plaintiff had also sued; refusing "to insist that these foreign appellants become guinea pigs in an effort to overturn Louisiana's erroneous rule"). Since the Court now makes *forum non conveniens* something of a derelict in maritime law, perhaps it is unconcerned that federal courts may now be required to alter their own *forum non conveniens* determinations to accommodate the policy of the State in which they sit. Under federal maritime principles, I should have thought that the required accommodation was the other way around. The Supreme Court of Texas so understood the force of admiralty; it has ruled that its state courts must entertain a *forum non conveniens* objection despite a Texas statute mandating an open forum. *Exxon Corp. v. Chick Kam Choo*, No. D-1693, ___ S.W.2d ___ (Sup. Ct. Tex., Jan. 12, 1994).

The Court does seem to leave open the possibility for a different result if those who raise the *forum non conveniens* objection are of foreign nationality. The Court is entitled, I suppose, to so confine its holding, but no part in its reasoning gives hope for a different result in a case involving foreign parties. The Court's substance-procedure distinction takes no account of the identity of the litigants, nor does the statement that *forum non conveniens* remains "nothing more or less than a supervening venue provision," ante, at 988. The Court ought to face up to the consequences of its rule in this regard.

* * *

Notes

1. In *Byrd v. Byrd,* 657 F.2d 615, 1981 AMC 2563 (4th Cir. 1981), the court faced a question of first impression, namely whether interspousal immunity applied within the federal admiralty jurisdiction to preclude a tort action by a wife against her husband for injuries sustained by her while on the husband's pleasure boat in navigable waters. No federal statute spoke to the question, and no federal court had previously even considered the question, much less established a federal admiralty rule answering it. The court did not do as the majority in *Jensen* did, concluding that the previous silence of federal law meant that there should be no federal rule on the issue. The court also did not do as the dissenting Justice Holmes would have done in *Jensen,* supplementing the silence of federal maritime law with state law. Instead, the court established a new rule of federal maritime law, that there should be no interspousal immunity in tort actions.

2. In *Green v. Industrial Helicopters, Inc.*, 593 So.2d 634, 1992 AMC 1426 (La. 1992), *cert. denied,* 506 U.S. 819, 113 S. Ct. 65, 121 L. Ed. 2d 32 (1992), a helicopter passenger brought action against a pilot and his employer to recover for injuries sustained when the helicopter made a crash landing on the high seas 150 miles off the coast of Louisiana. The Louisiana Supreme Court found the state statute which imposed strict liability was not preempted by federal maritime law.

> The proper inquiry is whether in this setting strict liability under Louisiana law thwarts the purpose of any specific Congressional pronouncement, or "work[s] material prejudice to the characteristic features of maritime law or interfere[s] with the proper harmony or uniformity of that law in its international and interstate relations". *Western Fuel Co. v. Garcia,* 257 U.S. 233, 42 S. Ct. 89, 66 L. Ed. 210 (1921); *Southern Pacific Co. v. Jensen,* 244 U.S. 205, 37 S. Ct. 524, 61 L. Ed. 1086 (1917).
>
> * * *
>
> Absent a clearly applicable act of Congress—and there is none here—we next look to the general maritime law to determine if application of La. C.C. art. 2317 would materially prejudice the "characteristic features of maritime law".
>
> * * *
>
> Given the lack of maritime rule clearly applicable to a helicopter crash on the high seas and the recognition of liability in the absence of fault in the general maritime law, strict custodial liability embodied in Louisiana Civil Code article 2317 cannot be said to "materially prejudice" characteristic features of the general maritime law.
>
> * * *
>
> In summary we conclude that there is no applicable contrary federal legislation and that La. C.C. art. 2317 neither prejudices the characteristic features of the general maritime law nor interferes impermissibly with any required uniformity in such law.

3. In *Yamaha Motor Corp. U.S.A. v. Calhoun,* 516 U.S. 199, 116 S. Ct. 619, 1996 AMC 305 (1996), a twelve year old girl was killed while operating a jet ski in state territorial waters. Her parents filed suit under both diversity and admiralty in federal district court but base their claim on the state wrongful death statute in order to enhance the amount of damages that could be recovered. Defendants contended that as the general maritime law recognized a wrongful death action for deaths occurring in state territorial waters, the court should apply federal maritime law. The Supreme Court first determined that the case fell within admiralty jurisdiction. The Court then concluded that inasmuch as the decedent had not been a "seafarer" the federal interest in uniformity was not controlling. It also observed that there was no controlling federal statute. Finally, the court concluded "the damages available for the jet ski death of Natalie Calhoun are properly governed by state law."

4. The United States Supreme Court has held that the savings clause in the Federal Boat Safety Act, 46 U.S.C. §§ 4301-4311 that saves state common law actions is not preempted by the Act or by the decision of the Coast Guard, which is given regulatory authority under the Act, not to promulgate a regulation requiring propeller guards on motorboats. *Sprietsma v. Mercury Marine,* 537 U.S. 51, 123 S.Ct. 518 (2002). In a wrongful death action in products liability and negligence based on an recreational boating accident on navigable waters, what is the source of the "common law action" that is saved, federal maritime law or state law?

E. Federal Judicial System

1. Admiralty Jurisdiction

ROMERO v. INTERNATIONAL TERMINAL OPERATING CO.

358 U.S. 354, 79 S. Ct. 468, 3 L. Ed. 2d 368 (1959)

Mr. Justice FRANKFURTER delivered the opinion of the Court

Petitioner Francisco Romero, a Spanish subject, signed on as a member of the crew of the *S.S. Guadalupe* for a voyage beginning about October 10, 1953. The *Guadalupe* was of Spanish registry, sailed under the Spanish flag and was owned by respondent Compania Trasatlantica (also known as Spanish Line), a Spanish corporation. At the completion of the voyage for which he signed, Romero continued uninterruptedly to work on the *Guadalupe.* Thereby, under the law of Spain, the terms and conditions of the original contract of hire remained in force. Subsequently the *S.S. Guadalupe* departed from the port of Bilbao in northern Spain, touched briefly at other Spanish ports, and sailed to the port of New York at Hoboken. From here the ship made a brief trip to the ports of Vera Cruz and Havana returning to Hoboken where, on May 12, 1954, Romero was seriously injured when struck by a cable on the deck of the *Guadalupe.* Thereupon petitioner filed suit on the law side of the District Court for the Southern District of New York.

The amended complaint claimed damages from four separate corporate defendants. Liability of Compania Trasatlantica and Garcia & Diaz, Inc., a New York corporation which acted as the husbanding agent for Compania's vessels while in the port of New York, was asserted under the Jones Act, 41 Stat. 1007, 46 U.S.C. § 688, and under the general maritime law of the United States for unseaworthiness of the ship, maintenance and cure[1] and a maritime tort. Liability for a maritime tort was alleged against respondents International Terminal Operating Co. and Quin Lumber Co. These two companies were working on board the *S.S. Guadalupe* at the time of the injury pursuant to oral contracts with Garcia & Diaz, Inc. Quin, a New York corporation, was engaged in carpentry work preparatory to the receipt of a cargo of grain. International Terminal, incorporated in Delaware, was employed as stevedore to load the cargo. The jurisdiction of the District Court was invoked under the Jones Act and §§ 1331[2] and 1332[3] of the Judicial Code, 28 U.S.C.

---

[1] The claim for maintenance and cure under the general maritime law included an amount for wages to the end of the voyage. We have not before us an independent claim for wages due and therefore need express no opinion on such a claim by one in petitioner's position.

[2] The district courts shall have original jurisdiction of all civil actions wherein the matter in controversy ... arises under the Constitution, laws or treaties of the United States.

[3] (a) The district courts shall have original jurisdiction of all civil actions where the matter in controversy ... is between:

* * *

(2) Citizens of a State, and foreign states or citizens or subjects thereof;

Following a pre-trial hearing the District Court dismissed the complaint. 142 F. Supp. 570.[4] The court held that the action under the Jones Act against Compania Trasatlantica must be dismissed for lack of jurisdiction since that Act provided no right of action for an alien seaman against a foreign shipowner under the circumstances detailed above. The claims under the general maritime law against Compania also were dismissed since the parties were not of diverse citizenship and 28 U.S.C. § 1331 did not confer jurisdiction on the federal law courts over claims rooted in federal maritime law. The District Court dismissed the Jones Act claim against Garcia & Diaz, Inc., pursuant to its finding that Garcia was not the employer of Romero nor, as a husbanding agent for Compania, did it have the operation and control of the vessel. The remaining claims, including those against the other respondents, were dismissed because of lack of the requisite complete diversity under the rule of *Strawbridge v. Curtiss*, 3 Cranch 267. Upon examination of the Spanish law the district judge also declined jurisdiction "even in admiralty as a matter of discretion." 142 F. Supp., at 574. The Spanish law provides Romero with a lifetime pension of 35% to 55% of his seaman's wages which may be increased by one-half if the negligence of the shipowner is established; it also allows the recovery of the Spanish counterpart of maintenance and cure. These rights under the Spanish law may be enforced through the Spanish consul in New York.

The Court of Appeals affirmed the dismissal of the complaint, 244 F.2d 409. We granted certiorari, 355 U.S. 807, because of the conflict among Courts of Appeals as to the proper construction of the relevant provision of the Judiciary Act of 1875 (now 28 U.S.C. § 1331) and because of questions raised regarding the applicability of *Lauritzen v. Larsen*, 345 U.S. 571, to the situation before us. The case was argued during the last Term and restored to the calendar for reargument during the present Term. 356 U.S. 955.

I. Jurisdiction

(a) Jurisdiction under the Jones Act

The District Court dismissed petitioner's Jones Act claims for lack of jurisdiction. "As frequently happens where jurisdiction depends on subject matter, the question whether jurisdiction exists has been confused with the question whether the complaint states a cause of action." *Montana-Dakota Utilities Co. v. Northwestern Public Service Co.*, 341 U.S. 246, 249. Petitioner asserts a substantial claim that the Jones Act affords him a right of recovery for the negligence of his employer. Such assertion alone is sufficient to empower the District Court to assume jurisdiction over the case and determine whether, in fact, the

---

[4] Prior to the commencement of the trial respondents moved to dismiss the complaint on the ground that the District Court lacked "jurisdiction" over the subject matter. The answers of some of the respondents also contained motions to dismiss for failure to state a claim upon which relief can be granted. A pre-trial hearing on the issue of "jurisdiction" was held and the complaint was dismissed. Although the trial court viewed the issues as jurisdictional in the correct sense, the procedure followed was precisely that provided for a preliminary hearing to determine whether a claim was stated upon which relief can be granted. Fed. R. Civ. P., 12 (d). Although the court considered evidence outside the pleadings, Federal Rule 12 (c) allows such evidence to be admitted, requiring the court then to treat the motion as one for summary judgment under Rule 56. Summary judgment is proper if "there is no genuine issue as to any material fact and ... the moving party is entitled to a judgment as a matter of law." Fed. R. Civ. P., 56 (c). The determinations made by the District Court, in the course of its hearing on jurisdiction, insofar as they are relevant to our disposition, were within the properly conceived scope of Rule 56. Since all the requirements of Rule 12 (c), relating to a hearing on a motion for judgment on the pleadings, were satisfied and the findings made were properly relevant to such a hearing, we need not restrict our disposition to the issue of "jurisdiction" merely because the proceedings below were inartistically labeled.

Act does provide the claimed rights. "A cause of action under our law was asserted here, and the court had power to determine whether it was or was not well founded in law and in fact." *Lauritzen v. Larsen*, 345 U.S. 571, 575.

(b) Jurisdiction under 28 U.S.C. § 1331.

Petitioner, a Spanish subject, asserts claims under the general maritime law against Compania Trasatlantica, a Spanish corporation. The jurisdiction of the Federal District Court, sitting as a court of law, was invoked under the provisions of the Judiciary Act of 1875 which granted jurisdiction to the lower federal courts "of all suits of a civil nature at common law or in equity, ... arising under the Constitution or laws of the United States,...." (now 28 U.S.C. § 1331).[5] Whether the Act of 1875 permits maritime claims rooted in federal law to be brought on the law side of the lower federal courts has recently been raised in litigation and has become the subject of conflicting decisions among Courts of Appeals.

* * *

Article III, § 2, cl. 1 (3d provision) of the Constitution and section 9 of the Act of September 24, 1789, have from the beginning been the sources of jurisdiction in litigation based upon federal maritime law. Article III impliedly contained three grants. (1) It empowered Congress to confer admiralty and maritime jurisdiction on the "Tribunals inferior to the Supreme Court" which were authorized by Art. I, § 8, cl 9. (2) It empowered the federal courts in their exercise of the admiralty and maritime jurisdiction which had been conferred on them, to draw on the substantive law "inherent in the admiralty and maritime jurisdiction," *Crowell v. Benson*, 285 U.S. 22, 55, and to continue the development of this law within constitutional limits. (3) It empowered Congress to revise and supplement the maritime law within the limits of the Constitution. *See Crowell v. Benson*, *supra*, at 55.

* * *

Section 9 not only established federal courts for the administration of maritime law; it recognized that some remedies in matters maritime had been traditionally administered by common-law courts of the original States.[12] This role of the States in the administration of maritime law was preserved in the famous "saving clause"—"saving to suitors, in all cases, the right of a common-law remedy, where the common law is competent to give it."[13] Since the original Judiciary Act also endowed the federal courts with diversity jurisdiction, common-law remedies for maritime causes could be enforced by the then Circuit Courts when the proper diversity of parties afforded access.

---

[5] Act of March 3, 1875, § 1, 18 Stat. 470. The modifications of language to be found in the present version of this Act, 28 U.S.C. § 1331, were not intended to change in any way the meaning or content of the Act of 1875. *See Reviser's Note* to 28 U.S.C. § 1331. The recent amendments to this Act, 72 Stat. 415, affected only jurisdictional amount and are not relevant here. *See* 958 U.S. CODE CONG. & ADMIN. NEWS 2333, 85th Cong., 2d Sess.

[12] *See New Jersey Steam Navigation Co. v. Merchants' Bank of Boston*, 6 How. 344, 390; *The Hamilton*, 207 U.S. 398, 404; 2 STORY, COMMENTARIES ON THE CONSTITUTION OF THE UNITED STATES, § 1672. *See also* Dodd, *The New Doctrine of the Supremacy of Admiralty Over the Common Law*, 21 COL. L. REV. 647 (1921); Black, *Admiralty Jurisdiction: Critique and Suggestions*, 50 COL. L. REV. 259 (1950).

[13] Act of Sept. 24, 1789, § 9, 1 Stat. 76.

Up to the passage of the Judiciary Act of 1875[14] these jurisdictional bases provided the only claim for jurisdiction in the federal courts in maritime matters.[15] The District Courts, endowed with "exclusive original cognizance of all civil causes of admiralty and maritime jurisdiction," sat to enforce the comprehensive federal interest in the law of the sea which had been a major reason for their creation. This jurisdiction was exercised according to the historic procedure in admiralty, by a judge without a jury. In addition, common-law remedies were, under the saving clause, enforcible in the courts of the States and on the common-law side of the lower federal courts when the diverse citizenship of the parties permitted. Except in diversity cases, maritime litigation brought in state courts could not be removed to the federal courts.[16]

The Judiciary Act of 1875 effected an extensive enlargement of the jurisdiction of the lower federal courts. For the first time their doors were opened to "all suits of a civil nature at common law or in equity, ... arising under the Constitution or laws of the United States, or treaties made, or which shall be made, under their authority...."[17] From 1875 to 1950 there is not to be found a hint or suggestion to cast doubt on the conviction that the language of that statute was taken straight from Art. III, § 2, cl. 1, extending the judicial power of the United States "to all Cases, in Law and Equity, arising under this Constitution, the Laws of the United States, and Treaties made, or which shall be made, under their Authority." Indeed what little legislative history there is affirmatively indicates that this was the source.[18] Thus the Act of 1875 drew on the scope of this provision of Clause 1, just as the Judiciary Act of 1789 reflected the constitutional authorization of Clause 1 of Section 2, which extended the judicial power "to all Cases of admiralty and maritime Jurisdiction."

These provisions of Article III are two of the nine separately enumerated classes of cases to which "judicial power" was extended by the Constitution and which thereby authorized grants by Congress of "judicial Power" to the "inferior" federal courts. The vast stream of litigation which has flowed through these courts from the beginning has done so on the assumption that, in dealing with a subject as technical as the jurisdiction of the courts, the Framers, predominantly lawyers, used precise, differentiating and not redundant language. This assumption, reflected in The Federalist Papers,[19] was authoritatively confirmed by Mr. Chief Justice Marshall in *American Ins. Co. v. Canter*, 1 Pet. 511, 544:

> We are therefore to inquire, whether cases in admiralty, and cases arising under the laws and Constitution of the United States, are identical.
>
> If we have recourse to that pure fountain from which all the jurisdiction of the Federal Courts is derived, we find language employed which cannot well be misunderstood. The Constitution declares, that 'the judicial power shall extend to all cases in

[14] Act of Mar. 3, 1875, 18 Stat. 470.

[15] *The Belfast*, 7 Wall. 624, 644; *Leon v. Galceran*, 11 Wall. 185, 188.

[16] The removal provisions of the original Judiciary Act of 1789, 1 Stat. 79, conferred a limited removal jurisdiction, not including cases of admiralty and maritime jurisdiction. In none of the statutes enacted since that time have saving-clause cases been made removable.

[17] Of course federal question jurisdiction was granted in the abortive Act of Feb. 13, 1801, § 11, 2 Stat. 92, repealed by Act of March 8, 1802, 2 Stat. 132.

[18] *See* 2 Cong. Rec. 4986-4987; Frankfurter and Landis, The Business of the Supreme Court (1928), 65-69.

[19] *See* The Federalist, No. 80 (Hamilton), note 8, *supra*.

> law and equity, arising under this Constitution, the laws of the United States, and treaties made, or which shall be made, under their authority; to all cases affecting ambassadors, or other public ministers, and consuls; to all cases of admiralty and maritime jurisdiction.
>
> The Constitution certainly contemplates these as three distinct classes of cases; and if they are distinct, the grant of jurisdiction over one of them does not confer jurisdiction over either of the other two. The discrimination made between them, in the Constitution, is, we think, conclusive against their identity.

See also The Sarah, 8 Wheat. 391.

This lucid principle of constitutional construction, embodied in one of Marshall's frequently quoted opinions, was never brought into question until 1952.[20] It had been treated as black-letter law in leading treatises.[21] It was part of the realm of legal ideas in which the authors of the Act of 1875 moved. Certainly the accomplished lawyers who drafted the Act of 1875[22] drew on the language of the constitutional grant on the assumption that they were dealing with a distinct class of cases, that the language incorporated in their enactment precluded "identity" with any other class of cases contained in Article III. Thus the grant of jurisdiction over "suits of a civil nature at common law or in equity ... arising under the Constitution or laws of the United States ... ," in the Act of 1875, as derived from Article III, could not reasonably be thought of as comprehending an entirely separate and distinct class of cases—"Cases of admiralty and maritime Jurisdiction."[23]

Of course all cases to which "judicial power" extends "arise," in a comprehensive, non-jurisdictional sense of the term, "under this Constitution." It is the Constitution that is the ultimate source of all "judicial Power"—defines grants and implies limits—and so "all Cases of admiralty and maritime Jurisdiction" arise under the Constitution in the sense that they have constitutional sanction. But they are not "Cases, in Law and Equity, arising under this Constitution, the Laws of the United States...."

Not only does language and construction point to the rejection of any infusion of general maritime jurisdiction into the Act of 1875, but history and reason powerfully support that rejection. The far-reaching extension of national power resulting from the victory of the North, and the concomitant utilization of federal courts for the vindication of that power in the Reconstruction Era, naturally led to enlarged jurisdiction of the federal courts over federal rights. But neither the aim of the Act of 1875 to provide a forum for the vindication of new federally created rights, nor the pressures which led to its enactment, suggest, even remotely, the inclusion of maritime claims within the scope of that statute. The provision of the Act of 1875 with which we are concerned was designed to give a new

---

[20] [Footnote omitted. *Eds.*]

[21] [Footnote omitted. *Eds.*]

[22] [Footnote omitted. *Eds.*]

[23] All suits involving maritime claims, regardless of the remedy sought, are cases of admiralty and maritime jurisdiction within the meaning of Article III whether they are asserted in the federal courts or, under the saving clause, in the state courts. Romero's claims for damages under the general maritime law are a case of admiralty and maritime jurisdiction. The substantive law on which these claims are based derives from the third provision of Art. III, § 2, cl. 1. Without that constitutional grant Romero would have no federal claim to assert. *Cf.* 2 STORY, COMMENTARIES ON THE CONSTITUTION OF THE UNITED STATES, § 1672.

content of jurisdiction to the federal courts, not to reaffirm one long-established, smoothly functioning since 1789.[24] We have uncovered no basis for finding the additional design of changing the method by which federal courts had administered admiralty law from the beginning. The federal admiralty courts had been completely adequate to the task of protecting maritime rights rooted in federal law. There is not the slightest indication of any intention, or of any professional or lay demands for a change in the time-sanctioned mode of trying suits in admiralty without a jury, from which it can be inferred that by the new grant of jurisdiction of cases "arising under the Constitution or laws" a drastic innovation was impliedly introduced in admiralty procedure, whereby Congress changed the method by which federal courts had administered admiralty law for almost a century. To draw such an inference is to find that a revolutionary procedural change had undesignedly come to pass. If we are now to attribute such a result to Congress the sole remaining justification for the federal admiralty courts which have played such a vital role in our federal judicial system for 169 years will be to provide a federal forum for the small number of maritime claims which derive from state law, and to afford the ancient remedy of a libel *in rem* in those limited instances when an *in personam* judgment would not suffice to satisfy a claim.[25]

* * *

Petitioner now asks us to hold that no student of the jurisdiction of the federal courts or of admiralty, no judge, and none of the learned and alert members of the admiralty bar were able, for seventy-five years, to discern the drastic change now asserted to have been contrived in admiralty jurisdiction by the Act of 1875. In light of such impressive testimony from the past the claim of a sudden discovery of a hidden latent meaning in an old technical phrase is surely suspect.

The history of archeology is replete with the unearthing of riches buried for centuries. Our legal history does not, however, offer a single archeological discovery of new, revolutionary meaning in reading an old judiciary enactment.[27] The presumption is powerful that such a far-reaching, dislocating construction as petitioner would now have us find in the Act of 1875 was not uncovered by judges, lawyers or scholars for seventy-five years because it is not there.

It is also significant that in the entire history of federal maritime legislation, whether before the passage of the Act of 1875 (*e.g.*, the Great Lakes Act—also a general jurisdictional statute and one often termed an anomaly in the maritime law because of its jury trial provision), or after (the Jones Act), Congress has not once left the availability of a trial on the law side to inference. It has made specific provision.[28] It is difficult to accept that in 1875, and in 1875 alone, a most far-reaching change was made subterraneously.

---

[24] *See* FRANKFURTER AND LANDIS, THE BUSINESS OF THE SUPREME COURT (1928), 64-65; Chadbourn and Levin, *Original Jurisdiction of Federal Questions*, 90 U. OF PA. L. REV. 639, 644-645 (1942).

[25] Of course, in a few instances, Congress has provided the federal admiralty courts with a specific statutory jurisdiction. *E.g.*, Death on the High Seas Act, 41 Stat. 537 (1920), 46 U.S.C. §§ 761-767.

[27] For reasons that would take us too far afield to discuss, *Erie R. Co. v. Tompkins*, 304 U.S. 64, is no exception.

[28] Such provisions are in the Jones Act, 41 Stat. 1007 (1920), 46 U.S.C. § 688, and in the Great Lakes Act, 5 Stat. 726 (1845), 28 U.S.C. § 1873. Neither the Suits in Admiralty Act of 1920, 41 Stat. 525, 46 U.S.C. § 741-752, nor the Death on the High Seas Act, 41 Stat. 537 (1920), 46 U.S.C. §§ 761-767, allows a jury trial in personal injury cases. When the Death on the High Seas Act was being debated it was stated that "That question was thrashed out and it was decided best not to incorporate into this bill a jury trial because of the difficulties in admiralty proceedings." Congressman Igoe, speaking for the Judiciary Committee, 59 Cong. Rec. 4482, 60th Cong., 2d Sess. (1920).

Not only would the infusion of general maritime jurisdiction into the Act of 1875 disregard the obvious construction of that statute. Important difficulties of judicial policy would flow from such an interpretation, an interpretation which would have a disruptive effect on the traditional allocation of power over maritime affairs in our federal system.

Thus the historic option of a maritime suitor pursuing a common-law remedy to select his forum, state or federal, would be taken away by an expanded view of § 1331,[29] since saving-clause actions would then be freely removable under § 1441 of Title 28.[30] The interpretation of the Act of 1875 contended for would have consequences more deeply felt than the elimination of a suitor's traditional choice of forum. By making maritime cases removable to the federal courts it would make considerable inroads into the traditionally exercised concurrent jurisdiction of the state courts in admiralty matters—a jurisdiction which it was the unquestioned aim of the saving clause of 1789 to preserve. This disruption of principle is emphasized by the few cases actually involved.[31] This small number of cases is only important in that it negatives the pressure of any practical consideration for the subversion of a principle so long-established and so deeply rooted. The role of the States in the development of maritime law is a role whose significance is rooted in the Judiciary Act of 1789 and the decisions of this Court.[32] Recognition of the part the States have played from the beginning has a dual significance. It indicates the extent to which an expanded view of the Act of 1875 would eviscerate the postulates of the saving clause, and it undermines the theoretical basis for giving the Act of 1875 a brand new meaning.

Although the corpus of admiralty law is federal in the sense that it derives from the implications of Article III evolved by the courts, to claim that all enforced rights pertaining to matters maritime are rooted in federal law is a destructive oversimplification of the highly intricate interplay of the States and the National Government in their regulation of maritime commerce. It is true that state law must yield to the needs of a uniform federal maritime law when this Court finds inroads on a harmonious system.[33] But this limitation still leaves the States a wide scope. State-created liens are enforced in admiralty.[34] State remedies for wrongful death and state statutes providing for the survival of actions, both historically absent from the relief offered by the admiralty,[35] have been upheld when applied to maritime causes of action.[36] Federal courts have enforced these statutes.[37] State rules for the partition and sale of ships,[38] state laws governing the specific performance of

---

[29] The policy of unremovability of maritime claims brought in the state courts was incorporated by Congress into the Jones Act. *See Pate v. Standard Dredging Corp.*, 193 F.2d 498 (C. A. 5th Cir. 1952).

[30] 28 U.S.C. § 1441 (b): "Any civil action of which the district courts have original jurisdiction founded on a claim or right arising under the Constitution, treaties or laws of the United States shall be removable without regard to the citizenship or residence of the parties."

[31] *See* the compilation of state court cases in Seventh 5-Year Index-Digest of American Maritime Cases, 1953-1957 (1957), XLIII-XLVIII.

[32] *See, e.g., Madruga v. Superior Court of California*, 346 U.S. 556, 560-561: "[T]he jurisdictional act [the Act of 1789] does leave state courts 'competent' to adjudicate maritime causes of action in proceedings '*in personam*'.... [T]his Court has said that a state, 'having concurrent jurisdiction, is free to adopt such remedies, and to attach to them such incidents, as it sees fit' so long as it does not attempt to make changes in the 'substantive maritime law.' *Red Cross Line v. Atlantic Fruit Co.*, 264 U.S. 109."

[33] *Southern Pacific Co. v. Jensen*, 244 U.S. 205; *Garrett v. Moore-McCormack Co.*, 317 U.S. 239; *Pope & Talbot, Inc., v. Hawn*, 346 U.S. 406. *See Maryland Casualty Co. v. Cushing*, 347 U.S. 409.

[34] *Vancouver S. S. Co., Ltd., v. Rice*, 288 U.S. 445; *Peyroux v. Howard*, 7 Pet. 324. *See also Edwards v. Elliott*, 21 Wall. 532.

[35] *The Harrisburg*, 119 U.S. 199. "Death is a composer of strife by the general law of the sea as it was for many centuries by the common law of the land." CARDOZO, J., in *Cortes v. Baltimore Insular Line*, Inc., 287 U.S. 367, 371.

[36] *The Hamilton*, 207 U.S. 398; *Western Fuel Co. v. Garcia*, 257 U.S. 233; *Just v. Chambers*, 312 U.S. 383.

[37] *The Hamilton, supra; Just v. Chambers, supra; Western Fuel Co. v. Garcia, supra.*

[38] *Madruga v. Superior Court of California*, 346 U.S. 556.

arbitration agreements,[39] state laws regulating the effect of a breach of warranty under contracts of maritime insurance[40]—all these laws and others have been accepted as rules of decision in admiralty cases, even, at times, when they conflicted with a rule of maritime law which did not require uniformity. "In the field of maritime contracts," this Court has said, "as in that of maritime torts, the National Government has left much regulatory power in the States.[41] Thus, if one thing is clear it is that the source of law in saving-clause actions cannot be described in absolute terms. Maritime law is not a monistic system. The State and Federal Governments jointly exert regulatory powers today as they have played joint roles in the development of maritime law throughout our history.[42] This sharing of competence in one aspect of our federalism has been traditionally embodied in the saving clause of the Act of 1789. Here, as is so often true in our federal system, allocations of jurisdiction have been carefully wrought to correspond to the realities of power and interest and national policy. To give a novel sweep to the Act would disrupt traditional maritime policies and quite gratuitously disturb a complementary, historic interacting federal-state relationship.

An infusion of general maritime jurisdiction into the "federal question" grant would not occasion merely an isolated change; it would generate many new complicated problems. If jurisdiction of maritime claims were allowed to be invoked under § 1331, it would become necessary for courts to decide whether the action "arises under federal law," and this jurisdictional decision would largely depend on whether the governing law is state or federal. Determinations of this nature are among the most difficult and subtle that federal courts are called upon to make.[43] Last Term's decision in *McAllister v. Magnolia Petroleum Co.*, 357 U.S. 221, illustrates the difficulties raised by the attempted application of a state statute of limitations to maritime personal injury actions. These problems result from the effort to fit state laws into the scheme of federal maritime law.

These difficulties, while nourishing academic speculation, have rarely confronted the courts. This Court has been able to wait until an actual conflict between state and federal standards has arisen, and only then proceed to resolve the problem of whether the State was free to regulate or federal law must govern. For example, if a State allowed the survival of a cause of action based on unseaworthiness as defined in the maritime law it was immaterial whether the standard was federal and governed by decisions of this Court, or was subject to state variations.[44] Thus we have been able to deal with such conceptual problems in the context of a specific conflict and a specific application of policy, as is so well illustrated by the *McAllister* case. However, such practical considerations for adjudication would be unavailable under an expanded view of § 1331. Federal courts would be forced to determine

[39] *Red Cross Line v. Atlantic Fruit Co.*, 264 U.S. 109.

[40] *Wilburn Boat Co. v. Fireman's Fund Ins. Co.*, 348 U.S. 310.

[41] *Id.*, at 313.

[42] [Footnote omitted. *Eds.*]

[43] *See, e.g., Caldarola v. Eckert*, 332 U.S. 155.

[44] Illustrative of this process is the recent case of *Allen v. Matson Navigation Co.*, 255 F.2d 273 (C. A. 9th Cir. 1958). The court remarked that "In discussing the question of the duty which the defendant owed to its passengers, all of the parties agreed that the law of California is to be applied. The trial court made a like assumption. We find it unnecessary to indicate any view as to whether in this the parties were correct for as we see it, no matter which law applies, the rule is the same, whether that of California, or that of the maritime law." *Id.*, at 277.

the respective spheres of state and federal legislative competence, the source of the governing law, as a preliminary question of jurisdiction; for only if the applicable law is "federal" law would jurisdiction be proper under § 1331. The necessity for jurisdictional determinations couched in terms of "state" or "federal law" would destroy that salutary flexibility which enables the courts to deal with source-of-law problems in light of the necessities illuminated by the particular question to be answered. Certainly sound judicial policy does not encourage a situation which necessitates constant adjudication of the boundaries of state and federal competence.

Typical also of the consequences that are implicit in this proposed modification of maritime jurisdiction, is the restriction of venue that would result from this novel interpretation of § 1331 of the Act of 1875. Litigants of diverse citizenship are now able to invoke the federal law forum for the trial of saving-clause cases. Such litigants are aided in their search for a federal forum by the liberality of the venue provisions applicable to actions based on diversity of citizenship. These provisions allow the action to be brought either "where all plaintiffs or all defendants reside."[45] If saving-clause actions were to be brought within the scope of § 1331, this choice could be no longer made. Plaintiffs would be subject to the rigid requirement that suit must be "brought only in the judicial district where all defendants reside ... ,"[46] and this would be so even where there is, in fact, diversity of citizenship.[47]

In the face of the consistent and compelling inferences to be drawn from history and policy against a break with a long past in the application of the Act of 1875, what justification is offered for this novel view of the statute? Support is ultimately reduced, one is compelled to say, to empty logic, reflecting a formal syllogism. The argument may thus be fairly summarized. It was not until recently, in a line of decision culminating in *Pope & Talbot, Inc., v. Hawn*, 346 U.S. 406, that it became apparent that the source of admiralty rights was a controlling body of federal admiralty law. This development led to a deepened consideration of the jurisdictional consequences of the federal source of maritime law. And so one turns to the Act of 1875. The Act of 1875 gave original jurisdiction to the federal courts over all cases arising under the Constitution and laws of the United States. Maritime law was federal law based on a constitutional grant of jurisdiction. Thus maritime cases arose under the Constitution or federal laws. By this mode of reasoning the words of the jurisdictional statute are found to "fit like a glove."[48]

Although it is true that the supremacy of federal maritime law over conflicting state law has recently been greatly extended, the federal nature of the maritime law administered in the federal courts has long been an accepted part of admiralty jurisprudence. The classic

---

[45] 28 U.S.C. § 1391(a).

[46] 28 U.S.C. § 1391(b).

[47] *Macon Grocery Co. v. Atlantic Coast Line R. Co.*, 215 U.S. 501. The more restrictive provisions apply in any action "wherein jurisdiction is not founded solely on diversity of citizenship...." 28 U.S.C. § 1391 (b).

There may also well be situations in which the venue provisions prevent the joinder of defendants in a Federal District Court and the state court rules of procedure do not allow their joinder, thus precluding suit altogether.

[48] *Jenkins v. Roderick*, 156 F. Supp. 299, 301 (U. S. D. C. Mass. 1957).

statement of Mr. Justice Holmes in *The Western Maid*, 257 U.S. 419, 432, summed up the accepted view that maritime law derived its force from the National Government and was part of the laws of the United States; and this was merely a restatement of a view which was clearly set forth in 1874 in *The Lottawanna*, 21 Wall. 558.[49] Thus the theory which underlies the effort to infuse general maritime jurisdiction into the Act of 1875 rests on no novel development in maritime law, but on premises as available in 1875 as they are today.

* * *

(c) "Pendent" and Diversity Jurisdiction.

Rejection of the proposed new reading of § 1331 does not preclude consideration of petitioner's claims under the general maritime law. These claims cannot, we have seen, be justified under § 1331. However, the District Court may have jurisdiction of them "pendent" to its jurisdiction under the Jones Act. Of course the considerations which call for the exercise of pendent jurisdiction of a state claim related to a pending federal cause of action within the appropriate scope of the doctrine of *Hurn v. Oursler*, 289 U.S. 238, are not the same when, as here, what is involved are related claims based on the federal maritime law. We perceive no barrier to the exercise of "pendent jurisdiction" in the very limited circumstances before us. Here we merely decide that a district judge has jurisdiction to determine whether a cause of action has been stated if that jurisdiction has been invoked by a complaint at law rather than by a libel in admiralty, as long as the complaint also properly alleges a claim under the Jones Act. We are not called upon to decide whether the District Court may submit to the jury the "pendent" claims under the general maritime law in the event that a cause of action be found to exist.

Respondents Garcia & Diaz and Quin Lumber Company, New York corporations, and International Terminal Operating Company, a Delaware corporation, are of diverse citizenship from the petitioner, a Spanish subject. Since the Jones Act provides an independent basis of federal jurisdiction over the non-diverse respondent, Compania Trasatlantica, the rule of *Strawbridge v. Curtiss*, 3 Cranch 267, does not require dismissal of the claims against the diverse respondents. Accordingly, the dismissal of these claims for lack of jurisdiction was erroneous.

* * *

[The dissenting opinions of Justices Black and Brennan have been omitted. eds.]

Note

As to the Outer Continental Shelf Lands Act as an independent basis for jurisdiction, *see Tennessee Gas Pipeline v. Houston Casualty Ins. Co.*, 87 F.3d 150, 1996 AMC 2296 (5th Cir. 1996).

---

[49] In *The Lottawanna*, the Court clearly recognized that maritime law was a body of uniform federal law drawing its authority from the Constitution and laws of the United States.

2. Supplemental Jurisdiction

28 U.S.C. § 1367. Supplemental Jurisdiction

(a) Except as provided in subsections (b) and (c) or as expressly provided otherwise by Federal statute, in any civil action of which the district courts have original jurisdiction, the district courts shall have supplemental jurisdiction over all other claims that are so related to claims in the action within such original jurisdiction that they form part of the same case or controversy under Article III of the United States Constitution. Such supplemental jurisdiction shall include claims that involve the joinder or intervention of additional parties.

(b) In any civil action of which the district courts have original jurisdiction founded solely on section 1332 of this title, the district courts shall not have supplemental jurisdiction under subsection (a) over claims by plaintiffs against persons made parties under Rule 14 [impleader], 19 [compulsory joinder], 20 [permissive joinder] , or 24 [intervention] of the Federal Rules of Civil Procedure, or over claims by persons proposed to be joined as plaintiffs under Rule 19 of such rules, or seeking to intervene as plaintiffs under Rule 24 of such rules, when exercising supplemental jurisdiction over such claims would be inconsistent with the jurisdictional requirements of section 1332.

(c) The district courts may decline to exercise supplemental jurisdiction over a claim under subsection (a) if—

(1) the claim raises a novel or complex issue of State law,
(2) the claim substantially predominates over the claim or claims over which the district court has original jurisdiction,
(3) the district court has dismissed all claims over which it has original jurisdiction, or
(4) in exceptional circumstances, there are other compelling reasons for declining jurisdiction.

(d) The period of limitations for any claim asserted under subsection (a), and for any other claim in the same action that is voluntarily dismissed at the same time as or after the dismissal of the claim under subsection (a), shall be tolled while the claim is pending and for a period of 30 days after it is dismissed unless State law provides for a longer tolling period.

(e) As used in this section, the term "State" includes the District of Columbia, the Commonwealth of Puerto Rico, and any territory or possession of the United States.

(Added Pub. L. 101-650, Title III, § 310(a), Dec. 1, 1990, 104 Stat. 5113.)

Note

The legislative history of the Judicial Improvements Act, P.L. 101-650, which added 28 U.S.C. §1367, explained that legislation was necessary to provide the federal courts with statutory authority to hear supplemental claims, to overcome the effect of the decision in *Finley v. U.S.*, 490 U.S. 545, 109 S.Ct. 2003 (1989), which had cast doubt on the authority of federal courts to hear some claims within supplemental jurisdiction. *See* House Report No. 101-734.

---

3. Right to Trial by Jury: Joinder of Jones Act and Traditional Maritime Claims

FITZGERALD v. UNITED STATES LINES CO.

374 U.S. 16, 83 S. Ct. 26, 11 L. Ed. 2d 99 (1963)

Mr. Justice BLACK delivered the opinion of the Court

Andres San Martin, a seaman, brought this action in the District Court for the Southern District of New York against the respondent United States Lines Company. His complaint alleged that he had twisted and strained his back while working for respondent on its ship. He claimed $75,000 damages based on the negligence of respondent and on the unseaworthiness of the ship and $10,000 based on respondent's failure to provide him with medical attention, maintenance and cure, and wages as required by law.[1] Martin's negligence claim invoked a remedy created by Congress in § 33 of the Jones Act, 46 U.S.C. § 688, which explicitly provides that a seaman can have a jury trial as of right; but the actions for unseaworthiness and for maintenance and cure are traditional admiralty remedies which in the absence of a statute do not ordinarily require trial by jury. The complainant here did demand a jury, however, for all the issues growing out of the single accident. The trial judge granted a jury trial for the Jones Act and the unseaworthiness issues but held the question of recovery under maintenance and cure in abeyance to try himself after jury trial of the other two issues. The jury returned a verdict for United States Lines on the negligence and unseaworthiness issues; the court then, after hearing testimony in addition to that presented to the jury, awarded Martin $224 for maintenance and cure. Sitting *en banc*, the Court of Appeals for the Second Circuit affirmed, four judges stating that it would be improper to submit a maintenance and cure claim to the jury, two believing it to be permissible but not required, and three maintaining that a seaman is entitled, as of right, to a jury trial of a maintenance and cure claim joined with a Jones Act claim. 306 F.2d 461. The lower courts are at odds on this issue.[2] We granted certiorari to decide it.[3] 371 U.S. 932.

For years it has been a common, although not uniform,[4] practice of District Courts to grant jury trials to plaintiffs who join in one complaint their Jones Act, unseaworthiness, and maintenance and cure claims when all the claims, as here, grow out of a single transac-

---

[1] Martin died while his appeal was pending and a public administrator was substituted for him.

[2] *See* notes 4 and 5, *infra*.

[3] Because of our limited grant of certiorari, we do not consider petitioner's argument that the complaint and trial record show diversity of citizenship jurisdiction and that therefore plaintiff was entitled to a jury trial. *See Atlantic & Gulf Stevedores, Inc., v. Ellerman Lines*, 369 U.S. 355, 360 (1962). Nor do we find it necessary to reach petitioner's argument that we should reconsider that part of the holding of *Romero v. International Terminal Operating Co.*, 358 U.S. 354 (1959), which concluded that claims based upon general maritime law cannot be brought in federal courts under the federal question jurisdiction of 28 U.S.C. § 1331.

[4] *See, e.g., Jesonis v. Oliver J. Olson & Co.*, 238 F.2d 307 (C. A. 9th Cir. 1956); *Stendze v. The Boat Neptune, Inc.*, 135 F. Supp. 801 (D. C. Mass. 1955); *cf. Jordine v. Walling*, 185 F.2d 662 (C. A. 3d Cir. 1950).

tion or accident.[5] This practice of requiring issues arising out of a single accident to be tried by a single tribunal is by no means surprising. Although remedies for negligence, unseaworthiness, and maintenance and cure have different origins and may on occasion call for application of slightly different principles and procedures, they nevertheless, when based on one unitary set of circumstances, serve the same purpose of indemnifying a seaman for damages caused by injury, depend in large part upon the same evidence, and involve some identical elements of recovery. Requiring a seaman to split up his lawsuit, submitting part of it to a jury and part to a judge, unduly complicates and confuses a trial, creates difficulties in applying doctrines of *res judicata* and collateral estoppel, and can easily result in too much or too little recovery.[6] The problems are particularly acute in determining the amount of damages. For example, all lost earnings and medical expenses are recoverable on a negligence count, but under the Jones Act they are subject to reduction by the jury if the seaman has been contributorily negligent. These same items are recoverable in part on the maintenance and cure count, but the damages are measured by different standards[7] and are not subject to reduction for any contributory negligence. It is extremely difficult for a judge in trying a maintenance and cure claim to ascertain, even with the use of special interrogatories, exactly what went into the damages awarded by a jury—how loss of earning power was calculated, how much was allowed for medical expenses and pain and suffering, how much was allowed for actual lost wages, and how much, if any, each of the recoveries was reduced by contributory negligence. This raises needless problems of who has the burden of proving exactly what the jury did.[8] And even if the judge can find out what elements of damage the jury's verdict actually represented, he must still try to solve the puzzling problem of the bearing the jury's verdict should have on recovery under the different standards of the maintenance and cure claim. In the absence of some statutory or constitutional obstacle, an end should be put to such an unfortunate, outdated, and wasteful manner of trying these cases.[9] Fortunately, there is no such obstacle.

While this Court has held that the Seventh Amendment does not require jury trials in admiralty cases,[10] neither that Amendment nor any other provision of the Constitution forbids them.[11] Nor does any statute of Congress or Rule of Procedure, Civil or Admiralty,

---

[5] *See, e.g.*, *Nolan v. General Seafoods Corp.*, 112 F.2d 515 (C. A. 1st Cir. 1940); *Lykes Bros. S.S. Co. v. Grubaugh*, 128 F.2d 387, *modified on rehearing*, 130 F.2d 25 (C. A. 5th Cir. 1942); *Bay State Dredging & Contracting Co. v. Porter*, 153 F.2d 827 (C. A. 1st Cir. 1946); *Gonzales v. United Fruit Co.*, 193 F.2d 479 (C. A. 2d Cir. 1951); *Rosenquist v. Isthmian S.S. Co.*, 205 F.2d 486 (C. A. 2d Cir. 1953); *Mitchell v. Trawler Racer, Inc.*, 265 F.2d 426 (C. A. 1st Cir. 1959), *rev'd on other grounds*, 362 U.S. 539 (1960); *McDonald v. Cape Cod Trawling Corp.*, 71 F. Supp. 888, 891 (D. C. Mass. 1947); GILMORE AND BLACK, THE LAW OF ADMIRALTY (1957), 262.

[6] For an illuminating discussion of the practical problems, *see Jenkins v. Roderick*, 156 F. Supp. 299, 304-306 (D. C. Mass. 1957) (WYZANSKI, J.).

This Court has held that recovery of maintenance and cure does not bar a subsequent action under the Jones Act, *Pacific S.S. Co. v. Peterson*, 278 U.S. 130 (1928), but of course, where such closely related claims are submitted to different triers of fact, questions of *res judicata* and collateral estoppel necessarily arise, particularly in connection with efforts to avoid duplication of damages.

[7] Maintenance and cure allows recovery for wages only to the end of the voyage on which a seaman is injured or becomes ill. *The Osceola*, 189 U.S. 158, 175 (1903). Medical expenses need not be provided beyond the point at which a seaman becomes incurable. *Farrell v. United States*, 336 U.S. 511 (1949).

[8] *See, e.g.*, *Bartholomew v. Universe Tankships, Inc.*, 279 F.2d 911, 915-916 (C. A. 2d Cir. 1960); *Stendze v. The Boat Neptune, Inc.*, 135 F. Supp. 801 (D. C. Mass. 1955). For another example of some of the difficulties involved in separate trials, *compare Claudio v. Sinclair Ref. Co.*, 160 F. Supp. 3 (D. C. E. D. N. Y. 1958), with *Lazarowitz v. American Export Lines*, 87 F. Supp. 197 (D. C. E. D. Pa. 1949).

[9] *See generally* Currie, *The Silver Oar and All That: A Study of the Romero Case*, 27 U. OF CHI. L. REV. 1 (1959); Kurland, *The Romero Case and Some Problems of Federal Jurisdiction*, 73 HARV. L. REV. 817, 850 (1960); Note, 73 HARV. L. REV. 138 (1959).

[10] *Waring v. Clarke*, 5 How. 441, 460 (1847).

[11] *The Genesee Chief v. Fitzhugh*, 12 How. 443, 459-460 (Dec. Term, 1851) (upholding constitutionality of jury trial provision in Great Lakes Act).

forbid jury trials in maritime cases. Article III of the Constitution vested in the federal courts jurisdiction over admiralty and maritime cases, and, since that time, the Congress has largely left to this Court the responsibility for fashioning the controlling rules of admiralty law. This Court has long recognized its power and responsibility in this area and has exercised that power where necessary to do so.[12] Where, as here, a particular mode of trial being used by many judges is so cumbersome, confusing, and time consuming that it places completely unnecessary obstacles in the paths of litigants seeking justice in our courts, we should not and do not hesitate to take action to correct the situation. Only one trier of fact should be used for the trial of what is essentially one lawsuit to settle one claim split conceptually into separate parts because of historical developments. And since Congress in the Jones Act has declared that the negligence part of the claim shall be tried by a jury, we would not be free, even if we wished, to require submission of all the claims to the judge alone. Therefore, the jury, a time-honored institution in our jurisprudence, is the only tribunal competent under the present congressional enactments to try all the claims. Accordingly, we hold that a maintenance and cure claim joined with a Jones Act claim must be submitted to the jury when both arise out of one set of facts. The seaman in this case was therefore entitled to a jury trial as of right on his maintenance and cure claim.

Judgment against the seaman on the Jones Act claim was affirmed by the Court of Appeals, and we declined to review it on certiorari. The shipowner points out that on remand the maintenance and cure claim would no longer be joined with a Jones Act claim and therefore, he argues, could be tried by a judge without a jury. We cannot agree. Our holding is that it was error to deprive the seaman of the jury trial he demanded, and he is entitled to relief from this error by having the kind of trial he would have had in the absence of error.

Reversed.

VODUSEK v. BAYLINER MARINE CORP.

71 F.3d 148, 1996 AMC 33 (4th Cir. 1995)

NIEMEYER, Circuit Judge:

This personal injury case presents two questions of first impression in this circuit: (1) whether a jury may decide all issues in a case involving both admiralty and law claims, and (2) whether a district court may properly permit a jury to draw an adverse inference from a party's spoliation of relevant evidence. We resolve both questions affirmatively.

I

In June 1989, Donald Vodusek, Sr., fueled his 28-foot cabin cruiser by siphoning gas from several gas cans in preparation for a family boat ride from Pasadena, Maryland, where

---

[12] *See, e.g., The John G. Stevens*, 170 U.S. 113 (1898); *Swift & Co. Packers v. Compania Colombiana Del Caribe*, S. A., 339 U.S. 684, 690, 691 (1950); *Warren v. United States*, 340 U.S. 523, 527 (1951); *Wilburn Boat Co. v. Fireman's Fund Ins. Co.*, 348 U.S. 310, 314 (1955); *Romero v. International Terminal Operating Co.*, 358 U.S. 354, 360-361 (1959); *The Tungus v. Skovgaard*, 358 U.S. 588, 597, 611 (1959) (opinion of BRENNAN, J., concurring in part and dissenting in part); *Mitchell v. Trawler Racer, Inc.*, 362 U.S. 539 (1960).

the boat was docked, to Baltimore's Inner Harbor. When he turned on the bilge pump roughly a half-hour later, the boat exploded and burned, causing Vodusek second and third degree burns over half of his body. Three months later, Vodusek died from burn-related complications.

Vodusek's boat was manufactured in 1978 by Bayliner Marine Corp. and sold to Stammer's Marine Center, Inc., a retail dealer. In 1984 Stammer's Marine performed a warranty repair for the boat's first owner, described on a warranty claim form: "Gas Tank Hose was kinked by Seat in Cabin. Remove Seat and Reroute Hose." Apparently, the repair was performed to the satisfaction of all parties involved. Four years later, Vodusek purchased the boat used from Stammer's Marine.

Following the death of her husband, Shirley Vodusek (hereinafter "Vodusek"), filed suit against Bayliner and Stammer's Marine contending that the fire resulted from a faulty bilge pump switch which sparked and ignited vapors from a leaking fuel system. In her complaint, she alleged an array of negligence and products liability claims for injuries sustained by her husband and for wrongful death. She sued Bayliner at law, relying on diversity jurisdiction, and Stammer's Marine in admiralty because the fire occurred on navigable waters.[1] The complaint included a demand for jury trial on all claims.

The district court submitted Vodusek's entire case to the jury, which returned a verdict in favor of the defendants. But, because the district court remained uncertain of whether this case should have been tried with or without a jury, it also rendered an independent decision on the merits as a court in admiralty. It, too, found in favor of the defendants. In arriving at its decision, the court disqualified Douglas Halsey, Vodusek's expert witness—even though his testimony had been considered by the jury—on the grounds that (1) Halsey's testimony was speculative and not based upon scientific principles; (2) Halsey was not qualified to render an expert opinion on the design of the boat's fuel system; and (3) Halsey participated in the spoliation of relevant evidence. This appeal followed.

Vodusek contends that the entire case should have been tried exclusively to the jury and therefore that the bench trial was improper and unnecessary. In connection with the jury trial, she contends that the district court erred in (1) submitting to the jury the question of whether she engaged in the spoliation of evidence; (2) allowing cross-examination of her expert witness by depositions of experts who did not testify; and (3) interpreting 33 C.F.R. § 183.554, a federal regulation requiring access to fuel system components on boats, as not covering fuel vent hoses. In connection with the bench trial, if found permissible, Vodusek contends that the court erred in disqualifying her expert witness and disregarding his testimony.

According to Bayliner and Stammer's Marine, this is an admiralty case that was properly decided by the court without a jury. Because the jury trial was unnecessary, they argue that this court need not review any issue arising from it.

---

[1] Vodusek alleged in her complaint:

5. As to the defendant Stammer's only, this is an admiralty or maritime claim within the meaning of Rule 9(h) of the Federal Civil Judicial Procedure and Rules. This Court has admiralty jurisdiction over defendant Stammer's pursuant to 18[28] U.S.C. § 1333 and 46 U.S.C.[App.] § 740.

6. This Court has diversity jurisdiction pursuant to 28 U.S.C. § 1332 as to defendant Bayliner. The citizenship of plaintiff and defendant Bayliner is diverse and the amount in controversy exceeds Fifty Thousand Dollars ($50,000.00), exclusive of interest and costs.

For the reasons that follow, we conclude that the district court properly submitted the entire case to the jury and therefore that the bench trial was superfluous. We also reject Vodusek's assignments of error regarding the jury trial. Accordingly, we affirm.

II

Because errors are assigned to both the jury and bench trials, we must first resolve whether all claims should have been submitted to a jury or some claims decided by the court without a jury.

In response to Vodusek's contention that this case was properly tried to the jury, Bayliner and Stammer's Marine contend that this case can be decided only in admiralty because the prerequisites of diversity jurisdiction, which formed the basis for allowing a jury trial, were not satisfied. Even though there was complete diversity between Vodusek and Bayliner to support the claims at law, Bayliner and Stammer's Marine argue that the court must consider the citizenship of all the parties to the action in deciding whether to submit a case to a jury, relying on *Powell v. Offshore Navigation*, 644 F.2d 1063 (5th Cir. Unit A.1981) (holding that citizenship of defendant named in admiralty claim must be considered in determining diversity jurisdiction over law claims in which admiralty defendant was not named), *cert. denied*, 454 U.S. 972, 102 S. Ct. 521, 70 L. Ed. 2d 391 (1981). Because Stammer's Marine and Vodusek both have Maryland citizenship for diversity purposes, Bayliner and Stammer's Marine argue that complete diversity as required by *Strawbridge v. Curtiss*, 7 U.S. (3 Cranch) 267, 2 L. Ed. 435 (1806), does not exist. Without jurisdiction to maintain any claim at law, they argue, the court was not required to submit the case to the jury because admiralty cases are traditionally tried to the bench.

Federal courts are authorized, in one civil action, to exercise several types of subject matter jurisdiction historically exercised by separate courts, including courts of law, equity, and admiralty. As a result, a single federal court has at least three separate departments—law, equity, and admiralty—each of which has its own traditional procedures. While the Seventh Amendment guarantees a jury trial in cases "at common law," no constitutional provision guarantees, or indeed prohibits, jury trials for cases tried in equity or in admiralty. Traditionally, however, admiralty courts and courts of equity did not rely on juries. *See generally Fitzgerald v. United States Lines Co.*, 374 U.S. 16, 83 S. Ct. 1646, 10 L. Ed. 2d 720 (1963).

When a civil action involves claims that historically would have been tried in different courts and a jury trial is demanded, the procedure for submitting part of the case to a jury can be complicated. *See, e.g., Ross v. Bernhard*, 396 U.S. 531, 90 S. Ct. 733, 24 L. Ed. 2d 729 (1970) ("[h]owever difficult it may have been to define with precision the line between actions at law dealing with legal rights and suits in equity dealing with equitable matters," the Seventh Amendment right to jury trial on legal claims must be preserved, even when complaint combines claims in equity with claims at law); *Dairy Queen, Inc. v. Wood*, 369 U.S. 469, 82 S. Ct. 894, 8 L. Ed. 2d 44 (1962) (holding that legal claims based on breach of contract must be determined by jury before final court determinations of equitable claims based on trademark infringement). While trials to different factfinders may be required in actions having law and equity components because of the jury's inability to fashion equitable remedies, that result is not compelled when claims at law and in admiralty, arising out of a single accident, are combined in a single complaint for damages. To render the trial process in that particular circumstance less cumbersome, confusing, and time-consuming, the Supreme Court has adopted the pragmatic procedural rule that both the admiralty claim and the law claim be decided by the jury so that "[o]nly one trier of fact [is] used for the trial of what is essentially one lawsuit to settle one claim split conceptually into separate parts because of historical developments." *Fitzgerald*, 374 U.S. at 21, 83 S. Ct. at 1650.

In *Fitzgerald*, an injured seaman sued his employer at law, alleging a claim for damages under the Jones Act, and in admiralty, alleging a claim for maintenance and cure. In ruling that both the admiralty and law claims should have been submitted to the jury, the Supreme Court focused on the confusion and complication that would result from trials before separate factfinders. The Court observed that the use of separate factfinders confounds the application of *res judicata* and collateral estoppel principles and unduly complicates damage calculations. With respect to the latter problem the Court explained:

> It is extremely difficult for a judge in trying a maintenance and cure claim to ascertain, even with the use of special interrogatories, exactly what went into the damages awarded by a jury—how loss of earning power was calculated, how much was allowed for medical expenses and pain and suffering, how much was allowed for actual lost wages, and how much, if any, each of the recoveries was reduced by contributory negligence. This raises needless problems of who has the burden of proving exactly what the jury did. And even if the judge can find out what elements of damage the jury's verdict actually represented, he must still try to solve the puzzling problem of the bearing the jury's verdict should have on recovery under the different standards of the maintenance and cure claim. In the absence of some statutory or constitutional obstacle, an end should be put to such an unfortunate, outdated, and wasteful manner of trying these cases. Fortunately, there is no such obstacle.

374 U.S. at 19-20, 83 S. Ct. at 1649-50 (footnotes omitted).

While we recognize that the circumstances in the case before us are somewhat different from those in *Fitzgerald*, we believe that the same pragmatic rule articulated in *Fitzgerald* should apply. In this case, the claims in admiralty and the claims at law name different defendants, each of whom is alleged to have contributed to liability through different conduct. Nevertheless, all of Vodusek's claims arise from the same boating accident and the same resulting injuries. Accordingly, the underlying reasons that motivated the Court's decision in *Fitzgerald* counsel us to extend the *Fitzgerald* rule to the circumstances here. Submitting both the admiralty and law claims to the jury better ensures that neither duplicative nor inadequate damages are awarded. Application of the *Fitzgerald* rule also avoids the substantial problems of applying principles of collateral estoppel when claims are tried separately. If, for example, the jury decided against Vodusek on her claims at law, determining the extent to which that verdict should bar aspects of her admiralty claims might require submitting detailed and therefore complicating interrogatories to the jury. We conclude that when the accident and injuries underlying the plaintiff's law and admiralty damage claims are the same, the considerations underlying the pragmatic rule of *Fitzgerald* dictate its application, even when the plaintiff has named different defendants in those claims.

Bayliner and Stammer's Marine argue that the *Fitzgerald* rule cannot apply here because the presence of Stammer's Marine destroys complete diversity and, along with it, the jurisdictional basis for the law claims. We reject this argument because it fails to recognize that the federal rules enable district courts to exercise their power in the three historically separate departments within a single case.

If Vodusek had filed separate suits against Bayliner at law and against Stammer's Marine in admiralty, she would have had a jurisdictional basis to proceed with each suit. Bayliner is a Delaware corporation with its principal place of business in Washington, and Vodusek is a Maryland citizen. Because the amount in controversy exceeds $50,000, Vodusek could have filed her claim at law against Bayliner in a federal court under the jurisdictional grant of 28 U.S.C. § 1332. Likewise, Vodusek's claim against Stammer's Marine could have been filed in admiralty under 28 U.S.C.App. § 1333 and 46 U.S.C.App. § 740 since the explosion and fire occurred on navigable waters. *See Sisson v. Ruby*, 497 U.S. 358, 110 S. Ct. 2892, 111 L. Ed. 2d 292 (1990); *Price v. Price*, 929 F.2d 131 (4th Cir.1991). That both of Vodusek's claims are combined in one complaint does not by itself defeat the subject matter jurisdiction the court would have had over separate suits. The federal rules preserve the right to invoke jurisdiction in the historically separate departments of the district court in a single action. *See* FED. R. CIV. P. 1 (explaining that federal rules are applicable to all suits "whether cognizable as cases at law or in equity or in admiralty"); FED. R. CIV. P. 9(h) (authorizing invocation of admiralty jurisdiction when claim could be based on some other jurisdictional ground as well); FED. R. CIV. P. 18(a) and 20(a) (permitting joinder of claims at law, in equity, and in admiralty and joinder of parties); FED. R. CIV. P. 82 (explaining that "[t]hese rules shall not be construed to extend or limit the jurisdiction of the United States district courts"). Because Vodusek's claims in law and admiralty can be joined without affecting the court's jurisdiction over the defendants in each historical department, we must yield to Vodusek's explicit election in naming a different defendant in the claims filed in each department.

We reject the Fifth Circuit's approach in *Powell v. Offshore Navigation, Inc.*, 644 F.2d 1063 (1981) (holding that existence of non-diverse defendants, notwithstanding court's admiralty jurisdiction, destroyed plaintiff's right to jury trial). That decision, we believe, fails to recognize the facility provided by the federal rules for joining law and admiralty claims without destroying the jurisdictional and procedural distinctions between them. The decision also frustrates the choices preserved to litigants to invoke admiralty jurisdiction for one claim and to sue at law for another, electing a jury trial. *See* Barbara B. Woodhouse, Comment, *Powell v. Offshore Navigation, Inc.: Jurisdiction Over Maritime Claims and the Right to Trial by Jury*, 82 COLUM. L. REV. 784 (1982). *See also Fitzgerald*, 374 U.S. at 21, 83 S. Ct. at 1650; *Hassinger v. Tideland Elec. Membership Corp.*, 627 F.Supp. 65 (E.D.N.C.1985), *aff'd only on related grounds*, 781 F.2d 1022 (4th Cir.), *cert. denied*, 478 U.S. 1004, 106 S. Ct. 3294, 92 L. Ed. 2d 709 (1986).

Because the district court properly submitted all claims to the jury, its decision rendered as a court in admiralty is superfluous, and any alleged error in the bench trial need not be reviewed.

* * *

AFFIRMED.

Note

Not all courts agree with *Vodusek, supra,* that a plaintiff may bring an *in rem* and an *in personam* claim together before a jury when the claims arise out of a single occurrence. In *T.N.T. Marine Service, Inc. v. Weaver Shipyards & Dry Dock, Inc.*, 702 F.2d 585, 1984 AMC 1341 (5th Cir. 1983), the U.S. Court of Appeals for the Fifth Circuit held that there was no right to a jury trial on a complaint that was designated as an admiralty and maritime claim, even though diversity jurisdiction existed and was alleged in the complaint as well.

---

4. Right to Trial by Jury: Joinder of Jones Act and Maritime Claims In rem

ZRNCEVICH v. BLUE HAWAII ENTERPRISES, INC.

738 F. Supp. 350; 1990 AMC 2450 (D. Hawaii 1990)

FONG, Chief Judge

Introduction

The issue before this court is whether plaintiff has a right to a jury trial where the plaintiff has asserted admiralty and maritime claims *in rem* as well as a claim under the Jones Act, 46 U.S.C. App. § 688.

Background

On September 28, 1989, plaintiff Robert Zrncevich, a seaman, brought this action against defendants Blue Hawaii Enterprises, Inc. ("Blue Hawaii") *in personam* and the vessel F/V Haida, O.N. 605147, her engines, tackle, stores and equipment *in rem*, alleging personal injury aboard ship. Plaintiff accepted a Stipulation of Undertaking in the amount of $150,000 security as the *res* in lieu of arresting the vessel. Plaintiff had not made an effort to arrest the vessel.

Plaintiff Zrncevich was hired by defendant Blue Hawaii to perform tasks on board ship related to Blue Hawaii's commercial fishing operation. Plaintiff's primary task was the handling of lobster cages. Plaintiff alleges that he received injuries to his hands while working on board ship, with symptoms including pain, tingling, numbness, contractures and loss of strength in his hands. Plaintiff further alleges that defendant Blue Hawaii refused him care for these injuries both on board ship and after plaintiff returned to Honolulu. In his suit, plaintiff alleges negligence, unseaworthiness and maintenance and cure, unpaid wages and breach of contract.

Plaintiff designated his case as filed "In Admiralty." Plaintiff pled "admiralty and maritime claims within the meaning of Federal Rules of Civil Procedure 9(h)" and asserted jurisdiction under 28 U.S.C. § 1333 (federal jurisdiction for admiralty and maritime claims). Plaintiff also asserted federal jurisdiction under the Jones Act, 46 U.S.C. App. § 688, and included a Demand for a Jury Trial "on all issues triable herein."

On January 12, 1990 plaintiff moved for leave to file a first amended complaint to clarify his jurisdictional assertion under the Jones Act. Defendants objected and filed a cross-motion to strike plaintiff's jury demand. Defendants asserted that in spite of the statutory right to a jury trial on the Jones Act claim, plaintiff had no right to a jury trial because plaintiff elected to proceed *in rem* in admiralty. Magistrate Daral G. Conklin denied both motions in his March 6, 1990 order.

The Magistrate found that plaintiff's original complaint properly alleged a claim under the Jones Act and that accordingly, it was unnecessary for plaintiff to amend his complaint. The Magistrate held that the plaintiff has a right to try at least his Jones Act claim, and possibly other claims, to the jury. Accordingly, the Magistrate also denied defendant's motion to strike plaintiff's jury demand.

The parties here appeal from those parts of the Magistrate's order denying their respective motions.

Discussion

In their Motion to Strike Jury Demand, defendants assert that plaintiff has no right to a jury trial on his Jones Act claim because plaintiff affirmatively asserted admiralty claims and admiralty jurisdiction in his complaint. Plaintiff asserted admiralty and maritime jurisdiction by pleading claims within the meaning of F.R.C.P. 9(h), which states that

> A pleading or count setting forth a claim for relief within the admiralty and maritime jurisdiction that is also within the jurisdiction of the district court on some other ground may contain a statement identifying the claim as an admiralty or maritime claim for the purposes of Rules 14(c), 38(e), 82, and the Supplemental Rules for Certain Admiralty and Maritime Claims.

F.R.C.P. 9(h).

Admiralty remedies such as actions for unseaworthiness and maintenance and cure do not ordinarily carry a right to trial by jury. While F.R.C.P. 38 generally preserves the Seventh Amendment right to a jury trial, Rule 38(e) provides that Rule 38 "shall not be construed to create a right to trial by jury of the issues in an admiralty or maritime claim within the meaning of Rule 9(h) ..."

At the same time, the Jones Act specifically allows a seaman to bring his Jones Act claim before a jury. The Jones Act reads in relevant part:

> Recovery for injury to or death of seaman. Any seaman who shall suffer personal injury in the course of his employment may, at his election, maintain an action for damages at law, with the right of trial by jury.

46 U.S.C. App. § 688. Plaintiff here asserted Jones Act claims and elected trial by jury by including a Demand for a Jury Trial in his pleadings.

Defendants argue that the statutory construction of the Jones Act demands an irrevocable election between an action at law (with a right to trial by jury) or in admiralty (without a jury trial). Defendants argue that plaintiff has elected to place his case in admiralty by (1) designating his claim in admiralty, and (2) utilizing remedies *in rem*. Defendants assert that plaintiff secured his claims *in rem* by naming the vessel as a defendant *in rem* and by accepting a stipulation of undertaking substituted as the *res* in lieu of the arrest of the vessel.

Plaintiff argues that his right to a jury trial under the Jones Act is statutorily guaranteed by his Demand for Jury Trial in his pleadings, and is not precluded or waived in any way by his assertion of admiralty claims.

This court must resolve two issues: (1) whether a plaintiff who has asserted claims in admiralty along with his Jones Act claim has a right to bring all his claims in admiralty and the Jones Act before a jury or (2) whether proceeding *in rem* precludes the plaintiff from bringing *any* claim before the jury.

Right to a Jury Trial For Joined Claims

The Jones Act gives seamen a statutory right to a jury trial for claims of personal injury. 46 U.S.C. App. § 688. However, bringing a Jones Act claim does not preclude a seaman from also asserting the traditional admiralty claims of unseaworthiness and maintenance and cure. *Haskins v. Point Towing Co.*, 395 F.2d 737, 742 (3d Cir. 1968). It is a common practice for district courts to grant jury trials to plaintiffs who join their Jones Act, unseaworthiness, and maintenance and cure claims in one complaint, when all claims arise out of a single transaction or occurrence. *Fitzgerald v. United States Lines Co.*, 374 U.S. 16, 18, 10 L. Ed. 2d 720, 83 S. Ct. 1646 (1963). Accordingly, hybrid actions consisting of both law claims (such as Jones Act claims) and admiralty claims abound.

Courts have struggled to find the best procedural tack to take when traditional admiralty and law claims are consolidated. In *Romero v. International Terminal Operating Co.*, 358 U.S. 354, 3 L. Ed. 2d 368, 79 S. Ct. 468 (1959), the Supreme Court held that the district court has pendent jurisdiction over unseaworthiness and maintenance and cure claims when joined with a Jones Act claim. However, the Court left unanswered the question whether all three claims could be submitted to the jury. This question, however, was addressed by the Second Circuit later that year, which held that maritime claims joined with Jones Act claims may be tried before the jury. *Bartholomew v. Universe Tankships, Inc.*, 263 F.2d 437 (2d Cir. 1959). The *Bartholomew* court discussed at length the legal and legislative history enabling joined Jones Act and maritime claims, and discussed the problems of evidence, *res judicata*, and judicial economy that would arise if the plaintiff were required to split claims so factually intertwined and of "fundamental singleness." *Bartholomew* 263 F.2d at 444-446.

The *Bartholomew* court's decision foreshadowed the Supreme Court's decision in the seminal *Fitzgerald* case. *Fitzgerald*, 374 U.S. 16, 10 L. Ed. 2d 720, 83 S. Ct. 1646. In *Fitzgerald*, a seaman brought an action against a shipowner for damages stemming from an alleged shipboard injury. *Id.* at 17. The seaman brought claims under the Jones Act, as well as actions for unseaworthiness and for maintenance and cure, and demanded a jury trial for all issues growing out of the single accident. *Id.* In holding that a traditional maritime maintenance and cure claim joined with a Jones Act claim must be submitted to the jury when both arise out of one set of facts, the court reasoned that:

> [r]equiring a seaman to split up his lawsuit, submitting part of it to a jury and part to a judge, unduly complicates and confuses a trial, creates difficulties in applying doctrines of *res judicata* and collateral estoppel, and can easily result in too much or too little recovery.

Id. at 18-19. The Court stated the principle, "Only one trier of fact should be used for the trial of what is essentially one lawsuit to settle one claim split conceptually into separate parts because of historical developments." *Id.* at 21.

The Court further stated that

> since Congress in the Jones Act has declared that the negligence part of the claim shall be tried by a jury, we would not be free, even if we wished, to require submission of all the claims to the judge alone.

Id.

Since *Fitzgerald* was decided, the majority of courts have held that traditional admiralty and maritime claims can be joined with claims having an independent basis of federal jurisdiction and brought together before the jury. In *Peace v. Fidalgo Island Packing Co.*, 419 F.2d 371 (9th Cir. 1969), the personal representative of a deceased seaman brought a claim for damages for negligence under the Jones Act and a claim for unseaworthiness under the Death On The High Seas Act, 46 U.S.C. App. § 761 *et seq. Citing Fitzgerald*, the Court of Appeals for the Ninth Circuit allowed plaintiff to join both claims and bring them before the jury. The appellate court held, "there is nothing in the Rules [of Civil Procedure] which prohibits a trial by jury on joined civil and admiralty claims." *Peace*, 419 F.2d at 371.

An appellate panel for the Ninth Circuit similarly held in *Owens-Illinois, Inc. v. U.S. District Court*, 698 F.2d 967 (9th Cir. 1983) that a jury trial is required where admiralty claims are joined with civil claims and common issues of fact are involved. The court would not allow defendant's right to a jury trial under diversity jurisdiction to be precluded by plaintiff's assertion of admiralty jurisdiction, since "when admiralty claims are joined with civil claims and the issues cannot be segregated for separate trial, a jury trial if timely demanded is required." *Id.* at 972.

Defendant cites *Trentacosta v. Frontier Pacific Aircraft Indus.*, 813 F.2d 1553 (9th Cir. 1987), as supporting the proposition that plaintiff must elect to proceed either in admiralty or at law when plaintiff joins his maritime and admiralty claims with a Jones Act claim. The *Trentacosta* plaintiff, however, did not properly invoke admiralty jurisdiction for his maritime claims in his amended complaint. *Id.* at 1555. In fact, the appellate court noted that if plaintiff amended his complaint to invoke admiralty jurisdiction, those claims could be joined with his Jones Act claim and all tried before a jury. *Id.* at 1561 n. 6.

It is the common rule in several districts that a seaman may bring unseaworthiness and maintenance and cure counts before the jury if joined with civil claims with independent federal jurisdictional basis, especially if the claims have arisen out of the same transaction or occurrence. *Duhon v. Koch Exploration Co.*, 628 F. Supp. 925 (W.D. La. 1986) (plaintiff's maritime claims may be joined with his Jones Act claim and tried to the jury and the maritime claims may still be governed according to the traditional rules of practice in admiralty); *Woosley v. Mike Hooks, Inc.*, 603 F. Supp. 1190 (W.D. La. 1985) (purely maritime claims "can and should" be tried to the jury when the Jones Act and maritime claims all arise out of the same transaction or occurrence); *Morrison v. United States Lines, Inc.*, 1983 A.M.C. 1769 (S.D.N.Y. 1983) (plaintiff seaman who withdrew his Jones Act claim no longer entitled to a jury trial on his maritime claim); *Red Star Towing & Transport Co. v. the Cargo Ship "Ming Giant"*, 552 F. Supp. 367 (S.D.N.Y. 1982) (a litigant in admiralty is not entitled as a matter of right to a non-jury trial; claims may be joined and tried before the jury); *Drakatos v. R.B. Denison, Inc.*, 493 F. Supp. 942 (D. Conn. 1980) (admiralty claims may be tried to the jury when linked to a civil claim with an independent basis for federal jurisdiction); *Rok v. Continental Seafoods, Inc.*, 462 F. Supp. 894 (S.D. Ala. 1978) (where jurisdiction in a seaman's action for personal injury was based, in part, on diversity of citizenship, plaintiff was entitled to trial by jury on both law claims and general maritime claims); *Mattes v. National Hellenic American Line, S.A.*, 427 F. Supp. 619 (S.D.N.Y. 1977) (where general maritime claims arise out of the same transaction as Jones Act claim, both may be tried to the jury although there is no diversity).

Accordingly, plaintiff is entitled to demand a jury trial on his joined Jones Act and admiralty and maritime claims.

In rem Proceedings

Although bringing hybrid law and admiralty claims before the jury is common, courts are divided on how to proceed in hybrid actions when traditional admiralty actions have been invoked, such as *in rem* proceedings, or when a Rule 9(h) election to proceed in admiralty has been made.

Defendants in the instant case assert that either of these actions by a plaintiff affirmatively determines the election to proceed in admiralty, traditionally without the right to a jury trial. Defendants assert that plaintiff here has forfeited his ability to try any of his claims to the jury by positively asserting Rule 9(h) admiralty jurisdiction and proceeding *in rem*. Defendants rely on *T.N.T. Marine Services Inc. v. Weaver Shipyards and Dry Docks, Inc.*, 702 F.2d 585, 587-88 (5th Cir.), *cert. den.* 464 U.S. 847, 78 L. Ed. 2d 141, 104 S. Ct. 151 (1983) (*in rem* claims are cognizable only in admiralty notwithstanding allegations of diversity jurisdiction), *Romero v. Bethlehem Steel Corporation*, 515 F.2d 1249 (5th Cir. 1975) (plaintiff not entitled to jury trial under diversity jurisdiction where he refused to withdraw 9(h) designation) and *Truehart v. Blandon*, 685 F. Supp. 956 (E.D. La. 1988) (complaint and proceeding *in rem* designates plaintiff's claim as one in admiralty and disallows jury demand asserted under diversity jurisdiction). However, the *T.N.T.*, *Romero*, and *Truehart* plaintiffs did not allege Jones Act claims. The Court in *Fitzgerald* specifically held that because of plaintiff's statutory right to a jury on the Jones Act claim, the Court is not free to take the joined claims away from the jury and try the case to the bench. *Fitzgerald*, 374 U.S. at 21.

Defendants also rely upon *Plamals v. the Pinar Del Rio*, 277 U.S. 151, 72 L. Ed. 827, 48 S. Ct. 457 (1927) which held that seamen may invoke remedies at law under the Jones Act or remedies in admiralty, but not both. In *Fernandes v. United Fruit Co.*, 303 F. Supp. 681 (D. Md. 1969), the district court followed *Plamals* in holding that plaintiff cannot utilize *in rem* proceedings when joining maritime and admiralty claims with Jones Act claims but must elect to place the whole case in either law or admiralty.

In contrast, several courts have held that the spirit of the Supreme Court's holding in Fitzgerald is best followed by allowing the plaintiff to bring the entire case to the jury regardless of the manner of assertion of claims in admiralty.

In *Haskins v. Point Towing Co.*, 395 F.2d 737 (3d Cir. 1968), the plaintiff seaman brought an action seeking recovery for personal injuries and asserted claims both *in rem* and *in personam*. *Id.* at 738. Notwithstanding the use of *in rem* proceedings, the *Haskins* court held that *Fitzgerald* gives a plaintiff, who demands a jury trial for his Jones Act claim, a right to join with it his claims under maritime law for unseaworthiness and maintenance and cure, and try them all before the jury. *Id.* at 743. The *Haskins* court stated further that *Fitzgerald* did not characterize the maritime claims as brought in law with the Jones Act claim, but specifically created a right to trial by jury for admiralty claims joined with a Jones Act claim. *Id.* at 741. The *Haskins* court also stated that the plaintiff should not have to bring the maritime claims at law just to secure the right to the jury trial:

> To require this would compel him to lose the advantages which inhere in the characteristic admiralty claims, such as *in rem* process, interlocutory appeals, admiralty attachment ... There is no reason to make relinquishment of the procedural advantages

> of these inherent admiralty claims for unseaworthiness and maintenance and cure the price for a jury trial.

Id. Although it did not mention *in rem* proceedings, the *Fitzgerald* opinion was not inapposite to the idea that maritime claims "may on occasion call for application of slightly different principles and procedures." *Fitzgerald, supra,* 374 U.S. at 18.

Similarly, in *Durden v. Exxon Corp.*, 803 F.2d 845 (5th Cir. 1986), plaintiff brought claims *in personam* and *in rem*. The court dismissed the plaintiff's Jones Act claim but noted that if it had not done so, *Fitzgerald* would have allowed plaintiff to bring maritime and admiralty claims to the jury along with his Jones Act claims. *Id.* at 848.

Neither is the Rule 9(h) assertion fatal to jury trial. In *Parfait v. Central Towing, Inc.*, 1979 A.M.C. 2485 (E.D. La. 1978), the court allowed the plaintiff to bring his maritime claims together with his Jones Act claim to the jury, even though plaintiff designated his unseaworthiness and maintenance and cure claims as admiralty claims pursuant to Rule 9(h) and also initiated an *in rem* seizure of the defendant's boat. The court held that it was "more consonant with the spirit of *Fitzgerald* to allow a jury trial for all claims of a Jones Act plaintiff when he sues only his employer notwithstanding a 9(h) designation and the use of admiralty procedures." *Id.* at 2489.

These latter cases are more in keeping with the spirit of *Fitzgerald* and its progeny where a Jones Act plaintiff brings a hybrid cause of action. The reasoning of the *Fitzgerald* Court in joining the claims before the jury centers on judicial economy, especially on the logistical and fairness problems which would be created by trying one case before two triers of fact. *Fitzgerald* 374 U.S. at 19. The Court describes in particular the potential problems in the determination of damages by two triers of fact. *Id.* The Court also reasons that it is important to avoid the problems of *res judicata* and collateral estoppel created when what is essentially one lawsuit is split. *Id.*

Importantly, *Fitzgerald* emphasizes that there is no explicit prohibition against jury trials for admiralty claims:

> While this Court has held that the Seventh Amendment does not require jury trials in admiralty cases, neither that amendment nor any other provision of the Constitution forbids them. Nor does any statute of Congress or Rule of Procedure, Civil or Admiralty, forbid jury trials in maritime cases.

Id. at 20. (Footnotes omitted).

The Ninth Circuit agreed that there is nothing to prohibit a jury trial on joined admiralty and Jones Act claims. In a cause of action brought by the widow of a deceased seaman under the Jones Act and the Death On the High Seas Act, the court held that

> [t]here is nothing in the present rules of Civil Procedure which grants a trial by jury in an admiralty or maritime claim ... But there is nothing in the Rules which prohibits a trial by jury on joined civil and admiralty claims. Rule 9(h) ... which pertains to identifying claims, does not modify this result.

Peace v. Fidalgo, supra, at 371.

There is nothing inherently incongruous about bringing an *in rem* and an *in personam* claim together before the jury when the claims arise out of a single occurrence. *Continental Grain Co. v. Barge FBL-585*, 364 U.S. 19, 4 L. Ed. 2d 1540, 80 S. Ct. 1470 (1960), concerned the § 1404 transfer of a federal case in which plaintiff had brought both an *in rem* action against a ship and an *in personam* action against the owner, stemming from the same occurrence and issues. The Court held that while the *in rem* and *in personam* claims were two methods invoked to bring the owner into court, the substance of what had to be done to adjudicate the rights of the parties in an *in rem* and an *in personam* claim was not different at all. *Continental Grain* at 26.

The majority of cases, including *Fitzgerald*, which hold that the plaintiff is entitled to bring joined maritime and civil claims before the jury, generally do not address the procedural steps taken by plaintiff in asserting the admiralty claims. Most cases allowing the joined claims do not describe whether the plaintiff simply stated admiralty claims, made a specific Rule 9(h) election, or initiated proceedings *in rem*. *Fitzgerald* does not indicate that it was intended to apply only to admiralty claims asserted informally, where no Rule 9(h) election or *in rem* assertions were made. These actions would not lessen the concerns enumerated by the *Fitzgerald* Court for judicial economy and the fairness problems when a single case is split and tried to two triers of fact. Neither can such actions reasonably be construed to indicate that a plaintiff elects to waive his statutory right to a jury trial under the Jones Act, when a demand for a jury trial is properly included in the complaint.

Therefore, allowing the plaintiff to join his Jones Act claim and maritime claims before the jury serves the principles of judicial economy and fairness that result from bringing the joined claims before a single trier of fact when the claims arise out of a single transaction or occurrence. The Jones Act guarantees the plaintiff a jury trial if timely elected, and there is no prohibition against a jury trial for the admiralty claims. Therefore, at the election of the plaintiff the one trier of fact will be the jury.

Conclusion

The Jones Act gives plaintiff a right to a trial by jury if plaintiff so elects. Plaintiff here asserted the Jones Act and demanded a jury trial. *Fitzgerald* holds that the seaman can join the traditional admiralty claims for unseaworthiness, maintenance and cure with Jones Act claims before the jury. This court now finds that this right to a jury trial is not precluded even if plaintiff has made a specific assertion of admiralty claims and utilized proceedings *in rem*.

Accordingly, defendants' appeal from the Magistrate's order is DENIED. As it is unnecessary for plaintiff to amend his complaint to maintain his right to a jury trial, plaintiff's appeal from the Magistrate's order is also DENIED.

IT IS SO ORDERED.

Note

Plaintiff who seeks to invoke the benefits of both an action at law (jury trial) and an action in admiralty (in rem remedy) must use care in pleading;

> The court finds well taken plaintiff's argument that the rule in *Fitzgerald* provides a right to jury trial of general maritime law claims brought in admiralty when they are joined with Jones Act claims brought on the law side with an election of trial by jury. However, the court in this case finds that plaintiff's complaint, designated under FED. R. CIV. P. 9(h), fails to make the requisite election because it does not invoke the court's federal question jurisdiction, 28 U.S.C. § 1331, over plaintiff's Jones Act claim. *See Plamals v. The Pinar Del Rio*, 277 U.S. 151, 156-57, 48 S. Ct. 457, 458, 72 L. Ed. 827 (1928); *Johnson v. Venezuelan Line Steamship Co.*, 314 F. Supp. 1403, 1406 (E.D. La. 1970). Accordingly, plaintiff must either move to amend his complaint to cure this defect or withdraw his jury demand.

Kathriner v. Unisea, Inc., 740 F. Supp. 768 D.C. Alaska (1990).

---

5. Counterclaims

Note

Under Rule 13(b) of the Federal Rules of Civil Procedure, a permissive counterclaim can be brought in an admiralty proceeding. If the claim is within the court's admiralty jurisdiction and the parties are diverse, the counterclaimant may identify its claim as maritime or bring it under the "saving to suitors" clause. If the original complaint and the counterclaim is one for which there would be a right to jury trial, if brought as independent action, is the counterclaimant entitled to a jury trial? *See, Wilmington Trust v. The United States District Court for the District of Hawaii*, 934 F.2d 1026, 1991 AMC 1849 (9th Cir. 1991), *cert. denied sub nom, Connecticut Bank & Trust Co. v. Wilmington Trust Co.*, 503 U.S. 966, 112 S. Ct. 1578, 118 L. Ed. 2d 220 (1992).

---

6. Impleader and Joinder of Parties Prior to the Supplemental Jurisdiction Act

Notes

1. *Impleader*

Prior to the enactment of the Supplemental Jurisdiction Act, the was a division of authority as to whether a defendant in an admiralty action could implead a third party defendant on a non-admiralty claim. Some courts held that this was impermissible primarily on two grounds. First, such practice if allowed could deny a third-party defendant his right to a jury trial. Second, because admiralty impleader allows a defendant (third-party plaintiff) to "tender" the third-party defendant directly to the plaintiff, enabling the court to enter judgment in favor of the plaintiff against the third—party defendant, the jurisdiction of the federal courts would be unconstitutionally enlarged if their was no admiralty jurisdiction or other independent federal jurisdictional ground to support plaintiff's claim against the third-party defendant. Consider a situation where plaintiff-seaman, a citizen of Texas, brings an action for unseaworthiness against his employer, also a Texas citizen. The employer then impleads the physician, another citizen of Texas, who treated plaintiff. Suppose the court should find that there was no unseaworthiness but that the doctor had been guilty of malpractice. *See,* for example *McCann v. Falgout Boat* Company, 44 F.R.D. 34 (S.D. Tex. 1968). Other courts relied on the doctrines of ancillary and pendent jurisdiction and permitted impleader of a third-party over whom there was no admiralty or independent basis of federal jurisdiction. *Joiner v. Diamond M. Drilling Co.*, 677 F.2d 1035 (5th Cir. 1982.

> The *Joiner* court specifically stated that because the rules of admiralty and civil procedure have merged, there is no impediment to the exercise of ancillary jurisdiction over state law claims appended to admiralty claims. *Id.* at 1040. It further "held" that a "third-party claim lacking independent grounds of jurisdiction may be appended to an admiralty action and is cognizable in federal court under the doctrine of ancillary jurisdiction as long as the ancillary claim arises out of the same core of operative facts as the main admiralty action." *Id.* at 1041.

Harcrest International, Ltd. v. M/V Zim Keelung, 681 F. Supp. 354 (E.D. La. 1988). *Also see, Gauthier v. Crosby Marine Service, Inc.*, 87 F.R.D. 353, 1981 AMC 1179 (E.D. La. 1980). *Cf. Harrison v. Glendel Drilling Company*, 679 F. Supp. 1413 W.D. 1988).

2. *Joinder of Parties*

Perhaps the most influential case on the use of the doctrines of ancillary and pendent jurisdiction in admiralty cases to exercise of jurisdiction over a party over whom there was no independent basis of federal jurisdiction was Chief Judge Friendly's decision in *Leather's Best, Inc. v. S.S. Mormaclynx*, 451 F.2d 800, 1971 AMC 2383 (2d Cir. 1971). In that cases shipper brought an admiralty action against a carrier and an action against the terminal operator (Tidewater) from which the goods disappeared. There was only a state claim against the latter as to which there was no independent basis of federal jurisdiction. The court used the following analysis:

> This conclusion raises the question whether the district court had jurisdiction with respect to the shipper's claim against Tidewater. In resolving this, we consider it appropriate to look to the doctrine of pendent jurisdiction.[10] We begin with the observation that the question of pendency in this instance hinges exclusively upon the identity of the facts in the state and federal claims, since Tidewater is a named defendant only with respect to the state claim.
>
> The question of pendent jurisdiction involves two discrete inquiries: whether the court has the "power" to hear the state claim; and whether, assuming the power, the court should, as a matter of "discretion," hear the state claim. As to the first issue, it is questionable whether this state claim could have been heard under the test of *Hurn v. Oursler*, 289 U.S. 238, 246, 53 S. Ct. 586, 589, 77 L. Ed. 1148 (1933), which restricted pendent jurisdictions to instances in which "two distinct grounds [one state, one federal] in support of a single cause of action [were] alleged." Joinder of the state claim against Tidewater would doubtless have been considered a second cause of action. But with the decision in *United Mine Workers v. Gibbs*, 383 U.S. 715, 86 S. Ct. 1130, 16 L. Ed. 2d 218 (1966), the Court abandoned such an "unnecessarily grudging" approach to the question of power to hear the pendent claim, and turned instead to a mode of analysis which focuses upon the relationship between the facts underlying the state and federal claims:

---

[10] From the pleadings it appears that Leather's Best is a New York corporation while Tidewater is a Delaware corporation. It further appears, however, that Tidewater's "principal place of business" is in the State of New York, which would foreclose the possibility of there being diversity jurisdiction with respect to the state claim. *See* 28 U.S.C. § 1332(c). In any event, the shipper's complaint failed to plead jurisdiction based upon diversity of citizenship and thus it is impossible to conclude that there is independent federal jurisdiction with respect to the shipper's claim against Tidewater.

On the other hand, the absence from the shipper's complaint of any allegation concerning pendent jurisdiction does not bar consideration of the issue by this court. Pendent jurisdiction is not matter which must be pleaded since the court already has jurisdiction over the case. *See* F.R.Civ.P. 8(a) (1); 5 Wright & Miller, Federal Practice and Procedure § 1207, at 82 (1969).

> The state and federal claims must derive from a common nucleus of operative facts. But if, considered without regard to their federal or state character, a plaintiff's claims are such that he would ordinarily be expected to try them all in one judicial proceeding, then, assuming substantiality of the federal issues, there is *power* in federal courts to hear the whole.

Id. at 725, 86 S. Ct. at 1138 (footnote omitted).

To be sure, the *Gibbs* Court was not confronted with the question whether pendent jurisdiction extended to a state claim against a party not named in the federal claim. But as we have recently observed in *Astor-Honor, Inc. v. Grosset & Dunlap, Inc.*, 441 F.2d 627, 629 (2 Cir. 1971), "Mr. Justice Brennan's language and the common sense considerations underlying it seem broad enough to cover that problem also. *See Note, UMW v. Gibbs and Pendent Jurisdiction*, 81 Harv.L.Rev. 657, 664 (1968)." In that decision, involving federal claims under the copyright laws and state claims of unfair trade practice and unfair competition, including a defendant not named in the copyright claims, we held that a federal court had power to hear a state claim against a party not named in the federal claim, provided the *Gibbs test* was met, noting that this conclusion was buttressed by our decisions concerning ancillary jurisdiction to entertain compulsory counterclaims under F.R.Civ.P.13(a), *United Artists Corp. v. Masterpiece Productions, Inc.*, 221 F.2d 213 (2 Cir. 1955), and third-party claims under F.R.Civ.P. 14(a), *Dery v. Wyer*, 265 F.2d 804 (2 Cir. 1959).

It is true that in those cases, as well as in *Astor-Honor*, the federal claim had arisen in the ordinary civil jurisdiction, whereas the federal claim in this action had been brought under the admiralty jurisdiction. At an earlier date, this difference might have affected our decision here. But the rules of procedure in the admiralty and civil jurisdictions were merged in 1966, and we are of the opinion that at least since that merger, the constitutional rationale which underlies the doctrine of ancillary jurisdiction in the context of Rule 13(a)[11] and Rule 14[12] may be applied to support the conclusion that a federal court has the power to hear a related state

---

[11] Prior to the 1966 merger, there was no rule of compulsory counterclaim, much less a doctrine of ancillary jurisdiction, in the maritime jurisdiction, and permissive cross-libels were limited to claims in admiralty arising out of the same contract or cause of action as the original claim. *Compare United States v. Isthmian S.S. Co.*, 359 U.S. 314, 320-323, 79 S. Ct. 857, 3 L. Ed. 2d 845 (1959); *Moore-McCormack Lines, Inc. v. McMahon*, 235 F.2d 142 (2 Cir. 1956). With merger, however, Rule 13 became applicable to proceedings brought in the admiralty jurisdiction. *See United States v. M/V Pitcairn*, 272 F. Supp. 518, 519 (E.D.La.1967); *cf. Upper Lakes Shipping, Ltd. v. International Longshoremen's Ass'n*, 293 F. Supp. 207, 208 (S.D.N.Y.1968). There is no evident reason why the doctrine of ancillary jurisdiction should not now be applicable as well to compulsory counterclaims which arise in the context of suits in admiralty. *See United States v. Shafter*, 49 F.R.D. 164, 167-168 (S.D.N.Y.1969), *aff'd on other grounds*, 424 F.2d 281 (2 Cir.), *cert. denied Kilarjan v. United States*, 400 U.S. 827, 91 S. Ct. 54, 27 L. Ed. 2d 57 (1970).

[12] With respect to third-party practice, too, admiralty practice differed from practice on the civil "side" prior to the 1966 merger. Under former Admiralty Rule 56, at least some independent basis of federal jurisdiction was always necessary to implead a third party. *See* 3 MOORE, FEDERAL PRACTICE PP. 14.20, at 669 (1970); 6 Wright & Miller, *Federal Practice and Procedure* § 1465, at 348-49 (1971). Indeed, there was substantial authority to the effect that the third-party claim had to come within the admiralty jurisdiction. *See Aktieselskabet Fido v. Lloyd Braziliero*, 283 F. 62, 72 (2 Cir.), *cert. denied*, 260 U.S. 737, 43 S. Ct. 97, 67 L. Ed. 489 (1922); *Rudy-Patrick Seed Co. v. Kokusai*, 1 F. Supp. 266 (S.D.N.Y. 1932). *But cf. Soderberg v. Atlantic Lighterage Corp.*, 19 F.2d 286, 287 (2 Cir.), *cert. denied*, 275 U.S. 542, 48 S. Ct. 37, 72 L. Ed. 416 (1927). With merger, a subsection (c) was added to Rule 14 with the intent of preserving certain features of admiralty impleader which were more liberal than civil impleader. *See* Colby, *Admiralty Unification*, 54 GEO.L.J. 1258, 1272-73 (1966). The effect of merger upon the former admiralty requirement of independent jurisdiction for impleader has not as yet been conclusively resolved. *Compare Gambino v. United Fruit Co.*, 48 F.R.D. 28 (S.D.N.Y. 1969), with *Young v. United States*, 272 F. Supp. 738, 742-743 (D.S.C. 1967), and *McCann v. Falgout Boat Co.*, 44 F.R.D. 34 (S.D.Tex. 1968). *See also Watz v. Zapata Off-Shore Co.*, 431 F.2d 100, 117-118 (5 Cir. 1970). But if we were presented with the question, it would be only with the greatest reluctance that we would conclude that under the merged rules the doctrine of ancillary jurisdiction did not extend to admiralty as well as to civil impleader. *Compare* 6 Wright & Miller, *supra*, § 1465, at 348-49. Certainly the practical considerations which support the doctrine of ancillary jurisdiction in the context of civil impleader are equally persuasive on the admiralty side. *Compare Dery v. Wyer, supra*, 265 F.2d at 806-807. In any event, we do not perceive the requirement of independent jurisdiction in pre-merger admiralty impleader to have had constitutional underpinings. Rather it reflected a judicial conception of the limited nature of Admiralty Rule 56 and the appropriate reach of the then distinct admiralty jurisdiction. *Compare Aktieselskabet Fido v. Lloyd Braziliero*, 283 F. 62, 72-73 (2 Cir.), *cert. denied*, 260 U.S. 737, 43 S. Ct. 97, 67 L. Ed. 489 (1922); *The Goyaz*, 281 F. 259, 260-261 (S.D.N.Y. 1922), *aff'd*, 3 F.2d 553 (2 Cir.), *cert. denied*, 267 U.S. 594, 45 S. Ct. 230, 69 L. Ed. 804 (1924); *Lamborn & Co. v. Compania Maritima Del Nervion*, 19 F.2d 155, 156 (2 Cir. 1927); *Rudy-Patrick Seed Co. v. Kokusai*, 1 F. Supp. 266 (S.D.N.Y. 1932).

To the extent that any possible constitutional considerations influenced judicial limitation of admiralty impleader, a major factor appears to have been concern with the denial of the jury trial right guaranteed by the Seventh Amendment. *See The Goyaz*, 281 F. 259, 261 (S.D.N.Y. 1922). This was, of course, a serious problem prior to the merger of the admiralty and civil jurisdictions. Nor has the problem been clearly resolved by the mere fact of merger. *See* F.R.Civ.P. 38(e). *Compare McCann v. Falgout Boat Co.*, 44 F.R.D. 34, 44 (S.D. Tex. 1968), with 6 Wright & Miller, *Federal Practice and Procedure* § 1465, at 350-52. However, insofar as third-party practice has relevance to the question of pendent jurisdiction in this case, we are not faced with any problem of denial of the right to jury trial since Tidewater made no such demand below. *See* F.R.Civ.P. 38(d).

In sum, then, we find the constitutional judgments reflected in the doctrine of ancillary jurisdiction in civil impleader to be of substantial relevance to the issue of pendent jurisdiction in this case.

claim against a defendant not named in the federal claim regardless of whether the federal claim arises in the civil or admiralty jurisdiction. Thus, we conclude that in a case such as this, where the facts underlying the state and federal claims are identical,[13] a federal court vested with admiralty jurisdiction over a shipper's claim against the carrier for breach of contract of carriage does have the "power" also to entertain its state tort claim against a pier operator.[14]

There remains, though, the further question whether this is an appropriate case for the court, in the exercise of its discretion, to hear the pendent claim. In this regard, the Supreme Court has indicated that the justification for the exercise of pendent jurisdiction "lies in the considerations of judicial economy, convenience and fairness to litigants." *United Mine Workers v. Gibbs, supra*, 383 U.S. at 726, 86 S. Ct. at 1139. In this case, the same facts are ultimately controlling with respect to both the state and federal claims; the desirability of having both claims tried in the same forum is self-evident. Moreover, while our conclusions in part II require us to remand the state claim for further proceedings, the evidentiary record compiled in the original proceeding will continue to be of substantial relevance, and we thus see no basis for declining jurisdiction over the state claim at this juncture.

Subsequently the court adhered to this approach in *Roco Carriers, Ltd. v. M/V NURNBERG EXPRESS*, 899 F.2d 1292, 1990 AMC 913 (2d Cir. 1990):

[U]nderlying admiralty jurisdiction is the sound policy of permitting claims arising in the admiralty or maritime context to be resolved in a single setting. *See British Transp. Comm'n v. United States*, 354 U.S. 129, 137-38, 1 L. Ed. 2d 1234, 77 S. Ct. 1103 (1957). This is not merely a matter of convenience for the parties. Rather, it stems from the historical recognition of the importance that maritime claims in particular be subjected to efficient and uniform procedures and treatment. *See In Re Oil Spill*, 699 F.2d at 913-14.

---

7. Removal

Notes

1. *Overview of Removal*

Where the plaintiff has brought suit in a state court, the defendant may, under specified circumstances, have the power to affect that choice by "removing" the suit to a federal court under 28 U.S.C. § 1441. Generally, a suit may be removed from a state court to a federal court only where it could have been commenced initially in a federal court; that is, where a federal court would have had original jurisdiction to entertain it. When a suit has been properly removed from a state court to a federal court, it will be resolved in the federal court as though it had been brought in the federal court from the very beginning.

As with most rules, there are exceptions to the removal rule, and there are circumstances where, even though federal jurisdiction is present, a defendant is not permitted to remove a case that has been brought in a state court. The right of a plaintiff under the "saving to suitors" clause to elect to bring his claim in a non-admiralty forum such

---

[13] The liability of the carrier under the contract of carriage turns ultimately upon the conduct of Tidewater which had charge of the container at the time of the loss. *See* PART II, *infra*.

[14] We do not regard certain decisions in which unsuccessful attempts have been made to join state claims against individual defendants, without diversity, in actions against the United States under the Federal Tort Claims Act for the same injury as opposed to our conclusion here. *See Wasserman v. Perugini*, 173 F.2d 305, 306 (2 Cir. 1949); *Williams v. United States*, 405 F.2d 951, 955 (9 Cir. 1969). *Wasserman* was a pre-*Gibbs* decision, and as we observed in *Astor-Honor, Inc. v. Grosset & Dunlap, Inc., supra*, 441 F.2d at 629, consequently is of little precedential value. As for *Williams*, we read that decision as not having reached the question whether the court had the "power" to hear the state claim in light of *Gibbs*, but rather to have declined as a matter of discretion to exercise jurisdiction over the state claims because the federal claim had been dismissed prior to trial. 405 F.2d at 955. In any case, we observed in *Astor-Honor, supra*, 441 F.2d at 630, that "we are not at all sure we would agree with [the *Williams* decision] insofar as [it] rested on a general theory of lack of power."

as a state court has been deemed to be a clear expression of Congressional intent which may not be defeated by removal. This means that, when a plaintiff has brought such a claim in a state court, the defendant may not remove it to a federal court even though initially it could have been commenced by the plaintiff in a federal court as an admiralty case under 28 U.S.C. § 1333. In other words, suits brought in a state court under the "saving to suitors" clause are exceptions to the right to remove. (*See Romero v. International Terminal Operating Co.*, 358 U.S. 354, 79 S. Ct. 468, 3 L.Ed.2d 368 (1959), *supra.*)

As further complication, however, if there is an alternative basis for federal jurisdiction, such as diversity of citizenship, then removal is permitted. The advantage of the state remedy is that a plaintiff may have his case tried to a jury. In a federal court, matters that proceed under admiralty jurisdiction are tried by the court alone without a jury. (An exception to this is actions brought under the Jones Act, which provides for trial by jury, or actions combined with a Jones Act count.) However, if the plaintiff and defendant are of diverse citizenship, instead of suing in a state court or suing in a federal court under its admiralty jurisdiction, the plaintiff may bring suit in a federal court by invoking the court's diversity of citizenship jurisdiction. In this situation, the plaintiff would also be able to have the matter resolved by a jury. Removal of a case in which there is a diversity of citizenship does not deprive a plaintiff of his right to a jury trial and does not undermine the "saving to suitors" provisions.

If there is diversity jurisdiction allowing the suit to be removed, will it be an admiralty action within Rule 9(h)? In *Scurlock v. American President Lines*, 162 F. Supp. 78 (N.D. Cal. 1958, the defendant was successful, because of diversity, in removing the case to admiralty. The court, however, granted that plaintiff's motion to transfer the case to the law side of the court where the plaintiff could have a jury trial. Doesn't present law merely allow forum shopping by the plaintiff? *See generally* Morse, *Removal of Saving Clause Suits as Civil Actions Within the Original Jurisdiction of the District Courts*, 4 MAR. LAW. 197 (1979).

By statute (28 U.S.C. § 1445(a)), Congress has provided that civil actions against a railroad under the Federal Employees' Liability Act (FELA) are not removable. This has been held to apply to actions by seamen under the Jones Act, which incorporates the provisions of the FELA. *Pate v. Standard Dredging Corp.*, 193 F.2d 498, 1952 AMC 287 (5th Cir. 1952). Thus, Jones Act claims are not removable even where there is diversity jurisdiction. But suppose a Jones Act claim is joined with general maritime claims for unseaworthiness and maintenance and cure. If there is no diversity, the Romero rule would prevent removal. If there is diversity, however, would the entire case be removable under § 1441(c) or at least the unseaworthiness and maintenance and cure claims? In *Pate*, the court stated that the unseaworthiness claim was not independent of the Jones Act claim for purposes of § 1441(c). The court further stated that although the maintenance and cure claim was independent, the jurisdictional amount prerequisite for diversity jurisdiction was not met so there could be no removal. But what if there is sufficient jurisdictional amount on the maintenance and cure claim? Compare *Sawyer v. Federal Barge Lines*, 510 F. Supp. 39, 1981 AMC 2688 (S.D. Ill. 1981) with *Consalves v. Amoco Shipping Co.*, 1982 AMC 1399 (S.D.N.Y. 1982), *reversed*, 733 F.2d 1020, 1984 AMC 2665 (2d Cir. 1984).

2. *Non-Removability*

> The principle of non-removability of maritime matters absent diversity has been followed frequently, *see, e.g.*, *Nesti v. Rose Barge Lines, Inc.*, 326 F. Supp. 170, 173 (N.D. Ill. 1971); *Harbor Boating Club v. Red Star Towing & Transportation Company, supra*, 179 F. Supp. at 756; *see also*, *Commonwealth of Puerto Rico v. Sea-Land Service, Inc.*, 349 F. Supp. 964, 977 (D.P.R. 1970); 1A MOORE'S FEDERAL PRACTICE P 0.167(3.-1), at 942-43 (2d ed. 1965). The Supreme Court's reading of "arising under" in § 1331 as not including maritime matters has also received extensive support, *see, e.g.*, *Dassigienis v. Cosmos Carriers & Trading Corporation*, 442 F.2d 1016, 1017 (2d Cir. 1971); *O.F. Shearer & Sons, Inc. v. Decher*, 349 F. Supp. 1214, 1217-1218 (S.D. W. Va. 1972). *See also* 1A MOORE'S FEDERAL PRACTICE P 0.167(3.-3), at 945-46 (2d ed. 1965).

Eastern Steel & Metal Company v. Hartford Fire Insurance Company, 376 F. Supp. 763, 1974 AMC 1701 (D. Conn. 1974).

POIRRIER v. NICKLOS DRILLING COMPANY

648 F.2d 1063, 1982 AMC 1514 (5th Cir. 1981)

TATE, Circuit Judge

Plaintiff Poirrier places a single issue before this court for resolution: Whether a maritime personal injury action, commenced in state court under the "saving to suitors" clause of 28 U.S.C. § 1333, can be removed to federal court on grounds of diversity of citizenship.

Poirrier was injured on an inland submersible drilling barge on the Atchafalaya River in Louisiana. Alleging the negligence of bargeowner Nicklos Drilling Co. (Nicklos) as the cause of his injuries, Poirrier filed suit in tort in the state courts of Louisiana. The defendant Nicklos, invoking the diversity jurisdiction of the federal courts, 28 U.S.C. § 1332, removed the action to the United States District Court for the Eastern District of Louisiana pursuant to the provisions of 28 U.S.C. § 1441. Poirrier then moved the district court to remand the case on grounds that its removal violated the express provisions of the "saving to suitors' clause. That motion was denied.

Poirrier now seeks review of the district court's order denying remand through the alternative vehicles of appeal or petition for a writ of mandamus.

An order denying remand of a case removed to federal court is not a final order within the meaning of 28 U.S.C. § 1291[2] and, standing by itself, it cannot be appealed unless certified by the district court according to the provisions of 28 U.S.C. § 1292(b).[2]

* * *

Such certification was not obtained in the present case and we are therefore without jurisdiction to review this order on appeal.

Where the circumstances are appropriate, appellate court review of an unappealable interlocutory order may be obtained through a petition for a writ of mandamus.

* * *

This case, however, does not present the "exceptional circumstances" that would "justify the invocation of this extraordinary remedy."

* * *

The district court did no more than deny remand where, on the face of the removal statute, 28 U.S.C. § 1441, and the grant of diversity jurisdiction, 28 U.S.C. § 1332, removal was entirely proper. Through his petition for mandamus, Poirrier challenges the power of a federal diversity court to retain jurisdiction of an action brought originally in state court under the "saving to suitors" clause of 28 U.S.C. § 1333—a challenge he would

---

[2] The courts of appeals shall have jurisdiction of appeals from all final decisions of the district courts of the United States, ... except where a direct review may be had in the Supreme Court. 28 U.S.C. § 1291.

[2] 28 U.S.C. § 1292(b) provides:

When a district judge, in making in a civil action an order not otherwise appealable under this section, shall be of the opinion that such order involves a controlling question of law as to which there is substantial grounds for difference of opinion and that an immediate appeal from the order may materially advance the ultimate termination of the litigation, he shall so state in writing in such order. The Court of Appeals may thereupon, in its discretion, permit an appeal to be taken from such order, if application is made to it within ten days after the entry of the order: *Provided, however,* That application for an appeal hereunder shall not stay proceedings in the district court unless the district judge or the Court of Appeals or a judge thereof shall so order.

characterize as raising a basic and as yet undecided question in this circuit. We do not believe the question here raised, however, is of a kind sufficient to justify the exercise of our "advisory" mandamus power.

* * *

This circuit has already recognized the removability, on diversity grounds, of maritime actions brought in state courts under the aegis of the "saving to suitors" clause:

> In *Romero v. International Terminal Operating Co.*, 1959, 358 U.S. 354, 79 S. Ct. 468, 3 L. Ed. 2d 368, which was decided since this action was commenced in the lower court, it was made clear that *except in diversity cases*, maritime litigation brought in state courts could not be removed to federal courts.

Gaitor v. Peninsular & Occidental S.S. Co., 287 F.2d 252, 254 (5th Cir. 1961) (ordering remand to state court of removed maritime action for lack of requisite jurisdictional amount) (emphasis added). *See also* 14 WRIGHT, MILLER & COOPER, *supra*, § 3674. Far from contradicting this view, the cases cited by Poirrier expressly support it. *See Pacific Far East Line, Inc. v. Ogden Corp.*, 425 F. Supp. 1239, 1242-43 (N.D.Cal.1977); *J. J. Ryan & Sons, Inc. v. Continental Ins. Co.*, 369 F. Supp. 692, 695 (D.S.C.1974); *Hill v. United Fruit Co.*, 149 F. Supp. 470, 472 (S.D.Cal.1957). The "saving to suitors" clause does no more than preserve the right of maritime suitors to pursue nonmaritime remedies. It does not guarantee them a nonfederal forum, or limit the right of defendants to remove such actions to federal court where there exists some basis for federal jurisdiction other than admiralty. *See* 14 WRIGHT, MILLER & COOPER, *supra*, § 3674.

The appeal is dismissed for lack of appellate jurisdiction; the petition for writ of mandamus is denied.

Note

As to the Outer Continental Shelf Lands Act as an independent basis for jurisdiction, *see Tennessee Gas Pipeline v. Houston Casualty Insurance Co.*, 87 F.3d 150, 1996 AMC 2296 (5th Cir. 1996).

Chapter 3

ADMIRALTY REMEDIES

A. Introductory Note: Enforcement of Maritime Claims, Liens and Mortgages in the United States*

1. *In rem* Actions

An action *in rem* is commenced by arresting property, typically a vessel, under Supplemental Rules C and E of the Federal Rules of Civil Procedure. The mere fact that the procedural device for instituting an *in rem* action is called an "arrest" does not mean that an *in rem* action in the United States is the same type of action which in other countries is commenced by an "arrest" procedure. An *in rem* action in the United States is an action against the named property itself. It need *not* be based on the personal liability of the owner of the property. It is *not* a means for obtaining *in personam* jurisdiction over a non-resident property owner. The law of the United States differentiates between a seizure of property by means of a judicial process called an "arrest" and a seizure of property by means of a judicial process called an "attachment". The arrest process is used to commence an *in rem* action. The attachment process, sometimes referred to as a "*quasi-in-rem*" proceeding, is used to commence an action *in personam.*

When Available—Maritime Liens

An *in rem* action may be brought to enforce maritime liens under the Commercial Instruments and Maritime Liens Act,[1] or to enforce other maritime liens created under the general maritime law. Generally actions for breach of maritime contracts and actions based on maritime torts give rise to maritime liens which may be enforced through an action *in rem.* Also statutes have conferred liens status in certain situations.

The following give rise to maritime liens.

1. Seamen's claim for wages
2. Master's claims for wages[3]
3. Salvage claims

---

* *Also see,* Steven F. Friedell and Nicholas J. Healy, *An Introduction to* In Rem *Jurisdiction and Procedure in the United States*, 20 J. Mar. L. & Com. 55 (1989) and Robert M. Jarvis, *An Introduction to Maritime Attachment Practice Under Rule B*, 20 J. Mar. L. & Com. 521 (1989).

[1] 46 U.S.C. §§ 31341 - 31343 (1989 Supp.). *See* Chapter 8.

[3] 46 U.S.C. § 11112 (1989 Supp.), master of a documented vessel.

4. Maritime torts including collision and personal injury claims
5. General Average claims
6. Preferred ship mortgage[4]
7. Supply and repair claims
8. Towage, wharfage, pilotage, stevedoring, etc. claims
9. Cargo damage caused by improper loading, stowage, custody, etc.
10. Ship's claim against cargo for unpaid freight
11. Breach of charter party

Arrest Procedures

When an *in rem* proceeding may be brought

Supplemental Rule C of the Federal Rules of Civil Procedure[5] specifies the rules applicable in *in rem* proceedings. It provides that an action *in rem* may be brought to enforce a maritime lien or whenever a federal statute provides for a maritime action *in rem*. Furthermore, an action *in rem* may be brought against the United States when authorized by statute, but the vessel in question may not actually be physically seized. Generally, a party who elects to proceed *in rem* also may proceed *in personam* against any party who may be liable.

The Complaint

In an *in rem* action plaintiff must file a "complaint" that describes the property that is subject to the action and states that it is in or will be in the judicial district during the pendency of the action. If the property is not within the district where the action is commenced and there is no prospect of it being so, an *in rem* action will not lie.[6]

Judicial Review—Notice

The complaint along with supporting papers must be reviewed by the court, and, if the conditions for an action *in rem* appear to exist, the court shall issue an order authorizing a warrant for the arrest of the vessel or other property that is the subject to the action. No notice other than execution is required. But if the property is not released within ten days, the plaintiff must give public notice of the action and the arrest in a newspaper of general circulation. This notice must specify the time within which the answer is required to be filed.

Claimant's Response

A claimant of property that is the subject of an action *in rem* must file its claim within ten days after process has been executed unless the court allows additional time. It must file its answer within twenty days after filing its claim. There are additional procedural matters

---

[4] As will be discussed later, preferred mortgages have been given a lien, may be enforced in an *in rem* proceeding, and are given priority over certain other claims.

[5] Unless stated otherwise or unless apparent from the context, the procedures referred to herein are prescribed in Supplemental Rule C of the Federal Rules of Civil Procedure.

[6] *But see infra*, NECESSITY FOR SEIZURE & RETENTION - EXCEPTIONS.

applicable to actions *in rem* contained in Supplemental Rule E, but as they are equally applicable to "attachments" they will be discussed *infra*.

Execution of Process

For an action *in rem* to be commenced the property that is the subject matter of the action must be subjected "physically" to the jurisdiction of the court.[7] It is not enough that the property is present in the judicial district where the court is located. A court officer, the United States Marshal, must physically seize the property, actually or figuratively, and take it into custody, if possible. In the case of an arrest of a vessel, however, service of the arrest papers on the master and placing a "keeper" on the vessel will suffice. In an *in rem* action jurisdiction over the property is required to give the court jurisdiction over the action, but as will be discussed this requirement has been weakened to some extent. Subject to the qualifications discussed below, seizure of the property is essential to give the court jurisdiction over the property.

---

2. *Admiralty Attachments and Garnishments*

There is an alternative method for obtaining *in personam* jurisdiction other than by service of process on the defendant or its agents authorized to receive process either in fact or by law. This procedure is sometimes referred to as *quasi-in-rem* jurisdiction and is accomplished by an attachment of defendant's property within a state. The presence of defendant's property within a state may be sufficient to constitute the "minimum contacts" required under the Due Process Clause. The seizure of the property may be sufficient to satisfy the service of process requirement. The nature and extent of the property, its use in the state, and the relationship, if any, between the property and the events that have given rise to the claim may assure that the due process fairness requirements have been satisfied.

Supplemental Rule B of the Federal Rules of Civil Procedure makes special provisions for bringing a maritime claim in federal court by commencing an *in personam* action by seizing property of the defendant by attachment or garnishment.

Attachment Procedures[8]

When Available—Complaint

A plaintiff who has asserted an admiralty or maritime claim *in personam* may include in its verified complaint a request for process to attach the defendant's goods and chattels, or credits and effects in the hands of garnishees named in the process up to the amount sued for. Rule B is available only where plaintiff has asserted a maritime or admiralty claim. The property plaintiff seeks to attach or garnish must be within the geographic boundaries of the federal judicial district wherein the action is brought.

---

[7] *But see infra*, NECESSITY FOR SEIZURE & RETENTION - EXCEPTIONS.

[8] Unless stated otherwise or unless apparent from the context, the procedures referred to herein are prescribed in Supplemental Rule B of the Federal Rules of Civil Procedure.

Defendant "not found within the district"

Attachment and garnishment are permissible under the Rule only "if the defendant shall not be found within the district." Note the use of the term "district". Most states because of their size or population have been divided by Congress into several federal judicial districts in order to facilitate the operation of the federal district courts. For example, the state of Louisiana contains three federal judicial districts, the Eastern District of Louisiana, the Middle District and the Western District, each with its own geographic boundaries.

Plaintiff must submit an affidavit to the effect that defendant cannot be found within the district where suit is brought. Usually plaintiff will set forth the steps it or its attorney took which support the allegation that defendant is not present within the district. An allegation that defendant cannot be found within the district has two dimensions:

1. defendant is not present for jurisdictional purposes;
2. defendant is not present for service of process.

To defeat an attachment and secure the release of property defendant must show that it is present in the district *both* in the jurisdictional sense (minimum contacts) and that it is amenable to service of process personally or through an agent authorized to accept service of process. The fact that defendant is present within the *state* is insufficient to bar a Rule B action if defendant is not present within the geographic area comprising the federal judicial district in which the action has been commenced.

Judicial Review—Notice

The procedures under Rule B are similar in many respects to the procedures required by Rule C. A court must review the complaint and affidavit and if it appears that plaintiff is entitled to have process issued, the court will so order. Notice is given to the garnishee or person in possession of the property when process, the attachment, is served on that person in order to secure physical control of the property by the court. Rule B provides that no default shall be taken unless there is proof that the plaintiff or the garnishee gave notice to the defendant. Notice may be given by mail with return receipt, or by actual service of process. Notice is not required if plaintiff or garnishee has been unable to give it despite diligent efforts to do so.

Answer

The garnishee has twenty days from service of process to file an answer. Plaintiff may serve interrogatories on the garnishee. The defendant has thirty days after process has been executed to file its answer.

Attachment and Arrest Distinguished

Rule B attachment differs from Rule C arrest in several respects. First, Rule C arrest may be used even though defendant can be found within the district.

Secondly, to invoke Rule C the property arrested must be related to the claim. The *in rem* action which is implemented by an arrest must be based on a maritime lien or be authorized by statute. By contrast Rule B attachment applies to *any* property of the defendant that is present within the district even though it is totally unrelated to the events giving rise to the claim. Unlike the rule of some countries a "sister ship" may not be arrested in the United States, *i.e.*, may not be the defendant in an *in rem* proceeding. Nevertheless, the "sister ship" doctrine would be applicable in a Rule B attachment as would any property of the defendant. Furthermore, an attachment need only be based on a maritime claim regardless of whether or not the claim gave rise to a maritime lien.

Third, in a Rule C *in rem* proceeding plaintiff's claim is predicated on the liability of the property itself. In rule B attachment, liability is always predicated on the personal liability of the defendant. If under the applicable substantive rules, a defendant is not personally liable, its property may not be attached. In an *in rem* proceeding, judgment is entered against the property which may be sold to satisfy the judgment against it. In such proceedings the purchaser takes free and clear of all maritime liens. In attachment proceedings judgment is entered against the owner of the property. The property may be sold to satisfy the judgment against the owner, but this does not necessarily affect the rights of other persons such as those who have maritime liens or a preferred ship mortgage on the property.

Rule B, however, specifically authorizes the plaintiff to use state provisions for attachment and garnishment in addition to or in the alternative to maritime attachment under the Rule, but the provisions of the Supplemental Rules are not applicable to such state actions. An action under a state attachment or garnishment procedure may also be brought in state court. Note, however, an admiralty action *in rem* may only be brought in federal court. A state court may not order the arrest of property in a case in which admiralty and maritime law is applicable.

3. Additional Provisions Applicable to Arrest and Attachment

Supplemental Rule E contains additional procedural provisions that are applicable to both maritime arrest and attachment proceedings.[9]

The Complaint

A complaint filed by a plaintiff under Rules B and C must state the circumstances under which the claim arose with such particularity that the defendant or claimant, without requesting additional information, will be able to begin investigating the facts and prepare a responsive pleading. The Federal Rules of Civil Procedure generally are not very demanding in regard to the facts pleaded as the basis for a complaint because they authorize parties to engage in extensive pre-trial discovery practices. Thus, the requirement of Supplemental Rule E that the facts be stated with sufficient particularity for the defendant

---

[9] Unless stated otherwise or unless apparent from the context, the procedures referred to herein are prescribed in Supplemental Rule E of the Federal Rules of Civil Procedure.

to begin its investigation of the incident on which the arrest or attachment is based is a more demanding standard. It should be noted that arrest warrants and writs of attachment are issued *ex parte* after the court has reviewed only the documents presented by the plaintiff. These documents must adequately inform the court that it should order process to be issued.

Security for Costs

The Rule also authorizes the court to require any party to post security for costs and expenses that may be awarded against him.

Property Not Within The District

Even where the property that is to be seized is not within the geographic bounds of the federal district court, the plaintiff may still apply for the issuance of process for its seizure. Plaintiff may then request that execution of process be delayed until the property is brought within the court's territorial jurisdiction or until some arrangement by way of stipulation may be agreed upon by the parties. Property may not be seized under Supplemental Rules B, C, and E unless it is within the district because process authorizing its seizure may only be served within the district.

Necessity for Seizure & Retention—General Rule

As a general proposition, jurisdiction *in rem* or *quasi-in-rem* is obtained by virtue of a seizure of defendant's property, or where the parties have stipulated the jurisdiction of the court, or where the defendant has waived any objection to the exercise of jurisdiction by the court. As stated previously if process issues but is not executed the court will not have jurisdiction. At one time it had been held that where property had been seized but was subsequently released without proper security, stipulation of the parties, or waiver, the court lost its *in rem* or *quasi-in-rem* jurisdiction over the matter. This applied not only to the initial proceedings in federal district court but on appeal as well. There was an exception to this rule, where property had been released and removed from the district by accident, fraud or improper conduct, jurisdiction was not lost as long as it once existed. The rule regarding retention of seized property by the court has been abrogated.

Necessity for Seizure

Under certain circumstances an action may proceed *in rem* or *quasi-in-rem* without an actual physical seizure or retention of the property in question. Supplemental Rule E states that where process of arrest or attachment and garnishment has issued "such process shall be stayed, or the property released, on the giving of security, to be approved by the court or clerk, or by stipulation of the parties, conditional to answer the judgment of the court ... ."

Under this provision, if property is seized, it may be released upon posting of a sufficient bond. In regard to the property that has been arrested, plaintiff's maritime lien is transferred from that property to the bond that has been given by way of security. Plaintiff no longer has a maritime lien on the property. Even where the property has not been seized the parties (plaintiff and defendant) may enter into a stipulation that:

1. the property will not be seized;
2. the matter may proceed *in rem* or *quasi-in-rem* as the case may be;
3. defendant undertakes to honor any judgment;
4. defendant consents to the court's continuing with the action;

In reality this means that the parties may confer *in rem* or *quasi-in-rem* jurisdiction upon the court by express agreement. *In rem* or *quasi-in-rem* jurisdiction may be conferred by waiver as well. Even where no property has been seized, a defendant who makes a general appearance and responds to the substance of plaintiff's complaint without clearly reserving an objection to the courts' jurisdiction will be considered to have waived the jurisdictional defect. At the extreme point, this means that an action may proceed *in rem* notwithstanding the fact that the property was never seized within the court's jurisdiction or was never within the court's jurisdiction where the parties so agree such as by stipulation or where defendant waives the right to object to the court's jurisdiction such as by failure to promptly and properly make the objection.

Service of Process

Supplemental Rule E (4) specifies the method of serving process on both tangible and intangible property.

Expenses of seizing and keeping property

The expenses of seizing and keeping property are provided for by federal statute.[10]

Post Arrest / Post Attachment Hearing

Supplemental Rule E (4) (f) confers upon a person whose property has been arrested or attached and garnished the right to a prompt judicial hearing at which hearing the plaintiff has the burden of proving that the arrest or attachment was authorized and lawful.

Release of Property—Security

The nature and amount of security to release property that has been seized or to stay execution of process prior to seizure may be fixed by agreement of the parties. Where the parties fail to agree the court will fix the security at an amount sufficient to cover "the plaintiff's claim fairly stated with accrued interest and costs."[11] This amount of security may not exceed twice the amount of the plaintiff's claim or the value of the property as determined by appraisal. The bond or stipulation offered as security must provide for the payment of the principal sum and interest of 6% per year.

The owner of a vessel may file a general bond or stipulation, with sufficient surety, which undertakes to satisfy any judgment of that court in all actions which may be brought in that court subsequently in which the vessel is attached or arrested. Where such a bond is filed, execution of process shall be stayed as long as the amount secured by the bond or

---

[10] 28 U. S.C. § 1921 (1987 P.P.).

[11] FED. R. CIV. P. SUPP. R. E 5(a).

stipulation is at least double the aggregate amount claimed by all plaintiffs in actions begun and pending in which arrest or attachment process against the vessel has been issued.

Property attached and garnished or arrested shall be released by the marshal upon acceptance and approval of a stipulation, bond or other security, signed by the party in whose behalf the property is detained or its attorney which expressly authorizes its release. However, all costs and charges of the court and its officers, including the marshal, must first have been paid. The marshal may not release the property in any other circumstance except upon order of the court. However, the clerk of the court, upon the giving of approved security as provided by law and the Supplemental Rules may enter an order as of course releasing the property. Likewise where an action is dismissed or discontinued the clerk may enter an order as of course releasing the property. Notwithstanding that Federal Rule of Civil Procedure 62 provides for an automatic stay in situations where a court has dismissed an action, it has been held that this does not override the provision of Supplemental Rule E which authorizes the clerk to release property "as of course" when an action has been dismissed. In case of a dismissal the plaintiff should specifically request the court to order a stay of the release of the detained property.

Increase or Decrease of Security; Counter-Security

Supplemental Rule E provides for certain practical contingencies. Thus, the court may order either a reduction of or an increase in security where it is appropriate to do so. Furthermore, where a counterclaim, including a claim for wrongful seizure, arising out of the same transaction or occurrence is asserted by the defendant who has provided security on the original claim, the court may order the plaintiff to give security on the counterclaim.

Restricted Appearance

Sometimes a party whose property has been attached and garnished or arrested faces a dilemma because it may want to defend against that claim without submitting generally to the jurisdiction of the court in respect to other claims for which arrest and attachment and garnishment are not available. Supplemental Rule E specifically authorizes such a restricted appearance, but the restrictive nature of the appearance must be expressly stated.

Sale of Property

All sales of property shall be made by the marshal and the proceeds paid into the registry of the court, where they will be dispersed according to law.

---

4. Actions in State Courts

Under Title 28 of the United States Code § 1333 a plaintiff who has a maritime claim is authorized by the "saving to suitors" provision to seek a state remedy in a state court where the law of a state makes such remedy available. Thus, an ordinary breach of maritime contract case or maritime tort case may be brought in state court. In such cases the procedures described in Supplemental Rules, B, C and E are not applicable. Instead state procedures for the enforcement of claims will be followed. Generally, state law, unlike federal law, makes no special provision for the enforcement of maritime claims. The usual state procedures applicable to *in personam* civil proceedings would be followed and remedies in such proceedings would be granted.

The United States Supreme Court has determined that except in extraordinary situations where important state interests are implicated such as forfeiture proceedings, a plaintiff who seeks to enforce a maritime claim in an *in rem* proceeding may do so only in a federal court. A state court may not entertain a maritime claim in an *in rem* proceeding. However, a plaintiff may use the full range of *in personam* procedures including the attachment and garnishment procedures in an action *quasi-in-rem* to the extent they are available under the law of the particular state in which suit is brought.

B. Arrest—Supplemental Rule C—Federal Rules of Civil Procedure

Supplemental Rule C. Actions *in rem*: Special provisions

(1)**When Available.** An action *in rem* may be brought:

(a) To enforce any maritime lien;

(b) Whenever a statute of the United States provides for a maritime action *in rem* or a proceeding analogous thereto.

Except as otherwise provided by law a party who may proceed *in rem* may also, or in the alternative, proceed *in personam* against any person who may be liable.

Statutory provisions exempting vessels or other property owned or possessed by or operated by or for the United States from arrest or seizure are not affected by this rule. When a statute so provides, an action against the United States or an instrumentality thereof may proceed on *in rem* principles.

(2) **Complaint.** In an action *in rem* the complaint must:

(a) be verified;

(b) describe with reasonable particularity the property that is the subject of the action;

(c) in an admiralty and maritime proceeding, state that the property is within the district or will be within the district while the action is pending;

(d) in a forfeiture proceeding for violation of a federal statute, state:

(i) the place of seizure and whether it was on land or on navigable waters;

(ii) whether the property is within the district, and if the property is not within the district the statutory basis for the court's exercise of jurisdiction over the property; and

(iii) all allegations required by the statute under which the action is brought.

(3) Judicial Authorization and Process.

(a) Arrest Warrant.

(i) When the United States files a complaint demanding a forfeiture for violation of a federal statute, the clerk must promptly issue a summons and a warrant for the arrest of the vessel or other property without requiring a certification of exigent circumstances, but if the property is real property the United States must proceed under applicable statutory procedures.

(ii)(A) In other actions, the court must review the complaint and any supporting papers. If the conditions for an *in rem* action appear to exist, the court must issue an order directing the clerk to issue a warrant for the arrest of the vessel or other property that is the subject of the action.

(B) If the plaintiff or the plaintiff's attorney certifies that exigent circumstances make court review impracticable, the clerk must promptly issue a summons and a warrant for the arrest of the vessel or other property that is the subject of the action. The plaintiff has the burden in any post-arrest hearing under Rule E(4)(f) to show that exigent circumstances existed.

(b) Service.

(i) If the property that is the subject of the action is a vessel or tangible property on board a vessel, the warrant and any supplemental process must be delivered to the marshal for service.

(ii) If the property that is the subject of the action is other property, tangible or intangible, the warrant and any supplemental process must be delivered to a person or organization authorized to enforce it, who may be: (A) a marshal; (B) someone under contract with the United States; (C) someone specially appointed by the court for that purpose; or, (D) in an action brought by the United States, any officer or employee of the United States.

(c) Deposit in Court. If the property that is the subject of the action consists in whole or in part of freight, the proceeds of property sold, or other intangible property, the clerk must issue—in addition to the warrant—a summons directing any person controlling the property to show cause why it should not be deposited in court to abide the judgment.

(d) Supplemental Process. The clerk may upon application issue supplemental process to enforce the court's order without further court order.

(4) Notice. No notice other than execution of process is required when the property that is the subject of the action has been released under Rule E(5). If the property is not released within 10 days after execution, the plaintiff must promptly—or within the time that the court allows—give public notice of the action and arrest in a newspaper designated by

court order and having general circulation in the district, but publication may be terminated if the property is released before publication is completed. The notice must specify the time under Rule C(6) to file a statement of interest in or right against the seized property and to answer. This rule does not affect the notice requirements in an action to foreclose a preferred ship mortgage under 46 U.S.C. §§ 31301 et seq., as amended.
(5) **Ancillary Process.** In any action *in rem* in which process has been served as provided by this rule, if any part of the property that is the subject of the action has not been brought within the control of the court because it has been removed or sold, or because it is intangible property in the hands of a person who has not been served with process, the court may, on motion, order any person having possession or control of such property or its proceeds to show cause why it should not be delivered into the custody of the marshal or other person or organization having a warrant for the arrest of the property, or paid into court to abide the judgment; and, after hearing, the court may enter such judgment as law and justice may require.

(6) **Responsive Pleading; Interrogatories.**

(a) Civil Forfeiture. In an *in rem* forfeiture action for violation of a federal statute:

(i) a person who asserts an interest in or right against the property that is the subject of the action must file a verified statement identifying the interest or right:

(A) within 30 days after the earlier of (1) the date of service of the Government's complaint or (2) completed publication of notice under Rule C(4), or
(B) within the time that the court allows.

(ii) an agent, bailee, or attorney must state the authority to file a statement of interest in or right against the property on behalf of another; and
(iii) a person who files a statement of interest in or right against the property must serve and file an answer within 20 days after filing the statement.

(b) Maritime Arrests and Other Proceedings. In an *in rem* action not governed by Rule C(6)(a):

(i) A person who asserts a right of possession or any ownership interest in the property that is the subject of the action must file a verified statement of right or interest:

(A) within 10 days after the earlier of (1) the execution of process, or (2) completed publication of notice under Rule C(4), or
(B) within the time that the court allows:

(ii) the statement of right or interest must describe the interest in the property that supports the person's demand for its restitution or right to defend the action;

(iii) an agent, bailee, or attorney must state the authority to file a statement of right or interest on behalf of another; and
(iv) a person who asserts a right of possession or any ownership interest must serve an answer within 20 days after filing the statement of interest or right.

(c) Interrogatories. Interrogatories may be served with the complaint in an *in rem* action without leave of court. Answers to the interrogatories must be served with the answer to the complaint.

(As amended Apr. 17, 2000, eff. Dec. 1, 2000; Apr. 29, 2002, eff. Dec. 1, 2002.)

C. Supplemental Rule E—Federal Rules of Civil Procedure

Rule E. Actions *In rem* and *Quasi In rem*: General Provisions

(1) **Applicability.** Except as otherwise provided, this rule applies to actions *in personam* with process of maritime attachment and garnishment, actions *in rem*, and petitory, possessory, and partition actions, supplementing Rules B, C, and D.

(2) **Complaint; Security.**
(a) *Complaint.* In actions to which this rule is applicable the complaint shall state the circumstances from which the claim arises with such particularity that the defendant or claimant will be able, without moving for a more definite statement, to commence an investigation of the facts and to frame a responsive pleading.
(b) *Security for Costs.* Subject to the provisions of Rule 54(d) and of relevant statutes, the court may, on the filing of the complaint or on the appearance of any defendant, claimant, or any other party, or at any later time, require the plaintiff, defendant, claimant, or other party to give security, or additional security, in such sum as the court shall direct to pay all costs and expenses that shall be awarded against the party by any interlocutory order or by the final judgment, or on appeal by any appellate court.

(3) **Process.**
(a) *Territorial Limits of Effective Service.* Process *in rem* and of maritime attachment and garnishment shall be served only within the district.
(b) *Issuance and Delivery.* Issuance and delivery of process *in rem*, or of maritime attachment and garnishment, shall be held in abeyance if the plaintiff so requests.

(4) **Execution of Process; Marshal's Return; Custody of Property; Procedures for Release.**

(a) *In General.* Upon issuance and delivery of the process, or, in the case of summons with process of attachment and garnishment, when it appears that the defendant cannot be found within the district, the marshal shall forthwith execute the process in accordance with this subdivision (4), making due and prompt return.

(b) *Tangible Property.* If tangible property is to be attached or arrested, the marshal shall take it into the marshal's possession for safe custody. If the character or situation of the property is such that the taking of actual possession is impracticable, the marshal shall execute the process by affixing a copy thereof to the property in a conspicuous place and by leaving a copy of the complaint and process with the person having possession or the person's agent. In furtherance of the marshal's custody of any vessel the marshal is authorized to make a written request to the collector of customs not to grant clearance to such vessel until notified by the marshal or a deputy marshal or by the clerk that the vessel has been released in accordance with these rules.

(c) *Intangible Property.* If intangible property is to be attached or arrested the marshal shall execute the process by leaving with the garnishee or other obligor a copy of the complaint and process requiring the garnishee or other obligor to answer as provided in Rules B(3)(a) and C(6); or the marshal may accept for payment into the registry of the court the amount owed to the extent of the amount claimed by the plaintiff with interest and costs, in which event the garnishee or other obligor shall not be required to answer unless alias process shall be served.

(d) *Directions with Respect to Property in Custody.* The marshal may at any time apply to the court for directions with respect to property that has been attached or arrested, and shall give notice of such application to any or all of the parties as the court may direct.

(e) *Expenses of Seizing and Keeping Property; Deposit.* These rules do not alter the provisions of Title 28, U.S.C., § 1921, as amended, relative to the expenses of seizing and keeping property attached or arrested and to the requirement of deposits to cover such expenses.

(f) *Procedure for Release from Arrest or Attachment.* Whenever property is arrested or attached, any person claiming an interest in it shall be entitled to a prompt hearing at which the plaintiff shall be required to show why the arrest or attachment should not be vacated or other relief granted consistent with these rules. This subdivision shall have no application to suits for seamen's wages when process is issued upon a certification of sufficient cause filed pursuant to Title 46, U.S.C. §§ 603 and 604 or to actions by the United States for forfeitures for violation of any statute of the United States.

(5) **Release of Property.**

(a) *Special Bond.* Except in cases of seizures for forfeiture under any law of the United States, whenever process of maritime attachment and garnishment or process *in rem* is issued the execution of such process shall be stayed, or the property released, on the giving of security, to be approved by the court or clerk, or by stipulation of the parties, conditioned to answer the judgment of the court or of any appellate court. The parties may stipulate the amount and nature of such security. In the event of the inability or refusal of the parties so to stipulate the court shall fix the principal sum of the bond or stipulation at an amount sufficient to cover the amount of the plaintiff's claim fairly stated with accrued interest and costs; but the principal sum shall in no event exceed (i) twice the amount of the plaintiff's claim or (ii) the value of the property on due appraisement, whichever is smaller. The bond or stipulation shall be conditioned for the payment of the principal sum and interest thereon at 6 per cent per annum.

(b) *General Bond.* The owner of any vessel may file a general bond or stipulation, with sufficient surety, to be approved by the court, conditioned to answer the judgment of such court in all or any actions that may be brought thereafter in such court in which the vessel is attached or arrested. Thereupon the execution of all such process against such vessel shall be stayed so long as the amount secured by such bond or stipulation is at least double the aggregate amount claimed by plaintiffs in all actions begun and pending in which such vessel has been attached or arrested. Judgments and remedies may be had on such bond or stipulation as if a special bond or stipulation had been filed in each of such actions. The district court may make necessary orders to carry this rule into effect, particularly as to the giving of proper notice of any action against or attachment of a vessel for which a general bond has been filed. Such bond or stipulation shall be indorsed by the clerk with a minute of the actions wherein process is so stayed. Future security may be required by the court at any time.

If a special bond or stipulation is given in a particular case, the liability on the general bond or stipulation shall cease as to that case.

(c) *Release by Consent or Stipulation; Order of Court or Clerk; Costs.* Any vessel, cargo, or other property in the custody of the marshal or other person or organization having the warrant may be released forthwith upon the marshal's acceptance and approval of a stipulation, bond, or other security, signed by the party on whose behalf the property is detained or the party's attorney and expressly authorizing such release, if all costs and charges of the court and its officers shall have first been paid. Otherwise no property in the custody of the marshal, other person or organization having the warrant, or other officer of the court shall be released without an order of the court; but such order may be entered as of course by the clerk, upon the giving of approved security as provided by law and these rules, or upon the dismissal or discontinuance of the action; but the marshal or other person or organization having the warrant shall not deliver any property so released until the costs and charges of the officers of the court shall first have been paid.

(d) *Possessory, Petitory, and Partition Actions.* The foregoing provisions of this subdivision (5) do not apply to petitory, possessory, and partition actions. In such cases the property arrested shall be released only by order of the court, on such terms and conditions and on the giving of such security as the court may require.

(6) Reduction or Impairment of Security.

(a) *In General.* Whenever security is taken the court may, on motion and hearing, for good cause shown, reduce the amount of any security given; and if the surety shall be or become insufficient, new or additional sureties may be required on motion and hearing.

(b) *Multiple Claims.* Should an incident or occurrence give rise to multiple claims *in rem* against a vessel in excess of its value and the vessel is attached or arrested, security shall be reduced to an amount as hereinafter set forth provided the owner, demise charterer or operator of the vessel shall enter a general appearance whereby such person shall become liable for any deficiency in excess of security filed. Upon such entry of appearance and the posting of a security equal to the value of the vessel plus pending freight, together with such sum as the court may fix to provide for the costs of the proceeding, conditioned to answer the judgment of the court or any appellate court with respect to all actions arising out of such incident or occurrence in which process for the attachment or arrest of the vessel has been or may thereafter be issued, such vessel shall be released. The filing of such security shall be deemed in the nature of an interpleader for the value of the vessel and the execution of further process against the vessel arising out of such incident or occurrence shall be stayed. Such stay shall not affect the right of a claimant to file an action *in personam* against any person with respect to such incident or occurrence in any forum in a jurisdiction in which he may be found or the right of any person to seek removal or transfer of any action under applicable rule or law.

(c) *Absent Claimants.* In an action under Rule E(6)(b), venue shall be the district the Vessel within which the Vessel is located. Where any lien claimant cannot be served within the State, or does not voluntarily appear, the court may order the absent claimant to appear and plead by a day certain. Such order, together with the stay issued under E(6)(B), shall be served on the absent claimant personally if practicable, wherever found. Where personal service is not practicable, the order and stay shall be published as the court may direct, not less than once a week for six consecutive weeks. If any absent claimant does not appear or plead within the time allowed, the court may proceed as if the absent claimant had been served with process within the State, but any adjudication shall, as regards the absent claimant without appearance, affect only his interest in the Vessel as a lien claimant in the action. Any defendant, not so personally notified may intervene at any time prior to final judgment.

(7) **Security on Counterclaim.** Whenever there is asserted a counterclaim arising out of the same transaction or occurrence with respect to which the action was originally filed, and the defendant or claimant in the original action has given security to respond in damages, any plaintiff for whose benefit such security has been given shall give security in the usual amount and form to respond in damages to the claims set forth in such counterclaim, unless the court, for cause shown, shall otherwise direct; and proceedings on the original claim shall be stayed until such security is given, unless the court otherwise directs. When

the United States or a corporate instrumentality thereof as defendant is relieved by law of the requirement of giving security to respond in damages it shall nevertheless be treated for the purposes of this subdivision E(7) as if it had given such security if a private person so situated would have been required to give it.

(8) Restricted Appearance. An appearance to defend against an admiralty and maritime claim with respect to which there has issued process *in rem*, or process of attachment and garnishment whether pursuant to these Supplemental Rules or to Rule 4(e), may be expressly restricted to the defense of such claim, and in that event shall not constitute an appearance for the purposes of any other claim with respect to which such process is not available or has not been served.

(9) Disposition of Property; Sales.

(a) *Actions for Forfeitures.* In any action *in rem* to enforce a forfeiture for violation of a statute of the United States the property shall be disposed of as provided by statute.

D. *In rem* Jurisdiction: Cases

1. Arrest Procedures: Post-Seizure Hearings/Release Bonds

SALAZAR v. THE "ATLANTIC SUN"

881 F.2d 73, 1989 AMC 2594 (3d Cir. 1989)

WEIS, Circuit Judge

* * *

Before docking at the port of Salem, New Jersey, a dispute had arisen between the captain and seamen aboard The Atlantic Sun and the ship's owner over alleged unpaid wages and the crew's failure to pick up cargo at a Brazilian port. After the vessel arrived at Salem, negotiations took place, but were unsuccessful.

At the instance of the captain, the district court ordered the ship arrested and ultimately set bond at $75,000. Apparently unable to secure a bond, the owner filed a petition in bankruptcy under Chapter 11. After a hearing, the bankruptcy judge lifted the automatic stay, and the district court scheduled a marshal's sale.

On the day set for sale, the owner presented a bond for $75,000, which the district court found defective in form and inadequate in amount because of increased charges resulting from the lapse of time. After the marshal's auction, the court set the time for a confirmation hearing. Near the conclusion of that hearing, the owner asked for a delay of two weeks to post a bond in the amount of $140,000, the high bid at the auction. The court denied the request, and instead confirmed the sale. When the owner did not present a supersedeas bond on the morning of the following day, the court refused a stay of confirmation. A panel of this Court denied a twenty-four hour stay.

On appeal, the owner argues that the sale should be set aside and the vessel returned. The owner asserts that the district court's failure to conduct an adversarial post-arrest hearing resolving challenges to the plaintiffs' claims amounts to a denial of due process and a violation of the Federal Rules of Civil Procedure. The owner also argues that the district judge denied it a reasonable opportunity to post a bond at the conclusion of the confirmation hearing.

* * *

Arrest of a vessel is an *in rem* procedure in admiralty law having an ancient lineage. Utilized even before the Elizabethan era, it had become a dominating feature of admiralty practice by the nineteenth century. *See generally* F. Wiswall, *The Development of Admiralty Jurisdiction and Practice Since 1800* 155-208 (1970), noted in *Merchants Nat'l Bank v. The Dredge Gen. G.L. Gillespie*, 663 F.2d 1338, 1342 n. 8 (5th Cir. Unit A Dec. 1981), *cert. dismissed*, 456 U.S. 966, 102 S. Ct. 2263, 72 L. Ed. 2d 865 (1982).

Seizure of a vessel by court officials at the instance of a complainant serves the dual purpose of securing jurisdiction and providing a source for the satisfaction of a maritime lien. In the English view—the so-called "procedural" theory—the arrest of a vessel is intended to force the owner to appear so as to give the court *in personam* jurisdiction. American courts, by and large, adopted a "personification" theory in which the vessel itself is a party and judgments are entered against her without the necessity of securing jurisdiction over the owner.

The Supreme Court in *Tucker v. Alexandroff*, 183 U.S. 424, 438, 22 S. Ct. 195, 201, 46 L. Ed. 264 (1902), described the personification theory in modern admiralty practice. *See also United States v. The Little Charles*, 26 F.Cas. 979, 981-82 (C.C.D.Va. 1818) (No. 15,612) (Marshall, C.J., sitting as Circuit Justice). Although subjected to academic criticism, *e.g.*, G. GILMORE & C. BLACK, THE LAW OF ADMIRALTY § 9-3 (2d ed. 1975), the personification theory has provided a useful jurisprudential concept in formulating procedures for the arrest process where maritime liens are in existence.

In 1844, the Supreme Court adopted the Rules of Practice in Causes of Admiralty and Maritime Jurisdiction, codifying *in rem* procedures then in practice. 44 U.S. (3 How.) iii-xiv (1844). The Court revised the rules in later years, and in 1966 admiralty practice was unified through amendments to the Federal Rules of Civil Procedure. Rules A-F of the Supplemental Rules for Certain Admiralty and Maritime Claims ("Supplemental Admiralty Rules") addressed the unique admiralty *in rem* action.

A few years later, common law *in rem* proceedings attracted the concern of the Supreme Court. In a series of decisions beginning with *Sniadach v. Family Fin. Corp.*, 395 U.S. 337, 89 S. Ct. 1820, 23 L. Ed. 2d 349 (1969), the Court outlined procedural due process requirements in attachment and garnishment, emphasizing particularly the need for a pre- or post-seizure hearing. *See Fuentes v. Shevin*, 407 U.S. 67, 92 S. Ct. 1983, 32 L. Ed. 2d 556 (1972); *Mitchell v. W.T. Grant Co.*, 416 U.S. 600, 94 S. Ct. 1895, 40 L. Ed. 2d 406 (1974); *North Georgia Finishing, Inc. v. Di-Chem Inc.*, 419 U.S. 601, 95 S. Ct. 719, 42 L. Ed. 2d 751 (1975). In another opinion affecting traditional *in rem* procedures, the Court insisted on the presence of a defendant's minimum contacts with the forum, *Shaffer v. Heitner*, 433 U.S. 186, 97 S. Ct. 2569, 53 L. Ed. 2d 683 (1977), a matter not at issue here.

None of these decisions by the Supreme Court arose in the admiralty context, and some federal courts reasoned that the unique historical and constitutional foundations of admiralty law may place maritime claims beyond the sweep of common law *in rem* cases. *See, e.g.*, *Merchants Nat'l Bank*, 663 F.2d at 1345-46; *Amstar Corp. v. S/S Alexandros T.*, 664 F.2d 904, 911-12 (4th Cir. 1981). At least two district courts, however, considered procedures under the Supplemental Admiralty Rules to be suspect. *Alyeska Pipeline Serv. Co. v. The Vessel Bay Ridge*, 509 F. Supp. 1115, 1120 (D. Alaska 1981), *appeal dismissed*, 703 F.2d 381 (9th Cir. 1983), *cert. dismissed*, 467 U.S. 1247, 104 S. Ct. 3526, 82 L. Ed. 2d 852 (1984); *Karl Senner Inc. v. M/V Acadian Valor*, 485 F. Supp. 287, 295 (E.D.La. 1980).

In Merchants National Bank, the Court of Appeals commented that local rules making a prompt post-seizure hearing available on request would cure any alleged constitutional defects in the arrest procedure. Where no such local rules exist, the Court declared that "every Admiralty Court has the inherent power to assure the protections contemplated." Merchants Nat'l Bank, 663 F.2d at 1344.

Despite the existence of local rules in many districts, the Maritime Law Association, concerned about the uncertainty over due process in attachment and arrest cases, presented to the Advisory Committee on Civil Rules proposals to amend Supplemental Admiralty Rules B, C, D, and E of the Federal Rules of Civil Procedure. These suggestions resulted in the 1985 adoption of amendments to the admiralty rules, providing for pre- and post-seizure procedures. In addition to these rules, many district courts, including New Jersey, have adopted complementary local rules.

We narrow our discussion to the Rules specifically addressing arrest procedures—Supplemental Admiralty Rules C and E and New Jersey Local Admiralty Rule (e). Supplemental Admiralty Rule C(3) provides that a complaint seeking the arrest of a vessel is to be reviewed by the court before a warrant is issued. Rule E(4)(f) states, with exceptions not pertinent here, that after an arrest, "any person claiming an interest in [the ship] shall be entitled to a prompt hearing at which the plaintiff shall be required to show why the arrest ... should not be vacated or other relief granted." In the District of New Jersey, Local Admiralty Rule (e)(8) ensures that "[a]n adversary hearing following arrest ... be conducted by the Court within three (3) court days after a request for such hearing, unless otherwise ordered."

Supplemental Admiralty Rule E(5)(a) permits the owner to secure the release of its vessel by posting a bond in an amount stipulated by the parties, or if they are unable to agree, in an amount fixed by the court that is "sufficient to cover the amount of the plaintiff's claim fairly stated with accrued interest and costs." The Supplemental Rules authorize the court to direct an interlocutory sale if the vessel is subject to deterioration, the expense of keeping her is disproportionate, or "if there is unreasonable delay in securing [her] release." FED. R. CIV. P. SUPP. ADM. R. E(9)(b).

Not specifically mentioned in the rules, but frequently used, is the plaintiff's agreement to the release of a vessel on the promise of the owner or its counsel to deliver a so-called Letter of Undertaking. This document is an agreement that the owner will enter an appearance, acknowledge ownership, and, whether the vessel be lost or not, pay any final decree entered against the ship. *See Continental Grain Co. v. Barge FBL-585*, 364 U.S. 19, 29, 80 S. Ct. 1470, 4 L. Ed. 2d 1540 (1960) (Whittaker, J., dissenting); McCreary, *Going for the Jugular Vein: Arrests and Attachments in Admiralty*, 28 OHIO ST. L.J. 19, 31 (1967).

With this general review of arrest procedures as background, we then come to the owner's assertion that the district court in this case did not conduct a post-arrest hearing.

* * *

The owner's argument on this appeal that the district court disposed of the case without a hearing or consideration of the necessary facts is a departure from its previous statements made in appeals to this Court. In its September 7, 1988 Emergency Petition for a Writ of Prohibition, the owner complained that the district judge did not explain the basis on which he set bond at $75,000. The owner speculated: "Presumably, [the district court] either rejected compelling proofs that the arrest had been improvident and the underlying claims specious, or it acted in the ... erroneous view that it ... must specially favor wards of admiralty ... ." Emergency Petition of Atlantic Sun, Ltd., for a Writ of Prohibition at 3. Thus, the owner itself confesses that evidence it considered at least "compelling" had been submitted to the district court.

Also in the petition, the owner acknowledged that from July 14 to August 24 the parties had attempted to agree on a bond amount, and that "[t]he district court was kept advised of the total lack of progress in these negotiations." *Id.* at 14 n. 14. It is remarkable, too, that in light of the owner's present emphasis on the lack of a post-arrest hearing, not one word referring to such an alleged deprivation was included in the Petition for a Writ of Prohibition, although all other bases were covered.

The district court record contains no entry showing that the owner requested a prompt post-arrest hearing—other than the August 5 proceeding—in which to submit other matters to the court. Supplemental Admiralty Rule E(4)(f) and Local Admiralty Rule(e)(8) state that the person claiming an interest is entitled to a hearing, but do not relieve the individual from asking for one. No such request appears in the record here.

To summarize, the owner had notice of the suit against the vessel on July 1, 1988, and filed a detailed defense on July 28, before counsel appeared in a court proceeding on August 5. Thereafter, counsel for both parties submitted memoranda before the district court fixed the bond amount on August 24.

It is pertinent that the owner has failed to present any evidence that the August 5, 1988 proceeding did not constitute a post-arrest hearing. What transpired that day could have been documented by the owner, which as appellant has the responsibility for presenting the full record on appeal. *See* FED. R. APP. P. 10(b)(1) ("the appellant shall order from the reporter a transcript of such parts of the proceedings not already on file as the appellant deems necessary").

Where no transcript of a hearing is prepared, FED. R. APP. P 10(c) allows the appellant to "prepare a statement of the ... proceeding[ ] from the best available means, including the appellant's recollection." The owner has not done so here. Moreover, we deem it significant that the owner's original counsel who were before the court on August 5, 1988 have not filed an affidavit or any other document asserting that the proceedings were not considered a post-arrest hearing or a satisfactory equivalent. *Cf. Bilmar Drilling, Inc. v. IFG Leasing Co.*, 795 F.2d 1194, 1200 (5th Cir. 1986) (mere recital by counsel of what happened during pre-trial conference is not enough).

The Supplemental Admiralty Rules do not specify what form the post-arrest hearing must follow. Consequently, the type of proceeding is left to the discretion of the district court. Whether a full adversary hearing with testimony and cross-examination of witnesses in open court is necessary depends on the nature of the issues in controversy.

The post-arrest hearing is not intended to resolve definitively the dispute between the parties, but only to make a preliminary determination whether there were reasonable grounds for issuing the arrest warrant, and if so, to fix an appropriate bond. Generally speaking, an exhaustive adversarial hearing is not necessary for resolution of those issues. Thus, in many instances we would expect that an informal proceeding, perhaps in the nature of a conference before the district court, supplemented by affidavits and legal memoranda as directed by the court might be sufficient.

It should be obvious at this point that a record should be made of whatever post-arrest hearing the district court may deem necessary under the circumstances. Where there is no record of a hearing or a summary of the necessary facts or evidence that the parties stipulated to certain facts, the appellate court is severely hampered in its review.

We are persuaded that the owner has not demonstrated that it was deprived of a post-arrest hearing. First, the owner failed to produce record evidence that the August 5 proceeding was not in fact an appropriate hearing. Second, although admitting that it had presented compelling proofs to the district court, the owner has not brought to our attention what other evidence it would have presented there, and thus has not demonstrated that injury has occurred. Finally, the owner did not comply with the Supplemental and Local Admiralty Rules by requesting another hearing, if in its view, the August 5 proceeding did not meet the requirement of the post-arrest hearing to which it was entitled. We also note that the district court reviewed the request for arrest before directing the clerk to issue a warrant. *See Mitchell*, 416 U.S. at 616-17.

Consequently, we reject the owner's claim of denial of due process.

* * *

The owner's second argument on appeal is that "[t]he owner of property seized *in rem* must be given a reasonable opportunity to obtain and post a release bond." Appellant's Brief at 28. As stated, the point might well be sustained. As the facts demonstrate, however, what is urged here is that after an auction has been held, an owner has the absolute right to possession of its vessel upon posting a bond equal to the amount of the highest bid. The owner cites no controlling authority for that proposition, but instead relies on two district court decisions that are not on point—*Gerard Constr. Co. v. Motor Vessel Virginia*, 480 F. Supp. 488 (W.D.Pa. 1979), and *Fair Ocean Co. v. Cargo of the Permina Samudra XII*, 423 F. Supp. 1037 (D. Guam 1976).

In effect, the owner is asking this Court to import into admiralty *in rem* proceedings a maritime version of the right of redemption familiar in the area of residential mortgage law. In the abstract, the idea is not without appeal. The central purpose of the arrest procedure, after all, is to provide the plaintiff with a means for satisfying his maritime lien. But penalizing the shipowner by wresting resources beyond those needed to meet a plaintiff's claim is neither helpful to commerce nor consistent with equitable considerations that influence admiralty jurisprudence.

Determining the shipowner's right to possession of its vessel by providing security for satisfaction of the plaintiff's lien, but yet giving due consideration to the bidder's position, is a task squarely within the discretionary powers of the court sitting in admiralty. Buoying up this point, Judge Brown wrote, "The Chancellor is no longer fixed to the woolsack. He may stride the quarter-deck of maritime jurisprudence and, in the role of admiralty judge, dispense, as would his landlocked brother, that which equity and good conscience impels." Compania *Anonima Venezolana de Navegacion v. A.J. Perez Export Co.*, 303 F.2d 692, 699 (5th Cir.), *cert. denied*, 371 U.S. 942, 83 S. Ct. 321, 9 L. Ed. 2d 276 (1962).

Generally speaking, a ship at auction will bring less than its actual value and less than replacement costs. Consequently, in many instances, the shipowner may emerge from a judicial sale with losses substantially in excess of the amount needed to satisfy the maritime lien. The party profiting in that situation is not the plaintiff who receives no more than his due, but the successful bidder at the auction who receives the vessel at a bargain price.

That is not to say that the successful bidder's interests are not worthy of consideration. As the Court of Appeals remarked in *Munro Drydock, Inc. v. M/V Heron*, 585 F.2d 13, 14 (1st Cir. 1978), "The policy of inspiring confidence in sales under the supervision of the court favors confirmation of a sale made to the highest bidder at a fairly conducted public auction." Recognizing that the purpose of a judicial sale is to benefit both creditors and debtors, courts must heed the aphorism that "[a]uctions should not be empty exercises." *First Nat'l Bank v. M/V Lightning Power*, 776 F.2d 1258, 1261 (5th Cir. 1985).

Nevertheless, the bidder at a sale is merely an offeror and has no rights to possession of the ship until the court's acceptance through the confirmation process. *Puget Sound Prod. Credit Ass'n v. Oil Screw Johnny* A., 819 F.2d 242, 246 (9th Cir. 1987) (*quoting The East Hampton*, 48 F.2d 542, 544 (2d Cir. 1931)). Giving the owner the opportunity to match the successful bid might well dampen the enthusiasm of prospective bidders, but is not likely to pose a formidable barrier to successful auctions. The history of mortgage redemption procedures would seem to provide adequate assurances on that score.

We do not overlook the fact that on two occasions, the owner failed to post a bond within the time set by court orders, and may thereby have waived its right to release of the vessel. We, however, choose not to steer that course here.

Having concluded that the owner's theory of a quasi right of redemption theory may have some merit, we assume, but only *arguendo*, its legitimacy. We next consider whether in the circumstances present here, such a right should be enforced. As noted before, the successful bidder at a judicial auction is in the position of an offeror, but becomes the owner of the vessel when the bid is accepted at confirmation. If the sale is held valid, the previous owner has no further interest in the property and the claims are transferred to the fund created. The sale price thus substitutes for the vessel as the *res*.

It follows that if the owner wishes to redeem the vessel, that action must take place, at the very latest, before confirmation of the sale. Because the owner's redemption would prevent—and is thus an obstacle to—confirmation, the intent to exercise any such right must be made known to the court in the form of an objection in advance, as is true with other challenges to the regularity of the sale.

Some elaboration of the facts is helpful at this point. After the court set bond at $75,000 in its August 24, 1988 order, plaintiffs asked, on September 1, that the amount be increased to $200,000. The district court did not act on this request. In rejecting the owner's offer to post $75,000 on November 9, 1988, the date set for the auction, the district court explained that "the passage of time and the play of events had rendered what may always have been an inadequate bond now hopelessly insufficient to cover plaintiffs' claims." Specifically, the court concluded that the plaintiffs' claim for penalty wages, although hotly contested, was "not as a matter of law foreclosed," and that administrative fees occasioned by the vessel's *in custodia legis* status had increased substantially. On November 10, 1988, the day following the auction, plaintiffs moved for an order to show cause why the bond should not be increased to $356,000.

Local Admiralty Rule (e)(12)(e) requires an interested person objecting to a sale to file a writing within three days following the sale and to deposit with the marshal an amount sufficient to pay the vessel's custodial expenses for at least one week. The owner here failed to do so, and thus the district judge held that it had no standing to contest confirmation. A disappointed bidder, however, did file an objection and the court scheduled a hearing. The judge then allowed testimony on alleged defects in the bidding procedure asserted by the disappointed bidder. After hearing the evidence, the district court rejected the objection and confirmed the sale.

During the same hearing on November 17, 1988, the court, acting on the plaintiffs' motion, decided that the bond should be raised to $140,000. This amount, the highest bid at the sale, represented the best record evidence of the value of the vessel. When the court inquired of the plaintiffs' counsel why it requested an increase of the bond after the auction, counsel explained that the purpose was to prevent the owner from making a claim for proceeds of the sale in excess of the $75,000 bond.

Toward the conclusion of the hearing, the owner asked for two weeks in which to raise the bond. The court denied this request, as well as one for a shorter period. The court instead stated that it would confirm the sale, but granted the owner until noon the following day to post a bond as a condition for a stay of confirmation pending appeal. When on the following morning the owner requested a further extension until 4:00 p.m. that day to post a bond—not as a supersedeas—but for the release of the vessel, the court refused. The court explained, "Vindication of the legitimate rights of the successful bidder on the vessel and of the legitimacy of a properly conducted judicial sale, coupled with the Court's familiarity with the long history of delays in this case, informed our denial of defendant's request."

Although in most cases one could expect the court to give an owner some time to post a bond, circumstances here were not of the usual nature. Granting the owner the right to post a release bond after confirmation would be, in effect, an abrogation of the confirmation proceeding. Because it had filed no objection, the owner had no standing at the time of the hearing to post a bond, and consequently, properly was not given time to do so.

The order raising the bond at that stage was probably unnecessary. The same result could have been more appropriately effected by the plaintiffs' requesting the court to deny any withdrawals from proceeds of the sale in the court's registry pending further examination of the actual amounts of the claims in controversy. The court had already decided that the $75,000 amount was inadequate; plaintiffs, therefore, need not have feared that the court would release to the owner any sums in excess of that amount without additional review. The situation here was quite unlike the instance where, absent fraud in appraisement or posting of a bond, a court loses the power to increase the bond on a vessel once it has been released on providing security. *See The Haytian Republic*, 154 U.S. 118, 126, 14 S. Ct. 992, 38 L. Ed. 930 (1894); *United States v. Ames*, 99 U.S. 35, 41-42, 25 L. Ed. 295 (1878).

Because we conclude that the owner had waived its right to release of the vessel upon posting of a bond, we find no error in the district court's decision to confirm the sale rather than to grant additional time to the owner.

The judgment of the district court will be affirmed.

---

2. *Intervention*

OVERSTREET v. THE WATER VESSEL "NORKONG"

706 F.2d 641, 1987 AMC 818 (5th Cir. 1983)

ALVIN B. RUBIN, Circuit Judge

We are urged to expand an ancient remedy to accommodate a new right. A seaman libelled a foreign vessel for injuries allegedly sustained while he was employed aboard the vessel. The owner supplied a release bond and the vessel was released from seizure. Over a year later the seaman's estranged wife sought to intervene in the suit on her own behalf and on behalf of the children of the marriage to assert the cause of action for loss of consortium first recognized by this court in 1981, on the thesis that the surety bond covered not only the seaman's claim but theirs. The district court, 538 F. Supp. 53, denied the intervention in reliance on an 1895 Supreme Court decision, *The Oregon*, 158 U.S. 186, 15 S. Ct. 804, 39 L. Ed. 943 (1895). Finding that, in principle, *The Oregon's* wake still controls our course, we affirm.

The seaman, Norman P. Overstreet, was injured while working aboard the M/V NORKONG, as a member of its crew, on February 16, 1980. Overstreet sued the NORKONG *in rem* under general maritime law on grounds of unseaworthiness.[1] He also sued her owner, Asiatic Drilling Company (Asiatic), and his employer, Scan Drilling Company (Scan), *in personam*, under the Jones Act, 46 U.S.C. § 688 (1976), for negligence. On the day Overstreet filed his complaint, the district court issued a warrant for the arrest of the NORKONG to answer to both the *in rem* and *in personam* claims. The warrant was executed, and the vessel brought to Pascagoula, Mississippi. Asiatic provided a bond issued by Insurance Company of North America (INA) in the amount of $750,000, the condition of which was that Asiatic and INA would "pay the said plaintiff the amount awarded by the final decree rendered in" the proceeding. The vessel was thereupon released and sailed away, never, perhaps, to return. After a hearing, the district court dismissed Overstreet's complaint against Asiatic and Scan for lack of personal jurisdiction. The district court also granted the NORKONG's motion to strike from the complaint Overstreet's allegations of negligence under the Jones Act. *Plamals v. The Pinar Del Rio*, 277 U.S. 151, 48 S. Ct. 457, 72 L. Ed. 827 (1928) (Jones Act claim based on negligence is solely *in personam* and may not be asserted against vessel).The bond must now answer only to Overstreet's unseaworthiness claim against the vessel.

Mrs. Overstreet, appearing individually and for her four minor children, seeks to assert an *in rem* claim under the same bond for what she indiscriminately describes as "loss of consortium, society and services" arising from her husband's injuries. She contends that she has a right to intervene under FED. R. CIV. P. 24(a)(2). It is a prerequisite of her intervention that she claim "an interest relating to the property or transaction which is the subject of the action," so we examine first whether she has such an interest in the sole property that is within the court's jurisdiction, the INA bond that stands in the place of the vessel.[2]

In 1981 we held that the spouse of an injured seaman has a cause of action for loss of the seaman's society separate from the seaman's claim for his injuries, and that the spouse's claim need not be asserted in the same proceeding as the seaman's claim.[3] Because the spouse's claim turns on the same facts and involves the same issues, presentation of both claims in the same action, when practicable, is desirable.[4] But the claim is not the seaman's. It is not a "latent development of [his] damages," as Mrs. Overstreet contends. It is a separate claim asserted by a separate party, for separate damages.

In *The Oregon*, after a libel had been filed against the vessel, the surety gave a stipulation for its release. The court refused to allow additional claimants to intervene, saying, "We know of no authority which permits the liability of sureties upon such a stipulation to be enlarged by the inclusion of claims other than the ones which the stipulators agree to

---

[1] *The Osceola*, 189 U.S. 158, 175, 23 S. Ct. 483, 487, 47 L. Ed. 760, 764 (1903) (vessel and her owner are liable for injuries to seaman in consequence of unseaworthiness).

[2] Once a vessel is released from arrest by a bond, the vessel itself can no longer be held to answer for the claims the bond is designed to meet. The bond is the claimant's sole source of recovery. *See The Oregon* (stipulation deemed substitute for vessel itself); G. GILMORE & C. BLACK, THE LAW OF ADMIRALTY § 9-89 (1975); Harmon, *Discharge and Waiver or Maritime Liens*, 47 TULANE L.R. 786, 795 (1973) ("The effect of the filing of a bond to release a vessel from seizure is to transfer the lien from the ship to the fund represented by the bond or stipulation.").

[3] *Cruz v. Hendy Int'l Co.*, 638 F.2d 719, 725-26 (5th Cir.1981).

[4] *Kotsiris v. Ling*, 451 S.W. 2d 411 (Ky. 1970) (joinder not required, although it is desirable and will probably occur in most cases).

pay."[5] It continued, explaining why it found the district court in error, "But if, after the stipulation is given, and the vessel is discharged from custody, other libels are filed, a new warrant of arrest must be issued, and the vessel again taken into custody."[6]

The rationale of *The Oregon* was in part that permitting the intervention might prejudice the original libellant if the sureties were unable to respond to the full amount of their stipulation, or to an amount sufficient to pay all the claims.[7] Mrs. Overstreet seeks to obviate the problem by conceding priority to her husband's claims. She has, therefore, persuaded us that this reason for the decision in *The Oregon* is not applicable here.

A second reason for refusing intervention in *The Oregon* was that "[t]he stipulators may be so well satisfied that the [owner of the vessel] has a defense to the original libel as to be willing to take upon themselves the contingency of a decree requiring its payment, but they may neither know, nor be able to conjecture, what other demands may be made against the property."[8] Mrs. Overstreet correctly points out that her claim stands or falls with her husband's and, if he fails, so does she. But this does not mean that INA should reasonably have anticipated, when it negotiated the bond, the interjection of her consortium claim and those of her four children into Overstreet's personal injury action, or that INA could estimate the amount that she and her children might claim. In all likelihood, INA was not apprised of Overstreet's family relationships, nor able to conjecture the degree to which his accident might impair those relationships, when it agreed to post bond for a certain premium. While neither the probability of losing the case nor INA's maximum exposure would be increased by the intervention of Mrs. Overstreet and her children, the amount of the possible award, up to the bond's maximum, would be enlarged. The evidence gives us no way to determine whether this would have affected INA's willingness to supply the bond on the fee charged.

The Supplemental Rules for Certain Admiralty and Maritime Claims of the Federal Rules of Civil Procedure provide for release of an arrested vessel on the giving of either a "special bond" [Rule E(5)(a)] or a "general bond" [Rule E(5)(b)]. The special bond is given for libels that have already issued. It the parties do not agree on an amount, it is to be "an amount sufficient to cover the amount of the plaintiff's claim fairly stated with accrued interest and costs." On the other hand, a general bond is given for actions that may subsequently be brought in which the vessel may be attached or arrested.[9] The bond given here was a special bond, and its effect is prescribed by the Rule. When a shipowner secures the release of a vessel seized pursuant to process *in rem*, the Supplemental Rules permit the shipowner to restrict, expressly, his appearance to the defense of that claim and that appearance does not constitute an appearance for the purpose of any other claim with respect to which process is not available or has not been served. FED. R. CIV. P. SUPP. R. E(5).Whatever the reason for the rule, it is explicit and categorical.

---

[5] *The Oregon*, 158 U.S. at 206, 15 S. Ct. at 812, 39 L. Ed. at 952.

[6] *Id.* at 210, 15 S. Ct. at 814, 39 L. Ed. at 954.

[7] *Id.* at 210, 15 S. Ct. at 814, 39 L. Ed. at 954.

[8] *Id.* at 206, 15 S. Ct. at 812, 39 L. Ed.at 952.

[9] 7A J. MOORE & A. PELAEZ, FEDERAL PRACTICE: ADMIRALTY ¶ E.13[1] & n. 7 (1982).

If a special bond is not obtained to secure the release of an arrested vessel, and the vessel is sold to meet the resulting judgment, the proceeds of the sale are deposited in the registry of the court. Third persons who claim an interest in the proceeds may then intervene.[10] This, however, is not an intervention in the suit leading to sale. It simply permits all those who did not participate in that proceeding, but who have claims against the vessel that were obliterated by the sale, to assert their claims against the fund into which the vessel has been converted. The proceeds remaining after the libel has been satisfied represent the vessel.[11] The surety bond provides no such residual fund for other claimants. It is posted to assure the payment of a single claim, not to stand in place of the vessel for all claims that might be asserted against her.

Mrs. Overstreet contends that the bond should be read in accordance with the intent of the court and that, because the magistrate who fixed the amount of the bond also held that her claim could be asserted against it, we should divine that it was his intention to require the bond to protect against her claims. There are several insurmountable obstacles to this conclusion. The first is that the bond is not ambiguous. The second is that the magistrate did not dictate the terms of the bond, only its amount. And the final one is that he has never suggested that this was his original intention.

We are unable to distinguish *The Oregon* on the basis that it involved a stipulation rather than a bond.[12]

Finally, Mrs. Overstreet argues that we are not bound by *The Oregon* in determining her right of intervention because the cause of action for loss of consortium did not exist when *The Oregon* was decided. She urges us to follow the example of the Supreme Court in *Moragne v. State Marine Lines, Inc.*, 398 U.S. 375, 90 S. Ct. 1772, 26 L. Ed. 2d 339 (1970), in which that Court concluded that the principles underlying the doctrine of *stare decisis* did not counsel against overruling a prior decision. The power to overrule the Supreme Court's decision lies in that court, not in us. While there may be occasional situations when subsequent Supreme Court opinions erode the authority of an earlier Supreme Court case without explicitly overruling it so that we may follow the Court's later lead,[13] no such change has occurred with regard to the posting of bonds to secure the release of vessels. While the few cases reported since 1895 involving the issue did not involve loss of

---

[10] *Jackson v. Inland Oil and Transport Co.*, 318 F.2d 802 (5th Cir.1963); *Crabtree v. The S.S. Julia*, 290 F.2d 478 (5th Cir.1961). *See* FED. R. CIV. P. SUPP. R. E. (9)(c) (proceeds of sale to be paid into registry and disposed of according to law).

[11] *The Oregon*, 158 U.S. at 211, 15 S. Ct. at 814, 39 L. Ed. at 954.

[12] 7A J. MOORE & A. PELAEZ, FEDERAL PRACTICE: ADMIRALTY ¶ E.13[1] & n. 17 (1982) ("[T]he terms "bond" and "stipulation" are used interchangeably in the admiralty ... ."). The distinction that once existed is explained by GILMORE & BLACK, THE LAW OF ADMIRALTY 796-97 (2d ed. 1975) (footnote omitted):

> The release of ships from arrest has been governed both by a statutory provision (which is now 28 U.S.C.A. § 2464) and by the former Admiralty Rules. The statute provided for the posting of bonds with the United States Marshal in specified amounts. The Rules provided for release on a stipulation for value entered into by the parties with the amount of the stipulation and the security therefor to be determined by the district judge if the parties could not agree. The stipulation for value was the procedure usually followed for the excellent reason (from the shipowner's point of view) that the release value under stipulation was less than the bonds required under § 2464.

The authors then explain that, "The matter is currently covered by Supplemental Rule E(5) (F.R.C.P.) which, according to the Advisory Committee's Note, restates the substance of the former Admiralty Rules and also incorporates 28 U.S.C.A. § 2464 'with changes of terminology, and with a substantial change as to the amount of the bond.' " "*Id.* at 797. They characterize the consolidation as a "light-hearted approach to § 2464." *Id.* Gilmore and Black state, "Bonds under § 2464 and stipulations for value under the former Admiralty Rules seem always to have been treated as identical in their legal effect. Presumably, bonds under subsection (a) and (b) of Rule E(5) will continue to be treated as having the same legal effect as stipulations under subsection (c)." *Id.* at 798.

[13] *Rowe v. Peyton*, 383 F.2d 709, 714 (4th Cir. 1967), *aff'd*, 391 U.S. 54, 88 S. Ct. 1549, 20 L. Ed. 2d 426 (1968).

consortium, *The Oregon* has been followed. *The Willamette*, 70 F. 874 (D.C.Ill.1892); *Norker v. The S/T Sister Katingo*, 201 F. Supp. 223 (D.Conn.1962). Indeed the Supplemental Rules, adopted in 1966, appear to confirm, not to undermine, *The Oregon*. The genesis of additional claims by new decisions does not alter the reading of the bond.

In view of the result we have reached, we do not decide whether the claims of a spouse and child for "loss of consortium and society and services" occasioned by a seaman's injury are supported by a maritime lien[14] or whether the Overstreet children, like their mother, have a cognizable claim separate from that of their father.

For these reasons, the judgment is AFFIRMED.

---

3. Waiver: Claim of Owner

CACTUS PIPE & SUPPLY CO., INC. v. M/V MONTMARTRE

756 F.2d 1103, 1985 AMC 2150 (5th Cir. 1985)

JOHN R. BROWN, Circuit Judge

This appeal arises from claims for damage to a cargo of steel tubing shipped aboard the M/V MONTMARTRE in July, 1979. Because we find that *in rem* jurisdiction was established in one case of this consolidated action, we reverse. We also reverse and remand for a determination of whether the vessel was liable *in rem*. We affirm the trial court's finding that appellee, vessel owner, was not liable as the carrier of cargo because there was no evidence that the vessel owner authorized issuance of the bills of lading either by actual or apparent authority.

How It All Began

Appellant, Cactus Pipe & Supply Co., Inc. (Cactus), contracted with Corinth Pipeworks, S.A. (Corinth) to purchase steel tubing. Under this agreement, the trial court found that Corinth was to arrange for shipment from Corinth, Greece to Houston, Texas. The cargo was shipped aboard the M/V MONTMARTRE owned by appellee Orient Leasing Co., Ltd. (Orient).

Before the carriage of cargo in issue, Orient bareboat chartered the MONTMARTRE to Eternity Navigation Co., S.A. (Eternity), in September, 1976. Eternity, as bareboat charter owner, time chartered the vessel to Iino Kaiun Kaisha, Ltd. (Iino). Iino in turn time chartered the MONTMARTRE to Canadian Forest Navigation Co., Ltd. (Canadian) in June, 1979. In July, 1979, Canadian voyage chartered the MONTMARTRE to Seanav International Co. (Seanav). Seanav in turn voyage chartered the vessel to Corinth.

Nine bills of lading covering the cargo were issued on July 14, 1979, signed by Delpa Shipping and Transportation Co., Ltd. (Delpa) "For The Master." The vessel arrived in Houston in August, 1979, and surveyors observed damage in the hold before unloading.

---

[14] Most maritime claims give rise to liens, but, *e.g.*, a seaman's statutory action for personal injury under the Jones Act, 46 U.S.C. § 688 (1976), does not. *See* G. GILMORE & C. BLACK, THE LAW OF ADMIRALTY § 9-20 & nn. 86, 95b (1975) (Jones Act claims based on shipowner's negligence do not give rise to liens, but on principle maritime torts should create liens).

In addition to damage, appellant Cactus contends that portions of the cargo were never delivered.

Cactus, consignee of the cargo of steel tubing, instituted two causes of action seeking recovery of its damages. The First action (District Court No. H-80-1721) was brought in Cactus' name by its subrogated underwriter against the MONTMARTRE, Orient and Corinth. The Second action (District Court No. H-80-1769) was instituted by Cactus seeking recovery of the uninsured portion of its loss (approximately $10,000) against the vessel and against Orient, the vessel owner. The MONTMARTRE was never arrested. However, a claim of owner was filed by Orient in both actions. Subsequently the two cases were consolidated pending trial.

On July 6, 1983, the district court, after a bench trial, entered its opinion finding that the cargo was damaged and short upon delivery in Houston, Texas. It also found that Corinth, the voyage charterer and shipper, was liable as a carrier of the cargo and that Orient, the vessel owner, was not liable because it was not the COGSA carrier. The trial court found that the MONTMARTRE, although the carrying vessel, was not liable to Cactus because it was not liable for the acts or omissions of the charterer/shipper, Corinth. The district court entered judgment in favor of Cactus and against Corinth for $28,673.51 plus interest. On August 11, 1983, the trial court issued amended conclusions of law determining that *in rem* jurisdiction over the vessel did not exist because the vessel was never arrested nor had any bond or letter of undertaking been filed in the court by the owner of the vessel. The court held that the claims of owner filed by the vessel owner, Orient, manifested only the vessel owner's interest in the vessel and did not establish *in rem* jurisdiction. The district court also determined that, although a voyage charterer such as Corinth may be liable as a carrier, the evidence was insufficient to hold Corinth liable as a carrier under the facts of this case. Accordingly, Cactus was awarded nothing.

The MONTMARTRE—In rem Jurisdiction

Cactus disputes the district court's conclusion that there was no *in rem* jurisdiction established over the MONTMARTRE. Specifically, Cactus urges that the claims of owner filed by Orient constituted an appearance on the part of the vessel thereby establishing *in rem* jurisdiction.

Generally, the power of the court to exercise jurisdiction over a vessel depends upon the arrest of the vessel within the court's territorial jurisdiction. *Reed v. The YAKA*, 307 F.2d 203, 204, 1962 A.M.C. 1226, 1228 (3d Cir.1962), *rev'd on other grounds*, 373 U.S. 410, 83 S. Ct. 1349, 10 L. Ed. 2d 448, 1963 A.M.C. 1373 (1963); *see also* Rule C, Supplemental Rules for Admiralty and Maritime Claims. A claimant, however, can waive the necessity of *in rem* seizure and consent to jurisdiction so far as its interest in the vessel is concerned. *The YAKA*, 307 F.2d at 204, 1962 A.M.C. at 1228. Thus in *Continental Grain Co. v. Federal Barge Lines, Inc.*, 268 F.2d 240, 1959 A.M.C. 2158 (5th Cir.1959), *aff'd sub nom. Continental Grain Co. v. Barge FBL*-585, 364 U.S. 19, 80 S. Ct. 1470, 4 L. Ed. 2d 1540, 1961 A.M.C. 1 (1960), we dealt with the issue of whether an *in rem* proceeding upon application of a willing claimant could be transferred under 28 U.S.C. 1404(a) to a district in which the *res* was not located. However, we initially determined that the issuance of a letter of undertaking on behalf of the vessel and a Non-Waiver of Rights Clause in the letter perfected the *in rem* jurisdiction of the court. On the filing of the action *in rem* and *in personam* for damage to a cargo of soybeans, the barge FBL-585 was not seized. We pointed out that in accordance with the practice in major seaports, a letter of undertaking was given by the vessel owner providing that in consideration of the barge not being seized and released on bond, the vessel owner would "file claim to Barge FBL-585, ... and that, vessel lost or not lost would pay any final decree which may be rendered against said vessel in said proceedings." 268 F.2d at 243, 1959 A.M.C. at 2160. We determined that the letter of undertaking, and particularly the Non-Waiver of Rights Clause, required that "we treat it as though, upon the libel being filed, the vessel had actually been seized, a Claim filed, a stipulation to abide decree with sureties executed and filed by Claimant, and the vessel formally released." *Id.* Essentially, the underlying rationale for all of this was the necessity of avoiding "needless costs, time, and inconvenience to litigants, counsel, ships, Clerks, Marshals, Keepers and court personnel...." *Id.* In *Associated Metals & Minerals Corp. v. S.S. PORTORIA*, 484 F.2d 460, 1973 A.M.C. 2095 (5th Cir.1973), no *in rem* process was issued, the vessel was not arrested, and the owner did not waive attachment of the vessel. We thus determined on those grounds that the district court erred in entering judgment against the vessel *in rem*.

In other contexts, a party can waive an objection to *in personam* jurisdiction. *See* F.R.Civ.P. 12. Rule 12(h)(1) provides that the defense of lack of jurisdiction over the person is waived (i) if omitted from a motion under 12(g), or (ii) if it is neither made by motion under Rule 12 nor included in a responsive pleading or an amendment. *See Golden v. Cox Furniture Mfg. Co.*, 683 F.2d 115 (5th Cir.1982) (objection to personal jurisdiction waived when answer and amended answer filed without raising *in personam* jurisdiction objection); *Jackson v. Hayakawa*, 682 F.2d 1344, 1347 (9th Cir.1982) (jurisdiction attaches if a defendant makes a voluntary general appearance, as by filing an answer through an attorney); *Familia De Boom v. Arosa Mercantil, S.A.*, 629 F.2d 1134, 1140, 1981 A.M.C. 2937, 2944 (5th Cir.1980), *cert. denied*, 451 U.S. 1008, 101 S. Ct. 2345, 68 L. Ed. 2d 861, 1981 A.M.C. 2100 (1981) (service of process and personal jurisdiction may be waived by a party); *United States v. Fishing Vessel MARY ANN*, 466 F.2d 63, 1972 A.M.C. 2652 (5th Cir.1972), *cert. denied sub nom. Walter v. United States*, 410 U.S. 929, 93 S. Ct. 1365, 35 L. Ed. 2d 590 (1973) (action to foreclose preferred ship mortgage—two defendants not served with process but answered asserting defenses on the merits).

Generally, an appearance in an action involves some presentation or submission to the court. *Port-Wide Container Co. v. Interstate Maintenance Corp.*, 440 F.2d 1195, 1196 (3rd Cir.1971) (no appearance found). An appearance may result from the filing of an answer without raising jurisdictional defects. An appearance may also arise by implication "from a defendant's seeking, taking, or agreeing to some step or proceeding in the cause beneficial to himself or detrimental to plaintiff other than one contesting only the jurisdiction or by reason of some act or proceedings recognizing the case as in court." 6 C.J.S. *Appearances* § 18 at 22 (1975); *see also Grammenos v. Lemos*, 457 F.2d 1067, 1070 (2d Cir.1972) (if a party enters a case and fails to object to jurisdiction, and requests the court to do some affirmative act on its behalf in some substantive way, the party will be held to have waived further objection).

In this case we must decide whether the filing of a claim of owner in a proceeding characterized expressly in the complaint as both *in rem* and *in personam* with the traditional prayer for issuance of process *in rem* against the vessel is sufficient to obtain *in rem* jurisdiction over the vessel. We hold that it does.

Some procedural background in this case is necessary to our analysis of *in rem* jurisdiction. In the First suit (District Court No. H-80-1721), the subrogated underwriter brought suit in the name of its assured, Cactus, against the vessel owner, vessel and charterer, Corinth. Cactus' prayer requested:

> that process in due form of law according to the practice of this Honorable Court in causes of admiralty and maritime jurisdiction may issue against the M/V MONTMARTRE, *citing* all persons having any interest in said vessel to appear and answer on oath all and singular the matters aforesaid.... That the said M/ VMONTMARTRE may be condemned and sold to pay the damages, with interest, costs and disbursements.

There was also a prayer for process against Orient and Corinth, and in fact, process was issued only as to Orient and Corinth. Orient answered for itself and there was no mention of an *in rem* jurisdiction challenge. Orient also filed several third party complaints and pursued discovery against all parties. On September 16, 1981, Orient filed its Claim of Owner to the MONTMARTRE and a motion for consolidation of the two pending cases.

In Second suit (District Court No. H-80-1769) the complaint was filed by Cactus against the MONTMARTRE and Orient for $10,000 on August 6, 1980 (recovery of the uninsured portion of its loss). Cactus' complaint prayed:

> that process in due form of law according to the practices of this Honorable Court in causes of admiralty and maritime jurisdiction may issue against M/V MONTMARTRE, her engines, boilers, tackle, etc., and that all persons having any right, title and interest therein be cited to appear and answer on oath all and singular the matters aforesaid, and that the said M/V MONTMARTRE may be condemned and sold to pay the damages of the aforesaid, with interest and cost.

No *in rem* process was issued by the Clerk. The only process issued was against Orient.

The Second case proceeded as a separate suit in a different district court. In November, 1980, an order of dismissal was entered by the trial judge for failure to prosecute. The judge later granted reinstatement of the case. Cactus moved for entry of a default judgment which the trial court later granted. The default judgment recites that both the vessel and vessel owner were defendants, were properly served, and they failed to appear and answer. Two months later on August 12, 1981, Orient and the MONTMARTRE filed in the

Second suit a motion to vacate and set aside the default judgment. Apparently the complaint was sent to Orient in Japan and there was some confusion with the First suit already on file. It is important to point out that in this motion, an objection to *in rem* jurisdiction was raised on the ground that the vessel was not arrested. The trial judge set aside the default judgment on September 8, 1981. On September 16, 1981, Orient filed its answer—only as to itself—and expressly asserted an objection to *in rem* jurisdiction. Orient also filed interrogatories and a third party complaint each raising the jurisdiction objection. On the same day, Orient filed its claim of owner specifically preserving its objection to the jurisdiction of the court.

On September 22, 1981, both trial judges in the two pending suits entered an order consolidating the cases "for all purposes." After the consolidation, on October 6, 1981, Orient as defendant and claimant and the MONTMARTRE as defendant moved for summary judgment on the merits and on the ground that there was no *in rem* jurisdiction. Thereafter, the trial judge entered his memorandum and order denying the motion for summary judgment. The trial court did state, however, that there was a colorable challenge to the *in rem* jurisdiction of the court. Since neither party had adequately briefed this issue, the defendant was permitted to resubmit a motion to dismiss for lack of *in rem* jurisdiction. The consolidated cases were tried before the judge, and he entered his findings in July, 1983, and amended conclusions of law in August, 1983. Initially the trial court determined that Corinth, the voyage charterer, was liable as the carrier but Orient and the MONTMARTRE were exonerated.

The trial court issued amended conclusions of law holding that there was no *in rem* jurisdiction over the vessel and the evidence was insufficient to hold Corinth responsible for the damage to the cargo.

Rule C(6), Supplemental Rules for Admiralty and Maritime Claims clearly defines the purpose of filing a claim of owner. The claimant must state his interest in the vessel by *virtue* of which the claimant demands *restitution* of the vessel and *the right to defend* it. The vessel owner's right to file an answer is predicated upon the filing of the claim of owner pursuant to Supplemental Rule C(6). "The right of answering in denial or avoidance of the libel, and all of it, in a suit *in rem* in the admiralty, depends upon the right to claim ... . [T]he claimant in admiralty may defend *in rem*, because he demands the redelivery to him of the arrested vessel." *The CARTONA*, 297 F. 827, 828, 1924 A.M.C. 771, 772 (2d Cir.1924). We thus agree with the trial court that claim of owner manifests the owner's interest in the vessel. We must disagree with the trial court's determination that an unconditional claim does not give rise to *in rem* jurisdiction. When the vessel owner lays claim to the vessel he has appeared on its behalf.

In The ROSALIE M, 12 F.2d 970, 1927 A.M.C. 999 (5th Cir.1926) a warrant of seizure was issued in a forfeiture proceeding and the vessel was seized. Appellant filed an answer and *claimed* the vessel as agent

for the owner. On appeal, the appellant contended that (i) the seizure of the vessel was unlawful because it was made beyond the territorial jurisdiction of the United States since the Volstead Act (a cargo of liquor was seized) had no effect beyond three miles from the shore and (ii) the Coast Guard had no authority outside the twelve mile limit under the Tariff Act of 1922.

We determined that, conceding that the Volstead Act was not in operation at the point where the vessel was initially seized, the vessel was nevertheless subject to seizure because she was engaged in an unlawful enterprise. We further conceded, without deciding, that the Coast Guard cutter was not authorized to operate outside the twelve mile limit. We reasoned that it did not necessarily follow that the judgment was illegal and that the objection to the authority of the Coast Guard to make the seizure was purely technical and without merit. We stated that "after a ship is brought into the custody of the marshal through proper admiralty process, any irregularity in the initial seizure is immaterial, and is *waived* by filing *a claim* or answer." 12 F.2d at 971, 1927 A.M.C. at 1002 (emphasis supplied). The Supreme Court similarly ruled in *The MERINO*, 22 U.S. (9 Wheat.) 391, 400, 6 L. Ed. 118, 120 (1824), in which the vessel owner questioned irregularities in the *in rem* process. The Court reasoned that all objections to the irregularities were waived by the appearance of the parties interested in the property seized and filing their claims to the *res*. *Id.*

In this case there were two claims of owner filed. In the First suit (District Court No. H-80-1721 suit brought by subrogated underwriter) the claim of owner stated: "Now appears Orient ... and makes claim to the [MONTMARTRE] ... and said claimant avers that it was ... owner ... wherefore it prays to defend accordingly." In the Second suit (District Court No. H-80-1769) the claim of owner was the same as that filed in the other case except it stated "... without waiving its defense that it is not subject to the jurisdiction of this Honorable Court."

We are persuaded that the claim of owner filed in the First suit (District Court No. H-80-1721) perfected the *in rem* jurisdiction of the district court. By the filing of this claim without any jurisdictional objection—and without any prior objection in the pleadings—the MONTMARTRE has appeared. The Claim of Owner does more than state the vessel owner's interest. The Claim specifically demands the return of the vessel—a substantive request that is detrimental to the plaintiff. The filing of the claim of owner also bears many of the earmarks of the filing of a claim of owner with a letter of undertaking in *Continental Grain*, 268 F.2d at 243, 1959 A.M.C. at 2160, and was effective under the circumstances of this case.

In the Second suit (District Court No. H-80-1769), however, the vessel owner adequately preserved its challenge to *in rem* jurisdiction. From Orient's and the MONTMARTRE's initial motion to vacate the default judgment through the consolidation of the cases, the objection to *in rem* jurisdiction was adequately raised and preserved. *See Aetna Business Credit, Inc. v. Universal Decor & Interior Design, Inc.*, 635 F.2d 434 (5th Cir.1981) (objections to adequacy of service of process preserved).

We hold therefore that the trial court incorrectly determined that there was no *in rem* jurisdiction over the vessel in the consolidated action insofar as that action relates to the allegations in the First suit (District Court No. H-80-1721). However, the action asserted by Cactus against the vessel and vessel owner in the Second suit (District Court No. H-80-1769) was correctly dismissed for lack of *in rem* jurisdiction.

* * *

PATRICK E. HIGGINBOTHAM, Circuit Judge, dissenting:

The majority has concluded that the filing of a Claim of Owner alone subjects a vessel to the *in rem* jurisdiction of the court. In my view, *in rem* jurisdiction over the vessel existed only if the owner intended to waive its arrest or if a waiver of arrest was the necessary legal consequence of the filing of a Claim of Owner. The owner did not intend to concede *in rem* jurisdiction, and nothing in the applicable rules of procedure contemplates the found waiver of arrest. There is, then, no legal basis for the implication of *in rem* jurisdiction, and I dissent.

I

The record leaves no doubt but that the vessel owner did not intend to concede *in rem* jurisdiction. As pointed out by the majority, there were two suits consolidated before the same judge. Claims of Owner were filed in both suits. The claims of ownership were identical except that in the second suit, the Claim of Owner stated "... without waiving its defense that it is not subject to the jurisdiction of this honorable court." The owner has always contested the absence of *in rem* jurisdiction. Yet, the majority concludes that the omission of the "without waiving its defense" qualifying language gave the court *in rem* jurisdiction in the first case. Even if an intent to waive arrest could be inferred from this plain inadvertence, it ought not be; certainly the district court was not required to do so. An admiralty court has the "power" to "withdraw from the extremes to which the general appearance rule ha[s] been pushed and to find no waiver when there [is] no *intentional* abandonment of the jurisdictional objection." *Giannakouros v. Oriental Tanker Corp.*, 338 F.2d 649, 650 (4th Cir. 1964), *cert denied*, 380 U.S. 979, 85 S. Ct. 1343, 14 L. Ed. 2d 272 (1965) (emphasis added). *See also Untersinger v. United States*, 172 F.2d 298, 301 (2d Cir. 1949) (no waiver where objection to venue in admiralty action made in answer that also pleaded to merits).

II

* * *

A Claim of Owner lacks "many of the earmarks" of the inherently consensual letter of undertaking. Admiralty courts have traditionally waived strict adherence to the jurisdictional requirement of arrest, and allowed release of a vessel from custody upon the posting of a bond or a stipulation for value. Such a bond confers jurisdiction even in the absence of arrest.... The Claim of Owner then, is an unlikely substitute for the arrested vessel, for it provides no affirmative "undertaking" from which an *in rem* judgment could be satisfied.

4. Release of Security: Effect on Jurisdiction

Notes

1. In *Republic National Bank of Miami v. U.S.*, 506 U.S. 80, 113 S. Ct. 554, 121 L. Ed. 2d 474, 1993 AMC 2010 (1992), the Supreme Court held in an *in rem* forfeiture action, the court is not divested of jurisdiction by the prevailing party's transfer of the *res* from the district. The applicable general principle is that jurisdiction, once vested, is not divested by a discontinuance of possession, although exceptions may exist where, for example, release of the *res* would render the judgment "useless" because the *res* could neither be delivered to the complainant nor restored to the claimant.
2. The Ninth Circuit has applied the rule of *Republic National Bank of Miami* to both admiralty arrest and attachment cases. *Stevedoring Services of America v. Ancora Transport*, 941 F.2d 1378, 1992 AMC 883 (9th Cir. 1991), *cert. granted and judgment vacated by*, 506 U.S. 1043, 113 S. Ct. 955, 122 L. Ed. 2d 112 (1993), *on remand to*, 59 F.3d 879, 1995 AMC 2688 (9th Cir. 1995) (attachment); *Edlin v. M/V Truthseeker*, 69 F.3d 392, 1996 AMC 1216 (9th Cir. 1994). In *Newpark Shipbuildng & Repair, Inc.*, 2 F.3d 572, 1994 AMC 133 (5th Cir. 1993), the Fifth Circuit, recognizing that rule formulated in *Republic National Bank* was applicable to admiralty cases, invoked the "useless judgment" exception to that rule, and dismissed the appeal.
3. Even before the *Republic National Bank of Miami* case, the rule of continuous control was not absolute. In *The Rio Grande*, 90 U.S. (23 Wall.) 458, 465, 23 L. Ed. 158 (1874), the Court stated:

> We hold the rule to be that valid seizure and actual control of the *res* by the marshal gives jurisdiction of the subject matter, and that an accidental or fraudulent or improper removal of it from his custody, or a delivery to the party upon security, does not destroy jurisdiction.

---

5. Pleading Requirements: Heightened Particularity

Note

Supplemental Rule E(2)(a) requires the complaint to "state the circumstances from which the claim arises with such particularity that the defendant or claimant will be able, without moving for a more definite statement, to commence an investigation of the facts and to frame a responsive pleading". This standard of particularity is higher than under the general Federal Rules of Civil Procedure. In *Riverway Co. v. Spivey Marine & Harbor Service Co.*, 598 F. Supp. 909, 912-13 (S.D. Ill. 1984), the court said:

> The construction placed upon Rule 9(b) of the Federal Rules of Civil Procedure requiring the circumstances of an action for fraud be stated with particularity, is helpful in determining the meaning of Supplemental Rule E(2)(a)...The purposes served by the heightened particularity in pleading requirements for an *in rem* maritime claim counsel for a similar reading of Supplemental Rule E(2)(a). The complaint should state the date, time, place, nature of the damaging incident, and the alleged wrongful action. Those usual requirements are, of course, always subject to the general standard that the complaint sufficiently notify the defendant of the incident in dispute and afford a reasonable belief that the claim has merit. The nature of an admiralty suit *in rem* compels such a standard. An admiralty action *in rem* involves arrest and seizure of the offending vessel simply upon filing a verified complaint. Supplemental Rule C(3). The drastic measure of seizing the vessel is demanded by the nature of maritime commerce, where the plaintiff's only security for his loss may at any time up anchor and sail for friendlier waters and less convenient forums, demands this drastic measure. Seizure of the *res*, therefore, has long been a necessary element of admiralty remedies. *See Manro v. Almeida*, 23 U.S. (10 Wheat.) 473 (1825). Inland riverway tugs do not usually steam to foreign ports, but the concern to maintain the plaintiff's security within the court's jurisdiction remains. The defendants, in turn, are entitled to freedom from

the threat of seizure of their livelihood upon conclusory allegations and dubious circumstances. Their fifth amendment rights protect them from arbitrary deprivation of property. Pleading specific circumstances is one part of the process which guards against the improper use of admiralty seizure proceedings. When the complaint posits sufficient facts so that the defendants may begin an investigation and prepare a responsive pleading, their interests are adequately protected.

---

6. Security on Counterclaims

TITAN NAVIGATION, INC. v. TIMSCO, INC.

808 F.2d 400, 1987 AMC 1396 (5th Cir. 1987)

POLITZ, Circuit Judge

This appeal involves the interpretation and application of Rule E(7) of the Supplemental Rules for Admiralty, in an instance in which a complainant possessed of a maritime lien secured the posting of security and, in turn, was ordered to post countersecurity for the defendant's counterclaim. For the reasons assigned, and with the caveats noted, we affirm.

Background

In late 1982 Timsco, Inc. contracted to furnish computer hardware and software for vessels owned by Titan Navigation, Inc. Titan preferred not to purchase the system outright, but opted to enter into a lease agreement with Marine Leasing, Inc., a corporation organized for the specific purpose of purchasing the systems and leasing them to vessels.

In July 1984, Titan and related corporations sued Timsco and Marine Leasing for recission of the contract and damages, contending that the computers were faulty. Timsco and Marine Leasing counterclaimed, seeking enforcement of the contract. Exercising its maritime lien rights, Marine Leasing arrested, or initiated an action to arrest vessels belonging to Titan. Titan secured the release of these vessels by posting the requisite security. Thereafter, Titan and its vessels counterclaimed, ultimately alleging breach of contract, misrepresentation, violation of the Texas Deceptive Trade Practices Act, breach of warranty, breach of indemnity, and violations of the Texas Uniform Commercial Code. Titan also requested that Timsco and Marine Leasing be ordered to post countersecurity under Rule E(7) of the Supplemental Rules for Admiralty.

The trial court ordered Timsco and Marine Leasing to either post countersecurity or release the security given in lieu of the arrest of Titan's vessels. Marine Leasing appealed and presented issues not brought to the attention of the district court. We remanded for reconsideration. After further discovery and proceedings, the district court again ordered the posting of countersecurity. Marine Leasing noticed the present appeal.

Analysis

* * *

This appeal turns on the language of Rule E(7), in light of its historical development. The pertinent language of this section is straightforward:

> 7) Security on Counterclaim. Whenever there is asserted a counterclaim arising out of the same transaction or occurrence with respect to which the action was originally filed, and the defendant or claimant in the original action has given security to respond in damages, any plaintiff for whose benefit such security has been given shall give security in the usual amount and form to respond in damages to the claims set forth in such counterclaim, unless the court, for cause shown, shall otherwise direct; ...

Marine Leasing first contends that the countersecurity provisions of the rule apply only to counterclaims in admiralty. In that regard it points out that Titan's counterclaim invokes only diversity and federal question jurisdiction. In support of this contention appellant relies on *United States v. Isthmian Steamship Co.*, 359 U.S. 314, 79 S. Ct. 857, 3 L. Ed. 2d 845 (1959). We find that reliance misplaced. Isthmian simply holds that the cross-libel referred to in Admiralty Rule 50 (the predecessor to Rule E(7)), included only those claims which related to the original libel. In the case at bar, all of the claims arise out of the same transaction and are at least within the pendent jurisdiction of the district court sitting in admiralty. In this resolution we are guided, as was the district court, by the scholarly opinion of Judge Friendly in *Leather's Best, Inc. v. S.S. MORMACLYNX*, 451 F.2d 800 (2d Cir. 1971). Titan was entitled to invoke the countersecurity provisions of Rule E(7) despite the fact that the counterclaim was not based in admiralty.

The more serious and difficult question posed by this appeal involves the ordering of the posting of countersecurity by one who possesses and has exercised an admiralty lien. The answer to that question requires a brief review of the historicity of this provision.

The concept of countersecurity is found in the first promulgation of rules in American admiralty courts, and it has continued to date with little substantive change.[2] With the merger of law and admiralty in 1966, admiralty's classic and ancient phraseology of libels and cross-libels was replaced with the more mundane terminology of claims and counterclaims, but Rule E(7) retained the essence of Admiralty Rule 50. *See* Advisory Committee's Note, Proposed Supplemental Rules for Certain Admiralty and Maritime Claims, reprinted in 39 F.R.D. 146, 160 (1966).

The rule is straightforward. When the defendant posts security to guarantee payment of an adverse judgment—typically the posting of a bond to secure release of a vessel—the

---

[2] The first countersecurity rule in admiralty was Admiralty Rule 54, adopted at 7 Wall. v (1868), which provided:

Whenever a cross-libel if filed upon any counter claim arising out of the same cause of action for which the original libel was filed, the respondents in the cross-libel shall give security in the usual amount and form, to respond in damages as claimed in said cross-libel, unless the court on cause shown, shall otherwise direct; and all proceedings upon the original libel shall be stayed until such security shall be given.

The same rule was re-adopted as Admiralty Rule 53 at 210 U.S. 562 (1907). In 1920 the provision became Admiralty Rule 50, 254 U.S. at 24 (Appendix), providing:

> Whenever a cross-libel is filed upon any counterclaim arising out of the same contract or cause of action for which the original libel was filed, and the respondent or claimant in the original suit shall have given security to respond in damages, the respondent in the cross-libel shall give security in the usual amount and form to respond in damages to the claims set forth in said cross-libel, unless the court, for cause shown, shall otherwise direct; and all proceedings on the original libel shall be stayed until such security be given unless the court otherwise directs.

complainant may be required to furnish security for the satisfaction of a counterclaim. Although the language of the rule is automatic it is not absolute, for the original seizing complainant may be excused by the court "for cause shown." Absent this relief by the court, the intent of the rule is manifest; it is "to place the parties on an equality as regards security." *Washington-Southern Navigation Co. v. Baltimore & Philadelphia Steamboat Co.*, 263 U.S. 629, 638-39, 44 S. Ct. 220, 223-24, 68 L. Ed. 480 (1924).[3]

The determination of "for cause shown" is relegated to the sound discretion of the district court. The extent of that discretion is critical to the resolution of this and similar appeals. We are persuaded that the discretion, although broad, is significantly cabined in some cases.

A survey of the jurisprudence reflects instances in which demands for countersecurity were carefully weighed and charily granted. Courts have recognized that seamen should not be forced to post countersecurity when they act to enforce their privileged position. *Washington-Southern Navigation Co. v. Baltimore & Philadelphia Steamboat Co.*; *Zubrod v. Associated Metals & Minerals Trade Co.*, 243 F. Supp. 340 (E.D. Pa. 1965); *Cudworth v. The St. Cuthbert*, 146 F. Supp. 857, 858 (E.D. Va. 1957) (action by seamen on salvage liens, holding seamen not required to post countersecurity because "to hold otherwise, salvage claims instituted by seamen could be effectively foreclosed.") The rationale for excusing seamen from posting security comes from their traditional role as wards of the court and the fact that Congress has long permitted them to prosecute civil actions without posting security. 28 U.S.C. § 1916.

Similarly, when a party is financially unable to post countersecurity, courts often dispense with the requirement of the rule, although the cases are not unanimous. The leading case on this point, with which we agree, remains *The Beaumont*, 8 F.2d 599 (4th Cir. 1925):

> The rule never contemplated, ... that, where the parties to the original libel had established their rights and obtained security, this should be lost to them, because of their inability, arising from insolvency or other good reason, to procure a bond to respond to a large claim asserted in the cross-libel, and that as a result their libel should be dismissed. This would not only be unjust, but would in effect negative and nullify the provision of the rule giving to the trial court full discretion to act upon the very subject involved.

8 F.2d at 601. *See also Spriggs v. Hoffstot*, 240 F.2d 76 (4th Cir. 1957) (finding no abuse of discretion in trial court's decision not to require countersecurity); *Whitney-Fidalgo Seafoods v. Miss Tammy*, 542 F. Supp. 1302 (W.D. Wash. 1982) (refusing counterclaimant's argument that the defendant on the counterclaim might be unable to pay a judgment and should therefore be required to post security); *cf. Flota Maritima Browning de Cuba v. M/V*

---

[3] *See, e.g., Seaboard & Caribbean Transp. Corp. v. Hafen-Dampfschiffahrt A.G.*, 329 F.2d 538 (5th Cir. 1964); *Spriggs v. Hoffstot*, 240 F.2d 76 (4th Cir. 1957); *Expert Diesel, Inc. v. Yacht "Fishin Fool"*, 627 F. Supp. 432 (S.D. Fla. 1986); *Williamett Transp., Inc. v. Cia. Anonima Venezolana de Navegacion*, 491 F. Supp. 442 (E.D. La. 1980); *Empresa Maritima a Vapor v. North & South American Steam Nav. Co.*, 16 F. 502 (S.D.N.Y. 1883).

Ciudad de la Habana, 245 F. Supp. 205 (D. Md. 1965); *Geotas Compania de Vapores v. S.S. Arie H.*, 237 F. Supp. 908 (E.D. Pa. 1964) (considering financial statements of cross libellant, requiring reduced countersecurity). We have recognized the pertinency of this consideration by concluding that financial difficulties would not automatically excuse the countersecurity requirement. *Seaboard & Caribbean Transp. Corp. v. Hafen-Dampfschiffahrt*, 329 F.2d 538 (5th Cir. 1964).

Finally, the court should not require countersecurity where the counterclaim is frivolous or so lacking in merit that the court can only conclude that the counterclaim was advanced solely to secure a negotiating advantage over the complainant.

In summary, we conclude that the exercise of the trial court's discretion to order countersecurity is to be guided by the essential and equitable purposes of the rule. In doing so, the court must weigh the importance of the security interest giving rise to the initial seizure, and the burden of posting countersecurity, against the potential injustice of requiring the defendant-counterclaimant to post security without affording reciprocal protection.

We believe the guidon for this analysis is the court's obligation to preserve the integrity of maritime liens. These vintage security devices endure and are protected because of their commercial usefulness. Despite the advent of instant communications, and the availability of sophisticated international financing, the ability of a ship's master to bind his vessel *in rem* continues to facilitate the prompt supply of goods and services. Similarly, liens under the law of general average permit the ship's master to make expeditious decisions regarding imperiled cargo; salvage liens encourage sailors to save property which would otherwise be lost; and liens arising out of collisions and other torts give innocent parties a source of financial responsibility, even though ultimate responsibility may lie with a distant and unreachable individual or corporation.

The considerable deference to be given maritime liens where countersecurity is requested was explained by Mr. Justice Brandeis in *Washington-Southern Navigation Co. v. Baltimore & Philadelphia Steamboat Co.*, where he discussed at length the history of Rule 50 and its predecessors, and rejected a rigid construction under which "a libellant may be automatically barred from prosecuting his suit, merely because he is unable or unwilling to give security to satisfy the claim made in the cross-libel." 263 U.S. at 632, 44 S. Ct. at 221.

* * *

We conclude that the ordering of countersecurity, under the particular facts presented, does no substantial harm to the sanctity or efficaciousness of maritime liens. In this case, the contract which gave rise to the lien was the result of careful negotiation between officials of the corporate parties. There is no indication whatsoever that Marine Leasing relied on the credit of any of the seized vessels in deciding to enter into the mesne contract between Timsco and Titan. We thus perceive no impairment of the fundamental utility of maritime liens, *i.e.*, as an inducer of credit for a ship's needed goods and services. Therefore, although we are loathe to approve what may develop to be a discharge of a maritime lien because of the lienholder's financial limitations, under the specific and narrowly defined facts of this particular case, we are not prepared to say that the trial court abused its discretion in ordering countersecurity.

The order requiring the posting of countersecurity is AFFIRMED.

E. Maritime Attachment

Note: The Process of Foreign Attachment: Historical Background and Purpose

In *Trans-Asiatic Oil Ltd., S.A. v. Apex Oil Co.*, 604 F. Supp. 4, 1984 AMC 2741 (D.P.R. 1983), *aff'd*, 804 F.2d 773, 1987 AMC 1115 (1st Cir. 1986), the history and purpose of maritime attachment were considered by the district court which stated the following:

> The process of foreign attachment which plaintiff used in this case has been recognized to be of ancient origin and preceding the founding of this Republic. As stated in *Manro v. Almeida*, 23 U.S. (10 Wheat.) 206, 6 L. Ed. 369 (1825):
>
>> Thus, this process has the clearest sanction in the practice of the civil law, and during the three years that the admiralty courts of these states were referred to the practice of the civil law for their "forms and modes of proceeding," there could have been no question that this process was legalized. Nor is there anything in the different phraseology adopted in the act of 1792, that could preclude its use. That it is agreeable to the "principles, rules and usages, which belong to courts of admiralty," is established, not only by its being resorted to in one at least of the courts of the United States, but by the explicit declaration of a book of respectable authority, and remote origin, in which it is laid down thus: "If the defendant has concealed himself, or has absconded from the kingdom, so that he cannot be arrested, if he have [*sic*] any goods, merchandise, ship or vessel, on the sea, or within the ebb or flow of the sea, and within the jurisdiction of the Lord High Admiral, a warrant is to be impetrated to this effect, viz., to attach such goods or ship of D., the defendant, in whose hands soever they may be; and to cite the said D. specially as the owner, and all others who claim any right to title to them, to be and appear on a certain day to answer unto P., in a civil and maritime cause".

The process of foreign attachment, developed to meet the necessities of those engaged in the multiple aspects of maritime commerce has two purposes as established in *Swift & Co. v. Compania Colombiana*, 339 U.S. 684, 70 S. Ct. 861, 94 L. Ed. 1206 (1949): (1) to secure the appearance of the respondents and (2) to secure satisfaction in case the suit is successful. *See also San Rafael Compania Naviera, S.A. v. American Smelting & Refining Co.*, 327 F.2d 581, 589 (9th Cir.1964). It should be noted that foreign attachment was originally found in Rule 2 of the former Rules of Admiralty which, after the unification of those rules with the F.R.C.P. in 1966, became Supplemental Rule B.

Federal Rules of Civil Procedure—Supplemental Rule B—Attachment

Supplemental Rule B. Attachment and Garnishment: Special Provisions

(1) When Available; Complaint, Affidavit, Judicial Authorization, and Process. In an in personam action:

> **(a)** If a defendant is not found within the district, a verified complaint may contain a prayer for process to attach the defendant's tangible or intangible personal property—up to the amount sued for—in the hands of garnishees named in the process.
> **(b)** The plaintiff or the plaintiff's attorney must sign and file with the complaint an affidavit stating that, to the affiant's knowledge, or on information and belief, the defendant cannot be found within the district. The court must review the complaint and affidavit and, if the conditions of this Rule B appear to exist, enter an order so stating and authorizing process of attachment and garnishment. The clerk may issue supplemental process enforcing the court's order upon application without further court order.
> **(c)** If the plaintiff or the plaintiff's attorney certifies that exigent circumstances make court review impracticable, the clerk must issue the summons and process of attachment and garnishment. The plaintiff has the burden in any post-attachment hearing under Rule E(4)(f) to show that exigent circumstances existed.
> **(d)(i)** If the property is a vessel or tangible property on board a vessel, the summons, process, and any supplemental process must be delivered to the marshal for service.
> **(ii)** If the property is other tangible or intangible property, the summons, process, and any supplemental process must be delivered to a person or organization authorized to serve it, who may be (A) a marshal; (B) someone under contract with the United States; (C) someone specially appointed by the court for that purpose; or, (D) in an action brought by the United States, any officer or employee of the United States.
> **(e)** The plaintiff may invoke state-law remedies under Rule 64 for seizure of person or property for the purpose of securing satisfaction of the judgment.

(2) Notice to Defendant. No default judgment may be entered except upon proof— which may be by affidavit—that:

> **(a)** the complaint, summons, and process of attachment or garnishment have been served on the defendant in a manner authorized by Rule 4;
> **(b)** the plaintiff or the garnishee has mailed to the defendant the complaint, summons, and process of attachment or garnishment, using any form of mail requiring a return receipt; or
> **(c)** the plaintiff or the garnishee has tried diligently to give notice of the action to the defendant but could not do so.

(3) Answer.

> **(a) By Garnishee.** The garnishee shall serve an answer, together with answers to any interrogatories served with the complaint, within 20 days after service of process upon

the garnishee. Interrogatories to the garnishee may be served with the complaint without leave of court. If the garnishee refuses or neglects to answer on oath as to the debts, credits, or effects of the defendant in the garnishee's hands, or any interrogatories concerning such debts, credits, and effects that may be propounded by the plaintiff, the court may award compulsory process against the garnishee. If the garnishee admits any debts, credits, or effects, they shall be held in the garnishee's hands or paid into the registry of the court, and shall be held in either case subject to the further order of the court.

(b) By Defendant. The defendant shall serve an answer within 30 days after process has been executed, whether by attachment of property or service on the garnishee.

CREDIT(S)

(Added Feb. 28, 1966, eff. July 1, 1966, and amended Apr. 29, 1985, eff. Aug. 1, 1985; Mar. 2, 1987, eff. Aug. 1, 1987; Apr. 17, 2000, eff. Dec. 1, 2000.)

F. Cases and Notes: The Nature of Rule B Jurisdiction

1. Quasi In rem *Proceedings*

EAST ASIATIC CO., LTD. v. INDOMAR, LTD.

422 F. Supp. 1335, 1976 AMC 2039 (S.D.N.Y. 1976)

Memorandum

TENNEY, District Judge

Indomar, Ltd. ("Indomar"), a Bahamian corporation, moves pursuant to Rule 60(b)(1) of the Federal Rules of Civil Procedure ("Rules") for an order correcting and amending a default judgment entered against it as defendant in an admiralty proceeding. The original action arose in connection with an alleged breach of a charter party between Indomar and East Asiatic Co., Ltd. ("East Asiatic"), the plaintiffs in the prior action and the current opponents to the motion to amend. Indomar defaulted, and judgment was had against it for $1,149,577.77, the entire amount claimed in East Asiatic's complaint, plus costs. Indomar moves to reduce that figure to $16,883.76, asserting that the lesser sum represents the maximum liability exposed to the Court's jurisdiction in the original proceedings. East Asiatic contends that the Court properly possessed jurisdiction to award the sum contained in the judgment and pleads that it be permitted to stand. For the reasons stated below, Indomar's motion to correct and amend the judgment is granted.

I

East Asiatic began its action against Indomar by process of maritime attachment levied against $16,883.76 of defendant's assets located within the Southern District of New York. Since the unification of admiralty and civil procedure, *see* ORDER OF SUPREME COURT OF

UNITED STATES, 383 U.S. 1031 (1966), maritime attachment procedure has been governed by Rule B of the Supplemental Rules for Certain Admiralty and Maritime Claims of the Federal Rules of Civil Procedure ("Supplemental Rules").[1] Maritime attachment is, however, a traditional remedy whose "origin is to be found in the remotest history, as well of the civil as of the common law." *Manro v. Almeida,* 23 U.S. (10 Wheat.) 473, 490, 6 L. Ed. 369 (1825). The remedy has "a dual purpose: (1) to obtain jurisdiction of the respondent *in personam* through his property and (2) to assure satisfaction of any decree in libelant's favor." *Seawind Compania, S.A. v. Crescent Line, Inc.*, 320 F.2d 580 (2d Cir. 1963) (*"Seawind"*); *see Swift & Company Packers v. Compania Columbiana Del Caribe, S.A.*, 339 U.S. 684, 70 S. Ct. 861, 94 L. Ed. 1206 (1950); *Chilean Line Inc. v. United States*, 344 F.2d 757, 760 (2d Cir. 1965); 2 E. BENEDICT, ADMIRALTY, § 288 (6th ed. A. Knauth 1940) ("Benedict"). The historic rule, which is followed in this Circuit, is that "[t]he two purposes may not be separated ... for security cannot be obtained except as an adjunct to obtaining jurisdiction." *Seawind, supra,* 320 F.2d at 582; 2 BENEDICT, *supra,* § 288.

East Asiatic overlooks this rule, however, and in substance contends that use of the maritime attachment process under Supplemental Rule B does not preclude the simultaneous assertion of pure in personam jurisdiction over defendant. Thus, East Asiatic alleges that this Court had in personam jurisdiction[2] over Indomar not only by virtue of the maritime attachment but also through compliance with the standard requirements for *in personam* jurisdiction, *i.e.*, that Indomar had sufficient contacts with the forum and that substituted service of process was made in accordance with Rule 4. Making this assertion, however, East Asiatic misapprehends the nature of maritime attachment and the relationship of Supplemental Rule B to the main body of the Federal Rules of Civil Procedure. Unification of admiralty and civil procedure has not abrogated the traditional jurisdictional function of maritime attachment, and compliance with Supplemental Rule B does not constitute service of process under Rule 4.

In admiralty, as in civil law, the court's direct *in personam* jurisdiction over defendant depends upon the latter's contacts with the forum and the correct service of process. *Ivanhoe*

---

[1] Supplemental Rule B reads in pertinent part:

> Attachment and Garnishment: Special Provisions
>
> (1) When Available; Complaint, Affidavit, and Process. With respect to any admiralty or maritime claim *in personam* a verified complaint may contain a prayer for process to attach the defendant's goods and chattels, or credits and effects in the hands of garnishees named in the complaint to the amount sued for, if the defendant shall not be found within the district. Such a complaint shall be accompanied by an affidavit signed by the plaintiff or his attorney that, to the affiant's knowledge, or to the best of his information and belief, the defendant cannot be found within the district. When a verified complaint is supported by such an affidavit the clerk shall forthwith issue a summons and process of attachment and garnishment. In addition, or in the alternative, the plaintiff may, pursuant to Rule 4(e), invoke the remedies provided by state law for attachment and garnishment or similar seizure of the defendant's property. Except for Rule E(8) these Supplemental Rules do not apply to state remedies so invoked.
>
> (2) Notice to Defendant. No judgment by default shall be entered except upon proof, which may be by affidavit, (a) that the plaintiff or the garnishee has given notice of the action to the defendant by mailing to him a copy of the complaint, summons, and process of attachment or garnishment, using any from of mail requiring a return receipt, or (b) that the complaint, summons, and process of attachment or garnishment have been served on the defendant in a manner authorized by Rule 4(d) or (i), or (c) that the plaintiff or the garnishee has made diligent efforts to give notice of the action to the defendant and has been unable to do so.

[2] All suits in admiralty are denominated either "*in personam*" or "*in rem.*" The *in rem* proceeding, which does not concern us here, is against the thing itself and operates after plaintiff has acquired a lien against the property. "The lien and the proceedings *in rem* are, therefore, correlative — where one exists, the other can be taken, and not otherwise." *The Rock Island Bridge,* 73 U.S. (6 Wall.) 213, 215, 18 L. Ed. 753 (1867); *see* Supplemental Rule C. Suits *in personam,* like the one at bar, are against an individual and do not depend upon the acquisition of a maritime lien. Benedict states that

> [m]ost actions may be maintained either *in rem* (if there is a maritime lien on a *res* in the jurisdiction) or *in personam* (if the defendant or respondent can be personally served with process or reached by means of an attachment proceeding), or both *in rem* and *in personam.* BENEDICT, *supra,* § 226.

Trading Co. v. M/S Bornholm, 160 F. Supp. 900 (S.D.N.Y.1957); *Arpad Szabo v. Smedvig Tankrederi A.S.*, 95 F. Supp. 519 (S.D.N.Y.1951); *Belgian Mission for Economic Cooperation v. Zarati Steamship Co., Ltd.*, 90 F. Supp. 741 (S.D.N.Y.1950). Maritime attachment, on the other hand, is available to the plaintiff only when the defendant is not "found" within the district. Supplemental Rule B(1). To determine whether defendant is "found" within the district "a two-pronged inquiry [is made]: first, whether [defendant] can be found within the district in terms of jurisdiction, and second, if so, whether it can be found for service of process." *United States v. Cia. Naviera Continental S.A.,* 178 F. Supp. 561, 563 (S.D.N.Y.1959); *see Chilean Line Inc. v. United States,* 344 F.2d 757, 760 (2d Cir. 1965); *Seawind, supra,* 320 F.2d at 582. If either inquiry produces a negative answer, attachment is permitted.[3] This two-pronged test results in a small group of cases where, in theory, plaintiff could acquire *in personam* jurisdiction either by traditional means or through maritime attachment. 2 BENEDICT, *supra*, §288; 7A MOORE'S FEDERAL PRACTICE ¶ B.03. For example, a defendant having an agent in the district and doing business within the state - but not within the district - would be subject either to maritime attachment jurisdiction or to pure *in personam* jurisdiction. However, there is no case cited to this Court wherein both methods of acquiring *in personam* jurisdiction were simultaneously employed. Nor can there logically be such a case, for such a holding would reduce maritime attachment to nothing more than a security lien. This cannot be done, for "[i]t is crystal clear that the historical purpose of the writ of foreign attachment is to compel the respondent's appearance. Although an incidental purpose thereof is to supply the libelant with security, this objective can only be obtained as an adjunct to jurisdiction." *D/S A/S Flint v. Sabre Shipping Corp.*, 228 F. Supp. 384, 388 (E.D.N.Y. 1964), *aff'd sub nom. Det Bergenske Dampskibesselskab v. Sabre Shipping Corp.,* 341 F.2d 50 (2d Cir. 1965) (*"Flint v. Sabre"*).

Unification of admiralty and civil procedure has done nothing to distort this basic principle, although East Asiatic apparently interprets the Notes of Advisory Committee on Supplemental Rule B ("Advisory Notes") as permitting the simultaneous acquisition of *in personam* jurisdiction by conventional process and by maritime attachment. This Court does not agree. The text in question reads as follows:

---

[3] Because maritime attachment operates on a defendant by tying up his property prior to the determination of his liability, *Thyssen Steel Corp. v. Federal Commerce & Navigation Co.*, 274 F. Supp. 18 (S.D.N.Y.1967), litigation in this area has largely turned on whether defendant could defeat an often onerous attachment by demonstrating that he is "found" within the district. The theory behind the typical maritime attachment controversy was expressed in *Federazione Italiana Dei Consorzi Agrari v. Mandask Compania De Vapores*, S.A., 158 F. Supp. 107, 111 (S.D.N.Y.1957):

> In the usual case it is the libelant who asserts that the respondent's activities in the district are sufficient to make it amenable to service, and the respondent in turn denies that it was doing business in the district in this sense. Here the reverse is true for it appears to the advantage of the libelant to claim that the respondent is not doing business within the district so that it may be free to attach the very substantial funds standing to respondent's credit here, whereas the respondent affirmatively asserts that it is doing business here, and that it could have been served had the libelant been so minded.

See Antco Shipping Company v. Yukon Compania Naviera, S.A., 318 F. Supp. 626 (S.D.N.Y.1970) (attempted attachment of defendant's ship); McCreary, *Going for the Jugular Vein: Arrests and Attachments in Admiralty*, 28 OHIO ST.L.J. 19 (1967).

The case at bar presents the unusual situation where plaintiff opts to commence proceedings by attaching a mere fraction of the claim asserted, and defendant chooses not to protect theses assets either by special appearance to dispute the attachment, Supplemental Rule E(8), or by general appearance to defend against the complaint.

> A change in the context of the practice is brought about by Rule 4(f), which will enable summons to be served throughout the state instead of, as heretofore, only within the district. The Advisory Committee considered whether the rule on attachment and garnishment should be correspondingly changed to permit those remedies only when the defendant cannot be found within the state and concluded that the remedy should not be so limited.
>
> The effect is to enlarge the class of cases in which the plaintiff may proceed by attachment or garnishment although jurisdiction of the person may be independently obtained. This is possible at the present time where, for example, a corporate defendant has appointed an agent within the district to accept service of process but is not carrying on activities there sufficient to subject it to jurisdiction ... or where, though the foreign corporation's activities in the district are sufficient to subject it personally to the jurisdiction, there is in the district no officer on whom process can be served.

(Citations omitted).

The enlargement of which the Advisory Notes speak refers to a situation which prevailed prior to the unification of admiralty and civil procedure in 1966. At that time an admiralty defendant doing sufficient business in the district but subject to service only beyond its borders, although within the state, could be subjected to the in personam jurisdiction of the court solely through process of maritime attachment. This class of defendants is now amenable to traditional *in personam* jurisdiction through the statewide service permitted by Rule 4(f). However, the Advisory Notes make it plain that these defendants remain vulnerable to attachment, and thus a plaintiff may proceed against them either by Rule 4(f) process or by maritime attachment. At the same time, Supplemental Rule B continues to permit attachment by a plaintiff proceeding against a foreign corporation which, although "present" in the district through its activities, can be reached for service only through extraterritorial process under Rule 4(e) or 4(i). In other words, the Advisory Notes recognize that attachment continues to be an option in certain cases where pure *in personam* jurisdiction might be alternatively achieved over the same defendants. But plaintiff cannot compel the defendant's appearance through Rule 4 and, at the same time, attach its property through Supplemental Rule B. Compelling defendant's appearance through extra-district process obviates the need to compel that appearance through maritime attachment. This Court cannot conclude that in widening a class of cases in which plaintiff may choose his approach, the Advisory Committee intended to undermine the venerable jurisdictional rationale of maritime attachment.

Moreover, even if it is assumed that use of maritime attachment does not preclude the simultaneous use of Rule 4 process to achieve pure *in personam* jurisdiction over the defendant, East Asiatic has not accomplished service upon Indomar as mandated by Rule 4. East Asiatic argues that in complying with the notice provisions of Supplemental Rule B(2) it satisfied the service requirements of Rule 4 and cites the various references to Rule 4 in Supplemental Rule B to support its contention that Supplemental Rule B is "a statute of the United States ... [which] provides for service of a summons ... upon a party not an inhabitant of or found within the state in which the district court is held," as provided for in Rule 4. Plaintiff overlooks the fact that Supplemental Rule B in no way concerns service of process, which, indeed, is not required to effect maritime attachment under Supplemental Rule B. The Rule is by its own terms a form of process, and its operation confers jurisdiction on the court. Supplemental Rule B does not even direct that notice be given to defendant until such time as default judgment is to be entered. And notice is then given purely on the ground of "fairness," since "none is required by the principles of due process." Advisory Notes, Subdivision (2). The method of communicating this default notice is governed internally by Supplemental Rule B(2).

Although East Asiatic did comply with Supplemental Rule B(2) in notifying Indomar before default was entered, this notification was no more than that necessary to permit execution thereafter on the property attached, and bears no significance with respect to service of process under Rule 4. Nor may East Asiatic state that it has conformed to any of the other provisions of Rule 4. It has not complied with the Rule 4(e) alternative which permits service as provided by "any statute or rule of the court of the state in which the district court is held." It has not satisfied the requirements of New York Business Corporation Law § 307 (McKinney Supp.1975), which, in conjunction with New York CPLR §302 (McKinney Supp.1975), permits service upon a non-domiciliary corporation transacting business within the state if service is made upon the Secretary of State. Finally, East Asiatic has not met any of the terms of Rule 4(i) relating to service in a foreign country, and it is not proceeding against an in state defendant within the contemplation of Rule 4(d)(3) and Rule 4(f).

II

Having determined that East Asiatic had but one base of *in personam* jurisdiction against Indomar, *i.e.*, that which it acquired through maritime attachment, it remains only to determine the effect of a default judgment in these circumstances. Although the jurisdiction achieved through maritime attachment is denominated *in personam*, it is clear that, absent an appearance by defendant, the judgment had is in the nature of *quasi in rem*. Indeed, the term "*quasi in rem*" is used in the title of Supplemental Rule E, which concerns actions commenced by maritime attachment. *See* Supplemental Rule E. The United States Court of Appeals for the Second Circuit has referred to Supplemental Rule B(1) as "a *quasi in rem* proceeding." *Maryland Tuna Corp. v. MS Benares,* 429 F.2d 307, 311 (2d Cir. 1970); *see Societe Commerciale de Transports Transatlantiques (S.C.T.T.) v. S.S. "African Mercury",* 366 F. Supp. 1347 (S.D.N.Y.1973).

Although attachment may issue against property held for the defendant in the district up to the amount sued for, *see* Supplemental Rule B(1), "execution in proceedings commenced by maritime *in personam* attachments in which defendant has not been personally served or appeared cannot exceed the value of the attached property." 7A *Moore's Federal Practice* ¶ B.03 n.6 (2d ed. 1972); *see* 2 BENEDICT, *supra,* § 288. The same proposition is well established outside admiralty. In *Cooper v. Reynolds,* 10 Wall. 308, 19 L. Ed. 931

(1870), the Supreme Court discussed the limits of a judgment based on jurisdiction over the *res* rather than over the persona. "[T]he judgment of the court, though in form a personal judgment against the defendant, has no effect beyond the property attached in that suit. No general execution can be issued for any balance unpaid after the attached property is exhausted." *Id.* at 318-19, 19 L. Ed. 931; *see Freeman v. Alderson,* 119 U.S. 185, 7 S. Ct. 165, 30 L. Ed. 372 (1886); *Pennoyer v. Neff,* 95 U.S. 714, 24 L. Ed. 565 (1878). The judgment in such a case is not entitled to full faith and credit in another district. *See Sherman v. Kirshman,* 369 F.2d 886, 889 (2d Cir. 1966).

Although it is possible that East Asiatic could have achieved pure *in personam* jurisdiction over Indomar in this Court through the defendant's contacts with the forum and receipt of perfected service, it elected to proceed by means of a Supplemental Rule B attachment, which then represented the sole basis of the Court's jurisdiction over Indomar. Since Indomar did not appear to perfect the Court's *in personam* jurisdiction, *see Atkins v. Fibre Disintegrating Co.*, 85 U.S. (18 Wall.) 272, 21 L. Ed. 841 (1873),[4] East Asiatic's recovery is limited according to the principles of *quasi in rem* jurisdiction. In order to avoid possible harassment of the defendant through improper registration of an unenforceable judgment in another district, *see* 28 U.S.C. § 1963,[5] the judgment against Indomar must be reduced to $16,883.76, the extent of the property subjected to the process of maritime attachment.

Submit amended judgment in conformity herewith.

So ordered.

Notes

1. *But see, Stevedoring Services of America v. Ancora Transport,* 941 F.2d 1378, 1992 AMC 883 (9th Cir. 1991), *cert. granted and judgment vacated by,* 506 U.S. 1043, 113 S. Ct. 955, 122 L. Ed. 2d 112 (1993), *on remand to,* 59 F.3d 879, 1995 AMC 2688 (9th Cir. 1995), where the court intimated that it is possible for a plaintiff to invoke both *quasi in rem* (via attachment) and *in personam* (via service of process) jurisdiction in the same proceeding:

> While it is true that SSA was free to assert both *quasi in rem* and *in personam* jurisdiction by serving the defendants not in that district but in the state, SSA alleged no facts in its complaint asserting appellees were subject to personal jurisdiction of the court, nor did they properly serve them to obtain personal jurisdiction.

2. ***The Nature of an Attachment Action***

> However, Teyseer argues that this is an *in personam* action, and that the release of the security is therefore irrelevant. It is true that an attachment under Rule B is available only "[w]ith respect to any admiralty or

---

[4] In a case commenced by maritime attachment, defendants made a general appearance. The court noted that "[t]his made their position just what it would have been if they had been brought in regularly by the service of process. In this aspect of the case all defects were cured and the jurisdiction of the court over their persons became complete. This warranted the decree *in personam* for the amount adjudged to the libellants." *Atkins v. Fibre Disintegrating Co., supra,* 85 U.S. at 298.

[5] Section 1963 reads as follows:

§1963. Registration in other districts

> A judgment in an action for the recovery of money or property now or hereafter entered in any district court which has become final by appeal or expiration of time for appeal may be registered in any other district by filing therein a certified copy of such judgment. A judgment so registered shall have the same effect as a judgment of the district court of the district where registered and may be enforced in like manner.
>
> A certified copy of the satisfaction of any judgment in whole or in part may be registered in like manner in any district in which the judgment is a lien.

maritime claim *in personam*." Rule B(1). But the filing of an admiralty or maritime *in personam claim* is not the equivalent of *in personam* jurisdiction over a party.[5] Attachment provides a limited substitute for the latter and the release of attached property affects only this latter jurisdiction.

A cause of action for damages because of the loss of cargo is normally *in personam* in the sense that the amount of damages to be awarded is not limited to the value of a particular asset if personal jurisdiction over the defendant exists. If personal jurisdiction cannot be obtained, however, and the personal appearance of a defendant is secured only by the arrest of his assets, the *in personam* character of the cause of action is largely meaningless. To our knowledge, all courts and commentators that have squarely addressed the question have stated that the nature of the jurisdiction the court acquires by a Rule B attachment is properly denominated "*quasi in rem*" because any judgment rendered is limited to the value of the attached property. *E.g.*, *Belcher Co. v. M/V Maratha Mariner*, 724 F.2d 1161, 1164 (5th Cir. 1984) (characterizing as "*quasi in rem*" actions that are begun by attachment when the court has no jurisdiction over the defendant's person but has jurisdiction over the thing belonging to the defendant); *Maryland Tuna Corp. v. MS Benares*, 429 F.2d 307, 311 (2d Cir. 1970) (proceeding begun under Rule B(1) is "*quasi in rem*" in nature); *Engineering Equipment Co. v. S.S. Selene*, 446 F. Supp. 706, 709 n.9 (S.D.N.Y. 1978) ("Although the jurisdiction achieved through maritime attachment is sometimes denominated *in personam*, there is no doubt that any judgment rendered is *quasi in rem* in nature and is limited to the value of the attached property."); *East Asiatic Co. v. Indomar, Ltd.*, 422 F. Supp. 1335, 1341-42 (S.D.N.Y. 1976) (same); 7A J. MOORE & A. PELAEZ, MOORE'S FEDERAL PRACTICE ¶ B.02, at B-103 n.6 (2d ed. 1983) (hereinafter Moore's) ("[E]xecution in proceedings commenced by maritime *in personam* attachments in which the defendant has not been personally served or appeared cannot exceed the value of the attached property."); Comment, *The Use of Maritime Attachment as a Jurisdictional Device*, 12 CORNELL INT'L L. J. 329, 332-33 (1979) (citation omitted) ("It should be emphasized that, despite the language in Rule B limiting its scope to claims brought "*in personam*," the Rule is in fact a classic example of *quasi in rem* jurisdiction ... .").

* * *

Thus, Teyseer's argument that its action is *in personam*, and that the release of the security is irrelevant, misses the mark. The filing of a purely *in personam* action does not determine jurisdiction over the defendant. Limited jurisdiction over the defendant may be acquired by the seizure of his assets. In that event, the *in personam* action takes on characteristics of an action *in rem*, and with respect to the consequences of a release of the security, is guided by *in rem* precedents.

Teyseer Cement Company v. Halla Maritime Corporation, 794 F.2d 472, 476-77, 1986 AMC 2705 (9th Cir. 1986).

3. ***Restricted appearance***

The defendant may enter a restricted appearance under Supplemental Admiralty Rule E(8) for the purpose of contesting the attachment without submitting to the court's jurisdiction.

Halla expressly entered a "restricted appearance" under Rule E(8). As noted earlier, the language of that Rule permits a defendant to restrict its appearance to the defense of the claim as to which there has issued process of attachment and garnishment. *See* MOORE'S ¶ E.16, at E-767. We have no reason to question the validity of restricted appearances, which have long been a part of admiralty proceedings. *See* Currie, *Attachment and Garnishment in the Federal Courts*. 59 MICH. L. REV. 337, 379 n.178 (1961). "It is clear that a defendant or owner entering a restricted appearance to an *in rem* or *quasi in rem* maritime proceeding can vigorously defend the merits of the claim against him without converting his restricted appearance into a general appearance."

---

[5] In *Polar Shipping*, we characterized as *in personam* the jurisdiction the court acquired *over a defendant* whose appearance has been secured by writ of attachment. *Id.* at 630. We cited *Swift & Co. Packers v. Compania Columbiana del Caribe*, 339 U.S. 684, 70 S. Ct. 861, 94 L. Ed. 1206 (1950) and 7 A MOORE'S FEDERAL PRACTICE. ¶ B.O2 at B-51 (2nd Ed. 1981) for that proposition. We believe both authorities more properly stand for the proposition that a writ of attachment is proper in an admiralty or maritime *in personam* cause of action, but that such a writ does not itself confer *in personam* jurisdiction over any party.

> *Moore's* ¶ E.16[1], at E-772. Rule E(8) permits a defendant whose appearance is obtained by attachment to avoid the dilemma of either defending the attached property by generally appearing and thus risking a loss greater than the value of the property, or letting it go by default. *Id.* at E-768.

Teyseer Cement Company v. Halla Maritime Corporation, 794 F.2d 472, 476-77, 1986 AMC 2705 (9th Cir. 1986).

---

2. *"Found Within the District": A Two-Prong Test*

SEAWIND COMPANIA, S.A. v. CRESCENT LINE, INC.

320 F.2d 580 (2d Cir. 1963)

WATERMAN, Circuit Judge

Seawind Compania, S.A., appeals from an order of the United States District Court for the Southern District of New York, Bonsal, J., sitting in the admiralty, by which the attachment of credits and effects of respondent-appellee, Crescent Lines, Inc., now known as Falcon Shipping Corp., was vacated. The attachment had been made pursuant to Rule 2 of the Rules of Practice in Admiralty and Maritime Cases promulgated by the United States Supreme Court. We affirm the order below.[1]

By its libel filed March 20, 1962, Seawind sought recovery of damages from Crescent Line and others for the alleged breach of a maritime agreement. The same day a citation *in personam* with a clause of foreign attachment in the usual form was issued to the United States Marshal for the Southern District of New York. The Marshal was directed to cite Crescent Line "if [it] shall be found in your District," and "if the said Respondent cannot be found," to attach its credits and effects in the hands of named garnishees. On March 21, 1962, a Deputy Marshal served the citation with clause of foreign attachment upon the named garnishees, and at the same time effected personal service upon the other respondents in the case. Although the Marshal's return certified that he was unable to find Crescent Line, Inc. "after due and diligent search," it is conceded that libelant did not inform the Marshal where Crescent Line, Inc., might be found and no attempt was made by him to locate or to serve this respondent.

By order to show cause dated March 29, 1962, Crescent Line moved pursuant to Rule 21 of the Admiralty Rules of the District Court for an order vacating the attachment. Appellee contended that it had been present and doing business in the Southern District of New York for several years, as Seawind well knew, and that the attachment was, therefore, illegally and improperly made. After a hearing, Judge Bonsal granted the motion and vacated the attachment on April 9, 1962. Reargument of the motion was held on April 17, 1962, and on the same day Judge Bonsal's Memorandum Decision was entered adhering to his original determination. This appeal followed.

---

[1] Our jurisdiction rests upon 28 U.S.C. § 1291; *Swift & Co. Packers v. Compania Columbiana Del Caribe, S.A.*, 339 U.S. 684, 689, 70 S. Ct. 861, 94 L. Ed. 1206 (1950).

An attachment under Rule 2 of the Admiralty Rules, customarily referred to as a foreign attachment, has a dual purpose: (1) to obtain jurisdiction of the respondent *in personam* through his property, and (2) to assure satisfaction of any decree in libelant's favor. 2 BENEDICT, ADMIRALTY § 288 (6th ed. 1940); *Swift & Company Packers v. Compania Columbiana Del Caribe, S.A.,* 339 U.S. 684, 70 S. Ct. 861, 94 L. Ed. 1206 (1950). The two purposes may not be separated, however, for security cannot be obtained except as an adjunct to obtaining jurisdiction.

Rule 2 provides, in pertinent part:

> In suits *in personam* the mesne process shall be by a simple monition in the nature of a summons to appear and answer to the suit, or by a simple warrant of arrest of the person of the respondent in the nature of a capias, as the libellant may, in his libel or information pray for or elect; in either case with a clause therein to attach his goods and chattels, or credits and effects in the hands of the garnishees named in the libel to the amount sued for, *if said respondent shall not be found within the district.*
>
> * * *

(Emphasis supplied.)

Thus, on motions to vacate foreign attachments, the essential issue before the district court is whether respondent could have been found within the district. We must affirm Judge Bonsal's determination that respondent-appellee could have been so found unless he applied an erroneous legal standard or his determination of subsidiary facts was clearly erroneous. *McAllister v. United States*, 348 U.S. 19, 75 S. Ct. 6, 99 L. Ed. 20 (1954); *cf.* Rule 52(a), FED. R. CIV. P.

The Admiralty Rules do not define the expression "found within the district." In the cases construing Rule 2, however, the requirement is said to present "a two-pronged inquiry: first, whether [the respondent] can be found within the district in terms of jurisdiction, and second, if so, whether it can be found for service of process." *United States v. Cia Naviera Continental S.A.*, 178 F. Supp. 561, 563 (S.D.N.Y.1959); *see American Potato Corp. v. Boca Grande S.S. Co.*, 233 F. 542 (E.D.Pa. 1916); *Insurance Co. of North America v. Canadian American Navigation Co. (The Melmay)*, 1933 A.M.C. 1057.

Considering the second question first, there is no doubt, we believe, that Crescent Line, Inc. (Falcon Shipping Corp.) could be found within the Southern District of New York on March 21, 1962, for service of process. In Admiralty, as under Rule 4(d) of the Federal Rules of Civil Procedure, service upon a corporation may properly be effected by service upon "an officer, a managing or general agent, or ... any other agent authorized by appointment or by law to receive service of process." *Ashcraft-Wilkinson Co. v. Compania De Navegacion Geamar, S.R.L.*, 117 F. Supp. 162, 164 (S.D.N.Y.1953); *Patel Cotton Co. v. Steel Traveler*, 107 F. Supp. 191, 193 (S.D.N.Y.1952); 2 BENEDICT, ADMIRALTY § 280 (6th ed. 1940).

Here, appellant does not deny that during the relevant period of time Crescent Line had a managing agent within the district, James W. Elwell & Co., Inc., with offices at 17

State Street in New York City; that the Elwell office was in the charge of David W. Swanson, president of both Elwell and Crescent Line (Falcon Shipping Corp.), who was present in his office at 17 State Street during normal business hours on March 21, 1962; and that the Secretary and proctor for both Crescent Line and Elwell was Henry P. Molloy, Jr., Esq., with offices at 26 Broadway in New York City.

Moreover, the district court could properly conclude that appellant knew, or ought to have known, the above facts, for both Swanson and Molloy signed the contract in suit, as President and Secretary of Crescent Line respectively; James W. Elwell & Co., Inc. was referred to in the contract as the Managing Agent of the respondent; and on February 19 and February 26, 1960, appellant, through its President, directed correspondence to "Crescent Line, Inc., James W. Elwell & Co., Inc., Agent, 17 State Street, New York 4, New York, Attention: Mr. David Swanson, President."

Appellant argues that because Crescent Line, on or about February 26, 1960, changed its corporate name to Falcon Shipping Corp., and sold its former name and good will, appellant no longer knew whether Swanson, Molloy, and James W. Elwell & Co., Inc. continued to serve as officers and agents of respondent-appellee. On March 16, 1960, however, invoices bearing the names of both Crescent Line and James W. Elwell & Co., Inc., were sent to appellant's attorney; and on April 7 and July 27, 1960, Henry P. Molloy, signing his name as "Secretary" of Falcon Shipping Corp., corresponded with appellant's attorney concerning Seawind Compania.

Even if appellant was ignorant, however, of the continuing relationships of Swanson, Molloy, and James W. Elwell & Co., Inc., to Falcon Shipping Corp., we must assume that appropriate inquires would have revealed these facts. No such inquiries were made. Judge Bonsal was clearly correct in ruling, therefore, that libelant failed to make a bona fide effort to locate respondent in the district, as we hold it was required to do. *Federazione Italiana Dei Consorzi Agrari v. Mandask Compania De Vapores, S.A.*, 158 F. Supp. 107, 111 (S.D.N.Y.1957); *Birdsall v. Germain Co.*, 227 F. 953 (S.D.N.Y.1915).

We turn, thus, to the question whether respondent-appellee was to be "found within" the Southern District of New York for the purpose of being subject to *in personam* jurisdiction in the court below. If foreign attachment in admiralty is permitted only as a means of enabling the libelant's suit to proceed, it might be supposed that the known presence of an agent authorized to accept process would suffice to preclude such an attachment under Rule 2. The cases, however, suggest an additional requirement, namely, that the respondent be engaged in sufficient activity in the district to subject it to jurisdiction even in the absence of a resident agent expressly authorized to accept process. *American Potato Corp. v. Boca Grande S.S. Co.*, 233 F. 542, 543 (E.D.Pa.1916); *Insurance Co. of North America v. Canadian American Navigation Co. (The Melmay),* 1933 A.M.C. 1057; *see Federazione Italiana D.C.A. v. Mandask Compania D.V., supra*; *United States v. Cia Naviera Continental S.A., supra*; *Sociedad Transoceanica Canopus, S.A. v. Interamerican Refining Corp.*, 185 F. Supp. 294 (D.N.J.1960). *But see The Valmar*, 38 F. Supp. 615 (E.D.Pa.1941).

Here, the minimum conditions necessary to a foreign corporation's being "found within the district" under Rule 2 need not be determined, for we believe that the district court's ruling was not clearly erroneous even under the rigorous standard suggested by the cases cited above.

Respondent-appellee is a Liberian corporation which, during 1962, was in the process of dissolution. Its major, and perhaps sole, business during that year was in the processing of cargo claims. Despite the fact that the corporate minutes and stock transfer books were kept in New York, and all of the corporation's officers were present in the district, this volume of activity would possibly not, by itself, qualify as "doing business" under ordinary tests *See Hanson v. Denckla*, 357 U.S. 235, 78 S. Ct. 1228, 2 L. Ed. 2d 1283 (1958); *Blount v. Peerless Chemicals, Inc.*, 316 F.2d 695 (2 Cir. 1963); and *see generally* Kurland, *The Supreme Court, the Due Process Clause and In personam Jurisdiction of State Courts*, 25 U.Chi.L.Rev. 569 (1958); Note, *Jurisdiction over Foreign Corporations—an Analysis of Due Process*, 104 U.Pa.L.Rev. 381 (1955).

What respondent-appellee's volume of business may lack under ordinary tests, however, appellant supplies by the nature of its claim. The contract in suit was made and allegedly breached by Crescent Lines in New York. For such activities respondent-appellee could clearly be made subject to suit in New York, even in the absence of a resident agent expressly authorized to accept process. *See McGee v. International Life Ins. Co.*, 355 U.S. 220, 78 S. Ct. 199, 2 L. Ed. 2d 223 (1957); *Travelers Health Ass'n v. Com. of Virginia*, 339 U.S. 643, 70 S. Ct. 927, 94 L. Ed. 1154 (1950); *International Shoe Co. v. Washington*, 326 U.S. 310, 66 S. Ct. 154, 90 L. Ed. 95 (1945).

Under these circumstances, we cannot say that Judge Bonsal's determination that Crescent Line could be found within the district was clearly erroneous.

The order of the district court vacating the attachment of appellee's credits and effects is affirmed, and the cause is remanded for further proceedings in the district court.

Notes

1. *"Jurisdictional Presence"*

In the context of Supplemental Admiralty Rule B, it is well established that a defendant is "found within the district" only if the defendant is able to accept process and engaged in sufficient activity in the district. Moreover, previous engagement in business activities in the district is not sufficient activity in the district for purpose of this maritime attachment rule. In *VTT Vulcan Petroleum, S.A. v. Langham-Hill Petroleum, Inc.*, 684 F. Supp. 389, 1989 AMC 1301 (S.D.N.Y. 1988), the court held that the prior activity in the district, though constituting past general jurisdiction, was not sufficient to preclude attachment under this special maritime rule. The court stated:

> Past general jurisdictional contacts, unrelated to the subject matter of the litigation, provide no security to a plaintiff who wants to ensure that any judgment in its favor might be satisfied. Unlike specific jurisdictional contacts which do not terminate when a defendant physically leaves the forum state, general jurisdictional contacts do terminate when the defendant physically ends all continuous and systematic contact with the forum. Although past general jurisdictional contacts might satisfy due process concerns in other contexts, such past general jurisdictional contacts cannot satisfy the "jurisdictional presence" prong of the test for vacating a maritime attachment.

In the present case, there is no contract—nor any other subject of the litigation—which was made, performed, or breached in New York. Under these circumstances, Langham-Hill's contacts with New York prior to March 22, 1988, are insufficient to provide the showing of "jurisdiction presence" necessary to allow this Court to vacate the attachment here. *See Seawind*, 320 F.2d at 583.

2. *Service of Process Via Agent*

The issue of whether service upon a local port agent constitutes valid service on a foreign shipowner was addressed in *Cobelfret-CIE Belge v. Samick Lines Co., Ltd.*, 542 F. Supp. 29, 1983 AMC 547 (W.D. Wash. 1982). The court determined the following:

> The test's second prong, whether Samick could be found for service of process within the district, is sharply contested. Defendant contends it was amenable to service of process through its local port agent, Olympic Steamship Company. Generally, in order to serve a party through its subagent, an agent's actions must be substantial, continual and on more than just a ship-to-ship basis. *Marvirason Compania Naviera, S.A. v. H. J. Baker & Bro.*, 1979 AMC 625, 628 (S.D.N.Y.1978). Although some courts have found that service upon a local port agent providing ordinary husbanding services on a ship-to-ship basis is valid service on a foreign shipowner, *see, e.g., Murphy v. Arrow Steamship*, 124 F. Supp. 199, 1954 AMC 1423 (E.D.Pa.1954), the majority of courts have held that subagents or husbanding agents are not authorized to accept service of process which will bind the vessel's owner. *See Serpe v. Eagle Ocean Transport Agency Co.*, 53 F.R.D. 21, 1971 AMC 748 (E.D.Wis.1971); *Amicale Industries, Inc. v. The S.S. Rantum*, 259 F. Supp. 534, 1967 AMC 96 (D.S.C.1966).
>
> Having reviewed the file and the briefs herein, I find that the defendant could not be found with reasonable diligence within the district for service. *Tug GO GETTER* at 398 F.2d 874. Before the SAMICK ATLANTIC was attached, plaintiff's counsel checked the following in an unsuccessful attempt to locate the defendant in the district: (1) the 1981 List of Active Corporations in the State of Washington, (2) the 1980 Coast Marine Transportation Directory, (3) the 1979-80 Pacific Coast Maritime Directory, (4) Pacific Northwest Bell telephone book and the Information operators, (5) Pacific Marine Directory, (6) Shipping News Directory, (7) Lloyd's Shipping Directory, (8) Northwest Shipping Directory, and (9) the Seattle City Directory. Counsel also contacted the Corporate Records Division of Washington's Secretary of State and was advised that Samick Lines was not qualified to do business in Washington and had not appointed a registered agent to receive process.
>
> Finally, neither the Affidavit of Gordon Cleverdon, Olympic Steamship's Vice President, nor his deposition and the exhibits attached indicated that Olympic had specific authority, express or implied, to receive service of process. *See generally* 2 MOORE'S FEDERAL PRACTICE P 4.22(1) (2d ed. 1982).

3. *Service of Process on Official Agent*

Many jurisdictions have a rule permitting service of process on a state official (often the Secretary of State) as the defendant's "appointed" representative when a non-resident defendant is not present in the jurisdiction for purposes of service. In such a jurisdiction, the second prong of the "found within the district" test is satisfied only if suit is brought in the district where service on the state official can be accomplished. See, e.g., *LaBanca v. Ostermunchner*, 664 F.2d 65, 1982 AMC 205 (5th Cir. 1981), where Rule B attachment in the Middle District of Florida was permitted despite plaintiff's ability to serve process on the Florida Secretary of State as defendant's agent, because service on the Secretary of State had to be made at the State Capitol, which was in the Northern District of Florida.

3. The Distinction Between Proceedings: Attachment and Actions In rem

BELCHER COMPANY OF ALABAMA, INC. v. M/V MARATHA MARINER

724 F.2d 1161, 1984 AMC 1679 (5th Cir. 1984)

ALVIN B. RUBIN, Circuit Judge

This *in rem* libel against a vessel to recover for fuel bunkers supplied to it was dismissed on the ground that a pending action in the Netherlands, in which jurisdiction had been obtained by attachment of the vessel, was the equivalent of an *in rem* action and hence was *lis alibis pendens*. Because the Netherlands permits no *in rem* actions, and, therefore, the suit pending there is *in personam*, and because the ultimate issues in the two suits are different, we reverse the judgment of dismissal.

Belcher Company of Alabama, Inc. (Belcher), filed an *in rem* libel against the vessel M/V Maratha Mariner of Bombay, India, and against all persons having or claiming any interest in the vessel, alleging that Belcher had supplied fuel bunkers to the vessel and had not been paid the amount due it, $99,344. The vessel had been chartered from its owner, Chowgule Steamship Company, Ltd. (Chowgule), by Armada Bulk Carriers of Denmark (Armada). Armada's broker had ordered fuel from Baymar, a California broker, and Baymar had, in turn, contracted with Belcher, which supplied the fuel to the vessel in Mobile, Alabama. Chowgule asserts that Armada paid Baymar for the fuel and that Baymar, in turn, made partial payment to Belcher and subsequently went out of business before paying the balance.

In 1979, Belcher had the vessel attached in the Netherlands to satisfy the alleged outstanding debt. Chowgule secured the release of the vessel by posting 275,000 Dutch guilders ($138,000 in U.S. dollars) in the form of a letter of undertaking, as security for its claim. That litigation is still pending in Rotterdam, the Netherlands. The vessel was later arrested in Houston, Texas, three years later, and this libel was initiated in the Southern District of Texas.

The Federal Maritime Lien Act provides, "[a]ny person furnishing ... necessaries, to any vessel, whether foreign or domestic, upon the order of the owner of such vessel, or of a person authorized by the owner, shall have a maritime lien on the vessel, which may be enforced by suit *in rem*...." 46 U.S.C. § 971. This lien attaches when necessaries are ordered by and supplied to a charterer,[1] unless the supplier has notice that the person who orders the necessaries lacked authority to do so.[2] Thus, when Belcher supplied fuel to the M/V Maratha Mariner, a maritime lien may have arisen by operation of law, and, if such a lien did arise, its enforceability may be subject to any defenses that may be available to the vessel owner, such as laches. The owner of the vessel is not itself liable for payment, however, unless it has entered into the contract for the supply of necessaries. It has no personal obligation even though a lien attaches to its vessel.[3]

---

[1] 46 U.S.C. § 973, as amended by Pub.L. No. 92-79, 85 Stat. 285 (1971); *Dampskibsselskzabet Dannebrog v. Signal Oil and Gas Company*, 310 U.S. 268, 60 S. Ct. 937, 84 L. Ed. 1197 (1939); G. Gilmore & C. Black, The Law of Admiralty 685 (2d ed. 1975) and cases cited therein.

[2] 46 U.S.C. §§ 972 & 973; G. Gilmore & C. Black, *supra* 685 *et seq.*

[3] *See generally* G. Gilmore & C. Black, *supra*, § 9-19; *but see infra* note 8.

Under the admiralty law of the United States, *in personam* and *in rem* actions may arise from the same claim, and may be brought separately or in the same suit. Supplemental Admiralty Rule C(1)(b). As its name implies, the *in personam* action is filed against the owner personally. An *in rem* action, on the other hand, is filed against the *res*, the vessel; and a maritime lien on the vessel is a prerequisite to an action *in rem*.[4] There is a third category of claims sometimes known as actions *quasi in rem*. Supplemental Admiralty Rule E. These are actions based on a claim for money begun by attachment or other seizure of property when the court has no jurisdiction over the person of the defendant, but has jurisdiction over a thing belonging to him or over a person who is indebted to, or owes a duty to the defendant.[5] A state has jurisdiction by an action *quasi in rem* to enforce a personal claim against a defendant to the extent of applying the property seized to the satisfaction of the claim.[6]

If American law had been applicable when the vessel was attached in the Netherlands, the supplier of fuel would have had a lien on the vessel and an action *in rem* could have been brought to enforce the maritime lien. The Netherlands action was, however, based on contract principles because Dutch law does not recognize the concept of maritime lien and, therefore, provides no mechanism by which such a lien can be enforced. The fact that an *in rem* action could not be brought in the Netherlands does not convert the attachment there filed into an *in rem* proceeding.

Chowgule contends that Belcher has admitted the foreign action to be in effect *in rem* because Belcher has asserted in the course of that action that, despite the difference in the two legal systems, "the position of the owner of the vessel is not essentially enhanced or changed [under Dutch law]. In the present [Netherlands] case the vessel was attached, whereupon by the law of the U.S.A. a lien could have been served. In order to withdraw this attachment, a guarantee was obtained. Possible judgment against Chowgule and possible non-compliance therewith will lead to compensation under guarantee and therewith indirectly on that item of property which by the law of the U.S.A. would be the debtor."

This is not, however, an admission that the foreign attachment is a libel *in rem*. As Belcher's pleading in the Netherlands case further states:

> By Dutch law of procedure which in effect does not provide for the action *in rem*, an action *in personam* must be brought therefore, whereby be it so, the owner of the vessel becomes debtor of the claim under section 321 paragraph 1 Wvk, whereas by the law of the U.S.A. the case itself, in the present instance the vessel, is the debtor.

Therein the true difference lies. In the *in rem* action, the issues are whether: (1) Belcher delivered the claimed quantity of fuel to the M/V Maratha Mariner; (2) the fuel delivered to the bunkers was a necessary within the meaning of the Maritime Lien Act, 46 U.S.C. §

---

[4] G. Gilmore & C. Black, § 1-12 at 35; *see, e.g.*, *The Rock Island Bridge*, 73 U.S. (6 Wall.) 213, 215, 18 L. Ed. 753, 754 (1862) (cited in G. Gilmore & C. Black at *id.*); *The Resolute*, 168 U.S. 437, 440, 18 S. Ct. 112, 113, 42 L. Ed. 533, 535 (1897); *Rainbow Line, Inv. v. M/V Tequila*, 480 F.2d 1024, 1028 (2d Cir.1973).

[5] Restatement (Second) of Judgments (1982) § 8; James, Civil Procedure 613 (1965).

[6] Restatement (Second) of Judgments (1982) § 9.

971; (3) the charges claimed are reasonable in amount; and (4) the person who placed the order had authority to do so, either real, apparent, or statutorily presumed. In the attachment action, the sole question is whether Chowgule became liable to Belcher contractually. While it is necessary to resolve a number of questions to determine that issue, the reasonableness of the charges and the status of the fuel as necessaries are irrelevant, and the methods of proving the authority of the person who placed the order differ.

The distinction between these types of proceedings is made clear by the Supplemental Rules. Attachment issues "with respect to any admiralty or maritime claim *in personam*" and its purpose is to "attach the defendant's goods and chattels" or other assets if the defendant shall not be found in the jurisdiction. Rule B. Attachment may be used for any debt. An action *in rem* on the other hand, is available only to enforce a maritime lien or when authorized by statute. Rule C. The arrest warrant extends only to the vessel "or other property that is the subject of the action." Rule C(3).

The Fourth Circuit has held that the judicial sale of a vessel in a Mexican bankruptcy action was sufficiently similar in substance to an American *in rem* action to remove an *in rem* lien on the vessel. *Gulf and Southern Terminal Corp. v. The SS President Roxas*, 701 F.2d 1110 (4th Cir.), *cert. denied*, — U.S. —, 103 S. Ct. 3115, 77 L. Ed. 2d 1369 (1983). In that case, the Mexican bankruptcy court had possession of the vessel, and sold it "free of encumbrances." The sale erased the lien despite the fact that Mexican law does not provide explicitly for an *in rem* proceeding both because the procedures employed were "virtually identical to those which are denominated as an *in rem* proceeding under American law" and because "the vessel was an asset of the bankrupt, under the control and proper jurisdiction of the Mexican court." *Id.* 701 F.2d at 1112. A bankruptcy court that has possession of any property has the power to sell the property free and clear of liens.[7]

Attachment does in many respects resemble arrest. In each proceeding the vessel is seized and it may later be sold to satisfy a judgment. In each, the vessel itself may be released and other security substituted. Nevertheless, not only do the issues in the two actions differ; the basic theory on which each is brought is different. In the *in rem* proceeding the owner bears no personal liability. The vessel is sold solely to satisfy the lien. If the proceeds of the sale are inadequate, there is no liability on the owner's part for the residue. Indeed the admiralty court will not render a personal judgment against the owner in excess of the amount of the release bond.[8] Only a personal action against the owner can establish such liability. In the attachment action, the object of the action is a personal judgment for the full sum due. The vessel is seized only to compel the owner's appearance by subjecting to the court's control property within its territorial jurisdiction. If the proceeds of sale of the vessel do not satisfy the judgment, the owner remains liable for the balance of the debt.

---

[7] *Matter of Buchman*, 600 F.2d 160, 165 (8th Cir.1979).

[8] *The Susana*, 2 F.2d 410, 412-13 (4th Cir.1924); *Red Star Towing & Transp. Co.*, 5 F. Supp. 502 (E.D.N.Y.1933); G. GILMORE & C. BLACK, *supra*, at 802.

In a few cases, however, owners appearing in an *in rem* action to contest the libelants' claims have been "treated as if they had been brought into court by personal process" and held personally liable for judgment in excess of the security. *The Fairisle*, 76 F. Supp. 27, 34 (D.Md.1947), *aff'd sub nom. Waterman S.S. Corp. v. Dean*, 171 F.2d 408 (4th Cir.1948)(quoted in *Treasure Salvors v. The Unidentified Wrecked and Abandoned Sailing Vessel*, 569 F.2d 330, 335 (5th Cir.1978)); *see also Mosher v. Tate*, 182 F.2d 475, 479-80 (9th Cir.1950); G. GILMORE & C. BLACK, *supra*, at 802-04.

Chowgule asserts that, when it provided security to release the vessel from attachment, this discharged the lien. With respect to the lien sought to be enforced, the release does transfer the lien from the vessel to the fund represented by the bond or letter of undertaking.[9] This does not imply that release from an attachment likewise clears the lien. An execution sale in an *in rem* proceeding clears the vessel of all liens.[10] An execution sale pursuant to a writ of attachment is not, however, the equivalent of a judicial sale in admiralty. The ship is not sold free of all liens; instead only the owner's interest, whatever it may be, is adjudicated.[11] Indeed, it could not do so, for the attachment bond does not substitute for a lien but only for the owner's personal liability.

In its analysis of the *lis alibis pendens* argument, the district court correctly stated the applicable rule: a court having jurisdiction should exercise it unless a compelling reason not to do so is demonstrated.[12] It found compelling reason, however, in the supposed hardship on Chowgule of defending two actions and in the possibility of double recovery. Both of these can readily be averted without the damage to Belcher that dismissal occasions. The Netherlands action has been tried and is awaiting decision. Staying proceedings in this action would avoid repetitive litigation of the issues there involved. If Belcher prevails, its judgment will be satisfied out of the security posted in that court. Thus both the expense of the second litigation and the possibility of double liability will be averted. If Chowgule prevails in the Netherlands action, its undertaking will be released and only those issues unique to the *in rem* action need be determined in the United States court. If, on the other hand, this action is dismissed and Belcher fails to prevail in the Netherlands action, it will be deprived of an opportunity to prove its claim *in rem*. No hardship is imposed on Chowgule by continuing the action, for the same undertaking posted in the Netherlands stands as security for the *in rem* action.

For these reasons the judgment is REVERSED and the case is REMANDED for further proceedings consistent with this opinion.

Question

If the defendant is not "found within the district" but is owed money by a debtor within the district, can the plaintiff garnish the debt? Is the debt an asset within the jurisdiction because the debtor is present there? *Day v. Temple Drilling Co.*, 613 F. Supp. 194 (S.D. Miss. 1985).

---

[9] *Gray v. Hopkins-Carter Hardware Co.* (The Lois), 32 F.2d 876, 878 (5th Cir.1929); G. Gilmore & C. Black, *supra*, at 799.

[10] *The Trenton*, 4 F. 657 (E.D.Mich.1880); *Zimmern Coal Co. v. Coal Trading Association of Rotterdam (The Totila x Harold)*, 30 F.2d 933 (5th Cir. 1929); G. Gilmore & C. Black, *supra*, at 787, *et seq.*

[11] G. Gilmore & C. Black, *supra*, at 802.

[12] *See Gulf Oil Corp. v. Gilbert*, 330 U.S. 501, 67 S. Ct. 839, 91 L. Ed. 1055 (1947); *The Belgenland*, 114 U.S. 355, 5 S. Ct. 860, 29 L. Ed. 152 (1885); *Chiazor v. Transworld Drilling Co. Ltd.*, 648 F.2d 1015, 1019 (5th Cir.1981); *Poseidon Schiffahrt, G.M.B.H. v. The M/S Netuno*, 474 F.2d 203, 204 (5th Cir.1973); *Perusahaan Umum Listrik Negara Pusat v. M/V Tel Aviv*, 711 F.2d 1231 (5th Cir.1983) (upholding conditional dismissal on *forum non conveniens* grounds because only connection with U.S. forum was in rem action and adequate alternative forum was substantially more convenient; conditional dismissal preserved plaintiff's rights and remedies).

4. Attachable property within the district

WINTER STORM SHIPPING, LTD v. TPI

310 F.3d 263 (2d Cir. 2002)

HAIGHT, Senior District Judge (sitting by designation)

Winter Storm Shipping, Ltd. ("Winter Storm") appeals from the January 11, 2002 Opinion and Order, 198 F.Supp.2d 385, and the January 16, 2002 Judgment of the District Court for the Southern District of New York (Shira A. Scheindlin, District Judge) vacating a maritime attachment of funds of defendants TPI, a/k/a Thai Petrochemical Industry Public Company Limited, Thai Petrochemical Industry PCl, TPI Oil (1997) Co., Ltd. and TPI Oil Co. Ltd. (collectively "TPI") in the hands of garnishee Bank of New York ("BNY") and dismissing Winter Storm's complaint for lack of jurisdiction over TPI. This appeal, involving the interplay between a centuries-old admiralty law procedure and present day banking technology, poses the question whether funds involved in electronic fund transfer ("EFT") between banks are subject to attachment under Rule B(1) of the Supplemental Rules for Certain Admiralty and Maritime Claims. The district court answered in the negative. We vacate the judgment of the district court and remand the case to that court with instructions to reinstate the attachment and retain jurisdiction.

BACKGROUND

Winter Storm, a foreign corporation with a place of business in Malta, chartered its vessel M/V NINEMIA to defendant-appellee TPI, a Thai corporation, to carry an oil cargo from Rabigh, Saudi Arabia, to Rayong, Thailand, in February and March, 2001. Winter Storm claims that TPI breached the charter party by failing to pay the full freight due and owes Winter Storm $361,621.58, an amount that includes interest and anticipated attorneys' and arbitrators' fees. The charter party provides for arbitration of disputes in London.

Winter Storm filed a complaint against TPI in the district court on June 21, 2001, and an amended complaint on June 26, 2001 (hereinafter the "complaint"), characterizing its claim as admiralty and maritime in nature under Rule 9(h), Fed.R.Civ.P., and invoking the district court's admiralty jurisdiction conferred by 28 U.S.C. § 1333. The complaint described the charter party of the NINEMIA, the voyage performed, and TPI's failure to pay the full freight, and asserted that "plaintiff has, or will shortly, nominate its arbitrator pursuant to the arbitration clause set forth in the contract of charter."

Winter Storm further alleged that TPI could not be "found within this District" within the meaning of Rule B of the Supplemental Rules for Certain Admiralty and Maritime Claims of the Federal Rules of Civil Procedure (the "Admiralty Rules") and sought an order directing the Clerk to issue process of maritime attachment and garnishment pursuant to Rule B and the Federal Arbitration Act ("FAA"), 9 U.S.C. § § 1, 8 attaching TPI's assets held by garnishees in the amount of $361,621.58.

Admiralty Rule B(1) provides:

> (a) If a defendant is not found within the district, a verified complaint may contain a prayer for process to attach the defendant's tangible or intangible personal property—up to the amount sued for—in the hands of garnishees named in the process.

The process of attachment prayed for by Winter Storm identified "Chase Manhattan Bank and/or Bank of New York" as potential garnishees.

Section 8 of the FAA, 9 U.S.C. § 8, which Winter Storm invoked in addition to Admiralty Rule B, makes maritime attachment available to parties to a maritime contract, such as a charter party, which contains an arbitration clause. The statute provides:

> If the basis of jurisdiction be a cause of action otherwise justiciable in admiralty, then, notwithstanding anything herein to the contrary, the party claiming to be aggrieved may begin his proceeding hereunder by libel and seizure of the vessel or other property of the other party according to the usual course of admiralty proceedings, and the court shall then have jurisdiction to direct the parties to proceed with the arbitration and shall retain jurisdiction to enter its decree upon the award.

The district court entered its *ex parte* order of attachment on June 22, 2002. Process of maritime attachment and garnishment was served upon BNY at 12:19 p.m. and 4:44 p.m. on June 28, 2001, and at 12:50 p.m. and 1:45 p.m. on June 29. At those times BNY did not hold any funds of TPI. However, as a result of these services of process BNY "not later than the close of business on June 28, 2001, placed a stop order on any funds relating to [TPI] passing through" BNY. Affidavit of David Rosenfield ("Rosenfield affidavit"), BNY's Manager—Legal Process and Senior Counsel, A-33.

TPI maintained an account with a Thai bank in Bangkok, the Bank of Ayudhya ("BA"), which in turn maintained an account at BNY. TPI entered into an unrelated commercial transaction with Oppsal Shipping Co., Ltd. ("Oppsal"), which maintained an account with the Royal Bank of Scotland in London ("RBS"). TPI's contract with Oppsal called for TPI to pay Oppsal in United States dollars. At 6:48 a.m. on July 2, 2001, BNY received from BA a payment order in respect of an EFT in the amount of $1,085,071.41 on behalf of TPI to the account of Oppsal at RBS. The transfer would be made electronically through BNY in New York City. BA was the originating bank and BNY acted as the intermediary bank.

Because BNY, in response to the earlier services of process of attachment procured by Winter Storm, had placed a stop order on TPI funds that might pass through it, BNY did not immediately execute BA's payment order that would have completed the electronic transfer of $1,085,071.41 by BA to RBS. Instead, BNY "placed $361,621.58 from the account of Bank of Ayudhya in a suspense account and issued a payment order in the amount of the balance of $723,449.83 to the account of Oppsal at The Royal Bank of

Scotland." Rosenfield affidavit, A-34. The deducted amount of $361,621.58 represents the total amount of Winter Storm's claims against TPI, as recited in the processes of attachment.

That sum was still anchored in BNY's suspense account when, at 10:59 a.m. on July 2, 2001, BNY was served with an additional process of maritime attachment on behalf of Winter Storm. BNY continued to hold these funds, now in obedience to the process. Had BNY not taken the earlier action of placing a stop order on any TPI funds that might pass through the bank, then "[i]n the ordinary course of business, The Bank would have executed the payment order well prior to the next service of process, which occurred at 10:59 a.m. on July 2, 2001." Rosenfield affidavit, A-35.

In these circumstances, TPI moved in the district court to vacate the attachment of the funds held by BNY in the suspense account. Winter Storm opposed TPI's motion. The district court granted TPI's motion to vacate the attachment and, since the attachment formed the sole basis for jurisdiction *quasi in rem* over TPI, dismissed Winter Storm's complaint for lack of jurisdiction. Judge Scheindlin held that an EFT intercepted at an intermediary bank is not "property" that can be attached under Admiralty Rule B. She reasoned principally that since the Admiralty Rules do not define "property" in this context, and "[t]here is no federal precedent on point," 198 F.Supp. at 388, recourse should be had to state law. That analysis led the district court to § 4-A-503 of the Uniform Commercial Code as adopted in New York, *see* N.Y. U.C.C. Art. 4A (McKinney 1991). Section 4-A-503 deals with court injunctions or restraining orders with respect to a "funds transfer," and provides that a court may "restrain" only the originator of a payment order (in this case TPI), the originator's bank (here, BA), or the beneficiary's bank (here, RBS). The section concludes: "A court may not otherwise restrain a person from issuing a payment order, paying or receiving payment of a payment order, or otherwise acting with respect to a funds transfer." The statutory scheme is intended to insulate an intermediary bank in a funds transfer bank from judicial restraint. *See* Official Comment, U.C.C. § 4-A-503 ("This section ... is designed to prevent interruption of a funds transfer after it has been set in motion[;] ... [i]n particular, intermediary banks are protected.").

Regarding U.C.C. § 4-A-503 as controlling, the district court vacated Winter Storm's maritime attachment and dismissed its complaint. This appeal followed.

DISCUSSION

I. Standard of Review

We review *de novo* the constructions of the statutes and rules and the conclusions of law upon which the district court based its opinion.

II. The History and Characteristics of Maritime Attachment

Maritime attachment is centuries old. "The use of the process of attachment in civil causes of maritime jurisdiction by courts of admiralty ... has prevailed during a period extending as far back as the authentic history of those tribunals can be traced." *Atkins v. Fibre Disintegrating Co.,* 85 U.S. (18 Wall.) 272, 303, 21 L.Ed. 841 (1873). As early as

1825, the Supreme Court was able to say of the right of attachment in *in personam* admiralty cases that "[t]his Court has entertained such suits too often, without hesitation, to permit the right now to be questioned." *Manro v. Almeida,* 23 U.S. (10 Wheat.) 473, 486, 6 L.Ed. 369 (1825). "[M]aritime attachment is a feature of admiralty jurisprudence that antedates both the congressional grant of admiralty jurisdiction to the federal district courts and the promulgation of the first Supreme Court Admiralty Rules in 1844." *Aurora Maritime Co. v. Abdullah Mohamed Fahem & Co.,* 85 F.3d 44, 47 (2d Cir.1996). Admiralty Rule B, quoted in part *supra,* contains the current provisions governing maritime attachment. [FN2] "Rule B is simply an extension of this ancient practice." *Aurora,* 85 F.3d at 47-48. A Rule B attachment is available only if the defendant "is not found within the district." "As developed by the courts, a defendant will be considered 'found within the district' in which the plaintiff brings its action if the defendant has sufficient contacts with the district to meet minimum due process standards *and* can be served with process in the district." Robert M. Jarvis, *An Introduction to Maritime Attachment Practice Under Rule B,* 20 Journal of Maritime Law and Commerce, No 4 (October 1989) at 521 (hereinafter "Jarvis").

"The rationale underlying maritime attachment is twofold. First, attachment provides a means to assure satisfaction if a suit is successful"; the second purpose is "to insure a defendant's appearance in an action, an aspect of attachment inextricably linked to a plaintiff's substantive right to recover." *Aurora,* 85 F.3d at 48 (internal citations omitted). *See also Manro v. Almeida,* 23 U.S. (10 Wheat.) at 489. The jurisdiction conferred by a maritime attachment is characterized as *quasi in rem. See Amoco Overseas Oil Co. v. Compagnie Nationale Algerienne de Navigation,* 605 F.2d 648, 654 (2d Cir.1979).

Maritime attachment is available whenever "the plaintiff has an *in personam* claim against the defendant which is cognizable in admiralty.... In other words, the plaintiff's claim must be one which will support a finding of admiralty jurisdiction under 28 U.S.C. § 1333." Jarvis, at 526 & n. 20.

The property attached need not have a direct connection to the claim sued upon, since Rule B(1)(a), broadly phrased, allows attachment of "the defendant's tangible or intangible personal property," limited only by "the amount sued for." The case at bar is illustrative; TPI's funds attached by Winter Storm in the hands of BNY were generated by a transaction bearing no relationship to the charter party underlying Winter Storm's claim.

III. Due Process

The district court vacated Winter Storm's attachment principally on the ground that U.C.C. § 4-A-503 precluded EFT funds in the hands of an intermediary bank from being regarded as TPI's "property" within the meaning of Admiralty Rule B. But Judge Scheindlin also said that "[p]ermitting wire transfer credits to be attached at unforeseen and unknown intermediary banks runs contrary to the (minimal) due process accorded maritime defendants." 198 F.Supp.2d at 391. The district court reasoned that a maritime defendant must be reasonably able to foresee being sued in the United States based on the location of its property, citing *Schiffahartsgesellschaft Leonhardt & Co. v. A. Bottacchi S.A. de Navegacion,*

773 F.2d 1528, 1536 (11th Cir.1985) (which relied in turn upon *Amoco,* 605 F.2d 648) and *Engineering Equipment Co. v. S.S. Selene,* 446 F.Supp. 706, 710 (S.D.N.Y.1978), and "decline[d] to endorse a rule stating that every time a foreign maritime entity initiates a wire transfer abroad, it must foresee attachment in New York and suit in the United States." *Winter Storm,* 198 F.Supp.2d at 391 n. 7. TPI urges this due process theory in resisting Winter Storm's appeal. We address the question first because if Winter Storm's attachment fails to pass constitutional due process muster the district court lacked jurisdiction and no other questions can arise.

We begin by noting that in the early days of American admiralty practice, plaintiffs (or "libelants," in the former parlance) simply obtained processes of maritime attachment from the clerk of the district court, without the participation of a judge. *See Manro v. Almeida,* 23 U.S. (10 Wheat.) 473, 6 L.Ed. 369, vintage 1825, where the Court, upholding the attachment, stated in matter-of-fact fashion that "[t]he clerk, it seems, issued the attachment as process of course," *id.* at 485. [FN3] That practice, formerly provided for by Admiralty Rule 2, was continued without substantive change when in 1966, 141 years after the Court decided *Manro v. Almeida,* the civil and admiralty rules were merged and Admiralty Rule 2 became Supplemental Rule B. *See* the Advisory Committee Notes to the 1966 adoption ("[Rule B(1)] preserves the traditional maritime remedy of attachment and garnishment, and carries forward the relevant substance of Admiralty Rule 2."). The Advisory Committee Notes go on to say:

> The former Admiralty Rules did not provide for notice to the defendant in attachment and garnishment proceedings. *None is required by the principles of due process,* since it is assumed that the garnishee or custodian of the property attached will either notify the defendant or be deprived of the right to plead the judgment as a defense in an action against him by the defendant. *Harris v. Balk,* 198 U.S. 215, 25 S.Ct. 625, 49 L.Ed. 1023 (1905); *Pennoyer v. Neff,* 95 U.S. 714, 24 L.Ed. 565 (1878). Modern conceptions of fairness, however, dictate that actual notice be given to persons known to claim an interest in the property that is the subject of the action where that is reasonably practicable. In attachment and garnishment proceedings the persons whose interests will be affected by the judgment are identified by the complaint. No substantial burden is imposed on the plaintiff by a simple requirement that he notify the defendant of the action by mail.

(emphasis added).

In 1966, then, the perception of the rules drafters was that the original maritime attachment rule posed no due process jurisdictional problems, and that the notice-by-mail requirement, new to the rule, satisfied the more generalized "modern conceptions of fairness."

That perception underwent something of a sea change "following various non-maritime decisions by the United States Supreme Court which mandated a reconsideration of traditional notions of due process." Jarvis at 523 (citing cases, among them *Shaffer v. Heitner,* 433 U.S. 186, 97 S.Ct. 2569, 53 L.Ed.2d 683 (1977)).

Shaffer, which did not involve a maritime claim, held that *quasi in rem* jurisdiction must satisfy the same due process requirements set with respect to *in personam* jurisdiction in *International Shoe Co. v. Washington,* 326 U.S. 310, 66 S.Ct. 154, 90 L.Ed. 95 (1945) and its progeny. *See Shaffer,* 433 U.S. at 207-12, 97 S.Ct. 2569. In *Shaffer,* the Delaware courts' assertion of jurisdiction was premised on the sequestration of stock that was conceptually located in Delaware because it was issued by a Delaware corporation; the Supreme Court reversed, noting, *inter alia,* that the stock was not the subject matter of the litigation and that the underlying cause of action did not relate to the stock. Thus, the constitutional requirement of at least minimal contacts was not met. *Id.* at 213-17, 97 S.Ct. 2569.

In *Amoco,* 605 F.2d 648, this Court considered the possible effect of *Shaffer* upon *quasi in rem* jurisdiction based upon the New York attachment statute, made applicable by Admiralty Rule B. Although the underlying claim for breach of charter party was maritime in nature, the validity of the attachment turned solely upon New York law, for reasons explained in *Amoco,* 605 F.2d at 650:

> The attachment was effected under state law, N.Y.C.P.L.R. § § 6201 *et seq.,* pursuant to Fed.R.Civ.P. Supplemental Rule B (for certain admiralty and maritime claims). By inadvertence, appellees did not also utilize the federal procedure which may be employed "in addition" under Rule B(1). Accordingly, it was incumbent upon them to perfect their state *quasi in rem* jurisdictional base by complying with New York statutory requirements. § 6214.

The *Amoco* court held that plaintiff had complied with the New York attachment statute. 605 F.2d at 652-54. The court then had to deal with defendant's "challenge to the jurisdiction of the court below," based upon "the due process clause as it restricts the assertion of personal jurisdiction through proceedings by attachment." *Id.* at 654. Defendant argued that plaintiff's attachment was invalid under the ruling in *Shaffer,* whose effect the *Amoco* court described:

> *Shaffer* completed the process of supplanting the old doctrine of personal jurisdiction based upon state sovereignty with a newer theory of personal jurisdiction stemming from notions of due process. Under the regime of *Shaffer,* the test of " 'fair play and substantial justice' " that governs in personam jurisdiction controls in rem jurisdiction as well. But this extension of the "fair play" test to the ostensible exercise of jurisdiction over property is not necessarily incompatible with the principle of jurisdiction quasi in rem because the presence of property in a State may bear on the existence of jurisdiction by providing contacts among the forum State, the defendant, and the litigation. The real teaching of *Shaffer* is that courts must look at realities and not be led astray by fictions.

Id. at 654-55 (citations and internal quotation marks omitted).

Analyzing *Shaffer* from that standpoint, and upholding the validity of the attachment in *Amoco,* the *Amoco* court discerned "several distinguishing [factors].... First, and most notable, is the fact that here, unlike *Shaffer,* the property attached is related to the matter in controversy. Far from being present in New York adventitiously, the freights that were attached were in [garnishee] Poten's accounts in New York pursuant to the Charter Party." *Id.* at 655 (citations omitted). *Amoco* also noted that "the parties to the Charter also specified that arbitration was to take place in New York," an agreement which "carries considerable weight in demonstrating that it is not unfair to require the parties to litigate in the forum in which arbitration was designated to take place." *Id.*

Although the *Amoco* court had said that the validity of the attachment turned solely upon the New York statute, the court went on to discuss *Shaffer* in the contexts of admiralty jurisdiction and maritime attachment:

> ... *Shaffer* did not consider assertion of jurisdiction over property in the admiralty context. Because the perpetrators of maritime injury are likely to be peripatetic, and since the constitutional power of the federal courts is separately derived in admiralty, U.S. Constitution Art. III § 2, suits under admiralty jurisdiction involve separate policies to some extent. This tradition suggests not only that jurisdiction by attachment of property should be accorded special deference in the admiralty context, but also that maritime actors must reasonably expect to be sued where their property may be found.

605 F.2d at 655 (citation omitted).

While the *Amoco* court found it unnecessary to decide whether, as "[a]t least one district court in another jurisdiction has held," *Shaffer* "does not affect jurisdiction obtained under Admiralty Rule B attachment," it went on to say that "even if the *Shaffer* rule of 'minimum contacts'/'fair play' applies in the realm of jurisdiction by attachment in admiralty, that application must be understood in the light of the special history and circumstances of that unique body of law." *Id.* at 655 n. 7 (citations omitted).

Given its procedural circumstances, *Amoco* cannot be regarded as a square holding, one way or the other, on the applicability of *Shaffer*-style due process requirements to maritime attachments. Such indications as may be gleaned from the opinion seem to point in the direction of subjecting admiralty attachments to less stringent requirements.

A number of district and circuit courts were required to confront head-on the possible effect of *Shaffer* and comparable non-maritime cases decided by the Supreme Court in the 1970s upon maritime attachment under Admiralty Rule B as it existed subsequent to the 1966 merger with the civil rules. Various maritime defendants contended that "Rule B was unconstitutional because it 1) permitted plaintiffs to proceed in an *ex parte* fashion; and, 2) authorized the clerk of the court to grant the plaintiff's attachment request." Jarvis at 523.

These constitutional challenges had only limited success. In his 1989 article Professor Jarvis was in a position to say: "Although some of these challenges succeeded at the district court level, every appellate court which had the opportunity to review the constitutionality of Rule B concluded that it was valid," citing as examples *Leonhardt,* 773 F.2d 1528, *Trans-Asiatic Oil, Ltd. S.A. v. Apex Oil Co.,* 743 F.2d 956 (1st Cir.1984), and *Polar Shipping Ltd. v. Oriental Shipping Corp.,* 680 F.2d 627 (9th Cir.1982).

Notwithstanding the unanimity of the post-*Shaffer* appellate decisions upholding the constitutionality of Admiralty Rule B, the drafters of the rules amended Rule B(1) in 1985 in order to address any possible due process concerns. While the practice of granting maritime attachments on an *ex parte* basis remains, Rule B(1) now requires the plaintiff to appear before a judge to procure an attachment. *See* Rule B(1)(b) ("The court must review the complaint and affidavit and, if the conditions of this Rule B appear to exist, enter an order so stating and authorizing process of attachment and garnishment."). The Advisory Committee Notes to the 1985 amendments explain their purpose:

> Rule B(1) has been amended to provide for judicial scrutiny before the issuance of any attachment or garnishment process. Its purpose is to eliminate doubts as to whether the Rule is consistent with the principles of procedural due process enunciated by the Supreme Court (citing cases). Such doubts were raised in *Grand Bahama Petroleum Co. v. Canadian Transportation Agencies, Ltd.,* 450 F.Supp. 447 (W.D.Wash.1978); and *Schiffahartsgesellschaft Leonhardt & Co. v. A. Bottacchi S.A. De Navegacion,* 552 F.Supp. 771 (S.D.Ga.1982), which was reversed, 732 F.2d 1543 (11th Cir.1984). But compare *Polar Shipping Ltd. v. Oriental Shipping Corp.,* 680 F.2d 627 (9th Cir.1982), in which a majority of the panel upheld the constitutionality of Rule B because of the unique commercial context in which it is invoked....

The 1985 amendments to the Admiralty Rules also included an addition to Rule E, which contains general provisions for practice in actions *in rem* and *quasi in rem.* New Rule E(4)(f) provides: "Whenever property is arrested or attached, any person claiming an interest in it shall be entitled to a prompt hearing at which the plaintiff shall be required to show why the arrest or attachment should not be vacated or other relief granted consistent with these rules." [FN6] The Advisory Committee notes explain that "Rule E(4)(f) is designed to satisfy the constitutional requirement of due process by guaranteeing to the shipowner a prompt post-seizure hearing at which he can attack the complaint, the arrest, the security demanded, or any other alleged deficiency in the proceedings."

It does not appear that any court subsequent to the 1985 amendments has questioned the constitutionality of maritime attachment under Rule B, let alone holding the Rule and the admiralty practice under it constitutionally infirm on due process grounds. In this Circuit *Aurora,* 85 F.3d 44, and *ContiChem LPG v. Parsons Shipping Co., Ltd.,* 229 F.3d 426 (2d Cir.2000), dealt with Rule B(1) maritime attachments after the 1985 amendments became effective on August 1 of that year. Neither decision evidences any due process concern, and the *ContiChem* court observed with seeming equanimity:

> Although a plaintiff seeking attachment must supply, along with its verified complaint, an affidavit stating that defendant cannot be found within the district, little else is required and there need only be a hearing after the attachment is served. *See* Rule B(1).

229 F.3d at 434. This Court also expressed no due process concerns in *Reibor International Ltd. v. Cargo Carriers (KACZ-CO.) Ltd.*, 759 F.2d 262 (2d Cir.1985), where the maritime attachment was procured under the original Admiralty Rule B; *Reibor* was decided in April 1985, four months before the 1985 amendments to Rules B and E became effective.

Due process concerns having been expressed in the case before us, they must be assessed in the light of the 1985 amendments to Admiralty Rules B and E. The district court did not refer to those amendments, and the cases the court cited antedate them. Under the rules as presently worded, process of maritime attachment cannot issue (absent exigent circumstances) unless a judge authorizes the process, and a defendant property owner is entitled to prompt notice of the attachment and a court hearing to test its validity. These amendments were fashioned for the stated purpose of addressing due process concerns. No court has subsequently suggested that the amendments were inadequate to that task.

The practical effect of the district court's analysis is that, in addition to the due process safeguards the 1985 amendments extended to defendants, funds in an EFT can never be subjected to maritime attachment unless the defendant also had specific advance knowledge of the name and address of the intermediary bank. We do not agree that so significant a restriction should be placed upon the traditional admiralty practice of maritime attachment. The use of EFTs, product of the modern electronic age, is widespread in international trade. Banking networks serving global commerce tend to use intermediary banks in the world's financial capitals such as New York, a wholly foreseeable arrangement that this Court noted in *Reibor,* 759 F.2d at 266: "Often, when a person in one foreign country makes a payment in U.S. dollars to someone in another foreign country, the payment clears through New York."

Indeed, the commercial and financial facts in *Reibor* closely resemble those in this case. The Spanish shipper of the cargo the chartered vessel carried to Jordan instructed its Madrid bank to transfer funds to the Canadian charterer's bank in Canada. "These funds passed through New York branch banks to effect the exchange into dollars." 759 F.2d at 264. The shipowner, claiming a breach of charter, served process of maritime attachment on the New York banks, taking the position that the funds in the EFT were property of the charterer and attachable under Admiralty Rule B. The attachments failed because at the time they were served the funds had not yet been transferred to the New York intermediary banks. We discuss *Reibor* in other contexts *supra,* but note for present purposes that *Reibor* voices no due process concerns in a case where the relevant circumstances are indistinguishable from the present case.

We regard the due process safeguards added by the 1985 amendments to Admiralty Rules B and E as sufficient to satisfy constitutional requirements, and discern in the due process clause no basis for rendering the traditional remedy of maritime attachment inapplicable to electronic transfers of funds familiar to those engaged in international trade and increasingly used by them. Accordingly we hold that when an individual or company transfers funds by means of an EFT, those funds may be subjected to maritime attachment in the hands of an intermediary bank without violating constitutional due process, whether or not the initiator of the transfer knew which intermediary bank would be used to effect it.

It is true that unlike *Amoco,* the funds of TPI attached in the hands of BNY bore no relationship to the underlying charter party, but maritime attachment has never required such a relationship. In *Manro v. Almeida,* 23 U.S. (10 Wheat.) 473, 6 L.Ed. 369, the property attached had nothing to do with the out-of-district defendant's maritime tort. More recently, *ContiChem,* 229 F.3d at 429, and *Aurora,* 85 F.3d at 46, involved the maritime attachment of defendants' bank accounts which, as in the present case, bore no relationship to the underlying claim.

It follows that if TPI's funds involved in the EFT constituted "property" of TPI within the meaning of Admiralty Rule B(1), those funds are subject to a valid maritime attachment, unless U.C.C. § 4-A-503 requires a different result. To those questions we now turn.

IV. EFT Funds as "Property" for Purposes of Maritime Attachment

In determining whether TPI's funds in the hands of BNY during the implementation of an EFT constituted "property" of TPI for purposes of Admiralty Rule B(1), we confront a question this Circuit left undecided in *Reibor,* 759 F.2d 262.

Plaintiff Reibor chartered its vessel to defendant Cargo, a Canadian company that could not be found within the Southern District of New York. Alleging breaches of charter by Cargo, Reibor served Admiralty Rule B writs of attachment on the New York branches of Manufacturers Hanover Trust Co. ("MHT/NY") and the Royal Bank of Canada ("RBC/NY"). Reibor was attempting to attach funds to be remitted to Cargo under a letter of credit calling for the transfer of funds from the Madrid branch of Manufacturers Hanover ("MHT/Madrid") to the Royal Bank of Canada at Montreal ("RBC/Montreal").

Reibor served two Rule B processes on MHT/NY, one on January 28 and the other on February 8, 1983. But it was not until February 11 that MHT/Madrid instructed MHT/NY to make an interbank transfer to RBC/NY through the Clearing House Interbank Payments System ("CHIPS"), a system for the electronic transfer of funds among member banks through a central computer. Reibor also served a process on RBC/NY at 10:25 a.m. on February 11, but RBC/NY did not receive the CHIPS credit until 2:21 p.m. on that day. A fourth process, served on February 14 or 15, "came too late: RBC/NY had wired the money to RBC/Montreal at 3:22 p.m. on February 11." 759 F.2d at 264.

In these circumstances, this Court identified the question on appeal as "the validity of a maritime garnishment served before the garnishee comes into possession of the property to be garnished." 759 F.2d at 263. In other words, the issue was whether a Rule B attachment covers "after-acquired property," that is, property of a defendant coming into the possession of a garnishee after service of process upon the garnishee.

The *Reibor* court concluded that on the question of after-acquired property, "the precedent in federal admiralty law is so thin that we should turn to state law more directly on point." 759 F.2d at 266. The court found that law in N.Y. C.P.L.R. § 6214(b), as explicated in McLaughlin's Practice Commentary: where the order of attachment is left with a third-party garnishee, "the levy is absolutely void unless the garnishee has some property belonging to the defendant or owes the defendant a debt at the time the order is left with him." N.Y. C.P.L.R. § 7B (McKinney 1980). Applying that state law principle to Reibor's Admiralty Rule B attachments, and given the chronology summarized above, this Court concluded that Reibor's processes were absolutely void.

As an alternative basis for vacating the attachments, both MHT/NY and RBC/NY argued that "a CHIPS credit is not property subject to attachment under the Admiralty Rules." *Reibor,* 759 F.2d at 264. This Court did not reach that question in *Reibor,* preferring to reserve it for "another day when somebody has served a writ of attachment on a bank either after it has received instructions from its forwarding bank to transfer a CHIPS credit but before it has made the transfer, or after it has received a CHIPS credit but before it has transferred any funds related thereto." *Id.* at 268-269. With the present case, that day has dawned.

As *Reibor* indicates, while "Federal law generally governs questions as to the validity of Rule B attachments," 759 F.2d at 265, state law may be borrowed if there is no federal admiralty law in point on the particular question presented. In support of this practice the *Reibor* court cited *Det Bergenske Dampskibsselskab v. Sabre Shipping Corp.,* 341 F.2d 50 (2d Cir.1965), an earlier example in this Circuit of looking to state law for guidance with respect to the effect of a maritime attachment. In *Reibor* the particular question presented was whether a writ of maritime attachment covered after-acquired property. In *Bergenske* the question was whether a writ of maritime attachment served on a branch office located in the Eastern District of New York was effective to attach a bank account at a branch office of the same bank located in the Southern District. The *Bergenske* court, while declaring that "[t]his argument must be dealt with according to federal law," also observed that "there is no established admiralty doctrine on this question, such as would reflect a predominant federal interest," and accordingly turned to state cases holding that "accounts in a foreign branch bank are not subject to attachment or execution by the process of a New York court served in New York on a main office, branch, or agency of the bank." 341 F.2d at 52-53 (citations omitted).

Reibor and *Bergenske* demonstrate that in order to decide whether TPI's funds involved in the EFT constituted TPI's property under Admiralty Rule B, we must first determine whether governing federal law provides the answer, in general terms or otherwise; or whether federal law is silent on the particular question presented, so that recourse may appropriately be had to state law. In Judge Scheindlin's view, "[t]he leading Second Circuit case on maritime attachment makes clear that whether a funds transfer at an intermediary bank constitutes property remains unanswered by federal courts," 198 F.Supp.2d at 389, citing credits, for some period of time before transferring them on to the destination banks. While claimants would have us believe that modern technology moved the funds from the originating bank through the intermediary bank to their ultimate destination without stopping, that was not the case. With each EFT at least two separate transactions occurred: first, funds moved from the originating bank to the intermediary bank; then the intermediary bank was to transfer the funds to the destination bank, a correspondent bank in Colombia. While the two transactions can occur almost instantaneously, sometimes they are separated by several days. Each of the amounts at issue was seized at the intermediary bank after the first transaction had concluded and before the second had begun.

6 F.3d at 54.

That is precisely what happened in the instant case. The processes of attachment Winter Storm seeks to enforce were served upon BNY after funds had moved from BA, the originating bank, to BNY as intermediary bank, but before BNY transferred the funds to RBS, the destination bank.

The *Daccarett* court's analysis of an EFT led to its conclusion that "an EFT while it takes the form of a bank credit at an intermediary bank is clearly a seizable *res* under the forfeiture statutes." 6 F.3d at 55. There is no principled basis for applying a different analysis or arriving at a different conclusion in the instant case. It is of no moment that *Daccarett* was a drug case and this is an admiralty case, or that the civil forfeiture statute and the Admiralty Rules differ in their descriptions of the circumstances justifying process against property, or that in *Daccarett* the government used Admiralty Rule C to arrest the funds while Winter Storm used Rule B to attach them. These are distinctions without a difference because they do not bear upon the decisive question presented, namely, whether EFT funds in the hands of an intermediary bank are subject to interdiction by legal process. *Daccarett's* holding that such funds are subject to Admiralty Rule C arrest furnishes authority for the conclusion that they are equally subject to Admiralty Rule B attachment. We reach that conclusion in this case.

It follows that the broad, inclusive language of Admiralty Rule B(1)(a) and the EFT analysis in *Daccarett* combine to fashion a rule in this Circuit that EFT funds in the hands of an intermediary bank may be attached pursuant to Admiralty Rule B(1)(a). Because that rule is derived from federal law, there is no occasion to look for guidance in state law. However, the district court looked to state law as embodied in U.C.C. § 4-A-503 and held it was fatal to Winter Storm's attachment. Even if, contrary to the conclusion we have just expressed, it was appropriate to consider state law, this provision of the U.C.C. cannot abrogate Winter Storm's right to a maritime attachment.

[The Court went on to hold that Supplemental Admiralty Rule B preempts the New York state enactment of U.C.C. § 4-A-503, which prohibits courts from restraining EFT funds in the hands of an intermediary bank. Eds.]

CONCLUSION

For the foregoing reasons, we vacate the judgment of the district court and remand the case to that court with instructions to reinstate the maritime attachment obtained by Winter Storm and to retain jurisdiction in the case in accordance with the principles and practices of federal admiralty law.

---

5. Questions of Constitutionality

Note: Due Process Requirements in a Maritime Context

Constitutional questions have been raised with respect to Supplemental Rules B, C and E. These include procedural due process issues involving lack of notice and hearing because of the ex parte nature of maritime arrest and attachment. They also include substantive considerations with regard to the exercise of jurisdiction through the seizure of the property of non-residence. Some of these issues are discussed in *Schiffahartsgesellschaft Leonhardt & Co. v. A. Bottacchi*, 773 F.2d 1528, 1986 AMC 1 (11th Cir. 1985).

Note: Federal Rules of Civil Procedure

Rule 4

(k) Territorial Limits of Effective Service

(1) Service of a summons or filing a waiver of service is effective to establish jurisdiction over the person of a defendant

(A) who could be subjected to the jurisdiction of a court of general jurisdiction in the state in which the district court is located, or
(B) who is a party joined under Rule 14 or Rule 19 and is served at a place within a judicial district of the United States and not more than 100 miles from the place from which the summons issues, or
(C) who is subject to the federal interpleader jurisdiction under 28 U.S.C. § 1335, or
(D) when authorized by a statute of the United States.

(2) If the exercise of jurisdiction is consistent with the Constitution and laws of the United States, serving a summons or filing a waiver of service is also effective, with respect to claims arising under federal law, to establish personal jurisdiction over the person of any defendant who is not subject to the jurisdiction of the courts of general jurisdiction of any state.

Note: Venue in Admiralty Cases

In ordinary admiralty *in personam* cases, unlike civil cases, venue is not statutorily prescribed. Rule 82 of the Federal Rules of Civil Procedure states:

> These rules shall not be construed to extend or limit the jurisdiction of the United States district courts or the venue of actions therein. An admiralty or maritime claim within the meaning of Rule 9(h) shall not be treated as a civil action for the purposes of Title 28, U.S.C. §§ 1391-93.[Venue provisions for civil cases.]

Thus, in ordinary *in personam* admiralty actions, venue lies in any place where defendant may be properly served. In rem actions and actions commenced by attachment may be brought in any place where defendants property may be seized. As the Supreme Court stated in *In re Louisville Underwriters*, 134 U.S. 488, 10 S. Ct. 587, 33 L. Ed. 991 (1890):

> By the ancient and settled practice of courts of admiralty, a libel *in personam* may be maintained for any cause of action within their jurisdiction, whenever a monition can be served on the libelee, or an attachment made of any personal property or credits of his; ...

The Jones Act provides that "Jurisdiction in such actions shall be under the court of the district in which the defendant employer resides or in which his principal office is located." 46 U.S.C.A. §§ 30104-30105 (formerly 46 app. U.S.C. § 688). This not only has been interpreted as a venue provision, but the Supreme Court has held that Jones Act plaintiffs may avail themselves of the liberalized venue provisions of 28 U.S.C. § 1391(c) which designates as the residence of a corporation "any judicial district in which it is subject to personal jurisdiction at the time the action is commenced." *Pure Oil Co. v. Suarez*, 384 U.S. 202, 86 S. Ct. 1394, 16 L. Ed. 2d 474 (1966).

28 U.S.C. § 1404 permits a court in which suit has been properly brought to transfer the case to another court where it could have been commenced for the convenience of the parties or in the interest of justice. This statute has been used in admiralty cases and seems to apply even where the action is brought *in rem*. *Continental Grain Co v. The FBL-585 and Federal Barge Lines, Inc.*, 364 U.S. 19, 80 S. Ct. 1470, 4 L. Ed. 2d 1450 (1960).

Chapter 4

CARRIAGE OF GOODS

A. Carriage Under Bills of Lading

1. Historical Introduction

From the General Maritime Law to the Carriage of Goods by Sea Act (COGSA)

During the eighteenth and nineteenth centuries, legislation and judicial practice in many countries in pursuit of "national" maritime policies displaced the venerable uniform "law of the sea" and gave rise to a sharp conflict of laws. By the end of the 19th century divergences in the regulation of sea-carriers' liability under contracts of affreightment evidenced by bills of lading had attracted attention and caused concern. The most spectacular conflict involved the question of the validity of "negligence" clauses, namely clauses designed to exonerate the carrier from liability for negligence in connection with damage to the cargo.

In some countries cargo interests prevailed and strict liability was imposed on carriers for loss or damage to the goods carried; in other countries hull interests prevailed, and carriers enjoyed an almost unlimited freedom of contract. Moreover, the national policy favoring either the shipper or the carrier was frequently extended through the adoption of choice of law rules designed to safeguard application of national law to bills of lading involving international contracts. Thus, due to varying substantive standards and conflicts rules, a negligence clause inserted in an international bill of lading could be valid in one country and invalid in another, and the liability of the carrier could differ with the forum. As a result, security in international transactions was endangered, the negotiability of bills of lading was imperiled, and world trade was seriously hampered.

Under the general maritime law of the United States as it existed until the middle of the 19th century, the contract of affreightment was generally enforceable according to its terms. Beginning in the 1880's, however, most state courts and federal courts consistently refused to enforce "unreasonable" stipulations inserted in domestic or international bills of lading. Soon it became "settled law" and "elementary doctrine" that exemptions limiting carriers from responsibility for the negligence of themselves or their servants were both "unjust and unreasonable, wanting in voluntary assent ... and in conflict with public policy."

See The Kensington, 183 U.S. 263, 268, 46 L.Ed. 190 (1902). This legal regime did not successfully safeguard American cargo interests, because most cargo to or from the United States was carried in British ships, and it did not encourage the growth of American shipping industries. In order to attain these aims, the Harter Act (46 U.S.C.A. §§ 30701-30707, formerly 46 U.S.C. §§ 190-196) was passed in 1893.

It has been said that the Harter Act was enacted as a result of pressure from American carriers by water who "were naturally unhappy with the decisions prohibiting bills of lading 'negligence' clauses and holding them liable for the consequences of unseaworthiness, even when caused by no fault on their part" and "pressed for legislation entitling them to do what their British competitors were allowed to do under the English decisions, *i.e.*, contract away their liability for cargo loss, damage and delay caused by fault and unseaworthiness." HEALY AND SHARPE, CASES AND MATERIALS ON ADMIRALTY 300 (2d ed. 1986). However, it has been also said that it was the discontent of shippers of cargo, of their underwriters and bankers, who "forced a statutory solution of the problem, at least to the extent of legislating 'certain rules' agreed to by all interested parties and of forbidding certain other clauses, and of leaving the remaining field of free contract for further consideration by the courts." KNAUTH, THE AMERICAN LAW OF OCEAN BILLS OF LADING 116 (4th ed. 1953).

Whether the Harter Act was originally conceived as an instrument of international trade war or as a concession to American cargo interests, it was in fact a compromise between shippers' and carriers' interests. Under the Act, clauses relieving the shipowner from liability for negligence were declared "null and void and of no effect," but the shipowner was relieved from liability for negligence "in navigation or in the management" of the vessel if he used due diligence to make his vessel "seaworthy." Initially designed to apply only to foreign trade, the Harter Act was extended to cover domestic trade as well and was declared applicable to all shipments to and from the ports of the United States. This Act still plays an important role in the regulation of both the domestic and the international trade of the United States.

The United States, having succeeded in reaching this compromise between the conflicting interests of shippers and carriers, took the lead in urging a uniform international regulation of the sea-carriers' liabilities along similar lines. The need for such regulation was generally felt, and action was taken by interested business groups and international organizations, such as the International Law Association and the Comité Maritime International. After several decades of preparatory work and backstage negotiations, the International Law Association adopted at its Hague meeting in 1921 a body of rules known as "Hague Rules, 1921." The Hague Rules were drafted in the form of a uniform bill of lading in the hope that the great shipping companies would adopt them voluntarily and that smaller operators would follow suit. The carriers, however, were not prepared to give up their extensive immunities under the then existing laws of several countries, and it became apparent that legislative action was necessary to make the new rules a part of bills of lading. Introduction of uniform legislation by a number of contracting states in accordance with the provisions of an international convention seemed to be the proper way, and a tentative Draft Convention incorporating the Hague Rules was submitted by the Belgian

Government to the Fifth Diplomatic Conference on Maritime Law (Brussels, October 1922). The original text of the Hague Rules was extensively discussed by the Conference in a number of sessions, and a final text was agreed upon. In the following year, the Rules were slightly amended by a committee appointed by the Conference, and finally, the movement for uniformity culminated in an International Convention for the Unification of Certain Rules of Law relating to Bills of Lading, signed in Brussels on August 25, 1924.

The Brussels Convention was not conceived as a comprehensive and self-sufficient code regulating the carriage of goods by sea; it was intended merely to unify certain rules relating to bills of lading, and only with regard to damages occurring to hull cargo (live animals excepted) between the time of loading and discharge. All bills of lading covered by the Convention were subject to certain standard clauses that define both the risks assumed by the carrier that cannot be altered by contrary agreement, and the immunities the carrier can enjoy unless the parties agree otherwise. In general, clauses relieving the carrier from liability for negligence in the loading, handling, stowing, keeping, carrying, and the discharge of the goods or diminishing his obligation to furnish a seaworthy vessel are declared null and void. The carrier is relieved from liability for negligence in "navigation or in the management" of the vessel and from the absolute warranty of seaworthiness. According to its Article X, the Convention applies to all bills of lading issued in any of the contracting States.

It was hoped that by balancing the conflicting policies of maritime nations and the interests of shippers and carriers, the Brussels Convention would standardize the liabilities of carriers on the international level. And it was expected that, as to matters regulated by the Convention, the outcome of litigation would be the same in the courts of any of the contracting states. The optimism that prevailed at the time the Convention was signed has largely been vindicated. Most of the maritime nations have ratified or adhered to the Brussels Convention; other countries, without formally adhering to the Convention, have enacted special legislation incorporating the rules agreed on in Brussels. In spite of this substantial formal uniformity of domestic legislation, however, problems in the determination of the carriers' liability and the validity of negligence clauses in bills of lading still persist. The very text of the Convention, as finally adopted, left the door open for subsequent variations to the prejudice of the desired uniformity. States adopted the rules with modifications and textual variations using various legislative methods; hence, conflicts among texts incorporating the uniform rules as well as conflicting interpretations are possible. Moreover, the area of application of the uniform rules and the choice of law applied to bills of lading outside the scope of the rules may differ from country to country. These divergences in domestic legislation and choice of law rules breed uncertainty. Depending on the place of litigation, the same bill of lading may or may not be subject to the uniform rules, even where the forum is a contracting country and the bill of lading involves contacts with another contracting nation. In certain cases the liability of the carrier may vary with the forum, and a negligence clause may be valid in one country and invalid in another, which is contrary to both the letter and spirit of the Brussels Convention.

In 1936 the United States enacted the Carriage of Goods by Sea Act (COGSA) (46 U.S.C. § 30701, Statutory Note, formerly 46 U.S.C. §§ 1300-1312), which adopted with some variation the text of Articles I to VIII of the Convention, and included provisions defining its area of application and its relation to other legislation of the United States. Less than a year after COGSA became effective, the United States deposited its ratification of the Brussels Convention (June 29, 1937). Textual variations between the Carriage of Goods by Sea Act and the Convention give rise to the question of the binding force of the latter on courts and individuals in the United States. Under the United States Constitution, an international treaty, if self-executing, is part of the law of the land. The Brussels Convention, however, was ratified subject to an "understanding" that, if the provisions of the Convention and the provisions of the Carriage of Goods by Sea Act should conflict, the Act shall prevail over the Convention. Thus, while a part of the law of the United States, the Convention is not directly binding upon courts and individuals; the law governing bills of lading is to be found in COGSA and related legislation.

2. Legislation

The Harter Act

46 U.S.C.A. §§ 30701 – 30707

§ 30701. Definition

In this chapter, the term "carrier" means the owner, manager, charterer, agent, or master of a vessel.

§ 30702. Application

(a) In General—Except as otherwise provided, this chapter applies to a carrier engaged in the carriage of goods to or from any port in the United States.

(b) Live Animals—Sections 30703 and 30704 of this title do not apply to the carriage of live animals.

§ 30703. Bills of Lading

(a) Issuance—On demand of a shipper, the carrier shall issue a bill of lading or shipping document.

(b) Contents—The bill of lading or shipping document shall include a statement of—

(1) the marks necessary to identify the goods;
(2) the number of packages, or the quantity or weight, and whether it is carrier's or shipper's weight; and
(3) the apparent condition of the goods.

(c) Prima Facie Evidence of Receipt—A bill of lading or shipping document issued under this section is prima facie evidence of receipt of the goods described.

§ 30704. Loading, stowage, custody, care, and delivery

A carrier may not insert in a bill of lading or shipping document a provision avoiding its liability for loss or damage arising from negligence or fault in loading, stowage, custody, care, or proper delivery. Any such provision is void.

§ 30705. Seaworthiness

(a) Prohibition—A carrier may not insert in a bill of lading or shipping document a provision lessening or avoiding its obligation to exercise due diligence to—

(1) make the vessel seaworthy; and
(2) properly man, equip, and supply the vessel.

(b) Voidness—A provision described in subsection (a) is void.

§ 30706. Defenses

(a) Due Diligence—If a carrier has exercised due diligence to make the vessel in all respects seaworthy and to properly man, equip, and supply the vessel, the carrier and the vessel are not liable for loss or damage arising from an error in the navigation or management of the vessel.

(b) Other Defenses—A carrier and the vessel are not liable for loss or damage arising from—

(1) dangers of the sea or other navigable waters;
(2) acts of God;
(3) public enemies;
(4) seizure under legal process;
(5) inherent defect, quality, or vice of the goods;
(6) insufficiency of package;
(7) act or omission of the shipper or owner of the goods or their agent; or
(8) saving or attempting to save life or property at sea, including a deviation in rendering such a service.

§ 30707. Criminal Penalty

(a) In General—A carrier that violates this chapter shall be fined under title 18.

(b) Lien—The amount of the fine and costs for the violation constitute a lien on the vessel engaged in the carriage. A civil action in rem to enforce the lien may be brought in the district court of the United States for any district in which the vessel is found.

(c) Disposition of Fine—Half of the fine shall go to the person injured by the violation and half to the United States Government.

THE HARTER ACT, 1893

(Superseded Version)

46 App. U.S.C. §§ 190, *et seq.*

§ 190. Stipulations relieving from liability for negligence

It shall not be lawful for the manager, agent, master, or owner of any vessels transporting merchandise or property from or between ports of the United States and foreign ports to insert in any bill of lading or shipping document any clause, covenant, or agreement whereby it, her, or they shall be relieved from liability for loss or damage arising from negligence, fault, or failure in proper loading, stowage, custody, care, or proper delivery of any and all lawful merchandise or property committed to its or their charge. Any and all words or clauses of such import inserted in bills of lading or shipping receipts shall be null and void and of no effect.

§ 191. Stipulations relieving from exercise of due diligence in equipping vessels

It shall not be lawful for any vessel transporting merchandise or property from or between ports of the United States of America and foreign ports, her owner, master, agent, or manager, to insert in any bill of lading or shipping document any covenant or agreement whereby the obligations of the owner or owners of said vessel to exercise due diligence [to] properly equip, man, provision, and outfit said vessel, and to make said vessel seaworthy and capable of performing her intended voyage, or whereby the obligations of the master, officers, agents, or servants to carefully handle and stow her cargo and to care for and properly deliver same, shall in any wise be lessened, weakened, or avoided.

§ 192. Limitation of liability for errors of navigation, dangers of the sea and acts of God

If the owner of any vessel transporting merchandise or property to or from any port in the United States of America shall exercise due diligence to make the said vessel in all respects seaworthy and properly manned, equipped, and supplied, neither the vessel, her owner or owners, agent, or charterers, shall become or be held responsible for damage or loss resulting from faults or errors in navigation or in the management of said vessel nor shall the vessel, her owner or owners, charterers, agent, or master be held liable for losses arising from dangers of the sea or other navigable waters, acts of God, or public enemies, or the inherent defect, quality, or vice of the thing carried, or from insufficiency of package, or seizure under legal process, or for loss resulting from any act or omission of the shipper or owner of the goods, his agent or representative, or from saving or attempting to save life or property at sea, or from any deviation in rendering such service.

§ 193. Bills of lading to be issued; contents

It shall be the duty of the owner or owners, masters, or agent of any vessel transporting merchandise or property from or between ports of the United States and foreign ports to issue to shippers of any lawful merchandise a bill of lading, or shipping document, stating, among other things, the marks necessary for identification, number of packages, or quantity, stating whether it be carrier's or shipper's weight, and apparent order or condition of such merchandise or property delivered to and received by the owner, master, or agent of the vessel for transportation, and such document shall be *prima facie* evidence of the receipt of the merchandise therein described.

§ 194. Penalties; lien; recovery

For a violation of any of the provisions of sections 190-193 of this title the agent, owner, or master of the vessel guilty of such violations, and who refuses to issue on demand the bill of lading provided for, shall be liable to a fine not exceeding $2,000. The amount of the fine and costs for such violation shall be a lien upon the vessel, whose agent, owner, or master is guilty of such violation, and such vessel may be libeled therefor in any district court of the United States, within whose jurisdiction the vessel may be found. One-half of such penalty shall go to the party injured by such violation and the remainder to the Government of the United States.

§ 196. Certain laws unaffected

Sections 190-195 of this title shall not be held to modify or repeal sections 181, 182, and 183 of this title, or any other statute defining the liability of vessels, their owners, or representatives.

§ 195. Certain provisions inapplicable to transportation of live animals

Sections 190 and 193 of this title shall not apply to the transportation of live animals.

CARRIAGE OF GOODS BY SEA ACT[1]

46 U.S.C. § 30701, Statutory Note

[Note]. **Bills of lading subject to chapter**

Every bill of lading or similar document of title which is evidence of a contract for the carriage of goods by sea to or from ports of the United States, in foreign trade, shall have effect subject to the provisions of this chapter.

§ 1. Definitions

When used in this chapter—

(a) The term "carrier" includes the owner or the charterer who enters into a contract of carriage with a shipper.

(b) The term "contract of carriage" applies only to contracts of carriage covered by a bill of lading or any similar document of title, insofar as such document relates to the carriage of goods by sea, including any bill of lading or any similar document as aforesaid issued under or pursuant to a charter party from the moment at which such bill of lading or similar document of title regulates the relations between a carrier and a holder of the same.

(c) The term "goods" includes goods, wares, merchandise, and articles of every kind whatsoever except live animals and cargo which by the contract of carriage is stated as being carried on deck and is so carried.

(d) The term "ship" means any vessel used for the carriage of goods by sea.

(e) The term "carriage of goods" covers the period from the time when the goods are loaded on to the time when they are discharged from the ship.

* * *

§ 2. Duties and rights of carrier

Subject to the provisions of section 1306 of this title, under every contract of carriage of goods by sea, the carrier in relation to the loading, handling, stowage, carriage, custody,

---

1 The Carriage of Goods by Sea Act was formerly codified in Title 46 U.S.C. §§ 1300-1315. When Congress began to re-codify Title 46, COGSA was placed in an Appendix to that title but retained the same section numbers and substantive content. Congress has recently completed the re-codification which does not contain COGSA. COGSA was originally enacted by the 74th Congress as: the law of April 16, 1936 C. 229, 49 Stat. 1207.

care, and discharge of such goods, shall be subject to the responsibilities and liabilities and entitled to the rights and immunities set forth in sections 1303 and 1304 of this title.

§ 3. Responsibilities and liabilities of carrier and ship

Seaworthiness

(1) The carrier shall be bound, before and at the beginning of the voyage, to exercise due diligence to—

(a) Make the ship seaworthy;
(b) Properly man, equip, and supply the ship;
(c) Make the holds, refrigerating and cooling chambers, and all other parts of the ship in which goods are carried, fit and safe for their reception, carriage, and preservation.

Cargo

(2) The carrier shall properly and carefully load, handle, stow, carry, keep, care for, and discharge the goods carried.

Contents of Bill

(3) After receiving the goods into his charge the carrier, or the master or agent of the carrier, shall, on demand of the shipper, issue to the shipper a bill of lading showing among other things—

(a) The leading marks necessary for identification of the goods as the same are furnished in writing by the shipper before the loading of such goods, starts, provided such marks are stamped or otherwise shown clearly upon the goods if uncovered, or on the cases or coverings in which such goods are contained, in such a manner as should ordinarily remain legible until the end of the voyage.
(b) Either the number of packages or pieces, or the quantity or weight, as the case may be, as furnished in writing by the shipper.
(c) The apparent order and condition of the goods: *Provided*, That no carrier, master, or agent of the carrier, shall be bound to state or show in the bill of lading any marks, number, quantity, or weight which he has reasonable ground for suspecting not accurately to represent the goods actually received, or which he has had no reasonable means of checking.

Bill as Prima Facie Evidence

(4) Such a bill of lading shall be *prima facie* evidence of the receipt by the carrier of the goods as therein described in accordance with paragraphs (3) (a), (b), and (c), of this section: *Provided*, That nothing in this chapter shall be construed as repealing or limiting the application of any part of sections 81-124 of Title 49.
(The Pomerence Act, *infra.*)

Guaranty of Statements

(5) The shipper shall be deemed to have guaranteed to the carrier the accuracy at the time of shipment of the marks, number, quantity, and weight, as furnished by him; and the shipper shall indemnify the carrier against all loss, damages, and expenses arising or resulting from inaccuracies in such particulars. The right of the carrier to such indemnity shall in no way limit his responsibility and liability under the contract of carriage to any person other than the shipper.

Notice of Loss or Damage; Limitation of Actions

(6) Unless notice of loss or damage and the general nature of such loss or damage be given in writing to the carrier or his agent at the port of discharge before or at the time of the removal of the goods into the custody of the person entitled to delivery thereof under the contract of carriage, such removal shall be *prima facie* evidence of the delivery by the carrier of the goods as described in the bill of lading. If the loss or damage is not apparent, the notice must be given within three days of the delivery.

Said notice of loss or damage may be endorsed upon the receipt for the goods given by the person taking delivery thereof.

The notice in writing need not be given if the state of the goods has at the time of their receipt been the subject of joint survey or inspection.

In any event the carrier and the ship shall be discharged from all liability in respect of loss or damage unless suit is brought within one year after delivery of the goods or the date when the goods should have been delivered: *Provided*, That if a notice of loss or damage, either apparent or concealed, is not given as provided for in this section, that shall not affect or prejudice the right of the shipper to bring suit within one year after the delivery of the goods or the date when the goods should have been delivered.

In the case of any actual or apprehended loss or damage the carrier and receiver shall give all reasonable facilities to each other for inspecting and tallying the goods.

"Shipped" Bill of Lading

(7) After the goods are loaded the bill of lading to be issued by the carrier, master, or agent of the carrier to the shipper shall, if the shipper so demands, be a "shipped" bill of lading: *Provided*, That if the shipper shall have previously taken up any document of title to such goods, he shall surrender the same as against the issue of the "shipped" bill of lading, but at the option of the carrier such document of title may be noted at the port of shipment by the carrier, master, or agent with the name or names of the ship or ships upon which the goods have been shipped and the date or dates of shipment, and when so noted the same shall for the purpose of this section be deemed to constitute a "shipped" bill of lading.

Limitation of Liability for Negligence

(8) Any clause, covenant, or agreement in a contract of carriage relieving the carrier or the ship from liability for loss or damage to or in connection with the goods, arising from negligence, fault, or failure in the duties and obligations provided in this section, or lessening such liability otherwise than as provided in this chapter, shall be null and void and of

no effect. A benefit of insurance in favor of the carrier, or similar clause, shall be deemed to be a clause relieving the carrier from liability.

§ 4. Rights and immunities of carrier and ship

Unseaworthiness

(1) Neither the carrier nor the ship shall be liable for loss or damage arising or resulting from unseaworthiness unless caused by want of due diligence on the part of the carrier to make the ship seaworthy, and to secure that the ship is properly manned, equipped, and supplied, and to make the holds, refrigerating and cool chambers, and all other parts of the ship in which goods are carried fit and safe for their reception, carriage, and preservation in accordance with the provisions of paragraph (1) of section 1303 of this title. Whenever loss or damage has resulted from unseaworthiness, the burden of proving the exercise of due diligence shall be on carrier or other persons claiming exemption under this section.

Uncontrollable Causes of Loss

(2) Neither the carrier nor the ship shall be responsible for loss or damage arising or resulting from—

(a) Act, neglect, or default of the master, mariner, pilot, or the servants of the carrier in the navigation or in the management of the ship;
(b) Fire, unless caused by the actual fault or privity of the carrier;
(c) Perils, dangers, and accidents of the sea or other navigable water;
(d) Act of God;
(e) Act of war;
(f) Act of public enemies;
(g) Arrest or restraint of princes, rulers, or people, or seizure under legal process;
(h) Quarantine restrictions;
(i) Act or omission of the shipper or owner of the goods, his agent or representative;
(j) Strikes or lockouts or stoppage or restraint of labor from whatever cause, whether partial or general: *Provided*, That nothing herein contained shall be construed to relieve a carrier from responsibility for the carrier's own acts;
(k) Riots and civil commotions;
(l) Saving or attempting to save life or property at sea;
(m) Wastage in bulk or weight or any other loss or damage arising from inherent defect, quality, or vice of the goods;
(n) Insufficiency of packing;
(o) Insufficiency or inadequacy of marks;
(p) Latent defects not discoverable by due diligence; and
(q) Any other cause arising without the actual fault and privity of the carrier and without the fault or neglect of the agents or servants of the carrier, but the burden of proof shall be on the person claiming the benefit of this exception to show that neither the actual fault or privity of the carrier nor the fault or neglect of the agents or servants of the carrier contributed to the loss or damage.

Freedom from Negligence

(3) The shipper shall not be responsible for loss or damage sustained by the carrier or the ship arising or resulting from any cause without the act, fault, or neglect of the shipper, his agents, or his servants.

Deviations

(4) Any deviation in saving or attempting to save life or property at sea, or any reasonable deviation shall not be deemed to be an infringement or breach of this chapter or of the contract of carriage, and the carrier shall not be liable for any loss or damage resulting therefrom: *Provided, however,* That if the deviation is for the purpose of loading or unloading cargo or passengers it shall, *prima facie*, be regarded as unreasonable.

Amount of Liability; Valuation of Cargo

(5) Neither the carrier nor the ship shall in any event be or become liable for any loss or damage to or in connection with the transportation of goods in an amount exceeding $500 per package lawful money of the United States, or in case of goods not shipped in packages, per customary freight unit, or the equivalent of that sum in other currency, unless the nature and value of such goods have been declared by the shipper before shipment and inserted in the bill of lading. This declaration, if embodied in the bill of lading, shall be *prima facie* evidence, but shall not be conclusive on the carrier.

By agreement between the carrier, master, or agent of the carrier, and the shipper another maximum amount than that mentioned in this paragraph may be fixed: *Provided,* That such maximum shall not be less than the figure above named. In no event shall the carrier be liable for more than the amount of damage actually sustained.

Neither the carrier nor the ship shall be responsible in any event for loss or damage to or in connection with the transportation of the goods if the nature or value thereof has been knowingly and fraudulently misstated by the shipper in the bill of lading.

Inflammable, Explosive, or Dangerous Cargo

(6) Goods of an inflammable, explosive, or dangerous nature to the shipment whereof the carrier, master or agent of the carrier, has not consented with knowledge of their nature and character, may at any time before discharge be landed at any place or destroyed or rendered innocuous by the carrier without compensation, and the shipper of such goods shall be liable for all damages and expenses directly or indirectly arising out of or resulting from such shipment. If any such goods shipped with such knowledge and consent shall become a danger to the ship or cargo, they may in like manner be landed at any place, or destroyed or rendered innocuous by the carrier without liability on the part of the carrier except to general average, if any.

§ 5. Surrender of rights; increase of liabilities; charter parties general average

A carrier shall be at liberty to surrender in whole or in part all or any of his rights and immunities or to increase any of his responsibilities and liabilities under this chapter, provided such surrender or increase shall be embodied in the bill of lading issued to the shipper.

The provisions of this chapter shall not be applicable to charter parties; but if bills of lading are issued in the case of a ship under a charter party, they shall comply with the terms of this chapter. Nothing in this chapter shall be held to prevent the insertion in a bill of lading of any lawful provision regarding general average.

§ 6. Special agreement as to particular goods

Notwithstanding the provisions of sections 1303-1305 of this title, a carrier, master or agent of the carrier, and a shipper shall, in regard to any particular goods be at liberty to enter into any agreement in any terms as to the responsibility and liability of the carrier for such goods, and as to the rights and immunities of the carrier in respect of such goods, or his obligation as to seaworthiness (so far as the stipulation regarding seaworthiness is not contrary to public policy), or the care or diligence of his servants or agents in regard to the loading, handling, stowage, carriage, custody, care, and discharge of the goods carried by sea: *Provided*, That in this case no bill of lading has been or shall be issued and that the terms agreed shall be embodied in a receipt which shall be a nonnegotiable document and shall be marked as such.

Any agreement so entered into shall have full legal effect: *Provided*, That this section shall not apply to ordinary commercial shipments made in the ordinary course of trade but only to other shipments where the character or condition of the property to be carried or the circumstances, terms, and conditions under which the carriage is to be performed are such as reasonably to justify a special agreement.

§ 7. Agreement as to liability prior to loading or after discharge

Nothing contained in this chapter shall prevent a carrier or a shipper from entering into any agreement, stipulation, condition, reservation, or exemption as to the responsibility and liability of the carrier or the ship for the loss or damage to or in connection with the custody and care and handling of goods prior to the loading on and subsequent to the discharge from the ship on which the goods are carried by sea.

§ 8. Rights and liabilities under other provisions of Title 46

The provisions of this chapter shall not affect the rights and obligations of the carrier under the provisions of the Shipping Act, 1916, or under the provisions of sections 175, 181-183, and 183b-188 of this title or of any amendments thereto; or under the provisions of any other enactment for the time being in force relating to the limitation of the liability of the owners of seagoing vessels.

§ 9. Discrimination between competing shippers

Nothing contained in this chapter shall be construed as permitting a common carrier by water to discriminate between competing shippers similarly placed in time and circumstances, either (a) with respect to their right to demand and receive bills of lading subject to the provisions of this chapter; or (b) when issuing such bills of lading, either in the surrender of any of the carrier's rights and immunities or in the increase of any of the carrier's rights and immunities or in the increase of any of the carrier's responsibilities and liabilities pursuant to section 1305 of this title; or (c) in any other way prohibited by the Shipping Act, 1916, as amended.

§ 10. Weight of bulk cargo

Where under the customs of any trade the weight of any bulk cargo inserted in the bill of lading is a weight ascertained or accepted by a third party other than the carrier or the shipper, and the fact that the weight is so ascertained or accepted is stated in the bill of lading, then, notwithstanding anything in this chapter, the bill of lading shall not be deemed to be prima facie evidence against the carrier of the receipt of goods of the weight so inserted in the bill of lading, and the accuracy thereof at the time of shipment shall not be deemed to have been guaranteed by the shipper.

§ 11. Liabilities before loading and after discharge; effect on other laws

Nothing in this chapter shall be construed as superseding any part of sections 190-196 of this title, or of any other law which would be applicable in the absence of this chapter, insofar as they relate to the duties, responsibilities, and liabilities of the ship or carrier prior to the time when the goods are loaded on or after the time they are discharged from the ship.

§ 12. Scope of Chapter; "United States; "foreign trade"

This chapter shall apply to all contracts for carriage of goods by sea to or from ports of the Unites States in foreign trade. As used in this chapter the term "United States" includes its districts, territories, and possessions. The term "foreign trade" means the transportation of goods between the ports of the United States and ports of foreign countries. Nothing in this chapter shall be held to apply to contracts for carriage of goods by sea between any port of the United States or its possessions, and any other port of the United States or its possessions: *Provided, however*, That any bill of lading or similar document of title which is evidence of a contract for the carriage of goods by sea between such ports, containing an express statement that it shall be subject to the provisions of this chapter, shall be subjected hereto as fully as if subject hereto by the express provisions of this chapter: *Provided further*, That every bill of lading or similar document of title which is evidence of a contract for the carriage of goods by sea from ports of the United States, in foreign trade, shall contain a statement that it shall have effect subject to the provisions of this chapter.

3. Bills of Lading

Introductory Note: Bills of Lading

Routine commercial activities often involve the formation of two kinds of contracts: sales contracts and transportation contracts. After having concluded a contract for the sale of goods either seller or purchaser may then enter into a contract of carriage, also referred to as a contract of affreightment, to provide for the transport of the goods to a particular place and delivery to a particular person. International sales transactions usually involve both sales and transportation contracts; interstate sales often do so as well. In such situations, not only must a seller sell goods to a purchaser, but the seller or the purchaser must arrange for someone to transport the goods to the purchaser or to the party who is ultimately to receive the goods.

Assume, for example, that Seller and Buyer have entered into a contract of sale and that the goods must be physically moved from Seller's place of business across a body of water, such as the Pacific Ocean, to Buyer's place of business. To this end, the services of a professional transporter are needed to accomplish this. Under the terms of this sales contract, Seller has the responsibility for arranging for transportation of the goods to Buyer. Seller has entered into a contract with a transporter, known as a "carrier," in which Carrier undertakes to deliver the goods on Seller's behalf to Buyer. This contract of carriage has given rise to new relationships. Seller who has arranged for the transport of the goods is no longer merely "the seller"; it has now also become "the shipper". Buyer is no longer just "the buyer"; it has now also become "the consignee". And a new party has entered the transaction, the company that has contracted to deliver the goods to the buyer-consignee is the "carrier".

In each aspect of the transaction, the participants have a variety of concerns. In the sales contract, Buyer wants the goods, title to the goods, and something like a bill of sale to show that it acquired the goods lawfully. Seller wants payment for the goods. The transportation contract raises a new set of concerns. Seller-as-shipper wants to assure that the goods will be delivered to the consignee or someone authorized to receive them—not anyone else. Buyer-as-consignee wants to assure that the goods will be released to it or its designee and to no one else. Carrier wants some method of identifying the buyer-consignee so that it can readily deliver the goods to the proper party. Carrier also wants to be paid for its services.

It is at this point that documents become an important factor in the transaction. How does the seller-shipper assure that it will be paid? How does the seller-shipper assure that the cargo will reach the consignee or its designee? How does the consignee lay proper claim to the cargo so the carrier will release it? How does the carrier assure itself that the person who claims the cargo has the right to receive it? The matter is made more complicated where buyer and seller have asked their respective banks to handle the payment and collection aspect of the sales transaction.

In these situations, a document, such as a bill of lading, may be used as a "link" between the sales part of the transaction and the transportation part of the transaction and may provide the assurances sought by the various parties. A bill of lading is a document issued by a carrier when goods have been received by it for transport from one port to another. Usually the shipper fills out the particulars on forms provided by the carrier. A bill of lading serves several purposes. It is a receipt which:

(1) shows that the carrier received specific goods from the shipper;
(2) evidences the contract of affreightment whereby the carrier agrees to transport shipper's goods from a specified place to another for a specified price;
(3) is a document of delivery which allows the carrier to identify the party to whom it should deliver the cargo, and allows the person who possesses the bill of lading to have the goods released to it; and
(4) may serve as a document of title, that is, by which it may prove ownership of the cargo.

After entering into the sales contract and promising to pay the sales price, Buyer notifies its bank, where it has established a line of credit, to expect a demand for payment from Seller's bank and, upon proper authorization, to pay the demand upon appropriate documentation from Seller's bank. Seller delivers goods to carrier and retains control of the goods by consigning the goods to itself. At Seller's request, Carrier issues a negotiable bill of lading to order of Seller. Seller then endorses the bill of lading in blank and gives the bill of lading to its bank to which is attached a document called a sight draft demanding payment. Seller's bank sends the bill of lading and draft to Buyer's bank which in turn notifies Buyer that it is in receipt of the bill of lading and draft. Buyer either pays the amount specified in the draft to its bank or through pre-arrangement with the bank authorizes the bank to debit its account in that amount. Buyer's bank then gives to Buyer the bill of lading and the draft. Buyer's bank forwards payment to Seller's bank which in turn deposits the amount in Seller's account or forwards the amount received to Seller depending on what arrangements have been made between Seller and its bank. Buyer gives Carrier the bill of lading and Carrier gives Buyer the goods, assuming that Carrier had been paid for transporting the goods.

Thus, in this transaction Seller is protected because the bill of lading will not be given to Buyer until the respective banks have assured that Seller will be paid the sales price. Carrier will not release the cargo to anyone except the person who presents the bill of lading. All parties are assured of delivery to the proper party, that is, the party who presents the bill of lading, because the transaction is structured so that only Buyer will have the bill of lading and then only after Seller has been assured of payment. Finally, inasmuch as Carrier has control of the goods, it can withhold delivery until it has been paid for its services. Of course, if freight (the charge for transporting the goods) has been pre-paid, there is no problem. If freight is to be paid by the buyer-consignee, then Carrier will insist on payment prior to releasing the cargo, for this right is invariably guaranteed in the bill of lading.

A carrier is not obliged to deliver the goods to any designated person but only to the person who presents the bill of lading. This makes it easy for the original buyer to transfer the bill to the person to whom it may have resold the goods, thereby enabling that party to receive them from the carrier. Some cargoes may be resold many times while in transit. Furthermore, banks which act as intermediaries are protected while they are in possession of the bill of lading. This is particularly important where a bank is extending credit to a buyer. Information contained in a bill of lading tells a bank that the cargo has been received by the carrier, loaded aboard a vessel and, the particulars about the cargo and its condition. Also, the bank can retain the bill of lading until the buyer has made satisfactory arrangements, if that had not been done beforehand.

There are alternatives to the use of negotiable bills of lading. The parties may use a straight (nonnegotiable) bill of lading or sea waybill to facilitate their transaction. Under these documents, the carrier delivers the goods to the person named in the document. Although it is not necessary for that person to produce a bill of lading, it will be necessary to produce proper identification. Likewise, a shipper may charter a vessel or part thereof in which case the charter party contract spells out the relations between shipper-charterer and the carrier.

FEDERAL BILLS OF LADING

49 U.S.C. §§ 80101-80116.

(The Pomerene Act Recodified)

Note

With respect to bills of lading which originate in the United States, the Federal Bills of Lading Act recognizes both negotiable and non-negotiable bills of lading. Is a non-negotiable bill of lading subject to the provisions of COGSA? *See, cf., J.C.B. Sales, Ltd. v. Wallenius Lines*, 124 F.3d 132, 1997 AMC 2705 (2d Cir. 1997). *Compare with* W. Tetley, Marine Cargo Claims, 944, 950, 962, 1001 (3d ed. 1988).

---

4. Developments Since the Enactment of COGSA

The Visby Amendments

In 1968 the so-called Visby Amendments (The Brussels Protocol of Amendments to the Hague Rules) were signed at a Diplomatic Conference called by the Belgian government in response to a request by the Comité Maritime International (CMI). The occasion for the call of this conference was the widespread belief among nations that were party to the Hague Rules that the per unit limitation of liability (£ 100 sterling per package) provided by those rules had become inadequate. The Visby Amendments adjusted the limits to 30 franc Poincaré per kilogram ($.09 U.S. per pound) and 10,000 franc Poincaré per package ($662 U.S.). The franc Poincaré is a unit of account consisting of 65.5 milligrams of gold at a standard fineness of .00009.

Many shipping nations, including the United Kingdom, have adopted the Visby Amendments, which entered into force in 1977. By their terms (Art. X), they apply to (1) bills of lading issued in a contracting state, (2) carriage from a port in a contracting state, and (3) bills of lading incorporating the rules, "whatever may be the nationality of the ship, the carrier, the shipper, the consignee, or any interested person." The Visby Amendments have not been ratified by the United States.

The adoption and application of the Visby Rules was further complicated by the fact that in 1971, by international agreement and domestic legislation in the United States, gold lost its monetary functions and no longer has an official price. Thus the franc Poincaré became no longer convertible to a fixed dollars amount. For solutions in another context—aviation—and the enforcement of the Warsaw Convention's limits on liability for loss of cargo, *see Franklin Mint Corporation v. Trans-World Airlines*, 466 U.S. 243 (1984).

In 1979, however, a protocol to the Visby Rules was adopted substituting the Special Drawing Right (SDR) for the franc Poincaré as a unit of account. An SDR is the unit of account used by the International Monetary Fund (IMF). Its value fluctuates and is published daily based on the weighted average of the values of a "basket" of key currencies. Since the value of an SDR is subject to daily fluctuations, many countries that have ratified both the Hague/Visby Rules or the Hague Rules only have adopted a "gold clause agreement" or other mechanism to fix the package limitation formula to a specific amount. Thus even among states that have ratified Visby, different limitations may apply.

The Hamburg Rules and UNCTAD

Unlike previous efforts to attain agreement on aspects of international shipping law, the most recent initiative for revision of the Brussels Conventions came from concerted action by the United Nations Conference for Trade and Development (UNCTAD) and the related United Nations Commission on Trade and Development (UNCITRAL). These forums were sought especially by developing countries who believed that organizations like the CMI did not suit their needs. The developing countries argued that the rules of international private maritime law had been written by traditional maritime states and were unfairly biased in favor of shipowners and carriers. UNCTAD has established a Permanent Committee on Shipping that has adopted as its mission a thoroughgoing review of virtually all the international conventions relating to shipping. This has created tension and disagreement with the more traditional organizations, the CMI and the International Maritime Organization (IMO), which consider themselves the guardians of the Brussels Conventions.

One of the first fruits of UNCTAD was the so-called Hamburg Rules, the United Nations Convention on the Carriage of Goods by Sea, 1978 (U.N. Doc. A/CONF. 89/13 (1978), reprinted in *17 Int'l Legal Materials 603 (1978))*. For a detailed history of the development of these rules, *see* SWEENEY, *The UNCITRAL Draft Convention on Carriage of Goods By Sea*, (Part I), 7 J. MAR. L. & COM. 69 (1975); (Part II), 7 J. MAR. L. & COM. 327 (1976); (Part III), 7 J. MAR. L. & COM. 487 (1976); (Part IV), 7 J. MAR. L. & COM. 615 (1976).

The Hamburg Rules allocate shipment risks between carriers and shippers in a fundamentally different way than the Hague Rules/Visby Amendments. The system the Hamburg Rules establish is, therefore, controversial. On November 1, 1991, the International Convention was ratified by Zambia, the twentieth nation. Thus, in accordance with the International Convention, the Hamburg Rules entered into effect in those twenty countries that ratified the International Convention on November 1, 1992. The Committee on Carriage of Goods of the Maritime Law Association of the United States commented:

> The list of 20 countries includes 15 countries in Africa, with the rest scattered about. Seven of the countries are landlocked states. Ten of the countries have never participated in any cargo convention before. That's not at all impressive. It represents a very small percentage of our foreign trade. It's an even smaller percentage of liner service trade into the United States. Thus, the opportunity for cargo subject to the Hamburg Rules, because it is in effect at the port of loading, to come here and thereby create a conflict with COGSA will be rare.

Fall 1991 Meeting of the MLA, Proceedings p. 9955 (1991).

Nevertheless, renewed activity to urge the United States Government to leapfrog the Visby Amendments and enact the Hamburg Rules into law is expected. The House Merchant Marine and Fisheries Committee has begun consideration of the Hamburg Rules. A key issue upon which there are differing views concerns the impact of the Hamburg Rules on marine insurance rates and practice. For a sympathetic view of this problem, *see* Selvig, *The Hamburg Rules, The Hague Rules and Marine Insurance Practice*, 12 J. MAR. L. & COM. 299 (1981). For an extensive commentary on the Hamburg Rules, *see The Hamburg Rules on the Carriage of Goods by Sea* (S. Mankabady ed. 1978). *See also* Note, *The Hamburg Rules Fault Concept and Common Carrier Liability under United States Law*, 19 VA. J. INT'L L. 433 (1979).

The Hamburg Rules introduce several new concepts, all of which tend to increase the liability of the carrier. First, in lieu of the "shopping list" of exceptions in the Hague Rules, there is a unitary concept of fault. The carrier is liable unless it proves that it took "all measures that could reasonably be required to avoid the occurrence and its consequences." Art. 5(1). This means that there is a continuing carrier duty for seaworthiness, and the exception to liability for negligence in the navigation and management of the ship in the Hague Rules is eliminated. Second, the fire exception is reduced, and the carrier will be liable for negligent acts of the crew in starting or fighting a fire. Art. 5(4)(a). Third, the carrier is liable for economic loss caused by delay in delivery up to a maximum of 2.5 times the freight charges on the shipment under that bill of lading. Arts. 5, 6(1)(b). Fourth, the liability limits are raised slightly above the Visby levels to 835 SDRs per package or 2.5 SDRs per kilogram, whichever is higher. Art. 6(1).

Note: MLA Proposed Compromise Between the Hague-Visby and the Hamburg Rules

The Maritime Law Association of the United States proposed a compromise between advocates of the status quo (the Hague Rules), the Hague-Visby Rules and the Hamburg Rules. Final Report: Revising the Carriage of Goods by Sea Act, Feb. 19, 1996, approved by the MLA on May 3, 1996. MLA Document No. 724, May 3, 1996. *See* Force, *A Comparison of the Hague, Hague-Visby, and Hamburg Rules: Much Ado About (?)*, 70 TUL.L.REV. 2051 (1996).

Note: Plans for a comprehensive new convention

On January 24th, 2008, the United Nations Commission on International Trade Law (UNCITRAL) Working Group on Transport Law adopted a *Draft convention on contracts for the international carriage of goods wholly or partly by sea*. It was presented to the annual session of UNCITRAL in June/July 2008 for a final round of negotiations and will be presented to the General Assembly later in 2008. It is reproduced as an Annex to the Working Group's *Report on the Work of its Twenty-First Session* (2008) A/CN.9/645 beginning at p 60. Whether it will ever come into force or be adopted by the United States is another matter.

---

5. *Period of Responsibility*

COGSA applies during "the period of time when the goods are loaded on to the time when they are discharged from the ship." This period is commonly referred to as "tackle to tackle", which Professor Tetley explains as follows:

> Tackle to tackle has traditionally meant from the moment when the ship's tackle is hooked on at the loading port until the moment when the ship's tackle is unhooked at discharge. If shore tackle is being used, that moment has traditionally been when the goods cross the ship's rail.

W. TETLEY, MARINE CARGO CLAIMS 14 (3d Ed. 1988).

Knauth suggests that COGSA "coverage ... depends on physical acts at the ship's side or on her decks which can be seen and which are usually the occasion for a record, a tally and an inspection." A. KNAUTH, OCEAN BILLS OF LADING 144 (4th Ed. 1953). He provides numerous examples of "loading" and "discharge". *Id.* at 145-146.

As will be seen, COGSA provides a carrier with absolute defenses in some situations and limited liability in others. Therefore, it may be in a carrier's best interest to have COGSA applicable during the entire period for which the carrier may be legally responsible for the goods. It is not uncommon for carrier's to include a provision in its bill of lading which makes COGSA applicable from the time the carrier receives the goods until the time the carrier delivers the goods.

Suppose a bill of lading specified that Carrier would deliver the goods to the port of "X" and Carrier's vessel either because of insufficient draft or port congestion is unable to reach or enter the port. The cargo is then unloaded onto a lighter (smaller vessel) for which

Carrier has contracted to bring the goods to the port of "X" and, as the lighter made its way to the port, the goods were damaged. Can Carrier invoke the benefits of COGSA? *See, e.g., U.S. v. Ultramar Shipping Co., Inc.*, 685 F. Supp. 887, 1988 A.M.C. 527 (S.D.N.Y. 1987). Suppose some of the goods had been loaded on the lighter by means of the lighter's gear and as more of the goods were being lowered onto the lighter the operator of the gear prematurely released the goods which fell upon the goods which had already been unloaded onto the lighter. Damage resulted both to the goods dropped and the goods struck. Can Carrier invoke the benefits of COGSA as to either or both? *See, e.g., Hoegh Lines v. Green Truck Sales, Inc.*, 298 F.2d 240 (9th Cir. 1962).

Outside the "tackle to tackle" period covered by COGSA, the contract of carriage is governed by the Harter Act, 46 U.S.C.A. §§ 30701-30707 (formerly 46 app. U.S.C. §§ 190-195). Under the Harter Act, the carrier's obligations are complete when "proper delivery" is made. 46 U.S.C.A. § 30704 (formerly 46 app. U.S.C. § 190). Thus, the Harter Act applies compulsorily in the period from when the goods are discharged from the ship's tackle until "proper delivery" is made. In *Mannesman Demag Corp. v. M/V Concert Express*, F.3d 587, 2000 AMC 2935 (5th Cir. 2000), the goods were carried from the port of Bremerhaven, Germany, to the port of Baltimore, Maryland, and from Baltimore to Terre Haute, Indiana, by land. The court held that "proper delivery" occurred for the purposes of the Harter Act when the goods were handed over to the land carrier for carriage from Baltimore to Terre Haute. Because the Harter Act is essentially a maritime statute, the court said it should not be interpreted to apply compulsorily to land carriage within the United States.

---

6. The Coverage of COGSA and the Multimodal and Container Revolution

COGSA and the Hague Rules have been criticized because of limits on their coverage. Note that live animals and cargo "which by the contract of carriage is stated as being carried on deck and is so carried" are expressly excluded from COGSA. § 1(c). Does this exclusion allow the carrier to avoid COGSA by the single expedient of moving all the cargo it can on deck? What was the purpose of the exclusion? Is there any reason for this today in the age of containerized cargo?

COGSA also is limited in its application to foreign trade; however the parties can agree to COGSA coverage for coastwise trade between ports in the United States as well. § 12.

By its terms COGSA only applies "tackle to tackle," from the point of loading to the point of discharge. § 1(e). It is, however, common for a clause in the bill of lading to provide for COGSA coverage for the "entire time the goods are in the custody of the carrier" before the goods are loaded and after discharge to the point of delivery, and this will be enforced. *See Brown & Root, Inc. v. M/V Peisander*, 648 F.2d 415, 1982 AMC 929 (5th Cir. 1981). Why would this be desirable from the carrier's point of view?

Since COGSA expressly saves the Harter Act from repeal, the Harter Act applies to the coastwise trade and to the period of custody before loading and after discharge from the vessel up to the point of delivery (unless COGSA coverage is provided by the parties). However, the question of which act applies is of little importance because they both impose the same duties to the carrier (due diligence in providing a seaworthy vessel and in the handling of cargo) and "except for unimportant differences in phraseology, the two acts come down to much the same thing." *Gordon H. Mooney Ltd. v. Farrell Lines,* 616 F.2d 619, 623 n.6, 1980 AMC 505, n.6 (2d Cir. 1980) (*citing* Gilmore & Black.)

The introduction of containers and other new shipping technology have created new problems of coverage under COGSA and the Harter Act. For example, is a LASH (lighter aboard ship) barge that is designed to be off-and on-loaded upon a mother ship "cargo" or "ship" under COGSA? In *Wirth Ltd. v. S/S Acadia Forest,* 537 F.2d 1272, 1976 AMC 2178 (5th Cir. 1976), the court held that these barges are ships engaged in foreign commerce under COSGA. What would be the consequence of denying them "ship" status?

Additional problems arise from the fact that while COGSA and the Hague Rules were designed to cover one mode of transport, carriage by water, it is increasingly common with containers and other "piggy back" traffic to handle goods "door to door." Sea carriers are now becoming multimodal transport operators, and freight forwarders act as cargo consolidators, taking responsibility for an entire integrated transport system. Such operators have developed combined transport bills of lading for these shipments. The legal problems and conflicts arising from this development have not been definitively settled. In May, 1980, after long preparation, the United Nations adopted a Convention on International Multimodal Transport of Goods, U.N. Doc. TD/16 (1980). Only a few states have signed this convention, however, and a unified approach to multimodal transport lies in the future. For an analysis see Driscoll & Larsen, *The Convention on International Multimodal Transport of Goods,* 57 TUL. L. REV. 193 (1982).

Both the MLA-drafted Senate Staff Working Draft of 1999 and the UNCITRAL Draft Convention (see Note above) propose an extension of the period of the carrier's responsibility beyond the "tackle to tackle" period. Under the UNCITRAL Draft Convention, the carrier's responsibility covers the whole period from the time when the carrier has received the goods for carriage until the time when the goods are delivered to the consignee. Thus, if the carrier issues a combined transport bill, or even if it simply takes delivery of the goods before they are put onto the ship, its liability under the draft convention begins when it takes delivery of the goods.

When loss of or damage to cargo occurs within the United States on the land leg of an international multimodal carriage, the carrier's liability may be governed by the Carmack Amendment, 49 U.S.C. § 11706, which regulates the liability of land carriers, particularly in relation to limitation of liability. Federal circuits disagree about whether the Carmack Amendment applies to the land leg of a multimodal carriage governed by a single combined transport bill of lading. In *Altadis USA, Inc. v. Sea Star Line L.L.C.,* 458 F.3d 1288, 2006 AMC 1846 (11th Cir. 2006), the Eleventh Circuit held that the Carmack Amendment applies only where the land carrier issues a separate bill of lading governing the land leg of the voyage. In direct contrast, in *Sompo Japan Insurance Co. of America v. Union Pacific Railroad Co.,* 456 F.3d 54, 2006 AMC 1817 (2d Cir. 2006), the Second Circuit held that the Carmack Amendment applies to the land transport leg even though only a single multimodal bill of lading has been issued to govern the whole transit, including both ocean and land legs. Under the *Altadis* view, the rules and limits of liability of COGSA apply throughout a multimodal carriage, including on the land leg, if that is what the bill of lading so provides. Under the *Sompo* view, the ocean-carriage regimes of COGSA and the Harter Act cannot be extended by contract to govern the land leg of multimodal carriage because the Carmack Amendment applies by its own force to the land leg, no matter what the bill of lading purports to provide. The U.S. Supreme Court granted certiorari in *Altadis* to resolve this issue, but later dismissed the writ because the case had settled, thereby leaving the circuit split unresolved. *Altadis USA, Inc. v. Sea Star Line L.L.C.,* 458 F.3d 1288, 2006 AMC 1846 (11th Cir. 2006), *cert. granted* 127 S.Ct. 853 (2007) (Mem.), *cert. dismissed* 127 S.Ct. 1209 (2007) (Mem.).

B. The Shipper's Prima Facie Case

According to controlling precedents in the United States, a person (shipper or consignee) who wishes to make a cargo claim against a carrier must make a *prima facie* case that the goods were damaged while in the carrier's custody. Plaintiff can make such a case by proving that the goods were delivered to the carrier in good condition and were damaged when they were delivered back to the shipper or consignee. *See Tenneco Resins, Inc. v. Davy International*, 881 F.2d 211, 1990 AMC 402 (5th Cir. 1989); *Blasser Brothers, Inc. v. Northern Pan-American Line*, 628 F.2d 376, 1982 AMC 84 (5th Cir. 1980). Plaintiff may prove his allegations by competent evidence, including inferences from established facts and other circumstantial evidence. Ordinarily, the carrier also introduces evidence tending to rebut the allegations of the plaintiff concerning the condition of the cargo when it was delivered to the carrier or when it was re-delivered to the shipper or consignee.

The bill of lading that was issued to the shipper may contain crucial information or may be determinative in the discharge of the plaintiff's burden of proof. *See* COGSA § 3(4). If the carrier issued a "clean" bill of lading, that is, one without exceptions as to the condition of the goods, the carrier may be estopped from denying the accuracy of the statements in the bill of lading. *See Trade Arbed, Inc. v. M/V Swallow*, 688 F. Supp. 1095, 1989 AMC 2218 (E.D. La. 1988). For what the carrier can do if there is a suspicion that false information has been given or if he is unable to verify the condition of the goods, *see* COGSA §§ 3(3)(c), 3(5), 10.

Bills of lading issued in the United States are subject to the Federal Bills of Lading Act, 49 U.S.C. § 1-24, known as the Pomerene Act. This law, passed in 1916 for the purpose of improving the negotiability of bills of lading, was expressly preserved by COGSA. Under 49 U.S.C. §§ 89, 90, the carrier is discharged by the delivery of the goods to the holder of the bill of lading. However, 49 U.S.C. § 102 provides that the carrier is liable to the holder of an "order" bill of lading for damages caused by non-receipt of all or part of the goods or by their failure to correspond with the description in the bill of lading. The holder of the bill is not required to prove that the misdescription was fraudulent, and full damages are recoverable because the Pomerene Act contains no provision limiting liability. *See Elgie & Co. v. Steamship Corporation of America*, 599 F.2d 1177, 1980 A.M.C. 231 (2d Cir. 1979).

If the shipper or consignee fails to establish a *prima facie* case, the action is dismissed. If, however, he is successful, the carrier may escape liability by proving that "he exercised due diligence to prevent the damage or that the harm was occasioned by one of the excepted causes delineated in § 1304 (2)." *Blasser Brothers, Inc. v. Northern Pan-American Line*, 628 F.2d 376, 381, 1982 AMC 84 (5th Cir. 1980). If the carrier succeeds in proving due diligence or an excepted cause, the shipper or consignee may still recover on proof that the negligence of the carrier was a *concurrent* cause of the loss. The burden then rebounds to the carrier who has the difficult task of proving the part of the loss that was caused by the excepted cause. If the carrier is unable to carry this burden, he is liable for the entire loss. This is just a broad outline of the detailed and complex scheme governing liability and the burden of proof in cargo claims. Variations and refinements are found in the cases that follow.

CAEMINT FOOD, INC. v. BRASILEIRO

647 F.2d 347, 1981 AMC 1801 (2nd Cir. 1981)

FRIENDLY, Circuit Judges

This is an appeal from a judgment of the District Court for the Southern District of New York in an admiralty case, 28 U.S.C. § 1333(1), for partial damage to a cargo of canned corned beef, 501 F. Supp. 791 (1980), transported by defendant Lloyd Brasileiro for plaintiff Caemint Food from Rio Grande, Brazil, to San Francisco, California. The appeal raises questions concerning the interplay of various provisions of §§ 3 and 4 of the Carriage of Goods by Sea Act (COGSA), 46 U.S.C. §§ 1303 and 1304. The district court entered judgment in favor of plaintiff for the full amount claimed. We are constrained to reverse and to direct dismissal of the complaint.

With respect to the facts we cannot improve on the statement of the district judge, 501 F. Supp. at 792-94:

> This is an action brought by plaintiff, Caemint Food, Inc., the consignee of a large shipment of canned corned beef from Brazil. Plaintiff brings this action against the defendant carrier, Lloyd Brasileiro Companhia De Navegacao, to recover for expenses and lost profits which plaintiff incurred as a result of mold and rust damage to a portion of the shipment. The total shipment, off-loaded in San Francisco, had been contained in 55,500 cartons. Each carton contained 24 or 48 cans. A total of 205,296 cans were found to contain mold on the labels and/or rust on the top and/or bottom rims. When placed in cartons the damaged cans amounted to 8,554 cartons.
>
> The shipment had been loaded onto defendant's vessel, Lloyd Altamira, in Rio Grande, Brazil between August 15 and August 18, 1977. Nineteen bills of lading had been issued to plaintiff, each of which stated that the goods had been received "in apparent good order and condition." Two certificates furnished by the Brazilian authorities also attested to the good order and condition of the shipment when loaded on board the vessel.

The shipment consigned to plaintiff had been loaded in the Nos. 3 and 4 holds of the vessel along with another shipment which was off-loaded prior to the shipment in question in Los Angeles. Between 5 and 7 percent of the cartons which had been off-loaded in Los Angeles were found to be damp to wet to the touch and to contain wet stains, although no claim for mold or rust damage was filed as to this shipment.

When the cartons were off-loaded in San Francisco on September 24, 1977, inspection revealed that some cartons had wet stains and corrugation and mold appeared on the outside of some cartons, as a result of which the shipment was denied entry, except for 10,000 cartons which passed initial inspection. The bulk of the shipment had been denied admission by the United States Department of Agriculture. An inspection conducted on behalf of plaintiffs was made by David Voss of the Bay Area Inspection Service. After the goods were denied entry, Voss initially segregated three (3) lots, or 12,000 cartons, as good for further inspection by the Department of Agriculture. These 12,000 cartons were again inspected and refused entry since individual cans were inspected and were shown to contain mold. Forty-five thousand (45,000) cartons were eventually opened at a warehouse in San Francisco and every tin examined. By this examination the 205,296 cans found to contain mold were segregated and placed into 8,554 cartons. The damaged cans came from cartons which showed evidence of having been wet as well as from cartons which appeared to be sound. Voss testified on the trial that in addition to mold on the labels he saw rust on the top and bottom rim of some cans. Thirty-six thousand nine hundred and forty-six (36,946) cartons were found to be good. These cartons, plus the 10,000 which originally passed inspection, were eventually shipped by plaintiff to Libby, the company for whom the goods had been purchased. The 8,554 bad cartons were sold as salvage.

Plaintiff incurred expenses of $67,936.17 in connection with the inspection services of Bay Area Inspection Service, the surveyor employed by plaintiff, and the sale of the damaged goods. Plaintiff's lost profit, less the amount realized in the salvage sale, was $61,059.22. The total of the damages sought by plaintiff is $128,995.39.

The cans of corned beef had been purchased by plaintiff from Swift Armour S.A. in Rio Grande, Brazil. They had been produced at two different plants owned by Swift Armour in Brazil on 31 different dates over a period of 68 days. They had been shipped to a warehouse in Rio Grande on 8 different dates—8 lots by truck, 11 lots by rail—and loaded aboard the vessel on 3 different dates.

The goods thus shipped to the warehouse remained there from June 25 until loading aboard the vessel commenced on August 15, 1977. The warehouse was brick. There is no evidence that the cartons got wet in the warehouse or en route. However, the weather report from Rio Grande showed that there had been heavy rain and very high humidity during much of the time that these cartons were stored in the warehouse awaiting loading. The evidence also discloses that part of the shipment traveled in what was described as "unstable weather."

The vessel left Rio Grande, on August 18. It stopped en route to the United States in Recife, Brazil for additional loading in the No. 4 hold. While the vessel was in port in Recife the weather report indicates that there was some light rain. The vessel log states that on August 31, 1977 at Recife the stevedores did not work because of rain. This was about three weeks before arrival in Los Angeles.

The photographs of the cartons off-loaded in San Francisco show the damaged condition of some of the cartons upon off-loading as testified to by Mr. Voss. These pictures show cartons with wet stain and corrugation. Significantly, the same pictures also reveal mold on the cartons. As noted above, inspection revealed that some of the cartons which were sound on the outside also contained from 2 to 6 moldy and rusted cans. Tests performed in San Francisco revealed that the water stains were the result of fresh water and not sea water. The 10,000 cartons which initially passed inspection were loaded on the very bottom of the No. 3 and No. 4 holds. The evidence shows that all the cartons were stowed in bulk and that a plastic covering and plywood had been placed at two-tier intervals.

Charts showing the temperature and humidity indexes in the holds during the voyage, as recorded by the ship's temperature and humidity control system, were destroyed by defendant more than a year after notice of the damage and four months after formal notice of the claim.

> The evidence established that the corn based paste which is used to secure the paper labels to each can of corned beef is susceptible to the development of mold which then appears on the labels. To avoid this problem a mold deterrent is used. The deterrent is manufactured by Dow Chemical Company and is known as Dowicide. The two Swift Armour Company plants in Brazil where the cans of corned beef involved here were produced, in mixing the paste for the labels, used twice the amount of Dowicide recommended by Dow in its literature. In addition, Dowicide was put on the varnish used on the cans.
>
> Expert testimony on the trial established that mold spores are everywhere, but at least three conditions are necessary for the growth and proliferation of mold—moisture, darkness and lack of ventilation. The court finds that the shipment here was subjected to these three conditions during two separate periods of time. The first time was during the six weeks that the cartons were stored in the warehouse in Brazil when there was heavy rain and very high humidity for many days. The second time was in the holds of the vessel on the voyage from Brazil to Los Angeles, after fresh water got on the cartons during loading either at Rio Grande or Recife or both.
>
> There is no direct proof that mold began to appear on the individual cans prior to loading. The court infers from the circumstantial evidence cited above that some mold developed during the time that the cartons were in the warehouse in Brazil.
>
> There was no water damage to the cartons before loading as the bills of lading attest. However, some of the cartons off-loaded in Los Angeles contained wet stains and some were damp to wet on touch, circumstantial evidence from which the court infers that the cartons were either exposed to rain on loading in Rio Grande or Recife or both and that there was poor ventilation in the holds which caused the corrugation and mold on the outside of some of the cartons off-loaded in San Francisco and contributed to the proliferation of mold on the individual cans.

In awarding judgment for the plaintiff, Judge Motley reasoned as follows: Plaintiffs made out a *prima facie* case under § 1303 by offering in evidence 19 bills of lading showing receipt of the cartons on board defendant's vessel in Rio Grande in apparent good order and condition; by demonstrating that upon delivery in San Francisco some of the cartons were wet, stained, or corrugated, that more than 200,000 cans, both in damaged and undamaged cartons, had developed mold on the labels affixed to them, and that some cans had developed rust on their rims; and by proving the amount of the loss sustained by selling the damaged cans at salvage. The burden then shifted to defendant to bring itself within one or more of the exceptions stated in § 1304(2). Judge Motley characterized defendant's case as raising the two § 1304(2) defenses of inherent vice and of a cause arising without the actual fault and privity of the carrier and without the fault or neglect of its agents. The judge stated that her finding "that mold began to develop on some of the cans prior to loading on board defendant's vessel because of the high humidity and heavy rain in Rio Grande during the long period of time that the cartons were stowed in the warehouse" brought the defendant within exception (m) and that this shifted to plaintiff the burden of showing that the fault or negligence of the defendant was a concurrent cause of the damage. 501 F. Supp. at 795. The court found that plaintiff had met this burden by producing evidence "that defendant's negligence caused some of the cartons to become wet and to remain wet because of high humidity and poor ventilation in the holds." *Id.* The situation was thus one of concurrent causes, for one of which, the "inherent defect, quality, or vice of the goods", defendant was not responsible and for the other of which it was, and the burden then shifted to defendant to show "what part of the loss was attributable to its fault and what part of the loss was attributable to some other cause for which it was not responsible". 501 F. Supp. at 796. Noting that we had characterized this as a "practically insuperable burden", *J. Gerber & Co. v. S.S. Sabine Howaldt*, 437 F.2d 580, 588 (1971), the court found that defendant had not discharged it by showing that following delivery in San Francisco plaintiff had estimated that only 1000 new cartons would be needed if the cans had been repacked and relabeled rather than sold as salvage merchandise. With respect, we are unable to accept this as the proper analysis.

Plaintiff's case is necessarily based on a breach by defendant of the duties imposed by § 1303(1)(c) and (2) of COGSA:

> (1) Seaworthiness. The carrier shall be bound, before and at the beginning of the voyage, to exercise due diligence to—
>
> * * *
>
> > (c) Make the holds, refrigerating and cooling chambers, and all other parts of the ship in which goods are carried, fit and safe for their reception, carriage, and preservation.
>
> (2) Cargo. The carrier shall properly and carefully load, handle, stow, carry, keep, care for, and discharge the goods carried.

In order to bring itself within these provisions, plaintiff has the burden, which remains with it throughout the case, of proving that "the goods were damaged while in the carrier's custody". *Pan-American Hide Co. v. Nippon Yusen (Kabushiki), Kaisha*, 13 F.2d 871 (S.D.N.Y. 1921) (L. Hand, J.). If plaintiff carries this burden, it establishes a *prima facie* case for recovery and will thus be entitled to prevail unless the carrier brings itself within one of the exceptions set forth in § 1304.

A shipper or consignee can prove that its goods were damaged while in the carrier's custody by proving "delivery of the goods to the carrier ... in good condition, and outturn by the carrier ... in damaged condition." *Vana Trading Co., Inc. v. S.S. "Mette Skou"*, 556 F.2d 100, 104 (2 Cir.), *cert. denied*, 34 U.S. 892 (1977); *Madow Co. v. S.S. Liberty Exporter*, 568 F.2d 1183, 1185 (2 Cir. 1978). Since it is undisputed that the cans of corned beef for which recovery is sought were damaged when the Lloyd Altamira arrived in San Francisco, the critical question is whether plaintiff proved that the cans were in good condition when the shipment was loaded in Rio Grande.

A clean bill of lading is ordinarily *prima facie* evidence of delivery in good condition. If plaintiff here were suing for damage to the cartons, the recitals of apparent good order and condition in the bills of lading issued by defendant would constitute *prima facie* evidence that the cartons were delivered in good condition. If defendant introduced no evidence to controvert the bills of lading, plaintiff would have carried its burden of proving delivery in good condition and, since damage to the cartons at outturn is conceded, would have established a *prima facie* case for recovery. Absent proof by defendant that the damage was attributable to one of the excepted causes enumerated in § 1304, plaintiff would have been entitled to recover for damage to the cartons. Here, however, plaintiff seeks to recover for damage to the cans, not to the cartons.

Although a clean bill of lading normally constitutes *prima facie* evidence that cargo was in good condition at the time of shipment, courts have long recognized that it does not have this probative force where, as here, the shipper seeks to recover for damage to goods shipped in packages that would have prevented the carrier from observing the damaged condition had it existed when the goods were loaded. The leading authority to this effect is Judge Augustus N. Hand's opinion in *The Niel Maersk*, 91 F.2d 932 (2d Cir.), *cert. denied*, 302 U.S. 753 (1937). That case involved sardine meal shipped in bags; on outturn much of the meal was found to be damaged. The district court awarded judgment for the consignees on the ground that heating and sweating caused by inadequate ventilation of the ship resulted in the deterioration of the fish meal. This court reversed, holding that though the ventilation may have been inadequate, the consignees had failed to prove the good condition of the fish meal when shipped. "The recitals of 'apparent good order and condition' in the bills of lading furnished only *prima facie* proof of the external condition of the bags. But their external condition would not show whether the contents were potentially subject to decay or had begun to heat up or deteriorate owing to excess of moisture or other causes such as excess of oil ... . The shippers had the burden of establishing that their merchandise was in actual good order and condition at the time of shipment ... . This burden was not sustained and libelants accordingly must fail in their effort to recover damages against the carrier." *Id.* at 933-34. Our case is *a fortiori* to *The Niel Maersk*, for the carrier since there was not only evidence submitted by the carrier that the cargo might have been damaged before shipment but an explicit finding by the court that some of the cans had already developed mold at that time.

* * *

This does not mean that a shipper or consignee that has shipped packaged goods under a clean bill of lading has no way to show the good condition of the contents at delivery in the face of a challenge by the carrier. Plaintiff may still satisfy its burden by producing credible evidence that the contents of the packages were in fact in good condition when loaded. Here the plaintiff introduced certificates of good condition issued by Brazilian authorities when the cargo was loaded aboard the vessel. However, there is no indication in the certificates that the officials issuing them opened any of the cartons to inspect their contents, and plaintiff did not introduce any evidence to suggest that such an inspection was conducted. The plaintiff also offered testimony that Swift Armour inspects its cans of corned beef for mold and rust before they leave its plants, that the shipper's railroad cars are inspected for leaks, and that cartons transported by truck are covered with nylon tarpaulins.

We need not decide whether the combination of the clean bills of lading, the certificates issued by Brazilian authorities, and the testimony concerning the handling of the goods prior to their arrival in Rio Grande constitute *prima facie* evidence of delivery in good condition. Even assuming that they did, "a *prima facie* case is one thing, and the burden of proof is another." *Pan-American Hide Co., supra*, 13 F.2d 871. The shipper "has that burden on the issue whether the goods were damaged while in the carrier's custody", *id.*, and the carrier is free to controvert the evidence of delivery in good condition introduced by the shipper. The shipper must "prove by a preponderance of the credible evidence that the [goods] were delivered to the vessel in good order and condition." *Vana Trading Co., Inc. v. S.S. Mette Skou*, 415 F. Supp. 884, 887 (S.D.N.Y. 1976), *rev'd on other grounds*, 556 F.2d 100 (2d Cir.), *cert. denied*, 434 U.S. 892 (1977). It is fair to impose on the plaintiff the burden of showing the condition of packaged goods on delivery because the shipper "has superior access to information as to the condition of goods when delivered to the carrier", *Commodity Service Corp. v. Hamburg-American Line, supra*, 354 F.2d 234; *The Katingo Hadjipatera, supra*, 81 F. Supp. at 447; *Elia Salzman Tobacco Co. v. S.S. Mormacwind, supra*, 371 F.2d at 539, just as the carrier has superior access to information as to what happened thereafter.

Lloyd Brasileiro introduced evidence showing that from the time the cargo began to arrive in Rio Grande until roughly six weeks later when it was loaded aboard the Lloyd Altamira, there were ten days of heavy rain and 26 days on which the humidity was 90% or higher. During the loading, some cartons were rejected because they were externally stained. The carrier also demonstrated that the corn based paste used to attach labels to the cans is a nutrient susceptible to the development of mold. Relying on this evidence, the district court expressly found that "some mold developed during the time that the cartons were in the warehouse in Brazil." 501 F. Supp. at 794.

Plaintiff does not challenge that finding here but argues that it nevertheless established a *prima facie* case for recovery. We cannot agree. Since at least some of the cans were damaged prior to shipment, plaintiff failed to carry its burden of proving that the cans were delivered free of the damage for which recovery is sought. Although plaintiff introduced uncontroverted evidence that the cans were damaged at outturn, it failed to prove that the cans were delivered in good condition and therefore failed to prove by a comparison of their condition at the beginning and end of the voyage that the damage occurred while they were in the carrier's custody.

This, however, still does not end the matter. A shipper or consignee who has not proved delivery in good condition may nevertheless establish a *prima facie* case for recovery by producing sufficient evidence that the nature of the damage suffered indicates that the damage occurred while the cargo was in the carrier's custody. As said in *Elia Salzman Tobacco Co. v. S.S. Mormacwind, supra*, 371 F.2d at 539:

> The shipper may also meet his burden by showing, from the condition of the cargo as delivered or otherwise, that the damage was caused by the carrier's negligence and not by any inherent vice of the cargo.

Plaintiff sought to bring itself within this principle by proof that many of the cartons turned out at San Francisco were wet, whereas the bills of lading negate their having been in such condition when loaded at Rio Grande, that the cargo was exposed to rain either during loading at Rio Grande or when the hatch was opened at Recife, and that the only cartons which immediately passed inspection were on the bottom of the holds. There are two difficulties with this. Although it was agreed in general that dampness facilitates the development and spread of mold, plaintiff failed to establish any correlation between the damage that some of the cartons suffered and the damage to the cans. There was thus no proof of a causal relation between the wetting of the cartons and the damage to the cans. In this respect the case differs significantly from Judge Weinfeld's decision in the *C. Itoh* case, *supra*, 470 F. Supp. 594, where the damaged boots all came from the wet stained cartons. Moreover, plaintiff submitted no evidence concerning how many of the molded cans came from the cartons that had suffered water damage as distinguished from the bulk of the cartons which were delivered in outwardly sound condition. The evidence on both these points was under the control of the plaintiff and there is no reason to excuse its failure to produce it.

The district court also predicated its decision on a finding that the formation of mold during the voyage had been promoted by improper ventilation of the ship. There was no direct evidence of this but the court drew an unfavorable inference from the fact that charts showing the temperature and humidity in the holds were destroyed more than a year after the damage and four months after formal notice of the claim, citing *Long Island R.R. Co. v. The New York Central No. 25*, 182 F. Supp. 100, 103-04 (S.D.N.Y. 1960). However, the force of the inference from destruction of the records is diminished by the agreement of the parties that it was the policy of Lloyd Brasileiro to destroy such records after a year and the absence of evidence that any issue as to the proper ventilation of the ship had been expressly raised before that time. It therefore seems doubtful that the routine destruction of the records, although admissible evidence, would supply sufficient proof that the vessel was improperly ventilated. *See* McCormick, Evidence § 273 at 662 (Cleary ed. 1972); *contra* 2 Wigmore, *Evidence* § 291 at 227-28 (Chadbourn rev. 1979). But even if there were sufficient evidence of improper ventilation, plaintiff still fails because, unlike the plaintiff in *Schnell v. The Vallescura, supra*, it did not establish that the cargo was in good condition when delivered and consequently defendant did not need to bring itself within exception (m), if indeed the carrier has the burden of bringing itself within this exception, and the problem of concurrent causation was thus never reached. Some argument is also made on the basis of testimony by plaintiff's surveyor that "[t]here was some rust on the top and bottom of the tin fold, where they folded the tin on the top and on the bottom", on the theory that the rust must have been caused by water seeping into the cartons during the voyage. Here again there was no evidence of a correlation between the presence of rust and water damage to the cartons, and the vague testimony of the surveyors would not support a damage award in any amount.

In sum plaintiff failed to bear the burden, imposed by § 1303 of COGSA, of proving that "the goods were damaged while in the carrier's custody", *Pan-American Hide Co.*, *supra*, 13 F.2d 871. As just indicated, under such circumstances there was no need for defendant to bring itself within one of the exceptions of § 1304(2), and the question of concurrent causation does not arise.

The judgment is reversed, with instructions to dismiss the complaint.

Note

In *Plastique Tags, Inc. v. Asia Trans Line, Inc.*, 83 F.3d 1367, 1370, 1996 A.M.C. 2304 (11th Cir. 1996), the court discussed the effect to be given to a bill of lading which contained "qualifying" terms.

> If a bill of lading contains no limiting language such as "shipper's load and count" then the bill of lading constitutes prima facie proof for each term. *See Nitram, Inc. v. Cretan Life*, 599 F.2d 1359 (5th Cir.1979) (though it was not possible for the carrier to actually count the goods loaded because of the rapidity of the loading process, where the carrier issued a bill of lading with no limiting language, the carrier was liable for a shortfall).
>
> If the bill of lading does contain limiting language, but the terms at issue in the bill of lading are verifiable by the carrier, then the bill of lading may constitute prima facie proof for those terms. *Westway Coffee Corp. v. M.V. Netuno*, 675 F.2d 30 (2d Cir.1982) (the weight of a sealed container is verifiable by a carrier and so the bill of lading constituted prima facie proof of the weight at delivery to the carrier, despite limiting language in the bill of lading).
>
> However, we agree with the conclusion of the Third Circuit that if the bill of lading contains limiting language, it does not constitute prima facie proof of terms not verifiable by the carrier. *See Bally, Inc. v. M.V. Zim America*, 22 F.3d 65 (2d Cir.1994) (while a bill of lading with limiting language constituted prima facie proof of the weight of a sealed container, it did not constitute prima facie proof of the number of items inside the sealed container).

Note: Proof of Good Condition

> The second way a plaintiff may discharge its burden of making out a prima facie case under COGSA is to show that the characteristics of the damage suffered by the goods justify the conclusion that the harm occurred while the goods were in the defendant's custody. As we have made clear, "the consignee's burden does not mean that it must always introduce direct evidence that the cargo was in good condition when shipped. It may additionally meet its burden by showing, as was also done here, from the condition of the cargo as delivered or otherwise, that the damage was caused by the carrier's negligence and not by any inherent vice in the cargo." *Vana Trading*, 556 F.2d at 105 n.8 (*citing Elia Salzman Tobacco Co. v. S.S. Mormacwind*, 371 F.2d 537, 539 (2d Cir.1967)) (emphasis added).
>
> > This second avenue is available because not infrequently a plaintiff who is unable to provide specific evidence as to the condition of the goods at delivery or outturn, can nonetheless show, by the nature of the damage, that the injury complained of happened to the cargo while it was in the carrier's custody. And the whole point of the prima facie requirements in COGSA, as our cases have repeatedly emphasized, is to establish that the damage to the goods occurred while under the supervision of the defendant. *See, e.g., Bally*, 22 F.3d at 69-70; *Caemint Food*, 647 F.2d at 354.

Transatlantic Marine Claims Agency, Inc. v. M/V "Oocl Inspiration", 137 F.3d 94, 1998 AMC 1327 (2d Cir. 1998).

Notes

1. *COGSA: Presumption of Good Delivery: § 3(6) [formerly 46 app. U.S.C. § 1303(6)]*

Section 3(6) of COGSA provides that the "removal of the goods into the custody of the person entitled to delivery thereof under the contract of carriage" is *prima facie* evidence of the delivery of the goods by the carrier as described in the bill of lading, unless notice of the loss or damage and the general nature of such loss or damage is given in writing to the carrier or his agent at the port of discharge before or at the time of the removal of the goods. This provision establishes what is known in practice as a *presumption of good delivery. See Pacific Employers Ins. Co. v. M/V Gloria*, 767 F.2d 229 (5th Cir. 1985). This presumption avails only in the absence of any other evidence on point. *See Socony Mobil Oil Co. v. Texas Coastal & International, Inc.*, 559 F.2d 1008 (5th Cir. 1977). When plaintiff provides sufficient evidence of the damage, the presumption disappears and the lack of notice "is accorded no special weight beyond that given other evidence concerning where the damage occurred." *Harbert International Establishment v. Power Shipping*, 635 F.2d 370, 373, 1983 AMC 785 (5th Cir. 1981).

2. *Delivery Under the Harter Act and COGSA*

Under the Harter Act, the carrier is required to make "proper delivery" of the goods in order to be discharged of his responsibilities toward the shipper or consignee. 46 U.S.C.A. § 30704 (formerly 46 U.S.C. § 190).

The words "proper delivery" have not been defined by statute. According to the courts, as a general rule, proper delivery by the carrier contemplates "delivery of the cargo to the consignee or designee set forth in the bill of lading, at a fit and proper wharf, with the duty upon the carrier to give reasonable notice to the consignee that the cargo has arrived, with a reasonable opportunity to pick it up, and a duty on the consignee to receive the goods at the place of outturn." *Farrell Lines, Inc. v. Highlands Ins. Co.*, 532 F. Supp. 77 (S.D.N.Y. 1982).

The general rule of proper delivery is subject to a well-recognized exception that a custom, regulation, or law at the port of discharge may provide otherwise. *See Black Sea & Baltic General Ins. Co. v. S.S. Hellenic Destiny*, 575 F. Supp. 685 (S.D.N.Y. 1983). The court stated that it is the obligation of the carrier "to deliver the goods from wharf to wharf, notify the consignee of the vessel's arrival, and to protect the cargo until the consignee has a reasonable opportunity to remove it ... unless these obligations are modified by local port law, custom, or regulation." Placement of the goods on the dock and under the custody of the local institution has been held to be proper delivery. In *Allstate Insurance Co. v. Imparca Lines*, 646 F.2d 166, 1982 AMC 423 (5th Cir. 1981), a container was stolen after being placed on the dock at Puerto Cabello, Venezuela, in the custody of the Instituto Nacional de Puertos (INP), which was the entity charged by law with the duty of receiving the cargo and distributing it to the consignee. The court held that this "constitutes delivery in accordance with the bill of lading and the custom and usage of the port." 646 F.2d at 169.

For discussion of the question of whether a discharge of the goods into lighters constitutes proper delivery, see *A/S Dampskibselskabet Torm v. McDermott, Inc.*, 788 F.2d 1103 (5th Cir. 1986); *Caterpillar Overseas, S.A. v. Steamship Expeditor*, 318 F.2d 720, 1964 AMC 1662 (2d Cir. 1963). For the question of whether the discharge of the goods on a vessel is lighterage or transshipment, *see U.S. v. Ultramar Shipping Co.*, 685 F. Supp. 887 (S.D.N.Y. 1988).

The Harter Act obligates the carrier to make proper delivery and holds the carrier liable for damage of or loss to cargo until proper delivery has been made. Delivery under COGSA, however, is important only because it marks the point at which the one year statute of limitation begins to run. The carrier's period of responsibility under COGSA is only from the time goods are loaded on the vessel until they are discharged. Nevertheless, the United States Court of Appeals for the Fifth Circuit has adopted the Harter Act rule of delivery for purposes of determining the point at which the COGSA limitation period begins to run. *See, Servicios-Expoarma, C.A. v. Industrial Maritime Carriers, Inc.*, 135 F.3d 984 (5th Cir. 1998). Other courts have held to the contrary. *See, Lithotip, C.A. v. S.S. Guarico*, 569 F. Supp. 837, 1985 AMC 1813 (S.D.N.Y. 1983).

In *Mannesman Demag Corp. v. M/V CONCERT EXPRESS*, 225 F. 3d 587, 2000 AMC 2935 (5th Cir., 2000), the court held that in the case of a "through" bill of lading for multimodal transport, "proper delivery" for Harter Act purposes took place when the goods were handed over to inland carrier. The Harter Act ceased to apply at that point, and the carriage thereafter was governed by the terms of the bill of lading and any law that might be compulsorily applicable to the land carriage.

C. Responsibilities of the Carrier

1. Due Diligence to Make Ship Seaworthy: 46 U.S.C.A. § 30706 (formerly 46 U.S.C. § 192); COGSA § 3(1)(a) [formerly 46 app. U.S.C. § 1303(1)(a)]

UNITED STATES v. ULTRAMAR SHIPPING CO.

685 F. Supp. 887, 1988 AMC 527 (S.D.N.Y. 1988), *aff'd*, 854 F.2d 1315, 1988 AMC 2408 (2d Cir. 1988)

BRIEANT, Chief Judge

* * *

The carrier's duty of due diligence to make the vessel seaworthy is a condition precedent to its enjoyment of any of the Harter Act's* exemptions. *Isbrandtsen Co. v. Federal Ins. Co.*, 113 F. Supp. 357 (S.D.N.Y. 1952), *aff'd*, 205 F.2d 679 (2d Cir.), *cert. denied*, 346 U.S. 866, 74 S. Ct. 106, 98 L. Ed. 377 (1953). The duty to exercise due diligence is not *pro forma*; the carrier is held to a high standard of care. *Peter Paul, Inc. v. Rederi A/B Pulp*, 258 F.2d 901 (2d Cir. 1958), *cert. denied*, 359 U.S. 910, 79 S. Ct. 586, 3 L. Ed. 2d 574 (1959); *Gold Dust Corp. v. Munson S.S. Line*, 55 F.2d 900 (2d Cir. 1932). This duty relates specifically to the inception of the voyage and applies to each vessel participating in the carriage.

In the case of *The Silvia*, 171 U.S. 462, 464, 19 S. Ct. 7, 43 L. Ed. 241 (1898), the Supreme Court announced that "[t]he test of seaworthiness is whether the vessel is reasonably fit to carry the cargo which she has undertaken to transport." *Atlantic Banana Co. v. M/V "Calanca"*, 342 F. Supp. 447, 452 (S.D.N.Y. 1972). This commonly accepted definition of seaworthiness was later explained in *The Southwark*, 191 U.S. 1, 9, 24 S. Ct. 1, 3, 48 L. Ed. 65 (1903):

> [S]eaworthiness is not an absolute but a relative term. It is to be considered in relation to the voyage undertaken, the cargo to be carried, and its stowage. Unless a vessel is reasonably fit to carry the cargo she has undertaken to transport, she is unseaworthy, but seaworthiness does not require perfection in a vessel.

Thus, a ship may be found seaworthy for lighterage but perhaps not fit for an ocean voyage, for lumber carriage but not for grain carriage, for summer travel but not for winter travel. *The Sagamore*, 300 F. 701 (2d Cir. 1924). Any doubt as to the seaworthiness of the vessel "must be resolved against the ship owner and in favor of the shipper." *The Southwark*, 191 U.S. at 24.

---

* The Harter Act was applicable because the cargo had been properly "discharged" onto "lighters" one of which was the CHERRY LAJU, therefore, COGSA was no longer applicable and the Harter Act applied until "delivery." Eds.

In an effort to establish the exercise of due diligence to render the CHERRY LAJU seaworthy, defendants introduced the testimony of naval architect Philip Kimball and Captains Edward P. Boyle and Scott Sammis of the National Cargo Bureau. These witnesses responded to plaintiff's claim that the CHERRY LAJU was rendered unseaworthy by her instability/improper stowage, unusable sailing directions, and broken fathometer. The Court finds that defendants failed to prove that they exercised the requisite diligence to make the CHERRY LAJU seaworthy.

Instability/Improper Stowage

Defendants failed to prove that the CHERRY LAJU complied with accepted safety rules for the carriage of bulk grain. The duty to make a vessel seaworthy requires that a vessel be safely loaded and properly stowed. *The Nidarholm*, 282 U.S. 681, 685, 51 S. Ct. 266, 268, 75 L. Ed. 614 (1931). "The law imposes upon owners of ships the duty of using due care to ascertain and consider the nature and characteristics of goods offered for shipment ... ." *The Poleric [Bank Line v. Porter]*, 25 F.2d 843, 845 (4th Cir. 1928). Section 1 of the Harter Act, 46 U.S.C. § 190, voids any provision in a bill of lading that attempts to relieve a carrier "from liability for loss or damage arising from negligence, fault, or failure in proper loading [or] stowage."

The rules and regulations of the National Cargo Bureau and SOLAS provide a measure of proper stowage. Even if these safety guidelines are not officially enforced as against vessels and voyages such as the CHERRY LAJU and her trip to Chalna, the Court must determine if the failure to abide by them was so dangerous or unreasonable under the circumstances as to be unacceptable. *The Silversandal [Bache v. Silver Line]*, 110 F.2d 60, 62 (2d Cir. 1940).

At trial, the National Cargo Bureau's current president, Captain Sammis, testified that he had participated in the drafting of the 1974 SOLAS requirements for grain carriage. Under these rules, a ship like the CHERRY LAJU was required to have shifting boards, to strap or lash down cargo in partly filled compartments such as the first hold, and to maintain throughout the voyage a minimum metacentric height ("GM"). Mr. Kimball testified that the SOLAS stability formula required the CHERRY LAJU to maintain a GM of 3.7 feet. (Kimball, Tr. 278; Ex. 23, 27, 27A, 33). Both he and Captain Boyle, Chief Deputy Surveyor of the National Cargo Bureau, conceded that the CHERRY LAJU's GM was well below that figure. The CHERRY LAJU had neither boards nor minimal stability and thereby exposed the cargo to undue risks.

Both Captain Sammis and Captain Boyle stated that the SOLAS regulations were not necessarily applicable to the CHERRY LAJU because she was engaged in a coastwise voyage and not an international voyage. (Sammis, Tr. 301; Ex. CC). However, Captain Boyle testified that during his career at sea he had never carried grain without shifting boards. (Tr. 272). He also testified that if the CHERRY LAJU had complied with the SOLAS regulations, the casualty would not have occurred. (Tr. 212). The Bangladesh Committee of Enquiry clearly considered the SOLAS guidelines applicable to the CHERRY LAJU.

(Ex. 17). Similarly, plaintiff's witness, Captain Rajnikant Jadhav, a master experienced in the carriage of grain and familiar with the Bay of Bengal, testified that in such bad weather, typical of the monsoon season, he would never have made the voyage without equipping the grain holds with shifting boards and calculating the GM. (Tr. 323-324).

Notwithstanding the SOLAS stability requirements, an experienced seaman should have realized that the ship's GM was dangerously low. Mr. Kimball calculated it to range between 1.47 and 1.61 feet at the time the CHERRY LAJU broke ground, finally settling on the figure 1.49 feet. (Tr. 147-153, 186-188). Although he also testified that such a GM was "sufficient," the Court concludes from general maritime usage that such a low GM was not sufficient and rendered the CHERRY LAJU unseaworthy for the carriage of grain during the monsoon season. By ignoring the GM guidelines, the CHERRY LAJU failed to comport with the settled principle that a vessel must be able to withstand expectable action of the seas and expectable vicissitudes. *The Cypria [Ore Steamship Corp. v. D/S A/S Hasse]*, 137 F.2d 326 (2d Cir. 1943).

Similarly, defendants have not met their burden of proving that the vessel was seaworthy in the absence of shifting boards of greater diligence in stowing and securing the cargo. It is clear that both Captain Sobhan and Captain Guerrero were familiar with the expectable weather and sea conditions at the time of the 200 mile voyage and the evidence is clear that under these circumstances the failure to protect stowed grain from shifting rendered the vessel unseaworthy.

Broken Fathometer/Unusable Sailing Directions

Plaintiff argues that the lack of an operational fathometer aboard the CHERRY LAJU deprived her master and officers of the knowledge that the vessel had no clearance at all and thereby rendered her unseaworthy. Defendants respond that the presence or absence of a fathometer does not determine seaworthiness. They claim that a fathometer would be useful to warn a vessel that it was entering shallow water when it did not intend to do so, but that it would not be helpful once a ship reached shallow water in which the ship intended to navigate. Defendants' witness Captain Boyle testified that the depth soundings recorded by a fathometer are used primarily to compare with those noted on depth charts and thereby pinpoint the ship's location: "It is not a grounding avoiding device. It is a navigational device when you're coming in and you have the gradient at the bottom. It is one more confirmation of where you are." (Boyle, Tr. 255-257). Defendants claim that the absence of a functional fathometer will not render a vessel unseaworthy when the vessel has other equipment which will fix her position.

Plaintiff relies on the testimony of defendants' own witnesses in its assertion that a working fathometer is imperative to a ship's seaworthiness. Captain Ostromogilisky testified that a fathometer is required for American flag vessels in the CHERRY LAJU's class. (Tr. 63). Captain Boyle testified that amendments to the 1974 SOLAS convention, which went into effect September 1, 1984, shortly after the sinking of the CHERRY LAJU, require a fathometer on board ships such as the CHERRY LAJU. (Tr. 257-258). Plaintiff's witness Captain Jadhav explained that aside from fixing a ship's position, a fathometer would assist when there is a risk of grounding because "it also gives you an idea as to whether your depth is increasing or decreasing as you go along the depth of water under your keel and as you're going along when you start realizing that it is decreasing to an extent where it becomes dangerous ... ." (Tr. 310-311).

The Court is guided by the rule that a vessel must be supplied with the means by which she may be safely navigated. *The Southwark*, 191 U.S. at 8-9, 24 S. Ct. at 3. She must "have on board a reliable compass or compasses, sextants and sounding apparatus" and be "equipped with adequate charts, light books, pilot books, lists of radio beacons, and notices to marines." 2A BENEDICT ON ADMIRALTY § 67. The case law is mixed as to whether a fathometer is required. *Compare Hurst v. City of Virginia Beach*, 1972 AMC 2346 (E.D. Va. 1971), with *Indian Towing Co. v. United States*, 182 F. Supp. 264, 270 (E.D.La. 1959).

Over fifty years ago, when radios were not required on harbor tugs and were infrequently supplied, Judge Learned Hand addressed the issue of whether they nevertheless are a condition of seaworthiness. *The T.J. Hooper*, 60 F.2d 737, 740 (2d Cir. 1932). He stated that

> in most cases reasonable prudence is in fact common prudence; but strictly it is never its measure; a whole calling may have unduly lagged in the adoption of new and available devices. It never may set its own tests, however persuasive be its usages. Courts must in the end say what is required; there are precautions so imperative that even their universal disregard will not excuse their omission.

Judge Hand concluded that, even though "there was no custom at all as to receiving sets," failure to supply tugs with them constituted unseaworthiness. Regardless of whether Judge Hand's decision was correct at the time it was uttered, in the instant case there does appear to exist a custom favoring the use of fathometers. At the time of the sinking of the CHERRY LAJU, it was believed "prudent" to have one on board. (Boyle, Tr. 258). However, this custom does not necessarily dictate the seaworthiness of the CHERRY LAJU for the lighterage voyage she undertook in this case.

Under different circumstances, on a longer voyage, in a larger ship a fathometer might be deemed imperative. Here, the CHERRY LAJU was able to fix her position absent a working fathometer because of the presence of direction finders, compasses, navigational charts, radio bearings, and radar. (Boyle, Tr. 255). And the testimony is uniform that a fathometer is neither the ordinary means for determining depth, nor the most accurate, especially as it does not operate efficiently in very shallow water. The absence of a working fathometer under the facts in this case and standing alone, probably did not render the vessel unseaworthy.

Nor did the presence of unreadable sailing directions render the CHERRY LAJU unseaworthy. It is true that the sailing directions, if readable, would have informed Captain Guerrero that he should not attempt to cross the Chalna bar in a southwest monsoon unless he had at least four feet of water under the keel. However, according to the CHERRY

LAJU's navigational and depth charts, at least that much of a margin was available to her. The Bangladesh Anticipated Drafts Chart (Ex. GG) indicated a tide of 29 feet 9 inches and the CHERRY LAJU's draft was 24 feet 6 inches. Under the circumstances of this case, a lighterage voyage in the Ganges River Delta, the instructions of the port's pilot would take precedence over any other sailing directions and thus, the absence of readable sailing directions standing alone, probably did not constitute unseaworthiness. However, as noted earlier, the CHERRY LAJU was unseaworthy due to her instability and improper stowage of cargo at the start of the voyage.

Because defendants have not established the seaworthiness of their vessel, the CHERRY LAJU, for the voyage she undertook in this case, they cannot avail themselves of the exceptions to liability under the Harter Act. They would rely on the Harter Act's exception for the damage or loss resulting from faults or errors in navigation or management of the vessel. 46 U.S.C.App. § 192. They blame the incident on the master's negligence and on the Bangladesh port authority's wrongful enticement of the CHERRY LAJU into a channel it should have known she could not navigate. However, in an Harter Act case, the faulty navigation exception is not available to unseaworthy vessels, regardless of whether the unseaworthy condition is related to the damage or loss. *The Isis*, 290 U.S. at 351, 54 S. Ct. at 167. Even if proof of a causal link were required, the unseaworthy condition in this case, the improper stowage of the cargo and the instability of the CHERRY LAJU, did proximately contribute to the loss.

* * *

Settle an appropriate judgment on five (5) days notice.

Note

The obligation of the carrier to exercise due diligence to make the ship seaworthy includes the duty of due care in the selection of the master and crew. If the master commits a navigational error that causes loss or damage to the goods, is there an inference of lack of due care in the selection of the master? See *In Re Ta Chi Navigation (Panama) Corp., S.A., as owner of the Steamship Eurybates*, 513 F. Supp. 155, 1981 AMC 2350 (E.D. La. 1981).

Is the carrier responsible for assuring the due diligence of his servants or independent contractors to whom the ship is entrusted for repairs? Is the obligation imposed on the carrier by § 3(1) of COGSA delegable? *See Riverstone Meat Co. v. Lancashire Shipping Co. (The Muncaster Castle)*, [1961] 1 Lloyds' Rep. 57, 1961 AMC 1357 (House of Lords, 1960). In *The Muncaster Castle*, the House of Lords held that the obligation to exercise due diligence is "an inescapable personal" one; the carrier is responsible if any employee or agent, including an independent contractor, fails to exercise due diligence in making the ship seaworthy before and at the beginning of the voyage. *Compare: Fireman's Fund Ins. Co. v. The Vignes*, 794 F.2d 1552, 1987 AMC 291 (11th Cir. 1986). In this case, the court held that a shipowner did not breach his obligation to exercise due diligence to make the ship seaworthy when he delegated a particular test to a qualified and careful contractor.

However, delegation of inspection to a qualified contractor such as a classification society does not always amount to due diligence. *Nissan Fire & Marine Insurance Co. Ltd v. M/V HYUNDAI EXPLORER*, 93 F.3d 641, 1996 AMC 2409 (9th Cir., 1996).

---

2. Due Diligence in the Handling of the Goods: 46 U.S.C.A. § 30705 (formerly 46 U.S.C. § 191); COGSA § 3(2) [formerly 46 app. U.S.C. § 1303(2)]

Note

The carrier's duty to "properly and carefully load, handle, stow, carry, keep, care for, and discharge the goods carried" under COGSA § 3(2) is a distinct and distinguished obligation that the law imposes on the carrier. As a practical matter, however, the question of the discharge of this obligation by the carrier arises in connection with excepted causes. It is often difficult to determine whether the loss or damage to the goods was caused by the breach of the carrier's obligation under COGSA § 3(2) or by some excepted cause that exonerates the carrier from responsibility.

Carriers may contract with shippers or consignees with respect to the responsibility for and control of loading and stowage operations. *Caterpillar Overseas, S.A. v. S.S. Expeditor*, 318 F.2d 720 (2d Cir. 1963).

COGSA § 3(2) imposes on the carrier a non-delegable duty to load and stow the goods. Unlike the duty under § 3(1), this duty does not cease with commencement of the voyage, but continues through to completion of discharge.

Because the carrier's duty under COGSA § 3(2) is non-delegable, the carrier cannot simply say that it is not liable because it did not contract to load, stow or discharge the goods. For example, if the shipper agrees with the carrier on FIO (Free In and Out) or FIOS (Free In and Out, Stowed) terms, the shipper undertakes to arrange and be responsible for loading and discharging. Nevertheless, the carrier has a non-delegable duty under COGSA to load and stow (and discharge), and remains responsible for loading and stowing even if those operations are performed by stevedores engaged by the shipper. In order to avoid liability for damage caused during loading or by faulty stowing, the carrier must raise the defenses conferred by COGSA § 4(2)(i),(q) (see below) by *proving* that the damage was caused by the shipper's fault, or without fault on its own part. See *Associated Metals & Minerals Corp. v. M/V ARKTIS SKY*, 978 F. 2d 47, 1993 AMC 509 (2d Cir. 1992).

D. Immunities of the Carrier

1. Loss Caused by Unseaworthiness Despite the Exercise of Due Diligence: COGSA § 4(1) [formerly 46 app. U.S.C. § 1304(1)]

Note

COGSA imposes on the carrier "before and at the beginning of the voyage" the obligation to *exercise due diligence* to make the ship "seaworthy." Any damage caused to the goods as a result of the carrier's breach of this obligation is compensable under COGSA. Note, however, that if the carrier fulfills his obligation under § 3(1) of COGSA, § 4(1) of the Act relieves the carrier of liability for the loss caused to the goods by the unseaworthiness of the vessel. *See Complaint of Tecomar, S.A.*, 765 F. Supp. 1150, 1991 AMC 2432 (S.D.N.Y. 1991). Thus, the carrier is exonerated when he proves that, despite the exercise of due diligence to make the ship seaworthy, the loss or damage resulted from the unseaworthy condition of the vessel. Such a condition may result from *latent defects*, that is, defects not discoverable by the exercise of due diligence, or from *transitory unseaworthiness*, that is, a condition that arose after the ship broke ground.

For a case in which the carrier was exonerated from liability under COGSA § 4(1) because the defect was latent, *see Tata, Inc. v. Farrell Lines, Inc.*, 1987 AMC 1764 (S.D.N.Y. 1987):

> Cargo owner sought to recover the amount a salvor was paid for towing a disabled feeder vessel to a port of refuge.

> The cargo was loaded on board the feeder vessel at Tuticorin for final carriage and delivery at Calcutta. Within 72 hours of its departure, steering was lost because the "keeper" securing the locknut threaded to the rudder post broke off. As the nut backed off the rudder post, so did the rudder.
>
> The court found the loss due to latent defect and denied recovery. The court noted the ship was designed and maintained to Lloyd's standards and that all inspections required were done. Further, ... that the Master and Chief Engineer had conducted an appropriate pre-departure check of the steering mechanism ... .
>
> The only way to check the condition of the "keeper" would have required cutting away an inspection window in the rudder blade. The court held that defendant was clearly not obliged to perform such an inspection before each voyage. Thus, the case fell "within the narrow class of latent defects ... [for] which a carrier is relieved of liability for a vessel's unseaworthiness."

The carrier may be exonerated from liability, quite apart from "excused" unseaworthiness, when the cause of the loss or damage to the goods is an "error in management or navigation." *See* COGSA § 4(2)(a). What happens if the carrier does not show that he exercised due diligence to make the ship seaworthy but proves that the loss or damage was caused by an error in management or navigation? In this respect, there is an important difference between COGSA and the Harter Act. Under the Harter Act, a carrier may not claim immunity unless he has shown that he has exercised due diligence to make the ship seaworthy. A carrier who cannot show that he has exercised due diligence to make the ship seaworthy is, therefore, liable for loss or damage to the goods regardless of the cause of the loss or damage. The carrier cannot be exonerated from liability on proof that the cause of the loss or damage is an excepted peril. *See The Isis*, 290 U.S. 333, 1933 AMC 1565 (1933). It is different under COGSA. In a cargo claim, the liability of the carrier always rests on proof of causal connection between the loss or damage to the goods and the breach of the carrier's obligation to make the ship seaworthy before and at the commencement of the voyage. *See United States v. Ultramar Shipping Co., supra.*

---

2. Burden of proof in relation to other cases

For unseaworthiness claims, COGSA § 4(1) expressly provides that the carrier bears the burden of proving due diligence. For the other defenses in COGSA § 4(2), burden of proof issues are more complex because the burden can shift several times. The relevant principles were memorably likened to a ping-pong game in *Nitram, Inc. v. Cretan Life*, 599 F.2d 1359, 1373 (5th Cir. 1979):

> To enforce their respective rights under [COGSA], litigants must engage in the ping-pong game of burden-shifting mandated by [§§1303, 1304]. The plaintiff serves, and must establish a prima facie case by proving both delivery of the goods to the carrier in good condition and outturn by the carrier in damaged condition. The ball is now in the carrier's court; he bears the burden of showing that the loss or damage falls within one of the COGSA exceptions set forth in 46 U.S.C.A. s 1304(2). Once that burden is satisfied, the burden shifts back to the plaintiff to show that the carrier's negligence contributed to the damage or loss. Once again, and for the final time, the burden then shifts to the carrier to segregate the portion of the damage due to the excepted cause from that portion resulting from its own negligence. With the volley thus complete, the trial judge must ultimately apportion responsibility for the loss or damage so proven.

To add to the confusion, not all of the defenses follow this sequence. The burden of proof shifts differently under COGSA § 4(2)(b) (fire), § 4(2)(c) (perils of the sea) and (in some circuits at least), § 4(2)(m) (inherent vice). The "serve" and the first two shifts of the burden of proof in typical cases are illustrated in the case extracted next, *Lekas & Drivas, Inc. v. Goulandris*, 306 F.2d 426 (2d Cir. 1962), which is concerned with the "restraint of princes" defense in COGSA § 4(2)(g). The third shift occurs because of the rule in *Schnell v. The Vallescura*, 293 U.S. 296, 555 S. Ct. 194, 79 L. Ed. 373 (1934), which is reproduced after *Lekas & Drivas*. The defenses with a different shifting of the burden are considered separately below.

LEKAS & DRIVAS, INC. v. GOULANDRIS

306 F.2d 426 (2d Cir. 1962)

FRIENDLY, Circuit Judge:

Mussolini's unprovoked attack on Greece on October 28, 1940, touched off a modern Odyssey whose legal consequences have occupied the courts in this circuit for more than twenty years; hopefully, this decision may end the epic.

Having taken on cargo at Izmir, Cavalla and Salonica, principally tobacco, the SS. Ioannis P. Goulandris docked at Piraeus on October 26, 1940, before her intended voyage to the United States via Gibraltar, a crossing ordinarily taking 25 to 28 days. Two days later, Italy attacked. The Ioannis was first requisitioned by the Greek Government for a short military mission. Transit of the Mediterranean having become impracticable, she was then directed by her government to proceed to the United States via Suez and the Cape of Good Hope. She sailed from Piraeus on November 10, 1940; she arrived in the United States in May, 1941, her cargo badly damaged during the long, hot voyage.

We have previously affirmed Chief Judge Ryan's dismissal, 173 F.Supp. 140, of large claims for damage to the tobacco, 281 F.2d 179 (2 Cir. 1960). The instant appeals relate to much smaller claims allowed by the judge in the same opinion, 173 F.Supp. at 179-180, for damage to a shipment of 308 cases and 7 barrels of a soft cheese known as "Kefalotyr" by libelant Lekas & Drivas, Inc. as consignor and consignee, and of 500 and 350 drums of olive oil, respectively, consigned to libelants Victor Cory Company and Pompeian Olive Oil Corporation.

The voyage took place under the difficulties expectable in wartime. The Greek Government had ordered the Ioannis to sail in convoy to Port Said and thereafter to follow the instructions of the British Admiralty; because these orders were confidential, the vessel was unable throughout the voyage to communicate directly with her owners, although communication by way of an intermediary in London did occur during stops in ports along the way. On December 14, the convoy the Ioannis had finally joined, after waiting 16 days at Port Said and three days at Great Bitter Lake, reached Aden. The Ioannis, drawing water uncontrollably through her stern gland and suffering severe vibrations in her tail-shaft, dropped out for repairs. Due to the needs of the British Navy, drydock facilities were unavailable, so the tail-shaft had to be drawn for inspection while the ship was afloat. To facilitate this, much cargo, including the cheese here in question, had to be removed and stored on lighters, where it was covered with tarpaulins; according to the agreed summary of the master's deposition, "There were no warehouse facilities at Aden where the cargo could be taken." By the uncontradicted deposition of the chief officer, the cheese had not begun to spoil when it was so removed. Wartime conditions caused the repairs, normally taking some three days, to require 35. The chief officer observed that, when the cheese was reloaded, it was spoiling—"it was leaking though the cases and barrels and had begun to develop a certain odor." Thereafter the Ioannis stopped in Durban for 13 days to take on bunkers and to make some condenser repairs; later, after a fire in the tobacco, she was at Barbados for 23 days. The Ioannis finally arrived at Norfolk on May 3, 1941, and in New York on May 8. A surveyor found the cheese to be "Melted with a terrible stench, and worthless"; it was subsequently sold for about a sixth of what its sound value would have been. Seventeen drums of the Cory shipment of olive oil and five of the Pompeian were cut and leaking; also, the latter was one drum short.

* * *

On April 9, 1959, Chief Judge Ryan filed a comprehensive opinion, 173 F.Supp. 140, denying the tobacco owners' claims, action which we subsequently affirmed, 281 F.2d 179, and granting those regarding the cheese and the olive oil. After referral of the latter to a Commissioner and dispute over the interest to be awarded, a resettled final decree was filed on July 25, 1961. Lekas & Drivas, Inc. recovered $24,780.21, plus interest at 4 1/2% from May 7, 1945, amounting to $18,083.36. Pompeian Olive Oil Corp. was awarded $1,472.46, with interest, similarly computed, totalling $1,074.53. Victor Cory Co. was allowed $1,089.82, with interest of $795.30. Respondents appeal from these awards, alleging error both as to liability (save as to the one drum missing from the Pompeian consignment) and as to the award of 16 years' interest.

We find no error in the granting of the claims as to the olive oil. . . .

* * *

The cheese claim presents a more difficult problem. We have concluded that as to this we must reverse.

When the cheese was loaded at Salonica, all 7 barrels and 67 of the cases were stowed in the after part of the No. 4 hold, and the other 241 cases in the poop, along with 704 other cases belonging to parties not in the present litigation. The judge found, 173 F.Supp. at 156, that the cheese "had melted and spoiled due to the high temperatures experienced on the voyage," and, id. at 179, that the poop was an improper place to stow cheese. The latter finding, which was the predicate of liability, was cast in terms of the poop's not being "a fit and proper place for carriage of the cheese from Greece to New York via the Mediterranean-Gibraltar route . . . " The reasoning was that if the voyage had been made as contemplated, the cheese would nevertheless have spoiled; that the legal cause of that spoilage would have been the stowage in the poop; and that the vessel was therefore liable for the damage which in fact occurred.

Respondents vigorously attack the judge's conclusion that the poop was an unfit place to stow the cheese. They say that if the voyage had been made via Gibraltar as contemplated, air temperatures would have ranged between 53° and 65° Fahrenheit and that, although the poop had no permanent ventilators, adequate ventilation was had through an open hatch. We find it unnecessary to pass on this challenge, for reasons that will shortly appear.

It cannot be disputed that the voyage of the Ioannis was affected by "restraint of princes, rulers, or people" under § 4(2)(g) of COGSA. Indeed, there was a double restraint—the threat of attack by an enemy government on the planned voyage through the Mediterranean and the order of the Greek Government to proceed via Suez and the Cape of Good Hope. "'Restraints of princes, rulers, and peoples' covers any forcible interference with the voyage or adventure at the hands of the constituted government, or ruling power of any country, whether done by it as an enemy of the State to which the ship belongs, or not." CARVER'S CARRIAGE OF GOODS BY SEA (10 ed.), 129. This "restraint" altered the voyage from a four week trip of 5000 miles through the Mediterranean and North Atlantic, in cool November weather, to a trip of 13,000 miles and five months around Africa, with two crossings of the Equator. Outside temperatures repeatedly hit 100° and above. Even with perfect ventilation in the poop, or with stowage elsewhere under adequate ventilation, the cheese would therefore, unless it were refrigerated, have been subject to extremely high temperatures for a period of time long enough to cause it to spoil. Whether stowage of some of the cheese in the poop was improper for the Gibraltar voyage is thus immaterial; "if the accident would have happened without defendant's negligent act, then such is not the cause of it." 2 HARPER & JAMES, THE LAW OF TORTS (1956) § 20.2, at p. 1114 fn. 18, and cases there cited; American Law Institute, Restatement of Torts, § 432, comment b and illustrations 1 and 2.

We could stop here were it not for the episode at Aden. As to this libelant makes two claims. One is that keeping the cheese on lighters for a month was negligent since respondents should have placed it under refrigeration. The other is that, spoilage having begun, respondents should have sold the cheese rather than reloaded it. We could remand for further consideration of these claims by the district judge who, on his view of the case, did not reach them. However, all the evidence is before us, most of it was given by deposition, and we think it best to bring this long litigation to an end.

It will be convenient first to consider the claim as to the master's duty to sell. We do not doubt that circumstances may arise when the master of a ship has not merely the authority but, under § 3(2) of COGSA, the duty to sell cargo that is at risk of further deterioration, communicating with the owner if that is feasible but still having both the authority and duty if it is not. . . . This duty exists even if the cause of the deterioration is an excepted cause, GILMORE AND BLACK, ADMIRALTY (1957) 149. If the spoilage had been detected early in the Ioannis' stay at Aden, the master would thus have been bound to endeavor to communicate with the owners via London and, failing contrary instructions, to try to sell the cheese since, even if the price at Aden were well below what had been expected at New York, it still might substantially exceed what would be realized after further spoilage. On the other hand, if the spoilage was not detected until the reloading, it would be imposing a rather heavy burden to say, "now in the peace of a quiet chamber," 277 F.2d at 13, that the master was required further to postpone the already long postponed departure from Aden in order to achieve some possible mitigation of the damages on this relatively small part of the Ioannis' cargo, at the cost of perhaps enhancing the risk to the larger part. The only evidence as to the time of detection of the spoilage is the chief officer's deposition; although far from conclusive, this tends rather to the view that the spoilage was discovered only when the cheese was reloaded. Very likely the foregoing should be further qualified in the sense that the Ioannis was bound to maintain some surveillance while the cargo was on the lighters. As to this the evidence is simply that there were four watchmen on each lighter to see that the cargo was properly ventilated and protected from the elements; whether due diligence on their part would have detected the spoilage before the reloading, the evidence does not disclose.

Decision therefore turns, as it so ofter does in claims of this sort, upon the burden of proof. The classic statement, in *Clark v. Barnwell,* 12 How. 272, 280, 53 U.S. 272, 280, 13 L.Ed. 985 (1851), is that when a carrier has discharged the burden of showing the existence of an excepting cause, "in this stage and posture of the case, the burden is upon the plaintiff to establish the negligence, as the affirmative lies upon him." From this respondents could argue that, they having shown the "cause" of the loss to be the restraint of princes, the burden of proof shifted back to the libelant. However, libelant might be expected to counter with the statement, in *Schnell v. The Vallescura*, 293 U.S. 296, 306, 55 S.Ct. 194, 197, 79 L.Ed. 373 (1934), that "Where the state of the proof is such as to show that the damage is due either to an excepted peril or to the carrier's negligent care of the cargo, it is for him to bring himself within the exception or to show that he has not been negligent."

In fact, neither Supreme Court decision is directly in point. The respondents in *Clark v. Barnwell* had not only established a peril of the sea as a cause but had negated all others; libelants in that case not merely failed to sustain a burden, but no evidence of negligence "is found in the record," 12 How. 283, 13 L.Ed. 985. *Schnell v. The Vallescura*, decided under the Harter Act, was a case in which the ship proved an excepted cause to have been at work and the libelant showed that negligence was also operative; the decision was that the carrier then had to show how much of the damage resulted from the excepted cause or suffer the whole liability. Here respondents proved the restraint of princes to be a cause in the important practical sense that otherwise the stop at Aden and the hot voyage around Africa would not have occurred. However, it might be argued that the possibility that diligence with respect to the cargo at Aden would have reduced the loss is sufficient to cancel recognition of the restraint as the "legal" cause unless the carrier also proves that it discharged its duty, under § 3(2) of COGSA, "properly and carefully [to] load, handle, stow, carry, keep, care for, and discharge the goods carried,"—in other words, that the mere raising of the issue as to the carrier's duty to sell places the burden of persuasion back where the shipper's evidence of delivery in good condition and outturn in bad had put it originally. *See* Note, *Cargo Damage at Sea: The Ship's Liability*, 27 Tex.L.Rev. 525, 534 (1949).

Such a contention gives inadequate weight to the division, made in § 4(2) of COGSA, between the specifically excepted causes (a)-(p) and the "catch-all" (q), to wit, "Any other cause arising without the actual fault and privity of the carrier and without the fault or neglect of the agents or servants of the carrier, but the burden of proof shall be on the person claiming the benefit of this exception to show that neither the actual fault or privity of the carrier nor the fault or neglect of the agents or servants of the carrier contributed to the loss or damage." To hold that when a carrier has shown that the loss arose as a consequence of restraint of princes, § 4(2)(g), it still has the burden of negating any other fault or neglect of its agents or servants would be to read the qualification of (q) into (a)-(p), although Congress did not put it there. It follows that libelant had the burden of showing circumstances from which a trier of the facts could properly conclude that the master's failure to dispose of the cheese at Aden was a breach of § 3(2). Had libelant done this, we would have a parallel to *Schnell v. The Vallescura*, with one cause proved to be excepted and the other not, and the teaching of that case, which we assume to be applicable to COGSA in this respect, would then place upon respondents the burden of showing how much of the damages came from the excepted as distinguished from the unexcepted cause. However, libelant did not sustain the burden required to bring it to that stage.

The same analysis disposes of the claim with respect to failure to refrigerate during the stay at Aden, even if we were to assume in libelant's favor that this omission, since it contributed to the spoilage, could be a basis of liability when it was already inevitable that the cheese would spoil, from an excepted cause, on the hot voyage around Africa. *See Peaslee, Multiple Causation and Damage*, 47 Harv.L.Rev. 1127 (1934); 2 HARPER & JAMES, *supra,* at 1123; American Law Institute, Restatement of Torts Second, Tentative Draft No. 7, § 433B; compare *Schroeder Bros., Inc. v. The Saturnia*, 226 F.2d 147 (2 Cir. 1955). The only evidence that refrigeration might have been obtainable was general testimony of a witness for libelant, clearly referring to normal conditions, that "they have refrigeration at Aden." Even assuming that this sufficed to raise an issue of negligence, clearly, in the face of the master's deposition that no warehouse facilities of any kind were available at Aden when the Ioannis was there, it did not meet a burden of proof.

The decree in favor of libelants Pompeian Olive Oil Corporation and Victor Cory is affirmed; the decree in favor of libelant Lekas & Drivas, Inc. is reversed and the libel dismissed.

THE VALLESCURA

293 U.S. 296, 555 S. Ct. 194, 79 L. Ed. 373 (1934)

Mr. Justice STONE delivered the opinion of the Court.

Petitioners brought suit in admiralty in the district court for Southern New York, to recover damages for injury to a shipment of onions on respondent's S.S. "Vallescura" from Spain to New York City. The onions, receipt of which in apparent good condition was acknowledged by the bill of lading, were delivered in New York damaged by decay. The vessel pleaded as a defense an exception, in the bill of lading, from liability for damage by "decay" and "perils of the seas," and that the damage "was not due to any cause or event arising through any negligence on the part of the vessel, her master, owner or agents."

On the trial there was evidence that the decay was caused by improper ventilation of the cargo during the voyage, and that the failure to ventilate was due in part to closing of the hatches and ventilators made necessary by heavy weather, and in part to the neglect of the master and crew in failing to keep them open at night in fair weather. The district court entered an interlocutory decree, adjudging that the libelants recover the amount of the damage sustained by them, caused by closing the hatches and ventilators during good weather, and appointing a special commissioner to ascertain and compute the amount of damage.

The commissioner, after hearing evidence, found that it was impossible to ascertain how much of the damage was due to want of ventilation in fair weather and how much to want of it in bad. But, after comparing the periods during which the ventilators were negligently closed with those during which they were open or properly closed, he stated: "It would seem, therefore, that the greater part of the damage must have been due to improper shutting of the hatches and ventilators." He concluded that as the vessel had failed to show what part of the damage was due to bad weather, the petitioner should recover the full amount of the damage. The district court, accepting the report of the commissioner as presumably correct ... found no basis for rejecting its conclusions and gave judgment to libelants accordingly. The Court of Appeals for the Second Circuit reversed, 70 F.2d 261, holding that as the damage was within the clause of the bill of lading exempting the vessel from liability for decay, the burden was on petitioner to show what part of the damage was taken out of the exception, due to respondent's negligence.

* * *

The failure to ventilate the cargo was not a "fault or error in navigation or management" of the vessel, from the consequences of which it may be relieved by § 3 of the Harter Act of February 13, 1893, § 3, c. 105, 27 Stat. 445; § 192, Tit. 46, U.S.C. The management was of the cargo, within the meaning of §§ 1 and 2 of the Act, and not of the vessel, to which § 3 relates. *The Germanic*, 196 U.S. 589, 597; *Knott v. Botany Mills*, 179 U.S. 69, 73, 74; *The Jean Bart*, 197 Fed. 1002, 1006 (D.C.). Hence, we pass to the decisive question whether, in view of the presumptions which aid the shipper in establishing the vessel's liability under a contract for carriage by sea, it was necessary for the petitioners to offer further evidence in order to recover the damage which they have suffered....

In general the burden rests upon the carrier of goods by sea to bring himself within any exception relieving him from the liability which the law otherwise imposes on him. This is true at common law with respect to the exceptions which the law itself annexed to his undertaking, such as his immunity from liability for act of God or the public enemy. *See* Carver, *Carriage by Sea* (7th ed.) Chap. I. The rule applies equally with respect to other exceptions for which the law permits him to stipulate. The reason for the rule is apparent. He is a bailee entrusted with the shipper's goods, with respect to the care and safe delivery of which the law imposes upon him an extraordinary duty. Discharge of the duty is peculiarly within his control. All the facts and circumstances upon which he may rely to relieve him of that duty are peculiarly within his know-ledge and usually unknown to the shipper. In consequence, the law casts upon him the burden of the loss which he cannot explain or, explaining, bring within the exceptional case in which he is relieved from liability.

To such exceptions the law itself annexes a condition that they shall relieve the carrier from liability for loss from an excepted cause only if in the course of the voyage he has used due care to guard against it. This rule is recognized and continued in the first section of the Harter Act, which makes it unlawful to insert any clause in a bill of lading whereby the carrier shall be relieved of liability for negligence.

It is commonly said that when the carrier succeeds in establishing that the injury is from an excepted cause, the burden is then on the shipper to show that that cause would not have produced the injury but for the carrier's negligence in failing to guard against it. Such we may assume the rule to be, at least to the extent of requiring the shipper to give evidence of negligence where the carrier has sustained the burden of showing that the immediate cause of the loss or injury is an excepted peril.

But this is plainly not the case where the efficient cause of the injury for which the carrier is *prima facie* liable is not shown to be an excepted peril. If he delivers a cargo damaged by causes unknown or unexplained, which had been received in good condition, he is subject to the rule applicable to all bailees, that such evidence makes out a *prima facie* case of liability. It is sufficient, if the carrier fails to show that the damage is from an excepted cause, to cast on him the further burden of showing that the damage is not due to failure properly to stow or care for the cargo during the voyage.

Here the stipulation was for exemption from liability for a particular kind of injury, - decay. But the decay of a perishable cargo is not a cause; it is an effect. It may be the result of a number of causes, for some of which, such as the inherent defects of the cargo, or, under the contract, sea peril making it impossible to ventilate properly, the carrier is not liable. For others, such as negligent stowage, or failure to care for the cargo properly during the voyage, he is liable. The stipulation thus did not add to the causes of injury from which the carrier could claim immunity. It could not relieve him from liability for want of diligence in the stowage or care of the cargo.

It is unnecessary for us to consider whether the effect of the clause is to relieve the carrier from the necessity, in the first instance, of offering evidence of due diligence in caring for a cargo received in good condition, and delivered in a state of decay. For here want of diligence in providing proper ventilation is established and it is found that the failure to ventilate has caused the damage. It is enough that the clause plainly cannot be taken to relieve the vessel from bringing itself within the exception from liability for damage by sea peril where the shipper has carried the burden of showing that the decay is due either to sea peril, in that bad weather prevented ventilation, or to the vessel's negligence. Where the state of the proof is such as to show that the damage is due either to an excepted peril or to the carrier's negligent care of the cargo, it is for him to bring himself within the exception or to show that he has not been negligent.

Similarly, the carrier must bear the entire loss where it appears that the injury to cargo is due either to sea peril or negligent stowage, or both, and he fails to show what damage is attributable to sea peril.

The vessel in the present case is in no better position because, upon the evidence, it appears that some of the damage, in an amount not ascertainable, is due to sea peril. That does not remove the burden of showing facts relieving it from liability. If it remains liable for the whole amount of the damage because it is unable to show that sea peril was a cause of the loss, it must equally remain so if it cannot show what part of the loss is due to that cause.

Since the respondent has failed throughout to sustain the burden, which rested upon it at the outset, of showing to what extent sea peril was the effective cause of the damage, and as the petitioners are without fault, no question of apportionment or division of the damage arises.

Reversed.

---

3. *Other defenses*

a. Errors in Navigation or Management: COGSA § 4(2)(a) [formerly 46 app. U.S.C. § 1304(2)(a)]

i. Unseaworthiness (COGSA §§ 3(1)(a), 4 [formerly 46 app. U.S.C. §§ 1303(1)(a), 1304]) v. Error in Management or Navigation (COGSA § 4(2)(a) [formerly 46 app. U.S.C. § 1304(2)(a)])

INTERNATIONAL NAV. CO. v. FARR & BAILEY MFG. CO.

181 U.S. 218, 21 S. Ct. 591, 45 L. Ed. 830 (1901)

Mr. Chief Justice FULLER, after stating the case as above, delivered the opinion of the court.

Counsel for petitioner states that the question raised on this record is: "Was the Indiana unseaworthy at the time of beginning her voyage from Liverpool to Philadelphia, or was the failure to securely fasten the port covers and keep them fastened a fault or error in the management of the vessel under the exemption of the 'Harter Act?'"

The courts below concurred in the conclusion that the Indiana was unseaworthy when she sailed because of the condition of the port hole, but the District Judge on the re-argument felt constrained to yield his individual convictions to the rule he understood to have been laid down in *The Silvia*, 171 U.S. 462.

The Silvia was decided, as all these cases must be, upon its particular facts and circumstances. The case is thus stated by Mr. Justice Gray, who delivered the opinion of the court:

> The Silvia, with the sugar in her lower hold, sailed from Matanzas for Philadelphia on the morning of February 16, 1894. The compartment between decks next the forecastle had been fitted up to carry steerage passengers, but on this voyage contained only spare sails and ropes, and a small quantity of stores. This compartment had four round ports on each side, which were about eight or nine feet above the water line when the vessel was deep laden. Each port was eight inches in diameter, furnished with a cover of glass five eighths of an inch thick, set in a brass frame, as well as with an inner cover or dummy of iron. When the ship sailed, the weather was fair, and the glass covers were tightly closed, but the iron covers were left open in order to light the compartment should it become necessary to get anything from it, and the hatches were battened down, but could have been opened in two minutes by knocking out the wedges. In the afternoon of the day of sailing, the ship encountered rough weather, and the glass cover of one of the ports was broken—whether by the force of the seas or by floating timber or wreckage, was wholly a matter of conjecture—and the water came in through the port, and damaged the sugar.
>
> And again:
>
> But the contention that the Silvia was unseaworthy when she sailed from Matanzas is unsupported by the facts. The test of seaworthiness is whether the vessel is reasonably fit to carry the cargo which she has undertaken to transport. The port holes of the compartment in question were furnished both with the usual glass covers and with the usual iron shutters or dead lights; and there is nothing in the case to justify an inference that there was any defect in the construction of either. When she began her voyage, the weather being fair, the glass covers only were shut, and the iron ones were left open for the purpose of lighting the compartment. Although the hatches were battened down they could have been taken off in two minutes, and no cargo was stowed against the ports so as to prevent or embarrass access to them in case a change of weather should make it necessary or proper to close the iron shutters. Had the cargo been so stowed as to require much time and labor to shift or remove it in order to get at the ports, the fact that the iron shutters were left open at the beginning of the voyage might have rendered the ship unseaworthy. *But as no cargo was so stowed, and the ports were in a place where these shutters would usually be left open for the admission of light, and could be speedily got at and closed if occasion should require, there is no ground for holding that the ship was unseaworthy at the time of sailing.*

In the present case the compartment in which the burlaps were stowed was used exclusively as a cargo hold; the glass and iron covers were intended to be securely closed before any cargo was received; the person whose duty it was to close them or see that they were closed, supposed that that had been properly done; and the hatches were battened down with no expectation that any more attention would be given to the port covers during the voyage; but in fact the port was not securely covered, and there was apparently nothing to prevent the influx of water, even under conditions not at all extraordinary, the port being only two or three feet above the water line.

But it is contended that in spite of the fact that the condition of the port hole rendered the ship unseaworthy when she sailed, the omission to securely cover it was a fault or error in management and within the exemption of the third section of the Harter Act ... .

We cannot accede to a view which so completely destroys the general rule that seaworthiness at the commencement of the voyage is a condition precedent, and that fault in management is no defence when there is lack of due diligence before the vessel breaks ground.

We do not think that a ship owner exercises due diligence within the meaning of the act by merely furnishing proper structure and equipment, for the diligence required is diligence to make the ship in all respects seaworthy, and that, in our judgment, means due diligence on the part of all the owners' servants in the use of the equipment before the commencement of the voyage and until it is actually commenced.

* * *

It is, of course, not to be understood as intimated that failure to close port holes necessarily creates unseaworthiness. That depends on circumstances, and we accept the finding of the District Court, and of the Court of Appeals, that it did so under the circumstances of this case.

* * *

Decree affirmed.

---

ii. Proper Care of the Cargo (COGSA § 3(2) [formerly 46 app. U.S.C. § 1303(2)]) v. Error in Navigation (COGSA § 4(2)(a) [formerly 46 app. U.S.C. § 1304(2)(a)])

KNOTT v. BOTANY WORSTED MILLS

179 U.S. 69, 21 S. Ct. 30, 45 L. Ed. 90 (1900)

Mr. Justice GRAY delivered the opinion of the court

The Botany Worsted Mills, a corporation of New Jersey, and Winter and Smillie, a firm of merchants in the city of New York, respectively owners of two separate lots of bales of wool, shipped at Buenos Aires for New York on board the steamship Portuguese Prince, severally filed libels in admiralty *in personam* in the District Court of the United States for the Southern District of New York, against James Knott, the owner of the vessel, to recover the damage caused to the wool by contact with drainage from wet sugar which also formed part of her cargo.

The Portuguese Prince was a British vessel, belonging to a line trading between New York and ports in the River Plata, Brazil, and the West Indies, loading and discharging cargo and having a resident agent at each port. The bills of lading of the wool, signed at Buenos Aires, December 21, 1894, gave her liberty to call at any port or ports to receive and discharge cargo, and for any other purpose whatever; and purported to exempt the carrier from liability for "negligence of masters or mariners;" "sweating, rust, natural decay, leakage or breakage, and all damage arising from the goods by stowage, or contact with, or by sweating, leakage, smell or evaporation from them;" "or any other peril of the seas, rivers, navigation, or of land transit, of whatsoever nature or kind; and whether any of the perils, causes or things above mentioned, or the loss or injury arising therefrom, be occasioned by the wrongful act, default, negligence, or error in judgment of the owners, masters, officers, mariners, crew, stevedores, engineers and other persons whomsoever in the service of the ship, whether employed on the said steamer or otherwise, and whether before, or after, or during the voyage, or for whose acts the shipowner would otherwise be liable; or by unseaworthiness of the ship at the beginning, or at any period of the voyage, provided all reasonable means have been taken to provide against such unseaworthiness."

The facts of the case are substantially undisputed. The bales of wool of the libelants were taken on board at Buenos Aires, December 21-24, 1894, and were stowed on end, with proper dunnage, between decks near the bow, and forward of a temporary wooden bulkhead, which was not tight. The vessel, after touching at other ports, touched on February 19, 1895, at Pernambuco, and there took on board two hundred tons of wet sugar, (from which there is always drainage,) which was stowed, with proper dunnage, between decks, aft of the wooden bulkhead. At that time the vessel was trimmed by the stern, and all drainage from the sugar, flowing aft, was carried off by the scuppers, which were sufficient for the purpose when the vessel was down by the stern, or on even keel in calm weather. There was no provision for carrying off the drainage in case it ran forward. She discharged other cargo at Para; and on March 10, when she left that port, she was two feet down by the head. She continued in this trim until she took on additional cargo at Port of Spain, where the error in trim was corrected, and she left that port on March 18, loaded one foot by the stern. It was agreed by the parties that there was no damage to the wool by sugar drainage until she was trimmed by the head at Para; that the wool was damaged, by sugar drainage finding its way through the bulkhead and reaching the wool, at Para, or between Para and Port of Spain, and not afterwards; that, after she was again trimmed by the stern at Port of Spain, none of the drainage from the sugar found its way forward; and that the court might draw inferences.

Upon the facts of this case, there can be no doubt that the ship was seaworthy, and that the damage to the wool was caused by drainage from the wet sugar through negligence of those in charge of the ship and cargo. The questions upon which the decision of the case turns are:

> Whether this damage to the wool was "loss or damage arising from negligence, fault or failure in proper loading, stowage, custody, care or proper delivery" of cargo, within the first section of the Harter Act; or was "damage or loss resulting from faults or errors in navigation or in the management of said vessel," within the third section of that act?

We fully concur with the courts below that the damage in question arose from negligence in loading or stowage of the cargo, and not from fault or error in the navigation or management of the ship—for the reasons stated by the District Judge, and approved by the Circuit Court of Appeals, as follows:

> The primary cause of the damage was negligence and inattention in the loading or stowage of the cargo, either regarded as a whole, or as respects the juxtaposition of wet sugar and wool bales placed far forward. The wool should not have been stowed forward of the wet sugar, unless care was taken in the other loading, and in all subsequent changes in the loading, to see that the ship should not get down by the head. There was no fault or defect in the vessel herself. She was constructed in the usual way, and was sufficient. But on sailing from Para she was a little down by the head, through inattention, during the changes in the loading, to the effect these changes made in the trim of the ship and in the flow of the sugar drainage. She was not down by the head more than frequently happens. It in no way affected her sea-going qualities; nor did the vessel herself cause any damage to the wool. The damage was caused by the drainage of the wet sugar alone. So that no question of the unseaworthiness of the ship arises. The ship herself was as seaworthy when she left Para, as when she sailed from Pernambuco. The negligence consisted in stowing the wool far forward, without taking care subsequently that no changes of loading should bring the ship down by the head. I must, therefore, regard the question as solely a question of negligence in the stowage and disposition of cargo, and of damage consequent thereon, though brought about by the effect of these negligent changes in loading on the trim of the ship. "The change of trim was merely incidental, the mere negligent result of the changes in the loading, no attention being given to the effect on the ship's trim, or on the sugar drainage.

* * *

---

iii. Perils of the sea

COGSA § 4(2)(c) [formerly 46 app. U.S.C. § 1304(2)(c)]

TAISHO MARINE & FIRE INS. CO., LTD. v. M/V SEA-LAND ENDURANCE

815 F.2d 1270, 1987 AMC 1730 (9th Cir. 1987)

BOOCHEVER, Circuit Judge:

Overview

Taisho Marine and Fire Insurance Company (Taisho) appeals the district court's judgment in favor of Sea-Land Service Incorporated (Sea-Land). The court held that the peril of the sea defense under the Carriage of Goods by Sea Act (COGSA), 46 U.S.C. App. § 1304(2)(c) (Supp. III 1985), prevented Taisho from recovering payments made to a shipper for cargo lost by Sea-Land. Taisho contends that the district court (1) reached a conclusion of law not supported by the facts, (2) improperly considered Taisho's status as an insurer, and (3) incorrectly placed the burden of proof on Taisho. We affirm.

Facts

In March 1984, a forty-foot aluminum cargo container packed with Sony stereo equipment was loaded aboard the M/V Sea-Land Endurance (Endurance) in Kobe, Japan. The container was stowed on the vessel's deck on the starboard side near her stern. The owner of the vessel, Sea-Land, issued bills of lading which are contracts of carriage subject to COGSA, 46 U.S.C. § 1300-1315. Sony insured the cargo with Taisho.

The vessel encountered adverse weather conditions en route to Long Beach, California. Between midnight and 9:00 A.M. on March 16, 1984, the cargo and the storage container were destroyed. Taisho paid the assured's claim for loss of cargo and brought this action as subrogee against the vessel Endurance and its owner, Sea-Land. The vessel was dismissed as Sea-Land agreed to be responsible for any liability imposed on the vessel.

The district court found that there was "no evidence of unseaworthiness on the part of the vessel or incompetent management of the ship by its Master." Further, the court concluded that Taisho did not fulfill its burden of proof to show that the loss of the cargo resulted from some fault of the crew or the vessel. The proof showed that the loss was caused by the weather alone. The court held that the peril of the sea defense, 46 U.S.C. § 1304(2)(c) was established by Sea-Land thereby exonerating Sea-Land from liability. The court wrote a Memorandum of Intended Decision and adopted Sea-Land's findings of fact and conclusions of law.

Taisho appeals.

Discussion

1) The Peril of the Sea Defense

Taisho argues that the district court's factual findings fail to meet the statutory requirements of the affirmative defense of peril of the sea provided by COGSA, 46 U.S.C. § 1304(2)(c). We review the court's determination of whether the established facts fall within the parameters of the peril of the sea defense under the deferential, clearly erroneous standard. *See United States v. McConney*, 728 F.2d 1195, 1202 (9th Cir.) (*en banc*), *cert. denied*, 469 U.S. 824, 83 L. Ed. 2d 46, 105 S. Ct. 101 (1984).

COGSA, 46 U.S.C. § 1304(2)(c) provides in pertinent part that "[n]either the carrier nor the ship shall be responsible for loss or damage arising or resulting from — ... (c) Perils, dangers, and accidents of the sea."

While "perils of the sea" is a term of art not uniformly defined, the generally accepted definition is "a fortuitous action of the elements at sea, of such force as to overcome the strength of a well-found ship or the usual precautions of good seamanship." G. GILMORE & C. BLACK, THE LAW OF ADMIRALTY, § 3-32 at 162 (2d ed. 1975); *States S.S. Co. v. United States*, 259 F.2d 458, 460-61 (9th Cir. 1958), *cert. denied*, 358 U.S. 933, 79 S. Ct. 316, 3 L. Ed. 2d 305 (1959); *R.T. Jones Lumber Co. v. Roen S.S. Co.*, 213 F.2d 370, 373 (7th Cir. 1954); *Philippine Sugar Centrals Agency v. Kokusai Kisen Kabushiki Kaisha*, 106 F.2d 32, 34-

35 (2d Cir. 1939). Case law fails to set out a bright line test to determine whether cargo was lost by a peril of the sea. Rather, the cases indicate that the validity of the statutory defense depends on the nature and cause of the loss under the particular facts of a case.

Taisho cites *J. Gerber & Co. v. S.S. Sabine Howaldt*, 437 F.2d 580 (2d Cir. 1971), for the proposition that a series of factors must be established in order to use the peril of the sea affirmative defense. Taisho contends that the peril of the sea defense only exists upon proof of several of the following factors: (1) the extent of structural damage to the vessel, (2) the extent of any speed reduction, (3) the extent of any cross-seas, (4) how far the vessel was blown off course, and (5) to what extent other vessels in the same storm experienced cargo-related damage. Taisho fails to note that these factors are not the cumulative total of all the indicia that can be used to determine the existence of a peril of the sea.

In *Gerber*, the court stated that in deciding whether a case falls within the statutory purview of peril of the sea, the central inquiry is into the measure of the violence of the winds and tempestuousness of the sea. "These are matters of degree and not amenable to precise definition." *Id.* at 596. Gerber was a shipper seeking recovery for damage caused by sea water to cargo transported by the S.S. Sabine Howaldt. The court held that the vessel was seaworthy, there was no negligence on the part of the carrier, and that the damage was caused by hurricane force winds and resulting cross-seas which forced up hatch covers admitting sea water to the holds. The loss was from a peril of the sea and the vessel owner was exonerated from any liability.

Gerber states that a very important measure considered on the peril of the sea issue is the wind velocity on the Beaufort Scale because of direct relationship between wind velocity and the size and shape of the waves. *Id.* at 596. No Beaufort Scale index exists which divides cases into those qualifying for the peril of the sea exception and those which do not. Nevertheless, courts have almost always found a peril of the sea where the force has been 11 or greater and very few cases are found to qualify where the winds are force 9 or less. *Id.* Wind velocity, however, is only a rough measure and must be considered with other indicia such as nature and extent of damage to the ship, cross-seas and other factors.

> While the seaworthiness of a ship presupposes that she is designed, built and equipped to stand up under reasonably expectable conditions this means no more than the usual bad weather which is normal for a particular sea area at a particular time. It does not, however, include an unusual combination of the destructive forces of wind and sea which a skilled and experienced ship's master would not expect and which the ship encountered as a stroke of bad luck. Hurricane force winds and turbulent cross-seas generating unpredictable strains and pressures on a ship's hull are an example.

Id. (footnote omitted).

The district court found that the vessel Endurance encountered at least four waves in excess of 60 feet which rolled the vessel more than 40 degrees. A substantial number of waves between 40 and 60 feet in height battered the vessel. During the storm, between

0200 and 0900 hours, the sustained winds remained between Beaufort Force 10 (Whole Gale, 48-55 knots) and 12 (Hurricane force, 64-71 knots) with gusts in excess of 95 knots. Throughout this period, the master maintained a reduced speed of 17 knots (normal operating speed is 21.5 knots) to minimize the risk of damage to the vessel, cargo, and personnel while maintaining rudder control. The court found that only a few vessels in the area between 1946 and 1984 reported seas of equal or greater height and that the sustained winds of 65 knots were the highest ever recorded in the area.

On March 17, the crew noted that (1) the port gangway was washed overboard, (2) two firehoses and nozzles were missing, (3) the port lifeboat embarkation ladder was damaged, and (4) the starboard pilot ladder was damaged. In addition, containers at Hatch 10, portside and Hatch 11, starboard (the container in question) were lost overboard and eight other containers were found damaged, four severely and four slightly. Neither the stacking frame cargo system nor the locking devices used to secure the container were damaged or failed during the storm. Taisho does not dispute the validity of these findings or the finding that the vessel was seaworthy and that Sea-Land exercised due diligence to render the Endurance seaworthy.

Taisho's cited cases fail to support the contention that unless the district court finds several factors existed out of the five previously enumerated, the court cannot conclude that the peril of the sea defense exonerated Sea-Land. Taisho's cites the following cases in support of its proposition: *Virgin Island Corp. v. Merwin Lighterage Co.*, 251 F.2d 872 (3d Cir.), *cert. denied*, 357 U.S. 929, 78 S. Ct. 1369, 2 L. Ed. 2d 1372 (1958) (*No Peril*—Two barges next to each other, one with cargo lashed down—the other without its cargo lashed down, court said lashing could have saved cargo); *States S.S. Co.*, 259 F.2d 458 (*No Peril*—Beaufort Force 9, mountainous seas, inherent condition of the hull rather than the sea caused the sinking); *Ore S.S. Corp. v. D/S A/S Hassel*, 137 F.2d 326 (2d Cir. 1943) (*No Peril*—Beaufort Force 9-10 for 3 days, two windows knocked in, lifeboat damaged, reduced speed, rivet missing, *winds not extraordinary*); *Philippine Sugar*, 106 F.2d 32 (*Peril*—3 days at Beaufort Force 9-10, lifeboat crushed, steel superstructure broken or carried away, blown 160 miles off course); *American Int'l Ins. Co. v. S.S. Fortaleza,* 446 F. Supp. 221 (D.P.R.), *aff'd*, 585 F.2d 22 (1978) (*Peril*—Winds Beaufort Force 6-11 for 24 hours, vessel rolled 40 degrees and continued rolling 30-40 degrees, seas in excess of 40 feet, lost 30 trailers, foremast snapped off, railing and steel deck curbing destroyed); *Freedman & Slater Inc. v. M/V Tofevo*, 222 F. Supp. 964 (S.D.N.Y. 1963) (*No Peril*—Alteration in log book showing higher Beaufort Forces not supported by other evidence); *Palmer Distrib. Corp. v. S.S. American Counselor*, 158 F. Supp. 264 (S.D.N.Y. 1957) (*No Peril*—Beaufort Force 9-10 for 3 days, *not unusual weather for North Atlantic*, no structural damage, other cargo not damaged).

The district court's findings of unusually high winds and seas, the rolling of the ship, the damage to the ship, the loss and damage of other containers, and Sea-Land's due diligence in making the vessel and cargo system seaworthy support the conclusion that the cargo was lost because of a peril of the sea.

3) Burden of Proof

Taisho argues that the court placed the burden of proof as to the issue of negligence on the wrong party as the peril of the sea affirmative defense requires the showing of an absence of negligence. Sea-Land contends that once they have proved that the loss was from the sea alone, the burden then shifts to Taisho to show a concurrent act to defeat Sea-Land's peril of the sea affirmative defense. The selection of the appropriate burden of proof is a question of law reviewed *de novo*. *See McConney*, 728 F.2d at 1201-04.

Generally, under COGSA, a shipper establishes a *prima facie* case against the carrier by showing that the cargo was delivered in good condition to the carrier but was discharged in a damaged condition. 46 U.S.C. §§ 1302, 1303; *Gerber*, 437 F.2d at 584; Gilmore & Black, *supra*, § 3-43 at 183. The burden of proof then shifts to the vessel owner to establish that the loss came under a statutory exception to COGSA....

The burden then returns to the shipper to show, at a minimum, concurrent causes of loss in the fault and negligence of the carrier, unless it is a type of negligence excluded under COGSA. *Gerber*, 437 F.2d at 588; Gilmore & Black, *supra*, § 3-43 at 184. The carrier then has the burden of allocating the loss between (1) the loss caused by his fault and negligence and (2) the loss covered under the exception. *Vana Trading Co. v. S.S. Mette Skou*, 556 F.2d 100, 105 (2d Cir.), *cert. denied*, *Flota Mercante Grancolombiana, S.A. v. Vana Trading Co., Inc.*, 434 U.S. 892, 98 S. Ct. 267, 54 L. Ed. 2d 177 (1977). Failure of the carrier to do so results in the carrier bearing the full loss. *Gerber*, 437 F.2d at 588.

The burden of proof, however, alters when a carrier seeks exoneration under the peril of the sea exception. 46 U.S.C. § 1304(2)(c).

> [I]n a sense, the absence of negligence as a concurring cause may be said to enter into the very definition of a sea peril, so that, in order to establish an exception under this clause, the ship would have to establish freedom from negligence.

Gilmore & Black, *supra*, § 3-32 at 162. Thus, under the peril of the sea exception, the carrier acquires the additional burden of showing freedom from negligence.

A prima facie case against Sea-Land was established by the stipulated facts that the cargo was delivered in good condition to the Endurance and never returned. The burden then shifted to Sea-Land to prove the loss fell under one of the statutory exceptions of COGSA. In choosing the peril of the sea defense, Sea-Land acquired the additional burden of proving freedom from negligence. The district court concluded that "[t]he proof establishes that the loss was caused by the weather alone." By finding that Sea-Land had established that the weather was the sole cause of the loss, the court inferredly found that Sea-Land had sustained its burden of proving that negligence was not a cause of the loss. At that point, the burden was placed on Taisho to show a concurrent cause of the loss. Taisho failed to meet this burden. We conclude that the district court correctly allocated the burdens of proof.

Conclusion

Taisho's argument that without proof of several enumerated factors there can be no peril of the sea defense is without merit. Taisho's second argument fails to show that the district court considered Taisho's rights as an insurer differently from that of a subrogee. Finally, Sea-Land sustained its burden of proving that the loss was caused solely by the perils of the sea and Taisho failed to rebut that evidence. Accordingly, we affirm the judgment of the district court.

AFFIRMED.

Note

There was no question in *Taisho Marine & Fire Ins. Co., Ltd. v. M/V Sea-Land Endurance, supra*, that the carrying ship was in seaworthy condition before it encountered the storm. In many cases, however, the ship's inability to carry the cargo safely through heavy weather raises questions about the ship's seaworthiness (or lack of it). For example, in *Edmond Weil, Inc. v. American West African Line, Inc.*, 147 F.2d 363, 1945 AMC 191 (2d Cir. 1945), cargo was damaged by water that entered the holds when "kick tubes" on the deck were broken off by deck cargo during a storm. The court said:

> The first question is whether the ship was unseaworthy. *Arguendo*, we will assume that the "kick tubes" did not make her so if she had carried no deck cargo; and, perhaps also, even when she carried certain kinds of deck cargo. Indeed, we might go still further, and assume that she was seaworthy, just as she rode, for a summer voyage, for example in the Mediterranean. But she was to cross the Atlantic in January, ending in latitudes over 40 degrees; and the question is whether, with the deck cargo she actually did carry and the "kick tubes" in her deck, she was reasonably fitted for such a voyage... The case comes down to whether a ship proves that she is well found for a winter Atlantic voyage, when her stow breaks apart under such conditions. We do not see how less can be asked of her upon such a voyage, than that she shall successfully meet such weather, for surely gales—indeed even "whole gales"—are to be expected in such waters at such a season.

Some of the water that entered the holds had come through "goosenecks" on the bridge deck. The carrier would not have been liable for damage caused from that source. Nevertheless, the carrier was held to be liable in full, because of the *Vallescura* rule, considered above at 237-238 [in the 2006 edition]. The court continued:

> [T]he seas which washed out the plugs [in the "goosenecks"] were either too strong to be resisted by ordinary means, or the plugs were driven home improperly; in either event the ship would be excused. Nevertheless the excuse will not serve her for several reasons. The greater part of the water which entered the bunker came over the sill of the open doorway from No. 4 'tween-deck [ie, from the "kick tubes"]; and for that the ship is liable in any event. How she could distinguish between the damage caused by that water, and the damage caused by the water which came from the storeroom [ie, from the "goosenecks"], it is impossible to imagine. Yet that would be her duty. *Schnell v. The Vallescura*, supra.

Questions

1. Compare the burden of proof on "negligence" allocated by the court in *Taisho Marine & Fire Ins. Co., Ltd. v. M/V Sea-Land Endurance, supra*, with that stated in *Complaint of Tecomar S.A.*, 765 F. Supp. 1150, 1175, 1991 AMC 2432 (S.D.N.Y. 1991):

> Accordingly, the burdens of proof in this case are allocated as follows: Tecomar [carrier] must establish that the weather encountered by the ship constituted a peril of the sea and that the peril caused the loss. If Tecomar succeeds, the burden shifts to Claimants to establish that the vessel was unseaworthy and that the unseaworthiness was at least a concurrent cause of the loss. Even if this is proven, however, Tecomar can still avoid liability under COGSA if it shows that it exercised due diligence in attempting to make the *Tuxpan* seaworthy.

2. Suppose a court rejects a "perils of the sea" defense because the storm which the vessel encountered was of a magnitude that was common for that time of year. Should the shipowner prevail on an "errors in navigation" defense if the court finds that the master erred in his decision as to what action the vessel should take in response to the storm? *See, Yawata Iron & Steel Co., Ltd. v. Anthony Shipping Co., Ltd.*, 396 F. Supp. 619, 1975 AMC 1602, (S.D.N.Y. 1975), *aff'd*, 538 F.2d 317, 1976 AMC 2685 (2d Cir. 1976).

---

b. Other Immunities

In addition to the three immunities that have already been considered—errors in navigation or management, perils of the sea and restraint of princes—there are fourteen other carrier immunities specifically enumerated in COGSA § 4, all of which by the terms of the Act must be proved by the carrier. Most of these are self-explanatory and present little difficulty conceptually, although there are many overlaps among them.

Most of the carrier immunities can be grouped into three general categories: (1) overwhelming outside human forces (*i.e.*, acts of war; acts of public enemies; arrest or restraint of princes; quarantines; strikes or lockouts; and riots and civil commotions), (2) overwhelming natural forces (*i.e.*, perils of the sea and acts of God), and (3) faults of the shipper (*i.e.*, act or omission of the shipper or his agents; wastage in bulk or weight and losses due to inherent vice; insufficiency of packaging or marking; and latent defects). An important question is what is the effect of carrier contributory or concurrent fault here? This is a complex question and the answer depends upon the precise nature of the carrier fault involved. Logically there are three possible solutions: first, the carrier can be totally excused if the fault itself is immune as an error of navigation or management; second, the fault can completely prevent the application of the immunity if, as in act of God, the absence of human negligence is part of the definition of the immunity, third, the presence of concurrent carrier fault can make it incumbent on the carrier to prove which part of the loss was caused by the immunity as distinguished from the fault.

Of the remaining immunities, fire presents special problems and is treated separately below. Likewise saving or attempting to save life or property at sea is best thought of in the nature of a deviation, which is treated below.

---

i. Inherent Vice: COGSA § 4(2)(m) [formerly 46 app. U.S.C. § 1304(2)(m)]

Note and Question

There is some disagreement between circuits about the burden of proof in cases where the carrier alleges that the loss or damage to the goods arose "from inherent defect, quality or vice of the goods". In the Second Circuit, the shipper must disprove inherent vice as part of its showing that the cargo was in good order and condition upon delivery. *See American Tobacco Company v. Goulandris*, 281 F.2d 179, 182 (2d Cir. 1960); *Hecht Lewis & Kahn, Inc. v. The S. S. President Buchanan*, 236 F.2d 627, 631 (2d Cir. 1956); *American Tobacco Company v. The Hadjipatera*, 81 F. Supp. 438, 446 (S.D.N.Y. 1948), *modified on other grounds*, 194 F.2d 449 (2d Cir. 1951); *United States Steel International, Inc. v. M.T. Granheim*, 540 F. Supp. 1326, 1982 AMC 2770 (S.D.N.Y. 1982). In the Fifth Circuit, however, the burden is on the carrier to prove inherent vice. *Quaker Oats Co. v. M/V Torvanger*, 734 F.2d 238, 241 n.3, 1984 AMC 2943 (5th Cir. 1984), *cert. denied*, 469 U.S. 1189, 105 S. Ct. 959, 83 L.Ed.2d 965, 1985 AMC 2398 (1985).

A chemical cargo has a natural tendency to form peroxides when exposed to oxygen. There is uncontradicted testimony that the chemical was properly treated by an inhibitor and protected from oxygenization by a nitrogen blanket during shipment and, thus, should not have formed peroxides. There is also uncontradicted evidence that the peroxide content of the chemical was well within commercially acceptable levels at the time of loading. Nevertheless, on discharge, the chemical was contaminated with peroxides. In such a case, where there is no apparent explanation for the damage to the cargo, who should lose, carrier or cargo? *See Quaker Oats Co. v. M/V Torvanger*, 734 F.2d 238, 241 n.3, 1984 AMC 2943 (5th Cir. 1984).

---

ii. "Q" Clause

COGSA § 4(2)(q) [formerly 46 app. U.S.C. § 1304(2)(q)]

IN RE INTERCONTINENTAL PROPERTIES MANAGEMENT

604 F.2d 254, 1979 AMC 1680 (4th Cir. 1979)

James Dickson PHILLIPS, Circuit Judge:

* * *

I. Background

This litigation to decide whether the economic loss resulting from destruction of a ship's cargo shall be borne by the cargo owners or the shipowner grew out of a stark tragedy involving the destruction as well of several human lives.

The M/V Mimi sailed from Miami, Florida, at around 10:30 P.M., October 9, 1975, bound for ports of call in Venezuela and Guyana. Her cargo consisted of bagged fertilizer and other general cargo stowed below and containers of general cargo stowed on deck. A small vessel, just under 500 gross registered tons, the MIMI was owned at the time by the appellee-appellant International Properties Management, S.A., a Panamanian corporation (Shipowner) and was under time charter to two joint venturers, All-Caribbean, Inc. and High Watch Shipping Company, Ltd. (Charterers). She carried a complement of four German officers, four Indonesian seamen, and a Filipino cook. Among the seamen was one Gun Gun Supardi who had signed aboard five months before in Hamburg, Germany, and had since served continuously as a member of the crew.

During loading operations just before departure from Miami, Gun Gun Supardi was cut above one eye when a cable snapped and lashed him. He was taken to a hospital after the MIMI had left the dock, given four stitches and then returned to the vessel. The captain sent him to his cabin to rest and Supardi stayed there for about twenty-four hours.

Shortly before midnight on October 10, having left his quarters he encountered the Chief Engineer in another part of the vessel. Words were exchanged, Supardi struck the officer with what he later described as an "iron," then knifed him. When another officer came to the rescue, Supardi knifed him. The berserk seaman then proceeded to seek out and knife in turn each of the other two officers. Those who survived the knife wounds were bludgeoned into submission. Supardi then awakened the sleeping crew members and forced them at knife-point to provision and lower a lifeboat. At some point in this process he shut down the engines and opened the sea-valves in the engine room. At about 4:00 A.M., October 11, 1975, while Supardi stood by in the lifeboat with his captive fellow crew members, the MIMI sank, carrying with it all its cargo and its already dead or incapacitated officers. Later that morning the lifeboat occupants were picked up by a passing ship, and at this point the author of the catastrophe passes from this factual account of the litigation's background.

* * *

Cargo's *prima facie* case of delivery and failure to return was stipulated. Similarly, the actual cause of loss was plain and undisputed: the ship was willfully scuttled by a member of its crew. Cargo adduced a great deal of evidence designed in various ways to establish that Shipowner had breached its obligation under § 3(1) to provide a seaworthy ship and that these breaches proximately caused the loss. This evidence went essentially to failures "properly [to] man" the ship, 46 U.S.C. § 1303(3)(1)(b), by pointing to carelessness in employing Gun Gun Supardi and in providing a crew adequate to have restrained him or otherwise prevented the scuttling. Shipowner countered with evidence designed to establish its § 4(1) "immunity" under the unseaworthiness theory by showing its "due diligence" in manning the ship in all the many respects challenged by Cargo and the lack of proximate causation between any of its acts or omissions respecting its "proper manning" obligation and the loss. The evidence of record supporting these opposing contentions respecting the unseaworthiness theory is voluminous, but its details need not be further described, for decision turns on whether or not shipowner successfully overcame by proof the *prima facie* imputation to it of fault in failing under § 3(2) "properly and carefully [to] carry, keep, care for, and discharge the goods carried."

As indicated in our general analysis of the proof scheme, this could only have been done by proof that established the cause of loss as one of those specifically excepted in § 4(2)(a)-(p), or as "[any] other cause arising without the actual fault ... of the carrier and without the fault or neglect of the agents or servants of the carrier," under § 4(2)(q) (the "Q-Clause"). In attempting to carry this burden, the Shipowner was of course constrained by indisputable evidence that the direct cause was the willful act of its seaman employee.

In summary, this was the proof laid before the district court and upon which it concluded that the Shipowner was entitled to exoneration. From that court's memorandum opinion it appears that although the parties argued and the court was advertent to the possible application of both theories of recovery, the court's legal conclusion of exoneration was related only to the unseaworthiness theory.

In attempting to exculpate itself from the breach of its general duty of care under § 3(2) that had been established *prima facie*, Shipowner expressly relied upon both § 4(2)(a) (errors in management) and § 4(2)(q) (the omnibus clause). The district court rightly rejected the "errors in management" exception and Shipowner has abandoned any reliance upon it on appeal. When the court then turned to the "Q-clause" omnibus exception, it revealed its critical misapprehension of the proper application of COGSA to the facts of the case, saying:

> The exception provided in § 1304(2)(q) appears to provide the same burden given in 46 U.S.C. § 1304(1), namely, that [Shipowner] prove that its fault, if any, did not contribute to or proximately cause the loss complained of. Thus, the one question before this Court is whether [Shipowner] has successfully proven that the cargo loss sustained from the sinking of the MIMI was not proximately caused by its negligence, if any.

The court then proceeded to analyze the evidence as it tended to prove or disprove proximate causal connection between the specific breaches of the seaworthiness obligation urged by Cargo and the loss. Finding no proximate cause, it held the Shipowner exonerated.

In this analysis, the district court wrongly equated the defensive proof requirements of §§ 4(1) and 4(2). While both do clearly relate to the question of Shipowner's fault, they are addressed, as our general analysis of COGSA has shown, to two distinctly different theories of recovery, and consequently have different substantive content. Specifically, the court's equating of the two led it completely to disregard the "Q-clause" requirement that the carrier prove not only that the identified cause of loss arose "without the actual fault and privity of the carrier" but also "without the fault or neglect of the agents or servants of the carrier" [emphasis supplied]. These dual requirements are plainly stated conjunctively in COGSA's "Q-clause."

Rightly applied to the undisputed facts of the case, COGSA posed a narrow question of law that the district court failed to identify as decisive. It is whether the loss of the MIMI's cargo by Supardi's act resulted from a cause "arising without the fault or neglect of the agents or servants of the carrier" within the meaning of the Q-clause, 46 U.S.C. § 1304(2)(q). Stated more abstractly, the question, apparently one of first impression under COGSA, is whether under the "Q-clause" a seaman's willful act of scuttling a ship is an excepted cause of cargo loss that exculpates the carrier/employer from liability.

Unless the plain language of the statute is to be disregarded, the answer seems equally plain: that it is not. Only one narrow interpretive problem may be thought left open by the quoted language. Applied to this case, it is whether Supardi, whose fault clearly caused the loss, was at the time of the scuttling an agent or servant of the Shipowner. That he was at the time employed by Shipowner is undisputed. He was therefore a "servant" of Shipowner unless there is to be read into the statute a "scope of employment" qualification outside whose reach his causative act fell.

Recognizing the problem posed for it by the literal language of this critical provision, Shipowner on this appeal argues that such a "scope of employment" qualification should be read into the Q-clause, citing an English case, *Leesh River Tea Co. v. British India Steam Navigation Co.*, [1966] 2 Q.B. 250 (C.A.), as persuasive authority for the proposition. Because the question is novel and because of the general policy favoring uniformity of interpretation of the various national counterparts to the Hague Rules, we have given careful consideration to the *Leesh River* decision.

We need neither adopt nor reject the *Leesh River* rule as one of general application in order to decide that Supardi's act in this case was that of a servant under the Q-clause, for his act lay within the scope of employment contemplated by *Leesh River* in any event. In *Leesh River* a carrier was sued for damage to cargo caused by seawater entering the hold of its ship. Stevedores employed by the carrier to transfer cargo had removed and stolen a brass plate from the hull, leaving a hole through which the water entered after the voyage resumed. Applying the English counterpart to pertinent provisions of COGSA, the *Leesh River* court held the carrier exculpated from liability under the Q-clause.

* * *

Obviously the very terms "agent and servant" imply at the minimum a temporal coincidence of general employment with causative act, and any rational interpretation of the Q-clause must start with that interpretation. *Leesh River* reads in only a modest further qualification: that the causative act shall have occurred at a place and time, and in respect of an object related to the general duties of the employment. It does not read in any further qualification related to the servant's culpability or state of mind, a qualification of the Q-clause that Shipowner here has contended for....

We are reinforced in this construction of the Q-clause by two other considerations than the plain meaning analysis. First, we think the result dictated by this construction conforms to the general policy that must underlie COGSA's careful allocation of proof burdens in respect of loss of goods at sea. In the proof scheme earlier analyzed appears a frequently used procedural device to force a preferred substantive result where proof is in equipoise or unavailable, or where only very specific exceptions to generally assumed liability are to be recognized. Where such a device is used it ordinarily reflects an intention that in the case where both parties are without direct fault but one must suffer the loss, it is ordinarily fairer that the loss shall fall upon the party in the better position to have controlled, and to produce evidence of, the operative facts. The device used is the evidentiary presumption (*prima facie case, res ipsa loquitur*) that casts the burden, hence the loss, on that disfavored party. That such a policy may well also cast the loss upon the disfavored party in some situations not precisely contemplated nor adequately described in a statute is itself likely to be an intended consequence. As between carrier and shipper of goods by sea, carrier is obviously the party more likely to be in control both of events and of evidence of events. So, we think is the result dictated by our construction of the Q-clause likely to conform to congressional policy in enacting COGSA.

Finally, the construction is suggested by considering Supardi's act as one of classic barratry. It meets the definition. *See, e.g., Carver's Carriage of Goods by Sea* § 185, at 159 (12th ed. R. Colinvaux 1971); and *see National Union Fire Insurance Co. v. Republic of China*, 254 F.2d 177, 182-84 (4th Cir. 1958) (insurance coverage). Before cargo damage law was codified, barratry was one of the exceptions to liability traditionally listed by the carrier in bills of lading. Many of these exceptions were carried into the specific exceptions in § 4(2) of COGSA. Barratry was not; and as perhaps the most obvious conceivable example of "fault" of a seaman servant, its intended inclusion within the general Q-Clause reference to servant fault seems a construction compelled by any common sense reading. From this, it would appear that barratry was simply not intended to be an exculpating cause of loss under COGSA. *See* SCRUTTON ON CHARTER PARTIES art. 113, at 239 (18th ed. A. Mocatta, M. Mustill & S. Boyd 1974).

* * *

Vacated and remanded for further proceedings.

---

iii. Fire

COGSA § 4(2)(b) [formerly 46 app. U.S.C. § 1304(2)(b)]; 46 U.S.C. § 30504 (formerly 46 U.S.C. § 182) (1851)

COMPLAINT OF TA CHI NAVIGATION (PANAMA), CORP., S.A.

677 F.2d 225, 1982 AMC 1710 (2d Cir. 1982)

VAN GRAAFEILAND, Circuit Judge:

This is an appeal from an order of the United States District Court for the Southern District of New York, C.H. TENNEY, J., denying the petition of a shipowner for exoneration from or limitation of liability for cargo damage claims resulting from a shipboard explosion and fire. Because the district court erred in fixing the elements and burdens of proof, we reverse and remand for further proceedings.

Judge Tenney's opinion, reported at 504 F. Supp. 209, contains a comprehensive statement of the facts. A short summary will therefore suffice for our purpose. The stricken ship was the *S.S. Eurypylus*, owned by Ta Chi Navigation (Panama) Corp., and the fire occurred on November 10, 1975 while she was en route from Japan to Panama. The ship was gutted and sold for scrap, and most of her cargo was destroyed. The district court found that the fire began when acetylene gas escaping from a welding hose in the ship's engine room was ignited by a spark. Cylinders containing oxygen and acetylene, stored in a port tonnage alleyway near the engine room, two of which were feeding the torch, promptly exploded, and the fire was almost immediately out of control. The district court predicated its finding of liability upon the presence of the cylinders in the alleyway, and the propriety of such storage was the most vigorously contested issue on the trial.

Cargo claimants produced two expert witnesses in support of their contention that the storage was improper. The shipowner produced substantial evidence to the contrary. That evidence showed that the ship was built in Scotland in 1958 and carried a 100 A-1 classification with Lloyds Register of Shipping from the time it was built, indicating thereby that the ship was of the best quality. There was also testimony that a storage rack for the oxygen and acetylene cylinders was installed in the alleyway when the ship was built. From time to time thereafter, the ship was checked by representatives of Lloyds, and safety equipment certificates were issued in accordance with Safety of Life at Sea regulations [SOLAS], which were prepared under the auspices of the Intergovernmental Maritime Consultive Organization (IMCO).

* * *

It is in the light of this testimony that the district court's discussion of the elements and burdens of proof must be examined. The district judge said that "the [shipowner] is required to prove that the vessel was seaworthy at the commencement of the voyage." 504 F. Supp. at 229. He continued, "If the petitioner failed to use due and proper care, *i.e.*, due diligence, to provide a competent master and crew and to see that the ship was seaworthy at the commencement of the voyage, then any loss occurring by reason of fault or neglect in these particulars is within its privity, and it may not avail itself of the fire exemption statutes." *Id.* at 230. He went on:

> In the instant case we are concerned with whether the carrier had exercised due diligence under § 1303 before and at the commencement of the voyage to make *S.S. Eurypylus* seaworthy, to properly man, equip, and supply her, and to make her holds fit and safe for the reception, carriage, and preservation of cargo. (*Id.*)

He then concluded that the storage of the oxyacetylene cylinders in the port tonnage alleyway rendered the *Eurypylus* unseaworthy at the commencement of the voyage. *Id.* at 233.

The district court's approach to the burden of proof is not as straightforward as we have presented it. It is clear, however, that the entire approach reflects a misunderstanding of the terms of the Fire Statute as they have been applied by the Supreme Court and the courts of this Circuit. The Fire Statute, 46 U.S.C. § 182, exonerates the shipowner from liability for fire damage to cargo unless the fire was caused by the "design or neglect" of the owner. "Neglect", as thus used, means negligence, not the breach of a non-delegable duty. *Consumers Import Co. v. Kabushiki Kaisha Kawasaki Zosenjo*, 320 U.S. 249, 252 (1943); *Earle & Stoddart, Inc. v. Ellerman's Wilson Line, Ltd.*, 287 U.S. 420, 427 (1932). "If the carrier shows that the damage was caused by fire, the shipper must prove that the carrier's negligence caused the damage." *Asbestos Corp. Ltd. v. Compagnie De Navigation Frais-Sinet Et Cyprien Fabre*, 480 F.2d 669, 673 (2d Cir. 1973).

* * *

The shipper can prove that the carrier caused the damage either by proving that a negligent act of the carrier caused the fire or that such an act prevented the fire's extinguishment. *Asbestos Corp. Ltd., supra,* 480 F.2d at 672.

This delineation of the carrier's liability did not change with the 1936 enactment of the Carriage of Goods by Sea Act (COGSA), ch. 229 § 1-16, 49 Stat. 1207 (current version at 46 U.S.C. §§ 1300-1315). Congress specifically provided that COGSA shall not affect the rights and obligations of the carrier under the Fire Statute. 46 U.S.C. § 1308. Congress also included in COGSA a provision that the carrier shall not be responsible for fire damage resulting from fire "unless caused by the actual fault or privity of the carrier." 46 U.S.C. § 1304(2) (b).

When COGSA was under consideration by the House Committee on Merchant Marine and Fisheries, the suggestion was made that "since this bill itself in section 8 disclaims all intent to modify the fire statute, and there is no apparent reason why it should be modified," the words "design or neglect of the carrier" as used in the Fire Statute be substituted for the words "fault or privity of the carrier" in the proposed Act. *Hearings on S. 1152 before the House Committee on Merchant Marine and Fisheries,* 74th Cong. 2d Sess. 13 (1936). However, it was pointed out that "the word 'fault' corresponds generally to the word 'neglect' and the word 'privity' to the word 'design,' " *id.* at 141, and the words "fault" and "privity" were retained in the statute.

We have adopted that reasoning in this Circuit and treat the COGSA fire exemption as being the same as that of the Fire Statute. *Asbestos Corp. Ltd. v. Compagnie De Navigation Frais-Sinet Et Cyprien Fabre, supra,* 480 F.2d at 672.

* * *

Unfortunately, the district court patterned its holding upon that of the Ninth Circuit in *Sunkist Growers, Inc. v. Adelaide Shipping Lines, Ltd.*, 603 F.2d 1327 (9th Cir. 1979), cert. denied, 444 U.S. 1012 (1980). In *Sunkist,* the Ninth Circuit held that the burden of proof is on the carrier to show that it exercised due diligence to provide a seaworthy ship in order to invoke the provisions of either section 1304(2) (b) or the Fire Statute. *Id.* at 1336. Commenting on this Court's holding in *Asbestos Corp. Ltd. v. Compagnie De Navigation, supra,* 480 F.2d 669, that the shipper must prove that the carrier's negligence caused the fire damage, the Ninth Circuit stated that the "use of this language was entirely unnecessary" and constituted a "casual treatment of the burden of proof by the author of the appellate court opinion." 603 F.2d at 1335. Strangely enough, the author of Sunkist did not fault the district court judge in *Asbestos* for holding that "[o]nce the defendant has sustained the burden of proving that it comes within the exemption of COGSA § 1304 (2) (b) or the Fire Statute the burden then shifts to the shipper to prove that the fire was caused by the 'design or neglect' or 'actual fault or privity' of the carrier". 345 F. Supp. 814, 821.

We disagree not only with *Sunkist's* unflattering characterization of Judge Timbers' opinion in *Asbestos,* an opinion that was concurred in by Judges Smith and Hayes, but also with the Ninth Circuit's interpretation of the interrelation between the Fire Statute and

COGSA, an interpretation that is concurred in by no other Circuit. The "ping pong" effect of the shifting burden of proof under section 1304(2), *Nitram, Inc. v. Cretan Life*, 599 F.2d 1359, 1373 (5th Cir. 1979) did not receive its first recognition by this Court in *Asbestos Corp. v. Compagnie De Navigation Frais-Sinet Et Cyprien Fabre, supra.* In *American Tobacco Co. v. The Katingo Hadjipatera, supra*, decided twenty-two years prior to Asbestos Corp., Judge Frank, writing for himself, Judge Swan, and Judge Learned Hand, said that, once a shipowner established loss by fire, "[n]o liability could be imposed unless the owners of [cargo] carried the burden of proving that the fire was caused by the shipowner's design or negligence or the carriers' actual fault or privity." 194 F.2d at 450.

When Congress wanted to put the burden of proving freedom from fault on a shipowner claiming the benefit of an exemption, it specifically said so. *See* 46 U.S.C. § 1304(2)(q). The Sunkist court would read the language of subsection (q) into subsection (b), "although Congress did not put it there." *See Lekas & Drivas, Inc. v. Goulandris, supra*, 306 F.2d at 432. This Court has not put it there either. We adhere to our prior holdings that, if the carrier shows that the damage was caused by fire, the shipper must prove that the carrier's negligence caused the fire or prevented its extinguishment. If on remand the shipper fails to meet this burden, the action must be dismissed. Only if the shipper sustained the burden would the carrier have the obligation to establish what portion of the damage was not attributable to its fault.

* * *

Reversed and remanded.

NISSAN FIRE & MARINE INS. CO., LTD. v. M/V HYUNDAI EXPLORER

93 F.3d 641, 1996 AMC 2409 (9th Cir. 1996)

D.W. NELSON, Circuit Judge:

I.

Introduction

This case arises out of an engine room fire aboard the M/V HYUNDAI EXPLORER (the "Vessel"), a Korean flag container cargo ship, on or about January 2, 1992. Defendant-appellant Hyundai Merchant Marine Co., Ltd. ("HMM"), the bareboat charterer[1] and operator of the Vessel when she experienced the fire, appeals the district court's grant of summary judgment for plaintiffs-appellees Nissan Fire & Marine Insurance Co., Ltd., Taiko Bussan Kaisha, Ltd., Fireman's Fund Insurance Co. and American Home Assurance Co., (collectively, "Cargo Interests"). Cargo Interests are the subrogated insurers or consignees of cargo that suffered damage because of the fire. We reverse the summary judgment for Cargo Interests and remand to the district court with instructions to enter judgment for HMM.

---

[1] A bareboat charterer is one who charters or leases a vessel without a crew. The charterer assumes full possession and control of the vessel and is deemed the owner of the vessel for purposes of the U.S. Carriage of Goods by Sea Act ("COGSA") during the period of the charter. 46 U.S.C.App. § 186.

II.

Factual and Procedural Background

The parties stipulated to most of the relevant facts in their Agreed Statement of Facts, which they filed with the district court. During the voyage at issue, the Vessel loaded and discharged cargo at Long Beach, Oakland and Seattle. It departed Seattle for Pusan, Korea on December 22, 1991. During the cargo operations in the United States ports and on the voyage to Korea, both of the Vessel's generators operated with no apparent problems until a fire was discovered on the morning of January 2, 1992.

The Vessel has an automated control room and was therefore manned only between 0800 and 1730 hours. The Third Engineer, who was the duty officer on the night of January 1, noted nothing out of the ordinary when he visited the engine room at 2200 hours as part of his routine. At 0700 hours on January 2, however, an alarm alerted him to a fire in the engine room. Although the crew was able to extinguish the fire, the engine control room sustained significant damage, and the Vessel required a salvage tug to tow her to Pusan. While under tow, she was unable to provide refrigeration to the refrigerated ("reefer") cargo, and much of it spoiled.

The fire resulted from the failure of a compression coupling on a fuel oil line to the No. 2 generator fuel pressure alarm. When the coupling failed, the line separated from the main fuel line and sprayed oil, which ignited when it contacted the engine exhaust system. The line was not original, but had been replaced at some unknown time in the past. Inspection of the coupling indicated that it was not defective, but that it had been improperly fitted. Inspection also revealed that a rubber "O" ring and some thread sealing tape were attached to the coupling. Presumably, the ring and tape were used to repair a previous leak, but it is not known when they were applied.

Both parties' expert witnesses opined that the repair to the coupling was of the type normally performed by a crewmember and that the curves on the replacement line indicated that a crewmember, rather than a shipyard, most likely made the repair in question. None of the engineers aboard at the time of the fire, each of whom had joined the Vessel between March and August, 1991, fitted the coupling in question or had ever seen the coupling leak. Only the engine room log books and maintenance records might have reflected repairs made by prior crew members, and these were destroyed in the fire.

While assembled, the coupling completely concealed the "O" ring, sealing tape and its poor fit. Indeed, both experts agreed that the defective fitting would not have been visually apparent to even a trained engineer or surveyor while assembled. Moreover, Cargo Interests' expert testified that engineers and surveyors normally do not open compression couplings in an engine room for inspection purposes and that disassembly is not part of routine maintenance or inspection. These observations held true in this case as HMM's port engineer in charge of the Vessel's maintenance and repair failed to discover the defect in the coupling assembly before the Vessel departed on the voyage in issue.

In addition, official inspections of the Vessel had failed to discover the defective coupling if, in fact, it existed when they were performed. The Vessel is certified ("classed") by the Korean Register of Shipping ("KRS"), which inspects vessels' safety for governmental insurance purposes. In September, 1990, the KRS surveyed the Vessel's No. 2 generator and its safety devices and alarms and found them to be in order. The KRS made another hull/machinery survey in August, 1991 and issued a report stating that it had inspected the safety devices and alarms for the generators and again found them to be in order. The No. 2 generator was next due for survey in 1995.

Cargo Interests brought suit against the Vessel and HMM for damages they incurred due to the spoiled reefer cargo. This case originally was brought as two separate suits, each against HMM in personam as claimant to the Vessel and against the Vessel in rem. After the cases were consolidated, the district court heard the parties' cross motions for summary judgment. HMM moved for summary judgment on the basis of its assertion that the "fire defenses" insulated it from liability. The fire defenses are comprised of two statutes that limit a shipowner's liability for cargo damage caused by fire aboard a vessel: the "Fire Statute," 46 U.S.C.app. § 182,[2] and the COGSA Fire Exemption, 46 U.S.C.app. § 1304(2)(b).[3]

The court determined, and HMM concedes, that the defective coupling responsible for the fire was an unseaworthy condition. The court then ruled that under the law of this Circuit, HMM had the burden of proving it had exercised due diligence to make the Vessel seaworthy before it could invoke the fire defenses. Further, the district court held that HMM's duty of due diligence was "absolute or non-delegable" and that HMM had failed to meet its burden. We reverse.

* * *

---

[2] 46 U.S.C.App. § 182 [the Fire Statute], enacted as part of the original Limitation of Liability Act of 1851, provides:
No owner of any vessel shall be liable to answer for or make good to any person any loss or damage, which may happen to any merchandise whatsoever, which shall be shipped, taken in, or put on board any such vessel, by reason or by means of any fire happening to or on board the vessel, unless such fire is caused by the design or neglect of such owner.

[3] Congress enacted COGSA in 1936 to partially replace the Harter Act of 1893, 46 U.S.C.App. §§ 190-196, and to make the law more favorable to shipowners. See In re Damodar Bulk Carriers, Ltd., 903 F.2d 675, 684 (9th Cir.1990). 46 U.S.C.App. §§ 1303 and 1304, part of COGSA, provide in relevant part:

> § 1303. Responsibilities and liabilities of carrier and ship
> Seaworthiness
> (1) The carrier shall be bound, before and at the beginning of the voyage, to exercise due diligence to -
> (a) Make the ship seaworthy;
> (b) Properly man, equip, and supply the ship;
>
> * * *
>
> § 1304. Rights and immunities of carrier and ship
> Unseaworthiness
> (1) Neither the carrier nor the ship shall be liable for loss or damage arising or resulting from unseaworthiness unless caused by want of due diligence on the part of the carrier to make the ship seaworthy, and to secure that the ship is properly manned, equipped, and supplied.... Whenever loss or damage has resulted from unseaworthiness, the burden of proving the exercise of due diligence shall be on the carrier or other persons claiming exemption under this section.
> Uncontrollable causes of loss
> (2) Neither the carrier nor the ship shall be responsible for loss or damage arising or resulting from -
>
> * * *
>
> (b) Fire, unless caused by the actual fault or privity of the carrier.

IV.

Discussion

A. Burden of proof on due diligence.

"Fire is the peril most dreaded by all mariners, and a peril most difficult to combat in a fully laden ship." *In re Liberty Shipping Corp.*, 509 F.2d 1249, 1250 (9th Cir.1975). That being so, the maritime law has developed unique provisions embodied in the fire defenses which govern a shipowner's liability in connection with a fire aboard his vessel. This court has held, however, that where unseaworthiness[4] caused the fire, a carrier[5] bears the burden of showing that it exercised due diligence to make the ship seaworthy before it can invoke the fire defenses to exonerate it from liability. *See Sunkist Growers, Inc. v. Adelaide Shipping Lines*, 603 F.2d 1327, 1340 (9th Cir.1979), *cert. denied*, 444 U.S. 1012, 100 S.Ct. 659, 62 L.Ed.2d 640 (1980); cf. *In re Damodar Bulk Carriers, Ltd.*, 903 F.2d 675, 686 (9th Cir.1990). Because the improperly fitted coupling on the Vessel was an unseaworthy condition, the district court correctly assigned to HMM the burden of proving its due diligence as a prerequisite to invoking the fire defenses.

B. The standard of due diligence under the fire defenses.

HMM contends that even if it bore the burden of showing that it acted with due diligence, the district court erred in holding that this duty was non-delegable.[6] Cargo Interests contend that the court imposed the proper standard and that HMM's duty of due diligence was in fact non-delegable.

This claim is without merit and manifests Cargo Interests' failure to recognize the different standards of due diligence that apply in the fire defenses and other COGSA exemptions. While the carrier's duty of due diligence is non-delegable for exoneration under the non-fire COGSA exemptions, a different standard of due diligence, one derived from the Fire Statute, governs fire cases and eliminates vicarious liability imputed to the carrier. Under the fire defenses, a carrier is liable only for "his personal negligence, or in case of a corporate owner, negligence of its managing officers and agents as distinguished from that of the master or subordinates." *Consumers Import Co. v. Kabushiki Kaisha*, 320 U.S. 249, 252, 64 S.Ct. 15, 16, 88 L.Ed. 30 (1943); *see also Earle & Stoddart v. Ellerman's Wilson Line*, 287 U.S. 420, 427, 53 S.Ct. 200, 201, 77 L.Ed. 403 (1932) ("The courts have been careful not to thwart the purpose of the fire statute by interpreting as 'neglect' of the

---

[4] The legal test for seaworthiness is "whether the vessel is reasonably fit to carry the cargo which she has undertaken to transport." The Silvia, 171 U.S. 462, 464, 19 S.Ct. 7, 8, 43 L.Ed. 241 (1898). Courts have held that a broad range of conditions may render a vessel unseaworthy: crew error, a defect in the vessel's construction or equipment, improper loading or stowage of cargo and various sorts of dangerous conditions.

[5] "The term 'carrier' includes the owner or the charterer who enters into a contract of carriage with the [cargo] shipper." 46 U.S.C.App. § 1301(a). In this case, HMM is the carrier and Cargo Interests are the shippers.

[6] The court stated at the hearing on the cross motions for summary judgment:

> [T]he shipowner has this duty of putting the vessel in a seaworthy condition at the beginning of the voyage.
>
> So we do not really have an issue of whether the shipowner is being held vicariously liable for the act of the crew, as this was a condition of the vessel at the time that it embarked upon the voyage. And this was the duty of the shipowner.
>
> And whether one calls it ... absolute or nondelegable, or whatever term you use, it is a duty that the shipowner owed where I don't think it's entitled to step behind the, quote, no liability for the acts of the crew, close quote, principle.

* * *

owners the breach of what in other connections is held to be a non-delegable duty."); *Westinghouse Elec. Corp. v. M/V "LESLIE LYKES"*, 734 F.2d 199, 209 (5th Cir.), *cert. denied*, 469 U.S. 1077, 105 S.Ct. 577, 83 L.Ed.2d 516 (1984); *Hasbro Indus. v. M/S St. Constantine*, 705 F.2d 339, 342 (9th Cir.1983) (holding that the negligence of the "shipowner's supervisory or managing employees" was sufficient to find personal negligence); *In re Ta Chi Navigation Corp.*, S.A., 677 F.2d 225, 228 (2d Cir.1982) (" 'Neglect' ... means negligence, not the breach of a non-delegable duty."); *Sunkist,* 603 F.2d at 1336 (stating that " 'neglect of the owner' under the Fire Statute refers to 'the neglect of the managing officers and agents as distinguished from that of the master or other members of the crew' ") (quoting *Albina Engine & Machine Works v. Hershey Chocolate Corp.*, 295 F.2d 619, 621 (9th Cir.1961)); *In re Liberty Shipping Corp.*, 509 F.2d 1249, 1252 (9th Cir.1975); *Asbestos Corp. Ltd. v. Compagnie De Navigation Fraissinet et Cyprien Fabre et al.*, 480 F.2d 669, 673 n. 7 (2d Cir.1973).

Although a carrier generally is not liable for the negligence or lack of due diligence of its crew or other lower level employees, it still may be liable for the actions of an employee responsible for starting the fire or preventing its spread if the carrier was personally negligent, for example, by not adequately training the employee or by failing to provide sufficient fire fighting equipment. *See, e.g., Hasbro,* 705 F.2d at 342; *Asbestos Corp.*, 480 F.2d at 672. Under the facts of this case, however, there was nothing to implicate the crew's training, the Vessel's fire-fighting equipment, or any other personal duties of HMM. The district court improperly focused on the unseaworthy condition rather than assessing whether any personal negligence by HMM was responsible for that condition. As we have discussed above, however, the fire defenses impose a burden of personal due diligence. Because the district court applied the wrong standard of due diligence in determining whether HMM had carried its burden, the court erred in granting summary judgment for Cargo Interests.

C. Proving due diligence

Exoneration under the fire defenses is not voided by an unseaworthy condition, but rather by an "inexcusable" unseaworthy condition, i.e., one that existed because of the carrier's lack of due diligence. *See Hasbro,* 705 F.2d at 341; *Sunkist,* 603 F.2d at 1335 (quoting *Asbestos Corp.*, 480 F.2d at 672). To carry its burden of proving due diligence, HMM had to prove that it had done all that was "proper and reasonable" to make the Vessel seaworthy. *See Martin v. The Southwark,* 191 U.S. 1, 15-16, 24 S.Ct. 1, 5-6, 48 L.Ed. 65 (1903). All of the evidence indicates that a crewmember made the repair in question; indeed, Cargo Interests' expert witness agreed with that assessment. Because the facts do not suggest any theory under which the defective repair could be imputed to HMM personally, it is irrelevant whether HMM can identify the specific circumstances surrounding the repair.

The evidence also demonstrates that HMM inspected the Vessel and/or had it inspected regularly. We are aware that compliance with classification society requirements does not necessarily establish due diligence. *See Louis Dreyfus Corp. v. 27,946 Long Tons of Corn,* 830 F.2d 1321, 1327 (5th Cir.1987); *Fireman's Fund Ins. Cos. v. M/V VIGNES,* 794

F.2d 1552, 1556 (11th Cir.1986). Nevertheless, the testing of the Vessel in accordance with classification society requirements is a factor tending to prove due diligence. The failure of regular KRS surveys of the engine room and generators to reveal any problems with the coupling provides strong evidence of HMM's due diligence because it shows how difficult it would have been to detect the unseaworthy condition and that HMM was not on notice of any problem concerning the coupling. The undisputed evidence indicates that the coupling had functioned without leaking for at least the previous nine months and that the defective assembly was hidden from even a trained eye.

There is no evidence that the defect could have been discovered without disassembly of the coupling. Even the Cargo Interests' own expert testified that disassembly of the coupling is normally not a part of routine inspections. There is no credible evidence that could establish the personal lack of due diligence by HMM. Therefore, we hold that HMM carried its burden of proving due diligence and that the defectively repaired coupling was an excusable condition of unseaworthiness.

V.

Conclusion

The fire defenses do not hold shipowners or other carriers liable for an unseaworthy condition that contributed to a vessel fire unless that unseaworthy condition was preventable by the carrier in the exercise of due diligence. We are satisfied that HMM has carried its burden of proving its due diligence to make the Vessel seaworthy. Unfortunately for Cargo Interests, the defectively repaired coupling was the sort of rare condition that was not remedied despite the exercise of due diligence. For the foregoing reasons, we reverse the district court's grant of summary judgment for Cargo Interests and remand to the district court with instructions to enter judgment for HMM.

REVERSED and REMANDED.

Notes

1. The Fifth and Eleventh Circuits agree with the Second Circuit (and thus disagree with the Ninth Circuit) that the onus is on the cargo-owner to prove that the cause of the fire was due to the "actual fault or privity" of the carrier. *Westinghouse Elec. Corp. v. M/V Leslie Lykes*, 734 F.2d 199, 1985 AMC 247 (5th Cir. 1985); *Banana Services Inc. v. M/V Tasman Star*, 68 F. 3d 418, 1996 AMC 260 (11th Cir. 1995).

2. All circuits agree that the carrier only loses the right to rely on the fire defense if it itself was guilty of "actual fault or privity". In the case of corporate carriers, this involves consideration of whether the relevant fault was at a sufficiently high level in the corporate hierarchy to be regarded as the fault of the company itself, rather than one of its employees. For example, in *Westinghouse Elec. Corp. v. M/V Leslie Lykes*, 734 F.2d 199, 1985 AMC 247 (5th Cir. 1985), the fire was caused by poor stowage of cargo. The court held that the carrier was not liable for the ignition of the fire:

> [T]he burden of proof was on the cargo to show that this stowage decision was within the "design or neglect" of the "managing officers and agents as distinguished from the master or subordinates" of Lykes. Despite this burden, Cargo failed to present any evidence as to who within the layout department prepared this cargo plan

and which, if any, supervisors checked and approved this person's work. There was no evidence of how many persons worked in this department, the various job categories and their corresponding spheres of authority, or the structure of the hierarchy leading from the layout personnel to the highest officers of the corporation... Without such evidence showing a broad range of corporate authority in a person involved in the stowage decision, the District Court could not properly conclude that the improper stowage was within the personal "design or neglect" of the corporate owner. The evidence was only that some employee or employees in the layout department designed the stowage in this case. This is not sufficient to defeat the Carrier's defense under the Fire Statute.

Problems: The Fire Exemption: A Theme With Variations

Facts: There was a shipment of goods on board the M/V Good Hope from Italy to the United States governed by the United States Carriage of Goods by Sea Act. In transit, a fire broke out. The goods carried were damaged. The shipper made his prima facie case.

1. In response to the shipper's claim, the carrier pleaded the fire exemption under COGSA § 4(2)(b). What should the carrier prove in order to be exonerated?
2. Suppose that the carrier proved that the loss resulted from the fire. Is this the end of the matter? Is there anything the shipper should do to prevent the carrier's exoneration?
3. Suppose that the shipper claimed that the carrier should not be allowed to assert the fire exemption, unless he proved first that he exercised due diligence to make the vessel seaworthy. How should the court rule?
4. Suppose that the shipper proved that the cause of the fire that damaged the goods was the *unseaworthiness of the vessel.* The shipper then claimed that the carrier should not be allowed to claim the fire exemption unless he first proved that he exercised due diligence to make the vessel seaworthy. How should the court rule?
5. *Variation*: Suppose the shipper proved that the vessel was unseaworthy and that the cause of the damage to the goods was the unseaworthiness of the vessel rather than the fire. Example: A fire broke out and fresh water was used to combat the fire. Bales of cotton untouched by the fire were found soaked in sea water. The carrier pleaded the fire exemption. What result?
6. *Variation*: Suppose that the shipper proved that the vessel was unseaworthy and that the unseaworthiness of the vessel was the cause of the fire. The carrier pleaded the fire statute and proved that the fire was the cause of the damage to the goods. Should the carrier be exonerated? Is there anything the shipper should do?
7. *Variation*: Suppose that the shipper proved that the vessel was unseaworthy and that the unseaworthiness of the vessel was the cause of the fire. The carrier pleaded the fire statute and proved that the fire was the cause of the damage and that he exercised due diligence to make the vessel seaworthy. The shipper claimed that, in order to be exonerated, the carrier must also prove that the fire had not been caused by the carrier' "actual fault or privity". How should the court rule?
8. What is "actual fault or privity" of the carrier?
9. Suppose that there is convincing evidence that the damage to the goods was caused by negligent fire fighting operations of the crew and master. Should the carrier be exonerated?
10. What happens when the cause of the fire is not established?

E. Damages and Limitation of Liability

Notes: Measure of Damages

1. *Market value*

SANTIAGO v. SEA-LAND SERVICE, INC.

United States District Court for the District of Puerto Rico, 1973.

366 F. Supp. 1309, 1974 AMC 673

* * *

In general, the measure of damages in cargo claims has been market value at the port of destination. . . . In the event goods are damaged rather than lost entirely, the measure would be the difference between sound market value at the port of destination and the market value of the goods in the damaged condition. . . . When cargo is wrongfully delayed rather than actually damaged, the proper measure of damages is the difference between the market value of the goods at the time and place they should have arrived and the market value of the goods when they arrived. This principle is very well illustrated by the case of *Atlantic Mutual Insurance Co. v. Poseidon Schiffahrt*, 313 F.2d 872 (7th Cir. 1963), cert. den. 375 U.S. 819, 84 S.Ct. 56, 11 L.Ed.2d 53 (1963), which discusses generally the measure of damages in all three situations, that is, loss, damage and delay.

* * *

An obvious exception arises where there exists no market value at the destination port for the commodity damaged. In such event the nearest market is often used with the addition of the cost of getting the goods to that market. In *Sanib Corp. v. United Fruit Co.*, 74 F. Supp. 64 (S.D.N.Y. 1947), there was damage to a shipment of banana powder upon its arrival at Tampa, Florida. The District Court found that there was no market value for banana powder at Tampa, so the court applied the New York market price with proper adjustment for the difference in freight and other necessary expenses.

Another rule is to apply when reconditioning of the damaged merchandise is feasible. Despite the fact that the market value of the commodity was decreased substantially by voyage damage, if restoration can be made at a modest cost so that the shipper realizes the market value of the product, the courts sometimes limit damages to such reconditioning costs. In *Weirton Steel Co. v. Isbrandtsen-Moller Co.*, 126 F.2d 593 (2nd Cir. 1942) tin plate was reconditioned for about 10% of its depreciation in value, and the shipper was able to use it for its intended purpose. Even though the tin plate was not completely restored in appearance, only the reconditioning costs were awarded as damages since the shipper was able to dispose of the merchandise without economical loss.

* * *

Various methods have been used to determine market value and the determination of said market value is not always a simple task for a judge or jury in a cargo claim. Thus, there is always the problem of proving market value prices at ports all over the world often on theoretical dates when goods should have arrived which can be the source of prolonged litigation. The solution to the problem is, of course the responsibility of the plaintiff, since he has the burden of proof as to the amount of the damages. . . . On occasions published listings for commodities such as sugar, grain, cotton or rubber constitute the best proof of market listings at the port of destination. On other occasions comparable sales are the best evidence of market value and in a large number of cases market value is actually determined by testimony of expert witnesses; the shipper himself which is familiar with the market, marine surveyors who have familiarized themselves with market conditions, etc. . . .

Whether the basis for market value set in a particular case is retail, wholesale, replacement, or even invoice value, it is not always susceptible of easy explanation. The courts usually select the value that is most in accord with basic principles of compensating or restoring the shipper, of making him whole. As a general provision, if goods are intended to be added to stock and no need exists for immediate replacement at retail costs or if no loss of sales at retail is shown the term market value would contemplate wholesale price. . . .

* * *

Retail values, including anticipated profits, have been awarded where it has been satisfactorily shown that these were in fact the sums lost. . . .

* * *

In addition to the actual loss of market value involved, there usually arise necessary expenses incidental to the loss sustained. These include survey fees (to determine the quantum of damage or to render expert assistance in restoration or salvage), necessary transportation, warehousing, and the like. *See Continental Distrib. Co. v. Reading Co.*, 168 F.2d 967 (3rd Cir. 1948). These charges are recoverable if they were reasonably considered necessary at the time they were incurred, although later developments indicate they were not really needed. . . .

Closely akin to the right to recover necessary incidental expenses is the obligation imposed upon the shipper to minimize his own damages. . . .

* * *

---

2. In *B.P. North American Petroleum v. Solar S/T*, 250 F.3d 307, 2001 AMC 1844 (5th Cir. 2001), the court held that in calculating the measure of damages, any price fluctuations or futures trading after discharge must be ignored. The court said:

> As we have noted, because of the applicability of the market value rule to this case, any futures trading by BP following the date of discharge does not affect a proper damages calculation. Because the market value rule considers the diminished value of the cargo on the date of discharge, later price fluctuations or changes in value beyond the date of discharge are irrelevant to the damages calculation. This principle was stated about as well as it can be said in 1878 by a California district court in *The Compta,* 6 F. Cas. 233, 234 (D. Cal. 1878) (No. 3070):
>
>> Where goods are delivered in a damaged condition, the damage sustained is the difference between their market value, if sound, and their market value in their unsound condition. Both values to be ascertained as of the time when the goods were, or should have been, delivered...If the shipper has seen fit to hold the goods for a better market, he has entered into a speculation the result of which can in no way affect the liability of the ship. If he has obtained a higher price than could have been realized at the time of the breach, the ship's liability is not thereby diminished. If he has sold them at a lower price, her liability is not increased.
>
> In sum, BP's futures trading is inapposite to a "market value" damages calculation in this case, and BP's damages should be calculated as the difference between the market value of sound oil on the date of discharge and an estimated valuation of the contaminated oil on the date of discharge.

250 F. 3d at 314; 2001 AMC at 1851.

Notes: Package limitation

1. *What is a "package" for limitation purposes?*

(a) *Non-containerized Cargo: Fully Enclosed Goods*

The first step in determining what constitutes a COGSA package is to ascertain the intent of the parties. This is done by evaluating the contents of the bill of lading. *Seguros "Illimani" S.A. v. M/V Popi P*, 929 F.2d 89, 1991 AMC 1521 (2d Cir. 1991); *Binladen BSB Landscaping v. M/V Nedlloyd Rotterdam*, 759 F.2d 1006, 1985 AMC 2113 (2d Cir.), *cert. denied*, 474 U.S. 902, 106 S. Ct. 229, 88 L. Ed. 2d 229 (1985); *Fireman's Fund Insurance Co. v. Tropical Shipping and Construction Co. Ltd.*, 254 F.3d 987; 2001 AMC 2474 (11th Cir. 2001). It is only in the event of ambiguity in the bill of lading that it becomes necessary to look elsewhere. However, some courts begin their inquiry by asking whether the cargo was packaged or prepared for shipment in any way, regardless of what the bill of lading might say. If not, the goods are "not shipped in packages" for the purposes of COGSA § 4(5), and so the customary freight unit is used. *Aggreko Inc. v. L.E.P. International, Ltd*, 780 F. Supp. 429, 1992 AMC 1127 (S.D. Tex. 1991); *G.E. Power Systems Inc. v. Industrial Maritime Carriers (Bahamas), Inc.*, 89 F. Supp. 2d 782 (E.D. La. 2000) (both holding that a large unpackaged item did not constitute a "package" for limitation purposes, notwithstanding the entry "one" in the "number of packages or units" column on the bill of lading). This argument was unsuccessful in *Fireman's Fund, supra.*

When the bill of lading does not provide a solution, and the cargo is not containerized, the general rule is that cargo must be "sufficiently wrapped, bundled or tied" (*Mitsui & Co. v. American Export Lines, Inc.*, 636 F.2d 807, 822, 1981 AMC 331 (2d Cir. 1981)) in order to be a COGSA package. The cases indicate that when cargo is fully boxed or crated and the identity of the goods concealed, it is a package, regardless of its size, shape or weight. *Hartford Fire Insurance Co. v. Pacific Far East Line, Inc.*, 491 F.2d 960, 1974 AMC 1475 (9th Cir.), *cert. denied*, 419 U.S. 873, 955 S. Ct. 134, 42 L. Ed. 2d 112 (1974). The theory behind this rule is that carriers and their agents, for their own insurance purposes, need to know the nature and value of the cargo they carry and should not be required to guess the value of the cargo carried, when they have not been provided with an opportunity to examine the cargo themselves. In order to protect carriers who cannot confirm the value of the cargo, because it is concealed, the courts find that concealed cargo is a single COGSA package. *General Electric Co. v. Inter-Ocean Shipping*, 862 F. Supp. 166, 1995 AMC 871 (S.D. Tex. 1994).

(b) *Non-containerized Cargo: Partially Enclosed Goods*

The most difficult package cases are those in which the cargo is partially packaged. However, it is not clear how much packaging is required before the goods will be considered a COGSA "package". Generally, if goods are fully exposed to plain view they will not be a COGSA package, but, if goods are completely concealed, they will be considered a package. When faced with cases involving partially packaged goods, most courts rely heavily upon the expression of the parties in the bill of lading, but this is not always true.

In *Tamini v. Salen Dry Cargo AB*, 866 F.2d 741, 743, 1989 AMC 892 (5th Cir. 1989), it was held that a drilling rig was not a package because it was "for the most part fully exposed; no appurtenances or packaging were attached to facilitate its handling during transportation .... ." The Court noted that freight charges were calculated on a weight basis rather than per package and limited carrier's liability by reference to the customary freight unit.

In *Hartford Fire* the court held that an electric transformer on a skid was not a package. This decision is contrary to another court's finding that a toggle press on a skid *was* a package, *Aluminios Pozuelo Ltd. v. S.S. Navigator*, 407 F.2d 152, 1968 AMC 2532 (2d Cir. 1968). In *Hartford Fire*, the Court reasoned that an unpackaged transformer does not become a package simply because it is attached to a skid. By contrast, in *Aluminios* the Court relied heavily on the parties' description of the skid as a package in the bill of lading, but also stated that packaged cargo was "a class of cargo, irrespective of size, shape or weight, to which some packaging preparation for transportation has been made which facilities handling, but which does not necessarily conceal or completely enclose the goods." *Aluminos*, 407 F.2d at 155. Surprisingly, the Court did not comment on the contents of the bill of lading in *Hartford Fire*.

Pallets have also been held to be packages. *Standard Electrica, S.A. v. Hamburg Sudamerikanische Dampfschiffahrts-Gessellschaft*, 375 F.2d 943, 1967 AMC 881 (2d Cir.), *cert. denied*, 389 U.S. 831, 88 S.Ct. 97, 19 L.Ed. 2d 89 (1967). In *Standard Electrica*, the bill of lading, dock receipt, commercial invoice and claim letter, all indicated that the parties intended the pallets would be considered packages for the purpose of carriage. Although a container case, the court's decision in *Seguros "Illimani"* similarly advocates heavy reliance upon the unit listed in the "NO OF PKGS" column in the bill of lading in order to determine the parties' intentions.

However, some courts begin their inquiry by asking whether the cargo was packaged or prepared for shipment in any way, regardless of what the bill of lading might say. If not, the goods are "not shipped in packages" for the purposes of COGSA § 4(5), and so the customary freight unit is used. *Aggreko, Inc. v. L.E.P. International, Ltd.*, 780 F. Supp. 429, 1992 AMC 1127 (S.D. Tex. 1991); *G.E. Power Systems, Inc. v. Industrial Maritime Carriers (Bahamas), Inc.*, 89 F. Supp. 2d 782 (E.D. La. 2000).

(c) ***Containerized Cargo***

MONICA TEXTILE CORPORATION v. S.S. TANA

952 F.2d 636, 1992 AMC 609 (2d Cir. 1991)

McLAUGHLIN, Circuit Judge:

We are (once again) presented with "the latest skirmish in the age old war between shippers and carriers over their respective rights and liabilities." *Matsushita Elec. Corp. v. S.S. Aegis Spirit*, 414 F. Supp. 894, 897 (W.D. Wash. 1976). This case requires us to revisit the issue whether a massive shipping container is a "package" for purposes of the $500 per-package limitation on liability of the Carriage of Goods by Sea Act ("COGSA"), 46 U.S.C. App. § 1304(5).

Holding that the single shipping container was the relevant COGSA package, the district court entered a $500 judgment for the shipper. We now reverse and hold that each of the 76 bales of cloth stowed inside the container is a separate package for COGSA purposes.

Background

Monica Textile Corporation ("Monica" or the "shipper") engaged the defendants-carriers to transport a single 20-foot shipping container from Africa to Savannah, Georgia. The parties' bill of lading disclosed that the container, which Monica had stuffed and sealed, held 76 bales of cotton cloth. The goods were damaged in transit and Monica brought suit in the District Court for the Southern District of New York (SAND, J.) to recover for the loss.

The carriers moved for partial summary judgment limiting their liability to $500 pursuant to COGSA's liability limitation provision, 46 U.S.C. App. § 1304(5). The district court initially denied the motion, holding "that where the bill of lading prepared by the carrier's agent discloses a specific number of identifiable units as the contents of the container, those units [the bales of cloth] constitute the package" for purposes of COGSA's limitation on liability. *Monica Textile Corp. v. S.S. Tana*, 731 F. Supp. 124, 127 (S.D.N.Y. 1990) ["*Monica I*"].

Shortly thereafter, this court decided *Seguros "Illimani" S.A. v. M/V Popi P*, 929 F.2d 89 (2d Cir. 1991), which held that for COGSA purposes the number of packages specified in the "No. of Pkgs." column of the bill of lading is generally controlling. *Id.* at 94. In the present case, though the "DESCRIPTION OF GOODS" column of the bill of lading stated that the contents of the container consisted of 76 bales of cotton cloth, the "No. of Pkgs." column of the bill of lading had the number "1" typed in, and a line labeled "Total Number of Packages or Units in Words (Total Column 19 [No. of Pkgs. column])," had the word "ONE" typed in. In light of these facts, Judge Sand permitted the carriers to renew their summary judgment motion to limit their liability to $500, and the district court reversed itself, holding that our intervening decision in Seguros compelled a finding that the single container, rather than the 76 bales stowed therein, was the relevant COGSA package. *See Monica Textile Corp. v. S.S. Tana*, 765 F. Supp. 1194, 1195-96 (S.D.N.Y. 1991) ["*Monica II*"]. Because the carriers conceded liability, the district court entered judgment for Monica in the amount of $500.

Monica appeals the judgment of the district court, maintaining that the 76 individual bales of cloth, not the solitary shipping container, were the appropriate COGSA packages. We agree and therefore reverse the judgment of the district court.

Discussion

The district court reversed itself in *Monica II* on the basis of *Seguros*, which it read

> as establishing a bright-line rule for determining the number of COGSA packages from the bill of lading. The number of packages is the number appearing in the "No. of Pkgs." column of the bill, unless other evidence of the parties' intent plainly contradicts the applicability of that number, or unless the item referred to by that number is incapable of qualifying as a COGSA package.

Monica II, 765 F. Supp. at 1195-96. The district court's characterization of the *Seguros* rule is accurate, as far as it goes. Seguros, however, involved 600 separate steel-strapped bundles, each containing 15 tin ingots. The issue therefore was whether there were 600 "packages" or 9,000 (600 x 15) "packages". Most significantly, our Seguros decision did not purport to apply to containers, and the district court's application of the Seguros rule to the container context was erroneous. An understanding of the "container" cases is necessary to appreciate our present holding that Seguros should not be extended to containers.

The Container Cases

Long before COGSA was enacted, industrialized nations recognized the need to reconcile the desire of carriers to limit their potential liability with their vastly superior bargaining power over shippers. *See* H.R. Rep. No. 2218, 74th Cong., 2d Sess. 6-9 (1936); *Mitsui & Co. v. America Export Lines, Inc.*, 636 F.2d 807, 814-15 (2d Cir. 1981); *Comment, Containerization, the Per Package Limitation, and the Concept of "Fair Opportunity,"* 11 MAR. LAW. 123, 124 (1986). The nations at the Brussels Convention of 1924 balanced these competing concerns with a per-package limitation on liability. *See* International Convention for the Unification of Certain Rules Relating to Bills of Lading, Aug. 25, 1924, 51 Stat. 233, 120 L.N.T.S. 155 (1931-32), *reprinted in* A. KNAUTH, THE AMERICAN LAW OF

OCEAN BILLS OF LADING 37-72 (4th ed. 1953); Note, *Defining "Package" in the Carriage of Goods by Sea Act*, 60 TEX. L. REV. 961, 964-66 (1982). The principles established by the Brussels Convention became the template for COGSA. *See Robert C. Herd & Co. v. Krawill Mach. Corp.*, 359 U.S. 297, 301, 79 S. Ct. 766, 769, 3 L. Ed. 2d 820 (1959) ("[t]he legislative history of the Act shows that it was lifted almost bodily from the Hague Rules of 1921, as amended by the Brussels Convention of 1924").

Unhappily, neither the statute nor its legislative history provides any clue as to the meaning of "package" in the Act. *See Aluminios Pozuelo Ltd. v. S.S. Navigator*, 407 F.2d 152, 154 (2d Cir. 1968). Despite the difficulties this lack of guidance engendered,[1] courts managed to muddle through this oft-litigated issue by generally deferring to the intent of the contracting parties when that intent was both clear and reasonable. This intent-approach later became strained by technological advances in the shipping industry. Indeed, "[f]ew, if any, in 1936 could have foreseen the change in the optimum size of shipping units...." *Standard Electrica, S.A. v. Hamburg Sudamerikanische Dampfschifffahrts-Gesellschaft*, 375 F.2d 943, 945 (2d Cir.), *cert. denied*, 389 U.S. 831, 88 S. Ct. 97, 19 L. Ed. 2d 89 (1967).

We first addressed COGSA's application to shipping innovations in *Standard Electrica*, which required us to determine which was the relevant COGSA package: each 60-pound carton or the pallets on which the cartons were bound together. Divining the parties' intent, we held the pallet to be the relevant COGSA package. *See id.* at 946.

The so-called "container revolution", however, "added a new dimension to the problem." *Mitsui*, 636 F.2d at 816. *See generally* Schmeltzer & Peavy, *Prospects and Problems of the Container Revolution*, 1 J. MAR. L. & COM. 203 (1970). Shippers, carriers and industry commentators "speculated at the time whether the courts would adopt the analysis of *Standard Electrica* or fashion a new rule to apply to containers." Note, *The Shipping Container as a COGSA Package: The Functional Economics Test is Abandoned*, 6 MAR. LAW. 336, 340 n.16 (1981) (collecting citations). Our decision in *Leather's Best, Inc. v. S.S. Mormaclynx*, 451 F.2d 800 (2d Cir. 1971) (FRIENDLY, C.J.), settled the issue, distinguishing *Standard Electrica* and veering away from our pre-container cases because of our

> belief that the purpose of s 4(5) of COGSA was to set a reasonable figure below which the carrier should not be permitted to limit his liability and that "package" is thus more sensibly related to the unit in which the shipper packed the goods and described them than to a large metal object, functionally a part of the ship, in which the carrier caused them to be "contained."

Id. at 815 (footnote omitted). *Leather's Best* thus stood foursquare for the proposition " 'that a container rarely should be treated as a package.' " *Smythgreyhound v. M/V "Eurygenes"*, 666 F.2d 746, 748 n.5 (2d Cir. 1981) (quoting *Croft & Scully Co. v. M/V Skulptor Vuchetich*,

---

[1] *Compare, e.g., Hartford Fire Ins. Co. v. Pacific Far East Line, Inc.*, 491 F.2d 960, 965 (9th Cir.) (holding that 18-ton electrical transformer bolted to a skid was not a COGSA package), *cert. denied*, 419 U.S. 873, 95 S. Ct. 134, 42 L. Ed. 2d 112 (1974) with *Aluminios Pozuelo Ltd. v. S.S. Navigator*, 407 F.2d 152, 155 (2d Cir.1968) (holding that a 3-ton toggle press bolted to a skid was a COGSA package). *See generally id.* at 154-56 (discussing pre-container cases).

508 F. Supp. 670, 678 (S.D. Tex. 1981), *aff'd in relevant part*, 664 F.2d 1277 (5th Cir. 1982)).

Although other courts subsequently embraced *Leather's Best*, *see, e.g.*, *Matsushita Elec. Corp. v. S.S. Aegis Spirit*, 414 F. Supp. 894, 907 (W.D. Wash. 1976), *cited with approval in Mitsui*, 636 F.2d at 819-20, we began to stray from it, in favor of a so-called "functional economics test." Whereas *Leather's Best* held that treating a container as a COGSA package is inconsistent with congressional intent and therefore strongly disfavored, *see Leather's Best*, 451 F.2d at 815; *accord Mitsui*, 636 F.2d at 820-21, the functional economics approach ignored congressional intent in favor of a "law and economics" analysis. *See, e.g.*, *Royal Typewriter Co. v. M/V Kulmerland*, 483 F.2d 645, 648-49 (2d Cir. 1973) (container is presumptively the package where the units inside are not suitable for breakbulk shipment); *Cameco, Inc. v. S.S. American Legion*, 514 F.2d 1291, 1298-99 (2d Cir. 1974).

The reaction to our functional economics approach was swift and overwhelmingly negative, as courts and commentators roundly criticized us for it. *See Croft & Scully Co. v. M/V Skulptor Vuchetich*, 664 F.2d 1277, 1281 n.10 (5th Cir. 1982) (functional economics test "necessitated much judicial guessing work, and we are well rid of it"); *Allstate Ins. Co. v. Inversiones Navieras Imparca, C.A.*, 646 F.2d 169, 172 (5th Cir. Unit B May 1981) (test "was subject to severe criticism from all corners"); *Matsushita*, 414 F. Supp. at 906 (rejecting the test "as contrary to the statute, commercially impracticable and unwise"); DeOrchis, *The Container and the Package Limitation—The Search for Predictability*, 5 J. MAR. L. & COM. 251, 257 (1974); Simon, *The Law of Shipping Containers (pt. 1)*, 5 J. MAR. L. & COM. 507, 522 (1974).

Recognizing that the functional economics test was "basically inconsistent with the holding of *Leather's Best*," and acknowledging the criticism the new approach had drawn, we eventually abandoned it. *See Mitsui*, 636 F.2d at 818-21. Judge Friendly, who had earlier written *Leather's Best*, also authored the *Mitsui* decision, and circulated it to the entire court. *Mitsui* held that when a bill of lading discloses on its face what is inside the container, and those contents may reasonably be considered COGSA packages, then the container is not the COGSA package. *See id.*; *Smythgreyhound*, 666 F.2d at 753. Mitsui settled the law in container cases for this Circuit and has been steadfastly followed. *See, e.g.*, *Binladen BSB Landscaping v. M.V. "Nedlloyd Rotterdam"*, 759 F.2d 1006, 1013 (2d Cir.), *cert. denied*, 474 U.S. 902, 106 S. Ct. 229, 88 L. Ed. 2d 229 (1985); *Smythgreyhound*, 666 F.2d at 753. *Mitsui* and its progeny, moreover, have been followed by courts in other circuits; *see* 2A E. FLYNN & G. RADUAZZO, BENEDICT ON ADMIRALTY § 167, at 16-34 (7th ed. 1991) ("the *Mitsui-Binladen* approach seems to be gaining favor in the rest of the country"); *see, e.g.*, *Hayes-Leger Assocs., Inc. v. M/V Oriental Knight*, 765 F.2d 1076, 1080 (11th Cir. 1985); *Allstate Ins.*, 646 F.2d at 172; *International Adjusters, Inc. v. Korean Wonis-Son*, 682 F. Supp. 383, 385-86 (N.D. Ill. 1988); and it has been praised by courts and commentators. *See, e.g.*, *Allstate Ins.*, 646 F.2d at 172 & n.1 ("we believe that the rule developed in *Mitsui* and *Leather's Best* is the best judicial solution, in the absence of a legislative solution"); 2A E. FLYNN & G. RADUAZZO, BENEDICT ON ADMIRALTY § 167, at 16-34 (7th ed.

1991) ("[a]mong other benefits, the *Mitsui-Binladen* approach is consistent with the position of the international community"); Note, *The Shipping Container as a COGSA Package: The Functional Economics Test is Abandoned*, 6 MAR. LAW. 336, 345 (1981) ("In terms of predictability and judicial economy, the decision in *Mitsui* is a realistic approach in an area in desperate need of legislative reform.").

Although Mitsui was concerned with containers, a district court later extended it to pallets. *See Allied Int'l Am. Eagle Trading Corp. v. S.S. "Yang Ming"*, 519 F. Supp. 187, 190 (S.D.N.Y. 1981), *rev'd*, 672 F.2d 1055 (2d Cir. 1982). We reversed, holding that containers and pallets are quite different and that "*Standard Electrica* ... is still the law with regard to pallets." *Yang Ming*, 672 F.2d at 1061. In so doing, we methodically documented why our decisions in *Standard Electrica* and *Leather's Best* required distinct analyses for container and non-container cases. *See id.* at 1058-61. We explained:

> [T]he container cases involve factors not found in pallet cases. Because of their size and their function in the shipping industry, containers are ordinarily not considered "packages."
>
> * * *
>
> ... In *Mitsui* ... as in other container cases, the courts must look askance at an agreement which purports to define a container as a "package" because the results of such a limitation can be ludicrous.

Id. at 1061, 1062

We thus rejected any notion that container and non-container cases were interchangeable; they were then and remain now separate lines of authority. They had been uniformly so construed until the present case. *See, e.g., St. Paul Fire & Marine Ins. Co. v. Sea-Land Serv., Inc.*, 735 F. Supp. 129, 133 (S.D.N.Y. 1990) ("containers present different considerations than pallets"); E. FLYNN & G. RADUAZZO, BENEDICT ON ADMIRALTY § 167, at 16-28 (7th ed. 1991) ("These standards [for determining the relevant COGSA package] vary according to whether or not the cargo is shipped in a container, and the discussion here will therefore treat non-containerized and containerized shipments separately.").

Seguros "Illimani"

We now turn to *Monica II's* application of our *Seguros* decision. The dispute in *Seguros* was whether each bundle of 15 tin ingots, or each individual ingot, constituted the relevant COGSA package. *See Seguros "Illimani" S.A. v. M/V Popi P*, 929 F.2d 89, 92 (2d Cir. 1991). We therefore adopted the following test to settle such controversies:

> The number appearing under the heading "NO. OF PKGS." is our starting point for determining the number of packages for purposes of the COGSA per-package limitation, and unless the significance of that number is plainly contradicted by contrary evidence of the parties' intent, or unless the number refers to items that cannot qualify

> as "packages," it is also the ending point of our inquiry. "Package" is a term of art in the ocean shipping business, and parties to bills of lading should expect to be held to the number that appears under a column whose heading so unmistakably refers to the number of packages.

Seguros, 929 F.2d at 94.[2] As between bales, boxes, bundles, cartons, cases, crates and other COGSA packages, the *Seguros* rule is as sensible as it is straightforward. But all "packages" were not created equal, as our container cases make plain. Containers raise unique issues which we have addressed in a distinct line of case law.

In light of our significant container jurisprudence, the *Seguros* rule is inapposite in the container context. In *Seguros*, the parties disputed whether the ingots or the bundles containing the ingots should be considered the relevant COGSA packages. No one even questioned the district court's holding that "[i]t is clear that the container is not the appropriate 'package' in this case." *Seguros "Illimani" S.A. v. M/V Popi P*, 735 F. Supp. 108, 111 (S.D.N.Y. 1990), *aff'd*, 929 F.2d 89 (2d Cir. 1991). Viewed in context, then, *Seguros* simply does not purport to apply when a container is alleged to be the relevant COGSA package. Indeed, that *Seguros* would, in dictum, overrule *sub silentio* a long line of Second Circuit precedent is inconceivable. Notwithstanding the insertion in the number-of-packages column(s) of the bill of lading of a number reflecting the number of containers, where the bill of lading discloses on its face what is inside the container(s) and those contents may reasonably be considered COGSA packages, the latter, not the container(s), are the COGSA packages. The district court's holding to the contrary in *Monica II* is erroneous.

Parties' Intent and Bill of Lading

We next consider the carriers' argument that the bill of lading manifests the parties' agreement that the container is the relevant COGSA package.

In non-container cases we have generally deferred to the parties' intent, as manifested by their bill of lading, in determining what unit is the relevant COGSA package. *See, e.g.*, *Seguros*, 929 F.2d at 95; *Standard Electrica*, 375 F.2d at 946. Such deference to the parties' wishes permits commercial flexibility without offending the statute.

COGSA, however, requires that we view container cases through a different prism. Thus, in container cases we must " 'take a critical look' " at clauses purporting to define the container as the COGSA package, *Smythgreyhound*, 666 F.2d at 750 (quoting *Mitsui*, 636 F.2d at 815). Accordingly, we have consistently cast a jaundiced eye upon language purporting to embody such an agreement.

The reason for this skepticism is that such agreements run against the grain of COGSA. *See id.*; *Binladen*, 759 F.2d at 1012-13 ("classification of [the container] as a 'package' would violate the purpose of s 4(5) by permitting the carrier to limit its liability unduly");

---

[2] *Compare Smythgreyhound*, 666 F.2d at 748 n.4 & 751 ("on their face the bills of lading reflect the lack of agreement, insofar as they refer to both 'containers' and 'cartons'") *and Matsushita*, 414 F. Supp. at 906 (no mutual understanding with resect to what constitutes COGSA package where carrier and shipper had no direct or indirect dealings). Other container cases have accorded little or no weight to the number in the "number of packages" column. *See, e.g.*, *Binladen*, 759 F.2d at 1009 & 1016 n.11; *Leather's Best*, 451 F.2d at 804.

Yang Ming, 672 F.2d at 1062 ("the courts must look askance at an agreement which purports to define a container as a 'package' "); *Mitsui*, 636 F.2d at 817 (*Leather's Best* "acknowledg[ed] that treating the containers as packages ... was precluded by the underlying purpose of [COGSA] § 4(5)"). Thus, "our repeatedly-expressed reluctance for sound reasons to treat a container as a package", *Binladen*, 759 F.2d at 1015, compels us to scrutinize the carriers' claim that they agreed with Monica to treat the container as the COGSA package.

The bill of lading in this case discloses on its face that 76 bales of cloth were stowed in the container. Even though that disclosure triggers *Mitsui's* presumption that the container is not the COGSA package, *see Mitsui*, 636 F.2d at 821; *see also Smythgreyhound*, 666 F.2d at 752 ("[*Mitsui*] adopted a general rule that where the bill of lading discloses the contents of the container, then the container is not the COGSA package.") (brackets in original), the carriers maintain that the bill of lading nevertheless discloses an agreement with Monica that the single container was the relevant package.

They emphasize two clauses appearing on the reverse of the carriers' standard bill of lading forms.[3] Clause 2 of the bill of lading provides, in relevant part:

> The word "package" shall include each container where the container is stuffed and sealed by the Merchant or on his behalf, although the Shipper may have furnished in the Particulars herein the contents of such sealed container. (See Clause 11).

Clause 11 states:

> Neither the Carrier nor the vessel shall in any event be or become liable for any loss or damage to or in connection with the transportation of goods in an amount exceeding U.S. $500 per package.... Where container(s) is stuffed by Shipper or on his behalf, and the container is sealed, the Carrier's liability will be limited to U.S. $500 with respect to the contents of each container, except when the Shipper declares value on the face hereof (Box 26) and pays additional charges on such declared value (Box 23). The freight charged on sealed containers when no higher valuation is declared by the Shipper is based on a value of U.S. $500 per container.

The carriers maintain that these clauses articulate an agreement between them and Monica to treat the container as the package.

The carriers' argument is premised on dicta in our container cases suggesting that parties to a bill of lading have the right to agree to treat a container as the relevant COGSA package. For example, in *Smythgreyhound*, we remarked in a footnote that parties may

[3] The district court was generous in its characterization of the typeface on the reverse of the bill of lading as "miniscule [sic]." *Monica I*, 731 F. Supp. at 126. Whereas standard typeface (like the body of this opinion) has six lines per inch, the carriers' boilerplate has sixteen lines per inch.

> agree between themselves that the container will be the COGSA "package," especially in cases where COGSA does not apply *ex proprio vigore*.... [W]e hold today that in the absence of clear and unambiguous language indicating agreement on the definition of "package," then we will conclusively presume that the container is not the package where the bill of lading discloses the container's contents.

Smythgreyhound, 666 F.2d at 753 n.20 (emphasis in original). Thus, the otherwise "clear rule that where the contents of the container are disclosed in the bill of lading then the container is not the COGSA package", *id.* at 753, seemingly has an exception: we will treat the container as the "package" if the bill of lading discloses that the parties have so agreed in terms that are explicit and unequivocal.

This supposed exception to the *Mitsui* rule, however, is more apparent than real. No appellate precedent has been found applying this exception to a bill of lading like the one before us now. And for good reason: our container cases recognize that when a bill of lading refers to both containers and other units susceptible of being COGSA packages, it is inherently ambiguous. In *Smythgreyhound*, we candidly admitted "that no shipper ever actually intends that its recovery will be limited to $500 per container, or that any carrier, in the absence of an express agreement, intends that the recovery should exceed $500 per container." *Smythgreyhound*, 666 F.2d at 748 n.4; *see also id.* at 751 ("on their face the bills of lading reflect the lack of agreement, insofar as they refer to both 'containers' and 'cartons' "); *Matsushita*, 414 F. Supp. at 906 ("it is clear that there was not and, realistically, could not have been any mutual understanding between [the shipper and carrier] with respect to the COGSA package"). *Mitsui* and its progeny resolve this ambiguity against the carriers. *See Mitsui*, 636 F.2d at 822-23.

It is not without significance that the two boilerplate clauses upon which the carriers rely have consistently failed to persuade us in the past that the container is intended to be the package. Clause 11, for example, is essentially the same one we ignored in *Leather's Best*, even though in *Leather's Best* the clause appeared on the front of the bill of lading in capital letters:

> shipper hereby agrees that carrier's liability is limited to $500 with respect to the entire contents of each container except when shipper declares a higher valuation and shall have paid additional freight on such declared valuation pursuant to appropriate rule in the continental north atlantic westbound freight conference tariff.

Leather's Best, 451 F.2d at 804. *Compare Monica I*, 731 F. Supp. at 126 (similar clause "in miniscule [sic] type face" on reverse of bill of lading).

Similarly, Clause 2 is virtually indistinguishable from one rejected in *Matsushita* which provided:

> where the cargo has been either packed into container(s) or unitized into similar article(s) of transport by or on behalf of the Merchant, it is expressly agreed that the number of such container(s) or similar article(s) of transport shown on the face hereof shall be considered as the number of the package(s) or unit(s) for the purpose of the application of the limitation of liability provided for herein.

Matsushita, 414 F. Supp. at 899;[4] *see also St. Paul Fire & Marine Ins.*, 735 F. Supp. at 132 ("Allowing the carrier ... to insert an essentially unbargained-for definition of 'package' in the bill of lading would effectively eliminate the protection COGSA was meant to afford shippers."); *Monica I*, 731 F. Supp. at 127 (*Mitsui* and its progeny "control[ ] despite the language of clause 11").

Because the bill of lading in this case is ambiguous on its face and Clauses 2 and 11 are unbargained-for boilerplate, we cannot say that Monica and the carriers unequivocally agreed to treat the container as the COGSA package. Thus, the exception to *Mitsui's* rule is not applicable; and the 76 bales, not the container, are the relevant units for determining the extent of the carriers' liability under the statute.

This conclusion is consistent with our longstanding recognition of what every shipper knows: that "bills of lading are contracts of adhesion ambiguities in which must be resolved against the carrier...." *Mitsui*, 636 F.2d at 822-23. Clauses 2 and 11, like others printed on the back of a form bill of lading, "carr[y] little weight toward establishing intent, being [ ] unilateral, self-serving declaration[s] by the carrier which w[ere] not negotiated by the parties and could scarcely be discerned by the unaided eye in the maze of microscopic and virtually illegible provisions on the back[ ] of the bill[ ] of lading." *Matsushita*, 414 F. Supp. at 906 n.52; *see also St. Paul Fire & Marine Ins. Co. v. Sea-Land Serv., Inc.*, 735 F. Supp. 129, 132 & n.4 (S.D.N.Y. 1990).

Conclusion

Seguros provides a bright-line rule in non-container cases that, "the more consistently it is followed, the more it should minimize disputes." *Seguros*, 929 F.2d at 94. Similarly, *Mitsui* and its progeny continue to provide a simple rule in container cases, a rule that is easily administered by the courts and readily amenable to *ex ante* application by contracting parties. Together, these rules foster predictability in this nettlesome area of the law. Applied faithfully and consistently, they should assist carriers, shippers and the courts to "avoid the pains of litigation." *Standard Electrica*, 375 F.2d at 945.

Monica I correctly construed and applied our continer jurisprudence; *Monica II* did not. Accordingly, the judgment of the district court in *Monica II* is reversed.

---

[4] Judge Friendly praised *Matsushita* and adopted its reasoning in *Mitsui*. *See* 636 F.2d at 819-21 (quoting Judge Beeks' "outstanding" *Matsushita* opinion); *see also Smythgreyhound*, 666 F.2d at 750 n.11 (quoting *Matsushita* and repeating *Mitsui's* reference to Judge Beeks as " 'an experienced admiralty lawyer before his appointment to the bench'").

Note: Unpackaged items within containers.

In both *Alternative Glass Supplies v. M/V NOMZI*, 1999 AMC 1080 (S.D.N.Y. 1999) and *Orient Overseas Container Line (U.K.), Ltd. v. Sea-Land Service, Inc.*, 122 F. Supp. 2d 481, 2001 AMC 1005 (S.D.N.Y. 2000), it was held that the container was the "package" for limitation purposes because the contents of the container were unpackaged. Both cases focused on the following words used by the *Monica Textile* court: "when a bill of lading discloses on its face what is inside the container, *and those contents may reasonably be considered COGSA packages*, the container is not the COGSA package" (emphasis added). Although the bills of lading referred to the number of items inside the container, those items were not sufficiently "wrapped, bundled or tied" to be COGSA packages. As a result, the container itself was held to be the package in both cases.

(d) *Customary Freight Unit*

1. *Introductory Note*

Consideration of the meaning of "customary freight unit" is only called for when the goods are not shipped in a package. *See, e.g., Waterman S.S. Corp. v. United States S.R. & M. Co.*, 155 F.2d 687, 693 (5th Cir., 1946), *cert. denied*, 329 U.S. 761 (1946) (pieces of structural steel shipped unpackaged); *The Bill*, 55 F. Supp. 780 (D. Md. 1944), *aff'd.* 145 F.2d 470 (4th Cir. 1944) (bulk oil); and *Caterpillar Americas Company v. S. S. Sea Roads*, 231 F. Supp. 647 (S.D. Fla. 1964) (tractor delivered to vessel under its own power); *Vistar, S.A. v. M/V Sealand Express*, 680 F. Supp. 855, 1987 AMC 2881 (S.D. Tex. 1987).

COGSA provides that carriers may limit their liability for goods not shipped in packages to $500 per customary freight unit. The customary freight unit is usually the actual unit of measurement which was used by the parties to calculate freight. The bill of lading and published tariff schedule should provide this information. However, if this information is not available, the usual unit of measurement used by the industry for cargo of that type will be applied. *Granite State Insurance Co. v. M/V Caraibe*, 825 F. Supp. 1113, 1994 AMC 680 (D. Puerto Rico 1993). In *Petition of Isbrandtsen Co.*, 201 F.2d 281, 286, 1953 AMC 86, 92 (2d Cir. 1953), the court held that uncrated locomotives were not packages, and applied the $500 per customary freight unit limitation. As freight for the shipment of 10 locomotives had been calculated at $10,000 per locomotive, the court limited the carrier's liability to $500 per locomotive. Total liability was $5,000.

Cargo which has been held not to have been shipped in packages includes cargo shipped: free standing and not enclosed in a box or crate, *Hartford Fire*, 491 F.2d 960, 1974 AMC 1475; without any packaging at all; *Binladen*, 759 F.2d 1006, 1985 AMC 2113 (2d Cir.), *cert. denied*, 474 U.S. 902, 106 S. Ct. 229 (1985); in its permanently enclosed condition, *Solar Turbines, Inc. v. S.S. "Al Shiadiah"*, 575 F. Supp. 939, 1984 AMC 2002 (S.D.N.Y. 1983); and cargo which is "for the most part fully exposed," *Tamini*, 866 F.2d 741, 743, 1989 AMC 892. Unboxed motor vehicles are not packages, *Aetna Ins. v. M/V Lash Italia*, 858 F.2d 190, 1989 AMC 135 (4th Cir. 1988); and neither are loose tractors, *Caterpillar Americas Co. v. S.S. Sea Roads*, 231 F. Supp. 647, 1964 AMC 2646 (S.D. Fla. 1964), *aff'd*, 364 F.2d 829, 1967 AMC 290 (5th Cir. 1966); nor are free standing locomotives, *Petition of Isbrandtsen Co.*, 201 F.2d at 286, 1953 AMC at 92.

2. *Application of the Customary Freight Unit*

In *Ulrich Ammann Building Equipment, Ltd. v. M/V Monsun*, 609 F. Supp. 87, 1985 AMC 1965 (S.D.N.Y. 1985), court had to decide how to apply the "customary freight unit" standard to 20 tractors that had been carried and lost.

* * *

The "guiding policy" of COGSA is "to limit liability of common carriers for damaged cargo where the value of the cargo is not known to the carrier." *THE MORMACOAK*, 451 F.2d 24, 26 (2d Cir. 1971). The statute was designed "to protect the shipping industry and to throw the burden to the shipper to declare the value of the goods and pay a higher tariff if he wished to have higher liability on the part of the carrier." *Caterpillar Americas Company v. Steamship Sea Roads*, 231 F. Supp. 647, 650 (S.D. Fla. 1964), *aff'd*, 364 F.2d 829 (5th Cir. 1966).

The words "customary freight unit", which describe the unit as to which the shipper's liability is limited to $500, refer not to the physical shipping unit but to the unit of cargo "customarily used as the basis for the calculation of the freight rate to be charged." *The MORMACOAK, supra*, 451 F.2d at 25; *The Edmund Fanning*, 201 F.2d 281, 286 (2d Cir. 1953). Thus, where a freight charge is computed on a lump sum basis for each of several pieces of equipment, the relevant customary freight unit is each piece of equipment. *Caterpillar Americas Co., supra*, 231 F. Supp. at 650. If a freight charge is computed on a lump sum basis for an entire shipment, the relevant customary freight unit is the entire shipment.

In the case at hand, the parties agree that the tractors were shipped in an unpackaged form and are in a disagreement only as to the relevant customary freight unit. If the customary freight unit is held to be the entire shipment of thirty tractors, Ammann's recovery is limited to $500 under both COGSA and the terms of the bill of lading. Similarly, if the customary freight unit is held to be each piece of equipment shipped, Ammann's recovery is limited to $500 for each tractor. If, however, the customary freight unit is per measurement ton, as it would be if the ordinary tariff rates rather than the amended rates were held to control, Ammann would be entitled to recover $500 for each measurement ton shipped or approximately $65,000 per tractor.

The Ship Defendants assert that the parties agreed to a lump sum rate for the entire shipment of thirty scrapers on one or more vessels. They contend that there was no weight or measurement basis for the freight charge and that the customary freight unit agreed upon by the parties was instead the entire shipment. They point to both the filed amended tariff and the freight list, which states that the twenty tractors were shipped under a lump sum rate, as evidence of this agreement. They argue that Ammann took a calculated risk in agreeing to the lump sum freight basis because while it reduced the amount of COGSA coverage to which Ammann would be entitled, it also gave them a considerable savings on freight cost.

In response, Ammann asserts that the Ship Defendants have failed to prove that the customary freight unit to be applied was the special amended rate rather than the regular weight/measurement tariff. It claims that there is no evidence as to what the phrase "Freight as Agreed" was intended to mean. The thrust of Ammann's argument is that because the shipment in question was for twenty rather than thirty tractors, this court cannot assume that the shipment was covered by the rates listed in the amended tariff. It argues that while the lump sum rate was for thirty units, the bill of lading covers a shipment of only twenty units and that there is no actual evidence of the freight actually charged for the shipment. It also points to the fact that like the regular tariff, the bill of lading used kilograms and centimeters to describe the shipment, whereas the filed amended tariff used tons and feet.

Despite Ammann's contentions, the Ship Defendants have successfully met their burden of establishing that the shipment of twenty tractors was made on a lump sum basis. The amended tariff expressly lists the tractors as being on a lump sum rather than weight/measurement rate basis. *See The MORMACOAK, supra*, 327 F. Supp. at 669 (flat rate in filed amended tariff applied despite plaintiff's claim that missing bill of lading computed freight on weight basis). Ammann claims that because of the discrepancies in numbers the amended tariff pertaining to thirty tractors should not be applicable to a shipment of only twenty tractors. However, there is an express statement in the tariff that the tractors were to be shipped on one or two vessels. Furthermore, there is nothing on either the bill of lading or the freight list or in this record to suggest that the parties intended the shipment to be dealt with on a different basis than that listed in the amended tariff. The listing of weight and measurement and a measurement different from that on the tariff, does not obviate the implications of a lump sum payment. *See Freedman & Slater, Inc. v. M.V. TOFEVO*, 222 F. Supp. 964, 973 (S.D.N.Y. 1963). Courts have held that even where a lump sum rate is arrived at by using weight and measurement, the weight/measurement does not become the freight unit for the transaction. *See General Motors Corp. v. Moore-McCormack Lines, Inc.*, 451 F.2d 24, 25-26 (2d Cir. 1971); *Barth v. Atlantic container Line*, 597 F. Supp. 1254 (D. Md. 1984). In addition, there is no validity to Ammann's claim that a temporary rate cannot be a "customary" rate. A customary freight unit is one that is "known to the immediate parties." *Freedman & Slater, Inc. v. M/V TOFEVO*, 222 F. Supp. 964 (S.D.N.Y. 1963).

A tariff validly filed "is not a mere contract but is the law ..." *The Peisander*, 648 F.2d 415, 421 (5th Cir. 1981). Thus the rate basis listed in the amended tariff, which was in effect at the time of the shipment, must be applied. Because the freight charged for the shipment of twenty tractors was computed on a lump sum for the entire shipment rather than for each piece of equipment or on a weight/measurement basis, the relevant customary freight unit is the entire shipment. Ammann is therefore limited under both COGSA and the bill of lading to a recovery of $500. While this result seems harsh given the actual value of the cargo, it is consistent with the intent of the statute. Ammann could have paid a higher tariff if it wished to impose a higher liability on the carrier. *See Caterpillar Americas Co. v. Steamship Sea Roads, supra*, 231 F. Supp. at 650; *Petition of Isbrandtsen*, 201 F.2d 281 (2d Cir. 1953). Because the bill of lading contained language providing for limitation of liability and also incorporated COGSA, the burden is on Ammann to prove that an opportunity to declare a higher value did not exist. *Barth v. Atlantic Container Line, supra*, at 1257. Ammann has not met this burden.

* * *

3. *The amount of the limit*

(a) *The $500 Limitation*

COGSA § 4(5) provides that by agreement the carrier and the shipper may agree to *increase* (not decrease) the $500 limitation on liability. Presumably in this case a higher freight will be charged. Courts have declared that the shipper must be provided with a fair opportunity to declare a higher value. *See Komatsu, Ltd. v. States Steamship*, 764 F.2d 806, 1982 AMC 2151 (9th Cir. 1986). Recent cases have focused on the meaning of "fair opportunity." *See Couthino Caro and Co., Inc. v. M/V Sava*, 849 F.2d 166, 1988 AMC 2941 (5th Cir. 1988); *Sony Magnetic Products of America v. Merivienty O/Y*, 668 F. Supp. 1505, 1988 AMC 718 (S.D. Ala. 1987); *MacSteel International U.S.A. Corp. v. M/V Ibn Abdoun*, 154 F. Supp. 2d 826 (S.D.N.Y. 2001). See Note 3 below.

The "fair opportunity" requirement is discussed in Sturley, *The Fair Opportunity Requirement under COGSA Section 4(5): A Case Study in the Misinterpretation of the Carriage of Goods by Sea Act*, 19 J. Mar. L. & Com. 1 (pt. I), 157 (pt. II) (1988); Sturley, *The Future of the COGSA Fair Opportunity Requirement: Is There Life after Carman Tool and Chan?*, 20 J. Mar. L. & Com. 559 (1989).

Is there any liability under COGSA for the consequential damages of the carrier's breach?

COGSA does not preclude a carrier from offering to limit its liability in an amount in excess of $500. What happens when a bill of lading provides that the Visby Amendments to the Hague Rules apply? The Visby Amendments provide higher limits than the $500 per package limit contained in COGSA. Some courts have held that the Visby Amendments may be enforced because they are consistent with the provision of COGSA which permits a valuation in excess of $500 per package. *Francosteel Corp. v. M/V Pal Marinos*, 885 F. Supp. 86, 1995 AMC 2327 (S.D.N.Y. 1995); *Daval Steel Prods. v. M/V Acadia Forest*, 683 F. Supp. 444, 1988 AMC 1669 (S.D.N.Y. 1988); *J.C.B. Sales, Ltd., v. Wallenius Lines*, 124 F.3d 132, 1997 AMC 2705 (2d Cir. 1997). Others have refused to hold that incorporation of the Visby Amendments amounts to a voluntary increase of the carrier's liability, particularly if that incorporation is by way of a generally-worded Clause Paramount. *Acciai Speciali Terni U.S.A., Inc. v. M/V BERANE*, 182 F. Supp. 2d 503, 2002 AMC 519 (D. Md. 2002).

(b) *Fair Opportunity to Declare a Higher Value*

Suppose a seller-shipper is shipping an expensive piece of equipment worth $100,000 fully encased so that it qualifies as a COGSA package. Assuming that none of the Section 4 defenses are available to the carrier, if the package is lost or its contents totally destroyed, its liability would be limited to $500 under COGSA. What are shipper's options? As a practical matter most shippers carry their own cargo insurance. Thus, shipper could collect $500 from carrier and the remainder from shipper's insurance company.

COGSA's limitation of liability provision, Section 4(5) fixes the limit at $500 per package "unless the nature and value of such goods have been declared by the shipper before shipment and inserted in the bill of lading. This declaration, if embodied in the bill of lading, shall be *prima facie* evidence, but shall not be conclusive on the carrier."

The latter provision has spawned the "fair opportunity" doctrine, whereby a carrier may not invoke the COGSA limitation provision unless the carrier has provided the shipper with a fair opportunity to declare the actual value of the goods, or at least, a value in excess of $500 per package. Of course, carriers are justified in changing a higher freight rate to reflect the increased risk, *i.e.*, the increased value of the goods beyond $500 per package. As a practical matter, it is cheaper for shippers to accept the COGSA $500 per package limitation and to procure their own insurance to cover the difference between that amount and the actual value of the goods, and this is what invariably occurs.

Nevertheless, a carrier who has failed to provide a shipper with a fair opportunity to declare a higher value on the goods will be precluded from invoking COGSA's $500 per package limit. Thus, a carrier must notify shipper that liability is limited under COGSA to $500 per package and provide shippers with an opportunity to opt out of the limitation. Courts seem generally in agreement with this proposition. The language in the bill of lading is crucial in establishing that a fair opportunity was provided. Courts, however, are not necessarily in complete agreement as to the specific provisions necessary to satisfy the requirement. Certainly a statement that the carriage is subject to the $500 per package limitation as provided in COGSA coupled with a statement that shipper may declare a higher value for a higher freight rate with space provided to insert the higher declared value would satisfy the requirement. *Nippon Fire & Marine Ins. Co. v. M/V Tourcoing*, 167 F.3d 99, 1999 AMC 913 (2d Cir. 1999).

Once the carrier has made a prima facie case that it has offered fair opportunity by pointing to bill of lading wording, the onus shifts to the shipper to show that fair opportunity did not in fact exist. In that context, the identity of the shipper may be relevant. In *Intercargo Ins. Co. v. Container Innovations, Inc.*, 100 F. Supp. 2d 198, 2000 AMC 2395 (S.D.N.Y. 2000), the shipper named on the bill of lading was Panalpina, one of the world's largest freight forwarders, a sophisticated party familiar with all the relevant statutes and international conventions. The court held that there was every reason to believe that Panalpina had knowledge of COGSA's actual liability limitation, and there was no evidence whatever to the contrary. See also *Vision Air Flight Service, Inc. v. M/V National Pride*, 155 F. 3d 1165, 1999 AMC 1168 (9th Cir. 1998) (sophisticated shipper could not be taken to say it had not had "fair opportunity" when it had bought cargo insurance).

The Third Circuit stands alone in rejecting the "fair opportunity" doctrine. In *Ferrostaal, Inc. v. M/V Sea Phoenix*, 447 F. 3d 212, 2006 AMC 1217 (3d Cir. 2006), the Third Circuit held that the "fair opportunity" doctrine is not consistent with either the text or the underlying policies of COGSA and is not required by Supreme Court precedent. The court rejected the position taken in each of the seven sister circuits that have adopted some version of the doctrine.

3. *The Harter Act and package limitation*

In cases covered by the Harter Act, no limitation figure is specified, so the actual value rule would be applicable. If the contract contains a limitation of liability, courts will require such contractual limitations to be reasonable. *See Hanover Insurance Co. v. Shulman Transport Enterprise, Inc.*, 581 F.2d 268, 1979 AMC 520 (1st Cir. 1978) [$50 limit held violative of public policy and unenforceable]; *Gold Metal Trading Corp. v. Atlantic Overseas Corp.*, 580 F. Supp. 610, 1984 AMC 2052 (S.D.N.Y. 1984) [$500 per package limitation applied under Harter Act]. A crucial factor in these cases seems to be whether or not the shipper is given an opportunity to declare a higher value. Where a bill of lading provides for a "reduced" freight rate for goods which the shipper agrees to value at $50, one court held that this was a reasonable exchange for the lower rate. In this context, the contractual limitation was given effect. *Antilles Ins. Co. v. Transconex, Inc.*, 862 F.2d 391, 1989 AMC 984 (1st Cir. 1988). However, in *Colgate Palmolive v. S.S. Dart Canada*, 724 F.2d 313, 1984 AMC 305 (2d Cir. 1983), the bill of lading incorporated COGSA including the $500 limitation and made it applicable before loading and after discharge. The damage occurred before loading but while the carrier was in custody of the goods. The court held that the limitation was invalid under New Jersey law and that COGSA was not applicable by its own terms. Thus, the contractual incorporation of COGSA had to meet the standards of state law. The Harter Act was not discussed.

COMMONWEALTH PETROCHEMICALS, INC. v. S/S PUERTO RICO

607 F.2d 322, 1979 AMC 2772 (4th Cir. 1979)

James Dickson PHILLIPS, Circuit Judge:

En route from Baltimore, Maryland to San Juan, Puerto Rico, an electrical transformer aboard the S.S. Puerto Rico was damaged. The covering bill of lading incorporated the provisions of the Carriage of Goods by Sea Act (COGSA), 46 U.S.C. §§ 1300-1315, and limited the carrier's liability to $500 per package. The transformer was defined as being one package in the long form bill of lading that was incorporated by reference into the short form bill given to the shippers. The district court refused to give effect to this definition and held the carrier liable for the full amount of the damage to the transformer, $13,901.01.

On the carrier's appeal, three issues are presented for decision. May the parties to a domestic contract of ocean carriage incorporate the provisions of COGSA and at the same time define a term of that statute in a manner that may be inconsistent with the interpretation that has been placed upon it by the courts? If so, may this be done through the use of two bills of lading, a short form given to the shipper incorporating COGSA and a long form incorporated by reference in the short form which provides the possibly inconsistent definition? And finally, was this effectively done in the case at bar? We answer all three issues in the affirmative and reverse.

I

The pertinent facts and the proceeding below may be briefly stated. The transformer measured more than 10 feet in each dimension and weighed 47,700 pounds. It was bolted to an iron skid and then loaded, with a second such transformer, on a special flat-bed trailer for the land journey from Rome, Georgia to Baltimore. The iron skids were in turn bolted to the trailer and the transformers were further fixed in place with heavy chains. When it arrived in Baltimore, the trailer was loaded on the S.S. Puerto Rico and during the voyage to San Juan one of the transformers was damaged.

The shippers, Commonwealth Petrochemicals, Inc. and Fluor Engineers and Constructors, Inc., then brought this action against the S.S. Puerto Rico *in rem* and its owner *pro hac vice*, Puerto Rico Maritime Shipping Authority, *in personam* to recover for the damage. The carrier admitted liability and the case was submitted to the district court on the pleadings and a stipulated set of facts, the only issue for decision being the measure of damages. The carrier sought to limit recovery to $500 on the theory that the bill of lading and the Carriage of Goods by Sea Act incorporated by reference therein, permitted limitation to $500 per package and that the partially enclosed transformer had been defined as one package. The district court concluded that by incorporating COGSA, the parties had also incorporated the judicial construction of the term "package" as used in 46 U.S.C. § 1304(5), and that under those constructions the transformer did not constitute a package. *Commonwealth Petrochemicals, Inc. v. S/S Puerto Rico*, 455 F. Supp. 310 (D. Md. 1978). It therefore entered judgment in the full amount of the damage and this appeal followed.

* * *

Relying on the language that COGSA should apply to contacts of domestic carriage when incorporated therein "as fully as if subject hereto by the express provisions of this chapter," the district court reasoned that the transformer did not constitute a "package" within the meaning of § 1304(5) of COGSA and that to give effect to the contractual definition would lessen the carrier's liability in violation of 46 U.S.C. § 1303(8). In this we conclude the district court erred.

We have held that when COGSA does not apply of its own force but is incorporated into a maritime contract by reference, it does not have "statute rank"; rather, it is merely part of the contract, a term like any other. *United States v. M/V Marilena P*, 433 F.2d 164, 170 (4th Cir. 1969). In *Pannell v. United States Lines Co.*, 263 F.2d 497, 498 (2d Cir. 1959), the United States Court of Appeals for the Second Circuit held that when COGSA does not apply *ex proprio vigore*, effect should be given to the parties' definition of package even if that definition is contrary to that which would control if COGSA were directly applicable. We find Pannell's reasoning compelling.

This seems to be simply an application of the principle of construction applicable to ocean bills of lading that as between a general and a specific provision, effect is to be given to the more specific. *See, e.g., Farr v. Hain S.S. Co.*, 121 F.2d 940 (2d Cir. 1941) (L. HAND, J.) (Harter Act); *In re Petterson Lighterage & Towing Corp.*, 154 F. Supp. 461 (S.D.N.Y. 1957), *aff'd per curiam*, 253 F.2d 952 (2d Cir. 1958) (COGSA). The term "package" is not defined in COGSA except insofar as one may consider judicial construction of the term to be definition. That construction, furthermore, is not uniform with partially encased items such as the transformer involved here. 2A BENEDICT ON ADMIRALTY § 167 at 16-19 to -20 (7th ed. I. Hall, A. Sann & M. Katzman 1977) (collecting cases). Under this principle the COGSA usage would be deemed the more general and the specific contractual usage therefore controlling.

A number of lower courts, in opinions that are not officially published, have reached the same result as did the Second Circuit in *Pannell*.

* * *

The language in the *Pannell* bill of lading incorporating COGSA as well as the definition of package was in all pertinent parts identical to that of the long form bill of lading in the appeal before us. *Pannell* does differ from the case at bar, however, in one particular which shippers contend is critically distinguishing: it did not involve incorporation of COGSA into a contract of domestic carriage and therefore was not subject to the language of § 1312 that COGSA should apply "as fully as if subject hereto by the express provisions of this chapter." Likewise, none of the other cases reaching the same result were subject to § 1312's proviso; all involved incorporation of COGSA outside its statutory time frame, *see* 46 U.S.C. §§ 1307, 1311, or with respect to items that were not "goods" within the provisions of COGSA, *see* 46 U.S.C. § 1301(c).

As tenable as that distinction may appear at first blush, the weight of reported authority does not accept it. The Third Circuit has noted that COGSA can apply to domestic commerce "only as a matter of contract and only to the extent that the parties have manifested an intent that it should apply." *PPG Industries, Inc. v. Ashland Oil Co.—Thomas Petroleum Transit Division*, 527 F.2d 502, 507 (3d Cir. 1975) (footnote omitted). In a related context, the District Court for the District of Puerto Rico has expressly rejected such a distinction. *Empacadora Puertorriquena De Carnes, Inc. v. Alterman Transport Line, Inc.*, 303 F. Supp. 474, 479 n.10 (D.P.R. 1969).

The fact that Congress expressly provided for the incorporation of COGSA into domestic contracts of carriage to which it does not apply *ex proprio vigore* may be explained by the existence of the Harter Act. As noted earlier, Congress viewed the need for amendment of the Harter Act to present distinct problems for foreign and domestic commerce. The other mercantile nations were subscribing to the Hague Rules and to bring our law into uniformity with theirs Congress adopted our version of the Rules, COGSA. The need for uniformity was felt to be less strong with domestic trade, but Congress concluded that the option of following COGSA should be available to domestic carriers and shippers as well. Since the Harter Act was to be expressly preserved for the domestic trade, statutory authority for the incorporation of COGSA had to be provided and since the Harter Act and COGSA do differ in some particulars the language upon which the district court in the instant matter relied was used. As indicated, we do not believe that this merely authorizing language is properly read to alter the ordinary rules of contract interpretation when, pursuant to it, COGSA is incorporated.

III

Shippers argue that public policy precludes enforcement of a clause in a long form bill of lading when only the short form is actually given to the shipper and the clause is one that is not typically found in bills of lading.

The use of a long form bill of lading that is incorporated by reference into the short form given the shipper is specifically provided for in sections 2 and 5 of the Inter-coastal Shipping Act, 46 U.S.C. §§ 844, 845b. The long form must be posted in certain places and be available upon request, but no suggestion is made that that was not done in this case. The practice has received judicial approval, *e.g., Zifferer v. Atlantic Lines, Ltd.*, 278 F. Supp. 736 (D.P.R. 1968), and seems to be customary in the industry.

Several courts, however, have refused to give effect to provisions included in the long form when the provision was such that the shipper could not be expected to have anticipated its existence. *Encyclopaedia Britannica, Inc. v. SS Hong Kong Producer*, 422 F.2d 7 (2d Cir. 1969); *Caribbean Produce Exchange, Inc. v. Sea Land Service, Inc.*, 415 F. Supp. 88 (D.P.R. 1976). We do not think that the case at bar falls within this qualification to the permissible use of two bills of lading. As a leading commentator on ocean-carriage has stated, "[T]he key to determining what is a package or unit for purposes of limitation is the intention of the parties, particularly as declared on the bill of lading...." W. Tetley, Marine Cargo Claims 435 (2d ed. 1978) (emphasis omitted). A clause defining the term package should be expected. In fact the *Pannell* decision involved a definition of "package" in language essentially identical to that involved in this case.

IV

Remaining for determination is the question whether the provisions of the bill of lading in this case define the transformer as one package. The clause of the long form bill of lading which purports to limit liability to $500 per package, continues: "It is agreed that the meaning of the word 'package' includes animals, pieces and all articles of any description except goods shipped in bulk." That definition is for all practical purposes identical to that involved in *Pannell* where the Second Circuit held that a yacht shipped in a cradle was a package within its terms. The transformer involved here is also a package under that definition. We note, although it is not conclusive, *Nichimen v. M. V. Farland*, 462 F.2d 319, 335 (2d Cir. 1972), that in the space in the bill of lading entitled "No. of Pkgs." each transformer is designated as a separate package.

The shippers contend that to permit the incorporation of COGSA while at the same time allowing the carrier to redefine its provisions to limit its liability is unreasonable. When incorporated into a domestic contract of carriage, COGSA is just another term of the agreement. It must be construed, within reason, in harmony with the other provisions of the contract. The term involved here is clearly valid under the Harter Act, the statute applicable *ex proprio vigore*, *see Reid v. Fargo*, 241 U.S. 544, 551 (1916); *Venezuelan Meat Export Co. v. United States*, 12 F. Supp. 379, 387-88 (D. Md. 1935), so the danger posed by permitting the parties to supersede an Act of Congress by their agreement is not present. While more than minimal compliance with the Harter Act may be demanded in some circumstances, this is not one of them. Had shippers wanted to obtain greater coverage than that provided by the terms of the bill of lading, that bill permitted them to declare a greater value for their goods. They did not do so.

Finally, shippers suggest that the definition of "package" contained in the bill of lading is ambiguous, pointing to other places in the bill where assertedly the definition may not easily be transposed for the word it defines. An adequate response is that of Judge Learned Hand:

> [I]t is idle to invoke the canon against redundancy in the interpretation of such a maritime document as this. Courts have again and again observed the curious, often the fantastic, incongruities in charter parties, bills of lading and insurance policies, composed, as they so often are, of a motley patchwork of verbiage thrown together apparently at random, often in an unfamiliar diction three hundred years old. Particularly in a document meant to do service in varying situations each word of such a discordant medley need not be made to count as we seek to make all the words count of carefully prepared contracts drawn for a particular occasion.

Farr v. Hain S.S. Co., 121 F.2d at 945. The definition is unambiguous in the context of the clause in which it was included and which alone is the subject of this litigation. It should be enforced, according to its plainly intended meaning there.

The judgment of the district court is reversed and the case is remanded for entry of judgment in favor of plaintiffs in the amount of $500.

REVERSED AND REMANDED.

Problems on the Applicability of Limitation of Liability

Two yachts and their equipment were shipped from Australia to the Untied States on the deck of the *M/V Prosperity* under a clean bill of lading that incorporated the United States Carriage of Goods by Sea Act. The yachts and equipment were damaged in transit due to the negligence of the carrier. The shipper/consignee filed suit in the United States District Court for the Southern District of New York seeking damages. *Cf. Sail America Foundation v. M/V T.S. Prosperity*, 778 F. Supp. 1282, 1992 AMC 1617 (S.D.N.Y. 1991).

1. The carrier admitted liability and claimed application of the $500 per package limitation under the United States Carriage of Goods by Sea Act. Does this act apply by its own force to the above shipment?
2. What is the effect of the incorporation of the United States Carriage of Goods by Sea Act into the bill of lading?
3. Does the Harter Act come into consideration as to the above shipment?
4. Should the carrier be entitled to the $500 per package limitation under the given facts? See *Enterprise, Inc. v. M/V Sam Houston*, 706 F. Supp. 451, 1988 AMC 2745 (E.D. La. 1988).
5. *Variation*: Suppose that the parties had agreed that the yachts and equipment would be carried on deck but the carrier stowed them under deck. Suppose, further, that the yachts and equipment were damaged by perils of the sea (*e.g.*, non-negligent stranding). Had the yachts and equipment been carried on deck, they would not have sustained any damage. Should the carrier be entitled to the $500 per package limitation?
6. *Variation*: Suppose that the bill of lading from Australia to the United States had provided for on deck carriage "at shipper's risk", that the yacht and equipment were carried on deck, and that they were damaged due to the carrier's negligence. Would the shipper be entitled to any recovery?

F. Who Is the COGSA Carrier?

Introductory Note on the COGSA Carrier

A shipowner which enters into a contract of carriage and issues a bill of lading to a shipper is a COGSA carrier. The shipowner may be liable *in personam* under COGSA for loss or damage to the goods. *Associated Metals & Minerals Corp. v. S.S. Portoria*, 484 F.2d 460, 1973 AMC 2095 (5th Cir. 1973). The shipowner's vessel may also be liable *in rem. Industria Nacional Del Papel, CA. v. M/V Albert F*, 730 F.2d 622, 1985 AMC 1437 (11th Cir.), *cert. denied* 469 U.S. 1037, 105 S. Ct. 515, 83 L. Ed. 2d 404, 1985 AMC 2397 (1984); *Cavcar Co. v. M/V SUZDAL*, 723 F.2d 1096, 1984 AMC 609 (3rd Cir. 1983).

A charterer (bareboat, time or voyage) which issues its own bill of lading to a consignee, will be regarded as a COGSA carrier and subject to *in personam* liability regardless of whether or not the shipowner might also be classified as a COGSA carrier. *Nitram, Inc. v. Cretan Life*, 599 F.2d 1359 (5th Cir. 1979); *Joo Seng Hong Kong Co., Ltd. v. S.S. Unibulkfir*, 483 F. Supp. 43 (S.D.N.Y. 1979); *Joseph L. Wilmotte & Co., Inc. v. Cobelfret Lines, S.P.R.L.*, 289 F. Supp. 601 (M.D. Fla. 1968).

Generally, when a shipowner carries goods for a person who has chartered its vessel, the charter party is the contract is of carriage. Such contracts of carriage (charter parties) are not subject to COGSA (unless the parties expressly agree to incorporate the terms of COGSA into the charter party). In charter party situations, it may be customary for the shipowner to issue a bill of lading to the charterer. As long as that bill of lading remains in the hands of the charterer, it will be regarded merely as a receipt and the charter party remains the contract of carriage which controls the legal relations between the shipowner and the charterer. Again, COGSA does not apply to such contracts of carriage or "receipts" issued thereunder. *Vanol, U.S.A., Inc. v. M/T CORONADO*, 663 F. Supp. 79, 1988 AMC 560 (S.D.N.Y. 1987). In such circumstances, however, if the charterer transfers or negotiates the bill of lading to a third party, such as a consignee, to whom the charterer may, for example, have sold the goods, the bill of lading will be regarded not as a mere receipt but as a contract of carriage between the shipowner and the person to whom the bill has been transferred. Under these circumstances, the shipowner is regarded as a COGSA carrier and may be held liable *in personam*.

In a charter party situation where the charterer (rather than the shipowner) has issued a bill of lading printed on its own form, the shipowner, nevertheless, may be liable *in personam* under agency principles to a consignee where the master signed the bill of lading as authorized or required by the terms of the charter party or where another person signed "for the master" as authorized by the terms of the charter party. *Instituto Cubano De Est. Del Azucar v. T/V GOLDEN WEST*, 246 F.2d 802 (2d Cir.) *cert. denied*, 355 U.S. 884, 78 S. Ct. 152, 2 L. Ed. 2d 114 (1957); *Ross Industries v. M/V GRETKE OLDENDORFF*, 483 F. Supp. 195, 1980 AMC 1397 (E.D. Tex. 1980). However, a consignee will not be able to prevail *in personam* against a vessel owner even where the bill of lading was signed by the master unless it introduces evidence that the master was authorized or required by the charter party to sign bills of lading and thereby bind the owner. *Sail America Foundation v. M/V T.S. PROSPERITY*, 778 F. Supp. 1282, 1992 AMC 1617 (S.D.N.Y. 1991); *Centennial Insurance Co. v. M/V CONSTELLATION ENTERPRISE*, 639 F. Supp. 1261, 1987 AMC 1155 (S.D.N.Y. 1986).

Ordinarily, liability *in rem* is grounded on the fiction that when the goods are loaded on board the vessel the shipowner has ratified the bill of lading. *Cf., Insurance Company of North America v. S.S. AMERICAN ARGOSY*, 732 F.2d 299, 1984 AMC 1547 (2d Cir. 1984) where the court held that the "ratification" fiction would not apply to an unauthorized agreement of which the shipowner was unaware. In this case, the bill of lading had been issued by a freight forwarder.

A NVOCC (Non-Vessel Operating Common Carrier) or freight forwarder who issues a bill of lading whereby it undertakes the responsibilities of a carrier will be treated as a COGSA carrier. *Sabah Shipyard SDN, Bhd. v. M/V Harbel Tapper*, 178 F.3d 400, 2000 AMC 163 (5th Cir. 1999), *Fireman's Fund Amerrican Ins. Companies v. Puerto Rican Forwarding Co., Inc.*, 492 F.2d 1294 (1st Cir. 1974); *M. Prusman Ltd. v. M/V Nathanel*, 670 F.Supp. 1141, 1988 AMC 296 (S.D.N.Y. 1987).

PACIFIC EMPLOYERS INS. CO. v. M/V GLORIA

767 F.2d 229 (5th Cir. 1985)

THORNBERRY, Circuit Judge

This case arises out of a shipment of bagged soybean meal from New Orleans, Louisiana, to Puerto Limon, Costa Rica. When the cargo arrived in Puerto Limon, tallies of the cargo showed that some of the bags were wet, some torn and slack, and some short-landed. Plaintiffs-appellees brought two admiralty actions under the Carriage of Goods by Sea Act, 46 U.S.C. § 1300, *et seq.* (West 1975) ("COGSA"), in which they sought to recover for the cargo damage, slackage, and shortage. The district court consolidated the two actions. The plaintiffs were: Cargill, Inc. ("Cargill"), the shipper of the cargo; Ternerina, S.A., Central Agricola De Cartago, S.A., Fabrica De Alimentos Para Animales, and Industria National De Alimentos Gibbons, S.A., the Costa Rican consignees and receivers of the cargo; and Pacific Employers Insurance, the cargo underwriter. Pursuant to a stipulation of the parties, Pacific Employers Insurance was subrogated to the rights of the owners of the cargo.

The plaintiffs sought recovery against the M/V GLORIA, Aquarius, Ltd., and Transportation Maritima Mexicana, S.A. The defendant M/V GLORIA is a three-hatch bulk and general cargo vessel of Liberian registry owned by the defendant Aquarius, Ltd. ("Aquarius"). The GLORIA was under a long-term time charter to the defendant Transportation Maritima Mexicana, S.A. ("TMM").

For the voyage in issue, TMM entered into a voyage charter with Greenwich Marine, Inc. ("Greenwich"), a subsidiary of plaintiff Cargill. Greenwich was not an original defendant in the action but was tendered as a party defendant by Aquarius and TMM pursuant to FED. R CIV. P. 14(c). Aquarius and TMM also filed third-party actions against Greenwich seeking contribution and indemnity.

Cargill entered into contracts to sell soybean meal to certain parties in Costa Rica. Pursuant to these contracts Cargill engaged Greenwich to find a vessel to carry the soybean meal from New Orleans to Puerto Limon, Costa Rica. Greenwich then entered into a voyage charter of the M/V GLORIA for this purpose. Loading of the bagged soybean meal began in New Orleans on August 5, 1980. Rogers Terminal and Shipping Corp. ("Rogers Terminal") was responsible for bagging, clerking, tallying, and stowing the cargo. Rogers Terminal completed stowage on August 11, and seven bills of lading covering the cargo were issued by "ROGERS TERMINAL & SHIPPING CORPORATION, AS AGENTS BY AUTHORITY OF THE MASTER." Each bill of lading indicates that the cargo was being shipped in apparent good order by Cargill, shipper's weight, quantity and quality, unknown. Further, each bill of lading incorporated the terms of the voyage charter party and the provisions of the Carriage of Goods by Sea Act. Cargill subsequently negotiated the bills of lading.

The GLORIA sailed from New Orleans on August 11 and arrived in Puerto Limon on August 16. Tallies of the cargo conducted by employees of the Puerto Limon Port Authority (the Japdeva) disclosed that the discharged cargo contained wet and torn bags and that the cargo was slack and short. Subsequently, the owners of the cargo and the cargo underwriter, as subrogee, brought this action to recover for the alleged damage, slackage, and shortage. Only the cargo carried under bills of lading 1, 2, 3, 5, and 7 is at issue in this litigation.

The defendants-appellants, Aquarius and TMM, brought Greenwich into the action as a defendant to the main demand and as a third-party defendant to their claims for contribution and indemnity. The district court ordered that the third-party action by TMM against Greenwich be stayed pending arbitration as required by the voyage charter party. The parties then agreed to submit the case to the district court on written briefs, depositions, exhibits, and proposed findings of fact and conclusions of law. No oral evidence was taken.

On January 26, 1984, the district court entered judgment in favor of plaintiffs and against the GLORIA, *in rem*, and Aquarius and TMM, *in personam*, in the amount of $59,540.24 plus legal interest from the date of judicial demand. In a written opinion the district court found that the vessel, Aquarius, and TMM were carriers under COGSA and that Greenwich was not a carrier. The court also found that plaintiffs established a *prima facie* case against the carriers for recovery of the cargo damage, slackage, and shortage, and that defendants failed to rebut the plaintiffs' evidence. On February 23, the district court entered an amended judgment dismissing the claims against Greenwich. Aquarius and TMM appeal from the judgment and the amended judgment.

* * *

II. COGSA Carriers

Plaintiffs may recover under COGSA only from the "carriers" of the cargo. COGSA defines "carrier" to include "the owner or the charterer who enters into a contract of carriage with a shipper." 46 U.S.C. § 1301(a). Accordingly, the plaintiffs must establish that a party defendant executed a contract of carriage. *Associated Metals*, 484 F.2d at 462. COGSA defines a "contract of carriage" as follows:

> The term "contract of carriage" applies only to contracts of carriage covered by a bill of lading or any similar document of title, insofar as such document relates to the carriage of goods by sea, including any bill of lading or any similar document as aforesaid issued under or pursuant to a charter party from the moment at which such bill of lading or similar document of title regulates the relations between a carrier and a holder of the same.

46 U.S.C. § 1301(b). The district court found that TMM and Aquarius entered into a contract of carriage with Cargill and thus were carriers under COGSA, and that Greenwich did not enter into a contract of carriage as defined by the Act and thus was not a carrier.

* * *

TMM

The bills of lading were issued by Rogers Terminal and were signed: "ROGERS TERMINAL & SHIPPING CORPORATION, AS AGENTS BY AUTHORITY OF THE MASTER." The district court found that in issuing the bills of lading, Rogers Terminal acted as agent for TMM and therefore TMM entered into a contract of carriage. TMM contends that this finding is clearly erroneous. We disagree and hold that there was sufficient evidence before the district court to support its finding. The voyage charter party entered into by TMM and Greenwich was incorporated into the bills of lading and provided, in part; that:

> Owners [TMM] to instruct their New York bank to advise Owners' agents at loading port immediately freight received by cable that freight payment has been received and Owners to instruct their agents to release Bill/s of Lading immediately on receipt of such advice. If release of Bill/s of Lading should be delayed, the Owners shall pay interest at one per cent over the New York Prime Rate on Bill/s of Lading date/s, on the cost and freight value of the cargo from the day on which the freight payment is re-

> ceived by the Owners' New York bank until the day on which the Bill/s of Lading are actually released by the Owners' agents.

The evidence before the district court did not clearly disclose for whom Rogers Terminal acted when it issued the bills of lading. Under the voyage charter party, Greenwich was obligated to appoint and employ stevedores at the loading port. Rogers Terminal performed stevedoring services in New Orleans. However, the National Cargo Bureau's Certificate of Loading, issued after loading of the GLORIA was completed, stated, "AGENT—ROGERS TERMINAL & SHIPPING CO.—T.M.M. CHARTERING." Moreover, the charter party states that TMM and/or its agents would be responsible for issuance of the bills of lading. The master of the GLORIA testified by deposition that he authorized Rogers Terminal to issue the bills of lading on his behalf. He also testified, however, that it was his belief that Rogers Terminal was acting on behalf of Greenwich.

The district court considered all of the evidence before it, and, relying primarily on the voyage charter party provision that TMM would issue the bills of lading upon payment of freight by Greenwich, the court found that the bills were issued by TMM through its agent, Rogers Terminal. The district court's finding, in light of the conflicting evidence, is not clearly erroneous and we Affirm the holding that TMM entered into a contract of carriage with respect to the soybean cargo and is thus a carrier under the provisions of COGSA.

Greenwich

The district court held that Greenwich was not a COGSA carrier because Greenwich did not issue the bills of lading and did not otherwise enter into a contract of carriage with Cargill. The court found that "Greenwich acted simply on behalf of the shipper in finding a vessel to carry the cargo and paying the appropriate freight." Greenwich did not enter into a contract that was "covered by a bill of lading or any similar document of title." *See* 46 U.S.C. § 1301(b).

In addition to contending that Greenwich issued the bills of lading, appellants argue that Greenwich is a COGSA carrier because the bills of lading were issued in connection with the voyage charter and because, under the voyage charter party, Greenwich was responsible for loading, stowage, and discharge—duties which COGSA places on the carrier. *See* 46 U.S.C. § 1303(2). First, we note that the voyage charter party merely states, "Charterers to appoint and employ stevedores at loading port/s," and "Charterers/Receivers Stevedores to be employed at discharging port/s." The charter party is not so explicit as appellants would have us believe. Moreover, even if Greenwich bore the responsibility under the voyage charter party for loading, stowage, and discharge, we do not believe this fact, alone, would make Greenwich a COGSA carrier. In *Dempsey & Associates v. S.S. SEA STAR*, 461 F.2d 1009 (2d Cir. 1972), the time charterer issued bills of lading in connection with a voyage charter. The court held that the time charterer was a COGSA carrier but that the voyage charterer was not. The court further held that the fact that the charter party required the voyage charterer to load, stow, and discharge the cargo created a duty running from the voyage charterer to the time charterer but did not affect the time charterer's obligations under COGSA and did not operate to make the voyage charterer a COGSA carrier. *Id.* at 1018-1019. We agree with the Second Circuit and we affirm the district court's finding that Greenwich is not a COGSA carrier.

Aquarius

Appellants also argue that the district court erred by finding that Aquarius is a COGSA carrier. Since appellees' causes of action were based on COGSA, there can be *in personam* liability against the vessel owner only if the owner is a carrier. *Associated Metals*, 484 F.2d at 462. Appellants contend that Aquarius did not enter into a contract of carriage and did not become bound by the bills of lading merely because they were signed "by authority of the master."

"A contract of carriage with an owner may either be direct between the parties, or by virtue of a charterer's authority to bind the owner by signing bills of lading 'for the master.'" *Matter of Intercontinental Properties Management, S.A.*, 604 F.2d 254, 258 n. 3 (4th Cir. 1979) . Appellees argue that the bills of lading were issued by Rogers Terminal—TMM's agent—with the actual authority of the vessel owner and that Aquarius is therefore bound. The circumstances under which the vessel owner may be bound by the bills of lading were well-stated by the First Circuit in *EAC Timberlane v. Pisces, Ltd.*, 745 F.2d 715 (1st Cir. 1984):

> Generally, when a bill of lading is signed by the charterer or its agent "for the master" with the authority of the shipowner, this binds the shipowner and places the shipowner within the provisions of COGSA. *E.g., Gans S.S. Line v. Wilhelmsen (The Themis)*, 2 Cir. 1921, 275 F. 254, 262; *Tube Products of India v. S.S. Rio Grande*, 1971, S.D.N.Y., 334 F. Supp. 1039, 1041; *see generally* Bauer, *Responsibilities of Owner and Charterer to Third Parties—Consequences Under Time and Voyage Charters*, 49 Tul. L. Rev. 995, 997-1001 (1975). When, however, a bill of lading is signed by the charter or its agent "for the master" but without the authority of the shipowner, the shipowner is not personally bound and does not by virtue of the charterer's signature become a COGSA carrier. *E.g., Associated Metals and Minerals Corp. v. S.S. Portoria*, 5 Cir. 1973, 484 F.2d 460, 462; *Dempsey & Associates, Inc. v. S.S. Sea Star*, 2 Cir. 1972, 461 F.2d 1009, 1015.

Id. at 719. Aquarius' liability depends on the effect of the signature caption "by authority of the master." In order to determine the effect we must examine Rogers Terminal's authority to sign on behalf of the master and the master's authority to bind Aquarius. *See Yeramex International v. S.S. TENDO*, 595 F.2d 943, 946 (4th Cir. 1979).

The district court's finding that the master authorized Rogers Terminal to issue the bills of lading on his behalf is not clearly erroneous. The captain of the GLORIA testified by deposition that he "gave Rogers Terminal an undertaking that they should sign the bills of lading." Appellants presented no conflicting evidence. This case is therefore unlike those cited by appellants in which there was no evidence that the master authorized the charterer or its agent to sign on his behalf. *See Dempsey & Associates v. S.S. SEA STAR*, 461 F.2d 1009, 1012-15 (2d Cir. 1972); *Thyssen Steel Corp. v. S.S. ADONIS*, 364 F. Supp. 1332, 1335 (S.D.N.Y. 1973); *United Nations Children's Fund v. S/S NORDSTERN*, 251 F. Supp. 833, 838 (S.D.N.Y. 1965).

We must next determine whether the master had actual authority to bind the vessel owner to the terms of the bills of lading. The charter party between Aquarius and TMM contained the following provisions:

> 8. [T]he Captain shall prosecute his voyages with the utmost despatch, and shall render all customary assistance with ship's crew and boats. The Captain (although appointed by the Owners), shall be under the orders and directions of the Charterers [TMM] as regards employment and agency; and Charterers are to load, stow, and trim and discharge the cargo at their expense under the supervision of the Captain, who is to sign Bills of Lading for cargo as presented, in conformity with Mate's or Tally Clerk's receipts.
>
> Rider 37. If required by Charterers and/or their Agents, Master to authorize Charterers or their Agents to sign Bills of Lading on his behalf in accordance with mates and/or tally clerks receipt without prejudice to this Charter Party.

We hold that Rider 37 to the charter party empowered the master to authorize TMM's agent to sign the bills of lading and thereby bind Aquarius. The case cited by appellants, *Yeramex International v. S.S. TENDO*, 595 F.2d 943 (4th Cir. 1979), is distinguishable. In *Yeramex* the charter party between the vessel owner and the time charterer contained a provision identical to clause 8 above. It also contained a provision that stated, in part: "Charterers shall indemnify Owners from all consequences arising out of Master or agents signing Bills of Lading in accordance with Charterers' instructions, or from complying with any orders or directions of Charterers in connection therewith." *Id.* at 947. The court in *Yeramex* found that under the provisions of the charter party the charterer assumed exclusive responsibility for handling of cargo and for issuance of bills of lading. The court further stated:

> In particular, we think all authority conferred by these provisions upon the vessels' masters for bills of lading issued by [time charterer] was authority which flowed, in fact, from [the time charterer] as principal to the masters as its agents, rather than as authority granted to [the time charterer] from the masters as the traditional personal agents of the owner ... . No authority in fact existed for [the time charterer] to bind the owner to the terms of the bill of lading as a contracting party, and no liability in personam under COGSA will lie against the owner in favor of third parties.

Id. at 948. The Aquarius/TTM charter party did not contain a provision requiring TMM to indemnify Aquarius from all consequences arising out of the master or agents signing bills of lading. Moreover, Rider 37 to the charter party contains an express authorization that was not present in the *Yeramex* charter party. The district court's findings that TMM was authorized to bind Aquarius to the terms of the bills of lading and that Aquarius is a COGSA carrier are not clearly erroneous.

* * *

Note

Compare, Yeramex International v. S.S. Tendo, 595 F.2d 943, 1979 AMC 1282 (4th Cir. 1979) which held under its facts of that case, that only the time charterer and not the ship owner was liable *in personam.*

Note: Ratification: The ship in rem *as COGSA carrier*

Regardless of who is liable *in personam* as contracting carrier, the ship itself may be held liable *in rem* under the doctrine of ratification. By sailing with the goods on board, the ship is taken to have ratified any bill of lading contracts for carriage on that voyage, whether those contracts were made by the shipowner or a charterer. In *Cactus Pipe & Supply Co., Inc. v. M/V Montmartre*, 756 F.2d 1103, 1113, 1985 AMC 2150 (5th Cir. 1985), the doctrine was explained as follows:

> When cargo has been stowed on board the vessel and bills of lading are issued, the bills of lading become binding contracts of the vessel *in rem* upon the sailing of the vessel with the cargo. The sailing of the vessel constitutes a ratification of the bills of lading. *Compagnie De Navigation Fraissinet & Cyprien Fabre, S.A. v. Mondial United Corp.*, 316 F.2d 163, 173, 1963 AMC 946, 956 (5th Cir. 1963); *see Cavcar Co. v. M/V SUZDAL*, 723 F.2d 1096, 1101, 1984 AMC 609, 617 (3d Cir. 1983); *Demsey & Assoc. v. The S.S. SEA STAR*, 461 F.2d 1009, 1015, 1972 AMC 1440, 1447 (2d Cir. 1972); *cf. Insurance Co. of North America v. The S/S AMERICAN ARGOSY*, 732 F.2d 299, 303, 1984 AMC 1547, 1553 (2d Cir. 1984); *see also*, H. LONGLEY, COMMON CARRIAGE OF CARGO, § 3.05[1][b] at 26 (1967). This action gives rise to a maritime lien which is the basis of the *in rem* recovery. Even though the vessel is operating under charter parties, the lien against the vessel is not affected. *Demsey*, 461 F.2d at 1014, 1972 AMC at 1446. Therefore, the sailing of the MONTMARTRE with the cargo of steel pipes aboard constituted a ratification of the bills of lading.

G. Extension of COGSA defenses, immunities and limitations to non-carriers

Note: The Himalaya Clause

A Himalaya Clause seeks to extend to non-carriers partial immunity or other protections afforded to the carrier by the bill of lading. *See* Healy, *Carriage of Goods by Sea: Application of the Himalaya Clause to Subdelegees of the Carrier*, 2 MAR. LAW. 91 (1977). Stevedores and others as bailees for hire owe a duty of reasonable care of the cargo and may also be held to a warranty of workman-like performance. *See*, for example, *Vitol Trading S.A., Inc. v. SGS Control Services, Inc.*, 680 F. Supp. 559, 1987 AMC 1995 (S.D.N.Y. 1987) [inspection company found in breach of warranty of workman-like performance because chemical analysis testing was deficient]. Absent contract, stevedores and terminal personnel are neither bound by the terms of a bill of lading nor regulated by contract. *ITT Rayonier, Inc. v. Southeastern Maritime Co.*, 620 F.2d 512, 1981 AMC 854 (5th Cir. 1980). A clear and unequivocal Himalaya Clause in the bill of lading, however, will be given effect to extend to the stevedore, who is the agent or subcontractor of the carrier, the benefit of the $500 limitation of liability. *See Miller Yacht Sales, Inc. v. M/V Vishva Shobha*, 494 F. Supp. 1005, 1981 AMC 2479 (S.D.N.Y. 1980).

Until recently, it was thought that Himalaya Clauses should be strictly construed. Where a clause applied by its terms to "agents and independent contractors" it did not extend to a trucker who was an agent or independent contractor of the consignee. *Taisho Marine & Fire Ins. Co. v. The Vessel Gladiolus*, 762 F.2d 1364, 1987 AMC 2047 (11th Cir. 1985). Also, where a stevedore is an agent of the shipper or consignee it was not covered by a clause that extended to agents of the carrier. *Ram Metals & Building Industries, Ltd. v. Zim Israel Navigation Company, Ltd.*, 732 F. Supp. 106, 1989 AMC 2215 (S.D. Fla. 1989).

However, in *Norfolk Southern Railway Co. v. Kirby*, 125 S. Ct. 385, 2004 AMC 2705 (2004), the Supreme Court recently held that there is no rule requiring especially strict interpretation of Himalaya clauses. The Court said:

> Kirby and ICC made a contract for the carriage of machinery from Sydney to Huntsville, and agreed to limit the liability of ICC and other parties who would participate in transporting the machinery. The bill's Himalaya Clause states:
>
> These conditions [for limitations on liability] apply whenever claims relating to the performance of the contract evidenced by this [bill of lading] are made against *any servant, agent or other person (including any independent contractor) whose services have been used in order to perform the contract.*" App. to Pet. for Cert. 59a, cl. 10.1 (emphasis added).
>
> The question presented is whether the liability limitation in Kirby's and ICC's contract extends to Norfolk, which is ICC's sub-subcontractor. The Circuits have split in answering this question. Compare, *e.g., Akiyama Corp. of America v. M.V. Hanjin Marseilles,* 162 F.3d 571, 574 (C.A.9 1998) (privity of contract is not required in order to benefit from a Himalaya Clause), with *Mikinberg v. Baltic S.S. Co.,* 988 F.2d 327, 332 (C.A.2 1993) (a contractual relationship is required).
>
> This is a simple question of contract interpretation. It turns only on whether the Eleventh Circuit correctly applied this Court's decision in *Robert C. Herd & Co. v. Krawill Machinery Corp.,* 359 U.S. 297, 79 S.Ct. 766, 3 L.Ed.2d 820 (1959). We conclude that it did not. In *Herd,* the bill of lading between a cargo owner and carrier said that, consistent with COGSA, " 'the Carrier's liability, if any, shall be determined on the basis of $500 per package.' " *Id.,* at 302, 79 S.Ct. 766. The carrier then hired a stevedoring company to load the cargo onto the ship, and the stevedoring company damaged the goods. The Court held that the stevedoring company was not a beneficiary of the bill's liability limitation. Because it found no evidence in COGSA or its legislative history that Congress meant COGSA's liability limitation to extend automatically to a carrier's agents, like stevedores, the Court looked to the language of the bill of lading itself. It reasoned that a clause limiting "'the Carrier's liability'" did not "indicate that the contracting parties intended to limit the liability of stevedores or other agents.... If such had been a purpose of the contracting parties it must be presumed that they would in some way have expressed it in the contract." *Ibid.* The Court added that liability limitations must be "strictly construed and limited to intended beneficiaries." *Id.,* at 305, 79 S.Ct. 766.
>
> The Eleventh Circuit, like respondents, made much of the *Herd* decision. Deriving a principle of narrow construction from *Herd,* the Court of Appeals concluded that the language of the ICC bill's Himalaya Clause is too vague to clearly include Norfolk. 300 F.3d, at 1308. Moreover, the lower court interpreted *Herd* to require privity between the carrier and the party seeking shelter under a Himalaya Clause. *Id.,* at 1308. But nothing in *Herd* requires the linguistic specificity or privity rules that the Eleventh Circuit attributes to it. The decision simply says that contracts for carriage of goods by sea must be construed like any other contracts: by their terms and consistent with the intent of the parties. If anything, *Herd* stands for the proposition that there is no special rule for Himalaya Clauses.
>
> The Court of Appeals' ruling is not true to the contract language or to the intent of the parties. The plain language of the Himalaya Clause indicates an intent to extend the liability limitation broadly—to "*any* servant, agent or other person (including *any* independent contractor)" whose services contribute to performing the contract. App. to Pet. for Cert. 59a, cl. 10.1 (emphasis added). "Read naturally, the word 'any' has an expansive

> meaning, that is, 'one or some indiscriminately of whatever kind.' " *United States v. Gonzales,* 520 U.S. 1, 5, 117 S.Ct. 1032, 137 L.Ed.2d 132 (1997) (quoting Webster's Third New International Dictionary 97 (1976)). There is no reason to contravene the clause's obvious meaning. See *Green v. Biddle,* 8 Wheat. 1, 89-90, 5 L.Ed. 547 (1823) ("[W]here the words of a law, treaty, or contract, have a plain and obvious meaning, all construction, in hostility with such meaning, is excluded"). The expansive contract language corresponds to the fact that various modes of transportation would be involved in performing the contract. Kirby and ICC contracted for the transportation of machinery from Australia to Huntsville, Alabama, and, as the crow flies, Huntsville is some 366 miles inland from the port of discharge. See G. Fitzpatrick & M. Modlin, Direct-Line Distances 168 (1986). Thus, the parties must have anticipated that a land carrier's services would be necessary for the contract's performance. It is clear to us that a railroad like Norfolk was an intended beneficiary of the ICC bill's broadly written Himalaya Clause. Accordingly, Norfolk's liability is limited by the terms of that clause.

Norfolk Southern, 125 S. Ct. 385, 396-98 (2004).

GRACE LINE, INC. v. TODD SHIPYARDS CORPORATION

500 F.2d 361, 1974 AMC 1136 (9th Cir. 1974)

James M. CARTER, Circuit Judge:

This case arises out of a collision between a steamship and a drydock. We are presented with issues of negligence, the propriety of prejudgment interest, the scope of the United States Carriage of Goods by Sea Act, the interpretation and validity of so-called 'Himalaya' clauses in bills of lading, and laches. Notwithstanding the number and complexity of the legal issues and the number of parties involved, the facts are rather simple.

Facts

The Santa Ana is a 10,000-ton cargo steamship owned and operated by Grace Lines, Inc. (hereafter Grace). On December 8, 1967, the steamship arrived in San Francisco Bay laden with cargo of coffee, lumber, corned beef and quebracho. These goods were insured, respectively, by Home Insurance Company (hereafter Home), Atlantic Mutual Insurance Company (hereafter Atlantic Mutual), Royal Globe Insurance Co. (hereafter Royal Globe), and Commercial Insurance Company of Newark (hereafter Commercial).

During a voyage by a cargo steamship, it is customary for the vessel to enter a drydock for inspection and repair. With this purpose, the Santa Ana steamed into the Oakland Estuary where its intended drydock was located. This was Drydock No. 2, operated by Todd Shipyards Corporation (hereafter Todd).

Ordinarily, Captain Fillipow commanded the Santa Ana, but a special pilot named Carlier took the helm in order to perform the delicate operation of entering the drydock. Pilot Carlier was an employee of Shipowners & Merchants Towboat Company, Ltd. (hereafter S & M Towboat), which also supplied tugboats to assist in the maneuvers.

The Oakland Estuary runs generally east to west, and Drydock No. 2 is on the south shore. After heading east up the estuary until reaching the drydock, the steamship made a 90 degrees turn to the south and aimed towards the drydock's entry.

* * *

At the time Pilot Carlier proceeded to navigate the steamship into the submerged drydock, an eastward breeze and a flowing tide pushed against the vessel on the starboard (*i.e.*, right hand) side. No finding was made, and nobody can say for certain, whether this starboard pressure was what made the steamship enter the drydock as it did, off-center, towards the port (*i.e.*, left hand) side. The port side hull rammed into the unseen recessed wall, ripping a hole in the vessel beneath the water line. Besides damaging the steamship, the collision caused injury to the drydock and allowed flooding water to injure the cargo. The steamship, however, was ultimately drydocked and repaired by Todd.

Out of this accident arose four law suits. (1) Grace, the owner of the steamship sued Todd, the operator of the drydock, for the damages to the vessel and resultant damages. Todd filed a counterclaim against Grace for the damages to the drydock and for the money Todd had spent in repairing the ripped hull. Todd also filed a third-party complaint for the dock damage against S & M Towboat, which employed Pilot Carlier and the tugboats. (2) Two cargo insurers, Home and Atlantic Mutual, joined in suit against Grace, the Santa Ana itself, Todd and S & M Towboat for damage to the coffee and lumber. (3) Commercial brought a separate suit against the same defendants for damage to the quebracho. (4) Royal Globe likewise brought a separate suit against the same defendants for damage to the corned beef.

The suits were consolidated and tried to the district court. In its findings and conclusions, the court held that Todd was negligent and hence liable to Grace in the net amount of $17,265.03; that Todd, though negligent, was entitled to immunity against the cargo insurers; and that neither Grace nor S & M Towboat were negligent or liable to any party.

In the two appeals (by Todd and the cargo insurers) and the two cross-appeals (by Grace and Todd), we face the following questions:

(1) Did the trial court err in finding Todd negligent?
(2) Did the trial court err in finding that there was no negligence on the part of the Santa Ana, Grace or S & M Towboat?
(3) Did the trial court err in refusing to grant pre-judgment interest to Grace?
(4) Did the trial court err in holding that Todd is entitled to the same exemptions and immunities from and limitations of liability which Grace has against the cargo interests (these exemptions, immunities and limitations primarily being those that the United States Carriage of Goods by Sea Act provides specifically for carriers)?

As elaborated below, we answer questions (1), (2) and (3) in the negative, affirming the district court on those points. We conclude, however, that question (4) should be answered in the affirmative; we therefore reverse the district court's holding that Todd is entitled to immunity from liability to the cargo insurers.

* * *

IV. *The 'Himalaya' Clause and COGSA*

The district court held that Todd was entitled to the same exemptions and immunities from and limitations of liability which Grace had against the cargo insurers. We disagree, holding that Todd was entitled to some but not all, of the exemptions and immunities and limitations which Grace had, as detailed below.

A. *The Provisions of the 'Himalaya' Clause*

The bills of lading constituting the contract of carriage between Grace and the cargo interest contain a so-called 'Himalaya' clause, which reads in pertinent part as follows:

'The Carrier shall be discharged from all liability in respect of loss, damage and every claim whatsoever with respect to the goods unless suit is brought within one year after delivery of the goods or the date when the goods should have been delivered.... It is expressly agreed between the parties (the Carrier and the cargo owners) hereto that the master, officers, crew members, contractors, stevedores, longshoremen, agents, representatives, employees or others used, engaged or employed by the carrier in the performance of such work or services (undertaken in this contract), shall each be the beneficiaries of and shall be entitled to the same, but no further exemptions and immunities from and limitations of liability which the carrier has under this bill of lading, whether printed, written, stamped thereon or incorporated by reference.... Without limitation or restriction of the exemptions and immunities from and limitations of liability provided for (above), the persons and companies mentioned therein shall be entitled to the same, but no further, benefits which the carrier has under the U.S. Carriage of Goods by Sea Act, including but not limited to Sections 3(6), 4(1), 4(2)(a), 4(2)(q) and 4(5) of said Act.'

As will be further discussed below, the United States Carriage of Goods by Sea Act (hereafter COGSA), 49 Stat. 1207 (1936), 46 U.S.C. §§ 1300-1315, grants certain immunities, exemptions and limitations to carriers of cargo by sea. Although the Act does not itself extend these protections to non-carriers, the bills of lading purport to incorporate certain of COGSA's provisions into the contract and thereby protect certain non-carriers as well. As we discuss below. Todd was a contractor engaged in the performance of work undertaken in the bills of lading, and hence the following of COGSA's protections are purportedly extended to Todd contractually:

> The one-year period of limitations for instituting suit and a notice-of-damage requirement (see COGSA, § 3(6), 46 U.S.C. § 1303(6)).

The immunity from liability for unseaworthiness of the vessel unless caused by want of due diligence (see COGSA, § 4(1), 46 U.S.C. § 1304(1));

The immunity from liability for negligent acts in the navigation or management of the ship (see COGSA, § 4(2)(a), 46 U.S.C. § 1304(2)(a));

The immunity from liability for damage caused by fire, unless caused by the actual fault or privity of the carrier (see COGSA, § 4(2)(b), 46 U.S.C. § 1304(2)(b));

The immunity from liability for damage arising from any cause without actual fault or privity (see COGSA, § 4(2)(q), 46 U.S.C. § 1304(2)(q)); and

The limited liability of $500 per package or freight unit unless the nature and value of the goods have been declared by the shipper before shipment and inserted in the bill of lading (see COGSA, § 4(5), 46 U.S.C. § 1304(5)).

The exemptions, immunities and limitations which are pertinent to the instant case are the complete exemption from liability (see COGSA, § 4(2)(a), 46 U.S.C. § 1304(2)(a)); the $500 limitation on liability (see COGSA, § 4(5), 46 U.S.C. § 1304(5)); and the one-year period of limitations for instituting suit (see COGSA, § 3(6), 46 U.S.C. § 1303(6)).

B. *The $500 Limitation on Amount of Liability*

In *Tessler Brothers (B.C.) Ltd. v. Italpacific Line and Matson Terminals, Inc.* (9 Cir. 1974) 494 F.2d 438, this court squarely faced the issue of whether a 'Himalaya' clause was valid which purported clearly and expressly to extend to a non-carrier to $500 limitation on liability which COGSA, § 4(5), 46 U.S.C. § 1304(5), provides for carriers. That clause was held valid, and Tessler Brothers is binding authority as regards the inclusion in bills of lading of limitations on amount of non-carrier's liability.

C. *The Complete Immunity from Liability for Negligence in Navigation and Management*

* * *

It will be noted that COGSA's provisions regulate the liability of carriers, but not non-carriers. Since the Act, in balance, is more protective than the common law, it is not surprising that noncarriers have nonetheless sought to place themselves under COGSA's shelter. This has been attempted by arguing in the courts that COGSA should be construed to protect parties other than carriers, despite the Act's language to the contrary; and since this argument has failed, the extension of COGSA has been attempted contractually, by providing in bills of lading that certain non-carriers would be subject to COGSA's protections.

In *Robert C. Herd & Co. v. Krawill Machinery Corp.*, 359 U.S. 297, 79 S.Ct. 766, 3 L.Ed.2d 820 (1959), the Supreme Court considered whether the provisions of COGSA should apply to a stevedore, either by virtue of the Act itself or by contractual extension in the bills of lading.

The Court held that nothing in the language, history, or environment of the Act showed a congressional intent to regulate by statute the liability of stevedores or other agents of the carrier.

The Court further noted that the bills of lading in that case did not expressly extend the provisions of COGSA to the stevedore.

In language of significance here, the Court stated as follows:

'This Court has several times held that an agent's only shield from liability 'for conduct harmful to the plaintiff ... is a constitutional rule of law that exonerates him.' ...Any such rule of law, being in derogation of the common law, must be strictly construed, for 'no statute is to be construed as altering the common law, farther than its words import. It is not to be construed as making any innovation upon the common law which it does not fairly express.' ...Similarly, contracts purporting to grant immunity from, or limitation of, liability must be strictly construed and limited to intended beneficiaries, for they 'are not to be applied to alter familiar rules visiting liability upon a tortfeasor for the consequences of his negligence, unless the clarity of the language used expresses such to be the understanding of the contracting parties."

The above quotation from the Herd opinion is of special import here. It suggests that the sole reason the Court refused to allow the contractual extension of COGSA's protections to stevedores was that the bill of lading in that case was not clear and express in its intent to make this extension; the Herd opinion might be interpreted to mean that a bill of lading, if it clearly and expressly extends a COGSA exemption, immunity or limitation to a non- carrier who is an agent of the carrier, is a valid derogation of the common law and will be given effect.

Thus the Court of Appeals for the Ninth Circuit in Tessler Brothers, supra, held on the basis of Herd that a bill of lading, if clear and express, was effective to extend the $500 limitation on the amount of liability, as provided in COGSA, § 4(5), 46 U.S.C. § 1304(5), to stevedores.

Our concern, however, is not with the contractual extension of the Act's limitation on amount of liability, but rather with an extension to non-carriers of the complete exemption from negligence in navigation and management as provided in COGSA, § 4(2)(a), 46 U.S.C. § 1304(2)(a).

3. Does the bill of lading clearly extend COGSA, § 4(2)(a), 46 U.S.C. § 1304(2) (a), to Todd? The bills of lading in our case expressly extended COGSA, § 4(2)(a), 46 U.S.C. § 1304(2)(a), to the master, officers, crewmembers, contractors, stevedores, longshoremen, agents, representatives, employees or others used, engaged or employed by the carrier in the performance of such work or services undertaken in the bills of lading. Although drydock operators were not expressly listed as persons covered, Todd would seem to be a 'contractor,' as the district court so held.

Less clear is whether Todd's services were part of the work or services undertaken in the bills of lading. The district court held that they were, and we are disposed to agree. The primary work undertaken in the bills of lading is the transporting of cargo. But implicit in the undertaking is the agreement to take reasonable steps to ensure the safety of the cargo in transport. Thus it is customary for cargo vessels to drydock in transit for routine inspections and repairs. The work performed by the drydock operator, although directly affecting the ship only, aids the carrier in safely transporting the cargo. We therefore hold that Todd was a contractor employed by Grace in performing the work undertaken in the bills of lading and hence was clearly intended by the parties thereto to be entitled to the immunities of COGSA, § 4(2)(a),46 U.S.C. § 1304(2)(a).

4. Was the 'Himalaya' clause an adhesion contract unenforceable against the cargo insurers? There is a general rule of contract law that when there is a gross disparity of bargaining power between two parties to a contract such that one party has no choice but to adhere to unfavorable and unfair terms, those terms will not be enforced against him unless he was given his understanding consent to be bound. See *Henningsen v. Bloomfield Motors*, 32 N.J. 358, 161 A.2d 69 (1960). The cargo insurers contend that the bills of

lading are contracts of adhesion, see *Cabot Corp. v. S S. Mormacscan*, (2 Cir. 1971) 441 F.2d 476, 478, and that since they gave no 'understanding consent,' they are not bound.

We recognize, as said in *Tessler Brothers, supra*, p. 445, 'that the content of ocean bills of lading is for all practical purposes completely within the carrier's power, subject to the provisions of COGSA, and that contracts purporting to limit liability must be strictly construed.' But we are not persuaded that we should refuse to enforce the bills of lading simply because they are in this respect contracts of adhesion. The cases refusing to enforce contracts because they were contracts of adhesion have generally involved special circumstances, such as a grossly unfair bargain foisted by a noncompetitive industry upon the ordinary consumer on a 'take-it-or-leave-it' basis, with the terms often buried in fine print unlikely to be understood or even read by the consumer. *See, e.g., Henningsen, supra.* There is no binding authority for likewise refusing to enforce bills of lading. The shipper or insurer of cargo, while not equal in bargaining power to the carrier, is not in the position of the ordinary man facing an enormous, impersonal industry. Surely the cargo insurers were aware of the 'Himalaya' clauses. As a group they perhaps could muster the bargaining power necessary to alter the terms in the bills of lading. Therefore, although we might find the bills of lading sufficiently adhesive to warrant a strict construction against the carrier and his agents, we are not moved by their adhesive character to interfere with the freedom of contract to the extent of refusing entirely to give effect to the 'Himalaya' clause. *Cf. Tessler Brothers, supra*, p. 445.

5. Does COGSA, § 6, 46 U.S.C. § 1306, prohibit the extension of the Act to non-carriers? Section 6, 46 U.S.C. § 1306, provides that a carrier and a shipper may enter into any agreement in any terms as to the liability of the carrier's agents for negligence in respect to cargo, but may do so only if no bill of lading has been or shall be issued and the shipments are not ordinary commercial shipments made in the ordinary course of trade. Since in our case there is a bill of lading and the shipment is in ordinary commerce, § 6, 46 U.S.C. § 1306, does not apply.

But the cargo interests argue that § 6, 46 U.S.C. § 1306, prohibits by implication any agreement to which the Section does not apply. This argument was presented in *Tessler Brothers, supra*, p. 444, and found wanting. Although § 6, 46 U.S.C. § 1306, describes certain situations, none of which is present here, in which any exculpatory agreement is permissible, we see no implication in the Section that in all other situations, such as ours, no exculpatory agreement is permissible.

6. Does an extension of COGSA, § 4(2)(a), 46 U.S.C. § 1304(2)(a), to non-carriers impermissibly derogate a common law principle against exculpation? There is a controlling rule of the common law, stated in perhaps its clearest form in *United States v. Atlantic Mutual Insurance Co.*,343 U.S. 236, 72 S.Ct. 666, 69 L.Ed. 907 (1952), that 'without congressional authority (carriers) cannot stipulate against their own negligence or that of their agents or servants.' *Atlantic Mutual, supra*, at p. 242.

In COGSA, § 4(2)(a), 46 U.S.C. § 1304(2)(a), Congress has immunized carriers from liability for negligence in navigation or management. It has not, however, altered the common law rule as regards agents or servants. We must therefore inquire whether Todd was an 'agent' or 'servant' of the carrier. We have already held Todd to be a 'contractor' but that of course does not necessarily make Todd an 'agent.' Restatement (Second) of Agency § 14N, Comment b (1957). If Todd is an agent, we must further inquire whether cases such as Herd and Tessler Brother, both decided after Atlantic Mutual, indicate a development in the common law such that it no longer forbids carriers from contractually exculpating their agents and servants from negligence.

"Agency' has been commonly defined as 'the fiduciary relation which results from the manifestation of consent by one person to another that the other shall act on his behalf and subject to his control, and consent by the other so to act.' Restatement (Second) of Agency § 1 (1957). The agent is the one who is to act. Restatement, *supra.*

From the facts of this case it is apparent that Todd was the carrier's agent within the meaning of the above definition. There was an agreement between the two that Todd should act on the carrier's behalf in maintaining the vessel in a seaworthy condition. Upon taking control of the vessel, Todd assuredly had a fiduciary duty to exercise skill and care in its work. This work, of course, would be subject to the ultimate control of the carrier as owner of the vessel.

As an 'agent,' Todd could not contractually be exculpated from its negligence, unless case law has modified the old common law rule. We do not think is has. Herd stands for the proposition that clear and express language in the contract is the sine qua non for altering the common law; but when that requirement is met, it is still left open for the courts to decide whether a particular alteration is repugnant to public policy. Herd did not imply that a contract, if clear and express in its intent, would be adequate to alter any familiar rule of tort liability whatsoever.

It is the holding of this court that a contract, no matter how clear and express, which purports wholly to immunize a non-carrier from liability for its negligence, is repugnant to traditional law and to sound policy. *Tessler Brothers*, which upheld the contractual monetary limitation of a non-carrier's (stevedore's) liability, is not inconsistent with our holding here, for as said in that case (at p. 443), 'This distinction between a limitation on liability and an exemption from liability is crucial. A limitation, unlike an exemption, does not induce negligence.'

Tessler Brothers, while stating that *Atlantic Mutual* was inapposite to a discussion of a 'Himalaya' clause that merely limits the amount of recovery for negligence, recognized that *Atlantic Mutual* '(invalidates) clauses that exempt carriers or their agents from liability for their negligence.' This language, of course, was not essential to the holding in *Tessler Brothers* and is therefore dictum; yet we believe it accurately states the law of *Atlantic Mutual.* Since the 'Himalaya' clause in this case purports to exempt non- carriers completely from any liability for negligence, and thereby strongly tends to induce negligence, the bill of lading is to that extent void.

7. Assuming that COGSA, § 4(2)(a), 46 U.S.C. § 1304(2)(a), could validly be extended to Todd, does the language of that provision apply to Todd's conduct? There is an alternate ground for holding that Todd is not immunized from liability—even if § 4(2)(a),

46 U.S.C. § 1304(2)(a), could validly be extended to protect non-carriers, its protection does not cover the sort of negligence of which Todd was culpable.

That section provides immunity only for 'Act, neglect, or default ... in the navigation or in the management of the ship....' A reading of the many cases giving content to the words 'navigation' and 'management' makes it evident that Todd was doing something else.

None of the cases actually gives a precise definition of the words, for the courts, eschewing abstractions, have been satisfied with determining on a case- to-case basis whether a particular act was or was not in 'navigation' or 'management.' Most of the cases have involved drawing the line between negligence in care of the cargo, for which there is liability, and negligence in navigation or management of the vessel, for which no liability attaches.] Obviously, carelessness in navigating or managing a cargo-laden ship would simultaneously create a foreseeable danger to the cargo; hence, it is not easy to draw a distinct line. Yet read as a whole, the cases would seem to support this test: If the act in question has the primary purpose of affecting the ship, it is 'in navigation or in management'; but if the primary purpose is to affect the cargo, it is not 'in navigation or in management.'

This test can be applied to our case by rough analogy only, for Todd's negligence—a failure to maintain a safe drydock—was in omission, not commission, and hence had no primary purpose. But the omission-commission distinction presents no difficulty if we assume hypothetically that Todd, instead of omitting to make the drydock safe, had undertaken to repair it, and had performed the job negligently. If Todd had thereby caused damage to a ship that later used the facilities, then we would hold that such act of negligence would have the primary purpose of affecting the drydock, not of affecting the ship.

True, acts affecting the drydock would ultimately affect the ship, just as acts affecting a ship would indirectly affect the cargo inside, But we are not looking for ultimate and indirect effects when trying to determine whether an act is in navigation or management of the ship. What we are looking for is whether the act which is negligently done, or not done, is primarily directed at the ship itself, or at something else. It seems apparent that Todd's negligence was not primarily directed at the Santa Ana, for Todd had been negligent as regards the drydock long before the Santa Ana contracted to enter it. We therefore hold that Todd's negligent maintenance of the drydock was not 'in navigation or management' of the vessel and that § 4(2)(a), 46 U.S.C. § 1304(2) (a), has no relevance to this case.

D. *The Time Limitation Under COGSA, § 3(6), 46 U.S.C. § 1303(6)*

Tessler Brothers, supra, p. 443, stated that *Atlantic Mutual* while invalidating clauses that completely exempt the agents of carriers, is inapposite to clauses that merely limit the amount of liability. In a similar vein, we believe that *Atlantic Mutual* is inapposite to clauses merely limiting the time limit in which suit must be brought. We might hold differently if the time limit provided were so short that it created an unreasonable risk to the plaintiff that he would lose his cause of action. But such is not the case. COGSA indicates the congressional determination that one year is a reasonable time limit for instituting suit against a carrier, and we see no factors necessitating more time for suit against the carrier's agents.

Since the extension of § 3(6), 46 U.S.C. § 1303(6), to agents of the carriers is clear and express, and since it creates a reasonable limitation on the common law liability of agents, and since there is no binding authority for holding such clauses void, we uphold the validity of this portion of the bills of lading.

This necessarily moots the holding of the district court that Royal Globe's suit was barred by laches. Since Royal Globe commenced its suit well after the one-year limit of § 3(6), 46 U.S.C. § 1303(6), had passed, and was thus barred by that fixed period of limitations, there is no need to decide if laches provides an additional time-bar. We leave it for the district court to determine on remand whether any other plaintiffs are affected by § 3(6), 46 U.S.C. § 1303(6).

Affirmed in part, and reversed in part and remanded for further proceedings not inconsistent with this opinion.

H. Deviation

GENERAL ELECTRIC CO. v. STEAMSHIP "NANCY LYKES"

536 F. Supp. 687, 1982 AMC 1726 (S.D.N.Y. 1982), *aff'd* 706 F.2d 80, 1983 AMC 1947 (2d Cir.), *cert. denied*, 464 U.S. 849, 104 S. Ct. 157, 78 L. Ed. 2d 145, 1984 AMC 2403 (1983)

LASKER, District Judge

General Electric Company International Sales Division ("GE") sues to recover for two locomotive cabs which were shipped by Lykes Bros. Steamship Company ("Lykes") via its liner service aboard the vessel the S.S. Nancy Lykes from New Orleans, Louisiana, destination Keelung, Taiwan. The locomotives were lost at sea on May 5, 1978, when the vessel encountered gale winds and rough seas off the coast of California.

The relevant voyage of the Nancy Lykes commenced in Mobile, Alabama on April 10, 1978, and proceeded to New Orleans, its first port of call. The advertised itinerary for the vessel listed Yokohama, Japan ("Kobe") as the next port of call, with an estimated arrival date of May 11, 1978. Instead of proceeding directly to Kobe after passing through the Panama Canal, however, the vessel next went to San Pedro, California, to secure fuel (bunkers). San Pedro was not listed on the published itinerary of the voyage. Lykes candidly acknowledges that the stop was made to take advantage of the low fuel prices then available at San Pedro and that its operations department directed the master to make the stop while the vessel was still in the Gulf area.

I

GE contends that the bunkers call at San Pedro constituted an unreasonable deviation from the published itinerary of the vessel and that the deviation caused the vessel to encounter the gales which precipitated the loss of the locomotives. In addition, GE alleges that the locomotives, which were stowed on deck, were not properly secured.

* * *

II

Lykes contends that it is customary for liner services to stop for bunkers in ports that are not advertised in their published itineraries; that Lykes established a custom beginning in 1978 of using San Pedro as a bunkers only port; that the bill of lading liberty clause encompassed such a step; that the locomotives were properly secured on the deck of the Nancy Lykes; and that the diversion to San Pedro did not involve a substantial risk of encountering unfavorable weather.

* * *

III

GE has failed to establish that the locomotives were not properly secured on the deck of the Nancy Lykes. The only evidence presented on this point was Patterson's opinion that more chains should have secured the locomotives. This conclusion, however, is contradicted by the National Cargo Bureau Certificate of Inspection which followed an actual inspection of the locomotives on deck. It is undisputed that this Certificate is generally relied on in the maritime industry to establish proper stowage.

GE has established, however, that the decision to proceed to San Pedro for bunkers was unreasonable. It is undisputed that sufficient bunkers were available in the Gulf ports and in the Panama Canal ports to carry the vessel to Kobe. It is also clear that the ordinary and customary trade route from the Panama Canal to the Far East is within the area described by Raguso. This conclusion is confirmed by the testimony of Kaciak that, if he had been asked to route the vessel from the Panama Canal to Kobe, rather than from San Pedro to Kobe, he would have recommended a course on the northern portion of the area described by Raguso, at least for the first part of the voyage. Moreover, the evidence established that vessels on liner service ordinarily take bunkers at an advertised port of call. Most importantly, we are persuaded that the diversion to San Pedro created an increased risk that unfavorable weather would be encountered. Raguso and Kaciak agreed at least that the statistical probability of encountering gale or near gale winds, of whatever variety or designation, increases in the springtime in the region the more northerly one goes from a latitude of approximately 30 degrees. By leaving from San Pedro rather than the Panama Canal, the vessel was assured of passing through the region north of 30 degrees whatever routing was chosen from San Pedro. Furthermore, we accept Raguso's estimate that the statistical probability of gale winds during this time of year is approximately 5 or 6 percent off the coast of California since, in addition to the expert testimony of the weather routers, every mariner with experience on these seas who testified acknowledged that gale or near gale northerly winds are known among mariners to occur in the region in the winter and spring months. Accordingly, we find that whatever the precise percentage of increased probability of unfavorable weather, the decision to go to San Pedro created a significantly greater risk of encountering unfavorable weather. Indeed, the two prior Lykes' vessels which made the San Pedro stop prior to the Nancy Lykes both encountered such weather, one from Gulf of Tehuantepec winds, the other from winds off the coast after departing from

San Pedro. At the least, this prior experience should have forewarned Lykes of the potential dangers in diverting to San Pedro.

Moreover, while it has not been demonstrated that the locomotives were improperly stowed on deck, the fact that such weighty cargo was being carried on deck should have been a significant consideration militating in favor of a route on the calmest seas possible. By directing the vessel to take on bunkers at San Pedro, Lykes foreclosed safer options and thrust the vessel into areas where the probability was increased that unfavorable weather would be encountered. This added risk of damage or loss to cargo solely for the benefit of the vessel must be deemed unreasonable. Indeed, there is no evidence that Lykes considered any factor other than its fuel cost savings in directing its vessels to take on bunkers at San Pedro.

Lykes' contention that the stop at San Pedro was not a deviation in light of the broad liberty clause contained in the bill of lading is unpersuasive. Paragraph III of the applicable bill of lading defines the permissible scope of the voyage as including "usual, customary or advertised ports, whether herein named or not, and ports in or out of the advertised, geographic or usual route or order ... ." In reference to a similarly broad liberties clause it has been noted that "[i]t would seem hard to 'deviate' from such a voyage." GILMORE & BLACK, THE LAW OF ADMIRALTY, 178 (2d Ed. 1975). Such a construction would undercut the policy and statutory provisions forbidding a carrier from contracting out of liability for his own wrongdoing and would be inconsistent with § 3(2) of the Carriage of Goods by Sea Act ("COGSA") which imposes upon the carrier a duty to " ... properly ... carry the goods." *Id.* at 178. Furthermore, § 4(4) of COGSA implies as clearly as possible that any unreasonable deviation is to be treated as a breach of the Act and the contract of carriage:

> Any deviation in saving or attempting to save life or property at sea, or any reasonable deviation shall not be deemed to be an infringement or breach of this Act or of the contract of carriage, and the carrier shall not be liable for any loss or damage resulting therefrom: Provided, however, That if the deviation is for the purpose of loading or unloading cargo or passengers as it shall, *prima facie*, be regarded as unreasonable. [Emphasis supplied]

Indeed, § 4(4) confirms that a carrier may not define the voyage in such broad language as to render it impossible for any deviation to be found no matter how far the vessel wanders from the specified route. Lykes' proposed construction of the liberty clause is at odds with § 4(4)'s concept of reasonable and unreasonable deviations. The liberty clause must therefore be construed to permit only reasonable deviations from the anticipated journey. *Id.* at 179. Moreover, the reasonableness of the deviation may not be judged merely from the point of view of the carrier. As § 4(4)'s proviso suggests, the carrier may not justify a deviation merely because it was to his benefit. "The carrier, throughout the performance of the voyage, is always subject to the Section 3(2) duty to care for and carry the goods properly, and his decision on a route would seem to be improper and unreasonable whenever it is made in disregard of that duty." *Id; see Spartus Corp. v. S.S. Yafo*, 590 F.2d 1310

(5th Cir. 1979); *Encyclopedia Britannica Inc. v. S.S. Hong Kong Producer*, 422 F.2d 7, 18 (2d Cir. 1969), *cert. denied*, 397 U.S. 964, 90 S. Ct. 998, 25 L. Ed. 2d 255 (1970).

Nor are we persuaded that Lykes' prior stops at San Pedro rendered that practice "customary" so that the Nancy Lykes' stop was not a deviation or was a justified deviation. The evidence established that, at least for liner services, bunkers are ordinarily secured at one of the ports of call advertised in the Journal of Commerce. Indeed, Kohler, in his long experience as a bunkers broker, had never been asked by a liner operator to secure bunkers in a port that was not an advertised port of call. Despite GE's evidence of instances where such stops were made, it is clear that, at the least, such stops are extraordinary for liner service vessels.

Similarly, Lykes' contention that the stop at San Pedro was a customary one for vessels going to the Far East is without merit. Lykes relies on the facts that, prior to the Nancy Lykes, it had directed two other vessels to stop at San Pedro for bunkers and that it used San Pedro frequently in the years following, as did other lines. However, the critical element as to "custom" in the cases relied on by Lykes is the knowledge on the part of the shipper that a particular port was a customary port for the voyage. *See, e.g., W. R. Grace & Co. v. Toyo Kisen Kabushiki Kaisha*, 12 F.2d 519 (9th Cir. 1926); *The Frederick Luckenbach*, 15 F.2d 241 (S.D.N.Y. 1926); *The San Guiseppe*, 122 F.2d 579 (4th Cir. 1941). Of course, where the shipper has knowledge that a particular stop will be made and consents either explicitly or implicitly, as in the cited cases, the particular stop can hardly be labeled a deviation from the contemplated voyage. In such circumstances, the shipper is logically held to have consented to any greater risks to his cargo imposed by the additional stop. By contrast, in the present case there were only two such diversions before the voyage in question; regardless of the later practice of Lykes or other liner services, knowledge on the part of GE that Lykes would be bunkering at San Pedro cannot be inferred, and all the evidence indicates that GE did not in fact know that such a stop was planned. In these circumstances, GE cannot be held to have consented to whatever added risks that were occasioned by the San Pedro deviation. In addition, in light of the finding that liner services ordinarily only bunker at advertised ports of call and that the ordinary trade route to the Far East from the Panama Canal is significantly further south than San Pedro, it cannot be said, as in *The San Guiseppe, supra*, that the bunkering stop was merely ancillary to the contemplated voyage.

In sum, the stop of the Nancy Lykes at San Pedro for bunkers was a deviation from the ordinary route for a liner service vessel since San Pedro was not an advertised port of call and was not along the ordinary trade route from the Panama Canal to the Far East. In light of the fact that the deviation exposed the vessel to significantly greater risks of adverse weather, and was made solely for the benefit of the vessel, it was unreasonable. As an unreasonable deviation, the vessel is liable for any damage to cargo caused by the diversion and recovery is not limited to the $500 per package limitation contained in the Bill of Lading and in COGSA.

Accordingly, GE is entitled to recover the $1,709,000 it cost it to replace the locomotive cabs lost overboard.

Submit judgment.

Notes

1. ***Consequences of deviation***

The Second Circuit has led the way in holding that an unreasonable deviation from the contract of carriage deprives the carrier of the benefit of section 4(5)'s liability limitation. *See Sedco, Inc. v. S.S. Strathewe*, 800 F.2d 27, 1986 AMC 2801 (2d Cir. 1986). Both the Ninth and Fifth Circuits agree with this view. *See Nemeth v. General Steamship Corp.*, 694 F.2d 609, 1983 AMC 885 (9th Cir. 1982); *Vision Air Flight Service, Inc. v. M/V National Pride*, 155 F.3d 1165, 1999 AMC 1168 (9th Cir. 1998); *Spartus Corp. v. S/S Yafo*, 590 F.2d 1310 (5th Cir. 1979). The Third and Eleventh Circuits have agreed with the Second, Fifth and Ninth Circuits in *dicta. S.P.M. Corp. v. M/V Ming Moon*, 965 F. 2d 1297, 1992 AMC 2409 (3d Cir. 1992); *Unimac Co., Inc. v. C.F. Ocean Service, Inc.*, 43 F.3d 1434, 1995 AMC 1484 (11th Cir. 1995). The Seventh Circuit, on the other hand, has concluded that the limitation applies regardless of whether there has been an unreasonable deviation. *Atlantic Mutual Insurance Co. v. Poseidon Schiffahrt*, 313 F.2d 872, 875, 1963 AMC 2697 (7th Cir. 1963). Which view is correct? The matter is analyzed in Friedell, *The Deviating Ship*, 32 HAST. L.J. 1535 (1981).

2. ***Basis for Liability***

Historically, a geographic deviation from the agreed upon or customary route ousted the terms of the bill of lading and the carrier was liable as an insurer for the loss of goods. A deviation was considered to be a fundamental breach of the contract of carriage. The carrier was not allowed plead any of the exceptions in the bill of lading. These consequences were imposed on the carrier because a deviation revoked the shipper's insurance coverage, and, as a matter of fairness, the shipper was allowed to recover its loss from the carrier. COGSA, however, provides that "any reasonable deviation" shall not be an infringement of that statute or a breach of a contract of carriage, and that the carrier shall not be liable for any loss or damage resulting therefrom. It has been suggested that COGSA has thus abolished the strict insurer's liability. Furthermore, changes in insurance law lend support to this result because today "held covered" insurance clauses protect the cargo regardless of deviation. G. GILMORE & C. BLACK, THE LAW OF ADMIRALTY § 3-40 (2d Ed. 1975).

Although there is no doubt (except in the Third Circuit: see note 1 *supra*) that the doctrine of deviation still applies despite enactment of COGSA, the historic "deprived of insurance rationale" has fallen out of favor. In *Vision Air Flight Service, Inc. v. M/V National Pride*, 155 F.3d 1165, 1174 n.10, 1999 AMC 1168 (9th Cir. 1998), the U.S. Court of Appeals for the Ninth Circuit said:

> Another fundamental objection to expansion of the doctrine seems to be that the doctrine is outmoded because modern insurance contracts now cover losses resulting from deviation. *See, e.g.,* Black and Gilmore [sic], *supra* at 181-82. Yet, historically, application of the deviation doctrine did not turn on whether the goods were insured. *See* Steven F. Friedell, *The Deviating Ship,* 32 Hastings L.J. 1535, 1545 n. 45 (1981). Moreover, to the extent the deviation doctrine is concerned with providing an incentive for carriers not to undertake certain actions that impose unreasonable risks on cargo, insurance is irrelevant.

3. ***Causal Relationship***

Must there be a causal relationship between deviation and the loss and if so, who has the burden of proving causal relationship or lack thereof? It appears that there must be some causal relationship between the deviation and the loss. Lack of causation seems to be treated as a defense which must be sustained by the carrier. *Hellenic Lines v. U.S.*, 512 F.2d 1196, 1975 AMC 697 (2d Cir. 1975); *Calmaquip Engineering West Hemisphere Corporation v. West Coast Carriers, Ltd.*, 650 F.2d 633, 1984 AMC 839 (5th Cir. 1981); *Mobil Sales & Supply Corp. v. M/V BANGLAR KAKOLI*, 588 F. Supp. 1134 (S.D.N.Y. 1984).

4. *Quasi-Deviation*

Originally, the doctrine of deviation was applied against the carrier only when it deviated geographically from the agreed upon route or the customary route. Some courts, however, found that when there were other fundamental breaches of the contract of carriage that these were analogous to deviation, hence, they characterize such breaches as "quasi-deviations." The effect of quasi-deviation has been to deprive a carrier of the benefit of a limitation of liability clause in its bill of lading and the $500 per package limitation of COGSA. *St. Johns N.F. Shipping Corp. v. S.A. Companhia Geral Commercial*, 263 U.S. 119, 44 S.Ct. 30, 68 L.Ed. 201 (1923) (stowage on deck despite clean bill of lading); *Encyclopaedia Britannica, Inc. v. S.S. Hong Kong Producer*, 422 F.2d 7 (2d Cir. 1969) *cert. denied*, 397 U.S. 964 (1970) (stowage on deck despite clean bill of lading); *Calmaquip Engineering West Hemisphere Corporation v. West Coast Carriers, Ltd.*, 650 F.2d 633, 1984 AMC 839 (5th Cir. 1981) (stowage on deck in contravention of shipper's express instruction to carry below deck).

More recently, however, some courts have begun to question the categorical conclusion that carrying cargo on deck constitutes a quasi-deviation in the face of a clean bill of lading. Courts have concluded that proof that goods were stowed in the customary manner for the particular trade precludes a finding of deviation and thereby makes an examination of the reasonableness of such stowage unnecessary. This is particularly significant in relation to cargo in containers, where carriage on the deck of a specially constructed container ship pursuant to a port or trade custom would not constitute a deviation. *Electro-Tec Corporation v. S.S. Dart Atlantica*, 598 F. Supp. 929, 1985 AMC 1606 (D. Md. 1984); *DuPont de Nemours International S.A. v. S.S. Mormacvega*, 367 F. Supp. 793, *aff'd.* 493 F.2d 97, 1972 AMC 2366 (2d Cir. 1974); *Konica Business Machines, Inc. v. Sea-Land Consumer, Vessel*, 153 F.3d 1076, 1998 AMC 2705 (9th Cir. 1998); *Vision Air Flight Service, Inc. v. M/V National Pride*, 155 F.3d 1165, 1172 n.8, 1999 AMC 1168 (9th Cir. 1998); *American Home Assurance Co. v. M/V Tabuk*, 170 F.Supp.2d 431, 2002 AMC 184 (S.D.N.Y. 2001) *aff'd* 45 Fed.Appx. 12 (2d Cir. 2002).

Moreover, the Second Circuit has also limited the doctrine of deviation to situations involving geographic deviation and unauthorized on-deck stowage of cargo (quasi-deviation), and has indicated that the doctrine should not be extended beyond these categories. "[M]ere negligence, lack of due diligence, or a failure to properly handle, stow, care, or deliver cargo never has constituted deviation" that would deprive a carrier of either a contractual or statutory limitation of liability. *Sedco, Inc. v. S.S. Strathewe*, 800 F.2d 27, 32, 1986 AMC 2801 (2d Cir. 1986). See also *Styling Plastics Co., Ltd. v. The Neptune Orient Lines, Ltd.*, 666 F. Supp. 1406, 1988 AMC 351 (N.D. Cal. 1987) and *C.A. Articulos Nacionales de Goma Gomaven v. M/V Aragua*, 756 F.2d 1156, 1986 AMC 2087 (5th Cir. 1985), where the court held that misdelivery of goods could not be considered an unreasonable deviation.

Although the doctrine of quasi-deviation is generally in retreat, another line of cases holds that a carrier who falsely issues a clean on-board bill of lading for goods that were never shipped, or who falsely issues a clean bill of lading for goods known to be shipped in damaged condition, is liable for misrepresentation and is precluded from limiting its liability under COGSA. *Berisford Metals Corporation v. S/S Salvadore*, 779 F.2d 841 (2d Cir. 1985) *cert. denied*, 476 U.S. 1188 (1986) (misrepresentation that cargo was loaded on ship); *Mitsui Marine Fire and Ins. Co. Ltd v. Direct Container Line, Inc.*, 119 F.Supp.2d 412, 416-17 (S.D.N.Y. 2000) (same); *Leather's Best Internat'l, Inc. v. M/V Lloyd Sergipe*, 760 F.Supp. 301, 311 (S.D.N.Y. 1991) (same); *Condor Indus. Internat'l, Inc. v. M/V Am. Express*, 667 F.Supp. 99, 100 (S.D.N.Y. 1987) (clean bill of lading for cargo known to be damaged).

Authorized deck carriage is not governed by COGSA but it is governed by the Harter Act. COGSA does not apply to "cargo which by the contract of carriage is stated as being carried on deck and is so carried". COGSA § 1(c). Because COGSA does not apply to authorized deck carriage, § 3(8) of COGSA does not strike down a bill of lading clause that exonerates the carrier from liability for damage to cargo carried on deck, if the bill of lading states that the cargo is to be carried on deck or if it is obvious from the circumstances that it must be so carried. *Chester v. Maritima del Litoral, S.A.*, 586 F.Supp. 192, 198, 1985 AMC 2831 (E.D.Wis. 1984) ("The plaintiffs'...argument that the use of a clause refusing liability for damage to goods carried on deck violates § 1303(8) of COGSA is circular. That provision prevents a carrier from relieving or lessening his liability for 'goods...as provided in this Act'. As explained above, § 1301(c) of COGSA explicitly excludes deck cargo from the category of 'goods' to which the Act's provisions apply, thereby neutralizing § 1303(8)".) However, the Harter Act strikes down such a clause to the extent that it purports to exonerate the carrier from liability for negligence. *Blanchard Lumber Co. v. S.S. Anthony II*, 259

F.Supp. 857 (S.D.N.Y. 1966). In this case, a shipment of lumber was agreed to be carried on deck and it was so carried from British Columbia to Providence, Rhode Island, under bills of lading providing that the shipment was "at shipper's risk." In an action by consignees against the carriers for damage caused to the cargo by negligent stowage, the court held that when shipments to or from ports of the United States in foreign trade are not covered by COGSA, the Harter Act applies during the entire voyage and exoneration clauses for negligence are invalid. Accordingly, because it had been agreed that the lumber would be carried on deck and it was so carried, it was not covered by the COGSA. Nevertheless, the Harter Act applied and the "at shipper's risk" clause in the bill of lading was null and void.

5. ***Land-Based Deviation***

When the parties extend the application of COGSA to the entire transportation including the land portion does the doctrine of deviation apply? *See Asahi America, Inc. v. The M/V Arild Maersk*, 602 F. Supp. 25, 1986 AMC 53 (S.D.N.Y. 1985) where the court found a land-based deviation.

6. ***Statute of Limitations***

An unreasonable course deviation does not oust COGSA's one year statute of limitation. *Mesocap Ind. Ltd. v. Torm Lines*, 194 F.3d 1342, 2000 AMC 370 (11th Cir. 1999).

I. Exoneration Clauses

Note: Exculpatory Clauses and the Harter Act

In simplified form, the following was the situation before the enactment of the Harter Act. Assume that a shipper and carrier entered into a contract of affreightment and the goods were damaged because the vessel was unseaworthy. This unseaworthy condition was known both to the shipowner and the master. The shipper would have several options. First, it could allege a breach of the bailment contract which would subject the carrier to strict liability if it were a common carrier. Second, it could allege a breach of the warranty of seaworthiness which was implied in the contract of carriage. Third, it could allege that the carrier breached its duty to exercise due care for the cargo. Although all of these various contract and tort claims might not be available in all fact situations, a shipper ordinarily would have been in a reasonably good position to recover for loss or damage to cargo. It is significant to observe that some of the bases for liability are grounded grounded in strict liability while others are based on fault.

Carriers sought to counter such claims by introducing exculpatory clauses into the contract of carriage, namely the bill of lading. These clauses negated the warranty of seaworthiness and purported to relieve the carrier from any:

(1) liability as bailee,
(2) duty to exercise due diligence to provide a seaworthy vessel,
(3) liability for loss caused by unseaworthiness,
(4) duty to care for cargo, etc.

In essence, these exculpatory clauses purported to exculpate a carrier from liability for all damage and loss to cargo resulting from any cause—including the carrier's own negligence. These clauses placed the entire risk of loss and damage on the shipper.

If the principle of "freedom of contract" had held sway in the courts, the exculpatory clauses would have been upheld and carriers would have contracted their way out of liability. However, the courts in the United States, unlike others such as in England, held that it was against public policy to allow carriers to exempt themselves from liability for loss or damage caused by their own fault. The Harter Act was intended to prohibit such exculpatory clauses subject to certain exceptions and defenses which were concessions to keeping the United States fleet competitive with those of other countries, principally England. Thus, the Harter Act does not impose strict liability. It does not prohibit a carrier from contracting-out of strict liability. Generally, these statutes prohibit a carrier from contracting-out of liability for loss or damage caused by its negligence. However, the statute exonerates the carrier for damage or loss to cargo caused by "errors in navigation and management" of the vessel by master and crew, if the carrier exercised due diligence to make the vessel seaworthy.

ASSOCIATED METALS & MINERALS CORP. v. M/V ARKTIS SKY

978 F.2d 47, 1993 AMC 509 (2nd Cir. 1992)

LAY, Senior Circuit Judge

This appeal involves an action in rem brought in the district court by Associated Metals & Minerals Corp. against the vessel M/V Arktis Sky; its operator, Erhversinvestering K/S; as well as its owner, Elite Shipping I/S. Elite Shipping entered into a charter party agreement with Altos Hornos De Vizcaya, S.A., a non-party to this action, to ship a cargo of galvanized steel sheets in 398 coils from Bilbao, Spain to Port Elizabeth, New Jersey. The shipper/charterer, Altos Hornos, sold the coils to Associated Metals. Altos Hornos contracted with its own stevedore, Maritime Candida, to load and stow the coils aboard the vessel in Spain. After the cargo was loaded, the chief mate of the Arktis signed with the vessel's stamp a lashing statement which noted that the lash had been "performed under chief mate instructions and satisfactory."

When the vessel arrived in Port Elizabeth it was discovered that some of the cargo had shifted during the voyage. The coils were damaged in the sum of $249,629.76. Associated Metals brought an action against the vessel, its operator and its owner. Associated Metals moved for summary judgment. The district court granted summary judgment in favor of the defendants and dismissed the complaint. This appeal followed.

Both parties agree that the Carriage of Goods by Sea Act, 46 U.S.C. app. §§ 1300-1314 (1988) (COGSA), applies to the liability questions raised in this case. The district court found that the defendants (the vessel, the operator and owner) established as a matter of law two of the exceptions under COGSA and therefore were exonerated from any damage. We respectfully disagree with the court's analysis; we reverse and remand for further proceedings.

* * *

The district court started with the assumption that Associated Metals had established a prima facie case against the vessel under 46 U.S.C. app. § 1303(2) (1988), which obligates a carrier to "properly and carefully load, handle, stow, carry, keep, care for, and discharge the goods carried." Although this circuit has held that section 1303(2) creates a non-delegable duty on behalf of the vessel,[1] the district court found that these statements were dicta and that the better reasoned cases hold that an "FIOS" or "free in and out, stowed" clause in a bill of lading, binding on the parties, shifts liability to the shipper for improper stowage or discharge without violating COGSA. According to the defendants,

---

[1] *See Nichimen Co. v. M.V. Farland*, 462 F.2d 319, 330 (2d Cir.1972); *Demsey & Assoc., Inc. v. S.S. Sea Star*, 461 F.2d 1009, 1014-15 (2d Cir.1972).

the FIOS terms shift both the risk and expense of loading, stowing, and discharging cargo to the shipper and the consignee. The district court thus held that the carrier's duty to load and stow cargo properly and carefully under section 1303(2) is not genuinely non-delegable.

In so holding, the district court rejected the reasoning of *Nichimen Co. v. M.V. Farland*, 462 F.2d 319, 330 (2d Cir. 1972), and *Demsey & Assoc., Inc. v. S.S. Sea Star*, 461 F.2d 1009, 1014-15 (2d Cir. 1972), and followed the reasoning of two district court cases in *Sigri Carbon Corp. v. Lykes Bros. S.S. Co.*, 655 F. Supp. 1435 (W.D. Ky. 1987), and *Sumitomo Corp. of America v. M/V "Sie Kim"*, 632 F. Supp. 824 (S.D.N.Y.1985). These cases construe COGSA to mean that vessels can be held liable for cargo damage only in cases where the vessel exercised control over the stowage or the stevedores. The district court quoted *Sigri Carbon* which held "[t]he inclusion of a FIOS term in a bill of lading should not be disregarded as inconsistent with COGSA so long as it is understood that the term in no way relieves the carrier of responsibility for its own acts or for the acts of others under its control." 655 F. Supp. at 1438. Thus, the district court held "that a carrier is not responsible for the consequences of improper stowage by agents of the shipper pursuant to an FIOS bill of lading."

We find this reasoning directly contrary to 46 U.S.C. app. § 1303(8) (1988):

> Any clause, covenant, or agreement in a contract of carriage relieving the carrier or the ship from liability for loss or damage to or in connection with the goods arising from negligence, fault, or failure in the duties and obligations provided in this section, or lessening such liability otherwise than as provided in this chapter, shall be null and void and of no effect.

In *Demsey*, this court observed:

> Under Sections 1303(1) and (2) of COGSA, the carrier is bound to exercise due diligence to make the ship seaworthy, to make the ship fit and safe for the reception, carriage and preservation of the cargo, and to properly load, handle, stow and discharge the goods being shipped. Every claim for cargo damage creates a maritime lien against the ship which may be enforced by a libel in rem. COGSA, Section 1303(8) prohibits a shipowner from contracting out of this liability. The fact that the [vessel] was operated under charter to [the charterer] does not affect the liability of the vessel.

Demsey, 461 F.2d at 1014 (citations omitted).

As in this lawsuit, the plaintiff in *Demsey* purchased steel coils that were damaged during shipping. In *Demsey*, the shipowner had arranged for the charterers "to load, stow, and trim the cargo at their expense under the supervision of the Captain... ." 461 F.2d at 1012. A voyage charter stated that the "cargo was 'to be loaded, stowed and discharged free of risk and expense to the vessel.'" *Id.* This court held that these advance arrangements did not shield the vessel from liability because COGSA forbids a shipowner from contracting out of liability for improper stowage of cargo. *Id.* at 1014-15. The court did, however, give some effect to the agreements, ultimately determining that both the vessel owner and the time charterer should be indemnified by the voyage charterer. *Id.* at 1019.

Similarly, in *Nichimen*, the plaintiff sued a vessel owner and a charterer over damage to steel coils that occurred while the steel was in transit. 462 F.2d at 322. Examining the relationships between the parties, the district court rejected a factual assertion that the plaintiff's agent had stowed the cargo. *Id.* at 330. This court expressed its approval of the district court's factual finding and stated that "in any event, under § 3(2) of COGSA, the carrier's duty to 'properly and carefully load ... [and] stow ... the goods carried' is non-delegable." *Id.* As in *Demsey*, the court ultimately determined that the charterer must indemnify the vessel for cargo damage. *Id.* at 332-33.

We find *Nichimen* and *Demsey*'s statutory analysis to be persuasive. Under the district court's enforcement of the FIOS clause, 46 U.S.C. app. § 1303(8) would have no meaning. The plain language of section 1303(8) forbids enforcement of agreements to relieve carriers of liability for negligence in carrying out the duties set forth in section 3 of COGSA. *See* Anthony N. Zock, *Charter Parties in Relation to Cargo*, 45 TUL.L.REV. 733, 747-48 (1975) (stating that "any provision in the charter party or the bill of lading that stipulates for an obligation, liability, or exemption that conflicts with the terms of either COGSA or the Harter Act will have no effect"). One of the duties assigned to carriers is that of properly and carefully loading cargo. *See* 46 U.S.C. app. § 1303(2) (1988). Thus, an agreement such as the one in question here is "null and void" under the statute because it purports to relieve a carrier of liability for negligence in one of its duties, the stowing of cargo.[2] It is of no consequence that unlike in *Demsey* and *Nichimen*, indemnification for damages is not in issue here.

The defendants suggest an alternative reading of the statute. They suggest that 46 U.S.C. app. § 1303(8) "specifically permits a carrier to limit its liability for its statutory duties, so long as such a limitation is consistent with other provisions of COGSA." (Br. for Defs.-Appellees at 24). This argument is girded on the portion of 46 U.S.C. app. § 1303(8) which states carriers may not contractually lessen their liability "otherwise than as provided in this chapter...." Defendants contend this language suggests that the duties of section 1303 are limited by the immunities of section 1304(2). A more accurate reading of the phrase suggests that "otherwise than as provided in this chapter... ." modifies the damage limitations ("lessening such liability") set forth in COGSA, which provides a $500 per package ceiling on damages. *See* 46 U.S.C. app. § 1304(5). The phrase does not affect the statute's prohibition on agreements relieving carriers of liability for negligence in carrying out their duties under the Act.

Section 1304(2)(i)

The district court held that the vessel had also established a second defense by carrying its burden of proof under section 1304(2)(i), which explicitly provides that a carrier shall

[2] In a recent opinion, the United States Court of Appeals for the First Circuit held that "parties are free ... to alter the general rule" that "the duty to load, stow, trim, and ultimately discharge a vessel's cargo generally falls on the shipowner who also bears the consequences of any failure." *Continental Grain Co. v. Puerto Rico Maritime Shipping Auth.*, 972 F.2d 426, 430 (1st Cir.1992). This case involved a private carriage of goods, *see id.* at 430, and thus COGSA did not apply, *see Zock, supra*, at 738.

not be liable for an act or omission of a shipper or owner of goods, his agent or representative.[3] The district court reasoned that its holding under the FIOS clause was consistent with this second defense. The result may be consistent but the analysis cannot be the same.

The liability provisions set forth in 46 U.S.C. app. § 1303(2) create a prima facie case against the vessel when a plaintiff (here a non-signator to the charter agreement) establishes that the carrier received the cargo in good condition and that the cargo arrived at its destination in a damaged condition. *See, e.g., Demsey*, 461 F.2d at 1014. Once a prima facie case is created, the burden shifts to the carrier to show, under section 1304(2)(i) and section 1304(2)(q), that the cargo loss or damage results from an act or omission of the shipper or owner of goods, his agent or representative; or if the loss or damage results from any other cause arising without the actual fault and privity of the carrier and without the fault or neglect of the agents or servants of the carrier. As previously discussed, this burden cannot be carried by contract terms or language of FIOS contained in a bill of lading. Both are barred by the non-delegable provisions of COGSA under section 1303(8).

* * *

There should be little dispute that the purpose of COGSA is to place primary responsibility for the safety of the cargo upon the vessel, its operators and owners. The parties cannot by private agreement circumvent the legislative purpose of the Act. 46 U.S.C. app. § 1303(8). The vessel may exonerate its responsibility by carrying its burden of proof that the damage did not occur because of its own acts. However, we find that the documentary proof and conflicting affidavits submitted in this case create a genuine dispute of material fact and that the defendants are not entitled at this stage of the proceeding to a judgment as a matter of law. Thus, we find the court has erred in granting a summary judgment in favor of the defendants.

The judgment is vacated and the case remanded for further proceedings in accord with this opinion.

Note

In *Tubacex, Inc. v. M/V Risan*, 45 F.3d 951, 1995 AMC 1305 (5th Cir. 1995), cargo was damaged during unloading operations undertaken by stevedores hired by the shipper. In a suit by the shipper for recovery of damages, the carrier defended on the ground that the damage to the cargo was not caused by the negligence of the carrier but it was caused by the negligence of stevedores hired by and under the control of the shipper. The shipper argued, however, that Sections 2(3) and 3(8) of the Carriage of Goods by Sea Act preclude the defenses that the carrier made. The court of appeals, purporting to follow the *Arktis Sky* decision but in effect distinguishing it, affirmed a summary judgment in favor of the carrier. In the opinion of the court, there were no overreaching bill of lading clauses and the carrier should be exonerated from liability because he met the burden of proof of the q clause defense.

The *Arktis Sky* decision has been noticed by the United States Supreme Court. In *Vimar Seguros Y Reaseguros, S.A. v. M/V Sky Reefer*, 515 U.S. 528, 115 S.Ct. 2322, 2329, 132 L.Ed.2d 462, 1995 AMC 1817(1995), the Court stated:

---

[3] Section 1304(2)(i) reads:

> Neither the carrier nor the ship shall be responsible for loss or damage arising or resulting from: (i) Act or omission of the shipper or owner of the goods, his agent or representative.

> The Japanese version of the Hague Rules, it is said, provides the carrier with a defense based on the acts or omissions of the stevedores hired by the shipper, Galaxie, *see* App. 112, Article 3(1), (carrier liable "when he or the persons employed by him" fail to take due care), while COGSA, according to petitioner, makes nondelegable the carrier's obligation to "properly and carefully ... stow ... the goods carried," COGSA § 3(2), 46 U.S.C.App. § 1303(2); *see Associated Metals & Minerals Corp. v. M/V Arktis Sky*, 978 F.2d 47, 50 (CA2 1992). But *see* COGSA § 4(2)(i), 46 U.S.C. § 1304(2)(i) ("[N]either the carrier nor the ship shall be responsible for loss or damage arising or resulting from ... [a]ct or omission of the shipper or owner of the goods, his agent or representative"); COGSA § 3(8), 46 U.S.C.App. § 1303(8) (agreement may not relieve or lessen liability "otherwise than as provided in this chapter"); Hegarty, A COGSA Carrier's Duty to Load and Stow Cargo is Nondelegable, or Is It?: *Associated Metals & Minerals Corp. v. M/V Arktis Sky*, 18 TUL. MAR. L.J. 125 (1993).

British case law does not follow such a strict prohibition of private agreements shifting the primary responsibility for the safety of the cargo. *Pyrene Company, Ltd. v. Scindia Steam Navigation Company, Ltd.*, 2 Q.B. 403 (1954), 2 All E.R. 158, acknowledges this fact.

> The extent to which the carrier has to undertake the loading of the vessel may depend not only upon the different systems of law but upon the custom and practice of the port and the nature of the cargo. It is difficult to believe that the Rules were intended to impose a universal rigidity in this respect, or to deny freedom of contract to the carrier. The carrier is practically bound to play some part in the loading and discharging, so that both operations are naturally included in those covered by the contract of carriage. But [there is] no reason why the Rules should not leave the parties free to determine by their own contract the part which each has to play. On this view the whole contract of carriage is subject to the Rules, but the extent to which loading and discharging are brought within the carrier's obligations is left to the parties themselves to decide.

[1954] 1 Ll.L.Rep. 321. *See also Jindal Iron & Steel Co. Ltd v. Islamic Solidarity Shipping Co. Jordan Inc. (The Jordan II)* [2004] UKHL 49 (reaffirming British approach in preference to the American approach).

2. *Rust Clauses*

The Ninth Circuit, in *Tokio Marine & Fire Insurance Co. v. Retla Steamship Co.*, 426 F.2d 1372, 1970 AMC 1611 (9th Cir. 1970), approved the use of rust clauses which would explicitly relieve the carrier from delivering iron or steel goods in a rust-free condition. In *Sumitomo Corp. of America v. M/V Saint Venture*, 683 F. Supp. 1361 (M.D. Fla. 1988), the court disallowed the application of the "Retla rust clause" because the clause in question, unlike the clause in *Retla*, was buried in fine print on the bill of lading and did not offer to substitute an alternative bill of lading without the rust language. However, in *Acwoo Steel Corp. v. Toko Kaiun Kaisha, Ltd.*, 840 F.2d 1284, 1988 AMC 2922 (6th Cir. 1988), the court upheld the use of a rust clause similar to the clause in *Sumitomo*.

3. *Lumber Clauses*

As to a Lumber Clause which is similar to the Rust Clause, *compare G.F. Co. v. Pan Ocean Shipping Co., Ltd.*, 23 F.3d 1498, 1994 AMC 1739 (9th Cir. 1994) *with Plywood Panels, Inc. v. M/V Sun Valley*, 804 F. Supp. 804, 1993 AMC 516 (E.D. Va. 1992).

Question

Can the carrier contract out of liability by getting the cargo-owner to agree that the carrier has exercised due care? What if the bill of lading for carriage of a bulk liquid cargo contains a clause stating "Vessel to clean tanks, lines and pumps to [cargo-owner's] surveyor's satisfaction" and the cargo-owner's surveyor inspects the tanks, lines and pumps and declares them to be suitable? If the cargo is contaminated during the voyage, can the carrier rely on the cargo-owner's surveyor's report to argue that its obligation under COGSA § 3(2) was fulfilled? See *Jamaica Nutrition Holdings Ltd v. United Shipping Co. Ltd*, 643 F.2d 376, 1981 AMC 2883 (5th Cir. 1981).

J. Forum Selection Clauses

VIMAR SEGUROS Y REASEGUROS, S.A. v. M/V SKY REEFER

515 U.S. 528, 115 S. Ct. 2322, 132 L. Ed. 2d 462, 1995 AMC 1817 (1995)

Justice KENNEDY delivered the opinion of the Court.

This case requires us to interpret the Carriage of Goods by Sea Act (COGSA), 46 U.S.C. App. § 1300 *et seq.*, as it relates to a contract containing a clause requiring arbitration in a foreign country. The question is whether a foreign arbitration clause in a bill of lading is invalid under COGSA because it lessens liability in the sense that COGSA prohibits. Our holding that COGSA does not forbid selection of the foreign forum makes it unnecessary to resolve the further question whether the Federal Arbitration Act (FAA), 9 U.S.C. § 1 *et seq.* (1988 ed. and Supp. V), would override COGSA were it interpreted otherwise. In our view, the relevant provisions of COGSA and the FAA are in accord, not in conflict.

I

The contract at issue in this case is a standard form bill of lading to evidence the purchase of a shipload of Moroccan oranges and lemons. The purchaser was Bacchus Associates (Bacchus), a New York partnership that distributes fruit at wholesale throughout the Northeastern United States. Bacchus dealt with Galaxie Negoce, S.A. (Galaxie), a Moroccan fruit supplier. Bacchus contracted with Galaxie to purchase the shipload of fruit and chartered a ship to transport it from Morocco to Massachusetts. The ship was the M/V Sky Reefer, a refrigerated cargo ship owned by M.H. Maritima, S.A., a Panamanian company, and time-chartered to Nichiro Gyogyo Kaisha, Ltd., a Japanese company. Stevedores hired by Galaxie loaded and stowed the cargo. As is customary in these types of transactions, when it received the cargo from Galaxie, Nichiro as carrier issued a form bill of lading to Galaxie as shipper and consignee. Once the ship set sail from Morocco, Galaxie tendered the bill of lading to Bacchus according to the terms of a letter of credit posted in Galaxie's favor.

Among the rights and responsibilities set out in the bill of lading were arbitration and choice-of-law clauses. Clause 3, entitled "Governing Law and Arbitration," provided:

> (1) The contract evidenced by or contained in this Bill of Lading shall be governed by the Japanese law.
> (2) Any dispute arising from this Bill of Lading shall be referred to arbitration in Tokyo by the Tokyo Maritime Arbitration Commission (TOMAC) of The Japan Shipping Exchange, Inc., in accordance with the rules of TOMAC and any amend-

ment thereto, and the award given by the arbitrators shall be final and binding on both parties. App. 49.

When the vessel's hatches were opened for discharge in Massachusetts, Bacchus discovered that thousands of boxes of oranges had shifted in the cargo holds, resulting in over $1 million damage. Bacchus received $733,442.90 compensation from petitioner Vimar Seguros y Reaseguros (Vimar Seguros), Bacchus' marine cargo insurer that became subrogated *pro tanto* to Bacchus' rights. Petitioner and Bacchus then brought suit against Maritima *in personam* and M/V Sky Reefer *in rem* in the District Court for the District of Massachusetts under the bill of lading. These defendants, respondents here, moved to stay the action and compel arbitration in Tokyo under clause 3 of the bill of lading and § 3 of the FAA, which requires courts to stay proceedings and enforce arbitration agreements covered by the Act. Petitioner and Bacchus opposed the motion, arguing the arbitration clause was unenforceable under the FAA both because it was a contract of adhesion and because it violated COGSA § 3(8). The premise of the latter argument was that the inconvenience and costs of proceeding in Japan would "lesse[n] ... liability" as those terms are used in COGSA.

The District Court rejected the adhesion argument, observing that Congress defined the arbitration agreements enforceable under the FAA to include maritime bills of lading, 9 U.S.C. § 1, and that petitioner was a sophisticated party familiar with the negotiation of maritime shipping transactions. It also rejected the argument that requiring the parties to submit to arbitration would lessen respondents' liability under COGSA § 3(8). The court granted the motion to stay judicial proceedings and to compel arbitration; it retained jurisdiction pending arbitration; and at petitioner's request, it certified for interlocutory appeal under 28 U.S.C. § 1292(b) its ruling to compel arbitration, stating that the controlling question of law was "whether [COGSA § 3(8)] nullifies an arbitration clause contained in a bill of lading governed by COGSA." Pet. for Cert. 30a.

The First Circuit affirmed the order to arbitrate. 29 F.3d 727 (1994). Although it expressed grave doubt whether a foreign arbitration clause lessened liability under COGSA § 3(8), 29 F.3d, at 730, the Court of Appeals assumed the clause was invalid under COGSA and resolved the conflict between the statutes in favor of the FAA, which it considered to be the later enacted and more specific statute, *id.*, at 731-733. We granted certiorari, 513 U.S. —, 115 S. Ct. 571, 130 L. Ed. 2d 488 (1994), to resolve a Circuit split on the enforceability of foreign arbitration clauses in maritime bills of lading. Compare the case below (enforcing foreign arbitration clause assuming *arguendo* it violated COGSA), with *State Establishment for Agricultural Product Trading v. M/V Wesermunde*, 838 F.2d 1576 (CA11) (declining to enforce foreign arbitration clause because that would violate COGSA), cert. denied, 488 U.S. 916, 109 S. Ct. 273, 102 L. Ed. 2d 262 (1988). We now affirm.

II

The parties devote much of their argument to the question whether COGSA or the FAA has priority. "[W]hen two statutes are capable of co-existence," however, "it is the duty of the courts, absent a clearly expressed congressional intention to the contrary, to regard each as effective." *Morton v. Mancari*, 417 U.S. 535, 551, 94 S. Ct. 2474, 2483, 41 L. Ed. 2d 290 (1974); *Pittsburgh & Lake Erie R. Co. v. Railway Labor Executives' Assn.*, 491 U.S. 490, 510, 109 S. Ct. 2584, 2596-2597, 105 L. Ed. 2d 415 (1989). There is no conflict unless COGSA by its own terms nullifies a foreign arbitration clause, and we choose to address that issue rather than assume nullification *arguendo*, as the Court of Appeals did. We consider the two arguments made by petitioner. The first is that a foreign arbitration clause lessens COGSA liability by increasing the transaction costs of obtaining relief. The second is that there is a risk foreign arbitrators will not apply COGSA.

A

The leading case for invalidation of a foreign forum selection clause is the opinion of the Court of Appeals for the Second Circuit in *Indussa Corp. v. S.S. Ranborg*, 377 F.2d 200 (1967) (en banc). The court there found that COGSA invalidated a clause designating a foreign judicial forum because it "puts 'a high hurdle' in the way of enforcing liability, and thus is an effective means for carriers to secure settlements lower than if cargo [owners] could sue in a convenient forum," *id.*, at 203 (citation omitted). The court observed "there could be no assurance that [the foreign court] would apply [COGSA] in the same way as would an American tribunal subject to the uniform control of the Supreme Court," *id.*, at 203-204. Following *Indussa*, the Courts of Appeals without exception have invalidated foreign forum selection clauses under § 3(8). See *Union Ins. Soc. of Canton, Ltd. v. S.S. Elikon*, 642 F.2d 721, 723-725 (CA4 1981); *Conklin & Garrett, Ltd v. M/V Finnrose*, 826 F.2d 1441, 1442-1444 (CA5 1987); *see also* G. Gilmore & C. Black, Law of Admiralty 145-146, n.23 (2d ed. 1975) (approving *Indussa* rule). As foreign arbitration clauses are but a subset of foreign forum selection clauses in general, *Scherk v. Alberto-Culver Co.*, 417 U.S. 506, 519, 94 S. Ct. 2449, 2457, 41 L. Ed. 2d 270 (1974), the *Indussa* holding has been extended to foreign arbitration clauses as well. See *State Establishment for Agricultural Product Trading, supra*, at 1580-1581; *cf. Vimar Seguros Y Reaseguros, supra*, at 730 (assuming *arguendo Indussa* applies). The logic of that extension would be quite defensible, but we cannot endorse the reasoning or the conclusion of the *Indussa* rule itself.

The determinative provision in COGSA, examined with care, does not support the arguments advanced first in *Indussa* and now by the petitioner. Section 3(8) of COGSA provides as follows:

> Any clause, covenant, or agreement in a contract of carriage relieving the carrier or the ship from liability for loss or damage to or in connection with the goods, arising from negligence, fault, or failure in the duties or obligations provided in this section, or lessening such liability otherwise than as provided in this chapter, shall be null and void and of no effect. 46 U.S.C. App. § 1303(8).

The liability that may not be lessened is "liability for loss or damage ... arising from negligence, fault, or failure in the duties or obligations provided in this section." The statute thus addresses the lessening of the specific liability imposed by the Act, without addressing the separate question of the means and costs of enforcing that liability. The difference is that between explicit statutory guarantees and the procedure for enforcing them, between applicable liability principles and the forum in which they are to be vindicated.

The liability imposed on carriers under COGSA § 3 is defined by explicit standards of conduct, and it is designed to correct specific abuses by carriers. In the 19th century it was a prevalent practice for common carriers to insert clauses in bills of lading exempting themselves from liability for damage or loss, limiting the period in which plaintiffs had to present their notice of claim or bring suit, and capping any damages awards per package. *See* 2A M. STURLEY, BENEDICT ON ADMIRALTY § 11, pp. 2-2 to 2-3 (1995); 2 T. SCHOENBAUM, ADMIRALTY AND MARITIME LAW § 10-13 (2d ed. 1994); Yancey, *The Carriage of Goods: Hague, COGSA, Visby, and Hamburg*, 57 TULANE L. REV. 1238, 1239-1240 (1983). Thus, § 3, entitled "Responsibilities and liabilities of carrier and ship," requires that the carrier "exercise due diligence to ... [m]ake the ship seaworthy" and "[p]roperly man, equip, and supply the ship" before and at the beginning of the voyage, § 3(1), "properly and carefully load, handle, stow, carry, keep, care for, and discharge the goods carried," § 3(2), and issue a bill of lading with specified contents, § 3(3). 46 U.S.C. App. § 1303(1), (2), and (3). Section 3(6) allows the cargo owner to provide notice of loss or damage within three days and to bring suit within one year. These are the substantive obligations and particular procedures that § 3(8) prohibits a carrier from altering to its advantage in a bill of lading. Nothing in this section, however, suggests that the statute prevents the parties from agreeing to enforce these obligations in a particular forum. By its terms, it establishes certain duties and obligations, separate and apart from the mechanisms for their enforcement.

Petitioner's contrary reading of § 3(8) is undermined by the Court's construction of a similar statutory provision in *Carnival Cruise Lines, Inc. v. Shute*, 499 U.S. 585, 111 S. Ct. 1522, 113 L. Ed. 2d 622 (1991). There a number of Washington residents argued that a Florida forum selection clause contained in a cruise ticket should not be enforced because the expense and inconvenience of litigation in Florida would "caus[e] plaintiffs unreasonable hardship in asserting their rights," *id.*, at 596, 111 S. Ct., at 1528-1529, and therefore " 'lessen, weaken, or avoid the right of any claimant to a trial by court of competent jurisdiction on the question of liability for ... loss or injury, or the measure of damages therefor' " in violation of the Limitation of Vessel Owner's Liability Act, 499 U.S., at 595-596, 111 S. Ct., at 1528 (quoting 46 U.S.C. App. § 183(c). We observed that the clause "does not purport to limit petitioner's liability for negligence," *id.*, at 596-597, 111 S. Ct., at 1529, and enforced the agreement over the dissent's argument, based in part on the *Indussa* line of cases, that the cost and inconvenience of traveling thousands of miles "lessens or weakens [plaintiffs'] ability to recover." 499 U.S., at 603, 111 S. Ct., at 1532 (STEVENS, J., dissenting).

If the question whether a provision lessens liability were answered by reference to the costs and inconvenience to the cargo owner, there would be no principled basis for distinguishing national from foreign arbitration clauses. Even if it were reasonable to read § 3(8) to make a distinction based on travel time, airfare, and hotels bills, these factors are not susceptible of a simple and enforceable distinction between domestic and foreign forums. Requiring a Seattle cargo owner to arbitrate in New York likely imposes more costs and burdens than a foreign arbitration clause requiring it to arbitrate in Vancouver. It would be unwieldy and unsupported by the terms or policy of the statute to require courts to proceed case by case to tally the costs and burdens to particular plaintiffs in light of their means, the size of their claims, and the relative burden on the carrier.

Our reading of "lessening such liability" to exclude increases in the transaction costs of litigation also finds support in the goals of the Brussels Convention for the Unification of Certain Rules Relating to Bills of Lading, 51 Stat. 233 (1924) (Hague Rules), on which COGSA is modeled. Sixty-six countries, including the United States and Japan, are now parties to the Convention, *see* Department of State, Office of the Legal Adviser, Treaties in Force: A List of Treaties and Other International Agreements of the United States in Force on January 1, 1994, p. 367 (June 1994), and it appears that none has interpreted its enactment of § 3(8) of the Hague Rules to prohibit foreign forum selection clauses, *see* Sturley, *International Uniform Laws in National Courts: The Influence of Domestic Law in Conflicts of Interpretation*, 27 Va. J. Int'l L. 729, 776-796 (1987). The English courts long ago rejected the reasoning later adopted by the *Indussa* court. *See Maharani Woollen Mills Co. v. Anchor Line*, [1927] 29 Lloyd's List L. Rep. 169 (C.A.) (SCRUTTON, L.J.) ("[T]he liability of the carrier appears to me to remain exactly the same under the clause. The only difference is a question of procedure—where shall the law be enforced?—and I do not read any clause as to procedure as lessening liability"). And other countries that do not recognize foreign forum selection clauses rely on specific provisions to that effect in their domestic versions of the Hague Rules, *see, e.g.*, Sea-Carriage of Goods Act 1924, § 9(2) (Australia); Carriage of Goods by Sea Act, No. 1 of 1986, § 3 (South Africa). In light of the fact that COGSA is the culmination of a multilateral effort "to establish uniform ocean bills of lading to govern the rights and liabilities of carriers and shippers inter se in international trade," *Robert C. Herd & Co. v. Krawill Machinery Corp.*, 359 U.S. 297, 301, 79 S. Ct. 766, 769, 3 L. Ed. 2d 820 (1959), we decline to interpret our version of the Hague Rules in a manner contrary to every other nation to have addressed this issue. See Sturley, *supra*, at 736 (conflicts in the interpretation of the Hague Rules not only destroy aesthetic symmetry in the international legal order but impose real costs on the commercial system in the Rules govern).

It would also be out of keeping with the objects of the Convention for the courts of this country to interpret COGSA to disparage the authority or competence of international forums for dispute resolution. Petitioner's skepticism over the ability of foreign arbitrators to apply COGSA or the Hague Rules, and its reliance on this aspect of *Indussa*, *supra*, must give way to contemporary principles of international comity and commercial practice. As the Court observed in *The Bremen v. Zapata Off-Shore Co.*, 407 U.S. 1, 92 S. Ct. 1907, 32 L. Ed. 2d 513 (1972), when it enforced a foreign forum selection clause, the historical judicial resistance to foreign forum selection clauses "has little place in an era when ... businesses once essentially local now operate in world markets." *Id.*, at 12, 92 S. Ct., at

1914. "The expansion of American business and industry will hardly be encouraged," we explained, "if, notwithstanding solemn contracts, we insist on a parochial concept that all disputes must be resolved under our laws and in our courts." *Id.*, at 9, 92 S. Ct., at 1912. *See Mitsubishi Motors Corp. v. Soler Chrysler-Plymouth, Inc.*, 473 U.S. 614, 638, 105 S. Ct. 3346, 3359-3360, 87 L. Ed. 2d 444 (1985) (if international arbitral institutions "are to take a central place in the international legal order, national courts will need to 'shake off the old judicial hostility to arbitration,' and also their customary and understandable unwillingness to cede jurisdiction of a claim arising under domestic law to a foreign or transnational tribunal") (citation omitted); *Scherk v. Alberto-Culver Co.*, 417 U.S., at 516, 94 S. Ct., at 2456 ("A parochial refusal by the courts of one country to enforce an international arbitration agreement" would frustrate "the orderliness and predictability essential to any international business transaction"); *see also* Allison, *Arbitration of Private Antitrust Claims in International Trade: A Study in the Subordination of National Interests to the Demands of a World Market*, 18 N.Y.U. J. INT'L LAW & POLITICS 361, 439 (1986).

That the forum here is arbitration only heightens the irony of petitioner's argument, for the FAA is also based in part on an international convention, 9 U.S.C. § 201 *et seq.* (codifying the United Nations Convention on the Recognition and Enforcement of Foreign Arbitral Awards, June 10, 1958, [1970] 21 U.S.T. 2517), T.I.A.S. No. 6997, intended "to encourage the recognition and enforcement of commercial arbitration agreements in international contracts and to unify the standards by which agreements to arbitrate are observed and arbitral awards are enforced in the signatory countries," *Scherk, supra,* at 520, n.15, 94 S. Ct., at 2457, n.15. The FAA requires enforcement of arbitration agreements in contracts that involve interstate commerce, see *Allied-Bruce Terminix Cos. v. Dobson*, 513 U.S. —, 115 S. Ct. 834, 130 L. Ed. 2d 753 (1995), and in maritime transactions, including bills of lading, see 9 U.S.C. §§ 1, 2, 201, 202, where there is no independent basis in law or equity for revocation. *Cf. Carnival Cruise Lines,* 499 U.S., at 595, 111 S. Ct., at 1528 ("forum-selection clauses contained in form passage contracts are subject to judicial scrutiny for fundamental fairness"). If the United States is to be able to gain the benefits of international accords and have a role as a trusted partner in multilateral endeavors, its courts should be most cautious before interpreting its domestic legislation in such manner as to violate international agreements. That concern counsels against construing COGSA to nullify foreign arbitration clauses because of inconvenience to the plaintiff or insular distrust of the ability of foreign arbitrators to apply the law.

B

Petitioner's second argument against enforcement of the Japanese arbitration clause is that there is no guarantee foreign arbitrators will apply COGSA. This objection raises a concern of substance. The central guarantee of § 3(8) is that the terms of a bill of landing may not relieve the carrier of the obligations or diminish the legal duties specified by the Act. The relevant question, therefore, is whether the substantive law to be applied will reduce the carrier's obligations to the cargo owner below what COGSA guarantees. See *Mitsubishi Motors, supra,* 473 U.S. at 637, n.19, 105 S. Ct., at 3359, n.19.

Petitioner argues that the arbitrators will follow the Japanese Hague Rules, which, petitioner contends, lessen respondents' liability in at least one significant respect. The Japanese version of the Hague Rules, it is said, provides the carrier with a defense based on the acts or omissions of the stevedores hired by the shipper, Galaxie, *see* App. 112, Article 3(1), (carrier liable "when he or the persons employed by him" fail to take due care), while COGSA, according to petitioner, makes nondelegable the carrier's obligation to "properly and carefully ... stow ... the goods carried," COGSA § 3(2), 46 U.S.C. App. § 1303(2); *see Associated Metals & Minerals Corp. v. M/V Arktis Sky*, 978 F.2d 47, 50 (CA2 1992). But see COGSA § 4(2)(i), 46 U.S.C. § 1304(2)(i) ("[N]either the carrier nor the ship shall be responsible for loss or damage arising or resulting from ... [a]ct or omission of the shipper or owner of the goods, his agent or representative"); COGSA § 3(8), 46 U.S.C. App. § 1303(8) (agreement may not relieve or lessen liability "otherwise than as provided in this chapter"); Hegarty, *A COGSA Carrier's Duty to Load and Stow Cargo is Nondelegable, or Is It?: Associated Metals & Minerals Corp. v. M/V Arktis Sky*, 18 Tulane Mar. L.J. 125 (1993).

Whatever the merits of petitioner's comparative reading of COGSA and its Japanese counterpart, its claim is premature. At this interlocutory stage it is not established what law the arbitrators will apply to petitioner's claims or that petitioner will receive diminished protection as a result. The arbitrators may conclude that COGSA applies of its own force or that Japanese law does not apply so that, under another clause of the bill of lading, COGSA controls. Respondents seek only to enforce the arbitration agreement. The district court has retained jurisdiction over the case and "will have the opportunity at the award-enforcement stage to ensure that the legitimate interest in the enforcement of the ... laws has been addressed." *Mitsubishi Motors*, 473 U.S., at 638, 105 S. Ct., at 3359; *cf.* 1 Restatement (Third) of Foreign Relations Law of the United States § 482(2)(d) (1986) ("A court in the United States need not recognize a judgment of the court of a foreign state if ... the judgment itself, is repugnant to the public policy of the United States"). Were there no subsequent opportunity for review and were we persuaded that "the choice-of-forum and choice-of-law clauses operated in tandem as a prospective waiver of a party's right to pursue statutory remedies ..., we would have little hesitation in condemning the agreement as against public policy." *Mitsubishi Motors*, *supra*, at 637, n.19, 105 S. Ct., at 3359, n.19. *Cf. Knott v. Botany Mills*, 179 U.S. 69, 21 S. Ct. 30, 45 L. Ed. 90 (1900) (nullifying choice-of-law provision under the Harter Act, the statutory precursor to COGSA, where British law would give effect to provision in bill of lading that purported to exempt carrier from liability for damage to goods caused by carrier's negligence in loading and stowage of cargo); *The Hollandia*, [1983] A.C. 565, 574-575 (H.L. 1982) (noting choice of forum clause "does not ex facie offend against article III, paragraph 8," but holding clause unenforceable where "the foreign court chosen as the exclusive forum would apply a domestic substantive law which would result in limiting the carrier's liability to the sum lower than that to which he would be entitled if [English COGSA] applied"). Under the circumstances of this case, however, the First Circuit was correct to reserve judgment on the choice-of-law question, 29 F.3d, at 729, n.3, as it must be decided in the first instance by the arbitrator, *cf. Mitsubishi Motors*, *supra*, 473 U.S., at 637, n.19, 105 S. Ct., at 3359, n.19.

As the District Court has retained jurisdiction, mere speculation that the foreign arbitrators might apply Japanese law which, depending on the proper construction of COGSA, might reduce respondents' legal obligations, does not in and of itself lessen liability under COGSA § 3(8).

Because we hold that foreign arbitration clauses in bills of lading are not invalid under COGSA in all circumstances, both the FAA and COGSA may be given full effect. The judgment of the Court of Appeals is affirmed, and the case is remanded for further proceedings consistent with this opinion.

It is so ordered.

Justice BREYER took no part in the consideration or decision of this case.

Justice O'CONNOR, concurring in the judgment.

I agree with what I understand to be the two basic points made in the Court's opinion. First, I agree that the language of the Carriage of Goods by Sea Act (COGSA), 46 U.S.C. App. § 1300 *et seq.*, and our decision in *Carnival Cruise Lines, Inc. v. Shute*, 499 U.S. 585, 111 S. Ct. 1522, 113 L. Ed. 2d 622 (1991), preclude a holding that the increased cost of litigating in a distant forum, without more, can lessen liability within the meaning of COGSA § 3(8). *Ante*, at 2327-2328. Second, I agree that, because the District Court has retained jurisdiction over this case while the arbitration proceeds, any claim of lessening of liability that might arise out of the arbitrators' interpretation of the bill of lading's choice of law clause, or out of their ap-plication of COGSA, is premature. *Ante*, at 2329-2330. Those two points suffice to affirm the decision below.

Because the Court's opinion appears to do more, however, I concur only in the judgment. Foreign arbitration clauses of the kind presented here do not divest domestic courts of jurisdiction, unlike true foreign forum selection clauses such as that considered in *Indussa Corp. v. S.S. Ranborg*, 377 F.2d 200 (CA2 1967) (en banc). That difference is an important one—it is, after all, what leads the Court to dismiss much of petitioner's argument as premature—and we need not decide today whether *Indussa*, insofar as it relied on considerations other than the increased cost of litigating in a distant forum, retains any vitality in the context of true foreign forum selection clauses. Accordingly, I would not, without qualification, reject "the reasoning [and] the conclusion of the *Indussa* rule itself," *ante*, at 2326, nor would I wholeheartedly approve an English decision that "long ago rejected the reasoning later adopted by the *Indussa* court," *ante*, at 2328. As the Court notes, "[f]ollowing *Indussa*, the Court of Appeals without exception have invalidated foreign forum selection clauses under § 3(8)," *ante*, at 2326. I would prefer to disturb that unbroken line of authority only to the extent necessary to decide this case.

Justice STEVENS, dissenting

* * *

I

* * *

Thus, our interpretation of maritime law prior to the enactment of the Harter Act, our reading of that statute in *Knott*, and the federal courts' consistent interpretation of COGSA, buttressed by scholarly recognition of the commercial interest in uniformity, demonstrate that the clauses in the Japanese carrier's bill of lading purporting to require arbitration in Tokyo pursuant to Japanese law both would have been held invalid under COGSA prior to today.[7]

The foreign arbitration clause imposes potentially prohibitive costs on the shipper, who must travel—and bring his lawyers, witnesses and exhibits—to a distant country in order to seek redress. The shipper will therefore be inclined either to settle the claim at a discount or to forgo bringing the claim at all. The foreign-law clause leaves the shipper who does pursue his claim open to the application of unfamiliar and potentially disadvantageous legal standards, until he can obtain review (perhaps years later) in a domestic forum under the high standard applicable to vacation of arbitration awards.[8] *See Wilko v. Swan*, 346 U.S. 427, 436-437, 74 S. Ct. 182, 187-88, 98 L. Ed. 168 (1953). Accordingly, courts have always held that such clauses "lessen" or "relieve" the carrier's liability, *see, e.g.*, *State Establishment for Agricultural Product Trading v. M/V Wesermunde*, 838 F.2d 1576, 1580-1582 (CA11), *cert. denied*, 488 U.S. 916, 109 S. Ct. 273, 102 L. Ed. 2d 262 (1988), and even the Court of Appeals in this case assumed as much, 29 F.3d 727, 730, 732, n.5 (CA1 1994). Yet this Court today holds that carriers may insert foreign-arbitration clauses into bills of lading, and it leaves in doubt the validity of choice-of-law clauses.

Although the policy undergirding the doctrine of *stare decisis* has its greatest value in preserving rules governing commercial transactions, particularly when their meaning is well understood and has been accepted for long periods of time,[9] the Court nevertheless has concluded that a change must be made. Its law-changing decision is supported by three arguments: (1) the statutory reference to "lessening such liability" has been misconstrued; (2) the prior understanding of the meaning of the statute has been "undermined" by the *Carnival Cruise* case; and (3) the new rule is supported by our obligation to honor the 1924 "Hague Rules." None of these arguments is persuasive.

II

The Court assumes that the words "lessening such liability" must be narrowly construed to refer only to the substantive rules that define the carrier's legal obligations. *Ante*, at 2327. Under this view, contractual provisions that lessen the amount of the consignee's

---

[7] Of course, the objectionable feature in the instant bill of lading is a foreign arbitration clause, not a foreign forum selection clause. But this distinction is of little importance; in relevant respects, there is no difference between the two. Both impose substantial costs on shippers, and both should be held to lessen liability under COGSA. The majority's reasoning to the contrary thus presumably covers forum selection as well as arbitration. *See ante*, at 2326; *ante*, at 2330-2331 (O'CONNOR, J., concurring in judgment). The only ground on which one might distinguish the two types of clauses is that another federal statute, the Federal Arbitration Act, makes arbitration clauses enforceable, whereas no analogous federal statute exists for forum selection clauses. For the reasons expressed *infra*, at 2336-2337, this distinction is unpersuasive.

[8] I am assuming that the majority would not actually uphold the application of disadvantageous legal standards—these, even under the narrowest reading of COGSA, surely lessen liability. *See ante*, at 2329-330. Nonetheless, the majority is apparently willing to allow arbitration to proceed under foreign law, and to determine afterwards whether application of that law has actually lessened the carrier's formal liability. As I have discussed above, this regime creates serious problems of delay and uncertainty. Because the majority's holding in this case is limited to the enforceability of the foreign arbitration clause—it does not actually pass upon the validity of the foreign law clause—I will not discuss the foreign law clause further except to say that it is an unenforceable lessening of liability to the extent it gives an advantage to the carrier at the expense of the shipper.

[9] *See* Eskridge v. Frickey, *The Supreme Court 1993 Term—Foreword: Law as Equilibrium*, 108 HARV. L. REV. 26, 81 (1994).

net recovery, or that lessen the likelihood that it will make any recovery at all, are beyond the scope of the statute.

In my opinion, this view is flatly inconsistent with the purpose of COGSA § 3(8). That section responds to the inequality of bargaining power inherent in bills of lading and to carriers' historic tendency to exploit that inequality whenever possible to immunize themselves from liability for their own fault. A bill of lading is a form document prepared by the carrier, who presents it to the shipper on a take-it-or-leave-it basis. *See* Black, *The Bremen, COGSA and the Problem of Conflicting Interpretation*, 6 VAND. J. TRANSNAT'L L. 365, 368 (1973); *Liverpool Steam*, 129 U.S., at 441, 9 S. Ct., at 471-72. Characteristically, there is no arms-length negotiation over the bill's terms; the shipper must agree to the carrier's standard-form language, or else refrain from using the carrier's services. Accordingly, if courts were to enforce bills of lading as written, a carrier could slip in a clause relieving itself of all liability for fault, or limiting that liability to a fraction of the shipper's damages, and the shipper would have no recourse. COGSA represents Congress' most recent attempt to respond to this problem. By its terms, it invalidates any clause in a bill of lading "relieving" or "lessening" the "liability" of the carrier for negligence, fault, or dereliction of duty.

When one reads the statutory language in light of the policies behind COGSA's enactment, it is perfectly clear that a foreign forum selection or arbitration clause "relieves" or "lessens" the carrier's liability. The transaction costs associated with an arbitration in Japan will obviously exceed the potential recovery in a great many cargo disputes. As a practical matter, therefore, in such a case no matter how clear the carrier's formal legal liability may be, it would make no sense for the consignee or its subrogee to enforce that liability. It seems to me that a contractual provision that entirely protects the shipper from being held liable for anything should be construed either to have "lessened" its inability or to have "relieved" it of liability.

Even if the value of the shipper's claim is large enough to justify litigation in Asia, contractual provisions that impose unnecessary and unreasonable costs on the consignee will inevitably lessen its net recovery. If, as under the Court's reasoning, such provisions do not affect the carrier's legal liability, it would appear to be permissible to require the consignee to pay the costs of the arbitration, or perhaps the travel expenses and fees of the expert witnesses, interpreters, and lawyers employed by both parties. Judge Friendly and the many other wise judges who shared his opinion were surely correct in concluding that Congress could not have intended such a perverse reading of the statutory text.

More is at stake here than the allocation of rights and duties between shippers and carriers. A bill of lading, besides being a contract of carriage, is a negotiable instrument that controls possession of the goods being shipped. Accordingly, the bill of lading can be sold, traded, or used to obtain credit as though the bill were the cargo itself. Disuniformity in the interpretation of bills of lading will impair their negotiability. See *Union Ins. Soc. of Canton, Ltd. v. S.S. Elikon*, 642 F.2d, at 723, GILMORE & BLACK, LAW OF ADMIRALTY 146-147 (2d ed. 1975). Thus, if the security interests in some bills of lading are enforceable only through the courts of Japan, while others may be enforceable only in Liechtenstein, the negotiability of bills of lading will suffer from the uncertainty. COGSA recognizes that this negotiability depends in part upon the financial community's capacity to rely on the enforceability, in an accessible forum, of the bills' terms. Today's decision destroys that capacity.

* * *

I respectfully dissent.

Notes and Questions

1. How realistic is the Court's conclusion that the District Court may provide relief if the arbitration panel refuses to apply U.S. COGSA? Suppose the arbitrators simply announce their decision without explaining the legal basis for it. What should the District Court do? Suppose the goods had been shipped from Japan to the United States and that, under Japanese law, the law of the place where the cargo had been shipped controls the transaction. Also the bill of lading provided for the application of Japanese law. What law would you expect the arbitrator apply? If under those circumstances, the arbitrator applied Japanese law, what should the U.S. District Court do?

2. In *Central National-Gottesman, Inc. v. M/V GERTRUDE OLDENDORFF*, 204 F. Supp. 2d 675, 682, 2002 AMC 1477 (S.D.N.Y. 2002), the court refused to apply *Sky Reefer* to a clause providing for disputes to be resolved in a foreign *court*, citing the impossibility of the U.S. court retaining jurisdiction. The court said:

> An integral component of the Court's reasoning in *Sky Reefer* was that there existed a subsequent opportunity for the district court to review the foreign court's decision to ensure that it comported with the interest in enforcement of the laws in the United States and was not violative of public policy. *Sky Reefer*, 515 U.S at 540, 115 S. Ct. 2322. Absent this opportunity for review, it is readily apparent that the Court would have had a much harder time enforcing the forum selection clause and transferring the case to Japan. *See id.* ("Were there no subsequent opportunity for review [and foreign law operated to waive COGSA protection] ..., we would have little hesitation in condemning the agreement as against public policy.") (internal quotations omitted). However, this option of retaining jurisdiction is simply not available with respect to the dispute at hand. *Sky Reefer* involved a dispute over enforcement of a foreign arbitration clause. "The safeguard of retained jurisdiction is therefore not applicable here because this case involves a foreign jurisdiction clause". *In re Rationis Enterprises, Inc.*, No. 97 CV 9052, 1999 WL 6364 at *3 (S.D.N.Y. Jan. 7, 1999) ... Since this precaution, to which *Sky Reefer* accorded substantial weight, is missing here, the court is reluctant to enforce the forum selection clause and dismiss this action for improper venue.

See also, to similar effect, *Nippon Fire & Marine Ins. Co. v. M/V Spring Wave*, 92 F. Supp. 2d 574, 577, 2000 AMC 1717 (E.D. La. 2000).

3. *Progeny of SKY REEFER*

Following the *SKY REEFER* decision, courts have consistently upheld foreign arbitration clauses. Citing dicta from *SKY REEFER*, several courts have also upheld forum selection clauses reasoning that "foreign arbitration clauses are but a subset of foreign forum selection clauses in general...." *Mitsui & Co. (USA) Inc. v. MIRA M/V*, 111 F.3d 33, 36, 1997 AMC 2126 (5th Cir. 1997) (quoting *Vimar Seguros Y Reaseguros v. M/V SKY REEFER*, 515 U.S. 528, 533). See also *Talatala v. Nippon Yusen Kaisha Corp.*, 974 F. Supp. 1321, 1324 n. 4, 1997 AMC 1398 (D. Haw. 1997); *Pasztory v Croatia Line*, 918 F. Supp. 961, 965, 1996 AMC 1189 (E.D. Va. 1996); *Nippon Fire & Marine Ins. Co.v M/V EGASCO STAR*, 899 F. Supp. 164, 170 n. 8 (S.D.N.Y. 1995), *aff'd*, 104 F.3d 351 (2d Cir. 1996) (Table), all applying *Sky Reefer* to choice of court clauses. Compare, however, *In re Rationis Enterprises, Inc. of Panama*, 1999

AMC 889 (S.D.N.Y. 1999); *Nippon Fire & Marine Ins. Co. v. M/V Spring Wave*, 92 F. Supp. 2d 574, 577, 2000 AMC 1717 (E.D. La. 2000); *Central National-Gottesman, Inc. v. M/V GERTRUDE OLDENDORFF*, 204 F. Supp. 2d 675, 682, 2002 AMC 1477 (S.D.N.Y. 2002), all declining to dismiss on *Sky Reefer* grounds in cases involving choice of court clauses.

The Ninth Circuit even upheld a foreign forum selection clause that provided for litigation in Korea, despite findings that the plaintiff would be seriously inconvenienced and that in rem proceedings were not available under Korean law. *See Fireman's Fund Insurance Co. v. M.V. DSR ATLANTIC*, 131 F.3d 1336, 1338, 1998 AMC 583 (9th Cir. 1998). But compare *Union Steel America Co. v. M/V SANKO SPRUCE*, 14 F. Supp. 2d 682, 1999 AMC (D.N.J. 1998); *Allianz Ins. Co. of Canada v. Cho Yang Shipping Co., Ltd*, 131 F. Supp. 2d 787, 2000 AMC 2947 (E.D. Va. 2000), refusing to follow *DSR Atlantic*. For other cases applying the *SKY REEFER* rule, see *G.A. Pasztory v. Croatia Line*, 918 F. Supp 961 (E.D. Va. 1996) (upholding a clause selecting Croatia as the forum for the settlement of disputes despite arguments that Croatia was "politically unstable and jurisprudentially immature"); *Talatala v. Nippon Yusen Kaisha Corp.*, 974 F. Supp 1321, 1997 AMC 1398 (D. Hawaii 1997) (upholding a bill of lading provision that all actions be brought in Tokyo under the laws of Japan).

4. *Stipulation of the Applicable Law*

It is well settled that the provisions of the Harter Act and of the Carriage of Goods by Sea Act express the public policy of the United States and are mandatory. Accordingly, any clause in a bill of lading covered by these acts that purports to exonerate the carrier from liability for negligence or to lessen his liability otherwise than as provided by these acts is null and void. It is another question whether the same result may be achieved indirectly by a clause stipulating the application of a more favorable foreign law, granting exclusive jurisdiction to the courts of a foreign country, or providing for the settlement of disputes by arbitration in a foreign country.

Bills of lading issued in countries that have enacted the Visby Rules may incorporate these rules expressly or by implication. *See, e.g., Daval Steel Products v. The Acadia Forest*, 1988 AMC 1669 (S.D.N.Y 1988): *I.N.A. v. The Atlantic Corona*, 704 F. Supp. 528, 1989 AMC 875 (S.D.N.Y. 1989). When the Visby Rules are expressly incorporated in a bill of lading, the higher Visby limit of recovery ought to be allowed; there is no conflict with COGSA, because parties are free to increase the liabilities of the carrier. In the absence of an express incorporation of the Visby Rules, a question of contractual interpretation arises as to the intent of the parties. If the court concludes that the parties intended to adopt the higher Visby limits, their intent ought to be given effect. *See Francosteel Corp. v. The Deppe Europe*, 1990 AMC 2962 (S.D.N.Y. 1990) (higher limit allowed); *I.N.A. v. The Sealand Developer*, 1990 AMC 2967 (S.D.N.Y. 1989) (higher limit *not* allowed); *J.C.B. Sales, Ltd. v. Wallenius Lines*, 124 F.3d 132, 1997 AMC 2705 (2d Cir. 1997) (higher limit allowed). Compare *Acciai Speciali Terni U.S.A., Inc. v. M/V BERANE*, 182 F. Supp. 2d 503, 2002 AMC 519 (D.Md. 2002) (generally-worded Clause Paramount held not sufficient to give effect to higher limit).

Prior to the enactment of the Harter Act, contracts of affreightment involving foreign contacts were, in principle, governed by the law selected by the parties and, in absence of agreement, by the law of the place of contracting as impliedly intended. Nevertheless, unreasonable limitations of liability contained in contracts which were to be performed in part or in whole in the United States were considered contrary to public policy and of no effect, whether American or foreign law governed. Thus, it was held, not without good reason, that "the objections to the validity of stipulations exempting common carriers from responsibility for negligence ... apply precisely the same to a stipulation for the adoption of the law of another country.... That stipulation is plainly nothing but a further device." *The Energia*, 56 F. 124, 127 (S.D.N.Y. 1893), *aff'd*, 66 F. 604 (2d Cir. 1895). Similar results were reached much more readily after the enactment of the Harter Act, which included provisions defining its area of application. The act was thus declared applicable as a matter of law to all shipments to or from the ports of the United States, and party autonomy to select the applicable law was excluded.

Following the long-established precedent of the Harter Act, § 12 (first paragraph) of the Carriage of Goods by Sea Act has been considered by certain decisions to be a rule of public policy that precludes any other choice of law for bills of lading coming under it. Thus a stipulation providing for application of foreign law to a bill of lading covered by the Carriage of Goods by Sea Act has been disregarded, and the liability of the carrier has been determined under the Act. *See, e.g., The Steel Inventor*, 35 F. Supp., 986, 997, 1941 AMC 169 (D. Md. 1940); *The Bill*, 47 F. Supp. 969, 975, 1942 AMC 1607 (D. Md. 1942). Ordinarily, the choice of law clause is coupled with a forum selection clause. *See, e.g., Conklin & Garrett Ltd. v. M/V Finnrose*, 826 F.2d 1441, 1988 AMC 318 (5th Cir. 1987) (clause providing that any disputes under the bill of lading "shall be decided in Finland under Finnish law"; *held*, this clause conflicts with COGSA § 3(8) and, therefore, is not enforceable).

According to consistent theory, private parties ought to have contractual freedom to choose the applicable law with respect to cases and matters not governed by the Harter Act or the Carriage of Goods by Sea Act. Contracts of affreightment lying outside the scope of these acts are generally governed by the conflicts of law rules that federal courts apply in maritime cases. It is thus with regard to matters and contracts not regulated by either act, such as carriage between foreign ports, carriage under charter-party rather than a bill of lading, or with regard to shipments of live animals or deck cargo, that resort to the general conflicts rules is made. Such contracts in the United States, as in all other countries, are primarily subject to the law selected by the parties. *See Teyseer Cement Co. v. Halla Maritime Corporation*, 583 F. Supp. 1268, 1985 AMC 356 (W.D. Wash. 1984) (shipment between foreign ports; choice of Korean law and forum upheld). For the enforceability for forum selection clauses in general and an elaboration on *The Bremen v. Zapata Off-Shore Co.*, 407 U.S. 1, 92 S.Ct. 1907, 32 L.Ed.2d 513, 1972 AMC 1407 (1972), *see Carnival Cruise Lines v. Shute*, 499 U.S. 585, 111 S. Ct. 1522, 113 L.Ed.2d 622, 1991 AMC 1697 (1991); *North River Insurance Co. v. Federal Seal/Federal Pacific Line*, 647 F.2d 985, 1982 AMC 2963 (9th Cir. 1981); *Sanko Steamship Co. v. Newfoundland Refining Co.*, 411 F. Supp. 285, 1976 AMC 417 (S.D.N.Y. 1976). The United States Supreme Court has indicated that "except as forbidden by some public policy, the tendency of the law is to apply in contract matters the law which the parties intended to apply". *Lauritzen v. Larsen*, 345 U.S. 571, 588, 73 S.Ct. 921, 97 L.Ed. 1254 (1953) (1953).

K. Statute of Limitations

Note

COGSA provides for a one year statute of limitation that commences upon delivery for goods that have been damaged (for goods that are lost, the period runs from the date they should have been delivered). COGSA does not define the term "delivery". The Fifth Circuit has held that "'[d]elivery' occurs when the carrier places the cargo into the custody of whoever is legally entitled to receive it from the carrier." *Servicios-Expoarma, C.A. v. Industrial Maritime Carriers, Inc.*, 135 F.3d 984, 992, 1998 AMC 1453 (5th Cir. 1998). The court adopted the common definitions of delivery which courts have used to determine the meaning of term "delivery" under the Harter Act.

> General maritime law requires that a carrier "unload the cargo onto a dock, segregate it by bill of lading and count, put it into place of rest on the pier so that it is accessible to the consignee, and afford the cosignee a reasonable opportunity to come and get it." (at 993)

There is an exception to this rule where customs or port regulations provide otherwise. Where a port regulation requires that cargo be delivered to an authorized customs warehouse, the carrier had "delivered" the cargo when it placed the goods in the hands of the customs officials. Some courts have held otherwise, *see, e.g., Lithotip, C.A. v. S.S. Guarico*, 569 F. Supp. 837, 1985 AMC 1813 (S.D.N.Y. 1983).

Chapter 5

CHARTER PARTIES

A. Definitions and Introductory Note

1. Definitions

> *Charterparty*: in medieval Latin, *carta partita*, an instrument written in duplicate on a single sheet and then divided by indented edges so that each part fitted the other (whence the term 'indenture'); only now used for this particular kind of shipping document.

STEWART BOYD, ANDREW BURROWS AND DAVID FOXTON, SCRUTTON ON CHARTERPARTIES AND BILLS OF LADING, 3 n.19 (20th ed. 1996).

There are several different types of charter party. The different types of contract have very different functions.

> *Voyage Charters*. A voyage charter is a contract for the carriage of goods on a ship on a single voyage. Usually, the charterer charters the whole of the carrying capacity of the ship to carry a full cargo, but voyage charter parties for part cargoes are possible. The carrying ship is operated by the owner or disponent owner (a term that is explained further below) and not by the charterer. The charterer does not bear any of the ship's running costs directly. It simply pays freight to the owner for use of the ship to carry cargo.
>
> *Time Charters*. A time charter is an agreement to divide responsibility for the navigational and commercial operations of the chartered ship. The shipowner (or disponent owner) remains responsible for the navigational operation of ship, along with its master and crew, without having to worry about finding commercial employment for it. The charterer finds commercial employment for the ship without having to worry about the technical and navigational aspects of running it, such as employing the master and crew. The charterer pays for the commercial use of the ship, and in return it is entitled to keep the freight paid by the cargo-owners for carriage of their goods on the ship. The shipowner is guaranteed payment for the use of the ship without having to find cargoes in the market; the charterer makes profits in the cargo market (the freights it receives from cargo-owners minus the hire it has to pay the shipowner) without having to run the ship itself.

Time and Voyage Charters Distinguished

> Under a voyage charter the owner or disponent owner is using the vessel to trade for his own account. He decides and controls how he will exploit the earning capacity of the vessel, what trades he will compete in, what cargoes he will carry. He bears the full commercial risk and expense and enjoys the full benefit of the earnings of the vessel. A time charter is different. The owner still has to bear the expense of maintaining the ship and the crew. He still carries the risk of marine accidents and has to insure his interest in the vessel appropriately. But, in return for the payment of hire, he transfers the right to exploit the earning capacity of the vessel to the time charterer. The time charterer also agrees to provide and pay for the fuel consumed and to bear disbursements which arise from the trading of the vessel.
> *Whistler International Ltd v. Kawasaki Kisen Kaisha Ltd (The Hill Harmony)* [2001] 1 App. Cas. 638, 652 (H.L.).

Demise or Bareboat Charters. Like a time charter, a demise charter is a contract for the use of a ship for a period of time. Unlike a time charterer, a demise charterer takes over possession of the ship in the legal sense. It becomes owner of the ship *pro hac vice*, the ship's disponent owner, rather than merely a hirer of the services of ship and crew. Because a demise charterer hires the ship without the services of master and crew, demise charters are also known as bareboat charters. Demise charter parties are not as commonly found as they were in the nineteenth century. In modern shipping practice, they are usually used as a vehicle for ship financing arrangements that split ownership of the ship as capital asset from entitlement to the stream of income it generates, for the purposes of avoiding tax.

> All charterers of ships, by virtue of the charter party, have some control over the ship. Such control may relate only to a particular voyage; it may operate during a specified period. If the charter party is by way of demise, property in the ship temporarily passes to the charterer - for the duration of the charter. If possession, as well as some degree of control, passes to the charterer, then the property passes to the charterer and he is *pro tempore* the owner. But no property in the ship passes if possession is not given to the charterer by virtue of the terms of the charter. If the control of the master and crew in the navigation of the ship passes to the charterer he has possession. If, on the other hand, he acquires only a right to the use of the ship - a right to use her carrying capacity...there is no demise, but only a contract for services - *locatio operis vehendarum mercium. Australasian United Steam Navigation Co. Ltd v. Shipping Control Board*, 71 C.L.R. 508, 521 (High Ct. Austl. 1945).

Although only a demise charterer can properly be called "disponent owner", that term is often used loosely to describe anyone who charters a ship to another. Thus, for example, a time charterer who sub-charters the ship to a voyage sub-charterer may be described as the "disponent owner", even though that is not strictly accurate to describe its rights over the ship.

Slot Charters. Slot charters are a relatively recent device for sharing the carrying capacity of a ship. They are commonly made between ocean carriers who form vessel-sharing alliances despite the fact that they are ostensibly competitors.

> In such arrangements, two or more operators, usually of similarly sized vessels in a particular geographic trade, will agree to share space on one another's vessels. The attraction of such arrangements is evident. Space is utilized more efficiently and operating costs are reduced while service is expanded. Usually, space on all vessels in an alliance is shared among carriers in proportion to space contributed by each operator to the alliance. Each operator continues its own marketing efforts, booking cargo under its name. Each operator services its own customers, furnishing stuffing and lashing, and, depending on the terms of the arrangement, loading and discharging its own containers.
>
> Vessel-sharing arrangements are implemented by charter parties known as slot charters, so named because space on container vessels is usually chartered by "slot," each slot representing the space required to accommodate one TEU [twenty-foot equivalent unit]. While members of an alliance may be parties to an overall operating agreement, the slot charter is the contract which governs the relationship on each voyage between only the Owner (i.e., the alliance member whose tonnage is performing the voyage) and the Slot Charterer (i.e., the alliance member who is chartering space from the Owner).
>
> Mary T. Reilly, *Identity of the Carrier: Issues Under Slot Charters*, 25 TUL. MAR. L.J. 505, 506 (2001).

---

2. Introductory Note

In Chapter 4, you observed how legal disputes arising from loss and damage to goods which occur during water transport are resolved by reference to the specific terms of the bill of lading and by the application of COGSA. In Chapter 5 you will see how legal relations between a shipowner and a charterer usually are controlled by the terms of the charter party. Because charter parties *per se* are excluded from the terms of COGSA, the principle of "freedom of contract" is generally applied by the courts. Under this principle, the parties are free to strike their bargain in any terms mutually agreeable to them. This permits them to incorporate the terms of COGSA in the charter party if they choose. When the parties incorporate COGSA, the various provisions of COGSA become terms of the charter party contract. In these situations, the parties may modify or even exclude some provisions of COGSA. These modifications are permissible because the parties are not bound by COGSA in the first place.

Nevertheless, there may be circumstances in which COGSA is applicable to a transaction as a matter of law, notwithstanding the fact that the carrying vessel in under charter. These situations invariably involve the assertion of rights by a third party. Thus, if Owner charters its vessel for 10 years to "X" Shipping Company (Charterer) and "X" Shipping agrees to carry the goods of "Y" Products Company (Shipper) on the vessel to a designated port, any bill of lading which is issued to "Y" or its consignee is subject to the provisions of COGSA. In this situation, under

COGSA either the charterer or the shipowner or both of them may be the COGSA carrier depending on the circumstances. Those circumstances include on whose form (letterhead) the bill of lading was issued, who is designated as the carrier in the bill, who signed the bill, on whose behalf was the form signed, etc. The legal relations between the shipowner and charterer are controlled by the charter party. The legal relations between the shipper or its consignee and the carrier, owner and/or charterer are controlled by the bill of lading and COGSA. Likewise where a shipper has entered into a voyage charter party with a shipowner to have its goods carried to a designated port, the legal relations between the owner and the charterer are governed by the charter party. Even if a bill of lading is also issued, it is regarded as a mere receipt as between those parties. But if that bill of lading is transferred to a third party such as a consignee, then the legal relations between the carrier, owner or charterer, and the third party are controlled by the terms of the bill of lading and COGSA. The cases in this Chapter raise legal disputes mostly between vessel owners and charterers, consequently the terms of the charter party itself are usually controlling.

B. Demise Charters

1. *Introductory Note*

In *United States v. Shea,* 152 U.S. 178, 189-90, 14 S. Ct. 519, 522, 38 L. Ed. 403 (1894), the Supreme Court said:

> No technical words are necessary to create a demise. It is enough that the language used shows an intent to transfer the possession, command, and control... [T]he conduct of the parties in the execution of the contract removes all obscurity as to its scope and meaning. As the findings show, the vessel, the James Bowen, was furnished by petitioner, and was accepted and used by the defendants. During the time of its use it was under the exclusive management and control of the defendants. The very condition resulted which is the purpose and effect of a demise—the transfer of the exclusive possession, management, and control. The vessel was not, when injured, returned to the petitioner, but when the repairs were finished, "resumed work." It is insisted by the defendants that there was no demise because, as claimed, the petitioner did not contract to furnish one vessel for any length of time, and could, if he wished, change vessels. It is doubtful whether that is a correct interpretation of the instrument, and whether it was in the power of the petitioner, after a vessel had been tendered and accepted by the government, to substitute another therefor. But even if it were so, the substituted vessel would pass into the exclusive possession of the government, the same as the vessel for which it was substituted.

DANT & RUSSELL, INC. v. DILLINGHAM TUG & BARGE CORP.

877 F.2d 1404, 1989 AMC 1896 (9th Cir. 1989)

Before Skopil, Hall and O'Scannlain, Circuit Judges

Per Curiam:

We are presented with the maritime law question of whether a vessel owner is liable to a cargo owner for damages in the absence of privity. We reverse the district court's finding that the vessel owner was negligent and its further finding that the vessel owner breached a warranty of seaworthiness. As a result, the district court's determination of damages owed by Pacific to

Fireman's Fund cannot stand. We remand to the district court the issue of the barge's in rem liability to Dant & Russell.

Facts

In December 1981, appellant Pacific Hawaiian ("Pacific"), owner of the Barge NORTON SOUND, demise chartered the barge to Hvide Marine Transport, Inc. ("Hvide"). As demise charterer, Hvide assumed possession, control, and "temporary ownership" of the barge. Hvide then voyage chartered the barge to Terminal Steamship Co. ("Terminal"), a wholly-owned subsidiary of appellee Dant & Russell ("D & R"), to carry D & R's lumber from Astoria, Oregon to Florida. As voyage charterer, Terminal obtained the use of the barge for carriage, but responsibility and control remained with Hvide.

D & R insured the lumber with appellee Fireman's Fund Insurance Co. ("Fireman's Fund"). By endorsement, the policy named Hvide as an additional assured with waiver of subrogation. Hvide also added an endorsement to its own Protection and Indemnity ("P & I") policy to extend coverage to the barge during the voyage.

In accord with the terms of the demise charter which called for various inspections and surveys, the NORTON SOUND was dry-docked at Dillingham Ship Repair ("DSR") on Swan Island in Portland, Oregon, for repairs necessary to meet inspection standards. Pacific retained Hughes to consult with and assist Bartholomew, Hvide's representative at DSR. Bartholomew acted as port engineer and was authorized by Hvide to direct the repairs.

Both Hughes and Bartholomew knew that on previous voyages, a portable pump had been needed to suction water out of the cargo hold of the barge, and that major parts of the barge's bilge and ballast system did not work.

DSR tested the system, recommended substantial repairs, and gave Bartholomew and Hughes an estimate for the work. Bartholomew and Hughes then agreed, in a letter signed by Tennant, a Pacific vice-president, and by Santos, a vice- president of Hvide, to defer repairs until after the voyage.

The tug crew loaded and stowed the cargo of lumber under Hughes' instruction. Bartholomew then helped to ballast the barge, and the barge left Astoria. During the voyage, ballast water leaked through the ballast lines and into void tanks in the cargo hold. This caused the barge to list so that water washed over the open afterdeck and entered the deckhouse.

When the cargo was unloaded in Florida, ten to fifteen percent of the lumber was stained by water, oil, rust, and debris. Fireman's Fund paid D & R $169,981.23 under the policy. D & R absorbed the $25,000 deductible under the policy.

Litigation ensued between Hvide and D & R: Hvide sought to recover its voyage charter hire and D & R sought to recover for the cargo damage. That litigation ended with a settlement agreement under which, inter alia, the claims of each were waived and released.

D & R and Fireman's Fund then filed this action against Pacific and the barge. Upon motion, the trial court dismissed the barge in rem.

At trial, Pacific stipulated that the barge was unseaworthy when she left Portland, but contended as barge owner, it had exercised due diligence to make the barge seaworthy and that it did not know, or should it have known as a matter of law, of the unseaworthiness.

The district court entered summary judgment against Pacific for breach of warranty of seaworthiness. After trial on the issues of negligence and damages, the district court also found Pacific negligent and assessed damages. It held that Pacific was not relieved of liability by virtue of various indemnity and hold harmless agreements in the charters and the insurance policies. Pacific now appeals the district court's findings; D & R cross-appeals the dismissal of the barge and the district court's calculation of damages.

The parties agree there is no dispute of material fact. This court, therefore, reviews de novo the district court's application of law to facts. *Darring v. Kincheloe*, 783 F.2d 874, 876 (9th Cir.1986).

Discussion

I

The district court found that Hughes and Tennant were negligent for failing to have the bilge and ballast system repaired before the voyage when they knew or should have known the barge was unseaworthy. Since they were acting as agents of Pacific, their actions were imputed to Pacific. *W.R. Grace & Co. v. Western U.S. Indus., Inc.*, 608 F.2d 1214, 1218 (9th Cir.1979), *cert. denied*, 446 U.S. 953, 100 S.Ct. 2920, 64 L.Ed.2d 810 (1980).

Pacific contests the finding of liability, saying that it owed no duty to D & R. It argues that scant precedent exists for holding a vessel owner liable to a cargo owner for negligent conduct predating a chain of charters.

Generally, during a demise charter, the vessel owner surrenders possession and control of the vessel to the charterer, who succeeds to most of the owner's rights and obligations and becomes the owner pro hac vice, i.e., for the term of the charter. *Reed v. S.S. YAKA*, 373 U.S. 410, 412-13, 83 S.Ct. 1349, 1351-52, 10 L.Ed.2d 448 (1963). Once the demise charter is perfected, the owner is relieved of its obligations for the term of the charter; liability for the contracts and torts of the master, crew and vessel falls upon the charterer and upon the vessel in rem. *Id.*; *Agrico Chem. Co. v. M/V BEN W. MARTIN*, 664 F.2d 85, 91 (5th Cir.1981). Thus, Hvide, the demise charterer, bears the owner's responsibility for events aboard the NORTON SOUND during the charter term. In short, Hvide decided to gamble that the barge would safely transport the lumber, and it lost. Pacific had no duty to pay the cost of Hvide's wager.

Therefore, the finding of negligence against Pacific is reversed.

II

The district court also found that Pacific had violated the warranty of seaworthiness. Pacific, however, claims waiver and points out that the warranty of seaworthiness is waived "where full inspection was made by those seeking to charter the vessels ... and the alleged defects or weaknesses were either patent or were especially called to such charterers' attention by the vessel owners." *Thomas Jordan, Inc. v. Mayronne Drilling Mud, Chem. & Eng'g Serv.*, 214 F.2d 410, 413 (5th Cir.1954) (quoting *Dempsey v. Downing*, 11 F.2d 15, 17 (4th Cir.1926)).

Here, Hvide, the demise charterer, supervised the inspection and took an active part in the repairs. Hvide had full knowledge of the vessel's unseaworthiness and assumed all risks. In similar cases, owners have been absolved of liability. *See id.*; *Nat G. Harrison Overseas Corp. v.*

American Tug Titan, 516 F.2d 89, 96 (5th Cir.) (owner is not responsible for conditions which demise charter could have ascertained by reasonable inspection), *modified on other grounds*, 520 F.2d 1104 (5th Cir.1975). Hvide's conduct constitutes waiver of any warranty claims against Pacific.

Pacific cannot be held liable under a warranty theory for a second reason. The owner and the voyage charterer are not in privity and the owner does not owe a duty to the voyage charterer. *Martin v. Walk, Haydel & Assocs., Inc.*, 742 F.2d 246, 249 (5th Cir.1984) (since no demise charter, owner was held liable for unseaworthiness); *Kerr-McGee Corp. v. Law*, 479 F.2d 61, 63 (4th Cir.1973) (demise charterer liable for seaworthiness); *Uni-Petrol Gesellschaft Fur Mineraloel Produkte M.B.H. v. M/T Lotus Maru*, 615 F.Supp. 78, 81 (S.D.N.Y.1985). "'An owner who has demised his ship is not indeed liable to anyone but the demisee under his warranty of seaworthiness for any loss or injury suffered during the demise. Such liabilities sound in contract and he has not made any contract with anyone else.'" *M/T/ Lotus Maru*, 615 F.Supp. at 81 (quoting *Cannella v. Lykes Bros. S.S. Co.*, 174 F.2d 794, 796 (2d Cir.), *cert. denied*, 338 U.S. 859, 70 S.Ct. 102, 94 L.Ed. 526 (1949)).

The finding that Pacific was liable for breach of warranty must, therefore, also be reversed.

III

In their cross-appeal, D & R and Fireman's Fund argue that the district court improperly dismissed the NORTON SOUND from this action.

The original complaint was filed against the barge in rem as well as against Pacific in personam. Such a claim attempts to recover from Pacific's property if D & R cannot recover from Pacific personally. D & R's and Fireman's Fund's claim relies on the venerable dictum of *The Barnstable*, 181 U.S. 464, 467, 21 S.Ct. 684, 685, 45 L.Ed. 954 (1901), which held that "the law in this country is well settled, that the ship itself is to be treated in some sense as a principal, and as personally liable for the negligence of anyone who is lawfully in possession of her, whether as owner or charterer." *See* GILMORE & BLACK, THE LAW OF ADMIRALTY, 600 (2d ed. 1975).

By order, the district court held that a waiver of subrogation by Fireman's Fund to D & R also applied to the barge. The waiver clause provided that:

> no right of subrogation ... shall lie against any craft belonging in part or on [sic] whole to the Assured or a subsidiary and/or affiliated company of the Assured. This clause, however, does not extend to exclude recoveries that may be had under Protection and Indemnity Insurance.

An endorsement to the policy named Hvide as an additional assured, and waived Fireman's Fund's rights of subrogation against Hvide.

The district court reasoned that the barge was a "craft belonging" to Hvide under D & R's policy because a demise charterer is generally treated as the owner of the chartered vessel pro hac vice. *See, e.g., Marr Enters. v. Lewis Refrig. Co.*, 556 F.2d 951, 957-58 (9th Cir.1977). It therefore dismissed the barge as a defendant because D & R's policy with Fireman's Fund excluded rights of subrogation against vessels "belonging ... to the Assured."

However, the district court failed to note that this release did not operate against D & R, but only against Fireman's Fund. Therefore, with regard to the $25,000 deductible on the insurance policy, this clause is inoperative and does not prevent D & R's cross claim.

Fireman's Fund further argues that the exclusion in the policy with regard to protection and indemnity insurance should preclude the dismissal of the barge in rem. We are not persuaded that the exclusion precludes dismissal of the barge. At most, it allows Fireman's Fund to make a claim in personam against Hvide only if Hvide has protection and indemnity insurance. It does not give Fireman's Fund the right to make a claim against the barge in rem.

Fireman's Fund makes the further argument that even if the waiver of subrogation might have protected the NORTON SOUND, Hvide's non-disclosure of the unseaworthiness of the barge was a breach of good faith. Such a breach makes Hvide's coverage under the policy voidable. However, Hvide's breach of good faith should not be imputed to the barge which became a third party beneficiary by virtue of the waiver of subrogation. See *Everglades Marina, Inc. v. American Eastern Dev. Corp.*, 374 So.2d 517 (Fla.1979). Therefore, Fireman's Fund's claims against the NORTON SOUND, in rem, were properly dismissed.

Finally, D & R's claim for $25,000 may also be untenable. As Pacific notes, paragraph 21 of the voyage charter between Hvide and D & R provides:

> All privileges, rights, exemptions and defenses provided for the benefit of Owner herein ["Owner" being defined in this policy as Hvide] shall be equally available to and for the benefit of every vessel used in the transportation, including the named tug and any substitute tug, as well as the owners, operators, officers and crews thereof.

Thus, Pacific can claim any defenses for the barge that Hvide could claim for itself. If the settlement agreement in Florida between Hvide and D & R released Hvide from all liability, it will also have released the barge. We remand this issue to the district court to determine if D & R is barred from asserting any cause of action against Hvide because of the settlement. If so, this is fatal to D & R's claim against the barge.

Conclusion

Since we have found that Pacific neither was negligent nor breached a warranty of the barge's seaworthiness, we reverse the district court's findings on those issues and thereby reverse its finding on damages. We affirm the district court's dismissal of the barge in rem with regard to Fireman's Fund, but not with regard to D & R. We remand the issue of the barge's in rem liability to D & R to the district court.

AFFIRMED in part, REVERSED in part, and REMANDED.

The dissenting opinion of Judge Hall is omitted [eds.]

Notes

1. When a vessel has been demise chartered, the master and crew may remain on the vessel and operate the vessel for the charterer. Under the circumstances the master and crew are subject to the orders of the charterer and are its

employees. In some demise charters the owner turns over to the charterer its vessel without master and crew. These charters are frequently referred to as "bareboat" charters.

2. Can the owner of vessel which has been demise chartered be liable to a third party with whom it is not in privity for damages caused by the unseaworthiness of the vessel or its negligent operation? Compare; *American Commercial Lines, Inc. v. Valley Line Co.*, 529 F.2d 921, 1977 AMC 2265 (8th Cir. 1976) with *Dant & Russell, Inc. v. Dillingham Tug & Barge Corp.*, 895 F.2d 507, 1990 AMC 1372 (9th Cir. 1989). See also *Siderius v. M/V Amilla*, 880 F.2d 662, 665, 1989 AMC 2533 (2d Cir. 1989), where the U.S. Court of Appeals for the Second Circuit said:

> [W]e agree with the district court's determination that Siderius [the cargo owner] may recover directly from Amilla [the shipowner] given that the ship was unseaworthy. We have long held that "when the charterer of a ship is liable to a cargo owner", and that liability results because the vessel owner has violated its warranty of seaworthiness, the "cargo owner" may hold the shipowner on his warranty to the charterer". *New York Cent. R.R. v. New York, N.H. & H.R.R.*, 275 F.2d 865, 866 (2d Cir. 1960).

3. The demise, in practical effect and in important legal consequence, shifts the possession and control of the vessel from one person to another, just as the shoreside lease of real property shifts many of the incidents of ownership from lessor to lessee." Gilmore & Black, *supra*, Chapter IV, page 215. Then, the authors proceed to discuss typical characteristics of a demise or bareboat charterer. "The test is one of 'control', if the owner retains control over the vessel, merely carrying the goods furnished or designated by the charter, the charter is not a demisee." (Sec. 4-21). Put another way, "to create a demise the owner of the vessel must completely and exclusively relinquish 'possession, command and navigation' thereof to the demise" *Guzman v. Pichirilo*, 369 U.S. 698, 699 82 S. Ct. 1095, 1096, 8 L. Ed. 2d 205 (1962), and further "it is therefore tantamount to, though just short of, an outright transfer of ownership." 369 U.S. at 700, 82 S. Ct. at 1096. That case, moreover, states that "courts are reluctant to find a demise when the dealings between the parties are consistent with a lesser relationship." *See Reed v. United States*, 78 U.S. (11 Wall.) 591, 601, 20 L. Ed. 220 (1871). The words "demise" or "bareboat" are not used in the charter agreement in controversy, although no technical words are absolutely necessary to create a demise.

* * *

> This Court is mindful that circumstances pertaining to a barge without an independent power source may differ from that of a vessel with its own means of propulsion. Some courts have indicated that charter of a barge without power is, in fact, a demise. *See R. Lenahan*, 48 F.2d 110 (2nd Cir., 1931); *Ira S. Bushey & Sons v. Hedger & Co.*, 40 F.2d 417 (2nd Cir., 1930); *The Nat E. Sutton*, 42 F.2d 229 (E.D.N.Y., 1930); *Moran Towing v. New York*, 36 F.2d 417 (S.D.N.Y. 1929); *Dailey v. Carroll*, 248 F. 466 (2nd Cir. 1917); *The Daniel Burns*, 52 F. 159 (S.D.N.Y., 1892). These cases and their holdings are noted in *The Doyle*, 105 F.2d 113, 114 (3rd Cir., 1939), but in the latter case which held a barge charterer to become the "owner pro hac vice", it was important that the charterer was a towing company with the right of and in the exercise of navigation of the barge, which caused damage to its cargo. (Its liability was held, however, to be less than the owners). *R.D. Wood Co. v. Phoenix Steel Corp.*, 211 F. Supp. 924, 927 (E.D. Pa., 1962) also comments on the latter aspect of Doyle, observing that "¼the towing company had clearly taken over *complete control of the vessel* and was, therefore, correctly treated as the owner." It was also observed, moreover, that there was "some indication that peculiar conditions at New York" required the second circuit rule pertaining to barge charters. It is concluded that whether or not the charter in controversy here is or is not a demise depends upon the facts of the case in light of effective control of the vessel and the charter provisions. *Leary v. United States*, 14 Wall. 607, 610, 20 L. Ed. 756 (1972). Where the charterer receives, in effect, only the *service* of a vessel (the word "use" is employed in *Leary*) without entire possession and control, it is less than a demise. *United States v. Shea*, 152 U.S. 178, 188, 14 S. Ct. 518, 38 L. Ed. 403 (1894).

* * *

Complaint of Cook Transp. System, Inc., 431 F. Supp 437, 443-44 (W.D. Tenn. 1976).

4. The liability of a charterer for damage to or loss of cargo is discussed in the Introductory Note to *Who is the COGSA Carrier?* in Chapter 4, section G.

5. Of course, a time charterer is liable to third persons for his own faults. However, in *Hasbro Industries, Inc. v. M/S St. Constantine*, 705 F.2d 339, 1983 AMC 1841 (9th Cir. 1983), the court found that charterers did not have a duty to exercise due diligence to make the ship seaworthy. In a similar vein, in *Haluapo v. Akashi Kaiun, K.K.*, 748 F.2d 1363, 1365, 1985 AMC 1107 (9th Cir. 1984), the court refused to hold a time charterer liable for injuries sustained by a longshoreman while unloading the vessel. The court distinguished other cases where liability had been extended either because the time charterer had hired a foreign stevedore and supervised its work and the charterer had actual control of the vessel. In the case at bar, the time charterer had "no involvement of the operation of the vessel or the loading of the cargo other than providing pilotage and tug boat service and arranging for the berthing of the vessel. The time charterer had neither knowledge of the defects on board the ship nor the ability to control the actions of the crew."

C. Relationship between charters and bills of lading

Understanding liability issues in charter party situations requires one to distinguish between those situations where the only parties involved in the transaction and ensuing dispute are the shipowner and the charterer from those where a third party, such as a shipper or consignee, is involved. In the two-party situation (involving only shipowner and charterer) legal relations between them are controlled by their contract—the charter party. COGSA is not applicable *ex proprio vigore*. The parties, nevertheless, may agree that COGSA or certain parts of COGSA shall apply to their transaction by incorporating the terms of COGSA into their charter party. This may be done by expressly including the text of COGSA in the charter party or by incorporating it by reference. In contrast, where a claim is made by a third-party shipper or consignee to whom a bill of lading has been transferred, COGSA usually will apply of its own force, regardless of whether or not it is incorporated by the charter party.

Charter party transactions do not in themselves fall within the ambit of COGSA. 46 app. U.S.C.A. § 1305; *Vanol, USA, Inc. v. M/T Coronado*, 663 F. Supp. 79, 1988 AMC 560 (S.D.N.Y. 1987). Where a shipowner enters into a demise or time charter with a charterer, the relationship is controlled by the terms of the charter party. Demise and time charters are not contracts of carriage but merely arrangements for the use of the carrying space on a vessel. In contrast to a contract of carriage, in a demise or time charter, the shipowner does not undertake to carry anyone's goods from one port to another; there is no third party such as a shipper, and, as no bill of lading or similar document is issued in these transactions, COGSA is not applicable.

Where a demise charterer uses the vessel to engage in the transportation business and enters into contracts of carriage with shippers, the vessel is not under the control of the shipowner. The charterer may issue bills of lading to a shipper and these will control the relationship between charterer-as-carrier and the shipper. Thus, COGSA may apply to cargo disputes between the charterer-carrier and shipper. However, because the shipowner has no contractual relationship with the shipper or its consignee, and has no control over the use of the vessel, the shipowner is not liable for acts of the charterer or its crew which result in loss of or damage to cargo.

The time charter party situation may be more complicated than explained above. Where a time charterer who enters into a contract of carriage with a shipper and issues to the shipper its own bill of lading signed by the charterer or its agent, the *charterer* is a COGSA carrier and the transaction is subject to COGSA. Under the facts as stated, however, the *shipowner* is not a COGSA carrier and is not personally liable for loss or damage to cargo. Neither it nor anyone acting on its behalf has issued a bill of lading. There is no contractual link between the shipowner and the shipper or its consignee.

In contrast to a demise charterer, however, a shipowner who time charters its vessel, has not given up control of its vessel. Although a demise charterer is regarded in law as owner *pro hac vice*, this is not so in the case of a time charterer. In a time charter, the shipowner and the charterer share responsibility for the operations of the vessel. In this respect, a charter party may contain a provision which purports to designate the master of the vessel as the agent of the charterer, at least with respect to cargo operations. This provision is often accompanied by another provision which obligates the master to sign bills of lading when requested by the charterer or which specifically authorizes the charterer or the charterer's agent to sign "for the master."

These provisions which are intended to insulate the shipowner from liability for cargo claims have not been given that effect by the courts. Thus, where a bill of lading obligates the master to sign bills of lading or authorizes the charterer or its agent to sign "for the master," the courts have generally held, in the absence of special circumstances, that the master still acts on behalf of the shipowner. *Pacific Emp. Ins. Co. v. M/V Gloria*, 767 F.2d 229 (5th Cir. 1985); *Insituto Cubano De Est. Del Azucar v. T/V Golden West*, 246 F.2d 802 (2d Cir.), *cert. denied*, 355 U.S. 884, 78 S. Ct. 152, 2 L. Ed. 2d 114 (1957). In such situations, the master is considered to be the shipowner's agent. Thus, if a shipowner has given its master authority to sign bills of lading at the request of the charterer and the master has, in fact, signed the bill of lading, the owner may be held liable *in personam* for damage or loss to cargo. Likewise, if a shipowner has given the charterer or charterer's agent authority to sign "for the master," the owner may be held liable. In these situations the bill of lading that has been signed by person authorized by the shipowner to do so provides a contractual link between the shipowner and the shipper and its consignee.

A voyage charter party is different from the demise and time charters discussed above in that it is, in reality, a contract of carriage. In some contracts of carriage, a shipper contracts with a carrier for the carrier to transport the shippers goods from one place to another. Ordinarily, the selection of the carrying vessel, ports of destination, etc., are at the discretion of the carrier. By contrast, in a voyage charter party, the charterer contracts with the shipowner for space on board a vessel for the purpose of transporting a particular cargo on a particular voyage. The charter party may specify a named vessel and/or vessel characteristics. It may give the charterer the right to select from a range of loading and discharge ports, etc. In this respect, a voyage charter may give the charterer greater flexibility and control. It may also be more economically advantageous because a charterer may have greater negotiating strength than an ordinary shipper.

Notwithstanding the differences between voyage charters on the one hand and demise and time charters on the other, there is an important similarity among them: in two party situations, disputes between the shipowner and the voyage charterer will be resolved by the terms of their contract—the voyage charter party. COGSA specifically states that it is not applicable in such situations. 46 app. U.S.C.A. § 1305. Thus, in case of loss or of damage to cargo, the shipper-charterer's rights will be determined under the charter party. Of course, the parties may have elected to incorporate the terms of COGSA, but then COGSA is merely another provision of their contract. Even where shipowner has given to the shipper-charterer a document called a bill of lading, the rights of the shipper-charterer are determined under the charter party. The charter party is the contract of carriage—not the bill of lading. The bill of lading will be regarded as being merely a receipt which shows that the shipowner-carrier received the goods.

Suppose the following has occurred. Shipowner (Carrier) and Charterer (Shipper) have entered into a voyage charter party and Carrier has given Shipper a negotiable bill of lading. Shipper has sold the goods to Buyer and has transferred the bill of lading to Buyer. The goods arrived in damaged condition. What remedies does Buyer have? Buyer has no rights under the charter party because it is not a party to it. Buyer, however, is in possession of a bill of lading issued by Carrier which obligates Carrier to deliver the goods to the person in possession of the bill of lading. COGSA states it is applicable "to any bill of lading ... issued under or pursuant to a charter party from the moment at which such bill of lading ... regulates the relations between a carrier and a holder of the same." 46 app. U.S.C.A. § 1301(b). Buyer is entitled to invoke the provisions of COGSA against Carrier, which in this case is the shipowner. The charter party is irrelevant to the legal status of Buyer. Buyer would not have a COGSA action against Shipper (Charterer) because it is not a COGSA carrier. Owner has Charterer's (Shipper's) goods on its vessel, therefore, it is the carrier. Buyer, however, may have a breach of contract action against the seller, who in this situation is also the shipper-charterer, depending on which party to the contract of sale, seller or buyer, had the risk of loss.

Finally, under the law of the United States, vessels are "personified" and may be liable in an action *in rem*. Therefore, where goods are loaded aboard a vessel, this is considered a ratification of the contract of carriage by the vessel, and the vessel, itself, may be liable *in rem* if cargo is damaged or lost.

D. Contract Formalities

Note

In *E.A.S.T., Inc. of Stamford, Conn. v. M/V Alaia*, 673 F.Supp. 796, 799, 1988 AMC 1396 (E.D. La. 1987) *aff'd* 876 F.2d 1168, 1989 AMC 2024 (5th Cir. 1989), the court observed that: "A charter comes into existence when the parties have a meeting of the minds on the *essential terms* of the charter." (emphasis added). Support for this view can be found in *Great Circle Lines, Ltd. v. Matheson & Co.*, 681 F.2d 121, 1982 AMC 2321 (2d Cir. 1982). There the parties had agreed upon the principal terms "subject details NYP 46," the latter abbreviation being a reference the 1946 New York Produce Exchange time charter form. The court stated:

> Certain long-standing customs of the shipping industry are crucial factors to be considered when deciding whether there has been a meeting of the minds on a maritime contract.

* * *

The shipping industry is a fast moving and ever changing business, where dealings between the parties called "trade" are usually conducted with a sense of urgency under severe time constraints. To bring owners and charterers together, it is the custom of the industry to deal through brokers who receive and send telex traffic all over the world.

Charter parties are formed in two stages. First, significant "main" terms are negotiated through brokers. These terms usually include the name of the charterer, name of owner, ship and its characteristics, time and place of delivery, duration of charter, place of redelivery, hire rate, printed form upon which the contract is based, and any other term that a party deems important. These are considered the "bare-bones" of the contract. The "main" terms when agreed upon are entitled a "fixture." Second, after a "fixture" has been reached, the parties continue to negotiate "details" amending the form contract specified in the "fixture." These minor or side issues "flesh-out" the original agreement or fixture. The "details" include a wide variety of matters, for example: fuel used, speed of vessel, condition of ship's holds, exact time of ship's delivery to charterer, brokerage, breakdown, bunkering, option to extend charter, cargo capacity, demurrage and whatever else is deemed by the parties to be of minor importance. The details are not meaningful to the trade in the same way that the main terms of the fixture are, inasmuch as the fixture affects the trade directly and determines whether it will be a successful piece of business. Where no amendment of details is agreed upon, however, the terms of the printed form govern.

A quite different conclusion was reached in *The "Junior K"* [1988] 2 Lloyd's Rep. 583. There the court reasoned:

In the context of an issue between the parties as to whether a binding charter-party was concluded, this case raises directly the question of the meaning and effect of a stipulation in telex exchanges that there is a fixture "subject to details."*

* * *

[I]n negotiations parties are free to stipulate that no binding contract shall come into existence, despite agreement on all essentials, until agreement is reached on yet unmentioned and unconsidered detailed provisions. And the law should respect such a stipulation in commercial negotiations. That seems to me to be exactly what happened in this case. The Gencon charter-party is, of course, a detailed and well-known standard form. It is plain that the parties had in mind a contract on the Gencon form but that they had not yet considered the details of it. By the expression, "Subject to details of the Gencon charterparty" the owners made clear that they did not wish to commit themselves contractually until negotiations had taken place about the details of the charter-party. Such discussions might have covered a number of clauses. It does not follow that the owners were willing to accept all

---

* The court's opinion reveals that various telexes were exchanged between the broker for the respective parties. The last telex stated:

Junior K
Confirm telcons here recap fixture *sub details.*
Vessel as described before as per our earlier recap (tc) 2 Oct acct Beogradska Plovidba Beograd
Min 6000 tons chopt up to full cargo of vessels capacity agprods stowed 55 cuft pmt
Laycan Spot/7 Oct (vsl could ETA Mersin tomo pm)
1 sb Mersin aaaa/1 sb Bombay aaaa
650 tons per wwd shexeiu free in
Disch cop free out
Dem USD 2000 per hdwts loadport
Frt USD 180,000 lsum FIO basis 6000 tons of cargo. Any additional cargo loaded to be settled at the rate of USD 25 pmt FIO.
90 pct freight within 3 banking days of issuing and releasing bsl balance after right and true delivery latest within 7 days completion discharge.
Freight deemed earned on shipment discountless ship and or cargo lost or not lost
Taxes/dues and or fees on freight and vessel owners account
Taxes/dues and or fees on cargo including primage if any max 5 pct charterers account
For primage/freight tax calculations, authorities to be shown lumpsum freight as USD 120,000
Any overage premia chts account BS/l dated 30 Sept will be issued and delivered chasbe
3.75 pct
SUB DETS GENCON CP *(Eds.).*

the detailed provisions of the standard form document. After all, it is a common occurrence for some of the detailed provisions of the Gencon form to be amended during the process of negotiation. In any event, the Gencon standard form contains within it alternative provisions which require a positive selection of the desired alternative.

* * *

My conclusion is, therefore, that no contract was concluded in this case.

E. Time Charters

1. Failure of the Shipowner or Vessel to Comply with the Terms of the Charter Party: Misrepresentations, Conditions, Warranties, Etc.

Introductory Note

What options, if any, does a charterer have when the statements made by the shipowner in a charter party do not comport with the true facts? For example, a charter party may state that the vessel will be delivered by a certain date and owner fails to do so. A vessel may be described as having a carrying capacity of so many tons, for example, and inspection by charterer's agent reveals that it has less than that capacity. Similarly, the charter party may state that the vessel can sail at certain speeds under normal conditions and during the voyage it is unable to maintain that speed. Finally suppose the vessel is unseaworthy when it is presented to charterer for acceptance or develops an unseaworthy condition during he voyage. In each of these situations, does charterer have the right to rescind, *i.e.*, cancel the charter party contract? Does charterer have the right to waive recission and recover damages for any losses it may have incurred as a result of the discrepancy? Are there situations where a charterer can both rescind and recover damages?"

In order for a discrepancy to create any rights in a charterer, it must be something more than *de minimis*. Unless an owner has absolutely guaranteed a specific fact, any negligible divergence from compliance will be disregarded by the courts. *Margaronis Navigation v. Peabody*, [1964] 2 Lloyd's Rep. 153. M. Wilford, T. Coglin, J. Kimball, Time Charters 86 (Lloyd's of London Press, 4th ed. 1995). Even where the discrepancy is substantial, the charterer's remedies may depend on whether the specific term is classified as a "condition" which would give rise to a right to rescind, or a "warranty" which creates a right to damages, or as "intermediate" or "inominate" terms where the right to either rescind or to recover damages depends on the circumstances of each cases. M. Wilford, T. Coglin, J. Kimball, Time Charters 88-96 (Lloyd's of London Press, 4th ed. 1995).

---

a. Size and Speed

GIANNELIS v. THE ATLANTA

82 F. Supp. 218, 1948 AMC 1769 (S.D. Ga. 1948)

* * *

The focal point of conflict in the litigation centers about the libel of Caravan Shipping Corporation as charterer of the "Atlanta" and Corinthian's cross-libel as owner. An amendment filed by Caravan alleges that the balance due it for cash advances, dry-docking costs, etc., is

$8,585.72. During the course of the trial the elimination of certain items reduced this amount to $7696.03.

Corinthian Steamship Company claims, on the other hand, that, rather than being indebted to Caravan, the charterer is indebted to it in the amount of $16,884.15. This figure represents the charter hire from January 10, to March 31, 1948, when the ship was libelled, a total of $25,650, against which admitted credits to the charterer by way of cash advances and sums paid on account of charter hire are conceded to the extent of $9033.63, leaving a balance of $16,884.15 allegedly due Corinthian.

In this dispute two questions imperiously demand solution. They are:

(1) Was there a breach of the warranties (or representations) made in the time charter respecting the capacity of the ship and as to her approximate speed and fuel consumption?

(2) (The second question relating to agency is omitted. Eds.)

* * *

Breach of Warranties

(1) Capacity of Ship

The "Atlanta" was chartered for the purpose of moving steel pipe out of Tampico where Caravan had more than 2,000 tons which it desired to transport to Venezuela. Capacity of the vessel was important to the charterer. The charter provided: "Owners guarantee vessel to carry 550 gross tons of 4 to 12 inch mixed standard steel or iron pipe in lengths not exceeding 18 feet." Proctor for Corinthian has suggested that this was a most unusual provision. Nasios, the owner's representative, testified that he was not acquainted with the fact that it had been inserted in the charter, in fact had objected to its inclusion in the first instance. (Tr. of Evidence, p. 118.) However, we are not concerned with whether or not Georgaros made a bad bargain for his principal. The time charter which he signed for Corinthian is binding on the owner in all its terms and conditions, however onerous. It guaranteed a definite capacity. This provision constituted an express warranty. *Metropolitan Coal Co. v. Howard*, 2 Cir., 155 F.2d 780(4). A breach thereof permits the charterer to sue for damages. *Wood v. Sewall's Adm'rs, D.C.*, 128 F. 141, affirmed 3 Cir., 135 F. 12, a case holding that a warranty of 3400 gross tons of iron pipe was not fulfilled by a shipment of 3258 tons. Or, at the election of the charterer, the breach of such a covenant may permit a rescission of the Charter Party. *Clydesdale Shipowners' Co. v. William W. Brauer Steamship Co., D.C.*, 120 F. 854.

The "Atlanta" carried 487 tons of pipe as loaded—a difference of some 63 tons from the capacity specified or approximately a 12% deficiency below the guarantee. The owner contends that the pipe was improperly loaded. It says that the pipe should have been "nested," that is, smaller pipes placed inside the larger ones. In this connection they rely, among other things, on "Modern Ship Stowage" published by the United States Department of Commerce where it is said (p. 382): "When a large quantity of cast iron pipes of varying sizes is shipped it is often possible to nest them by putting the smaller ones inside the larger, and so save considerable space."

The evidence as to this point is in sharp conflict. Captain Pantazopoulos himself was apparently uncertain whether it was proper procedure to nest or not to nest the pipe although he was of the opinion that the cargo was improperly loaded and that the stevedores were in "too much of a hurry." (Tr. of Evidence, p. 29, 32.)

As a matter of fact, about 1/3 to 1/2 of the pipe in the forward hold was nested. None was so loaded in the aft hatch. (Tr. of Evidence, p. 35, 136.) The exact reason why the stevedores stopped this method of stowage does not appear from the evidence. The Master testified that the pipes were slipping inside each other.

W. P. Jones testified for Caravan as an expert. He referred to the nesting of pipe as a "very abnormal practice." (Tr. of Evidence, p. 75.) On a ship with an aft hatch such as the "Atlanta" where the pipe had to be nested on the dock he thought such a procedure very unsafe. "The nesting of pipe is not good stowage; we never plan it," he said. From his personal examination of the aft hold of the "Atlanta" it would not have been possible under any conditions, he thought, to nest pipes in 18 foot lengths. (Tr. of Evidence, p. 146.)

Expert testimony on this subject was also produced by the owner. Mr. Martin Roberts testified that he would have nested the pipe in No. 2 hatch. However, the nesting there would have to have been done within the hatch, he said, as otherwise the pipe inside would slide out. Nesting is ordinary procedure "if you get in a jam for space." (Tr. of Evidence, p. 90.) However, he had never had any experience in discharging nested pipes and admitted that "it was not a normal stevedoring operation." He estimated that nesting pipes increases the time of labor about 20%. (Tr. of Evidence, p. 93.)

A diagram prepared by Mr. Jones shows that the stanchions in the aft hold of the "Atlanta" would have made it extremely difficult, if not impossible, to move 18 foot pipe therein for the purpose of nesting same. There was no space to swing the pipe. Mr. Nasios, the owner's representative, admitted that the vessel would not be seaworthy with pipe nested in the forward hatch and not in the aft hatch. (Tr. of Evidence, p. 137.) Captain Pantazopoulos also conceded that this was true. The fact was that when the "Atlanta" sailed from Tampico she was somewhat "down by the head." Some change of loading was made in order to trim her.

The question of fact involved is not an easy one. Certainly the "Atlanta" as loaded at Tampico did not comply with the owner's warranty as to capacity. The deficiency was a substantial and material one. In my opinion, a stevedore is not required to adopt out-of-the-ordinary methods of loading a ship, involving considerably more expense. There is nothing in the evidence suggesting that the stevedores were incompetent or that the "Atlanta" was not loaded according to the usual practices and standards prevailing at Tampico. The Agent under whom they operated was concededly one of the best. (Tr. of Evidence, p. 29.)

Clause 8 of the Charter Party provided that the charterers were to "load, stow and trim cargo at their expense under the supervision of the captain." Under such a charter the owner has a definite share of the responsibility and control as to the manner of loading. *Knohr & Burchard v. Pacific Creosoting Co., D.C.*, 181 F. 856; *The Giles Loring, D.C.*, 48 F. 463. Where the owner's guaranty of the ship's capacity is at stake the duty of the Master, even beyond precautions as to seaworthiness, is manifest. Captain Pantazopoulos and Nasios were present and observed the loading operations at Tampico. If they made any real objections to the manner of stowage the record fails to reflect them. Pantazopoulos says that he told the stevedores that the ship was being loaded "very badly." (Tr. of Evidence, p. 29.) But there his protests died though the charter definitely conferred upon him the right to do something about the situation. As I appraise the facts, I must and do hold that there was a breach of the warranty as to the "Atlanta's" capacity to lift cargo.

(2) Warranty as to Speed and Fuel Consumption.

The charter represented that the "Atlanta" was capable of steaming, fully laden, under good weather conditions at about 10 knots on a consumption of about 10 tons of the best grade fuel oil. Owners contend that such a statement is a representation and not a warranty, citing *The Beechpark* (*Denholm Shipping Co. v. W.E. Hedger Co. Inc.*), D.C., 34 F.2d 572, 1929 A. M. C. 880. However, that was a District Court decision which was reversed on appeal. The Circuit Court of Appeals for the Second Circuit, in reversing the decision, held that where a steamer is described as being "capable of steaming about 11 knots to 12 knots an hour in good weather in smooth water on a consumption of about 32 to 34 tons best Welsh coal"—a warranty results rather than a representation, even though the statement is not expressly designated as a warranty. *Denholm Shipping Co., Ltd. v. W.E. Hedger Co., Inc.*, 2 Cir., 47 F.2d 213. *The Beechpark* was cited in *Romano v. West India Fruit & Steamship Co., Inc.*, 5 Cir., 151 F.2d 727 where the Court ruled in a decision by Judge Hutcheson that a charter representation that a ship has a speed of 9 knots per hour is a warranty and that it was breached when the vessel did not attain it between Cristobal and Miami.

The "Atlanta" had not been drydocked in about five months. She was admittedly foul, with some 5 feet of scale. Her speed was retarded as a result. Enroute to Tampico she averaged only 6 or 7 knots, steaming light. She arrived more than a day late at Tampico. Nasios testified that the ship did not try to make speed as her fuel was short and bad weather might arise. (Tr. of Evidence, p. 131.) But this is hardly a satisfactory explanation in view of the warranty that the ship would be at Tampico on January 8th at 4:00 P.M. If I should give credence to the testimony of Nasios in this respect it would tend to solve the troublesome question as to waiver of the warranty of speed by Caravan's accepting the ship knowing of the deficiency in her speed. But independently of Nasios' explanation I am of the opinion that under the peculiar circumstances of emergency confronting both charterer and owner at Tampico there was no waiver of the warranty by Caravan.

Undoubtedly the "Atlanta" was delayed by extremely bad weather out of Tampico. The log shows storm conditions prevailing for all except a few days of the voyage to Puerto Cabello. But I am satisfied that it was not the storm that kept the "Atlanta" from making 10 knots enroute to that port. She may have been prevented by it from making 7 or 8 knots but not 10 or even 9 knots as she was incapable of the latter, fully laden. Moreover the "Atlanta" consumed considerably more fuel than the owners warranted. She was burning up to 5 tons more fuel per day than had been stipulated.

The admissions of Georgaros and the owners are entitled to much weight in considering any question as to Corinthian's compliance with the warranties. Whether valid or not, the "Addendum"* is a deliberate admission by an agent authorized to deal with the charterer that there had been a breach as to capacity to lift cargo as well as in respect to speed and fuel oil consumption. On January 21st he writes Nasios telling him "The way the ship is now is no good at all." In his letter of February 17th to Nasseof, Georgaros goes into detail with respect to the "Atlanta's" failure to perform. On February 12th he had telegraphed the owners: "We guaranteed ship 10 knots on 10 tons of fuel and capacity minimum 550 tons. However ship did 6 knots on 15 tons and capacity is 480 tons." Nasios informed Georgaros: "The speed of the ship will be right after it goes to drydock." Neither Nasseof nor Nasios ever really challenged the assertions of Georgaros. Indeed, on February 16th the former clearly admitted the ship's inability to live up to the original specifications when he instructed Georgaros to reduce speed 8-9 knots on "new contracts" and to increase fuel "about 11-12."

To overcome the effect of such admissions is a large order. In the opinion of the Special Commissioner the owner has failed to do so. Aside from the admissions, however, the evidence shows a material breach of the charter provision as to a warranted speed of "about 10 knots" on "about 10 tons" of fuel. Under the circumstances Caravan was justified in rescinding the contract upon discharge of the ship at Puerto Cabello.

* * *

Note

In addition to the fault of deviation, however, libelant has all along relied on (1) the lateness of the ship's sailing from Mayaguez to Cristobal, and (2) breach of warranty as to the vessel's speed. As to the claimed late sailing, the record will not support a finding that any of the damage was due to this cause. It is true that, in chartering the Sonia, "West India" did state, "It is understood the vessel now is in Mayaguez and is to sail not later than Thursday noon for Cristobal," and the proof shows that the Sonia did not sail on that day but a day or so later. But the sailing date was not warranted, the libelant was notified of the delay in ample time to have protected itself from a too early cutting of the bananas, and such damage, if any, as might have been caused by the too early cutting could not be said to be the proximate result of the delay. Besides there was no exception to the notation of the bill of lading that the bananas were loaded green, and we do not find that the damage suffered can be laid to the late sailing or to a too early cutting.

As to the speed of the vessel, however, the matter stands differently. The charter party contained this positive and unequivocal declaration: "Speed of nine knots per hours," and the evidence shows that she did not make this speed from Cristobal, with the result that she was many hours late, enough hours, indeed, in view of the condition of the bananas on arrival, to account, with the consequences of the deviation, for all the loss that occurred. If, then, this statement is a warranty, the judgment must be affirmed. The owner, agreeing that the speed of a vessel may be warranted, insists that the inserted clause was not a warranty at all because not expressly declared to be. But this will not stand up under the authorities. As *Denholm Shipping Co. v. W. E. Hedger Co.*, 2 Cir., 47 F.2d 213 points out, the failure to use the word 'warranty' in a statement of this kind is

---

* On 8 February 1948 the time charter was drastically modified by a so-called Addendum. In the Addendum the owners conceded the failure of the vessel to measure upto the charter specifications as to lifting capacity, speed, and fuel oil consumption.

unimportant. What is important is whether the statement was positively and unequivocally made as a statement of fact and whether the natural tendency of its making was to induce the chartering of the ship. The charter showed that the trade for which the ship was engaged, that is that she was to run in, was between ports in Florida, the West Indies, Central America, the Caribbean Sea, Mexico, and certain ports in the northern part of South America. In subchartering, there was discussion of the speed of the vessel, and to support his assurance that she could and would make nine knots, the charterer drew to the subcharterer's attention the affirmation of the written charter that the vessel was of that speed. The statement was a warranty and the ship is liable for damages resulting from its breach.

Romano v. West India Fruit & Steamship Co., Inc., 151 F.2d 727, 1946 AMC 90 (5th 1945).

---

b. Seaworthiness

Notes

1. *Implied Warranty of Seaworthiness*

In *Neubros Corporation v. Northwestern National Insurance Co.*, 359 F. Supp. 310, 1972 AMC 2443, 1973 AMC 511 (E.D.N.Y. 1972) owner sued Hull Underwriters and charterers for damage to chartered barge which it alleged had been overloaded by charterer. The defense was based on allegations that the owner had been aware of the purpose for which the barge was to be used and that the damage was caused by the unseaworthiness of barge, in that it was not fit for its intended purpose. The court upheld charterer's reliance on the "warranty" of seaworthiness.

The Warranty of Seaworthiness to the Charterer

The general rule is that every charter implies a warranty by the owner that the vessel is seaworthy unless the parties agree to the contrary. *The Caledonia*, 157 U.S. 124, 131, 15 S. Ct. 537, 540, 39 L. Ed. 644 (1895); *McAllister Lighterage Line, Inc. v. Insurance Co. of North America*, 244 F.2d 867, 871 (2d Cir. 1957); *Jordan, Inc. v. Mayronne Drilling Service*, 214 F.2d 410 (5th Cir. 1954), Gilmore and Black, The Law of Admiralty, p. 182. Knowledge by the charterer of an unseaworthy condition will not deny him the right to rely on the owner's implied warranty of seaworthiness. *Church Cooperage Co. v. Pinkney*, 170 F. 266 (2d Cir. 1909), *cert. denied*, 214 U.S. 526, 29 S. Ct. 704, 53 L. Ed. 1068. Agreements relieving the owner of obligation under the implied warranty of seaworthiness are not favored. *The Carib Prince*, 170 U.S. 655, 659, 18 S. Ct. 753, 755, 42 L. Ed. 1181 (1898). In the *Carib Prince* the Court said:

> ... clauses exempting the owner from the general obligation of furnishing a seaworthy vessel must be confined within strict limits, and were not to be extended by latitudinarian construction or forced implication so as to comprehend a state of unseaworthiness, whether patent or latent existing at the commencement of the voyage.

* * *

Seaworthiness

Seaworthiness is a relative term. "[It] expresses a relation between the state of the ship and the perils it has to meet in the situation it is in." 2 Arnould, Marine Insurance (14th Ed.), p. 630. It is the fitness in design, structure and condition to perform the task for which the vessel is chartered. *The Caledonia, supra*, 15 S. Ct. at p. 540; *McAllister Lighterage Lines, Inc. v. Insurance Company of North America, supra*, 244 F.2d at p. 870; 1 Carver, Carriage by Sea (12th Ed.), p. 98.

2. *Waiver of the Warranty of Seaworthiness*

After reviewing drafts of the agreement with Kemp's attorney, Bumble Bee sent the final bare boat Charter Agreement late in March. Louis Kemp, the charterer's president, found that the agreement differed from his understanding of the arrangement. Specifically, he understood that Bumble Bee had agreed that the engines would be in good working order and had represented orally that the freezing system would meet Kemp's specific needs. The agreement contained no such provisions and in fact, disclaimed all warranties, express or implied. Despite his reservations, Kemp signed it without voicing his concerns to Bumble Bee. He took the vessel in early April and sailed to Alaska for the May herring season.

* * *

Kemp argues that even if Bumble Bee did not expressly warrant the vessel's seaworthiness, the warranty is implied in every charter unless clearly and unequivocally waived. It claims that Bumble Bee failed to waive the implied warranty.

California provides that waivers of warranties may be enforced if they "clearly communicate that a particular risk falls on the [charterer]. *Hauter v. Zogarts*, 120 Cal. Rptr. 681, 690 (Cal. S. Ct. 1975). Such waivers are construed strictly against the maker. *Zogarts, id.* Federal maritime law is similar. *See* BENEDICT at 3-9; and *In Compania De Navigacion La Flecha v. Brauer*, 168 U.S. 104, 118 (1897).

Sub-paragraph 3E provides that after accepting delivery, Kemp "shall not be entitled to make or assert any claim against Owner on account of any representations or warranties, express or implied, with respect to the Vessel." Sub-paragraph 3F provides that Kemp's acceptance of the vessel is conclusive evidence that it inspected the vessel and "deemed" it seaworthy and suitable for its needs.

These clauses clearly and unequivocally communicate that the risk of unseaworthiness would fall on Kemp once it accepted the vessel. Similar disclaimers have been found to be clear and unequivocal and have been enforced in admiralty. *See, e.g., McAllister Lighterage Line v. Insurance Co.*, 244 F.2d 867, 871 (2d Cir.) *cert. denied sub nom.* 355 U.S. 871 (1957) ("The acceptance of said scow by charterer is to be conclusive evidence of the seaworthy condition of said scow at the commencement of this charter" is clear and unequivocal.) [Kemp] effectively waived the implied warranty of seaworthiness. The court erred in refusing to enforce its waiver.

A. Kemp Fisheries, Inc. v. Castle & Cooke, Inc., 852 F.2d 493, 1989 AMC 236 (9th Cir. 1988).

3. *Remedies of Charterer—English Law*

A charter party which describes the vessel as, *inter alia*, "with hull, machinery and equipment in a thoroughly efficient state," is an undertaking of seaworthiness. A charter party may provide "that on delivery the ship is to be 'tight, staunch, strong and in every way fitted for the service.'" This is an undertaking that the vessel is seaworthy at the time of delivery. As Notes 1 & 2, *supra*, demonstrate, in absence of any of any express undertaking or waiver of the as to seaworthiness, an undertaking of seaworthiness will be implied. These undertakings are not on their own continuing obligations. However, if the charter party also contains terms to the affect that the ship will be "maintained in a thoroughly efficient state during service," then the undertaking will be considered as continuing one. M. WILFORD, T. COGLIN, J. KIMBALL, TIME CHARTERS 96-97 (Lloyd's of London Press, 4th ed. 1995).

The English cases seem to treat the "undertaking" of seaworthiness as an "intermediate" term and not as a condition. As such, charterer's right to rescind the contract depends on the facts and circumstances of the breach. The undertaking of seaworthiness is so far-reaching that it would be unreasonable for a minor breach in some trivial way to allow the charterer to terminate the charter. Charterers, however, need not accept an unseaworthy vessel, but they may require owner to correct the defect. If owner fails to do so, this could be considered a repudiation of the charter party which would give charterer the right to terminate. M. WILFORD, T. COGLIN, J. KIMBALL, TIME CHARTERS 97-99 (Lloyd's of London Press, 4th ed. 1995).

4. ***Remedies of Charterer—U.S. Law***

> The approach to discrepancies in the description of a ships characteristics in U.S. case law is not clear. [S]tatements may be called 'representations", "warranties" or "conditions", although the term may not well dispose of the underlying issue of whether the ship's failure to comply entitles the charterer to treat the contact as terminated or merely to recover damages resulting from the breach. Rather than focus on the proper terminology, it is more useful to consider the inherent materiality of the representation or undertaking in question, the in time at which a breach or default occurs, and the consequences thereof to the charter.
>
> Under the American precedents, it is more important to distinguish between cases involving a misdescription determined prior to delivery of the vessel and one occurring after delivery. In he former a refusal to accept the vessel has been held justified even where the deviation from the represented characteristic is relatively small.
>
> * * *
>
> Once delivery of the vessel has been accepted, however, the charterer is entitled to refuse to perform the charter only if there is a material breach on the part of the owner which frustrates the essential purpose of the contract.

M. Wilford, T. Coglin, J. Kimball, Time Charters 108 (Lloyd's of London Press, 4th ed. 1995).

This is illustrated in *Aaby v. States Marine Corporation*, 181 F.2d 383 (2d Cir.) *cert. denied*, 340 U.S. 829, 71 S. Ct. 66, 95 L. Ed. 609 (1950) where the court stated:

> With respect to the undertaking of seaworthiness on the part of the owner of a vessel, it is usually said that it is a "warranty," implied in the absence of an express and unambiguous stipulation or a controlling statute to the contrary. Scrutton, however, speaks of it as being a "condition" similarly implied. Charterparties and Bills of Lading (12th ed.) p. 95. And it has sometimes been spoken of as simply a "covenant." *The Steel Navigator*, 2 Cir. 23 F.2d 590; *Franklin Fire Ins. Co. v. Royal Mail Steam Packet Co.*, 2 Cir. 58 F.2d 175, *certiorari denied* 287 U.S. 630, 53 S. Ct. 82, 77 L. Ed. 546; *Wilson v. Griswold*, C.C.S.D.N.Y., Fed. Cas. No. 17,806. Williston considers that "The basis of the undertaking of seaworthiness is the same as that of implied warranties in the sale of goods; the shipowner is in a position to know the condition of his ship and the charterer justifiably relies upon his judgment." 4 Williston on Contracts § 1078. But this would not seem to explain the unquestioned line of authority that the undertaking of seaworthiness is absolute in the sense that the owner's exercise of due diligence to discover defects is immaterial. As Lord Blackburn, in *Steel v. State Line S.S. Co.*, (1887) 3 A.C. 72, 86, put it, the obligation is not merely that the owners "should do their best to make the ship fit, but that the ship should really be fit. The problem is not made any simpler when, as here, there is an express stipulation of seaworthiness but that stipulation is not made one of the express "conditions" to the contract, and is contained in the preliminary recital of agreements between the parties.
>
> In the midst of this confusion, however, one thing rather clearly appears: that repudiation by a charterer is permissible only where the breach of the owner's undertaking of seaworthiness is so substantial as to defeat or frustrate the commercial purpose of the charter. The English authorities speak in these terms. *Tarrabochia v. Hickey*, (1856) 1 H. & N. 183, 156 Eng. Rep. 1168; *Tully v. Howling*, (1877) 2 Q.B.D. 182; *Stanton v. Richardson*, (1872) L.R. 7 C.P. 421, *aff'd*, (1875) L.R. 9 C.P. 390 (Exch), *aff'd* H.L., *see* (1875) 1 Q.B.D. 381; *see Scrutton, supra* at pp. 96, 103; Carver, *supra*, § 145. There are no American cases to the contrary. Thus, it has been said that "the stipulation of seaworthiness is not so far a condition precedent that the hirer is not liable in such case for any of the charter money. If he uses her, he must pay for the use to the extent to which it goes." *Work v. Leathers*, 97 U.S. 379, 380, 24 L. Ed. 1012; *The Toledo*, 2 Cir., 122 F.2d 255, 257, *certiorari denied Isbrandtsen-Moller Co. v. The Toledo*, 314 U.S. 689, 62 S. Ct. 302, 86 L. Ed. 551. The preliminary statement in a charter party as to the vessel's registered tonnage has been similarly treated, substantial compliance therewith

> being held sufficient, at least where the vessel has been designated by name and the kind and quantity of cargo has been specified. *Watts v. Camors*, 115 U.S. 353, 6 S. Ct. 91, 29 L. Ed. 406. Thus also, breach of a provision that the vessel shall sail with all convenient speed, "reasonable dispatch," or the like has been held not to justify repudiation unless delay has been so great as to frustrate the object of the charter. *Clipsham v. Vertue*, (1843) 6 Q.B. 265, 114 Eng. Rep. 1249; *see* 4 WILLISTON ON CONTRACTS, § 1079.
>
> We take it, then, that the undertaking of seaworthiness is to be treated like any other contractual undertaking not expressly made a condition precedent to a party's performance of his obligations: an insubstantial breach of it, not going to defeat the object of the contract, will not justify repudiation.

* * *

In *Aaby, supra*, the court concluded that charterer could not terminate the charter. The unseaworthy condition manifested itself shortly after the voyage commenced. The vessel returned to port where the condition was repaired. The vessel was ready to sail after a delay of two and one half days. The charter party which had just commenced was for a term of 12 months Suppose the unseaworthy condition had been discovered during a joint inspection prior to charterer's acceptance of the vessel. Could charterer have rescinded the contract? If not, what remedy could charterer invoke.

---

2. Off Hire

a. Unseaworthiness — Off-hire or Repudiation

UNITED STATES v. M/V MARILENA P

433 F.2d 164, 1969 AMC 1155 (4th Cir. 1969)

Albert V. BRYAN, Circuit Judge

In admiralty asking damages, the United States complained of the M/V Marilena P [of Greek Registry] and her owner, Marilena Compania Naviera, S.A., for nullifying a charter party. The controversy grew out of the crew's refusal to sail.* As the ad-port was within the Viet Nam war theatre and the ship's lading was combat materials, they declined the voyage, either as too perilous or for some other reason not clearly recorded. The charterer argues that the ship thus became unseaworthy, in violation and dissolution of the charter. The shipowner, responding for itself and as the vessel's claimant, traversed the libel, and also counter-demanded damages upon the assertion that the Government had reneged on its agreement.

Appealing against a wholly adverse judgment, the shipowner persuades us to its view ... .

* * *

I

In our judgment no breach of the charter was committed by the respondent shipowner. The admiralty judge concluded that when presented to the charterer at Seattle on September 1, the Marilena P was unseaworthy because she was then "without a crew willing to sail the vessel to South Viet Nam". This determination, we think, is not altogether precise.

---

* The members of the crew were Greek nationals. Eds.

A few minutes past midnight of August 31-September 1 at Seattle she was an arrived ship. An MSTS** Deputy Operations Officer there boarded her, and with the first officer and a marine surveyor "made a thorough tour of the ship"—an on-hire survey. Thereafter, about 8 o'clock A.M. September 1, the Marilena P was accepted by the Government. She was then fueled by the charterer and, at its direction the vessel was moved to Tacoma.

At her new berth, loading commenced about 7:30 P.M. September 1. Neither before nor during that day did the crew protest the scheduled passage to South Viet Nam, although the log notes some grumblings. There was no cessation in the loading until between 2 and 3 o'clock on the afternoon of September 2nd. The record indicates no reluctance of the longshoremen to carry on the cargo.

Hence, MSTS can hardly be heard to say that the vessel was unseaworthy on September 1. The owner at that time had no warning or premonition of the group's recalcitrance. They had signed on for a definite period, including August and September 1965, without restriction of destination. It was not incumbent upon the owner or master to ask if they were willing to ship to Viet Nam. Their defiance was in violation of Greek law, and on return to Athens some of them were punished for their disobedience.

But, conceding arguendo the strike created unseaworthiness amounting to an infraction of the charter, no right of repudiation was automatically conferred upon the United States. The promises of seaworthiness in the charter were not made conditions, nor did the crew's inaction constitute a frustration of the hiring of the ship.[1] From the context of the contract it is plain that their breach did not give an election forthwith to the charterer to wind up the arrangement on account of this development.

The parties quite explicitly evidenced their understanding that a contingency of this kind should not, ex proprio vigore, end it. They foresaw the possibility and stipulated a remedy, at least for a temporary wait in the departure. This is the stipulation:

> Article 17. Off-Hire.
> (a) In the event of loss of time *from deficiency of men including but not limited to strikes* ... the payment of hire shall cease from the time thereby lost ... (Emphasis added)

This provision refutes the option claimed by the Government to withdraw immediately from its contract upon inception of a strike. The conclusively manifested intention of the parties was that a breach of this nature was not to be accompanied by such grave results. Consequently, we need not and do not decide the much debated question of when unseaworthiness or what degree thereof, without more, justifies renunciation by the charterer. *See Aaby v. States Marine Corporation*, 181 F.2d 383, 386 (2 Cir. 1950).

Of course, cancellation might have been imposed if the strike so plainly appeared unsolvable as to be a frustration, but that was not the appearance here. This, the United States acknowledged by indulging the owner additional time to obtain a full company.

** Military sea Transportation Service of the United States. Eds.

[1] Frustration of a charter party is a change of conditions so radical that accomplishment of the commercial object of the charter is made impossible. *See* Gilmore & Black, Admiralty at 198.

Tolerance in this respect is not uncommon; in the Government's charter of the Mormacrigel, 12 days waiting time was permitted. Further, nowhere in the charter was time declared of the essence. Indeed, it has not been stressed at any stage of the case. Overtopping all considerations, however, it must be recalled that the hindering event was not of the owner's making or neglect.

Finally, the assurance of seaworthiness was not absolute as it would be in the absence of qualification. Each assurance is modified in terms of due diligence. Therefore, the duty to maintain a crew was not unconditional. Once reasonable care was exerted, unseaworthiness non obstante was not a transgression of the charter. This understanding is punctuated by the following charter clauses:

> Article 4. Delivery of the Vessel:
> (b) ... Vessel on delivery shall be, *insofar as due diligence can make her so*, seaworthy, tight, staunch, strong, and in every way suitable and adequately fitted for and in all respects ready to receive and transport lawful cargo. (Emphasis added)
>
> * * *
>
> Article 18. Owner's Obligation:
> (a) ... The Owner shall use *due diligence* ... to keep the Vessel in a thoroughly efficient state in ... *personnel* ... relating to the seaworthiness of the Vessel ..." (Accent added)

While the due diligence must be established by the shipowner, we think the proof here abrim in this demonstration. Nothing prior to presentation of the ship for service, as earlier noted, even remotely indicated intransigence of the crew. Vigilance in its discovery could not be expected without some prior clue of the men's dispositions. At once upon learning on September 4 of the revolt, respondent's port captain left Greece and went to Seattle. He offered the crew double pay. Ten replacements were recruited in Athens and the earliest available flight reservations for them obtained. Four more were secured in New York. The ship's company had consisted of 40, but the captain could not induce enough of the insubordinates to make up the requisite complement.

Furthermore, the Government cannot fairly charge lack of diligence. As heretofore stated, on September 3 the United States allowed the owner until September 8 to make good the deficiency of crew. Nevertheless, on September 4—within an hour or two after it issued this deadline—the Government arranged with the Mormacrigel to pick up the freight intended for the Marilena P. At that moment 400 tons of it were in her holds. On the same day, September 4, this laden was removed by the Government. Before September 8 the substitute vessel sailed away with the entire tonnage.

In *Aaby v. States Marine Corporation, supra*, 181 F.2d 383, 386, the Court refused to allow such impetuous action. Noting the differences among the authorities, at home and aboard, on the remedies for charter infringements or defaults, the opinion stated:

> in the midst of this confusion, however, one thing rather clearly appears; that repudiation by a charterer is permissible only where the breach of the owner's undertaking of seawor-

thiness is so substantial as to defeat or frustrate the commercial purpose of the charter. The English authorities speak in these terms.

In *Hong Kong Fir Shipping Co. v. Kawasaki Kisen Kaishe*, 1 All E.R. 474 (1962) the British Court of Appeal met and answered the questions here. There a time charter of December 26, 1956 let a vessel for 24 months to the charterer, with delivery at Liverpool. The agreement required the ship to be "in every way fitted for ordinary cargo service". On the day of delivery, February 13, 1957, she sailed for Newport News, Virginia to take on coal for Osaka. When accepted by the charterers at Liverpool, "her engineroom was undermanned and her engineroom staff incompetent". Because of this deficiency, her engines broke down and she lost several months of working time. Nevertheless, the charterer was denied the power to cancel the agreement.

Although the British courts may seem more lenient on this point than the American, the reasoning of the Court pertinently is notable. As a member of the unanimous Court, Upjohn, L.J. observed:

> Yet with all respect to counsel's argument, it seems to me quite clear that the seaworthiness clause is *not in general treated as a condition* [accent added] for breach of which the charterer is at once entitled to repudiate. This is established by a number of authorities over a long period of years and I mention them without quoting from them.
>
> * * *
>
> Why is this apparently basic and underlying condition of seaworthiness not, in fact, treated as a condition? It is for the simple reason that the seaworthiness clause is breached by the slightest failure to be fitted 'in every way' for service. Thus, to take examples from the judgments in some of the cases I have mentioned above, if a nail is missing from one of the timbers of a wooden vessel, or if proper medical supplies or two anchors are not on board at the time of sailing, the owners are in breach of the seaworthiness stipulation. It is contrary to common sense to suppose that, in such circumstances, the parties contemplated that the charterer should at once be entitled to treat the contract as at an end for such trifling breaches.

1 All E.R. 474, 482-83 (1962).

In summary, on September 3 when the Government served its demand upon the owner to man the ship or be declared in default, and on September 4 when the loaded cargo was removed, the shipowner had not breached the contract. Consequently, the Government could not then terminate the agreement and cannot successfully claim, as it does in this action, damages for a breach at that time.

* * *

WINTER, Circuit Judge (dissenting)

* * *

From the scope of the undertaking, *i.e.*, to provide a ship to carry the cargo to Vietnam, it follows that the failure to do so, whether blameworthy or not, was a breach of the charter party. *Work v. Leathers*, 97 U.S. 379, 380, 24 L. Ed. 1012 (1878); *Davison v. Von Lingen*, 113 U.S. 40, 5 S. Ct. 346, 28 L. Ed. 885 (1885); *Pendleton v. Benner Line*, 246 U.S. 353, 357, 38 S. Ct. 330, 62 L. Ed. 770 (1918). *See also*, *Norrington v. Wright*, 115 U.S. 188, 203, 6 S. Ct. 12, 29 L. Ed. 366 (1885); *The March*, 25 F. 106 (D.Md. 1885); *Pedersen v. Pagenstecher*, 32 F. 841 (S.D.N.Y.1887); *Dexter & Carpenter Co. v. United States*, 13 F.2d 498 (S.D.N.Y.1926). The majority view notwithstanding, it is difficult to imagine a more substantial, basic default in a time charter than the failure to provide a crew, unless it be the failure to supply a ship and a crew. The entire purpose of the charter party was totally frustrated.

* * *

---

b. "Preventing the Working of the Vessel"

Note

Not all "off-hire" or "breakdown" clauses are worded the same. Therefore, under some circumstances a vessel may go "off-hire" under the wording of a clause in one charter party form and yet may be "off-hire" not under the language of a clause in another form. Even in interpreting a clause contained in one form judges do not always in agree as to the circumstances in which a vessel will be "off-hire" under the clause before them. In *Steamship Knutsford Co. v. Barber & Co.*, 261 F. 866 (2d Cir. 1919), *cert. denied*, 252 U.S. 586, 40 S. Ct. 396, 64 L. Ed. 729 (1920), clause 16 of the charter party provided:

> That in the event of loss of time from deficiency of men or stores, breakdown of machinery, stranding, or damage preventing the working of the vessel for more than twenty-four (24) consecutive hours, payment of hire shall cease until she shall be again in an efficient state to resume her service; but should the vessel be driven into port or to anchorage by stress of weather, or from any accident to cargo, such detention or loss of time shall be at the charterer's risk and expense.

In that case there was a fire while the vessel was in port. Its cargo was removed and repairs were made to the vessel. The majority of the court concluded that during this time the vessel was no longer "off-hire."

> The evidence is far from clear, but it sufficiently appears that the sugar was taken out because it had to be. The hold had been flooded, and the charterer must examine and restow it before the ship could proceed. The same apparently was true of the cases of machinery, and possibly of the carbon, too, although the record is silent as to the last. But as regards the steel billets and the spelter it must be assumed that they were not injured. These being the circumstances, we think that the time necessary to examine and restow the sugar was not "loss of time" within the meaning of article 16, but that the charterer was using the ship at that time for a purpose which, though it necessarily delayed her, was still his own, and was not due to any "damage" to the ship. It seems to us that article 16 does not justify a deduction during that period, or until the charterer began to lose the use of the ship after he again wished to load her.

* * *

> *The Canadia*, 241 Fed. 233, 154 C.C.A. 153 (C.C.A. 3d Cir.), squarely supports our ruling. In that case the vessel was held to be off hire during the period of a fire, but on hire while being discharged, though in an unseaworthy condition, being available for the purposes required by the charterer. We see no substantial difference between that form of expression and the one which we somewhat prefer; *i.e.*, that the charterer has lost no time because of the damage.

Judge Manton dissented stating:

> The vessel was not fit to receive cargo while she was afire, or while the fire was being extinguished, nor while the hold was flooded; and she was not in an efficient state to resume her service until the repairs found necessary were completed. To say that it is incumbent upon the charterer to remove the cargo, because that was damaged, is ignoring the effect of the *Hogarth v. Miller* and *Lake Steamship Co. v. Bacon Cases, supra.* Moreover, it appears that through the period while the fire was in progress, while it was being extinguished, and while the vessel was being repaired and the hold cleared in consequence thereof, there was a loss of time from damage preventing the working of the ship, and if, during part of the time, the charterer was in fact shifting cargo for his own account, the fire and its consequences were nevertheless, throughout the entire period, a concurring cause of the loss of time. Here the vessel itself was actually on fire. There is no evidence to bear out the suggestion, made upon the argument, that it originated in the cargo. A consequence was the flooding of the hold, that created the need for shifting the cargo, all being occasioned by the fire, and also the necessity for repairs after the fire.

---

c. Third Party Liability

Note

As a result of the negligence of a third party, a vessel under time charter was damaged and had to undergo repairs. The charter party provided not only that the vessel would be "off-hire" during this period, but also that the charterer, at its option, could extend the length of the charter period at the charter party rate of hire by the amount of time the vessel was off-hire. At the expiration of the period of time stated in the charter party, the market rate of hire was higher than the charter rate, consequently charterer elected to extend the charter for a period equal to the time the vessel had been off-hire. Owner was permitted to recover form the third-party tortfeasor, the difference between the charter rate paid by the charterer and the market rate it could have received if the charter party had not been extended. *Compania-Pelinean De Navegacion, S.A. v. Texas Petroleum Co.*, 540 F.2d 53, 1976 AMC 1745 (2d Cir. 1976), *cert. denied*, 429 U.S. 1041, 97 S. Ct. 741, 50 L. Ed. 2d 753 (1977).

---

3. Mutual Exceptions

Note

Charter parties often contain exoneration clauses stating that losses caused by certain causes are "mutually excepted". Such clauses must be read in the context of the other provisions of the charter party, particularly the off-hire clause. For example, in *Clyde Commercial S.S. Co. v. West India S.S. Co,* 169 F. 275 (2d Cir. 1909), clause 17 of the charter party provided that "The act of God, enemies, fire, restraint of princes, rulers and people and all dangers and accidents of the seas, rivers, machinery, boilers and steam navigation and errors of navigation throughout this charter party always mutually excepted". Clause 15 was a typical off-hire clause, which put the ship off-hire "in the event of the loss of time from deficiency of men or stores, breakdown of machinery, stranding, fire or damage preventing the working of the vessel for more than 24 hours". The court said:

> If the causes enumerated in article 15 for which payment of hire is suspended were wholly different from the exceptions in article 17, it might be fairly contended that those exceptions applied to them, but they include many categories exactly alike. If hire is to be suspended for delay over 24 hours caused by breakdown of machinery, that delay is immediately excused by the exception of accidents to machinery in article 17. Suspension in case of stranding is immediately excused, whether the owner is at fault or not, by the exception of accidents of the sea or errors in navigation; suspension in case of fire by the exception of fire. This leads us to the conclusion that article 15 must be understood to state absolute categories in which the parties intended the hire to be suspended whether the owner was at fault or not, and therefore that article 17 does not apply to them at all.

---

4. Frustration

Notes

1. [F]rustration occurs whenever the law recognizes that without default of either party a contractual obligation has become incapable of being performed because the circumstances in which performance is called for would render it a thing radically different from that which was undertaken by the contract. *Non haec in foedera veni*—it was not that I promised to do.

The Newa, [1981] 2 Lloyd's L. Rep. 239, 253.

2. In *The Claveresk*, 264 F. 276 (2d Cir. 1920), the ship *Claveresk* was requisitioned by the British Government during the First World War while under time charter to the plaintiff (the libelant). More than 20 ships owned by the same owner were requisitioned at the same time and it was obvious from the evidence that the requisitioning was intended to be of indefinite duration. The U.S. Court of Appeals for the Second Circuit held that the contract was frustrated at the moment of requisitioning. The court said:

> [I]t being true that government on February 10, 1917, made it impossible for either Sutherland, Earn Line, or any other private individual to use the Claveresk, and did this under circumstances clearly showing to any sensible man that such indefinite taking would almost certainly outlast the life of the charter, it further appearing that the boat was so retained far beyond the charter period, and indeed (by admission at bar) still is kept by government (*cf. Bank Line Case*, at page 454), it follows as a conclusion of law that the charter party was terminated by frustration on February 10, 1917.

The Claveresk, 264 F. 276, 283 (2d Cir. 1920),

3. *Transatlantic Financing Corporation v. United States*, 363 F.2d 312, 66 AMC 1455 (D.C. Cir. 1966) involved a voyage charter party entered into on October 2, 1956, covering carriage of a cargo of wheat from a United States Gulf Port to a safe port in Iran. On October 29, 1956, Israel invaded Egypt. On October 31, 1956, Great Britain and France invaded the Suez Canal Zone. On November 2, 1956, the Egyptian Government obstructed the Suez Canal with sunken vessels and closed it to traffic. Although the Suez Canal was generally regarded as the customary route for the voyage, the charterer told the owner that it expected it to carry out its obligations under the charter. The owner made the voyage via the Cape of Good Hope. The use of this route entailed more expense for the owner. Owner sued charterer in *quantum meruit.* Its theory of recovery was that the original charter had been frustrated and that when it complied with charterer's demand that the cargo be delivered it was entitled to additional compensation. The Court of Appeals affirmed the dismissal of the owner's claim.

The Court drew an analogy with and relied heavily on the rules used to decide ordinary land based contractual disputes, namely the doctrine of impossibility of contract.

> When the issue is raised, the court is asked to construct a condition of performance based on the changed circumstances, a process which involves at least three reasonably definable steps. First, a contingency—something unexpected—must have occurred. Second, the risk of the unexpected occurrence must not have been allocated either by agreement or by custom. Finally, occurrence of the contingency must have rendered performance commercially impracticable. Unless the court finds these three requirements satisfied, the plea of impossibility must fail.
>
> The first requirement was met here. It seems reasonable, where no route is mentioned in a contract, to assume the parties expected performance by the usual and customary route at the time of contract. Since the usual and customary route from Texas to Iran at the time of contract was through Suez, closure of the Canal made impossible the expected method of performance. But this unexpected development raises rather than resolves the impossibility issue, which turns additionally on whether the risk of the contingency's occurrence had been allocated and, if not, whether performance by alternative routes was rendered impracticable.
>
> Proof that the risk of a contingency's occurrence has been allocated may be expressed in or implied from the agreement. Such proof may also be found in the surrounding circumstances, including custom and usages of the trade. The contract in this case does not expressly condition performance upon availability of the Suez route. Nor does it specify "via Suez" or on the other hand, "via Suez or Cape of Good Hope." Nor are there provisions in the contract from which we may properly imply that the continued availability of Suez was a condition of performance. Nor is there anything in custom or trade usage, or in the surrounding circumstances generally, which would support our constructing a condition of performance.
>
> * * *
>
> If anything, the circumstances surrounding this contract indicate that the risk of the Canal's closure may be deemed to have been allocated to Transatlantic. We know or may safely assume that the parties were aware, as were most commercial men with interests affected by the Suez situation, *see The Eugenia, supra*, that the Canal might become a dangerous area. No doubt the tension affected freight rates, and it is arguable that the risk of closure became part of the dickered terms. We do not deem the risk of closure so allocated, however. Foreseeability or even recognition of a risk does not necessarily prove its allocation. Parties to a contract are not always able to provide for all the possibilities of which they are aware, sometimes because they cannot agree, often simply because they are too busy. Moreover, that some abnormal risk was contemplated is probative but does not necessarily establish an allocation of the risk of the contingency which actually occurs. In this case, for example, nationalization by Egypt of the Canal Corporation and formation of the Suez Users Group did not necessarily indicate that the Canal would be blocked even if a confrontation resulted. The surrounding circumstances do indicate, however, a willingness by Transatlantic to assume abnormal risks, and this fact should legitimately cause us to judge the impracticability of performance by an alternative route in stricter terms than we would were the contingency unforeseen.
>
> We turn then to the question whether occurrence of the contingency rendered performance commercially impracticable under the circumstances of this case. The goods shipped were not subject to harm from the longer, less temperate Southern route. The vessel and crew were fit to proceed around the Cape. Transatlantic was no less able than the United States to purchase insurance to cover the contingency's occurrence. If anything, it is more reasonable to expect owner-operators of vessels to insure against the hazards of war. They are in the best position to calculate the cost of performance by alternative routes (and therefore to estimate the amount of insurance required), and are undoubtedly sensitive to international troubles which uniquely affect the demand for and cost of their services. The only factor operating here in appellant's favor is the added expense, allegedly $43,972.00 above and beyond the contract price of $305,842.92, of extending a 10,000 mile voyage by approximately 3,000 miles. While it may be an overstatement to say that increased cost and difficulty of performance never

constitute impracticability, to justify relief there must be more of a variation between expected cost and the cost of performing by an available alternative than is present in this case, where the promisor can legitimately be presumed to have accepted some degree of abnormal risk, and where impracticability is urged on the basis of added expense alone

We conclude, therefore, as have most other courts considering related issues arising out of the Suez closure that performance of this contract was not rendered legally impossible. [...]

4. Depending on their duration, delays during the charter period may frustrate the charterparty contract. If the delay appears at the outset to be only temporary (unlike that in *The Claveresk*, supra, which appeared from the outset to be of indefinite duration), the question of whether the contract is frustrated depends on the probable length of delay, considered as a proportion of the time that the charter period has left to run. The delay must be of sufficient duration to deprive the parties of the commercial benefit of their original bargain. For example, many charterparties were frustrated by the outbreak of hostilities between Iran and Iraq in 1980, which trapped some 60 ships in the Shatt-al-Arab waterway leading to the port of Basrah. The outbreak of hostilities did not *ipso facto* frustrate time charterparties of the trapped ships, as initially it was possible that it might be of short duration only. The charterparties were frustrated only when it became clear that the conflict would continue for a sufficient period to bring an end to the contracts as commercial propositions. *International Sea Tankers Inc. v. Hemisphere Shipping Co. Ltd (The Wenjiang)(No. 2)* [1983] 2 Lloyd's Rep. 400; *Vinava Shipping Co. Ltd v. Finelvet A.G. (The Chrysalis)* [1983] 2 Lloyd's Rep. 503.

---

*5. Redelivery**

a. Overlap and Underlap

PREBENSENS DAMPSKIBSSELSKABET A/S v. MUNSON S.S. LINE

258 F. 227 (2d Cir. 1919)

WARD, Circuit Judge

October 31, 1912, her owners chartered the steamer Falk to the Munson Line "for a period of about 36 calendar months (term of charter party to be understood to mean a month more or less)" from the time of delivery. The charter party was of the usual time charter form and contained the following articles:

> 4. That the charterers shall pay for the use and hire of the said vessel nine hundred and fifty pounds British sterling (£950) per calendar month, commencing on and from the day of her delivery, as aforesaid, and at and after the same rate for any part of a month; hire to continue until her delivery, with clean holds to the owners (unless lost) at a port in the United Kingdom or on the continent between Bordeaux and Hamburg, both inclusive (Rouen excluded), at charterers' option.
>
> 5. That should the steamer be on her voyage towards the port of return delivery at the time a payment of hire becomes due, said payment shall be made for such length of time as the owners or their agents and charterers or their agents may agree upon as the estimated

* Redelivery problems occur in time and bareboat charter situations. (Eds.)

time necessary to complete the voyage, and when the steamer is delivered to owner's agents any difference shall be refunded by steamer or paid by charterers, as the case may require.

January 20, 1913, the steamer was delivered to the charterer and redelivered by it to the owners March 1, 1916, to which date the charterer paid hire at the charter rate.

The owners contend that the term ended January 20, 1916, with a permissible overlap or underlap of one month, so that the charterer was liable until February 20, 1916, at the charter rate of freight, and for the 10 days thereafter until redelivery at the market rate of freight; the same amounting to about $9,000, to recover which this libel was filed. The charterer, on the other hand, contends that it is liable only at the charter rate of freight until the actual redelivery, March 1, 1916. Judge Mayer sustained the owner's contention and entered a decree for the libelant.

We think the construction of these articles is made clear by former decisions in this circuit. In the case of charters for a fixed time Judge Addison Brown held that the charterer was entitled to a reasonable overlap at the charter rate of freight. Straits of *Dover S.S. Co. v. Munson (D.C.)* 95 Fed. 690; *Anderson v. Munson (D.C.)* 104 Fed. 915. In the case of charters for "about" a named time, we have held that the charterer is entitled to a reasonable underlap as well as overlap. *The Rygja*, 161 Fed. 106, 88 C.C.A. 270; *Trechmann S.S. Co. v. Munson Line*, 203 Fed. 692, 121 C.C.A. 650.

* * *

But we construe the charter in this case as being for a term of 36 months, with a permitted underlap or overlap of 1 month. It is an "about" term charter, with the "about" period defined to be 1 month. Accordingly for any overlap beyond 37 months the charterer must pay at the market rate. The owners contend that the reasoning as to the difficulty of estimating the market rate of freight at a time of redelivery in the future is the same in this case as it was in the case of *Ropner v. S.S. Co.* But this subordinate consideration, which was consistent with the primary ground of decision in that case, must yield to the primary ground of decision in this case, with which it is not consistent. The charterer being liable to pay the market rate of freight after the expiration of the term of 36 months and the permitted overlap of 1 month, and the last installment falling due before the time of actual redelivery, the natural estimate as to the rate of freight would seem to have been the rate prevailing at the time the installment fell due. Both the estimated time and the estimated freight were to be corrected, if necessary, at the time of redelivery.

The decree is affirmed.

BRITAIN S.S. CO. v. MUNSON S.S. LINE

31 F.2d 530 (2d Cir.), *cert. denied*, 280 U.S. 574, 50 S. Ct. 29, 74 L. Ed. 625 (1929)

From a decree in admiralty, awarding damages to the owner of the British steamship Putney for a redelivery of the vessels before the expiration of a time charter, and for a wrongful deduction from the charter hire of expenses of fumigation, the charterer has appealed. Modified.

By the terms of the charter party the Putney was let to the Munson Steamship Line "from the time of delivery, for about two (2) to about three (3) consecutive calendar months," to be employed between ports within specified geographical limits, and to be redelivered at a safe United States Atlantic port north of Cape Hatteras. The ship was delivered on March 20, 1925, at Matanzas, Cuba. She loaded there a cargo of sugar, discharged it at New York, and returned to Cuba for a second cargo, which she discharged at New York by May 7th. On that date, which was 13 days before the expiration of 2 months from the date of delivery, the charterer tendered redelivery of the vessel, which the owner accepted under protest. On May 9th a new charter was made between the parties, without prejudice to the rights of either, for one round trip from the United States to the West Indies, within limits as specified in the original charter, but at a lower rate of hire. Under this second charter the Putney was delivered May 13th, and made a voyage to Cuba and return. She was redelivered on June 23d, which was 3 months and 3 days after her original delivery on March 20th.

During the charterer's operation of the vessel in April, 1925, she was required by the quarantine officer at New York to under go fumigation. This was demanded under sections 102 and 103 of the Quarantine Laws and Regulations, because she had not been fumigated in nearly 2 years and had visited a Mediterranean port within the previous 4 months (before chartered to the appellant). The cost of fumigation and charter hire for the time it took were deducted by the charterer from the hire.

By a libel *in personam* the owner sought to recover these deductions for fumigation, as well as charter hire at the original rate from May 7 to June 23, less credit for hire paid under the second charter. On conflicting testimony the court found that a reasonable estimate of the time required for a voyage from New York to Cuba and return was 21 to 24 days. It was held that the redelivery on May 7th was premature, that hire at the original rate was payable until redelivery on June 23d, and that the expense of fumigation was upon the charterer. The opinion is reported in (D.C) 25 F.(2d) 868.

* * *

SWAN, Circuit Judge (after stating the facts as above)

When a charter party is for a term of "about six months," or other stated period, the use of the word "about" is interpreted as signifying an intention to allow the charterer a reasonable leeway in respect to the date on which the vessel shall be surrendered. It is a recognition, based on the necessities of practical business, that her voyages cannot be planned so accurately as to bring her home on an exact date, and that the parties have contemplated the possibility of a reasonable shortening or lengthening of the stated term. Hence, if a voyage terminates in a port of redelivery before the end of the stated term, the charterer may require the vessel to make another "reasonable" voyage, even though it is certain to overlap the stated term. If however, the time remaining before the end of the stated term is so short as to render another voyage "unreasonable," then the vessel may be surrendered by the charterer, or withdrawn by the owner, thus creating an underlap. These rules have been often stated by this court. *The*

Rygja (C. C. A.) 161 F. 106; *Trechmann S. S. Co., Limited v. Munson S. S. Line (C. C. A.)* 203 F. 692; Munson S. S. *Line v. Elswick Steam Shipping Co.*, 207 F. 984 (D.C. N.Y), affirmed (C. C. A.) 214 F. 84 *Damp Skibs, Etc., v. Tropical Fruit Co.* (C. C. A.) 281 F. 749; *The Negus*, 298 F. 747 (D. C. N. Y.), *affirmed* (C. C. A.) 298 F. 752.

In the case at bar the District Court held that the phrase "for about two (2) to about three (3) consecutive calendar months" permitted no surrender of the vessel before May 20th; in other words, that there could be no underlap to the term of two months from her delivery. There is much force in the charterer's argument that the use of two "abouts" shows an intention to allow latitude at each end of the two to three month term, and that the court's construction gives no effect whatever to the first "about." But even if the charterer's construction be adopted, and it be conceded that an underlap would have been permissible under some circumstances, the option to surrender could be validly exercised on May 7th only if no "reasonable" voyage were then available. On conflicting evidence the court found that a reasonable estimate of the time required for a voyage from New York to Cuba and return was from 21 to 24 days. This finding is sufficiently supported to be accepted on appeal. It shows that the probable overlap from undertaking the voyage would be less than the 13-day underlap which would result from surrendering her on May 7th. Under such surrendering we think the voyage was reasonable in respect to its probable duration. So much is at least implied, if not decided, in *The Negus* and in *Trechmann v. Munson, supra.* That the voyage was commercially practicable and available to the charterer seems to be sufficiently demonstrated by the actual voyage under the charter of May 9th. Hence we agree with the court's conclusion that the redelivery on May 7th was premature and ineffective.

So we come to the question of damages. Where the charterer is privileged to make a voyage which will result in an overlap, and actually makes it, he must pay hire at the charter rate until redelivery. *Straits of Dover S.S. Co. v. Munson*, 95 F. 690 (D.C.) affirmed 100 F. 1005 (C.C.A. 2); *Anderson v. Munson*, 104 F. 913 (D.C.); *Ropner v. Inter-American S.S. Co.*, 243 F. 549 (C.C.A. 2). The instant case presents the problem of what hire is payable where an overlapping voyage is privileged, but is not made; for the voyage performed under the second charter was without prejudice. The owner argues that, where an overlapping voyage is permissible, it is compulsory.

It is true that, in *Munson S.S. Line v. Elswick Steam Shipping Co., Supra*, Judge Veeder says (page 991): "... If the voyage be reasonable its is compulsory; that is, the charter hire must be paid." And similar language, relying upon the *Elswick* Case, may be found in Judge Hough's opinion in *Dampskibs, etc., v. Tropical Fruit Co., supra*, at page 742. Both of these statements, however, were plain obiter, and it is clear that Judge Veeder's dictum cannot have the meaning ascribed to it by the appellee, because later in the same paragraph he adds: "... The owner either gets his vessel back if no such voyage is practicable, or, if it is practicable and not ordered by the charterer, his charter hire to the end of the specified term."

In affirming Judge Veeder's opinion, we expressly reserved a decision on this point. It was, however, decided in *Trechmann v. Munson, supra.* That case held that, where the charterer could have set out upon an overlapping voyage, but refused to do so, such refusal did not entitle the owner to hire during the assumed duration of such a voyage, but only to the date when the vessel could be legally redelivered. There a vessel chartered for "about 12 months" was surrendered 29 days before the expiration of the 12-month period. A voyage which would take 43 days was available to her. To reduce the loss, the parties made a second charter, without prejudice, at a lower rate. This voyage took 59 days. The owner claimed hire at the original charter rate for the full 59 days. The District Court allowed the original rate for 43 days. On appeal, the owner was awarded the original rate for only 29 days; that is, until the expiration of the stated term of the charter.

It is clear that the charterer is under no duty to the owner to employ the vessel; his full duty is performed by paying hire to the end of the term agreed upon. On May 20th, the charterer could have made a valid redelivery. The option which the charterer had to use her beyond May 20th cannot give the owner the right to insist that the charterer shall do so. To say that it does is to put the charterer's arrangements at the owner's mercy, which is precisely the opposite of what is intended by the charter. So the damages should be limited to the difference between the two charter hires until the expiration of two months; that is, until May 20th.

* * *

Note

The position taken by the parties in an overlap/underlap dispute is driven primarily by the relationship between the charterparty rate of hire and the prevailing market rate at the end of the charter period. In *Torvald Klaveness A/S v. Arni Maritime Corp. (The Gregos)* [1995] 1 Lloyd's Rep. 1, 4 (H.L.), Lord Mustill said:

> Where the charter-party is for a period of time rather than a voyage, and the remuneration is calculated according to the time used rather than the service performed, the risk of delay is primarily on the charterer. For the shipowner, so long as he commits no breach and nothing puts the ship off-hire, his right to remuneration is unaffected by a disturbance of the charterer's plans. It is for the latter to choose between cautious planning, which may leave gaps between employments, and bolder scheduling with the risk of setting aims which cannot be realized in practice.
>
> This distribution of risk holds good during for most of the chartered service. As the time for redelivery approaches things become more complicated. (The word 'redelivery' is inaccurate, but it is convenient, and I will use it). If the market is rising, the charterer wants to have the use of the vessel at the chartered rate for as long as possible. Conversely, the shipowner must think ahead to the next employment, and if as is common he has made a forward fixture he will be in difficulties if the vessel is retained by the charterer longer than had been foreseen. This conflict of interest becomes particularly acute when there is time left for only one more voyage before the expiry of the charter, and disputes may arise if the charterer orders the ship to perform a service which the shipowner believes will extend beyond the date fixed for redelivery.

Conversely, if the market is falling, the charterer wants to redeliver the vessel as soon as possible so as to get out of the now disadvantageous charter rate and take advantage of the new, low, market rate. That is the sub-text that explains cases like *Britain S.S. Co. v. Munson S.S. Line*, *supra*.

6. Remedies: Damages — Withdrawal

1. *Note – When Withdrawal Becomes Effective*

In *Diana Co. Maritima, S.A. of P. v. Subfreights of S.S. Adm. F.*, 280 F. Supp. 607, 612 (S.D.N.Y. 1968), the court said:

> The effect of withdrawal of a vessel is to terminate the charter party. *Ocean Cargo Lines, Ltd. v. North Atlantic Marine Co.*, 227 F.Supp. at 881. There is no dispute that the Admiralty Flyer was withdrawn; the only question is *when* was the withdrawal "effective." The significance of the date when the withdrawal became effective is that the amount of the Owner's lien is computed as of that date.
>
> The notice of withdrawal herein clearly speaks in "present" terms. It states that "... you are hereby notified that the vessel is withdrawn ... and owner is taking steps to mitigate damages."
>
> * * *
>
> In the leading case of *Luckenbach v. Pierson*, 229 F. 130 (2nd Cir. 1915), the time charter provided that hire was to be paid semi-monthly in advance, with the shipowner having the "faculty of withdrawing the said steamer" upon default of such payment. Hire due on June 11, 1906 was already in arrears when the shipowner, on June 27, wrote the charterer that, if the arrears were not paid "... by four o'clock this afternoon, I *will withdraw* said steamer from your service ..." At that time, the vessel was being loaded in port. However, the shipowner did not withdraw the vessel on that date. Instead, the vessel sailed; and, on June 30th, the shipowner informed the charterer that the vessel would be withdrawn at the end of the trip.
>
> The Court held that the vessel was not withdrawn on June 27, the date of the notice of withdrawal, because the shipowner allowed the vessel to "proceed on her voyage, a proceeding entirely inconsistent with a then withdrawal" (229 F. at 132). The Court observed that the shipowner could have withdrawn the vessel on the date of the notice of withdrawal by relanding the cargo.
>
> It should be noted that the notice of withdrawal in *Luckenbach* clearly contained "present language"; however, that fact was not deemed controlling. *Cf. Jebsen v. A Cargo of Hemp*, 228 F. 143, 149 (D. Mass.1915) (date of withdrawal determined from owner's conduct controls despite contrary indication in notice of withdrawal).
>
> Judge Ward, writing for the Court of Appeals for this Circuit in *Luckenbach*, stated the rule to be applied:
>
>> [The] withdrawal of a vessel from a charter party means that the owner shall deprive the charterer of any further enjoyment or use of the vessel and take it into his own exclusive possession. This can be presently done, even where the vessel is at sea, *provided she is light; but if there be any cargo on board no withdrawal can be made until the cargo be relanded if the vessel is at the loading port, or until it be discharged if she is at sea or at destination.* (229 F. at 132) (Emphasis added)
>
> The rule of *Luckenbach v. Pierson* has recently been followed and approved in this circuit, *Ocean Cargo Lines, Ltd. v. North Atlantic Marine Co.*, 227 F. Supp. 872, 881 (S.D.N.Y.1964), and in the Ninth Circuit, *Schirmer Stevedoring Co., Ltd. v. Seaboard Stevedoring Corp.*, 306 F.2d 188, 193 (9th Cir. 1962).[7]
>
> Applying the rule of *Luckenbach v. Pierson* to the instant case, the Court holds that withdrawal of the Admiralty Flyer did not become effective until the cargoes were discharged at the United States Gulf ports in December of 1965. As *Luckenbach* makes clear, the language of the notice of withdrawal is not controlling.

---

[7] The Trustee places some reliance on *Italian State Ry. v. Mavrogordatos*, [1919] 2 K.B. 305, which held that a withdrawal was effective immediately even though a vessel was on the high seas. Italian State Ry. represents the English rule as to when a notice of withdrawal is effective. *See* SCRUTTON, CHARTERPARTIES AND BILLS OF LADING (17th ed. 1964) 355; CARVER, CARRIAGE BY SEA (11th ed. Colinvaux 1963) 388. But the English rule is clearly contrary to that which is the law in the Second Circuit. Moreover, Italian State Ry. is factually distinguishable: the vessel had no cargo aboard and was proceeding toward the point of redelivery when the notice of withdrawal was sent.

2. The key to understanding the parties' motivation in relation to withdrawal is consideration of the prevailing market rate of hire at the time the shipowner's right of withdrawal arises. In a rising market, the shipowner is keen to withdraw the vessel from the charterer's service as early as possible, to take advantage of the new, higher, market rate. In a falling market, the shipowner is reluctant to withdraw, preferring to keep the vessel at the charterer's service under the existing contract with its higher-than-market hire rate.

3. Under English law, withdrawal of a ship for non-payment of hire is effective immediately. If the ship is in the middle of a carrying voyage when withdrawal occurs (as it was in *Diana Co. Maritima*, supra), the charterer is left with little choice but to charter the vessel back from the shipowner at the new, higher, market rate, or even at a rate higher than the market. The English courts have refused to intervene in such cases, saying that there is no basis for equity to intervene to relieve commercial parties from the consequences of an unfavorable bargain. *Mardorf Peach & Co. Ltd v. Attica Sea Carriers Corp. of Liberia (The Laconia)* [1977] A.C. 850 (H.L.).

F. Safe Port — Safe Berth

ORDUNA S.A. v. ZEN-NOH GRAIN CORPORATION

913 F.2d 1149, 1991 AMC 346 (5th Cir. 1990)

W. Eugene DAVIS, Circuit Judge

While loading a ship, a loading arm fell from a grain elevator tower causing the ship damage. The district court found the elevator operator, the designer of the tower, and the ship's charterer liable for that damage. The various parties have filed multiple appeals and cross-appeals raising several issues. We affirm in part, reverse in part, and remand the case to the district court.

I. Facts

In March 1984, a steel loading arm fell from a grain elevator on the Mississippi River onto the deck of the M/V TREBIZOND which was loading cargo in the berth below. This incident damaged the ship and delayed its departure. The shipowners, Orduna, S.A. and Transglobal Maritime Corporation (collectively Orduna), sued its voyage charterers, Euro-Frachtkontor G.m.b.H. (Euro); the owner and operator of the grain elevator, Zen-Noh Grain Corporation (Zen-Noh); the design engineering firm of the collapsed structure, F & P Engineers, Inc. (collectively, with its insurers, F & P); and the loading arm manufacturer, Buhler-Miag, Inc. (Buhler). These defendants filed a flurry of cross-claims and third-party claims among themselves.

Following a bench trial, the district court found Zen-Noh and F & P jointly and severally liable to Orduna. The district court awarded Orduna $378,528.75 in damages with interest running from date of judgment. The court also found Euro liable to Orduna, but granted Euro full indemnification from Zen-Noh and F & P. The court apportioned fault between Zen-Noh and F & P at one-third and two-thirds respectively.

The parties raise several issues on appeal. Zen-Noh argues that the trial court erred in finding it negligent in not inspecting and maintaining its grain elevator properly. Zen-Noh also argues that the trial court should have found that the exculpatory clause of Zen-Noh's dock tariff relieved it from liability. Zen-Noh further argues that the trial court erred in failing to allow it to submit rebuttal testimony, and it questions the damages awarded to plaintiff.

F & P argues that because its inadequate design of the tower did not *cause* the accident, the judgment against it cannot stand. Euro argues that it should not be liable to Orduna based solely on the safe berth clause in the charter party. Orduna also challenges the district court's denial of prejudgment interest. We will address all these issues in turn.

* * *

V. Euro's Appeal

Euro, the vessel charterer, argues that the district court erred in imposing liability against it in the face of the finding that its conduct was unrelated to the tower's collapse. The district court predicated liability against Euro on the charter party between Euro and Orduna which contained a standard "safe berth" clause.[6] The trial court held that the clause made Euro the warrantor of the safety of the berth it selected for the vessel. Euro argues that at most this clause imposed upon it the obligation to use due diligence to select a safe berth.

In imposing liability against Euro, the trial court relied on three Second Circuit cases. These cases hold that a charterer warrants the safety of the berth it selects when the charter party includes a safe berth clause. *See Venore Transp. Co. v. Oswego Shipping Corp.*, 498 F.2d 469, 472-73 (2d Cir.), *cert. denied,* 419 U.S. 998, 95 S. Ct. 313, 42 L. Ed. 2d 272 (1974); *Ore Carriers of Liberia, Inc. v. Navigen Co.*, 435 F.2d 549, 550 (2d Cir.1970) (per curiam); *Paragon Oil Co. v. Republic Tankers, S.A.*, 310 F.2d 169 (2d Cir.1962), *cert. denied,* 372 U.S. 967, 83 S. Ct. 1092, 10 L. Ed. 2d 130 (1963). *But see Hastorf v. O'Brien*, 173 F. 346, 347 (2d Cir.1909) (charterer held to reasonable man standard); *accord The TERNE,* 64 F.2d 502 (2d Cir.) (charterer not liable when ship caught in ice and damaged), *cert. denied,* 290 U.S. 635, 54 S. Ct. 53, 78 L. Ed. 552 (1933).

The commentators have strongly criticized these Second Circuit decisions which impose liability without fault on the charterer under a safe berth clause. Gilmore and Black argue that "these authorities go too far" for several reasons. G. GILMORE & C. BLACK, THE LAW OF ADMIRALTY § 4-4, at 204-06 (2d ed.1975). First, the master on the scene, rather than a distant charterer, is in a better position to judge the safety of a particular berth. The master is an expert in navigation, knows the draft and trim of his vessel, and is on the spot. Conversely, the charterer, who is usually a merchant, may know nothing about navigation or the vessel and is ordinarily far from the scene. Moreover, the charterer customarily chooses ports and berths based on commercial as opposed to nautical grounds. *Id.*

Second, requiring negligence as a predicate for the charterer's liability does not increase the risk that the vessel will be exposed to an unsafe berth. The standard safe berth clause does not compel the master to take a vessel into an unsafe berth. *Id.* Because courts have interpreted safe berth clauses to free the master from any obligation to enter an unsafe port

---

[6] The safe berth clause provided that the charterers should designate "safe discharging berths [the] vessel being always afloat."

or berth, "it is by no means necessary that they be given the quite different meaning of creating an affirmative liability of charterer to ship, in case of mishap." *Id.* at 205; *see also* J. RAMBERG, UNSAFE PORTS AND BERTHS § 17, at 664 (1967) ("[A]n evaluation of the arguments *pro et contra* does not lead to a strict liability for the charterer."); Smith, *Time and Voyage Charters: Safe Port/Safe Berth*, 49 TUL.L.REV. 860, 868 (1975) ("[C]ourts are placing an undeserved burden on the charterer in holding him to a warrantor's liability.").

Moreover, Euro and the commentators (*see* G. GILMORE & C. BLACK, *supra*, § 4-4, at 205-06; Smith, *supra*, at 862-63) argue that a Supreme Court decision which has never been overruled or weakened supports their position. In *Atkins v. Fibre Disintegrating Co.*, 2 F. Cas. 78 (E.D.N.Y.1868) (No. 601), *aff'd*, 85 U.S. (18 Wall.) 272, 21 L. Ed. 841 (1873), the district court confronted a claim for damages to a vessel that resulted when she entered an unsafe port. Judge Benedict held:

> [I]t is said that the master was induced to accept [the port] as within the terms of the contract by the representations of the charterers' agent that it was a safe port; and that his acceptance was a qualified acceptance, given upon representations which amounted to warranty.
>
> * * *
>
> I do not think it could be justly held ... that any thing said or done by the master was calculated to lead the charterers' agent to suppose that [the port] was not within the privilege given by the charter party, or to inform him that the charterer was to be held responsible in case the vessel received injury in using that port.

Id. at 79.

On appeal of a jurisdictional issue, the Supreme Court affirmed Judge Benedict's decision on the merits:

> In regard to the merits—after a careful examination of the record—we have found no reason to dissent from the views of the learned district judge by whom the case was heard. However full might be our discussion, we should announce the same conclusions. They are clearly expressed and ably vindicated in his opinion. To go again through the process by which they were reached would be a matter rather of form than substance.

85 U.S. (18 Wall.) at 299 (citation omitted). Several district courts have at least in dicta expressed a preference for this view. *See In re Jubilant Voyager Corp. of Pan.* (The COCKROW), 1984 AMC 1725, 1726 (E.D.Va.1983) (citing GILMORE AND BLACK) (the proposition that a safe berth clause holds a charterer liable regardless of fault "may not be a sound one"); *California through Dep't of Transp. v. The S/T NORFOLK*, 435 F. Supp. 1039, 1047-49 (N.D.Cal.1977) (charterer not liable to shipowner under safe berth clause when charterer exercised due diligence); *National Marine Serv., Inc. v. Gulf Oil Co.*, 433 F. Supp. 913, 917-18 (E.D.La.1977)

(quoting Gilmore and Black) (charterer not liable to shipowner under safe berth clause for shipowner's own negligence), *aff'd mem. per curiam*, 608 F.2d 522 (5th Cir.1979); *see also International Tank Terminals, Ltd. v. M/V ACADIA FOREST*, 579 F.2d 964, 967 (5th Cir.1978) (citing Gilmore and Black) (noting that use of safe berth clause "to impose liability upon the charter party who directs the vessel to a certain port ... has been under attack recently").

We agree with the commentators cited above that no legitimate legal or social policy is furthered by making the charterer warrant the safety of the berth it selects. Such a warranty could discourage the master on the scene from using his best judgment in determining the safety of the berth. Moreover, avoiding strict liability does not increase risks because the safe berth clause itself gives the master the freedom not to take his vessel into an unsafe port.

In conclusion, we hold that a charter party's safe berth clause does not make a charterer the warrantor of the safety of a berth. Instead the safe berth clause imposes upon the charterer a duty of due diligence to select a safe berth. Thus because the district court did not find Euro negligent, we must vacate the district court's judgment in favor of Orduna and against Euro.[7]

Notes

1. *Port Rendered Unsafe by Subsequent Political Events*

In *The "Evia" (No. 2)*, 1982 2 Lloyd's Rep. 311, Lord Roskill delivered the following speech:

> My Lords, as a result of the outbreak of hostilities between Iran and Iraq in September, 1980, a large number of ships were trapped in the Shatt-al-Arab waterway. The appellants had the misfortune to be the owners of such a ship, *Evia*, registered in Liberia. The respondents were the time charterers of *Evia* under a time charter-party for a period of 18 months, two months more or less at the respondents' option, concluded in Greece and dated Nov. 12, 1979. This time charter-party was in the Baltime 1939 form as amended in 1950, that form being as is usual substantially amended and with a large number of typed clauses attached.
>
> * * *
>
> My Lords, I propose to consider first the question which arises on cl. 2. It will be convenient to quote again those few words in that clause which are relevant—
>
> The vessel to be employed ... between good and safe ports ...
>
> * * *
>
> In order to consider the scope of the contractual promise which these eight words impose upon a charterer, it must be determined how a charterer would exercise his undoubted right to require the shipowner to perform his contractual obligations to render services with his ship, his master, officers and crew, the consideration for the performance of their obligation being the charterer's regular payment of time-charter hire. The answer must be that a charterer will exercise that undoubted contractual right by giving the shipowner orders to go to a particular port or place of loading or discharge. It is clearly at that point of time when that order is given that that contractual promise by the charterer regarding the safety of that intended port or place must be fulfilled. But that contractual promise cannot mean that that port or place must be safe when that order is given, for

---

[7] Euro also argues that the berth was "safe" at the time it directed the vessel to it and became "unsafe" only at a later time. Our disposition of this issue makes it unnecessary for us to reach this argument....

were that so, a charterer could not legitimately give orders to go to an ice-bound port which he and the owner both knew in all human probability would be ice-free by the time that vessel reached it. Nor, were that the nature of the promise, could a charterer order the ship to a port or place the approaches to which were at the time of the order blocked as a result of a collision or by some submerged wreck or other obstacles even though such obstacles would in all human probability be out of the way before the ship required to enter. The charterer's contractual promise must, I think, relate to the characteristics of the port or place in question, and in my view, means that when the order is given that port or place is prospectively safe for the ship to get to, stay at, so far as necessary, and in due course, leave. But if those characteristics are such as to make that port or place prospectively safe in this way, I cannot think that if in spite of them, some unexpected and abnormal event thereafter suddenly occurs which creates conditions of unsafety where conditions of safety had previously existed and as a result the ship is delayed, damaged or destroyed, that contractual promise extends to making the charterer liable for any resulting loss or damage, physical or financial. So to hold would make the charterer the insurer of such unexpected and abnormal risks which in my view should properly fall upon the ship's insurers under the policies of insurance the effecting of which is the owner's responsibility under cl. 3 unless, of course, the owner chooses to be his own insurer in these respects.

* * *

My Lords, on the view of the law which I take, since Basrah was prospectively safe at the time of nomination, and since the unsafety arose after her arrival and was due to an unexpected and abnormal event, there was at the former time no breach of cl. 2 by the respondents, and that is the first ground upon which I would dismiss this appeal.

* * *

My Lords, in the case of a time charterer, I cannot bring myself to think that he has no further obligation to the owner even though for the reasons I have given earlier he is not the insurer of the risks arising from the unsafety of the nominated port. Suppose some event has occurred after nomination which has made or will or may make the nominated port unsafe. Is a time charterer obliged to do anything further? What is a voyage charterer to do in similar circumstances? My Lords, this problem seems never to have been judicially considered in any detail; indeed, as I have already stated, in *The Houston City* the Privy Council expressly declined to consider it.

In my opinion, while the primary obligation of a time charterer under cl. 2 of this charter-party is that which I have already stated, namely, to order the ship to go only to a port which, at the time when the order is given, is prospectively safe for her, there may be circumstances in which, by reason of a port, which was prospectively safe when the order to go to it was given, subsequently becoming unsafe, cl. 2, on its true construction, imposes a further and secondary obligation on the charterer.

In this connection two possible situations require to be considered. The first situation is where, after the time charter has performed his primary obligation by ordering the ship to go to a port which, at the time of such order, was prospectively safe for her, and while she is still proceeding towards such port in compliance with such order, new circumstances arise which render the port unsafe. The second situation is where, after the time charterer has performed his primary obligation by ordering the ship to go to a port which was, at the time of such order, prospectively safe for her, and she has proceeded to and entered such port in compliance with such order, new circumstances arise which render the port unsafe.

In the first situation it is my opinion that cl. 2, on its true construction, (unless the cause of the new unsafety be purely temporary in character) imposes on the time charterer a further and secondary obligation to cancel his original order and, assuming that he wishes to continue to trade the ship, to order her to go to another port which, at the time when such fresh order is given, is prospectively safe for her. This is because cl. 2 should be construed as requiring the time charterer to do all that he can effectively do to protect the ship from the new danger in the port which has arisen since his original order for her to go to it was given.

In the second situation the question whether cl. 2, on its true construction, imposes a further and secondary obligation on the time charterer will depend on whether, having regard to the nature and consequences of the new danger in the port which has arisen, it is possible for the ship to avoid such danger by leaving the port. If, on the one hand, it is not possible for the ship so to leave, then no further and secondary obligation is imposed on the time charterer. This is because cl. 2 should not be construed as requiring the time charterer to give orders with which it is not possible for the ship to comply, and which would for that reason be ineffective. If, on the other hand, it is possible for the ship to avoid the new danger in the port which has arisen by leaving, then a further and secondary obligation is imposed on the time charterer to order the ship to leave the port forthwith, whether she has completed loading or discharging or not, and, assuming that he wishes to continue to trade the ship, to order her to go to another port which, at the time when such fresh order is given, is prospectively safe for her. This is again because cl. 2 should be construed as requiring the time charterer to do all that he can effectively do to protect the ship from the new danger in the port which has arisen since his original order for her to go to it was given.

My Lords, what I have said with regard to these further and secondary obligations under cl. 2 of this charter-party will apply to any other similarly worded "safe port" clauses.

* * *

My Lords, before leaving this part of the case, I would mention three further matters. First, with all respect to Sir Sebag Shaw, I cannot accept (still ignoring cl. 21) that cl. 2 only applies to physical unsafety. I think that both as a matter of construction and on the authorities, of which *Ogden v. Graham* is but an example, though an impressive one, it covers political unsafety as well. Secondly, it will have been observed that throughout this judgment I have eschewed the use of the phrases "safe port warranty" and "warranty of safety" though the word "warranty" is often used in the cases to which I have referred. As with the so-called warranty of seaworthiness, so with this so-called warranty, its use is historic but as well-known recent decisions have shown, inaccurate. So long as it is realized that it is used as a matter of convenience, and not an expression of the legal consequences of its breach and is not a definition of the character of the provision under consideration, that use may be convenient. But since your Lordships are here concerned with statements of principle, I have ventured, at the risk of accusations of pedantry, to call the obligation under discussion a contractual promise for in truth that is what it is rather than a warranty. Thirdly, if it be said that the imposition of these further and secondary obligations upon a time charterer may put him in difficulties with any sub time charterer or voyage charterer from him or under any bills of lading issued by him or at his behest, my answer is that a time charterer would be prudent to protect himself against the consequences of such possible inconsistencies by including suitable wording into whatever further contracts he chooses himself to make or into which the owners, the master or other agent of the owners, wish to enter.

* * *

2. *Unsafe Port and Master's Negligence*

Negligence on the part of the master may relieve a charterer of its liability under the safe port provision. The master's negligence may permit the fact-finder to conclude either that the port was safe because peril could have been avoided by prudent seamanship, or, even where the port is found to be unsafe, the master's conduct may be regarded as supervening cause. But not every risk taken by the master will be considered to be a superseding cause. As explained in *American President Lines, Ltd. v. United States*, 208 F. Supp. 573, 577-78 (N.D. Cal. 1961):

The decisions involving the so-called "safe-port" and "safe-berth" provisions in charter party agreements make it very clear that a charterer cannot escape liability for damage ultimately resulting from a directive that the chartered vessel go to an unsafe port or berth merely because the captain in attempting to comply, follows an obviously risky course of action in preference to an available alternative which might have avoided the damage. In most of the decisions finding liability on the part of the charterer there was a danger foreseeable to the captain and an available alternative.[1]

The decisions recognize that when a charterer directs a vessel to a port the captain believes to be unsafe, he is confronted with a difficult dilemma. He may refuse to comply, thus thwarting the desires of the charterer and assuming the risk of an ultimate determination that the port was not in fact unsafe. Or, he may attempt to comply, and run the risk of making a miscalculation in seeking to avoid the danger to which the charterer's directive has subjected the vessel. When a captain has been placed in such a dilemma by a charterer's breach of contract in directing the vessel to an unsafe port, the entire burden of responsibility for the safety of the ship cannot legally be shifted to the captain. If the captain elects to attempt to comply with the charterer's directive, it would be inequitable to relieve the charterer of liability for harm caused by the peril which his wrongful demand created merely because the captain's choice of alternative courses, which give promise of avoiding such peril, proves to be incorrect. Thus, the applicable decisions have established the principle that the charterer is not relieved of legal responsibility for the consequences of his breach of contract unless the course followed by the captain is so imprudent that it can fairly be said to be an intervening act of negligence.[2] It is not enough that the course followed by the captain entails some foreseeable risk of harm. For, some risk is inherent in any attempt to proceed to an unsafe port. To constitute an intervening act of negligence, the course followed by the captain must entail an unreasonable risk.

In the present case the Board of Contract Appeals found that the Government breached the charter party agreement by directing the PRESIDENT ARTHUR to load at the unsafe port of Villa do Porto. The master of the PRESIDENT ARTHUR was initially unable to enter Villa do Porto because of the hazardous weather conditions. But, in an effort to comply with the Government's demand that cargo be loaded there, he followed the Port Captain's suggestion that he anchor in Sao Lourenco Bay to await an improvement in the weather. The Board of Contract Appeals found that this course entailed a foreseeable risk of harm because of the very weather conditions which made Villa do Porto an unsafe port. It also found that the master had an available alternative in that he might have skirted the island until the weather improved. It concluded that it necessarily followed that the damage suffered by the PRESIDENT ARTHUR at Sao Lourenco Bay was not the proximate result of the Government's demand that she load cargo at Villa do Porto. In so concluding, the Board committed an error of law. For the law, as established by the cited decisions, is that action taken by a master in an effort to comply with the demand of a charterer that he proceed to an unsafe port does not constitute an intervening act of negligence merely because the action taken entails some foreseeable risk. To break the chain of causation, the master's action must entail a risk that is unreasonable under all the circumstances."

---

[1] *See e.g., Reardon Smith Line Ltd. v. Australian Wheat Board,* 1956 Appeal Cases 266; *Compania Naviera Maropan v. Bowaters,* 2 Q.B. 68 (1955); *G.W. Grace & Co., Ltd. v. General Steam Navigation Co., Ltd.,* 2 K.B. 383 (1950); *P. Dougherty Co. v. Bader Coal Co.,* 244 F. 267 (D.C. Mass.1917); *The Northman,* 189 F. 33 (2 Cir. 1911).

[2] *Reardon Smith Line Ltd. v. Australian Wheat Board,* 1956 Appeal Cases 266; *Compania Naviera Maropan v. Bowaters,* 2 Q.B. 68 (1955); *G.W. Grace & Co., Ltd. v. General Steam Navigation Co.,* Ltd. 2 K.B. 383 (1950).

G. Voyage Charters

1. Late Delivery—Cancellation

PAN CARGO SHIPPING CORPORATION v. UNITED STATES

234 F. Supp. 623, 1965 AMC 2649 (S.D.N.Y. 1964), *aff'd*, 373 F.2d 525 (2d Cir.), *cert. denied*, 389 U.S. 836, 88 S. Ct. 51, 19 L. Ed. 2d 98 (1967)

[Libelant Pan Cargo Shipping Corporation (Pan Cargo) entered into a voyage charter party with the U.S. Navy on 3 December 1957. Under the charter party, Pan Cargo's tanker "National Peace" was to carry oil to a Far East port from one or more safe ports in the Persian Gulf to be determined by the charterer.

At the time the parties fixed the charter, a boycott by the Arab nations against ships that traded with Israel was in effect. Though aware of this situation, no one for the libelant advised the Navy that the Peace, under her former name of Memory I, had made a prior voyage to Israel. Libelant believed and hoped that because the name of the vessel had been changed since her prior visits to Israel that Arab authorities would not be aware of that voyage.

According to the terms of the charter party, the Navy notified the libelant that the Peace should load its oil cargo at the Saudi Arabian port of Ras Tanura. On 17 December 1957 the vessel docked at Ras Tanura and began discharging her water ballast in preparation for taking on cargo. At this point, the ship was not allowed to conduct any other activity with the shore of the foreign port until it obtained "free practique", permission of the shore authorities.

Prior to completing the discharge of her ballast, an inspection of the ship's logs by a Saudi Arabian official revealed the prior voyage to Israel. Consequently, free practique was denied and the Peace was immediately ordered to lay offshore where she remained.

The charter specified January 5, 1958 as the "canceling date" and included the following provision:

> If the vessel is not ready to load by 4:00 p.m. (local time) on the canceling date named in the voyage order issued hereunder, the Charterer shall have the option of canceling the voyage order by giving the owner notice of such cancellation within twenty-for (24) hours after the canceling date; ...

On 6 January 1958 the Navy gave libelant written notice that it was exercising this option and canceling the charter party, among other things, for failure of the National Peace to be "ready in all respects to load with clearances required of vessel by custom of loading port and laws of Saudi Arabia".

Libelant sues for $160,110.16 as damages for a claimed wrongful cancellation by Navy of the charter party.

The issue is thus whether the consequences of the prohibition by the Saudi Arabian government against loading cargo are to be born by the libelant or by the Navy. Eds.]

* * *

Neither side is really at fault. The loss was occasioned by the refusal of Saudi Arabia to permit the cargo to be loaded.

As between the two parties thus situated, this loss should be borne by libelant, which knew the facts as to the voyage of Memory I to Israel and which deliberately took the risk thereby created. The loss should not be borne by respondent, which did not know the facts as to the voyage of Memory I to Israel and had no control over the events disabling Memory I from loading her cargo at Ras Tanura; respondent did not get the cargo carriage by the National Peace for which it had bargained.

It remains to be seen whether provisions of the charter party prevent a decision otherwise dictated by fairness and equity.

The charter plainly provides that the charterer may cancel if the vessel is not "ready to load" by January 5, 1958. The situation here was precisely covered by that provision.

It is obvious that the Peace was not "ready to load" at Ras Tanura. She had not obtained free pratique and never did obtain it. It was the responsibility of the vessel to secure free pratique. The reasons for its refusal are wholly irrelevant. The result is the same as if Asiatic cholera or some other contagious disease were rampant on board and on this account pratique had been refused. In that event, surely libelant could not claim the vessel as "ready to load". Here, the reason for refusing pratique was not, to our understanding, a reasonable one. But the reasons for the Saudi Arabian decision in this instance are beside the point. The fact is that pratique was refused, the ship was not an "arrived" ship, and did not have entry to the port. That lines were fast to the pier means nothing; no one was permitted to leave the ship; communication with the shore was refused. The vessel was promptly ordered away. She was never "ready to load".

* * *

It should be noted that the charter in suit requires that a notice of readiness be given; there is no option as to this. Whether any notice of readiness was given here is doubtful because the only such notice was addressed by the Master of the Peace to Aramco and not to the charterer. In any event, no effective notice of readiness could be given because the Peace was not in fact "ready to load". The leading case in this area is *Aktieselskabet Fido v. Lloyd Braziliero*, 283 F. 62 (2d Cir. 1922) where it was said (at 69):

> A notice of readiness when a vessel is not actually ready has no effect. A notice is without legal effect, if the facts it states are untrue.

It is laid down in CARVER, CARRIAGE OF GOODS BY SEA (10th ed.), 861-62, as follows:

> Before the lay days at the port of loading can begin to run against the charterer, he must have had notice of the ship's arrival, and of her readiness to receive cargo.

* * *

And such notice cannot be given until the ship is an 'arrived' ship, *i.e.*, has arrived at the stipulated place, and is, so far as she is concerned, ready to load.

* * *

The Austin Friars, 71 L.T. 27 (1894) is a decision of the President of the Probate, Divorce and Admiralty Division. The charterers had the option to cancel "if the ship does not arrive at port of loading and be ready to load on or before midnight of 10th Oct." The ship arrived at the loading port at 11 p.m. (2300) on October 10, "but no one could leave the ship or come on board until the doctor had visited her and pronounced her free from infection". The doctor came on board next morning (October 11); the ship was given medical clearance but the charterers cancelled the charter for failure to be ready to load by midnight, October 10. The registrar had held that the ship was ready to load on arrival at 11 p.m. on October 10. This was specifically disapproved, the President stating:

> If the ship is not in fact ready to load by the specified time, they [the charterers] are to be entitled to cancel the charter party.

* * *

Settle decree or decrees on notice.

Notes

1. In *Pan Cargo Shipping Corp., supra*, the ship never obtained free pratique and so could never give a valid notice of readiness (NOR). In ordinary circumstances, the granting of free pratique is a formality and the ship may give NOR before actually receiving the free pratique clearance. *Shipping Developments Corp. v. V/O Sojuzneftexport: The Delian Spirit* [1972] 1 Q.B. 103; *Logs & Timber Products (Singapore) Pte Ltd v. Keeley Granite (Pty) Ltd (The Freijo)* [1978] 2 Lloyd's Rep. 1. This situation is equivalent to the opening of the ship's hatch covers. The ship is not literally ready to load or discharge until the hatch covers are open, but it may give NOR on arrival at the port, even if the hatch covers are still closed, as they will usually be if the ship has to wait for berth. Lord Justice Parker of the English Court of Appeal described the position as follows in *Antclizo Shipping Corp. v. Food Corp. of India (The Antclizo) (No. 2)* [1992] 1 Lloyd's Rep 558, 564:

> "When the notice is given, the situation must be such that at the earliest time that the charterers or consignees can be ready to perform their part in loading or discharging, the vessel will, barring accidents, be ready at once to perform her part in such operations."

The situation is different if the charterparty specifically provides that laytime cannot commence until the ship is granted free pratique: *See, e.g., Sale Corp of Monrovia v Turkish Cargo Lines General Manager (The Amiral Fahri Engin)* [1993] 1 Lloyd's Rep. 75.

Since July 1st, 2004, when the International Ship and Port Facility Security Code (the ISPS Code) came into force, all ships must receive security clearance before entering port. Ships may be detained by the U.S. Coast Guard for inspection even if they are not actually in violation of the provisions of the Code: for example, if they are arriving from a port about which there are security concerns. Because the granting of security clearance under the ISPS Code is not routine, it may be a prerequisite to the giving of NOR unless the charterparty specifically provides that the ship can give NOR while waiting for clearance.

2. A charter party may provide that the charter has a right to cancel the charter if the vessel is not delivered by a specified date or within a specified period of time. This right, however, will be considered waived if the charterer agrees to an extension of time within which delivery may be made. *Fernales Shipping Co. v. Bonaire Petroleum Corp.*, 733 F.2d 381 (5th Cir. 1984). Where no date for delivery is specified the owner must tender the vessel "with reasonable dispatch." *Sanday v. United States Shipping Board Emergency Fleet Corporation*, 6 F.2d 384 (2d Cir.), *cert. denied*, 269 U.S. 556, 46 S. Ct. 19, 70 L. Ed. 409 (1925).

---

2. Laytime and Demurrage

Notes

1. Disputes about laytime and demurrage use a specialized vocabulary that can be confusing at times. Confusion can be compounded by the common habit of using abbreviations for terms that have technical meanings to begin with: for example, "WWDSSHEXUU", which means "weather working days, Saturdays, Sundays and holidays excluded, unless used". Interpretive assistance can be found in the Voyage Charter Party Laytime Interpretation Rules 1993 (known as Voylayrules 93), issued jointly by the Baltic and International Maritime Council (BIMCO), the Comité Maritime International (CMI), the Federation of National Associations of Ship Brokers and Agents (FONASBA) and the International Association of Dry Cargo Shipowners (INTERCARGO). The Voylayrules 93 are available on the Tulane Maritime Law Center website at www.tulanemaritimelaw.net/docs/voylayrules. The Voylayrules definitions of "laytime" and "demurrage" themselves are as follows:

> "LAYTIME" shall mean the period of time agreed between the parties during which the owner will make and keep the vessel available for loading or discharging without payment additional to the freight.
> "DEMURRAGE" shall mean an agreed amount payable to the owner in respect of delay to the vessel beyond the laytime, for which the owner is not responsible. Demurrage shall not be subject to laytime exceptions.

2. "Demurrage" should be distinguished from "detention." As has been seen demurrage is a charge imposed on the charterer for exceeding lay days or otherwise delaying the ultimate redelivery of the vessel to its owner. This should be distinguished from detention which is a penalty imposed on a charterer for a wrongful or unreasonable delay in redelivery of the vessel to its owner. A charter party may provide for demurrage for 10 days at $2,000 per day. If, however, the vessel is delayed beyond the specified 10 days, the owner may be entitled to *damages* for detention.

Also, where a charterer is able to expedite the redelivery to the owner such as by loading or unloading in less time than specified as laydays, the charter may be entitled to a financial credit or bonus called dispatch. *Government of Republic of Indonesia v. M/V Glapkos*, 553 F. Supp. 272, 1986 AMC 602 (E.D. La. 1982).

ORIENT SHIPPING ROTTERDAM B.V. v. HUGO NEU & SONS, INC.

918 F. Supp. 806, 1996 AMC 1366 (S.D.N.Y. 1996)

* * *

I

The charterparty between plaintiff and defendant, dated June 19, 1992, called for the Mastrogiorgis B to load a full cargo of shredded scrap at New York and then proceed to one safe berth in Bombay.

The charterparty provided in clause 18:

> Cargo is to be loaded, stowed, trimmed at the average rate of 10000 MT per weather working days of 24 consecutive hours, Saturdays after noon, Sundays and holidays excepted, even if used.
> Cargo is to be discharged at the average rate of 1500 MT per weather working day of 24 consecutive hours, Saturdays, Sundays and holidays excepted, even if used.
> Laytime is reversible.

The vessel loaded 21,262.8 metric tons of cargo at New York. She departed that port on June 25, 1992. On August 9, 1992, the vessel arrived at the port of Bombay.

The master tendered notice of readiness at 11:00 a.m. on August 9, which defendant's Bombay agent accepted on August 10. Upon arrival at the port, the Mastrogiorgis B anchored at the Bombay Floating Light. On August 21 the vessel shifted from the Bombay Floating Light to the anchorage. She was free of pratique on August 21. The vessel remained at the anchorage until August 25 when the port authorities ordered her to shift back to the Bombay floating light. The vessel did not berth until September 10, 1992, when discharging began.

The delay the Mastrogiorgis B encountered in berthing at Bombay resulted from port congestion. During the months of July and August, 1992, a total of eleven vessels with scrap cargoes arrived at the port. Seven scrap vessels arrived between July 13 and August 15. When the Mastrogiorgis B arrived at Bombay on August 9, there were three scrap vessels in berth and three earlier arriving vessels awaiting berth.

* * *

At midnight on June 30, 1992, an India-wide transporters' strike became effective. The strike ended on July 13. No trucks were available to receive scrap cargoes at Bombay during the strike and in point of fact, no scrap vessels discharged at the port during that time.

The parties dispute the effect, if any, of the transporters' strike on the delay encountered by the Mastrogiorgis B in obtaining a berth. I draw the logical inference that the strike, which made trucks unavailable to receive scrap cargoes, contributed to the number of vessels waiting in line to discharge when the Mastrogiorgis B arrived at Bombay. However, in the view I take of the case, that finding is not necessary to the decision.

II

The cargo receivers completed discharging the Mastrogiorgis B's cargo on October 4, 1992. The delay the vessel encountered in obtaining a berth caused her to exceed the reversible laytime for loading and discharging. Thus plaintiff asserts a claim for demurrage.

The liability of defendant charterer for demurrage turns upon the proper construction of clause 56 of the charterparty. That clause provides:

> Should the delivery of cargo to the place of loading, or shipment or loading or discharging of cargo be prevented or interfered with by reason of war, blockade, revolutions, insurrections, mobilizations, strikes, lockouts of any class of workers, civil commotions, riots, acts of God, plague or other epidemics, the time by which loading/discharging shall be prevented or interfered with by any such cause or causes, or by other cause or causes whatsoever, whether or not of a nature or kind as enumerated above, which shall be beyond the Charterers/Receivers control, shall not count, and demurrage shall not accrue unless the vessel is already on demurrage.

This exception clause is drafted in the broadest possible language. While "strikes" is one of the several identified exceptions, the phrase "or by other cause or causes whatsoever" takes the clause out of the doctrine of *ejusdem generis*. Accordingly the exception clause relieves defendant from liability for demurrage resulting from port congestion, so long as that congestion was "beyond the Charterers/Receiver's control," clearly the case here.

* * *

Following the alternative holding of the *Rutherglen*, I conclude that in the case at bar, the parties agreed that demurrage would not accrue during delay occasioned by port congestion that was beyond the control of the defendant charterer.

III

Given my construction of the exceptions clause in this charter party, I need not decide whether the congestion at Bombay resulted from the land transporters' strike. But it may be useful to recite my finding on that aspect of the case as well.

I find by a preponderance of the credible evidence that the transporters' strike, which made trucks unavailable to receive scrap cargoes at Bombay during the first two weeks in July, resulted in escalating congestion and delay.

* * *

The lingering effect upon the port of the transporters' strike, demonstrated by a preponderance of the evidence, is sufficient to bring the resulting delay of the Mastrogiorgis B in berthing within the strike exception in clause 56. That is the conclusion reached by Judge Learned Hand in *The Nordhvalen*, 1923 A. M. C. 398 (S.D.N.Y.1923) (not officially reported). Cargo at the discharge port in question had to be discharged into lighters. A strike of longshoreman had prevented the lighters from being discharged. The strike had been called off when the vessel arrived, but she had to wait for enough lighters to be discharged before her own cargo could be worked. Judge Hand held that the strike exception covered the case: "*The Nordhvalen* was as directly held up by the past strike as she might have been by a present one." 1923 A. M. C. at 399. In reaching that conclusion, Judge Hand cited and followed an English case, *Leonis S.S. Co. v. Joseph Rank, Ltd.*, 11 Asp.M.C. 162. He regarded *Leonis* as "precisely in point," saying of it: "There the strike and insurrection had ended before the *Leonis* arrived at Bahia, but the harbor was filled with vessels with full hulls. The consequent delay was held to fall within a similar [strike] clause." *Id.*

* * *

Note

In *United States v. Atlantic Refining Co.*, 112 F. Supp. 76 (D.N.J. 1951) the court discussed the impact of strikes on the charterer's obligation to pay demurrage:

> It is well recognized that demurrage is extended freight and that the risk of vicissitudes which prevent the loading or discharge of cargo within the stipulated lay days lies unconditionally with the charterers. *Yone Suzuki v. Central Argentine Ry.*, 2 Cir., 27 F.2d 795; *The Marpesia*, 2 Cir., 292 F. 957. But, this absolute liability to pay demurrage is subject to three exceptions: (1) specific exonerating clauses in the charter party; (2) the delay being attributed to the fault of the shipowner or those for whom he is responsible; and (3) a vis major amounting to "a sudden or unforeseen interruption or prevention of the act itself of loading or discharging, not occurring throughout the connivance or fault of the charterers. *Crossman v. Burrill*, 179 U.S. 100, 21 S. Ct. 38, 42 L. Ed. 106; *see also*, *The Marpesia*, *supra*.
>
> There is no question of vis major involved here for it can hardly be claimed that the strike referred to in the proof (particularly in view of the contention of respondent) was so unusual, extraordinary and unexpected a circumstance as to be equivalent to vis major.
>
> Respondent contends, assuming arguendo, that the vessel required the assistance of tugboats in order to dock at the Fort Mifflin terminal, and was unable to obtain tugboat assistance because of a strike, the respondent would not be answerable for the resulting delay for the reason that Clause 20(a) of Part II, the general "strike exception" clause of the charter party is a complete and sufficient excuse. However, it does not appear that respondent's exculpation would be so justified particularly in the light of the specific limitations in the demurrage clause (10). In an analogous situation in the case of *Continental Grain Co. v. Armour Fertilizer Works*, D.C., 22 F. Supp. 49, 53, the court said:
>
> The general 'strike exception' clause in the charter party* does not prevent the running of demurrage; some similar phrase is necessary in conjunction with the demurrage clause to free the charterer from the burden of paying demurrage when the delay is due to strikes, etc.
>
> A review of the cases, wherein the courts have held that charterers were not liable for demurrage for delays due to strikes, reveals that, in addition to the general 'strike exception' clause, the charters also contained stipulations exonerating the charters from liability, for demurrage when the delay was due to strikes, riots, etc., said stipulations being incorporated in or appurtenant to the 'lay day' or 'demurrage' clauses of the charter parties. [Cases cited.] *See also Yone Suzuki v. Central Argentine Ry.*, *supra.*

---

* This clause exculpated the vessel, owner, master and the charterer from, *inter alia*, "any loss or damage or failure in performing hereunder, arising from, ...; strike or lockout...."

a. Arrived Vessel

DEAN H.

Arbitration at New York, July 17, 1952

1953 AMC 593

* * *

The Dispute

The owner claims demurrage in the sum of $9,792.00 from the charterer of the vessel on the ground that the total laytime at loading and discharging from the *Dean H* was 343 hours and 12 minutes over the 180 hours of total laytime provided for in the charters party.

The charterer denies liability for any demurrage. It contends that the owner did not properly compute the laytime. In addition, it contends that it is entitled to damages in the amount of $12,420.05, from the owner for breach of the charter party, on the ground that through the fault of the owner and its agents, the cargo of molasses was discharged at an inadequate rate and was "contaminated by the addition of water." It also alleges a breach of contract by the owner in placing a lien upon the cargo for freight in violation of the provision in the charter party that payment for freight was to be in New York.

The charter party dated March 24, 1950 and executed by the parties is the determinative document in this matter. Under this agreement the Steamship *Dean H* was chartered to transport 10,000 tons of Black Strap Molasses from Cuba to Greece commencing in April of 1950. The record shows that the molasses was loaded at the ports of Caibarien and Havana in Cuba between April 20th and 25th and that the ship arrived at Piraeus Roads on May 17, 1950. Because her draft was too deep it was necessary to lighter part of the molasses before the ship could proceed to the named port in Greece, Eleusis. Unloading was finally completed at Eleusis on May 27, 1950.

* * *

B. *Unloading at Piraeus.* With respect to the laytime for unloading, the chief dispute concerns the question whether the owner was justified under the charter party in commencing computation from the time the Steamship *Dean H* anchored at Pireaus Roads. The charter party provides, in part 1, as follows:

> Discharging Port(s): One (1) safe port in Greece, probably Eleusis (near Piraeus) Charterer's Option.

It is noted that the discharging port is designated as "probably" Eleusis. There is nothing the charter party definitely naming Eleusis as the port of discharge. On the other hand, the charter party is equally silent as to any desire on the charterer's part to name some other port. There is some colloquy between counsel in the minutes of the hearing before the arbitrators as to which of the parties was responsible for designating Eleusis as the discharging port in the new bills of lading, signed May 2, 1950 (*See* S.M. 71-72). Other than the fact that these bills of lading named Eleusis, and in that respect were perfectly consistent with the charter party, it is not at all clear who was responsible. Colloquy between counsel, of course, can hardly be regarded as proper evidence. Considering that under the charter party it was in the charterer's option to name the discharging port, that preference was indicated in the charter party to unload at Eleusis, and that there was no notice from the charterer to substitute another port in Greece, it was reasonable for the Steamship *Dean H* to regard Eleusis as the intended port of discharge, and proceed to act accordingly.

In addition, when the vessel's agent sent a letter to the charterer's agent and the receivers, on May 16th, requesting them to arrange to take part of the cargo "in the open sea of Piraeus Harbor to enable her" to pass through the Salamis Canal for Eleusis because her draft was between 27 feet and 28 feet, the charterer's agent in acknowledging, stated:

> ... we have chartered the S/T *Leman* for partial discharge of the cargo of above mentioned tanker and consequently, we request you to proceed to the necessary formalities (Customs, etc.) for the carrying out of the above work.

There was nothing said in protest of Eleusis as the discharge port. Nor was there any stated desire of the charterer to change the discharge port to Piraeus or some other Greek port.

It is not disputed that no vessel with a draft exceeding 26 feet could reach Eleusis, because to reach the port it was necessary to pass through the Salamis Canal, and Greek Naval regulations prohibited vessels with a draft in excess of 26 feet from passing through the Canal. It is also beyond question that the charterer was on notice that the Steamship *Dean H's* loaded draft would exceed 26 feet. The description of the ship as contained in the charter party includes the following:

> Loaded draft of Vessel on assigned summer freeboard 27 ft. 7/8 in. in salt water.
> Capacity for cargo: 10,000 Tons (2240 lbs. each) of Molasses (10% more or less, Vessel's option).

Furthermore, the cargo was designated in the charter party as:

> BLACKSTRAP MOLASSES—TEN THOUSAND TONS (10,000) (2240 lbs.) MINIMUM/MAXIMUM
>
> Charterer's option.

In contending that the owner was in error in computing laytime from six hours after delivering its notice of readiness at the Piraeus anchorage, the charterer takes the position, *inter alia*, that, under the charter party, the Steamship *Dean H* could not be an "arrived ship" for purposes of unloading laytime, until she was inside the port of Eleusis. (*See* Exs. C and G attached to charterer's main brief). In other words, it argues that, under Clause 5 of the charter party, berth or no berth, laytime does not commence until the ship is within the port designated.

The charterer's argument, however, ignores or fails to consider the provisions of Clauses 1 (a) and 9 of the charter party. Clause 1 (a) states, in material part, as follows:

> ... and being so loaded shall forthwith proceed, as ordered on signing Bills of Lading, to the Discharging Port(s), *or so near thereunto as she may safely get* (*always afloat*) *and deliver said cargo*. (emphasis added)

Clause 9 provides:

> The Vessel shall load and discharge at any safe place or wharf, or alongside vessels or lighters reachable on her arrival, which shall be designated and procured by the Charterer, provided the Vessel can proceed thereto, lie at, and depart therefrom always safely afloat, any lighterage being at the expense, risk and peril of the Charterer. The Charterer shall have the right of shifting the Vessel at ports of loading and/or discharge from one safe berth to another on payment of all ... extra port charges and port expenses incurred by reason of using more than one berth. Time consumed on account of shifting shall count as used laytime except as otherwise provided in Clause 14.

That the anchorage at Pireaus was a safe place was never questioned by the charterer. Therefore, since the Steamship *Dean H* could not enter Eleusis "safely afloat," it was within the terms of the charter party for her to deliver the cargo at the Piraeus anchorage; and the notice of readiness to discharge was properly given.

Mencke vs. Cargo of Java Sugar, 187 U. S. 248, supports the owner's position here. There, the charter party provided, *inter alia*, as follows:

> ... or at option of charterers to order vessels ... to discharge at New York ... or so near the port of discharge as she may safely get and deliver the same, always afloat....
>
> * * *
>
> ... all goods to be brought to and taken from alongside of the ship, always afloat, at the said charterers' risk and expense, ... ; lighterage, if any, to reach the port of destination, or deliver the cargo at port of destination, remains for account of receivers, ...

The vessel was ordered to discharge at New York at a refinery above Brooklyn Bridge, but was unable to proceed directly there because the height of her masts was such that she could not pass under the bridge. Consequently, the cargo was discharged into lighters at a dock below the bridge. In contending that the expense of lighterage was upon the owners, the receivers of the cargo argued that the lighterage clause of the charter party did not relieve the owners of the ship from their obligation to proceed to a designated dock above the bridge, and to there deliver the cargo. In rendering judgment in favor of the owners, however, the Court at pages 253-254, stated:

In such a condition of affairs we think that resort to lighterage was natural and reasonable and within the obvious and fair import of the terms of the charter party. The clause, which is claimed to give the charterers or their assigns the right to appoint the dock in which to discharge cargo contains conditions that the port must be safe, and that the vessel must discharge, always afloat, either at a safe port or so near the port of discharge as she can safely get. ... A ship could not be said to be afloat, whether the obstacle encountered was a shoal or bar in the port over which she could not proceed, or a bridge under or through which she could not pass; nor could she be said to have safely reached a dock if required to mutilate her hull or her permanent masts."

In *The Gazelle and Cargo*, 128 U. S. 474, it was held that where a charter party provided for a voyage "to a safe, direct, Norwegian or Danish port, as ordered on signing bills of lading or as near thereunto as she can safely get and always lay and discharge afloat," it was the responsibility of the charterer to order the ship to a port which she could safely enter with her cargo, or which, at least, had a safe anchorage outside where she could lie and discharge afloat. In *The Edward T. Stotesbury*, 187 Fed. 111, the court ruled that, where by the terms of a charter party the charterer is to name the berth for discharging, he should be ready to receive the cargo when the vessel is ready to deliver, even if she cannot do so either because he has failed to name the berth, or because he has named a berth to which she cannot get, or to which she is prevented from getting through no fault of hers.

The charterer also contends that when the captain of the Steamship *Dean H* found that it was not safe to enter the port of Eleusis, he should have gone to the port of Piraeus instead of anchoring in Piraeus Roads. He cites *The Alhambra*, LR 6 Prob. Div. 68, in support of this contention. The case is distinguishable, however, for there the court held as inadmissible evidence sought to be presented of a custom of vessels which were too deep to enter the port in question to discharge a portion of their cargo in the roads outside, and that it could be done with reasonable safety. Therefore, according to the court, the vessel was justified in refusing to discharge at the unsafe port but in going to the nearest safe port. In the case at bar, as already noted, it is not disputed that the anchorage at Piraeus was a safe berth. That being so, the fact that the master did not take the more extreme step of discharging the entire cargo at some other port, rather than to lighten the ship by 1000 tons so he could unload the remaining 9000 tons at Eleusis as called for in the charter party and the bills of lading, cannot be regarded as a breach. Moreover, according to the Central Harbor Master of Piraeus, the anchorage in Piraeus Roads was considered to be within the legal and fiscal limits of the Port of Piraeus anyway.

C. *Unloading at Eleusis.* Charterer contends that the claim for demurrage must fail because of the inadequate rate of discharge of the cargo caused by, (1) inadequate facilities of the Steamship Dean H, (2) improper temperature, (3) insufficient pressure, and (4) neglect and default of the owner and its agents. The claim that the vessel's hose was inadequate because it was a 6 inch rather than an 8 inch hose, can be dismissed as being without merit. The charter party provides, in Special Provision #4, that the owner will furnish 130 feet of hose, but does not specify any particular dimension as being required.

In the absence of a showing of a custom and practice to furnish hose of a minimum diameter of 8 inches, it cannot be said that the owner was bound to furnish any hose other than that which constituted the regular equipment of the vessel.

The evidence shows that when the Steamship *Dean H* anchored at Eleusis and prepared to discharge to the shore installations, it was discovered that an additional 50 feet of hose was needed. The required hose was furnished by the captain from the vessel's extra equipment in the absence, according to the captain, of any available hose on shore. The captain testified that the extra length of hose was furnished on the condition that neither he nor the ship, "would be responsible for any loss of cargo if the hose broke because I wasn't sure what shape it was in." (SM 21-22). He also testified that after the charterer's representative refused to confirm in writing the above condition, he wrote and gave to the representative the following letter:

> As you have stated you did not have any hose available to make the connection from the vessels (*sic*) stern to the shore line I have complied with your request and loaned you the use of one fifty foot length of six inch hose belonging to the vessel.
>
> * * *
>
> As I informed you this hose is not new and I cannot guarantee it as to strength nor in any way at all but as you have requested that I loan you this hose under the circumstances as stated above I must also warn you that the vessel is not to be responsible for any loss of cargo or freight should this hose burst. I am complying with your request not to exceed 100 pounds pressure on the line also.

The charterer admits receiving the letter in question.

Under the circumstances, any inadequacy in the rate of discharge attributable to the extra length of hose, which was admittedly not in good condition, cannot be made the responsibility of the owner. Clause 10 of the charter party providing that the risk and peril of pumping out operations was on the vessel applies "only so far as the Vessel's permanent connections" are involved.

* * *

Notes

1. *"At or Off Port"*

In *Yone Suzuki v. Central Argentine Ry,* 27 F.2d 795 (2d Cir. 1928), *cert. denied,* 278 U.S. 652, 49 S. Ct. 178, 73 L. Ed. 563 (1929), the charter party provide

> 5. Lay days for discharging shall be as follows: "Commencing from twenty-four (24) hours after arrival at or off discharging port [Buenos Aires] whether steamer is in berth or not, cargo to be taken from alongside by the consignee named in the bill of lading at port of discharge as quickly as steamer can deliver, but in no case at less than 1,000 tons (of 2,240 pounds each) per running day, Sundays and legal holidays excepted, unless used.
>
> * * *

15. Steamer to be discharged at such wharf as party of the second part or their agents may designate, where steamer may always safely lie afloat.

Consignee argued that lay days did not begin to run until the vessel reached its designated wharves. Both the district court and the court of appeals disagreed.

But we agree with the District Court that the clause as to lay days for discharging cannot be explained in any such way. The time when lay days for discharging are to commence is clearly stated to be the time when the vessel is "at or off discharging port whether vessel is in berth or not." The difference in the language from that governing lay days for loading was doubtless intended to give vessels the benefit of delays in reaching berth in calculating demurrage. Vessels at the time were in enormous demand and could exact charter provisions strongly in their favor. Lay days do not necessarily begin when a ship is at or off her berth, but their beginning depends on the terms of the charter provisions. The port is ordinarily the place where the port authorities are exercising jurisdiction. Such a place was Buenos Aires Roads. *Sailing Ship Garston Company v. Hickie*, [1884] 15 Q.B.D. 580. As the District Judge said:

> No vessel can proceed beyond the roads without a permit. No permit is granted till an immediately available berth is designated. There is no stopping place between the roads and berths under ordinary circumstances. The roads are the place where vessels waiting for a berth usually lie. The time when the vessels arrived at the roads, therefore, must determine the beginning of lay days unless it was intended that they should not begin until after a vessel was actually in or at least off its berth.

* * *

We think that such explicit language as "at or off" the "discharging port" made Buenos Aires Roads the place where the lay days began to run. The distance from the docks is not so extraordinarily great, and little, if any, greater than the distance from quarantine in New York Harbor to some of the uptown docks.

* * *

Even if "readiness to discharge," and not arrival "at or off" the port, were the test of the beginning of the lay days, those days would begin when the vessel arrived at the port, and not when she arrived at or just off her berth. Such was the rule laid down by Judge Ward in The Edward T. Stotesbury, *supra*, who said:

When ... the charterer is to name the berth, he should be ready to receive the cargo when the vessel is ready to deliver, even if she cannot do so, either because he has not named the berth, or because he has named a berth to which she cannot get, or to which she is prevented from getting through no fault of hers." *Carbon Slate Co. v. Ennis* (C.C.A.) 114 F. 260; *Roney v. Talbot & Co.* (C.C.A.) 161 F. 309; *The Lake Yelverton* (C.C.A.) 300 F. 47; *Pyman Bros. v. Dreyfus Bros. & Co.*, 24 Q.B.D. 152.

Even a case that goes as far as *Tharsis v. Morel*, [1891] 2 Q.B. 647, does not apply to a charter party which provides that lay days shall begin 24 hours after arrival "whether steamer is in berth or not." *W. K. Niver Coal Co. v. Cheronea S.S. Co.* (C.C.A. 1st Cir. 1905) 142 F. 402, *cert. denied*, 201 U.S. 647, 26 S. Ct. 761, 50 L. Ed. 904 (1906), 5 L.R.A. (N.S.) 126; *Northfield S.S. Co. v. Compagnie L'Union des Gaz*, [1911] 1 K.B. 434. In such cases the lay days begin when the vessel is in port, and not when at her berth.

* * *

2. *Risk of Delay*

In *Brennan Corporation v. United States*, 641 F. Supp. 245, 1987 AMC 1955 (D.D.C. 1986) the United States had contracted with Refinery to provide deballasting services for a vessel, the *Anatoli*, the United States had chartered. Refinery was negligent in providing these services. As a result the vessel became contaminated and could not load the cargo. Another vessel had to be substituted. Owner claimed demurrage for the time lost during the deballasting operation and the time expended in cleaning the contaminated vessel. The court upheld the vessel owner's claim.

> It is recognized under charter party and maritime law that after the Anatoli tendered a notice of readiness, the defendant assumed all risks for delays suffered by the plaintiff. *United States v. Atlantic Refining Co.*, 112 F. Supp. 76, 80 (D. N.J. 1951); *Compagnie, D: Navigazione Mauritius Rome v. Kulukundis*, 182 F. Supp. 258, 263 (E.D. N.Y. 1959), *aff'd*, 277 F.2d 161 (2d Cir. 1960). Once the Anatoli announced a readiness to accept the cargo, the defendant was required to provide a safe berth, to assist in loading the cargo and not to interfere with the Anatoli's efforts in the performance of the loading process. Likewise, the Refinery, acting at the behest of the Sealift Command, had a duty not to prevent the Anatoli from completing the contract. When the Refinery caused the contamination of the Anatoli's ballast tanks, it interfered with the plaintiff's performance of the contract with Sealift Command.
>
> * * *
>
> The government's contention that it had a right to cancel the charter party contract because the Anatoli had contaminated tanks, irrespective of its origin, cannot be sustained. It should not have the right to cancel the agreement when the Refinery hired by the government to provide the cargo and to provide the deballasting facilities was the source of the contamination. "Charterers cannot, on the one hand, set up a barrier to the vessel's satisfying the charter party requirements for becoming an arrived ship and then seek to use this same barrier as a defense to avoid payment of demurrage.*Diamantis Gafos*, 1970 A.M.C. 945, 948 (Arb. N.Y. 1969).

---

3. *Vis Major*

The running of laytime and demurrage time may also be interrupted by *vis major*, which can be defined as "an unusual and extraordinary interruption that could not have been anticipated when the contract was made". *Crossman v. Burrill*, 179 U.S. 100, 21 S. Ct. 38, 45 L. Ed. 106 (1900).

> In the case at bar, the defence of *vis major*, as pleaded in the answer, was that the ship owners were prevented from discharging the cargo, and the charterers were prevented from receiving it, any sooner than they did, by reason of acts of the public enemy, to wit, certain vessels of war, then in the harbor of Rio Janeiro, were engaged in firing upon the forts in the harbor and in making war upon the government of Brazil; that the firing between those vessels and those forts made it impossible to discharge or to receive the cargo from the vessel any sooner than it was discharged or received; and that the detention alleged in the libel was caused by those acts of the public enemy, and not by any default of the charterers...Upon principle, and according to the general current of authority, the detention alleged was not caused by default of the charterers, and did not render them responsible for demurrage, under this charter-party.

Crossman v. Burrill, 179 U.S. 100, 108-09 (1900).

Although *Crossman* shows the effect of *vis major*, it should be noted that very few causes are likely to amount to *vis major* in practice. Very few events that might interrupt loading or discharging are so "unusual and extraordinary" that the parties could not have anticipated them when the contract was made. This is borne out by the fact that charter parties routinely contain provisions contemplating many different kinds of time interruption.

Chapter 6

PERSONAL INJURY AND DEATH CLAIMS

Section I. Remedies of Seamen

Part 1. Maintenance, Cure, and Wages: Cases and Notes

A. Recognition of Cause of Action

COX v. DRAVO CORP.

517 F.2d 620 (3d Cir.), *cert. denied* 423 U.S. 1020, 96 S. Ct. 475, 46 L. Ed. 2d 392 (1975)

GIBBONS, Circuit Judge

The obligation of the vessel to provide maintenance and cure first appeared in American maritime law in *Harden v. Gordon*, 11 F. Cas. 480 (No. 6,047) (C.C.D. Me. 1823). In that well-known decision Justice Story wrote:

> My opinion is that if the plaintiff is entitled to be cured at the expense of the ship, it is a claim in the nature of additional wages during the period of sickness, and is just as proper for a suit [in admiralty], as a claim for additional pay, while in port, or for subsistence in port, where that has been unjustly withheld. It stands upon the same analogy, as the compensation allowed by our laws in cases of short allowance of provisions and water, where it is expressly provided, that the amount shall be recoverable in the same manner as wages...

Id. at 482.

B. Elements of Cause of Action

WARREN v. UNITED STATES

340 U.S. 523, 71 S. Ct. 432, 95 L. Ed. 503, 1951 AMC 416 (1951)

Mr. Justice DOUGLAS delivered the opinion of the Court

Petitioner seeks in this suit maintenance and cure from the United States, as owner of *S.S. Anna Howard Shaw*. Petitioner was a messman who went ashore on leave while the vessel was at Naples in 1944. He and two other members of the crew first did some sightseeing. Then the three of them drank one bottle of wine and went to a dance hall, where they stayed an hour and a half, dancing. There was a room adjoining the dance hall that over looked the ocean. French doors opened onto an unprotected ledge which extended out from the building a few feet. Petitioner stepped to within 6 inches of the edge and leaned over to take a look. As he did so, he took hold of an iron rod which seemed to be attached to the building. The rod came off and petitioner lost his balance and fell, breaking a leg.

The District Court awarded maintenance. 75 F. Supp. 210, 76 F. Supp 735. The Court of Appeals disallowed it. 179 F.2d 919. The case is here on certiorari.

* * *

The Shipowner's Liability Convention, proclaimed by the President Sept. 29, 1939, 54 Stat. 1693, provides in Art. 2:

1. The shipowner shall be liable in respect of—
   (a) sickness and injury occurring between the date specified in the articles of agreement for reporting for duty and the termination of the engagement;
   (b) death resulting from such sickness or injury.
2. Provided that national laws or regulations may make exceptions in respect of:
   (a) injury incurred otherwise than in the service of the ship;
   (b) injury or sickness due to the wilful act, default or misbehavior of the sick, injured or deceased person;
   (c) sickness or infirmity intentionally concealed when the engagement is entered into.

Petitioner's argument is twofold. He maintains first that under paragraph 1 a shipowner's duty to provide maintenance and cure is absolute and that the exceptions specified in paragraph 2 are not operative until a statute is enacted which puts them in force. He argues in the second place that, even if paragraph 2 is operative without an Act of Congress, his conduct was not due to a "wilful act, default or misbehavior" within the meaning of that paragraph. An amicus curiae argues that the injury was not received "in the service of the ship" within the meaning of Paragraph 2 (a) of Art. 2.

There is support for petitioner's first point in the concurring opinion of Chief Justice Stone in *Waterman Steamship Corp. v. Jones*, 318 U.S. 724, 738. But we think the preferred view is opposed. Our conclusion is that the exceptions permitted by paragraph 2 are operative by virtue of the general maritime law and that no Act of Congress is necessary to give them force.

* * *

The District Court held that petitioner's degree of fault did not bar a recovery for maintenance and cure. The Court of Appeals thought otherwise. The question is whether the injury was "due to the wilful act, default or misbehavior" of petitioner within the meaning of Art. 2, paragraph 2 (b) of the Convention. The standard prescribed is not negligence but wilful misbehavior. In the maritime law it has long been held that while fault of the seamen will forfeit the right to maintenance and cure, it must be "some positively vicious conduct—such as gross negligence or willful disobedience of orders." *The Chandos*, 6 Sawy, 544, 549-550; *The City of Carlisle*, 39 F. 807, 813; *The Ben Flint*, 1 Bliss 562, 566. *And see Reed v. Canfield*, 1 Sumn. 195, 206. In *Aguilar v. Standard Oil Co.*, 318 U.S. 724, 731, we stated the rule as follows: "Conceptions of contributory negligence, the fellow-servant doctrine, and assumption of risk have no place in the liability or defense against it. Only some wilful misbehavior or deliberate act of indiscretion suffices to deprive the seaman of his protection."

The exception which some cases have made for injuries resulting from intoxication (*see*, *Aguilar v. Standard Oil Co.*, *supra*, p. 731) has no place in this case. As the District Judge rules, the amount of wine consumed hardly permits a finding of intoxication. Petitioner was plainly negligent. Yet we should have to strain to find the element of wilfulness or its equivalent. He sought to use some care when he looked down from the small balcony, as evidenced by his seizure of the iron bar for a handhold. His conduct did not measure up to a standard of due care under the circumstances. But we agree with the District Court that it was not wilful misbehavior within the meaning of the Convention.

Finally it is suggested that the injury did not occur "in the service of the ship," as that term is used in paragraph 2 (a) of Art. 2 of the Convention. We held in *Aguilar v. Standard Oil Co.*, *supra*, that maintenance and cure extends to injuries occurring while the seaman is departing on or returning from shore leave though he has at the time no duty to perform for the ship. It is contended that the doctrine of that case should not be extended to injuries received during the diversions of the seaman after he has reached the shore. Mr. Justice Rutledge, speaking for the Court in the *Aguilar* case, stated the reasons for extending maintenance and cure to shore leave cases as follows (pp. 733-734):

> To relieve the shipowner of his obligation in the case of injuries incurred on shore leave would cast upon the seaman hazards encountered only by reason of the voyage. The assumption is hardly sound that the normal uses and purposes of shore leave are 'exclusively personal' and have no relation to the vessel's business. Men cannot live for long cooped up board ship, without substantial impairment of their efficiency, if not also serious danger to discipline. Relaxation beyond the confines of the ship is necessary if the work is to go on, more so that it may move smoothly. No master would take a crew to sea if he could not grant shore leave, and no crew would be taken if it could never obtain it.... In short, shore leave is an elemental necessity in the sailing of ships, a part of the business as old as the art, not merely a personal diversion.

> The voyage creates not only the need for relaxation ashore, but the necessity that it be satisfied in distant and unfamiliar ports. If, in those surroundings, the seaman, without disqualifying misconduct, contracts disease or incurs injury, it is because of the voyage, the shipowner's business has separated him from his usual places of association. By adding this separation to the restrictions of living as well as working abroad, it forges dual and unique compulsions for seeking relief wherever it may be found. In sum, it is the ship's business which subjects the seaman to the risks attending hours of relaxation in strange surroundings. Accordingly, it is but reasonable that the business extend the same protections against injury from them as it gives for other risks of the employment.

This reasoning is as applicable to injuries received during the period of relaxation while on shore as it is to those received while reaching it. To restrict the liability along the lines suggested would be to whittle it down "by restrictive and artificial distinctions" as attempted in the *Aguilar* case. We repeat what we said there, "If leeway is to be given in either direction, all the considerations which brought the liability into being dictate it should be in the sailor's behalf." 318 U.S. at 735. *Reversed.*

Note: Fraud or Willful Misconduct as a Defense

Maintenance and cure must be paid regardless of fault or contributory negligence of the seaman. *Warren v. United States*, 340 U.S. 523, 71 S.Ct. 432, 95 L.Ed. 503 (1951). However, willful misconduct or fraudulent concealment of a pre-existing condition is a defense, *see Lancaster Towing, Inc. v. Davis*, 681 F. Supp 387 (N.D. Mass. 1987).

Note: Persons Liable to Pay Maintenance and Cure

Responsibility for maintenance and cure ordinarily lies with the vessel owner who is usually the seaman's employer. Charterers are normally not liable for maintenance and cure unless the plaintiff establishes the existence of a demise charterer. A demise charterer assumes not only full control over the vessel, but also the owner's responsibility for maintenance and cure. *Matute v. Lloyd Bermuda Lines, Ltd.*, 931 F.2d 231, 235, 1991 AMC 1830 (3d Cir. 1991).

Where a seaman is employed by one person and the vessel on which he is employed is owned by another, his employer is liable as employer and the vessel owner may be liable on an agency theory. For example, in *Archer v. Trans/American Services, Ltd.*, 834 F.2d 1570 (11th Cir. 1988), an assistant pantryman (Archer) was employed by the catering concessionaire (Trans/American) to work on a cruise ship owned and operated by Scandinavian. The district court held that he was entitled to maintenance and cure from both his employer (Trans/American) and the shipowner (Scandinavian). Only Trans/American appealed. The district court judgment was affirmed on appeal. The court said:

> In this case, an agency relationship exists between Trans/American and Scandinavian. Trans/American independent contractor status does not render the agency finding clearly erroneous or improper as a matter of law.
>
> If the law were to recognize this contractual arrangement as something other than an agency relationship, the result would be anomalous. In this case, a cruise ship has contracted for its entire food and beverage service,

> thus, completely insulating itself from any and all liability which might arise from that service. If the ship owner or operator can contract for its food and beverage service, then it may also contract for its crew members, its engineers, its maintenance, housekeeping, and hospitality staffs. The logical extension of this notion is that the ship owner or operator could contract for its entire operation. In such a manner, the ship owner or operator would escape all accountability for the ship's condition and the conduct of those working abroad. In every instance in which the ship owner or operator has historically been held accountable, an independent contractor allegedly unrelated to the ship would be the responsible party.

Archer v. Trans/American Services, Ltd., 834 F.2d 1570, 1573 (11th Cir. 1988)

In any event the vessel is liable *in rem* to pay maintenance and cure. *Solet v. M/V Captain H.V. Dufrene*, 303 F. Supp. 980, 1970 AMC 571 (E.D. La. 1969).

Notes on Injuries on Land and "Service of the Ship"

1. ***Blue Water Seaman: Shore Leave or Vacation***

> Shore Leave consisting of brief periods ashore in home or foreign ports in the course of a voyage, or perhaps even before a voyage begins or after it has terminated, is no doubt, a usual, traditional, and perhaps essential incident of a seaman's employment. Furthermore, during such leave the seaman in a sense is in the service of his ship, for, we suppose he could be called back on board, if he could be found, to cope with any shipboard emergency which might arise in port. But protracted vacations are not of 'elemental necessity in the sailing of ships, a part of the business as old as the art.' They are not traditional in maritime employment; they are the product of modern collective bargaining agreements now generally common both to sea and ashore. And, during vacation periods we cannot assume that the seaman is answerable to the call of duty; and hence in a sense is in the service of the ship.

Haskell v. Socony Mobil Oil Co., 237 F.2d 707, 710 (1st Cir. 1956).

2. ***Commuter Seaman***

Gilmore & Black in The Law of Admiralty 292 (2d ed. 1975) have observed that the extension of the maintenance and cure remedy to shore leave raises questions in cases involving "commuter seamen", those who live at home and commute to work or who serve for a fixed period of time on a vessel and are then on shore for a period of time fixed or otherwise. An example of the former would be a seaman employed on a ferry boat that crossed the Mississippi River going back and forth between the east bank of New Orleans to the west bank—a voyage that took but a few minutes. The latter are illustrated by off-shore workers who often work a 7 day shift on a drilling platform and then are on shore for their seven days off, or persons who work rotating shifts, that is they work a shift on a vessel until a particular job is finished and then they are on shore until their turn comes up to work another shift.

The Fifth Circuit has stated that there are two factors to be considered in the "commuter seaman" situation: (1) whether or not the seaman was on authorized shore leave when injured, and (2) whether or not the seaman was answerable to the call of duty. Shore leave status in the traditional sense refers to the seaman

> who, as a necessary incident of irregular shipboard employment, was authorized to go ashore from time to time and place to place for diversion and relax from the routine of the ship.
>
> * * *

> [N]ot only did the shipowner's business separate such a seaman from his usual places of association, but also, since he was not replaced while he was ashore, he remained at all times subject to his shipping articles and recallable at the will of his master.
>
> * * *
>
> Not so for this off-shore worker in the oil industry. Sellers employment was arranged into definite, equal periods on shore and on the rig. He was subjected to no foreign or irregular accommodations. Such a worker was to a large extent able to maintain the home life of ordinary shore dwellers. A separate crewman regularly replaced him and recall was not contemplated under any ordinary circumstances.

Sellers v. Dixilyn Corporation, 433 F.2d 446, 448, 1971 AMC 425 (5th Cir. 1970),

In another case the Fifth Circuit discussed in some detail the meaning of "in the service of the ship" the context of a land based injury: "The determination of whether a seaman is 'in the service of the vessel' and 'answerable to the call of duty' at the time of the accident depends on the particular facts and circumstances of each case. Nevertheless, it is clear as a matter of law that the seaman's answerability to the 'call of duty' imports at the very least some binding obligations on the part of the seaman to serve.

* * *

The fact that a seaman is 'answerable to the call of duty' imports a legal obligation both on the part of the seaman, enforceable by the shipowner, and on the part of the vessel, to pay him and provide maintenance and cure in terms of illness or injury, enforceable by the seaman in courts of admiralty. It is because the seaman remains bound to the vessel that the vessel and the shipowner are correspondingly obligated to him for maintenance and cure in case of injury. These reciprocal obligations determine an individual's status as a seaman, and whether the seaman is in the service of his vessel." *Baker v. Ocean Systems, Inc.*, 454 F.2d 379, 384-85 (5th Cir. 1972). The court found that an employee who worked a rotating shift was not "answerable to the call of duty" during the periods when he was "off shift."

C. Amount of maintenance

Notes

1. *Amount of Maintenance*

The amount of maintenance awarded will be determined by the court based on the evidence presented by the seaman. The seaman has the burden to prove the amount necessary, but the court may take into account the ordinary "costs of food and lodging in a particular area comparable to that received on board the vessel." *See Castro v. M/V Ambassador*, 657 F. Supp 886, 1989 AMC 128 (E.D. La. 1987). *See also Incandela v. American Dredging Co.*, 659 F.2d 11, 14, 1981 AMC 2401, 2404 (2d Cir. 1981):

> To fulfill its purpose, the maintenance rate should be set at a level which will "provide a seaman with food and lodging when he becomes sick or injured in the ship's service." *Vaughn v. Atkinson*, 369 U.S. 527, 531 (1962). Nevertheless, since at least the early 1950's many courts have fallen into the habit of awarding maintenance at the fixed rate of $8.00 per day, regardless of the gradual erosion of the purchasing power which the amount represents. 1B BENEDICT ON ADMIRALTY § 51 (1980); G. GILMORE & C. BLACK, THE LAW OF ADMIRALTY 307 (2d ed. 1975). On the other hand, some courts have awarded higher maintenance rates after seamen have introduced evidence of higher living costs.
>
> * * *

To fulfill its purpose, the maintenance rate should be set at a level which will "provide a seaman with food and lodging when he becomes sick or injured in the ship's service." *Vaughn v. Atkinson,* 369 U.S. 527, 531 (1962). Nevertheless, since at least the early 1950's many courts have fallen into the habit of awarding maintenance at the fixed rate of $8.00 per day, regardless of the gradual erosion of the purchasing power which the amount represents. 1B BENEDICT ON ADMIRALTY § 51 (1980); G. GILMORE & C. BLACK, THE LAW OF ADMIRALTY 307 (2d ed. 1975). On the other hand, some courts have awarded higher maintenance rates after seamen have introduced evidence of higher living costs.

* * *

In this case, plaintiff's uncontradicted testimony that he spent between $175 and $200 per week on maintenance costs made out a prima facie case for an award of $26.80 per day (one-seventh of $187.50, the mid-point between the two estimates). Defendant made no attempt to introduce rebuttal evidence on this point, and would have faced an uphill battle if it had tried; it was conceded at oral argument that the cheapest room at the Seamen's Institute in New York City now costs $18.00 per night. Therefore it was error for the district court to have refused to allow the jury to utilize the $26.80 figure in calculating the maintenance owed to plaintiff.

Once plaintiff's testimony was in the record, a *prima facie* case was made out and the burden shifted to the defendant to demonstrate that plaintiff's actual expenditures were excessive, in light of any realistic alternatives for room and board available to him in New York. Since the $26.80 figure was not disputed and was reasonable in view of living costs in New York the $13.50 figure merely represented defendant's arbitrary decision to pay plaintiff half of his regular salary, and was not intended to reflect in any way the cost of housing and food in New York. It was not rebuttal evidence on the issue of maintenance and can therefore be disregarded. Incandela is therefore entitled to a maintenance award calculated at the rate of $26.80 per day.

The seaman is entitled to recover the total cost of rent or mortgage of the home where he lives, but only a proportionate share of the other expenses if he lives there with his family. *Ritchie v. Grimm*, 724 F.Supp. 59, 61 (E.D.N.Y. 1989):

[T]he Court holds that the proper amount of maintenance should include the total cost of rent for Ritchie's apartment as well as his share of food and other costs testified to at the October 30 hearing. Specifically, the Court holds that Ritchie is entitled to receive $125 per week for rent, $47 per week for food (Ritchie's share of the weekly food expenses) and $209 per week for other expenses (Ritchie's share of all other expenses testified to). The payment of $125 is based upon the $500 monthly rental payment testified to by Mrs. Ritchie. Although the Court notes that Ritchie resides in the apartment with his wife and child, the Court holds that it is reasonable to award Ritchie the full monthly payment since it is likely that Ritchie would pay the same amount in rent even if he alone resided in the apartment.

In *Hall v. Noble Drilling (U.S.), Inc.*, 242 F.3d 582, 2001 AMC 1099 (5th Cir. 2001) the Fifth Circuit held that a seaman who pays the rent or mortgage of a home he shares with his family may recover the full amount of the rent or mortgage for purposes of calculation of a maintenance award, not a prorated amount. However, the costs of heat, electricity and water may be prorated.

2. *Damages for Failure to Pay Maintenance and Cure*

In most circuits, an employer's refusal or failure to pay maintenance and cure will give a seaman an independent cause of action for compensatory damages, attorney's fees and possibly punitive damages. *See Harper v. Zapata Off-Shore Co.*, 741 F.2d 87, 1985 AMC 979 (5th Cir. 1984). However, courts have struggled to define a clear legal standard for damage awards. In *Morales v. Garijak, Inc.*, 829 F.2d 1355, 1988 AMC 1075 (5th Cir. 1987), the court explained that only *unreasonable* behavior would be enough for a recovery of compensatory damages.

3. *Punitive Damages*

Since *Miles v. Apex Marine Corp.*, 498 U.S. 19, 111 S. Ct. 317, 112 L. Ed. 2d 275, 1991 AMC 1 (1990), punitive damages in maintenance and cure actions have been denied in the Fifth and Ninth Circuits. *Guevara v. Maritime Overseas Corporation*, 59 F.3d 1496, 1995 AMC. 2409 (5th Cir. 1995), *cert. denied*, 116 S. Ct. 706 (1996); and *Glynn v. Roy Al Boat Management Corp.*, 57 F.3d 1395, 1995 A.M.C. 2022 (9th Cir. 1995), *cert denied*, , 516 U.S. 1046, 116 S. Ct. 708 (1996).

D. Pre-existing Injury

GAUTHIER v. CROSBY MARINE SERVICE, INC.

499 F. Supp. 295, 1981 AMC 1170 (E.D. La. 1980), *aff'd*, 752 F.2d 1085, 1985 AMC 2477 (5th Cir. 1985)

CASSIBRY, District Judge

* * *

A vessel owner is obligated to furnish a seaman with maintenance and cure benefits with respect to an injury or illness that occurs or manifests itself while the seaman is in the service of the vessel. The origin or cause of the disability, the fact that it pre-existed the voyage, originated on another vessel, or even was due to the fault of another vessel are all irrelevant. *Meade v. Skip Fisheries, Inc.*, 385 F. Supp. 725 (D. Mass. 1974) and cases cited therein. As long as a seaman believes in good faith that he is fit for duty, he is entitled to maintenance and cure from his present employer notwithstanding that he falls ill from a pre-existing illness. *Gooden v. Sinclair Refining Co.*, 378 F.2d 576 (3rd Cir. 1967);... In fact, at least two courts would hold the present employer solely liable for all maintenance and cure under the "last ship" rule. *Meade*, 385 F. Supp. 725, 728, (D. Mass. 1974) (ALDRICH, J.); *Diaz*, 237 F. Supp. 261 (FEINBERG, J.). Mr. Gauthier, in the instant case, had a reasonable, good faith belief on September 22, 1978 that he was fit for duty with Griffin. Griffin was therefore liable to plaintiff for maintenance and cure for the hydrocele and the heart condition after plaintiff's groin symptoms recurred on September 25, *see Gooden*, 378 F.2d at 578 (prior injuries "heightened" on later ship although not involved in any other accidents), and the heart condition was subsequently discovered. Griffin was further liable for maintenance and cure during the period plaintiff was convalescing and he contracted hepatitis, continuing to the date of maximum cure. *Brahms v. Moore McCormack Lines, Inc.*, 133 F. Supp. 283 (S.D.N.Y. 1955) (new illness part of the progressive manifestation of plaintiff's present inability to care for himself which began aboard ship).

* * *

The testimony also established that plaintiff's heart condition was the result of many years of accumulation of fatty deposits and cholesterol in the arteries. Both these conditions afflicted plaintiff while he was in the employ of Crosby, and it is only fair that Crosby share the burden of maintenance and cure for them. Because the hepatitis was totally divorced from plaintiff's service for Crosby, Crosby is not liable for maintenance and cure associated with that illness.

I agree with my brethren who espouse the last ship rule that a seaman should not be required to ascertain, seek out, and pursue the proper employer to get his award. *See Meade*, 385 F. Supp. at 728; *Diaz*, 237 F. Supp. at 266. Yet both potentially liable employers are before me here, and it would be inequitable to force one or the other to shoulder the entire burden. I will therefore follow the Third Circuit and apportion liability equally between the two ostensibly innocent employers. *Gooden*, 378 F.2d 576. Of course, if Crosby is later found to be culpable for negligence or unseaworthiness, it will be liable for all of the maintenance and cure attributable to the groin injury. ÿ Because the heart condition would have needed immediate attention eventually, and its discovery in connection with the groin injury was coincidental (although apparently quite fortunate for Mr. Gauthier), those expenses will be shared equally regardless of the findings of the jury on the other causes of action.

E. Miscellaneous Notes

1. *Contracts for Maintenance and Cure*

What effect, if any, should a court give to the rate of maintenance which has been fixed in a collective bargaining agreement between a seaman's union and a shipowner? The Ninth Circuit has held that the rate is binding on the seaman despite the district court's determination that the amount is inadequate to obtain food and lodging. *Gardiner v. Sea-Land Service, Inc.*, 786 F.2d 943, 1986 AMC (9th Cir.), *cert. denied*, 479 U.S. 924, 107 S.Ct. 331 (1986). This approach was followed in *Macedo v. F/V Paul & Michelle*, 868 F.2d 519, 1990 AMC 1368 (1st Cir.) 1989), *Al-Zawkari v. American Steamship Co.*, 871 F.2d 585, 1990 AMC 1312 (6th Cir. 1989); *Baldassaro v. United States*, 64 F.3d 206, 1995 AMC 2947 (5th Cir. 1995) and *Frederick v. Kirby Tankships, Inc.,* 205 F.3d 1277, 2000 AMC 1839 (11th Cir. 2000). In contrast the Third Circuit has held that a seaman may challenge the rate stipulated in the collective bargaining agreement. *Barnes v. Andover Co., L.P.*, 900 F.2d 630, 1990 AMC 1265 (3rd Cir. 1990).

There were several decisions at District Court level in the Second Circuit agreeing with *Barnes* - see *Gilliken v. United States*, 764 F. Supp 261, 1992 AMC 111 (E.D.N.Y. 1991); *Brown v. United States*, 882 F. Supp. 1424, 1995 AMC 1801 (S.D.N.Y. 1995); *McMillan v. Tug Jane A. Bouchard*, 885 F. Supp. 452 (E.D.N.Y. 1995); *Covella v. Buchanan Marine, Inc.,* 1997 AMC 1192 (S.D.N.Y. 1996); *Durfor v. K-Sea Transportation Corp.*, 2001 AMC 2390 (S.D.N.Y. 2001) – but in *Ammar v. U.S.*, 342 F.3d 133, 1995 AMC 1801 (2d Cir. 2003), the U.S. Court of Appeals for the Second Circuit joined the Ninth Circuit in holding that the rate of maintenance should be limited to the amount fixed in the collective bargaining agreement.

In contrast, several state courts have sided with *Barnes* in holding that the collective bargaining agreement cannot abrogate the seaman's right to adequate maintenance and cure. *See Lundborg v. Keystone Shipping Co.*, 981 P.2d 854, 1999 AMC 2635 (Wash. 1999), *Daniels v. Standard Marine Transport Service, Inc.*, 680 N.Y.S.2d 41, 1999 AMC 2889 (C.A.N.Y. 1998). Some state courts apply the collective bargaining rate: *Jordan v. Intercontinental Bulktank Corp.*, 621 So. 2d 1141 (La. App., 1st Cir. 1993).

2. *Disability and Health Care Plans*

Does an employer satisfy its legal obligation to pay maintenance when it establishes a disability plan pursuant to a collective bargaining agreement? The answer seems to depend upon whether the "benefits" are regarded as a form of "deferred compensation," *Shaw v. Ohio River Company*, 526 F.2d 193, 200, 1976 AMC 1164 (1975), or as substitute for maintenance, *Thomas v. Humble Oil & Refining Company*, 420 F.2d 793, 794, 1970 AMC 25 (4th Cir. 1970) (where the collective bargaining agreement clearly provided that: "Maintenance shall not be paid concurrently with payments under the Disability Benefits Plan, ...") Benefits which are regarded as "deferred compensation" are not considered to be the payment of maintenance.

As to cure, it appears that an employer incurs no further obligation to pay for medical treatment which has already been paid by a welfare plan or by health insurance such as Blue Cross, pursuant to a collective bargaining agreement. The courts seem to have distinguished Jones Act and similar actions and rejected the application of the so-called "collateral source" rule. "[A] vessel owner's duty to provide maintenance and cure arises independently of any considerations of fault and without regard to whether or not the seaman's disability is causally related to his employment. Whatever justification there may be for the collateral source rule in situations where liability is based on fault, there is no perceivable basis for applying it to the no-fault obligation to furnish maintenances and cure. *Shaw v. Ohio River Company*, 526 F.2d 193, 201, 1976 AMC 1164 (3d Cir. 1975). *See also, Al Zawkari v. American S.S. Co.*, 871 F.2d 585, 1990 AMC 1312 (6th Cir. 1989).

3. *Public Health Hospitals*

In 1981, Congress enacted the Omnibus Budget Reconciliation Act, Pub. L. No 97-35, 95 Stat. 357 (1981), a comprehensive appropriations bill that adjusted the eligibility requirements and amounts budgeted for a large number of federal programs. Among its other provisions, the Act ordered the closure and transfer to nonfederal control of the Public Health hospitals and clinics. Section 986 of the Act terminated the right of outpatient seamen to obtain free medical care in the facilities after October 1, 1981, while Section 988 allowed continued free care for a maximum of one additional year for in-patient seamen hospitalized prior to October 1, 1981. In *Jones v. Reagan*, 748 F.2d 1331, 1985 AMC 944 (9th Cir. 1984), permanently disabled seamen filed suit challenging the validity of the sections of the Omnibus Budget Reconciliation Act of 1981 that terminated a seaman's right to free medical care in governmental facilities. The court held that the Act did not unconstitutionally deprive seamen of any right. A summary judgment for the government was affirmed on appeal.

4. *Medicare*

Several courts have held that the availability of free medical care to an injured seaman under the Medicaid Program satisfies the vessel owners obligation to furnish cure. *Moran Towing & Transportation Co. v. Lombas*, 58 F.3d 24, 1995 AMC 2113 (2d Cir. 1995). See *Blige v. M/V GEECHEE GIRL*, 180 F. Supp. 2d 1349, 1355, 2001 AMC 2425, 2431-32 (S.D. Ga. 2001), the court said:

> Historically, the availability of cost-free cure at the United States Public Health Services marine hospitals satisfied the shipowner's cure obligation. Today, the shipowner's cure obligation is satisfied by Medicare/Medicaid, since it is the functional equivalent of the previously available free treatment at Public Heath Services hospitals...Thus, the shipowner is not liable for medical expenses paid by Medicaid, although it remains liable for out of pocket expenses, such as premiums or co-payments.

5. *"Contribution and Indemnity"*

A shipowner who has paid maintenance and cure, may seek contribution or indemnity from a third party who was wholly or partially responsible for the injuries sustained by the seaman. In the past, a shipowner was barred from seeking indemnification for maintenance and cure payments. *See* THE FEDERAL No. 2, 21 F.2d 313, 1927 AMC 1471 (2d Cir. 1927). The decision, based on the idea that maintenance and cure is a contractual obligation of the shipowner-employer, was overruled by *Black v. Red Star Towing & Transp. Co., Inc.*, 860 F.2d 30, 1989 AMC 1 (2d Cir. 1988). Accordingly, an employer who pays maintenance and cure is entitled to complete indemnity from a third party tortfeasor whose fault was the sole cause of the seaman's injuries. If the third party tortfeasor was jointly negligent, the employer may recover only the amount for which the third party is proportionately liable. An employer may even recover from a previous employer, if the seaman's injuries resulted from work done for that employer. However, an employer may not claim contribution or indemnity from the injured seaman or from a fellow employee.

6. ***Distinction between Maintenance & Cure and "Found"***

Occasionally, a claim for "found" is made. In *Youn v. Maritime Overseas Corp.*, 623 So. 2d 1257, 1261 (La. 1993), plaintiff's injury was such that he was unable to work on his employers vessels. The Louisiana Supreme Court upheld an award for "found" in the amount of $10 per day for loss of past and future found. The court stated:

> 'Found' is an admiralty term which describes the element of damages representing the value of the living expenses provided to a seaman by his employer as a condition of employment while aboard ship. Found generally includes expenses for food, lodging and clothing. Frank L. Maraist, Admiralty in a Nutshell 194 (2d ed. 1988).
>
> Plaintiff clearly suffered this loss, inasmuch as he will never again receive these sums from his employer while aboard ship. The only issue is the precise value of the loss.

F. Duration of the Obligation

Introductory Note

The obligation to pay maintenance and cure extends only to the moment of "maximum possible cure". If the seaman's condition is incurable, the obligation does not extend for the whole of the remainder of the seaman's life. In *Farrell v. U.S.*, 336 U.S. 511, 69 S. Ct. 707, 93 L. Ed. 850 (1949), the seaman became totally and permanently blind while in the service of the ship. The Supreme Court held that he was not entitled to maintenance and cure for the rest of his life, saying:

> It is claimed, however, even if the basis for a lifetime award does not exist, that he is entitled to maintenance and cure beyond the period allowed by the courts below. This is based largely upon statements in the opinion of the Court in *Calmar Steamship Corp. v. Taylor*, 303 U.S. 525. There the question as stated by the Court was whether the duty of a shipowner to provide maintenance and cure for a seaman falling ill of an incurable disease while in its employ, extends to the payment of a lump-sum award sufficient to defray the cost of maintenance and cure for the remainder of his life. The Court laid aside cases where incapacity is caused by the employment and said, "We can find no basis for saying that, if the disease proves to be incurable, the duty extends beyond a fair time after the voyage in which to effect such improvement in the seaman's condition as reasonably may be expected to result from nursing, care, and medical treatment. This would satisfy such demands of policy as underlie the imposition of the obligation. Beyond this we think there is no duty, at least where the illness is not caused by the seaman's service.

336 U.S. 511, 515 (1949).

Similarly, the obligation to pay the seaman's wages extends only to the end of the seaman's contract. In *Farrell, supra*, the Court said:

> The two courts below have held the petitioner entitled to wages until the completion of the voyage at the port of New York on March 28, 1944. The petitioner contends that he has a right to wages for twelve months from December 16, 1943, the date he joined the vessel...It is not questioned that the general custom in ships, other than the coastwise trade, is to sign on for a voyage rather than for a fixed period. But it is contended that the last clause of this contract obligated the petitioner to serve for twelve calendar months, irrespective of the termination of the voyage, and therefore gave him the right to wages for a similar period. The contract is not an

> uncommon form and complied with war-time requirements as to voyage contracts. We think, in the light of the custom of the industry and the condition of the times, there is nothing ambiguous about it and that it obligated the petitioner only for the voyage on which the ship was engaged when he signed on and that, when it terminated at a port of discharge in the United States, he could not have been required to reembark for a second voyage. The twelve-month period appears as a limitation upon the duration of the voyage and not as a stated period of employment. We think the court below made no error in determining the wages.

336 U.S. 511, 520-21 (1949).

VELLA v. FORD MOTOR CO.

421 U.S. 1, 95 S. Ct. 1381, 43 L. Ed. 2d 682, 1975 AMC 563 (1974)

Mr. Justice BRENNAN delivered the opinion of the Court

We granted certiorari in this case limited to the question whether a shipowner's duty to furnish an injured seaman maintenance and cure continues from the date the seaman leaves the ship to the date when a medical diagnosis is made that the seaman's injury was permanent immediately after his accident and therefore incurable. 419 U.S. 894 (1974).

Petitioner was a seaman aboard respondent's Great Lakes vessel, S.S. Robert S. McNamara. He was discharged and left the ship on June 29, 1968. Thereafter he filed this suit in the District Court for the Eastern District of Michigan, Southern Division, based on a claim that on April 4, 1968, while replacing a lower engineroom deck plate, he slipped and fell on the oily floor plate causing his head to suffer a severe blow when it struck an electrical box. The complaint included a count, among others, for maintenance and cure. The medical testimony at the trial was that petitioner suffered from a vestibular disorder defined as damage to the balancing mechanism of the inner ear. The testimony of respondent's medical witness, Dr. Heil, an otolaryngologist, supplied the only medical diagnosis as to the time when the disorder became permanent and not susceptible of curative treatment. Dr. Heil testified on April 27, 1972, that he had recently examined petitioner. He conceded that a severe blow to the head, such as alleged by petitioner, could have caused the disorder. He said, however, that the disorder is not a condition that can be cured by treatment. The jury awarded petitioner maintenance and cure in the amount of $5,848. Respondent moved for a judgment notwithstanding the verdict on the ground that the award was not within the permissible scope of maintenance and cure. The District Court denied the motion and stated: "While it is true that maintenance and cure is not available for a sickness declared to be permanent, it is also true that maintenance and cure continues until such time as the incapacity is declared to be permanent." App. 20a. The Court of Appeals for the Sixth Circuit reversed without a published opinion, 495 F.2d 1374 (1974). The Court of Appeals held that "once the seaman reaches 'maximum medical recovery,' the shipowner's obligation to provide maintenance and cure ceases," App. 28a, and since "[t]he record in this case does not permit an inference other than that [petitioner's] condition was permanent immediately after the accident," *id.*, at 29a, the District Court's holding impermissibly extended the shipowner's obligation.

We disagree with the Court of Appeals and therefore reverse. The shipowner's ancient duty to provide maintenance and cure for the seaman who becomes ill or is injured while in the service of the ship derives from the "unique hazards [which] attend the work of seamen," and fosters the "combined object of encouraging marine commerce and assuring the well-being of seamen." *Aguilar v. Standard Oil Co.*, 318 U.S. 724, 727 (1943). To further that "combined object" we have held that the duty arises irrespective of the absence of shipowner negligence and indeed irrespective of whether the illness or injury is suffered in the course of the seaman's employment. *Calmar S.S. Corp. v. Taylor*, 303 U.S. 525, 527 (1938). And, "[s]o broad is the shipowner's obligation, ... negligence or acts short of culpable misconduct on the seaman's part will not relieve [the shipowner] of the responsibility." *Aguilar v. Standard Oil Co., supra*, at 730-731. Thus, the breadth and inclusiveness of the shipowner's duty assure its easy and ready administration for "[i]t has few exceptions or conditions to stir contentions, cause delays, and invite litigations." *Farrell v. United States*, 336 U.S. 511, 516 (1949).

Denial of maintenance and cure when the seaman's injury, though in fact permanent immediately after the accident, is not medically diagnosed as permanent until long after its occurrence would obviously diserve and frustrate the "combined object of encouraging marine commerce and assuring the well-being of seamen." A shipowner might withhold vitally necessary maintenance and cure on the belief, however well or poorly founded, that the seaman's injury is permanent and incurable. Or the seaman, if paid maintenance and cure by the shipowner, might be required to reimburse the payments, if it is later determined that the injury was permanent immediately after the accident. Thus uncertainty would displace the essential certainty of protection against the ravages of illness and injury that encourages seamen to undertake their hazardous calling. Moreover, easy and ready administration of the shipowner's duty would seriously suffer from the introduction of complexities and uncertainty that could "stir contentions, cause delays, and invite litigations."

The Shipowners' Liability Convention, made effective for the United States on October 29, 1939, *Farrell v. United States, supra*, at 517, buttresses our conclusion that the District Court correctly held that "maintenance and cure continues until such time as the incapacity is declared to be permanent."[4] That holding tracks the wording of Art. 4, P. 1, of the Convention which provides: "The shipowner shall be liable to defray the expense of medical care and maintenance until the sick or injured person has been cured, or until the sickness or incapacity has been declared of a permanent character." 54 Stat. 1696. (Emphasis supplied.) The aim of the Convention "was not to change materially American stan-

---

[4] On this record maintenance and cure could have been claimed to continue from June 29, 1968, the date petitioner left the vessel, to April 27, 1972, the date Dr. Heil testified that the vestibular disorder was permanent immediately after the accident and not susceptible of curative treatment. The jury, however, awarded petitioner maintenance and cure at $8 per day only for the period from June 29, 1968, to June 29, 1970. Petitioner's appeal to the Court of Appeals did not, however, draw into question a claim of entitlement to maintenance and cure for the longer period sought by him in this Court, Brief for Petitioner 19. *See Le Tulle v. Scofield*, 308 U.S. 415, 421-422 (1940). Moreover, in light of our holding that the shipowner's duty continued until Dr. Heil's testimony, it is not necessary to address the question whether the jury award might also be sustained on the ground that the shipowner's duty in any event obliged him to provide palliative medical care to arrest further progress of the condition or to reduce pain, and we intimate no view whatever upon the shipowner's duty in that regard. Compare *Ward v. Union Barge Line Corp.*, 443 F.2d 565, 572 (CA3 1971), with the opinion of the Court of Appeals in this case. App. 29a n.1. Nor do we express any view whether a seaman may forfeit his right to maintenance and cure by not reporting a known injury or malady, or by refusing from the outset to allow proper medical examination, or by discontinuing medical care made available.

dards but to equalize operating costs by raising the standards of member nations to the American level." *Warren v. United States*, 340 U.S. 523, 527 (1951). Thus Art. 4, P. 1, is declaratory of a longstanding tradition respecting the scope of the shipowner's duty to furnish injured seamen maintenance and cure, *Farrell v. United States*, *supra*, at 518, and therefore the District Court's interpretation was correct.

The judgment of the Court of Appeals is reversed, and the case is remanded for further proceedings consistent with this opinion.

So ordered.

Note

In *Cox v. Dravo Corp.*, 517 F.2d 620 (3d Cir. 1975), the court held that an award of maintenance and cure cannot be sustained on the ground of a shipowner's duty to provide medical care that can serve only to reduce pain. Further, the court announced that there is no duty to provide treatment that arrests the progress of a deteriorating condition. The plaintiff, relying on language in the *Vella* case, argued that the duty to provide maintenance and cure inevitably continues until such time as there has been a judicial determination of the permanency of the injury. The court declared (517 F.2d at 627):

> We can imagine a factual dispute as to when a diagnosis of permanency was made. If there is such a dispute it must be resolved by the trier of fact. When it is so resolved the date of diganosis so determined, not the date of the judicial determination, defines the end of the vessel's maintenance and cure obligation.

For a discussion of the case, *see,* Note, 17 B.C. Ind. & Com. L. Rev. 648 (1976).

What about a seaman who suffered a renal failure? The condition of his kidneys cannot be improved, *i.e.*, cannot be cured, but without regular dialysis treatment or a kidney transplant, he will die. Does this situation suggest that there is a type of therapeutic treatment that falls somewhere in between "cure" and mere "palliative treatment" which should qualify for an award of maintenance and cure? *See Costa Crociere, S.p.A. v. Rose*, 939 F. Supp. 1538 (S.D. Fla. 1996).

G. Wage Penalties

Notes

1. The penalty wage statute, 46 U.S.C. § 10313(g) (formerly 46 U.S.C. § 596) requires vessel owners to pay seamen promptly after their discharge and authorizes seamen to recover double wages for each day that payment is delayed without sufficient cause. In *Griffin v. Oceanic Contractors, Inc.*, 458 U.S. 564, 102 S. Ct. 3245, 73 L. Ed. 2d 973, 1982 AMC 2377 (1982), the Supreme Court held that the statute requires penalty wages to be paid for each day that payment is delayed. The Court held that the district court had erred in limiting the period of payment to the time when the seaman remained unemployed. The Court said:

> The District Court found that respondent had refused to pay petitioner the balance of earned wages promptly after discharge, and that its refusal was "without sufficient cause." Respondent challenges neither of these findings. Although the two statutory conditions were satisfied, however, the District Court obviously did not assess double wages "for each and every day" during which payment was delayed, but instead limited the assessment to the period of petitioner's unemployment. Nothing in the language of the statute vests the courts with the discretion to set such a limitation.

> It is highly probable that respondents are correct in their contention that a recovery in excess of $300,000 in this case greatly exceeds any actual injury suffered by petitioner as a result of respondent's delay in paying his wages. But this Court has previously recognized that awards made under this statute were not intended to be merely compensatory.

458 U.S. 564, 571 (1982).

2. What can an employer do if it believes that it has a defense to the wage claim? Can it pay the funds representing the disputed claims into the court registry? *See Mateo v. M/S Kiso* 805 F. Supp. 761, 1993 AMC 2278 (N.D. Cal. 1991). Also, *see Cohen v. S/S Consumer*, 746 F.2d 1069, 1985 AMC 1686 (5th Cir. 1985) for a discussion of the purpose of the penalty provision.

3. In *Governor and Co. of Bank of Scotland v. Sabay*, 211 F.3d 261, 2000 AMC 1532 (5th Cir. 2000) *rehearing and rehearing en banc denied* 218 F.3d 745 (5th Cir. 2000), it was held that the penalty wages action lies directly against the owner (and master) *in personam*. Thus, the seamen's preferred maritime lien for penalty wages could only be enforced against vessel sale proceeds in which the owner had an interest. Because there was a secured mortgagee whose claim exceeded the sale proceeds, the owner no longer had any interest to which the penalty wages lien could attach.

Part 2. Action for Negligence — The Jones Act, Injury but No Death:

Cases and Notes

THE OSCEOLA

189 U.S. 158, 23 S. Ct. 483, 47 L. Ed. 760 (1903)

This was a libel *in rem* filed in the District Court for the Eastern District of Wisconsin, in admiralty, against the propeller Osceola, to recover damages for a personal injury sustained by one Patrick Shea, a seaman on board the vessel, through the negligence of the master.

Upon a full review of English and American authorities, we think the law may be considered as settled upon the following propositions:

(1) That a vessel and her owners are liable, in case a seaman falls sick or is wounded in the service of the ship, to the extent of his maintenance and cure, and to his wages, at least so long as the voyage is continued.

(2) That the vessel and her owners are, both by English and American law, liable to an indemnity for injuries received by seamen in consequence of the unseaworthiness of the ship, or a failure to supply and keep in order the proper appliances appurtenant to such ship.

(3) That all the members of the crew, except perhaps the master, are, as between themselves, fellow servants, and hence seamen cannot recover for injuries sustained through the negligence of another member of the crew beyond the expense of their maintenance and cure.

(4) That the seaman is not allowed to recover an indemnity for the negligence of the master, or any member of the crew, but is entitled to maintenance and cure, whether the injuries were received from negligence or accident.

It will be observed in these cases that a departure has been made from the Continental codes in allowing an indemnity beyond the expense of maintenance and cure in cases arising from unseaworthiness. This departure originated in England in the Merchants' Shipping Act of 1876, ÿ and in this country, in a general consensus of opinion among the Circuit and District Courts, that an exception should be made from the general principle before obtaining, in favor of seamen suffering injury through the unseaworthiness of the vessel. We are not disposed to disturb so wholesome a doctrine by any contrary decision of our own.

Note

In suits against persons other than his employer, a seaman has the same rights against negligent third parties as anyone else. If a seaman is aboard his employers' vessel and is injured when another vessel negligently collides with the one on which he is aboard, he may bring an action for negligence under the general maritime law which has always provided a remedy in case of collision. The action may be brought in federal court in admiralty or at law if there is diversity of citizenship. It may be brought in state court under saving to suitors. Damages recoverable are those permitted under general maritime law and are enumerated in the discussion of unseaworthiness, *supra*.

A. The Statutes

The Jones Act

46 U.S.C.A. §§ 30104-5

§ 30104. Personal injury to or death of seamen

(a) Cause of Action—A seaman injured in the course of employment or, if the seaman dies from the injury, the personal representative of the seaman may elect to bring a civil action at law, with the right of trial by jury, against the employer. Laws of the United States regulating recovery for personal injury to, or death of, a railway employee apply to an action under this section.

(b) Venue—An action under this section shall be brought in the judicial district in which the employer resides or the employer's principal office is located.

§ 30105.Restriction on recovery by non-citizens and non-resident aliens for incidents in waters of other countries

(a) Definition—In this section, the term "continental shelf" has the meaning given that term in article I of the 1958 Convention on the Continental Shelf.

(b) Restriction—Except as provided in subsection (c), a civil action for maintenance and cure or for damages for personal injury or death may not be brought under a maritime law of the United States if—

(1) the individual suffering the injury or death was not a citizen or permanent resident alien of the United States at the time of the incident giving rise to the action;
(2) the incident occurred in the territorial waters or waters overlaying the continental shelf of a country other than the United States; and
(3) the individual suffering the injury or death was employed at the time of the incident by a person engaged in the exploration, development, or production of off-shore mineral or energy resources, including drilling, mapping, surveying, diving, pipelaying, maintaining, repairing, constructing, or transporting supplies, equipment, or personnel, but not including transporting those resources by a vessel constructed or adapted primarily to carry oil in bulk in the cargo spaces.

(c) Nonapplication—Subsection (b) does not apply if the individual bringing the action establishes that a remedy is not available under the laws of—
(1) the country asserting jurisdiction over the area in which the incident occurred; or

(2) the country in which the individual suffering the injury or death maintained citizenship or residency at the time of the incident.

Also relevant is 46 U.S.C.A. § 30510 (formerly 46 App. U.S.C. § 183g):

30510. Vicarious liability for medical malpractice with regard to crew
In a civil action by any person in which the owner or operator of a vessel or employer of a crewmember is claimed to have vicarious liability for medical malpractice with regard to a crewmember occurring at a shoreside facility, and to the extent the damages resulted from the conduct of any shoreside doctor, hospital, medical facility, or other health care provider, the owner, operator, or employer is entitled to rely on any statutory limitations of liability applicable to the doctor, hospital, medical facility, or other health care provider in the State of the United States in which the shoreside medical care was provided.

THE JONES ACT

(Superseded Version)

46 App. U.S.C.§ 688

§ 688. Recovery for injury to or death of seaman

(a) Application of railway employee statutes; jurisdiction

Any seaman who shall suffer personal injury in the course of his employment may, at his election, maintain an action for damages at law, with the right of trial by jury, and in such action all statutes of the United States modifying or extending the common-law right or remedy in cases of personal injury to railway employees shall apply; and in case of the death of any seaman as a result of any such personal injury the personal representative of such seaman may maintain an action for damages at law with the right of trial by jury, and in such action all statutes of the United States conferring or regulating the right of action for death in the case of railway employees shall be applicable. Jurisdiction in such actions shall be under the court of the district in which the defendant employer resides or in which his principal office is located. (Mar. 4, 1915, ch. 153, 20, 38 Stat. 1185; June 5, 1920, ch. 250 33, 41 Stat. 1007).

(b) Limitation for certain aliens; applicability in lieu of other remedy

(1) No action may be maintained under subsection (a) of this section or under any other maritime law of the United States for maintenance and cure or for damages for the injury or death of a person who was not a citizen or permanent resident alien of the United States at the time of the incident giving rise to the action if the incident occurred—

(A) while that person was in the employ of an enterprise engaged in the exploration, development, or production of off-shore mineral or energy resources—including but not limited to drilling, mapping, surveying, diving, pipelaying, maintaining, repairing, constructing, or transporting supplies, equipment or personnel, but not including transporting those resources by a vessel constructed or adapted primarily to carry oil in bulk in the cargo spaces; and
(B) in the territorial waters or waters overlaying the continental shelf of a nation other than the United States, its territories, or possessions. As used in this paragraph, the term "continental shelf" has the meaning stated in article I of the 1958 Convention on the Continental Shelf.

(2) The provisions of paragraph (1) of this subsection shall not be applicable if the person bringing the action establishes that no remedy was available to that person—

(A) under the laws of the nation asserting jurisdiction over the area in which the incident occurred; or
(B) under the laws of the nation in which, at the time of the incident, the person for whose injury or death a remedy is sought maintained citizenship or residency.

Note

The constitutionality of the Jones Act was upheld in *Panama Railroad Co. v. Johnson*, 264 U.S. 375, 44 S.Ct. 391, 68 L.Ed. 748, 1924 AMC 551 (1924). In that case, the Supreme Court held that the word "jurisdiction" in the last sentence of the Jones Act means "venue"; the words "at his election" in the first sentence of the same statute do not accord a choice to an injured seaman to seek relief under a nonmaritime system of law; and that these words allow any injured seaman to seek relief, either on the side of the court with a jury or in admiralty without a jury, under the rules of substantive maritime law as modified by the statute.

In *Plamals v. The Pinar Del Rio*, 277 U.S. 151, 48 S.Ct. 457, 72 L.Ed. 827, 1928 AMC 932 (1928), the Supreme Court held that the Jones Act does not give rise to a maritime lien in favor of an injured seaman. Plaintiff, accordingly, may not proceed *in rem* in a Jones Act suit; he must proceed *in personam* against his employer. He may proceed in admiralty though without jury trial. The employer, however, need not to be owner or operator of a vessel to be liable under the Jones Act. *Barrios v. Louisiana Construction Materials Co.*, 465 F.2d 1157, 1972 AMC 2659 (5th Cir. 1972).

If a Jones Act suit is commenced in a state court, it is not removable to the federal court. *See Pate v. Standard Dredging Co.*, 193 F.2d 498 (5th Cir. 1952).This is so even in the presence of complete diversity between the parties. *See* CHAPTER 3 for a review of the general law of removal in maritime cases.

In 1980, Congress established a uniform national statute of limitations of three years for suits "for recovery of damages for personal injury or death, or both, arising out of a maritime tort." 46 U.S.C.A. 30106 (formerly 46 U.S.C. § 763a).

Federal Employers' Liability Act

45 U.S.C. § 51, *et seq.*

§ 51. Liability of common carriers by railroad, in interstate or foreign commerce, for injuries to employees from negligence; employee defined

Every common carrier by railroad while engaging in commerce between any of the several States or Territories, or between any of the States and Territories, or between the District of Columbia and any of the States or Territories, or between the District of Columbia or any of the States or any of the States or Territories and any foreign nation or nations, shall be liable in damages to any person suffering injury while he is employed by such carrier in such commerce, or, in case of the death of such employee, to his or her personal representative, for the benefit of the surviving widow or husband and children of such employee; and, if none, then of such employee's parents; and, if none, then of the next of kin dependent upon such employee, for such injury or death resulting in whole or in part from the negligence of any of the officers, agents, or employees of such carrier, or by reason of any defect or insufficiency, due to its negligence, in its cars, engines, appliances, machinery, track, roadbed, works, boats, wharves, or other equipment.

Any employee of a carrier, any part of whose duties as such employee shall be the furtherance of interstate or foreign commerce; or shall, in any way directly or closely and substantially, affect such commerce as above set forth shall, for the purposes of this chapter, be considered as being employed by such carrier in such commerce and shall be considered as entitled to the benefits of this chapter.

§ 52. Carriers in Territories or other possessions of United States

Every common carrier by railroad in the Territories, the District of Columbia, the Panama Canal Zone, or other possessions of the United States shall be liable in damages to any person suffering injury while he is employed by such carrier in any of said jurisdictions, or, in case of the death of such employee, to his or her personal representative, for the benefit of the surviving widow or husband and children of such employee; and, if none, then of such employee's parents; and, if none, then of the next of kin dependent upon such employee, for such injury or death resulting in whole or in part from the negligence of any of the officers, agents, or employees of such carrier, or by reason of any defect or insufficiency, due to its negligence, in its cars, engines, appliances, machinery, track, roadbed, works, boats, wharves, or other equipment.

§ 53. Contributory negligence; diminution of damages

In all actions on and after April 22, 1908 brought against any such common carrier by railroad under or by virtue of any of the provisions of this chapter to recover damages for personal injuries to an employee, or where such injuries have resulted in his death, the fact that the employee may have been guilty of contributory negligence shall not bar a recovery, but the damages shall be diminished by the jury in proportion to the amount of negligence attributable to such employee: *Provided*, That no such employee who may be injured or killed shall be held to have been guilty of contributory negligence in any case where the violation by such common carrier of any statute enacted for the safety of employees contributed to the injury or death of such employee.

§ 54. Assumption of risks of employment

In any action brought against any common carrier under or by virtue of any of the provisions of this chapter to recover damages for injuries to, or the death of, any of its employees, such employee shall not be held to have assumed the risks of his employment in any case where such injury or death resulted in whole or in part from the negligence of any of the officers, agents, or employees of such carrier; and no employee shall be held to have assumed the risks of his employment in any case where the violation by such common carrier of any statute enacted for the safety of employees contributed to the injury or death of such employee.

§ 55. Contract, rule, regulation, or device exempting from liability; set-off

Any contract, rule, regulation, or device whatsoever, the purpose or intent of which shall be to enable any common carrier to exempt itself from any liability created by this chapter, shall to that extent be void: *Provided*, That in any action brought against any such common carrier under or by virtue of any of the provisions of this chapter, such common carrier may set off therein any sum it has contributed or paid to any insurance, relief benefit, or indemnity that may have been paid to the injured employee or the person entitled thereto on account of the injury or death for which said action was brought.

§ 56. Actions; limitations; concurrent jurisdiction of courts

No action shall be maintained under this chapter unless commenced within three years from the day the cause of action accrued.

Under this chapter an action may be brought in a district court of the United States, in the district of the residence of the defendant, or in which the cause of action arose, or in which the defendant shall be doing business at the time of commencing such action. The jurisdiction of the courts of the Untied States under this chapter shall be concurrent with that of the courts of the several States.

§ 57. Who included in term "common carrier"

The term "common carrier" as used in this chapter shall include the receiver or receivers or other persons or corporations charged with the duty of the management and operation of the business of a common carrier.

§ 58. Duty or liability of common carriers and rights of employees under other acts not impaired

Nothing in this chapter shall be held to limit the duty or liability of common carriers or to impair the rights of their employees under any other Act or Acts of Congress.

§ 59. Survival of right of action of person injured

Any right of action given by this chapter to a person suffering injury shall survive to his or her personal representative, for the benefit of the surviving widow or husband and children of such employee, and, if none, then of such employee's parents; and, if none, then of the next of kin dependent upon such employee, but in such cases there shall be only one recovery for the same injury.

§ 60. Penalty for suppression of voluntary information incident to accidents; separability of provisions

Any contract, rule, regulation, or device whatsoever, the purpose, intent, or effect of which shall be to prevent employees of any common carrier from furnishing voluntarily information to a person in interest as to the facts incident to the injury or death of any employee, shall be void, and whoever, by threat, intimidation, order, rule, contract, regulation, or device whatsoever, shall attempt to prevent any person from furnishing voluntarily such information to a person in interest, or whoever discharges or otherwise disciplines or attempts to discipline any employee for furnishing voluntarily such information to a person in interest, shall, upon conviction thereof, be punished by a fine of not more than $1,000 or imprisoned for not more than one year, or by both such fine and imprisonment, for each offense: *Provided,* That nothing herein contained shall be construed to void any contract, rule, or regulation with respect to any information contained in the files of the carrier, or other privileged or confidential reports.

If any provision of this chapter is declared unconstitutional or the applicability thereof to any person or circumstances is held invalid, the validity of the remainder of the chapter and the applicability of such provision to other persons and circumstances shall not be affected thereby.

---

1. Coverage: "Any Seaman ..."

a. Status

Introductory Note

Many different kinds of workers do work of many different kinds on vessels. This creates the perennial problem of deciding which kinds of maritime workers qualify as "seamen" for the purposes of the Jones Act. Before the decision of the Supreme Court in *McDermott Intern., Inc. v. Wilander,* 498 U.S. 337, 111 S. Ct. 807, 112 L. Ed. 2d 866, 1991 AMC 913 (1991), there was disagreement between circuit courts about whether a maritime worker could be a "seaman" without contributing in some way to the transportation function of the vessel. The *Wilander* Court said:

> Notwithstanding the aid in navigation doctrine, federal courts throughout the last century consistently awarded seamen's benefits to those whose work on board ship did not direct the vessel. Firemen, engineers, carpenters, and cooks all were considered seamen. *See, e.g., Wilson v. The Ohio*, 30 F. Cas. 149 (No. 17,825) (ED Pa. 1834) (firemen); *Allen v. Hallet*, 1 F. Cas. 472 (No. 223) (SDNY 1849) (cook); *Sageman v. The Brandywine*, 21 F. Cas. 149 (No. 12,216) (D Mich. 1852) (female cook); *The Sultana*, 23 F. Cas. 379 (No. 13,602) (D Mich. 1857) (clerk). *See generally* M. NORRIS, THE LAW OF SEAMEN § 2.3 (4th ed. 1985); Engerrand & Bale, *Seaman Status Reconsidered*, 24 S. TEX. L. J. 431, 432-433 (1983).
>
> * * *
>
> By the middle of the 19th century, the leading admiralty treatise noted the wide variety of those eligible for seamen's benefits: "Masters, mates, sailors, surveyors, carpenters, coopers, stewards, cooks, cabin boys, kitchen boys, engineers, pilots, firemen, deck hands, waiters,—women as well as men,—are mariners." E. BENEDICT, THE AMERICAN ADMIRALTY § 278, p. 158 (1850). Benedict concluded that American admiralty courts did not require that seamen have a connection to navigation. "The term mariner includes all persons employed on board ships and vessels during the voyage to assist in their navigation and preservation, *or to promote the purposes of the voyage.*" *Ibid.* (emphasis added). Moreover, Benedict explained, this was the better rule; admiralty courts throughout the world had long recognized that seamen's benefits were properly extended to all those who worked on board vessels in furtherance of the myriad purposes for which ships set to sea...
>
> * * *
>
> We believe the better rule is to define "master or member of a crew" under the LHWCA, and therefore "seaman" under the Jones Act, solely in terms of the employee's connection to a vessel in navigation. This rule best explains our case law, and is consistent with the pre-Jones Act interpretation of "seaman" and Congress' land-based/sea-based distinction. All who work at sea in the service of a ship face those particular perils to which the protection of maritime law, statutory as well as decisional, is directed. *See generally* Robertson, *A New Approach to Determining Seaman Status*, 64 TEXAS L. REV. 79 (1985). It is not the employee's particular job that is determinative, but the employee's connection to a vessel.
>
> * * *
>
> The key to seaman status is employment-related connection to a vessel in navigation. We are not called upon here to define this connection in all details, but we hold that a necessary element of the connection is that a seaman perform the work of a vessel...It is not necessary that a seaman aid in navigation or contribute to the transportation of the vessel, but a seaman must be doing the ship's work.

498 U.S. 337, 343-44, 354-55 (1991)

CHANDRIS, INC. v. LATSIS

515 U.S. 347, 115 S. Ct. 2172, 132 L. Ed. 2d 314, 1995 AMC 1840 (1995)

Justice O'CONNOR delivered the opinion of the Court

This case asks us to clarify what "employment-related connection to a vessel in navigation," *McDermott International, Inc. v. Wilander*, 498 U.S. 337, 355, 111 S. Ct. 807, 817, 112 L. Ed. 2d 866 (1991), is necessary for a maritime worker to qualify as a seaman under the Jones Act, 46 U.S.C.App. § 688(a). In *Wilander*, we addressed the type of activities that a seaman must perform and held that, under the Jones Act, a seaman's job need not be limited to transportation-related functions that directly aid in the vessel's navigation. We now determine what relationship a worker must have to the vessel, regardless of the specific tasks the worker undertakes, in order to obtain seaman status.

I

In May 1989, respondent Antonios Latsis was employed by petitioner Chandris, Inc., as a salaried superintendent engineer. Latsis was responsible for maintaining and updating the electronic and communications equipment on Chandris' fleet of vessels, which consisted of six passenger cruise ships. Each ship in the Chandris fleet carried between 12 and 14 engineers who were assigned permanently to that vessel. Latsis, on the other hand, was one of two supervising engineers based at Chandris' Miami office; his duties ran to the entire fleet and included not only overseeing the vessels' engineering departments, which required him to take a number of voyages, but also planning and directing ship maintenance from the shore. Latsis claimed at trial that he spent 72 percent of his time at sea, his immediate supervisor testified that the appropriate figure was closer to 10 percent.

On May 14, 1989, Latsis sailed for Bermuda aboard the S.S. Galileo to plan for an upcoming renovation of the ship, which was one of the older vessels in the Chandris fleet. Latsis developed a problem with his right eye on the day of departure, and he saw the ship's doctor as the Galileo left port. The doctor diagnosed a suspected detached retina but failed to follow standard medical procedure, which would have been to direct Latsis to see an ophthalmologist on an emergency basis. Instead, the ship's doctor recommended that Latsis relax until he could see an eye specialist when the Galileo arrived in Bermuda two days later. No attempt was made to transport Latsis ashore for prompt medical care by means of a pilot vessel or helicopter during the 11 hours it took the ship to reach the open sea from Baltimore, and Latsis received no further medical care until after the ship arrived in Bermuda. In Bermuda, a doctor diagnosed a detached retina and recommended immediate hospitalization and surgery. Although the operation was a partial success, Latsis lost 75 percent of his vision in his right eye.

Following his recuperation, which lasted approximately six weeks, Latsis resumed his duties with Chandris. On September 30, 1989, he sailed with the Galileo to Bremerhaven, Germany, where the vessel was placed in drydock for a 6-month refurbishment. After the conversion, the company renamed the vessel the S.S. Meridian. Latsis, who had been with the ship the entire time it was in drydock in Bremerhaven, sailed back to the United States on board the Meridian and continued to work for Chandris until November 1990, when his employment was terminated for reasons that are not clear from the record.

In October 1991, Latsis filed suit in the United States District Court for the Southern District of New York seeking compensatory damages under the Jones Act, 46 U.S.C.App. § 688, for the negligence of the ship's doctor that resulted in the significant loss of sight in Latsis' right eye... . The District Court instructed the jury that it could conclude that Latsis was a seaman within the meaning of the statute if it found as follows: "[T]he plaintiff was either permanently assigned to the vessel or performed a substantial part of his work on the vessel. In determining whether Mr. Latsis performed a substantial part of his work on the vessel, you may not consider the period of time the Galileo was in drydock in Germany, because during that time period she was out of navigation. You may, however, consider the time spent sailing to and from Germany for the conversion. Also, on this first element of being a seaman, seamen do not include land-based workers." The parties stipulated to the District Court's second requirement for Jones Act coverage—that Latsis' duties contributed to the accomplishment of the missions of the Chandris vessels... . The jury returned a verdict in favor of Chandris solely on the issue of Latsis' status as a seaman under the Jones Act.

Respondent appealed to the Court of Appeals for the Second Circuit, which vacated the judgment and remanded the case for a new trial. 20 F.3d 45 (1994). The court emphasized that its longstanding test for seaman status under the Jones Act required "'a more or less permanent connection with the ship,'" a connection that need not be limited to time spent on the vessel but could also be established by the nature of the work performed. The court thought that the alternate formulation employed by the District Court (permanent assignment to the vessel or performance of a substantial part of his work on the vessel), which was derived from *Offshore Co. v. Robison*, 266 F.2d 769, 779 (CA5 1959), improperly framed the issue for the jury primarily, if not solely, in terms of Latsis' temporal relationship to the vessel. With that understanding of what the language of the Robison test implied, the court concluded that the District Court's seaman status jury instructions constituted plain error under established circuit precedent. The court then took this case as an opportunity to clarify its seaman status requirements, directing the District Court that the jury should be instructed on remand as follows: "[T]he test of seaman status under the Jones Act is an employment-related connection to a vessel in navigation. The test will be met where a jury finds that (1) the plaintiff contributed to the function of or helped accomplish the mission of, a vessel; (2) the plaintiff's contribution was limited to a particular vessel or identifiable group of vessels; (3) the plaintiff's contribution was substantial in terms of its (a) duration or (b) nature; and (4) the course of the plaintiff's employment regularly exposed the plaintiff to the hazards of the sea." 20 F.3d, at 57. Elsewhere on the same page, however, the court phrased the third prong as requiring a substantial connection in terms of both duration and nature. Finally, the Court of Appeals held that the District Court erred in instructing the jury that the time Latsis spent with the ship while it was in drydock could not count in the substantial connection equation.

We granted certiorari, 513 U.S. —, 115 S. Ct. 354, 130 L. Ed. 2d 309 (1994), to resolve the continuing conflict among the Courts of Appeals regarding the appropriate requirements for seaman status under the Jones Act.

II

* * *

A

In *Wilander*, decided in 1991, the Court attempted for the first time in 33 years to clarify the definition of a "seaman" under the Jones Act....

* * *

Beyond dispensing with the "aid to navigation" requirement, however, *Wilander* did not consider the requisite connection to a vessel in any detail and therefore failed to end the prevailing confusion regarding seaman status.

B

Respondent urges us to find our way out of the Jones Act "labyrinth" by focusing on the seemingly activity-based policy underlying the statute (the protection of those who are exposed to the perils of the sea), and to conclude that anyone working on board a vessel for the duration of a "voyage" in furtherance of the vessel's mission has the necessary employment-related connection to qualify as a seaman. Such an approach, however, would run counter to our prior decisions and our understanding of the remedial scheme Congress has established for injured maritime workers. A brief survey of the Jones Act's tortured history makes clear that we must reject the initial appeal of such a "voyage" test and undertake the more difficult task of developing a status-based standard that, although it determines Jones Act coverage without regard to the precise activity in which the worker is engaged at the time of the injury, nevertheless best furthers the Jones Act's remedial goals.

Our Jones Act cases establish several basic principles regarding the definition of a seaman. First, "[w]hether under the Jones Act or general maritime law, seamen do not include land-based workers." *Wilander*, *supra*, at 348, *see also* Allbritton, *Seaman Status in Wilander's Wake*, 68 TULANE L. REV. 373, 387 (1994)... .

In addition to recognizing a fundamental distinction between land-based and sea-based maritime employees, our cases also emphasize that Jones Act coverage, like the jurisdiction of admiralty over causes of action for maintenance and cure for injuries received in the course of a seamen's employment, depends "not on the place where the injury is inflicted ... but on the nature of the seaman's service, his status as a member of the vessel, and his relationship as such to the vessel and its operation in navigable waters." Thus, maritime workers who obtain seaman status do not lose that protection automatically when on shore and may recover under the Jones Act whenever they are injured in the service of a vessel, regardless of whether the injury occurs on or off the ship... .

Our LHWCA cases also recognize the converse: land-based maritime workers injured while on a vessel in navigation remain covered by the LHWCA, which expressly provides compensation for injuries to certain workers engaged in "maritime employment" that are incurred "upon the navigable waters of the United States," 33 U.S.C. § 903(a). Thus, in Director, *OWCP v. Perini North River Associates*, 459 U.S. 297, 103 S. Ct. 634, 74 L. Ed. 2d 465 (1983), we held that a worker injured while "working on a barge in actual navigable waters" of the Hudson River, could be compensated under the LHWCA... .

* * *

We believe it is important to avoid "'engrafting upon the statutory classification of a "seaman" a judicial gloss so protean, elusive, or arbitrary as to permit a worker to walk into and out of coverage in the course of his regular duties.'" *Barrett v. Chevron, U.S.A., Inc.*, 781 F.2d 1067, 1075 (CA5 1986) (en banc) (quoting *Longmire v. Sea Drilling Corp.*, 610 F.2d 1342, 1347, n.6 (CA5 1980)). In evaluating the employment-related connection of a maritime worker to a vessel in navigation, courts should not employ "a 'snapshot' test for seaman status, inspecting only the situation as it exists at the instant of injury; a more enduring relationship is contemplated in the jurisprudence." Thus, a worker may not oscillate back and forth between Jones Act coverage and other remedies depending on the activity in which the worker was engaged while injured. Unlike Justice STEVENS, we do not believe that any maritime worker on a ship at sea as part of his employment is automatically a member of the crew of the vessel within the meaning of the statutory terms. Our rejection of the voyage test is also consistent with the interests of employers and maritime workers alike in being able to predict who will be covered by the Jones Act (and, perhaps more importantly for purposes of the employers' workers' compensation obligations, who will be covered by the LHWCA) before a particular work day begins.

To say that our cases have recognized a distinction between land-based and sea-based maritime workers that precludes application of a voyage test for seaman status, however, is not to say that a maritime employee must work only on board a vessel to qualify as a seaman under the Jones Act. In *Southwest Marine, Inc. v. Gizoni*, 502 U.S. 81, 112 S. Ct. 486, 116 L. Ed. 2d 405 (1991), decided only a few months after *Wilander*, we concluded that a worker's status as a ship repairman, one of the enumerated occupations encompassed within the term "employee" under the LHWCA, 33 U.S.C. § 902(3), did not necessarily restrict the worker to a remedy under that statute. We explained that, "[w]hile in some cases a ship repairman may lack the requisite connection to a vessel in navigation to qualify for seaman status, ... not all ship repairmen lack the requisite connection as a matter of law. This is so because '[i]t is not the employee's particular job that is determinative, but the employee's connection to a vessel.'" *Gizoni*, *supra*, at 89, 112 S. Ct., at 492 (quoting *Wilander*, 498 U.S., at 354, 111 S. Ct., at 817) (footnote omitted). Thus, we concluded, the Jones Act remedy may be available to maritime workers who are employed by a shipyard and who spend a portion of their time working on shore but spend the rest of their time at sea.

Beyond these basic themes, which are sufficient to foreclose respondent's principal argument, our cases are largely silent as to the precise relationship a maritime worker must bear to a vessel in order to come within the Jones Act's ambit. We have, until now, left to the lower federal courts the task of developing appropriate criteria to distinguish the "ship's company" from those members of the maritime community whose employment is essentially land-based.

C

The Court of Appeals for the First Circuit was apparently the first to develop a generally applicable test for seaman status. In *Carumbo v. Cape Cod S.S. Co.*, 123 F.2d 991 (CA1

1941), the court retained the pre-Swanson view that "the word 'seaman' under the Jones Act did not mean the same thing as 'member of a crew' under the [LHWCA]," *id.*, at 994. It concluded that "one who does any sort of work aboard a ship in navigation is a 'seaman' within the meaning of the Jones Act." The phrase "member of a crew," on the other hand, the court gave a more restrictive meaning. The court adopted three elements to define the phrase that had been used at various times in prior cases, holding that "[t]he requirements that the ship be in navigation; that there be a more or less permanent connection with the ship; and that the worker be aboard primarily to aid in navigation appear to us to be the essential and decisive elements of the definition of a 'member of a crew.'" Once it became clear that the phrase "master or member of a crew" from the LHWCA is coextensive with the term "seaman" in the Jones Act, courts accepted the Carumbo formulation of master or member of a crew in the Jones Act context. The Court of Appeals for the Second Circuit initially was among the jurisdictions to adopt the Carumbo formulation as the basis of its seaman status inquiry, *see Salgado v. M.J. Rudolph Corp.*, 514 F.2d, at 755, but that court took the instant case as an opportunity to modify the traditional test somewhat (replacing the "more or less permanent connection" prong with a requirement that the connection be "substantial in terms of its (a) duration and (b) nature"), 20 F.3d, at 57.

The second major body of seaman status law developed in the Court of Appeals for the Fifth Circuit, which has a substantial Jones Act caseload, in the wake of *Offshore Co. v. Robison*, 266 F.2d 769 (CA5 1959). At the time of his injury, Robison was an oil worker permanently assigned to a drilling rig mounted on a barge in the Gulf of Mexico. In sustaining the jury's award of damages to Robison under the Jones Act, the court abandoned the aid in navigation requirement of the traditional test and held as follows: "[T]here is an evidentiary basis for a Jones Act case to go to the jury: (1) if there is evidence that the injured workman was assigned permanently to a vessel ... or performed a substantial part of his work on the vessel; and (2) if the capacity in which he was employed or the duties which he performed contributed to the function of the vessel or the accomplishment of its mission, or to the operation or welfare of the vessel in terms of its maintenance during its movement or during anchorage for its future trips." Soon after Robison, the Fifth Circuit modified the test to allow seaman status for those workers who had the requisite connection with an "identifiable fleet" of vessels, a finite group of vessels under common ownership or control. *Braniff v. Jackson Avenue-Gretna Ferry, Inc.*, 280 F.2d 523, 528 (1960). *See also Barrett*, 781 F.2d, at 1074; *Bertrand v. International Mooring & Marine, Inc.*, 700 F.2d 240 (CA5 1983), *cert. denied*, 464 U.S. 1069, 104 S. Ct. 974, 79 L. Ed. 2d 212 (1984). The modified Robison formulation, which replaced the Carumbo version as the definitive test for seaman status in the Fifth Circuit, has been highly influential in other courts as well. *See* Robertson 95; *Miller v. Patton-Tully Transp. Co.*, 851 F.2d 202, 204 (CA8 1988); *Caruso v. Sterling Yacht & Shipbuilders, Inc.*, 828 F.2d 14, 15 (CA11 1987); *Bennett v. Perini Corp.*, 510 F.2d 114, 115 (CA1 1975).

While the Carumbo and Robison approaches may not seem all that different at first glance, subsequent developments in the Fifth Circuit's Jones Act jurisprudence added a strictly temporal gloss to the Jones Act inquiry. Under *Barrett v. Chevron, U.S.A., Inc.*, *supra*, if an employee's regular duties require him to divide his time between vessel and land, his status as a crew member is determined "in the context of his entire employment" with his current employer. In Barrett, the court noted that the worker "performed seventy to eighty percent of his work on platforms and no more than twenty to thirty percent of his work on vessels" and then concluded that, "[b]ecause he did not perform a substantial portion of his work aboard a vessel or fleet of vessels, he failed to establish that he was a member of the crew of a vessel." 781 F.2d, at 1076. Since Barrett, the Fifth Circuit consistently has analyzed the problem in terms of the percentage of work performed on vessels for the employer in question—and has declined to find seaman status where the employee spent less than 30 percent of his time aboard ship. See, *e.g.*, *Palmer v. Fayard Moving & Transp. Corp.*, 930 F.2d 437, 439 (CA5 1991); *Lormand v. Superior Oil Co.*, 845 F.2d 536, 541 (CA5 1987), *cert. denied*, 484 U.S. 1031, 108 S. Ct. 739, 98 L. Ed. 2d 774 (1988); *cf. Leonard v. Dixie Well Service & Supply, Inc.*, 828 F.2d 291, 295 (CA5 1987); *Pickle v. International Oilfield Divers, Inc.*, 791 F.2d 1237, 1240 (CA5 1986), *cert. denied*, 479 U.S. 1059, 107 S. Ct. 939, 93 L. Ed. 2d 989 (1987).

Although some courts of appeals have varied the applicable tests to some degree, *see, e.g.*, *Johnson v. John F. Beasley Constr. Co.*, 742 F.2d, at 1062-1063, the traditional Carumbo seaman status formulation and the subsequent Robison modification are universally recognized, and one or the other is applied in every federal circuit to have considered the issue. *See* Bull, *Seaman Status Revisited: A Practical Guide To Status Determination*, 6 U.S.F.MAR.L.J. 547, 562-572 (1994) (collecting cases). The federal courts generally require at least a significant connection to a vessel in navigation (or to an identifiable fleet of vessels) for a maritime worker to qualify as a seaman under the Jones Act. Although the traditional test requires a "more or less permanent connection" and the Robison formulation calls for "substantial" work aboard a vessel, "this general requirement varies little, if at all, from one jurisdiction to another," *id.*, at 587, and "[t]he courts have repeatedly held that the relationship creating seaman status must be substantial in point of time and work, and not merely sporadic," *id.*, at 587-588.

D

... [W]e think that the essential requirements for seaman status are twofold. First, as we emphasized in *Wilander*, "an employee's duties must 'contribut[e] to the function of the vessel or to the accomplishment of its mission.'" 498 U.S., at 355, 111 S. Ct., at 817 (quoting *Robison*, 266 F.2d, at 779). The Jones Act's protections, like the other admiralty protections for seamen, only extend to those maritime employees who do the ship's work. But this threshold requirement is very broad: "[a]ll who work at sea in the service of a ship" are eligible for seaman status. 498 U.S., at 354, 111 S. Ct., at 817.

Second, and most important for our purposes here, a seaman must have a connection to a vessel in navigation (or to an identifiable group of such vessels) that is substantial in terms of both its duration and its nature. The fundamental purpose of this substantial connection requirement is to give full effect to the remedial scheme created by Congress and to separate the sea-based maritime employees who are entitled to Jones Act protection from those land-based workers who have only a transitory or sporadic connection to a vessel in navigation, and therefore whose employment does not regularly expose them to the perils of the sea. *See* 1B A. JENNER, BENEDICT ON ADMIRALTY, § 11a, pp. 2-10.1 to 2-11 (7th ed. 1994) ("If it can be shown that the employee performed a significant part of his work on board the vessel on which he was injured, with at least some degree of regularity and continuity, the test for seaman status will be satisfied" (footnote omitted)). This requirement therefore determines which maritime employees in *Wilander*'s broad category of persons eligible for seaman status because they are "doing the ship's work," 498 U.S., at 355, 111 S. Ct., at 817, are in fact entitled to the benefits conferred upon seamen by the Jones Act because they have the requisite employment-related connection to a vessel in navigation.

It is important to recall that the question of who is a "member of a crew," and therefore who is a "seaman," is a mixed question of law and fact. Because statutory terms are at issue, their interpretation is a question of law and it is the court's duty to define the appropriate standard. On the other hand, "[i]f reasonable persons, applying the proper legal standard, could differ as to whether the employee was a 'member of a crew,' it is a question for the jury." The jury should be permitted, when determining whether a maritime employee has the requisite employment-related connection to a vessel in navigation to qualify as a member of the vessel's crew, to consider all relevant circumstances bearing on the two elements outlined above.

In defining the prerequisites for Jones Act coverage, we think it preferable to focus upon the essence of what it means to be a seaman and to eschew the temptation to create detailed tests to effectuate the congressional purpose, tests that tend to become ends in and of themselves. The principal formulations employed by the Courts of Appeals—"more or less permanent assignment" or "connection to a vessel that is substantial in terms of its duration and nature"—are simply different ways of getting at the same basic point: the Jones Act remedy is reserved for sea-based maritime employees whose work regularly exposes them to "the special hazards and disadvantages to which they who go down to sea in ships are subjected." *Sieracki*, 328 U.S., at 104, 66 S. Ct., at 882 (STONE, C.J., dissenting). Indeed, it is difficult to discern major substantive differences in the language of the two phrases. In our view, "the total circumstances of an individual's employment must be weighed to determine whether he had a sufficient relation to the navigation of vessels and the perils attendant thereon." *Wallace v. Oceaneering Int'l*, 727 F.2d 427, 432 (CA5 1984). The duration of a worker's connection to a vessel and the nature of the worker's activities, taken together, determine whether a maritime employee is a seaman because the ultimate inquiry is whether the worker in question is a member of the vessel's crew or simply a land-based employee who happens to be working on the vessel at a given time.

Although we adopt the centerpiece of the formulation used by the Court of Appeals in this case—that a seaman must have a connection with a vessel in navigation that is substantial in both duration and nature—we should point out how our understanding of the import of that language may be different in some respects from that of the court below. The Court of Appeals suggested that its test for seaman status "does not unequivocally require a

Jones Act seaman to be substantially connected to a vessel" in terms of time if the worker performs important work on board on a steady, although not necessarily on a temporally significant, basis. 20 F.3d, at 53. Perhaps giving effect to this intuition, or perhaps reacting to the temporal gloss placed on the Robison language by later Fifth Circuit decisions, the court phrased its standard at one point as requiring a jury to find that a Jones Act plaintiff's contribution to the function of the vessel was substantial in terms of its duration or nature. *Id.*, at 57. It is not clear which version ("duration or nature" as opposed to "duration and nature") the Court of Appeals intended to adopt for the substantial connection requirement—or indeed whether the court saw a significant difference between the two. Nevertheless, we think it is important that a seaman's connection to a vessel in fact be substantial in both respects.

We agree with the Court of Appeals that seaman status is not merely a temporal concept, but we also believe that it necessarily includes a temporal element. A maritime worker who spends only a small fraction of his working time on board a vessel is fundamentally land-based and therefore not a member of the vessel's crew, regardless of what his duties are. Naturally, substantiality in this context is determined by reference to the period covered by the Jones Act plaintiff's maritime employment, rather than by some absolute measure. Generally, the Fifth Circuit seems to have identified an appropriate rule of thumb for the ordinary case: a worker who spends less than about 30 percent of his time in the service of a vessel in navigation should not qualify as a seaman under the Jones Act. This figure of course serves as no more than a guideline established by years of experience, and departure from it will certainly be justified in appropriate cases. As we have said, "[t]he inquiry into seaman status is of necessity fact specific; it will depend on the nature of the vessel and the employee's precise relation to it." *Wilander*, 498 U.S., at 356, 111 S. Ct., at 818. Nevertheless, we believe that courts, employers, and maritime workers can all benefit from reference to these general principles. And where undisputed facts reveal that a maritime worker has a clearly inadequate temporal connection to vessels in navigation, the court may take the question from the jury by granting summary judgment or a directed verdict. *See, e.g.*, *Palmer*, 930 F.2d, at 439.

On the other hand, we see no reason to limit the seaman status inquiry, as petitioners contend, exclusively to an examination of the overall course of a worker's service with a particular employer. When a maritime worker's basic assignment changes, his seaman status may change as well. *See* Barrett, 781 F.2d, at 1077 (RUBIN, J., dissenting) ("An assignment to work as a crew member, like the voyage of a vessel, may be brief, and the *Robison* test is applicable in deciding the worker's status during any such employment"); *Longmire*, 610 F.2d, at 1347, n.6. For example, we can imagine situations in which someone who had worked for years in an employer's shoreside headquarters is then reassigned to a ship in a classic seaman's job that involves a regular and continuous, rather than intermittent, commitment of the worker's labor to the function of a vessel. Such a person should not be denied seaman status if injured shortly after the reassignment, just as someone actually transferred to a desk job in the company's office and injured in the hallway should not be entitled to claim seaman status on the basis of prior service at sea. If a maritime employee receives a new work assignment in which his essential duties are changed, he is entitled to have the assessment of the substantiality of his vessel-related work made on the basis of his activities in his new position. *See* Cheavens, 64 TULANE L. REV., at 389-390. Thus, nothing in our opinion forecloses Jones Act coverage, in appropriate cases, for Justice STEVENS' paradigmatic maritime worker injured while reassigned to "a lengthy voyage on the high seas," post, at 2198. While our approach maintains the status-based inquiry this Court's earlier cases contemplate, we recognize that seaman status also should not be some immutable characteristic that maritime workers who spend only a portion of their time at sea can never attain.

III

One final issue remains for our determination: whether the District Court erred in instructing the jurors that, "[i]n determining whether Mr. Latsis performed a substantial part of his work on the vessel, [they could] not consider the period of time the Galileo was in drydock in Germany, because during that time period she was out of navigation." We agree with the Court of Appeals that it d*id*.

The foregoing discussion establishes that, to qualify as a seaman under the Jones Act, a maritime employee must have a substantial employment-related connection to a vessel in navigation. Of course, any time Latsis spent with the Galileo while the ship was out of navigation could not count as time spent at sea for purposes of that inquiry, and it would have been appropriate for the District Court to make this clear to the jury. Yet the underlying inquiry whether a vessel is or is not "in navigation" for Jones Act purposes is a fact-intensive question that is normally for the jury and not the court to decide... . Based upon the record before us, we think the court failed adequately to justify its decision to remove the question whether the Galileo was "in navigation" while in Bremerhaven from the jury.

Under our precedent and the law prevailing in the circuits, it is generally accepted that "a vessel does not cease to be a vessel when she is not voyaging, but is at anchor, berthed, or at dockside," even when the vessel is undergoing repairs. At some point, however, repairs become sufficiently significant that the vessel can no longer be considered in navigation. In *West v. United States*, 361 U.S. 118, 80 S. Ct. 189, 4 L. Ed. 2d 161 (1959), we held that a shoreside worker was not entitled to recover for unseaworthiness because the vessel on which he was injured was undergoing an overhaul for the purpose of making her seaworthy and therefore had been withdrawn from navigation. We explained that, in such cases, "the focus should be upon the status of the ship, the pattern of the repairs, and the extensive nature of the work contracted to be done." The general rule among the Courts of Appeals is that vessels undergoing repairs or spending a relatively short period of time in drydock are still considered to be "in navigation" whereas ships being transformed through "major" overhauls or renovations are not. See Bull, 6 U.S.F. MAR. L.J., at 582-584 (collecting cases).

... Our review of the record in this case uncovered relatively little evidence bearing on the Galileo's status during the repairs, and even less discussion of the question by the District Court. On the one hand, the work on the Chandris vessel took only about six months, which seems to be a relatively short period of time for important repairs on oceangoing vessels. On the other hand, Latsis' own description of the work performed suggests that the modifications to the vessel were actually quite significant, including the removal of the ship's bottom plates and propellers, the addition of bow thrusters, overhaul of the main engines, reconstruction of the boilers, and renovations of the cabins and other passenger areas of the ship. On these facts ... it is possible that Chandris could be entitled to partial summary judgment or a directed verdict concerning whether the Galileo remained in navigation while in drydock; the record, however, contains no stipulations or findings by the District Court to justify its conclusion that the modifications to the Galileo were sufficiently extensive to remove the vessel from navigation as a matter of law. On that basis, we agree with the Court of Appeals that the District Court's drydock instruction was erroneous.

* * *

IV

* * *

On remand, the District Court should charge the jury in a manner consistent with our holding that the "employment-related connection to a vessel in navigation" necessary to qualify as a seaman under the Jones Act, *id.*, at 355, 111 S. Ct., at 817, comprises two basic elements: the worker's duties must contribute to the function of the vessel or to the accomplishment of its mission, and the worker must have a connection to a vessel in navigation (or an identifiable group of vessels) that is substantial in terms of both its duration and its nature. As to the latter point, the court should emphasize that the Jones Act was intended to protect sea-based maritime workers, who owe their allegiance to a vessel, and not land-based employees, who do not. By instructing juries in Jones Act cases accordingly, courts can give proper effect to the remedial scheme Congress has created for injured maritime workers.

It is so ordered.

Justice STEVENS, with whom Justice THOMAS and Justice BREYER join, concurring in the judgment

The majority has reached the odd conclusion that a maritime engineer, injured aboard ship on the high seas while performing his duties as an employee of the ship, might not be a "seaman" within the meaning of the Jones Act. This decision is unprecedented. It ignores the critical distinction between work performed aboard ship during a voyage—when the members of the crew encounter "the perils of the sea"—and maritime work performed on a vessel moored to a dock in a safe harbor. In my judgment, an employee of the ship who is injured at sea in the course of his employment is always a "seaman." I would leave more ambiguous, shore-bound cases for another day. Accordingly, though I concur in the Court's disposition of this case, returning it to the District Court for a new trial, I disagree with the standard this Court directs the trial court to apply on remand.

* * *

II

Despite the language, history, and purpose of the Jones Act, the Court today holds that seaman status may require more than a single ocean voyage. The Court's opinion thus obscures, if it does not ignore, the distinction between the perils of the sea and the risks faced by maritime workers when a ship is moored to a dock. The test that the Court formulates may be appropriate for the resolution of cases in the latter category. The Court fails, however, to explain why the member of the crew of a vessel at sea is not always a seaman.

Respondent's argument, "that any worker who is assigned to a vessel for the duration of a voyage and whose duties contribute to the vessel's mission must be classified as a seaman respecting injuries incurred on that voyage," Brief for Respondent 14, is not inconsistent with the Court's view, *ante*, at 2185-2186, that an employee must occupy a certain status in order to qualify as a seaman. It merely recognizes that all members of a ship's crew have that status while the vessel is at sea. In contrast, when the ship is in a harbor, further inquiry may be necessary to separate land-based from sea-based maritime employees. The Court is therefore simply wrong when it states that a "'voyage test' would conflict with our prior understanding of the Jones Act as fundamentally status-based, granting the negligence cause of action to those maritime workers who form the ship's company," *ante*, at 2186. The "ship's company" is readily identifiable when the ship is at sea; the fact that it may be less so when the ship is in port is not an acceptable reason for refusing to rely on the voyage test in a case like this one.

The Court is also quite wrong to suggest that our prior cases "indicate that a maritime worker does not become a 'member of a crew' as soon as a vessel leaves the dock," *ante*, at 2186. In neither of the two cases on which it relies to support this conclusion did the injured workman even claim the status of a seaman. In *Director, Office of Workers' Compensation Programs v. Perini North River Associates*, 459 U.S. 297, 103 S. Ct. 634, 74 L. Ed. 2d 465 (1983), we held that an employee of a firm that was building the foundation of a sewage treatment plant, which extended over the Hudson River adjacent to Manhattan, was covered by the LHWCA because he was injured while working on a barge in navigable waters. The Court of Appeals had denied coverage on the ground that this worker was not engaged in maritime employment. Thus, Perini had nothing to do with any possible overlap between the Jones Act and the LHWCA; this Court's reversal merely found a sufficient maritime connection to support LHWCA coverage of an admittedly shore-based worker.

The other case that the Court cites, *Parker v. Motor Boat Sales, Inc.*, 314 U.S. 244, 62 S. Ct. 221, 86 L. Ed. 184 (1941), involved a janitor who had drowned while riding in a motor boat on the James River near Richmond. The Court of Appeals had held that his widow was not entitled to compensation under the LHWCA on the alternative grounds (1) that the janitor was not acting in the course of his employment when the boat capsized, and (2) that the LHWCA did not apply because Virginia law could provide compensation. *See id.*, at 245, 62 S. Ct., at 222-223. As in Perini, our opinion reversing that decision did not discuss the Jones Act, because no one had even mentioned the possibility that the janitor might be a "seaman." ...

The Court's only other justification for refusing to apply a voyage test is its purported concern about a worker who might "walk into and out of coverage in the course of his regular duties." *Ante* at 2187 (internal quotation marks omitted). Because the only way that a seaman could walk out of Jones Act coverage during a voyage would be to quit his job and become a passenger (or possibly jump overboard), I take the majority's argument to mean that a single voyage is not a long enough time to establish seaman status. I simply do not understand this argument. Surely a voyage is sufficient time to establish an employment-related, status-based connection to a vessel in navigation that exposes the employee to the perils of the sea. The majority cannot explain why an employee who signs on for a single journey is any less a "seaman" or "member of a crew" if he intends to become an insurance agent after the voyage than if he intends to remain with the ship. What is important is the employee's status at the time of the injury, not his status a day, a month, or a year beforehand or afterward.

Apparently, the majority's real concern about walking in and out of coverage is that an employer will be unable to predict which of his employees will be covered by the Jones Act, and which by the LHWCA, on any given day. I think it is a novel construction of the Jones Act to read it as a scheme to protect employers. But even if Congress had shared the Court's concern, this case does not implicate it in the least. We are talking here about a lengthy voyage on the high seas. The employer controls who goes on that voyage; he knows, more or less, when that voyage will begin and when it will end. And, but for the majority's decision today, he would know that while the ship is at sea, all his employees thereon would be covered by the Jones Act and not by the LHWCA. Thus, no one is walking out of Jones Act coverage and into LHWCA coverage (or vice versa) without the employer's knowledge and control. Once again, the majority's concern—and its method of determining seaman status—is properly directed at injuries occurring while the ship is at port.

* * *

Notes

1. The *Chandris* court spoke of the employee's "connection with a vessel in navigation" (515 U.S. 347, 370, emphasis added), many maritime workers who spend a substantial amount of time at sea work on different vessels at different times. That was the situation in *Harbor Tug and Barge Co. v. Papai,* 520 U.S. 548, 117 S. Ct. 1535, 137 L. Ed. 2d 800, 1997AMC 1817 (1997), where the plaintiff was injured on the defendant's vessel during a one-day job obtained through a union "hiring hall". The plaintiff had worked for the defendant 12 times in the previous 2½ months, receiving all of those jobs through the "hiring hall". The Supreme Court reversed the circuit court's decision that the plaintiff was a Jones Act "seaman" because he did not work on an identifiable fleet of vessels in common ownership or control. The Court said:

> In deciding whether there is an identifiable group of vessels of relevance for a Jones Act seaman status determination, the question is whether the vessels are subject to common ownership or control. The requisite link is not established by the mere use of the same hiring hall which draws from the same pool of employees.
>
> Considering prior employments with independent employers in making the seaman status inquiry would undermine "the interests of employers and maritime workers alike in being able to predict who will be covered

> by the Jones Act (and, perhaps more importantly for purposes of the employers' workers' compensation obligations, who will be covered by the LHWCA) before a particular work day begins." Chandris, supra, at 363, 115 S. Ct., at 2187. There would be no principled basis for limiting which prior employments are considered for determining seaman status. The Court of Appeals spoke of a "relevant time period" but, as noted above, it did not define this term. Since the substantial connection standard is often, as here, the determinative element of the seaman inquiry, it must be given workable and practical confines. When the inquiry further turns on whether the employee has a substantial connection to an identifiable group of vessels, common ownership or control is essential for this purpose.

520 U.S. 548, 557-58 (1997).

2. *Pilots*

In *Bach v. Trident Steamship Co.*, 920 F.2d 322, 1991 AMC 928, *vacated & remanded*, 500 U.S. 949, *aff'd.*, 947 F.2d 1290 (1991), *cert. denied*, 504 U.S. 931, 112 S. Ct. 199 (1992), the Fifth Circuit refused to grant "seaman" status to a compulsory river pilot.

Eugene G. Bach, Jr., a compulsory river pilot between New Orleans and Pilottown, suffered a fatal heart attack shortly after boarding the M/V JAYMAT TRIDENT, a small pilot boat. His survivors brought suit under the Jones Act, the LHWCA and the general maritime law. The court, reciting the two-prong test for seaman status—permanent attachment to a vessel or fleet of vessels and contribution to the function or mission of a vessel or fleet of vessels—concluded that Bach had failed to meet the first prong requiring attachment. Bach's survivors argued that since the total of the vessels that he piloted and controlled, including the M/V JAYMAT TRIDENT, constituted a fleet in their aggregate, he fulfilled the required connection. The court rejected this argument stating that a fleet is more than a "group of vessels an employee happened to work aboard." 920 F.2d at 324. Rather, a fleet is an identifiable group of vessels under one common ownership.

The court considered whether an exception for the attachment to a vessel test should be made for workers who perform traditional maritime work onboard various unconnected vessels. They answered this question in the negative:

> [T]o create an exception for a worker such as Bach who has the duties and faces the risks of a traditional seaman but who lacks requisite vessel connection would include all sorts of workers we have previously excluded, would widen the divergence of views between our circuit and others, and would make our seaman test unnecessarily uncertain and ambiguous. We therefore decline to make such a radical change in this circuit's test for Jones Act coverage.

920 F.2d at 326.

Judge Brown, in his dissent, argued that it was "simply inconceivable that Congress ... would exclude from the broad term 'seaman' one so vital, so indispensable, so legislatively recognized as a compulsory pilot". Calling the compulsory pilot "the very essence of maritime commerce," 920 F.2d at 332, Brown concluded that compulsory pilots should not be excluded from Jones Act protection while aboard and directing the navigation of a vessel. 920 F.2d at 332.

Bach was appealed to the Supreme Court, which granted certiorari, vacated the judgment and remanded to the Fifth Circuit for reconsideration in light of the *Wilander* decision. *Bach v. Trident S.S. Co.*, 11 S. Ct. 2253 (1991). On remand, the Fifth Circuit noted that the holding in *Wilander* was that a maritime worker need not aid in the navigation of the vessel to be a seaman. The court held that since its original decision was not based upon whether *Bach* aided in the navigation of the vessel but upon his lack of a permanent relationship to any vessel or fleet of vessels, the *Wilander* decision did not affect the conclusion originally reached by the court in Bach. The Fifth Circuit therefore reinstated its earlier judgment. *Bach v. Trident S.S. Co.*, 947 F.2d 1290, 1992 AMC 643 (5th Cir. 1991), and certiorari was denied, 504 U.S. 931, 112 S. Ct. 1996, 118 L. Ed. 2d 592 (1992).

3. *Divers*

In *Wisner v. Professional Divers of New Orleans*, 731 So. 2d 200, 1999 AMC 1189 (La. 1999), *cert. denied*, 120 S. Ct. 285, 145 L. Ed. 2d 238 (1999), the Supreme Court of Louisiana held that a diver doing 90% of his work at sea from different vessels was entitled to Jones Act remedies from his employer. Is this consistent with the Supreme Court's *Wilander/Chandris/Papai* trilogy?

4. *Who is the Employer?*

For determination of the question of who is the employer of an injured seaman, see *Wheatley v. Gladden*, 660 F.2d 1024, 1982 AMC 618 (4th Cir. 1981):

> The trial court also held that Wheatley could not recover on his Jones Act claim and his "maintenance and cure" claim against Gladden because each required an employer/employee relationship which was absent in this case as a matter of law.
>
> It is true that an employer/employee relationship is a necessary antecedent to a Jones Act negligence claim. *Cosmopolitan Shipping Co. v. McAllister*, 337 U.S. 783 (1949), and to a "maintenance and cure" claim, *Cortes v. Baltimore Insular Line*, 287 U.S. 367, 371 (1932). The existence of such an employer/employee relationship must be determined under maritime law, *United States v. Webb, Inc.*, 397 U.S. 179 (1970), and the burden of proof is on the seaman to establish the employment relationship. Among the factors to be considered in determining whether a party is an employer are the degree of control exercised over the details of the operation, the amount of supervision, the amount of investment in the operation, the method of payment and the parties' understanding of the relationship. *United States v. Webb, Inc. supra; Kirkconnell v. United States*, 347 F.2d 260, 171 Ct. Cl. 43 (1965). The resolution of the issue is normally a factual one within the province of a jury. *The Norland*, 101 F.2d 967, 9 Alaska 471 (9th Cir. 1939); *Claussen v. Gulf Oil Corp.*, 136 F. Supp. 110 (W.D. Pa. 1955); 2 M. NORRIS, THE LAW OF SEAMEN § 670 (3d ed. 1970).
>
> * * *
>
> A boat owner may retain sufficient control over his property to be charged with the duties of an employer even though another party actually is in charge of the vessel's operation.

Because an employer/employee relationship is a necessary antecedent to a Jones Act claim, "only one person, firm, or corporation can be sued as employer". *Cosmopolitan Shipping Co. v McAllister*, 337 U.S. 783, 791, 69 S. Ct. 1317, 1322 (1949).

5. *Borrowed Servant Doctrine*

A person may be a member of the crew of a vessel, and, therefore, a Jones Act seaman even though he is employed by an independent contractor rather than the shipowner. In such a case, the seaman is a *borrowed servant* of the shipowner and the shipowner occupies the position of an employer under the Jones Act. In *Ruis v. Shell Oil*, 413 F.2d 310, 312-13 (5th Cir. 1969), the court said that the crucial element is "control" and suggested several factors that were helpful in determining who had control. These are:

1) who has control over the employee and work he is performing, beyond mere suggestion of details or cooperation?
2) whose work is being performed?
3) was there an agreement, understanding or meeting of the minds between the original employer and the subsequent person for whom the employee performed services?
4) did the employee acquiesce in the new work situation?
5) did the original employer terminate his relationship with the employee?

6) who furnished the tools and place for performance?
7) was the new employment over a period of time?
8) who had the right to discharge the employee?
9) who had the obligation to pay the employee?

The borrowed servant doctrine is also important for purposes of LHWCA. *See West v. Kerr-McGee Corporation*, 765 F.2d 526, 1986 AMC 150 (5th Cir. 1985).

6. *Substantiality—Length of Employment*

The requirements formulated in *Chandris* that a person have "a connection to a vessel in navigation (or to an identifiable group of such vessels) that is substantial in terms of both its duration and nature" presents particular difficulties in light of current employment practices.

How should courts apply the durational test to an employee who is injured within a relatively short time after commencing his duties on the vessel?

> Because it found that Rig 3 was not a vessel as a matter of law, the district court did not consider whether Manuel satisfied the other requisite for seaman status—a substantial employment-related connection to a vessel in navigation. *Chandris*, 515 U.S. at 368, 115 S. Ct. at 2189. Ordinarily, seaman status is a fact-specific inquiry better left to MC the province of the jury. *Ducote*, 953 F.2d at 1002; *see also Offshore Co. v. Robison*, 266 F.2d 769, 779-80 (5th Cir.1959). However, "[w]hen the underlying facts are established, and the rule of law is undisputed, the issue is whether the facts meet the statutory standard." *McDermott Int'l. v. Wilander*, 498 U.S. 337, 356, 111 S. Ct. 807, 817, 112 L. Ed.2d 866 (1991).
>
> The summary judgment evidence established that Manuel was assigned to and worked aboard Rig 3 the entire two months he worked for P.A.W. Also, it is undisputed that Manuel's duties contributed to the function of Rig 3. P.A.W.'s argument that Manuel does not have the requisite connection to a vessel is limited to the assertion that the possibility that Manuel could have been assigned to other work locations renders his assignment to Rig 3 less than permanent. This argument is seriously flawed. In *Chandris*, the Supreme Court makes it clear that the adequacy of the plaintiff's connection to a vessel is properly assessed on the basis of his work assignment at the time of his injury:
>
>> Such a person should not be denied seaman status if injured shortly after the reassignment [to a vessel], just as someone actually transferred to a desk job in the company's office and injured in the hallway should not be entitled to claim seaman status on the basis of prior service at sea.
>
> *Chandris*, 515 U.S. at 372, 115 S. Ct. at 2191. At the time of his injury, Manuel was assigned to work aboard a vessel in navigation. The fact that Manuel was subject to reassignment by P.A.W. at some later time is of no moment. As the Supreme Court pointed out in *Chandris*, "[w]hen a maritime worker's basic assignment changes, his seaman status may change as well." *Chandris*, 515 U.S. at 372, 115 S. Ct. at 2191. Manuel's basic assignment never changed; he remained assigned to Rig 3 for the entire two months leading up to his injury. Therefore, we conclude that Manuel satisfies *Chandris*' two-prong test for seaman status as a matter of law.
>
> * * *

Manuel v. P.A.W. Drilling & Well Service, 135 F.3d 344, 1988 AMC 1390 (5th Cir. 1998).

How should courts apply the durational test to an employee whose work is clearly seaman's work, but whose employment on that job is of a relatively short duration?

In *Foulk v. Donjon Marine Co., Inc.*, 144 F.3d 252, 1998 AMC 2926 (3d Cir. 1998) the court reversed the grant of summary judgment which had held that a person hired to work on a project for ten days, as a matter of law, could not satisfy the durational test. The appellate court concluded "that the durational element cannot be answered by an absolute measure. It is the temporal element and the nature of the activities performed that, taken together, determine seaman status." 144 F.3d 259. Specifically that court found that it was "inappropriate to determine the minimum durational element by an absolute number, such as 10 days." *Id.*

How should courts apply the durational test to an employee whose employer owns no vessels but who assigns the employee to work on vessels owned by other persons where those vessels are not under common ownership, control, or operation?

See, Wisner v. Professional Divers of New Orleans, 731 So. 2d 200 (La. 1999), *cert. denied,* 120 S. Ct. 285, 145 L. Ed. 2d 238 (1999), where the Louisiana Supreme Court held that a diver whose employment placed him on vessels for ninety percent of his work life, qualified as a Jones Act seaman.

How should courts apply the durational test to an employee who initially worked for employer X, then left to work for employer Y, and finally, returned to work for the original employer, X, at which time he sustained an injury?

One court has held "that evidence of an employee's prior assignment with the same employer is not admissible under the Fleet Seaman Doctrine if those assignments were not part of a continuous employment relationship between the employer and employee." *Shade v. Great Lakes Dredge & Dock Co.*, 154 F.3d 143, 154 (3d Cir. 1998).

---

b. Vessel in Navigation

Introductory Note

The vessel on which the seaman serves must be "in navigation" for the seaman to fall within the protection of the Jones Act. A vessel does not cease to be "in navigation" the moment that it stops sailing, but any substantial lay-up will take the vessel out of navigation. In *Desper v. Starved Rock Ferry Co.*, 342 U.S. 187, 72 S. Ct. 216, 96 L. Ed. 205, 1952 AMC 12 (1951), the plaintiff was injured while assisting with the process of returning to the water a fleet of boats that had been laid up for the winter. The Supreme Court held that he was not entitled to Jones Act protection:

> The ... question is whether ... decedent was a "seaman" at the time of his death. The many cases turning upon the question whether an individual was a "seaman" demonstrate that the matter depends largely on the facts of the particular case and the activity in which he was engaged at the time of injury. The facts in this case are unique. The work in which the decedent was engaged at the time of his death quite clearly was not that usually done by a "seaman." The boats were not afloat and had neither captain nor crew. They were undergoing seasonal repairs, the work being of the kind that, in the case of larger vessels, would customarily be done by exclusively shore-based personnel. For a number of reasons the ships might not be launched, or he might not operate one. To be sure, he was a probable navigator in the near future, but the law does not cover probable or expectant seamen but seamen in being. It is our conclusion that while engaged in such seasonal repair work Desper was not a "seaman" within the purview of the Jones Act. The distinct nature of the work is emphasized by the fact that there was no vessel engaged in navigation at the time of the decedent's death. All had been "laid up for the winter."

Similarly, in *Wixom v. Boland Marine & Mfg. Co. Inc.*, 614 F.2d 956, 1980 AMC 2992 (5th Cir. 1980), the plaintiff was injured when he fell to the deck of a U.S. Navy ship that had been under repair at the defendant's shipyard for almost two years at the time of the accident. The court held that the plaintiff was not a seaman because the ship was not "in navigation" at the time of the accident.

Notes

1. *Vessels Undergoing Repairs*

As to vessel status, the Supreme Court adopted the general rule in the lower court that "vessels undergoing repairs or spending a relatively short period of time in dry dock are still considered to be 'in navigation' whereas ships being transformed through 'major' overhauls or renovation are not." *Chandris, Inc. v. Latsis*, 515 U.S. 347, 115 S. Ct. 2172, 132 L. Ed. 2d 314, 1995 AMC 1840 (1995).

2. *Vessel in Navigation*

In a Jones Act action, the question of whether a vessel has been *withdrawn* from navigation is, ordinarily, one of fact. *See Abshire v. Seacoast Products, Inc.*, 668 F.2d 832 (5th Cir. 1982). Likewise, the question of whether a floating structure has acquired the status of a vessel in navigation for purposes of a Jones Act action is ordinarily one of fact. *Cf. Garrett v. Dean Shank Drilling Co.*, 799 F.2d 1009 (5th Cir. 1986). In this case, a drilling barge was launched on navigable waters and delivered to its owner. However, before the barge could operate as a drilling rig, it required the addition of living quarters for the crew, a derrick, navigational lights, and other accoutrements. While these additions were being made, a worker was injured on the barge. In due course, the injured worker filed a Jones Act action against the owner of the barge rather than his employer, the shipbuilder. The jury found the plaintiff to be a Jones Act seaman. The Court of Appeal conceded that the question of whether a vessel is in navigation is one of fact but reversed on the ground that the matter here should be determined as a question of law: a structure that is being outfitted for its intended purpose cannot be a vessel in navigation. *See also Reynolds v. Ingalls Shipbuilding Division, Litton Systems, Inc.*, 788 F.2d 264, 1986 AMC 2839 (5th Cir. 1986), in which the court held that "a ship undergoing sea trials is not 'in navigation' for purposes of the Jones Act." For the question whether a floating structure is a vessel in navigation for purposes of LHWCA, *see Stewart v. Dutra Construction Co.* 543 U.S. 481; 125 S.Ct. 1118 (2005), *infra*.

3. *Vessel or Work Platform*

STEWART v. DUTRA CONSTRUCTION CO.

543 U.S. 481; 125 S.Ct. 1118 (2005)

Justice THOMAS delivered the opinion of the Court.

I

As part of Boston's Central Artery/Tunnel Project, or "Big Dig," the Commonwealth of Massachusetts undertook to extend the Massachusetts Turnpike through a tunnel running beneath South Boston and Boston Harbor to Logan Airport. The Commonwealth employed respondent Dutra Construction Company to assist in that undertaking. At the time, Dutra owned the world's largest dredge, the *Super Scoop*, which was capable of digging the 50-foot-deep, 100-foot-wide, three-quarter-mile-long trench beneath Boston Harbor that is now the Ted Williams Tunnel.

The *Super Scoop* is a massive floating platform from which a clamshell bucket is suspended beneath the water. The bucket removes silt from the ocean floor and dumps the sediment onto one of two scows that float alongside the dredge. The *Super Scoop* has certain characteristics common to seagoing vessels, such as a captain and crew, navigational lights, ballast tanks, and a crew dining area. But it lacks others. Most conspicuously, the *Super Scoop* has only limited means of self-propulsion. It is moved long distances by tugboat. (To work on the Big Dig, it was towed from its home base in California through the Panama Canal and up the eastern seaboard to Boston Harbor.) It navigates short distances by manipulating its anchors and cables. When dredging the Boston Harbor trench, it typically moved in this way once every couple of hours, covering a distance of 30-to-50 feet each time.

Dutra hired petitioner Willard Stewart, a marine engineer, to maintain the mechanical systems on the *Super Scoop* during its dredging of the harbor. At the time of Stewart's accident, the *Super Scoop* lay idle because one of its scows, Scow No. 4, had suffered an engine malfunction and the other was at sea. Stewart was on board Scow No. 4, feeding wires through an open hatch located about 10 feet above the engine area. While Stewart was perched beside the hatch, the *Super Scoop* used its bucket to move the scow. In the process, the scow collided with the *Super Scoop,* causing a jolt that plunged Stewart headfirst through the hatch to the deck below. He was seriously injured.

Stewart sued Dutra in the United States District Court for the District of Massachusetts under the Jones Act, 38 Stat. 1185, 46 U.S.C.App. § 688(a), alleging that he was a seaman injured by Dutra's negligence. He also filed an alternative claim under § 5(b) of the LHWCA, 33 U.S.C. § 905(b), which authorizes covered employees to sue a "vessel" owner as a third party for an injury caused by the owner's negligence.

Dutra moved for summary judgment on the Jones Act claim, arguing that Stewart was not a seaman. The company acknowledged that Stewart was "a member of the [*Super Scoop's*] crew," 230 F.3d 461, 466 (1st Cir. 2000); that he spent "[n]inety-nine percent of his time while on the job" aboard the *Super Scoop,* App. 20 (Defendant's Memorandum in Support of Summary Judgment); and that his "duties contributed to the function" of the *Super Scoop, id.,* at 32. Dutra argued only that the *Super Scoop* was not a vessel for purposes of the Jones Act. Dutra pointed to the Court of Appeals' en banc decision in *DiGiovanni v. Traylor Brothers, Inc.,* 959 F.2d 1119 (1st Cir. 1992), which held that "if a barge ... or other float's purpose or primary business is *not* navigation or commerce, then workers assigned thereto for its shore enterprise are to be considered seamen only when it is in actual navigation or transit" at the time of the plaintiff's injury. *Id.,* at 1123 (internal quotation marks omitted). The District Court granted summary judgment to Dutra, because the *Super Scoop's* primary purpose was dredging rather than transportation and because it was stationary at the time of Stewart's injury.

On interlocutory appeal, the Court of Appeals affirmed, concluding that it too was bound by *DiGiovanni.* 230 F.3d, at 467-468. The court reasoned that the *Super Scoop's* primary function was construction and that "[a]ny navigation or transportation that may be required is incidental to this primary function." *Id.,* at 468. The court also concluded that the scow's movement at the time of the accident did not help Stewart, because his status as a seaman depended on the movement of the *Super Scoop* (which was stationary) rather than the scow. *Id.,* at 469.

On remand, the District Court granted summary judgment in favor of Dutra on Stewart's alternative claim that Dutra was liable for negligence as an owner of a "vessel" under the LHWCA, 33 U.S.C. § 905(b). The Court of Appeals again affirmed. It noted that Dutra had conceded that the *Super Scoop* was a "vessel" for purposes of § 905(b), explaining that "the LHWCA's definition of 'vessel' is 'significantly more inclusive than that used for evaluating seaman status under the Jones Act.' " 343 F.3d 10, 13 (1st Cir. 2003) (quoting *Morehead v. Atkinson-Kiewit,* 97 F.3d 603, 607 (1st Cir. 1996) (en banc)). The Court of Appeals nonetheless agreed with the District Court's conclusion that Dutra's alleged negligence was committed in its capacity as an employer rather than as owner of the vessel under § 905(b).

We granted certiorari to resolve confusion over how to determine whether a watercraft is a "vessel" for purposes of the LHWCA. 540 U.S. 1177, 124 S.Ct. 1414, 158 L.Ed.2d 76 (2004).

II

Prior to the passage of the Jones Act, general maritime law usually entitled a seaman who fell sick or was injured both to maintenance and cure (or the right to be cared for and paid wages during the voyage, see, *e.g., Harden v. Gordon,* 11 F. Cas. 480, 482-483 (No. 6,047) (CC Me. 1823) (Story, J.)), and to damages for any "injuries received ... in consequence of the unseaworthiness of the ship," *The Osceola,* 189 U.S. 158, 175, 23 S.Ct. 483, 47 L.Ed. 760 (1903). Suits against shipowners for negligence, however, were barred. Courts presumed that the seaman, in signing articles of employment for the voyage, had assumed the risks of his occupation; thus a seaman was "not allowed to recover an indemnity for the negligence of the master, or any member of the crew." *Ibid.*

Congress enacted the Jones Act in 1920 to remove this bar to negligence suits by seamen. See *Chandris, Inc. v. Latsis,* 515 U.S. 347, 354, 115 S.Ct. 2172, 132 L.Ed.2d 314 (1995). Specifically, the Jones Act provides:

> "Any seaman who shall suffer personal injury in the course of his employment may, at his election, maintain an action for damages at law, with the right of trial by jury, and in such action all statutes of the United States modifying or extending the common-law right or remedy in cases of personal injury to railway employees shall apply." 46 U.S.C.App. § 688(a).

Although the statute is silent on who is a "seaman," both the maritime law backdrop against which Congress enacted the Jones Act and Congress' subsequent enactments provide some guidance.

First, "seaman" is a term of art that had an established meaning under general maritime law. We have thus presumed that when the Jones Act made available negligence remedies to "[a]ny seaman who shall suffer personal injury in the course of his employment," Congress took the term "seaman" as the general maritime law found it. *Chandris, supra,* at 355, 115 S.Ct. 2172 (citing *Warner v. Goltra,* 293 U.S. 155, 159, 55 S.Ct. 46, 79 L.Ed. 254 (1934)); G. Gilmore & C. Black, Law of Admiralty § 6-21, pp. 328-329 (2d ed.1975).

Second, Congress provided further guidance in 1927 when it enacted the LHWCA, which provides scheduled compensation to land-based maritime workers but which also excepts from its coverage "a master or member of a crew of any vessel." 33 U.S.C. § 902(3)(G). This exception is simply "a refinement of the term 'seaman' in the Jones Act." *McDermott Int'l, Inc. v. Wilander,* 498 U.S. 337, 347, 111 S.Ct. 807, 112 L.Ed.2d 866 (1991). Thus the Jones Act and the LHWCA are complementary regimes that work in tandem: The Jones Act provides tort remedies to *sea*-based maritime workers, while the LHWCA provides workers' compensation to *land*-based maritime employees. *Ibid.; Swanson v. Marra Bros., Inc.,* 328 U.S. 1, 6-7, 66 S.Ct. 869, 90 L.Ed. 1045 (1946).

Still, discerning the contours of "seaman" status, even with the general maritime law and the LHWCA's language as aids to interpretation, has not been easy. See *Chandris, supra,* at 356, 115 S.Ct. 2172. We began clarifying the definition of "seaman" in a pair of cases, *McDermott Int'l, Inc. v. Wilander, supra,* and *Chandris, supra,* that addressed the relationship a worker must have to a vessel in order to be a "master or member" of its crew. We now turn to the other half of the LHWCA's equation: how to determine whether a watercraft is a "vessel."

A

Just as Congress did not define the term "seaman" in the Jones Act,[1] it did not define the term "vessel" in the LHWCA itself.[2] However, Congress provided a definition elsewhere. At the time of the LHWCA's enactment, § § 1 and 3 of the Revised Statutes of 1873 specified:

> "In determining the meaning of the revised statutes, or of any act or resolution of Congress passed subsequent to February twenty-fifth, eighteen hundred and seventy-one, ... [t]he word 'vessel' includes every description of water-craft or other artificial contrivance used, or capable of being used, as a means of transportation on water."[3] 18 Stat., pt. 1, p. 1.

Sections 1 and 3 show that, because the LHWCA is an Act of Congress passed after February 25, 1871, the LHWCA's use of the term "vessel" "includes every description of

[1] The Shipping Act of 1916 defines the term "vessel" for purposes of the Jones Act. See 46 U.S.C.App. § 801. However, the provision of the Jones Act at issue here, § 688(a), speaks not of "vessels," but of "seamen." In any event, because we have identified a Jones Act "seaman" with reference to the LHWCA's exclusion, see 33 U.S.C. § 902(3)(G) ("a master or member of a crew of any vessel"), it is the LHWCA's use of the term "vessel" that matters. And, as we explain, the context surrounding Congress' enactment of the LHWCA suggests that Rev. Stat. § 3, now 1 U.S.C. § 3, provides the controlling definition of the term "vessel" in the LHWCA.

[2] As part of its 1972 Amendments to the LHWCA, Congress amended the Act with what appears at first blush to be a definition of the term "vessel": "Unless the context requires otherwise, the term 'vessel' means any vessel upon which or in connection with which any person entitled to benefits under this chapter suffers injury or death arising out of or in the course of his employment, and said vessel's owner, owner pro hac vice, agent, operator, charter or bare boat charterer, master, officer, or crew member." 33 U.S.C. § 902(21). However, Congress enacted this definition in conjunction with the third-party vessel owner provision of § 905(b). Rather than specifying the characteristics of a vessel, § 902(21) instead lists the parties liable for the negligent operation of a vessel. See *McCarthy v. The Bark Peking,* 716 F.2d 130, 133 (C.A.2 1983) (§ 902(21) is "circular" and "does not provide precise guidance as to what is included within the term 'vessel' ").

[3] Congress had used substantially the same definition before, first in an 1866 antismuggling statute, see § 1, 14 Stat. 178, and then in an 1870 statute "provid[ing] for the Relief of sick and disabled Seamen," § 7, 16 Stat. 170.

[4] During the 1947 codification, the hyphen was removed from the word "watercraft." § 3, 61 Stat. 633.

water-craft or other artificial contrivance used, or capable of being used, as a means of transportation on water." *Ibid.*

Section 3's definition, repealed and recodified in 1947 as part of the Rules of Construction Act, 1 U.S.C. § 3, has remained virtually unchanged from 1873 to the present.[4] Even now, § 3 continues to supply the default definition of "vessel" throughout the U.S.Code, "unless the context indicates otherwise." 1 U.S.C. § 1. The context surrounding the LHWCA's enactment indicates that § 3 defines the term "vessel" for purposes of the LHWCA.

Section 3 merely codified the meaning that the term "vessel" had acquired in general maritime law. See 1 S. Friedell, Benedict on Admiralty § 165 (rev. 7th ed.2004). In the decades following its enactment, § 3 was regularly used to define the term "vessel" in maritime jurisprudence. Taking only the issue presented here—whether a dredge is a vessel—prior to passage of the Jones Act and the LHWCA, courts often used § 3's definition to conclude that dredges were vessels.[5]

From the very beginning, these courts understood the differences between dredges and more traditional seagoing vessels. Though smaller, the dredges at issue in the earliest cases were essentially the same as the *Super Scoop* here. For instance, the court could have been speaking equally of the *Super Scoop* as of *The Alabama* when it declared:

> "The dredge and scows have no means of propulsion of their own except that the dredge, by use of anchors, windlass, and rope, is moved for short distances, as required in carrying on the business of dredging. Both the dredge and the scows are moved from place to place where they may be employed by being toweb, and some of the tows have been for long distances and upon the high seas. The dredge and scows are not made for or adapted to the carriage of freight or passengers, and the evidence does not show that, in point of fact, this dredge and scows had ever been so used and employed." *The Alabama,* 19 F. 544, 545 (S.D.Ala.1884).

See also *Huismann v. The Pioneer,* 30 F. 206 (E.D.N.Y.1886). None of this prevented the court from recognizing that dredges are vessels because they are watercraft with "the capacity to be navigated in and upon the waters." *The Alabama, supra,* at 546; see also *The Pioneer, supra,* at 207; *The International,* 89 F. 484, 485 (C.A.3 1898).

This Court also treated dredges as vessels prior to the passage of the Jones Act and the LHWCA. It did so in a pair of cases, first implicitly in *The "Virginia Ehrman" and the "Agnese,"* 97 U.S. 309, 24 L.Ed. 890 (1878), and then explicitly in *Ellis v. United States,* 206 U.S. 246, 27 S.Ct. 600, 51 L.Ed. 1047 (1907). In *Ellis,* this Court considered, *inter alia,* whether workers aboard various dredges and scows were covered by a federal labor law. Just as in the present case, one of the *Ellis* appellants argued that the dredges at issue were

---

[5] See, *e.g., The Alabama,* 19 F. 544, 546 (S.D.Ala.1884) (dredge was a vessel and subject to maritime liens); *Huismann v. The Pioneer,* 30 F. 206, 207 (E.D.N.Y.1886) (dredge was a vessel under § 3); *Saylor v. Taylor,* 77 F. 476, 477 (C.A.4 1896) (dredge was a vessel under § 3, and its workers were seamen); *The International,* 89 F. 484, 484-485 (C.A.3 1898) (dredge was a vessel under § 3); *Eastern S.S. Corp. v. Great Lakes Dredge & Dock Co.,* 256 F. 497, 500-501 (C.A.1 1919) (type of dredge called a "drillboat" was a vessel under § 3); *Los Angeles v. United Dredging Co.,* 14 F.2d 364, 365-366 (C.A.9 1926) (dredge was a vessel under § 3 and its engineers were seamen).

"vessels" within the meaning of Rev. Stat. § 3, now 1 U.S.C. § 3. 206 U.S., at 249, 27 S.Ct. 600. The United States responded that dredges were only vessels, if at all, when in actual navigation as they were "towed from port to port." *Id.*, at 253, 27 S.Ct. 600. Citing § 3, Justice Holmes rejected the Government's argument, stating that "[t]he scows and floating dredges were vessels" that "were within the admiralty jurisdiction of the United States." *Id.*, at 259, 27 S.Ct. 600.

These early cases show that at the time Congress enacted the Jones Act and the LHWCA in the 1920's, it was settled that § 3 defined the term "vessel" for purposes of those statutes. It was also settled that a structure's status as a vessel under § 3 depended on whether the structure was a means of maritime transportation. See R. Hughes, Handbook of Admiralty Law § 5, p. 14 (2d ed.1920). For then, as now, dredges served a waterborne transportation function, since in performing their work they carried machinery, equipment, and crew over water. See, *e.g.*, *Butler v. Ellis*, 45 F.2d 951, 955 (C.A.4 1930) (finding the vessel status of dredges "sustained by the overwhelming weight of authority"); *The Hurricane*, 2 F.2d 70, 72 (E.D.Pa.1924) (expressing "no doubt" that dredges are vessels), *aff'd*, 9 F.2d 396 (C.A.3 1925).

This Court's cases have continued to treat § 3 as defining the term "vessel" in the LHWCA, and they have continued to construe § 3's definition in light of the term's established meaning in general maritime law. For instance, in *Norton v. Warner Co.*, 321 U.S. 565, 64 S.Ct. 747, 88 L.Ed. 931 (1944), the Court considered whether a worker on a harbor barge was "a master or member of a crew of any vessel" under the LHWCA, 33 U.S.C. § 902(3)(G). In finding that the "barge [was] a vessel within the meaning of the Act," the Court not only quoted § 3's definition of the term "vessel," but it also cited in support of its holding several earlier cases that had held dredges to be vessels based on the general maritime law. 321 U.S., at 571, and n. 4, 64 S.Ct. 747. This Court therefore confirmed in *Norton* that § 3 defines the term "vessel" in the LHWCA and that § 3 should be construed consistently with the general maritime law. Since *Norton*, this Court has often said that dredges and comparable watercraft qualify as vessels under the Jones Act and the LHWCA.[6]

B

Despite this Court's reliance on § 3 in cases like *Ellis* and *Norton*, Dutra argues that the Court has implicitly narrowed § 3's definition. Section 3 says that a "vessel" must be "used, or capable of being used, as a means of transportation on water." 18 Stat., pt. 1, p. 1. In a pair of cases, the Court held that a drydock, *Cope v. Vallette Dry-Dock Co.*, 119 U.S. 625, 630, 7 S.Ct. 336, 30 L.Ed. 501 (1887), and a wharfboat attached to the mainland, *Evansville & Bowling Green Packet Co. v. Chero Cola Bottling Co.*, 271 U.S. 19, 22, 46 S.Ct. 379,

[6] See, *e.g.*, *Jerome B. Grubart, Inc. v. Great Lakes Dredge & Dock Co.*, 513 U.S. 527, 535, and n. 1, 115 S.Ct. 1043, 130 L.Ed.2d 1024 (1995) (indicating that a stationary crane barge was a "vessel" under the Extension of Admiralty Jurisdiction Act); *Southwest Marine, Inc. v. Gizoni*, 502 U.S. 81, 92, 112 S.Ct. 486, 116 L.Ed.2d 405 (1991) (holding that a jury could reasonably find that floating platforms were "vessels in navigation" under the Jones Act); *Jones & Laughlin Steel Corp. v. Pfeifer*, 462 U.S. 523, 528-530, 103 S.Ct. 2541, 76 L.Ed.2d 768 (1983) (treating coal barge as a "vessel" under the LHWCA, 33 U.S.C. § 905(b)); cf. *Senko v. LaCrosse Dredging Corp.*, 352 U.S. 370, 372, 77 S.Ct. 415, 1 L.Ed.2d 404 (1957) (assuming that a dredge was a Jones Act vessel); *id.*, at 375, n. 1, 77 S.Ct. 415 (Harlan, J., dissenting) (same).

70 L.Ed. 805 (1926), were not vessels under § 3, because they were not *practically* capable of being used to transport people, freight, or cargo from place to place. According to Dutra, *Cope* and *Evansville* adopted a definition of "vessel" narrower than § 3's text.

Dutra misreads *Cope* and *Evansville.* In *Cope,* the plaintiff sought a salvage award for having prevented a drydock from sinking after a steamship collided with it. 119 U.S., at 625-626, 7 S.Ct. 336. At the time of the accident, the drydock, a floating dock used for repairing vessels, was "moored and lying at [the] usual place" it had occupied for the past 20 years. *Id.,* at 626, 7 S.Ct. 336. In those circumstances, the drydock was a "fixed structure" that had been "permanently moored," rather than a vessel that had been temporarily anchored. *Id.,* at 627, 7 S.Ct. 336. *Evansville* involved a wharfboat secured by cables to the mainland. Local water, electricity, and telephone lines all ran from shore to the wharfboat, evincing a "permanent location." 271 U.S., at 22, 46 S.Ct. 379. And the wharfboat, like the drydock in *Cope,* was neither "taken from place to place" nor "used to carry freight from one place to another." 271 U.S., at 22, 46 S.Ct. 379. As in *Cope,* the Court concluded that the wharfboat "was not practically capable of being used as a means of transportation." 271 U.S., at 22, 46 S.Ct. 379.

Cope and *Evansville* did no more than construe § 3 in light of the distinction drawn by the general maritime law between watercraft temporarily stationed in a particular location and those permanently affixed to shore or resting on the ocean floor. See, *e.g., The Alabama,* 19 F., at 546 (noting that vessels possess "mobility and [the] capacity to navigate," as distinct from fixed structures like wharves, drydocks, and bridges). Simply put, a watercraft is not "capable of being used" for maritime transport in any meaningful sense if it has been permanently moored or otherwise rendered practically incapable of transportation or movement.

This distinction is sensible: A ship and its crew do not move in and out of Jones Act coverage depending on whether the ship is at anchor, docked for loading or unloading, or berthed for minor repairs, in the same way that ships taken permanently out of the water as a practical matter do not remain vessels merely because of the remote possibility that they may one day sail again. See *Pavone v. Mississippi Riverboat Amusement Corp.,* 52 F.3d 560, 570 (C.A.5 1995) (floating casino was no longer a vessel where it "was moored to the shore in a semi-permanent or indefinite manner"); *Kathriner v. UNISEA, Inc.,* 975 F.2d 657, 660 (C.A.9 1992) (floating processing plant was no longer a vessel where a "large opening [had been] cut into her hull," rendering her incapable of moving over the water). Even if the general maritime law had not informed the meaning of § 3, its definition would not sweep within its reach an array of fixed structures not commonly thought of as capable of being used for water transport. See, *e.g., Leocal v. Ashcroft,* 543 U.S. —, —, 125 S.Ct. 377, 382, 160 L.Ed.2d 271 (2004) ("When interpreting a statute, we must give words their 'ordinary or natural' meaning" (quoting *Smith v. United States,* 508 U.S. 223, 228, 113 S.Ct. 2050, 124 L.Ed.2d 138 (1993))).

Applying § 3 brings within the purview of the Jones Act the sorts of watercraft considered vessels at the time Congress passed the Act. By including special-purpose vessels like dredges, § 3 sweeps broadly, but the other prerequisites to qualifying for seaman status under the Jones Act provide some limits, notwithstanding § 3's breadth. A maritime worker seeking Jones Act seaman status must also prove that his duties contributed to the vessel's function or mission, and that his connection to the vessel was substantial both in nature and duration. *Chandris,* 515 U.S., at 376, 115 S.Ct. 2172. Thus, even though the *Super Scoop* is a "vessel," workers injured aboard the *Super Scoop* are eligible for seaman status only if they are "master[s] or member[s]" of its crew.

C

The Court of Appeals, relying on its previous en banc decision in *DiGiovanni v. Traylor Brothers, Inc.,* 959 F.2d 1119 (1st Cir. 1992), held that the *Super Scoop* is not a "vessel," because its primary purpose is not navigation or commerce and because it was not in actual transit at the time of Stewart's injury. 230 F.3d, at 468-469. Neither prong of the Court of Appeals' test is consistent with the text of § 3 or the established meaning of the term "vessel" in general maritime law.

Section 3 requires only that a watercraft be "used, or capable of being used, as a means of transportation on water" to qualify as a vessel. It does not require that a watercraft be used *primarily* for that purpose. See *The Alabama, supra,* at 546; *The International,* 89 F., at 485. As the Court of Appeals recognized, the *Super Scoop's* "function was to move through Boston Harbor, ... digging the ocean bottom as it moved." 343 F.3d, at 12. In other words, the *Super Scoop* was not only "capable of being used" to transport equipment and workers over water—it *was* used to transport those things. Indeed, it could not have dug the Ted Williams Tunnel had it been unable to traverse the Boston Harbor, carrying with it workers like Stewart.

Also, a watercraft need not be in motion to qualify as a vessel under § 3. Looking to whether a watercraft is motionless or moving is the sort of "snapshot" test that we rejected in *Chandris.* Just as a worker does not "oscillate back and forth between Jones Act coverage and other remedies depending on the activity in which the worker was engaged while injured," *Chandris,* 515 U.S., at 363, 115 S.Ct. 2172, neither does a watercraft pass in and out of Jones Act coverage depending on whether it was moving at the time of the accident.

Granted, the Court has sometimes spoken of the requirement that a vessel be "in navigation," *id.,* at 373-374, 115 S.Ct. 2172, but never to indicate that a structure's locomotion at any given moment mattered. Rather, the point was that structures may lose their character as vessels if they have been withdrawn from the water for extended periods of time. *Ibid.; Roper v. United States,* 368 U.S. 20, 21, 23, 82 S.Ct. 5, 7 L.Ed.2d 1 (1961); *West v. United States,* 361 U.S. 118, 122, 80 S.Ct. 189, 4 L.Ed.2d 161 (1959). The Court did not mean that the "in navigation" requirement stood apart from § 3, such that a "vessel" for purposes of § 3 might nevertheless not be a "vessel in navigation" for purposes of the Jones Act or the LHWCA. See, *e.g., United States v. Templeton,* 378 F.3d 845, 851 (C.A.8 2004) ("[T]he definition of 'vessel in navigation' under the Jones Act is not as expansive as the general definition of 'vessel' " (citations omitted)).

Instead, the "in navigation" requirement is an element of the vessel status of a watercraft. It is relevant to whether the craft is "used, or capable of being used" for maritime transportation. A ship long lodged in a drydock or shipyard can again be put to sea, no less than one permanently moored to shore or the ocean floor can be cut loose and made to sail. The question remains in all cases whether the watercraft's use "as a means of transportation on water" is a practical possibility or merely a theoretical one. *Supra,* at — - — 11-12. In some cases that inquiry may involve factual issues for the jury, *Chandris, supra,* at 373, 115 S.Ct. 2172, but here no relevant facts were in dispute. Dutra conceded that the *Super Scoop* was only temporarily stationary while Stewart and others were repairing the scow; the *Super Scoop* had not been taken out of service, permanently anchored, or otherwise rendered practically incapable of maritime transport.

Finally, although Dutra argues that the *Super Scoop* is not a "vessel" under § 902(3)(G), which is the LHWCA provision that excludes seamen from the Act's coverage, Dutra conceded below that the *Super Scoop* *is* a "vessel" under § 905(b), which is the LHWCA provision that imposes liability on vessel owners for negligence to longshoremen. The concession was necessary because the Court of Appeals had previously held that § 905(b)'s use of the term "vessel" is " 'significantly more inclusive than that used for evaluating seaman status under the Jones Act.' " 343 F.3d, at 13 (quoting *Morehead v. Atkinson-Kiewit,* 97 F.3d, at 607). The Court of Appeals' approach is no longer tenable. The LHWCA does not meaningfully define the term "vessel" as it appears in either § 902(3)(G) or § 905(b), see n. 2, *supra,* and 1 U.S.C. § 3 defines the term "vessel" throughout the LHWCA.

III

At the time that Congress enacted the LHWCA and since, Rev. Stat. § 3, now 1 U.S.C. § 3, has defined the term "vessel" in the LHWCA. Under § 3, a "vessel" is any watercraft practically capable of maritime transportation, regardless of its primary purpose or state of transit at a particular moment. Because the *Super Scoop* was engaged in maritime transportation at the time of Stewart's injury, it was a vessel within the meaning of 1 U.S.C. § 3. Despite the seeming incongruity of grouping dredges alongside more traditional seafaring vessels under the maritime statutes, Congress and the courts have long done precisely that:

> "[I]t seems a stretch of the imagination to class the deck hands of a mud dredge in the quiet waters of a Potomac creek with the bold and skillful mariners who breast the angry waves of the Atlantic; but such and so far-reaching are the principles which underlie the jurisdiction of the courts of admiralty that they adapt themselves to all the new kinds of property and new sets of operatives and new conditions which are brought into existence in the progress of the world." *Saylor v. Taylor,* 77 F. 476, 479 (C.A.4 1896).

The judgment of the Court of Appeals is reversed, and the case is remanded for further proceedings consistent with this opinion.

It is so ordered.

THE CHIEF JUSTICE took no part in the decision of this case.

Notes

1. *Pre-Dutra cases*

Before *Stewart v. Dutra Construction Co., supra,* the broad definition of "vessel" in 1 U.S.C. § 3 was applied to actions for recovery under the Jones Act and quite a few special purpose structures have been found to be vessels. *See Colomb v. Texaco,* 736 F.2d 218 (5th Cir. 1984) (a submersible drilling barge); *Hicks v. ODECO,* 512 F. 2d 817, 1975 AMC 1378 (5th Cir. 1975) (a submersible oil storage facility); *Marathon Pipe Line Co. v. Drilling Rig ROWAN/ ODESSA,* 761 F.2d 229, 1986 AMC 2343 (5th Cir. 1985) (a jack-up rig). Certain courts, however, sought to narrow this definition. *See Bernard v. Binnings Constr. Co., Inc.,* 741 F.2d 824, 1985 AMC 784 (5th Cir. 1984) (finding a work punt not to be a vessel); *Barger Petroleum Helicopters, Inc.,* 692 F.2d 337, 1983 AMC 2854 (5th Cir. 1982) (holding that a helicopter, though equipped with floaters and serving in the Gulf of Mexico, is not a vessel for Jones Act purposes); *Cook v. Beldon Concrete Products, Inc.,* 472 F.2d 999, 1973 AMC 285 (5th Cir. 1973) (finding that a floating construction platform was not a vessel).

In *Manuel v. P.A.W. Drilling & Well Service, Inc.,* 135 F.3d 344, 1998 AMC 1390 (5th Cir. 1998), the court engaged in an extensive examination of the prior jurisprudence, contrasting "special purpose vessel" cases with "work platform" cases. The Fifth Circuit view was that vessels were required to have some transportation function or at least be in navigation at the time of injury. *Michel v. Total Transportation, Inc.,* 957 F.2d 186, 189, 1993 AMC 2406 (5th Cir. 1992), 1993 AMC 2406 and *Manuel v. P.A.W. Drilling & Well Service, Inc.,* 135 F.3d 344, 1998 AMC 1390 (5th Cir. 1998). In contrast, the Ninth Circuit in *Gizoni v. Southwest Marine Incorporated,* 56 F.3d 1138, 1995 AMC 2093 (9th Cir.), *cert. denied,* 516 U.S. 944, 116 S. Ct. 381 (1995) held that "unusual-looking crafts whose purpose is not the transportation of persons or things can be considered vessels under the Jones Act".

2. *Transportation Function*

In *Fields v. Pool Offshore, Inc.,* 182 F.3d 353, 357-59 (5th Cir. 1999), the Fifth Circuit elaborated further on its approach to the work platform issue.

> Courts have long recognized a distinction between "work platforms" that are designed for primarily stationary residence and true vessels. . . . Looking to the language of the statute, we have consistently defined vessel status in reference to the importance of transportation as the craft's purpose. . . . In particular, we have focused on three factors when trying to determine whether a structure is a work platform beyond the realm of the Jones Act. First, we ask whether the structure was constructed to serve primarily as a work platform. Second, we look to whether or not the structure was moored or otherwise secured at the time of the accident. Lastly, we attempt to ascertain whether the transportation function of the structure went beyond theoretical mobility and occasional incidental movement. . . .
>
> In applying the three-factor test of work-platform status to the Neptune Spar, it becomes apparent that it cannot be a vessel. As the defendants' affidavits indicated, there are no plans to even consider moving the Neptune Spar until the current field is exhausted. While nothing can ever be certain in the petroleum industry, the unchallenged prediction of defendants is that the field will remain productive for the next fifteen years. This distinguishes the Neptune Spar from the types of specialized mobile drilling craft that we have previously classified as vessels. As we have taken care to point out, while such drilling craft may stay on a particular site, they always move on to the next location when their work is done. *See Manuel,* 135 F.3d at 346 (noting that drilling vessel had been deployed at nineteen different sites over the course of two years); *Colomb v. Texaco, Inc.,* 736 F.2d 218, 221 (5th Cir. 1984) ("highly mobile" submersible drilling barge was "routinely" refloated and moved to the next location). *See also Blanchard v. Engine and Gas Compressor Services, Inc.,* 575 F.2d 1140, 1143 (5th Cir. 1978) (distinguishing work platform from drilling barge rigs because there was no intention to move structures "on a regular basis, as is done with submersible drilling rigs"). Unlike these vessels, the Neptune Spar is designed not only to discover and open a field, but also to exploit it—a goal that requires considerably greater commitment to a particular location. Given these undisputed facts, it would seem readily apparent that the

primary, indeed only, purpose of the Neptune Spar is to serve as a work platform in a specific, fixed location for the foreseeable future.

The work platform status of the Neptune Spar is reinforced by reference to the second factor. The Neptune Spar was not only secured to the ocean floor at the time of the accident, it was secured using an elaborate system that guarantees movement will be a difficult and expensive undertaking. We are not talking about a case in which a structure merely rests on the bottom or is secured by a run-of-the-mill anchor. Here, the defendants have at presumably considerable expense sunk massive (180 foot) pilings into the ocean floor, and attached the spar to these pilings by means of similarly impressive chain lines. And like its sibling conventional fixed production platforms, the Neptune Spar is further anchored in position by the underwater infrastructure of extraction and exportation pipes that transport the petroleum from wellhead to the platform and from the platform to the shore. In this case, the infrastructure consists of two eight-inch pipelines and seven nine-and-a-half- inch casing risers. This distinguishes it from other structures whose commitment to a particular location is less firmly evidenced by the strength of their physical attachment. *Cf. Hicks v. Ocean Drilling and Exploration Co.*, 512 F.2d 817, 823-24 (5th Cir. 1975) (evidence sufficient to sustain jury finding that submersible petroleum storage barge sunk to the bottom and then connected to nearby platform by pipe and catwalk, but not in any way affixed into seabed, was a vessel) with *Blanchard,* 575 F.2d at 1143 (5th Cir. 1978) (compressor building mounted on submersible barge was distinguishable from structure in *Hicks* because barge was anchored with steel cables attached to fixed pilings); *Hemba v. Freeport McMoran Energy Partners, Ltd.*, 811 F.2d 276, 278 (5th Cir. 1987) (rig attached by pilings driven two hundred feet into the seabed was not a vessel).

Any lingering doubt would seemingly be eradicated by examination of the third factor. While the Neptune Spar remains in its current position, it will have extremely limited and purely incidental mobility. According to the defendants' unchallenged affidavits, the Neptune Spar can be moved by tightening and slackening the chain lines connected to the pilings. This procedure is used to place the structure over one of the site's seven closely packed wellheads to perform needed work. Because of the location of the pilings, however, this movement is limited to 250 feet in any direction. This tightly-constrained range of motion is not inconsistent with work platform status. *See Burchett,* 48 F.3d at 177-78 (loading barge was a work platform despite the fact it was regularly moved to align itself with boat receiving goods); *Cook v. Belden Concrete Products, Inc.,* 472 F.2d 999, 1002 (5th Cir. 1973) (construction barge that was regularly towed into open water to launch completed craft was not a vessel). While there remains some theoretical possibility of more lengthy movement when the current field is exhausted, the mere possibility of movement so many years hence cannot render irrelevant the structure's current and long-term immobility. [some citations omitted.]

The Fifth and Ninth Circuit disagree as to the definition of the term "vessel." Although the court in *Gizoni v. Southwest Marine Incorporated,* 56 F.3d 1138, 1995 AMC 2093 (9th Cir.), *cert. denied,* 516 U.S. 944, 116 S. Ct. 381 (1995) held that "unusual-looking crafts whose purpose is not the transportation of persons or things can be considered vessels under the Jones Act," the Fifth Circuit requires vessels have some transportation function or at least be in navigation at the time of injury. *Michel v. Total Transportation, Inc.*, 957 F.2d 186, 189, 1993 AMC 2406 (5th Cir. 1992), 1993 AMC 2406 and *Manuel v. P.A.W. Drilling & Well Service, Inc.*, 135 F.3d 344, 1998 AMC 1390 (5th Cir. 1998).

3. *Oceanographic Research Vessel*

The Oceanographic Research Vessels Act (formerly 46 U.S.C. app. § 444) provided that scientific personnel on oceanographic research vessels shall not be considered seamen under the provisions of the merchant seamen statutes. This section was removed because scientific personnel are excluded from the definition of "seamen" by operation of 46 U.S.C.A. § 10101(3). In *Presley v. The Carribean Seal,* 709 F.2d 406, 1984 AMC 2307 (5th Cir. 1983), 1984 AMC 2307, the court held that the Oceanographic Research Vessels Act did not prevent plaintiff, a member of the scientific personnel of an oceanographic vessel, from being considered a seaman under the general maritime law but the Act prevented him from being considered a seaman under the provisions of the Jones Act. *Cf., Sennet v. Shell Oil Co.,* 325 F. Supp. 1, 1972 AMC 1346 (E.D. La. 1971).

4. ***Gambling Structures***

Many different kinds of structures are currently placed in navigable waters to function as gambling casinos. Some of these structures regularly sail on gambling cruises, others never sail and some sail only infrequently or sporadically. Furthermore, some of these structures are incapable of independent movement in the water and some may not be capable of moving even with the assistance of a vessel. The issue as to whether or not these structures are "vessels" is discussed in *Pavone v. Miss. Riverboat Amusement Corp.*, 52 F.3d 560, 1995 AMC 2038 (5th Cir. 1995). The recent trend has been to hold that permanently moored riverboat casinos are not "vessels in navigation" for the purposes of the Jones Act, even if they were originally built as vessels and are capable of sailing. *Martin v. Boyd Gaming Corp.*, 374 F.3d 375, 2004 AMC 1944 (5th Cir. 2004); *Howard v. Southern Ill. Riverboat Casino Cruises, Inc.*, 364 F.3d 854, 2004 AMC 956 (7th Cir. 2004).

---

c. *"In the Course of His Employment"*

HOPSON v. TEXACO, INC.

383 U.S. 262, 86 S. Ct. 756, 15 L. Ed. 2d 740, 1966 AMC 281 (1966)

PER CURIAM

These actions were brought under the Jones Act, as amended (41 Stat. 1007, 46 U.S.C. § 688 (1964 ed.)), to recover damages for injuries sustained by one seaman, and for the death of another, as a result of an automobile accident on the island of Trinidad. Judgment on the jury's verdict was entered in United States District Court in favor of the plaintiffs, but the Court of Appeals reversed. 351 F.2d 415. We grant the petition for a writ of certiorari and reverse.

The facts are not in dispute. The two seamen were members of the crew of respondent's tanker which was docked at respondent's refinery at Pointe-a-Pierre on the island of Trinidad. Both fell ill and it was determined that they would be unable to continue the voyage. In order to discharge an incapacitated seaman in a foreign port, federal law requires that he be taken to a United States Consul where arrangements for his return to the United States can be made. The United States Consul's Office was located in Port of Spain, some 38 miles distant. Although respondent had a fleet of motor vehicles used for transportation in the immediate vicinity of the refinery and docking area, its practice was to utilize either of two local taxi companies for journeys to more distant points. The ship's Master procured one of these cabs which set out for Port of Spain with the two ill seamen. En route, the taxi collided with a truck, killing the Master and one of the seamen; the other seaman was seriously injured. The jury found that the taxi driver had been negligent—a finding challenged neither in the Court of Appeals nor here. The Court of Appeals reversed the District Court's determination that respondent is liable to petitioners for this negligence of the taxi operator.

The Jones Act incorporates the standards of the Federal Employers' Liability Act, as amended, which renders an employer liable for the injuries negligently inflicted on its employees by its "officers, agents, or employees." We noted in *Sinkler v. Missouri Pac. R. Co.*, 356 U.S. 326, that the latter Act was "an avowed departure from the rules of the common law" (*id.*, at 329), which, recognizing "[t]he cost of human injury, an inescapable expense of railroading," undertook to "adjust that expense equitably between the worker and the carrier." *Ibid.* In order to give "an accommodating scope... to the word 'agents'" (*id.*, at 330-331), we concluded that "when [an] ... employee's injury is caused in whole or in part by the fault of others performing, under contract, operational activities of his employer, such others are 'agents' of the employer within the meaning of § 1 of FELA." (*Id.*, at 331-332).

We think those principles apply with equal force here. These seamen were in the service of the ship and the ill-fated journey to Port of Spain was a vital part of the ship's total operations. The ship could not sail with these two men, nor could it lawfully discharge them without taking them to the United States Consul. Indeed, to have abandoned them would have breached the statutory duty to arrange for their return to the United States. Getting these two ill seamen to the United States Consul's office was, therefore, the duty of respondent. And it was respondent—not the seamen—which selected, as it had done many times before, the taxi service. Respondent—the law says—should bear the responsibility for the negligence of the driver which it chose. This is so because, as we said in *Sinkler*, "justice demands that one who gives his labor to the furtherance of the enterprise should be assured that all combining their exertions with him in the common pursuit will conduct themselves in all respects with sufficient care that his safety while doing his part will not be endangered." 356 U.S., at 330. *Reversed.*

Note

When does the Jones Act coverage commence? When the seaman signs a contract of employment? When he reports for service on board the ship? When he signs articles and commences to serve? Does it make any difference if the master has the right to reject the seaman? What if the employer furnishes transportation to the seaman from his home city to the ship? *See Vincent v. Harvey Well Service*, 441 F.2d 146, 1970 AMC 560 (5th Cir. 1971).

In *Mounteer v. Marine Transport Lines, Inc.*, 463 F. Supp. 715, 1979 AMC 313 (S.D.N.Y. 1979), plaintiff, a Third Assistant Marine Engineer, was being transported from Cairo to Port Said, Egypt, at the expense of the defendant, to serve on defendant's vessel. Plaintiff was injured in an accident caused by the negligence of the taxi driver who was driving plaintiff across the desert. Plaintiff brought a Jones Act claim for his injuries, loss of wages and maintenance and cure. Defendant argued that the plaintiff was not "in the service of the vessel," because his employment with the defendant had not yet begun. Relying on the Supreme Court's decision in *Hopson v. Texaco*, the court held that the defendant's transportation of the plaintiff across the Egyptian desert to join its stranded vessel (which could not leave port without the plaintiff on board) was for the service of the vessel from the defendant's standpoint.

---

2. Standard of Care and Causation

GAUTREAUX v. SCURLOCK MARINE, INC.

107 F.3d 331 (5th Cir. 1997)

DUHE, Circuit Judge

Defendant-Appellant Scurlock Marine, Inc. moves this En Banc Court to consider whether seamen, in Jones Act negligence cases, are bound to a standard of ordinary prudence in the exercise of care for their own safety, or whether they are bound to a lesser duty of slight care. On appeal to a panel of this Court, Scurlock Marine had assigned as error, *inter alia*, the district court's instructions to the jury charging that seamen were bound only to a duty of slight care for their own safety. The panel denied Scurlock Marine relief on this point because the jury instructions were consistent with what the panel considered was the settled law of this Circuit. *Gautreaux v. Scurlock Marine, Inc.*, 84 F.3d 776, 780-81 (5th Cir. 1996). A review of our Jones Act case law reveals, however, that this "settled law" obtains from doubtful parentage. We thus now overrule cases contrary to the principles embraced in this opinion and AFFIRM in part, VACATE in part and REMAND for further proceedings as to comparative fault consistent with our decision today.

Background

Archie Scurlock, as President and owner of Scurlock Marine, Inc., ("Scurlock Marine") purchased the M/V BROOKE LYNN in May, 1993, and retained Lance Orgeron as her first and permanent captain. Scurlock hired Charles Gautreaux as the BROOKE LYNN's relief captain in October, 1993. Gautreaux was qualified for the position, having worked as a tanker man since the early 1980s and having recently earned a United States Coast Guard master's license.

The BROOKE LYNN is a standard inland push boat, equipped with two towing winches on her bow, which are used to secure lines joining the BROOKE LYNN to the barges in her tow. The starboard side winch is hydraulic, and the port side winch is electric. Upon being hired, Gautreaux was taken to the BROOKE LYNN and instructed on her operation by Archie Scurlock. Orgeron took Gautreaux on a tour of the vessel, showing him her layout and familiarizing him with her equipment. Orgeron showed Gautreaux the manual crank handle that accompanied the port side electric winch and told him that it was to be used to override the electric switches on the winch if they failed. Orgeron explained that, if the winch became "bound up" and failed to engage by use of the electric ignition switch, the manual crank should be attached to the winch motor and turned a few times to "unbind" the winch, and then the electric ignition switch should be used to try to engage the winch. Neither Scurlock nor Orgeron told Gautreaux that if he needed to use the manual crank handle to unbind the winch, he should not leave it on the winch motor when attempting to engage the winch by use of the electric ignition switch.

About four months after he was hired, Gautreaux, serving as captain of the BROOKE LYNN, relieved the tanker man on duty and began off loading of the barge in tow. As the barge discharged its cargo, it began to rise in the water, eventually causing the towing wires to become taut. Noticing this, Gautreaux attempted to relieve the tension in the wires by unwinding them from the winches. He released the starboard wire first, which caused that side of the BROOKE LYNN to drop and the port side towing wire to become even tighter. Gautreaux then attempted to release the port side wire, but the electric winch would not work. He attached the manual crank to the winch motor, and began turning the crank while simultaneously pressing the electric ignition switch. When the motor started, the manual crank handle flew off and struck Gautreaux on the right side of his face, crushing his right eye and inflicting other severe injuries.

Gautreaux sued Scurlock Marine, alleging that his injuries were caused by its negligence and the unseaworthiness of the BROOKE LYNN. Gautreaux's primary complaint was that Scurlock Marine failed to properly train him in the use and operation of the electric towing winch and its manual crank handle, thereby not providing him a safe place to work. Scurlock Marine answered and sought exoneration from or limitation of its liability. After a two-day trial, the jury returned a verdict in favor of Gautreaux on his Jones Act negligence claim, but found the BROOKE LYNN seaworthy. The jury apportioned fault 95% to Scurlock Marine and 5% to Gautreaux and awarded a total of $854,000 in damages.

* * *

On appeal to this Court, Scurlock Marine argued, *inter alia*, that in its instructions regarding contributory negligence, the district court erred by charging the jury that a Jones Act seaman need exercise only "slight care" for his own safety. Scurlock Marine maintained that the standard to which Gautreaux, and all seamen, should be held is that of a reasonably prudent person exercising ordinary or due care under like circumstances. Accordingly, Scurlock Marine urged this Court to abandon the slight care standard in Jones Act cases, contending the standard "has evolved from this Court's blind adherence to an incorrect statement of the law." *Gautreaux*, 84 F.3d at 781 n.7. The panel acknowledged that the viability of the slight care standard has recently been questioned but considered it the settled law of this Circuit. It thus refused to hold that the district court erred in giving the "slight care" instruction, noting that "settled law of this Circuit, such as the slight care standard in a Jones Act case, can only be changed, absent action by the United States Supreme Court, by this Court sitting en banc." *Id.* The panel accordingly affirmed the district court's judgment and this en banc rehearing followed.

* * *

Discussion

The district court's instruction, consistent with the Fifth Circuit's Pattern Jury Instructions, informed the jurors that "[i]n determining whether the plaintiff was contributorily negligent, you must bear in mind that a Jones Act seaman does not have a duty to use ordinary care under the circumstances for his own safety. A Jones Act seaman is obliged to exercise only slight care under the circumstances for his own safety at the time of the accident." Scurlock Marine asserts that this charge is defective, maintaining that historically, Jones Act seamen had been expressly bound to a standard of ordinary prudence under like circumstances. In support of its contention, Scurlock Marine cites early Supreme Court opinions to illustrate that the phrase "slight negligence" or "slight care" stood not for the duty of care owed by employers and employees, as the phrase is now understood, but for that quantum of evidence necessary to sustain a jury verdict on review. The duty of care owed by both parties, Scurlock Marine contends, had always been, and should remain, that of the reasonable person.

We acknowledge there is much confusion in this Circuit as to the proper standard of care by which juries should measure a plaintiff's duty under the Jones Act to protect himself. While some courts have instructed juries that a plaintiff's duty is only one of slight care, as did the district court in the instant case, others charge that the duty is one of ordinary prudence. Admittedly, this Court has been less than clear in its articulation of the proper standard of care to which seamen are bound. We granted this *en banc* rehearing to eliminate the uncertainty and to consider returning, as Scurlock Marine requests, to the reasonable person standard.

A. The Development of the Slight Care, or Slight Negligence, Standard

The language chosen by Congress to determine the responsibility of both employers and employees under the Jones Act is simple and direct. Nothing in the statute indicates Congress's intention to hold Jones Act employees to a standard of slight duty of care in the exercise of concern for their own safety. Below, we explain the statutory scheme and Supreme Court precedent interpreting it before we illustrate our departure from their clear mandates.

1. The Statutory Scheme and Supreme Court Precedent

Under the Jones Act, seamen are afforded rights parallel to those of railway employees under the Federal Employers' Liability Act ("FELA"). 46 U.S.C. § 688. Section 51 of the FELA provides, in pertinent part, that "[e]very common carrier by railroad ... shall be liable in damages ... for such injury or death *resulting in whole or in part* from the negligence of any of the officers, agents, or employees of such carrier." 45 U.S.C. § 51 (emphasis added). A seaman is entitled to recovery under the Jones Act, therefore, if his employer's negligence is the cause, in whole or in part, of his injury. In their earlier articulations of § 51 liability, courts had replaced the phrase "in whole or in part" with the adjective "slightest." In *Rogers v. Missouri Pacific R. Co.*, 352 U.S. 500, 506, 77 S. Ct. 443, 448, 1 L. Ed. 2d 493 (1957), the Supreme Court used the term "slightest" to describe the reduced standard of causation between the employer's negligence and the employee's injury in FELA § 51 cases. In *Ferguson v. Moore-McCormack Lines, Inc.*, 352 U.S. 521, 523, 77 S. Ct. 457, 458, 1 L. Ed. 2d 511 (1957), the Court applied the same standard to a Jones Act case, writing, "'Under this statute the test of a jury case is simply whether the proofs justify with reason the conclusion that employer negligence played any part, even the slightest, in producing the injury or death for which damages are sought.'" (quoting *Rogers*, 352 U.S. at 506, 77 S. Ct. at 448).

Nothing in these cases, then, supports the proposition that the duty of care owed is slight. Rather, the phrase "in whole or in part" as set forth in the statute, or, as it has come to be known, "slightest," modifies only the causation prong of the inquiry. The phrase does not also modify the word "negligence." The duty of care owed, therefore, under normal rules of statutory construction, retains the usual and familiar definition of ordinary prudence. *See Texas Food Indus. Assoc. v. United States Dept. of Agriculture*, 81 F.3d 578, 582

(5th Cir. 1996) (stating it is a "cardinal canon of statutory construction ... that [in interpreting a statute,] the words of a statute will be given their plain meaning").

Despite the clarity of the Supreme Court's decisions, the word "slightest," used initially to refer to the quantum of evidence of an employer's breach of duty necessary to sustain a jury verdict, soon took on a different referent. Once the Supreme Court had reduced the statutory language "in whole or in part" to "any part, even the slightest," it was not long before our court further reduced the phrase "any part, even the slightest" to a shorthand expression of "slight negligence" or "slight evidence of negligence." Thereafter we used the phrase "slight negligence" uncritically. Justice Frankfurter's comment on the (mis)use of the phrase "assumption of the risk" in FELA actions aptly applies to our discussion today: "A phrase begins life as a literary expression; its felicity leads to its lazy repetition; and repetition soon establishes it as a legal formula, undiscriminatingly used to express different and sometimes contradictory ideas." *Tiller v. Atlantic Coast Line R. Co.*, 318 U.S. 54, 68, 63 S. Ct. 444, 452, 87 L. Ed. 610 (1943) (FRANKFURTER, J., concurring). The same holds true of our use of the phrase "slight negligence" or "slight care" in Jones Act negligence cases.

Guided by the Supreme Court, we initially employed the phrase "slight negligence" as a shorthand expression for the standard by which we measure, in our review of a jury verdict, the sufficiency of evidence to establish a causal link between an employer's negligence and a seaman's injury. Significantly, an employer's duty of care always remained that of *ordinary* negligence. Soon, however, we began using the phrase "slight negligence" to refer not only to the sufficiency of the evidence inquiry but also to that duty of care Jones Act employers owed to their employees. A plaintiff, therefore, could now reach the jury not only with "slight evidence" of his employer's negligence, but also with slight evidence of his employer having been only "slightly negligent." Once we had characterized the phrase "slight negligence" as shorthand to depict a duty of care owed by an employer to its employee, it was not long before we also used the phrase to represent the plaintiff's duty of care to protect himself from work-related injuries. We did so by rephrasing "slight negligence" to "slight care."

Historically, then, Jones Act employers and seamen were expressly bound to a standard of ordinary prudence; when the phrase "slight negligence" came to stand for the duty of care owed by employers and employees, however, employers were understood to be held to a higher degree of personal responsibility as to their employees, and plaintiff-seamen were understood to be held to a lower degree of personal responsibility for themselves. We hold that the historical interpretation always should have been, and should now be, applied in this Circuit. We offer the following survey of our case law, however, to illustrate just how we devolved from the Supreme Court's pronouncements in *Rogers* and *Ferguson* to our "settled law" today.

2. Our Departure from the Standard of Reasonable Care

In *Page v. St. Louis Southwestern Railway Co.*, 349 F.2d 820, 823 (5th Cir. 1965), we kept the standards for determining duty of care and causation distinct when we clarified that in FELA cases, the traditional standard for determining negligence applied:

> As to both attack or defense, there are two common elements, (1) negligence, *i.e.*, the standard of care, and (2) causation, *i.e.*, the relation of the negligence to the injury. So far as negligence is concerned, that standard is the same—ordinary prudence—for both Employee and Railroad alike.

In *Boeing Co. v. Shipman*, 411 F.2d 365 (5th Cir. 1969) (en banc), however, the standards became more nebulous. We misinterpreted *Rogers*'s "any part, even the slightest" language to refer not to the evidence necessary to support a jury verdict, but to an employer's duty of care. We concluded that "[s]light negligence, necessary to support an [sic] FELA action, is defined as 'a failure to exercise *great* care,' and that burden of proof, obviously, is much less than the burden required to sustain recovery in ordinary negligence actions." *Id.* at 371. Thus, in *Boeing*, we broadened the scope of a FELA—and by implication Jones Act—action insofar as we exposed employers to a higher degree of care and thus more liability than they otherwise would be exposed to in ordinary negligence actions.

In the following years, we vacillated considerably in our pronunciations of the proper standard of care.

* * *

B. Ordinary Prudence

The above survey of our decisions shows the confused start and the diverted path leading to the "settled law" in this Circuit that a Jones Act employer is bound by a greater-than-ordinary standard of care towards its employees and that a seaman owes only a slight duty to look after his own safety. We agree with the Third Circuit that nothing in the text or structure of the FELA-Jones Act legislation suggests that the standard of care to be attributed to either an employer or an employee is anything different than ordinary prudence under the circumstances. *Fashauer v. New Jersey Transit Rail Operations, Inc.*, 57 F.3d 1269, 1283 (3d Cir. 1995). In addressing a seaman's duty to act with reasonable care, the Third Circuit reasoned:

> By its very terms, the FELA provides that "the damages shall be diminished by the jury in proportion to the amount of negligence attributable to such employee." 45 U.S.C. § 53. The statute does not distinguish between degrees of negligence; the statute does not say that the plaintiff only has a slight duty of care. Under the statute, a plaintiff's recovery is reduced to the extent that he is negligent and that such negligence is responsible for the injury. In such a situation, one must assume that Congress intended its words to mean what they ordinarily are taken to mean—a person is negligent if he

> or she fails to act as an ordinarily prudent person would act in similar circumstances. Such a reading also is in accord with the FELA's pure comparative negligence scheme; and to adopt [plaintiff's] argument would be to abandon the clear dictate of the statute in favor of a policy decision to favor employees over employers.

Id.; *see also Tiller v. Atlantic Coast Line R. Co.*, 318 U.S. 54, 67, 63 S. Ct. 444, 451, 87 L. Ed. 610 (1943) (holding that "the employer's liability is to be determined under the general rule which defines negligence as the lack of due care under the circumstances; or the failure to do what a reasonable and prudent man would ordinarily have done under the circumstances of the situation"). Our sister circuits have similarly held. *See, e.g., Smith v. Tow Boat Serv. & Management, Inc.*, 66 F.3d 336 (9th Cir. 1995) (unpublished) (rejecting "slight care" standard); *see also Karvelis v. Constellation Lines, S.A.*, 806 F.2d 49, 52-53 & n. 2 (2d Cir. 1986), *cert. denied*, 481 U.S. 1015, 107 S. Ct. 1891, 95 L. Ed. 2d 498 (1987), (approving jury instruction informing that both employer and employee under Jones Act are charged with duty of reasonable care under the circumstances); *Ybarra v. Burlington N., Inc.*, 689 F.2d 147, 150 (8th Cir. 1982) (approving jury instruction that railroad has duty to exercise reasonable care for protection of employees); *Joyce v. Atlantic Richfield Co.*, 651 F.2d 676, 681 (10th Cir. 1981) (defining negligence as failure to use reasonable care).

We find further support for our position in Supreme Court precedent. In *Urie v. Thompson*, 337 U.S. 163, 174, 69 S. Ct. 1018, 1027, 93 L. Ed. 1282 (1949), the Court emphasized that the term "negligence" is to be defined "by the common law principles as established and applied in the federal courts." (internal quotations and citation omitted). Although the Court's discussion refers specifically to § 51 "negligence," it would defy logic not to extend this reasoning to the term as used in § 53, which discusses a plaintiff's contributory negligence. *See also Consolidated Rail Corp. v. Gottshall*, 512 U.S. 532, —, 114 S. Ct. 2396, 2404, 129 L. Ed. 2d 427 (1994) (holding that common law principles are entitled to great weight in FELA analysis unless expressly rejected in text of statute).

A seaman, then, is obligated under the Jones Act to act with ordinary prudence under the circumstances. The circumstances of a seaman's employment include not only his reliance on his employer to provide a safe work environment but also his own experience, training, or education. The reasonable person standard, therefore, under the Jones Act becomes one of the reasonable *seaman* in like circumstances. To hold otherwise would unjustly reward unreasonable conduct and would fault seamen only for their gross negligence, which was not the contemplation of Congress. *See* Robert Force, *Allocation of Risk and Standard of Care Under the Jones Act: "Slight Negligence," "Slight Care"?*, 25 J. MAR. L. & COM. 1, 31 (1994).

By ascribing to seamen a slight duty of care to protect themselves from the negligence of their employers, *Spinks* and its progeny, specifically *Brooks*, are repugnant to the principles we espouse today and are therefore overruled. Moreover, by attributing to Jones Act employers a higher duty of care than that required under ordinary negligence, *Allen* and its progeny repudiate the reasonable person standard and are also overruled.

Conclusion

In light of the foregoing discussion about the appropriate standards of care that should guide employers and employees under the Jones Act, we hold that the jurors in the instant case were improperly instructed as to Gautreaux's duty to exercise care for his own safety. We, however, express no opinion as to the proper apportionment of fault between the two parties. We accordingly AFFIRM the district court's determination of the amount of damages, VACATE the district court's judgment as to comparative fault and REMAND for proceedings to determine the comparative fault (if any) of the plaintiff and apportionment of the damages consistent with this opinion. In all other respects, we reinstate the panel's opinion.

AFFIRMED IN PART, VACATED IN PART, AND REMANDED.

Notes

1. The doctrine of negligence is utilized in many areas of the law. Maritime law is no exception. As a general proposition "negligence is negligence" whether the doctrine is being applied in tort law, contract law, etc. or whether it is being applied as a matter of land based law or maritime law. Also, as a general proposition, with a few exceptions, American law does not distinguish among "degrees" of negligence. Thus, in tort law, for example, usually it does not matter whether or not defendant's negligence was only "slight" or whether it was "ordinary" or whether it was "great". It is in this sense that one may say "negligence is negligence." All negligence, regardless of the context in which the doctrine is being applied, is premised on a finding of a breach of a duty to act as reasonable person under the circumstances. A finding of a breach of duty is generally insufficient to justify recovery unless it is also found that the breach of duty contributed to the injury or damage in question. The "standard of care" required in maritime law can be stated generically as being that of a reasonable person under the circumstances.

Under the Jones Act, however, the courts have often characterized the seaman-plaintiff's burden of proof as "featherweight". The language of "slight" negligence is only appropriate when referring to the quantum of proof plaintiff needs to adduce to withstand defendant's motion for judgment as a matter of law (formerly known as motion for directed verdict and motion for judgment notwithstanding the verdict).

> As this Court has held in countless cases cases presenting the Jones Act "featherweight" burden, directed verdict is justified "[o]nly when there is a complete absence of probative facts to support the verdict." *Thornton v. Gulf Fleet Marine Corp.*, 752 F.2d 1074, 1076 (5th Cir. 1985) (quoting *Lavender v. Kurn*, 327 U.S. 645, 652, 66 S. Ct. 740, 743, 90 L. Ed. 916, 922 (1946)); *see also Comeaux v. T.L. James & Co.*, 702 F.2d 1023, 1024 (5th Cir. 1983), modifying 666 F.2d 294 (5th Cir. 1982); *Alvarez v. J. Ray McDermott & Co.*, 674 F.2d 1037, 1042 (5th Cir. 1982). The jury's verdict must be allowed to stand unless the plaintiff failed to put forth at least a marginal claim for relief. *See id.*; *Holmes v. J. Ray McDermott & Co.*, 734 F.2d 1110, 1120 (5th Cir. 1984); *Leonard v. Exxon Corp.*, 581 F.2d 522, 524 (5th Cir.), *cert. denied*, 411 U.S. 923, 99 S. Ct. 2032, 60 L. Ed. 2d 397 (1979). Like the trial court, we review all evidence in the light most favorable to the party (*Bommarito*) opposing the motion. *Day v. South Park Independent School Dist.*, 768 F.2d 696, 699-700 (5th Cir. 1985); *Brewer v. Blackwell*, 692 F.2d 387, 391 (5th Cir. 1982).

Bommarito v. Penrod Drilling Corp., 929 F.2d 186, 188 (5th Cir. 1991).

Thus, even in a Jones Act case it is necessary for the seaman-plaintiff to introduce some evidence from which a jury could find that his employer's conduct fell below the standard of care that a reasonable employer would have used under the circumstances. However, the introduction of virtually any evidence regardless of how slight is sufficient to have the jury resolve the issue of negligence. Stated otherwise, the introduction of even the slightest evidence that the employer's conduct fell below the reasonable person standard precludes the trial judge from taking the case away from the jury or from setting aside a plaintiff's verdict.

> Likewise, courts have often referred to plaintiff's burden of proving causation as being "featherweight" because FELA and the Jones Act only require a seaman to prove that his employer's negligence was *a* cause, sometimes referred to as the "producing cause", and not *the* cause of his or injury. *Landry v. Oceanic Contractors, Inc.*, 731 F.2d 299, 1986 AMC 865 (5th Cir. 1984). In *Norfolk Southern Ry. Co. v. Sorrell*, 127 S.Ct. 799, 2007 AMC 192 (2007), a FELA case, the Supreme Court held that the same causation standard should be applied to both employer and employee, but declined to consider what that causation standard should be. The Court said:
>
> Sorrell argues that FELA does contain an explicit statutory alteration from the common-law rule: Section 1 of FELA - addressing railroad negligence - uses the language "in whole or in part," 45 U.S.C. § 51, while Section 3 - covering employee contributory negligence - does not, § 53. This, Sorrell contends, evinces an intent to depart from the common-law causation standard with respect to railroad negligence under Section 1, but not with respect to any employee contributory negligence under Section 3.
>
> The inclusion of this language in one section and not the other does not alone justify a departure from the common-law practice of applying a single standard of causation. It would have made little sense to include the "in whole or in part" language in Section 3, because if the employee's contributory negligence contributed "in whole" to his injury, there would be no recovery against the railroad in the first place. The language made sense in Section 1, however, to make clear that there could be recovery against the railroad even if it were only partially negligent.

Norfolk Southern Ry. Co. v. Sorrell, 127 S.Ct. 799, 808 (2007).

Thus, the effect of *Sorrell* in conjunction with such decisions as *Landry* is presumably that both employee *and* employer need only prove that the other's fault was a "producing cause".

FERGUSON v. MOORE-MCCORMACK LINES, INC.

352 U.S. 521, 77 S. Ct. 457, 1 L. Ed. 2d 511, 1957 AMC 647 (1957)

Mr. Justice Douglas announced the judgment of the Court and an opinion in which The Chief Justice, Mr. Justice CLARK and Mr. Justice BRENNAN join.

Petitioner was injured in 1950 while serving as a second baker on respondent's passenger ship *Brazil*. Among his duties, he was required to fill orders of the ship's waiters for ice cream. On the day of the accident, he had received an order from a ship's waiter for 12 portions of ice cream. When he got half way down in the two-and-one-half-gallon ice-cream container from which he was filling these orders, the ice cream was so hard that it could not be removed with the hemispherical scoop with which he had been furnished. Petitioner undertook to remove the ice cream with a sharp butcher knife kept nearby, grasping the handle and chipping at the hard ice cream. The knife struck a spot in the ice cream which was so hard that his hand slipped down onto the blade of the knife, resulting in the loss of two fingers of his right hand.

Petitioner brought this suit under the Jones Act, 41 Stat. 1007, 46 U.S.C. § 688, to recover for his injuries, which were alleged to be the result of respondent's negligence. At the close of petitioner's case, respondent's motion for a directed verdict was denied. Respondent offered no evidence. After the jury returned a verdict of $17,500 for the petitioner, respondent moved to set aside the verdict. This motion was also denied and judgment entered for the petitioner in accordance with the jury verdict. The Court of Appeals reversed, holding that it was "not within the realm of reasonable foreseeability" that petitioner would use the knife to chip the frozen ice cream. 228 F.2d 891, 892. We granted certiorari. 351 U.S. 936.

We conclude that there was sufficient evidence to take to the jury the question whether respondent was negligent in failing to furnish petitioner with an adequate tool with which to perform his task.

Petitioner testified that the hard ice cream could have been loosened safely with an ice chipper. He had used such an instrument for that purpose on other ships. He was not, however, furnished such an instrument. There was evidence that the scoop with which he had been furnished was totally inadequate to remove ice cream of the consistency of that which he had to serve. And, there was evidence that its extremely hard consistency was produced by the failure of another member of the crew to transfer it from the deep freeze to a tempering chest in sufficient time to allow all of it to become disposable by means of the scoop when the time came for it to be served. There was no showing that any device was close at hand which would have safely performed the task. Finally, there was evidence that petitioner had been instructed to give the waiters prompt service.

Respondent urges that it was not reasonably foreseeable that petitioner would utilize the knife to loosen the ice cream. But the jury, which plays a pre-eminent role in these Jones Act cases (*Jacob v. New York City*, 315 U.S. 752; *Schulz v. Pennsylvania R. Co.*, 350 U.S. 523), could conclude that petitioner had been furnished no safe tool to perform his task. It was not necessary that respondent be in a position to foresee the exact chain of circumstances which actually led to the accident. The jury was instructed that it might consider whether respondent could have anticipated that a knife would be used to get out the ice cream. On this record, fairminded men could conclude that respondent should have foreseen that petitioner might be tempted to use a knife to perform his task with dispatch, since no adequate implement was furnished him. *See Schulz v. Pennsylvania R. Co.*, 350 U.S. 523, 526. Since the standard of liability under the Jones Act is that established by Congress under the Federal Employers' Liability Act, what we said in *Rogers v. Missouri Pacific R. Co., ante*, p. 500, decided this day, is relevant here:

> Under this statute the test of a jury case is simply whether the proofs justify with reason the conclusion that employer negligence *played any part, even the slightest*, in producing the injury or death for which damages are sought.

Because the jury could have so concluded, the Court of Appeals erred in holding that respondent's motion for a directed verdict should have been granted. "Courts should not assume that in determining these questions of negligence juries will fall short of a fair performance of their constitutional function." *Wilkerson v. McCarthy*, 336 U.S. 53, 62.

Reversed.

KERNAN v. AMERICAN DREDGING CO.

355 U.S. 426, 78 S. Ct. 394, 2 L. Ed. 2d 382, 1958 AMC 251 (1958)

Mr. Justice BRENNAN delivered the opinion of the Court

In this ÿ proceeding ÿ the District Court for the Eastern District of Pennsylvania denied the petitioner's claim for damages filed on behalf of the widow and other dependents of a seaman who lost his life on respondent's tug in a fire caused by the violation of a navigation rule. 141 F. Supp. 582. The Court of Appeals for the Third Circuit affirmed. 235 F.2d 618, rehearing denied, 235 F.2d 619. We granted certiorari. 352 U.S. 965.

The seaman lost his life on the tug *Arthur N. Herron*, which, on the night of November 18, 1952, while towing a scow on the Schuylkill River in Philadelphia, caught fire when an open-flame kerosene lamp on the deck of the scow ignited highly inflammable vapors lying above an extensive accumulation of petroleum products spread over the surface of the river. Several oil refineries and facilities for oil storage, and for loading and unloading petroleum products, are located along the banks of the Schuylkill River. The trial court found that the lamp was not more than three feet above the water. Maintaining the lamp at a height of less than eight feet violated a navigation rule promulgated by the Commandant of the United States Coast Guard. The trial court found that the vapor would not have been ignited if the lamp had been carried at the required height.

The District Court held that the violation of the rule, "whether ÿ [it] be called negligence or be said to make the flotilla unseaworthy," did not impose liability because "the Coast Guard regulation had to do solely with navigation and was intended for the prevention of collisions, and for no other purpose. In the present case there was no collision and no fault of navigation. True, the origin of the fire can be traced to the violation of the regulation, but the question is not causation but whether the violation of the regulation, of itself, imposes liability." 141 F. Supp., at 585.

* * *

The petitioner also urges that, since the violation of the rule requiring the lights to be eight feet above the water resulted in a defect or insufficiency in the flotilla's lighting equipment which in fact caused the seaman's death, liability was created without regard to negligence under the line of decisions of this Court in actions under the FELA based upon violations of either the Safety Appliance Acts or the Boiler Inspection Act. That line of decisions interpreted the clause of § 1 of the FELA, 45 U.S.C. § 51, which imposes liability on the employer "by reason of any defect or insufficiency, due to its negligence, in its cars, engines, appliances, machinery, track, roadbed, works, boats, wharves, or other equipment." The cases hold that under this clause, a defect resulting from a violation of either statute which causes the injury or death of an employee creates liability without regard to negligence. *San Antonio & A.P.R. Co. v. Wagner*, 241 U.S. 476, 484. Here the defect or insufficiency in the flotilla's lighting equipment due to a violation of the statute resulted in the death of the seaman. The question for our decision is whether, in the absence of any showing of negligence, the Jones Act—which in terms incorporates the provisions of the FELA—permits recovery for the death of a seaman resulting from a violation of a statutory duty. We hold that it does.

In denying the claim the lower courts relied upon their views of general tort doctrine... . In the railroad and shipping industries, however, the FELA and Jones Act provide the framework for determining liability for industrial accidents. But instead of a detailed statute codifying common-law principles, Congress saw fit to enact a statute of the most general terms, thus leaving in large measure to the courts the duty of fashioning remedies for injured employees in a manner analogous to the development of tort remedies at common law. But it is clear that the general congressional intent was to provide liberal recovery for injured workers, *Rogers v. Missouri Pacific R. Co.*, 352 U.S. 500, 508-510, and it is also clear that Congress intended the creation of no static remedy, but one which would be developed and enlarged to meet changing conditions and changing concepts of industry's duty toward its workers.

The FELA and the Jones Act impose upon the employer the duty of paying damages when injury to the worker is caused, in whole or in part, by the employer's fault. This fault may consist of a breach of the duty of care, analogous but by no means identical to the general common-law duty, or of a breach of some statutory duty. The tort doctrine which the lower courts applied imposes liability for violation of a statutory duty only where the injury is one which the statute was designed to prevent. However, this Court has repeatedly refused to apply such a limiting doctrine in FELA cases. In FELA cases based upon violations of the Safety Appliance Acts or the Boiler Inspection Act, the Court has held that a violation of either statute creates liability under FELA if the resulting defect or insufficiency in equipment contributes in fact to the death or injury in suit, without regard to whether the injury flowing from the breach was the injury the statute sought to prevent. Since it appears in this case that the defect or insufficiency of the flotilla's lighting equipment resulting from the violation of 33 U.S.C. § 157 actually caused the seaman's death, this principle governs and compels a result in favor of the petitioner's claim.

* * *

The decisive question in this case, then, is whether the principles developed in this line of FELA cases permit recovery for violation of this navigation statute or are limited, as the dissenting opinion would have it, to cases involving the Safety Appliance and Boiler Inspection Acts. Our attention is directed to the provisions of § 4 of the FELA, which makes reference to "any statute enacted for the safety of employees ... ," and it is urged that this phrase, in some unexplained manner, creates a special relationship between the FELA and the Safety Appliance and Boiler Inspection Acts. Several answers may be given to this contention.

First, § 4 relates entirely to the defense of assumption of risk, abolishing this defense where the injury was caused by the employer's negligence or by "violation ... of any statute enacted for the safety of employees...." It is § 1 of the FELA which creates the cause of action and this section, on its face, is barren of any suggestion that injuries caused by violation of *any* statute are to be treated specially. In formulating the rule that violation of the Safety Appliance and Boiler Inspection Acts creates liability for resulting injuries without proof of negligence, the Court relied on judicially evolved principles designed to carry out the general congressional purpose of providing appropriate remedies for injuries incurred by railroad employees. For Congress, in 1908, did not crystallize the application of the Act by enacting specific rules to guide the courts. Rather, by using generalized language, it created only a framework within which the courts were left to evolve, much in the manner of the common law, a system of principles providing compensation for injuries to employees consistent with the changing realities of employment in the railroad industry.

Second, it is argued that the Safety Appliance and Boiler Inspection Acts are special safety statutes and thus may easily be assimilated to the FELA under general common-law principles. But there is no magic in the word "safety." In the cases we have discussed it was regarded as irrelevant that the defects in the appliances did not disable them from performing their intended safety function. For instance, in *Gotschall* the coupling defect parting the cars resulted in the automatic setting of the emergency brakes as a safety measure. In *Coray* the train stopped due to the operation of the very safety mechanism required by the statute. In *Urie* the defect in the sanders which caused sand to come into the locomotive cabs in no wise impaired the designed safety function of the sanders—to provide sand for traction. We think that the irrelevance of the safety aspect in these cases demonstrates that the basis of liability is a violation of statutory duty without regard to whether the injury flowing from the violation was the injury the statute sought to guard against. It must therefore be concluded that the nature of the Acts violated is not a controlling consideration; the basis of liability is the FELA.

The courts, in developing the FELA with a view to adjusting equitably between the worker and his corporate employer the risks inherent in the railroad industry, have plainly rejected many of the refined distinctions necessary in common-law tort doctrine for the purpose of allocating risks between persons who are more nearly on an equal footing as to financial capacity and ability to avoid the hazards involved. Among the refinements developed by the common law for the purpose of limiting the risk of liability arising from wrongful conduct is the rule that violation of a statutory duty creates liability only when the statute was intended to protect those in the position of the plaintiff from the type of injury in fact incurred. This limiting approach has long been discarded from the FELA. Instead, the theory of the FELA is that where the employer's conduct falls short of the high standard required of him by this Act, and his fault, in whole or in part, causes injury, liability ensues. And this result follows whether the fault is a violation of a statutory duty or the more general duty of acting with care, for the employer owes the employee, as much as the duty of acting with care, the duty of complying with his statutory obligations.

We find no difficulty in applying these principles, developed under the FELA, to the present action under the Jones Act, for the latter Act expressly provides for seamen the cause of action—and consequently the entire judicially developed doctrine of liability—granted to railroad workers by the FELA. The deceased seaman here was in a position perfectly analogous to that of the railroad workers allowed recovery in the line of cases we have discussed, and the principles governing those cases clearly should apply here.

The judgment of the Court of Appeals is reversed with direction to remand to the District Court for further proceedings not inconsistent with this opinion. *Reversed.*

Mr. Justice HARLAN, whom Mr. Justice FRANKFURTER, Mr. Justice BURTON, and Mr. Justice WHITTAKER joined, dissented.

Notes

1. *Kernan* was distinguished by the Second Circuit in *Jones v. Spentonbush-Red Star Co.*, 155 F.3d 587, 1999 AMC 324 (2d Cir. 1998), where the court refused to regard a breach of an Occupational Safety and Health Act (OSHA) regulation as establishing negligence *per se* for Jones Act purposes, even though the regulation was a safety one, requiring a grinding wheel to have a guard.

> In contrast to the defendants in *Kernan* ... however, Spentonbush did not violate a Coast Guard regulation or maritime statute. Instead, it violated an OSHA regulation. This distinction in the source of defendant's statutory duty is key to this appeal. Unlike Coast Guard regulations and maritime statutes that are specifically aimed at shipping activities, Jones relies on a general workplace safety regulation to attain the same results in a maritime context. We do not think it was Congress' purpose for the Occupational Safety and Health Act (the Act) to have such an all- encompassing effect. ... Congress provides the following limitation to the Act's applicability:
>
> > Nothing in this chapter shall be construed to supersede or in any manner affect any workmen's compensation law or *to enlarge or diminish or affect in any other manner the common law or statutory rights, duties, or liabilities of employers and employees under any law with respect to injuries, diseases, or death of employees* arising out of, or in the course of, employment. 29 U.S.C. § 653(b)(4) (1994) (emphasis added).
>
> Imposing negligence *per se*, shifting the burden of proof and barring a finding of comparative negligence for an OSHA violation would all "enlarge or diminish or affect in any other manner" the liability of a maritime employer.

155 F. 3d 587, 595, 1999 AMC 324, 334.

2. In *Sentilles v. Inter-Caribbean Corporation*, 361 U.S. 107, 80 S. Ct. 173, 4 L. Ed. 2d 142 (1959), a seaman sued his employer, the shipowner, seeking damages under the Jones Act for injuries sustained in consequence of a seaboard accident. As the vessel encountered a heavy sea, plaintiff was pitched into the air and fell back to the deck, where, upon landing, a wave washed him a considerable distance. Shortly after the accident, plaintiff became ill, was

hospitalized and treated for a serious case of tuberculosis. His theory was that the accident aggravated a previously latent tubercular condition.

The case was submitted to a jury, a verdict was returned for plaintiff, and the District Court rendered judgment in his favor. The Court of Appeal reversed on the ground that the evidence did not justify the jury's conclusion that the accident caused aggravation of the pre-existing tubercular condition. The United States Supreme Court granted certiorari and reversed; the Court of Appeal had applied an improper standard in reviewing the medical evidence and in examining the judgment rendered on the jury's verdict.

The medical evidence was not conclusive. A specialist had testified that the aggravation of plaintiff's tubercular condition "might be a consequence of the accident." Another specialist had testified that the trauma and plaintiff's pre-existing diabetic condition were "the most likely causes of the aggravation of the tuberculosis." A third specialist, who had never examined plaintiff, answered when questioned hypothetically that the accident "probably aggravated his condition." The United States Supreme Court held that the jury's power to draw the inference that the aggravation of plaintiff's condition was in fact caused by the accident "was not impaired by the failure of any medical witness to testify that it was in fact the cause." "The members of the jury," the Court declared, "not the medical witnesses, were sworn to make a legal determination of the question of causation. They were entitled to take all the circumstances, including the medical testimony, into consideration.... The focal point of judicial review is the reasonableness of the particular inference or conclusion drawn by the jury.... The proofs here justified with reason the conclusion of the jury that the accident caused the petitioner's serious subsequent illness."

Has the Court dispensed with proof of proximate causation in Jones Act cases? *See Landry v. Oceanic Contractors, Inc.*, 731 F.2d 299, 1986 AMC (5th Cir. 1984), *rehearing denied* 746 F.2d 812 (5th Cir. 1984). For a case in which the court dismissed a claim for lack of causation under the Jones Act standard, *see Martin v. John W. Stone Oil Distributor, Inc.*, 819 F.2d 547, 1988 AMC 1689 (5th Cir. 1987).

3. *Proof of Causation*

In a Jones Act case, plaintiff need not show that the negligence of the employer is the sole cause of his injuries. *Gajewski v. United States*, 540 F. Supp. 381, 1982 AMC 2830 (S.D.N.Y. 1982). Moreover, plaintiff need not prove proximate cause in the traditional sense. *See Sentilles v. Inter-Caribbean Shipping Corp.*, 361 U.S. 107, 80 S.Ct. 173, 4 L.Ed.2d 142 (1959). For a case in which no causation was found, *see Martin v. John W. Stone Oil Distributor, Inc.*, 819 F.2d 547, 1988 AMC 1689 (5th Cir. 1987).

Likewise it has been stated that:

> The "producing cause" FELA standard, used for Jones Act negligence, facilitates proof by the employee, incorporating any cause regardless of immediacy. Plaintiff's burden of proving such cause is "featherweight," *Davis v. Hill Engineering, Inc.*, 549 F.2d 314, 331 (5th Cir. 1977), and all that is required is a showing of "slight negligence," *Allen v. Seacoast Products, Inc.*, 623 F.2d 355, 361 (5th Cir. 1980). In keeping with this less demanding standard of proof of causation, the test for sufficiency of evidence in a Jones Act case also requires less evidence to support a finding and directed verdicts and j.n.o.v. motions are granted "only when there is a complete absence of probative facts" to support a verdict. *Lavender v. Kurn*, 327 U.S. 645, 652-53, 66 S. Ct. 740, 743, 90 L. Ed. 2d 916, 922 (1946) (construing standard for FELA cases, applicable to Jones Act cases, *Ferguson v. Moore-McCormick Lines, Inc.*, 352 U.S. 521, 523, 77 S. Ct. 457, 458, 1 L. Ed. 2d 511, 513 (1957)); *Kendrick v. Illinois Central Gulf Railroad Co.*, 669 F.2d 341, 343 n.1 (5th Cir. 1982); *Comeaux v. T.L. James & Co.*, 666 F.2d at 298 n.3; *Allen v. Seacoast Products, Inc.*, 623 F.2d 355, 3359-60 (5th Cir. 1980).
>
> Similarly, we have applied the same standards of proof, causation, and review to the issue of the plaintiff's contributory negligence. *See Campbell v. Seacoast Products, Inc.*, 581 F.2d 98, 99 n.2 (5th Cir. 1978) (applying *Lavender* standard of review to Jones Act case where jury verdict favors plaintiff or defendant); *McBride v. Loffland Brothers Co.*, 422 F.2d 363, (5th Cir. 1970).

Comeaux v. T.L. James & Co., 702 F.2d 1023, 1024, 1984 AMC 2805 (5th Cir. 1983).

> The burden to prove causation in a Jones Act case is "very light" or "featherweight." *Landry v. Two R. Drilling Co.*, 511 F.2d 138, 142 (5th Cir. 1975). Under the Jones Act, a defendant must bear the responsibility for any negligence, however slight, that played a part in producing the plaintiff's injury. *See Landry v. Oceanic Contractors, Inc.*, 731 F.2d 299, 302 (5th Cir. 1984). Although in Jones Act cases a "jury is entitled to make permissible inferences from unexplained events," summary judgment is nevertheless warranted when there is a complete absence of proof of an essential element of the nonmoving party's case. *See Martin v. John W. Stond Oil Distrib., Inc.*, 819 F.2d 547, 549 (5th Cir. 1987). The standard for negligence under general maritime law [not applicable in Jones Act cases] is higher. The plaintiff must demonstrate that there was a duty owned by the defendant to the plaintiff, breach of that duty, injury sustained by plaintiff, and a causal connection between defendant's conduct and the plaintiff's injury. *See Thomas v. Express Boat Co.*, 759 F.2d 444, 448 (5th Cir. 1985). Furthermore, the resultant harm must be reasonably foreseeable. *Daigle v. Point Landing, Inc.*, 616 F.2d 825, 827 (5th Cir. 1980).

In re Cooper/T. Smith, 929 F.2d 1073, 1077, 1991 AMC 2169 (5th Cir. 1991).

4. *Standard of proof in Jones Act v. standard of proof in unseaworthiness cases*

In *Chisholm v. Sabine Towing & Transp. Co., Inc.,* 679 F.2d 60, 62 (5th Cir. 1982), the court said:

> Jones Act negligence and unseaworthiness are two separate and distinct claims. This court recognizes two different standards of causation. The "producing cause" standard utilized for Jones Act negligence is the F.E.L.A. Standard. The language selected by Congress to fix liability is simple and direct. Defendant must bear responsibility if his negligence played any part, even the slightest, in producing the injury. *Rogers v. Missouri Pacific R. Co.*, 352 U.S. 500, 506. The standard of causation for unseaworthiness is a more demanding one and requires proof of proximate cause.

5. *Recovery for Fright*

The Court in *Consolidated Rail Corp. v. Gottshall,* 114 S. Ct. 2396, 2408, 129 L.Ed.2d 427, 1994 AMC 2113 (1994) held that actions for fright are available under FELA and presumably under the Jones Act. The Court adopted the zone of danger test is the standard of recovery. Actions for fright under FELA are judged according to the common law development of emotional distress. Most states use the "bystander" test and some use the "physical impact" test, but only 14 use the "zone of danger" test adopted by the Supreme Court.

6. *Aggravation of Original Injury by Negligent Medical Treatment*

A negligent employer is liable not only for the initial injury but for subsequent negligent medical care necessitated by the original injury. *Alholm v. American S.S. Co.*, 144 F.3d 1172, 1998 AMC 2352 (8th Cir. 1998).

B. Conflict of Laws

Introductory Note

When a legal relationship involves foreign contacts, a question arises as to the applicable law. This question is resolved by resorting to *choice of law* rules that may be established by statute, judicial precedents, or by agreement of the parties. The choice of law rules are a part of the law of the forum. Thus, when a foreign seaman is injured aboard a foreign-flag vessel in a United States port, and the action is brought in a federal district court under the grant of admiralty jurisdiction, the court is bound to apply federal law.

The process of choice of law may be simplified by statutes that define their own area of application. For example, the words "any seaman" in the Jones Act were at first taken to require application of the statute to causes of action for personal injuries sustained by a seaman regardless of the nationality of the plaintiff, the flag of the vessel, or the place of the injury. Such an extremely broad application of the Jones Act was impractical and undesirable. The Supreme Court, therefore, sought to establish guidelines for a choice of law process in *Lauritzen v. Larsen*, 345 U.S. 571, 73 S.Ct. 921, 97 L.Ed. 1254, 1953 AMC 1210 (1953), discussed below.

Presumably, questions of choice of law arise *after* the question of jurisdiction is settled. If a court has subject matter jurisdiction of a controversy, and the parties are properly before the court, then it is proper for the court to decide the question of the applicable law. After the choice of law determination, the third step in the analysis is a *forum non conveniens* determination. One would be hard-pressed, however, to find a case involving an injured seaman in which the court decided that foreign law was applicable and retained jurisdiction.

In 1982, Congress amended the Jones Act to bar suits for maintenance and cure or personal injury and death by a person not a citizen or resident of the United States who is employed in the production of off-shore mineral or energy resources of nations other than the United States. An exception to this bar can be established by showing that no remedy is available under the laws of the nation asserting jurisdiction. 46 U.S.C.A. § 30105 (formerly 46 U.S.C. § 688(b)).

HELLENIC LINES LTD. v. RHODITIS

398 U.S. 306, 90 S. Ct. 1731, 26 L. Ed. 2d 252, 1970 AMC 994 (1970)

Mr. Justice DOUGLAS delivered the opinion of the Court

This is a suit under the Jones Act by a seaman who was injured aboard the ship *Hellenic Hero* in the Port of New Orleans. The District Court, sitting without a jury, rendered judgment for the seaman, 273 F. Supp. 248. The Court of Appeals affirmed. 412 F.2d 919. The case is here on petition for a writ of certiorari which we granted, 396 U.S. 1000, in light of the conflict between the decision below and *Tsakonites v. Transpacific Carriers Corp.*, 368 F.2d 426, in the Second Circuit.

Petitioner Hellenic Lines Ltd. is a Greek corporation that has its largest office in New York and another office in New Orleans. More than 95% of its stock is owned by a United States domiciliary who is a Greek citizen—Pericles G. Callimanopoulos (whom we call Pericles). He lives in Connecticut and manages the corporation out of New York. He has lived in this country since 1945. The ship *Hellenic Hero* is engaged in regularly scheduled runs between various ports of the United States and the Middle East, Pakistan, and India. The District Court found that its entire income is from cargo either originating or terminating in the United States.

Respondent, the seaman, signed on in Greece, and he is a Greek citizen. His contract of employment provides that Greek law and a Greek collective-bargaining agreement apply between the employer and the seaman and that all claims arising out of the employment contract are to be adjudicated by a Greek court. And it seems to be conceded that respondent could obtain relief through Greek courts, if he desired.

The Jones Act speaks only of "the defendant employer" without any qualifications. In *Lauritizen v. Larsen*, 345 U.S. 571, however, we listed seven factors to be considered in determining whether a particular shipowner should be held to be an "employer" for Jones Act purposes:

> (1) the place of the wrongful act; (2) the law of the flag; (3) the allegiance or domicile of the injured seaman; (4) allegiance of the defendant shipowner; (5) the place where the contract of employment was made; (6) the inaccessibility of a foreign forum; and (7) the law of the forum.

Of these seven factors it is urged that four are in favor of the shipowner and against jurisdiction: the ship's flag is Greek; the injured seaman is Greek; the employment contract is Greek; and there is a foreign forum available to the injured seaman.

The *Lauritizen* test, however, is not a mechanical one. 345 U.S. at 582. We indicated that the flag that a ship flies may, at times, alone be sufficient. *Id.*, at 585-586. The significance of one of more factors must be considered in light of the national interest served by the assertion of Jones Act jurisdiction. Moreover, the list of seven factors in *Lauritizen* was not intended as exhaustive. As held in *Pavlou v. Ocean Traders Marine Corp.*, 211 F. Supp. 320, 324, and approved by the Court of Appeals in the present case, 412 F.2d at 923, the shipowner's *base of operations* is another factor of importance in determining whether the Jones Act is applicable; and there well may be others.

In *Lauritizen* the injured seaman had been hired in and was returned to the United States, and the shipowner was served here. Those were the only contacts of that shipping operation with this country.

The present case is quite different.

Pericles became a lawful permanent resident alien in 1952. We extend to such an alien the same constitutional protections of due process that we accord citizens. *Kwong Hai Chew v. Colding*, 344 U.S. 590, 596. The injury occurred here. The forum is a United States court. Pericles' base of operations is New York. The *Hellenic Hero* was not a casual visitor; rather, it and many of its sister ships were earning income from cargo originating or terminating here. We see no reason whatsoever to give the Jones Act a strained construction so that this alien owner, engaged in an extensive business operation in this country, may have an advantage over citizens engaged in the same business by allowing him to escape the obligations and responsibility of a Jones Act "employer." The flag, the nationality of the seaman, the fact that his employment contract was Greek, and that he might be compensated there are in the totality of the circumstances of this case minor weights in the scales compared with the substantial and continuing contacts that this alien owner has with this country. If, as stated in *Bartholomew v. Universe Tankships Inc.*, 263 F.2d 437, the liberal purposes of the Jones Act are to be effectuated, the facade of the operation must be considered as minor, compared with the real nature of the operation and a cold objective look at the actual operational contacts that this ship and this owner have with the United States. By that test the Court of Appeals was clearly right in holding that petitioner Hellenic Lines was an "employer" under the Jones Act. *Affirmed.*

Mr. Justice HARLAN, with whom The Chief Justice and Mr. Justice STEWART join, dissenting

I dissent from today's decision holding that a Greek seaman who signs articles in Greece for employment on a Greek-owned, Greek-flag vessel may recover under the Jones Act for shipboard injuries sustained while the vessel was in American territorial waters. This result is supported neither by precedent, nor realistic policy, and in my opinion is far removed from any intention that can reasonably be ascribed to Congress.

Note: Forum Selection Clauses

The Court of Appeals for the Fifth Circuit has held that a forum selection clause in a foreign seaman's employment contract was enforceable. *Marinechance Shipping, Ltd. v. Sebastian*, 143 F.3d 216, 1998 AMC 2819 (5th Cir. 1998). The same court has held that an arbitration clause in a foreign seaman's employment contract is enforceable, despite the fact that seamen's employment contracts are excluded from the operation of the Federal Arbitration Act by 9 U.S.C. §1. The Fifth Circuit held that that exclusion does not apply to cases where a stay of proceedings is sought pursuant to the part of Title 9 (*i.e.*, 9 U.S.C. §§ 201-208) that implements the Convention on the Recognition and Enforcement of Foreign Arbitral Awards (the New York Convention). *Francisco v. M/T Stolt Achievement*, 293 F.3d 270, 2002 AMC 1529 (5th Cir. 2002).

In *Bodzai v. Arctic Fjord, Inc.*, 990 P.2d 616, 2000 AMC 266 (Ak. 1999), the Supreme Court of Alaska distinguished *Marinechance*, holding claims for maintenance and cure, unseaworthiness and Jones Act did not arise from contract and so could not be affected by a forum selection clause in contract relating to "Any dispute which may arise under the terms of this contract".

Part 3. Actions for Unseaworthiness: Cases and Notes

Introductory Notes

1. The origin of a seaman's right to recover for injuries caused by an unseaworthy ship is far from clear. The earliest codifications of the law of the sea provided only the equivalent of maintenance and cure—medical treatment and wages to a mariner wounded or falling ill in the service of the ship. Markedly similar provisions granting relief of this nature are to be found in the Laws of Oleron, promulgated about 1150 A.D. by Eleanor, Duchess of Guienne; in the Laws of Wisbuy, published in the following century; in the Laws of the Hanse Towns, which appeared in 1597; and in the Marine Ordinances of Louis XIV, published in 1681.

For many years American courts regarded these ancient codes as establishing the limits of a shipowner's liability to a seaman injured in the service of his vessel. During this early period the maritime law was concerned with the concept of unseaworthiness only with reference to two situations quite unrelated to the right of a crew member to recover for personal injuries. The earliest mention of unseaworthiness in American judicial opinions appears in cases in which mariners were suing for their wages. They were required to prove the unseaworthiness of the vessel to excuse their desertion or misconduct which otherwise would result in a forfeiture of their right to wages. The other route through which the concept of unseaworthiness found its way into the maritime law was via the rules covering marine insurance and the carriage of goods by sea.

Not until the late nineteenth century did there develop in American admiralty courts the doctrine that seamen had a right to recover for personal injuries beyond maintenance and cure. During that period it became generally accepted that a shipowner was liable to a mariner injured in the service of a ship as a consequence of the owner's failure to exercise due diligence. The decisions of that era for the most part treated maritime injuries cases on the same footing as cases involving the duty of a shoreside employer to exercise ordinary care to provide his employees with a reasonably safe place to work.

This was the historical background behind Mr. Justice Brown's much quoted second proposition in *The Osceola*, 189 U.S. 158, 175, 23 S.Ct. 483, 47 L.Ed. 760 (1903): "That the vessel and her owner are, both by English and American law, liable to an indemnity for injuries received by seamen in consequence of the unseaworthiness of the ship, or a failure to supply and keep in order the proper appliances appurtenant to the ship." In support of this proposition the Court's opinion noted that "[i]t will be observed in these cases that a departure has been made from the Continental codes in allowing an indemnity beyond the expense of maintenance and cure in cases arising from unseaworthiness. This departure originated in England in the Merchants' Shipping Act of 1876 ... and in this country, in a general consensus of opinion among the Circuit and District Courts, that an exception should be made from the general principle before obtaining, in favor of seamen suffering injury through the unseaworthiness of the vessel. We are not disposed to disturb so wholesome a doctrine by any contrary decision of our own." 189 U.S. at 175.

It is arguable that the import of the above-quoted second proposition in *The Osceola* was not to broaden the shipowner's liability, but, rather, to limit liability for negligence to those situations where his negligence resulted in the vessel's unseaworthiness. Support for such a view is to be found not only in the historic context in which *The Osceola* was decided, but in the discussion in the balance of the opinion, in the decision itself (in favor of the shipowner), and in the equation which the Court drew with the law of England, where the Merchant Shipping Act of 1876 imposed upon the owner only the duty to use "all reasonable means" to "insure the seaworthiness of the ship." This limited view of *The Osceola's* pronouncement as to liability for unseaworthiness may be the basis for subsequent decisions of federal courts exonerating shipowners from responsibility for the negligence of their agents because that negligence had not rendered the vessel unseaworthy. Such a reading of the *Osceola* opinion also finds arguable support in several subsequent decisions of the Supreme Court. *Baltimore S.S. Co. v. Phillips*, 274 U.S. 316, 47 S.Ct. 600, 71 L.Ed. 1069 (1927); *Plamals v. The Pinar Del Rio*, 277 U.S. 151, , 48 S.Ct. 457, 72 L.Ed. 827 (1928); *Pacific Co. v. Peterson*, 278 U.S. 130, , 49 S.Ct. 75, 73 L.Ed. 220 (1928). In any event, with the passage of the Jones Act in 1920, 41 Stat. 1007, 46 U.S.C.A. §§ 30104-5 (formerly 46 U.S.C. § 688), Congress effectively obliterated all distinctions between the kinds of negligence for which the shipowner is liable, as well as limitations imposed by the fellow-servant doctrine, by extending to seamen the remedies made available to railroad workers under the Federal Employers' Liability Act.

The United States Supreme Court began to develop the ancient doctrine of unseaworthiness in *Mahnich v. Southern Steamship Co.*, 321 U.S. 96, 64 S.Ct. 455, 88 L.Ed. 561,1944 AMC 1 (1944). That case involved the claim of a seaman who was a member of the crew of a vessel. Soon thereafter, the Court extended a warranty of seaworthiness to longshoremen and harbor workers. *Seas Shipping Co. v. Sieracki*, 328 U.S. 85, 66 S.Ct. 872, 90 L.Ed. 1099 1956 AMC 698 (1946); *Pope & Talbot, Inc. v. Hawn*, 346 U.S. 406, 74 S.Ct. 202, 98 L.Ed. 143 1954 AMC 1 (1953). During the 1950's and 1960's, most of the cases elaborating on the notion of unseaworthiness involved claims of longshoremen and harbor workers. However, the 1972 amendments to the Longshoremen's and Harbor Workers' Compensation Act (see *infra*) eliminated the unseaworthiness action that longshoremen and harbor workers covered by the Act had against a shipowner. Once again, therefore, the warranty of seaworthiness is largely confined to seamen who are members of the crew of a vessel. Pre-1972 decisions defining the scope of unseaworthiness, even if rendered for claims by longshoremen and harbor workers, continue to be controlling, however, for the determination of claims of seamen.

2. The warranty of seaworthiness applies to the hull of a ship, the ship's cargo-handling machinery, hand tool aboard the ship, ropes and tackle, and, in general, all sorts of equipment either belonging to the ship or brought aboard by stevedores. *See Italia Societa per Azioni di Navigazione v. Oregon Stevedoring Co.*, 376 U.S. 315, 84 S.Ct. 748, 11 L.Ed.2d 732, 1964 AMC 1075 (1964); *Michalic v. Cleveland Tankers, Inc.* , 364 U.S. 325, 81 S.Ct. 6, 5 L.Ed.2d 20, 1960 AMC 2251 (1960); *Crumady v. The J.H. Fisser*, 358 U.S. 423, 79 S.Ct. 445, 3 L.Ed.2d 413, 1959 AMC 580 (1959). Cargo that is improperly packaged or improperly stowed may render a vessel unseaworthy. *See Gutierrez v. Waterman Steamship Corp.*, 373 U.S. 206, 83 S.Ct. 1185, 10 L.Ed.2d 297,1963 AMC 1649 (1963); *Atlantic & Gulf*

Stevedores, Inc. v. Ellerman Lines, 369 U.S. 355, 82 S.Ct. 780, 7 L.Ed.2d 798,1962 AMC 565 (1962); *Waterman Steamship Corp. v. Dugan & McNamara, Inc.*, 364 U.S. 421, 81 S.Ct. 200, 5 L.Ed.2d 169,1960 AMC 2260 (1960). Even the ship's stores and their wrapping can make the ship unseaworthy. *Martinez v. Sea-Land Services, Inc.*, 763 F.2d 26, 1986 AMC 851 (1st Cir. 1985). Finally, the crew of a vessel is warranted as seaworthy. *See Waldron v. Moore-McCormick Lines,* 386 U.S. 724, , 87 S.Ct. 1410, 18 L.Ed.2d 482, 1967 AMC 579 (1967); *Boudoin v. Lykes Brothers Steamship Co.*, 348 U.S. 336, 75 S.Ct. 382, 99 L.Ed. 354, 1955 AMC 488 (1955).

3. A ship may be unseaworthy if it does not have certain types of equipment, such as maps or lifesaving gear. However, the Supreme Court has held that a ship lacking a forced cargo ventilation system is not unseaworthy. *Morales v. City of Galveston,* 370 U.S. 165, 82 S.Ct. 1226, 8 L.Ed.2d 412, 1962 AMC 1450 (1962). The question whether a ship is unseaworthy is ordinarily one of fact. An instruction to the jury that a ship is unseaworthy as a matter of law may be reversible error. *See Dunlap v. G. & C. Towing, Inc.*, 613 F.2d 493, 1980 AMC 1874 (4th Cir. 1980).

4. A seaman employed by the bareboat charterer of a vessel may sue his employer under the Jones Act for negligence and the shipowner *in rem* for unseaworthiness. *See The Barnstable,* 181 U.S. 464 21 S.Ct. 684, 45 L.Ed. 954 (1901). According to *Baker v. Raymond International,* 656 F.2d 173, 1982 AMC 2752 (5th Cir. 1981), the seaman may also sue the shipowner *in personam* for unseaworthiness (subject to any ceiling established by the Limitation of Liability Act).

A. Application of the Doctrine

MITCHELL v. TRAWLER RACER, INC.

362 U.S. 539, 80 S. Ct. 926, 4 L. Ed. 2d 941, 1960 AMC 1503 (1960)

Mr. Justice STEWART delivered the opinion of the Court

The petitioner was a member of the crew of the Boston fishing trawler *Racer*, owned and operated by the respondent. On April 1, 1957, the vessel returned to her home port from a 10-day voyage to the North Atlantic fishing grounds, loaded with a catch of fish and fish spawn. After working that morning with his fellow crew members in unloading the spawn, the petitioner changed his clothes and came on deck to go ashore. He made his way to the side of the vessel which abutted the dock, and in accord with recognized custom stepped onto the ship's rail in order to reach a ladder attached to the pier. He was injured when his foot slipped off the rail as he grasped the ladder.

To recover for his injuries he filed this action for damages in a complaint containing three counts: the first under the Jones Act, alleging negligence; the second alleging unseaworthiness; and the third for maintenance and cure. At the trial there was evidence to show that the ship's rail where the petitioner had lost his footing was covered for a distance of 10 or 12 feet with slime and fish gurry, apparently remaining there from the earlier unloading operations.

The district judge instructed the jury that in order to allow recovery upon either the negligence or unseaworthiness count, they must find that the slime and gurry had been on the ship's rail for a period of time long enough for the respondent to have learned about it and to have removed it. Counsel for the petitioner requested that the trial judge distinguish between negligence and unseaworthiness in this respect, and specifically requested him to instruct the jury that notice was not a necessary element in proving liability based upon unseaworthiness of the vessel. This request was denied. The jury awarded the petitioner maintenance and cure, but found for the respondent shipowner on both the negligence and unseaworthiness counts.

An appeal was taken upon the sole ground that the district judge had been in error in instructing the jury that constructive notice was necessary to support liability for unseaworthiness. The Court of Appeals affirmed, holding that at least with respect to "an unseaworthy condition which arises only during the progress of the voyage," the shipowner's obligation "is merely to see that reasonable care is used under the circumstances... incident to the correction of the newly arisen defect." 265 F.2d 426, 432.

* * *

In its present posture this case thus presents the single issue whether with respect to so-called "transitory" unseaworthiness the shipowner's liability is limited by concepts of common-law negligence. There are here no problems, such as have recently engaged the Court's attention, with respect to the petitioner's status as a "seaman." The *Racer* was in active maritime operation, and the petitioner was a member of her crew.

* * *

The first reference in this Court to the shipowner's obligation to furnish a seaworthy ship as explicitly unrelated to the standard of ordinary care in a personal injury case appears in *Carlisle Packing Co. v. Sandanger*, 259 U.S. 255. There is was said "we think the trial court might have told the jury that without regard to negligence the vessel was unseaworthy when she left the dock ÿ and that if thus unseaworthy and one of the crew received damage as the direct result thereof, he was entitled to recover compensatory damages." 259 U.S. at 259. This characterization of unseaworthiness as unrelated to negligence was probably not necessary to the decision in that case, where the respondent's injuries had clearly in fact been caused by failure to exercise ordinary care (putting gasoline in a can labeled "coal oil" and neglecting to provide the vessel with life preservers). Yet there is no reason to suppose that the Court's language was inadvertent.

During the two decades that followed the *Carlisle* decision there came to be a general acceptance of the view that *The Osceaola* had enunciated a concept of absolute liability for unseaworthiness unrelated to principles of negligence law. Personal injury litigation based upon unseaworthiness was substantial. See, Gilmore and Black, The Law of Admiralty (1957), p. 316. And the standard texts accepted that theory of liability without question. *See* Benedict, The Law of American Admiralty (6th ed., 1940), Vol. I, § 83; Robinson, Admiralty Law (1939), p. 303 *et seq.* Perhaps the clearest expression appeared in Judge Augustus Hand's opinion in *The H.A. Scandrett*, 87 F.2d 708:

> In our opinion the libelant had a right of indemnity for injuries arising from an unseaworthy ship even though there was no means of anticipating trouble.
>
> The ship is not freed from liability by mere due diligence to render her seaworthy as may be the case under the Harter Act (46 U.S.C.A. §§ 190-195) where loss results from faults in navigation, but under the maritime law there is an absolute obligation to

> provide a seaworthy vessel and, in default thereof, liability follows for any injuries caused by breach of the obligation.

87 F.2d. at 711.

In 1944 this Court decided *Mahnich v. Southern S.S. Co.*, 321 U.S. 96. While it is possible to take a narrow view of the precise holding in that case, the fact is that *Mahnich* stands as a landmark in the development of admiralty law. Chief Justice Stone's opinion in that case gave an unqualified stamp of solid authority to the view that *The Osceola* was correctly to be understood as holding that the duty to provide a seaworthy ship depends not at all upon the negligence of the shipowner or his agents. Moreover, the dissent in *Mahnich* accepted this reading of *The Osceola* and claimed no more than that the injury in *Mahnich* was not properly attributable to unseaworthiness. See 321 U.S., at 105-113.

In *Seas Shipping Co. v. Sieracki*, 328 U.S. 85, the Court effectively scotched any doubts that might have lingered after *Mahnich* as to the nature of the shipowner's duty to provide a seaworthy vessel. The character of the duty, said the Court, is "absolute." "It is essentially a species of liability without fault, analogous to other well known instances in our law. Derived from and shaped to meet the hazards which performing the service imposes, the liability is neither limited by conceptions of negligence nor contractual in character ÿ . It is a form of absolute duty owing to all within the range of its humanitarian policy." 328 U.S., at 94-95. The dissenting opinion agreed as to the nature of the shipowner's duty. "[D]ue diligence of the owner," it said, "does not relieve him from this obligation." 328 U.S., at 104.

* * *

There is no suggestion in any of the decisions that the duty is less onerous with respect to an unseaworthy condition arising after the vessel leaves her home port, or that the duty is any less with respect to an unseaworthy condition which may be only temporary. Of particular relevance here is *Alaska Steamship Co. v. Petterson, supra.* In that case the Court affirmed a judgment holding the shipowner liable for injuries caused by defective equipment temporarily brought on board by an independent contractor over which the owner had no control. That decision is thus specific authority for the proposition that the shipowner's actual or constructive knowledge of the unseaworthy condition is not essential to his liability. That decision also effectively disposes of the suggestion that liability for a temporary unseaworthy condition is different from the liability that attaches when the condition is permanent.

There is ample room for argument, in the light of history, as to how the law of unseaworthiness should have or could have developed. Such theories might be made to fill a volume of logic. But, in view of the decisions in this Court over the last 15 years, we can find no room for argument as to what the law is. What has evolved is a complete divorcement of unseaworthiness liability from concepts of negligence. To hold otherwise now would be to erase more than just a page of history.

What has been said is not to suggest that the owner is obligated to furnish an accident-free ship. The duty is absolute, but it is a duty only to furnish a vessel and appurtenances reasonably fit for their intended use. The standard is not perfection, but reasonable fitness; not a ship that will weather every conceivable storm or withstand every imaginable peril of the sea, but a vessel reasonably suitable for her intended service. *Boudoin v. Lykes Bros. S.S. Co.*, 348 U.S. 336.

The judgment must be reversed, and the case remanded to the District Court for a new trial on the issue of unseaworthiness.

Reversed and remanded.

[Dissenting opinion of Justice FRANKFURTER, with whom Justices HARLAN and WITTAKER join, is omitted.]

USNER v. LUCKENBACH OVERSEAS CORP.

400 U.S. 494, 91 S. Ct. 514, 27 L. Ed. 2d 562, 1971 AMC 277 (1971)

Mr. Justice STEWART delivered the opinion of the Court

The petitioner, a longshoreman* employed by an independent stevedoring contractor, was injured while engaged with his fellow employees in loading cargo aboard the *S.S. Edgar F. Luckenbach*. He brought this action for damages against the respondents, the owner and the charterer of the ship, in a federal district court, alleging that his injuries had been caused by the ship's unseaworthiness.

In the course of pretrial proceedings the circumstances under which the petitioner had been injured were fully disclosed, and they are not in dispute. On the day in question the ship lay moored to a dock in New Orleans, Louisiana, receiving cargo from a barge positioned alongside. The loading operations were being performed by the petitioner and his fellow longshoremen under the direction of their employer. Some of the men were on the ship, operating the port winch and boom at the No. 2 hatch. The petitioner and others were on the barge, where their job was to "break out" the bundles of cargo by securing them to a sling attached to the fall each time it was lowered from the ship's boom by the winch operator. The loading operations had been proceeding in this manner for some time, until upon one occasion the winch operator did not lower the fall far enough. Finding the sling beyond his reach, the petitioner motioned to the flagman standing on the deck of the ship to direct the winch operator to lower the fall further. The winch operator then lowered the fall, but he lowered it too far and too fast. The sling struck the petitioner, knocking him to the deck of the barge and causing his injuries. Neither before nor after this occurrence was any difficulty experienced with the winch, boom, fall, sling, or any other equipment or appurtenance of the ship or her cargo.

---

* [At one time the warranty of seaworthiness had been extended to longshoremen engaged on loading and unloading a vessel. Congress eliminated this action in the 1972 amendments to the Longshoremen's and Harbor Worker's Compensation Act. However, decisions in cases involving longshoremen are still relevant to the law of unseaworthiness as applied to seamen. Eds.]

The respondents moved for summary judgment in the District Court, upon the ground that a single negligent act by a fellow longshoreman could not render the ship unseaworthy. The District Court denied the motion, but granted the respondents leave to take an interlocutory appeal under 28 U.S.C. § 1292(b). The United States Court of Appeals for the Fifth Circuit allowed the appeal and, reversing the District Court, directed that the respondents' motion for summary judgment be granted. 413 F.2d 984. It was the appellate court's view that "'[i]nstant unseaworthiness' resulting from 'operational negligence' of the stevedoring contractor is not a basis for recovery by an injured longshoreman." 413 F.2d, at 985-986. We granted certiorari, 397 U.S. 933, because of a conflict among the circuits on the basic issue presented.

The development in admiralty law of the doctrine of unseaworthiness as a predicate for a shipowner's liability for personal injuries or death has been fully chronicled elsewhere, and it would serve no useful purpose to repeat the details of that development here.

* * *

A major burden of the Court's decisions spelling out the nature and scope of the cause of action for unseaworthiness has been insistence upon the point that it is a remedy separate from, independent of, and additional to other claims against the shipowner, whether created by statute or under general maritime law. More specifically, the Court has repeatedly taken pains to point out that liability based upon unseaworthiness is wholly distinct from liability based upon negligence. The reason, of course, is that unseaworthiness is a *condition*, and how that condition came into being—whether by negligence or otherwise—is quite irrelevant to the owner's liability for personal injuries resulting from it.

We had occasion to emphasize this basic distinction again in *Mitchell v. Trawler Racer*, 362 U.S. 539. There the unseaworthy condition causing the plaintiff's injury was a ship's rail made slippery by the presence of fish gurry and slime.

* * *

Trawler Racer involved the defective condition of a physical part of the ship itself. But our cases have held that the scope of unseaworthiness is by no means so limited. A vessel's condition of unseaworthiness might arise from any number of circumstances. Her gear might be defective, her appurtenances in disrepair, her crew unfit. The number of men assigned to perform a shipboard task might be insufficient. The method of loading her cargo, or the manner of its stowage, might be improper. For any of these reasons, or others, a vessel might not be reasonably fit for her intended service.

What caused the petitioner's injuries in the present case, however, was not the condition of the ship, her appurtenances, her cargo, or her crew, but the isolated, personal negligent act of the petitioner's fellow longshoreman. To hold that this individual act of negligence rendered the ship unseaworthy would be to subvert the fundamental distinction between unseaworthiness and negligence that we have so painstakingly and repeatedly emphasized in our decisions. In *Trawler Racer, supra*, there existed a condition of unseaworthiness, and we held it was error to require a finding of negligent conduct in order to hold the shipowner liable. The case before us presents the other side of the same coin. For it would be equally erroneous here, where no condition of unseaworthiness existed, to hold the shipowner liable for a third party's single and wholly unforeseeable act of negligence. The judgment of the court of Appeals is affirmed.

It is so ordered.

[Dissenting opinion of Justice DOUGLAS, with whom Justice BLACK and Justice BRENNAN concur, is omitted.]

B. Damages: Comparative Fault

Note

In *Lewis v. Timco, Inc.*, 716 F.2d 1425, 1984 AMC 191 (5th Cir. 1983) (en banc), Alfred Lewis, a worker aboard a drilling barge, was injured by a design defect in hydraulic tongs used to "make up" tubing joints to be placed in a well. The tongs were manufactured by Joy Manufacturing, Inc. The trial court found that the liability in this action should be apportioned as follows: 50% to Lewis, 20% to Joy Manufacturing, and 20% and 10% to Rebel Rentals and Edwards Rentals (companies which had supplied the tongs and/or instructed Lewis on the use of the tongs).

The main issue presented was whether the doctrine of comparative fault applies in a products liability suit under maritime jurisdiction. The court held that it did. Recognizing that the majority of state and federal courts have held comparative liability applicable to strict liability cases, the court concluded that the same result was appropriate for maritime cases. The court was further persuaded by the fact that comparative liability had long been accepted in other actions under maritime jurisdiction such as in unseaworthiness, the Jones Act, DOHSA and LHWCA. In short, the court concluded that "general considerations of fairness and efficiency support a comparative fault defense in products liability actions. In maritime suits, these considerations are bolstered by the historical reliance on comparative fault as integral to an essentially uniform and unitary body of law."

Judge Politz, joined by Judges Johnson and Williams, dissented. He argued that Lewis' award should not be reduced based simply on his own negligence in operation of the faulty product. Instead reductions in an award of damages should have been based on an assessment of causation, such as how much Lewis contributed to the cause of the accident rather than how blameworthy he was.

In *Lewis v. Timco, Inc.*, 736 F.2d 163, 1984 AMC 1185 (5th Cir. 1984), the original Fifth Circuit panel, on remand, faced the issue of whether the trial court had acted clearly erroneously in its determination that Lewis was 50% at fault in the accident. The court held that the district court's findings were clearly erroneous and "involve[d] an erroneous application of law." Thus, the court held as a matter of law that Lewis was not guilty of any negligence and, therefore, no reduction in quantum damages was necessary.

Section II. Longshoremen and Harbor Workers: Cases and Notes

Introductory Note

The notion of "maritime employment" applies to seamen, members of the crew of a vessel, and to a great number of land based workers usually designated as longshoremen and harbor workers. Work is "maritime" when it relates to the shipping industry or when it is done in the hazardous zone over or adjacent to navigable waters. Seamen, *i.e.*, members of the crew of a vessel, have the remedies of maintenance and cure, a Jones Act claim, and a claim for unseaworthiness. Maritime workers other than seamen have remedies under state and federal workers' compensation statutes and, in certain circumstances, actions for negligence. For a proper understanding of the remedies available to such maritime workers against their employers and third persons a historical introduction is necessary.

The movement to provide a system of guaranteed compensation to workers injured in the course of their employment began in the United States in the early twentieth century. Proponents of this legislation concentrated their efforts at the state level, but most legislative bodies proceeded cautiously for fear that workmen's compensation laws might infringe on the due process clause of the federal Constitution. In 1917, the Supreme Court dispelled such apprehensions by upholding the constitutionality of the workmen's compensation laws of New York, Iowa, and Washington. *New York Central Railroad v. White*, 243 U.S. 188, 37 S.Ct. 247, 61 L.Ed. 667 (1917). However, in the companion case of *Southern Pacific Co. v. Jensen*, 244 U.S. 205, 37 S.Ct. 524, 61 L.Ed. 1086, 1996 A.M.C. 2076 (1917), which arose under the New York transit workers' compensation statute, Justice McReynolds declared for the majority that the statute could not constitutionally be applied to a longshoreman who was fatally injured on the gangway of a ship while assisting in unloading operations. He reasoned that the matter was within the admiralty jurisdiction of the United States because the deceased was doing maritime work under a maritime contract and was injured on navigable waters; that the constitutional grant of admiralty jurisdiction contemplates a uniform system of maritime laws; that the power to modify the existing maritime laws is necessarily vested in the Congress; that the inaction of Congress demonstrates an intent to preserve the status quo; and that the saving to suitors clause in the Judiciary Act does not apply to workmen's compensation laws because the remedies under these laws are wholly unknown to the common law. He concluded:

> If New York can subject foreign ships coming into her ports to such obligations as those imposed by her Compensation Statute, other States may do likewise. The necessary consequence would be destruction of the very uniformity in respect to maritime matters which the Constitution was designed to establish; and freedom of navigation between the States and with foreign countries would be seriously hampered and impeded. A far more serious injury would result to commerce than could have been inflicted by the Washington statute authorizing a materialman's lien condemned in *The Roanoke*. The legislature exceeded its authority in attempting to extend the statute under consideration to conditions like those here disclosed. So applied, it conflicts with the Constitution and to that extent is invalid.

Justice Holmes filed a celebrated dissenting opinion:

> The Southern Pacific Company has been held liable under the statutes of New York for an accidental injury happening upon a gang-plank between a pier and the company's vessel and causing the death of one of its employees. The company not having insured as permitted, the statute may be taken as if it simply imposed a limited but absolute liability in such a case. The short question is whether the power of the State to regulate the liability in that place and to enforce it in the State's own courts is taken away by the conferring of exclusive jurisdiction of all civil causes of admiralty and maritime jurisdiction upon the courts of the United States.
>
> There is no doubt that saving to suitors of the right of a common-law remedy leaves open the common-law jurisdiction of the state courts, and leaves some power of legislation at least, to the States.
>
> The statute having been upheld in other respects, *New York Central R. R. Co. v. White*, 243 U.S. 188, I should have thought these authorities conclusive. The liability created by the New York act ends in a money judgment, and the mode in which the amount is ascertained, or is to be paid, being one that the State constitutionally might adopt, cannot matter to the question before us if any liability can be imposed that was not known to the maritime law.
>
> The common law is not a brooding omnipresence in the sky but the articulate voice of some sovereign or quasi-sovereign that can be identified; although some decisions with which I have disagreed seem to me to have forgotten the fact. It always is the law of some State, and if the District Courts adopt the common law of torts, as they have shown a tendency to do, they thereby assume that a law not of maritime origin and deriving its authority in that territory only from some particular State of this Union also governs maritime torts in that

> territory–and if the common law, the statute law has at least equal force, as the discussion in *The Osceola* assumes. On the other hand the refusal of the District Courts to give remedies coextensive with the common law would prove no more than that they regarded their jurisdiction as limited by the ancient lines–not that they doubted that the common law might and would be enforced in the courts of the States as it always has been. This court has recognized that in some cases different principles of liability would be applied as the suit would happen to be brought in a common-law or admiralty court. Compare *The Max Morris*, 137 U.S. 1, with *Belden v. Chase*, 150 U.S. 674, 691. But hitherto it has not been doubted authoritatively, so far as I know, that even when the admiralty had a rule of its own to which it adhered, as in *Workman v. New York City*, 179 U.S. 552, the state law, common or statute, would prevail in the courts of the State. Happily such conflicts are few.
>
> It might be asked why, if the grant of jurisdiction to the courts of the United States imports a power in Congress to legislate, the saving of a common-law remedy, *i.e.*, in the state courts, did not import a like if subordinate power in the States. But leaving that question on one side, such cases as *Steamboat Co. v. Chase*, 16 Wall. 522. *The Hamilton*, 207 U.S. 398, and *Atlantic Transport Co. v. Imbrovek*, 234 U.S. 52, show that it is too late to say that the mere silence of Congress excludes the statute or common law of a State from supplementing the wholly inadequate maritime law of the time of the Constitution, in the regulation of personal rights, and I venture to say that it never has been supposed to do so, or had any such effect.

The *Jensen* decision meant that a longshoreman injured on navigable waters was denied a no-fault remedy against his employer; of course, he could have an action for negligence, but this would be subject to the defenses of assumption of risk and the fellow-servant doctrine. Contributory negligence would not bar recovery, but would result in mitigation of damages. Congress sought to make state no-fault remedies available to longshoremen and harbor workers by a 1917 amendment to the saving suitors clause in the Judiciary Act. The Supreme Court, however, struck down the amendment in *Knickerbocker Ice Co. v. Stewart*, 253 U.S. 149 40 S.Ct. 438, 64 L.Ed. 834 (1920), on the ground that Congress cannot delegate legislative authority to the states in matters falling within the admiralty jurisdiction of the United States.

Subsequently, in *Western Fuel Co. v. Garcia*, 257 U.S. 233, 42 S.Ct. 89, 66 L.Ed. 210 (1921), the Court held that the California wrongful death statute could be applied to a suit seeking damages for the death of a longshoreman on navigable waters because the subject of the litigation was "maritime but local." Further in *Grant Smith-Portership Co. v. Rhode*, 257 U.S. 469, 42 S.Ct. 157, 66 L.Ed. 321 (1922), the Court held that an action in admiralty for damages brought by a carpenter against his employer on account of injuries sustained on a partially completed ship lying in navigable waters was barred by the Oregon workmen's compensation statute. This statute could be constitutionally applied because the matter was "maritime but local" and the application of state law did not derogate from the uniformity of the maritime workers other than masters and members of the crew of a vessel. In 1922, Congress once again amended the saving to suitors clause to put longshoremen under state workmen's compensation statutes, but exempting the master and the crew of any vessel. The Congressional intent was to preserve the uniformity of maritime law as to seamen and permit the application of state statutes to other maritime workers. The Supreme Court struck down this amendment in *Washington v. Dawson & Co.*, 264 U.S. 219, 44 S.Ct. 302, 68 L.Ed. 646 (1924) as an unconstitutional delegation of power to the states. In the course of its opinion, the Court indicated that the appropriate solution would be the enactment of a workmen's compensation statute by Congress.

In 1926, the legal status of longshoremen and harbor workers was improved by their recognition as "seamen" within the meaning of the Jones Act if they were injured on navigable waters while doing work traditionally done by seamen. *International Stevedoring Co. v. Haverty*, 272 U.S. 50, 47 S.Ct. 19, 71 L.Ed. 157, 1926 AMC 1638 (1926). This decision, however, was soon superseded by the Longshoremen's anc Harbor Workers' Compensation Act of 1927, enacted by Congress.

A. Territorial Application of the Longshore and Harbor Workers' Compensation Act (LHWCA): Relationship with State Compensation Acts

Background Note

Section 903 (a) of the LHWCA originally provided:

> Compensation shall be payable under this chapter in respect of disability or death of an employee, but only if the disability or death results from an injury occurring upon the navigable waters of the United States (including any dry dock) and if recovery for the disability or death through workmen's compensation proceedings may not validly be provided by State law...

Compensation was thought to be limited to injuries occurring on navigable waters, and the limitation concerning recovery through state workmen's compensation proceedings was thought to be a reference to the "maritime but local" rule that decisions of the Supreme Court had established. If the matter was maritime but local, state statutes could constitutionally apply and there was no need for a federal remedy. As a result of these limitations, if a remedy could be provided by state law for injuries occurring on navigable waters, a claim for compensation under the LHWCA would be dismissed under the act; conversely, if a remedy could not validly be provided by state law, a claim for compensation under state law would be dismissed under that law.

In this form, the legislation proved difficult to apply. Many workers fell into what became known as the "twilight zone" between federal and state systems, where it was not clear which system governed until there had been some judicial determination of the question. In *Davis v. Department of Labor & Industries*, 317 U.S. 249, 63 S. Ct. 225, 87 L. Ed. 246, 1942 AMC 1653 (1942), the Court said:

> Since 1917, Congress and the states have sought to restore order out of the confusion which resulted from the *Jensen* decision. That success has not finally been achieved is illustrated by the present case. The Longshoremen's Act, passed with specific reference to the *Jensen* rule, provided a partial solution. The Washington statute represents a state effort to clarify the situation. Both of these laws show clearly that neither was intended to encroach on the field occupied by the other. But the line separating the scope of the two being undefined and undefinable with exact precision, marginal employment may, by reason of particular facts, fall on either side.
>
> > There is, in the light of the cases referred to, clearly a twilight zone in which the employees must have their rights determined case by case, and in which particular facts and circumstances are vital elements. That zone includes persons such as the decedent who are, as a matter of actual administration, in fact protected under the state compensation act.

317 U.S. 249, 256 (1942).

Notes

1. ***Injuries on the Pier***

In *Nacirema Operating Company v. Johnson*, 396 U.S. 212, 90 S. Ct. 347, 24 L. Ed. 2d 1971 (1969), the United States Supreme Court held as a matter of statutory construction that injuries to longshoremen occurring on piers permanently affixed to shore were not compensable under LHWCA. Therefore, state law only applied landward of the *Jensen* line. However, the *Johnson* case was legislatively overruled by the 1972 Amendment to Section 3(a) of LHWCA.

A question has arisen as to the existence of admiralty jurisdiction when longshoremen sustain injuries on the pier on account of the fault of a person other than their land-based employer. LHWCA coverage is broader than the current view of United Stated courts concerning the reach of admiralty jurisdiction under 28 U.S.C. § 1333. *See Parker v. South Louisiana Contractors, Inc.*, 537 F.2d 113, 1976 AMC 2201 (5th Cir. 1976); Note, *infra.*

2. *Injuries on the High Seas*

The LHWCA applies to the high seas since § 39 of the LHWCA calls for compensation districts for injuries sustained on the high seas, and because U.S. navigable waters includes the high seas. *Kollias v. D & G Marine Maintenance*, 29 F.3d 67, 1995 AMC 609 (2d Cir. 1994).

LONGSHORE AND HARBOR WORKERS' COMPENSATION ACT: AMENDMENTS EXPANDING SITUS

33 U.S.C. § 903 (a) (1972 Amendment)

(a) Compensation shall be payable under this chapter in respect of disability or death of an employee, but only if the disability or death results from an injury occurring upon the navigable waters of the United States (including any adjoining pier, wharf, dry dock, terminal, building way, marine railway, or other adjoining area customarily used by an employer in loading, unloading, repairing, or building a vessel).

SUN SHIP, INC. v. PENNSYLVANIA

447 U.S. 715, 100 S. Ct. 2432, 65 L. Ed. 2d 458, 1980 AMC 1930 (1980)

Mr. Justice BRENNAN delivered the opinion of the Court

The single question presented by these consolidated cases is whether a State may apply its workers' compensation scheme to land-based injuries that fall within the coverage of the Longshoremen's and Harbor Workers' Compensation Act (LHWCA), as amended in 1972. 33 U.S.C. §§ 901-950. We hold that it may.

Appellees are five employees of appellant Sun Ship, Inc., a shipbuilding and ship repair enterprise located on the Delaware River, a navigable water of the United States in Pennsylvania. Each employee was injured after the effective date of the 1972 amendments to the LHWCA while involved in shipbuilding or ship repair activities. Although the LHWCA applied to the injuries sustained, each appellee filed claims for benefits under the Pennsylvania Workmen's Compensation Act with state authorities. Appellant contended that the federal compensation statute was the employee's exclusive remedy. In upholding awards to each respondent, the Pennsylvania Workmen's Compensation Appeal Board ruled that the LHWCA did not pre-empt state compensation laws. The Commonwealth Court affirmed, and the Supreme Court of Pennsylvania denied petitions for allowance of appeal.

* * *

Before 1972, ... marine-related injuries fell within one of three jurisdictional spheres as they moved landward. At the furthest extreme, *Jensen* commanded that nonlocal maritime injuries fall under the LHWCA. "Maritime but local" injuries "upon the navigable waters of the United States," 33 U.S.C. § 903(a), could be compensated under the LHWCA or under state law. And injuries suffered beyond navigable waters—albeit within the range of federal admiralty jurisdiction—were remediable only under state law.

* * *

The language of the 1972 amendments cannot fairly be understood as pre-empting state workers' remedies from the field of the LHWCA, and thereby resurrecting the jurisdictional monstrosity that existed before the clarifying opinions in *Davis* and *Calbeck*. Appellant focuses our attention upon the deletion from amended § 903 (a) of the phrase: "[if] recovery ... through workmen's compensation proceedings may not validly be provided by State law." But, if anything, that change reinforces our previous interpretation of that section as contemplating concurrent jurisdiction. *Calbeck, supra* 370 U.S., at 126. For it was that reference to state law which provided the strongest (although ultimately unsuccessful) argument for reading the pre-1972 § 903 (a) as an exclusive jurisdictional provision. *Calbeck, supra,* at 132 (STEWART, J., dissenting). Whether Congress accepted *Calbeck's* view that the state-law clause was *consonant* with concurrent jurisdiction, or the dissenters' construction of the clause as *inconsistent* with concurrent jurisdiction, the deletion of that language in 1972—if it indicates anything—may logically only imply acquiescence in *Calbeck's* conclusion that the LHWCA operates within the same ambit as state workers' remedies.[2] It would be a *tour de force* of statutory misinterpretation to treat the *removal* of phrasing that arguably establishes exclusive jurisdiction as manifesting the intent to command such exclusivity.

Nor does the legislative history suggest a congressional decision to exclude state laws from the terrain newly occupied by the post-1972 Longshoremen's Act. Appellant can draw little support from general expressions of intent to alleviate unjust disparities in recovery conditioned upon the location of marine laborers at the time of an accident; as Part IV, *infra*, demonstrates, concurrency of jurisdiction in no way undercuts that commendable policy. And appellant is not much assisted by fixing upon the sentence in the bill Reports that declares:

> It is apparent that if the Federal benefit structure embodied in Committee bill is enacted, there would be a substantial disparity in benefits payable to a permanently disabled longshoreman, depending on which side of the water's edge the accident occurred, *if State laws are permitted to continue to apply to injuries occurring on land.*

S. Rep. No. 1125 92d Cong., 2d Sess., 13 (1972); H.R. Rep. No. 1441, 92d Cong., 2d Sess. 10 (1972), U.S. Code Cong. & Admin.News 1972, pp. 4698, 4707 (emphasis added).

---

[2] If Congress joined in *Calbeck's* understanding that the phrase underscored the LHWCA's application where state law compensability had been drawn into question by *Jensen*, then the striking of the language may be explained on the ground of its superfluity once Congress had pushed the federal Act landward beyond the *Jensen* line. If the Court took the dissenters' position that the state law clause imposed jurisdictional exclusivity, then its deletion indicates repeal of any such exclusivity. Finally, Congress may simply have endeavored to reaffirm the correctness of the existing law.

That statement likely means only that state laws should not be permitted to apply *exclusively* to injuries occurring upon land; the "substantial disparity in benefits" that troubled Congress is eliminated once federal law provides a concurrent or supplementary route to compensation. And, in any event, as Professors Gilmore and Black have noted, "the statement does not appear to be entitled to much weight," since the "p+art of the Committee Report which is devoted to the shoreward extension of [LHWCA] coverage does not so much as mention the pre-1972 case law on 'maritime but local' and the 'twilight zone.'... G. GILMORE & C. BLACK, THE LAW OF ADMIRALTY 425 (2d ed. 1975) (hereafter GILMORE & BLACK). In particular, there is no intimation of intent to overrule *Davis* and *Calbeck*—a significant omission in light of the care which the Reports elsewhere take in identifying the Supreme Court cases to be overturned by the abolition of longshoremen's actions for unseaworthiness. *See* S. REP. No. 92-1125, *supra*, at 8-12; H.R. Rep. No. 92-1441, *supra*, at 4-8; GILMORE & BLACK 425.

We therefore find no sign in the 1972 amendments to the LHWCA that Congress wished to alter the accepted understanding that federal jurisdiction would coexist with state compensation laws in that field in which the latter may constitutionally operate under the *Jensen* doctrine.

Appellant vigorously contends, nevertheless, that jurisdictional exclusivity is—in "fact" or in "law"—implied in the LHWCA. Pointing to declarations of congressional policy to eliminate disparities in compensation to marine workers depending on whether they were injured on land or over water, S. Rep. No. 92-1125, *supra*, at 12-13; H. R. Rep. No. 92-1441, *supra*, at 10-11, appellant urges that concurrent remedial jurisdiction on land would defeat the uniformity principle underlying the statute.

As the Reports make clear, the disparities which Congress had in view in amending the LHWCA lay primarily in the paucity of relief under state compensation laws. The thrust of the amendments was to "upgrade the benefits." S. Rep. No. 92-1125, *supra*, at 1; *see Northeast Marine Terminal Co. v. Caputo*, 432 U.S. 249, 261-262 (1977). Concurrent jurisdiction for state and federal compensation laws is in no way inconsistent with this policy of raising awards to a federal minimum. When laborers file claims under the LHWCA, they are compensated under federal standards. And workers who commence their actions under state law will generally be able to make up the difference between state and federal benefit levels by seeking relief under the Longshoremen's Act, if the latter applies.[6]

To be sure, if state remedial schemes are more generous than federal law, concurrent jurisdiction could result in more favorable awards for workers' injuries than under an exclu-

---

[6] Most often, state workmen's compensation laws will not be treated as making awards thereunder final or conclusive. *See Calbeck v. Travelers Insurance Co., supra*, at 131-132; *Industrial Comm'n v. McCartin*, 330 U.S. 622 (1947); GILMORE & BLACK, *supra*, at 431-433; 4 A. Larson, Law of Workmen's Compensation §§ 85.20, 89.53(a) and (b) (1979); Larson, *The Conflict of Laws Problem Between the Longshoremen's Act and State Workmen's Compensation Acts*, 45 S. CAL. L. REV. 699, 729-730 (1972). Admittedly, if a particular state compensation law provision does indisputably declare its awards final, a conflict with the LHWCA may possibly arise where a claimant seeks inferior state benefits in the first instance. But the consequences to the claimant of this error would be less drastic than those of a mistake under the rule appellant contemplates—under which a misstep could result in no benefits. At any rate, although the question is not directly before us, we observe that if federal preclusion ever need be implied to cope with this remote contingency, a less disruptive approach would be to pre-empt the state compensation exclusivity clause, rather than to pre-empt the entire state compensation statute as appellant suggests.

sively federal compensation system. But we find no evidence that Congress was concerned about a disparity between adequate federal benefits and *superior* state benefits....

Finally, we are not persuaded that the bare fact that the federal and state compensation systems are different gives rise to a conflict that, from the employer's standpoint, necessitates exclusivity for each compensation system within a separate sphere. Mandating exclusive jurisdiction will not relieve employers of their distinct obligations under state and federal compensation law. The line that circumscribes the jurisdictional compass of the LHWCA—a compound of "status" and "situs"—is no less vague than its counterpart in the pre-"twilight zone" *Jensen* era. Thus, even were the LHWCA exclusive within its field, many employers would be compelled to abide by state-imposed responsibilities lest a claim fall beyond the scope of the LHWCA....

Of one thing we may be certain. The exclusivity rule which appellant urges upon us would thrust employees into the same jurisdictional peril from which they were rescued by *Davis* and *Calbeck v. Travelers Insurance Co. See* GILMORE & BLACK, *supra*, at 425. The legislative policy animating the LHWCA's landward shift was remedial; the amendments' framers acted out of solicitude for the workers. *See P. C. Pfeiffer Co., supra*, at 74-75; *Northeast Marine Terminal Co.*, 432 U.S., at 268. To adopt appellant's position, then, would blunt the thrust of the 1972 amendments, and frustrate Congress' intent to aid injured maritime laborers. We decline to do so in the name of "uniformity."

Accordingly, we affirm.

Note: Mutual Exclusivity of the LHWCA and the Jones Act

The LHWCA and the Jones Act are mutually exclusive. State workers' compensation acts do not apply to seamen because of the *Jensen* doctrine. *See Knickerbocker Ice Co. v. Stewart*, 253 U.S. 149 (1920); *Bearden v. Leon C. Breaux Towing Co.*, 365 So. 2d 1192 (La. App. 3d Cir. 1978). However, there is authority for the proposition that state compensation schemes may operate concurrently with the Jones Act; that is, there is a "twilight zone" in which either remedy may be available. *See Maryland Cas. Co. v. Toups*, 172 F.2d 542, 1949 AMC 994 (5th Cir. 1949). According to 33 U.S.C. § 903(a)(1), the LHWCA does not apply to "a master or member of the crew of any vessel." *See also id.* § 902(3); *Mcdermott, Inc. v. Boudreaux*, 679 F.2d 452 (5th Cir. 1982). Conversely, the Jones Act does not apply to longshoremen or harborworkers covered by the LHWCA. Thus, a master or member of the crew of a vessel is not entitled to benefits under the LHWCA, and a longshoreman or harborworker may not sue his employer for recovery under the Jones Act (or for maintenance and cure under the general maritime law).

Despite the mutual exclusivity of the LHWCA and the Jones Act, courts have recognized the existence of a "twilight zone," or area of uncertainty in which either statute may apply. *See McDermott, Inc. v. Boudreaux*, 679 F.2d 452, 459 (5th Cir. 1982):

> [W]e, realize that, in a practical sense, a "zone of uncertainty" inevitably connects the two Acts. Confronted by conflicting evidence concerning a worker's duties or undisputed evidence concerning an occupation that exhibits the characteristics of both traditional land and sea duties, a factfinder might be able to draw reasonable inferences to justify coverage under *either* statute.
>
> *Abshire* offers a classic instance of the case that could have gone either way. Plaintiff produced evidence that he was a marine welder and mechanic permanently assigned to a fleet of fishing vessels and spent most of his time performing repairs aboard the employer's boats; defendant produced evidence that plaintiff was a shore-based maintenance employee who never went to sea and whose only contact with vessels under way "was

in testing them in connection with repairs and maintenance." *Id.* at 836. The district court properly submitted the issue to a jury, which found that the welder/mechanic was entitled to damages as a Jones Act seaman. Although we affirmed the judgment, we just as easily could have approved a jury's finding that *Abshire* was restricted to compensation under the Longshoremen's Act. Incidentally, the judgment for Abshire under the Jones Act also ordered repayment of two insurers that already had compensated him under the Longshoremen's Act.

Note: State workers' compensation schemes

State workers' compensation acts do not apply to seamen because of the *Jensen* doctrine. *See Knickerbocker Ice Co. v. Stewart*, 253 U.S. 149, 40 S.Ct. 438, 64 L.Ed. 834 (1920); *Bearden v. Leon C. Breaux Towing Co.*, 365 So. 2d 1192 (La. App. 3d Cir. 1978). However, there is authority for the proposition that state compensation schemes may operate concurrently with the Jones Act; that is, there is a "twilight zone" in which either remedy may be available. *See Maryland Cas. Co. v. Toups*, 172 F.2d 542, 1949 AMC 994 (5th Cir. 1949); *Haire v. Devcon Int'l Corp.*, 668 So.2d 775 (Ala. Ct. App. 1995). Conversely, there is a considerable body of authority in state and federal courts to the effect that there is no "twilight zone", and that Jones Act seamen are not entitled to state workers' compensation remedies even if their work is "maritime but local". *Benders v. Board of Governors*, 636 A.2d 1313 (R.I. 1994); *Indiana & Michigan Electric Co. v. Workers' Comp. Comm'r*, 403 S.E.2d 416 (W.Va. 1991); *Bearden v. Leon C. Breaux Towing Co.*, 365 So. 2d 1192 (La. App. 3d Cir. 1978); *Green v. Industrial Com'n*, 717 N.E.2d 457 (Ill. App. 3 Dist. 1999).

SOUTHWEST MARINE, INC. v. GIZONI

502 U.S. 81, 112 S. Ct. 486; 116 L. Ed. 2d 405; 1992 AMC 305 (1991)

Justice WHITE delivered the opinion of the Court

The question presented is whether a maritime worker whose occupation is one of those enumerated in the Longshore and Harbor Workers' Compensation Act (LHWCA), 44 Stat. 1424, as amended, 33 U.S.C. § 901 *et seq.*, may yet be a "seaman" within the meaning of the Jones Act, 46 U.S.C. App. § 688, and thus be entitled to bring suit under that statute.

I

Petitioner Southwest Marine, Inc., operates a ship repair facility in San Diego, California. In connection with its ship repair activities, Southwest Marine owns several floating platforms, including a pontoon barge, two float barges, a rail barge, a diver's barge, and a crane barge. These platforms by themselves have no power, means of steering, navigation lights, navigation aids, or living facilities. They are moved about by tugboats, which position the platforms alongside vessels under repair at berths or in drydock at Southwest Marine's shipyard or at the nearby Naval Station. The platforms are used to move equipment, materials, supplies, and vessel components around the shipyard and on to and off of the vessels under repair. Once in place, the platforms support ship repairmen engaged in their work.

Southwest Marine employed respondent Byron Gizoni as a rigging foreman. Gizoni worked on the floating platforms and rode them as they were towed into place. Gizoni occasionally served as a lookout and gave maneuvering signals to the tugboat operator when the platforms were moved. He also received lines passed to the platforms by the ships' crews to secure the platforms to the vessels under repair. Gizoni suffered disabling leg and back injuries in a fall when his foot broke through a thin wooden sheet covering a hole in the deck of a platform being used to transport a rudder from the shipyard to a floating drydock.

Gizoni submitted a claim for, and received, medical and compensation benefits from Southwest Marine pursuant to the LHWCA. He later sued Southwest Marine under the Jones Act in the United States District Court for the Southern District of California, alleging that he was a seaman injured as a result of his employer's negligence. Gizoni also pleaded causes of action for unseaworthiness and for maintenance and cure. App. IV-4, IV-5. In addition to the above facts, Gizoni alleged in his complaint that Southwest Marine's floating platforms were "a group of vessels ... in navigable waters," and that as a rigging foreman, he was "permanently assigned to said group of vessels." *Id.*, at IV-3.

The District Court granted Southwest Marine's motion for summary judgment on two grounds. The District Court determined as a matter of law that Gizoni was not a Jones Act seaman, finding that Southwest Marine's floating platforms were not "vessels in navigation," and that Gizoni was on board to perform work as a ship repairman, not to "aid in navigation." App. to Pet. for Cert. I-1, I-2. More important to our purposes here, the District Court further concluded that Gizoni was a harbor worker precluded from bringing his action by the exclusive remedy provisions of the LHWCA, 33 U.S.C. § 905(a). App. to Pet. for Cert I-2.

The United States Court of Appeals for the Ninth Circuit reversed the determination that Gizoni was not a seaman as a matter of law, 909 F.2d 385, 387 (1990), holding that questions of fact existed as to seaman status, *e.g.*, whether the floating platforms were vessels in navigation, whether Gizoni's relationship to those platforms was permanent, and whether he aided in their navigation. *Id.*, at 388. The Ninth Circuit also reversed the District Court's determination that the exclusive remedy provisions of the LHWCA precluded Gizoni from pursuing his Jones Act claim. The court concluded that the LHWCA by its terms does not cover "a master or member of a crew of any vessel," 33 U.S.C. § 902(3)(G), that this phrase is the equivalent of "seaman" under the Jones Act, and that the question of his seaman status should have been presented to a jury. 909 F.2d at 389. The Ninth Circuit thus rejected the notion that any employee whose work involved ship repair was necessarily restricted to remedy under the LHWCA, reasoning that coverage under the Jones Act or the LHWCA depended not on the claimant's job title, but on the nature of the claimant's work and the intent of Congress in enacting these statutes. *Ibid.*

We granted certiorari, 498 U.S. — (1991), to resolve the conflict among the Circuits on this issue.[1] We now affirm the judgment of the Ninth Circuit.

---

[1] The Ninth Circuit in this case followed a decision by the Sixth Circuit, which held that "[a] plaintiff is not limited to the remedies available under the LHWCA unless he is unable to show that a genuine factual issue exists as to whether he was a seaman at the time of his injury." *Petersen v. Chesapeake & Ohio R. Co.*, 784 F.2d 732, 739 (1986). To the contrary, the Fifth Circuit has previously held that because longshoremen, shipbuilders and ship repairers are engaged in occupations enumerated in the LHWCA, they are unqualifiedly covered by that Act if they meet the Act's situs requirements; coverage of these workmen by the LHWCA renders them ineligible for consideration as seamen or members of the crew of a vessel entitled to claim the benefits of the Jones Act." *Pizzitolo v. Electro-Coal Transfer Corp.*, 812 F.2d 977, 9883 (1987). A later decision by the Fifth Circuit undercut much of the reasoning in Pizzitolo by limiting it to cases where "the evidence is insufficient to warrant a finding of seaman's status." *Legros v. Panther Services Group, Inc.*, 863 F.2d 345, 349 (1988). The Fifth Circuit granted rehearing en banc, but the parties later settled and the appeal was dismissed. *Legros v. Panther Services Group, Inc.*, 874 F.2d 953 (1989). With the opinion in *Legros* vacated, *Pizzitolo* remains the law in the Fifth Circuit, although its breadth may be in some question.

II

The Jones Act and the LHWCA each provide a remedy to the injured maritime worker; however, each specifies different maritime workers to be within its reach. In relevant part, the Jones Act provides that "any seaman who shall suffer personal injury in the course of his employment may, at his election, maintain an action for damages at law, with the right of trial by jury, and in such action all statutes of the United States modifying or extending the common-law right or remedy in cases of personal injury to railway employees shall apply ... ." 46 U.S.C. App. § 688(a). Under the LHWCA, the exclusiveness of liability provision in part states that the liability of an employer "shall be exclusive and in place of all other liability of such employer to the employee ... ." 33 U.S.C. § 905(a). However, the term "employee", as defined in the LHWCA does not include "a master or member of a crew of any vessel." 33 U.S.C. § 902(3)(G). The District Court was therefore plainly wrong in holding that, as a matter of law, the LHWCA provided the exclusive remedy for all harbor workers. That cannot be the case if the LHWCA and its exclusionary provision do not apply to a harbor worker who is also a "member of a crew of any vessel," a phrase that is a "refinement" of the term "seaman" in the Jones Act. *McDermott Int'l, Inc. v. Wilander*, 498 U.S. ___, ___ (1991).[3]

The determination of who is a "member of a crew" is "better characterized as a mixed question of law and fact," rather than as a pure question of fact. *Id.*, at ___. Even so, "the inquiry into seaman status is of necessity fact-specific; it will depend on the nature of the vessel, and the employee's precise relation to it." *Ibid.* Our decision in *Wilander* jettisoned any lingering notion that a maritime worker need aid in the navigation of a vessel in order to qualify as a "seaman" under the Jones Act. "The key to seaman status is employment-related connection to a vessel in navigation.... It is not necessary that a seaman aid in navigation or contribute to the transportation of the vessel, but a seaman must be doing the ship's work." *Id.*, at ___. In arriving at this conclusion, we again recognized that "the Jones Act and the LHWCA are mutually exclusive," *id.*, at ___ (*citing Swanson v. Marra Brothers, Inc.*, 328 U.S. 1 (1946)), for the very reason that the LHWCA specifically precludes from its provisions any employee who is "a master or member of a crew of any vessel."

Southwest Marine suggests, in line with Fifth Circuit precedent, that this fact-intensive inquiry may always be resolved as a matter of law if the claimant's job fits within one of the enumerated occupations defining the term "employee" covered by the LHWCA. However, this argument ignores the fact that some maritime workers may be Jones Act seamen

---

[3] Southwest Marine points as well to a separate exclusiveness of liability provision regarding the negligence of a vessel, 33 U.S.C. § 905(b), and places great emphasis on a passage that states:

> If such person was employed to provide shipbuilding, repairing, or breaking services and such person's employer was the owner, owner pro hac vice, agent, operator, or charterer of the vessel, no such action shall be permitted, in whole or in part or directly or indirectly, against the injured person's employer (in any capacity, including as the vessel's owner, owner pro hac vice, agent, operator, or charterer) or against the employees of the employer.

This exclusivity provision applies, however, only "in the event of injury to a person covered under this chapter [the LHWCA] caused by the negligence of a vessel." 33 U.S.C. § 905(b). As we have already noted, the question whether Gizoni is "a person covered under this chapter" depends upon whether he is a "seaman" under the Jones Act. Like the companion exclusivity provision of § 905(a), § 905(b) does not dictate sole recourse to the LHWCA unless Gizoni is found not to be "a master or member of a crew of any vessel."

performing a job specifically enumerated under the LHWCA. Indeed, Congress foresaw this possibility, and we have previously quoted a portion of the legislative history to the 1972 amendments to the LHWCA that states: "'The bill would amend the Act to provide coverage of longshoremen, harbor workers, ship repairmen, ship builders, shipbreakers, and other employees engaged in maritime employment (excluding masters and members of the crew of a vessel).'" *Northeast Marine Terminal Co. v. Caputo*, 432 U.S. 249, 266, n.26 (1977) (quoting S. Rep. No. 92—1125, p. 13 (1972)) (emphasis added). As we observed in *Wilander*: "There is no indication in the Jones Act, the LHWCA, or elsewhere, that Congress has excluded from Jones Act remedies those traditional seamen who owe allegiance to a vessel at sea, but who do not aid in navigation." 498 U.S., at ___. While in some cases a ship repairman may lack the requisite connection to a vessel in navigation to qualify for seaman status, *see, e.g.*, *Sun Ship, Inc. v. Pennsylvania*, 447 U.S. 715 (1980) (ship repairmen working and injured on land); *P. C. Pfeiffer Co. v. Ford*, 444 U.S. 69, 80, and n.12 (1979), not all ship repairmen lack the requisite connection as a matter of law.[4] This is so because "it is not the employee's particular job that is determinative, but the employee's connection to a vessel." *Wilander, supra*, at ___. By its terms the LHWCA preserves the Jones Act remedy for vessel crewmen, even if they are employed by a shipyard. A maritime worker is limited to LHWCA remedies only if no genuine issue of fact exists as to whether the worker was a seaman under the Jones Act.

Southwest Marine submits several arguments in an attempt to foreclose this Jones Act suit. First, Southwest Marine contends that our decision above will conflict with decisions holding that the LHWCA provides the exclusive remedy for certain injured railroad workers otherwise permitted by the Federal Employers' Liability Act, 45 U.S.C. § 51 *et seq.*, to pursue a negligence cause of action. *See, e.g.*, *Chesapeake & Ohio R. Co. v. Schwalb*, 493 U.S. 40 (1989); *Pennsylvania R. R. v. O'Rourke*, 344 U.S. 334 (1953). Such cases, however, can provide no meaningful guidance on the issue here, for the LHWCA contains no exclusion for railroad workers comparable to that for Jones Act seamen.

Next, Southwest Marine advances a "primary jurisdiction" argument suggesting that, where a maritime worker is "arguably covered" by the LHWCA, the district court should stay any Jones Act proceeding pending a final LHWCA "administrative agency" determination that the worker is, in fact, a "master or member of a crew." We find no indication in the LHWCA that Congress intended to preclude or stay traditional Jones Act suits in the district courts. Indeed, the LHWCA anticipates that such suits could be brought. Title 33 U.S.C. § 913(d) tolls the time to file LHWCA claims "where recovery is denied to any person, in a suit brought at law or in admiralty to recover damages in respect of injury or death, on the ground that such person was an employee and the defendant was an employer within the meaning of this chapter and that such employer had secured compensation to such employee under this chapter."

---

[4] Gizoni stipulates that he was a ship repairman for Southwest Marine and correctly notes that many ship repairmen are excluded from LHWCA coverage, even though ship repairmen are expressly enumerated as a category of "harborworker" included within its coverage. *See* 33 U.S.C. § 902(3)(F) (individuals employed to repair recreational vessels under 65 feet in length); § 902(3)(H) (persons engaged to repair small vessels under 18 tons net). We find it significant that such clear exclusions of certain ship repairmen fall on either side of the exclusion here at issue for "a master or member of a crew of any vessel." § 902(3)(G).

Southwest Marine seeks to support its primary jurisdiction argument by pointing to the relation between the Federal Employees Compensation Act (FECA), 5 U.S.C. § 8101 *et seq.*, and the Federal Tort Claims Act (FTCA), 28 U.S.C. § 2671 *et seq.* But FECA contains an "unambiguous and comprehensive" provision barring any judicial review of the Secretary's determination of FECA coverage. *Lindahl v. OPM*, 470 U.S. 768, 780, and n.13 (1985); *see* 5 U.S.C. § 8128(b). Consequently, the courts have no jurisdiction over FTCA claims where the Secretary of Labor determines that FECA applies. The LHWCA contains no such provision. Likewise, we reject Southwest Marine's argument that agency proceedings under the LHWCA require the jurisdictional limitations we have found the National Labor Relations Act (NLRA), 29 U.S.C. § 151 *et seq.*, to place on state and federal courts in favor of the proceedings conducted by the National Labor Relations Board. *See, e.g., Longshoremen v. Davis*, 476 U.S. 380, 389-390 (1986); *San Diego Building Trades Council v. Garmon*, 359 U.S. 236, 243-245 (1959). The administrative proceedings outlined under the LHWCA in no way approach "the NLRA's 'complex and interrelated federal scheme of law, remedy, and administration'" requiring pre-emption in those cases. *Longshoremen, supra*, at 389 (quoting Garmon, *supra*, at 243)). Neither is it "essential to the administration" of the LHWCA that resolution of the question of coverage be left "'in the first instance'" to agency proceedings in the Department of Labor. *Longshoremen, supra*, at 390 (quoting Garmon, *supra*, at 244-245)).

Finally, Southwest Marine suggests that an employee's receipt of benefits under the LHWCA should preclude subsequent litigation under the Jones Act. To the contrary, however, we have ruled that where the evidence is sufficient to send the threshold question of seaman status to the jury, it is reversible error to permit an employer to prove that the worker accepted LHWCA benefits while awaiting trial. *Tipton v. Socony Mobil Oil Co.*, 375 U.S. 34, 37 (1963). It is by now "universally accepted" that an employee who receives voluntary payments under the LHWCA without a formal award is not barred from subsequently seeking relief under the Jones Act. G. GILMORE & C. BLACK, LAW OF ADMIRALTY 435 (2d ed. 1975); *see* 4 A. LARSON, WORKMEN'S COMPENSATION LAW § 90.51, p. 16-507 (1989) (collecting cases); *Simms v. Valley Line Co.*, 709 F.2d 409, 412, and nn. 3 and 5 (CA5 1983). This is so, quite obviously, because the question of coverage has never actually been litigated. Moreover, the LHWCA clearly does not comprehend such a preclusive effect, as it specifically provides that any amounts paid to an employee for the same injury, disability, or death pursuant to the Jones Act shall be credited against any liability imposed by the LHWCA.[5] 33 U.S.C. § 903(e). *See* GILMORE & BLACK, *supra*, at 435.

III

Because a ship repairman may spend all of his working hours aboard a vessel in furtherance of its mission—even one used exclusively in ship repair work—that worker may qualify as a Jones Act seaman. By ruling as a matter of law on the basis of job title or occupation

---

[5] For this same reason, equitable estoppel arguments suggested by amicus Shipbuilders Council of America must fail. Where full compensation credit removes the threat of double recovery, the critical element of detrimental reliance does not appear. *See Heckler v. Community Health Services*, 467 U.S. 51, 59 (1984); *Lyng v. Payne*, 476 U.S. 926, 935 (1986). Argument by amicus would force injured maritime workers to an election of remedies we do not believe Congress to have intended.

alone, the District Court foreclosed Gizoni's ability to make this showing. "If reasonable persons, applying the proper legal standard, could differ as to whether the employee was a 'member of a crew,' it is a question for the jury." *Wilander*, 498 U.S., at ___. The Ninth Circuit concluded that questions of fact existed regarding whether the floating platforms were vessels in navigation, and whether Gizoni had sufficient connection to the platforms to qualify for seaman status.[6] Gizoni alleges facts in support of each of these propositions—facts which Southwest Marine disputes. *Compare* Brief for Respondent 11, with Brief for Petitioner 3. Summary judgment was inappropriate.

The judgment of the Court of Appeals is *Affirmed.*

Problems

1. Suppose plaintiff brought suit against his employer claiming recovery under the Jones Act but the court found that he was a longshoreman or harbor worker. If the period of limitations has not run, the plaintiff may claim benefits under the LHWCA (or under a state statute, if applicable).

Suppose, however, that plaintiff brought suit against his employer claiming recovery under the Jones Act and the court found that he was a seaman but not entitled to any recovery because, for example, the employer was free of fault. Can plaintiff now claim benefits under the LHWCA, claiming that he is a longshoreman? Strong argument may be made that such a claim is barred by res judicata or collateral estoppel. However, it has been held that the finding of a seaman's status in the Jones Act suit does not bar a later claim for compensation. *Strachan Shipping Co. v. Shea*, 406 F.2d 521, 1969 AMC 67 (5th Cir. 1969), *cert. denied*, 395 U.S. 920 (1969); *Young v. Shea*, 397 F.2d 185, 1969 AMC 560 (5th Cir. 1968), *cert. denied*, 395 U.S. 920 (1969).

2. Suppose plaintiff claimed benefits under the LHWCA and the administrative law judge found that he was a seaman, *i.e.*, a member of the crew of a vessel. He may now sue his employer under the Jones Act, provided that the period of limitation has not run. It is the same when an administrative law judge finds that plaintiff is a longshoreman or harbor worker but the federal court sets aside the award of benefits on the ground that the plaintiff is a seaman. *See McDermott Inc. v. Boudreaux*, 679 F.2d 452 (5th Cir. 1982).

Suppose, however, that plaintiff recovered compensation under the LHWCA. May he now sue for recovery under the Jones Act? *See Papai v. Harbor Tug and Barge Company*, 67 F.3d 203, 1995 AMC 2888 (9th Cir. 1995), *rvsd. on other grounds*, 520 U.S. 548 (1997); *Biggs v. Norfolk Dredging Co.*, 360 F.2d 360, 1966 AMC 578 (4th Cir. 1966); *Figueroa v. Campbell Industries*, 45 F.3d 311 (9th Cir. 1995); and *C.N.A. Ins. Co. v. Workers' Comp. Appeals Bd.*, 68 Cal. Rptr 2d 115, 1998 AMC 534 (Cal. App. 2d Dist. 1997). In those cases the court held that the plaintiff was not estopped from claiming recovery under the Jones Act, and that there is no need to accord finality to the administrative finding with regard to the status of the plaintiff. *But see Welch v. Elevating Boats, Inc.*, 516 F. Supp. 1245 (E.D. La. 1982), where suit under the Jones Act was dismissed on the grounds that plaintiff was collaterally estopped from claiming seaman's status and, as a matter of law, that he was not a seaman. See also *Sharp v. Johnson Bros. Corp.*, 973 F.2d 423, 426, 1995 AMC 912 (5th Cir. 1992), holding that an administrative determination of LHWCA entitlement precludes Jones Act action if it amounts to a "formal award". In *Reyes v. Delta Dallas Alpha Corp.*, 199 F.3d 626, 2000 AMC 776 (2d Cir. 1999) and *Mooney v. City of New York*, 219 F.3d 123, 2001 AMC 38 (2d Cir. 2000), the

---

[6] The Ninth Circuit also found questions of fact to remain concerning whether Gizoni aided in the navigation of these platforms. After *McDermott Int'l, Inc. v. Wilander*, 498 U.S. ___, 111 S. Ct. 807, 112 L. Ed. 2d 866 (1991), however, only "employment-related connection to a vessel in navigation" is required. *Id.*, at ___, 111 S. Ct., at 817. To be a seaman, the employee need not aid in navigation.

Second Circuit held that receipt of *State* workers' compensation benefits by the plaintiff did not constitute a waiver of Jones Act claims, but that waiver would arise if there were a "formal award".

B. Coverage of the Longshore and Harbor Workers' Compensation Act (LHWCA): Status and Situs Requirements

Background Note

The 1927 LHWCA was generally applicable to persons engaged in "maritime employment," subject to certain exclusions. The term "employee" applied to longshoremen and harbor workers, but not to "a master or member of the crew of any vessel" (33 U.S.C. §§ 902(3), 903(A)(1)), "an officer or employee of the United States or any agency thereof or of any state or foreign government, or any political subdivision thereof" (33 U.S.C. § 903(a)(2)), or "any person engaged by the master to load or unload or repair any small vessel under eighteen tons net" (33 U.S.C. §§ 903 (3), 903(A)(1)). These exclusions have been carried forward without change.

However, the coverage of the act was broadened in 1972 and in 1984. Addition of language to § 903(a) specifies that the term navigable waters of the United States includes "any adjoining pier, wharf, dry dock, terminal, building way, marine railway, or other adjoining area customarily used by an employer in loading, unloading, repairing, or building a vessel." Furthermore, the word "employer" in § 902(4) has been broadened by the addition of the same words.

---

33 U.S.C. §§ 902 and 903

as amended in 1984

§ 902. Definitions

When used in this chapter—

* * *

(2) The term "injury" means accidental injury or death arising out of and in the course of employment, and such occupational disease or infection as arises naturally out of such employment or as naturally or unavoidably results from such accidental injury, and includes an injury caused by the willful act of a third person directed against an employee because of his employment.

(3) The term "employee" means any person engaged in maritime employment, including any longshoreman or other person engaged in longshoring operations, and any harbor-worker including a ship repairman, shipbuilder, and ship-breaker, but such term does not include—

(A) individuals employed exclusively to perform office clerical, secretarial, security, or data processing work;

(B) individuals employed by a club, camp, recreational operation, restaurant, museum, or retail outlet;

(C) individuals employed by a marina and who are not engaged in construction, replacement, or expansion of such marina (except for routine maintenance);

(D) individuals who (i) are employed by suppliers, transporters, or vendors, (ii) are temporarily doing business on the premises of an employer described in paragraph (4), and (iii) are not engaged in work normally performed by employees of that employer under this chapter;
(E) aquaculture workers;
(F) individuals employed to build, repair, or dismantle any recreational vessel under sixty-five feet in length;
(G) a master or member of a crew of any vessel; or
(H) any person engaged by a master to load or unload or repair any small vessel under eighteen tons net;

if individuals described in clauses (A) through (F) are subject to coverage under a State workers' compensation law.
(4) The term "employer" means an employer any of whose employees are employed in maritime employment, in whole or in part, upon the navigable waters of the United States (including any adjoining pier, wharf, dry dock, terminal, building way, marine railway, or other adjoining area customarily used by an employer in loading, unloading, repairing, or building a vessel).

* * *

§ 903. Coverage
(a) Disability or death; injuries occurring upon navigable waters of United States
Except as otherwise provided in this section, compensation shall be payable under this chapter in respect of disability or death of an employee, but only if the disability or death results from an injury occurring upon the navigable waters of the United States (including any adjoining pier, wharf, dry dock, terminal, building way, marine railway, or other adjoining area customarily used by an employer in loading, unloading, repairing, dismantling, or building a vessel).
(b) Governmental officers and employees
No compensation shall be payable in respect of the disability or death of an officer or employee of the United States, or any agency thereof, or of any State or foreign government, or any subdivision thereof.
(c) Intoxication; willful intention to kill
No compensation shall be payable if the injury was occasioned solely by the intoxication of the employee or by the willful intention of the employee to injure or kill himself or another.
(d) Small vessels

(1) No compensation shall be payable to an employee employed at a facility of an employer if, as certified by the Secretary, the facility is engaged in the business of building, repairing, or dismantling exclusively small vessels (as defined in paragraph (3) of this subsection), unless the injury occurs while upon the navigable waters of the

United States or while upon any adjoining pier, wharf, dock, facility over land for launching vessels, or facility over land for hauling, lifting, or drydocking vessels.

(2) Notwithstanding paragraph (1), compensation shall be payable to an employee—

(A) who is employed at a facility which is used in the business of building, repairing, or dismantling small vessels if such facility receives Federal maritime subsidies; or

(B) if the employee is not subject to coverage under a State workers' compensation law.

(3) For purposes of this subsection, a small vessel means—

(A) a commercial barge which is under 900 lightship displacement tons; or

(B) a commercial tugboat, towboat, crew boat, supply boat, fishing vessel, or other work vessel which is under 1,600 tons gross.

(e) Credit for benefits paid under other laws

Notwithstanding any other provision of law, any amounts paid to an employee for the same injury, disability, or death for which benefits are claimed under this chapter pursuant to any other workers' compensation law or section 688 of Title 46 (relating to recovery for injury to or death of seamen) shall be credited against any liability imposed by this chapter.

P.C. PFEIFFER CO., INC. v. FORD

444 U.S. 69, 100 S. Ct. 32, 62 L. Ed. 2d 225, 1979 AMC 2319 (1979)

Mr. Justice POWELL delivered the opinion of the Court

The question in this case is whether two workers were engaged in "maritime employment," as defined by § 2(3) of the Longshoremen's and Harbor Workers' Compensation Act, 44 Stat. 1425, as amended, 86 Stat. 1251, 33 U.C.S. § 902(3), when they sustained injuries for which they sought compensation.

I

On April 12, 1973, Diverson Ford accidentally struck the middle finger of his left hand with a hammer while working on a public dock in the Port of Beaumont, Tex. On the day of his injury, Ford was employed by the P. C. Pfeiffer Co. to fasten military vehicles onto railroad flatcars. The vehicles had been delivered to the port by ship a number of days before the accident, stored, and then loaded onto flatcars the day before. The flatcars would take the vehicles to their inland designation.

Ford was working out of the warehousemen's local on the day of the accident. Agreements between employers, the warehousemen's union, and the longshoremen's union limit the tasks that warehousemen may perform in the Port of Beaumont. Warehousemen may not move cargo directly from a vessel either to a point of rest in storage or to a railroad car. Nor may they move cargo from a shoreside point of rest directly onto a vessel. These jobs are reserved for longshoremen.

On May 2, 1973, Will Bryant was injured while unloading a bale of cotton from a dray wagon into a pier warehouse. Bryant was working as a cottonheader for the Ayers Steamship Co. in the Port of Galveston, Tex. Cotton arrives at the port from inland shippers and enters storage in cotton compress-warehouses. The cotton then goes by dray wagon to pier warehouses where a driver and two cotton headers unload and store it. Longshoremen later move the cotton from the pier warehouses onto ships.

Contractual agreements between employers, the cotton headers' union, and the longshoremen's union distinguish the work that cotton headers may perform from the tasks assignable to longshoremen. Cotton headers may only load cotton off dray wagons into the pier warehouses or move cotton within a pier warehouse. Cargo moved directly from the ship to shoreside transportation, or directly from shoreside transportation to the ship, is handled solely by longshoremen.

II

Before 1972, neither Ford nor Bryant could have received compensation under the Longshoremen's and Harbor Workers' Compensation Act because his injury occurred on land. The pre-1972 Act was simply an effort to fill the gap in workmen's compensation coverage created by this Court's decision in *Southern Pacific Co. v. Jensen*, 244 U.S. 205 (1917), which held that state compensation systems could not reach longshoremen injured seaward of the water's edge. A single situs requirement in § 3(a) of the Act governed the scope of its coverage. That requirement limited coverage to workers whose "disability or death [resulted] from an injury occurring upon the navigable waters of the United States (including any dry dock)... ." 44 Stat. 1426. In light of Jensen and the limited purpose of the Act, the situs test was understood to draw a sharp line between injuries sustained over water and those suffered on land. Thus, in *Nacirema Operating Co. v. Johnson*, 396 U.S. 212, 218-220 (1969), this Court held that the Act did not extend to injuries occurring on a pier attached to the land. Although the Court recognized that inequities might result from rigid adherence to the Jensen line,the Court concluded that "[the] invitation to move that line landward must be addressed to Congress, not to this Court." 396 U.S., at 224.

Congress responded with the Longshoremen's and Harbor Workers' Compensation Act Amendments of 1972 (1972 Act). The Act now extends coverage to more workers by replacing the single-situs requirement with a two-part situs and status standard. The newly broadened situs test provides compensation for an "employee" whose disability or death "results from an injury occurring upon the navigable waters of the United States (including any adjoining pier, wharf, dry dock, terminal, building way, marine railway, or other adjoining area customarily used by an employer in loading, unloading, repairing, or building a vessel)." § 3(a), 33 U.S.C. § 903(a). The status test defines an employee as "any person engaged in maritime employment, including any longshoreman or other person engaged in longshoring operations, and any harbor worker including a ship repairman, shipbuilder, and shipbreaker... ." § 2(3), 33 U.S.C. § 902(3). To be eligible for compensation, a person must be an employee as defined by § 2(3) who sustains injury on the situs defined by § 3(a).

III

This Court first considered the scope of § 2(3)'s status requirement in *Northeast Marine Terminal Co. v. Caputo*, 432 U.S. 249 (1977). That case concerned the claims of two workers, Blundo and Caputo. Blundo was on a pier checking cargo as it was removed from a container when he suffered a fall. Caputo sustained injury while rolling a loaded dolly into a consignee's truck. We recognized that neither the 1972 Act nor its legislative history states explicitly whether workers like Blundo and Caputo, who handle cargo between sea and land transportation, are employees within the meaning of § 2(3). The Court found, however, that consideration of the legislative history in light of the remedial purposes behind the expansion of coverage reveals a clear intent to cover such workers. 432 U.S., at 267-278.

One of the reasons Congress expanded coverage in 1972 was that containerization permits loading and unloading tasks traditionally conducted aboard ship to be performed on the land. Such tasks are "longshoring operations." *Id.*, at 270-271. Blundo's job of checking and marking goods as they were removed from a container was an integral part of the unloading process even though the container had been removed from a ship and trucked to a different pier before being emptied. Therefore, Blundo was an employee within the meaning of § 2(3). 432 U.S., at 271.

Caputo, working as part of the traditional process of moving goods from ship to land transportation, was unaffected by the advent of containerization. But the Court recognized another congressional purpose relevant to the resolution of Caputo's claim. Congress wanted to ensure that a worker who could have been covered part of the time by the pre-1972 Act would be completely covered by the 1972 Act. By enlarging the covered situs and enacting the status requirement, Congress intended that a worker's eligibility for federal benefits would not depend on whether he was injured while walking down a gangway or while taking his first step onto the land. Congress therefore counted as "longshoremen" persons who spend "at least some of their time in indisputably longshoring operations." *Id.*, at 273. Caputo, who could have been assigned to loading containers and barges as well as trucks, was such a person. *Ibid.* Accordingly, the Court did not have to decide whether Caputo's work was "maritime employment" simply because he "engaged in the final steps of moving cargo from maritime to land transportation: putting it in the consignee's truck." *Id.*, at 272.

In holding that Blundo and Caputo were covered by the Act, Northeast Marine Terminal explicitly rejected the "point of rest" theory. Under that test, maritime employment would include only the portion of the unloading process that takes place before the stevedoring gang places cargo onto the dock. For example, a worker who carried cargo directly from a ship to a warehouse or a truck would be engaged in maritime employment, but one who carried cargo from a warehouse to a truck would not. In loading operations, only workers employed to the seaside of the last point of rest would be covered.

We explained that application of the point-of-rest test would be inconsistent with congressional intent. First, the concept, although well known in the maritime industry, was not mentioned in the Act or its legislative history. Second, the standard excludes from coverage employees like Blundo whose work was shifted landward by the use of containers. Third, the test conflicts with the express purpose of the Act because it allows workers to walk in and out of coverage as their work moves to different sides of a point of rest. *Id.*, at 275-276. In sum, "[a] theory that nowhere appears in the Act, that was never mentioned by Congress during the legislative process, that does not comport with Congress' intent, and that restricts the coverage of a remedial Act designed to extend coverage [was] incapable of defeating our conclusion that Blundo and Caputo [were] 'employees.'" *Id.*, at 278-279.

Most of the litigation in the present case took place before our decision in Northeast Marine Terminal. At the initial administrative level, both Ford's and Bryant's claims for coverage were denied by Administrative Law Judges applying the point-of-rest doctrine. The Benefits Review Board reversed both decisions. The Court of Appeals for the Fifth Circuit affirmed. *Jacksonville Shipyards, Inc. v. Perdue*, 539 F.2d 533 (1976). The court rejected the point-of-rest theory, holding instead that the 1972 Act covers all workers directly involved in the work of loading, unloading, repairing, building, or breaking a vessel. *Id.*, at 539-540. The court found that "Ford's work of fastening the vehicles to the flat cars was ... the last step in transferring this cargo from sea to land transportation," *id.*, at 543, and that Bryant's work "was an integral part of the ongoing process of moving cargo between land transportation and a ship," *id.*, at 544. Accordingly, the Court of Appeals concluded that both men were covered by the 1972 Act.

We granted certiorari, vacated, and remanded for reconsideration in light of *Northeast Marine Terminal.* 433 U.S. 904 (1977). On remand, the Fifth Circuit reaffirmed the reasoning of its earlier opinion. 575 F.2d 79, 80 (1978) (*per curiam*). We again granted certiorari, 439 U.S. 978 (1978), and we now affirm.

IV

Petitioners urge that Ford and Bryant are not covered by the 1972 Act because they were not engaged in "maritime employment." Petitioners suggest that a person is engaged in maritime employment only if, on the day of his injury, he could have been assigned to perform work upon the navigable waters of the United States. By navigable waters, the petitioners do not mean the broad situs defined in § 3(a), as amended by the 1972 Act; rather they refer to places seaward of the Jensen line. In other words, petitioners argue that the 1972 Act covers only workers who are working or who may be assigned to workover the water itself. They say that this formulation follows congressional intent to cover all workers who, before 1972, could have walked in and out of coverage during any given day.

Petitioners' position is plainly inconsistent with the language and structure of the 1972 Act. The Act, as noted above, contains distinct situs and status requirements. The situs test of § 3(a) allows recovery for an injury suffered on navigable waters or certain adjoining areas landward of the Jensen line. This test defines the broad geographic coverage of the Act.

Section 2(3) restricts the scope of coverage by further requiring that the injured worker must have been engaged in "maritime employment." This section defines the Act's occupational requirements. The term "maritime employment" refers to the nature of a worker's activities. Thus, § 2(3) uses the phrase "[longshoremen] or other [persons] engaged in longshoring operations" as one example of workers who engage in maritime employment no matter where they do their job. Since § 3(a) already limits the geographic coverage of the Act, § 2(3) need not provide that longshoremen are covered only if they work in certain places. The use of the term "maritime employment" in § 2(3), therefore, provides no support for the proposition that the statutory definition of an employee imports a geographic limitation narrower than the one defined in § 3(a).

The difficulty with petitioners' position becomes even plainer when their interpretation is applied to a single statutory provision that contains both the status and the situs requirement. Section 2(4), 33 U.S.C. § 902(4), defines an "employer" as one "any of whose employees are employed in maritime employment, in whole or in part, upon the navigable waters of the United States" as broadly defined by § 3(a). If the term "maritime employment" referred only to work that might take employees seaward of the Jensen line, then the broader situs test in the final clause of this section would become virtually superfluous. We decline the invitation to construe "maritime employment" so as to create two differing situs requirements in a single sentence. By understanding the term "maritime employment" to embody an occupational rather than a geographic concept, we give the two phases in § 2(4) distinct and consistent meanings.

The discussion of coverage in the legislative history also shows that Congress intended the term "maritime employment" to refer to status rather than situs. Committees in both Houses of Congress recognized:

> [To] take a typical example, cargo, whether in break bulk or containerized form, is typically unloaded from the ship and immediately transported to a storage or holding area on the pier, wharf, or terminal adjoining navigable waters. The employees who perform this work would be covered under the bill for injuries sustained by them over the navigable waters or on the adjoining land area. The Committee does not intend to cover employees who are not engaged in loading, unloading, repairing, or building a vessel, just because they are injured in an area adjoining navigable waters used for such activity. Thus, employees whose responsibility is only to pick up stored cargo for further trans-shipment would not be covered, nor would purely clerical employees whose jobs do not require them to participate in the loading or unloading of cargo.

This legislative history discusses workers solely in terms of what they are doing and never in terms of where they are working.

In adopting an occupational test that focuses on loading and unloading, Congress anticipated that some persons who work only on land would receive benefits under the 1972 Act. An obvious example of such a worker is Blundo. He was checking and marking cargo from a container that had been removed from a ship and moved over land to another pier before it was opened. Without any indication that he ever would be required to set foot on a ship, this Court held that he was covered by the 1972 Act because this type of work was maritime employment. *Northeast Marine Terminal Co.*, 432 U.S., at 271.

Land-based workers who do not handle containerized cargo also may be engaged in loading, unloading, repairing, or building a vessel. The Senate Subcommittee on Labor heard testimony that 30%-35% of ship repair work is done on land. Furthermore, the usual longshoring crew includes some men whose duties may be carried out solely on the land. A typical loading gang consists of persons who move cargo from a warehouse to the side of a ship, front men who attach the load to the ship's gear for lifting aboard the vessel, and a hold gang which stores cargo inside the ship. Although the workers who carry the cargo to shipside and the front men who attach the cargo to the lifting devices need not board a ship to carry out their duties, they are incontestably longshoremen directly engaged in the loading process. Even the petitioners concede that some land-based workers are covered by the 1972 Act.

V

The issue in this case thus becomes whether Ford and Bryant are the kind of land-based employees that Congress intended to encompass within the term "maritime employment." Both men engaged in the type of duties that longshoremen perform in transferring goods between ship and land transportation. If the cotton that Bryant was unloading had been brought directly from the compress-warehouse to a ship, his task of moving cotton off a dray wagon would have been performed by a longshoreman. Similarly, longshoremen—not warehousemen like Ford—would fasten military vehicles onto railroad flatcars if those vehicles went directly from a ship to the railroad cars. The only basis for distinguishing Bryant or Ford from longshoremen who otherwise would perform the same work is the point-of-rest theory. That is, longshoremen in the Ports of Beaumont and Galveston would have performed the work done by Bryant and Ford had the cargo moved without interruption between land and sea transportation. Our unanimous opinion in *Northeast Marine Terminal* expressly decided that application of the point-of-rest test to define the scope of maritime employment would be contrary to congressional intent. *Id.*, at 275-279. Thus, there is no principled basis for distinguishing Ford and Bryant from longshoremen who have been injured while performing the same tasks.

We believe that § 2(3)'s explicit use of the terms "longshoreman" and "other person engaged in longshoring operations" to describe persons engaged in maritime employment demonstrates that workers doing tasks traditionally performed by longshoremen are within the purview of the 1972 Act. We do not suggest that the scope of maritime employment depends upon the vagaries of union jurisdiction. 432 U.S., at 268, n.30. Instead, the crucial factor is the nature of the activity to which a worker may be assigned. Persons moving cargo directly from ship to land transportation are engaged in maritime employment. *Id.*, at 267. A worker responsible for some portion of that activity is as much an integral part of the process of loading or unloading a ship as a person who participates in the entire process. We therefore hold that Ford and Bryant were engaged in maritime employment because they were engaged in intermediate steps of moving cargo betweenship and land transportation.

Our decision serves the intent of Congress in creating the status requirement. First, it focuses upon the nature, not the location, of employment. Second, it does not extend coverage to all workers in the situs area. There is no doubt for example, that neither the driver of the truck carrying cotton to Galveston nor the locomotive engineer transporting military vehicles from Beaumont was engaged in maritime employment even though he was working on the marine situs. Such a person's "responsibility is only to pick up stored cargo for further trans-shipment." S. Rep. No. 92-1125, p.13 (1972); H. R. Rep. No. 92-1441, p. 11 (1972); *see Northeast Marine Terminal Co. v. Caputo*, 432 U.S., at 267, 275.

Our decision today also serves the broader congressional purpose of expanding coverage. Congress intended to apply a simple, uniform standard of coverage. Adoption of the petitioners' test would conflict with that goal, because any individual worker's coverage would depend upon the assignment policies of his employer. For example, a land-based worker would be covered if his employer allowed him to alternate assignments with co-workers who work on the water, but he would not be covered if the employer never allowed him to board a ship. Congress did not intend the Act's coverage to shift with the employer's whim. *See id.*, at 276, n.38. In contrast, a definition of maritime employment that reaches any worker who moves cargo between ship and land transportation will enable both workers and employers to predict with reasonable assurance who on the situs is protected by the 1972 Act.

Because the Court of Appeals correctly determined that Ford and Bryant were engaged in maritime employment at the time of their injuries, its judgment is

Affirmed.

Notes: Status and Situs Requirements

1. To recover benefits under the LHWCA, an employee must satisfy both the *status* requirement under § 902(3) and the *situs* requirement under § 903(a). The status test, as discussed in *Pfeiffer*, requires that the employee be engaged in "maritime employment." The situs test requires that the injury take place on the "navigable waters of the United States." The 1972 and 1984 amendments to the act specify that the term "navigable waters" includes "any adjoining pier, wharf, drydock, terminal building way, marine railway, on other adjoining area customarily used by an employer in loading, unloading, repairing, dismantling, or building a vessel."

Courts have struggled to define the parameters of the status and situs requirements. In *Director v. Perini North River Associates*, 459 U.S. 297, 103 S. Ct. 634, 74 L. Ed. 465, 1983 AMC 609 (1983), the Court held that an employee injured on "actual" navigable waters of the United States, as distinguished from the expanded situs under the 1972 amendment to § 903(a), is not bound to show that his employment bears a direct and substantial relation to navigation or commerce to be covered. The standard that situs alone suffices or that the status requirement is satisfied when an employee is injured on "actual" navigable waters of the United States is the same as under the prior law. The Court concluded that Congress in adopting the 1972 Amendments intended to expand coverage and not to exclude anyone who had been covered by prior law. Because the expanded coverage for the first time included workers whose duties may be performed solely on land, it was necessary to apply both a status and situs test to these workers. As to those who work on navigable waters, the Court concluded:

> We hold only that when a worker is injured on the actual navigable waters in the course of his employment on those waters, he satisfies the status requirement in § 2(3), and is covered under the LHWCA, providing, of course, that he is the employee of a statutory "employer," and is not excluded by any other provision of the Act. We consider these employees to be "engaged in maritime employment" not simply because they are injured in a historically maritime locale, but because they are required to perform their duties upon navigable waters. (at p. 323).

Conversely, the status test focuses on the type of occupation rather than the location of employment. The employee must show that the occupation was in some way related to loading, unloading, construction, repair or dismantling of vessels. For example, in *Sanders v. Alabama Dry Dock and Shipbuilding Co.*, 841 F.2d 1085 (11th Cir. 1988), the appeals court held that an industrial relations specialist who oversaw activities in a shipyard *was* engaged in maritime employment because the purpose of his job was to keep the shipyard running smoothly. Yet, the court in *Dorris v. Director, OWCP*, 808 F.2d 1362, 1987 AMC 2730 (9th Cir. 1987) denied that a truck driver who transported cargo to the docks and engaged in a longshore work on an "episodic basis" was involved in maritime employment.

2. The Fifth Circuit has qualified the rule that a worker injured in the course of employment on navigable waters is engaged in maritime employment and meets the status test by excluding those situations where the worker's presence on the water at the time of the injury was either "transient or fortuitous" even though technically in the course of employment. These situations should be distinguished from a worker who spends a "not in substantial amount of time" working on water. For example, the court found that spending 8.3 percent of work time on a vessel was "not in substantial." *Bienvenu v. Texaco, Inc.*, 164 F.3d 901, 1999 AMC 1255 (5th Cir. 1999).

3. Courts have also refused to extend LHWCA coverage to a worker who satisfies the status, but not the situs requirement of the act. *See, Humphries v. Director, O.W.C.P.*, 834 F.2d 372 (4th Cir. 1987). In *Humphries*, the plaintiff worked as a shift foreman for Cargill, Inc. As part of his employment responsibilities, plaintiff was required to pick up food for employees working overtime. Cargill imposed this responsibility on the shift foreman in order to prevent delays in loading and unloading operations. On the night of the accident, plaintiff drove to a restaurant approximately one and one-half miles from the Cargill terminal to get a meal for an employee working overtime. As he left the restaurant, plaintiff experienced car trouble. Humphries was seriously injured when hit by a passing automobile as he left his car to check under the hood. The Benefits Review Board held that plaintiff's injuries were not covered under the LHWCA because, at the time of his injury, he was not on a maritime situs. The Fourth Circuit first noted that "as a shift foreman supervising and facilitating a loading operation Humphries was clearly 'engaged in maritime employment;'" and therefore met the status requirement. While agreeing with Humphries that the maritime situs requirement should be interpreted broadly, the court held that "[w]ere we to read the situs requirement so broadly as to embrace this claim, however, we would come perilously close to eliminating it entirely."

HERB'S WELDING, INC. v. GRAY

470 U.S. 414, 105 S. Ct. 1421, 84 L. Ed. 2d 406, 1985 AMC 1700 (1985)

Justice WHITE delivered the opinion of the Court

The Longshoremen's and Harbor Workers' Compensation Act (LHWCA or Act), 44 Stat. 1424, as amended, 33 U.S.C. § 901 *et seq.*, provides compensation for the death or disability of any person engaged in "maritime employment," § 902(3), if the disability or death results from an injury incurred upon the navigable waters of the United States or any adjoining pier or other area customarily used by an employer in loading, unloading, repairing, or building a vessel, § 903(a). Thus, a worker claiming under the Act must satisfy both a "status" and a "situs" test. The court below held that respondent Robert Gray, a welder working on a fixed offshore oil-drilling platform in state territorial waters, was entitled to benefits under the Act. We reverse for the reason that Gray was not engaged in maritime employment.

I

Respondent Gray worked for Herb's Welding, Inc., in the Bay Marchand oil and gas field off the Louisiana coast. Herb's Welding provided welding services to the owners of drilling platforms. The field was located partly in Louisiana territorial waters, *i.e.*, within three miles of the shore, and partly on the Outer Continental Shelf. Gray ate and slept on a platform situated in Louisiana waters. He spent roughly three-quarters of his working time on platforms in state waters and the rest on platforms on the Outer Continental Shelf. He worked exclusively as a welder, building and replacing pipelines and doing general maintenance work on the platforms.

On July 11, 1975, Gray was welding a gas flow line on a fixed platform located in Louisiana waters. He burnt through the bottom of the line and an explosion occurred. Gray ran from the area, and in doing so hurt his knee. He sought benefits under the LHWCA for lost wages, disability, and medical expenses.[3] When petitioner United States Fidelity & Guaranty Co., the workers' compensation carrier for Herb's Welding, denied LHWCA benefits, Gray filed a complaint with the Department of Labor. The Administrative Law Judge (ALJ), relying on our decision in *Rodrigue v. Aetna Casualty & Surety Co.*, 395 U.S. 352 (1969), ruled that because Gray's work was totally involved in the exploration for, and development and transmission of, oil and gas from submerged lands, it was not relevant to traditional maritime law and lacked any significant maritime connection. Gray therefore did not satisfy the LHWCA's status requirement.

The Benefits Review Board reversed on other grounds. 12 BRBS 752 (1980). By a vote of 2-1, it concluded that irrespective of the nature of his employment, Gray could recover by virtue of a provision of the Outer Continental Shelf Lands Act, 67 Stat. 462, 43 U.S.C. § 1331 *et seq.* (Lands Act), that grants LHWCA benefits to offshore oil workers injured on the Outer Continental Shelf[4] Although Gray had been injured in state waters, the Board felt that his injury nonetheless could be said to have occurred, in the words of the statute, "as a result of" operations on the outer shelf. It considered his work "integrally related" to such operations. 12 BRBS, at 757. The dissenting Board member argued that the Lands Act provides LHWCA benefits only for injuries actually occurring in the geographic area of the outershelf. *Id.*, at 761-763.

---

[3] Gray did recover under the Louisiana workers' compensation scheme, receiving weekly benefits totalling $3,172.50 over two years as well as $1,696.14 for medical expenses. These payments were credited against his later LHWCA recovery. *See* App. to Pet. for Cert. A-45. State workers' compensation and the LHWCA are not mutually exclusive remedies. *Sun Ship, Inc.v. Pennsylvania*, 447 U.S. 715 (1980).

[4] The relevant section provides:

With respect to disability or death of an employee resulting from any injury occurring as the result of operations conducted on the Outer Continental Shelf for the purpose of exploring for, developing, removing or transporting by pipeline the natural resources, or involving rights to the natural resources, of the subsoil and seabed of the outer Continental Shelf, compensation shall be payable under the provisions of the Longshoremen's and Harbor Workers' Compensation Act. 67 Stat. 463, as amended, 43 U.S.C. § 1333(b).

The Board reaffirmed its position after the case was remanded to the ALJ for entry of judgment and calculation of benefits, and petitioners sought review in the Court of Appeals for the Fifth Circuit. That court affirmed, relying directly on the LHWCA rather than on the Lands Act. 703 F.2d 176 (1983). With regard to the Act's situs requirement, it noted that this Court had compared drilling platforms to wharves in *Rodrigue v. Aetna Casualty & Surety Co., supra.* Given that the 1972 Amendments to the LHWCA extended coverage to accidents occurring on wharves, it would be incongruous if they did not also reach accidents occurring on drilling platforms. Also, since workers injured on movable barges, on fixed platforms on the Outer Continental Shelf, or en route to fixed platforms, are all covered, there would be a "curious hole" in coverage if someone in Gray's position was not. 703 F.2d, at 177-178. As for Gray's status, the Court of Appeals, differing with the ALJ, held that Gray's work bore "a realistically significant relationship to traditional maritime activity involving navigation and commerce on navigable waters," *id.*, at 179-180, because it was an integral part of the offshore drilling process, which, the court had held in *Pippen v. Shell Oil Co.*, 661 F.2d 378 (1981), was itself maritime commerce. We granted certiorari. 465 U.S. 1098 (1984).

II

A

When extractive operations first moved offshore, all claims for injuries on fixed platforms proceeded under state workers' compensation schemes. *See Hearings*, at 396, 409, 411. *See also Robertson* 993. With the 1953 passage of the Lands Act, Congress extended LHWCA coverage to oil workers more than three miles offshore. 43 U.S.C. § 1333(b). Because until 1972 the LHWCA itself extended coverage only to accidents occurring on navigable waters, 33 U.S.C. § 903 (1970 ed.), and because stationary rigs were considered to be islands, *Rodrigue v. Aetna Casualty & Surety Co., supra,* oil rig workers inside the 3-mile limit were left to recover under state schemes. *See, e.g.*, *Freeman v. Chevron Oil Co.*, 517 F.2d 201 (CA5 1975); *Gifford v. Aurand Mfg. Co.*, 207 So. 2d 160 (La. App. 1968). Any worker, inside or outside the 3-mile limit, who qualified as a seaman was not covered by the LHWCA, but could sue under the Jones Act, 46 U.S.C. § 688, the Death on the High Seas Act, 46 U.S. C. § 761 *et seq.*, and the general maritime law. Hearings, at 411-414, 450-459, 487; *see* n.1, *supra. See also* Wright, *Jurisdiction in the Tidelands*, 32 TULANE L. REV. 175, 186 (1958).

So matters stood when Congress amended the LHWCA in 1972. What is known about the congressional intent behind that legislation has been amply described in our prior opinions. *See, e.g., Director, OWCP v. Perini North River Associates*, 459 U.S. 297 (1983); *Sun Ship, Inc. v. Pennsylvania*, 447 U.S. 715, 717-722 (1980); *Northeast Marine Terminal Co. v. Caputo*, 432 U.S. 249, 256-265 (1977). The most important of Congress' concerns, for present purposes, was the desire to extend coverage to longshoremen, harbor workers, and others who were injured while on piers, docks, and other areas customarily used to load and unload ships or to repair or build ships, rather than while actually a float. Whereas prior to 1972 the Act reached only accidents occurring on navigable waters, the amended

33 U.S.C. § 903 expressly extended coverage to "adjoining [areas]." At the same time, the amended definition of an "employee" limited coverage to employees engaged in "maritime employment."

The Act, as amended, does not mention offshore drilling rigs or the workers thereon. The legislative history of the amendments is also silent, although early in the legislative process, a bill was introduced to extend the Act to all offshore oil workers. The bill died in Committee. While hardly dispositive, it is worth noting that the same Committee considered the 1972 Amendments to the LHWCA, and the possible extension of the Lands Act's application of the LHWCA to drilling platforms, apparently without it ever occurring to anyone that the two might have been duplicative. The concurrent but independent reconsideration of both the Lands Act and the LHWCA, the congressional view that the amendments to the latter involved the "[extension] of [coverage] to [shoreside] [areas]," H.R.Rep. No. 92-1441, p. 10 (1972), and the absence of any mention of drilling platforms in the discussion of the LHWCA, combine to suggest that the 1972 Congress at least did not intentionally extend the LHWCA to workers such as Gray.

B

The rationale of the Court of Appeals was that offshore drilling is maritime commerce and that anyone performing any task that is part and parcel of that activity is in maritime employment for LHWCA purposes. Since it is doubtful that an offshore driller will pay and maintain a worker on an offshore rig whose job is unnecessary to the venture, this approach would extend coverage to virtually everyone on the stationary platform. We think this construction of the Act is untenable.

The Act does not define the term "maritime employment," but our cases and the legislative history of the amendments foreclose the Court of Appeals' reading. *Rodrigue* involved two men killed while working on an offshore drilling rig on the Outer Continental Shelf. Their families brought third-party negligence suits in federal court, claiming recovery under both the Death on the High Seas Act and the state law of Louisiana. The District Court ruled that resort could not be had to state law and that the High Seas Act provided the exclusive remedy. The Court of Appeals for the Fifth Circuit affirmed, holding that the men had been engaged in maritime activity on the high seas and that maritime law was the exclusive source of relief. We reversed. First, the platforms involved were artificial islands and were to be treated as though they were federal enclaves in an upland State. Federal law was to govern accidents occurring on these islands; but, contrary to the Court of Appeals, we held that the Lands Act and borrowed state law, not the maritime law, constituted the controlling federal law. The platforms "were islands, albeit artificial ones, and the accidents had no more connection with the ordinary stuff of admiralty than do accidents on piers." 395 U.S., at 360. Indeed, observing that the Court had previously "held that drilling platforms are not within admiralty jurisdiction," we indicated that drilling platforms were not even suggestive of traditional maritime affairs. *Id.*, at 360-361.

We also went on to examine the legislative history of the Lands Act and noted (1) that Congress was of the view that maritime law would not apply to fixed platforms unless a statute expressly so provided; and (2) that Congress had seriously considered applying maritime law to these platform but had rejected that approach because it considered maritime law to be inapposite, a view that would be untenable if drilling from a fixed platform is a maritime operation. The history of the Lands Act at the very least forecloses the Court of Appeals' holding that offshore drilling is a maritime activity and that any task essential thereto is maritime employment for LHWCA purposes.

We cannot assume that Congress was unfamiliar with *Rodrigue* and the Lands Act when it referred to "maritime employment" in defining the term "employee" in 1972. It would have been a significant departure from prior understanding to use that phrase to reach stationary drilling rigs generally.

The Fifth Circuit's expansive view of maritime employment is also inconsistent with our prior cases under the 1972 Amendments to the LHWCA. The expansion of the definition of navigable waters to include rather large shoreside areas necessitated an affirmative description of the particular employees working in those areas who would be covered. This was the function of the maritime employment requirement. But Congress did not seek to cover all those who breathe salt air. Its purpose was to cover those workers on the situs who are involved in the essential elements of loading and unloading; it is "clear that persons who are on the situs but not engaged in the overall process of loading or unloading vessels are not covered." *Northeast Marine Terminal Co. v. Caputo*, 432 U.S., at 267. While "maritime employment" is not limited to the occupations specifically mentioned in § 2(3), neither can it be read to eliminate any requirement of a connection with the loading or construction of ships. As we have said, the "maritime employment" requirement is "an occupational test that focuses on loading and unloading." *P.C. Pfeiffer Co. v. Ford*, 444 U.S. 69, 80 (1979). The Amendments were not meant "to cover employees who are not engaged in loading, unloading, repairing, or building a vessel, just because they are injured in an area adjoining navigable waters used for such activity." H. R. Rep. No. 92-1441, p. 11 (1972); S. Rep. No. 92-1125, p. 13 (1972). We have never read "maritime employment" to extend so far beyond those actually involved in moving cargo between ship and land transportation. Both Caputo and *P.C. Pfeiffer Co.* make this clear and lead us to the conclusion that Gray was not engaged in maritime employment for purposes of the LHWCA.[10]

Gray was a welder. His work had nothing to do with the loading or unloading process, nor is there any indication that he was even employed in the maintenance of equipment used in such tasks. Gray's welding work was far removed from traditional LHWCA activities, notwithstanding the fact that he unloaded his own gear upon arriving at a platform by

---

[10] This view of "maritime employment" does not preclude benefits for those whose injury would have been covered before 1972 because it occurred "on navigable waters." *Director, OWCP v. Perini North River Associates*, 459 U.S. 297 (1983). No claim is made that Gray was injured "on navigable waters." Indeed, it was agreed by all counsel at oral argument that prior to 1972 Gray would not have been covered, except arguably by operation of the Lands Act. *See* Tr. of Oral Arg. 11, 46, 52-54. *See also* 703 F.2d, at 179.

In light of the dissent's reliance on *Perini, post*, at 442-443, we point out that that decision was carefully limited to coverage of an employee "injured while performing his job upon actual navigable waters." 459 U.S., at 299; *see id.*, at 305, 311-312, 315, 324. The Court's rationale was that, first, any employee injured on navigable waters would have been covered prior to 1972, and, second, Congress did not intend to restrict coverage in adopting its "maritime employment" test. The holding was, "of course," limited to workers covered prior to 1972, *id.*, at 325, n. 34, a group to which Gray does not belong. The opinion says nothing about the contours of the status rquirement as applied to a worker, like Gray, who was not injured on navigable waters. To hold that enactment of the status requirement did not constrict prior coverage is wholly different from refusing to view that requirement as a meaningful limit on the Act's extended coverage.

boat. Tr. of Oral Arg. 56. He built and maintained pipelines and the platforms themselves. There is nothing inherently maritime about those tasks. They are also performed on land, and their nature is not significantly altered by the marine environment, particularly since exploration and development of the Continental Shelf are not themselves maritime commerce.

The dissent emphasizes that Gray was generally on or near the water and faced maritime hazards. Post, at 445-449. To the extent this is so, it is relevant to "situs," not "status." To hold that Gray was necessarily engaged in maritime employment because he was on a drilling platform would ignore Congress' admonition that not everyone on a covered situs automatically satisfies the status test. *See* S. Rep. No. 92-1125, p. 13 (1972). The dissent considers "[the] maritime nature of the occupation ... apparent from examining its location in terms of the expanded situs coverage of the 1972 Amendments." Post, at 446. We recognize that the nature of a particular job is defined in part by its location. But to classify Gray's employment as maritime because he was on a covered situs, post, at 448, or in a "maritime environment," post, at 450, would blur together requirements Congress intended to be distinct. We cannot thus read the status requirement out of the statute.

III

Respondents, and the dissenters, object that denying coverage to someone in Gray's position will result in exactly the sort of inconsistent, checkered coverage that Congress sought to eliminate in 1972. In the words of the court below, it creates a "curious hole" in coverage, 703 F.2d, at 178, because Gray would have been covered had he been injured on navigable waters or on the outer shelf.

We do not find the argument compelling. First, this submission goes far beyond Congress' undoubted desire to treat equally all workers engaged in loading or unloading a ship, whether they were injured on the ship or on an adjoining pier or dock. The former were covered prior to 1972; the latter were not. Both are covered under the 1972 Amendments. Second, there will always be a boundary to coverage, and there will always be people who cross it during their employment. *Nacirema Operating Co. v. Johnson*, 396 U.S. 212, 223-224 (1969). If that phenomenon was enough to require coverage, the Act would have to reach much further than anyone argues that it does or should. Third, the inconsistent coverage here results primarily from the explicit geographic limitation to the Lands Act's incorporation of the LHWCA. Gray would indeed have been covered for a significant portion of his work-time, but because of the Lands Act, not because he fell within the terms of the LHWCA. Congress' desire to make LHWCA coverage uniform reveals little about the position of those for whom partial coverage results from a separate statute. This is especially true because that statute draws a clear geographical boundary that will predictably result in workers moving in and out of coverage.

As we have said before in this area, if Congress' coverage decisions are mistaken as a matter of policy, it is for Congress to change them. We should not legislate for them. *See Victory Carriers, Inc. v. Law*, 404 U.S. 202, 216 (1971).

IV

Because Gray's employment was not "maritime," he does not qualify for benefits under the LHWCA. We need not determine whether he satisfied the Act's situs requirement. We express no opinion on his argument that he is covered by 43 U.S.C. § 1333(b). The judgment is reversed, and the case is remanded to the Court of Appeals for further proceedings consistent with this opinion.

It is so ordered.

Justice MARSHALL, with whom Justice BRENNAN, Justice BLACKMUN, and Justice O'CONNOR join, dissenting

Today the Court holds that a marine petroleum worker is not covered by the Longshoremen's and Harbor Workers' Compensation Act (LHWCA or Act), 44 Stat. 1424, as amended, 33 U.S.C. § 901 *et seq.*, when pursuing his occupation on a fixed offshore rig within the 3-mile limit of a State's territorial waters. Although such an individual routinely travels over water as an essential part of his job and performs the rest of his job adjacent to and surrounded by water, he is not covered because, in the Court's view, his occupation is not "maritime employment." *See* § 2(3), 33 U.S.C. § 902(3). The Court reaches this conclusion even though a worker of the same occupation, working in the same industry, and performing the same tasks on a rig located in the same place, would be covered if that rig were one that was capable of floating. Neither the Court nor any of the parties have identified any reason why Congress might have desired this distinction. To the contrary, a principal congressional goal behind the 1972 Amendments was to rid the Act of just such arbitrary distinctions derived from traditional admiralty jurisprudence. Because the coverage pattern that the Court adopts is at odds with the Act's 1972 Amendments, and because the accident here meets the Amendments' status and situs tests, I respectfully dissent.

* * *

Note: Sieracki Seamen

In *Blancq v. Hapag-Lloyd A.G.*, 986 F. Supp. 376, 1998 AMC 1440 (E.D. La. 1997), the court concluded:

> River pilots are maritime workers who do not qualify as Jones Act "seamen" and who do not fit comfortably within the LHWCA. Both of these statutory schemes were created in favor of an employee against his employer. In this case, the parties do not dispute that Captain Blancq was self-employed and acted as an independent contractor, with no connection to a particular vessel. Captain Blancq was not employed by the vessel owner. Rather, he is a member and a shareholder of the Crescent River Port Pilots' Association (the "Pilots' Association"). According to its charter, the Pilots' Association is a non- profit corporation, the purpose of which is "[t]o effect the corporate association of licensed and commissioned Louisiana Crescent River Port Pilots, for their mutual benefit and social betterment." Pl.'s Supplemental Mem., Attach., Art. III. Further, another objective of the corporation is "[t]o provide for a pension and welfare plan for retired shareholders of this corporation, and for their families." *Id.* Each pilot-member holds one share in the corporation, which functions to collect pilotage fees and distribute them to the membership "in their just proportion" after deduction of costs and expenses. *Id.*, Art. VII. Additionally, the Pilots' Association makes rules for the assignment of members to pilot jobs. The charter and by-laws do not characterize pilots as employees of the Pilots'

> Association, but refers to them as shareholders and members. Given plaintiff's unique employment status, and in the absence of Fifth Circuit authority to the contrary, this Court concludes that it is consistent with the purposes behind the LHWCA and general maritime law to exclude a river pilot from coverage under the LHWCA.

---

3. Sieracki Liability

The warranty of seaworthiness is a duty that is generally owed to those employees covered under the Jones Act. *See* 1 SCHOENBAUM, *supra,* § 6-27, at 345. However, for those workers who "fall into the crack between seamen and longshore workers," the *Sieracki* doctrine and the warranty of seaworthiness "still rule[ ] the sea." *Id.*, § 6-27, at 347. In *Seas Shipping v. Sieracki*, 328 U.S. 85, 99, 66 S. Ct. 872, 880, 90 L. Ed. 1099 (1946), the Supreme Court extended the remedy of unseaworthiness to longshoremen "doing a seaman's work and incurring a seaman's hazards." The *Sieracki* doctrine was expanded by the Supreme Court in *Pope & Talbot, Inc. v. Hawn*, 346 U.S. 406, 413, 74 S. Ct. 202, 207, 98 L.Ed. 143 (1953), to include independent contractors who were subject to the same dangers as those crew members directly employed by the vessel. A river pilot who aids in the vessel's navigation is engaged in seaman's work and exposed to typical seaman's dangers.

The 1972 Amendments to the LHWCA eliminated the unseaworthiness remedy from any employee covered under the LHWCA. *See* 33 U.S.C. § 905(b). Although some courts have concluded that the 1972 Amendments entirely abolished the *Sieracki* doctrine, *see, e.g., Normile v. Maritime Co. of Philippines*, 643 F.2d 1380 (9th Cir.1981), the Fifth Circuit has made clear that persons excluded from the LHWCA's coverage may qualify as *Sieracki* seamen for the warranty of seaworthiness. *See Aparicio v. Swan Lake*, 643 F.2d 1109 (5th Cir.1981) (holding that under circumstances in which the maritime worker is not covered by the LHWCA, he may invoke the *Sieracki* unseaworthiness action against the vessel owner); *see also Cormier v. Oceanic Contractors, Inc.*, 696 F.2d 1112, 1113 (5th Cir.1983) (foreign worker outside of LHWCA's coverage entitled to unseaworthiness remedy), *cert. denied*, 464 U.S. 821, 104 S. Ct. 85, 78 L. Ed. 2d 94 (1983); *Coats v. Penrod Drilling Corp.*, 785 F. Supp. 614, 622-24 (S.D. Miss.1992) (shore-based worker testing equipment on offshore rig entitled to *Sieracki* claim), *aff'd*, 61 F.3d 1113, 1118 n.2 (*en banc*) (noting that viability of *Sieracki* seaman status was not before the court); *Laakso v. Mitsui & Co. USA, Inc.*, Civ. A. No.88-2450, 1989 WL 149186 at *8-*9 (Dec. 6, 1989 E.D.La.) (worker outside of LHWCA's coverage retains his *Sieracki* unseaworthiness action); *Clark*, 631 F. Supp. at 1283 (pilot not covered under LHWCA is clearly due his remedy for unseaworthiness).

Having concluded that Captain Blancq falls outside of both the Jones Act and the LHWCA, he is eligible for the warranty of seaworthiness.[9]

* * *

---

[9] The Court notes that Captain Blancq also has a cause of action for negligence under the general maritime law. The duty of care owed to Captain Blancq by the defendants is one of reasonable care under the particular circumstances. *See Kermarec v. Compagnie Generale Transatlantique*, 358 U.S. 625, 79 S. Ct. 406, 3 L. Ed. 2d 550 (1959).

C. Exclusive Liability of the Employer

33 U.S.C. §§ 904-5, 933

§ 904. Liability for compensation

(a) Every employer shall be liable for and shall secure the payment to his employees of the compensation payable under sections 907, 908, and 909 of this title. In the case of an employer who is a subcontractor, only such subcontractor fails to secure the payment of compensation shall the contractor be liable for and be required to secure the payment of compensation. A subcontractor shall not be deemed to have failed to secure the payment of compensation if the contractor has provided insurance for such compensation for the benefit of the subcontractor.

(b) Compensation shall be payable irrespective of fault as a cause for the injury.

§ 905. Exclusiveness of liability

(a) Employer liability; failure of employer to secure payment of compensation

The liability of an employer prescribed in section 904 of this title shall be exclusive and in place of all other liability of such employer to the employee, his legal representative, husband or wife, parents, dependents, next of kin, and anyone otherwise entitled to recover damages from such employer at law or in admiralty on account of such injury or death, except that if an employer fails to secure payment of compensation as required by this chapter, an injured employee, or his legal representative in case death results from the injury, may elect to claim compensation under the chapter or to maintain an action at law or in admiralty for damages on account of such injury or death. In such action the defendant may not plead as a defense that the injury was caused by the negligence of a fellow servant, or that the employee assumed the risk of his employment, or that the injury was due to the contributory negligence of the employee. For purposes of this subsection, a contractor shall be deemed the employer of a subcontractor's employees only if the subcontractor fails to secure the payment of compensation as required by section 904 of this title.

(b) Negligence of vessel

In the event of injury to a person covered under this chapter caused by the negligence of a vessel, then such person, or anyone otherwise entitled to recover damages by reason thereof, may bring an action against such vessel as a third party in accordance with the provisions of section 933 of this title, and the employer shall not be liable to the vessel for such damages directly or indirectly and any agreements or warranties to the contrary shall be void. If such person was employed by the vessel to provide stevedoring services, no such action shall be permitted if the injury was caused by the negligence of persons engaged in providing stevedoring services to the vessel. If such person was employed to provide shipbuilding, repairing, or breaking services and such person's employer was the owner, owner pro hac vice, agent, operator, or charterer of the vessel, no such action shall be permitted, in whole or in part or directly or indirectly, against the injured person's employer (in any capacity, including as the vessel's owner, owner pro hac vice, agent, operator, or charterer) or against the employees of the employer. The liability of the vessel under this subsection shall not be

based upon the warranty of seaworthiness or a breach thereof at the time the injury occurred. The remedy provided in this subsection shall be exclusive of all other remedies against the vessel except remedies available under this chapter.
(c) Outer Continental Shelf
In the event that the negligence of a vessel causes injury to a person entitled to receive benefits under this chapter by virtue of section 1333 of Title 43, then such person, or anyone otherwise entitled to recover damages by reason thereof, may bring an action against such vessel in accordance with the provisions of subsection (b) of this section. Nothing contained in subsection (b) of this section shall preclude the enforcement according to its terms of any reciprocal indemnity provision whereby the employer of a person entitled to receive benefits under this chapter by virtue of section 1333 of Title 43 and the vessel agree to defend and indemnify the other for cost of defense and loss or liability for damages arising out of or resulting from death or bodily injury to their employees.

* * *

§ 933. Compensation for Injuries Where Third Persons Are Liable

(a) Election of remedies

If on account of a disability or death for which compensation is payable under this chapter the person entitled to such compensation determines that some person other than the employer or a person or persons in his employ is liable in damages, he need not elect whether to receive such compensation or to recover damages against such third person.

Notes

1. ***Relationship Between 33 U.S.C. § 905(b) and 33 U.S.C. § 933***

§ 905(b) (*see, supra*) provides a cause of action to a longshoreman injured due to the negligence of a vessel. § 905(b) allows the injured longshoreman or a "third party in accordance with the provisions of § 933 of this title..." to bring a negligence action against the vessel. § 933(a) provides that where a longshoreman is injured due to the negligence of another he does not need to choose either to receive benefits from his employer under the LHWCA or to sue the negligent third party. Under § 933(b), acceptance of compensation from the employer under the LHWCA operates as an assignment to the employer of all rights of the injured longshoreman, unless the longshoreman commences an action against the third party within six months of the acceptance of compensation. However, if the employer fails to bring the action within ninety days of the assignment, he loses the right to bring any such action and the right reverts to the injured employee. If the employer brings the action, he is entitled to reasonable attorney's fees incurred in bringing the action plus any amounts actually paid to the injured employee and the present value of any amounts that will have to be paid in the future. An recovery exceeding that amount is to be paid to the party entitled to compensation. (§ 933(e)).

2. *Actions Under State Law*

In *Garvin v. Alumax of South Carolina*, 787 F.2d 910 , 1987 AMC 402, (4th Cir. 1987) *cert. denied*, 479 U.S. 915 (1986), the court stated:

> As initially enacted, when the application of the LHWCA stopped at the water's edge, the third party claim would usually be one in admiralty. When application of the federal statute was moved inland to supplement state workmen's compensation statutes without displacing them, a third party claim under state law by a recipient of benefits under the LHWCA was not converted into a maritime claim. Its scope, including available defenses, is governed by state law. Thus in *Holland v. Sea-Land Service*, 655 F.2d 556 (4th Cir. 1981), *cert. denied* 455 U.S. 919 (1982), we held that the defendant, in an action brought by a recipient of benefits under the LHWCA for damages on account of injury for which he was receiving compensation, could defend on the basis of the state's contributory negligence rule.
>
> A similar result was reached in *Millspaugh v. Port of Portland*, 25 Ore. App. 389, 671 P. 2d 743 (1983), in which it was held that Oregon's rule of municipal immunity is applicable to such a claim.
>
> The Supreme Court itself left no doubt about the matter in *Victory Carriers, Inc. v. Law*, 404 U.S. 202 (1971). The third party action, when founded on state law, is a creature of state law and is to be governed entirely by it. Indeed, in *Ferri v. Ackerman*, 444 U.S. 1983 (1979), the Supreme Court stated with respect to such a third party claim by an LHWCA compensation recipient:
>
> When state law creates a cause of action, the state is free to define the defenses to the claim, including the defense of immunity, unless the state rule is in conflict with federal law.
>
> The South Carolina rule of immunity of a contractor in the position of Alumax is different from that under the LHWCA, but not in conflict with it, for Congress has not purported to prescribe the immunity rules to be applied by states in actions brought upon state law claims. The federal immunity rule is to be applied when the third party claim is a federal claim; when the third party claim is a state law claim, the immunity rules of that state are to be applied. The federal and state statutes are readily harmonized, and each may function in its own sphere without interference with the other.

In *Grantham v. Avondale Industries, Inc.*, 964 F.2d 471, 1993 AMC 1671 (5th Cir. 1992), Fred Grantham, a painter, was employed by International Marine Industrial Applicators. International Marine contracted with Avondale Industries to paint portions of a ship being constructed. Grantham fell and was injured while painting the ship. Grantham received benefits from International Marine under LHWCA and sued Avondale for negligence and strict liability in federal district court. His suit was based on diversity of citizenship. The district court dismissed his case holding that Avondale, as an employer of Grantham, was entitled to immunity from tort claims.

Under the LHWCA, an employee may not sue his employer in tort for work related injuries. But, under § 905(b), tort remedies are available against negligent third parties. Therefore, the court needed to first determine whether Avondale qualified as a third party subject to suit, or was immunized as an employer of Grantham.

Under federal law, since International Marine provided benefits, Avondale was not the statutory employer of Grantham: "[A] contractor shall be deemed the employer of a subcontractor's employees only if the subcontractor fails to secure the payment of compensation as required by ... this title." *See* 33 U.S.C. § 905(a). Louisiana State law provides, to the contrary, that a contractor is a "statutory employer" and, therefore, immune from tort liability. *See* La. Rev. Stat. 23:1032. Thus, the more important question was whether the federal or state immunity rule should be applied when an employee receives benefits under the LHWCA.

The Fifth Circuit held that the issue of whether the state or federal immunity rule should be applied is a question of federal law and, thus, the decisions of the Fifth Circuit controlled in this case. The rule applied in the Fifth Circuit is that "the LHWCA's immunity rule control[s] in a diversity action in which an employee of a subcontractor sue[s] the contractor on a state law negligence theory." Therefore, the court found that Avondale was not immune from a state tort claim, and, thus, Grantham's suit was improperly dismissed.

In *Brown v. Avondale Industries, Inc.*, 617 So. 2d 482 (La. 1993), the Supreme Court of Louisiana held that a Louisiana statute providing immunity was not available where the plaintiff was proceeding under LHWCA because the issue was governed by federal law, not state law. By doing so, the court implicitly followed *Grantham* and disagreed with *Garvin*.

D. Suits Against Shipowners

Notes

1. A shipowner who negligently inflicts injuries on a maritime worker commits a maritime tort. *See Pope & Talbot v. Hawn*, 346 U.S. 406, 1954 AMC 1 (1953); *see alsoInternational Stevedoring Co. v. Haverty*, 272 U.S. 40, 1926 AMC 1638 (1926). The matter is within the admiralty jurisdiction and subject to federal maritime law. In such a case, contributory negligence is not a bar to the action by the injured worker but results in mitigation of damages. *Pope v. Talbot v. Hawn, supra.*

2. In *Seas Shipping Co. v. Sieracki*, 328 U.S. 85, 66 S.Ct. 872, 90 L.Ed. 1099, 1946 AMC 689 (1946), the Supreme Court held that the warranty of seaworthiness extends to longshoremen and other harbor workers. Thus, an injured longshoreman could proceed directly against a shipowner to recover for injuries sustained as a result of the unseaworthiness of the vessel. In turn, the shipowner could proceed against the employer of the longshoreman for indemnity under the *Ryan* doctrine.

The 1972 amendments to the LHWCA purport to eliminate the action for unseaworthiness that was available to a longshoreman or harbor worker under the *Sieracki* doctrine. However doubts continue to be voiced as to the viability of *Sieracki* with respect to longshoremen and harbor workers *not* covered by the LHWCA. For this reason the following subsection addresses actions brought against a shipowner under the theory of unseaworthiness as well as negligence.

3. In *Gutierrez v. Waterman Steamship Corporation*, 373 U.S. 206, 83 S.Ct. 1185, 10 L.Ed.2d 297, 1963 AMC 1649 (1963), the United States Supreme Court allowed recovery for personal injuries sustained by a longshoreman on a pier on grounds of the unseaworthiness of the vessel. Beans had spilled on the pier from defective sacks, found to be an instrumentality of the vessel, and plaintiff slipped and fell when he stepped on loose beans. In *Victory Carriers v. Law*, 404 U.S. 202, 92 S.Ct. 418, 30 L.Ed.2d 383, 1972 AMC 1 (1971), a longshoreman was likewise injured on the pier while driving a forklift loaded with cargo. The forklift belonged to his land-based employer; it was not an instrumentality of the ship. In an action brought by the longshoreman against the shipowner on grounds of unseaworthiness of the vessel, the Court held that because the injury occurred on the pier, admiralty jurisdiction was lacking. Accordingly, the matter was governed by state law.

After the 1972 Amendments to LHWCA, a longshoreman's action under the statute cannot be grounded on unseaworthiness. However, question remains as to the existence of admiralty jurisdiction in an action by a longshoreman grounded on negligence for injuries sustained on the pier. According to § 903(a) of LHWCA, for purposes of compensation, a pier is considered to be "navigable waters" of the United States. However, LHWCA coverage is broader than the current view concerning the limits of admiralty tort jurisdiction under 28 U.S.C. § 1333. In this respect, the *Law* case still controls. *See Parker v. South Louisiana Contractors, Inc.*, 537 F.2d 113, 1976 AMC 2201 (5th Cir. 1976); *Holland v. Sea-Land Service, Inc.*, 655 F.2d 556, 1981 AMC 2474 (4th Cir. 1981). *Gutierrez* may still be pertinent when injuries on the pier are negligently caused by operations involving an instrumentality of the ship.

1. Negligence: Duty and Standard of Care

SCINDIA STEAM NAVIGATION CO., LTD. v. DE LOS SANTOS

451 U.S. 156, 101 S.Ct. 1614, 68 L.Ed.2d 1, 1981 A.M.C. 601 (1981)

Justice WHITE delivered the opinion of the Court.

Respondent Santos, a longshoreman and an employee of respondent Seattle Stevedore Co., was injured while he was helping load the M/S *Jalaratna*, a vessel owned by petitioner Scindia Steam Navigation Co., Ltd. He later brought an action against Scindia pursuant to § 5(b) of the Longshoremen's and Harbor Workers' Compensation Act (Act), as amended in 1972, which, as set forth in 33 U.S.C. § 905(b), ...

* * *

The District Court granted petitioner's motion for summary judgment; the Court of Appeals, disagreeing with the District Court on both the facts and the law, reversed and remanded for further proceedings. 598 F.2d 480 (CA9 1979). We granted certiorari, 446 U.S. 934, 100 S.Ct. 2150, 64 L.Ed.2d 786, because the Courts of Appeals are in considerable disagreement as to the meaning and application of § 905(b).

I

For present purposes, we take the facts from the opinion of the Court of Appeals, which properly viewed the case in the light most favorable to Santos, against whom summary judgment had been granted.

On December 10, 1972, Seattle Stevedore Co., pursuant to its undertaking with Scindia, was engaged in loading a cargo of wheat into a hold of the M/S *Jalaratna*. A winch, part of the ship's gear, was being used to lower wooden pallets, each containing seventy 50-pound sacks of wheat, into the hold. Because of the location of the winch controls, the longshoreman operator relied on the hatch tender, another longshoreman, to signal him when to start and stop the winch while lowering a pallet of sacks into the hold. Santos and three other longshoremen were in the hold. Their task was to remove sacks of wheat from the pallet and properly stow them.

On the day of the accident, as it had for the two previous days, the braking mechanism of the winch was malfunctioning in that it would not quickly stop the descent of a loaded pallet, which would continue to drop for several feet before coming to a stop. At the time important here, while a pallet was being lowered, the hatch tender signaled the winch operator to stop the descent of the load. The brake was applied, but the pallet did not stop before striking a pallet jack[5] with some force and spilling about half the sacks of wheat from the pallet. The hatch tender signaled the operator to raise the pallet about 15 feet and, believing that the remaining sacks on the pallet were secure enough not to fall, permitted Santos and the other men to clear away the spilled sacks then lying below in the hold. Some minutes later, however, more sacks fell from the pallet, striking and injuring Santos.

[5] A pallet jack is a small, wheeled, cartlike vehicle with prongs on the front like a forklift with which the longshoremen in the hold would cart the pallet load to the wings of the hold where they would then remove the sacks and stow them by hand. Record 77.

There was dispute as to whether the additional sacks fell because the suspended pallet was swinging back and forth or because while the pallet was suspended the braking mechanism slipped on three or four occasions, each time requiring the operator to raise it again, thus working loose the additional sacks that fell on Santos.

Relying on the legislative history of the 1972 Amendments to the Act, the District Court held that the negligence standards governing the longshoreman's action against a shipowner under § 905(b) are best expressed in Restatement (Second) of Torts §§ 343 and 343A (1965), which purport to state the prevailing or preferred rules governing the liability of a possessor of land to an invitee.[6] Under these land-based negligence standards, the District Court thought

> "a shipowner is not liable for dangerous conditions created by the stevedore's negligence while the stevedore [is] in exclusive control over the manner and area of the work ..., nor is the shipowner under a duty to warn the stevedore or his employees of dangers or open and obvious defects which are known to the stevedore or his employees or which are so obvious and apparent that they may reasonably be expected to discover them." 1976 A.M.C. 2583, 2585.

Based on the admissions of the parties and the depositions available to the court, the District Court concluded (1) that there was no dispute that the premises were in the exclusive control of Seattle during the loading operation and that (2) even if Scindia knew or should have known of the defective winch,[7] the condition of the winch "was open and obvious to the plaintiff" and "the fact that plaintiff undertook his actions free from any direction by the defendant while recognizing that the circumstances were so dangerous, is such that the defendant cannot be held liable as a matter of law." *Id.*, at 2586-2587. In addition, the District Court found that "the alleged defective condition of the winch had only a remote cause-in-fact relationship to plaintiff's accident and could not have been the proximate cause thereof as a matter of law." *Id.*, at 2587. Hence, summary judgment was granted.

---

[6] Restatement (Second) of Torts § 343 provides:

"§ 343. Dangerous Conditions Known to or Discoverable by Possessor

"A possessor of land is subject to liability for physical harm caused to his invitees by a condition on the land if, but only if, he

"(a) knows or by the exercise of reasonable care would discover the condition, and should realize that it involves an unreasonable risk of harm to such invitees, and

"(b) should expect that they will not discover or realize the danger, or will fail to protect themselves against it, and

"(c) fails to exercise reasonable care to protect them against the danger."

Restatement (Second) of Torts § 343A provides:

"§ 343A. Known or Obvious Dangers

"(1) A possessor of land is not liable to his invitees for physical harm caused to them by any activity or condition on the land whose danger is known or obvious to them, unless the possessor should anticipate the harm despite such knowledge or obviousness.

"(2) In determining whether the possessor should anticipate harm from a known or obvious danger, the fact that the invitee is entitled to make use of public land, or of the facilities of a public utility, is a factor of importance indicating that the harm should be anticipated."

[7] The District Court stated, 1976 A.M.C., at 2586, that "[p]laintiff does not controvert defendant's claim that no one from the ship's crew was ever informed of the winch's condition prior to the accident" and further stated that if the winch was defective, it was a "condition [about] which the Court finds the shipowner did not know nor should it reasonably have been expected to know, given the exclusive control of the gear by the stevedores during the relevant time period." *Ibid.* Scindia contended in any event that the winch was not defective but concedes that for present purposes the case should be judged on the assumption that it was.

Reversing, the Court of Appeals disagreed with the District Court and with other Courts of Appeals with respect to the applicable law. Sections 343 and 343A of the Restatement were improper measures of the shipowner's liability for negligence under § 905(b)[9] because those sections in effect incorporated notions of contributory negligence and assumption of risk that were inapplicable under the maritime law. Instead, the Court of Appeals declared the controlling standard under § 905(b) to be the following:

> "A vessel is subject to liability for injuries to longshoremen working on or near the vessel caused by conditions on the vessel if, but only if, the shipowner
> "(a) knows of, or by the exercise of reasonable care would discover, the condition, and should realize that it involves an unreasonable risk of harm to such longshoremen, and
> "(b) the shipowner fails to exercise reasonable care under the circumstances to protect the longshoremen against the danger." 598 F.2d, at 485.

Under this standard, Scindia's duty to inspect did not end even if the vessel was turned over to the stevedore in safe condition. If conditions dangerous to the longshoremen subsequently developed, in light of the vessel's practical opportunities to discover the dangers and remedy them, failure to do so could be negligence on its part.

Under the Court of Appeals' view of the law there were several material facts in dispute that were for a jury to resolve: whether the shipowner knew or should have known of the defective winch; whether Seattle was in exclusive control of the loading in the sense that only Seattle could have repaired the winch; whether the defective operation of the winch had caused the initial spillage of the sacks, thus necessitating a cleanup, or had later been the proximate cause of the additional sacks falling from the pallet and injuring Santos. Accordingly, the Court of Appeals set aside the judgment of the District Court and remanded for further proceedings.

II

Initially, we must briefly revisit the 1972 Amendments to the Act. Prior to 1972, a longshoreman injured while loading or unloading a ship could receive compensation payments and also have judgment against the shipowner if the injury was caused by the ship's unseaworthiness or negligence. *Seas Shipping Co. v. Sieracki*, 328 U.S. 85, 66 S.Ct. 872, 90 L.Ed. 1099 (1946). Proof of unseaworthiness required no proof of fault on the part of the shipowner other than an unsafe, injury-causing condition on the vessel. This was true even though the condition was caused, created, or brought into play by the stevedore or its employees. In the latter event, the shipowner could recover over against a stevedore for

---

[9] The Court of Appeals acknowledged that the Courts of Appeals for the Second, Fourth, and Fifth Circuits had relied on these sections in § 905(b) suits. See, *e. g., Canizzo v. Farrell Lines, Inc.*, 579 F.2d 682 (CA2 1978); *Gay v. Ocean Transport & Trading, Ltd.*, 546 F.2d 1233 (CA5 1977); *Anuszewski v. Dynamic Mariners Corp., Panama*, 540 F.2d 757 (CA4 1976); *Napoli v. Hellenic Lines, Ltd.*, 536 F.2d 505 (CA2 1976). The Court of Appeals for the Second Circuit has recently reaffirmed its position. *Evans v. S.S. "Campeche,"* 639 F.2d 848 (1981). On the other hand, the First and Third Circuits, like the Ninth Circuit, have held that these sections should not apply in § 905(b) suits since they might bar a longshoreman from recovery because he was contributorily negligent or because he voluntarily encountered a known or obvious risk. See *Sarauw v. Oceanic Navigation Corp.*, 622 F.2d 1168 (CA3 1980); *Johnson v. A/S Ivarans Rederi*, 613 F.2d 334 (CA1 1980); *Griffith v. Wheeling Pittsburgh Steel Corp.*, 610 F.2d 116 (CA3 1979); *Lawson v. United States*, 605 F.2d 448 (CA9 1979); *Bachtel v. Mammoth Bulk Carriers, Ltd.*, 605 F.2d 438 (CA9 1979); 598 F.2d 480 (CA9 1979) (case below).

breach of express or implied warranty to handle the cargo in a reasonably safe manner. *Ryan Stevedoring Co. v. Pan-Atlantic S.S. Corp.*, 350 U.S. 124, 76 S.Ct. 232, 100 L.Ed. 133 (1956).

The 1972 Amendments, particularly by adding § 905(b), radically changed this scheme of things. The compensation payments due the longshoreman from the stevedore for injuries incurred in the course of his employment were substantially increased; the longshoreman's right to recover for unseaworthiness was abolished; his right to recover from the shipowner for negligence was preserved in § 905(b), which provided a statutory negligence action against the ship; and the stevedore's obligation to indemnify the shipowner if the latter was held liable to the longshoreman was abolished.

Section 905(b) did not specify the acts or omissions of the vessel that would constitute negligence. In light of the differences among the lower federal courts as to the construction and application of § 905(b), neither can it be said that the legislative history, which has been analyzed and reanalyzed in the course of these cases, furnishes sure guidance for construing § 905(b).[13] Much was left to be resolved through the "application of accepted principles of tort law and the ordinary process of litigation." Rep., p. 11.

III

We held in *Marine Terminals v. Burnside Shipping Co.*, 394 U.S. 404, 415, 89 S.Ct. 1144, 1150, 22 L.Ed.2d 371 (1969), that the vessel owes to the stevedore and his longshoremen employees the duty of exercising due care "under the circumstances." This duty extends at least to exercising ordinary care under the circumstances to have the ship and its equipment in such condition that an expert and experienced stevedore will be able by the exercise of reasonable care to carry on its cargo operations with reasonable safety to persons and property, and to warning the stevedore of any hazards on the ship or with respect to its equipment that are known to the vessel or should be known to it in the exercise of reasonable care, that would likely be encountered by the stevedore in the course of his cargo operations and that are not known by the stevedore and would not be obvious to or anticipated by him if reasonably competent in the performance of his work. *Id.*, at 416, n. 18, 89 S.Ct., at 1151. The shipowner thus has a duty with respect to the condition of the

[13] Section 905(b) itself negates the vessel's liability for unseaworthiness, and the Committee Reports state that the purpose of eliminating this remedy was to place the injured longshoreman "in the same position he would be if he were injured in non-maritime employment ashore ... and not to endow him with any special maritime theory of liability or cause of action under whatever judicial nomenclature it may be called, such as 'unseaworthiness', 'non-delegable duty', or the like." S.Rep.No.92-1125, p. 10 (1972) (hereafter Rep.). (H.R.Rep.No.92- 1441 (1972), U.S.Code Cong. & Admin.News 1972, 4698, is in all relevant respects identical to the Senate Report.) The vessel was not to be liable on the theory of unseaworthiness for the acts or omissions of stevedores, or of the employees of stevedores, for the manner in which the stevedore performed its work, or for its defective gear or equipment. Rep., p. 10. Its liability was to be "based on its own negligence" and could be proved only if it was shown "to have acted or have failed to act in a negligent manner such as would render a land-based third party in non-maritime pursuits liable under similar circumstances." *Id.*, at 11.

At the same time, the Committees observed that the statutory cause of action for negligence would "meet the objective of encouraging safety because the vessel would still be required to exercise the same care as a land-based person in providing a safe place to work." *Id.*, at 10. Nothing was intended "to derogate from the vessel's responsibility to take appropriate corrective action where it knows or should have known about a dangerous condition" as long as the vessel was not "chargeable with the negligence of the stevedore or employees of the stevedore." *Id.*, at 10, 11.

The Committees also anticipated that in § 905(b) cases, as in other admiralty cases, the rule of comparative negligence would apply and the defense of assumption of risk would be barred. Furthermore, the Reports emphasized that the amendments were not intended to relieve any person from his duties and obligations under the Occupational Safety and Health Act of 1970.

Otherwise, the definition of the vessel's negligence and its resulting liability were left to be "resolved through the application of accepted principles of tort law and the ordinary process of litigation--just as they are in cases involving alleged negligence by land-based third parties." Rep., p. 11. It was anticipated, however, that questions arising in § 905(b) cases "shall be determined as a matter of Federal law." Rep., p. 12.

ship's gear, equipment, tools, and work space to be used in the stevedoring operations; and if he fails at least to warn the stevedore of hidden danger which would have been known to him in the exercise of reasonable care, he has breached his duty and is liable if his negligence causes injury to a longshoreman. ... It is also accepted that the vessel may be liable if it actively involves itself in the cargo operations and negligently injures a longshoreman or if it fails to exercise due care to avoid exposing longshoremen to harm from hazards they may encounter in areas, or from equipment, under the active control of the vessel during the stevedoring operation.

The parties, however, like the District Court and the Court of Appeals, are in sharp disagreement as to the vessel's duty under § 905(b) once the stevedore's cargo operations have begun. Scindia contends that the shipowner has no duty to supervise or inspect the stevedore's cargo operations or to take reasonable care to discover dangerous conditions that develop or come to light during the loading or unloading. Scindia also submits that even if the vessel learns of the hazard, it has no duty to correct it and is entitled as a matter of law to rely on the stevedore to protect his employees from injury. This is true, Scindia argues, even though the hazard is an obviously defective ship's winch being used by the stevedore and his longshoremen employees,[14] and even if the winch was defective when the stevedore came aboard and the vessel is charged with knowledge of the condition. Respondents, on the other hand, defend the view of the Court of Appeals that the vessel is subject to a continuing duty to use reasonable care to discover dangerous conditions exposing longshoremen to unreasonable risk of harm and to exercise reasonable care under the circumstances to protect them. We are unable to agree wholly with either of these submissions.

Considering first the position of the Court of Appeals, we cannot agree that the vessel's duty to the longshoreman requires the shipowner to inspect or supervise the stevedoring operation. Congress intended to make the vessel answerable for its own negligence and to terminate its automatic, faultless responsibility for conditions caused by the negligence or other defaults of the stevedore. Cases holding the vessel liable on the ground that it owed nondelegable duties to protect the longshoremen from injury were rejected.[15] It would be inconsistent with the Act to hold, nevertheless, that the shipowner has a continuing duty to take reasonable steps to discover and correct dangerous conditions that develop during the loading or unloading process. Such an approach would repeatedly result in holding the shipowner solely liable for conditions that are attributable to the stevedore, rather than the

---

[14] Because the legislative history suggests that the shipowner's liability is to be judged by land-based standards, see n. 13, *supra*, it is urged that the District Court properly turned to and applied §§ 343 and 343A of the Restatement (Second) of Torts. But the legislative history does not refer to the Restatement and also states that land-based principles of assumption of risk and contributory negligence are not to be applied in § 905(b) cases. This strongly suggests, as *Kermarec v. Compagnie Generale Transatlantique*, 358 U.S. 625, 79 S.Ct. 406, 3 L.Ed.2d 550 (1959), indicated, that maritime negligence actions are not necessarily to be governed by principles applicable in nonmaritime contexts. Furthermore, since the lower courts are in disagreement not only as to the applicability of §§ 343 and 343A but also as to their import and meaning when applied in the maritime context, those sections, while not irrelevant, do not furnish sure guidance in cases such as this.

[15] "Thus a vessel shall not be liable in damages for acts or omissions of stevedores or employees of stevedores subject to this Act. *Crumedy vs. The J. H. Fisser*, 358 U.S. 423 [79 S.Ct. 445, 3 L.Ed. 413]; *Albanese vs. Matts [Maats]*, 382 U.S. 283 [86 S.Ct. 429, 15 L.Ed.2d 327], *Skibinski vs. Waterman SS Corp.*, [360] F.2d 539; for the manner or method in which stevedores or employees of stevedores subject to this Act perform their work, *A. N. G. [A. & G.] Stevedores vs. Ellerman Lines*, 369 U.S. 355 [82 S.Ct. 780, 7 L.Ed.2d 798], *Blassingill vs. Waterman SS Corp.*, 336 F.2d 367; for gear or equipment of stevedores or employees of stevedores subject to this Act whether used aboard ship, or ashore, *Alaska SS Co. vs. Peterson*, 347 U.S. 396 [74 S.Ct. 601, 98 L.Ed. 798], *Italia Societa vs. Oregon Stevedoring Co.*, 376 U.S. 315 [84 S.Ct. 748, 11 L.Ed.2d 732], or for other categories of unseaworthiness which have been judicially established. This listing of cases is not intended to reflect a judgment as to whether recovery on a particular actual setting could be predicated on the vessel's negligence." Rep., p. 10.

ship. True, the liability would be cast in terms of negligence rather than unseaworthiness, but the result would be much the same. "[C]reation of a shipowner's duty to oversee the stevedore's activity and insure the safety of longshoremen would ... saddle the shipowner with precisely the sort of nondelegable duty that Congress sought to eliminate by amending section 905(b)." *Hurst v. Triad Shipping Co.*, 554 F.2d 1237, 1249-1250, n. 35 (CA3 1977); *Evans v. S.S. "Campeche,"* 639 F.2d 848, 856 (CA2 1981).[16]

As a general matter, the shipowner may rely on the stevedore to avoid exposing the longshoremen to unreasonable hazards. Section 41 of the Act, 33 U.S.C. § 941, requires the stevedore, the longshoremen's employer, to provide a "reasonably safe" place to work and to take such safeguards with respect to equipment and working conditions as the Secretary of Labor may determine to be necessary to avoid injury to longshoremen. The ship is not the common employer of the longshoremen and owes no such statutory duty to them. Furthermore, as our cases indicate, the stevedore normally warrants to discharge his duties in a workman-like manner; and although the 1972 Amendments relieved the stevedore of his duty to indemnify the shipowner for damages paid to longshoremen for injuries caused by the stevedore's breach of warranty, they did not otherwise disturb the contractual undertaking of the stevedore nor the rightful expectation of the vessel that the stevedore would perform his task properly without supervision by the ship.

The approach of the indemnity cases in this Court, beginning with *Ryan Stevedoring Co. v. Pan-Atlantic S.S. Corp.*, 350 U.S. 124, 76 S.Ct. 232, 100 L.Ed. 133 (1956), was that the stevedore was in the best position to avoid accidents during cargo operations and that the shipowner could rely on the stevedore's warranty to perform competently. In *Italia Societa v. Oregon Stevedoring Co.*, 376 U.S. 315, 84 S.Ct. 748, 11 L.Ed.2d 732 (1964), for example, the vessel was found liable for injuries to a longshoreman caused by an unseaworthy condition arising when the stevedore, without negligence, supplied defective equipment used in handling the cargo. We held the vessel entitled to recover over against the stevedore, saying:

> "Oregon, a specialist in stevedoring, was hired to load and unload the petitioner's vessels and to supply the ordinary equipment necessary for these operations. The defective rope which created the condition of unseaworthiness on the vessel and rendered the shipowner liable to the stevedore's employee was supplied by Oregon, and the stevedoring operations in the course of which the longshoreman was injured were in the hands of the employees of Oregon. Not only did the agreement between the shipowner place control of the operations on the stevedore company, but Oregon was also

---

[16] Much is made of the Committees' statement that nothing in the bill "is intended to derogate from the vessel's responsibility to take appropriate corrective action where it knows or should have known about a dangerous condition." *Ibid.* But the statement did not explain what the vessel's "responsibility" is and what "appropriate" action might be, or when it "should have known" of the condition. The Committees did offer an example:

"So, for example, where a longshoreman slips on an oil spill on a vessel's deck and is injured, the proposed amendments to Section 5 would still permit an action against the vessel for negligence. To recover, he must establish that: 1) the vessel put the foreign substance on the deck, or knew that it was there, and willfully or negligently failed to remove it; or 2) the foreign substance had been on the deck for such a period of time that it should have been discovered and removed by the vessel in the exercise of reasonable care by the vessel under the circumstances." *Id.*, at 10-11.

However, when the failure to remove the oil spill would be "willful" or "negligent" or what the exercise of reasonable care under the circumstances would require was not explicated except to say that the "vessel will not be chargeable with the negligence of the stevedore or employees of the stevedore." *Id.*, at 11.

charged under the contract with the supervision of these operations. Although none of these factors affect the shipowner's primary liability to the injured employee of Oregon, since its duty to supply a seaworthy vessel is strict and nondelegable, and extends to those who perform the unloading and loading portion of the ship's work, *Seas Shipping Co. v. Sieracki*, 328 U.S. 85 [66 S.Ct. 872, 90 L.Ed. 1099], cf. *Pope & Talbot v. Hawn*, 346 U.S. 406 [74 S.Ct. 202, 98 L.Ed. 143], they demonstrate that Oregon was in a far better position than the shipowner to avoid the accident. The shipowner defers to the qualification of the stevedoring contractor in the selection and use of equipment and relies on the competency of the stevedore company." *Id.*, at 322-323, 84 S.Ct., at 752-753.

The 1972 Amendments foreclosed indemnity of the shipowner by the stevedore in § 905(b) cases; but they also rejected the notion of a nondelegable duty on the shipowner to provide a safe place to work and did not undermine the justifiable expectations of the vessel that the stevedore would perform with reasonable competence and see to the safety of the cargo operations.

We are of the view that absent contract provision, positive law, or custom to the contrary--none of which has been cited to us in this case--the shipowner has no general duty by way of supervision or inspection to exercise reasonable care to discover dangerous conditions that develop within the confines of the cargo operations that are assigned to the stevedore. The necessary consequence is that the shipowner is not liable to the longshoremen for injuries caused by dangers unknown to the owner and about which he had no duty to inform himself. This conclusion is plainly consistent with the congressional intent to foreclose the faultless liability of the shipowner based on a theory of unseaworthiness or nondelegable duty. The shipowner, within limits, *is* entitled to rely on the stevedore, and owes no duty to the longshoremen to inspect or supervise the cargo operations. To the extent that the judgment of the Court of Appeals rested on a contrary view, we disagree.

IV

We arrive at the more difficult and recurring issue involved in this case: What are the shipowner's duties when he learns that an apparently dangerous condition exists or has developed in the cargo operation, which is known to the stevedore and which may cause injury to the longshoreman? Must the owner take some action? Scindia and the District Court would have it that the vessel is entitled to rely on the expertise and responsibility of the stevedore and is not liable for injuries caused by dangers known by or obvious to the stevedore, who, if he fails to take proper precautions, is necessarily the sole and proximate cause of the injury. There is arguable support for this position in our cases.

* * *

In *Crumady*, the Court declared that "those acting for the vessel owner" had adjusted the winch "in a way that made it unsafe and dangerous for the work at hand." *Id.*, at 427, 79 S.Ct., at 447. It thus appeared that the vessel had at least been negligent, yet it was entitled to shift its entire liability to the stevedore because it was entitled to rely on the stevedore's undertaking to perform in a workmanlike manner. Arguably, Scindia should likewise be justified in expecting Seattle to perform its undertaking and should therefore have no duty or responsibility with respect to the ship's winch, which, if defective, was obviously so and which the stevedore continued to use.

The court below rejected this position, holding that if the vessel should realize that the condition presents an unreasonable risk of harm, it is liable if it "fails to exercise reasonable care under the circumstances" to protect the longshoremen. The court did not suggest how to recognize an "unreasonable risk" of harm from an obvious danger or suggest what reasonable care under the circumstances might be.

The Court of Appeals for the Second Circuit, while disagreeing with the duty-to-inspect thesis of the Court of Appeals in the present case, has also rejected this position, ruling that although the shipowner is normally entitled to rely on the stevedore to guard against hazards to its employees, "there may be circumstances in which it would not be reasonable for the shipowner to assume that the stevedore will correct the problem." *Evans v. S.S. "Campeche,"* 639 F.2d, at 856. As that court sees it, mere knowledge of the danger would not be sufficient in itself to fasten such a duty on the shipowner, but if the shipowner should anticipate that the stevedore will not or cannot correct the danger and that the longshoremen cannot avoid it, then the shipowner's duty is triggered to take steps, reasonable in the circumstances, to eliminate or neutralize the hazard. We are presently unprepared to agree that the shipowner has precisely the duty described by the Court of Appeals for the Second Circuit, but for the reasons that follow we agree that there are circumstances in which the shipowner has a duty to act where the danger to longshoremen arises from the malfunctioning of the ship's gear being used in the cargo operations.

On the facts posited here, for two days prior to the accident, it had been apparent to those working with the winch that this equipment was malfunctioning. Even so, whether it could be safely used or whether it posed an unreasonable risk of harm to Santos or other longshoremen was a matter of judgment committed to the stevedore in the first instance. The malfunctioning being obvious and Seattle having continued to use it, Scindia submits that if it was aware of the condition or was charged with knowledge of it, it was nevertheless entitled to assume that Seattle, the specialist in loading and unloading, considered the equipment reasonably safe and was entitled to rely on that judgment.

Yet it is quite possible, it seems to us, that Seattle's judgment in this respect was so obviously improvident that Scindia, if it knew of the defect and that Seattle was continuing to use it, should have realized the winch presented an unreasonable risk of harm to the longshoremen, [FN22] and that in such circumstances it had a duty to intervene and repair the ship's winch. The same would be true if the defect existed from the outset and Scindia must be deemed to have been aware of is condition.

As we have indicated, the legal duties placed on the stevedore and the vessel's justifiable expectations that those duties will be performed are relevant in determining whether the shipowner has breached its duty. The trial court, and where appropriate the jury, should thus be made aware of the scope of the stevedore's duty under the positive law. But an equally necessary inquiry is whether the pertinent statutes, regulations, or custom place or assume a continuing duty on the vessel to repair defective ship's gear being used by the stevedore in the cargo operation.

... Even in the absence of other statutory or regulatory law placing on the shipowner the obligation to repair a defective winch, a possible inference from the provisions already described is that when a defective winch is discovered, it should not be repaired by the stevedore but should be reported to and repaired by the shipowner. If this is the case, the situation comes down to this: If Scindia was aware that the winch was malfunctioning to some degree, and if there was a jury issue as to whether it was so unsafe that the stevedore should have ceased using it, could the jury also have found that the winch was so clearly unsafe that Scindia should have intervened and stopped the loading operation until the winch was serviceable?

... Based on our own examination of the record, we agree with the Court of Appeals in this respect and with its conclusion that the District Court erred in granting summary judgment. The case should be returned to the District Court and, if necessary, tried to a jury under appropriate instructions.

Accordingly, we affirm the judgment of the Court of Appeals and remand the case to that court for further proceedings consistent with this opinion.

So ordered.

* * *

Justice POWELL, with whom Justice REHNQUIST joins, concurring.

* * *

The difficulty with a more general reasonableness standard like that adopted by the court below is that it fails to deal with the problems of allocating responsibility between the stevedore and the shipowner. It may be that it is "reasonable" for a shipowner to rely on the stevedore to discover and avoid most obvious hazards. But when, in a suit by longshoreman, a jury is presented with the single question whether it was "reasonable" for the shipowner to fail to take action concerning a particular obvious hazard, the jury will be quite likely to find liability. If such an outcome were to become the norm, negligent stevedores would be receiving windfall recoveries in the form of reimbursement for the statutory benefit payments made to the injured longshoremen.[2] This would decrease significantly the incentives toward safety of the party in the best position to prevent injuries, and undercut the primary responsibility of that party for ensuring safety.

---

[2] Under 33 U.S.C. § 905(b), the shipowner is liable in damages to the longshoreman if it was negligent, and it may not seek to recover any part of this liability from the stevedore. The longshoreman's recovery is not reduced to reflect the negligence of the stevedore. *Edmonds v. Compagnie Generale Transatlantique*, 443 U.S. 256, 99 S.Ct. 2753, 61 L.Ed.2d 521 (1979). Under 33 U.S.C. § 933, the stevedore--even if concurrently negligent-receives reimbursement for its statutory benefit payments to the longshoreman, up to the full amount of those payments. See also *Bloomer v. Liberty Mutual Ins. Co.*, 445 U.S. 74, 100 S.Ct. 925, 63 L.Ed. 215 (1980) (stevedore's lien is not reduced by its proportional share of the costs of litigating the negligence suit). As a result of this automatic reimbursement, there is a danger that "concurrently negligent stevedores will be insulated from the obligation to pay statutory workmen's compensation benefits, and thus will have inadequate incentives to provide a safe working environment for their employees." *Edmonds, supra*, 443 U.S., at 274, 99 S.Ct., at 2764 (BLACKMUN, J., dissenting). In cases involving obvious and avoidable hazards, this danger will be realized unless the shipowner's liability is limited to the unusual case in which it should be anticipated that the stevedore will fail to act reasonably. Any more stringent, or less defined, rule of shipowner liability will skew the statutory scheme in a way Congress could not have intended. Cf. *Canizzo v. Farrell Lines, Inc.*, 579 F.2d 682, 687-688 (CA2 1978) (Friendly, J., dissenting).

Notes on the Scindia Rules

1. The Supreme Court again examined the relative duties of the shipowner and the stevedore with regard to the safety of longshoremen in *Howlett v. Birkdale Shipping Co., S.A.*, 512 U.S. 92, 114 S.Ct. 2057, 129 L.Ed. 2d 78, 1194 AMC 1817 (1994). In *Scindia*, the Court articulated three duties that the law imposes on shipowners, succinctly summarized in *Howlett* as:

> The starting point in this regard must be our decision in *Scindia Steam,* which outlined the three general duties shipowners owe to longshoremen. The first, which courts have come to call the "turnover duty," relates to the condition of the ship upon the commencement of stevedoring operations. The second duty, applicable once stevedoring operations have begun, provides that a shipowner must exercise reasonable care to prevent injuries to longshoremen in areas that remain under the "active control of the vessel." The third duty, called the "duty to intervene," concerns the vessel's obligations with regard to cargo operations in areas under the principal control of the independent stevedore.

In *Howlett,* a longshoreman engaged in unloading cargo was injured allegedly because the foreign stevedore improperly loaded the cargo. Howlett asserted that the shipowner was negligent in not supervising the work of the loading stevedore and for not inspecting the stow after the loading had been completed. The Supreme Court rejected these contentions and concluded:

> In sum, the vessel's turnover duty to warn of latent defects in the cargo stow and cargo area is a narrow one. The duty attaches only to latent hazards, defined as hazards that are not known to the stevedore and that would be neither obvious to nor anticipated by a skilled stevedore in the competent performance of its work. Furthermore, the duty encompasses only those hazards that "are known to the vessel or should be known to it in the exercise of reasonable care." Contrary to Howlett's submission, however, the exercise of reasonable care does not require the shipowner to supervise the ongoing operations of the loading stevedore (or other stevedores who handle the cargo before its arrival in port) or to inspect the completed stow.

2. ***Open and Obvious hazards.***

The court in *Kirsh v. Plovida*, 971 F. 2d 1036 (3d Cir. 1992) engaged in an extensive discussion of the "turnover duty" as it related to open and obvious conditions. In some circumstances such as where longshoremen cannot avoid the hazard, the open and obvious rule may not be a bar to recovery. The approach to the open and obvious situation is important because if a shipowner has no duty with respect to such conditions then the issue of comparative negligence does not come into play. Approaching the issue in terms of "duty" is much like the common law approach to contributory negligence and assumption of risk. The case also reveals a possible link between the turnover duty and the duty to intervene. For example, in a situation where a shipowner is aware of a hazardous condition and relies on the stevedore to "work around" it, what if any is the shipowner's duty when it learns that the stevedore has not does so?

It has also been suggested that the open and obvious rule should not apply where a longshoreman's only alternative is to continue to work despite knowledge of the hazard or "to leave his job or face trouble for delaying the work. *Stass v. American Commercial Lines, Inc.* 720 F.2d 879, 5th Cir. 879 (1983).

3. ***The "operational control" duty.***

A shipowner's duty when it has retained operational control of an area or has involved itself in the cargo loading or unloading process is examined extensively in *Davis v. Portline Transportes Internacional,* 16 F.3d 532 (3d Cir. 1994).

4. ***Scindia and other maritime employees.***

The *Scindia* rationale and duties have been applied in cases involving maritime worker other than longshoremen such as ship repairmen. *Mayer v. Lykes Bros. S.S. Co., Inc.*, 585 F. Supp. 1222 (E.D. La. 1984).

Notes

1. *Vessel for Purposes of Section 905 Actions*

Section 902(21) of LHWCA provides generally:

> Unless the context requires otherwise, the term "vessel" means any vessel upon which or in connection with which any person entitled to benefits under this chapter suffers injury or death arising out of or in the course of his employment, and said vessel's owner, owner pro hac vice, agent, operator, charter or bareboat charterer, master, officer, or crew member.

For the definition of the word "vessel" for purposes of Section 905 of LHWCA, *see Stewart v. Dutra Construction Co.* 543 U.S. 481; 125 S.Ct. 1118, *supra,* pp. 412-20 [2006 edition].

2. *The Character of the Section 905(b) Action*

The question has arisen whether an action under 33 U.S.C. § 905(b) is a tort action under principles of land law or under principles of maritime law. Numerous appeals courts initially held that § 905(b) was intended to establish liability under "land-based principles of negligence." *Griffith v. Wheeling Pittsburgh Steel Corp.*, 610 F.2d 116 (3d Cir. 1979), *vacated*, 451 U.S. 965, *reinstated*, 657 F.2d 25, 1981 AMC 2974 (3d Cir. 1981); *Gay v. Ocean Transport and Trading, Ltd.*, 546 F.2d 1233, 1977 AMC 996 (5th Cir. 1977).

Courts have recently emphasized that the § 905(b) action is for maritime tort only. *See Richendollar, supra; see also May v. Transword Drilling Co.*, 786 F.2d 1261, 1987 AMC 971 (5th Cir. 1986) ("injury on navigable waters is a *sina qua non* of the maritime tort"). Thus, a plaintiff in a § 905(b) action must show that the case falls within admiralty jurisdiction: the tort must involve a vessel on navigable waters (or in accordance with the Admiralty Extension Act) and have a significant relationship with traditional maritime activity. For its basis in jurisdiction, the plaintiff's action arises under the general maritime law and not the LHWCA. *Stevenson v. Point Marine, Inc.*, 697 F. Supp. 285 (E.D. La. 1988); *see also Comment, Jurisdiction in Section 905(b) Actions—Wrong Test Doomed to Wrong Results*, 13 TUL. MAR. L.J. 121 (1988).

3. *The Land-based Employer as Shipowner*

Certain land-based employers, such as stevedores and ship repairers, own or operate vessels in the course of their business. In such cases, the question arises whether the liability of the land-based employer is limited to the payment of benefits under the LHWCA or whether the injured employee may sue his employer in his capacity as shipowner for damages under the general maritime law. The problem is the same when a shipowner chooses to undertake certain operations, such as stevedoring or ship repairing, instead of engaging the services of an independent contractor. *See Smith v. M/V Captain Fred*, 546 F.2d 119, 1977 AMC 353 (5th Cir. 1977); *Fanetti v. Hellenic Lines, Ltd.*, 678 F.2d 424, 1982 AMC 1521 (2d Cir. 1982).

In *Reed v. Yaka*, 373 U.S. 410, 83 S.Ct. 1349, 10 L.Ed.2d 448, 1963 AMC 1373 (1963), a longshoreman filed a label *in rem* against the steamship *Yaka* to recover for injuries he sustained due to the unseaworthiness of the vessel in the process of loading operations. The shipowner impleaded plaintiff's land-based employer, who was the bareboat charterer of the *Yaka*, alleging that the employer's negligence was the sole cause of the injury. The Supreme Court declared that a bareboat charterer as owner *pro hac vice* incurs the liabilities of a shipowner. And, since the unseaworthiness of the *Yaka* was not in dispute, the court held that the plaintiff was not barred by the Longshoremen's Act from relying on his employer's liability as shipowner for the *Yaka's* unseaworthiness in order to support his label *in rem* against the vessel.

The 1972 Amendments to the LHWCA eliminated the unseaworthiness action that an employee covered by the Act had against a shipowner. 33 U.S.C. § 905(b). However, the question arose whether a land-based employee of an independent contractor could still have a negligence action against his employer under § 905(b) if the employer was also shipowner or owner *pro hac vice, see Bossard v. Port Allen Marine Service, Inc.*, 624 F.2d 671, 1984 AMC 303

(5th Cir. 1980). The court held that a ship repairer, though having control of the vessel, is not an owner *pro hac vice*; only a bareboat charterer has this status. Hence, an injured employee does not have a § 905(b) action against the ship repairer-employer. *See also Ducote v. International Operating Co.*, 678 F.2d 543, 1985 AMC 2405 (5th Cir. 1981) [a terminal operator was found, as a matter of law, not to be an owner *pro hac vice*]. Did Congress mean to overrule the *Yaka* case legislatively in all respects?

The Supreme Court resolved this question in *Jones & Laughlin Steel Corp. v. Pfeifer*, 462 U.S. 523, 103 S. Ct. 2541, 2546-57, 76 L. Ed. 2d 768, 1983 AMC 1881 (1983), stating as follows:

> Most longshoremen who load and unload ships are employed by independent stevedores, who have contracted with the vessel owners to provide such services. In this case, however, the respondent longshoreman was employed directly by the petitioner vessel owner. Under § 4 of the Act, a longshoreman who is injured in the course of his employment is entitled to a specified amount of compensation from his employer, whether or not the injury was caused by the employer's negligence. Section 5(a) of the Act appears to make that liability exclusive. It reads, "The liability of an employer prescribed in § 4 of this act shall be exclusive and in place of all other liability of such an employer to the employee...." 44 Stat. 1526, 33 U.S.C. § 905(a). Since the petitioner was the respondent's employer and paid him benefits pursuant to § 4 of the Act, it contends that § 5(a) absolves it of all other responsibility for damages.
>
> Although petitioner's contention is, indeed, supported by the language of § 5(a), it is undermined by the plain language of § 5(b). The first sentence of § 5(b) authorizes a longshoreman whose injury is caused by the negligence of a vessel to bring a separate action against such a vessel as a third party. Thus, in the typical tripartite situation, the longshoreman is not only guaranteed the statutory compensation from his employer; he may also recover tort damages if he can prove negligence by the vessel. The second sentence of § 5(b) makes it clear that such a separate action is authorized against the vessel even when there is no independent stevedore and the longshoreman is employed directly by the vessel owner. That sentence provides, "If such person was employed by the vessel to provide stevedoring services, no such action shall be permitted if the injury was caused by the negligence of persons engaged in providing stevedoring services to the vessel." If § 5(a) had been intended to bar all negligence suits against owner-employes, there would have been no need to put an additional sentence in § 5(b) barring suits against owner-employers for injuries caused by fellow servants.
>
> The history of the Act further refutes petitioner's contention that § 5(a) of the Act bars respondent's suit under § 5(b). Prior to 1972, this Court had construed the Act to authorize a longshoreman employed directly by the vessel to obtain a recovery from his employer in excess of the statutory schedule even though § 5 of the Act contained the same exclusive liability language as today. *Reed v. The Yaka*, 373 U.S. 410 (1963); *Jacksonville v. Lykes Brothers Steamship Co.*, 386 U.S. 731 (1967). Although the 1972 Amendments changed the character of the longshoreman's action against the vessel by substituting negligence for unseaworthiness as the basis for liability, Congress clearly intended to preserve the rights of longshoremen employed by the vessel to maintain such an action.

Employees not covered by the LHWCA may still have an action for unseaworthiness against then land-based employer who also happens to be a shipowner.

4. *Vessel Negligence*

The question of whether a longshoreman's injuries are attributed to the negligence of his employer in his capacity as shipowner or in his capacity as land-based employer is not always easy to determine. In *White v. Cooper/T. Smith Corporation*, 690 F. Supp. 534 (E.D. La. 1988), a longshoreman injured in two separate accidents brought suit against his employer in his capacity as shipowner, and his wife joined in the suit seeking recovery for loss of consortium. The court ruled as a matter of law that under the facts alleged in the complaint with respect to the first accident, there was no vessel negligence. In the first incident plaintiff slipped while working on a mooring buoy after he had left his employer's vessel. As to the second accident, however, the court found that the petition stated sufficient facts to engage the liability of the employer under § 905(b), that is, in his capacity as shipowner. In this incident, plaintiff was injured on his employer's vessel while turning its steering wheel. The court found that the first incident lacked "vessel negligence" but there was a material fact in issue with respect to "vessel negligence" as to the second incident. The court also held that when an action under § 905(b) is available to a longshoreman, his spouse may institute action for loss of consortium.

5. *Unseaworthiness*

A longshoreman, assigned by his land-based employer to work on board a vessel belonging to the employer may qualify as a member of the crew of that vessel under the *Robison* test or may retain the status of a longshoreman. In the latter situation, he may recover from his employer damages for personal injuries in accordance with § 905(b) of the LHWCA. *See Jones & Laughlin Steel Corporation v. Pfeiffer*, 462 U.S. 523, 103 S. Ct. 2541, 76 L. Ed. 2d 768, 1983 AMC 1881 (1983), *supra.* A longshoreman, assigned by his land-based employer to work on board a vessel belonging to another person, may also be a seaman, a member of the crew of that vessel, if he meets the *Robison* test. In such a case, the longshoreman, in his capacity as a *borrowed servant,* may bring a Jones Act action or an action for unseaworthiness under the general maritime law against the shipowner. *See Wheatly v. Gladden*, 660 F.2d 1024, 1982 AMC 618 (4th Cir. 1981); Note, *supra.* A question remains, however, as to whether a longshoreman who is not covered by the LHWCA may bring an action grounded on *unseaworthiness* against a non-employer shipowner. In *Aparicio v. Swan Lake*, 643 F.2d 1109, 1981 AMC 1887 (5th Cir. 1981), the court held that a longshoreman who is *not* covered by LHWCA may bring an action against a shipowner for the recovery of damages caused by the unseaworthiness of the vessel. *But see Normile v. Maritime Company*, 643 F.2d 1380, 1981 AMC 2470 (9th Cir. 1981). In this case, the court held that the 1972 Amendments to the LHWCA suppressed the unseaworthiness action as to *all* longshoremen whether or not covered by the act. There is a general agreement that the unseaworthiness action is no longer available to a longshoreman who is covered by the LHWCA. *See Burks v. American River Transportation Company*, 679 F.2d 69, 1985 AMC 2208 (5th Cir. 1982). In this case, a longshoreman was injured on a vessel belonging to a person other than his employer while performing stevedoring work and sued the shipowner on grounds of unseaworthiness. Plaintiff claimed that he was a seaman, permanently assigned by his employer to do the work of a seaman on a vessel belonging to his employer but a longshoreman as to the vessel on which he was injured. The court held that whether or not plaintiff was a seaman as to his employer, he was a longshoreman covered by the LHWCA as to the defendant shipowner; therefore, after the 1972 Amendments to the LHWCA, plaintiff was not entitled to sue the shipowner for unseaworthiness.

May a seaman, member of the crew of a vessel, assigned to perform stevedoring duties on a vessel belonging to a person other than his employer claim from the non-employer shipowner benefits under the LHWCA? *See Smith v. Harbor Towing & Fleeting, Inc.*, 910 F.2d 312, 1991 AMC 986 (5th Cir. 1990). In this case, a seaman was injured on a vessel belonging to a person other than his employer while assisting in loading and unloading operations. He sued his employer under the Jones Act and under the general maritime law for unseaworthiness. He also sued the owner of the vessel on which he was injured for negligence and unseaworthiness under the general maritime law. Cognizant of the rule that the remedy of unseaworthiness is reserved for members of the crew of a vessel, plaintiff argued that, as to the vessel on which he was injured, he was a longshoreman not covered by LHWCA and, therefore, entitled to a remedy for unseaworthiness. The court granted a motion for partial summary judgment in favor of the non-employer shipowner, on the authority of *Bridges v. Penrod Drilling Co.*, 740 F.2d 361, 1986 AMC 1777 (5th Cir. 1984). The court concluded:

> In summary, we hold that a Jones Act seaman, who possesses the full range of traditional seamen's rights and remedies, cannot maintain a *Sieracki* seaworthiness action against a vessel on which he is not a crew member. In reaching this conclusion, we are not unmindful of the fact that longshoremen performing a seaman's task on a nonemployer's vessel are entitled to an unseaworthiness remedy while seamen performing the same task are not. Although this court may wish to reexamine this issue en banc, until then the holding in *Bridges* controls this case. Thus, we hold that Smith may not assert a *Sieracki* unseaworthiness claim against Chotin, and the judgment of the district court is hereby affirmed.

6. *Products Liability and Unseaworthiness*

The law of products liability, including strict liability, is a part of the general maritime law. *See East River Steamship Corporation v. Transamerica Delaval, Inc.*, 476 U.S. 858, 106 S. Ct. 2295, 90 L. Ed. 2d 865, 1986 AMC 2027 (1986). Unseaworthiness gives rise to a liability without negligence that is often called "absolute" or "strict liability." The 1972 Amendments to LHWCA suppressed the action for unseaworthiness that was available to longshoremen against shipowners under the general maritime law, and question has arisen as to whether *all* actions brought by longshoremen on grounds of strict liability were suppressed. In *Streach v. Associated Container Transportation, Ltd.*, 388 F. Supp. 953 (C.D. Cal. 1975), the court held that a strict products liability suit by a longshoreman is not the same as a proscribed action grounded on unseaworthiness and that such an action is not barred by the 1972 Amendments to LHWCA. Of course, a shipowner would then be liable in his capacity as manufacturer, designer, or distributor of a defective product.

Occasionally, injured longshoremen allege that their injuries on board the vessel were caused by a *negligently designed product* rather than the unseaworthiness of the vessel in order to prevent a summary dismissal of the action by application of LHWCA. Courts, however, can see through the pleadings. *See Bilderbeck v. World Wide Shipping Agency*, 776 F.2d 817 (9th Cir. 1985). The court affirmed a judgment discussing the action, stating:

> In the absence of specific allegations of negligence, the trial court acted within its discretion in disregarding the generalizations as simply another attempt to get seaworthiness into the case in the face of clear Congressional intent to remove it. There was no reversible error.
>
> We leave for later cases the question left open in *Scindia*, whether the functional equivalent of unseaworthiness can be brought back into these cases by pleading and proving that the vessel carried a negligently created defect that made the vessel hazardous to longshoremen and that the shipowner knew or reasonably should have known of the hazard, and nonetheless failed to warn the stevedore company so that it could take steps to protect its workmen. That was not this case.

E. Contribution and Indemnity

Background Note

Section 5 (33 U.S.C. § 905) of the LHWCA originally provided:

> *The liability of an employer prescribed in section 4* [for compensation] *shall be exclusive and in place of all other liability of such employer to the employee*, his legal representative, husband or wife, parents, dependents, next of kin, *and any one otherwise entitled to recover damages from such employer at law or in admiralty on account of such injury or death*. [Emphasis added.]

Nevertheless, the Supreme Court imposed *tort* liability on the land-based employer of a longshoreman or harbor worker in two situations: (a) when a longshoreman or harbor worker injured aboard a ship recovered damages from the shipowner, and the shipowner brought a suit for indemnity or contribution against the land-based employer; and (b) when the land-based employer also qualified as an owner *pro hac vice* of a vessel.

Frequently a longshoreman or harbor worker is injured in circumstances implicating the liability of a person other than his land-based employer. For example, the injuries sustained by a longshoreman may have been caused, in whole or in part, by the negligence of a shipowner. If the shipowner is solely liable under principles of tort law, the injured longshoreman or harbor worker may receive compensation under the LHWCA from his employer and sue the shipowner for damages. The employer of the injured worker may also sue the third-party tortfeasor to recover the payments made to the employee under LHWCA. This suit for indemnity may be based on a statutory assignment under 33 U.S.C. § 933 or on the general maritime law. For a discussion of actions for indemnity, as distinguished from actions for contribution, *see Federal Marine Terminals, Inc. v. Burnside Shipping Co.*, 394 U.S. 404, 1969 AMC 745 (1969). There, an employer brought an action against a shipowner claiming indemnity for payments made to an injured employee under the LHWCA on the ground that the injury had been caused by the negligence of the shipowner. The court held that the employer was not limited to the right of subrogation under the LHWCA but could maintain a direct action against the vessel for indemnity.

If the longshoreman or harbor worker is injured through the concurrent fault of his employer and a third party, questions arise as to the liability of each party toward the injured worker and toward each other. Matters become more complex when the liability of one party is based on negligence or products liability, whereas the liability of the other party is limited to benefits under the LHWCA.

In *Halcyon Lines v. Haenn Ship Ceiling & Refitting Corp.*, 342 U.S. 282, 72 S.Ct. 277, 96 L.Ed. 318, 1952 AMC 1 (1952), a ship repairman employed by Haenn was injured aboard a vessel belonging to Halcyon, and brought suit against Halcyon for negligence and unseaworthiness. Halcyon impleaded Haenn, and the jury found that plaintiff's injuries were attributable seventy-five percent to the fault of Haenn and twenty-five percent to the fault of Halcyon. Before the Supreme Court, Halcyon claimed contribution in proportion to the fault of each defendant. Haenn, however, maintained that there is no contribution among joint tortfeasors under the general maritime law in cases other than collisions, and the Court agreed. As a result, an injured longshoreman was able to recover his entire loss from the shipowner in an action based on negligence and unseaworthiness, and the shipowner had no recourse against the employer of the longshoreman, even if the injury had been proximately caused by the fault of the employer. The liability of the employer was limited to that established by the LHWCA. In *Cooper Stevedoring Co. v. Fritz Kopke, Inc.*, 417 U.S. 106, 94 S.Ct. 2174, 40 L.Ed.2d 694, 1974 AMC 537 (1974), a case governed by the law as it existed prior to the 1972 amendments to the LHWCA, the Supreme Court restricted the *Halcyon* case to its own facts. The Court held that the general maritime law provided a rule for contribution among joint tortfeasors in cases other than collisions and in which the employer could not claim exclusive liability under the LHWCA. Thus, in a suit by an injured longshoreman against a shipowner and a third-party stevedore (other than plaintiff's employer), the Court allowed contribution between joint tortfeasors. For an action for contribution against the United States for injuries compensable under the Federal Employees Compensation Act, *see Galimi v. Jetco, Inc.*, 514 F.2d 949, 1975 AMC 681 (2d Cir. 1975).

Subsequently, however, the Supreme Court held that a right to contribution or indemnity, though nonexistent under tort theory, may be based on the breach of an express or implied warranty of workmanlike service when the unseaworthiness of the vessel was produced by the fault of the contracting stevedoring company. *Ryan Stevedoring Co. v. Pan-Atlantic Steamship Co.*, 350 U.S. 124, 76 S.Ct. 232, 100 L.Ed. 133 (1956) [implied warranty]. Further, in *Italia Societa per Azioni di Navigazione v. Oregon Stevedoring Co.*, 376 U.S. 315, 84 S.Ct. 748, 11 L.Ed.2d 732, 1964 AMC 1075 (1964), the Supreme Court found breach of warranty where equipment furnished by the stevedore failed because of a latent defect. In the framework of the tripartite relationship among a longshoreman, his employer, and the shipowner, these decisions meant that the liability of the employer was no longer exclusively governed by the LHWCA. Instead, liability for the payment of damages rested entirely on the employer, even if the injuries had been caused to a large extent by the fault of the shipowner.

Then the 1972 amendments to the LHWCA were enacted. According to the provisions of 33 U.S.C. § 905(b) a shipowner may not recover damages he has paid to a longshoreman from the longshoreman's employer under any theory of warranty, express or implied, in tort or in contract. It should be noted, however, that the 1972 amendments to the LHWCA do not affect the applicability of the warranty of workmanlike service to persons other than employers of longshoremen and harbor workers. *See Stevens v. East-West Towing Co.*, 649 F.2d 1104, 1982 AMC 2820 (5th Cir. 1981) [charter party]; *Leckelt v. Superior Oil Co.*, 608 F.2d 592, 1980 AMC 2097 (5th Cir. 1979) [vessel manufacture]; *Fairmont Shipping Corp. v. Clevron International Oil Co.*, 511 F.2d 1252, 1975 AMC 261 (5th Cir. 1979) [towage]. Thus, pre-1972 decisions extending the *Ryan* doctrine to a variety of maritime contracts continue to be valid. *See, e.g., Parfait v. Jahncke Service, Inc.*, 484 F.2d 296, 1974 AMC 1892 (5th Cir. 1973) [diesel dredge repair contract]; *Whisenant v. Brewster-Bartle Offshore Co.*, 446 F.2d 394, 1970 AMC 1713 (4th Cir. 1969) [towage]; *Lusich v. Bloomfield Steamship Co.*, 355 F.2d 770, 1966 AMC 191 (5th Cir. 1966) [ship repair]; *United States v. Tug Manzanillo*, 310 F.2d 220, 1963 AMC 365 (9th Cir. 1062) [towage]; *McWilliams Blue Line, Inc. v. Esso Standard Oil*

Co., 245 F.2d 84, 1957 AMC 1213 (2d Cir. 1957) [towage]. *But see General Construction Co. v. Umpqua River Navigation Co.*, 458 F.2d 1186, 1972 AMC 1615 (9th Cir. 1972) [dredging contract].

EDMONDS v. COMPAGNIE GENERALE TRANSATLANTIQUE

443 U.S. 256, 99 S. Ct. 2753, 61 L. Ed. 2d 521, 1979 AMC 1167 (1979)

Mr. Justice WHITE delivered the opinion of the Court

On March 3, 1974, the S.S. *Atlantic Cognac*, a containership owned by respondent, arrived at the Portsmouth Marine Terminal, Va. Petitioner, a longshoreman, was then employed by the Nacirema Operating Co., a stevedoring concern that the shipowner had engaged to unload cargo from the vessel. The longshoreman was injured in the course of that work, and he received benefits for that injury from his employer under the Longshoremen's and Harbor Workers' Compensation Act. 44 Stat. 1424, as amended, 33 U.S.C. § 901 *et seq*. In addition, the longshoreman brought this negligence action against the shipowner in Federal District Court.

A jury determined that the longshoreman had suffered total damages of $100,000, that he was responsible for 10% of the total negligence resulting in his injury, that the stevedore's fault, through a co-employee's negligence, contributed 70%, and that the shipowner was accountable for 20%. Following an established principle of maritime law, the District Court reduced the award to the longshoreman by the 10% attributed to his own negligence. But also in accordance with maritime law, and the common law as well, the court refused further to reduce the award against the shipowner in proportion to the fault of the employer.

The United States Court of Appeals for the Fourth Circuit, with two judges dissenting, reversed en banc, holding that the 1972 Amendments to the Act, 86 Stat. 1251, had altered the traditional admiralty rule by making the shipowner liable only for that share of the total damages equivalent to the ratio of its fault to the total fault. 577 F.2d 1153, 1155-1156 (1978). Other Courts of Appeals have reached the contrary conclusion. We granted certiorari to resolve this conflict

I

Admiralty law is judge-made law to a great extent, and a longshoreman's maritime tort action against a shipowner was recognized long before the 1972 Amendments, *see Pope & Talbot, Inc. v. Hawn*, 346 U.S. 406, 413-414 (1953), as it has been since. As that law had evolved by 1972, a longshoreman's award in a suit against a negligent shipowner would be reduced by that portion of the damages assignable to the longshoreman's own negligence; but, as a matter of maritime tort law, the shipowner would be responsible to the longshoreman in full for the remainder, even if the stevedore's negligence contributed to the injuries. This latter rule is in accord with the common law, which allows an injured party to sue a tortfeasor for the full amount of damages for an indivisible injury that the tortfeasor's negligence was a substantial factor in causing, even if the concurrent negligence of others contributed to the incident.

The problem we face today, as was true of similar problems the Court has dealt with in the past, is complicated by the overlap of loss-allocating mechanisms that are guided by somewhat inconsistent principles. The liability of the ship to the longshoreman is determined by a combination of judge-made and statutory law and, in the present context, depends on a showing of negligence or some other culpability. The longshoreman-victim, however, and his stevedore-employer—also a tortfeasor in this case—are participants in a workers' compensation scheme that affords benefits to the longshoreman regardless of the employer's fault and provides that the stevedore's only liability for the longshoreman's injury is to the longshoreman in the amount specified in the statute. 33 U.S.C. § 905. We have more than once attempted to reconcile these systems.

We first held that the shipowner could not circumvent the exclusive-remedy provision by obtaining contribution from the concurrent tortfeasor employer. *Halcyon Lines v. Haenn Ship Ceiling & Refitting Corp.*, 342 U.S. 282 (1952); *Pope & Talbot, Inc. v. Hawn, supra*; *see Cooper Stevedoring Co. v. Fritz Kopke, Inc.*, 417 U.S. 106, 111-113 (1974). As a matter of maritime law, we also held that a longshoreman working on a vessel was entitled to the warranty of seaworthiness, *Seas Shipping Co. v. Sieracki*, 328 U.S. 85, 94 (1946), which amounted to liability without fault for most onboard injuries. However, we went on to hold, as a matter of contract law, that the shipowner could obtain from the stevedore an express or implied warranty of workman like service that might result in indemnification of the shipowner for its liability to the longshoreman. *Ryan Stevedoring Co. v. Pan-Atlantic S.S. Corp.*, 350 U.S. 124 (1956).

Against this background, Congress acted in 1972, among other things, to eliminate the shipowner's liability to the longshoreman for unseaworthiness and the stevedore's liability to the shipowner for unworkmanlike service resulting in injury to the longshoreman—in other words, to overrule *Sieracki* and *Ryan*. *See Northeast Marine Terminal Co. v. Caputo*, 432 U.S. 249, 260-261, and n.18 (1977); *Cooper Stevedoring Co. v. Fritz Kopke, Inc., supra*, at 113 n.6. Though admitting that nothing in either the statute or its history expressly indicates that Congress intended to modify as well the existing rules governing the longshoreman's maritime negligence suit against the shipowner by diminishing damages recoverable from the latter on the basis of the proportionate fault of the nonparty stevedore, 577 F.2d, at 1155, and n.2, the en banc Court of Appeals found that such a result was necessary to reconcile two sentences added in 1972 as part of 33 U.S.C. § 905 (b). The two sentences state:

> In the event of injury to a person covered under this chapter caused by the negligence of a vessel, then such person, or anyone otherwise entitled to recover damages by reason thereof, may bring an action against such vessel as a third party in accordance with the provisions of section 933 of this title, and the employer shall not be liable to the vessel for such damages directly or indirectly and any agreements or warranties to the contrary shall be void. If such person was employed by the vessel to provide stevedoring services, no such action shall be permitted if the injury was caused by the negligence of persons engaged in providing stevedoring services to the vessel.

33 U.S.C. § 905 (b).
The Court of Appeals described the perceived conflict in this fashion:

> The first sentence says that if the injury is caused by the negligence of a vessel the longshoreman may recover, but the second sentence says he may not recover anything of the ship if his injury was caused by the negligence of a person providing stevedoring services. The sentences are irreconcilable if read to mean that any negligence on the part of the ship will warrant recovery while any negligence on the part of the stevedore will defeat it. They may be harmonized only if read in apportioned terms.

577 F.2d, at 1155.
For a number of reasons, we are unpersuaded that Congress intended to upset a "long-established and familiar [principle]" of maritime law by imposing a proportionate-fault rule.

A

In the first place, the conflict seen by the Court of Appeals is largely one of its own creation. Both sides admit that each sentence may be read so as not to conflict with the other. The first sentence addresses the recurring situations, reflected by the facts in this case, where the party injured by the negligence of the vessel is a longshoreman employed by a stevedoring concern. In these circumstances, the longshoreman may sue the vessel as a third party, but his employer, the stevedore, is not to be liable directly or indirectly for any damages that may be recovered. This first sentence overrules *Ryan* and prevents the vessel from recouping from the stevedore any of the damages that the longshoreman may recover from the vessel. But the sentence neither expressly nor implicitly purports to overrule or modify the traditional rule that the longshoreman may recover the total amount of his damages from the vessel if the latter's negligence is a contributing cause of his injury, even if the stevedore, whose limited liability is fixed by statute, is partly to blame.

The second sentence of the paragraph is expressly addressed to the different and less familiar arrangement where the injured longshoreman loading or unloading the ship is employed by the vessel itself, not by a separate stevedoring company—in short, to the situation where the ship is its own stevedore. In this situation, the second sentence places some limitations on suits against the vessel for injuries caused during its stevedoring operations. Whatever these limitations may be, there is no conflict between the two sentences, and one arises only if the second sentence is read, as the Court of Appeals read it, as applying to all injured longshoremen, whether employed by the ship or by an independent stevedore. Nothing in the legislative history advises this construction of the sentence, and we see no reason to depart from the language of the statute in this respect.

Respondent insists that, even though the two sentences may deal with different business arrangements, problems still arise. If under the first sentence a third-party suit against the vessel is authorized when *any* part of the negligence causing the injury is that of the vessel, it is argued that suit against the vessel under the second sentence should be barred when *any* part of the negligence causing the injury is that of a co-worker also providing stevedoring services to the vessel. Under this interpretation, the employee of the independent stevedore could recover from the ship where the stevedore was responsible for 99% of the negligence, though a ship's employee performing stevedoring services could not hold the vessel liable if his co-worker's negligence was the slightest cause of the injury. This is said to be preposterous and contrary to the legislative intent to treat the vessel that provides its own stevedoring services just like other shipowners when and if it negligently causes injury in its capacity as a shipowner and just like other stevedores when it negligently injures in the course of providing its own loading or unloading services.

Aside from the fact that the problem suggested would arise only in the application of the second sentence, which is not involved in this case, the argument that the words "caused by the negligence of" in the two sentences must be given the same meaning and that they cannot have the meaning ascribed to them by petitioner's construction of the first sentence, logically leads to the conclusion that the injured longshoreman should *never* be able to bring suit against the vessel unless it is the sole cause of the injury. This is a doubly absurd conclusion. It is supported by no one, and to avoid it, it is necessary only to construe the second sentence to permit a third-party suit against the vessel providing its own loading and unloading services when negligence in its nonstevedoring capacity contributes to the injury. The second sentence means no more than that all longshoremen are to be treated the same whether their employer is an independent stevedore or a shipowner-stevedore and that all stevedores are to be treated the same whether they are independent or an arm of the shipowner itself.

This leaves the question of the measure of recovery against a shipowner, whether or not it is doing its own stevedoring, when as shipowner it is only partially responsible for the negligence, but we are quite unable to distill from the face of the obviously awkward wording of the two sentences any indication that Congress intended to modify the pre-existing rule that a longshoreman who is injured by the concurrent negligence of the stevedore and the ship may recover for the entire amount of his injuries from the ship.

B

The legislative history strongly counsels against the Court of Appeals' interpretation of the statute, which modifies the longshoreman's pre-existing rights against the negligent vessel. The reports and debates leading up to the 1972 Amendments contain not a word of this concept. This silence is most eloquent, for such reticence while contemplating an important and controversial change in existing law is unlikely. Moreover, the general statements appearing in the legislative history concerning § 905(b) are inconsistent with what respondent argues was in the back of the legislators' minds about this specific issue. The Committees repeatedly refer to the refusal to limit the shipowner's liability for negligence, which they felt left the vessel in the same position as a land-based third party whose negligence injures an employee. Because an employee generally may recover in full from a third-party concurrent tortfeasor, these statements are hardly indicative of an intent to modify the law in the respect found by the Court of Appeals. At the very least, one would expect some hint of a purpose to work such a change, but there was none.

The shipowner denies that the legislative history is so one-sided, relying upon statements that vessels "will not be chargeable with the negligence of the stevedore or [the] employees of the stevedore." S. Rep. 11; *see* 577 F.2d, at 1156 n.2. But in context these declarations deal only with removal of the shipowner's liability under the warranty of seaworthiness for acts of the stevedore—even nonnegligent ones.

C

Finally, we note that the proportionate-fault rule adopted by the Court of Appeals itself produces consequences that we doubt Congress intended. It may remove some inequities, but it creates others and appears to shift some burdens to the longshoreman.

As we have said, § 905 permits the injured longshoreman to sue the vessel and exempts the employer from any liability to the vessel for any damages that may be recovered. Congress clearly contemplated that the employee be free to sue the third-party vessel, to prove negligence and causation on the vessel's part, and to have the total damages set by the court or jury without regard to the benefits he has received or to which he may be entitled under the Act. Furthermore, under the traditional rule, the employee may recover from the ship the entire amount of the damages so determined. If he recovers less than the statutory benefits, his employer is still liable for the statutory amount.

Under this arrangement, it is true that the ship will be liable for all of the damages found by the judge or jury; yet its negligence may have been only a minor cause of the injury. The stevedore-employer may have been predominantly responsible; yet its liability is limited by the Act, and if it has lien rights on the longshoreman's recovery it may be out-of-pocket even less.

Under the Court of Appeals' proportionate-fault rule, however, there will be many circumstances where the longshoreman will not be able to recover in any way the full amount of the damages determined in his suit against the vessel. If, for example, his damages are at least twice the benefits paid or payable under the Act and the ship is less than 50% at fault, the total of his statutory benefits plus the reduced recovery from the ship will not equal his total damages. More generally, it would appear that if the stevedore's proportionate fault is more than the proportion of compensation to actual damages, the longshoreman will always fall short of recovering the amount that the factfinder has determined is necessary to remedy his total injury, even though the diminution is due not to his fault, but to that of his employer.

But the impact of the proportionate-fault rule on the longshoreman does not stop there. Under § 933(b), an administrative order for benefits operates as an assignment to the stevedore-employer of the longshoreman's rights against the third party unless the longshoreman sues within six months. And a corresponding judicially created lien in the employer's favor operates where the longshoreman himself sues. In the past, this lien has been for the benefits paid up to the amount of the recovery. And under § 933(c), which Congress left intact in 1972, where the stevedore-employer sues the vessel as statutory assignee it may retain from any recovery an amount equal in general to the expenses of the suit, the costs of medical services and supplies it provided the employee, all compensation benefits paid, the present value of benefits to be paid, plus one-fifth of whatever might remain. Under the Court of Appeals' proportionate-fault system, the longshoreman would get very little, if any, of the diminished recovery obtained by his employer. Indeed, unless the vessel's proportionate fault exceeded the ratio of compensation benefits to total damages, the longshoreman would receive nothing from the third-party action, and the negligent stevedore might recoup all the compensation benefits it had paid.

Some inequity appears inevitable in the present statutory scheme, but we find nothing to indicate and should not presume that Congress intended to place the burden of the inequity on the longshoreman whom the Act seeks to protect. Further, the 1972 Amendments make quite clear that "the employer shall not be liable to the vessel for such damages *directly or indirectly*," 33 U.S.C. § 905(b) (emphasis supplied), and that with the disappearance of the ship's contribution and indemnity right against the stevedore the latter should no longer have to appear routinely in suits between longshoreman and shipowner. Consequently, as we have done before, we must reject a "theory that nowhere appears in the Act, that was never mentioned by Congress during the legislative process, that does not comport with Congress' intent, and that restricts ... a remedial Act ... ." *Northeast Marine Terminal Co. v. Caputo*, 432 U.S., at 278-279.

II

Of course, our conclusion that Congress did not intend to change the judicially created rule that the shipowner can be made to pay all the damages not due to the plaintiff's own negligence does not decide whether we are free to and should change that role so as to make the vessel liable only for the damages in proportion to its own negligence. Indeed, some amici in support of respondent share the view that Congress did not change the rule but argue that this Court should do so. We disagree.

Though we recently acknowledged the sound arguments supporting division of damages between parties before the court on the basis of their comparative fault, *see United States v. Reliable Transfer Co.*, 421 U.S. 397 (1975), we are mindful that here we deal with an interface of statutory and judge-made law. In 1972 Congress aligned the rights and liabilities of stevedores, shipowners, and longshoremen in light of the rules of maritime law that it chose not to change. "One of the most controversial and difficult issues which [Congress was] required to resolve ... [concerned] the liability of vessels, as third parties, to pay damages to longshoremen who are injured while engaged in stevedoring operations." S.Rep. 8. By now changing what we have already established that Congress understood to be the law, and did not itself wish to modify, we might knock out of kilter this delicate balance. As our cases advise, we should stay our hand in these circumstances. *Cooper Stevedoring Co. v. Fritz Kopke, Inc.*, 417 U.S., at 112; *Halcyon Lines v. Haenn Ship Ceiling & Refitting Corp.*, 342 U.S., at 285-286. Once Congress has relied upon conditions that the courts have created, we are not as free as we would otherwise be to change them. A change in the conditions would effectively alter the statute by causing it to reach different results than Congress envisioned. Indeed, Congress might have intended to adopt the existing maritime rule even for third-party actions under the Act that are not within the admiralty jurisdiction, though we need not and do not reach that issue today.

Accordingly, we reverse the judgment below and remand for proceedings consistent with this opinion.

Mr. Justice POWELL took no part in the consideration or decision of this case.

Mr. Justice BLACKMUN, with whom Mr. Justice MARSHALL and Mr. Justice STEVENS join, dissenting.

The jury in this case found that the shipowner, the stevedore, and the longshoreman were each partially responsible for the latter's (petitioner Stanley Edmonds) injury. A member of the ship's crew instructed Edmonds to remove a jack from the rear wheel of a large cargo container. As Edmonds went behind the container to remove the jack, another longshoreman backed a truck into the container, causing it to roll backwards and pin Edmonds against the bulkhead. The jury concluded that the shipowner, as the employer of the crewman, was 20% responsible for the accident; the stevedore, as the employer of the longshoreman driving the truck, was 70% responsible; and Edmonds himself was 10% responsible.

The Court holds that the shipowner, who was 20% negligent, must pay 90% of Edmonds' damages. Edmonds, because of his comparative negligence, must absorb 10% of the damages himself. But the stevedore, who, the jury determined, was 70% at fault, will recoup its statutory compensation payments out of the damages payable to Edmonds, and thus will go scot-free.

The Court does not, and indeed could not, defend this result on grounds of reason or fairness. Today's ruling means that concurrently negligent stevedores will be insulated from the obligation to pay statutory workmen's compensation benefits, and thus will have inadequate incentives to provide a safe working environment for their employees. It also means that shipowners in effect will be held vicariously liable for the negligence of stevedores, and will have to pay damages far out of proportion to their degree of fault. Nor does the Court suggest that its holding is compelled by the language or legislative history of § 5(b) of the Longshoremen's and Harbor Workers' Compensation Act (LHWCA), 33 U.S.C. § 905(b). The Court appears to advance two justifications for its decision: first, that principles of comparative negligence did not apply under the traditional law of admiralty, and Congress intended to preclude judicial modification of that law when it passed the 1972 Amendments to the LHWCA; and second, that a rule of comparative negligence would be unfair to injured longshoremen. Since I find both purported justifications wholly inadequate to support the Court's decision, I respectfully dissent.

Notes

1. ***Contribution and Indemnity when LHWCA Does Not Apply***

Is a land-based employer immune to suits for contribution or indemnity in situations in which the LHWCA does *not* apply? In *White v. Johns-Manville Corp.*, 662 F.2d 243, 1982 AMC 1770 (4th Cir. 1981), harbor workers brought suit against a manufacturer for injuries caused by asbestos, and the manufacturer impleaded the land-based employer, seeking indemnity. The court held that contractual indemnity is governed by state law, but noncontractual (tort) indemnity is within admiralty jurisdiction. The court held that no indemnity was due under any theory advanced by the manufacturers but reserved decision as to the exclusivity of the liability of the employer under § 905(b).

2. ***Contribution and indemnity when some but not all defendants settle***

In all cases, maritime or non-maritime, a question arises of the effect that settlement by some defendants has on the liability of the remaining, non-settling defendants. For example, if the plaintiff suffers $1,000,000 of harm and sues three defendants, A, B and C, then settles with A for $600,000, what impact should that have on the liability of B and C if the case goes to trial? Should B and C get credit for the $600,000 paid by A, so that they are only liable for the remaining $400,000 of the plaintiff's loss? That approach is known as the "pro tanto" approach. Alternatively, should liability be apportioned between B and C according to their proportionate share of responsibility, regardless of the amount paid by A? That is known as the "proportionate share" approach. If B is found to be 20% to blame and C only 10%, then B has to pay $200,000 and C has to pay $100,000. The end result will be that the plaintiff will receive only $900,000, because he or she settled for only $600,000 with A, who was 70% responsible for the plaintiff's injuries. Conversely, if B is found to be 40% to blame and C 20%, then B has to pay $400,000 and C has to pay $200,000, that being the share of the plaintiff's $1,000,000 loss corresponding to their respective shares of responsibility. The end result will be that the plaintiff will receive $1,500,000, more than his or her loss, because he or she made a good settlement of $600,000 with A, who was only 40% to blame.

In *McDermott, Inc. v. AmClyde*, 511 U.S. 202, 114 S. Ct. 1461, 1994 AMC 1521 (1994), a maritime case not involving personal injury, the Supreme Court held that the "proportionate share" rule should be used in preference to the "pro tanto" rule. Furthermore, the Court held that the non-settling defendants should not be entitled to any contribution from the settling defendants. To hold otherwise would be to discourage settlement, said the Court.

3. A panel of the Court of Appeals for the Fifth Circuit in *Coats v. Penrod Drilling Corporation*, 61 F.3d 1113, 1996 AMC 1 (5th Cir. 1995) reiterating that joint and several liability is the rule in maritime personal injury cases, rejected one defendant's proposed modification of the rule. Under the proposal a contributorily negligent plaintiff would bear his proportionate share of the risk that part of the judgment in his favor may be uncollectible from one or more of the defendants.

F. Stevedore's Lien and Assignment of the Employee's Action

33 U.S.C. § 933. Compensation for injuries where third persons are liable

(a) Election of remedies

If on account of a disability or death for which compensation is payable under this chapter the person entitled to such compensation determines that some person other than the employer or a person or persons in his employ is liable in damages, he need not elect whether to receive such compensation or to recover damages against such third person.

(b) Acceptance of compensation operating as assignment

Acceptance of compensation under an award in a compensation order filed by the deputy commissioner, an administrative law judge, or the Board shall operate as an assignment to the employer of all rights of the person entitled to compensation to recover damages against such third person unless such person shall commence an action against such third person within six months after such acceptance. If the employer fails to commence an action against such third person within ninety days after the cause of action is assigned under this section, the right to bring such action shall revert to the person entitled to compensation. For the purpose of this subsection, the term "award" with respect to a compensation order means a formal order issued by the deputy commissioner, an administrative law judge, or Board.

(c) Payment into section 944 fund operating as assignment

The payment of such compensation into the fund established in section 944 of this title shall operate as an assignment to the employer of all right of the legal representative of the deceased (hereinafter referred to as "representative") to recover damages against such third person.

(d) Institution of proceedings or compromise by assignee

Such employer on account of such assignment may either institute proceedings for the recovery of such damages or may compromise with such third person either without or after instituting such proceeding.

(e) Recoveries by assignee

Any amount recovered by such employer on account of such assignment, whether or not as the result of a compromise, shall be distributed as follows:

(1) The employer shall retain an amount equal to—

(A) the expenses incurred by him in respect to such proceedings or compromise (including a reasonable attorney's fee as determined by the deputy commissioner or Board);

(B) the cost of all benefits actually furnished by him to the employee under section 907 of this title;

(C) all amounts paid as compensation;

(D) the present value of all amounts thereafter payable as compensation, such present value to be computed in accordance with a schedule prepared by the Secretary, and the present value of the cost of all benefits thereafter to be furnished under section 907 of this title, to be estimated by the deputy commissioner, and the amounts so computed and estimated to be retained by the employer as a trust fund to pay such compensation and the cost of such benefits as they become due, and to pay any sum finally remaining in excess thereof to the person entitled to compensation or to the representative; and

(2) The employer shall pay any excess to the person entitled to compensation or to the representative.

(f) Institution of proceedings by person entitled to compensation

If the person entitled to compensation institutes proceedings within the period prescribed in subsection (b) of this section the employer shall be required to pay as compensation under this chapter a sum equal to the excess of the amount which the Secretary determines is payable on account of such injury or death over the net amount recovered against such third person. Such net amount shall be equal to the actual amount recovered less the expenses reasonably incurred by such person in respect to such proceedings (including reasonable attorneys' fees).

(g) Compromise obtained by person entitled to compensation

(1) If the person entitled to compensation (or the person's representative) enters into a settlement with a third person referred to in subsection (a) of this section for an amount less than the compensation to which the person (or the person's representative) would be entitled under this chapter, the employer shall be liable for compensation as determined under subsection (f) of this section only if written approval of the settlement is obtained from the employer and the employer's carrier, before the settlement is executed, and by the person entitled to compensation (or the person's representative). The approval shall be made on a form provided by the Secretary and shall be filed in the office of the deputy commissioner within thirty days after the settlement is entered into.

(2) If no written approval of the settlement is obtained and filed as required by paragraph (1), or if the employee fails to notify the employer of any settlement obtained from or judgment rendered against a third person, all rights to compensation and medical benefits under this chapter shall be terminated, regardless of whether the employer or the employer's insurer has made payments or acknowledged entitlement to benefits under this chapter.

(3) Any payments by the special fund established under section 944 of this title shall be a lien upon the proceeds of any settlement obtained from or judgment rendered against a third person referred to under subsection (a) of this section. Notwithstanding any other provision of law, such lien shall be enforceable against such proceeds, regardless of whether the Secretary on behalf of the special fund has agreed to or has received actual notice of the settlement or judgment.

(4) Any payments by a trust fund described in section 917 of this title shall be a lien upon the proceeds of any settlement obtained from or judgment recorded against a third person referred to under subsection (a) of this section. Such lien shall have priority over a lien under paragraph (3) of this subsection.

(h) Subrogation

Where the employer is insured and the insurance carrier has assumed the payment of the compensation, the insurance carrier shall be subrogated to all the rights of the employer under this section.

(i) Right to compensation as exclusive remedy

The right to compensation or benefits under this chapter shall be the exclusive remedy to an employee when he is injured, or to his eligible survivors or legal representatives if he is killed, by the negligence or wrong of any other person or persons in the same employ: *Provided.* That this provision shall not affect the liability of a person other than an officer or employee of the employer.

Notes

1. In *Bloomer v. Liberty Mutual Ins. Co.*, 445 U.S. 74, 100 S.Ct. 925, 63 L.Ed.2d 215, 1980 AMC 338, 1980 AMC 338 (1980), the issue was "whether the stevedore's lien must be reduced by a proportionate share of the longshoremen's expenses in obtaining a recovery from the shipowner, or whether the stevedore is instead entitled to be reimbursed for the full amount of the compensation" on the vessel, *S.S. Pacific Breeze*. He received $17,152.83 in compensation from Liberty Mutual, his employer's insurance carrier. Plaintiff thereafter brought a diversity action against the vessel owner under 33 U.S.C. § 905(b), in which plaintiff and the vessel owner settled for $60,000. Liberty Mutual sought to recover the full amount it had paid to *Bloomer* in compensation, while *Bloomer* argued that the stevedore's lien should be reduced by an amount representing a proportionate share of the expenses of the suit against the shipowner. The court denied plaintiff's request, holding that under the legislative history and clear provisions of 33 U.S.C. § 933, Congress intended "that the longshoreman's attorney's fees would be paid by the lonshoreman alone."

The *Bloomer* rule was applied by the United States Fifth Circuit Court of Appeals in *Bartholomew v. CNG Producing Co.*, 862 F.2d 555, 1989 AMC 741 (5th Cir. 1989). The plaintiff in that case argued (1) that an amendment of 33 U.S.C. § 933(f) in 1984 overruled the *Bloomer* holding, and (2) that it was not equitable to allow a stevedore's insurance company to gain from a longshoreman's suit against a negligent third party without having to pay its proportionate share of the costs. The court held that that 1984 amendment to 33 U.S.C. § 933(f), rather of overruling the *Bloomer* holding, actually reinforced it. While sympathizing with the plaintiff's equity argument, the court stated that "Congress' intent that the compensation carrier's lien remain inviolate, ... seems ... to be clear." The court therefore felt that only Congress had the power to change its decision, and accordingly awarded to the insurance company the full amount it paid in compensation to the plaintiff.

2. In *Pallas Shipping Agency, Ltd. v. Duris*, 461 U.S. 529, 103 S.Ct. 1991, 76 L.Ed.2d 120, 1983 AMC 1724, the Supreme Court held that in the absence of a formal award, an employee's acceptance of compensation payments cannot lead to an assignment of his right of action against third parties.

> Petitioner contends that the requirement of a formal compensation order prior to the assignment of an injured longshoreman's claims will frustrate the Act's aims of ensuring prompt payment to injured workers and of relieving burden of litigating compensation claims. It is said that employers who desire to seek indemnification from the negligent third party will be encouraged to contest their liability in order to obtain a compensation order instead of making voluntary payments. We do not find this contention persuasive. Employers are not required to contest their liability in order to obtain a formal compensation award. Department of Labor regulations permit an employer who makes voluntary payments to obtain a compensation order upon request if there is not disagreement among the parties. 20 CFR 702.315(a) (1982).. Moreover, even without a statutory assignment of the longshoreman's claims, an employer can seek indemnification from negligent third parties for payments it has made to the longshoreman. *See Federal Marine Terminals v. Burnside Shipping Co.*, 394 U.S. 404 (1969); *Crescent Wharf & Warehouse Co. v. Barracuda Tanker Corp.*, 696 F.2d 703 (CA9 1983). For these reasons, the employer who seeks to bring an action against a shipowner, charterer, or other third person has little to gain from contesting his liability to the longshoreman under the LHWCA.

We therefore conclude that respondent's acceptance of voluntary compensation payments did not constitute "[a]cceptance of such compensation under an award in a compensation order" so as to give rise to the assignment of respondent's claims against third persons.

Section III. Remedies for Wrongful Death

Part 1. Death on the High Seas: Cases and Notes

A. Introduction

Note

In *The Harrisburg*, 119 U.S. 199, 7 S.Ct. 140, 30 L.Ed. 358 (1886), the Supreme Court held that the general maritime law does not afford a cause of action for wrongful death. However, in *The Hamilton*, 207 U.S. 398, 28 S.Ct. 133, 52 L.Ed. 264 (1907), the Court declared that the lacuna in maritime law created by the lack of a cause of action for wrongful death could be filled by the application of a state wrongful death statute. Thus, dependents of persons wrongfully killed on state territorial waters or, perhaps, on the high seas had remedies under state laws.

In 1920, Congress enacted the Death on the High Seas Act (DOHSA), now 46 U.S.C.A. §§ 30301-30308 (formerly 46 U.S.C. §§ 761-768), which established a cause of action for death "caused by wrongful act, neglect, or default occurring on the high seas beyond a marine league from the shore of any State," dependency, or territory (46 U.S.C.A. § 30302, formerly 46 U.S.C. § 761). In the same year, Congress also enacted the Jones Act, which incorporated the wrongful death provision of the Federal Employers' Liability Act (FELA), now 45 U.S.C. §§ 51-60. The two statutes are not entirely consistent as to the nature of the wrongful death recovery and as to the classes of persons entitled to recovery.

Subsequently jurisprudence established that DOHSA furnished the exclusive remedy for the wrongful death of a person other than a seaman on the high seas, and state statutes furnished remedies for wrongful death on territorial waters. The Jones Act provided the exclusive remedy for the death of a seaman in territorial waters, and both DOHSA (unseaworthiness) and the Jones Act (negligence) offered remedies for the death of a seaman on the high seas.

In 1946, in *Seas Shipping Co. v. Sieracki*, 328 U.S. 85, 66 S.Ct. 872, 90 L.Ed. 1099, 1956 AMC 698 (1946), the warranty of seaworthiness, which theretoforce was applicable to seamen only, was extended to longshoremen and other harbor workers. It was not clear, however, whether state wrongful death statutes gave recovery for wrongful death caused by the unseaworthiness of a vessel, and the extent to which state law applied to matters within the admiralty jurisdiction of the United States. The Supreme Court, in initial attempts to resolve practical questions concerning the extent to which state law imposed substantive limitations on recovery, instead engaged in metaphysical discussion concerning the distinction between "right" and "remedy." *See The Tungus v. Skovgaard*, 358 U.S. 588, 79 S.Ct. 503, 3 L.Ed.2d 524, 1959 AMC 813; *Hess v. United States*, 361 U.S. 314, 80 S.Ct. 341, 4 L.Ed.2d 305, 1960 AMC 527 (1960); *Goett v. Union Carbide Corp.*, 361 U.S. 340, 1960 AMC (1960). Faced with confusion and uncertainty, the Supreme Court overruled *The Harrisburg* in *Moragne v. States Marine Lines, Inc.* 398 U.S. 375, 90 S.Ct. 1772, 26 L.Ed.2d 339, 1970 AMC 967 (1970). These matters are explored in the following materials.

Wrongful-death statutes are to be distinguished from survival statutes. The latter have been separately enacted to abrogate the common-law rule that an action for tort abated at the death of either the injured person or the tortfeasor. Survival statutes permit the deceased's estate to prosecute any claims for personal injury the deceased would have had, but for his death. They do not permit recovery from harms suffered by the deceased' family as a result of his death. *See Michigan C. R. Co. v. Vreeland*, 227 U.S. 59, 33 S.Ct. 192, 57 L.Ed. 417 (1913).

B. The Death on the High Seas Act: 46 U.S.C.A. §§ 30301-30308

§ 30301. Short title

This chapter may be cited as the "Death on the High Seas Act".

§ 30302. Cause of action

When the death of an individual is caused by wrongful act, neglect, or default occurring on the high seas beyond 3 nautical miles from the shore of the United States, the personal representative of the decedent may bring a civil action in admiralty against the person or vessel responsible. The action shall be for the exclusive benefit of the decedent's spouse, parent, child, or dependent relative.

§ 30303. Amount and apportionment of recovery

The recovery in an action under this chapter shall be a fair compensation for the pecuniary loss sustained by the individuals for whose benefit the action is brought. The court shall apportion the recovery among those individuals in proportion to the loss each has sustained.

§ 30304. Contributory negligence

In an action under this chapter, contributory negligence of the decedent is not a bar to recovery. The court shall consider the degree of negligence of the decedent and reduce the recovery accordingly.

§ 30305. Death of plaintiff in pending action

If a civil action in admiralty is pending in a court of the United States to recover for personal injury caused by wrongful act, neglect, or default described in section 30302 of this title, and the individual dies during the action as a result of the wrongful act, neglect, or default, the personal representative of the decedent may be substituted as the plaintiff and the action may proceed under this chapter for the recovery authorized by this chapter.

§ 30306. Foreign cause of action

When a cause of action exists under the law of a foreign country for death by wrongful act, neglect, or default on the high seas, a civil action in admiralty may be brought in a court of the United States based on the foreign cause of action, without abatement of the amount for which recovery is authorized.

§ 30307. Commercial aviation accidents

(a) Definition—In this section, the term "nonpecuniary damages" means damages for loss of care, comfort, and companionship.

(b) Beyond 12 Nautical Miles—In an action under this chapter, if the death resulted from a commercial aviation accident occurring on the high seas beyond 12 nautical miles from the shore of the United States, additional compensation is recoverable for nonpecuniary damages, but punitive damages are not recoverable.

(c) Within 12 Nautical Miles—This chapter does not apply if the death resulted from a commercial aviation accident occurring on the high seas 12 nautical miles or less from the shore of the United States.

§ 30308. Nonapplication

(a) State Law—This chapter does not affect the law of a State regulating the right to recover for death.

(b) Internal Waters—This chapter does not apply to the Great Lakes or waters within the territorial limits of a State.

46 U.S.C. App. §§ 761-768

(Superseded Version)

§ 761. Right of action; where and by whom brought

(a) subject to subsection (b), whenever the death of a person shall be caused by wrongful act, neglect, or default occurring on the high seas beyond a marine league from the shore of any State, or the District of Columbia, or the Territories or dependencies of the United States, the personal representative of the decedent may maintain a suit for damages in the district courts of the United States, in admiralty, for the exclusive benefit of the decedent's wife, husband, parent, child, or dependent relative against the vessel, person, or corporation which would have been liable if death had not ensued.

(b) In the case of a commercial aviation accident, whenever the death of a person shall be caused by wrongful act, neglect, or default occurring on the high seas 12 nautical miles or closer to the shore of any State, or the District of Columbia, or the Territories or dependencies of the United States, this Act shall not apply and the rules applicable under Federal, State, and other appropriate law shall apply.

§ 762. Amount and apportionment of recovery

(a) The recovery in such suit shall be a fair and just compensation for the pecuniary loss sustained by the persons for whose benefit the suit is brought and shall be apportioned among them by the court in proportion to the loss they may severally have suffered by reason of the death of the person by whose representative the suit is brought.

(b) (1) If the death resulted from a commercial aviation accident occurring on the high seas beyond 12 nautical miles from the shore of any State, or the District of Columbia, or the Territories or dependencies of the United States, additional compensation for nonpecuniary damages for wrongful death of a decedent is recoverable. Punitive damages are not recoverable.

(2) In this subsection, the term "nonpecuniary damages" means damages for loss of care, comfort, and companionship.

§ 763a. Limitations

[This section was not enacted as part of the Death on the High Seas Act and is obviously broader in application. Eds.]

Unless otherwise specified by law, a suit for recovery of damages for personal injury or death, or both, arising out of a maritime tort, shall not be maintained unless commenced within three years from the date the cause of action accrued.

§ 764. Rights of action given by laws of foreign countries

Whenever a right of action is granted by the law of any foreign State on account of death by wrongful act, neglect, or default occurring upon the high seas, such right may be maintained in an appropriate action in admiralty in the courts of the United States without abatement in respect to the amount for which recovery is authorized, any statute of the United States to the contrary notwithstanding.

§ 765. Death of plaintiff pending action

If a person die as the result of such wrongful act, neglect, or default as is mentioned in section 761 of this title during the pendency in a court of admiralty of the United States of a suit to recover damages for personal injuries in respect of such act, neglect, or default, the personal representative of the decedent may be substituted as a party and the suit may proceed as a suit under this chapter for recovery of the compensation provided in section 762 of this title.

§ 766. Contributory negligence

In suits under this chapter the fact that the decedent has been guilty of contributory negligence shall not bar recovery, but the court shall take into consideration the degree of negligence attributable to the decedent and reduce the recovery accordingly.

§ 767. Exceptions from operation of chapter

The provisions of any State statute giving or regulating rights of action or remedies for death shall not be affected by this chapter. Nor shall this chapter apply to the Great Lakes or to any waters within the territorial limits of any State, or to any navigable waters in the Panama Canal Zone.

Note: Coverage of DOHSA

DOHSA permits recovery for wrongful death caused by negligence or unseaworthiness. *Bodden v. American Offshore, Inc.*, 681 F.2d 319, 1982 AMC 2409 (5th Cir. 1982). Plaintiffs under DOHSA may recover only their pecuniary loss, including loss of services and loss of support. *Mobile Oil Corp. v. Higginbotham*, 436 U.S. 618, 1978 AMC 1059 (1978); *Smith v. Ithaca Corp.*, 612 F.2d 215, 1981 AMC 1029 (5th Cir. 1980). Punitive damages are not recoverable under DOHSA. *Bergen v. F/V St. Patrick*, 816 F.2d 1345, 1987 AMC 2024 (9th Cir. 1987); *Jennings v. The Boeing Co.*, 660 F. Supp. 796 (E.D. Pa. 1987).

DOHSA applies in foreign territorial waters as well as the high seas. *See Howard v. Crystal Cruise Line*, 41 F.3d 527 (9th Cir.), 1995 AMC 305 (1994); *Public Administrator v. Angela Compania Naviera*, 592 F.2d 58, 1979 AMC 106 (2d Cir. 1979). Moreover, DOHSA applies to maritime torts only. Thus, if a tort is not within the purview of admiralty jurisdiction, DOHSA does not apply. *See Brons v. Beech Aircraft Corp.*, 627 F. Supp 230 (S.D. Fla. 1985). But compare *Kunreuther v. Outboard Marine Corp.*, 757 F. Supp. 633, 1991 AMC 1812 (E.D. Pa. 1991).

C. State Remedies

OFFSHORE LOGISTICS, INC. v. TALLENTIRE

477 U.S. 207, 106 S. Ct. 2485, 91 L. Ed. 2d 174, 1986 AMC 2113 (1986)

Justice O'CONNOR delivered the opinion of the Court

Respondents' husbands were killed when petitioner Air Logistic's helicopter, in which the decedents were traveling crashed in the high seas. The issues presented is whether the Death on the High Seas Act (DOHSA), 41 Stat. 537, 46 U.S.C. § 761 *et seq.*, provides the exclusive remedy by which respondents may recover against petitioner for the wrongful death of their husbands, or whether they may also recover the measure of damages provided by the Louisiana wrongful death statute, La. Civ. Code Ann., Art 2315 (West Supp. 1986), applying either of its own force or as surrogate federal law under the Outer Continental Shelf Lands Act (OCSLA), 67 Stat. 462, as amended, 43 U.S.C. § 1331 *et seq.*

I

The husbands of respondents Corrine Taylor and Beth Tallentire worked on drilling platforms in the Gulf of Mexico, off the coast of Louisiana. On August 6, 1980, respondents' husbands were killed while being transported in a helicopter owned and operated by petitioner Air Logistics (hereafter petitioner), a Division of Offshore Logistics, Inc., from a drilling platform to Houma, Louisiana. The crash occurred approximately 35 miles off the coast of Louisiana, well over the 3-mile limit that separates Louisiana's territorial waters from the high seas for purposes of DOHSA.

Respondents each filed wrongful death suits in United States District Court, raising claims under DOHSA, OCSLA, and the law of Louisiana. These actions were later consolidated in the Eastern District of Louisiana. Upon petitioner's pretrial motion for partial summary judgment, the District Court ruled that DOHSA provides the exclusive remedy for death on the high seas, and it therefore dismissed respondents' claims based upon the Louisiana wrongful death statute. Petitioner admitted liability and the trial was limited to the question of damages. Because DOHSA limits recovery to "fair and just compensation for ... pecuniary loss," the District Court's awards to respondents did not include damages for nonpecuniary losses. 46 U.S.C. § 762.

Respondents appealed the District Court's dismissal of their OCSLA and state law wrongful death claims, contending that they were entitled to nonpecuniary damages under the Louisiana wrongful death statute. *See* La. Civ. Code Ann., Art. 2315(B) (West Supp. 1986) (permitting recovery for both pecuniary and nonpecuniary damages, "[including] loss of consortium, service, and society"). They argued that the Louisiana statute applied to this helicopter crash on the high seas, either of its own force by virtue of the saving provision in § 7 of DOHSA, 46 U.S.C. § 767, or as adopted federal law through OCSLA. *See* 43 U.S.C. § 1333(a)(2)(A). The Court of Appeals for the Fifth Circuit reversed the District Court's denial of benefits recoverable under Louisiana law, with one judge specially concurring and another judge dissenting. *See* 754 F.2d 1274 (1985).

* * *

Because the Fifth Circuit's decision creates the potential for disunity in the administration of wrongful death remedies for causes of action arising from accidents on the high seas and is in conflict with the prevailing view in other courts that DOHSA pre-empts state law wrongful death statutes in the area of its operation, we granted certiorari. 474 U.S. 816 (1985). We now hold that neither OCSLA nor DOHSA requires or permits the application of Louisiana law in this case, and accordingly reverse the judgment of the Court of Appeals for the Fifth Circuit.

II

* * *

In 1920, Congress enacted DOHSA, in which it finally repudiated the rule of *The Harrisburg* for maritime deaths occurring beyond state territorial waters by providing for a federal maritime remedy for wrongful deaths more than three miles from shore.[1] DOHSA limits the class of beneficiaries to the decedent's "wife, husband, parent, child, or dependent relative," 46 U.S.C. § 761, establishes a 3-year statute of limitations period, § 763a, allows a suit filed by the victim to continue as a wrongful death action if the victim dies of his injuries while suit is pending, § 765, provides that contributory negligence will not bar recovery, § 766, and declares that "recovery ... shall be a fair and just compensation for the pecuniary loss sustained by the persons for whose benefit the suit is brought...." § 762.

* * *

III

As explained above, DOHSA is intended to provide a maritime remedy for deaths stemming from wrongful acts or omissions "occurring on the high seas." 46 U.S.C. § 761. OCSLA, by contrast, provides an essentially nonmaritime remedy and controls only on "the subsoil and seabed of the outer Continental Shelf, and artificial islands and fixed structures" erected thereon. 43 U.S.C. § 1333(a)(2)(A). By its terms, OCSLA must be "construed in such a manner that the character of the waters above the outer Continental Shelf as high seas ... shall not be affected." § 1332(2). Within the area covered by OCSLA, federal law controls but the law of the adjacent State is adopted as surrogate federal law to the extent that it is not inconsistent with applicable federal laws or regulations. § 1333(a)(2)(A).

The intent behind OCSLA was to treat the artificial structures covered by the Act as upland islands or as federal enclaves within a landlocked State, and not as vessels, for purposes of defining the applicable law because maritime law was deemed inapposite to these fixed structures. *See Rodrigue v. Aetna Casualty & Surety Co.*, 395 U.S. 352, 361-366 (1969). This Court endorsed the congressional assumption that admiralty law generally would not apply to the lands and structures covered by OCSLA in *Rodrigue*, noting that accidents on the artificial islands covered by OCSLA "had no more connection with the ordinary stuff of admiralty than do accidents on piers." *Id.*, at 360. *See also Herb's Welding, Inc. v. Gray*, 470 U.S. 414, 422 (1985). Thus, in *Rodrigue*, the Court held that an admiralty action under DOHSA does not apply to accidents "actually occurring" on these artificial islands, and that DOHSA therefore does not preclude the application of state law as adopted federal law through OCSLA to wrongful death actions arising from accidents on offshore platforms. *Rodrigue v. Aetna Casualty Co.*, *supra*, at 366, 89 S. Ct., at 1842.

Respondents argue that because the decedents were platform workers being transported from work to the mainland, OCSLA, not DOHSA, governs their cause of action.

* * *

[1] DOSHA does not include a survival provision authorizing recovery for pain and suffering before death. We do not address the issue whether the DOSHA recovery for the beneficiaries' pecuniary loss may be "supplemented" by a recovery of the decedent's pain and suffering before death under the survival provision of some conceivably applicable state statute that is intended to apply on the high seas. *See generally Barbe v. Drummond*, 507 F.2d 794, 797-798 (CAI 1974); *Dugas v. National Aircraft Corp.*, 438 F.2d 1386 (CA3 1971).

We do not interpret § 4 of OCSLA, 43 U.S.C. § 1333, to require or permit us to extend the coverage of the statute to the platform workers in this case who were killed miles away from the platform and on the high seas simply because they were platform workers. Congress determined that the general scope of OCSLA's coverage, like the operation of DOHSA's remedies, would be determined principally by locale, not by the status of the individual injured or killed.

* * *

In the circumstances presented, then, the conclusion is inescapable that the remedies afforded by DOHSA, not OCSLA, govern this action. Thus, respondents may secure the nonpecuniary damages made available by Louisiana's wrongful death statute only if it is found that DOHSA preserves, or does not pre-empt, state remedies on the high seas.

IV

Respondents argue that the first sentence of § 7 of DOHSA was intended to ensure the applicability of state wrongful death statutes to deaths on the high seas. We conclude that provision will not bear respondents' reading when evaluated in light of the language of the Act as a whole, the legislative history of § 7, the congressional purposes underlying the Act, and the importance of uniformity of admiralty law. *See Mastro Plastics Corp. v. NLRB*, 350 U.S. 270, 285 (1956) ("'In expounding a statute, we must not be guided by a single sentence or member of a sentence, but look to the provisions of the whole law, and to its object and policy'") (quoting *United States v. Heirs of Boisdoré*, 8 How. 113, 122 (1849)). These references persuade us that the first sentence of § 7 was intended only to serve as a jurisdictional saving clause, ensuring that state courts enjoyed the right to entertain causes of action and provide wrongful death remedies both for accidents arising on territorial waters and, under DOHSA, for accidents occurring more than one marine league from shore.

The first sentence of § 7 of DOHSA, as originally drafted, provided that "the provisions of any State statute giving or regulating rights of action or remedies for death shall not be affected by this act as to causes of action accruing within the territorial limits of any State." *See* 59 Cong. Rec. 4482 (1920). During the House debate, Representative Mann proposed an amendment deleting the words "as to causes of action accruing within the territorial limits of any state." Although at first blush the language of the amended § 7 seems to support respondents' position, a closer comparison of the language of § 7, both before and after its amendment, with the language of § 4 of the Act belies respondents' facial argument.

* * *

In sum, the language of § 7 and its legislative history, as well as the congressional purposes underlying DOHSA, mandate that § 7 be read not as an endorsement of the application of state wrongful death statutes to the high seas, but rather as a jurisdictional saving clause. Viewed in this light, § 7 serves not to destroy the uniformity of wrongful death remedies on the high seas but to facilitate the effective and just administration of those remedies. The recognition of concurrent state jurisdiction to hear DOHSA actions makes available to DOHSA beneficiaries a convenient forum for the decision of their wrongful death claims. *See* Note, *Admiralty: Death on the High Seas by Wrongful Act*, 47 CORNELL L. Q. 632, 638 (1962) (hereinafter Note). Because the resolution of DOHSA claims does not normally require the expertise that admiralty courts bring to bear, DOHSA actions are clearly within the competence of state courts to adjudicate. *See* ALI Study, at 237; Note, at 637. Also, the availability of concurrent jurisdiction prevents disunity in the provision of forums to survivors of those killed on the high seas; it ensures that if a seaman and a passenger are killed at sea in the same accident, the beneficiaries of both are able to choose the forum in which they prefer to proceed. *See Engel v. Davenport*, 271 U.S. 33 (1926) (state and federal courts have concurrent jurisdiction over Jones Act claims). *See also* ALI Study § 1316(b), at 237; Note, at 638. *Cf. also Gulf Offshore Co. v. Mobil Oil Corp.*, 453 U.S. 473 (1981) (recognizing state courts' concurrent jurisdiction over OCSLA claims).

Once it is determined that § 7 acts as a jurisdictional saving clause, and not as a guarantee of the applicability of state substantive law to wrongful deaths on the high seas, the conclusion that the state statutes are pre-empted by DOHSA where it applies is inevitable. As we held in *Higginbotham*, Congress has "struck the balance for us" in determining that survivors should be restricted to the recovery of their nonpecuniary losses, and when DOHSA "does speak directly to a question, the courts are not free to 'supplement' Congress' answer so thoroughly that the Act becomes meaningless." 436 U.S., at 625, 98 S. Ct. at 2015.

Admittedly, in the circumstances of this case, the recognition of a state damages remedy for loss of society would bring respondents' DOHSA recovery into line with the damages available to a beneficiary of a federal *Moragne* maritime cause of action arising from a death on territorial waters. *See Sea-Land Services, Inc. v. Gaudet*, 414 U.S. 573 (1974) (holding that awards under the general federal maritime cause of action for wrongful death could include compensation for loss of society). However, the questionable practical significance of this difference in recovery, *see Mobil Oil Corp. v. Higginbotham, supra*, at 624, and n.20, is far overshadowed by the potential for serious conflicts between DOHSA and state substantive law in such areas as limitations periods, classes of beneficiaries, and the definition of potential defenses. We defer to Congress' purpose in making a uniform provision for recovery for wrongful deaths on the high seas, an area where the federal interests are primary.

The judgment of the Court of Appeals for the Fifth Circuit is reversed, and the case is remanded for further proceedings consistent with this opinion.

It is so ordered.

Justice POWELL, with whom Justice BRENNAN, Justice MARSHALL, and Justice STEVENS join, concurring in Part III and dissenting

The Court today holds that § 7 of the Death on the High Seas Act (DOHSA), 41 Stat. 538, 46 U.S.C. § 767, forecloses application of state remedies for wrongful deaths on the high seas. Thus, the Court confines state courts to the adjudication of causes of action brought under DOHSA. Because I believe that the Court's reading of § 7 is at odds with the language of the statute and its legislative history, I dissent.

* * *

II

The starting point in statutory construction is, of course, the language of the statute itself. *Blue Chip Stamps v. Manor Drug Stores*, 421 U.S. 723, 756 (1975) (POWELL, J., concurring). *See Consumer Product Safety Comm'n v. GTE Sylvania, Inc.*, 447 U.S. 102 (1980). The language of § 7, given scant attention by the Court, reads as codified:

> § 767. Exceptions from operation of chapter
> The provisions of any State statute *giving or regulating rights of action or remedies for death* shall not be affected by this chapter. Nor shall this chapter apply to the Great Lakes or to any waters within the territorial limits of any State, or to any navigable waters in the Panama Canal Zone.

46 U.S.C. § 767 (emphasis added). The terms of the provision are clear. The provision preserves state rights of action and state remedies for wrongful death without any territorial qualification. It encompasses not only jurisdiction, but also "rights of action" and "remedies." The geographic reach of these traditional rights of action is therefore undiminished by DOHSA.

The congressional debate and other legislative history cast no doubt on the plain meaning of § 7.

* * *

It is not easy to understand how § 7 was transformed from a provision that preserved both state jurisdiction and state rights of action in territorial waters, into a mere "jurisdictional saving clause" with no power to preserve state rights of action on the high seas. The Mann Amendment did nothing more than remove a territorial restriction; all other clauses of § 7 remained intact. As Representative Mann stated: "If the amendment which I have suggested should be agreed to, the bill *would not interfere in any way with rights now granted by any State statute*, whether the cause of action accrued within the territorial limits of the State or not." 59 Cong. Rec. 4484 (1920) (emphasis added). Moreover, as already noted, construing § 7 as preserving only state jurisdiction on the high seas is at odds with the terms of the provision itself. The language plainly refers to "[the] provisions of any State statute giving or regulating rights of action or remedies for death."

* * *

IV

The Court argues that preserving state rights of action for death on the high seas, in accordance with the plain language of § 7, would undermine a uniform federal remedy and conflict with the *exclusive*, federal character of most aspects of admiralty law. I agree that such a result undercuts a federal uniformity that seems desirable here, but it is not the role of this Court to reconsider the wisdom of a policy choice that Congress has already made. Congress enacted the Mann Amendment to remove the territorial restriction from § 7's preservation of state-law rights of action for wrongful death. The Court now holds that those rights of action may not be enforced on the high seas, and thereby imposes an exclusive federal remedy that Congress declined to enact. We should respect the outcome of the legislative process and preserve State rights of action for wrongful death on the high seas until Congress legislates otherwise. Accordingly, I dissent.

Note: Jury Trial

Is there a possibility for a jury trial in a suit under DOHSA? In *Friedman v. Mitsubishi Aircraft International, Inc.*, 678 F. Supp. 1064 (S.D.N.Y. 1988), an aircraft crashed on the high seas and plaintiff moved for a trial by jury. The motion was grounded on the theory that DOHSA was inapplicable in the absence of a traditional maritime activity and, in the alternative, if DOHSA was applicable, on the assertion that Section 7 of DOHSA preserves the right to a jury trial, especially when diversity jurisdiction exists. The court denied the motion. In the opinion of the court, DOHSA provides the exclusive remedy for all deaths on the high seas, regardless of any traditional maritime activity, and substantive state wrongful death remedies are preempted outside the territorial waters of a state. "It follows, therefore," the court concluded that "since DOHSA provides a remedy in admiralty, admiralty principles are applicable and a DOHSA plaintiff has no right to a jury trial of wrongful death claims."

Is the right to a jury trial a "substantive" remedy or a part of procedural law? If Section 7 of DOHSA is a jurisdictional saving clause that preserves the jurisdiction of a state court to hear DOHSA claims, what prevents the state court from granting a motion for a jury trial? *See Favaloro v. S.S. Golden Gate*, 687 F. Supp. 475, 1988 AMC 818 (N.D. Cal. 1987); *In re Korean Airlines Disaster of September 1, 1983*, 704 F. Supp. 1135 (Dist. Colum. 1988), *aff'd* in part, 932 F.2d 1475 (D. Col. Cir. 1991).

Part 2. Wrongful Death Actions Under General Maritime Law — (Within State Territorial Waters): Cases and Notes

A. Creation of a Cause of Action

MORAGNE v. STATES MARINE LINES, INC.

398 U.S. 375, 90 S. Ct. 1772, 26 L. Ed. 2d 339, 1970 AMC 967 (1970)

Mr. Justice HARLAN delivered the opinion of the Court

We brought this case here to consider whether *The Harrisburg*, 119 U.S. 199, in which this Court held in 1886 that maritime law does not afford a cause of action for wrongful death, should any longer be regarded as acceptable law.

The complaint sets forth that Edward Moragne, a longshoreman, was killed while working aboard the vessel *Palmetto State* in navigable waters within the State of Florida. Petitioner, as his widow and representative of his estate, brought this suit in a state court against respondent States Marine Lines, Inc., the owner of the vessel, to recover damages for wrongful death and for the pain and suffering experienced by the decedent prior to his death. The claims were predicated upon both negligence and the unseaworthiness of the vessel.

* * *

I

The Court's opinion in *The Harrisburg* acknowledged that the result reached had little justification except in primitive English legal history—a history far removed from the American law of remedies for maritime deaths.

II

We need not, however, pronounce a verdict on whether *The Harrisburg*, when decided, was a correct extrapolation of the principles of decisional law then in existence. A development of major significance has intervened, making clear that the rule against recovery for wrongful death is sharply out of keeping with the policies of modern American maritime law. This development is the wholesale abandonment of the rule in most of the areas where it once held sway, quite evidently prompted by the same sense of the rule's injustice that generated so much criticism of its original promulgation.

* * *

In the United States, every State today has enacted a wrongful-death statute. *See Smith*, *supra*, 44 N.C. L. Rev. 402. The Congress has created actions for wrongful deaths of railroad employees, Federal Employers' Liability Act, 45 U.S.C. §§ 51-59; of merchant seamen, Jones Act, 46 U.S.C. § 688; and of persons on the high seas, Death on the High Seas Act, 46 U.S.C. §§ 761, 762. Congress has also, in the Federal Tort Claims Act, 28 U.S.C. § 1346(b), made the United States subject to liability in certain circumstances for negligently caused wrongful death to the same extent as a private person. *See, e.g., Richards v. United States*, 369 U.S. 1 (1962).

These numerous and broadly applicable statutes, taken as a whole, make it clear that there is no present public policy against allowing recovery for wrongful death. The statutes evidence a wide rejection by the legislatures of whatever justifications may once have existed for a general refusal to allow such recovery.

This legislative establishment of policy carries significance beyond the particular scope of each of the statutes involved. The policy thus established has become itself a part of our law, to be given its appropriate weight not only in matters of statutory construction but also in those of decisional law.

* * *

III

Our undertaking, therefore, is to determine whether Congress has given such a direction in its legislation granting remedies for wrongful deaths in portions of the maritime domain. We find that Congress has given no affirmative indication of an intent to preclude the judicial allowance of a remedy for wrongful death to persons in the situation of this petitioner.

From the date of *The Harrisburg* until 1920, there was no remedy for death on the high seas caused by breach of one of the duties imposed by federal maritime law. For deaths with state territorial waters, the federal law accommodated the humane policies of state wrongful-death statutes by allowing recovery whenever an applicable state statute favored such recovery. Congress acted in 1920 to furnish the remedy denied by the courts for deaths beyond the jurisdiction of any State, by passing two landmark statutes. The first of these was the Death on the High Seas Act, 41 Stat. 537, 46 U.S.C. § 761 *et seq.*

... The second statute was the Jones Act, 41 Stat. 1007, 46 U.S.C. § 688, which, by extending to seamen the protections of the Federal Employers' Liability Act, provided a right of recovery against their employers for negligence resulting in injury or death. This right follows from the seamen's employment status and is not limited to injury or death occurring on the high seas.

The United States, participating as *amicus curiae*, contended at oral argument that these statutes, if construed to forbid recognition of a general maritime remedy for wrongful death within territorial waters, would perpetuate three anomalies of present law. The first of these is simply the discrepancy produced whenever the rule of *The Harrisburg* holds sway: within territorial waters, identical conduct violating federal law (here the furnishing of an unseaworthy vessel) produces liability if the victim is merely injured, but frequently not if he is killed. As we have concluded, such a distinction is not compatible with the general policies of federal maritime law.

The second incongruity is that identical breaches of the duty to provide a seaworthy ship, resulting in death, produce liability outside the three-mile limit—since a claim under the Death on the High Seas Act may be founded on unseaworthiness, *see Kernan v. American Dredging Co.*, 355 U.S. 426, 430 n.4 (1958)—but not within the territorial waters of a State whose local statute excludes unseaworthiness claims. The United States argues that since the substantive duty is federal, and federal maritime jurisdiction covers navigable waters within and without the three-mile limit, no rational policy supports this distinction in the availability of a remedy.

The third, and assertedly the "strangest" anomaly is that a true seaman—that is, a member of a ship's company, covered by the Jones Act—is provided no remedy for death caused by unseaworthiness within territorial waters, while a longshoreman, to whom the duty of seaworthiness was extended only because he performs work traditionally done by seamen, does have such a remedy when allowed by a state statute.

There is much force to the United States' argument that these distinctions are so lacking in any apparent justification that we should not, in the absence of compelling evidence, presume that Congress affirmatively intended to freeze them into maritime law. There should be no presumption that Congress has removed this Court's traditional responsibility to vindicate the policies of maritime law by ceding that function exclusively to the States.

* * *

Read in light of the state of maritime law in 1920, we believe this legislative history indicates that Congress intended to ensure the continued availability of a remedy, historically provided by the States, for deaths in territorial waters; its failure to extend the Act to cover such deaths primarily reflected the lack of necessity for coverage by a federal statute, rather than an affirmative desire to insulate such deaths from the benefits of any federal remedy that might be available independently of the Act. The void that existed in maritime law up until 1920 was the absence of any remedy for wrongful death on the high seas. Congress, in acting to fill that void, legislated only to the three-mile limit because that was the extent of the problem. The express provision that state remedies in territorial waters were not disturbed by the Act ensured that Congress' solution of one problem would not create another by inviting the courts to find that the Act pre-empted the entire field, destroying the state remedies that had previously existed.

The beneficiaries of persons meeting death on territorial waters did not suffer at that time from being excluded from the coverage of the Act. To the contrary, the state remedies that were left undisturbed not only were familiar but also may actually have been more generous than the remedy provided by the new Act... .

* * *

We conclude that the Death on the High Seas Act was not intended to preclude that availability of a remedy for wrongful death under general maritime law in situations not covered by the Act. Because the refusal of maritime law to provide such a remedy appears to be jurisprudentially unsound and to have produced serious confusion and hardship, that refusal should cease unless there are substantial countervailing factors that dictate adherence to *The Harrisburg* simply as a matter of *stare decisis*. We now turn to a consideration of those factors.

V

* * *

The one aspect of a claim for wrongful death that has no precise counterpart in the established law governing nonfatal injuries is the determination of the beneficiaries who are entitled to recover. General maritime law, which denied any recovery for wrongful death, found no need to specify which dependents should receive such recovery. On this question, petitioner and the United States argue that we may look for guidance to the expressions of Congress, which has spoken on this subject in the Death on the High Seas Act, the Jones Act, and the Longshoremen's and Harbor Workers' Compensation Act. Though very similar, each of these provisions differs slightly in the naming of dependent relatives who may recover and in the priority given in their claims.

The United States contends that, of the three, the provision that should be borrowed for wrongful-death actions under general maritime law is that of the Death on the High Seas Act. It is the congressional enactment that deals specifically and exclusively with actions for wrongful death, and that simply provides a remedy—for deaths on the high seas—for breaches of the duties imposed by general maritime law. In contrast, the beneficiary provisions of the Jones Act are applicable only to a specific class of actions—claims by seamen against their employers—based on violations of the special standard of negligence that has been imposed under the Federal Employers' Liability Act. That standard appears to be unlike any imposed by general maritime law. Further, although the Longshoremen's and Harbor Workers' Compensation Act is applicable to longshoremen such as petitioner's late husband, its principles of recovery are wholly foreign to those of general maritime law—like most workmen's compensation laws, it deals only with the responsibilities of employers for death or injury to their employees, and provides standardized amounts of compensation regardless of fault on the part of the employer.

The only one of these statutes that applies not just to a class of workers but to any "person," and that bases liability on conduct violative of general maritime law, is the Death on the High Seas Act. The borrowing of its schedule of beneficiaries, argues the United States, will not only effectuate the expressed congressional preferences in this area but will also promote uniformity by ensuring that the beneficiaries will be the same for identical torts, rather than varying with the employment status of the decedent. There is no occasion, according to this argument, to borrow from the law of the relevant coastal State, since the underlying duties to be effectuated are entirely federal and Congress has expressed its preference of beneficiaries for violations of maritime law.

We do not determine this issue now, for we think its final resolution should await further sifting through the lower courts in future litigation. For present purposes we conclude only that its existence affords no sufficient reason for not coming to grips with *The Harrisburg*. If still other subsidiary issues should require resolution, such as particular questions of the measure of damages, the courts will not be without persuasive analogy for guidance. Both the Death on the High Seas Act and the numerous state wrongful-death acts have been implemented with success for decades. The experience thus built up counsels that a suit for wrongful death raises no problems unlike those that have long been grist for the judicial mill.

* * *

We accordingly overrule *The Harrisburg*, and hold that an action does lie under general maritime law for death caused by violation of maritime duties. The judgment of the Court of Appeals is reversed, and the case is remanded to that court for further proceedings consistent with this opinion.

It is so ordered.

Notes

1. *The Moragne Action*

The *Moragne* decision itself was concerned with death caused by unseaworthiness. However, the *Moragne* action also provides a remedy for wrongful death caused to a maritime worker by negligence within territorial waters. *Garris v. Norfolk Shipbuilding & Drydock Corp.*, 532 U.S. 811, 121 S. Ct. 1927, 2001 AMC 1817 (2001).

The *Moragne* action survives the death of the decedent. *McKeithen v. M/V Frosta*, 435 F. Supp. 584, 1978 AMC 51 (E.D. La. 1977). The claim gives rise to a maritime lien, and the suit may be brought *in rem* and *in personam*. *Palmer v. Ribax, Inc.*, 407 F. Supp. 974, 1976 AMC 1056 (M.D. Fla. 1976). Suit may be brought by a stepchild. *Spiller v. Lowe & Associates*, 466 F.2d 903 1972 AMC 2510 (8th Cir. 1972). It may also be brought by the parents of a seaman, even if the deceased is survived by closer relatives, such as children, legitimate or illegitimate, when the parents cannot recover under the Jones Act. *Hamilton v. Canal Barge Co.*, 395 F. Supp. 978 (E.D. La. 1975); *Palmer v. Ribax, Inc., supra.* A fiancée has no standing to sue under *Moragne*. *Hamilton v. Canal Barge Co., supra.* Questions of filiation in a *Moragne* suit are determined under state law, as incorporated into the maritime law. *In re Industrial Transportation Corp.*, 344 F. Supp. 1371, 1972 AMC 2380 (E.D.N.Y. 1972).

When a seaman is fatally injured in territorial waters, the *Moragne* action applies along with the Jones Act. Application of the *Moragne* action is particularly desirable when death results from unseaworthiness rather than negligence. *Ivy v. Security Barge Lines, Inc.*, 606 F.2d 524, 1980 AMC 356 (5th Cir. 1979). In any case, however, the Jones Act precludes recovery under the general maritime law for the non-pecuniary loss sustained by the seaman's survivors. *See Miles v. Apex Marine Corp.*, 498 U.S. 19, 111 S. Ct. 317, 112 L. Ed. 2d 275, 1991 AMC 1 (1990).

When a person dies in state territorial waters, the issue arises as to whether state law or rules of general maritime law govern the remedies for such action. In such circumstance, DOHSA only provides for deaths which occur on the high seas, and the Jones Act only provides for the wrongful deaths of seamen caused by employer negligence. After the enactment of DOHSA, the Supreme Court in *Moragne v. State Marine Lines*, 398 U.S. 375, 90 S. Ct. 1772, 26 L. Ed. 2d 339 (1970) provided a general maritime law cause of action for a longshoreman (Sieracki seaman) killed in the territorial waters of the United States.

In *Miles v. Apex Marine Corp., supra*, the Supreme Court "extended" the *Moragne* general maritime wrongful death action to seamen killed in territorial waters.

Subsequently, in *Norfolk Shipbuilding & Drydock Corp. v. Garris*, 532 U.S. 811, 121 S.Ct. 1927, 150 L. Ed. 2d 34, 2001 AMC 1817 (2001), the Supreme Court held that a general maritime law action for deaths that occur in state waters may be maintained for the negligent breach of a maritime duty of care. In other words, the Court extended *Moragne* which was an unseaworthiness case to apply to negligence actions as well.

Prior to *Moragne*, the Supreme Court had held that state wrongful death statutes could be invoked for deaths that occur in state waters under the "maritime but local" doctrine. *Western Fuels v. Garcia*, 257 U.S. 233 (1921). In fact, such actions could be brought in federal court under admiralty jurisdiction. These state wrongful death statutes were available to all classes of persons, including maritime workers, except that the Jones Act provided the exclusive remedy for seamen. *Lindgren v. United States*, 281 U.S. 38, 50 S.Ct. 207, 74 L.Ed. 686 (1930).

The question after *Moragne* was whether or not the general maritime law action created by *Moragne* displaced state law. *See Yamaha Motor Corp., U.S.A. v. Calhoun, infra.*

2. *DOHSA and the Moragne Action*

In *Mobil Oil Corp. v. Higginbotham*, 436 U.S. 618 , 98 S. Ct. 2010, 56 L. Ed. 2d 581 (1978), the Supreme Court was faced with the question as to whether to extend *Moragne* and *Gaudet* line of authorities to a death on the high seas. The Court held that the congressionally provided remedy contained in the Death on the High Seas Act was the exclusive remedy and is not supplemented by the general maritime law.

YAMAHA MOTOR CORP., U.S.A. v. CALHOUN

516 U.S. 199, 116 S. Ct. 619, 133 L. Ed. 2d 578, 1996 AMC 305 (1996)

Justice GINSBURG delivered the opinion of the Court

Twelve-year-old Natalie Calhoun was killed in a jet ski accident on July 6, 1989. At the time of her death, she was vacationing with family friends at a beach-front resort in Puerto Rico. Alleging that the jet ski was defectively designed or made, Natalie's parents sought to recover from the manufacturer pursuant to state survival and wrongful death statutes. The manufacturer contended that state remedies could not be applied because Natalie died on navigable waters; federal, judge-declared maritime law, the manufacturer urged, controlled to the exclusion of state law.

Traditionally, state remedies have been applied in accident cases of this order—maritime wrongful death cases in which no federal statute specifies the appropriate relief and the decedent was not a seaman, longshore worker, or person otherwise engaged in a maritime trade. We hold, in accord with the United States Court of Appeals for the Third Circuit, that state remedies remain applicable in such cases and have not been displaced by the federal maritime wrongful death action recognized in *Moragne v. States Marine Lines, Inc.*, 398 U.S. 375, 90 S. Ct. 1772, 26 L. Ed. 2d 339 (1970).

I

Natalie Calhoun, the twelve-year-old daughter of respondents Lucien and Robin Calhoun, died in a tragic accident on July 6, 1989. On vacation with family friends at a resort hotel in Puerto Rico, Natalie had rented a "WaveJammer" jet ski manufactured by Yamaha Motor Company, Ltd., and distributed by Yamaha Motor Corporation, U.S.A. (collectively, "Yamaha"), the petitioners in this case. While riding the WaveJammer, Natalie slammed into a vessel anchored in the waters off the hotel frontage, and was killed.

The Calhouns, individually and in their capacities as administrators of their daughter's estate, sued Yamaha in the United States District Court for the Eastern District of Pennsylvania. Invoking Pennsylvania's wrongful death and survival statutes, 42 Pa. Cons. Stat. §§ 8301-8302 (1982 and Supp.1995), the Calhouns asserted several bases for recovery (including negligence, strict liability, and breach of implied warranties), and sought damages for lost future earnings, loss of society, loss of support and services, and funeral expenses, as well as punitive damages. They grounded federal jurisdiction on both diversity of citizenship, 28 U.S.C. § 1332,[2] and admiralty, 28 U.S.C. § 1333.

Yamaha moved for partial summary judgment, arguing that the federal maritime wrongful death action this Court recognized in *Moragne v. States Marine Lines, Inc.*, 398 U.S. 375, 90 S. Ct. 1772, 26 L. Ed. 2d 339 (1970), provided the exclusive basis for recovery, displacing all remedies afforded by state law. Under *Moragne*, Yamaha contended, the Calhouns could recover as damages only Natalie's funeral expenses. The District Court agreed with Yamaha that *Moragne*'s maritime death action displaced state remedies; the

---

[2] The Calhouns are citizens of Pennsylvania. Yamaha Motor Corporation, U.S.A. is incorporated and has its principal place of business in California; Yamaha Motor Company, Ltd. is incorporated and has its principal place of business in Japan.

court held, however, that loss of society and loss of support and services were compensable under *Moragne*.

* * *

Although the Court of Appeals granted the interlocutory review petition, the panel to which the appeal was assigned did not reach the questions presented in the certified order, for it determined that an anterior issue was pivotal. The District Court, as just recounted, had concluded that any damages the Calhouns might recover from Yamaha would be governed exclusively by federal maritime law. But the Third Circuit panel questioned that conclusion and inquired whether state wrongful death and survival statutes supplied the remedial prescriptions for the Calhouns' complaint. The appellate panel asked whether the state remedies endured or were "displaced by a federal maritime rule of decision." 40 F.3d 622, 624 (1994). Ultimately, the Court of Appeals ruled that state law remedies apply in this case. *Id.*, at 644.

II

* * *

We therefore proceed to the issue on which certiorari was granted: Does the federal maritime claim for wrongful death recognized in *Moragne* supply the exclusive remedy in cases involving the deaths of nonseafarer[3] in territorial waters?

III

Because this case involves a watercraft collision on navigable waters, it falls within admiralty's domain. *See Sisson v. Ruby*, 497 U.S. 358, 361-367, 110 S. Ct. 2892, 2895-2898, 111 L. Ed. 2d 292 (1990); *Foremost Ins. Co. v. Richardson*, 457 U.S. 668, 677, 102 S. Ct. 2654, 2659, 73 L. Ed. 2d 300 (1982). "With admiralty jurisdiction," we have often said, "comes the application of substantive admiralty law." *East River S.S. Corp. v. Transamerica Delaval Inc.*, 476 U.S. 858, 864, 106 S. Ct. 2295, 2298-2299, 90 L. Ed. 2d 865 (1986). The exercise of admiralty jurisdiction, however, "does not result in automatic displacement of state law." *Jerome B. Grubart, Inc. v. Great Lakes Dredge & Dock Co.*, 513 U.S. ___, ___, 115 S. Ct. 1043, 1046, 130 L. Ed. 2d 1024 (1995). Indeed, prior to *Moragne*, federal admiralty courts routinely applied state wrongful death and survival statutes in maritime accident cases.[4] The question before us is whether *Moragne* should be read to stop that practice.

Our review of maritime wrongful death law begins with *The Harrisburg*, 119 U.S. 199, 7 S. Ct. 140, 30 L. Ed. 358 (1886), where we held that the general maritime law (a species of judge-made federal common law) did not afford a cause of action for wrongful death. The *Harrisburg* Court said that wrongful death actions are statutory and may not be created by judicial decree. The Court did not question the soundness of this view, or examine the historical justifications that account for it. Instead, the Court merely noted that com-

[3] By "nonseafarers," we mean persons who are neither seamen covered by the Jones Act, 46 U.S.C.App. § 688 (1988 ed.), nor longshore workers covered by the Longshore and Harbor Workers' Compensation Act, 33 U.S.C. § 901 *et seq.*

[4] Throughout this opinion, for economy, we use the term wrongful death remedies or statutes to include survival statutes.

mon law in the United States, like the common law of England, did not allow recovery "for an injury which results in death," *id.*, at 204, 7 S. Ct., at 142 (internal quotation marks omitted), and that no country had "adopted a different rule on this subject for the sea from that which it maintains on the land," *id.*, at 213, 7 S. Ct., at 146. The Court did not consider itself free to chart a different course by crafting a judge-made wrongful death action under our maritime law.

Federal admiralty courts tempered the harshness of *The Harrisburg*'s rule by allowing recovery under state wrongful death statutes. *See, e.g.*, *The Hamilton*, 207 U.S. 398, 28 S. Ct. 133, 52 L. Ed. 264 (1907); *The City of Norwalk*, 55 F. 98 (S.D.N.Y.1893).[5] We reaffirmed this practice in *Western Fuel Co. v. Garcia*, 257 U.S. 233, 42 S. Ct. 89, 66 L. Ed. 210 (1921), by holding that California's wrongful death statute governed a suit brought by the widow of a maritime worker killed in that State's territorial waters. Though we had generally refused to give effect to state laws regarded as inconsonant with the substance of federal maritime law, we concluded that extending state wrongful death statutes to fatal accidents in territorial waters was compatible with substantive maritime policies: "The subject is maritime and local in character and the specified modification of or supplement to the rule applied in admiralty courts ... will not work material prejudice to the characteristic features of the general maritime law, nor interfere with the proper harmony and uniformity of that law in its international and interstate relations." *Id.*, at 242, 42 S. Ct., at 90.[6] On similar reasoning, we also held that state survival statutes may be applied in cases arising out of accidents in territorial waters. *See Just v. Chambers*, 312 U.S. 383, 391-392, 61 S. Ct. 687, 692-693, 85 L. Ed. 903 (1941).

State wrongful death statutes proved an adequate supplement to federal maritime law, until a series of this Court's decisions transformed the maritime doctrine of unseaworthiness into a strict liability rule. Prior to 1944, unseaworthiness "was an obscure and relatively little used" liability standard, largely because "a shipowner's duty at that time was only to use due diligence to provide a seaworthy ship." *Miles v. Apex Marine Corp.*, 498 U.S. 19, 25, 111 S. Ct. 317, 322, 112 L. Ed. 2d 275 (1990) (internal quotation marks omitted). *See also Moragne*, 398 U.S., at 398-399, 90 S. Ct., at 1786-1787. *Mahnich v. Southern S.S. Co.*, 321 U.S. 96, 64 S. Ct. 455, 88 L. Ed. 561 (1944), however, notably expanded a shipowner's liability to injured seamen by imposing a nondelegable duty "to furnish a vessel and appurtenances reasonably fit for their intended use." *Mitchell v. Trawler Racer, Inc.*, 362 U.S. 539, 550, 80 S. Ct. 926, 933, 4 L. Ed. 2d 941 (1960). The duty imposed was absolute; failure to supply a safe ship resulted in liability "irrespective of fault and irrespective of the intervening negligence of crew members." *Miles*, 498 U.S., at 25, 111 S. Ct., at 322. The unseaworthiness doctrine thus became a "species of liability with-

[5] Congress also mitigated the impact of *The Harrisburg* by enacting two statutes affording recovery for wrongful death. In 1920, Congress passed the Death on the High Seas Act (DOHSA), 46 U.S.C.App. § 761 *et seq.* (1988 ed.), which provides a federal claim for wrongful death occurring more than three nautical miles from the shore of any State or Territory. In that same year, Congress also passed the Jones Act, 46 U.S.C.App. § 688 (1988 ed.), which provides a wrongful death claim to the survivors of seamen killed in the course of their employment, whether on the high seas or in territorial waters.

[6] Indeed, years before *The Harrisburg*, this Court rendered a pathmarking decision, *Steamboat Co. v. Chase*, 83 U.S. 522, 21 L. Ed. 369, 16 Wall. 522 (1873). In *Steamboat*, the Court upheld, under the "saving-to-suitors" proviso of the Judiciary Act of 1789 (surviving currently in 28 U.S.C. § 1333(1)), a state court's application of the State's wrongful death statute to a fatality caused by a collision in territorial waters between defendants' steamboat and a sailboat in which plaintiff's decedent was passing.

out fault," *Seas Shipping Co. v. Sieracki*, 328 U.S. 85, 94, 66 S. Ct. 872, 877, 90 L. Ed. 1099 (1946), and soon eclipsed ordinary negligence as the primary basis of recovery when a seafarer was injured or killed. *Miles*, 498 U.S., at 25-26, 111 S. Ct., at 321-322.[7]

The disparity between the unseaworthiness doctrine's strict liability standard and negligence-based state wrongful death statutes figured prominently in our landmark *Moragne* decision. Petsonella *Moragne*, the widow of a longshore worker killed in Florida's territorial waters, brought suit under Florida's wrongful death and survival statutes, alleging both negligence and unseaworthiness. The district court dismissed the claim for wrongful death based on unseaworthiness, citing this Court's decision in *The Tungus v. Skovgaard*, 358 U.S. 588, 79 S. Ct. 503, 3 L. Ed. 2d 524 (1959). There, a sharply-divided Court held that "when admiralty adopts a State's right of action for wrongful death, it must enforce the right as an integrated whole, with whatever conditions and limitations the creating State has attached." *Id.*, at 592, 79 S. Ct., at 506. Thus, in wrongful death actions involving fatalities in territorial waters, state statutes provided the standard of liability as well as the remedial regime. Because the Florida Supreme Court had previously held that Florida's wrongful death statute did not encompass unseaworthiness as a basis of liability, the Court of Appeals affirmed the dismissal of *Moragne*'s unseaworthiness claim. *See Moragne*, 398 U.S., at 377, 90 S. Ct., at 1775-1776.

The Court acknowledged in *Moragne* that *The Tungus* had led to considerable uncertainty over the role state law should play in remedying deaths in territorial waters, but concluded that "the primary source of the confusion is not to be found in *The Tungus*, but in *The Harrisburg*." 398 U.S., at 378, 90 S. Ct., at 1776. Upon reexamining the soundness of The Harrisburg, we decided that its holding, "somewhat dubious even when rendered, is such an unjustifiable anomaly in the present maritime law that it should no longer be followed." 398 U.S., at 378, 90 S. Ct., at 1776. Accordingly, the Court overruled *The Harrisburg* and held that an action "lie [s] under general maritime law for death caused by violation of maritime duties." 398 U.S., at 409, 90 S. Ct., at 1792.

IV

Yamaha argues that *Moragne*—despite its focus on "maritime duties" owed to maritime workers—covers the waters, creating a uniform federal maritime remedy for all deaths occurring in state territorial waters, and ousting all previously available state remedies. In Yamaha's view, state remedies can no longer supplement general maritime law (as they routinely did before *Moragne*), because *Moragne* launched a solitary federal scheme.[8] Yamaha's reading of *Moragne* is not without force; in several contexts, we have recognized

---

[7] The Court extended the duty to provide a seaworthy ship, once owed only to seamen, to longshore workers in *Seas Shipping Co. v. Sieracki*, 328 U.S. 85, 66 S. Ct. 872, 90 L. Ed. 1099 (1946). Congress effectively overruled this extension in its 1972 amendments to the Longshore and Harbor Workers' Compensation Act, 33 U.S.C. § 901 *et seq. See* 33 U.S.C. § 905(b). We have thus far declined to extend the duty further. *See Kermarec v. Compagnie Generale Transatlantique*, 358 U.S. 625, 629, 79 S. Ct. 406, 409, 3 L. Ed. 2d 550 (1959) (unseaworthiness doctrine inapplicable to invitee aboard vessel).

[8] If *Moragne*'s wrongful death action did not extend to nonseafarers like Natalie, one could hardly argue that Moragne displaced the state law remedies the Calhouns seek. Lower courts have held that *Moragne*'s wrongful death action extends to nonseafarers. *See, e.g., Sutton v. Earles*, 26 F.3d 903 (C.A.9 1994) (recreational boater); *Wahlstrom v. Kawasaki Heavy Industries, Ltd.*, 4 F.3d 1084 (C.A.2 1993) (jet skier), *cert. denied*, 510 U.S. ___, 114 S. Ct. 1060, 127 L. Ed. 2d 380 (1994). We assume, for purposes of this decision, the correctness of that position. Similarly, as in prior encounters, we assume without deciding that *Moragne* also provides a survival action. *See Miles v. Apex Marine Corp.*, 498 U.S. 19, 34, 111 S. Ct. 317, 326-327, 112 L. Ed. 2d 275 (1990). The question we confront is not what Moragne added to the remedial arsenal in maritime cases, but what, if anything, it removed from admiralty's stock.

that vindication of maritime policies demanded uniform adherence to a federal rule of decision, with no leeway for variation or supplementation by state law. *See, e.g., Kossick v. United Fruit Co.*, 365 U.S. 731, 742, 81 S. Ct. 886, 894, 6 L. Ed. 2d 56 (1961) (federal maritime rule validating oral contracts precluded application of state Statute of Frauds); *Pope & Talbot, Inc. v. Hawn*, 346 U.S. 406, 409, 74 S. Ct. 202, 204-205, 98 L. Ed. 143 (1953) (admiralty's comparative negligence rule barred application of state contributory negligence rule); *Garrett v. Moore-McCormack Co.*, 317 U.S. 239, 248-249, 63 S. Ct. 246, 252-253, 87 L. Ed. 239 (1942) (federal maritime rule allocating burden of proof displaced conflicting state rule).[9] In addition, Yamaha correctly points out that uniformity concerns informed our decision in *Moragne*.

The uniformity concerns that prompted us to overrule *The Harrisburg*, however, were of a different order than those invoked by Yamaha. *Moragne* did not reexamine the soundness of *The Harrisburg* out of concern that state damage awards in maritime wrongful death cases were excessive, or that variations in the remedies afforded by the States threatened to interfere with the harmonious operation of maritime law. Variations of this sort had long been deemed compatible with federal maritime interests. *See Western Fuel*, 257 U.S., at 242, 42 S. Ct., at 90-91. The uniformity concern that drove our decision in *Moragne* related, instead, to the availability of unseaworthiness as a basis of liability.

By 1970, when *Moragne* was decided, claims premised on unseaworthiness had become "the principal vehicle for recovery" by seamen and other maritime workers injured or killed in the course of their employment. *Moragne*, 398 U.S., at 399, 90 S. Ct., at 1786-1787. But with *The Harrisburg* in place, troubling anomalies had developed that many times precluded the survivors of maritime workers from recovering for deaths caused by an unseaworthy vessel. The *Moragne* Court identified three anomalies and concluded they could no longer be tolerated.

First, the Court noted that "within territorial waters, identical conduct violating federal law (here the furnishing of an unseaworthy vessel) produces liability if the victim is merely injured, but frequently not if he is killed." *Id.*, at 395, 90 S. Ct., at 1785. This occurred because in nonfatal injury cases, state substantive liability standards were superseded by federal maritime law, *see Kermarec v. Compagnie Generale Transatlantique*, 358 U.S. 625, 628, 79 S. Ct. 406, 408-409, 3 L. Ed. 2d 550 (1959); *Pope & Talbot*, 346 U.S., at 409, 74 S. Ct., at 204-205, which provided for maritime worker recovery based on unseaworthiness. But if the same worker met death in the territorial waters of a State whose wrongful death statute did not encompass unseaworthiness (as was the case in *Moragne* itself), the survivors could not proceed under that generous standard of liability. *See The Tungus*, 358 U.S., at 592-593, 79 S. Ct., at 506-507.

---

[9] The federal cast of admiralty law, we have observed, means that "state law must yield to the needs of a uniform federal maritime law when this Court finds inroads on a harmonious system[,] [b]ut this limitation still leaves the States a wide scope." *Romero v. International Terminal Operating Co.*, 358 U.S. 354, 373, 79 S. Ct. 468, 480, 3 L. Ed. 2d 368 (1959). Our precedent does not precisely delineate that scope. As we recently acknowledged, "[i]t would be idle to pretend that the line separating permissible from impermissible state regulation is readily discernible in our admiralty jurisprudence." *American Dredging Co. v. Miller*, 510 U.S. ___, ___, 114 S. Ct. 981, 987, 127 L. Ed. 2d 285 (1994). We attempt no grand synthesis or reconciliation of our precedent today, but confine our inquiry to the modest question whether it was *Moragne*'s design to terminate recourse to state remedies when nonseafarers meet death in territorial waters.

Second, we explained in *Moragne* that "identical breaches of the duty to provide a seaworthy ship, resulting in death, produce liability outside the three-mile limit ... but not within the territorial waters of a State whose local statute excludes unseaworthiness claims." *Moragne*, 398 U.S., at 395, 90 S. Ct., at 1785. This occurred because survivors of a maritime worker killed on the high seas could sue for wrongful death under the Death on the High Seas Act (DOHSA), 46 U.S.C.App. § 761 *et seq.* (1988 ed.), which encompasses unseaworthiness as a basis of liability. *Moragne*, 398 U.S., at 395, 90 S. Ct., at 1784-1785 (citing *Kernan v. American Dredging Co.*, 355 U.S. 426, 430, n.4, 78 S. Ct. 394, 397 n.4, 2 L. Ed. 2d 382 (1958)).

Finally, we pointed out that "a true seaman [a member of a ship's company] ... is provided no remedy for death caused by unseaworthiness within territorial waters, while a longshoreman, to whom the duty of seaworthiness was extended only because he performs work traditionally done by seamen, does have such a remedy when allowed by a state statute." 398 U.S., at 395-396, 90 S. Ct., at 1785. This anomaly stemmed from the Court's rulings in *Lindgren v. United States*, 281 U.S. 38, 50 S. Ct. 207, 74 L. Ed. 686 (1930), and *Gillespie v. United States Steel Corp.*, 379 U.S. 148, 85 S. Ct. 308, 13 L. Ed. 2d 199 (1964), that the Jones Act, 46 U.S.C.App. § 688 (1988 ed.), which provides only a negligence-based claim for the wrongful death of seamen, precludes any state remedy, even one accommodating unseaworthiness. As a result, at the time *Moragne* was decided, the survivors of a longshore worker killed in the territorial waters of a State whose wrongful death statute incorporated unseaworthiness could sue under that theory, but the survivors of a similarly-situated seaman could not.[10]

The anomalies described in *Moragne* relate to ships and the workers who serve them, and to a distinctly maritime substantive concept—the unseaworthiness doctrine. The Court surely meant to "assure uniform vindication of federal policies," 398 U.S., at 401, 90 S. Ct., at 1788, with respect to the matters it examined. The law as it developed under *The Harrisburg* had forced on the States more than they could bear—the task of "provid[ing] the sole remedy" in cases that did not involve "traditional common-law concepts," but "concepts peculiar to maritime law." 398 U.S., at 401, n.15, 90 S. Ct., at 1788, n.15 (internal quotation marks omitted). Discarding *The Harrisburg* and declaring a wrongful death right of action under general maritime law, the Court concluded, would "remov[e] the tensions and discrepancies" occasioned by the need "to accommodate state remedial statutes to exclusively maritime substantive concepts." 398 U.S., at 401, 90 S. Ct., at 1788.[11]

---

[10] As noted earlier, unseaworthiness recovery by longshore workers was terminated by Congress in its 1972 amendments to the Longshore and Harbor Workers' Compensation Act, 33 U.S.C. § 901 *et seq. See* 33 U.S.C. § 905(b).

[11] The Court might have simply overruled *The Tungus*, *see supra* pp. 624-625, thus permitting plaintiffs to rely on federal liability standards to obtain state wrongful death remedies. The petitioner in Moragne, widow of a longshore worker, had urged that course when she sought certiorari. *See Moragne v. States Marine Lines, Inc.*, 398 U.S. 375, 378, n. 1, 90 S. Ct. 1772, 1776, n. 1, 26 L. Ed. 2d 339 (1970). But training *Moragne* solely on *The Tungus* would have left untouched the survivors of seamen, who remain blocked by the Jones Act from pursuing state wrongful death claims—whether under a theory of negligence or unseaworthiness. *See Gillespie v. United States Steel Corp.*, 379 U.S. 148, 154-155, 85 S. Ct. 308, 312-313, 13 L. Ed. 2d 199 (1964). Thus, nothing short of a federal maritime right of action for wrongful death could have achieved uniform access by seafarers to the unseaworthiness doctrine, the Court's driving concern in *Moragne*. *See* 398 U.S., at 396, n. 12, 90 S. Ct., at 1785, n. 12.

Moragne, in sum, centered on the extension of relief, not on the contraction of remedies. The decision recalled that " 'it better becomes the humane and liberal character of proceedings in admiralty to give than to withhold the remedy, when not required to withhold it by established and inflexible rules.' " *Id.*, at 387, 90 S. Ct., at 1781 (quoting *The Sea Gull,* 21 F.Cas. 909, 910 (C.C.Md.1865) (CHASE, C. J.)). The Court tied Petsonella *Moragne's* plea based on the unseaworthiness of the vessel to a federal right-of-action anchor,[12] but notably left in place the negligence claim she had stated under Florida's law. *See* 398 U.S., at 376-377, 90 S. Ct. at 1775-1776.[13]

Our understanding of *Moragne* accords with that of the Third Circuit, which Judge Becker set out as follows:

> *Moragne* ... showed no hostility to concurrent application of state wrongful death statutes. Indeed, to read into *Moragne* the idea that it was placing a ceiling on recovery for wrongful death, rather than a floor, is somewhat ahistorical. The *Moragne* cause of action was in many respects a gap-filling measure to ensure that seamen (and their survivors) would all be treated alike. The 'humane and liberal' purpose underlying the general maritime remedy of *Moragne* was driven by the idea that survivors of seamen killed in state territorial waters should not have been barred from recovery simply because the tort system of the particular state in which a seaman died did not incorporate special maritime doctrines. It is difficult to see how this purpose can be taken as an intent to preclude the operation of state laws that do supply a remedy.

40 F.3d, at 641-642 (citation omitted).

We have reasoned similarly in *Sun Ship, Inc. v. Pennsylvania,* 447 U.S. 715, 100 S. Ct. 2432, 65 L. Ed. 2d 458 (1980), where we held that a State may apply its workers' compensation scheme to land-based injuries that fall within the compass of the Longshore and Harbor Workers' Compensation Act, 33 U.S.C. § 901 *et seq. See Sun Ship,* 447 U.S., at 724, 100 S. Ct., at 2438-2439 (a State's remedial scheme might be "more generous than federal law" but nevertheless could apply because Congress indicated no concern "about a disparity between adequate federal benefits and superior state benefits") (emphasis in original).[14]

---

[12] While unseaworthiness was the doctrine immediately at stake in *Moragne,* the right of action, as stated in the Court's opinion, is "for death caused by violation of maritime duties." *Moragne,* 398 U.S., at 409, 90 S. Ct., at 1792. *See East River S.S. Corp. v. Transamerica Delaval Inc.*, 476 U.S. 858, 865, 106 S. Ct. 2295, 2299, 90 L. Ed. 2d 865 (1986) (maritime law incorporates strict product liability); *Kermarec,* 358 U.S., at 630, 79 S. Ct., at 409-410 (negligence). *See also* G. GILMORE & C. BLACK, THE LAW OF ADMIRALTY 368 (2d ed.1975).

[13] *Moragne* was entertained by the Court of Appeals pursuant to a 28 U.S.C. § 1292(b) certification directed to the District Court's order dismissing the unseaworthiness claim. *See* 398 U.S., at 376, 90 S. Ct., at 1775.

[14] Federal maritime law has long accommodated the States' interest in regulating maritime affairs within their territorial waters. See, *e.g., Just v. Chambers,* 312 U.S. 383, 390, 61 S. Ct. 687, 692, 85 L. Ed. 903 (1941) ("maritime law [is] not a complete and perfect system"; "a considerable body of municipal law ... underlies ... its administration"). States have thus traditionally contributed to the provision of environmental and safety standards for maritime activities. *See, e.g., Askew v. American Waterways Operators, Inc.*, 411 U.S. 325, 93 S. Ct. 1590, 36 L. Ed. 2d 280 (1973) (oil pollution); *Huron Portland Cement Co. v. Detroit,* 362 U.S. 440, 80 S. Ct. 813, 4 L. Ed. 2d 852 (1960) (air pollution); *Kelly v. Washington ex rel. Foss Co.*, 302 U.S. 1, 58 S. Ct. 87, 82 L. Ed. 3 (1937) (safety inspection); *Cooley v. Board of Wardens of Port of Philadelphia ex rel. Soc. for Relief of Distressed Pilots,* 53 U.S. 299, 13 L. Ed. 996, 12 How. 299 (1852) (pilotage regulation). Permissible state regulation, we have recognized, must be consistent with federal maritime principles and policies. *See Romero,* 358 U.S., at 373- 374, 79 S. Ct., at 480-481.

When Congress has prescribed a comprehensive tort recovery regime to be uniformly applied, there is, we have generally recognized, no cause for enlargement of the damages statutorily provided. *See Miles*, 498 U.S., at 30-36, 111 S. Ct., at 324-328 (Jones Act, rather than general maritime law, determines damages recoverable in action for wrongful death of seamen); *Offshore Logistics, Inc. v. Tallentire*, 477 U.S. 207, 232, 106 S. Ct. 2485, 2499, 91 L. Ed. 2d 174 (1986) (DOHSA, which limits damages to pecuniary losses, may not be supplemented by nonpecuniary damages under a state wrongful death statute); *Mobil Oil Corp. v. Higginbotham*, 436 U.S. 618, 624-625, 98 S. Ct. 2010, 2014-2015, 56 L. Ed. 2d 581 (1978) (DOHSA precludes damages for loss of society under general maritime law). But Congress has not prescribed remedies for the wrongful deaths of nonseafarers in territorial waters. *See Miles*, 498 U.S., at 31, 111 S. Ct., at 325. There is, however, a relevant congressional disposition. Section 7 of DOHSA states: "The provisions of any State statute giving or regulating rights of action or remedies for death shall not be affected by this chapter." 46 U.S.C.App. § 767. This statement, by its terms, simply stops DOHSA from displacing state law in territorial waters. *See Miles*, 498 U.S., at 25, 111 S. Ct., at 321-322; *Tallentire*, 477 U.S., at 224-225, 106 S. Ct., at 2495-2496; *Moragne*, 398 U.S., at 397-398, 90 S. Ct., at 1785-1786. Taking into account what Congress sought to achieve, we preserve the application of state statutes to deaths within territorial waters.

* * *

For the reasons stated, we hold that the damages available for the jet ski death of Natalie Calhoun are properly governed by state law.[15] The judgment of the Court of Appeals for the Third Circuit is accordingly

Affirmed.

Note

1. The Supreme Court in *Calhoun* left open the question of *which* state law would govern the remedies available. On remand, the District Court held, and on appeal, the Third Circuit confirmed, that Pennsylvania law governed the determination of compensatory damages, Puerto Rico law governed determination of punitive damages, and federal maritime law governed determination of liability. *Calhoun v. Yamaha Motor Corp., U.S.A.*, 216 F.3d 338, 2000 AMC 1865 (3d Cir. 2000). This determination proved fatal to the bulk of the parents' claim, because Puerto Rico law does not permit the award of punitive damages. The Calhouns applied to the Supreme Court again for certiorari, but this time they were unsuccessful (*Calhoun v. Yamaha Motor Corp., U.S.A.*, 531 U.S. 1037, 121 S. Ct. 627 (2000)) despite an application for rehearing of the cert. application (*Calhoun v. Yamaha Motor Corp., U.S.A.*, 531 U.S. 1105, 121 S. Ct. 797 (2001)). When the suit finally went to trial, the jury entered a verdict for the defendant, holding that the jet ski was not a defective product. The Calhouns appealed unsuccessfully. *Calhoun v. Yamaha Motor Corp., U.S.A.*, 350 F.3d 316 (3d Cir. 2003). Thus, the 14-year saga of their lawsuit ended with them receiving no damages for Natalie Calhoun's death.

---

[15] The Third Circuit left for initial consideration by the District Court the question whether Pennsylvania's wrongful death remedies or Puerto Rico's apply. 40 F.3d 622, 644 (1994). The Court of Appeals also left open, as do we, the source—federal or state—of the standards governing liability, as distinguished from the rules on remedies. We thus reserve for another day reconciliation of the maritime personal injury decisions that rejected state substantive liability standards, and the maritime wrongful death cases in which state law has held sway. Compare *Kermarec*, 358 U.S., at 628, 79 S. Ct., at 408-409 (personal injury); *Pope & Talbot, Inc. v. Hawn*, 346 U.S. 406, 409, 74 S. Ct. 202, 204-205, 98 L. Ed. 143 (1953) (same), with *Hess v. United States*, 361 U.S. 314, 319, 80 S. Ct. 341, 345-346, 4 L. Ed. 2d 305 (1960) (wrongful death); *The Tungus v. Skovgaard*, 358 U.S. 588, 592-594, 79 S. Ct. 503, 506-508, 3 L. Ed. 2d 524 (1959) (same).

2. Following *Calhoun*, the Court of Appeals for the Eleventh Circuit approved application of Florida law, which allows recovery of non-pecuniary damages, in a wrongful death action where a non-seaman was killed in state waters. *American Dredging Co. v. Lambert*, 81 F.3d 127, 1996 AMC 2929 (11th Cir. 1996). However, state law provides only the remedy; uniformity demands that federal general maritime law determines the standard of liability. *In re Amtrak "Sunset, Ltd." Train Crash*, 121 F.3d 1421, 1997 AMC 2962 (11th Cir. 1997); *Calhoun v. Yamaha Motor Corp., U.S.A.*, 216 F.3d 338, 2000 AMC 1865 (3d Cir. 2000). Thus, in *In re Amtrak*, the Eleventh Circuit held that although punitive damages were available under Alabama state law to non-seafarers killed in state waters, the standard of liability for recovery of those punitive damages was determined by federal law ("intentional or wanton and reckless conduct" necessary), rather than Alabama state law (by which simple negligence sufficed).

B. Survival Actions

DOOLEY v. KOREAN AIR LINES CO., LTD.

524 U.S. 116, 118 S. Ct. 1890, 141 L. Ed. 2d 102, 1998 AMC 1940 (1998)

Justice THOMAS delivered the opinion of the Court

In a case of death on the high seas, the Death on the High Seas Act, 46 U.S.C.App. § 761 *et seq.*, allows certain relatives of the decedent to sue for their pecuniary losses, but does not authorize recovery for the decedent's pre-death pain and suffering. This case presents the question whether those relatives may nevertheless recover such damages through a survival action under general maritime law. We hold that they may not.

I

On September 1, 1983, Korean Air Lines Flight KE007, en route from Anchorage, Alaska, to Seoul, South Korea, strayed into the airspace of the former Soviet Union and was shot down over the Sea of Japan. All 269 people on board were killed.

Petitioners, the personal representatives of three of the passengers, brought lawsuits against respondent Korean Air Lines Co., Ltd. (KAL), in the United States District Court for the District of Columbia. These cases were consolidated in that court, along with the other federal actions arising out of the crash. After trial, a jury found that KAL had committed "willful misconduct," thus removing the Warsaw Convention's $75,000 cap on damages, and in a subsequent verdict awarded $50 million in punitive damages. The Court of Appeals for the District of Columbia Circuit upheld the finding of willful misconduct, but vacated the punitive damages award on the ground that the Warsaw Convention does not permit the recovery of punitive damages. *In re Korean Air Lines Disaster of Sept. 1, 1983*, 932 F.2d 1475, *cert. denied*, 502 U.S. 994, 112 S. Ct. 616, 116 L. Ed. 2d 638 (1991).

The Judicial Panel on Multidistrict Litigation thereafter remanded, for damages trials, all of the individual cases to the District Courts in which they had been filed. In petitioners' cases, KAL moved for a pretrial determination that the Death on the High Seas Act (DOHSA), 46 U.S.C.App. § 761 *et seq.*, provides the exclusive source of recoverable damages. DOHSA provides, in relevant part:

> Whenever the death of a person shall be caused by wrongful act, neglect, or default occurring on the high seas beyond a marine league from the shore of any State, or the District of Columbia, or the Territories or dependencies of the United States, the personal representative of the decedent may maintain a suit for damages in the district courts of the United States, in admiralty, for the exclusive benefit of the decedent's wife, husband, parent, child or dependent relative ... § 761.
>
> The recovery in such suit shall be a fair and just compensation for the pecuniary loss sustained by the persons for whose benefit the suit is brought.... § 762.

KAL argued that, in a case of death on the high seas, DOHSA provides the exclusive cause of action and does not permit damages for loss of society, survivors' grief, and decedents' pre-death pain and suffering. The District Court for the District of Columbia disagreed, holding that because petitioners' claims were brought pursuant to the Warsaw Convention, DOHSA could not limit the recoverable damages. The Court determined that Article 17 of the Warsaw Convention "allows for the recovery of all 'damages sustained,'" meaning any "actual harm" that any party "experienced" as a result of the crash. App. 59.

While petitioners' cases were awaiting damages trials, we reached a different conclusion in *Zicherman v. Korean Air Lines Co.*, 516 U.S. 217, 116 S. Ct. 629, 133 L. Ed. 2d 596 (1996), another case arising out of the downing of Flight KE007. In *Zicherman*, we held that the Warsaw Convention "permit[s] compensation only for legally cognizable harm, but leave[s] the specification of what harm is legally cognizable to the domestic law applicable under the forum's choice-of-law rules," and that where "an airplane crash occurs on the high seas, DOHSA supplies the substantive United States law." *Id.*, at 231, 116 S. Ct., at 637. Accordingly, the petitioners could not recover damages for loss of society: "[W]here DOHSA applies, neither state law, *see Offshore Logistics, Inc. v. Tallentire*, 477 U.S. 207, 232-233, 106 S. Ct. 2485, 2499-2500, 91 L. Ed. 2d 174 (1986), nor general maritime law, *see Mobil Oil Corp. v. Higginbotham*, 436 U.S. 618, 625-626, 98 S. Ct. 2010, 2015, 56 L. Ed. 2d 581 (1978), can provide a basis for recovery of loss-of-society damages." *Id.*, at 230, 106 S. Ct., at 2498. We did not decide, however, whether the petitioners in *Zicherman* could recover for their decedents' pre-death pain and suffering, as KAL had not raised this issue in its petition for certiorari. *See id.*, at 230, n.4, 116 S. Ct., at 636, n.4.

After the *Zicherman* decision, KAL again moved to dismiss all of petitioners' claims for nonpecuniary damages. The District Court granted this motion, holding that United States law (not South Korean law) governed these cases; that DOHSA provides the applicable United States law; and that DOHSA does not permit the recovery of nonpecuniary damages—including petitioners' claims for their decedents' pre-death pain and suffering. *In Re Korean Air Lines Disaster of Sept. 1, 1983*, 935 F. Supp. 10, 12-15 (1996).

On appeal, petitioners argued that although DOHSA does not itself permit recovery for a decedent's pre-death pain and suffering, general maritime law provides a survival action that allows a decedent's estate to recover for injuries (including pre-death pain and suffering) suffered by the decedent. The Court of Appeals rejected this argument and affirmed. *In Re Korean Air Lines Disaster of Sept. 1, 1983*, 117 F.3d 1477 (C.A.D.C.1997). Assuming arguendo that there is a survival cause of action under general maritime law, the court held that such an action is unavailable when the death is on the high seas:

> For deaths on the high seas, Congress decided who may sue and for what. Judge-made general maritime law may not override such congressional judgments, however ancient those judgments may happen to be. Congress made the law and it is up to Congress to change it." *Id.*, at 1481.

We granted certiorari, 522 U.S. —, 118 S. Ct. 679, 139 L. Ed. 2d 628 (1998), to resolve a Circuit split concerning the availability of a general maritime survival action in cases of death on the high seas. *Compare, e.g., In Re Korean Air Lines Disaster*, 117 F.3d, at 1481, *with Gray v. Lockheed Aeronautical Systems Co.*, 125 F.3d 1371, 1385 (C.A.11 1997).

II

Before Congress enacted DOHSA in 1920, the general law of admiralty permitted a person injured by tortious conduct to sue for damages, but did not permit an action to be brought when the person was killed by that conduct. *See generally* R. HUGHES, HANDBOOK OF ADMIRALTY LAW 222-223 (2d ed.1920). This rule stemmed from the theory that a right of action was personal to the victim and thus expired when the victim died. Accordingly, in the absence of an act of Congress or state statute providing a right of action, a suit in admiralty could not be maintained in the courts of the United States to recover damages for a person's death. *See The Harrisburg*, 119 U.S. 199, 213, 7 S. Ct. 140, 146-147, 30 L.Ed. 358 (1886); *The Alaska*, 130 U.S. 201, 209, 9 S. Ct. 461, 463, 32 L.Ed. 923 (1889).[1]

Congress passed such a statute, and thus authorized recovery for deaths on the high seas, with its enactment of DOHSA. DOHSA provides a cause of action for "the death of a person ... caused by wrongful act, neglect, or default occurring on the high seas," § 761; this action must be brought by the decedent's personal representative "for the exclusive benefit of the decedent's wife, husband, parent, child, or dependent relative," *ibid.* The Act limits recovery in such a suit to "a fair and just compensation for the pecuniary loss sustained by the persons for whose benefit the suit is sought." § 762. DOHSA also includes a limited survival provision: In situations in which a person injured on the high seas sues for his injuries and then dies prior to completion of the suit, "the personal representative of the decedent may be substituted as a party and the suit may proceed as a suit under this chapter for the recovery of the compensation provided in section 762." § 765. Other sections establish a limitations period, § 763a, govern actions under foreign law, § 764, bar contributory negligence as a complete defense, § 766, exempt the Great Lakes, navigable waters in the Panama Canal Zone, and state territorial waters from the Act's coverage, § 767, and preserve certain state law remedies and state court jurisdiction, *ibid.* DOHSA

---

[1] We later rejected this rule in *Moragne v. States Marine Lines, Inc.*, 398 U.S. 375, 408-409, 90 S. Ct. 1772, 1791-1792, 26 L. Ed. 2d 339 (1970), by overruling *The Harrisburg*, 119 U.S. 199, 7 S. Ct. 140, 30 L.Ed. 358 (1886), and holding that a federal remedy for wrongful death exists under general maritime law. *In Sea-Land Services, Inc. v. Gaudet*, 414 U.S. 573, 574, 94 S. Ct. 806, 809-810, 39 L. Ed. 2d 9 (1974), we further held that such wrongful death awards could include compensation for loss of support and services and for loss of society.

does not authorize recovery for the decedent's own losses, nor does it allow damages for non-pecuniary losses.

In *Mobil Oil Corp. v. Higginbotham*, 436 U.S. 618, 98 S. Ct. 2010, 56 L. Ed. 2d 581 (1978), we considered whether, in a case of death on the high seas, a decedent's survivors could recover damages under general maritime law for their loss of society. We held that they could not, and thus limited to territorial waters those cases in which we had permitted loss of society damages under general maritime law. *Id.*, at 622-624, 98 S. Ct., at 2013-2014; see n. 1, *supra*. For deaths on the high seas, DOHSA "announces Congress' considered judgment on such issues as the beneficiaries, the limitations period, contributory negligence, survival, and damages." 436 U.S., at 625, 98 S. Ct., at 2015. We thus noted that while we could "fil[l] a gap left by Congress' silence," we were not free to "rewrit[e] rules that Congress has affirmatively and specifically enacted." *Ibid.* Because "Congress ha[d] struck the balance for us" in DOHSA by limiting the available recovery to pecuniary losses suffered by surviving relatives, *id.*, at 623, 98 S. Ct., at 2014, we had "no authority to substitute our views for those expressed by Congress." *Id.*, at 626, 98 S. Ct., at 2015. Higginbotham, however, involved only the scope of the remedies available in a wrongful death action, and thus did not address the availability of other causes of action.

Conceding that DOHSA does not authorize recovery for a decedent's pre- death pain and suffering, petitioners seek to recover such damages through a general maritime survival action. Petitioners argue that general maritime law recognizes a survival action, which permits a decedent's estate to recover damages that the decedent would have been able to recover but for his death, including pre-death pain and suffering. And, they contend, because DOHSA is a wrongful death statute—giving surviving relatives a cause of action for losses they suffered as a result of the decedent's death—it has no bearing on the availability of a survival action.

We disagree. DOHSA expresses Congress' judgment that there should be no such cause of action in cases of death on the high seas. By authorizing only certain surviving relatives to recover damages, and by limiting damages to the pecuniary losses sustained by those relatives, Congress provided the exclusive recovery for deaths that occur on the high seas. Petitioners concede that their proposed survival action would necessarily expand the class of beneficiaries in cases of death on the high seas by permitting decedents' estates (and their various beneficiaries) to recover compensation. They further concede that their cause of action would expand the recoverable damages for deaths on the high seas by permitting the recovery of non-pecuniary losses, such as pre-death pain and suffering. Because Congress has already decided these issues, it has precluded the judiciary from enlarging either the class of beneficiaries or the recoverable damages. As we noted in *Higginbotham*, "Congress did not limit DOHSA beneficiaries to recovery of their pecuniary losses in order to encourage the creation of nonpecuniary supplements." 436 U.S., at 625, 98 S. Ct., at 2015.

The comprehensive scope of DOHSA is confirmed by its survival provision, see supra, at 1894, which limits the recovery in such cases to the pecuniary losses suffered by surviving relatives. The Act thus expresses Congress' "considered judgment," *Mobil Oil Corp. v.*

Higginbotham, supra, at 625, 98 S. Ct., at 2015, on the availability and contours of a survival action in cases of death on the high seas. For this reason, it cannot be contended that DOHSA has no bearing on survival actions; rather, Congress has simply chosen to adopt a more limited survival provision. Indeed, Congress did so in the same year that it incorporated into the Jones Act, which permits seamen injured in the course of their employment to recover damages for their injuries, a survival action similar to the one petitioners seek here. *See* Act of June 5, 1920, § 33, 41 Stat. 1007 (incorporating survival action of the Federal Employers' Liability Act, 45 U.S.C. § 59). Even in the exercise of our admiralty jurisdiction, we will not upset the balance struck by Congress by authorizing a cause of action with which Congress was certainly familiar but nonetheless declined to adopt.

In sum, Congress has spoken on the availability of a survival action, the losses to be recovered, and the beneficiaries, in cases of death on the high seas. Because Congress has chosen not to authorize a survival action for a decedent's pre-death pain and suffering, there can be no general maritime survival action for such damages.[2] The judgment of the Court of Appeals is

Affirmed.

Note

Although *Dooley* did not expressly reject the possibility that DOHSA could be supplemented by a *State* survival action (as opposed to a general maritime law one) that was implicit. See *Jacobs v. Northern King Shipping Co., Ltd.*, 180 F.3d 713, 1999 AMC 2341 (5th Cir. 1999). *Offshore Logistics v. Tallentire, supra*, had previously held that DOHSA pre-empted recovery of non-pecuniary losses under State *wrongful death* states. *Tallentire* left open the possibility of a state *survival* action supplementing DOHSA, but that possibility has been foreclosed by *Jacobs*.

C. Restrictions on Damages

MILES v. APEX MARINE CORP.

498 U.S. 19, 111 S. Ct. 317, 112 L. Ed. 2d 275, 1991 AMC 1 (1990)

Justice O'CONNOR delivered the opinion of the Court

We decide whether the parent of a seaman who died from injuries incurred aboard respondents' vessel may recover under general maritime law for loss of society, and whether a claim for the seaman's lost future earnings survives his death.

I

Ludwick Torregano was a seaman aboard the vessel *M/V Archon*. On the evening of July 18, 1984, Clifford Melrose, a fellow crew member, stabbed Torregano repeatedly, killing him. At the time, the ship was docked in the harbor of Vancouver, Washington.

---

[2] Accordingly, we need not decide whether general maritime law ever provides a survival action.

Mercedel Miles, Torregano's mother and administratrix of his estate, sued Apex Marine Corporation and Westchester Marine Shipping Company, the vessel's operators, Archon Marine Company, the charterer, and Aeron Marine Company, the *Archon's* owner (collectively Apex), in United States District Court for the Eastern District of Louisiana. Miles alleged negligence under the Jones Act, 46 U.S.C. App. § 688, for failure to prevent the assault on her son, and breach of the warranty of seaworthiness under general maritime law for hiring a crew member unfit to serve. She sought compensation for loss of support and services and loss of society resulting from the death of her son, punitive damages, and compensation to the estate for Torregano's pain and suffering prior to his death and for his lost future income.

At trial, the District Court granted Apex's motion to strike the claim for punitive damages, ruled that the estate could not recover Torregano's lost future income, and denied Miles' motion for a directed verdict as to negligence and unseaworthiness. The court instructed the jury that Miles could not recover damages for loss of society if they found that she was not financially dependent on her son.

The jury found that Apex was negligent and that Torregano was 7% contributorily negligent in causing his death, but that the ship was seaworthy. After discounting for Torregano's contributory negligence, the jury awarded Miles $7,254 for the loss of support and services of her son and awarded the estate $130,200 for Torregano's pain and suffering. The jury also found that Miles was not financially dependent on her son and therefore not entitled to damages for loss of society. The District Court denied both parties' motions for judgment notwithstanding the verdict and entered judgment accordingly.

The United States Court of Appeals for the Fifth Circuit affirmed in part, reversed in part, and remanded. 882 F.2d 976 (1989). The court affirmed the judgment of negligence on the part of Apex, but held that there was insufficient evidence to support the contributory negligence finding. *Id.*, at 983-985. Miles was therefore entitled to the full measure of $7,800 for loss of support and services, and the estate entitled to $140,000 for Torregano's pain and suffering. The court also found that Melrose's extraordinarily violent disposition demonstrated that he was unfit, and therefore that the Archon was unseaworthy as a matter of law. *Id.*, at 983. Because this ruling revived Miles' general maritime claim, the court considered two questions concerning the scope of damages under general maritime law. The court reaffirmed its prior decision in *Sistrunk v. Circle Bar Drilling Co.*, 770 F.2d 455 (CA5 1985), holding that a nondependent parent may not recover for loss of society in a general maritime wrongful death action. 882 F.2d, at 989. It also held that general maritime law does not permit a survival action for decedent's lost future earnings. *Id.*, at 987.

We granted Miles' petition for certiorari on these two issues, 494 U.S. ___, 110 S. Ct. 1295, 108 L. Ed. 2d 472 (1990), and now affirm the judgment of the Court of Appeals.

II

We rely primarily on *Moragne v. States Marine Lines, Inc.*, 398 U.S. 375 , 90 S. Ct. 1772, 26 L. Ed. 2d 339 (1970).

* * *

III

* * *

The Jones Act provides an action in negligence for the death or injury of a seaman. It thereby overruled *The Osceola*, 189 U.S. 158, 23 S. Ct. 483, 47 L. Ed. 760 (1903), which established that seamen could recover under general maritime law for injuries resulting from unseaworthiness, but not negligence. The Jones Act evinces no general hostility to recovery under maritime law. It does not disturb seamen's general maritime claims for injuries resulting from unseaworthiness, *Pacific Steamship Co. v. Peterson*, 278 U.S. 130, 139, 49 S. Ct. 75, 78, 73 L. Ed. 220 (1928), and it does not preclude the recovery for wrongful death due to unseaworthiness created by its companion statute DOHSA. *Kernan v. American Dredging Co.*, 355 U.S. 426, 430, n.4, 78 S. Ct. 394, 397, n.4, 2 L. Ed. 2d 382 (1958). Rather, the Jones Act establishes a uniform system of seamen's tort law parallel to that available to employees of interstate railway carriers under FELA. As the Court concluded in *Moragne*, the extension of the DOHSA wrongful death action to territorial waters furthers rather than hinders uniformity in the exercise of admiralty jurisdiction. *Moragne, supra*, 398 U.S., at 396, n.12, 90 S. Ct., at 1785, n.12.

There is also little question that *Moragne* intended to create a general maritime wrongful death action applicable beyond the situation of longshoremen. For one thing, *Moragne* explicitly overruled *The Harrisburg*. *Moragne, supra*, 398 U.S., at 409, 90 S. Ct., at 1792. *The Harrisburg* involved a true seaman. *The Harrisburg*, 119 U.S., at 200, 7 S. Ct., at 141. In addition, all three of the "anomalies" to which the *Moragne* cause of action was directed involved seamen. The "strangest" anomaly—that recovery was available for the wrongful death in territorial waters of a longshoreman, but not a true seaman—could only be remedied if the *Moragne* wrongful death action extended to seamen. It would be strange indeed were we to read *Moragne* as not addressing a problem that in large part motivated its result. If there has been any doubt about the matter, we today make explicit that there is a general maritime cause of action for the wrongful death of a seaman, adopting the reasoning of the unanimous and carefully crafted opinion in *Moragne*.

IV

Moragne did not set forth the scope of the damages recoverable under the maritime wrongful death action. The Court first considered that question in *Sea-Land Services, Inc. v. Gaudet*, 414 U.S. 573, 94 S. Ct. 806, 39 L. Ed. 2d 9 (1974). Respondent brought a general maritime action to recover for the wrongful death of her husband, a longshoreman. The Court held that a dependent plaintiff in a maritime wrongful death action could recover for the pecuniary losses of support, services, and funeral expenses, as well as for the nonpecuniary loss of society suffered as the result of the death. *Id.*, at 591, 94 S. Ct., at 818. *Gaudet* involved the death of a longshoreman in territorial waters.[1] Consequently, the Court had no need to consider the preclusive effect of DOHSA for deaths on the high seas, or the Jones Act for deaths of true seamen.

---

[1] As with *Moragne*, the 1972 amendments to LHWCA have rendered *Gaudet* inapplicable on its facts. *See supra*, at 323; 33 U.S.C. § 905(b). Suit in *Gaudet* was filed before 1972. *Gaudet v. Sea-Land Services, Inc.*, 463 F.2d 1331, 1332 (CA5 1972).

We considered DOHSA in *Mobil Oil Corp v. Higginbotham*, 436 U.S. 618, 98 S. Ct. 2010, 56 L. Ed. 2d 581 (1978). That case involved death on the high seas and, like *Gaudet*, presented the question of loss of society damages in a maritime wrongful death action. The Court began by recognizing that *Gaudet*, although broadly written, applied only in territorial waters and therefore did not decide the precise question presented. *Id.*, at 622-623, 98 S. Ct., at 2013-2014. Congress made the decision for us. DOHSA, by its terms, limits recoverable damages in wrongful death suits to "*pecuniary* loss sustained by the persons for whose benefit the suit is brought." 46 U.S.C. App. § 762 (emphasis added). This explicit limitation forecloses recovery for non-pecuniary loss, such as loss of society, in a general maritime action.

Respondents argued that admiralty courts have traditionally undertaken to supplement maritime statutes. The Court's answer in *Higginbotham* is fully consistent with those principles we have here derived from *Moragne:* Congress has spoken directly to the question of recoverable damages on the high seas, and "when it does speak directly to a question, the courts are not free to 'supplement' Congress' answer so thoroughly that the Act becomes meaningless." *Higginbotham, supra*, at 625, 98 S. Ct., at 2015. *Moragne* involved gap-filling in an area left open by statute; supplementation was entirely appropriate. But in an "area covered by the statute, it would be no more appropriate to prescribe a different measure of damages than to prescribe a different statute of limitations, or a different class of beneficiaries." *Higginbotham, supra*, at 625, 98 S. Ct., at 2015.

The logic of *Higginbotham* controls our decision here. The holding of Gaudet applies only in territorial waters, and it applies only to longshoremen. *Gaudet* did not consider the preclusive effect of the Jones Act for deaths of true seamen. We do so now.

Unlike DOHSA, the Jones Act does not explicitly limit damages to any particular form. Enacted in 1920, the Jones Act makes applicable to seamen the substantive recovery provisions of the older FELA. *See* 46 U.S.C. App. § 688. FELA recites only that employers shall be liable in "damages" for the injury or death of one protected under the Act. 45 U.S.C. § 51. In *Michigan Central R. Co. v. Vreeland*, 227 U.S. 59, 33 S. Ct. 192, 57 L. Ed. 417 (1913), however, the Court explained that the language of the FELA wrongful death provision is essentially identical to that of Lord Campbell's Act, 9 & 10 Vict. ch. 93 (1846), the first wrongful death statute Lord Campbell's Act also did not limit explicitly the "damages" to be recovered, but that Act and the many state statutes that followed it consistently had been interpreted as providing recovery only for pecuniary loss. *Vreeland, supra*, at 69-71. The Court so construed FELA. *Ibid.*

When Congress passed the Jones Act, the *Vreeland* gloss on FELA, and the hoary tradition behind it, were well established. Incorporating FELA unaltered into the Jones Act, Congress must have intended to incorporate the pecuniary limitation on damages as well. We assume that Congress is aware of existing law when it passes legislation. *See Cannon v. University of Chicago*, 441 U.S. 677, 696-697, 99 S. Ct. 1946, 1957, 60 L. Ed. 2d 560 (1979). There is no recovery for loss of society in a Jones Act wrongful death action.

---

[2] In *Offshore Logistics, Inc. v. Tallentire*, 477 U.S. 207, 215, n. 1, 106 S. Ct. 2485, 2490, n. 1, 91 L. Ed. 2d 174 (1986), we declined to approve or disapprove the practice of some courts of applying state survival statutes to cases involving death on the high seas.

The Jones Act also precludes recovery for loss of society in this case. The Jones Act applies when a seaman has been killed as a result of negligence and it limits recovery to pecuniary loss. The general maritime claim here alleged that Torregano had been killed as a result of the unseaworthiness of the vessel. It would be inconsistent with our place in the constitutional scheme were we to sanction more expansive remedies in a judicially-created cause of action in which liability is without fault than Congress has allowed in cases of death resulting from negligence. We must conclude that there is no recovery for loss of society in a general maritime action for the wrongful death of a Jones Act seaman.

Our decision also remedies an anomaly we created in *Higginbotham*. Respondents in that case warned that the elimination of loss of society damages for wrongful deaths on the high seas would create an unwarranted inconsistency between deaths in territorial waters, where loss of society was available under *Gaudet*, and deaths on the high seas. We recognized the value of uniformity, but concluded that a concern for consistency could not override the statute. *Higginbotham*, 436 U.S., at 624, 98 S. Ct., at 2014. Today we restore a uniform rule applicable to all actions for the wrongful death of a seaman, whether under DOHSA, the Jones Act, or general maritime law.

V

We next must decide whether, in a general maritime action surviving the death of a seaman, the estate can recover decedent's lost future earnings. Under traditional maritime law, as under common law, there is no right of survival; a seaman's personal cause of action does not survive the seaman's death. *Cortes v. Baltimore Insular Line, Inc.*, 287 U.S. 367, 371, 53 S. Ct. 173, 174, 77 L. Ed. 368 (1932); *Romero v. International Terminal Operating Co.*, 358 U.S. 354, 373, 79 S. Ct. 468, 480, 3 L. Ed. 2d 368 (1959); *Gillespie*, 379 U.S., at 157, 85 S. Ct., at 313-314.

Congress and the States have changed the rule in many instances. The Jones Act, through its incorporation of FELA, provides that a seaman's right of action for injuries due to negligence survives to the seaman's personal representative. *See* 45 U.S.C. § 59; *Gillespie, supra*, at 157, 85 S. Ct., at 313. Most States have survival statutes applicable to tort actions generally, *see* 1 S. Speiser, Recovery for Wrongful Death 2d § 3.2, (1975 and Supp. 1989), 2 *id.*, §§ 14.1, 14.3, App. A., and admiralty courts have applied these state statutes in many instances to preserve suits for injury at sea. *See, e.g., Just v. Chambers* 312 U.S. 383, 391, 61 S. Ct. 687, 693, 85 L. Ed. 903 (1941). *See also Kernan v. American Dredging Co.*, 355 U.S. 426, 430, n.4, 78 S. Ct. 394, 397, n.4, 2 L. Ed. 2d 382 (1958); *Kossick v. United Fruit Co.*, 365 U.S. 731, 739, 81 S. Ct. 886, 892, 6 L. Ed. 2d 56 (1961); *Gillespie, supra*, 379 U.S., at 157, 85 S. Ct., at 313-314; Comment, *Application of State Survival Statutes in Maritime Causes*, 60 Colum. L. Rev. 534, 535, n.11 (1960); Nagy, *The General Maritime Law Survival Action: What are the Elements of Recoverable Damages?*, 9 U. Haw. L. Rev. 5, 27 (1987). Where these state statutes do not apply,[2] however, or where there is no state survival statute, there is no survival of unseaworthiness claims absent a change in the traditional maritime rule.

Several Courts of Appeals have relied on *Moragne* to hold that there is a general maritime right of survival. *See Spiller v. Thomas M. Lowe, Jr., & Assocs., Inc.*, 466 F.2d 903, 909 (CA8 1972); *Barbe v. Drummond*, 507 F.2d 794, 799-800 (CA1 1974); *Law v. Sea Drilling Corp.*, 523 F.2d 793, 795 (CA5 1975); *Evich v. Connelly*, 759 F.2d 1432, 1434 (CA9 1985). As we have noted, *Moragne* found that congressional and state abrogation of the maritime rule against wrongful death actions demonstrated a strong policy judgment, to which the court deferred. *Moragne*, 398 U.S., at 388-393, 90 S. Ct., at 1781-1784. Following this reasoning, the lower courts have looked to the Jones Act and the many state survival statutes and concluded that these enactments dictate a change in the general maritime rule against survival. *See, e.g., Spiller, supra*, at 909; *Barbe, supra*, at 799-800, and n.6.

Miles argues that we should follow the Courts of Appeals and recognize a general maritime survival right. Apex urges us to reaffirm the traditional maritime rule and overrule these decisions. We decline to address the issue, because its resolution is unnecessary to our decision on the narrow question presented: whether the income decedent would have earned but for his death is recoverable. We hold that it is not.

Recovery of lost future income in a survival suit will, in many instances, be duplicative of recovery by dependents for loss of support in a wrongful death action; the support dependents lose as a result of a seaman's death would have come from the seaman's future earnings.

* * *

The Jones Act/FELA survival provision limits recovery to losses suffered during the decedent's lifetime. *See* 45 U.S.C. § 59. This was the established rule under FELA when Congress passed the Jones Act, incorporating FELA. *see St. Louis, I. M. & S. R. Co., supra*, 237 U.S., at 658, 35 S. Ct., at 706, and it is the rule under the Jones Act. *See Van Beeck, supra*, at 347 Congress has limited the survival right for seamen's injuries resulting from negligence. As with loss of society in wrongful death actions, this forecloses more expansive remedies in a general maritime action founded on strict liability. We will not create, under our admiralty powers, a remedy disfavored by a clear majority of the States and that goes well beyond the limits of Congress' ordered system of recovery for seamen's injury and death. Because Torregano's estate cannot recover for his lost future income under the Jones Act, it cannot do so under general maritime law.

VI

Cognizant of the constitutional relationship between the courts and Congress, we today act in accordance with the uniform plan of maritime tort law Congress created in DOHSA and the Jones Act. We hold that there is a general maritime cause of action for the wrongful death of a seaman, but that damages recoverable in such an action do not include loss of society. We also hold that a general maritime survival action cannot include recovery for decedent's lost future earnings. Accordingly, the judgment of the Court of Appeals is

Affirmed.

Notes

Courts are divided about whether *Miles* controls the decision in *Gaudet* where loss of consortium was available under general maritime law to beneficiaries of maritime workers, non-seamen, and seamen in actions against non-employers. Although some courts allow loss of consortium to relatives of maritime workers and non-maritime plaintiffs, other courts refuse to allow relatives of non-seamen to collect greater recovery than relatives of true seamen because seamen were traditionally the wards of the courts. The latter courts have focused on an interest in uniformity.

The conflicting cases are discussed at length in Force, *The Curse of* Miles v. Apex Marine Corp.*: The Mischief of Seeking "Uniformity" and "Legislative Intent" in Maritime Personal Injury Cases*, 55 LA. L. REV. 745 (1995).

1. Punitive Damages

May punitive damages be recovered in a seaman's action brought under the general maritime law or the Jones Act? *Complaint of Merry Shipping, Inc.*, 650 F.2d 622, 1981 AMC 2839 (5th Cir. 1981) which allowed such recovery was overruled in dictum on the authority of *Miles* in *Guevara v. Maritime Overseas Corporation*, 59 F.3d 1496, 1995 AMC 2409 (5th Cir. 1995), *cert. denied*, 116 S. Ct. 706 (1996).

2. *Loss of Consortium in Injury Cases*

In *American Export Lines, Inc. v. Alvez*, 446 U.S. 274, 100 S.Ct. 1673, 64 L.Ed.2d 284 (1980), the Supreme Court held that the wife of a harbor worker who was injured non-fatally aboard a vessel in state territorial waters could recover for loss of society. Has this decision been overruled impliedly by *Miles v. Apex Marine Corp., supra*?

Although *American Export Lines* has never been expressly overruled, it is wise to ask if it is good law. The holding that the wife of an injured longshoreman may recover non-pecuniary damages was based on an extension of the rule in *Sea-Land Services, Inc. v. Gaudet*, 414 U.S. 573, 94 S.Ct. 806, 39 L.Ed.2d 9, 1973 AMC 2572 (1974). Yet, *Gaudet* has since been severely limited in two subsequent Supreme Court cases. *See Miles v. Apex Marine Corp.*, 498 U.S. 19, 1991 A.M.C. 1 (1990); *Mobil Oil Co. v. Higginbotham*, 436 U.S. 618 (1978). Many have argued that *Gaudet's* continued presence creates a wrinkle in the uniformity of maritime law that should soon be resolved. *See* C. Taylor Simpson, *Sailing the Statutory Seas Toward Uniformity in Maritime Tort Law:* Miles v. Apex Marine Corp. 15 TUL. MAR. L.J. 449 (1991).

The decision in *American Export Lines* conflicts with all other remedies available under the maritime law. Non-pecuniary damages are not available under the Jones Act nor under the LHWCA when a seaman or worker is injured. To provide such damages under the general maritime law, when a longshoreman sues a vessel owner under 905(b), would give claimants a remedy that is not available to any seaman nor to any longshoreman injured while not aboard a ship. There seems to be no policy reason for making the availability of non-pecuniary damages dependent solely on the basis of where the longshoreman was injured. Thus, an argument for uniformity in the remedies available to injured workers seems to be warranted.

Nevertheless, in *Moore v. M/V Angela*, 353 F.3d 376, 2004 AMC 59 (5th Cir. 2003), the court held that an award of damages for loss of consortium to the widow of a longshoreman was permissible in a §905(b) action. The court said:

> Despite the illogical discrepancies between the law governing injuries to longshoremen in territorial waters and persons governed by the Death on the High Seas Act or the Jones Act, we must apply the law as it is.

Moore v. M/V Angela, 353 F.3d 376, 383 (5th Cir. 2003).

In *In re Amtrak "Sunset, Ltd" Train Crash*, 121 F.3d 1421, 1997 AMC 2962 (11th Cir. 1997), the Eleventh Circuit held that punitive damages and damages for loss of society or consortium are not available in personal injury actions under maritime law; they are unaffected by *Yamaha v. Calhoun, supra*, which dealt only with death cases.

3. ***Discounting: Inflation and Interest***

When calculating damages, the court or jury should take into account both the anticipated rate of inflation and the fact that the lump sum award can be invested to earn interest. In *Jones & Laughlin Steel Corp. v. Pfeifer*, 462 U.S. 523, 538-47, 103 S. Ct. 2541, 2551-55, 76 L. Ed. 768 (1983), the Supreme Court rejected the "total offset method", which regards any investment gains as being effectively canceled out by the effect of inflation. As a result, the award should be discounted to some extent, to reflect the present value of the future loss (i.e., the sum which, if given now, would produce the required figure over the period of years remaining in the plaintiff's life). The Court reviewed several different approaches taken by lower courts to the process of discounting, but refused to adopt any one of them "and establish it for all time as the exclusive method in all federal trials for calculating an award for lost earnings in an inflationary economy". *Id.* at 546, 2555.

Section IV. Remedies of Non-Maritime Persons

1. Duty and Standard of Care Generally

A variety of individuals other than seamen and other maritime employees may be lawfully present on a vessel. Every day, passengers board cruise ships, merchant ships are inspected by various government officials, and seamen receive visitors aboard the vessel. These persons are entitled to be protected by a certain standard of care notwithstanding their non-maritime status.

As a general rule, the shipowner owes a duty of exercising reasonable care toward the persons lawfully present aboard the vessel, *see Leathers v. Blessing*, 105 U.S. 626, 26 L.Ed. 1192 (1881); *The Max Morris*, 137 U.S. 1, 11 S.Ct. 29, 34 L.Ed. 586 (1890); *The Admiral Peoples*, 295 U.S. 649, 55 S.Ct. 885, 79 L.Ed. 1633 (1935). In *Kermarec v. Companie Generale Transatlantique*, the Supreme Court also refused to elaborate a standard of care which depends upon whether the injured person is a licensee or invitee on the vessel. The Court held that "the owner of a ship in navigable waters owes to all who are on board for purposes not inimical to his legitimate interests the duty of exercising reasonable care under the circumstances of each case." *Kermarec v. Compagnie Generale Transatlantique*, 358 U.S. 625, 79 S.Ct. 406, 3 L.Ed.2d 550 (1959). Nevertheless, such standard of care is only applicable where the injured person was lawfully present aboard the vessel. Stowaways and all individuals who have no legal right to remain aboard the vessel are entitled only to a lessened standard of care limited to humane treatment, *see The Laura Madsen*, 112 F. 72 (W.D. Wash. 1901). In such situations the shipowner is only liable for his willful or wanton misconduct towards stowaways, *see Taylor v. Alaska Rivers Navigations Co.*, 391 P. 2d 15 (Ala. 1964).

The issue of liability is to be determined upon principles not foreign to the common law of torts notwithstanding its maritime flavor. A shipowner is liable when he, or an employee (under the doctrine of respondeat superior) negligently caused an injury to a person lawfully present aboard the vessel, namely, when he has breached his duty to exercise reasonable care, *see Monteleone v. Bahama Cruise Line, Inc.*, 838 F.2d 63, 64, 1988 AMC 1146 (2d Cir. 1988).

In determining the standard of care to which a shipowner is held accountable, "the extent to which the circumstances surrounding maritime travel are different from those encountered in daily life and involve more danger to the passenger, will determine how high a degree of care is reasonable in each case." *See Rainey v. Paquet Cruises, Inc.*, 709 F.2d 169, 172, 1983 AMC 2100 (2d Cir. 1983). Early case law considered the shipowner accountable to a heightened standard of care. This position was based upon the premise that "... when carriers undertake to convey persons by the powerful and dangerous agency of steam, public policy and safety require that they be held to the greatest possible care and diligence,—that the personal safety of passengers should not be left to the sport of chance, or the negligence of careless agents," *see Pennsylvania Co. v. Roy*, 102 U.S. 451, 453, 26 L.Ed. 141 (1880); *see also Ludena v. the Santa Luisa*, 112 F. Supp. 401 (D.C.N.Y. 1953) (duty of care characterized as "... the greatest possible care ... ."); *Moore-McCormack Lines, Inc. v. Russack*, 266 F.2d 573 (9th Cir. 1959). The Supreme Court, however, in *Kermarec*, concluded that a shipowner is accountable to no more than a duty to exercise reasonable care, as a reasonable shipowner. A court's inquiry should focus on the amount of control the shipowner and the crew of the vessel possessed or should have possessed over a given situation. For example, in *Monteleone v. Bahama Cruise Lines, Inc.*, the court refused to hold a shipowner liable when a passenger tripped on a protruding screw and sustained injuries when she fell down a flight of stairs on a cruise ship. Taking into consideration the fact that the shipowner had demonstrated that the stairs were regularly inspected to guard against such defects, the court held that the "(shipowner's) liability properly turns on whether it had notice of the screw's protrusion [and that] merely allowing the screw to protrude did not constitute a breach of duty." *Id.* at 65.

The standard of care which is owed to passengers and other non-seafarers was recently discussed by the Ninth Circuit which stated:

> We conclude that the district court applied the proper standard of care. The district court correctly noted that a shipowner owes a duty of reasonable care to those aboard the ship who are not crew members. *See Kermarec v. Compagnie Generale Transatlantique*, 358 U.S. 625, 630, 79 S. Ct. 406, 409-10, 3 L. Ed. 2d 550 (1959). In *Kermarec*, the Supreme Court held that "the owner of a ship in navigable waters owes to all who are on board for purposes not inimical to his legitimate interests the duty of exercising reasonable care under the circumstances of each case." *Id.* at 632, 79 S. Ct. at 410; accord *Morton v. De Oliveira*, 984 F.2d 289, 291 (9th Cir.), *cert. denied*, 510 U.S. 907, 114 S. Ct. 289, 126 L. Ed. 2d 238 (1993).
>
> The degree of care required is always that which is reasonable, but the application of reasonable will of course change with the circumstances of each particular case. The Second Circuit has described the standard accurately:
>
> > What is required ... is merely the conduct of the reasonable man of ordinary prudence under the circumstances, and the greater danger, or the greater responsibility, is merely one of the circumstances, demanding only an increased amount of

> care. In some instances, reasonable care under the circumstances may be a very high degree of care; in other instances, it may be something less.

Rainey v. Paquet Cruises, Inc., 709 F.2d 169, 170-71 (2d Cir.1983) (internal quotations and citations omitted). The district court correctly determined that the standard of care is one of reasonableness, but in a situation such as this, where the risk is great because of high seas, an increased amount of care and precaution is reasonable.

> Furthermore, the district court's finding that Catalina Cruises breached this standard of reasonable care is not clearly erroneous. The crew of the COUNTESS had significant information regarding the weather they would encounter when crossing. The conditions had steadily deteriorated throughout the morning hours and had not shown any signs of improving. Captain Martin and Dennis were aware that the crossing would be rough and that they could be facing rather severe wind gusts. Knowing all this, Captain Martin ventured into this weather with over 300 passengers on board, many of them young campers.
>
> During the voyage, the MONARCH radioed the COUNTESS and informed Dennis that the MONARCH'S crossing had been miserable. Dennis failed to inform Captain Martin of the conditions the MONARCH reported. The COUNTESS continued to encounter rough seas, until a large wave caused one of the vessel's windows to shatter. After the window shattered, and water literally washed many passengers from their seats, Captain Martin slowed the vessel and changed course so the ride would be more comfortable. Many on board noticed an extreme change in the smoothness of the ride.
>
> A person exercising reasonable care under the circumstances would have slowed the vessel sooner, sought refuge at Long Point once he realized the severity of the conditions, or decided not to risk venturing out into the hazardous conditions at all. Accordingly, we hold that the district court did not commit clear error in determining that Catalina Cruises did not act with reasonable care under the circumstances of this case.

In re: Catalina Cruises, Inc., 137 F.3d 1422, 1998 AMC 1282 (9th Cir. 1998).

The shipowner, however, may be absolutely liable for the intentional torts of the members of its crew, *see Morton v. De Oliveira*, 984 F.2d 289, 1993 AMC 843 (9th Cir. 1993). In *Morton*, a passenger was allegedly raped by a crew member. The court held that the passenger could recover against a shipowner without showing any negligence on the part of the the shipowner.

The shipowner's liability to non-maritime persons has also been held to not be limited to the confines of the ship, *see Gillmor v. Caribbean Cruise Line. Ltd.*, 789 F. Supp. 488, 1994 AMC 1329 (D. P.R. 1992) (Vessel owner liable if the crew knew or should have known about the high probability of criminal activity in the area adjacent to the vessel's moorage and failed to warn the passengers of the danger).

The principles of comparative negligence may also be used by a shipowner to reduce the amount of damages. *See Carey v. Bahama Cruise Lines*, 864 F.2d 201, 1989 AMC 852 (1st Cir. 1988).

---

2. *Wrongful Death Actions*

a. *Deaths on the High Seas*

When a tort on the high seas causes the death of a passenger, the court applies the Death On the High Seas Act, 46 U.S.C.A. § 30302 (DOHSA, formerly 46 U.S.C. § 761). State law is displaced in such action since DOHSA has been held to provide the exclusive federal remedy, *see Offshore Logistics v. Tallentire*, 477 U.S. 207, 106 S.Ct. 2485, 91 L.Ed.2d 174, 1986 AMC 2113 (1986) (Dependents of offshore workers killed in a helicopter crash on the high seas held to be limited to DOHSA remedies. Such remedies may not be supplemented by any state law). Courts have also determined that wrongful deaths which occur in foreign territorial waters are considered as within the ambit of DOHSA, *see Howard v. Crystal Cruises, Inc.*, 41 F.3d 527, 1995 AMC 305(9th Cir. 1994) (Dependents of a passenger who had been injured in foreign territorial waters and from which he subsequently died held to be limited to DOHSA's pecuniary damages although the accident causing the death of the passenger occurred in foreign territorial waters. The court considered that the primary purpose of DOHSA was to create a remedy for deaths occurring outside the reach of the state courts of the United States).

---

b. *Deaths in Territorial Waters*

See Yamaha Motor Corp., U.S.A. v. Calhoun, and accompanying Note, *supra*.

---

3. *Choice of Law: Choice of Forum Clauses*

Many nations have accepted the Athens Convention Relating to the Carriage of Passengers and Their Luggage By Sea (1974), which deals with the recovery of damages by passengers for personal injury and death as well as loss of baggage. Under the Convention, the carrier is liable for losses caused by the fault or neglect of the shipowner or his employees. Fault or neglect is presumed (although subject to rebuttal evidence) in the case of death, injury or loss of baggage due to shipwreck, collision, standing, explosion, fire, or a defect in the ship. No contractual alteration of these rules is permitted. Under the Convention liability is limited to 70,000 gold francs per passenger for death or injury; 50,000 gold francs for loss or damage to a vehicle; 12,5000 gold francs for loss of cabin baggage; and 18,000 gold francs for any other loss.

The United States has not ratified the Athens Convention. Liability for death, personal injury or loss of baggage is based upon common-law negligence, but a generally high standard of care is applied. *See Allen v. Matson Navigation Co.*, 255 F.2d 273, 1958 AMC 1343 (9th Cir. 1958). Contract clauses that relieve a carrier from liability for negligence or limit damages are void by statute. 46 U.S.C.A. § 30509 (formerly 46 U.S.C. § 183c). Contract provisions placing limits on liability for loss of passenger baggage are valid if reasonable under the circumstances. *See The Leviathan*, 4 F. Supp. 918, 1933 AMC 1394 (E.D.N.Y. 1933); *Miller v. International Freighting Corp.*, 97 F. Supp. 60, 1951 AMC 944 (S.D.N.Y. 1951).

Is a provision on the contract of passage specifying a time limit for suit valid? *Compare DeNicola v. Cunard Line, Inc.*, 642 F.2d 5, 1981 AMC 1388 (1st Cir. 1981) with *Raskin v. Compania de Vapores Realma*, 521 F. Supp. 337, 1983 AMC 814 (S.D.N.Y. 1981).

Is a forum selection clause contained in a form passage contract valid? In *Carnival Cruise Lines, Inc. v. Shute*, 499 U.S. 585, 111 S. Ct. 1522, 113 L. Ed. 2d 622, 1991 AMC 1697 (1991), a Washington state couple, the Shutes, purchased passage on a ship owned by Carnival Cruise Lines which sent the Shutes tickets that contained a clause designating courts in Florida as the agreed-upon forum for the resolution of any disputes. The Shutes boarded the ship in Los Angeles and, while in international waters off the Mexican coast, Mrs. Shute suffered injuries when she slipped and fell. The Shutes filed suite in a Washington Federal District Court, which granted summary judgment for the cruise line. The Court of Appeals reversed, holding, *inter alia*, that the forum selection clause should not be enforced because it was not freely bargained for and because its enforcement would deprive the Shutes of their day in court since the couple was physically and financially incapable of pursuing litigation in Florida.

The Supreme Court, reversing the judgment of the Court of Appeals, emphasized that forum-selection clauses contained in form passage contracts are subject to judicial scrutiny for fundamental fairness. In the instant case the Court held that the forum selection clause at issue was reasonable and enforceable. Florida was not a "remote alien forum" nor, given the fact that the accident occurred off the Mexican coast, was Washington inherently more suited to resolution of the dispute than Florida. Further, the Court found no indication that the cruise line designated Florida as the forum in order to discourage cruise passengers from pursuing legitimate claims, no evidence that the Company obtained passengers' assent to the clause by fraud or overreaching, and the passengers conceded that they were given notice of the provision. Finally, the Court ruled that the forum selection clause did not violate 46 U.S.C.A. § 30509 (formerly 46 U.S.C. App. § 183c) which prohibits a vessel owner from inserting in any contract a provision depriving a claimant of trial by a court of competent jurisdiction for loss of life or personal injury resulting from negligence. The Court characterized the forum selection clause as merely stating that actions arising out of passage contracts were to be brought, if at all, in court located in Florida which would be a court of competent jurisdiction within the meaning of the statute.

The result in Carnival Cruise Lines, Inc. was legislatively overruled with an amendment to 46 U.S.C.A. § 30509 (formerly 46 U.S.C.A. § 183c) which precludes a carrier from limiting a passengers choice of an otherwise valid forum by a forum selection clause. This amendment was itself overruled, presumably reinstating the effect of Carnival Cruise Lines, Inc.

Section V. Products Liability

In *East River Steamship Corp. v. Transamerica Delaval, Inc.*, 476 U.S. 858, 106 S. Ct. 2295, 90 L. Ed. 2d 865, 1986 AMC 2027 (1986), the Supreme Court held that the general maritime law recognizes strict liability for harm done or injury caused by defective products. The Court went on to consider the question whether there can be tort liability for "injury to the product itself": i.e., for the defect in the product. The Court rejected the argument that there should be liability for damage to the product itself, holding that there could only be liability for harm done or injury caused by the product. When rejecting tort liability in those the cases where the product injures only itself (i.e., is defective but does no harm to others), the Court said:

> [S]ince by definition no person or other property is damaged, the resulting loss is purely economic. Even when the harm to the product itself occurs through an abrupt, accident-like event, the resulting loss due to repair costs, decreased value, and lost profits is essentially the failure of the purchaser to receive the benefit of its bargain—traditionally the core concern of contract law. *See* E. FARNSWORTH, CONTRACTS § 12.8, pp. 839-840 (1982).

476 U.S. 858, 870 (1986).

Chapter 7

COLLISION AND OTHER ACCIDENTS

A. Liability

1. Inevitable Accident

THE JUMNA

149 F. 171 (2d Cir. 1906)

On appeal and cross-appeal from a decree of the District Court for the Southern District of New York dismissing the libel and cross-libels and deciding that the collision between barge No. 19, in tow of the tug Gypsum King, and the steamship Jumna, and the subsequent collision of said barge and the schooner Gypsum Emperor with the New Haven Railroad's pier No. 38, East River, was the result of inevitable accident.

The opinion of Judge Holt in the District Court is reported in 140 F. 743....

COXE, Circuit Judge

It is conceded on all hands that, except in a few unimportant details, the facts are fully and accurately stated in the opinion of the district judge. He has carefully considered the conflicting theories of fault and has reached the conclusion that negligence has not been established as to any of the vessels participating in the collision. To arrive at this result it was necessary for him to determine several disputed questions of fact regarding which it is sufficient to say that in many instances he was unquestionably right and in no instance is the finding so clearly against the preponderance of proof as to warrant us in setting it aside.

For instance, was the Jumna's hawser sufficient and in proper condition? Was the tow of the Gypsum King properly made up? Did the McCaldin Brothers make proper effort to reach the port side of the Jumna? Did the Dalzell put a sudden strain on the hawser?

In each of these instances the district judge found against the asserted negligence and we think the weight of testimony sustains these findings. Like him we are unable to localize the blame for the collision. We had some doubt as to whether the tugs in charge of the Jumna, and particularly the McCaldin Brothers, can be exculpated but, after an examination of the testimony, we incline to the opinion that they did everything which could be reasonably expected of them and that the McCaldin Brothers started to make fast to the port quarter of the Jumna as soon as the latter cleared the pier and it was possible to get around her stern.

The judge of the District Court has found that the collision was the result of an inevitable accident. Such an accident usually happens when it is not possible to prevent it by the exercise of due care, caution and nautical skill. It is generally, though not invariably, attributed to an act of God, as where a tremendous tempest arises, such as devastated Galveston a few years ago, or more recently destroyed the shipping in the harbor of Havana. So, where a dense fog or falling snow obstructs the vision, where a gale and high seas unite to make navigation difficult, or where a severe storm is prevailing upon a dark night, a collision happening in such circumstances, the colliding vessels exercising the care, skill and caution required by prudent navigation, would be attributed to inevitable accident. Such accidents usually occur when safe navigation is rendered impossible from causes which no human foresight can prevent; when the forces of nature burst forth in unforeseen and uncontrollable fury so that man is helpless, and the stoutest ship and the most experienced mariner are at the mercy of the winds and waves.

In admiralty law, however, the phrase has a more comprehensive meaning. It is not necessary that the accident should be the result of a vis major. If no negligence can be imputed to either vessel there is a presumption that they are navigating in a lawful manner and where no fault can be shown the accident may be said to be inevitable.

* * *

The test is, could the collision have been prevented by the exercise of ordinary care, caution and maritime skill? In the case at bar we are unable upon the testimony before us to specify any particular fault, to put our finger upon any act or omission and assert that to it the accident was attributable. Fault may exist, but we are unable to discover it; it is inscrutable. Where the evidence is so conflicting that it is impossible to determine to what direct and specific acts the collision is attributable, it is a case of damage arising from a cause that is inscrutable. *The Fern and The Swann*, Newb. 158, Fed. Cas. No. 8,588. Whether the case at bar be thus classified, or whether it be held to come within the admiralty definition of inevitable accident is not material; in either event the loss must be borne by the party on whom it falls... .

Note

Fault in a collision case may arise because of (1) negligence on the part of the navigators, lack of proper care or skill; (2) violation of the rules of the road, the applicable rules of navigation laid down by or under the authority of statute: or (3) failure to comply with local navigational customs or usage.

THE LOUISIANA

70 U.S. (3 Wall.) 164, 18 L. Ed. 85 (1865)

[The steamship LOUISIANA broke free from its moorings in a strong gale and drifted until it collided with the steamship FLUSHING, which was hard aground on a sandbar. The owners of the FLUSHING sued the LOUISIANA *in rem*. The District Court held that the LOUISIANA was not at fault. The Circuit Court for Maryland reversed, holding the LOUISIANA to be entirely at fault. Eds.]

* * *

Mr. Justice GRIER delivered the opinion of the court

The steamer Flushing being aground on Hampton Bar, out of the channel or course of vessels navigating the bay or harbor, and incapable of motion, cannot be justly charged with any participation in causing the collision.

The collision being caused by the Louisiana drifting from her moorings, she must be liable for the damages consequent thereon, unless she can show affirmatively that the drifting was the result of inevitable accident, or a *vis major*, which human skill and precaution, and a proper display of nautical skill could not have prevented.

Now the facts show that the Louisiana has entirely failed to establish her defence.

1. The drifting of this vessel was not caused by any sudden hurricane which nautical experience could not anticipate. None of the other numerous vessels, at that time in the harbor, were driven from their moorings. The wind which arose was only of such a character that its effects might have been anticipated, and, by proper precaution, prevented;—"a half gale," "a stiff breeze," "a little more than ordinary."

The fact that the steamer was ordered by the government officers to take in coal at the old wharf, which had a narrow front when compared with the great length of the vessel, could not relieve the officers of the boat from the duty of securing her in such a manner as to prevent her drifting when the change of the tide and winds changed the direction of the forces acting upon the vessel. And the fact that under these circumstances she *did* drift, is conclusive evidence that she was not sufficiently and properly secured.

It requires no assumption or affectation of any very great nautical skill in this court to point out the defects of the management of this vessel by the mate, who was left in charge of her. If the tide and wind could have been reasonably expected to remain as it was when, according to the mate's idea, the vessel was lying so "*very nice to the wharf*," we should probably not have heard of this case.

So long as things were in the condition in which they were when the vessel was first moored, she was sufficiently secured to meet any stress or force likely to be opposed to her in that direction. But when the tide changed so as to strike the stern with a momentum increased by a high wind, and multiplied by the leverage resulting from the length of the vessel exposed below the wharf, the "necessity" for a change of position ought to have suggested itself to a person of nautical skill, as a proper precaution against a danger which might justly have been anticipated. The fact that the captain and mate "did not anticipate the breaking away of the vessel, and thought the lines sufficient to hold her," may prove their want of judgment, but not that "the accident was unavoidable;" and this more especially, as other person of nautical skill—disinterested witnesses in this case—found no difficulty in securing their vessels at the same place, and under similar circumstances.

2. It is not necessary to a decision of the cause to show that this collision might have been averted by a proper use of the anchors of the Louisiana, after she had broken away from her mooring at the wharf, or by a proper use of her steam power, further than to say, that the testimony in the case would well justify that conclusion.

We are of opinion, therefore, that the appellant has failed to show that the collision is the result of inevitable accident, and that the decree of the Circuit Court should be

AFFIRMED WITH COSTS.

Note

Like other presumptions, the presumption in *The Louisiana,* 70 U.S. (3 Wall.) 164, 18 L. Ed. 85 (1865) is rebuttable. Thus, in a case where a vessel struck a bridge, evidence that the Coast Guard had determined pursuant to an investigation that the bridge was an obstruction to navigation may be sufficient to overcome the presumption. *I & M Rail Link, LLC v. Northstar Navigation, Inc.*, 198 F.3d 1012, 2000 AMC 736 (7th Cir. 1999), *cert. denied,* 531 U.S. 917, 121 S. Ct. 276, 148 L. Ed. 2d 201 (2000).

---

2. Error in Extremis

Note

Generally speaking, a ship must be navigated with reasonable care and skill at all times. However, errors of navigation may be excused if committed "*in extremis*": that is, in a position of great danger caused by the acts or omissions of another ship. For example, in *Puerto Rico Ports Auth. v. M/V Manhattan Prince*, 897 F.2d 1, 1990 AMC 1475 (1st Cir. 1990), the tug *Borinquen* was held to have acted reasonably, despite the fact that it dropped the lines by which it was attached to the ship *Manhattan Prince* and allowed *Manhattan Prince* to allide with the wharf, causing damage to both ship and wharf. The tug *Borinquen* was in danger itself as a result of negligent navigation of the *Manhattan Prince* by the master and pilot. The court said:

> The doctrine of *in extremis* has long been a part of admiralty law. In *The Blue Jacket*, 144 U.S. 371, 392, 12 S. Ct. 711, 719, 36 L. Ed. 469, (1892), the rule was stated as follows:
>
> > As was held in *The Bywell Castle*, 4 Prob.Div. 219, "where one ship has, by wrong manoeuvres, placed another ship in a position of extreme danger, that other ship will not be held to blame if she has done something wrong, and has not been manoeuvred with perfect skill and presence of mind."
>
> There was no misapplication of the *in extremis* doctrine here. The captain of the tug Borinquen testified in effect as follows: He had no problem communicating with the pilot. After the ship cleared the Catano dock, the pilot told him to stop pushing. At that time, the tug was between the head of the Catano dock and the bulkhead of the terminal pier. He told the pilot that he was about 50 feet from the pier, that there would be a collision, and he was going to release the lines because the tug was in danger. It was his judgment that if the tug had not backed away from the tanker, it would have been sandwiched between the tanker and the Catano pier.
>
> * * *

From this evidence the court could have found that the tug did not do anything to create the emergency, that the safety of the tug and its crew was put in peril as the ship continued forward towards the piers and that casting off the lines was a reasonable response to the danger thrust upon the tug by the tanker.

The testimony is more than sufficient to sustain the district court's finding that the tug Borinquen was *in extremis* when it cast off the lines and therefore did not act negligently.

Puerto Rico Ports Auth. v. M/V Manhattan Prince, 897 F.2d 1, 6-7 (1990).

---

3. Vicarious Liability

Note: Vicarious Liability for Acts of Compulsory/Noncompulsory Pilots

The rule in *The China*, 74 U.S. (7 Wall.) 53, 19 L. Ed. 67 (1868) is that a shipowner is not vicariously liable *in personam* for the negligence of a compulsory pilot, but the ship is vicariously liable *in rem*. The rule in *The China* is still in force. *See Afran Transport Co. v. Steamship Transcolorado*, 468 F.2d 772, 1974 AMC 2034 (5th Cir. 1972); *State of California v. Italian Motorship Ilice*, 534 F.2d 836, 1976 AMC 2290 (9th Cir. 1976); *Hogge v. Steamship Yorkman*, 434 F. Supp. 715, 1977 AMC 805 (D. Md. 1977); *Logue Stevedoring Corp. v. The Dalzellance*, 198 F.2d 369, 1952 AMC 1297 (2d Cir. 1952); *Homer Ramsdell Transportation Co. v. La. Compagnie Generale Transatlantique*, 182 U.S. 406, 21 S. Ct. 831, 45 L. Ed. 1155 (1901).

When the pilot is voluntarily taken aboard ship and his or her fault is the cause of injury or damage, the ship operator is liable both *in rem* and *in personam* under the generally recognized rules of *respondeat superior*. The rule in *The China* applies only to compulsory pilots. When is a pilot "compulsory" for these purposes? What if the services of a pilot are required by the private owner of a port facility? *See Texaco Trinidad, Inc. v. Afran Transport Co.*, 538 F. Supp. 1038, 1983 AMC 1582 (E.D. Pa. 1982) (pilot compulsory when required by berth or terminal owner even though pilotage not required by law or regulation).

If an onshore terminal employs a mooring master to assist in the docking of vessels, can the risk of liability from negligent mooring of the vessel be shifted from the terminal to the vessel through a pilotage clause in the agreement between the terminal and the ship that makes the mooring master the servant of the ship? *See Kane v. Hawaiian Independent Refinery, Inc.*, 690 F.2d 722, 1984 AMC 1323 (9th Cir. 1982) (the validity of pilotage clause upheld). For pilotage clauses in towing contracts, see Chapter 5, on Towage, Pilotage and Salvage.

In *Guanco v. Edward Shipping & Mercantile, S.A.*, 705 F.2d 360 (9th Cir. 1983), a crew member aboard the *M/V Pacific Queen* was injured while the ship was being docked in Apra Harbor, Guam, by a compulsory pilot. In the resulting litigation, the pilot company denied liability, relying on a clause in the pilotage agreement that the shipowner ["Edward"] would indemnify the pilot company for any injury resulting from the pilot's negligence. The court upheld the pilotage clause, stating as follows:

For the first argument, Edward relies upon Guam Civil Code § 2384, which provides:

> The owner or master of a ship is not responsible for the negligence of a pilot whom he bound by law to employ; but if he is allowed an option between pilots, some of whom are competent, or is required only to pay compensation to a pilot, whether he employs him or not, he is also responsible to third persons.

It codifies the common law rule that a shipowner will not be held liable when the selection of a pilot is not a voluntary act. *Homer Ramsdell Transportation Co. v. La Compagnie Generale Transatlantique*, 182 U.S. 406 (1901). The rule grew out of the traditional pilotage system in which a shipmaster was required to accept the first pilot to offer his services to the vessel as it entered the harbor.

In *Apra Harbor*, however, a shipmaster has a choice among pilots. There are two companies providing local pilotage service. And under the plain language of Guam Civil Code § 2384, as long as the shipmaster can reject a pilot, he will be held responsible if he accepts the services of that pilot. This responsibility is reinforced by an administrative regulation, which imposes on a shipmaster the duty to relieve any incompetent or negligent pilot on board his ship. 9 GUAM ADMIN. R. § 8004.8. If the pilot aboard the Pacific Queen was negligent, Edward' shipmaster had a duty to replace that pilot.

... The exculpatory clause is reasonable. When the pilot boards the ship and takes over direction of its movement, he becomes independent of his employer, the pilotage company. He must serve the interest of the shipowner, and not of the pilotage company. Consequently the shipowner, who has a right to the best efforts of the pilot, bears the responsibility for the acts of the pilot.

... Because of the particular nature of the pilot's duties, it is fair and reasonable to indemnify the company which employs the pilot for that period when the pilot is on board another vessel, directing the movements of that vessel. The contract which Edward signed with Cabras is enforceable, even if Edward did not and could not bargain over the exculpatory clause. The clause is fair and reasonable in the light of the customary business practices of pilotage companies in Guam and elsewhere throughout the United States.

4. Allocation of Fault — The Modern Rule

UNITED STATES v. RELIABLE TRANSFER CO., INC.

421 U.S. 397, 95 S. Ct. 1708, 44 L. Ed. 2d 251, 1975 AMC 541 (1975)

Mr. Justice STEWART delivered the opinion of the Court

More than a century ago, in *The Schooner Catharine v. Dickinson*, 17 How. 170, this Court established in our admiralty law the rule of divided damages. That rule, most commonly applied in cases of collision between two vessels, requires the equal division of property damage whenever both parties are found to be guilty of contributing fault, whatever the relative degree of their fault may have been. The courts of every major maritime nation except ours have long since abandoned that rule, and now assess damages in such cases on the basis of proportionate fault when such an allocation can reasonably be made. In the present case we are called upon to decide whether this country's admiralty rule of divided damages should be replaced by a rule requiring, when possible, the allocation of liability for damages in proportion to the relative fault of each party.

On a clear but windy December night in 1968, the Mary A. Whalen, a coastal tanker owned by the respondent Reliable Transfer Co., embarked from Constable Hook, N.J., for Island Park, N. Y., with a load of fuel oil. The voyage ended, instead, with the vessel stranded on a sand bar off Rockaway Point outside New York Harbor.

The Whalen's course led across the mouth of Rockaway Inlet, a narrow body of water that lies between a breakwater to the southeast and the shoreline of Coney Island to the northwest. The breakwater is ordinarily marked at its southernmost point by a flashing light maintained by the Coast Guard. As, however, the Whalen's captain and a deckhand observed while the vessel was proceeding southwardly across the inlet, the light was not operating that night. As the Whalen approached Rockaway Point about half an hour later, her captain attempted to pass a tug with a barge in tow ahead, but, after determining that he could not overtake them, decided to make a 180 degree turn to pass astern of the barge. At this time the tide was at flood, and the waves, whipped by northwest winds of gale force, were eight to ten feet high. After making the 180 degree turn and passing astern of the barge, the captain headed the Whalen eastwardly, believing that the vessel was then south of the breakwater and that he was heading her for the open sea. He was wrong. About a minute later the light structure on the southern point of the breakwater came into view. Tuning to avoid rocks visible ahead, the Whalen ran aground in the sand.

The respondent brought this action against the United States in Federal District Court, under the Suits in Admiralty Act, 41 Stat. 525, 46 U.S.C. § 741 *et seq.*, and the Federal Tort Claims Act, 28 U.S.C. § 1346 *et seq.*, seeking to recover for damages to the Whalen caused by the stranding. The District Court found that the vessel's grounding was caused 25% by the failure of the Coast Guard to maintain the breakwater light and 75% by the fault of the Whalen. In so finding on the issue of comparative fault, the court stated:

> The fault of the vessel was more egregious than the fault of the Coast Guard. Attempting to negotiate a turn to the east, in the narrow space between the bell buoy No. 4 and the shoals off Rockaway Point, the Captain set his course without knowing where he was. Obviously, he would not have found the breakwater light looming directly ahead of him within a minute after his change of course, if he had not been north of the point where he believed he was.
>
> Equipped with look-out, chart, searchlight, radio-telephone, and radar, he made use of nothing except his own guesswork judgment. After ... turning in a loop toward the north so as to pass astern of the tow, he should have made sure of his position before setting his new 73 degree course. The fact that a northwest gale blowing at 45 knots with eight to ten foot seas made it difficult to see, emphasizes the need for caution rather than excusing a turn into the unknown... .
>
> The court held, however, that the settled admiralty rule of divided damages required each party to bear one-half of the damages to the vessel.[1]

The Court of Appeals for the Second Circuit affirmed this judgment. 497 F.2d 1036.... We granted certiorari, 419 U.S. 1018, to consider the continued validity of the divided damages rule.

The precise origins of the divided damages rule are shrouded in the mists of history. In any event it was not until early in the 19th century that the divided damages rule as we know it emerged clearly in British admiralty law. In 1815, in *The Woodrop-Sims*, 2 Dods. 83, 165 Eng. Rep. 1422, Sir William Scott, later Lord Stowell, considered the various circumstances under which maritime collisions could occur and stated that division of damages was appropriate in those cases "where both parties are to blame." *Id.*, at 85, 165 Eng. Rep., at 1423. In such cases the total damages were to be "apportioned between" the parties "as having been occasioned by the fault of both of them." *Ibid.* Nine years later the divided damages rule became settled in English admiralty law when the House of Lords in a maritime collision case where both ships were at fault reversed a decision of a Scottish court that had apportioned damages by degree of blame, and, relying on The Woodrop-Sims, ordered that the damages be divided equally. *Hay v. Le Neve*, 2 Shaw H.L. 395.

It was against this background that in 1855 this Court adopted the rule of equal division of damages in *The Schooner Catharine v. Dickinson*, 17 How. 170. The rule was adopted because it was then the prevailing rule in England, because it had become the

---

[1] The operation of the rule was described in *The Sapphire*, 18 Wall. 51, 56. 21 L. Ed. 814:

> It is undoubtedly the rule in admiralty that where both vessels are in fault the sums representing the damage sustained by each must be added together and the aggregate divided between the two. This is in effect deducting the lesser from the greater and dividing the remainder.... If one in fault has sustained no injury, it is liable for half the damages sustained by the other, though that other was also in fault.
>
> Similarly, in *The North Star*, 106 U.S. 17, 22, the rule was thus stated:
>
> [A]ccording to the general maritime law, in cases of collision occurring by the fault of both parties, the entire damage to both ships is added together in one common mass and equally divided between them, and thereupon arises a liability of one party to pay to the other such sum as is necessary to equalize the burden.

* * *

> It has long been settled that the divided damages rule applies not only in cases of collision between two vessels, but also in cases like this one where a vessel party at fault is damaged in collision or grounding because of the mutual contributing fault of a nonvessel party....

majority rule in the lower federal courts, and because it seemed the "most just and equitable, and ... best [tended] to induce care and vigilance on both sides, in the navigation." *Id.*, at 177-178. There can be no question that subsequent history and experience have conspicuously eroded the rule's foundations.

It was true at the time of The Catharine that the divided damages rule was well entrenched in English law. The rule was an ancient form of rough justice, a means of apportioning damages where it was difficult to measure which party was more at fault. *See* 4 R. MARSDEN, BRITISH SHIPPING LAWS, *COLLISIONS AT SEA* §§ 119-147 (11th ed. 1961); Staring, *Contribution and Division of Damages in Admiralty and Maritime Cases*, 45 CALIF. L. REV. 304, 305-310 (1957). But England has long since abandoned the rule and now follows the Brussels Collision Liability Convention of 1910 that provides for the apportionment of damages on the basis of "degree" of fault whenever it is possible to do so. Indeed, the United States is now virtually alone among the world's major maritime nations in not adhering to the Convention with its rule of proportional fault—a fact that encourages transoceanic forum shopping. *See* G. GILMORE & C. BLACK, THE LAW OF ADMIRALTY 529 (2d ed. 1975) (hereinafter GILMORE & BLACK).

While the lower federal courts originally adhered to the divided damages rule, they have more recently followed it only grudgingly, terming it "unfair," "illogical," "arbitrary," "archaic and frequently unjust." Judge Learned Hand was a particularly stern critic of the rule. Dissenting in *National Bulk Carriers v. United States*, 183 F.2d 405, 410 (CA2), he wrote: "An equal division [of damages] in this case would be plainly unjust; they ought to be divided in some such proportion as five to one. And so they could be but for our obstinate cleaving to the ancient rule which has been abrogated by nearly all civilized nations." And Judge Hand had all but invited this Court to overturn the rule when, in an earlier opinion for the Court of Appeals for the Second Circuit, he stated that "we have no power to divest ourselves of this vestigial relic; we can only go so far as to close our eyes to doubtful delinquencies." *Oriental Trading & Transport Co. v. Gulf Oil Corp.*, 173 F.2d 108, 111. Some courts, even bolder, have simply ignored the rule. *See* J. Griffin, *The American Law of Collision* 564 (1949); *Staring, supra*, at 341-342. *Cf. The Margaret*, 30 F.2d 923 (CA3).

It is no longer apparent, if it ever was, that this Solomonic division of damages serves to achieve even rough justice. An equal division of damages is a reasonably satisfactory result only where each vessel's fault is approximately equal and each vessel thus assumes a share of the collision damages in proportion to its share of the blame, or where proportionate degrees of fault cannot be measured and determined on a rational basis. The rule produces palpably unfair results in every other case. For example, where one ship's fault in causing a collision is relatively slight and her damages small, and where the second ship is grossly negligent and suffers extensive damage, the first ship must still make a substantial payment to the second. "This result hardly commends itself to the sense of justice any more appealingly than does the common law doctrine of contributory negligence... ." GILMORE & BLACK 528.

And the potential unfairness of the division is magnified by the application of the rule of *The Pennsylvania*, 19 Wall. 125, whereby a ship's relatively minor statutory violation will require her to bear half the collision damage unless she can satisfy the heavy burden of showing "not merely that her fault might not have been one of the causes, or that it probably was not, but that *it could not have been.*" *Id.*, at 136 (emphasis added).

The Court has long implicitly recognized the patent harshness of an equal division of damages in the face of disparate blame by applying the "major-minor" fault doctrine to find a grossly negligent party solely at fault. But this escape valve, in addition to being inherently unreliable, simply replaces one unfairness with another. That a vessel is primarily negligent does not justify its shouldering all responsibility, nor excuse the slightly negligent vessel from bearing any liability at all... .

The divided damages rule has been said to be justified by the difficulty of determining comparative degrees of negligence when both parties are concededly guilty of contributing fault. *The Max Morris*, 137 U.S. 1. Although there is some force in this argument, it cannot justify an equal division of damages in every case of collision based on mutual fault. When it is impossible fairly to allocate degrees of fault, the division of damages equally between wrongdoing parties is an equitable solution. But the rule is unnecessarily crude and inequitable in a case like this one where an allocation of disparate proportional fault has been made. Potential problems of proof in some cases hardly require adherence to an archaic and unfair rule in all cases. Every other major maritime nation has evidently been able to apply a rule of comparative negligence without serious problems, *see* Mole & Wilson, *A Study of Comparative Negligence*, 17 CORN. L.Q. 333, 346 (1932); *In re Adams' Petition*, 125 F. Supp. 110, 114 (SDNY), *affd.* 237 F.2d 884 (CA2), and in our own admiralty law a rule of comparative negligence has long been applied with no untoward difficulties in personal injury actions. *See, e.g., Pope & Talbot, Inc. v. Hawn,* 346 U.S. 406, 409. *See also* Merchant Marine (Jones) Act, 38 Stat. 1185, as amended, 41 Stat. 1007, 46 U.S.C. § 688; Death on the High Seas Act, 41 Stat. 537, 46 U.S.C. § 766.

The argument has also been made that the divided damages rule promotes out-of-court settlements, because when it becomes apparent that both vessels are at fault, both parties can readily agree to divide the damages—thus avoiding the expense and delay of prolonged litigation and the concomitant burden on the courts. It would be far more difficult, it is argued, for the parties to agree on who was more at fault and to apportion damages accordingly. But the argument is hardly persuasive. For if the fault of the two parties is markedly disproportionate, it is in the interest of the slightly negligent party to litigate the controversy in the hope that the major-minor fault rule may eventually persuade a court to absolve it of all liability. And if, on the other hand, it appears after a realistic assessment of the situation that the fault of both parties is roughly equal, then there is no reason why a rule that apportions damages would be any less likely to induce a settlement than a rule that always divides damages equally. Experience with comparative negligence in the personal injury area teaches that a rule of fairness in court will produce fair out-of-court settlements. But even if this argument were more persuasive than it is, it could hardly be accepted. For, at bottom, it asks us to continue the operation of an archaic rule because its facile application out of court yields quick, though inequitable, settlements, and relieves the courts of some litigation. Congestion in the courts cannot justify a legal rule that produces unjust results in litigation simply to encourage speedy out-of-court accommodations.

Finally, the respondent suggests that the creation of a new rule of damages in maritime collision cases is a task for Congress and not for this Court. But the Judiciary has traditionally taken the lead in formulating flexible and fair remedies in the law maritime, and "Congress has largely left to this Court the responsibility for fashioning the controlling rules of admiralty law." *Fitzgerald v. United States Lines Co.*, 374 U.S. 16, 20. *See also Moragne v. States Marine Lines*, 398 U.S. 375, 405 n. 17; *Kermarec v. Compagnie Generale Transatlantique*, 358 U.S. 625, 630-632. No statutory or judicial precept precludes a change in the rule of divided damages, and indeed a proportional fault rule would simply bring recovery for property damage in maritime collision cases into line with the rule of admiralty law long since established by Congress for personal injury cases. *See* the Jones Act, 46 U.S.C. § 688.

* * *

The rule of divided damages in admiralty has continued to prevail in this country by sheer inertia rather than by reason of any intrinsic merit. The reasons that originally led to the Court's adoption of the rule have long since disappeared. The rule has been repeatedly criticized by experienced federal judges who have correctly pointed out that the result it works has too often been precisely the opposite of what the Court sought to achieve in The Schooner Catharine—the "just and equitable" allocation of damages. And worldwide experience has taught that that goal can be more nearly realized by a standard that allocates liability for damages according to comparative fault whenever possible.

We hold that when two or more parties have contributed by their fault to cause property damage in a maritime collision or stranding, liability for such damage is to be allocated among the parties proportionately to the comparative degree of their fault, and that liability for such damages is to be allocated equally only when the parties are equally at fault or when it is not possible fairly to measure the comparative degree of their fault.

Accordingly, the judgment before us is vacated and the case is remanded for further proceedings consistent with this opinion.

---

5. *Proximate Cause*

Note

The adoption of the comparative fault rule in *United States v. Reliable Transfer Co.*, 421 U.S. 397, 95 S. Ct. 1708, 44 L. Ed. 2d 251, 1975 AMC 541 (1975) did not dispense with the need to make an analysis of proximate cause or the related "superseding cause" doctrine. In *Exxon Co., U.S.A. v. Sofec, Inc.*, 517 U.S. 830, 116 S. Ct. 1813, 135 L. Ed. 2d 113, 1996 AMC 1817 (1996), an oil tanker belonging to the plaintiff (Exxon) grounded after breaking free from a Single Point Mooring System (SPM) owned and operated by one of the defendants and manufactured by another. The tanker became a constructive total loss and the plaintiff sued the defendants alleging that the loss of the tanker was caused by their fault. The defendants argued that the negligence of the tanker's captain after the tanker had broken free was the sole and superseding proximate cause of the loss. The Supreme Court agreed with the defendants, saying:

> Exxon's primary argument is that the proximate causation requirement, and the related superseding cause doctrine, are not or should not be applicable in admiralty. In particular, Exxon asserts that the lower courts' refusal to allocate any share of damages to parties whose fault was a cause in fact of Exxon's injury conflicts with our decision in *Reliable Transfer*.
>
> We disagree. In *Reliable Transfer*, we discarded a longstanding rule that property damages in admiralty cases are to be divided equally between those liable for injury, "whatever the relative degree of their fault may have been," 421 U.S., at 397, 95 S. Ct., at 1709, and adopted the comparative fault principle in its stead. The proximate causation requirement was not before us in *Reliable Transfer*, and we did not suggest that the requirement was inapplicable in admiralty. (Nor, for that matter, did we consider whether the injury had been proximately caused by the defendant in that case.)
>
> There is nothing internally inconsistent in a system that apportions damages based upon comparative fault only among tortfeasors whose actions were proximate causes of an injury. Nor is there any repugnancy between the superseding cause doctrine, which is one facet of the proximate causation requirement, and a comparative fault method of allocating damages.

Exxon Co., U.S.A. v. Sofec, Inc., 517 U.S. 830, 836 (1990).

---

6. *Violation of Safety Standards: The Pennsylvania Rule*

Introductory Note

In *The Pennsylvania,* 86 U.S. (19 Wall) 125, 22 L. Ed. 148 (1873), a collision between the sailing bark MARY TROOP and the steamship PENNSYLVANIA occurred in very dense fog. The MARY TROOP was moving slowly, ringing a bell as a fog signal, although the collision regulations stipulated use of a foghorn. The PENNSYLVANIA was proceeding at a speed of seven knots, although the collision regulations required ships "to go at a moderate speed" in fog. The Supreme Court held that the PENNSYLVANIA was at fault by going too fast and the MARY TROOP by ringing a bell rather than sounding a foghorn. The Court said (*id.* at 136):

> Concluding then, as we must, that the bark was in fault, it still remains to inquire whether the fault contributed to the collision, whether in any degree it was the cause of the vessels coming into a dangerous position. It must be conceded that if it clearly appears the fault could have had nothing to do with the disaster, it may be dismissed from consideration. The liability for damages is upon the ship or ships whose fault caused the injury. But when, as in this case, a ship at the time of a collision is in actual violation of a statutory rule intended to prevent collisions, it is no more than a reasonable presumption that the fault, if not the sole cause, was at least a contributory cause of the disaster. In such a case the burden rests upon the ship of showing not merely that her fault might not have been one of the causes, or that it probably was not, but that it could not have been. Such a rule is necessary to enforce obedience to the mandate of the statute.

CANDIES TOWING CO., INC. v. M/V B & C ESERMAN

673 F.2d 91, 1983 AMC 2033 (5th Cir. 1982)

John R. BROWN, Circuit Judge

In this sugary sweet tale of oceangoing disaster, Candies Towing, owner of a sunken barge, and ProRico, owner of its cargo, sue the tug *M/V B&C Eserman*, and its owners, for the loss of barge and cargo. Trial before the District Court resulted in a judgment for the vessel. Ensnared in the rigging of the clearly erroneous rule, we affirm the factual findings and decree but modify in one important respect.

A. Cargo of Molasses for Neptune's Graveyard

Following in the wake of the District Court, which set forth all the important facts, we will but summarize. Candies Towing, a Louisiana corporation, owned a steel hull, oceangoing barge, OC-250. It measured 250 feet in length, 72 feet of beam, and a depth of 15 feet. Built in 1970 as a deck barge, OC-250 later was converted by its owners for use as a liquid bulk carrier. It carried an A-1 certification of the American Bureau of Shipping and satisfied Coast Guard standards for a seagoing barge. The Coast Guard, in fact, inspected the barge and gave its approval on March 24, 1977, less than nine months before it sank.

The tug *B&C Eserman* is an 80-foot, 1250 horsepower twin screw diesel tug that carries a crew of four. It routinely operated with OC-250 to carry cargoes of liquid molasses between Mobile, Alabama and West Palm Beach, Florida.

From October 15-25, 1977, the barge underwent substantial maintenance and repair work at Hunt's Shipyard in Harvey, Louisiana. Although OC-250 had not suffered any accident or casualty, Hunt's employees repaired deck cracks, separations of welds in the internal frame work, two splits in the bottom, damage to the longitudinal bulkhead, and repaired or replaced internal frames and supports. All this work concentrated on the forward section of the barge in way of the first two compartments. Following completion of the repairs and an inspection, OC-250 returned to service.

On November 27, 1977, *B&C Eserman,* while en route to Wilmington, North Carolina from West Palm Beach, grounded its laden tow, OC-250, on Frying Pan Shoal Reef. Although some question exists, it appears that the barge grounded stern-first on a hard sand reef, at a speed of 1 to 1½ miles per hour, in calm seas. At the time, OC-250 carried a cargo of molasses to a draft of 10½ feet forward and 11½ aft.

Captain Jones, at the conn, lacked a fathometer, channel charts, tide tables, light lists, or other such aids to navigation. It was his first trip to Wilmington. He had no offshore license and was not a qualified navigator. His prior experience on seagoing tugs was as a wheelman or mate, not as a captain. Nor did he have the requisite number of licensed watchstanders on board.

Approximately ten hours later, high tide freed OC-250 from its strand, and the tow proceeded into Wilmington. There Captain Leo Spooner, Candies' representative, met the vessel as usual. Spooner, already aware from radio communications that OC-250 had gone aground, checked it out. He inspected each of the tanks after unloading and found no water in any of them. Personnel from ProRico and American Molasses also inspected the barge. No one found any damage or cause for concern. Following these inspections, Captain Spooner cleared OC-250 as fit to resume travel. The tow thus returned to West Palm Beach for the next voyage.

Spooner and ProRico's representative again inspected OC-250 in West Palm Beach. After seeing its trim, freeboard and draft, Spooner found it fit. Despite deteriorating weather conditions, it set out for Mobile on December 4. After passing Dry Tortugas, the last point of land along the Florida Keys, Captain Jones noticed that the barge had sheered to the left. He had the tug circle the barge but found nothing wrong.

The weather indeed worsened. One winter storm, called a norther, hit on December 7, with seas of up to 15 feet. A second struck on December 9, with seas up to 20 feet and winds around 100 miles per hour. At dawn on December 10, Captain Jones noticed that the freeboard at the bow of the barge had increased, indicating that the stern was going down. Down, indeed, it went, in some 1300 feet of water, a total loss of both the barge and its cargo of 4248 short tons of bulk molasses.

Bittersweet Results in the District Court

The District Court made extensive findings of fact. It held that the tug did not breach a duty to Candies, Captain Jones acted reasonably in sailing for Mobile despite the bad weather, and Candies failed to show that any of the clear statutory violations with regard to crew qualifications and watchstanding at sea "were in any way connected to" the sinking of the barge. The Court specifically found that the rule of *The Pennsylvania*, 86 U.S. (19 Wall) 125, 22 L. Ed. 148 (1873) did not apply since no collision had occurred, citing *Garner v. Cities Service Tankers Corp.*, 456 F.2d 476, 1972 A.M.C. 1980 (5th Cir. 1972). It therefore granted a decree in favor of the tug *B&C Eserman*.

M/V Scope of Review

The findings of the District Judge, confronted with a mystery for which no apparent cause exists, float well above that Plimsoll Line. We affirm the findings and judgment of the District Court.

Accepting the factual findings does not yet put an end to this watery donnybrook, for we cannot anchor until we have addressed the District Court's treatment of the rule of The Pennsylvania, supra.

In simplest terms, that rule states that where a vessel is guilty of a statutory violation, the defaulting ship must show "not merely that her fault might not have been one of the causes, or that it probably was not, but that it could not have been." 86 U.S. (19 Wall) at 136, 22 L. Ed. at 151. *See also Allied Chemical, supra*, at 1052; G. Gilmore & C. Black, The Law of Admiralty (2d ed. 1975) § 10-25, at 898. It thus constitutes an evidentiary rule reversing the burden of proof. It does not render immaterial negligence, fault or damages but does impose a substantial burden upon the party at fault in proving its innocence.

The District Court simply erred as a matter of law in concluding that the rule of The Pennsylvania applies only in collision cases. The case on which the District Judge relied, *Garner, supra*, neither establishes nor supports any such holding. A hot water tank on the SS Bradford Island exploded, killing one employee and injuring two others. The vessel owners sought to apply the rule of *The Pennslyvania* to force the shipyard, which had connected its 125 pounds per square inch (PSI) saturated steam system to the vessel's 70 PSI system, to prove that its action could not have contributed to the cause of the accident. This court, per the late Judge Gewin, refused. We began by pointing out,

> Within the Fifth Circuit, the rule of *The Pennsylvania* has not been viewed as a rule of liability. The rule creates a shift in the burden of proof as to causation... . Although Cities Services cites authority in other circuits where the rule has been applied in cases not involving collisions between ships, we have found no instance where this court has done so.

456 F.2d at 480, 1972 A.M.C. at 1985 (citations omitted).

The inability to find such precedent, of course, by no means stamps such a possibility as incorrect. Indeed, our specific holding belied the District Court's broad generalization. We did not hold, nor have we ever held, that the rule of *The Pennsylvania* applies only to collision cases. Rather, we merely declined "to extend the rule of The Pennsylvania from its tort origins to the setting of contractual indemnity or breach of WWLP." *Id.* Thus, although the rule of *The Pennsylvania* rightfully has little application in a contractual indemnity action, an action far removed from its original port of call, Garner does not state and we do not interpret it to mean that in other tort actions, such as here, the rule does not apply.

The Appropriate Vantage Point

This Court recently spoke on the subject and clarified the ramifications of Garner. In *Reyes v. Vantage Steamship Co.*, 558 F.2d 238 (5th Cir. 1977), on rehearing, 609 F.2d 140 (5th Cir. 1980), we applied the rule of *The Pennsylvania* where a vessel lacked a required line-throwing device and its crew, in violation of the maritime rescue doctrine, made no effort to save a drowning sailor. The sailor, legally drunk at the time, decided to take a swim in the ocean and dived some 35 feet off the side of the vessel. He was spotted immediately by other crew members, who knew from the outset that he was in danger. Yet no one made any effort to rescue Reyes. These facts and the absence of the statutorily required line throwing device established negligence as a matter of law. Citing *In re Seaboard Shipping Corp.*, 499 F.2d 132, 136, 1971 A.M.C. 2145, 2152 (2d Cir. 1971), *cert. denied*, 406 U.S. 949, 92 S. Ct. 2038-39, 32 L. Ed. 2d 337 (1972), we explicitly held that the rule of *The Pennsylvania* extended to this man overboard situation:

> Nothing that has been said impairs the principle that ... in Jones Act cases ... cause in fact is still necessary ... Combining this slight standard of causation with the presumption of causation to which the plaintiff is here entitled means that on remand the ship owner must show that the ship's inaction and regulatory violations *could not have been* even a contributing cause of Reyes' death.

609 F.2d at 146, (emphasis added).

In *Seaboard Shipping, supra,* two crew members of a barge died during a wild storm on Lake Michigan. The Second Circuit found that the barge was unseaworthy in three respects: its radio was out of order, its lifeboat was damaged, and its inflatable liferaft was improperly stowed. Seaboard, the barge owner, argued that in all probability none of those defects caused the deaths. Yet the Court refused to exonerate Seaboard, declaring,

> We need go no further here than to say, however, that given the statutory violations alone (the liferaft stowage and the overloading), Seaboard is not entitled to exoneration. *The Pennsylvania* ... makes it clear that the burden is on a ship in violation of a safety statute—in this case the barge—to show "not merely that her fault might not have been one of the causes, or that it probably was not, but that it could not have been." Seaboard is wrong in its contention that admiralty applies their rule only in collision cases. *Kernan v. American Dredging Co.*, 355 U.S. 426 (1958) (fire on a tug caused by open-flame kerosene lamp carried on scow in statutory violation); *The Denali*, 112 F.2d 952 (9th Cir. 1940) (stranding case).

449 F.2d at 136, 1971 A.M.C. at 2152. These cases, we believe, establish beyond doubt that the rule of *The Pennsylvania* does apply in non-collision cases.

Nor does *U.S. v. Reliable Transfer Co.*, 421 U.S. 397, 95 S. Ct. 1708, 44 L. Ed. 2d 251, 1975 A.M.C. 541 (1975), in any way alter our conclusion. *Reliable Transfer*, a tidal wave case in the admiralty, overruled only the time honored policy practice of dividing damages in a case of mutual or joint fault on a 50/50 basis. It does not bring into question the rule shifting the burden of proof.

* * *

No Candy

Given our conclusion that the District Court erred in its discussion of *The Pennsylvania* rule, we necessarily must address its findings to determine whether we must remand. We conclude that we need not do so.

Two separate incidents took place: the grounding and the sinking. As to the first, we have fault but no damage; in the second, damage but no fault. While *The Pennsylvania* does impose a strenuous burden upon one guilty of statutory default, and we hesitate not a moment in declaring *B&C Eserman* negligent as to the grounding of the barge, it does not delete the requirement of causation with respect to the loss of the barge many days later under severe conditions of wave and weather. The District Court concluded, and we cannot disagree, that whatever *B&C Eserman's* statutory violations, whatever its negligence insofar as the grounding is concerned, neither had anything to do with the sinking. "Plaintiffs failed to show that any of the factors above, either individually or collectively, were in any way connected to the sinking of the barge." (emphasis supplied) *B&C Eserman* introduced testimony that the barge suffered from a weak internal framework. Such a weakness could cause the barge to "work", causing metal fatigue and, ultimately, breaking the internal structure. The extensive repair work done on OC-250, according to expert testimony, established such a weakness. The District Judge apparently credited this testimony and believed it furnished a more logical explanation for the sinking then the grounding two weeks previously. Thus, even if the District Court had correctly interpreted the rule of *The Pennsylvania*, it still would have granted judgment for the tug since neither the negligent grounding some two weeks before nor the statutory violations on the trip to Mobile could have caused the sinking.

The Court of Appeals, no less than Coke, does not require the performance of a useless act. We therefore modify the opinion of the District Court as regards the rule of The Pennsylvania and, as modified, affirm.

AFFIRMED AS MODIFIED.

Notes

1. It is possible for both vessels involved in a collision to be found to be at fault by application of the *Pennsylvania* rule. In *Otto Candies, Inc. v. M/V Madeline D*, 721 F.2d 1034, 1987 AMC 911 (5th Cir. 1983), the court rejected an argument that a party at fault under the *Pennsylvania* presumption was estopped from arguing that the other vessel involved in the collision was also at fault under the *Pennsylvania* presumption. The court said:

> Here, the district court was unable to determine the cause of the *Ferdie Candies'* collision and, for whatever reason, made no credibility determination as between the opposing contentions as to whether steering negligence by an unlicensed deckhand on the part of either one vessel or the other factually caused the accident. In that posture of the case, the invoked *Pennsylvania* rule required the district court to find that the statutory fault of both vessels contributed to the accident, unless it found that the fault of either (or of both, for that matter) could not have been a cause of the collision. The district court was in error of law in holding that one party or the other, because of mutual fault, was estopped from invoking the *Pennsylvania* rule, which is a rule of presumed causation not of clean hands-dirty hands moral blameworthiness.

Otto Candies, Inc. v. M/V Madeline D, 721 F.2d 1034, 1036 (5th Cir. 1983).

2. *The 1910 Brussels Collision Convention*

As stated in *Reliable Transfer*, the basic international law concerning collision is embodied in the 1910 Brussels Collision Convention. The basis for liability is fault, and the proportional fault rule applies (Arts. 3-4). The United States is one of the few nations of the world that has not adhered to this convention. Despite the adoption of the proportional fault rule in *Reliable Transfer*, important differences still exist between U.S. and the international law relating to collisions, as will be made clear below.

In *Otal Investments, Ltd. v. M/V Clary*, 494 F.3d 30, 2007 AMC 1817 (2d Cir. 2007), the Second Circuit applied the 1910 Collision Convention to a collision in international waters between vessels flying flags of signatory states. The Court also held that the *Pennsylvania* rule is substantive, not procedural, and therefore should not be applied to a collision governed by the Convention, which abolishes all presumptions of causative fault.

3. *The Rules of the Road*

The Basic Collision Regulations or International Rules were developed by the Intergovernmental Maritime Commission (IMCO) and agreed upon in the 1972 Convention on the International Regulations for Preventing Collisions at Sea, done at London in 1972. In 1977, these rules were adopted by statute in the United States. 33

U.S.C. §§ 1601-1608. In the internal waters of the United States the Inland Navigational Rules, 33 U.S.C. §§ 2001-2073, apply.

For an application of these rules in a recent case, *see Capt'n Mark v. Sea Fever Corp.*, 692 F.2d 163, 1983 AMC 2651 (1st Cir. 1982). *See also Partenreederei M.S. Bernd Leonhardt v. U.S.*, 393 F.2d 756, 1968 AMC 910 (4th Cir. 1968).

4. *The Wreck Act*

This statute, 33 U.S.C. §§ 409, 411, requires the owner of a vessel sunk "accidentally or otherwise" to visibly mark it and to remove it. The United States Supreme Court has held that this statute is not exclusive, and that under principles of tort liability a negligent non-owner may be liable for the costs of removal or may be required by the United States through injunctive relief to remove the vessel. *Wyandotte Transportation Co. v. United States*, 389 U.S. 191, 88 S. Ct. 379, 19 L. Ed. 2d 407 (1967).

Can the owner or negligent non-owner be liable from a post-sinking collision with an unmarked wreck? *See Nunley v. M/V Dauntless Colocotronis*, 696 F.2d 1141 (5th Cir. 1983) and *Ison v. Roof*, 698 F.2d 294 (6th Cir.), *cert. denied sub nom. Great Southwest Fire Ins. Co. v. Iron*, 461 U.S. 957, 103 S. Ct. 2429, 77 L. Ed. 2d 1316 (1983).

B. Damages

Note: Total and Partial Losses

When the vessel involved in a collision or accident is a total loss, the damages include (1) the market value of the vessel at the time of the loss (plus pending freight) and (2) pollution cleanup, salvage, wreck removal, and other incidental costs proximately resulting from the casualty. For problems of valuation of the vessel, *see Oliver J. Olson & Co. v. American Steamship Marine Leopard*, 356 F.2d 728, 1966 AMC 1064 (9th Cir. 1966). Loss of earnings and detention are not recoverable. *See The Umbria*, 166 U.S. 404, 17 S. Ct. 610, 41 L. Ed. 1053 (1897).

In a case of damage other than total loss, damages include (1) the cost of repairs (or diminution of value if no repairs are made), (2) detention, *i.e.* loss of earnings for the period the vessel is out of service, and (3) incidental costs such as wharfage, pilotage, and salvage costs. *See Skou v. United States*, 478 F.2d 343, 1973 AMC 1482 (5th Cir. 1973). In a repair—loss of use case, suppose the vessel owner uses the occasion to advance the regularly scheduled drydocking of the vessel? *See Bouchard Transp. Co., Inc. v. The Tug Ocean Prince*, 691 F.2d 609, 1982 AMC 2944 (2d Cir. 1982).

More difficult issues of damage recovery are raised in the following cases.

---

1. Economic Loss

VENORE TRANSPORTATION CO. v. M/V STRUMA

583 F.2d 708, 1978 AMC 2146 (4th Cir. 1978)

HAYNSWORTH, Chief Judge

Venore Transportation Company, time charterer of the 55,000 ton *S.S. Oswego Liberty*, sought damages from the 60,000 ton *M/V Struma* and her owner, Bulk Transport Corporation, for loss of use of the *Oswego Liberty* after the two vessels had been in a collision. The district court entered summary judgment for the defendants, reasoning that the claim was foreclosed by the Supreme Court's decision in *Robins Dry Dock and Repair Co. v. Flint*, 275

U.S. 279. Because there was no suspension in the payment of charter hire while the *Oswego Liberty* was being repaired, we conclude that Robins is inapplicable and that recovery of charter hire should be allowed.

In January 1972 the Oswego Shipping Corporation let the *Oswego Liberty* to Venore Transportation Company for a term of thirteen and a half years. The time charter party fixed the charter hire at monthly rates of more than $90,000.

* * *

On November 27, 1974 the *Oswego Liberty* and the *Struma* were in a collision, and the *Oswego Liberty* was withdrawn from service and laid up for repairs until January 17, 1975. During the time she was under repair, escalated charter hire of $225,380.64 accrued, which Venore has paid to the owner.

For the purpose of these proceedings, the *Struma* has conceded her fault, and the owner's claim against her has been settled. The owner's claim, however, consisted entirely of the expenses to which it was put to repair the physical damage sustained by the *Oswego Liberty.* It claimed nothing for its loss of use of the vessel. Indeed, it could not have made such a claim, for it had received the full charter hire for the period during which the vessel was under repair.

Robins Dry Dock was not a case arising out of a collision. The charter party there required that the vessel be dry docked periodically. While in dry dock, her propeller was negligently damaged and had to be replaced. That enlarged the time during which the vessel was out of service, and it was for the loss of use of the vessel during that period that the time charterer claimed. The Supreme Court reasoned that the dry dock's duty arose out of its contract with the owner, and that it had no such contractual duty to the time charterer. Since there had been no demise of the vessel, it was technically in the possession of the owner, and the time charterer had no property interest in it. Thus there was applicable the principle that one who unintentionally but negligently damages the property of another is not liable to others who may suffer economic loss because the owner is unable to perform contractual commitments to those others.

It is essentially a principle of disallowance of damages because of remoteness, and because of the concern that the number and the amount of potential claims in a given instance may be staggering. The time charterer in *Robins Dry Dock* had not paid charter hire for the period during which the vessel was out of service. The claim was essentially one for loss of anticipated profits.

The principle has found expression in a variety of cases since *Robins Dry Dock.*

* * *

The principle of *Robins Dry Dock* is perfectly defensible, if pragmatic considerations require the foreclosure of remote damage claims. The tort feasor, having paid the owner for its loss of use of the vessel, should not be required to pay additionally for the time charterer's loss of anticipated profits. A pragmatic approach would require that the offending vessel pay for loss of use of the damaged vessel once, but no more. Unless the offending vessel is required to pay for the loss of use of the *Oswego Liberty* in this case, however, it would never be required to pay at all. The owner lost no charter hire. It could not claim a loss it had not suffered, and it did not do so. But payment for loss of use of the damaged vessel is a conventional item of recovery, and the fact that the charter party has transferred the risk of loss of use from the owner to the time charterer should not extinguish the right to a recovery of a traditional item of damages. There is nothing remote about these damages; the only objection is that they were suffered by the time charterer rather than by the owner.

* * *

We do not intend, however, to suggest that the time charterer is entitled to lost profits. That kind of claim is foreclosed by *Robins Dry Dock*. The traditional item of recoverable damage is the owner's claim for loss of use. When the vessel is under a time charter, the starting point for the measurement of those damages is lost charter hire. Our only holding is that when there has been no suspension in the payment of charter hire during the period when the vessel is out of service, the time charterer who has paid the charter hire is entitled to recover what the owner would have been entitled to recover had those payments been suspended.

In *Robins Dry Dock*, Mr. Justice Holmes wrote broadly, as he customarily did, but there is no inconsistency in our holding and that of the Supreme Court in *Robins Dry Dock*. Nor do we enlarge in any way the types of damages which have been traditionally recoverable, nor the offending vessel's obligation of recompense. Under our holding, the STRUMA and her owner will pay no more than they would have if the charter had provided for a suspension of charter hire while the vessel was laid up.

Thus we conclude that either the owner or the time charterer, but not both, may claim damages for loss of use depending upon the charter's placement of the risk of loss of use.

Reversed and remanded.

WINTER, Circuit Judge, dissenting

... Recovery in *Robins Dry Dock* was denied, not on the ground that the damages were too remote, but on the ground that a time charterer has no standing or property interest to recover from an unintentional wrongdoer.... *Robins Dry Dock* thus establishes a rule of liability, not of damages, as the majority would read it.

The majority also justifies the result it reaches on the pragmatic ground that the tortfeasor, the offending vessel, should pay for loss of use of the damaged vessel once, but no more, and that where the owner suffers no loss of use because the time charterer, by the terms of the time charter, has not been excused from paying hire, the time charterer should be permitted to recover its direct loss, i.e. the hire it must pay, but not its loss of profits. This very argument was rejected in *Robins Dry Dock*... .

* * *

Notes

1. The *Robins Dry Dock* rule was applied by an *en banc* Fifth Circuit in *State of Louisiana, Ex Rel. Guste v. M/V Testbank*, 752 F.2d 1019, 1985 AMC 1521 (5th Cir. 1985). A collision between the *Sea Daniel* and the *Testbank* in the

Mississippi River Gulf Outlet (MR-GO) caused a spill of pentachlorophenol, PCP, into the water. Because of the highly toxic nature of PCP, the U.S. Coast Guard closed the outlet for three weeks, temporarily suspending all fishing, shrimping, and related activity in the outlet and four hundred square miles of surrounding marsh and waterways. Forty-one lawsuits were filed, presenting claims of shipping interests, marina and boat rental operators, wholesale and retail seafood enterprises not actually engaged in fishing, seafood restaurants, tackle and bait shops, and recreational fishermen. A majority of the court held that all claims but those of the commercial fishermen failed because of the *Robins Dry Dock* rule, as none of the plaintiffs had suffered physical damage to their property. In a famous dissent, Judge Wisdom argued that the *Robins Dry Dock* rule should be abandoned in favor of a rule modeled on the "special damage" requirement in public nuisance cases. Both the dissenting opinion and the concurring opinions pointed out the inconsistency in allowing recovery by commercial fishermen, who had not suffered damage to property.

2. *Lessees and "Proprietary Interest"*

An interesting application of the *Robins Drydock* doctrine was presented when the M/V Bright Field allided with the Riverwalk Shopping Center causing extensive physical damage to the structure of the center and to many shops. Lessees of various shops brought suit to recover not only for physical damages to their stock and equipment but for loss of business during the period the stores were closed for repairs. Does their status as "lessees" satisfy the *Robins Drydock* "proprietary interest" test? *Complaint of Clearsky Shipping Corp.*, 1998 WL 770498, 1999 AMC 531 (E.D. La. 1998).

---

2. *Total Loss*

Note

In *A & S Transportation Co. v. The Tug Fajardo*, 688 F.2d 1, 1983 AMC 10 (5th Cir. 1982), PCI International, Inc., a bareboat charterer, sued Puerto Rico Lighterage Co., the owner of a tug (the "Fajardo"), for consequential damages incurred when their barge become stranded due to the negligence of the tug. As a result of the stranding, the barge was deemed a constructive total loss.

PCI asserted that it was due consequential damages based on "the uniqueness of the barge and alleged expenses incurred in procuring a substitute." The Fifth Circuit affirmed the holding of the district court, which denied such damages. The court of appeals, reaffirming the traditional rule first found in *The Umbria*, 166 U.S. 404, 17 S. Ct. 610, 41 L. Ed. 1053 (1897), found that "[w]here a vessel is totally lost, the measure of damages is its value at the time of loss." 688 F.2d at 2. The court refused to create an exception to this rule for bareboat charterers calling such an idea "illogical" and concluding: "The liability of those responsible for the loss should not depend on whether the injured party is an owner or a bareboat charterer." 688 F.2d at 3.

---

3. *Cargo Losses*

UNITED STATES v. ATLANTIC MUTUAL INSURANCE CO.

343 U.S. 236, 72 S. Ct. 666, 96 L. Ed. 907, 1952 AMC 659 (1952)

Mr. Justice BLACK delivered the opinion of the Court

Respondents are cargo owners who shipped goods on the steamship *Nathaniel Bacon* owned by petitioner, the United States, and operated as a common carrier of goods for hire. It collided with the *Esso Belgium* and respondents' cargo was damaged. The ships were also damaged. This litigation was brought in the District Court to determine liability for the damages suffered by the cargo owners and for the physical damage caused the ships. It was agreed in the District Court that:

(a) The collision was due to negligent navigation by employees of both ships. The cargo owners were in no way at fault.
(b) *The Belgium*, as one of two joint tortfeasors, must pay "100%" of damages suffered by the Bacon's cargo owners.
(c) Because of § 3 of the Harter Act and § 4(2) of the Carriage of Goods by Sea Act, the cargo owners are barred from directly suing the Bacon for cargo damages.
(d) Since the two ships were mutually at fault, the aggregate of all damages to both should be shared by both.
(e) In computing the aggregate damages caused both ships, account should be taken of the cargo damages recovered from the *Belgium* by the cargo owners.
(f) The bill of lading issued by the Bacon to the cargo owners contained a "Both-to-Blame" clause.[5] This clause, if valid, requires the cargo owners to indemnify the carrier Bacon for any amounts the Bacon loses because damages recovered by the cargo owners from the *Belgium* are included in the aggregate damages divided between the two ships.

The only question presented to us is whether the "Both-to-Blame" clause is valid. Respondent cargo owners contend that it is void and unenforceable as a violation of the long-standing rule of law which forbids common carriers from stipulating against the consequences of their own or their employees' negligence. Petitioner, the United States, contends that § 3 of the Harter Act, as substantially reenacted in § 4(2) of the Carriage of Goods by Sea Act, provides special statutory authorization permitting ocean carriers to deviate from the general rule and to stipulate against their negligence as they did here. The District Court held the clause valid. 90 F. Supp. 836. The Court of Appeals reversed. 191 F.2d 370. Deeming the question decided of sufficient importance to justify our review, this Court granted certiorari.

There is a general rule of law that common carriers cannot stipulate for immunity from their own or their agents' negligence. While this general rule was fashioned by the courts, it has been continuously accepted as a guide to common-carrier relationships for more than a century and has acquired the force and precision of a legislative enactment. Considering the relationship of the rule to the Harter Act, this Court said in 1901 that "in view of the well-settled nature of the general rule at the time the statute was adopted, it must result that legislative approval was by clear implication

---

[5] The clause reads as follows:

> If the ship comes into collision with another ship as a result of the negligence of the other ship and any act, neglect or default of the Master, mariner, pilot or the servants of the Carrier in the navigation or in the management of the ship, the owners of the goods carried hereunder will indemnify the Carrier against all loss or liability to the other or non-carrying ship or her owners in so far as such loss or liability represents loss of, or damage to, or any claim whatsoever of the owners of said goods, paid or payable by the other or non-carrying ship or her owners to the owners of said goods and set-off, recouped or recovered by the other or non-carrying ship or her owners as part of their claim against the carrying ship or Carrier.

given to the general rule as then existing in all cases where it was not changed." *The Kensington*, 183 U.S. 263, 268-269. Our question therefore is whether the language of the Harter Act, substantially reenacted in the Carriage of Goods by Sea Act, has carved out a special statutory exception to the general rule so as to permit a carrier to deprive its cargo owners of a part of the fruits of any judgment they obtain in a direct action against a noncarrying vessel that contributes to a collision.

Prior to the passage of the Harter Act in 1893, cargo damages incurred in a both-to-blame collision could be recovered in full from either ship. *The Atlas*, 93 U.S. 302. The Harter Act, under some circumstances, took away the right of the cargo owner to sue his own carrier for cargo damages caused by the negligent navigation of the carrier's servants or agents. It did not deprive the cargo owner of his tort action against the noncarrying ship. *The Chattahoochee*, 173 U.S. 540, 549-550. Nor did the Harter Act go so far as to insulate the carrier from responsibility to another vessel for physical damages caused to the ship by negligent navigation of the carrier's servants or agents. In *The Delaware*, 161 U.S. 459, 471, 474, this Court declined to give the Harter Act such a broad interpretation even though the language itself, if "broadly construed" and considered alone, would have justified such an interpretation. In addition, the Harter Act does not exonerate the carrier from its obligation to share with the noncarrier one-half the damages paid by the noncarrier to the cargo owners... .

Apparently it was not until about forty years after the passage of the Harter Act that shipowners first attempted by stipulation to deprive cargo owners of a part of their recovery against noncarrying ships.... The present effort of shipowners appears to date from 1937 when the North Atlantic Freight Conference adopted the "Both-to-Blame" clause. So far as appears, this is the first test of the legality of the clause that has appeared in the courts. When Congress passed the Carriage of Goods by Sea Act in 1936, it indicated no purpose to bring about a change in the long-existing relationships and obligations between carriers and shippers which would be relevant to the validity of the "Both-to-Blame" clause.

Petitioner argues that the clause does nothing more than remove an "anomaly" which arises from this Court's construction of the Harter Act. It is said to be "anomalous" to hold a carrier not liable at all if it alone is guilty of negligent navigation but at the same time to hold it indirectly liable for one-half the cargo damages if another ship is jointly negligent with it. Assuming for the moment that all rules of law must be symmetrical, we think it would be "anomalous" to hold that a cargo owner, who has an unquestioned right under the law to recover full damages from a noncarrying vessel, can be compelled to give up a portion of that recovery to his carrier because of a stipulation exacted in a bill of lading. Moreover, there is no indication that either the Harter Act or the Carriage of Goods by Sea Act was designed to alter the long-established rule that the full burden of the losses sustained by both ships in a both-to-blame collision is to be shared equally.

Note

In *Amoco Transport Co. v. S/S. Mason Lykes*, 768 F.2d 659, 1986 AMC 563 (5th Cir. 1985), the MASON LYKES collided with the AMOCO CREMORA in a dense fog. The MASON LYKES was found to be 90% at fault and the AMOCO CREMORA 10%. The main issue in this case was whether the owners of cargo carried on the MASON LYKES could recover damages from AMOCO CREMORA.

The court of appeals rejected the district court's holding that cargo interests could not recover freight damages from the owners of the AMOCO CREMORA. Instead the court likened this case to the issue found in *Aktieselskabet Cuzco v. The Sucarseco ("The Toluma")*, 294 U.S. 394, 55 S. Ct. 467, 79 L. Ed. 942 (1935). In that case the court held that cargo owners could recover expenses paid for unloading, reloading and storage paid as a result of the vessel's owner's partial fault in a collision which placed the vessel in drydock for repairs. The *Toluma* decision was distinguished from that in *Robins Dry Dock & Repair Co. v. Flint* which stated that "a tort to the person or property of one man does not make the tort-feasor liable to another merely because the injured person was under a contract with that other, unknown to the doer of the wrong." 275 U.S. 303, 309, 48 S. Ct. 134, 72 L. Ed. 290 (1927). The *Amoco Transp.* court reasoned that recovery was warranted given "the common adventure nature of the relationship between the vessel owner and the cargo interests." 768 F.2d at 666. The court was influenced by the fact that "the expenses in question were expenses arising directly from the collision, expenses for which the negligent non-carrying vessel would have been liable even in the absence of a general average right by the vessel owners against the cargo interests." *Id.*

The court in the present case found the bills of lading from the voyage of the MASON LYKES to be a "common adventure between the vessel and cargo interests similar to the participants in the voyage of the *Toluma*." *Id.* at 667. Furthermore, as in *Toluma*, the bill of lading between cargo interests and the MASON LYKES contained a freight earned clause. The non-carrying vessel, however, would have been liable for the damages arising from the collision even in the absence of a freight earned clause. Therefore, the court concluded that "[t]he cargo interests are entitled to recover their damages from either Lykes or Amoco, for they have a valid cause of action against both." *Id.* at 669

In allowing the cargo's claim for damages against Amoco, the court denied that such a remedy would allow for "runaway recovery" by the cargo interests. Instead they found that "[t]he claim against Amoco by the cargo owners is in the nature of an equitable subrogation of Lykes' rights. So viewed, there would be no double recovery, much less runaway recovery." *Id.* at 668.

ALLIED CHEMICAL CORP. v. HESS TANKSHIP CO. OF DEL.

661 F.2d 1044, 1982 AMC 1271 (5th Cir. 1981)

John R. BROWN, Circuit Judge

It was a dark and stormy night. A patchy, low-lying fog covered the murky waters of the river and obscured the banks. Ships, passing in the night, were but phantoms, vague outlines disappearing into the mist. Ships' whistles, echoing across the dark expanse, seemed like mournful cries from another world. Then suddenly, looming out of the darkness, another ship appeared. The distance was too small; time too short; before anyone could do more than cry out, the unthinkable occurred. The ships collided. The tug, helpless, drifted downriver. Floundering like some giant behemoth wounded in battle, the tanker came to ground and impaled itself on some voracious underwater obstruction. And still the whistles, echoing, seemed like cries from another world.

This apparent screenplay for a Grade B film, in fact, came to Southwest Pass of the Mississippi River, about 3 miles below Head of Passes, in Louisiana, on February 1, 1973. The cast of characters included the *S.S. Hess Refiner (Refiner)*, a jumboized T-2 tanker approximately 605 feet in length and 75 feet in beam and drawing, that fateful night, 32 feet, 1 inch forward and 34 feet, 7 inches aft; the *Socrates*, a 125-foot seagoing tug drawing 14 feet, equipped with twin pilot-house-controlled engines boasting 3200 h.p.; and its tow, the barge *Allied Chemical No. 44 (AC-44)*, which measured some 340 feet in length, 68 feet in beam, drawing approximately 17 feet forward and 18 feet aft. *Refiner* is owned by Hess Tankship Company and was bareboat chartered to Amerada Hess Corporation (collectively Hess). SOCRATES is owned by Allied Towing Corporation (Allied Towing). AC-44 belongs to Allied Chemical Corporation (Allied Chemical), which, despite the apparent filial connection, bears no relation to Allied Towing.

* * *

The District Court found the parties equally to blame and allocated fault accordingly in conformity with *Reliable Transfer*.... The equal 50/50 allocation of fault finds ample support in the facts and the record, and we affirm.

Allied Towing labels as error the District Court's holding that Allied Chemical may recover its full damages from Hess. The reason for this counter-intuitive strategy is that, under long-standing admiralty practice, this loss goes into Hess' damage claim which, on striking the balance, means that Hess will be entitled to recover 50% of such amount against Allied Towing. *The Chattahoochee*, 173 U.S. 540, 19 S. Ct. 491, 43 L. Ed. 801 (1899); *The New York*, 175 U.S. 187 (1899); *Griffin on Collision* §§ 245, 246.

Allied Towing informs us that *Alamo Chemical Transportation Co. v. M/V Overseas Valdes*, 469 F.Supp. 203 (E.D. La.1979), interpreting the *Reliable Transfer* mandate, supplants that traditional rule. We disagree....

In arriving at that decision, the *Overseas Valdes* Court explicitly rejected prior contrary holdings. In *Complaint of Flota Mercante Grancolombiana, S.A.*, 440 F. Supp. 704, 725 (S.D.N.Y.1977), the Court, taking due notice of *Reliable Transfer*, stated:

> This Court believes that the better rule would be to allow ... a full recovery against the non-carrying vessel, allow the latter to add the payments it makes to cargo to its own damages, and then to permit it to recover this total from the carrying vessel in proportion to the fault of the carrying vessel. This resolution would be more in accord with the principles enunciated in *Reliable Transfer* [which] was intended to change the rule of damages so that the burden would fall more equitably on those parties whose fault contributed to the collision.

We believe that *Flota Mercante* more nearly charts a Reliable course. The Supreme Court acted to abolish the doctrine of mutual fault-equal contribution, an anachronism which every other maritime nation had already rejected. The decision only alters the proportions in which damages are fixed—it does not abolish the procedure by which an innocent cargo owner traditionally could recover his damages in full from the tortious non-carrying vessel no matter what the degree of fault between the tortious actors.[24]

The Supreme Court provides support for our view in *Edmonds v. Compagnie Generale Transatlantique*, 443 U.S. 256, (1979).... *Citing Reliable Transfer*, the Court observed "*Reliable Transfer* merely changed the apportionment from equal division to division on the basis of relative fault. But we did not upset the rule that the plaintiff may recover from one of the colliding vessels the damage concurrently caused by the negligence of both." 443 U.S. at 272 (n.30).

Overseas Valdes, decided before Edmonds, involved a Both-to-Blame clause that recovery under the traditional rule would sidestep. The Court, by confining Firestone to its percentage recovery against Maritime, did an end-run around the problem. In so doing, it created a greater problem.

The Court's decision in *Overseas Valdes* leaves the innocent cargo, "the one party both aggrieved and free to do something about it," *O/Y Finlayson-Forssa v. Pan Atlantic Steamship Co.*, 259 F.2d 11, 13 (5th Cir. 1958), *cert. denied*, 361 U.S. 882, (1959), in the lurch. Where a cargo suffers damages from a collision where both vessels were negligent, it is the only innocent party. *Reliable Transfer* certainly did not intend to shift the risk of loss away from the negligent parties. Yet *Overseas Valdes* does precisely that.

We reject Allied Towing's argument and the decision in *Overseas Valdes* to the extent it is inconsistent with out holding.[25] We therefore affirm the District Court's grant of full recovery against Hess, which automatically goes into its damages for ultimate division.

Notes

1. ***Damages Recoverable by Owners of Cargo***

Under Article 4 of the Collision Convention of 1910, cargo can only recover from the noncarrying vessel to the extent of that vessel's degree of fault. Compare this to the American rule in the foregoing cases. Is there a good argument that *Reliable Transfer* should be interpreted to overrule the American rule?

2. ***Damages Recoverable by Personal Injury and Death Claimants***

Personal injury and death claimants recover the full amount of their damages except where limitation of liability applies. In a both-to-blame collision each vessel is jointly and severally liable, and the amounts paid are included as collision damages. The matter of personal injury and death is covered extensively in Chapter 3, *supra.*

3. ***Prejudgment Interest***

This item is often an important aspect of a damage award in marine casualty cases. The law concerning when prejudgment interest will be given was set out by the court in *Alkmeon Naviera, S.A. v. M/V "Marina L,"* 633 F.2d 789, 793-94, 1982 AMC 153 (9th Cir. 1980):

---

[24] *See also Gulfcoast Transit v. ANCO PRINCESS*, 1978 A.M.C. 2471 (E.D.La. 1977), citing *Oriental Hero-Caster*, 1976 A.M.C. 1287, 1306 (S.D.N.Y. 1976) ("*The Reliable Transfer* decision has no application to an action between innocent cargo and one of the vessels in a collision."); *Florida East Coast Railway, supra*; *Samuels v. Empresa Lineas Maritimas Argentinas*, 573 F.2d 884, 887-888 (5th Cir. 1978), *cert. denied*, 443 U.S. 915, 99 S. Ct. 3106, 61 L. Ed. 2d 878 (1979).

[25] In proceedings fixing damages and striking the balance, Allied Towing, of course, may urge all contractual exemptions and limitations from liability to cargo.

While the award of prejudgment interest is in the discretion of the trial judge, this discretion must be "exercised with a view to the right to interest unless the circumstances are exceptional." [*The President Madison*, 91 F.2d 845,] 847. The rationale for restricting discretion to exceptional cases is that, in admiralty collisions, prejudgment interest is an element of compensation and not a penalty. *Federal Barge Lines, Inc. v. Republic Marine, Inc.*, 616 F.2d 372, 373 (8th Cir. 1980); *Rosa v. Insurance Co. of Pa.*, 421 F.2d 390, 393 (9th Cir. 1970). As such, it is usually denied only when a party "deprive[s] himself of interest." *The President Madison*, 91 F.2d at 847. Unwarranted delay by counsel is the most common ground for denial, *American Zinc Co. v. Foster*, 441 F.2d 1100, 1101 (5th Cir.), *cert. denied*, 404 U.S. 855 (1971); *The President Madison*, 91 F.2d at 847, but other cases arise. This circuit, for example, has denied prejudgment interest where there was less than actual loss and no proof of of deprivation of use, *Firemen's Fund Ins. Co., v. Standard Oil Co. of Cal.*, 339 F.2d 148, 159 (9th Cir. 1964); where the parties have excluded prejudgment interest in their stipulation of damages, *Grace Line, Inc. v. Todd Shipyards Corp.*, 500 F.2d 361, 366 (9th Cir. 1974); or where the parties assert claims or defenses in bad faith, *Darling v. Scheimer*, 444 F.2d 514, 515 (9th Cir. 1971). Other circuits have considered uncertainty regarding claims or damages as "peculiar circumstances." *Sinclair Refining Co. v. S/S Green Island*, 426 F.2d 260, 262 (5th Cir. 1970). *Contra: Ore Carriers of Liberia, Inc. v. Navigen Co.*, 305 F. Supp. 895, 897 (S.D.N.Y. 1969), *aff'd*, 435 F.2d 549, 551 (2d Cir. 1970).

In *City of Milwaukee v. Cement Div., Nat. Gypsum Co.*, 515 U.S. 189, 115 S. Ct. 2091, 132 L. Ed. 2d 148, 1995 AMC 1882 (1995), the Court confirmed that the general rule is that prejudgment interest should be awarded in maritime collision cases, subject to a limited exception for "peculiar" or "exceptional" circumstances.

Problem

Suppose two vessels, the Ajax and Bjax, are involved in a collision and it is determined that the Ajax is 20% at fault while the Bjax is 80% at fault. The following damages are proved:

Vessel Ajax		
1.	Cost of repairs and incidentals	$ 600,000
2.	Loss profits based on the charter rate	50,000
3.	Damage paid to injured seaman	50,000
	Total	**$ 700,000**
Vessel Bjax		
1.	Market value of vessel (total loss)	$ 950,000
2.	Wreck removal	50,000
	Total	**$ 1,000,000**

How would damages be allocated if it were determined that cargo aboard the Bjax was also a total loss valued at $300,000?

Chapter 8

MARITIME LIENS

A. The Nature of Maritime Liens

Note: Definition and Enforcement of Maritime Liens

A maritime lien is a secured right peculiar to maritime law. A lien is a charge on property for the payment of a debt, and a maritime lien is a special property right in a vessel given to a creditor by law as security for a debt or claim arising from some service rendered to the ship to facilitate her use in navigation or from an injury caused by the vessel in navigable waters.

Most maritime claims deriving form tort, contract, or from a peculiarly maritime operation, such as salvage, give rise to maritime liens. Exceptions may be established by precedents or by statute. For example, a seaman's claim for personal injuries under the Jones Act is not supported by a lien. *Plamals v. The Pinar Del Rio*, 277 U.S. 151, 48 S. Ct. 457, 72 L. Ed. 827, 1928 AMC 932 (1928). Historically, the premiums that are due under a contract of marine insurance were not supported by a lien. *In re Insurance Co. of Pennsylvania*, 22 F. 109 (N.D.N.Y. 1884), *aff'd*, 24 F. 559 (C.N.D.N.Y. 1885). However, in *Equilease Corp. v. M/V Sampson*, 793 F.2d 598, 1986 AMC 1826 (5th Cir.) (*en banc*), *cert. denied sub nom. Fred S. James & Co. of Texas, Inc. v. Equilease Corp.*, 479 U.S. 984, 107 S. Ct. 570, 93 L. Ed. 2d 575, 1987 AMC 2406 (1986), the Fifth Circuit held that unpaid insurance premiums did give rise to a maritime lien.

Other maritime claims that give rise to maritime liens include the following: seamen's claims for wages; salvage; claims under the general law of maritime tort; general average; the preferred ship mortgage; supplies, repairs, and other necessaries; towage, wharfage, pilotage, stevedoring; cargo damage caused by the fault of the carrier; ships claims for unpaid freight; and breach of charter parties. A maritime claim may be enforced by an action *in personam* in a federal district court or in a state court under the "saving to suitors" clause. Such an action presupposes that the court has subject-matter jurisdiction and that the defendant is properly before the court. A judgment in an *in personam* action may be enforced by the seizure and sale of the entire property of the judgment—debtor; his liability is unlimited unless jurisdiction was based on an attachment of defendant's property and the defendant made a limited appearance. In such a case, the judgment may be enforced only against the property that was attached.

Most maritime claims also may be enforced by an action *in rem*. Such an action must be brought in a federal district court in admiralty; state courts do not have concurrent jurisdiction under the "saving to suitors" clause. An *in rem* action presupposes the presence of the *res* before the court, and a judgment ordinarily may be enforced only against the *res*. Under the circumstances, the liability of the defendant is limited to the value of the *res*.

An action *in rem* is available for the enforcement of a *maritime lien*. All maritime liens may be "executed", that is, foreclosed, by an action *in rem*. A person entitled to a maritime lien is not necessarily limited to an action *in rem*; he may also have an action *in personam*. In such a case, he may proceed both *in rem* and *in personam* if the prerequisites for each action are met. Exceptionally, however, a maritime claim may be enforceable only by an action *in personam* or only by an action *in rem*.

An *in rem* action is theoretically addressed against the *res*, which in the framework of maritime law may be a vessel, its cargo, or earned freight. In this way, the *res* is personified. This fiction pervades nineteenth-century American jurisprudence, but its applications are questionable in modern law. *See Continental Grain Co. v. Barge FBL*-585, 364 U.S. 19, 80 S. Ct. 1470, 4 L. Ed. 2d 1540, 1961 AMC 1 (1960).

The question has arisen whether new forms of maritime liens may be created. Despite its decision in *Equilease*, *supra*, the Fifth Circuit has declared:

> But admiralty law has long ceased to create new liens. The only liens recognized today are those created by statute and those historically recognized by maritime law. There are no liens by analogy, and "maritime liens ... cannot be conferred on the theory of unjust enrichment or subrogation." This principle is summed up in the dictum that the maritime lien is "*stricti juris* and will not be extended by construction, analogy or inference."

In re Admiralty Lines, Ltd., 280 F. Supp. 601, 604-605 (E.D. La. 1968), *aff'd*, 410 F.2d 398 (5th Cir. 1969).

See also Nadle v. M/V Tequila, 1973 AMC 909 (S.D.N.Y. 1973); *Kane v. Motor Vessel Leda*, 355 F. Supp. 796, 1972 AMC 2094, 1973 AMC 2296 (E.D. La. 1972), *aff'd*, 491 F.2d 899, 1974 AMC 425 (5th Cir. 1974). In *Kane* the court declared:

> Admiralty will entertain a claim for unjust enrichment, or as it is sometimes called, quasi-contract ... . This claim does not however give rise to a lien. It is purely *in personam*.

---

1. The Law of Maritime Liens: Nineteenth Century Jurisprudence

THE BRIG NESTOR

18 F. Cas. 9 (Cir. Ct. D. Maine, 1831)

STORY, J

* * *

Now a lien by the maritime law is not strictly a Roman hypothecation, though it resembles it, and is often called a tacit hypothecation. It also somewhat resembles what is called a privilege in that law, that is, a right of priority of satisfaction out of the proceeds of the thing in a concurrence of creditors. Emerigon says, that this privilege was strictly personal, and gave only a preference upon simple contract creditors, and had no effect against those, who were secured by express hypothecations; and that this personal privilege given by the Roman law is unknown in the French jurisprudence; for by the law of France every privilege carries with it a tacit and privileged hypothecation, at least as to the thing which is the subject of it.

* * *

> Lord Tenterden has remarked, that a contract of hypothecation made by the master does not transfer the property of the ship; but only gives the creditor a privilege or claim upon it, to be carried into effect by legal process. And this is equally true, whether the hypothecation be express or tacit.

THE BOLD BUCCLEUGH

13 Eng. Rep. 884 [7 Moo. P.C. 267] (1851)

A maritime lien does not include or require possession. The word is used in Maritime Law not in the strict legal sense in which we understand it in Courts of Common Law, in which case there could be no lien where there was no possession, actual or constructive; but to express, as if by analogy, the nature of claims which neither presuppose nor originate in possession. This was well understood in the Civil Law, by which there might be a pledge with possession, and a hypothecation without possession, and by which in either case the right traveled with the thing into whosoever possession it came. Having its origin in this rule of the Civil Law, a maritime lien is well defined by Lord Tenterden, to mean a claim or privilege upon a thing to be carried into effect by legal process; and Mr. Justice Story (1 Sumner, 78) explains that process to be a proceeding *in rem*, and adds, that wherever a lien or claim is given upon the thing, then the Admiralty enforces it by a proceeding *in rem*, and indeed is the only Court competent to enforce it. A maritime lien is the foundation of the proceeding *in rem*, a process to make perfect a right inchoate from the moment the lien attaches: and whilst it must be admitted that where such a lien exists, a proceeding *in rem* may be had, it will be found to be equally true, that in all cases where a proceeding *in rem* is the proper course, there a maritime lien exists, which gives a privilege or claim upon the thing, to be carried into effect by legal process. This claim or privilege travels with the thing, into whosoever possession it may come. It is inchoate from the moment the claim or privilege attaches, and when carried into effect by legal process, by a proceeding *in rem*, relates back to the period when it first attached.

* * *

This rule, which is simple and intelligible, is, in our opinion applicable to all cases. It is not necessary to say that the lien is indelible, and may not be lost by negligence or delay where the rights of third parties may be compromised; but where reasonable diligence is used, and the proceedings are had in good faith, the lien may be enforced, into whosoever possession the thing may come.

THE BRIG MALEK ADHEL

43 U.S. (2 How.) 210, 11 L. Ed. 239 (1844)

Mr. Justice STORY delivered the opinion of the court

This is an appeal from a decree of the Circuit Court of the United States for the district of Maryland, sitting in admiralty, and affirming a decree of the District Court rendered upon an information *in rem*, upon a seizure brought for a supposed violation of the act of the 3d of March, 1819, ch. 75, (ch. 200,) to protect the commerce of the United States, and to punish the crime of piracy. The information originally contained five counts, each asserting a piratical aggression and restraint on the high seas upon a different vessel.

* * *

It was fully admitted in the court below, that the owners of the brig and cargo never contemplated or authorized the acts complained of; that the brig was bound on an innocent commercial voyage from New York to Guayamas, in California; and that the equipments on board were the usual equipments for such a voyage. It appears from the evidence that the brig sailed from the port of New York on the 30th of June, 1840, under the command of one Joseph Nunez, armed with a cannon and ammunition, and with pistols and daggers on board. The acts of aggression complained of, were committed at different times under false pretenses, and wantonly and willfully without provocation or justification, between the 6th of July, 1840, and the 20th of August, 1840, when the brig arrived at Bahia; where, in consequence of the information given to the American consul by the crew, the brig was seized by the United States ship Enterprize, then at that port, and carried to Rio Janeiro, and from thence brought to the United States.

* * *

The next question is, whether the innocence of the owners can withdraw the ship from the penalty of confiscation under the act of Congress. Here, again, it may be remarked that the act makes no exception whatsoever, whether the aggression be with or without the co-operation of the owners. The vessel which commits the aggression is treated as the offender, as the guilty instrument or thing to which the forfeiture attaches, without any reference whatsoever to the character or conduct of the owner. The vessel or boat (says the act of Congress) from which such piratical aggression, &c., shall have been first attempted or made shall be condemned. Nor is there any thing new in a provision of this sort. It is not an uncommon course in the admiralty, acting under the law of nations, to treat the vessel in which or by which, or by the master or crew thereof, a wrong or offense has been done as the offender, without any regard whatsoever to the personal misconduct or responsibility of the owner thereof. And this is done from the necessity of the case, as the only adequate means of suppressing the offense or wrong, or insuring an indemnity to the injured party. The doctrine also is familiarly applied to cases of smuggling and other misconduct under our revenue laws; and has been applied to other kindred cases, such as cases arising on embargo and non-intercourse acts. In short, the acts of the master and crew, in cases of this sort, bind the interest of the owner of the ship, whether he be innocent or guilty; and he impliedly submits to whatever the law denounces as a forfeiture attached to the ship by reason of their unlawful or wanton wrongs. In the case of the *United States v. The Schooner Little Charles*, 1 Brock. Rep. 347, 354, a case arising under the embargo laws, the same argument which has been addressed to us, was upon that occasion addressed to Mr. Chief Justice Marshall. The learned judge, in reply, said: "This is not a proceedings against the owner; it is a proceeding against the vessel for an offense committed by the vessel; which is not the less an offense, and does not the less subject her to forfeiture because it was committed without the authority and against the will of the owner. It is true that inanimate matter can commit no offense. But this body is animated and put in action by the crew, who are guided by the master. The vessel acts and speaks by the master. She reports herself by the master. It is therefore not unreasonable that the vessel should be affected by this report." The same doctrine was held by this court in the case of the *Palmyra*, 12 Wheat. R. 1, 14, where referring to seizures in revenue causes, it was said: "The thing is here primarily considered as the offender, or rather the offense is primarily attached to the thing; and this whether the offense be *malum prohibitum* or *malum in re*. The same thing applies to proceeding *in rem* or seizures in the Admiralty."

* * *

The ship is also by the general maritime law held responsible for the torts and misconduct of the master and crew thereof, whether arising from negligence or a willful disregard of duty; as for example, in cases of collision and other wrongs done upon the high seas or elsewhere within the admiralty and maritime jurisdiction, upon the general policy of that law, which looks to the instrument itself, used as the means of the mischief, as the best and surest pledge for the compensation and indemnity to the injured party.

* * *

The remaining question is, whether the cargo is involved in the same fate as the ship. In respect to the forfeiture under the act of 1819, it is plain that the cargo stands upon a very different ground from that of the ship. Nothing is said in relation to the condemnation of the cargo in the fourth section of the act; and in the silence of any expression of the legislature, in the case of provisions confessedly penal, it ought not to be presumed that their intention exceeded their language. We have no right to presume that the policy of the act reached beyond the condemnation of the offending vessel.

* * *

The present case seems to us fairly to fall within the general principle of exempting the cargo. The owners are confessedly innocent of all intentional or meditated wrong. They are free from any imputation of guilt, and every suspicion of connivance with the master in his hostile acts and wanton misconduct. Unless, then, there were some stubborn rule, which, upon clear grounds of public policy, required the penalty of confiscation to extend to the cargo, we should be unwilling to enforce it. We know of no such rule. On the contrary, the act of Congress, pointing out, as it does, in this very case, a limitation of the penalty of confiscation to the vessel alone, satisfies our minds that the public policy of our government in cases of this nature is not intended to embrace the cargo. It is satisfied by attaching the penalty to the offending vessel, as all that public justice and a just regard to private rights require. For these reasons, we are of opinion that the decrees condemning the vessel and restoring the cargo, rendered in both the courts below, ought to be affirmed.

* * *

Note: Functional Characteristics

In the United States, the law of maritime liens is largely the product of nineteenth-century jurisprudence. A maritime lien has been said to be a *jus in re* (rather than *ad rem*), that is, a *real* rather than a *personal* right. *The John G. Stevens*, 170 U.S. 113, 18 S. Ct. 544, 42 L. Ed. 969 (1898). In civil law terms, such a right confers direct and immediate authority over a thing, and may be asserted against subsequent acquirers of the thing, whether they are in good or in bad faith. *See* A. Yiannopoulos, Civil Law Property §§ 144-146 (2d ed. 1980). In order to explain the priority of liens of the same rank, admiralty courts have declared that a maritime lien is a "proprietary" interest and that the lienor is a part owner. However, in order to explain the ranking of maritime liens, courts have resorted to different rationalizations. *See* section on priority of liens, *infra.*

The best way to determine the nature of maritime liens is to focus attention on their function. A maritime lien is a nonpossessory security device that is created by operation of law. *The Bold Buccleugh, supra.* Parties do not enjoy contractual freedom to create new forms of maritime liens or to exclude the creation of certain forms of maritime liens (*e.g.*, liens for torts, wages, or salvage). The lienor has the right to follow the *res* and is entitled to preferential treatment from the proceeds of the sale of the *res* or from a release bond that is a substitute for the *res*.

A maritime lien is enforceable by process against the *res*. Thus, jurisdictional requirements are satisfied by the presence of the *res* before the court. Jurisdiction over the person of the defendant is not required.

A maritime lien also serves as a device for limitation of liability. In cases in which there is liability *in rem* though no liability *in personam*, the liability of the defendant is ordinarily limited to the value of the *res*. *See The China*, 74 U.S. (7 Wall.) 53, 19 L. Ed. 67 (1868).

---

2. Comparative Law

Note: Comparison: Civil and Common Law Jurisdictions

The law of maritime liens has developed along different lines in England and in civil law jurisdictions. All countries recognize that the vessel may be the object of security rights. The creditor of a shipowner may have a privilege against the proceeds of the sale of a ship for preferential satisfaction of his claim, whether the claim is based on tort, contract, or some other source of obligations. *See* John M. Kriz, *Ship Mortgages, Maritime Liens, and Their Enforcement: The Brussels Conventions of 1926 and 1952*, 1964 Duke L.J. 70 (1964).

According to the prevailing view on the continent, however, a privilege is not a real right as distinguished from a personal right; it is merely a cause of preference attached to a real or personal right. A privileged creditor cannot proceed against the vessel, an inanimate object. Legal process is always directed against a natural person or a legal entity, such as a partnership or a corporation. A ship, like any other thing that belongs to the debtor, may be seized by the creditor in order to compel the appearance of the owner before the court or in order to secure the execution and preferential satisfaction of a judgment. In this sense, the seizure of a vessel under continental law may be compared to a foreign attachment under American admiralty practice. However, the analogy would be misleading for a number of reasons.

In most continental countries, the mere seizure of a vessel does not establish jurisdiction for the adjudication of the merits of a claim. Exceptionally, legislation in certain countries establishes a *forum arresti*, and courts may adjudicate the merits of a claim for which the vessel was arrested. In the majority of countries, however, the seizure is a conservatory measure and if the court has no jurisdiction, the seizure will be lifted.

Also in contrast with American law, a judgment rendered by a continental court may be satisfied from the entire property of the defendant. The seizure does not result in a judgment that may be satisfied only from the proceeds of the thing seized.

Note: International Conventions

In spite of its great commercial importance, the matter of maritime liens and mortgages is characterized by a high degree of international uncertainty. National laws differ widely with respect to the creation and enforcement of maritime liens. In order to harmonize these uncertainties, the Comité Maritime International drafted and the Brussels Diplomatic Conference adopted three international conventions to establish a standard list of maritime liens and a common method of their enforcement. The first effort was the International Convention for the Unification of Certain Rules of Law Relating to Maritime Liens and Mortgages (Brussels, April 10, 1926). Enforcement problems were dealt with in the International Convention Relating to the Arrest of Seagoing Ships (Brussels, May 10, 1952). In 1967, a convention to replace the 1926 Convention was adopted by the Brussels Diplomatic Conference, but this has not gained widespread international acceptance. The principal innovation of the 1967 Convention was the elimination of the maritime lien for masters' contracts. *See generally*, Jan M. Sandström, *The Changing International Concept of the Maritime Lien as a Security Right*, 47 TUL. L. REV. 681 (1973).

Neither the 1926 Liens Convention nor the 1952 Arrest Convention nor the 1967 Liens Convention achieved widespread international acceptance. In response, the International Maritime Organization (an arm of the United Nations) has made further efforts to produce international uniformity of the law of maritime liens and mortgages. In 1993, yet another liens convention was made, the International Convention on Maritime Liens and Mortgages (Geneva, May 6, 1993). The 1993 Liens Convention entered into force internationally on September 5th, 2004, six months after 11 countries became party to it (Ecuador, Estonia, Monaco, Nigeria, Russia, St Vincent and the Grenadines, Spain, Syria, Tunisia, Ukraine and Vanuatu). Enforcement problems raised by the 1952 Arrest Convention were addressed in 1999, in the International Convention on Arrest of Ships (Geneva, March 12, 1999), which has not yet come into force internationally (it needs 10 parties to do so; it presently has seven).

The United States has not ratified any of the five conventions. There is no indication that it is likely to do so.

B. Vessels to Which Maritime Liens Attach

Notes

1. *Construction of Vessel*

Contracts to construct a vessel or to supply materials for the construction of vessels are not maritime contracts and do not create maritime liens. Likewise, only a "vessel" can be the subject of a "preferred ship mortgage" and the lien afforded thereby. *Chase Manhattan Fin. Serv., Inc. v. McMillian*, 896 F.2d 452, 1990 AMC 1702 (10th Cir. 1990).

2. *Component Parts and Accessories of a Vessel*

A vessel "is considered to consist of the hull, tackle, apparel and furniture." *The Joseph Warner*, 32 F. Supp. 532, 1940 AMC 217 (D. Mass. 1939). Thus as a general rule, when a maritime lien attaches to a vessel it also attaches to its component parts and accessories.

The *component parts* of a vessel are things attached to the vessel so as to become "an integral part" of it. A maritime lien on the vessel reaches these things even if they belong to a person other than the owner of the vessel, such as a charterer, a lessor, or a vendor under a conditional sale. *See In re Steamship Tropic Breeze*, 456 F.2d 137, 1972 AMC 1622 (1st Cir. 1972):

> The traditional admiralty rule is that the vessel itself and all equipment which is "an integral part of the vessel and [is] essential to its navigation and operation," are subject to preferred maritime liens on the vessel.
> The cement equipment involved in this case is clearly of the type that is subject of such claims. The Tropic Breeze became, with the installation of the equipment, a bulk cement carrier. The equipment was essential to its operation as such a carrier. It could not be removed without substantial cost, and the value of the ship would be substantially less without it. The fact that the equipment was owned by Tropical, a time charterer, does not change the result.

Id. at 141. (citations omitted).

For other cases in which things attached to a vessel were held to be an integral part of it, *see Turner v. United States*, 27 F.2d 134, 1928 AMC 1089 (2d Cir. 1928) (refrigeration equipment); *The Witch Queen*, 30 F. Cas. 396

(D.C. Cal. 1874) (No. 17,916) (diving bell and air pump); *The Hope*, 191 F. 243 (D. Mass. 1911) (net lifter and motor for its operation); *The Paraiso*, 226 F. 966 (W.D. Wash. 1915) (oil tanks); *First Suffolk National Bank of Huntington v. The Air Brant*, 125 F. Supp. 709, 1955 AMC 2130 (E.D.N.Y. 1954) (fish pumps, block, and fish boat davits).

Accessories are things that are placed on a vessel for its completion or ornamentation, but are not attached so as to become an integral part of it. When accessories belong to the owner of the vessel, they are clearly subject to the maritime liens that attach to the vessel. *See United States v. The Zarco*, 187 F. Supp. 371, 1961 AMC 78 (S.D. Cal. 1960) (generator armature). However, difficult questions arise when accessories belong to a person other than the shipowner. In these circumstances, admiralty courts tend to apply the rules that common-law courts have developed with respect to Fixtures. *See First National Bank & Trust Co. of Escanaba v. Oil Screw Olive L. Moore, Barge Wiltranco I*, 379 F. Supp. 1382, 1976 AMC 657 (W.D. Mich. 1973), *aff'd*, 521 F.2d 1401 (6th Cir. 1975); *The Joseph Warner*, 32 F. Supp. 532, 1940 AMC 217 (D. Mass. 1939).

In a number of cases, courts have held that maritime liens do not attach to leased thing. *See San Diego Trust & Savings Bank v. Oil Screw Linda Lee*, 1949 AMC 324 (S.D. Cal. 1947) (radio equipment); *C.I.T. Corp. v. Oil Screw Peggy*, 424 F.2d 767, 1970 AMC 1550 (5th Cir. 1970) (radar equipment); *United States v. F/V Golden Dawn*, 222 F. Supp. 186, 1964 AMC 691 (E.D.N.Y. 1963) (fishfinder); *W.R. Grace & Co. v. Charleston Lighterage & Transfer Co.*, 193 F.2d 539, 1952 AMC 689 (4th Cir. 1952) ("equipment"). *But see United States v. F/V Sylvester F. Whalen*, 217 F. Supp. 916, 1963 AMC 2389 (D. Me. 1963) (fathometer and radar equipment); *The Augusta*, 15 F.2d 727 (E.D. La. 1920) (wireless equipment).

In *First National Bank & Trust Co. of Escanada v. Oil Screw Olive L. Moore, supra*, the court held that leased equipment does not become subject to the lien of a preferred ship mortgage even if it could become subject to traditional maritime liens. *See also United States v. F/V Golden Dawn, supra; but see First Suffolk National Bank v. The Air Brant, supra; United States v. The Sylvester F. Whalen, supra.*

It has been held that accessories belonging to a vendor under a conditional sale are reached by maritime liens on the vessel. *See The Hope, supra*, and *The Showboat*, 47 F.2d 286, 1931 AMC 19 (D. Mass. 1930). In the latter case, the court held that furnishings provided under a conditional sale agreement for the operation of a vessel as a restaurant and dance hall were not subject to a maritime lien that attached on the vessel; however, portable fire extinguishers provided under a similar agreement were held to be subject to a maritime lien. What is the difference between the two types of equipment?

Prepaid freight is not a part of the vessel. *Galban Lobo Trading Co. S.A. v. The Diponegaro*, 103 F. Supp. 452, 1952 AMC 181 (S.D.N.Y. 1951). Likewise, cargo carried on a vessel is not a component part of the vessel, even if it belongs to the owner of the vessel. Thus, a maritime lien on the vessel does not extend to its cargo. *See Vlavianos v. The Cypress*, 171 F.2d 435, 1949 AMC 9 (4th Cir. 1948), *cert. denied*, 337 U.S. 924, 69 S. Ct. 1168, 93 L. Ed. 1732 (1949). Unpaid seamen, however, may have a lien for wages on earned freight. *Id.*

Does the case law governing accessories defy rational analysis? Does the distinction between things that are essential or necessary for the operation of a vessel and those that are not furnish a rational criterion? *Compare The Hope, supra;* United *States v. The Sylvester F. Whalen, supra; The Augusta, supra,* with *W.R. Grace & Co. v. Charleston L. & T. Co., supra; First Nat'l Bank & Trust Co. v. Oil Screw Olive L. Moore, supra.* Should the existence of a written agreement control the outcome? *See The Linda Lee, supra.* How about a process of "balancing equities" as under the common law of fixtures? Should the creditor under a preferred ship mortgage be given protection at the expense of a lessor or a conditional vendor of movable equipment?

3. *Interpretations of the Term "Vessel"*

Many different floating structures have been held to be "vessels" for the purposes of attachment of maritime liens. In *J.M.L. Trading Corp. v. Marine Salvage Corp.*, 501 F. Supp. 323 (E.D.N.Y. 1980), four floating wooden drydocks were held to be subject to maritime liens. In *McCarthy v. The Bark Peking*, 716 F.2d 130, 1984 AMC 1 (2d Cir. 1983), a museum vessel was held to be a "vessel", even though its rudder was welded in one position. The court said:

> The *Peking* may be fated to ride at anchor for the rest of her days. Her rudder is welded in place. Her owner has no intention of slipping her moorings and taking her again to the open seas, with the seagulls in her wake. But she retains at least this much of the dignity of her former venerable station: as long as she rides at anchor in the harbor, ready and able to head for the open seas, even in tow, she remains a vessel. Much as we should like to formulate a definition of "vessel" that captures the essence of the seagoing definiendum, no Platonic form suggests itself; hence we are left with the halting efforts of the common law. The *Peking*, despite her moorings and her role as a museum piece, still rests upon navigable waters and may be returned to the sea, if only in tow. Paraphrasing the late Mr. Justice Frankfurter in a different context, we "cannot keep the word of promise to [her] ear ... and break it to [her] hope."

McCarthy v. The Bark Peking, 716 F.2d 130, 136 (2d Cir. 1983).

---

1. Time of Attachment

ARQUES SHIPYARDS v. THE S.S. CHARLES VAN DAMME

175 F. Supp. 871 (N.D. Cal. 1959)

WOLLENBERG, District Judge

This libel *in rem* alleges a maritime lien (45 U.S.C.A. § 971) for "wharfage, berthage, dockage facilities, towing and materials to be used in and upon said vessel."

* * *

The affidavit in support of the exceptions states that on December 1, 1957, the respondent vessel was towed to Jack London Square, Oakland, California, where it was opened for business as a restaurant. The affidavit then sets forth facts showing that said vessel was permanently connected to the mainland.

However, it seems clear that admiralty jurisdiction does not depend on respondent's classification when in use as a restaurant, but rather on (1) whether the materials furnished and the services performed were capable of giving rise to a maritime lien, or (2) the respondent's status at such time.

* * *

Libelant's affidavit states that the maritime lien is based on materials and services furnished prior to December 1, 1957. If this is so, then such period is the crucial time for testing admiralty jurisdiction. The question of respondent's status when in use as a restaurant would be immaterial except in so far as the nature of the services and materials related to such use. If a maritime lien arose at the time such services and materials were furnished it seems clear that a Court of Admiralty could not be ousted from jurisdiction by subsequent changes in the character of the respondent S. S. Charles Van Damme.

* * *

Therefore, in accordance with the above opinion, the exceptions to the libel are hereby overruled.

Note: The "Dead Ship" Doctrine

Maritime liens may attach to "vessels". As a general rule, if a structure is a vessel for purposes of admiralty jurisdiction, it is also susceptible of maritime liens.

Under the "dead ship" doctrine, however, a vessel withdrawn from navigation, though still a vessel for purposes of admiralty jurisdiction, is not susceptible of maritime liens. Thus, persons rendering services to a vessel withdrawn from navigation are not entitled to maritime liens for wages. *See Slavin v. Port Service Corp.*, 138 F.2d 386, 1944 AMC 687 (3d Cir. 1943); *Hayford v. Doussony*, 32 F.2d 605, 1929 AMC 849 (5th Cir. 1929), *aff'd*, 42 F.2d 439 (5th Cir. 1930). Moreover, the contract of employment under which services are rendered may not be a maritime contract. *See The Sirius*, 65 F. 226 (N.D. Cal. 1895).

The determination of whether a vessel has been withdrawn from navigation is not always an easy matter. In *In re The Queen, Ltd.*, 1973 AMC 646 (Bankr. E.D. Pa. 1973), *aff'd*, 361 F. Supp. 1009, 1973 AMC 2510 (E.D. Pa. 1973), the court questioned the viability of the "dead ship" doctrine and seemingly held that as long as a floating structure is a vessel, it is susceptible of maritime liens. The court found that the S.S. Queen Elizabeth was a vessel to which maritime liens could attach, although it had been tied to the dock and not removed form its berth; it was not used for transportation or any maritime purpose; and it was actually used as a restaurant and hotel. In the course of its opinion, the court declared:

> There is a line of court decisions, known as "The Showboat" cases, in which ships were used as restaurants, dance halls, or the like, in which the courts have held that the mere restructuring of the watercraft for such purposes did not change their characters as "vessels", unless the structure was permanently attached to the land: *Ark* (D.C., Fla.), 17 F. 2d 444, 1927 A.M.C. 38; *Showboat* (D.C., Mass.), 47 F. 2d 286, 1931 A.M.C. 19; *Club Royale* (D.C., N.J.), 13 F. Supp. 123, 1936 A.M.C. 441. In *Miami River Boat Yard, Inc. v. 60' Houseboat* (5th Cir.), 390 F. 2d 596, 1968 A.M.C. 336, the Court held that, although the watercraft "has no motive power and must, as would the most lowly of dumb barges, be towed, does not deprive her of the status of a "vessel"". And, in the same circuit, in the case of M/V *Marifax v. McCrory* (5th Cir.), 391 F. 2d 909, 1968 A.M.C. 965, the court held that a landing craft which had been in mothballs for 15 years, was still a "vessel" because it was not "navigably impotent."

In *Johnson v. Oil Transport Co.*, 440 F.2d 109, 1971 AMC 1038, 1971 AMC 1837 (5th Cir.), *cert. denied*, 404 U.S. 868, 92 S. Ct. 109, 30 L. Ed. 2d 111 (1971), the court held that a vessel undergoing general overhaul in a dry dock is withdrawn from navigation. Thus, a person injured aboard such a vessel is not entitled to a maritime tort lien. Is there a lien for repairs?

---

2. Vessels in Custodia Legis*: Expenses of Justice*

NEW YORK DOCK CO. v. S.S. POZNAN

274 U.S. 117, 47 S. Ct. 482, 71 L. Ed. 955 (1927)

Mr. Justice STONE delivered the opinion of the Court

This case involves the right of a wharf owner to preferential payment from the proceeds of a vessel, for wharfage furnished the vessel while in the custody of a United States marshal under a warrant of arrest in admiralty. The owner of the S.S. Poznan entered into a contract with petitioner, the owner of a private pier in New York harbor, for the use of the pier for discharging cargo from December 1, 1920 until completion. The rate agreed upon was $250 per day, plus certain incidental charges not now material. On December 2, 1920, the Poznan was made fast to the pier. Later in the day, she was arrested by the United States marshal for the district upon libels, afterward consolidated into a single cause, for non-delivery of the vessel's cargo and for damages for breach of contracts of affreightment. The marshal allowed the vessel to remain at the pier. Later, on application of one of the libelling cargo owners, the district court ordered the delivery of a part of the cargo which that libellant had shipped, and made the order applicable to all other libellants who should make a like claim. The discharge of the cargo was then begun and deliveries were made to the several libellants in the consolidated cause, including respondent, the John B. Harris Co.

After the cargo had been about one-half discharged, the charterer applied to the district court for leave to move the vessel to another pier where the cargo could be removed more expeditiously. But, on request of some of the libellants and a committee representing the shippers, the application was denied on January 5, 1921. The vessel was unloaded by February 18, 1921. Delivery of the cargo from the pier was completed March 1, 1921, but the vessel remained fast to the pier to and including March 11, 1921, when she was removed.

Meanwhile, the marshal having declined to pay the bill for wharfage without an order of the court, petitioner, in April, 1921, filed its libel against the vessel for the balance of wharfage charges unpaid, aggregating $17,462. By order of the district court, the libellants in the consolidated cause were permitted to intervene. Respondent, the John B. Harris Co., served notice of intervention, and filed its answer denying the allegations in the libel and praying that it be dismissed on the ground, among others, that the wharfage was furnished while the vessel was in the custody of the marshal, and hence no maritime lien could arise. Respondent has since prosecuted the defense in behalf of all the other libellants in the consolidated cause.

The vessel was later sold under an order in the consolidated cause and the proceeds, which were not enough to satisfy the libellants, paid into the registry of the court. The libellants in the consolidated suit have made common cause by stipulation that the recovery under the final decree should be paid to trustees and distributed in accordance with the instructions of a committee representing all of them. The committee found the total claims of the libellants to exceed the amount of the proceeds of the ship. A pro rata distribution has been made to the claimants and an adequate amount reserved to pay the demand of the petitioner, if allowed in this suit. The marshal, although refusing petitioner's request for payment of the wharfage charge, nevertheless included it in his bill of costs and expenses in the consolidated cause and charged his commission on this amount. The court disallowed these items but "without prejudice to any rights of the New York Dock Company to have recourse against the proceeds of the vessel...."

The district court, in the present libel, allowed as a preferential payment from the proceeds of the ship, the reasonable value of the benefits resulting to the consolidated libellants from the wharfage and incidental service furnished by petitioner, to be determined by a special master. This was found by the master and held by the district court to be the reasonable value of the wharfage. A decree for this amount, less certain payments on account made by the owner of the ship, pursuant to the original contract of wharfage, 297 Fed. 345, was reversed by the circuit court of appeals for the second circuit. 9 F. 2d 838. This Court granted certiorari. 269 U.S. 547.

The court below held that as the wharfage was furnished after the arrest of the ship, and while it was in the custody of the law, no maritime lien could attach, and that a preferential payment could not be supported upon any other theory applicable to the facts of this case.

A question much argued, both here and below, was whether the case could be considered an exception to the general rule that there can be no maritime lien for services furnished a vessel while in *custodia legis*. *Cf. The Young America*, 30 Fed. 789; *The Nisseqogue*, 280 Fed. 174; *Paxson v. Cunningham*, 63 Fed. 132; *The Willamette Valley*, 66 Fed. 565. But, in the view we take, the case does not turn upon possible exceptions to that rule, as we think petitioner's right of recovery depends, as the district court ruled, not upon the existence of a maritime lien, but upon principles of general application which should govern whenever a court undertakes the administration of property or a fund brought into its custody for the benefit of suitors.

The libellants in the consolidated cause were not only concerned as owners in securing delivery of the cargo, but as lienors they were interested in the ship and, as eventually appeared, in the whole of her proceeds. Service rendered to the ship after arrest, in aid of the discharge of cargo, and afterward pending the sale, necessarily inured to their benefit, for it contributed to the creation of the fund now available to them. The most elementary notion of justice would seem to require that services or property furnished upon the authority of the court or its officer, acting within his authority, for the common benefit of those interested in a fund administered by the court, should be paid from the fund as an "expense of justice." *The Phebe*, 1 Ware 354, 359, Fed. Cases 11065. This is the familiar rule of courts of equity when administering a trust fund or property in the hands of receivers. The rule is extended, in making disposition of the earnings of the property in the hands of the receiver, to require payment of sums due for supplies furnished before the receivership, where their use by the debtor or receiver in the operation of the property has produced the earnings.

* * *

Such preferential payments are mere incidents to the judicial administration of a fund. They are not to be explained in terms of equitable liens in the technical sense, as is the case with agreements that particular property shall be applied as security for the satisfaction of particular obligations or vendors' liens and the like, which are enforced by plenary suits in equity. They result rather from the self-imposed duty of the court, in the exercise of its accustomed jurisdiction, to require that expenses which have contributed either to the preservation or creation of the fund in its custody shall be paid before a general distribution among those entitled to receive it.

* * *

Such a preferential payment from the proceeds of the ship, for wharfage furnished to her while in custody, was allowed by the court below in *The St. Paul*, 271 Fed. 265. But in the present case, that court thought that *The St. Paul* case was to be distinguished on the ground that there the wharfage service was furnished and the obligation incurred in accordance with an order made by the court and with the consent of the libellants. But here the court denied a motion to remove the ship from petitioner's wharf with the consent of some of the libellants and with full knowledge of all concerned that the wharfage was then being furnished. The libellants in the consolidated cause, who are united in interest with respondent in the present case, thus appear to have acquiesced in this determination. We are unable to perceive any basis for a distinction between action of the court in authorizing the ship to proceed to the wharf to enable it to discharge its cargo in the one case, and authorizing it to remain there for a like purpose in the other. It is enough if the court approves the service rendered or permits it to be rendered, and it inures to the benefit of the property or funds in its custody.

* * *

Notes

1. *Vessels in Custodia Legis*

In accord with *Poznan, supra,* maritime liens do not arise when the admiralty court permits a consent-keeper to operate the arrested vessel. *See Roy v. M/V Kateri Tek,* 238 F. Supp. 813, 1966 AMC 1830 (E.D. La. 1965). In such a case, however, supplymen are entitled to priority payment as an expense of justice. The same rule applies when a person makes advances for the maintenance of the vessel with the approval of the court or of the marshal. *See* 46 U.S.C. § 953(B)(2), which provides that a preferred ship mortgage shall be subordinated to "expenses and fees allowed costs taxed...." *Challenger, Inc. v. Durno,* 245 F.2d 815, 1958 AMC 125 (5th Cir. 1957); *United States v. The Audrey II,* 185 F. Supp. 777, 1960 AMC 1977 (N.D. Cal. 1960). As will be discussed, *infra,* 46 U.S.C. § 953(b)(2) has been recodified at 46 U.S.C. § 31326(b)(1) which continues to provide that a preferred ship mortgage is subordinate to "expenses and fees allowed by the court, costs imposed by the court...."

Expenses contracted in *custodia legis* must be based upon the credit of the vessel. Otherwise, all or part of such expenses may be denied. *See Larsen v. New York Dock Co.,* 166 F.2d 687, 1948 AMC 756 (2d Cir. 1948). It is preferable to obtain a court order prior to contracting expenses to ensure that the expenses will be given priority over earlier claims, including maritime liens and mortgages. *See The Audrey II,* 185 F. Supp. 777, 1960 AMC 1977 (N.D. Cal. 1960). However, *THE POZNAN* decision is authority for the position that reasonable expenses incurred for the common benefit of all creditors made without prior court order should nonetheless be given priority.

After a vessel has been arrested, other persons with lien claims may be permitted to intervene in the action and rearrest the vessel. The court may require intervenors to share in the expenses *custodia legis. Beauregard, Inc. v. Sword Services LLC,* 107 F.3d 351. 1997 AMC 1788 (5th Cir. 1997).

Maritime liens may arise, however, when a vessel is attached under state law. *See City of Erie v. Steamship North American,* 267 F. Supp. 875, 1968 AMC 500 (W.D. Pa. 1967); *The Pacific Hemlock,* 3 F. Supp. 305, 1933 AMC 298 (W.D. Wash. 1932); *but compare United States v. Oil Screw Ken Jr.,* 275 F. Supp. 792 (E.D. La. 1967).

2. *Vessels Owned or Operated by a Sovereign*

There is normally no reason to assert a maritime lien against a vessel operated by a sovereign because of the recognized availability of *in personam* relief against all levels of government. Furthermore, such vessels are normally immune from *in rem* process. Yet the issue may arise whether a lien can be asserted against such a vessel after it is sold or reverts to private ownership. In a well-known opinion by Justice Holmes, the Supreme Court answered no to this question. *See The Western Maid,* 257 U.S. 419, 42 S. Ct. 159, 66 L. Ed. 299 (1922).

C. Tort Liens

1. Marine Pollution

STATE OF CALIFORNIA, DEPT. OF FISH AND GAME v. S.S. BOURNEMOUTH

307 F. Supp. 922, 1970 AMC 642 (C.D. Cal. 1969)

FERGUSON, District Judge

The plaintiff, State of California, by and through its Department of Fish and Game, filed a complaint *in rem* against the vessel S.S. Bournemouth to recover damages incurred by discharging a quantity of bunker oil into the navigable waters of the State of California and of the United States.

The complaint alleges that the S.S. Bournemouth (hereinafter called "Bournemouth") is a ship of the Liberian Flag, Lloyds Registry Identification Number 516-2504, Official Number 720, owned and operated by Bournemouth Shipping Company, Monrovia, Liberia, and presently under charter to States Marine Lines, Inc., a Delaware corporation.

The acts complained of allegedly occurred on or about October 3, 1969, while the Bournemouth was moored in the navigable waters at Long Beach, California, Berth 10, Pier A, to discharge cargo. Plaintiff seeks relief in the form of damages to compensate for injury to property arising out of pollution to the water and for costs of abatement.

The Bournemouth, while lying at anchor at Berth 10, Pier A, Long Beach, California, was seized, arrested and taken into possession October 5, 1969, by the United States Marshal for the Central District of California subject to a warrant for arrest in an action *in rem*. A bond was posted, and the Bournemouth was permitted to leave the United States.

The defendant made a restricted appearance under Admiralty and Maritime Claims Rule E(8) and moved to dismiss for lack of jurisdiction....

Plaintiff ... urges that injury caused by oil pollution to its navigable waters states a maritime cause of action giving rise to a maritime lien and a suit *in rem* in admiralty independent of any statute. Defendant, on the other hand, contends that not every maritime tort results in a maritime lien, which lien both parties agree is a condition precedent to an action *in rem*. Defendant takes the position that only two types of maritime torts create maritime liens: collision claims and personal injury claims.

The issue before the court in ruling on defendant's motion to dismiss is therefore a narrow one. Stated simply, the issue is whether the tort of injury to plaintiff's property (navigable waters and marine life) will give rise to a maritime lien and thereby support an admiralty action *in rem* against the Bournemouth.

The court finds no merit in defendant's position and is of the opinion ... that a maritime lien against the Bournemouth arises in favor of the plaintiff which will support an admiralty action *in rem*, as a matter of general maritime law without the aid or necessity of a statutory lien.

* * *

The court acknowledges the fact that the great bulk of maritime tort litigation involving suits *in rem* which hold that a maritime lien arises against the vessel falls within the two broad categories: collision claims and personal injury claims, suggested by defendant. The cases do not, however, support the view that these categories are all inclusive or that the tort liability of a vessel for its unlawful acts should be so limited. Nor can the court find support in any public policy or set of reasons advanced by defendant for so limiting maritime liens.

* * *

It is the view of this court that the general maritime law has consistently provided *in rem* relief to the owner of property tortiously damaged by conversion while such property is upon the navigable waters. While here the alleged injury was to the water itself, and possibly the marine life also, efforts to distinguish between various types of injury which may occur to various types of property would serve no useful purpose … .

* * *

In the instant case it is admitted by defendant's counsel that the owners of the Bournemouth are not present and subject to personal service of process. It is further admitted that the vessel's present schedule does not call for her to return to the United States. The injury to property alleged to have been caused by defendant in discharging bunker oil into the navigable waters of the State of California is the basis for a claim of the same general merit as any conversion of property historically recognized by the general maritime law and is protected by the creation of a maritime lien.

Oil pollution of the nation's navigable waters by seagoing vessels both foreign and domestic is a serious and growing problem. The cost to the public, both directly in terms of damage to the water and indirectly of abatement is considerable. In cases where it can be proven that such damage to property does in fact occur, the governmental agencies charged with protecting the public interest have a right of recourse *in rem* against the offending vessel for damages to compensate for the loss.

* * *

---

2. Liability of the Vessel: Personification of the Res

Notes

1. In *The Barnstable* 181 U.S. 464, 21 S. Ct. 684, 45 L. Ed. 954 (1901), the Supreme Court held that the owner of a ship was not liable to indemnify the demise charterer (which was the employer of the master and crew) for its liability in damages as a result of a collision with another vessel. Dicta in the case suggested that the ship itself could be held liable *in rem* to the other vessel, even though the shipowner was not liable *in personam* because the ship was under demise charter. Those dicta continue to decide cases. A vessel may be arrested and judgment may be rendered *in rem* for torts committed by one lawfully in possession, such as a bareboat charterer. Typically, however, when the fault is attributed to the charterer only, the shipowner is entitled to full indemnity. *See Demsey & Associates, Inc. v. Steamship Sea Star*, 461 F.2d 1009, 1972 AMC 1440 (2d Cir. 1972); *United Nations Children's Fund v. Steamship*

Nordstern, 251 F. Supp. 833 (S.D.N.Y. 1965); *British West Indies Produce, Inc. v. Steamship Atlantic Clipper*, 353 F. Supp. 548, 1973 AMC 163 (S.D.N.Y. 1973).

2. The question whether there can be liability *in rem* without liability *in personam* may arise in a variety of contexts. *See Grillea v. United States*, 232 F.2d 919, 1956 AMC 1009 (2d Cir. 1956) (suit by injured longshoreman against the vessel *in rem* and against the bareboat charterer *in personam*). The United States Supreme Court avoided determination of the issue in *Guzman v. Pichirilo*, 369 U.S. 698, 82 S. Ct. 1095, 8 L. Ed. 2d 205, 1962 AMC 1142 (1962) by finding no demise and in *Reed v. The Yaka*, 373 U.S. 410, 83 S. Ct. 1349, 10 L. Ed. 2d 448, 1963 AMC 1373 (1963) by finding that the bareboat charterer was personally liable. In *Baker v. Raymond International, Inc.*, 656 F.2d 173, 1982 AMC 2752 (5th Cir. 1981), *cert. denied*, 456 U.S. 983, 102 S. Ct. 2256, 72 L. Ed. 2d 861 (1982), the court held that an injured seaman may sue the bareboat charterer, his employer, *in personam* and the shipowner both *in rem* and *in personam* for injuries occasioned by the unseaworthiness of the vessel. The court declared:

> We make explicit what was implicit in *The Barnstable*: a seaman may have recourse *in personam* against the owner of an unseaworthy vessel, without regard to whether owner or bareboat charterer is responsible for the vessel's condition. This personal liability is not, of course, unlimited. It is subject to the ceiling established by the Limitation Act, 46 U.S.C. sec. 183 (a). If the vessel's unseaworthiness is not the result of the owner's knowledge or privity, his total actual exposure may be limited to the value of the vessel.

656 F. 2d at 184.

Ordinarily, an *in rem* judgment may not exceed the value of the bond given for the release of the vessel. Under exceptional circumstances, however, a decree *in rem* may exceed the value of a bond fixed by the court. *See The Fairisle*, 76 F. Supp. 27 (D. Md. 1947), *aff'd*, *Waterman Steamship Corp. v. Dean*, 171 F.2d 408, 1948 AMC 794 (4th Cir. 1948), *cert. denied*, 337 U.S. 924, 69 S. Ct. 1168, 93 L. Ed. 1732 (1949). After a vessel is released on bond, there can be no new seizure *in rem* on the same cause of action. *The Cleveland*, 98 F. 631 (N.D. Wash. 1899). The Rule is otherwise when a vessel is attached and released on bond in an *in personam* action.

3. *Res Judicata*

If an *in rem* action is dismissed, the decree is a bar to a subsequent action *in personam* on the same cause of action. *Bailey v. Sundberg*, 49 F. 583 (2d Cir. 1892). Likewise, if an *in personam* action is dismissed, the decree is ordinarily a bar to a subsequent action *in rem* on the same cause of action. *See Burns Brothers v. Central Railroad*, 202 F.2d 910, 1953 AMC 718 (2d Cir. 1953). In this case, the court stated that a vessel is not a different party from its owner and declared:

> Disputes arise between human beings, not inanimate things; and it would be absurd to give the beaten party another chance because on second trial he appear as the claimant of a vessel that is, and can be nothing but the measure of his stake in the controversy.

Id. at 913.

However, on account of extraordinary circumstances, the court allowed plaintiff to proceed *in rem*. *See* G. Gilmore & C. Black, The Law of Admiralty, § 9-17 at 613-14 (2d ed. 1975).

In contrast, it was held in *Central Hudson Gas & Elec. Corp. v. Empresa Naviera Santa, S.A.*, 56 F.3d 359, 1996 AMC 163 (2d Cir. 1995) that judgment *in rem* against the ship did not preclude plaintiff from suing the demise charterer *in personam*.

When a judgment *in personam* remains unsatisfied, it has been held that the creditor may bring a new suit *in rem* on the same cause of action. *The Eastern Shore*, 24 F.2d 443, 1928 AMC 327 (D. Md. 1928); *see also*, *Pratt v. United States*, 340 F.2d 174 (1st Cir. 1964). In such a case, the decree *in personam* is not *res judicata*. *Baun v. The Ethel G.*, 125 F. Supp. 835, 1955 AMC 374 (D. Alaska 1954). It is the same when a judgment *in rem* remains unsatisfied; the creditor may proceed *in personam* on the same cause of action and the previous decree ought not to have the effect of *res judicata. See* G. GILMORE & C. BLACK, THE LAW OF ADMIRALTY § 9-90 at 801-805 (2d ed. 1975); *Central Hudson Gas & Elec. Corp. v. Empresa Naviera Santa, S.A.*, 56 F.3d 359, 1996 AMC 163 (2d Cir. 1995).

D. Contract Liens

Note: The Creation of Contract Liens

The law of maritime liens in the United States consists largely of rules developed by federal courts in order to meet the demands of the shipping industry. State courts did not have concurrent jurisdiction for the enforcement of maritime liens because an action *in rem* was not a remedy known to common law. States also did not have concurrent legislative jurisdiction to establish maritime liens except under the "home port" doctrine. State created maritime liens were enforceable only in admiralty and were accorded a low priority.

Dissatisfaction with the law governing service liens led to the enactment of the Federal Maritime Lien Act in 1910. Furthermore, the need for effective means of ship financing at the end of the First World War led to the enactment of the Federal Ship Mortgage Act in 1920. The Lien Act was amended in 1920 and reenacted as a part of the Ship Mortgage Act.

The Maritime Lien Act superseded all state statutes that established maritime liens for necessaries. Today, such statutes are either moribund or dead. *See* G. GILMORE & C. BLACK, THE LAW OF ADMIRALTY § 9-35 at 659 (2d ed. 1975). However, state created contract liens that are not for necessaries may be still enforceable in Admiralty. *See Burdine v. Walden*, 91 F.2d 321, 1937 AMC 1149 (5th Cir. 1937) (master's lien for wages); *Grow v. The Steel Gas Screw Loraine K.*, 310 F.2d 547, 1963 AMC 2044 (6th Cir. 1962) (maritime insurance premium). For liens for shipbuilding, a non-maritime contract, *see Armstrong v. United States*, 364 U.S. 40, 80 S. Ct. 1563, 4 L. Ed. 2d 1554, 1961 AMC 17 (1960).

Contract liens for necessaries are essentially statutory. The broad application given to the Federal Maritime Lien Act in this area has rendered nineteenth-century precedents obsolete. Other contract liens, however, are still governed by the general maritime law as altered by the federal statutes. Thus, to assume that statutes are "the sole repository of contract liens" is to disregard the long history of maritime jurisprudence. *Rainbow Line, Inc. v. M/V Tequila*, 341 F. Supp. 459, 1972 AMC 1540 (S.D.N.Y. 1972), *aff'd*, 480 F.2d 1024, 1973 AMC 1431 (2d Cir. 1973).

In this century, admiralty courts have been expanding the scope of their jurisdiction in matters of contract. *See Hinkins Steamship Agency, Inc. v. Freighters, Inc.*, 351 F. Supp. 373, 1973 AMC 348 (N.D. Cal. 1972), *aff'd*, 498 F.2d 411, 1974 AMC 1397 (9th Cir. 1974) (procuration of husbanding services); *Bergen Shipping Co., Ltd. v. Japan Marine Services, Ltd.*, 386 F. Supp. 430, 1975 AMC 490 (S.D.N.Y. 1974) (agreement to procure crew); *Ocean Science & Engineering, Inc. v. International Geomarine Corp.*, 312 F. Supp. 825, 1971 AMC 143 (D. Del. 1970) (oceanographic survey). This development, however, has not led to the recognition of new forms of contract liens.

---

1. Executory Contracts/Partial Execution

OSAKA SHOSEN KAISHA v. PACIFIC EXPORT LUMBER CO.

260 U.S. 490, 43 S. Ct. 172, 67 L. Ed. 364 (1923)

Mr. Justice McREYNOLDS delivered the opinion of the Court

March 19, 1917, through its agent at Tacoma, Wash., Osaka Shosen Kaisha, incorporated under the laws of Japan and owner of the Japanese steamer "Saigon Maru," then at Singapore, chartered the whole of that vessel, including her deck, to respondent Lumber Company to carry a full cargo of lumber from the Columbia or Willamette River to Bombay. In May, 1917, the vessel began to load at Portland, Ore. Having taken on a full under-deck cargo and 241,559 feet upon the deck, the captain refused to accept more. After insisting that the vessel was not loaded to capacity and ineffectively demanding that she receive an additional 508,441 feet, respondent libeled her, setting up the charter party and the captain's refusal, and claimed substantial damages. The owner gave bond; the vessel departed and safely delivered her cargo.

The Lumber Company maintains that it suffered material loss by the ship's refusal to accept a full load; that she is liable therefor under the general admiralty law.

* * *

Petitioner excepted to the libel upon the ground that the facts alleged showed no lien or right to proceed *in rem*.

* * *

Both courts below acted upon the view that while the ship is not liable *in rem* for breaches of an affreightment contract so long as it remains wholly executory, she becomes liable therefor whenever she partly executes it, as by taking on board some part of the cargo. In support of this view, it is said: Early decisions of our circuit and district courts held that under maritime law the ship is liable *in rem* for any breach of a contract of affreightment with owner or master. That *The Freeman* (1856), 18 How. 182, 188, and *The Yankee Blade* (1857), 19 How. 82, 89, 90, 91, modified this doctrine by denying such liability where the contract remains purely executory, but left it in full force where the vessel has partly performed the agreement, as by accepting part of the indicated cargo.

* * *

We think the argument is unsound.

* * *

The Freeman and *The Yankee Blade* distinctly rejected the theory of the earlier opinions. They are inconsistent with the doctrine that partial performance may create a privilege or lien upon the vessel. And in so far as the lower courts express approval of this doctrine in their more recent opinions, they fail properly to interpret what has been said here.

While, perhaps, not essential to the decision, this Court, through Mr. Justice Curtis, said in *The Freeman*: "Under the maritime law of the United States the vessel is bound to the cargo, and the cargo to the vessel, for the performance of a contract of affreightment; but the law creates no lien on a vessel as a security for the performance of a contract to transport cargo, until some lawful contract of affreightment is made, and a cargo shipped under it."

In *The Yankee Blade*, Mr. Justice Grier, speaking for the Court, declared:

> The maritime 'privilege' or lien is adopted from the civil law, and imports a tacit hypothecation of the subject of it. It is a '*jus in re*,' without actual possession or any right of possession. It accompanies the property into the hands of a bona fide purchaser. It can be executed and divested only by a proceeding *in rem*. This sort of proceeding against personal

property is unknown to the common law, and is peculiar to the process of courts of admiralty. The foreign and other attachments of property in the State courts, though by analogy loosely termed proceedings *in rem*, are evidently not within the category. But this privilege or lien, though adhering to the vessel, is secret one; it may operate to the prejudice of general creditors and purchasers without notice; it is therefore *'stricti juris,'* and cannot be extended by construction, analogy, or inference. 'Analogy,' says Pardessus, (Droit Civ., vol. 3, 597,) 'cannot afford a decisive argument, because privileges are of strict right. They are an exception to the rule by which all creditors have equal rights in the property of their debtor, and an exception should be declared and described in express words; we cannot arrive at it by reasoning from one case to another.

Now, it is a doctrine not to be found in any treatise on maritime law, that every contract by the owner or master of a vessel, for the future employment of it, hypothecates the vessel for its performance. This lien or privilege is founded on the rule of maritime law as stated by Cleirac, (597:) 'Le batel est obligee a la marchandise et la marchandise au batel.' The obligation is mutual and reciprocal. The merchandise is bound or hypothecated to the vessel for freight and charges, (unless released by the covenants of the charter-party,) and the vessel to the cargo. The bill of lading usually sets forth the terms of the contract, and shows the duty assumed by the vessel. Where there is a charter-party, its covenants will define the duties imposed on the ship. Hence it is said, (1 Valin, Ordon. de Mar., b. 3, tit. 1, art 11,) that 'the ship, with her tackle, the freight, and the cargo, are respectively bound (affectee) by the covenants of the charter-party.' But this duty of the vessel, to the performance of which the law binds her by hypothecation, is to deliver the cargo at the time and place stipulated in the bill of lading or charter-party, without injury or deterioration. If the cargo be not placed on board, it is not bound to the vessel, and the vessel cannot be in default for the non-delivery, in good order, of goods never received on board. Consequently, if the master or owner refuses to perform his contract, or for any other reason the ship does not receive cargo and depart on her voyage according to contract, the charterer has no privilege or maritime lien on the ship for such breach of the contract by the owners, but must resort to his personal action for damages, as in other cases ... .

* * *

Later opinions approve the same general rule.

The doctrine that the obligation between ship and cargo is mutual and reciprocal, and does not attach until the cargo is on board, or in the custody of the master, has been so often discussed and so long settled, that it would be useless labor to restate it, or the principles which lie at its foundation. The case of the *Schooner Freeman v. Buckingham*, decided by this court, is decisive of this case. *The Lady Franklin*, 8 Wall. 325, 329.

* * *

The maritime privilege or lien, though adhering to the vessel, is a secret one which may operate to the prejudice of general creditors and purchasers without notice and is therefore *stricti juris* and cannot be extended by construction, analogy or inference. *The Yankee Blade*, *supra*. The contract of affreightment itself creates no lien, and this Court has consistently declared that the obligation between ship and cargo is mutual and reciprocal and does not attach until the cargo is on board or in the master's custody. We think the lien created by the law must be mutual and reciprocal; the lien of the cargo owner upon the ship is limited by the corresponding and reciprocal rights of the ship owner upon the cargo. *See The Thomas P. Sheldon*, 113 Fed. 779, 782, 783.

The theory that partial acceptance of the designated cargo under a contract of affreightment creates a privilege or lien upon the ship for damages resulting from failure to take all, is inconsistent with the opinions of this Court and, we think, without support of adequate authority. In *The S. L. Watson*, 118 Fed. 945, 952, the court well said:

> The rule of admiralty, as always stated, is that the cargo is bound to the ship and the ship to the cargo. Whatever cases may have been decided otherwise disregarded the universal fact that no lien arises in admiralty except in connection with some visible occurrence relating to the vessel or cargo or to a person injured. This is necessary in order that innocent parties dealing with vessels may not be the losers by secret liens, the existence of which they have no possibility of detecting by any relation to any visible fact. It is in harmony with this rule that no lien lies in behalf of a vessel against her cargo for dead freight, or against a vessel for supplies contracted for, but not actually put aboard. *The Kiersage*, 2 Curt. 421, Fed. Cas. No. 7,762; *Pars. Ship. & Adm.* (1869), 142, 143. It follows out the same principle that Mr. Justice Curtis states in *The Kiersage*, 2 Curt. 424, Fed. Cas. No. 7,762, that admiralty liens are *stricti juris*, and that they cannot be extended argumentatively, or by analogy or inference. He says, 'They must be given by the law itself, and the case must be found described in the law'

Reversed.

Note: Breach of Executory Contract

A maritime lien does not attach for breach of an executory contract. May a time-charterer maintain an action *in rem* for prospective lost profits in connection with the breach of the charter party by the shipowner? In *Interocean Shipping Co. v. M/V Lygaria*, 512 F. Supp. 960, 1981 AMC 2244 (D. Md. 1981), the court held that the time charterer was not entitled to a lien for prospective lost profits because the cargo to be carried was never loaded on the vessel. *But see, E.A.S.T., Inc. of Stamford Conn. v. M/V Alaia*, 673 F. Supp. 796, 1988 AMC 1396, (E.D. La.) *aff'd*, 876 F.2d 1168, 1989 AMC 2024 (5th Cir. 1987) (action for breach of warranty of seaworthiness—Charterer had paid charter hire, advanced money to agent to pay port charges and had cargo on dock ready for shipment).

In *Krauss Brothers Lumber Co. v. Dimon Steamship Corp. (The Pacific Cedar)*, 290 U.S. 117, 54 S. Ct. 105, 78 L. Ed. 216 (1933), the Court considered whether a maritime lien attached to a claim by a shipper for the difference between the freight paid and the freight earned at the agreed rate. The Court state as follows:

> We see no distinction, either in principle or with respect to the practical operation or convenience of maritime commerce, between the lien asserted here for overpayment of freight by mistake and those for overpayments similarly made but induced by other means. Here, as there, the overpayment, made as the cargo was unloaded, occurred while the union of ship and cargo continued, and the liability asserted was determined by events contemporaneous with that union. The circumstances which called the lien into being do not differ in point of notoriety from those giving rise to other affreightment liens upon the vessel. While it is true that the maritime

> lien is secret, hence is *stricti juris* and not to be extended by implication, this does not mean that the right to the lien is not to be recognized and upheld, when within accepted supporting principles, merely because the circumstances which call for its recognition are unusual or infrequent.

Id. at 107.

Is this case consistent with the decision in *Osaka Shosen Kaisha v. Lumber Co.*?

---

2. Contracts of Passage

ACKER v. THE CITY OF ATHENS

177 F. 2d 961 (4th Cir. 1949)

PER CURIAM

Certain passenger-claimants seek an order from this court staying, without bond, the distribution of a fund of $400,000 derived from the sale of the steamship, City of Athens, now on deposit in the Registry of the District Court.... The claims are based upon a prepayment of passage money for a voyage which the ship failed to make. Hence the passengers did not board the ship nor was their baggage placed on board for the purposes of the voyage. When the claims were rejected in the District Court the passengers noted an appeal and prayed that the distribution of the fund to other claimants be stayed pending the action of this court....

The contentions of the passenger-claimants are: (1) that the failure of the ship to perform her obligations to them as a common carrier amounted to a tort which gave rise to a maritime lien in their favor; and (2) that they acquired a maritime lien by way of subrogation to the extent that the passenger monies were used to secure supplies for the ship and to pay the wages of the crew. Arguments have been made and briefs have been filed on behalf of the passengers and other lien claimants opposing the motion and have been considered by the court, and we have reached the conclusion upon the merits, for the reasons given in the opinion of the District Judge, *Todd Shipyards Corp. v. City of Athens*, D.C., 83 F. Supp. 67, that the claims of the passengers to a maritime lien cannot be sustained under the established rules of Admiralty law, and hence it would serve no good purpose to postpone further the distribution of the fund, already long delayed, to the claimants entitled thereto.

* * *

Note: Carriage of Passengers

Would a lien exist if the passengers on *The City of Athens* had gone on board the vessel before the voyage was cancelled? Does *in personam* liability exist?

---

3. Seamen's Liens for "Wages"

WEST WINDS, INC. v. M.V. RESOLUTE

720 F.2d 1097, 1984 AMC 319 (9th Cir. 1983)

REINHARDT, Circuit Judge

Appellants are 23 seamen and the trustees of their union's trust funds whose motion to intervene of right under FED. R. CIV. P. 24(a)(2) was denied by the district court. The sole issue on appeal is whether contributions to trust funds created for the benefit of the employees are "wages of the crew" that may serve as the basis for a preferred maritime lien under 46 U.S.C. § 953 (1976). We are compelled by precedent in this circuit to hold that they are not, at least in the absence of a loss of benefits. Accordingly, we affirm the district court's denial of the motion to intervene.

West Winds, Inc., Nautical Electric, Inc., and Schou-Gallis Co., Ltd., filed an admiralty complaint against the M/V RESOLUTE, *in rem*, and Coast Line Associates, the owner and operator of the vessel, *in personam*, under 46 U.S.C. § 971 (1976), to recover the costs of repairs, supplies, and other necessaries furnished to the vessel. The 23 seamen appellants were employed by Coast Line Associates between January and June 1982. Under the provisions of its collective bargaining agreement with the International Organization of Masters, Mates and Pilots, Coast Line was required to contribute to trust funds that provide health, retirement, pension, training, vacation, and similar benefits to the seamen. Coast Line failed to make the contributions for the 23 seamen as required by the collective bargaining agreement. To protect their interest in procuring the payment of the delinquent trust fund contributions, the trustees and the seamen sought to intervene of right in the underlying action under FED. R. CIV. P. 24(a)(2).

Appellants claim that the delinquencies give rise to a preferred maritime lien as "wages of the crew" under the Ship Mortgage Act of 1920, section 30, subsection M, 46 U.S.C. § 953 (1976). Under the Act, "a lien for ... wages of the crew of the vessel" is a "preferred maritime lien" that has priority over all other claims and may be asserted in any *in rem* proceeding brought against a vessel. *Id.* Appellants maintain that, because contributions to the trust funds are a form of compensation, they should be treated as "wages of the crew." They do not allege, however, that the failure to make contributions has caused or will cause any loss of benefits.

The district court issued a memorandum and order denying appellants' motion to intervene. Relying upon *Long Island Tankers Corp. v. S.S. Kaimana*, 265 F. Supp. 723 (N.D. Cal. 1967), the district court held that the delinquent trust fund contributions were not "wages of the crew" for purposes of section 953 and that therefore there was no basis for the assertion of a preferred maritime lien. Accordingly, the district court held that the applicants-in-intervention did not allege "an interest relating to the property or transaction which is the subject of the action" as required for intervention of right under FED. R. CIV. P. 24(a)(2).

* * *

II.

As appellees argue, there is Ninth Circuit precedent directly on point in this case. In *Cross v. S.S. Kaimana*, 401 F.2d 182 (9th Cir. 1968) (*per curiam*), *cert. denied*, 393 U.S. 1095, 89 S. Ct. 879, 21 L. Ed. 2d 785 (1969), in a one sentence opinion, we adopted the reasoning of the district court and held that contributions of employers to trust funds created pursuant to collective bargaining agreements to provide vacation, pension, and welfare benefits to seamen do not constitute "wages of the crew" under 46 U.S.C. § 953. The district court decision, *Long Island Tankers Corp. v. S.S. Kaimana*, 265 F. Supp. 723 (N.D. Cal. 1967), affirmed in *Cross*, addressed a factual situation strikingly similar to the one before us. In that case, as here, the employers were required to make contributions to the trust funds based upon the number of days and type of work performed by their employees. In *Long Island Tankers*, after several employers failed to make contributions the trustees of the funds brought an action seeking to assert preferred maritime liens to recover the contributions as "wages of the crew" under 46 U.S.C. § 953. The district court dismissed the action and held that the contributions were not "wages of the crew" that could serve as the basis for the trustees' assertion of preferred maritime liens. *See* 265 F. Supp. at 726-27.

Appellants contend that we should distinguish *Long Island Tankers* because seamen, as well as trustees of the trust funds, seek to assert the lien here. We decline to do so. Appellants correctly assert that *Long Island Tankers* reserved a question regarding the right of seamen to assert a preferred maritime lien. The question reserved, however, was only whether seamen could assert a preferred maritime lien for a *loss of benefits* caused by an employer's failure to make trust fund contributions. 265 F. Supp. at 727-28. The court did not reserve the question whether seamen could assert a preferred maritime lien for a failure to make contributions when no accompanying loss of benefits was claimed. In reserving the question it did, the court expressly relied on the distinction between contributions that merely serve to fund benefits and the benefits themselves. *Id.* at 727-29. Because the seamen here do not allege any loss of benefits due to Coast Line's failure to make the trust fund contributions, we hold that they fall within the rule established in *Long Island Tankers*. However, like the court in that case, we reserve to another day the question whether seamen may assert a preferred maritime lien for a loss of benefits caused by an employer's failure to make contributions.

Appellants challenge the present-day validity of the reasoning of *Long Island Tankers*. In *Long Island Tankers* the court relied heavily upon the Supreme Court's decision in *United States v. Embassy Restaurant, Inc.*, 359 U.S. 29, 79 S. Ct. 554, 3 L. Ed. 2d 601 (1959). *Embassy Restaurant* held that employer contributions to trust funds were not entitled to priority over other debts as "wages ... due to workmen" under the Bankruptcy Act. *See* 359 U.S. at 35, 79 S. Ct. at 558. Claiming that *Embassy Restaurant* was "overruled" by Congress in the Bankruptcy Reform Act, Pub. L. No. 95-598 § 507, 92 Stat. 2549, 2583-85 (1978), appellants argue that Long Island Tankers is no longer good law. We disagree.

In the Bankruptcy Reform Act, Congress placed "contributions to employee benefit plans" immediately below "wages, salaries, or commissions" on the hierarchy of debt priorities in bankruptcy proceedings. *See* 11 U.S.C. § 507(a)(3), (4).... In *Embassy Restaurant*, the Court declined to treat contributions as wages; when Congress adopted the Bankruptcy Reform Act, it, too, refused to treat contributions as wages. Instead, it created a completely new category, with a lesser priority than wages, for such claims. Under the Bankruptcy Reform Act, if there are insufficient funds to pay both wages and contributions, the wages are paid and the contributions are not. This type of lesser priority for contributions was not considered by the *Embassy* Court.

* * *

Although the Bankruptcy Reform Act changed the priority afforded to claimants like those in *Embassy*, Congress did not "overrule" *Embassy* or even reject its reasoning. *Long Island Tankers* therefore survives as precedent that is binding upon us.

Cross' affirmance of *Long Island Tankers* does not stand alone. Other courts addressing the issue have held that employer contributions to trust funds created to benefit employees are not "wages of the crew" under 46 U.S.C. § 953. *Barnouw v. S.S. Ozark*, 304 F.2d 717, 719-20 (5th Cir. 1962); *Brandon v. S.S. Denton*, 302 F.2d 404, 415-16 (5th Cir. 1962); *Irving Trust Co. v. The Golden Sail*, 197 F. Supp. 777, 778-79 (D. Or. 1961). Moreover, a recent Supreme Court decision defining "wages" under another maritime statute suggests the vitality of the holding in *Long Island Tankers*.

In *Morrison-Knudsen Construction Co. v. Director, Office of Workers' Compensation Programs*, 461 U.S. 624, 103 S. Ct. 2045, 2049, 76 L. Ed. 2d 194 (1983), the Supreme Court held that employer contributions to union health, welfare, pensions, and training trust funds are not "wages" for the purpose of computing compensation benefits under section 2(13) of the Longshoremen's and Harbor Workers' Compensation Act, 33 U.S.C. § 902(13) (1976). The Court emphasized that, because contributions are not "benefits with a present value that can be readily converted into a cash equivalent on the basis of their market values," they should not be treated as "wages." 103 S. Ct. at 2049. Rather than constituting benefits convertible to a cash equivalent, contributions generally accumulate in trust funds, which, after investment, finance future benefits that are non-convertible, and may vary according to an employee's needs. *See id.*; *Long Island Tankers*, 265 F. Supp. at 727.

Despite *Morrison-Knudsen*, appellants argue that, because contributions to trust funds are increasingly given by employers to employees as a form of compensation, "wages of the crew" should be read to include such contributions. Appellants point out that some courts interpreting other statutes have held that "wages" includes contributions because they are, in fact, part of the total compensation for employment. *See, e.g., W.W. Cross & Co. v. NLRB*, 174 F.2d 875, 877-78 (1st Cir. 1949); *Inland Steel Co. v. NLRB*, 170 F.2d 247, 251 (7th Cir. 1948), *cert. denied*, 336 U.S. 960, 69 S. Ct. 887, 93 L. Ed. 1112 (1949); *Dunlop v. Tremayne*, 62 Cal.2d 427, 431, 398 P.2d 774, 777, 42 Cal.Rptr. 438, 441 (1965). Although we are sympathetic to appellants' argument, we are not free to accept it here. Part of the reason lies in certain limits that we perceive to exist with respect to the function of statutory interpretation.

It has long been recognized that:

> increasingly as a statute gains in age ... its language is called upon to deal with circumstances utterly uncontemplated at the time of its passage. Here the quest is not properly for

> the sense originally intended by the statute, for the sense sought originally to be put into it, but rather for the sense which can be *quarried out of it* in the light of the new situation.

Llewellyn, *Remarks on the Theory of Appellate Decision and the Rules or Canons about How Statutes are to be Construed*, 3 VAND. L. REV. 395, 400 (1950) (emphasis in original); *see* H. HART & A. SACKS, THE LEGAL PROCESS 1410-11 (tent. ed. 1958) (unpublished manuscript). For this reason, generally, a court interpreting a statute should:

> ask itself not only what the legislation means abstractly, or even on the basis of legislative history, but also what it ought to mean in terms of the needs and goals of our present day society. This approach is required by the insuperable difficulties of readjusting old legislation by the legislative process and by the fact that it is obviously impossible to secure an omniscient legislature.

Phelps, *Factors Influencing Judges in Interpreting Statutes*, 3 VAND. L. REV. 456, 469 (1950); *see In re Grand Jury Subpoena of Persico*, 522 F.2d 41, 64-65 (2d Cir. 1975); *see also* G. CALABRESI, A COMMON LAW IN THE AGE OF STATUTES 163-66 (1982) (suggesting that courts explicitly turn to common law principles to update statutes); Note, *Intent, Clear Statements, and the Common Law: Statutory Interpretation in the Supreme Court*, 95 HARV. L. REV. 892, 913 (1982) (proposing a "common law model of statutory interpretation" that would allow courts to "view statutes as statements of consensually agreed upon principles").

Despite the general validity of this approach to statutory interpretation, the judiciary is not the proper branch of government to update complex statutes when legislative decisionmaking is necessary. For example, in the case of the Bankruptcy Reform Act's creation of a new intermediate level of debt priorities covering contributions, Congress was the only branch of government capable of making the necessary change; courts could only decide whether "wages" includes contributions and could not create a new, separate, and lesser priority category. *See* G. CALABRESI, *supra*, at 158-62 (recognizing inherent difficulties in courts' updating of detailed and technical statutes); G. GILMORE, THE AGES OF AMERICAN LAW 96 (1977) ("[T]he more tightly a statute was drafted originally, the more difficult it becomes to adjust the statute to changing conditions without legislative revision." (footnote omitted)). Here, as with the bankruptcy laws, in order to bring the Ship Mortgage Act up to date, it may be necessary to create a new, separate, and lesser priority category for contributions. That, as we have already said, we cannot do.

We must reject appellants' argument for another reason, as well. The Supreme Court recently refused to define "wages" as including contributions in another maritime act despite its recognition of the changes that have occurred in the methods of paying compensation. *See Morrison-Knudsen*, 103 S. Ct. at 2051-53. It did so partly because the legislative history and administrative practice under the Longshoremen's and Harbor Workers' Compensation Act did not reflect an intention to include contributions. *See id.* at 2050-51. In light of this reasoning, we do not believe that we are free to ignore the judicial history of the Ship Mortgage Act and *Long Island Tankers* simply because of those same changes.

In conclusion, Ninth Circuit precedent and other persuasive authority, as well as the complexities implicated by a judicial restructuring of lien priorities, compel the conclusion that contributions, at least in the absence of any actual loss of benefits, are not "wages of the crew" under 46 U.S.C. § 953 and therefore cannot serve as the basis for the assertion of a preferred maritime lien.

III.

Although we are not free to afford appellants the relief they seek, they have offered compelling reasons why employer contributions to trust funds should be afforded some form of priority treatment for maritime lien purposes. Demands for contributions to trust funds providing benefits to employees increasingly serve as a substitute for wage demands in collective bargaining negotiations. *See* S. Rep. No. 989, 95th Cong., 2d Sess. 69 (1978), *reprinted in* 1978 U.S. Code Cong. & Ad. News 5787, 5855; H. Rep. No. 533, 93d Cong., 2nd Sess. 2-3 (1974), *reprinted in* 1974 U.S. Code Cong. & Ad. News 4639, 4640-41; *see also* Employee Retirement Income Security Act, Pub. L. No. 93-406, 88 Stat. 829 (1974) (extensively regulating the increasing number of trust funds created pursuant to collective bargaining agreements). For this reason alone, contributions to seamen's trust funds would warrant some form of priority treatment similar to that afforded "wages of the crew." Moreover, affording priority treatment to trust fund contributions would further the purpose of the preferred maritime lien—to protect the compensation given seamen. *See* S. Rep. No. 573, 66th Cong., 2nd Sess. 9 (1920). Finally, there is somewhat of an anomaly in the fact that money given by an employer directly to an employee to spend on benefits is treated as "wages," but the same funds, if given to a trust fund that bestows identical benefits upon the employee, are not. *See Duncanson-Harrelson Co. v. Director, Office of Workers' Compensation Programs*, 686 F.2d 1336, 1345 (9th Cir. 1982), *vacated and remanded*, 462 U.S. 1101, 103 S. Ct. 2446, 77 L. Ed. 2d 1329 (1983).

As these arguments strongly suggest, Congress may, as it did in enacting the Bankruptcy Reform Act, wish to "recognize[ ] the realities of labor contract negotiations, where fringe benefits may be substituted for wage demands." S. Rep. No. 989, 95th Cong., 2d Sess. 69 (1978), *reprinted in* 1978 U.S. Code Cong. & Ad. News 5787, 5855. Significant changes in economic conditions suggest the inadequacies of the present debt priorities in the Ship Mortgage Act—priorities that have not been changed since the Act was originally adopted in 1920. Amending 46 U.S.C. § 953 to bring the lien priorities in line with modern economic reality would further the purpose of the section and avoid anomalous results.

IV.

We conclude that, at least absent any loss of benefits, seamen may not assert a preferred maritime lien for "wages of the crew" under 46 U.S.C. § 953 based on an employer's failure to make contributions to trust funds. Therefore, the district court's denial of appellants' motion to intervene of right is

Affirmed.

Note: Seamen's Wages

Seamen's wage claims are traditionally the most sacrosanct of transactions giving rise to maritime liens, 46 U.S.C. § 31301(5)(D). Under 46 U.S.C. § 11112 a wage lien is provided for masters of U.S. documented vessels as well. Nevertheless, troublesome questions arise. Are shares in the catch of a fishing vessel "wages"? *See Harison v. The Beverly Lynn*, 172 F. Supp. 719, 1960 AMC 921 (D.P.R. 1959). Would seamen have a lien for unpaid withholding taxes and F.I.C.A. payments? *See P.C. Pfeiffer Co. v. The Pacific Star*, 183 F. Supp. 932, 1960 AMC 1666 (E.D. Va. 1960). Should income tax on wages be paid ahead of maritime liens? *See Marine Midland Trust Co. of New York v. United States*, 299 F.2d 724 (4th Cir. 1962).

4. Contract for Sale vs. Contract to Charter Vessel

Question

Breach of a contract to sell a vessel does not give rise to a maritime lien because a contract to sell a ship is not a maritime contract. *S.C. Loveland, Inc. v. East West Towing, Inc.*, 608 F.2d 160, 164, 1980 AMC 2947 (5th Cir. 1979), *cert. denied sub nom. St. Paul Mercury Ins. Co. v. East West Towing, Inc.*, 446 U.S. 918, 100 S. Ct. 1852, 64 L. Ed. 2d 272 (1980). Breach of a charterparty contract to hire a vessel does give rise to a maritime lien because a charterparty contract is a maritime contract. *Natasha, Inc. v. Evita Marine Charters, Inc.*, 763 F.2d 468, 470, 1986 AMC 490 (1st Cir. 1985). Should there be a maritime lien for breach of a sale contract disguised as a charterparty contract? *See, e.g., Cary Marine, Inc. v. Motorvessel Papillon*, 872 F.2d 751, 1990 AMC 828 (6th Cir. 1989) (arrangement including bareboat charter with option to purchase held to be for sale rather than charter).

5. The Preferred Ship Mortgage

Note: The Ship Mortgage Act, 1920

In *Bogart v. The Steamboat John Jay*, 58 U.S. (17 How.) 399, 15 L. Ed. 95 (1854), the court held that admiralty did not have jurisdiction for the foreclosure of a ship mortgage. *See also McCorkle v. First Pennsylvania Banking & Trust Co.*, 459 F.2d 243, 1972 AMC 1596 (4th Cir. 1972). Such a mortgage could be established under state law and could be foreclosed in a state court, but not in an *in rem* action. If a vessel was arrested by a person having a maritime lien, a mortgage creditor could appear before the admiralty court to claim sums remaining after the satisfaction of maritime liens. In such a case, the mortgage creditor was in competition with other persons who did not enjoy the status of a lienor under the maritime law and, for all practical purposes, the security of the mortgage was worthless. In order to encourage investments in the shipping industry and to allow the United States to effectively dispose of the fleet of vessels that it had acquired in the war years, Congress enacted the Ship Mortgage Act in 1920, 46 U.S.C. §§ 911-916.

The constitutionality of the Ship Mortgage Act was upheld in *Detroit Trust Co. v. The Thomas Barlum*, 293 U.S. 21, 55 S. Ct. 31, 79 L. Ed. 176, 1934 AMC 1417 (1934). In the same case, the court established the proposition that a preferred ship mortgage need not secure a maritime claim. Thus, a preferred ship mortgage may be created for the construction of a vessel. *See State of Israel v. M/V Nili*, 435 F.2d 242, 1971 AMC 428 (5th Cir. 1970), *cert. denied*, 401 U.S. 994, 91 S. Ct. 1232, 28 L. Ed. 2d 532, 1971 AMC 1325 (1971).

By virtue of a 1954 amendment to 46 U.S.C. § 951, a preferred ship mortgage established in a foreign country may be foreclosed in the United States in the same way as a similar mortgage created under the laws of the United States; however, a mortgage on a foreign vessel is subordinated to claims for necessaries furnished in the United States. An anti-lien clause in the mortgage cannot circumvent this provision. *State of Israel v. M/V Nili, supra.*

The Ship Mortgage Act, 1920 has been amended and recodified at 46 U.S.C. §§ 31301 *et seq.* which became effective January 1, 1989.

Title 46 United States Code*

Chapter 313—Commercial Instruments and Maritime Liens

Subchapter I — General

§ 31301. Definitions

In this chapter—

* * *

(4) "necessaries" includes repairs, supplies, towage, and the use of a dry dock or marine railway;

(5) "preferred maritime lien" means a maritime lien on a vessel—

(A) arising before a preferred mortgage was filed under section 31321 of this title;

(B) for damage arising out of maritime tort;

(C) for wages of a stevedore when employed directly by a person listed in section 31341 of this title;

(D) for wages of the crew of the vessel;

(E) for general average; or

(F) for salvage, including contract salvage; and

(6) "preferred mortgage"—

(A) means a mortgage that is a preferred mortgage under section 31322 of this title; and

(B) also means in sections 31325 and 31326 of this title, a mortgage, hypothecation, or similar charge that is established as a security on a foreign vessel if the mortgage, hypothecation, or similar charge was executed under the laws of the foreign country under whose laws the ownership of the vessel is documented and has been registered under those laws in a public register at the port of registry of the vessel or at a central office.

Subchapter II — Commercial Instruments

§ 31321. Filing, recording, and discharge

(a) (1) A bill of sale, conveyance, mortgage, assignment, or related instrument, whenever made, that includes any part of a documented vessel or a vessel for which an application for documentation is filed, must be filed with the Secretary of Transportation to be valid, to the extent the vessel is involved, against any person except—

(A) the grantor, mortgagor, or assignor;

(B) the heir or devisee of the grantor, mortgagor, or assignor; and

(C) a person having actual notice of the sale, conveyance, mortgage, assignment, or related instrument.

(2) Each bill of sale, conveyance, mortgage, assignment, or related instrument that is filed in substantial compliance with this section is valid against any person from the time it is filed with the Secretary.

(3) The parties to an instrument or an application for documentation shall use diligence to ensure that the parts of the instrument or application for which they are responsible are in substantial compliance with the filing and documentation requirements.

(b) To be filed, a bill of sale, conveyance, mortgage, assignment, or related instrument must—

(1) identify the vessel;

(2) state the name and address of each party to the instrument;

(3) state, if a mortgage, the amount of the direct or contingent obligations (in one or more units of account as agreed to by the parties) that is or may become secured by the mortgage, excluding interest, expenses, and fees;

(4) state the interest of the grantor, mortgagor, or assignor in the vessel;

(5) state the interest sold, conveyed, mortgaged, or assigned; and

(6) be signed and acknowledged.

* * *

§ 31322. Preferred mortgages

(a) (1) A preferred mortgage is a mortgage, whenever made, that—

(A) includes the whole of a vessel;

(B) is filed in substantial compliance with section 31321 of this title;

(C) (i) covers a documented vessel; or

(ii) covers a vessel for which an application for documentation is filed that is in substantial compliance with the requirements of chapter 121 of this title and the regulations prescribed under that chapter; and

(D) has as the mortgagee—

(i) a State;

(ii) the United States Government;

(iii) a federally insured depository institution, unless disapproved by the Secretary;

(iv) an individual who is a citizen of the United States;

(v) a person qualifying as a citizen of the United States under section 2 of the Shipping Act, 1916 (46 App. U.S.C. 802); or

(vi) a person approved by the Secretary of Transportation.

(2) Paragraph (1)(D) of this subsection does not apply to a vessel operated only as a fishing vessel, fish processing vessel, or a fish tender vessel (as defined in section 2101 of this title) or to a vessel operated only for pleasure.

* * *

(d) (1) A mortgage or instrument granting a security interest perfected under State law covering the whole of a vessel titled in a State is deemed to be a preferred mortgage if—

(A) the Secretary certifies that the State titling system complies with the Secretary's guidelines for a titling system under section 13106(b)(8) of this title; and

(B) information on the vessel covered by the mortgage or instrument is made available to the Secretary under chapter 125 of this title.

(2) This subsection applies to mortgages or instruments covering vessels titled in a State after—

(A) the Secretary's certification under paragraph (1)(A) of this subsection; and

(B) the State begins making information available to the Secretary under chapter 125 of this title.

(3) A preferred mortgage under this subsection continues to be a preferred mortgage if the vessel is no longer titled in the State where the mortgage was made.

* * *

§ 31325. Preferred mortgage liens and enforcement

(a) A preferred mortgage is a lien on the mortgaged vessel in the amount of the outstanding mortgage indebtedness secured by the vessel.

(b) On default of any term of the preferred mortgage, the mortgagee may enforce the preferred mortgage lien in—

(1) a civil action *in rem* for a documented vessel, a vessel to be documented under chapter 121 of this title, or a foreign vessel and;

(2) a civil action *in personam* in admiralty against the mortgagor, comaker, or guarantor for the amount of the oustanding indebtedness secured by the mortgaged vessel or any deficiency in full payment of that indebtedness; and

(3) a civil action against the mortgagor, comaker, or guarantor for the amount of the outstanding indebtedness secured by the mortgaged vessel or any deficiency in full payment of that indebtedness.

(c) The district courts have original jurisdiction of a civil action brought under subsection (b)(1) or (2) of this section. However, for a documented vessel, a vessel to be documented under chapter 121 of this title, or a foreign vessel, this jurisdiction is exclusive of the courts of the States for a civil action brought under subsection (b)(1) of this section.

* * *

§ 31326. Court sales to enforce preferred mortgage liens and maritime liens and priority of claims

(a) When a vessel is sold by order of a district court in a civil action *in rem* brought to enforce a preferred mortgage lien or a maritime lien, any claim in the vessel existing on the date of sale is terminated, including a possessory common law lien of which a person is deprived under section 31325(e)(2) of this title, and the vessel is sold free of all those claims.

(b) Each of the claims terminated under subsection (a) of this section attaches, in the same amount and in accordance with their priorities to the proceeds of the sale, except that—

(1) the preferred mortgage lien has priority over all claims against the vessel (except for expenses and fees allowed by the court, costs imposed by the court, and preferred maritime liens); and

(2) for a foreign vessel, the preferred mortgage lien is subordinate to a maritime lien for necessaries provided in the United States.

Subchapter III — Maritime Liens

These provisions are found in Section 6 *infra*, Liens for Necessaries.

---

6. Liens for Necessaries

Note: The "Home Port" Doctrine and the Enactment of the Maritime Lien Act

Early admiralty decisions established the proposition that one who furnishes supplies or materials to a vessel in a foreign port acquires a maritime lien under the general maritime law. In *The General Smith*, 17 U.S. (4 Wheat.) 438, 4 L. Ed. 609 (1819), however, the United Sates Supreme Court established the converse proposition that there is no maritime lien under the general maritime law for the furnishing of supplies or repairs at the home port of a vessel. The court reasoned that in the home port suppliers and materialmen are presumed to rely on the credit of the owner of the vessel rather than on that of the vessel.

Under the "home port" doctrine, states had legislative jurisdiction to enact statutes establishing maritime liens for services furnished to vessels at the home port. In the course of the nineteenth century, many states enacted statutes designed to fill the lacuna in the general maritime law created by *The General Smith*. Such liens, however, could only be executed in federal district courts in admiralty, and their priority was low.

Determination of the home port of a vessel also proved to be a difficult matter and incongruous results were reached in practice. *See The St. Jago de Cuba*, 22 U.S. (9 Wheat.) 409, 6 L. Ed. 122 (1824). In *The Lottawanna*, 88 U.S. (21 Wall.) 558, 22 L. Ed. 654, 1996 AMC 2372 (1874), interested parties asked the United States Supreme Court to overrule *The General Smith*. In a celebrated opinion by Justice Bradley, the court decided to stay the course. According to the court, the general maritime law of the United States did not recognize a maritime lien for services in the home port of a vessel, and a change in the law was a matter that had to be addressed to the Congress.

Yielding to mounting pressures, Congress enacted the Maritime Lien Act in 1910. Ten years later, the act was amended and reenacted as a part of the Ship Mortgage Act of 1920. The purpose of the amendment was to broaden the scope of the lien act by expansion of the notion of "necessaries." As previously discussed, the Ship Mortgage Act has been amended and recodified. *See* 46 U.S.C. §§ 31301, *et seq.*, *infra*. It is important, however, to be familiar with the Maritime Lien Act since caselaw relying upon its provisions serves as the basis for interpreting the current statutory law regarding maritime liens.

The Federal Maritime Lien Act

Superseded Version
46 U.S.C. § 971 *et seq.*

§ 971. Persons entitled to lien

Any person furnishing repairs, supplies, towage, use of dry dock or marine railway, or other necessaries, to any vessel, whether foreign or domestic, upon the order of the owner of such vessel, or of a person authorized by the owner, shall have a maritime lien on the vessel, which may be enforced by suit *in rem*, and it shall not be necessary to allege or prove that credit was given to the vessel.

§ 972. Persons authorized to procure repairs, supplies, and necessaries

The following persons shall be presumed to have authority form the owner to procure repairs, supplies, towage, use of dry dock or marine railway, and other necessaries for the vessel:

The managing owner, ship's husband, master, or any person to whom the management of the vessel at the port of supply is intrusted. No person tortiously or unlawfully in possession or charge of a vessel shall have authority to bind the vessel.

§ 973. Notice to persons furnishing repairs, supplies, and necessaries

The officers and agents of a vessel specified in section 972 of this title shall be taken to include such officers and agents when appointed by a charterer, by an owner *pro hac vice*, or by an agreed purchaser in possession of the vessel.

§ 974. Waiver of right to lien

Nothing in this chapter shall be construed to prevent the furnisher of repairs, supplies, towage, use of dry dock or marine railway, or other necessaries, or the mortgagee, from waiving his right to a lien, or in the case of a preferred mortgage lien, to the preferred status of such lien, at any time by agreement or otherwise; and this chapter shall not be construed to affect the rules of law existing on June 5, 1920, in regard to (1) the right to proceed against the vessel for advances, (2) laches in the enforcement of liens upon vessels, (3) the right to proceed *in personam*, (4) the rank of preferred maritime liens among themselves, or (5) priorities between maritime liens and mortgages, other than preferred mortgage, upon vessels of the United States.

§ 975. State Statutes superseded

This chapter shall supersede the provisions of all State statutes conferring liens on vessels, insofar as such statutes purport to create rights of action to be enforced by suits *in rem* in admiralty against vessels for repairs, supplies, towage, use of dry dock or marine railway, and other necessaries.

---

a. Current Statutory Provisions Relating to Maritime Liens

Commercial Instruments and Maritime Liens

46 U.S.C. § 31301, *et seq.*

§ 31301. Definitions

(4) "Necessaries" includes repairs supplies, towage and the use of a dry dock or marine railway.

§ 31305. Waiver of lien rights

This chapter does not prevent a mortgagee or other lien holder from waiving or subordinating at any time by agreement or otherwise the lien holder's right to a lien, the priority or, if a preferred moortgage lien, the preferred status of the lien.

§ 31307. State statutes superseded

This chapter supersedes any State statute conferring a lien on a vessel to the extent the statute establishes a claim to be enforced by a civil action *in rem* against the vessel for necessaries.

Subchapter III — Maritime Liens

§ 31341. Persons presumed to have authority to procure necessaries

(a) The following persons are presumed to have authority to procure necessaries for a vessel:

(1) the owner;

(2) the master;

(3) a person entrusted with the management of the vessel at the port of supply; or

(4) an officer or agent appointed by—

(A) the owner;

(B) a charterer;

(C) an owner *pro hac vice*; or

(D) an agreed buyer in possession of the vessel.

(b) A person tortiously or unlawfully in possession or charge of a vessel has no authority to procure necessaries for the vessel.

§ 31342. Establishing maritime liens

(a) Except as provided in subsection (b) of this section, a person providing necessaries to a vessel on the order of the owner or a person authorized by the owner —

(1) has a maritime lien on the vessel;

(2) may bring a civil action in rem to enforce the lien; and

(3) is not required to allege or prove in the action that credit was given to the vessel.

(b) This section does not apply to a public vessel.

§ 31343. Recording and discharging liens on preferred mortgage vessels

(a) Except as provided under subsection (d) of this section, a person claiming a lien on a vessel covered by a preferred mortgage filed or recorded under this chapter may record with the Secretary of Transportation a notice of that person's lien claim on the vessel. To be recordable, the notice must—

(1) state the nature of the lien;

(2) state the date the lien was established;

(3) state the amount of the lien;

(4) state the name and address of the person; and

(5) be signed and acknowledged.

(b) The Secretary shall record a notice complying with subsection (a) of this section.

(c) On full and final discharge of the indebtedness that is the basis for a claim recorded under subsection (b) of this section, on request of the Secretary or owner, the person having the claim shall provide the Secretary with an acknowledged certificate of discharge of the indebtedness. The Secretary shall record the certificate.

(d) A person claiming a lien on a vessel covered by a preferred mortgage under section 31322(d) of this title must record and discharge the lien as provided by the law of the Sate in which the vessel is titled.

b. Interpretation of Current Statutory Provisions: Relevant Decisions Based Upon the Federal Maritime Lien Act.

i. 46 U.S.C. § 31342: "A Person Providing Necessaries to a Vessel ..."

PIEDMONT COAL CO. v. SEABOARD FISHERIES CO.

254 U.S. 1, 41 S. Ct. 1, 65 L. Ed. 97 (1920)

Mr. Justice BRANDEIS delivered the opinion of the court

The Atlantic Phosphate and Oil Corporation owned a fleet of nineteen fishing steamers. It owned also factories at Promised Land, Long Island, and Tiverton, Rhode Island, to which the fish caught were delivered and at which its vessels coaled. When the fishing season of 1914 opened the company was financially embarrassed. Its steamers and factories had been mortgaged to secure an issue of bonds. Bills for supplies theretofore furnished remained unpaid. The company had neither money nor credit. It could not enter upon the season's operations unless some arrangement should be made to supply its vessels and factories with coal. After some negotiations, the Piedmont and Georges Creek Coal Company, then a creditor for coal delivered during the year 1913, agreed to furnish the Oil Corporation such coal as it would require during the season of 1914—the understanding of the parties being that the coal to be delivered would be used by the factories as well as by the vessels, that the greater part would be used by the vessels, that the law would afford a lien on the vessels for the purchase price of the coal and that the Coal Company would thus have security. Shipments of coal were made under this agreement from time to time during the spring and summer as ordered by the Oil Corporation. In the autumn receivers for the corporation were appointed by the District Court of the United States for the District of Rhode Island, and later a suit was brought to foreclose the mortgage upon the vessels and factories. At the time the receivers were appointed five cargoes of coal shipped under the above agreement had not been paid for. The Coal Company libeled twelve of the steamers asserting maritime liens for the price and value of either all the coal or of such parts as had been used by the libeled vessels respectively. Meanwhile, the vessels were sold under the decree of foreclosure. The Seaboard Fisheries Company became the purchaser and, intervening as claimant in the lien proceedings, denied liability. The District Court held that the Coal Company had a maritime lien on each vessel for the coal received by it. *The William B. Murray*, 240 Fed. Rep. 147. The Circuit Court of Appeals reversed these decrees with costs and directed that the libels be dismissed. *The Walter Adams*, 253 Fed. Rep. 20. Then this court granted the Coal Company's petition for a writ of certiorari. 248 U.S. 556.

As to the facts proved there is no disagreement between the two lower courts. The substantial question presented is whether these facts constitute a furnishing of supplies by the Coal Company to the vessels upon order of the owner within the provisions of the Act of June 23, 1910, c. 373, § 1, 36 Stat. 604. That coal was furnished to the vessels to the extent to which they severally received it on board, is clear. The precise question, therefore, is: Was the coal furnished by the libelant, the Coal Company, or was it furnished by the Oil Corporation, the owner of the fleet? In determining this question additional facts must be considered:

No coal was delivered by the Coal Company directly to any vessel; and it had no dealings of any kind concerning the coal directly with the officers of any vessel. All the coal was billed by the Coal Company to the Oil Corporation and there was no reference on any invoice, or on its books, either to the fleet or to any vessel. There was no understanding between the companies when the agreement to supply the coal was made or when the coal was delivered that any part of it was specifically for any one of the several vessels libeled, or that it was for any particular vessel of the fleet, or even for the vessels then composing the fleet. Indeed, the first shipment was stated on the invoice to be "coal for factory." The negotiations of the Oil Corporation with the Coal Company did not relate to coal required at that time by the particular vessels subsequently libeled as distinguished from other vessels of the fleet.

The coal was sold f.o.b. at the Coal Company's piers which were at St. George, Staten Island, and Port Reading, New Jersey. At these piers it was loaded on barges which were towed either to the Oil Corporation's plant at Promised Land or to that at Tiverton. Some of these barges were supplied by the Oil Corporation, some by the Coal Company. If supplied by the latter, trimming and towing charges were added to the agreed price of the coal. Upon arrival of the coal at the factories it was placed in the Oil Corporation's bins. At Promised Land—which received four of the five shipments—the bins already contained other coal (1068 tons) which had been theretofore purchased by the Oil Corporation and had been paid for. With this coal on hand that delivered by libelant was commingled. At each plant both the vessels and the factory were from time to time supplied with coal from the same bins; but the greater part of the coal supplied from each plant was used by the vessels. Weeks, and in some instances months, elapsed between placing the coal in the bins and the delivery of it by the Corporation to the several vessels. When it made such deliveries it furnished coal to the vessels, as it did to the factories, not under direction of the Coal Company but in its discretion as owner of the coal and of the business.

The quantity of coal delivered to each vessel was proved; but to what extent the coal supplied to the several vessels which bunkered at Promised Land came from the 1068 tons previously purchased, and to what extent it came from the lots purchased from the Coal Company, it was impossible to determine. In making the computations which formed the basis of the decrees in the District Court, it was assumed that, of the coal supplied to the several vessels which bunkered at Promised Land, a proportionate part of that received by each had come from the coal purchased from libelant.

The Coal Company contends on these facts that it furnished necessary supplies to the several vessels within the meaning of § 1 of the Act of June 23, 1910. But the facts show that no coal was furnished by that company to any vessel "upon the order of the owner." The title to the coal had passed to the Oil Corporation when it was loaded on board the barges at the Coal Company's piers. It was delivered to Promised Land and Tiverton as the Oil Corporation's coal and placed in its bins. As its coal the later distribution was made in its discretion to vessels and factories. A large part of the coal so acquired by the Oil Corporation for use in its business was subsequently appropriated by it specifically to the use of the several vessels of the fleet and this use of the coal by vessels of the fleet was a use which had been contemplated by the parties when it was purchased. But the fact that such a use had been contemplated does not render the subsequent appropriation by the owner a furnishing by the coal dealer to the several vessels.

To hold that a lien for the unpaid purchase price of supplies arises in favor of the seller merely because the purchaser, who is the owner of a vessel, subsequently appropriates the supplies to her use would involve abandonment of the principle upon which maritime liens rest and the substitution therefor of the very different principle which underlies mechanics' and materialmen's liens on houses and other structures. The former had its origin in desire to protect the ship; the latter mainly in desire to protect those who furnish work and materials. The maritime lien developed as a necessary incident of the operation of vessels. The ship's function is to move from place to place. She is peculiarly subject to vicissitudes which would compel abandonment of vessel or voyage, unless repairs and supplies were promptly furnished. Since she is usually absent from the home port, remote from the residence of her owners and without any large amount of money, it is essential that she should be self-reliant—that she should be able to obtain upon her own account needed repairs and supplies. The recognition by the law of such inherent power did not involve any new legal conception, since the ship had been treated in other connections as an entity capable of entering into relations with others, of acting independently and of becoming responsible for her acts. Because the ship's need was the source of the maritime lien it could arise only if the repairs or supplies were necessary; if the pledge of her credit was necessary to the obtaining of them; if they were actually obtained; and if they were furnished upon her credit. The mechanic's and materialman's lien, on the other hand, attaches ordinarily although the labor and material cannot be said to have been necessary; although at the time they were furnished there was no thought of obtaining security upon the building; and although the credit of the owner or of others had in fact been relied upon. The principle upon which the mechanic's lien rests is, in a sense, that of unjust enrichment. Ordinarily, it is the equity arising from assumed enhancement in value resulting from work or materials expended upon the property without payment therefor which is laid hold of to protect workmen and others who, it is assumed, are especially deserving, would ordinarily fail to provide by agreement for their own protection and would often be unable to do so.

* * *

In the case at bar there was no understanding when the contract was made, or when the coal was delivered by the libelant, that any part of it was for any particular vessel or even for the vessels then composing the fleet. And it was clearly understood that the purchasing corporation would apply part of the coal to a nonmaritime use. The difficulty here (unlike that presented in *The Vigilancia*, 58 Fed. Rep. 698; *The Cimbria*, 156 Fed. Rep. 378, 382; and *The Curtin*, 165 Fed. Rep. 271) is not in failure to show that the coal was furnished to the vessels but in failure to prove that it was furnished by the libelant.

* * *

Affirmed.

FOSS LAUNCH & TUG CO. v. CHAR CHING SHIPPING U.S.A.

808 F.2d 697, 1987 AMC 913 (9th Cir. 1987)

GOODWIN, Circuit Judge

The only substantial question in this appeal is whether a lessor of container boxes to a company that operates a fleet of container ships can assert a maritime lien against a vessel pursuant to 46 U.S.C. §§ 971-975. The district court granted summary judgment for the lien claimant. We reverse.

The essential facts are not in dispute. Appellees leased containers to CC Line under a series of separate lease agreements. The containers were to be used by CC Line in connection with its transpacific shipping service between various ports in Asia and the United States. Under the lease agreements, containers were delivered to CC Line at different times in a variety of locations. The containers are substantially uniform in design and construction, and are treated by carriers as fungible. Some deliveries under the Flexivan agreements were apparently made to CC Line's own container yards that service its transpacific operations. The Transamerica, Nautilus, Genstar, and Itel leasing contracts, however, provided for the delivery of containers to CC Line at container manufacturing plants and at the lessor's own container depots. Once the CC Line took possession of the containers, CC Line had unrestricted authority to designate which containers would be placed aboard the particular vessels operating in its transpacific service.[1] The lease agreements likewise did not restrict the use of the leased containers to exclusive use in maritime transportation. These boxes are designed for intermodal transportation.

The vessel "C.C. San Francisco" entered CC Line's transpacific service in 1983. It was specially designed for carrying cargo packed in containers. One or more of each lessor's containers was actually used aboard the "C.C. San Francisco" for the transport of ocean cargo.

In late August, 1984, the vessel "C.C. San Francisco" was arrested in Los Angeles in an *in rem* maritime action by appellees. The registered owner of the vessel, "Char Yigh Marine (Panama) S.A.," thereafter appeared in district court and sought a post-seizure hearing to have plaintiffs-appellees justify their maritime lien claims. Cross-motions for summary judgment were filed with the district court and on August 20, 1985, the district court ruled in favor of plaintiffs' liens. The district court held:

> (1) that the plaintiffs' container leases with "CC Line" are maritime contracts; (2) that plaintiffs' containers served as the functional equivalent of the hold of the "CC San Francisco" and are therefore "necessaries" within the meaning of 46 U.S.C. § 971; (3) that plaintiffs "furnished" containers to the "CC San Francisco" within the meaning of 46 U.S.C. § 971; (4) that plaintiffs have valid maritime liens for necessaries against the vessel "CC San Francisco" for all containers carried aboard that vessel; and (5), that the maritime lien encompasses all periods plaintiffs' containers served as the functional equivalent of the hold of the "CC San Francisco," including incidental land use.

Flexivan Leasing, Inc. v. M/V C.C. San Francisco, 628 F. Supp. 1077, 1080 (C.D.Cal.1985).

---

[1] This practice is apparently consistent with the current industry practice with respect to containerization. Containers are leased in bulk lots so that they can be employed interchangably or sequentially in the conveyance of freight by means of various modes of transport including ships, airplanes, railroads, and trucks.

* * *

We have no difficulty in following the cases which have found similar container leases to be sufficiently related to maritime transportation to support the extension of federal admiralty jurisdiction. *CTI-Container Leasing Corp. v. Oceanic Operations Corp.*, 682 F. 2d 377, 380-81 (2d Cir.1982); *American President Lines, Ltd. v. Green Transfer & Storage, Inc.*, 568 F. Supp. 58, 60 (D.Or.1983); *Integrated Container Service, Inc. v. Starlines Container Shipping, Ltd.*, 476 F. Supp. 119, 125 (S.D.N.Y.1979).[2]

Of the remaining issues raised on appeal, each turns on an interpretation of the governing federal maritime lien statute, 46 U.S.C. § 971. That statute provides as follows:

> Any person furnishing repairs, supplies, towage, use of dry dock or marine railway, or other necessaries, to any vessel, whether foreign or domestic, upon the order of the owner of such vessel, or of a person authorized by the owner, shall have a maritime lien on the vessel, which may be enforced by suit *in rem*, and it shall not be necessary to allege or prove that credit was given to the vessel. 46 U.S.C. § 971 (1982).

A recent decision of this court, *Farwest Steel Corp. v. Barge Sea-Span*, 241, 769 F. 2d 620, 623 (9th Cir.1985), instructs that there are three requirements for the grant of a maritime lien under 46 U.S.C. § 971. A person lien claimant must have: (1) furnish[ed] repairs, supplies, or other necessaries, (2) to any vessel, (3) "upon the order of the owner of such vessel, or of a person authorized by the owner." 46 U.S.C. § 971.

* * *

The second requirement, that the lien claimant be a person "furnishing ... to any vessel," presents a closer question. Its resolution turns on the intent of Congress in drafting a form of the verb "to furnish" into the text of 46 U.S.C. § 971. There is no doubt that containers furnished by the lien claimant were carried on one of a group of vessels intended to carry such containers. The question is whether the lien claimant furnished the attached containers "to" that vessel under the Act. In other words, is it a condition precedent to a lien that containers which have been leased to managers of a fleet of container vessels also must have been specifically set apart for use on the particular vessel against which a lien is asserted?

The "furnishing" question has recently been faced in two other circuits. Apparently in an effort to accommodate the professed expectations and needs of the shipping industry, each court applied a broad construction of "furnishing." In the most recent decision, the Fifth Circuit noted the closeness of the question but nevertheless concluded: "We find no persuasive reason to read the term 'furnishing' ... narrowly.... The statute was intended to encourage private investment in the maritime industry. We will not begin now to defeat the purpose of the Act by layering technicalities onto its interpretation." *Equilease*, 793 F. 2d at 603. Similarly, a Florida district court noted that "for purposes of creating a valid

[2] We express no opinion on the effect of "incidental land uses" of containers employed in "inter-modal" freight conveyance, originating on maritime vessels, upon the proper boundaries of admiralty jurisdiction. We need not decide whether a creditor could permit maritime attachment of containers located far in the interior of the country even though they may have been subject to the preference accorded maritime liens while aboard ship.

maritime lien, it may not be essential, and indeed may not be desirable, that the container be delivered directly to the vessel, be sold rather than leased, or be earmarked for a particular vessel." *Transamerica ICS*, 1984 A.M.C. at 490.

We respect the reasoning of these courts. But we are reluctant to subject the heretofore relatively certain law of maritime liens to the uncertainty and flux of developing shipping industry practices when the controlling precedents governing interpretation of the Act favor a narrow construction of the "furnishing" requirement.

We begin with the plain meaning of 46 U.S.C. § 971. Stripped to its essentials, the statute states that "[a]ny person furnishing ... necessaries ... to any vessel...." We note initally that the verb "to furnish" as found in the statute appears in the form of the active and not the passive voice. For example, the statute could have been drafted to state that "necessaries that *are furnished* to any vessel" can support a maritime lien. In such circumstance, it would have been possible for even the fortuitous application or use of necessaries by a vessel to create a valid maritime lien against a vessel. In creating a preferred class of secured creditors, Congress chose not to draft the Act in the passive voice and we think the correct inference is that Congress intended "furnishing" to require active forethought or advance identification of particular vessels in relation to "necessaries" supplied.

This inference is consistent with the historical vessel-specific character of a maritime lien. Under the law of maritime liens, a vessel is considered to be a distinct entity responsible only for its own debts. *Riffe Petroleum Co. v. Cibro Sales Corp.*, 601 F. 2d 1385, 1389 (10th Cir.1979). As a consequence, maritime liens are enforced through *in rem* proceedings, *see* Rule C, Supplemental Rules for Certain Admiralty and Maritime Claims, FED. R. CIV. P., and jurisdiction lies only in the district where the vessel is located.

Our restrictive interpretation of "furnishing" is supported by longstanding precedents interpreting 46 U.S.C. § 971. *Piedmont & Georges Creek Coal Co. v. Seaboard Fisheries Co.*, 254 U.S. 1, 41 S. Ct. 1, 65 L. Ed. 97 (1920), and its progeny are particularly apposite to this action. In *Piedmont*, the Supreme Court denied maritime liens sought against vessels that had received coal which had been sold to the vessels' owner on credit. The defect was not "in failure to show that the coal was furnished to the vessels but in failure to prove that it was furnished *by* the libelant." *Piedmont*, 254 U.S. at 13, 41 S. Ct. at 5.

Appellees contend that *Piedmont* represents a case driven by a simple failure of proof as to the amounts of coal actually received by each vessel in a group of vessels supplied with coal. However, it is clear that *Piedmont* has not been interpreted in such a limited fashion. In *Bankers Trust Co. v. Hudson River Day Line*, 93 F. 2d 457 (2d. Cir.1937), maritime liens were denied a supplier of oil who had delivered oil to a buyer's barges under a single bulk supply contract. In denying the lien, the *Bankers Trust* court understood the holding of Piedmont on the "furnishing" question to require that "supplies, though delivered in mass to the owner of the fleet under a single contract, [must be] expressly ordered by the owner and delivered to him by the supplyman for the use of *named vessels in specified portions.*" *Id.* at 458 (emphasis supplied by Second Circuit) (*quoting The American Eagle*, 30 F. 2d 293, 295 (D.Del.1929)).

In *Dampskibsselskabet Dannebrog v. Signal Oil & Gas Co.*, 310 U.S. 268 (1940), the Supreme Court decided to grant a maritime lien only after distinguishing *Piedmont* in the following manner: "In the instant case, the oil was supplied exclusively for the vessels in question, was delivered directly to the vessels and was so invoiced; and there was nothing in the general contract to the effect that the supplies were to be furnished [to some degree] upon the credit of the vessels." *Id.* at 277. Thus, the holding of *Dampskibsselskabet* should be read to encompass only those cases in which a materialman has taken care, in an ascertainable manner, to designate the items or services he contracts to provide for use on the particular vessel against which a lien is subsequently sought. *See also The Everosa*, 93 F. 2d 732, 735 (1st Cir.1937) (lien granted) ("In the present case, the master of a particular vessel requisitioned for coal to the coal company; it was sent to a particular vessel, loaded on her by the coal company's representative and paid for by her master"); *Carr v. George E. Warren Corp.*, 2 F. 2d 333, 334 (4th Cir.1924) (lien granted) ("In this case, the coal was actually purchased on the credit of the steamers, billed to the steamers, and used by them.")

Piedmont was also responsible for the incorporation of the *stricti juris* principle, long a feature of the law of maritime liens, *see Vandewater v. Mills*, 60 U.S. 82, 19 How. 82, 89, 15 L. Ed. 554 (1857), into the law governing the interpretation of maritime liens under the Act. *Piedmont*, 254 U.S. at 12, 41 S. Ct. at 4. Because the maritime lien under 46 U.S.C. § 971 is secret and may operate to the prejudice of prior mortgagees and other creditors without notice, it will not be "extended by construction, analogy or inference." *Id.*; *See also W.A. Marshall & Co. v. S.S. "President Arthur"*, 279 U.S. 564, 568, 49 S. Ct. 420, 421, 73 L. Ed. 846 (1929); *Bankers Trust Co.*, 93 F. 2d at 459; *Bellingham Nat. Bank*, 587 F. Supp. at 28-29.

The facts and posture of the instant action parallel those found in Piedmont. In each case a materialman provided bulk supplies—coal in *Piedmont*, containers here—in circumstances where the final allocation of supplies, to any vessel of the group intended to be supplied, was left to the discretion of the procuring authority. Although, in both cases, it was understood that the supplies provided would predominantly be put to maritime use, in neither case was there any evident attempt to designate any individual vessel to receive any identifiable component of the supplies.

Appellees vainly attempt to distinguish *Piedmont*. First, they contend that their ability to identify precisely which containers were carried on board the "C.C. San Francisco" at which time adequately answers the concern in Piedmont over the grant of equally proportional liens against each of the vessels in the group that received coal. However, this is simply not a distinguishing characteristic. The *Piedmont* holding was not made contingent on the district court's inability to establish the exact amount of coal used by a particular vessel in the group. Rather, the defect was in the unstructured character of the contractual arrangements for the supply of coal to the *Piedmont* vessel group. *Piedmont*, 254 U.S. at 13, 41 S. Ct. at 4.

Second, appellees argue that the fact that the coal supplied in *Piedmont* was found to have been partially consumed in the owner's dockside factory instead of in vessels potentially subject to maritime liens is a distinguishing characteristic. While the Supreme Court did note that it was concerned about the potential for nonmaritime use of coal supplied to the owner's dock, *see Piedmont*, 254 U.S. at 13, 41 S. Ct. at 4, a similar problem is presented here by the potential for "inter-modal" use of containers. In an attempt to cure this deficiency, the district court granted maritime liens only to the extent that containers were the "functional equivalent of the hold" of the "C.C. San Francisco." However, under the leasing agreements entered into with CC Line, none of the appellees restricted the "inter-modal" use of their leased containers to exclusively maritime conveyance. Thus, despite the district court's holding below, it cannot be gainsaid that nonmaritime use analogous to that in *Piedmont*, was permitted under the container leasing agreements in issue here.

Finally, it is particularly instructive to compare the similarity in the reasoning supporting the holdings of both the district court in *Piedmont* and the district court in this action. The *Piedmont* district court, in its attempt to justify a broad interpretation of the "furnishing" requirement, stated:

> As supplies for fleets of vessels under a common ownership and management in the ordinary course of business are contracted for in view of the general requirements of the entire fleet, as supply men will thus be called upon to furnish supplies in advance of the arrival of the vessels, as at the time supplies are ordered there may be uncertainty as to which vessel may require them and use them, *the statute should receive a construction which will make it applicable to and consistent with modern business conditions.* A supply man who furnished supplies ready for any vessel of a fleet that may call for it should not be deprived of the same right to a lien as a supply man who is told the name of the vessel which is to require the supplies.

240 F. 147, 153 (D.R.I.1917) (emphasis added). The district court in this action similarly stated that

> In light of today's shipping practices [the bulk leasing of containers], defendant's contention that a container need be furnished to a specific vessel, rather than to a fleet of vessels, in order for a valid maritime lien to exist, is highly impractical.

Flexivan, 628 F. Supp at 1079 (emphasis added).

Like the Supreme Court in *Piedmont*, we are not persuaded that "modern business conditions" in the shipping industry are sufficient justification to expand the "furnishing to any vessel" requirement of 46 U.S.C. § 971.[4] Accordingly, we hold that cargo containers leased in bulk to a time-charterer of a group of vessels for unrestricted use on board the vessels in that group, are not furnished to any particular vessel of the group, on which they subsequently happen to be employed, within the meaning of 46 U.S.C. § 971.

We reverse the order of the district court with respect to the establishment of maritime liens under the Federal Maritime Lien Act, 46 U.S.C. § 971. This cause is remanded to the district court for further proceedings as may be necessary to discharge the lien.

Reversed and remanded.

---

[4] Appellees' contention that there is no substantive difference between a container company leasing 10 containers to steamship company A, pre-allocating them only for use on a group of 5 specified vessels, and that company leasing 10 other containers to steamship company B, without pre-allocation but where the containers actually were carried aboard five vessels, misses the mark. We are presented with a question of interpretation of the statute and under a narrow interpretation of "furnishing," in neither case would a maritime lien likely attach. The relevant comparison is between companies A & B and a company C which leases an identified set of containers specifically for use on a named vessel.

J. BLAINE ANDERSON, Circuit Judge, concurred in part and dissented in part. [Opinion omitted. Eds.]

Note

In *Freret Marine Supply v. Harris Trust & Savings Bank*, 73 Fed. Appx. 698 (5th Cir. 2003), a bank that had processed credit card transactions for a cruise ship operator sued two cruise ships *in rem* to recover sums that it had had to repay to credit card companies on behalf of the cruise ship operator when the cruise ship operator went bankrupt and ceased operations. The U.S. Court of Appeals for the Fifth Circuit held that the bank did not have a maritime lien over the cruise ships. The court held that the contract between the bank and the cruise ship operator was not a maritime contract, but even if it had been, the bank's services were provided to the cruise ship operator itself, not to the individual ships.

---

ii. 46 U.S.C. § 31301(4): "'Necessaries' Includes Repairs, Supplies, Towage, and the Use of a Dry Dock or Marine Railway...."

CLUBB OIL TOOLS, INC. v. M/V GEORGE VERGOTTIS

460 F. Supp. 835, 1980 AMC 556 (S.D. Tex. 1978)

Carl O. BUE, Jr., District Judge

* * *

Plaintiff contends, and the Court concludes, that the rental of the pipe to Trefalcon creates a lien in its favor against the GEORGE VERGOTTIS pursuant to 46 U.S.C.A. § 971.

* * *

Defendant Franconia Sea Transport urges the applicability of *J. Ray McDermott & Co. v. The Off-Shore Menhaden Company*, 262 F. 2d 523 (5th Cir. 1959), wherein Chief Judge John R. Brown held that a lien was not created in favor of the claimant for the cost of dredging a slip for use as a permanent berth. The capital nature of the facility led the court to conclude that it should not come within the purview of the Lien Act, for to do so would open the door to claims that the costs of constructing wharves, docks, warehouse sheds and other permanent capital improvements may also be the subject of maritime liens.

* * *

While plaintiff concedes the absence of case authority directly on point, it urges that the prevailing broad meaning given the phrase "other necessaries" and the reasoning behind the act combine to compel the conclusion that a lien exists in the instant case. In support of this position, plaintiff urges that the pipe rental is analogous to stevedoring services which may form the basis for a maritime lien. *Nacirema Operating Co., Inc. v. S.S. Al Kulsum*, 407 F. Supp. 1222 (S.D.N.Y.1975). After analyzing the briefs submitted by the parties and the relevant treatises and case authority, the Court concludes that the rental of oil pipe in the present case does come within the meaning of the term "other necessaries" and may give rise to a maritime lien.

While the Lien Act has in the past been strictly construed so as to avoid the creation of a lien, "the present state of the law is not far from the point where any service which is "convenient, useful and at times necessary' may qualify as a lien under the Lien Act." G. GILMORE & C. BLACK, THE LAW OF ADMIRALTY 658 (2nd ed. 1975). Thus, "other necessaries" has been defined to include "those items or services which a prudent owner or master would deem to be reasonably required to facilitate the use of the ship, save her from danger and enable her to perform those acts currently demanded of her.... (T)he furnished goals and services must be reasonably needed for the venture in which the ship is engaged." 2 I. HALL, A. SANN & S. BELLMAN, BENEDICT ON ADMIRALTY 3-27 (7th ed. 1975).

Application of this definition to the facts of the present case indicates that the furnishing of oil pipe was reasonably required to facilitate the vessel's mission. The unrebutted testimony at trial revealed that the only feasible means of loading the oil was through the use of a pipeline. Thus, the creation of a lien to cover the cost of the renting of the pipe to defendant Trefalcon is consistent with the purpose of the Lien Act "to keep the ship active, thereby facilitating the flow of commerce and protecting the interests of the owners and secured parties".

* * *

This Court concludes that the facts of this case are clearly distinguishable from *J. Ray McDermott & Co. v. The Off-Shore Menhaden Company* in that the pipe rental in the instant case was not in the nature of a permanent capital improvement as was the permanent slip dredged in *J. Ray McDermott.* The short duration of the rental agreement coupled with the temporary manner in which the pipeline was strung indicate that the clear intent of all the parties was a short-term rental designed to effectuate the loading of the vessel on this one-time basis. Thus, the fear expressed by Chief Judge John R. Brown that the allowance of a lien in *J. Ray McDermott* might set a dangerous precedent for the creation of liens in a multitude of situations where capital improvements are made to ports is not applicable to the instant case, which instead fits the category of cases in which the proper application of the Lien Act leads "to the allowance of maritime liens to new and infrequent situations".

* * *

Note: Liens for "Other Necessaries"

46 U.S.C. § 31301(4) defines "necessaries" furnished to a vessel as including certain specific services or supplies. The Federal Maritime Lien Act not only contained identical language but also the phrase "other necessaries". *See* 46 U.S.C. § 971, *supra.* Courts have given a broad application to 46 U.S.C. § 31342 and have held various sorts of services and supplies to be "necessaries." It has been said: "The present state of the law is not far from the point where any service that is 'convenient, useful and at times necessary' may qualify as a lien under the Lien Act." G. GILMORE & C. BLACK, THE LAW OF ADMIRALTY 543 (2d ed. 1975).

In *Blair v. M/V Blue Spruce*, 315 F. Supp. 555, 1970 AMC 1298 (D. Mass. 1970), it was held that pilotage services were a "necessary" for the purposes of the Federal Maritime Lien Act, thus entitling the pilot to a maritime lien, even though the ship had refused the pilot's services. In addition to addressing the issue of whether services were "furnished" to the vessel, the Court also had to determine whether pilotage which was tendered but refused was "necessary" within the meaning of the federal statute. In resolving this issue the Court stated:

> To effectuate the purposes of the statute, courts have held that the phrase "other necessaries" should be broadly interpreted. *See J. Ray McDermott & Co. v. The Off-Shore Menhaden Co.*, 1959, 5 Cir., 262 F.2d 523, *rehearing denied* Feb. 11, 1959; *City of Erie v. S.S. North American*, 1967, W.D. Pa., 267 F. Supp. 875; *Layton Industries, Inc. v. The Sport Fishing Cruiser Gladiator*, 1967, D. Mass., 263 F. Supp. 356 (FORD, J.); *Allen v. The M/V Contessa*, 1961, S.D. Tex., 196 F. Supp. 649. One recent case from this district has phrased the test as whether the services are reasonably needed in the ship's business. *See Layton Industries, Inc. v. The Sport Fishing Cruiser Gladiator*, 1967, D. Mass., 263 F. Supp. 356 (FORD, J.). Under this statute a variety of items have been found by courts to be "other necessaries." A sampling of the more unusual items includes *Colonial Press of Miami, Inc. v. The BMV Allen's Cay*, 1960, 5 Cir., 277 F.2d 540 (printing materials); *The Susquehanna*, 1923, D. Mass., 3 F.2d 1014 (fumigation of passengers' baggage); *In re Burton S.S. Co.*, 1925, D. Mass., 3 F.2d 1015 (Cape Cod Canal charges); *City of Erie v. S.S. North American*, 1967, W.D. Pa., 267 F. Supp. 875 (wharfage); *Allen v. The M/V Contessa*, 1961, S.D. Tex., 196 F. Supp. 649 (cigarettes). One item of personal service, fairly similar to piloting, which has been held to be an "other [necessary]" is stevedoring. *See In re North Atlantic and Gulf Steamship Co.*, 1962, S.D.N.Y., 204 F. Supp. 899, 907, *aff'd sub nom. Schilling v. Dannebrog*, 1963, 2 Cir., 320 F.2d 628; *The Little Charley*, 1929, D. Md., 31 F.2d 120; *United States v. Certain Subfreights Due S.S. Neponset*, 1924, D. Mass., 300 F. 981, *rev'd on other grounds, United States v. Robins Dry Dock and Repair Co.*, 1926, 13 F.2d 808; *The Henry S. Grove*, 1922, W.D. Wash., 285 F. 60; *International Terminal Operating Co., Inc. v. S.S. Valmas*, 1967, 4 Cir., 375 F.2d 586 [dictum].
>
> Although there is a dearth of cases squarely facing whether pilotage is an "other [necessary]," the cited instances of "necessaries" tend to support the view that pilotage is a necessary. Furthermore, the only references to the issue imply that pilotage services create a lien either under general maritime law, *The Alligator*, 1908, 3 Cir., 161 F. 37 [dictum], or under the Federal Maritime Lien Act, G. GILMORE & C. BLACK, THE LAW OF ADMIRALTY, p. 516 (1957).

* * *

Other services which have been held to be a "necessary" giving rise to a maritime lien include those of a marine architect who drew plans for the installation of new engines in a vessel although the installation did not take place. *Tug Miki Miki*, 1970 AMC 1828 (N.D. Cal. 1969). Advertising expense for a cruise ship is a necessary. *Stern, Hays & Lang, Inc. v. M/V Nili*, 407 F.2d 549, 1969 AMC 13 (5th Cir. 1969). *See also Atlantic Steamer Supply Co. v. The Steamship Tradewind*, 153 F. Supp. 354, 1957 AMC 2169 (D. Md. 1957). An expense incurred by a travel agency for the transportation of crew members to or from the vessel is also a necessary. *See Carl Enterprises v. Barge Hudson Handler*, 475 F. Supp. 42, 1980 AMC 1759 (S.D. Ala. 1979). However, in *J.H. Westerbeke Corp. v. The Golden Fleece*, 1970 AMC 1740 (D. Mass. 1970), the court held that the purchase of a generator was not necessary because the vessel already had two functional generators either of which was sufficient for its navigation. Likewise, in *McDermott & Co. v. The Off-Shore Menhaden Co.*, 262 F.2d 523, 1959 AMC 527 (5th Cir. 1959), the court held that the dredging out of a special slip for use as permanent berth of a vessel was not a necessary.

Are the services of the master of a vessel a "necessary"? An American citizen who serves as master of a vessel has a lien for wages under 46 U.S.C. § 11112. A foreign citizen, however, does not have a lien for master's wages; he may have a contract lien under 46 U.S.C. § 31301, § 31342. In *Medina v. Marvirazon Compania Naviera, S.A.*, 533 F. Supp. 1279, 1287, 1983 AMC 2116 (D. Mass. 1982), the court declared that "[s]urely a captain's services are necessary." *But see Vlavianos v. The Cypress*, 171 F.2d 435, 1949 AMC 9 (4th Cir. 1948), *cert. denied*, 337 U.S. 924, 69 S. Ct. 1168, 93 L. Ed. 1732 (1949). A passenger on the Cypress who had paid $300 in advance for his passage was so impatient at the failure of the vessel to sail on schedule that he had Captain Vlavianos arrested in order to secure the return of his money. A crewmember of the Cypress incurred a taxi bill of $5 to go to the Central Police Station in Baltimore where the captain was confined, and he also advanced the captain $300 with which to purchase his freedom. Subsequently, the crewmember claimed a lien on the ship for $305, asserting that the captain was necessary to a ship, basing his claim on 46 U.S.C. § 971. The court held: "It is obvious that the statute has no application to this situation," and denied the lien.

The issue of whether cargo containers are "necessaries" under the Federal Maritime Lien Act was addressed by the court in *Foss Launch & Tug Company v. Char Ching Shipping U.S.A. Ltd., supra.* Although the court concluded that the containers at issue were not furnished to the vessel, the Ninth Circuit had no difficulty in determining that the term "necessaries" included cargo containers. The court stated:

* * *

> The term, in modern interpretations, has been expanded to encompass any item which is "reasonably needed for the venture in which the ship is engaged." 2 S. FRIEDELL, S. BELLMAN, A. JENNER & J. LOO, BENEDICT ON ADMIRALTY § 37 at 3-27 (7th ed. 1986). *See also Farwest Steel Corp.*, 769 F.2d at 623 ("[t]he term 'necessaries' under section 971 refers to 'supplies which are necessary to keep the ship going' ").
>
> The wide range of items that can be characterized as "necessaries" under the Act is exemplified by the result in *Equilease Corp. v. M/V Sampson*, 793 F.2d 598, (5th Cir. 1986) (*en banc*). In *Equilease*, the court stated:
>
> The term 'necessary' under the FMLA [Act] includes most goods or services that are useful to the vessel, keep her out of danger, and enable her to perform her particular function.... What is a 'necessary' is to be determined relative to the requirements of the ship." *Equilease*, 793 F.2d at 603 (citations omitted). The court's resulting conclusion was that "because insurance is essential to keep a vessel in commerce, insurance is a 'necessary' under 46 U.S.C. § 971. 793 F.2d at 604.
>
> During all relevant periods of the operations of the "C.C. San Francisco," cargo containers of the type leased by appellees were more than reasonably necessary to the successful operation of the vessel. Although theoretically it might have been possible to convert the "C.C. San Francisco" from a container carrier to another type of cargo vessel, such transformation or modification was not attempted here. The vessel entered service in 1983 designed to transport cargo containers of the type supplied by appellees. It was engaged in container shipping throughout its time-charter period of operation by CC Line. We therefore hold that containers provided to the "C.C. San Francisco" under the leasing agreements were "necessaries" within the meaning of 46 U.S.C. § 971. *Accord Transamerica ICS, Inc. v. M/V Panatlantic*, 1984 A.M.C. 489, 490 (S.D. Fla. 1983) ("the Court is convinced that containers are 'necessaries' within the meaning of 46 U.S.C., sec. 971"); *Nautilus Leasing Services, Inc. v. M/V Cosmos, et al.*, 1983 A.M.C. 1483 (S.D.N.Y. 1983) ("we have no difficulty holding that the containers in the instant case are 'necessaries' within 46 U.S.C., sec. 971").

* * *

Note: Absence of Maritime Contract

Suppose a supplier of necessaries would qualify for a maritime lien because it literally satisfies the requirements of the Lien Act, would the lien be defeated if the underlying contract between the vessel owner and the supplier does not qualify as a "maritime contract"? *See Ventura Packers, Inc. v. F/V Jeanine Kathleen*, 305 F.3d 913, 2002 AMC 2248 (9th Cir. 2002).

---

iii. 46 U.S.C. § 31341: "Persons ... Presumed to Have Authority to Procure Necessaries for a Vessel...."

Note: "Presumed ... Authority" and "Authorized by the Owner"

Under the Federal Maritime Lien Act the owner of a vessel or a person authorized by the owner could establish maritime liens for necessaries. *See* 46 U.S.C. § 971. The persons presumed "to have authority from the owner to procure" necessaries "for the vessel" under § 972 were "the managing owner, ship's husband, master, or any person to whom the management of the vessel at the port of supply [was] intrusted." Section 973 further stated that "[t]he officers and agents of a vessel specified in section 972 ... include[d] such officers and agents when appointed by a charterer, by an owner *pro hac vice*, or by an agreed purchaser in possession of the vessel." In interpreting this statutory language, courts faced a myriad of issues. It was not always easy to determine whether the person who ordered the supplies or repairs was the owner of the vessel. *See "The Josephine Lanasa" (Findley v. Lanasa)*, 276 F.2d 907, 1960 AMC 1444 (5th Cir. 1960). Was the "economic owner" of a vessel or a person having an equitable title "owner" within the meaning of section 971? *See Diaz v. The Steamship Seathunder*, 191 F. Supp. 807, 1961 AMC 561 (D. Md. 1961). What about a prospective owner? *See Freedom Line, Inc. v. Glenrock*, 268 F. Supp. 7, 1968 AMC 507 (S.D. Fla. 1967). Were these persons presumed "to have authority from the owner" under section 972?

It has been held that for the determination of the question whether one was "a person authorized by the owner" under section 971, ordinary principles of agency, ratification, and estoppel were applicable. *See Esso International, Inc. v. Steamship Captain John*, 322 F. Supp. 314, 1970 AMC 2086 (S.D. Tex. 1970), *aff'd*, 443 F.2d 1144, 1971 AMC 2285 (5th Cir. 1971).

Under 46 U.S.C. § 31341 the persons presumed to have authority to procure necessaries are: "(1) the owner, (2) the master, (3) a person entrusted with the management of the vessel at the port of supply; or an officer or agent appointed by (A) the owner; (B) a charterer; (C) an owner *pro hac vice*; or (D) an agreed buyer in possession of the vessel." Under § 31342 a maritime lien arises in favor of "a person providing necessaries to a vessel ... on order of a person listed in section 31341 ... or a person authorized by the owner ..." Though the wording of sections 31341-2 and the applicable provisions of the Federal Maritime Lien Act differs, many of the issues addressed in interpreting the language of the Federal Maritime Lien Act are equally relevant when considering the current statutory provisions.

EPSTEIN v. CORPORACION PERUANA DE VAPORES

325 F. Supp. 535, 1971 AMC 1259 (S.D.N.Y. 1971)

Memorandum

CROAKE, District Judge

This is a suit in admiralty brought by the plaintiff, Stratford International Tobacco Company, against the Corporacion Peruana de Vapores to recover a balance of $7,206.50 due on a $13,436.50 purchase of cigarettes and liquor made on May 6, 1965. The facts of the case are as follows.

I

Plaintiff is a corporation engaged in the sale of tax-free cigarettes and liquor to vessels in the Port of New York (Transcript page 11, line 15). Alfred Parodi is a salesman in plaintiff's employ. On May 4, 1965 and May 5, 1965, Parodi had conversations with Luis E. Saavedra, the Captain of the S.S. NAPO (one of defendant's ships). On May 6, 1965, pursuant to these conversations, Saavedra agreed to purchase 2,270,000 cigarettes totalling $12,251.50 and 40 cases of liquor totalling $1,185.00 from plaintiff. Broken down, the cigarette sales consisted of 1,000,000 Salem cigarettes, 500,000 Kents, 300,000 Lucky Strikes, 200,000 Chesterfield Regulars, 100,000 Camels, 100,00 Half 'n Halfs and 70,000 Montclairs (plaintiff's exhibit #1). The liquor consisted of ten cases of Chivas Regal, ten cases of Old Parr, ten cases of Ye Monks Flagons, five cases of White Horse, two cases of Black & White, two cases of Drambuie and one case of B & B.

These goods were delivered to the S.S. NAPO on May 6, 1965, and copies of the invoices for them given to the captain. However, contrary to its usual practice of cash payment at the time of delivery, plaintiff reluctantly consented to a sale on partial credit as the result of Saavedra's simply not having enough cash to pay for the cigarettes and liquor he had ordered. As Parodi himself later testified, "We were more or less forced into granting credit.... I was not aware that credit would occur until the last moment when the captain did not receive the money that he was supposed to have received."

Following delivery of the goods, plaintiff made repeated demands of Saavedra for the $7,206.50 still due on the sale. However, these demands were met only by promises that the money would be forthcoming. When these promises were not met, copies of the original invoices were forwarded to defendant's home office in Peru with a demand for payment. Defendant received these invoices on November 2, 1965. Disclaiming all knowledge of the transaction, it refused to pay, and began an investigation into the conduct of Saavedra. On December 1, 1965, the captain was discharged by the company. He died shortly thereafter.

It is not disputed by either party that the master of a vessel possesses full authority to make purchases binding upon the vessel's owner for "necessaries" to be used on board his own ship unless the contrary is clearly stated to all concerned. In describing the origins of this authority, Benedict's THE LAW OF AMERICAN ADMIRALTY states—

> A ship is, of necessity, a wanderer. She visits shores where her owners are not known or are inaccessible. The master is the fully authorized agent of the distant owners, but is not usually of sufficient pecuniary ability to respond to unforeseen demands of the voyage. These and other kindred characteristics of maritime commerce underlie the practice....

BENEDICT, THE LAW OF AMERICAN ADMIRALTY, 6th Edition (1940), volume 1, pp. 19-20.

Also, it should be noted that cigarettes have been held to be "necessaries" within the meaning of maritime law. *Allen v. The M/V Contessa*, 196 F. Supp. 649 (S.D. Texas 1961).

However, the amount of cigarettes and liquor purchased by Captain Saavedra makes it clear that these supplies were not purchased for consumption by the S.S. NAPO alone. Indeed, plaintiff itself concedes that, in March of 1965 (some six weeks before the transaction in question), the same captain of the same vessel purchased 1,500,000 cigarettes, admittedly "more than what was necessary for the use of the ship."

However, while admitting that the sale in question did not constitute "necessaries" for the S.S. NAPO itself, plaintiff contends that the supplies were purchased by the captain as "necessaries" for other ships owned by the defendant corporation. These cigarettes and liquor, it is claimed, were to be carried by the S.S. NAPO to a home port in Peru where they were to be redistributed to other vessels which had no access to United States ports. Accordingly, it is argued, the captain had authority to make the purchase and defendant should be bound thereby.

Defendant, in turn, denies any knowledge of or authorization for the captain's conduct. It maintains that the captain was never authorized to purchase the supplies in question for his own or any other ship in defendant's fleet, and speculates that the real motive behind the purchase was the captain's participation in a scheme to smuggle tax-free, contraband cigarettes and liquor totally outside the scope of his duties as ship's captain. Accordingly, defendant refuses to be bound by the obligation owing from the captain to the plaintiff, and will not pay the balance due unless so ordered by this court. This court rules as follows.

II

The key question before the court in the instant matter is whether or not the captain of the S.S. NAPO had any kind of authority to purchase the cigarettes and liquor in question and bind the defendant thereby. Clearly, the owner of a vessel is liable for contractual obligations incurred by its master where such obligations were incurred pursuant to either express, apparent, or implied authority. But whether such authority existed in the case at bar is not an easy matter for resolution.

It is the judgment of this court that the captain of the S.S. NAPO was clearly without express authority to make the purchases in question. Express authority is that authority which a principal intentionally confers upon his agent by manifestations to him. In the instant case, not only were such overt manifestations lacking; the captain was specifically forbidden to make purchases such as the one in question by the internal regulations of defendant company (*See* Appendix for English language translations of these regulations—defendant's exhibits A and B). This prohibition was furthered bolstered by defendant's policy of not supplying the captains of its ships with American cash except for that supplied by Hansen & Tidemann (its American agent) for payroll purposes.

The absence of express authority, of course, does not rule out the possibility of apparent or implied authority. Apparent authority is that authority which a principal holds his agent out as possessing or which he permits the agent to represent that he possesses. However, in the instant case, one is hard-pressed to find any such conduct on the part of defendant.

Defendant did nothing to encourage the idea that the captain had authority to purchase the supplies in question. Indeed, the testimony of plaintiff's sole witness, Alfred Parodi, reveals that plaintiff never received any requisition forms directly from the defendant corporation nor did it receive purchasing requests from Hansen & Tidemann. Rather, it always dealt directly with the ship's master.

To counter this, plaintiff argues that past transactions of a similar nature established a pattern of apparent authority in the captain to make these purchases. But the evidence fails to link these transactions to the defendant company itself. In most instances, payment was by cash and, in those few cases where payment was by check, the check was not drawn on the account of defendant, but rather by a bank in Peru upon the Chase Manhattan Bank in New York. Thus the court finds apparent authority in the captain also lacking.

Plaintiff also claims that the captain of the S.S. NAPO had implied authority to bind defendant to the purchases in question. Implied authority is that authority which comes in conformity either with law or the general business customs of a particular trade.

Where conformity with law is concerned, the captain of a vessel has, as previously noted, implied authority to bind the owner thereof to the purchase of "necessaries" for the use of his ship. However, in the instant case, the court is concerned not with the purchase of necessaries for the captain's own vessel, but with the purchase of necessaries for other ships. Thus, the crucial question becomes one of whether or not a captain has implied authority to purchase "necessaries" for a ship other than his own.

This court holds that he does not. A captain is master of his own ship, not of any other. And no definition of "necesaries" dating back one hundred years that this court has been able to uncover holds to the contrary....

Thus, plaintiff is left with the contention that the captain had implied authority to purchase the supplies in question because said purchase was in conformity with general business customs. This proposition must also fail

Plaintiff's witness, Alfred Parodi, testified to the custom of captains purchasing more than their own ships' necessary requirements of cigarettes and liquor and distributing them to other vessels which do not reach the United States. But there is little else before this court to support the proposition that such a custom actually exists—a proposition which this court declines to accept in view of its earlier finding that a captain does not have implied authority to purchase necessaries for ships other than his own as a matter of case or statute law. And, even if such a custom did exist, one must doubt its applicability to the case at bar. For there is little to show that plaintiff sold the cigarettes and liquor in question to Saavedra in the belief that they would be transferred to other ships belonging to defendant. Indeed, the evidence is to the contrary. Parodi himself testified that, once the goods were cleared with customs and tax agents, his job was at an end and he was "not concerned" with the fate of the goods.

It is the conclusion of this court then, that the captain of the S.S. NAPO was without authority—express, apparent, or implied—to bind defendant to the purchase in question. The record supports the belief that, whatever the purpose of Captain Saavedra in making these purchases, it was outside the scope of his employment by defendant, and plaintiff had no reason to think otherwise....

(a) Authority to Lien a Vessel Under the General Maritime Law

Note

Under the general maritime law, a necessaries supplier did not acquire a maritime lien if it could by reasonable diligence have ascertained that the person ordering the necessaries did not have authority to lien the vessel.

> Under what circumstances, if under any, a charterer who has control and possession of a vessel under a charter party requiring him, at his own cost, to provide for necessary supplies and repairs, may pledge the credit of the vessel, it is not necessary now to determine. We mean only to decide, at this time, that one furnishing supplies or making repairs on the order simply of a person or corporation acquiring the control and possession of a vessel under such a charter party cannot acquire a maritime lien if the circumstances attending

> the transaction put him on inquiry as to the existence and terms of such charter party, but he failed to make inquiry, and chose to act on a mere belief that the vessel would be liable for his claim.

The Valencia v. Ziegler, 165 U.S. 264, 272-73, 17 S. Ct. 323, 326, 41 L. Ed. 710 (1897).

(b) Authority to Lien a Vessel Under the Federal Maritime Lien Act: Pre-1971

Note: The Original Language of 46 U.S.C. § 973

The Federal Maritime Lien Act was incorporated verbatim into the Ship Mortgage Act of 1920. Section 973 of that Act was amended in 1971. *See* version of statute, *supra*. Prior to 1971, § 973 contained language that barred the attachment of a maritime lien where the materialman "knew, or by exercise of reasonable diligence could have ascertained, that because of the terms of the charter party" the person ordering the materials "was without authority to bind the vessel therefor."

DAMPSKIBSSELSKABET DANNEBROG v. SIGNAL OIL & GAS CO. OF CALIFORNIA

310 U.S. 268, 60 S. Ct. 937, 84 L. Ed. 1197 (1940)

Mr. Chief Justice HUGHES delivered the opinion of the Court

The question is whether the respondent is entitled to maritime liens for fuel oil delivered to petitioners' vessels.

In September, 1932, respondent, Signal Oil and Gas Company, made a contract with the Anglo Canadian Shipping Company, Limited, agreeing to sell fuel oil to any vessel which the Anglo Canadian Company might own, charter or operate. In May, 1933, the parties modified the contract so as to include the fuel oil requirements of vessels owned, chartered or operated by W.L. Comyn & Sons. Later, the respective owners of the two vessels here in question, the "Stjerneborg" and the "Brand," chartered them to W.L. Comyn & Sons.

The charters were time charters on the so-called "Government form." The owners agreed "to let" and the charterers "to hire" the vessel "from the time of delivery" for a specified period, the vessel to be placed "at the disposal of the charterers" at such place as the charterers may direct, being on her delivery ready to receive cargo and to be employed in carrying merchandise as stated. The owners agreed to provide and pay for all provisions, wages and shipping and discharging fees of the captain, officers, engineers, firemen and crew; to pay for the insurance of the vessel, and to maintain her in a thoroughly efficient state in hull, machinery and equipment. The charterers agreed to "provide and pay for" coals and fuel oil, port charges, pilotages, etc., and all other usual expenses except as before stated. The charterers were to pay "for the use and hire" of the vessel a stipulated amount commencing "on and from the day of her delivery" and to continue until "the day of her redelivery in like good order and condition, ordinary wear and tear excepted, to the owners (unless lost) at a safe port" as designated. It was provided that the captain, although appointed by the owners, should be "under the orders and direction of the charterers as regards employment or agency"; and the charterers were to load, stow and trim the cargo at their expense under the supervision of the captain. If the charterers should have reason to be dissatisfied with the conduct of the captain, officers or engineers, the owners if necessary should make a change in the appointments. The charterers were allowed to appoint a supercargo to accompany the vessel and "see that voyages are prosecuted with the utmost despatch." It was further provided that nothing in the charter should be construed as a "demise" and that the owners were to remain responsible for the navigation of the vessel. The charters contained no prohibition against the creation of liens for necessary supplies ordered by the charterers.

Respondent libeled the vessels for fuel oil supplied to the vessels respectively on the charterers' order, and the owners appeared and filed answers alleging that the oil was furnished upon the charterers' credit and not upon that of the vessel.

* * *

Petitioners rely upon our decisions in *The Kate*, 164 U.S. 458, 464, and *The Valencia*, 165 U.S. 264, to the effect that where the charter party requires the charterer to provide and pay for supplies, the supplier being charged with knowledge of the provisions of the charter party was not entitled to a maritime lien for supplies furnished to the vessel upon the order of the charterer.

These decisions, however, were prior to the passage of the Act of June 23, 1910, 36 Stat. 604, which governs the present case.... Its purpose was to simplify and clarify the rules as to maritime liens as to which there had been much confusion. The Act did away with the artificial distinction between repairs, supplies, etc., furnished in home ports and those furnished in foreign ports. It did away with the doctrine that when the owner of a vessel contracted in person for necessaries or was present in the port when they were ordered, it was presumed that the material-man did not intend to rely upon the vessel's credit. It substituted a federal statute for numerous state statutes purporting to confer liens. *Piedmont Coal Co. v. Seaboard Fisheries Co.*, 254 U.S. 1, 11.

In so doing, the statute provided a series of simple and comprehensive rules. While it was said not to be intended to change the general principles of the law of maritime liens, it was intended to operate in aid of those who supply necessaries to ships and it correspondingly restricted the rights of the owners of the vessels.

* * *

Despite the aim thus to provide simple and clear rules, there has been no little contrariety of opinion in the application of the statute,—well illustrated by the conflicting decisions to which we have referred with respect to the existence of maritime liens where supplies have been ordered by a charterer who has agreed with the owner to provide and pay for them. As, in such a case, the supplies are furnished on the charterer's order, there is no question that the supplier is charged with knowledge of the provisions of the charter when he either knows them or by reasonable diligence could have ascertained them. So far, the principle of *The Kate* and *The Valencia, supra*, is embodied in the statute. But it does not follow that, in the light of the statute, *The Kate* and *The Valencia* can still be regarded as authority for the view that the mere fact that the charterer is bound to provide and pay for the supplies excludes the supplier from having a maritime lien when the charter party contains no prohibition against its creation.

We think that our decision in *The South Coast*, 251 U.S. 519, negatives such a conclusion.

* * *

We think that the fair import of our decision in *The South Coast* is that when the charterer has the direction and control of the vessel and it is his business to provide necessary supplies, and the charter party does not prohibit the creation of a maritime lien therefor, the material-man is entitled to furnish the supplies upon the credit of the vessel as well as upon that of the charterer and the lien is not defeated by the fact that the charterer has promised the owner to pay.

When, however, the charter party, with knowledge of which the material-man is charged, prohibits the creation of a lien for supplies ordered by the charterer or the charterer's representative, no lien will attach. This was decided in *United States v. Carver*, 260 U.S. 482.

* * *

As, in the instant case, the charter parties contained no provision prohibiting the creation of a maritime lien, we are of the opinion that the mere fact that they required the charterers to provide and pay for the supplies did not prevent the liens from attaching.

The argument is pressed that respondent was under a general contract to supply "the fuel oil requirements of any and all vessels owned, chartered, or operated" by W.L. Comyn & Sons. But this contract did not provide that the oil should be supplied on the sole credit of Comyn as the owner or charterer of the vessels or negative the creation of maritime liens for supplies actually furnished to the vessels in satisfying their requirements. The decisions which petitioner cites are not apposite. In *Piedmont Coal Co. v. Seaboard Fisheries Co.*, *supra*, the Coal Company had made a contract with a corporation, which owned both steamers and factories, to furnish such coal as should be required. The court observed that the difficulty which confronted the Coal Company in seeking to enforce a maritime lien did not lie in the fact that a contract had been made for the supply of coal. "A vessel," said the court, "may be liable *in rem* for supplies, although the owner can be made liable therefor *in personam*; since the dealer may rely upon the credit of both." So, the court recognized that if in that case "the coal had been furnished to the several vessels by the libellant, maritime liens would have arisen and could have been established under the statute without proof that credit was given to the vessels." The difficulty which blocked recovery by the Coal Company was "solely that it did not furnish coal to the vessels." There "was no understanding when the contract was made, or when the coal was delivered by the libellant, that any part of it was for any particular vessel or even for the vessels then composing the fleet. And it was clearly understood that the purchasing corporation would apply part of the coal to a non-maritime use." *Id.*, pp. 10, 11, 13. In the instant case, the oil was supplied exclusively for the vessels in question, was delivered directly to the vessels and was so invoiced; and there was nothing in the general contract to the effect that the supplies were to be furnished upon the exclusive credit of W.L. Comyn & Sons and not also upon the credit of the vessels.

* * *

There remains the contention that, apart from any prohibition of the creation of liens, the vessels could not be bound for supplies ordered by the charterers because of the nature of the charter parties. There is a plain distinction between a case of a bare-boat charter, where the charterer mans the vessel, and a case where the charter party is a mere contract for the carriage of goods. In the former there is a clear demise; in the latter, the charterer is in substance only a shipper. There is an intermediate class of charters which has given rise to many questions in various situations. Time charters of the sort now before us are in this class. The owner provides the master and crew and undertakes the navigation of the vessel and to maintain her in an efficient condition. But the master although appointed by the owner, is placed "under the orders and direction of the charterers as regards employment or agency." The owners agree "to let" the vessel and the charterers "to hire" her "from the time of delivery" until the date set for "her redelivery." The charterers are to provide and pay for fuel supplies, port charges, pilotages, etc. and all other expenses except those pertaining to the captain, officers or crew.

There is thus a distribution of responsibility, and liability or the legal consequences of particular conduct would be determined accordingly. While the owners assumed responsibility for the navigation of the vessels and their maintenance in an efficient state, we are not concerned with any questions relating to faults in navigation or failure in maintenance. The mere fact that the owners furnished the master and crew cannot be regarded as decisive of the question before us. *See United States v. Shea*, 152 U.S. 178, 190, 191; *United States v. Cornell Steamboat Co.*, 267 U.S. 281. Aside from the navigation of the vessels, they were placed under the control of the charterers and the master and crew were under their directions. The vessels by the terms of the charters were delivered to the charterers, and where the vessels were to go and what they were to carry, within the broad limits described in the charters, were determined by the charterers.

The question whether under a charter, containing these or similar provisions, the materialman may have a lien for supplies furnished on the order of the charterer has given rise to conflicting views and no little confusion has resulted.

We think that this conflict may be resolved by having due regard to the manifest purpose of the governing statute. The Act says nothing about types of charters. In speaking of those who shall be presumed to have authority to procure supplies, the statute expressly includes not only the "ship's husband" and the "master" but "any person to whom the management of the vessel at the port of supply is intrusted," and these persons are to be taken to include such officers and agents "when appointed by a charterer, by an owner *pro hac vice*, or by an agreed purchaser in possession of the vessel." We think that the purpose of the statute is not properly served by construing the term "management of the vessel" as referring to her "navigation." Management is a broader term connoting direction and control for the purposes for which the vessel is used. Where, as in this case, apart from mere navigation, the vessel is placed under the direction and control of the charterer as the hirer of the vessel, who as such may determine to what port she shall go and what she shall carry, subject only to specified exceptions, we think the charterer must be deemed to be intrusted with the vessel's management for the purpose of applying the statutory test of authority to obtain necessary supplies upon the credit of the vessel, in the absence of a provision to the contrary.

The origin of the maritime lien is the need of the ship. *Piedmont Coal Co. v. Seaboard Fisheries Co., supra.* The lien is given for supplies which are necessary to keep the ship going. The material-man when furnishing such supplies on the order of the charterer is charged with knowledge of the terms of the charter party when he can ascertain them, but when it appears that by these terms the charterer has direction and control of the vessel and that he is the one to obtain the essential supplies, and that there is no prohibition of the creation of a maritime lien, the material-man is protected by the terms of the statute. He furnishes the supplies on the order of the person authorized to obtain them and he is entitled to rely on the credit of the vessel as well as upon the credit of the one who gives the order.

We are of the opinion that it would thwart the purpose of the statute to compel the material-man furnishing supplies to the vessel to resolve the ambiguities which may be found in such charters as those here involved. The statute was intended to afford the material-man a reasonably certain criterion. The owner has a simple and ready means of protection. All that it is necessary for him to do, as the material-man in dealing with the charterer is charged with notice of the charter, is to provide therein that the creation of maritime liens is prohibited. When the owner does not do so, he should not be heard to complain when it appears that it is the charterer's business to obtain supplies to keep the vessel on her way and the charter has not prohibited reliance upon the credit of the vessel.

The judgment of the Circuit Court of Appeals is Affirmed.

(c) The Effect of the 1971 Amendment: No-Lien Clauses

Note: The 1971 Amendment

In 1971 Congress deleted the language from 46 U.S.C. § 973 that barred the attachment of a maritime lien where the materialman "knew, or by the exercise of reasonable diligence could have ascertained that because of the terms of the charter party" the person ordering the materials had no authority "to bind the vessel therefor."

In G. Gilmore & C. Black, The Law of Admiralty 687 (2d ed. 1975), the authors state that "the principal (and desirable) effect of the 1971 amendment will prove [to be] the abrogation of the absolute duty to make inquiry established in *Carver* and affirmed in *Signal Oil* and a return toward the general maritime theory announced in *The Kate* and *The Valencia*. That is, a materialman who neither knows nor has reason to know that he is dealing with a chartered ship will be entitled to rely on the presumption of authority established by § 972. If, under all the circumstances, he has reason to know that the she is chartered, and makes no further inquiry, the prohibition of lien clause in the charter should be effective against him."

In *Lake Union Dry Dock Co. v. M/V Polar Viking*, 446 F. Supp. 1286, 1978 AMC 1477 (W.D. Wash. 1978), Judge Beeks handed down the following opinion:

> In this case plaintiffs Lake Union Drydock Company (Lake Union) and Duwamish Shipyard, Inc. (Duwamish) seek to foreclose maritime liens against the M/V Polar Viking pursuant to the Maritime Lien Act. Plaintiffs supplied materials and/or rendered services to the vessel while she was under a sub-demise charter to Northland Marine Lines (NML) from her owner *pro hac vice* Red Circle Transport (Red Circle), claimant herein.

On December 10, 1975 Red Circle subchartered the Polar Viking to NML for a period of one year. Between January 17 and February 18, 1976 Duwamish fabricated a stern roller with hydraulic actuated pins for the Polar Viking at the request of NML for $14,153.53. Duwamish did not install the stern roller on the vessel nor was the vessel in Duwamish's yard. Red Circle alleges, and Duwamish does not dispute, that Duwamish knew that NML utilized chartered vessels prior to commencing such work.

In June and again in August, 1976 Lake Union performed certain repairs on the Polar Viking at the request of NML. The first services were invoiced on July 20 in the amount of $10,614.73. The August repairs were invoiced on September 24, 1976 at $3,481.23. According to the deposition of Mr. Stebbins, manager of Lake Union's drydock facility, NML generally hired Lake Union to perform emergency repairs only, as were those performed on the Polar Viking.

While the Polar Viking was in drydock, Lake Union learned that the vessel was under charter. Lake Union then attempted to discover the ownership of the vessel through listings in Dun & Bradstreet, which led to an interior design firm. (The vessel was apparently listed under its former name, Ocean Gulf). Its requests to see NML's charter and a financial statement were refused, but it was assured that NML was negotiating to purchase the vessel at that time and that the account would be paid in a matter of days.

* * *

The primary question, which arises from the undisputed fact that the charter agreement between Red Circle and NML contained a no-lien clause, is whether § 973 of the Maritime Lien Act, as amended in 1971, precludes the assertion of such clause against the plaintiffs, thus barring their maritime lien claims. This is a question of first impression.

* * *

Claimant adopts the contention of Professors Gilmore and Black that the amended statute merely reinstates the prestatutory general maritime law enunciated in *The Kate* and *The Valencia*. This argument discerns the materialman's general maritime duty of inquiry pursuant to *The Kate* and *The Valencia* to be perceptibly different form his pre-71 statutory duty as developed under *U.S. v. Carver*.

I find no such difference, however, and if there be one it is too ethereal for application. The materialmen on the *The Valencia* and those who supplied the vessel Clio in *U.S. v. Carver* possessed the same quantum of knowledge; neither had knowledge that the vessels were chartered. However, the Supreme Court imputed to them constructive knowledge of the charter and its terms. The Court found that the materialmen had a duty to inquire with "reasonable diligence," and that such inquiry would have revealed a lack of authority by the party requesting the services to bind the vessel. Thus, the materialman's duty to inquire under general maritime law was identical to his duty under the statute prior to amendment in 1971. The former duty provision of § 973 merely incorporated and codified the general maritime law.

Claimant essentially argues that the amended statute, which deleted a duty of reasonably diligent inquiry, requires a duty of reasonably diligent inquiry. It is clear, then, that Red Circle's argument cannot be accepted for it would render useless the Congressional intendment in amending the statute. Statutory amendments are usually intended to alter the law and I believe this to be such an amendment. The statement found in the legislative history that the amendment makes no change in the law of maritime liens is merely an attempt by Congress to serve notice that the effect of the amendment is limited. It is not intended to affect the law of maritime liens generally, but merely to enlarge the right of a materialman to assert a lien against a vessel when he has no knowledge that the person requesting necessaries is without authority to do so.

The meaning of § 973 cannot be determined solely on its face because Congress has unfortunately failed to clearly express itself. Rather, three factors must be evaluated to discern the meaning of the statute: language, history, and the relationship of the provision of the entire statutory scheme. The statute on its face demonstrates that the duty of inquiry has been eliminated. The legislative history indicates that a lien will be barred if the materialman has knowledge of the no-lien clause. In harmonizing these two factors, the statute must be construed to entitle a materialman to a maritime lien for necessaries furnished to a vessel unless he has actual knowledge that the vessel is operating under a charter which contains a no-lien provision. In other words, the assertion of a lien will be barred only if the materialman has actual knowledge of the no-lien clause. Since actual knowledge will bar the assertion of a lien, plaintiffs' contention that a materialman's lien vests absolutely is erroneous.

This interpretation is in harmony with the presumption of authority provisions of §§ 972 and 973. The owner of a vessel must now establish that the materialman had actual knowledge of a no-lien clause if he is to overcome the materialman's statutory presumption. The imposition of this burden is supported by the legislative history. Congress intended to place the greater burden upon the vessel owner: "As a practical matter, the owner can more easily protect himself contractually by bonds or otherwise at the time he charters the vessel, than can the American materialman who furnishes necessaries to a vessel under great economic pressure to put back to sea."

I believe that § 973, as here construed, will achieve the purpose desired by Congress. It recognized that an innocent materialman required greater protection than the pre-amendment statute provided. It also recognized that a materialman with actual knowledge needed no further protection; he could protect himself by refusing to service a vessel, by arranging for payment, or he could merely assume a known risk.

Claimant also contends that the intent of Congress was to deal solely with itinerant foreign flag vessels. While Congress certainly had this problem in mind when the statute was enacted, it did not so limit its application. Another motivation for favoring the materialman was to relieve him of the time pressures inherent in the requirement of reasonably diligent inquiry. "Granting the materialman a lien encourages the prompt furnishing of necessaries to vessels so that they can be speedily turned around and put to sea. This is especially significant today when the emphasis on vessel performance is reduced port time and increased speed." Surely itinerant foreign flag vessels have no monopoly on concern for vessel performance.

In light of the above, it is clear that the no-lien clause of the charter under which NML operated the Polar Viking is not binding upon plaintiffs. Neither had actual knowledge thereof.

Even if there is no lien, may the owner of the vessel be liable *in personam* on an unjust enrichment theory?

BELCHER OIL CO. v. M/V GARDENIA

766 F.2d 1508, 1986 AMC 1745 (11th Cir. 1985)

Daniel Holcombe THOMAS, District Judge

Appellants Belcher Oil Company and Belcher Towing Company (collectively "Belcher") brought an action *in rem* against the M/V GARDENIA pursuant to the Federal Maritime Lien Act, 46 U.S.C. § 971, *et seq.*, to recover for necessaries furnished to the M/V GARDENIA. Specifically, Belcher sought to recover that value of towage and bunkering services provided to the vessel upon the charterer's insolvency. Appellee M/V GARDENIA, through its owner, N.V. Stoomvaart Maatschappij Oostzee (hereinafter the "owner"), defended the action and asserted as affirmative defenses (1) that at all times material to Belcher's claim, Belcher had knowledge that Pan Atlantic Lines, the vessel's time-charterer, and Chester, Blackburn & Roeder ("CB&R"), its agent, lacked the authority to bind the vessel; (2) that at all times material to Belcher's claim, Belcher had knowledge of the prohibition of lien clause contained in the charter party for the M/V GARDENIA; and (3) assuming maritime liens against the vessel were created, Belcher waived those liens by their conduct indicating that they intended to rely exclusively on the credit of the time charterer Pan Atlantic Lines or its agent CB&R.

The action was tried without a jury on July 3, 1984. The owners did not contest that Belcher provided the necessaries. It was stipulated that Belcher had a *prima facie* case and that the M/V GARDENIA would present its defenses to rebut the statutory presumptions enjoyed by Belcher pursuant to 46 U.S.C. § 971, *et seq.* Final Judgment and written Findings of Fact and Conclusions of Law were entered in favor of the M/V GARDENIA on all three defenses. This appeal follows and we affirm.

In January 1983, the M/V GARDENIA was operating out of the Port of Miami, under time charter to Pan Atlantic Lines. CB&R acted as Pan Atlantic Lines' agent in the Port of Miami to handle Pan Atlantic Lines' accounts for the procurement of, and payment for, service and supplies required by its chartered vessel. During the time the M/V GARDENIA was operating in the Port of Miami, Belcher provided towage and bunkering services to the vessel.

Under the terms of the chapter party Pan Atlantic Lines, as charterers, were responsible for the various ports of the M/V GARDENIA. The charter party also contained a "prohibition of lien" clause which prohibited the charterer from incurring any maritime liens against the vessel and/or her owners for supplies or necessaries.

The facts, as found by the district court, are paraphrased below.

At all material times Pan Atlantic Lines was the time charterer of the M/V GARDENIA and CB&R was the agent for Pan Atlantic Lines. Belcher had a long-standing business relationship with both CB&R and Pan Atlantic Lines and was familiar with the intricacies of the operation of CB&R and Pan Atlantic Lines.

Upon the orders of Pan Atlantic Lines' agent, CB&R, Belcher provided fuel bunkers to the M/V GARDENIA on May 25, 1983, and towing services on March 5 and June 5, 1983. Prior to the time these "necessaries" were furnished, Belcher had knowledge that CB&R was an agent for Pan Atlantic Lines and that CB&R had no authority other than to act on behalf of Pan Atlantic Lines.

Belcher was advised by the manager of CB&R's Accounts Payable Department, prior to delivery of the services at issue, that Pan Atlantic Lines was the time charterer of the M/V GARDENIA and that the charter party prohibited Belcher from looking to the vessel and/or her owners for payment of these services. Therefore, Belcher knew that CB&R and Pan Atlantic Lines had no authority to bind the vessel or its owners and could only look to Pan Atlantic Lines for payment.

Belcher was further advised by the manager of CB&R's Accounts Payable Department that there was, in fact, a prohibition of lien clause contained in the charter party. Therefore, Belcher knew or certainly should have known that the charter party contained such a clause. The court further found that Belcher had actual knowledge of the prohibition of lien clause. The court's conclusion that Belcher had actual knowledge of the prohibition of lien clause was found to be corroborated by the fact that several of Belcher's previous bunkering certificates for the M/V GARDENIA, while time-chartered to Pan Atlantic Lines, contained the disclaimer language "for and/or in behalf of time-charterers without recourse to myself and/or Owners of the Vessel."

On May 25, 1983, a dispute arose on board the M/V GARDENIA among representatives of CB&R, Belcher and the officers of the vessel with respect to the execution of Belcher's bunkering certificates for the fuel bunkers delivered by Belcher on that day. The Master of the vessel informed CB&R's fuel coordinator that he would not sign the bunkering certificate without a disclaimer stamp. The district court found that, at this time, Belcher was again informed that the charter party contained a prohibition of lien clause which prohibited the vessel from being liened. Belcher subsequently consented to accepting the signature of CB&R's representative after being informed of the provisions of the charter party agreement.

The court further found, assuming *arguendo* that a lien had been created, Belcher waived any such lien by failing to withdraw the bunkers. Instead, Belcher elected to accept the signature of CB&R's representative in order to facilitate the sale of the bunkers, thereby waiving any lien it may have had against the vessel.

The Dispositive Issue

On appeal, Belcher enumerates six assignments of error. However, we need only address the question of whether actual knowledge of a prohibition of lien clause contained in a charter party is the only manner in which a vessel and/or her owners can establish a charterer's lack of authority to bind the vessel so as to defeat a maritime lien afforded the supplier pursuant to 46 U.S.C. § 971, *et seq.*

The Federal Maritime Lien Act

Section 971 of the Federal Maritime Lien Act provides:

> Any person furnishing repairs, supplies, towage, use of dry dock or marine railway, or other necessaries, to any vessel, whether foreign or domestic, *upon the order of the owner* of such vessel, *or of a person authorized by the owner*, shall have a maritime lien on the vessel, which may be enforced by suit *in rem*, and it shall not be necessary to allege or prove that the credit was given to the vessel. 46 U.S.C. § 971. (emphasis added).

Section 972 of the Act provides:

> The following persons shall be presumed to have authority from the owner to procure repairs, supplies, towage, use of dry dock or marine railway, and other necessaries for the vessel: The managing owner, ship's husband, master, or any person to whom the management of the vessel at the port of supply is intrusted. No person tortiously or unlawfully in possession or charge of a vessel shall have authority to bind the vessel. 46 U.S.C. § 972.

Section 973 of the Act was amended in 1971. Prior to 1971, this section provided:

> The officers and agents of a vessel specified in section 972 of this title shall be taken to include such officers and agents when appointed by a charterer, by an owner *pro hac vice*, or by an agreed purchaser in possession of the vessel; but nothing in this chapter shall be construed to confer a lien when the furnisher knew, or by exercise of reasonable diligence could have ascertained, that because of the terms of a charter party, agreement for sale of the vessel, or for any other reason, the person ordering the repairs, supplies, or other necessaries was without authority to bind the vessel. 46 U.S.C. § 973 (pre-1971).

The duty of inquiry imposed by 46 U.S.C. § 973, prior to 1971, eventually became a substantial obstacle for those persons furnishing supplies and other necessaries to maritime vessels. In virtually every instance the supplier was under a duty to ascertain the authority of the individual ordering supplies for a ship to incur liens on the vessel. *See United States v. Carver*, 260 U.S. 482, 43 S. Ct. 181, 67 L. Ed. 361 (1923); *Dampskibsselskabet Dannebrog v. Signal Oil & Gas Co.*, 310 U.S. 268, 60 S. Ct. 937, 84 L. Ed. 1197 (1940). Such a duty of inquiry became quite impractical in light of the various chartering and subchartering practices of foreign and domestic vessels. Furthermore, vessel owners and charterers engaged in sub-chartering activities began to insert "prohibition of lien" or "no lien" provisions in charter parties. This practice effectively shifted the risk of loss to the supplier since a reasonably diligent inquiry would almost certainly yield information which would effectively bar any lien.

In response to this problem, Congress amended 46 U.S.C. § 973 in 1971[1] by deleting the language imposing a duty of inquiry on the materialman. The 1971 amendment to the Federal Maritime Lien Act, 46 U.S.C. § 973, deleted the words "but nothing in this chapter shall be construed to confer a lien when the furnisher knew, or by exercise of reasonable diligence could have ascertained, that because of the terms of the charter party ... the person ordering the repairs, supplies, or other necessaries was without authority to bind the vessel."[2]

The primary concern of the legislators supporting the 1971 amendment was that suppliers were frequently unable to either ascertain the existence of a charter and determine if the charter party contained a prohibition of lien clause or to perform an adequate check on the entity ordering the supplies. *See* H.R. 92-340, 92 Cong., 1st Sess., *reprinted in* 1971 U.S. CODE CONG. & AD. NEWS 1363; 177 Cong. Rec. 25,762 (1971); *Id.* at 25,763; *Id.* at 25,764.

Knowledge of Lack of Authority v. Knowledge or Prohibition of Lien Clause

As noted above, the district court held, *inter alia*, that the presumption of a lien will be defeated if the vessel and/or her owners establish either that the supplier had actual knowledge that the person ordering the supplier or other necessaries lacked the authority to bind the vessel, or that the supplier had actual knowledge of a prohibition of lien clause in the charter party.

Belcher maintains that these two findings are inconsistent with the decided cases and defeat the intent of the 1971 amendment. Belcher contends that nothing short of *actual knowledge of a prohibition lien clause* will defeat the lien afforded under 46 U.S.C. § 71. (emphasis added). We disagree.

Section 971 of the Federal Maritime Lien Act clearly states that a maritime lien will arise in favor of one furnishing necessaries to a vessel when those necessaries are ordered by the owner or a *person authorized by the owner* to bind the vessel. (emphasis added) Section 972 of the Act provides that a charterer is *presumed* to have authority to bind the vessel. (emphasis added). The statute is clear that a lien will not arise when necessaries are ordered by one without authority to

---

[1] 46 U.S.C. § 973 now provides:
The officers and agents of a vessel specified in Section 972 of this title shall be taken to include such officers and agents when appointed by a charterer, by an owner, *pro hac vice*, or by an agreed purchaser in possession of the vessel.

[2] Due to the nature of the shipping business, materialmen furnishing supplies and other necessaries to a vessel rarely have sufficient time in which to ascertain whether a vessel is under charter or to review complicated charter provisions prior to entering into contracts for the furnishing of necessaries to a vessel which may be in port for only a brief period.

bind the vessel. Although a charterer is presumed to have authority to bind the vessel, the lien does not vest absolutely as a matter of law, but rather, "the burden is upon the owner to show that the supplier of necessaries had actual knowledge of the existence of any lack of authority relied upon as a defense." *Jan C. Uiterwhy Co., Inc. v. M/V MARE ARABICO*, 459 F. Supp. 1325, 1331 (D. Md. 1978). This was made even clearer in the case of *Belcher Co. of Alabama, Inc. v. M/V MARTHA MARINER*, 724 F.2d 1161 (5th Cir. 1984) in which it is stated, "This lien [46 U.S.C. § 971] attaches when necessaries are ordered by and supplied to the charterer, unless the supplier has notice that the person who orders the necessaries lacked authority to do so."

Gilmore & Black, in the 2nd Edition of THE LAW OF ADMIRALTY at page 685, give a very interesting discussion on the effect of the 1971 amendment to § 973. Among other things, Gilmore & Black state, "If the person who orders the services is not authorized by the owner to create liens and if the furnisher of the services has notice of the lack of authority, it is entirely clear that no lien will arise."

Belcher's emphasis upon the supplier obtaining actual knowledge of prohibition of lien clauses is misplaced. If a supplier has actual knowledge of prohibition of lien clause in a charter party then he certainly has actual knowledge of the charterer's lack of authority to bind the vessel. Actual knowledge of a prohibition of lien clause is merely one way of obtaining actual knowledge of one's lack of authority to bind the vessel.

The cases relied upon by Belcher do not support such a requirement. *TTT Stevedores of Texas, Inc. v. M/V JAGAT VIJETA*, 696 F.2d 1135 (5th Cir. 1983); *Gulf Oil Trading Co. v. M/V CARBIE MAR*, 757 F.2d 743 (5th Cir. 1985); *Jan C. Uiterwyk Co., Inc. v. M/V MARE ARABICO, supra*; *Lake Union Drydock Co. v. M/V POLAR VIKING*, 446 F. Supp. 1286 (W.D. Wash. 1978).

Belcher relies primarily upon *TTT Stevedores of Texas, Inc., v. M/V JAGAT VIJETA, supra.* In that case the Fifth Circuit Court of Appeals recognized that actual knowledge of a prohibition of lien clause would bar the lien. 696 F.2d at 1138. It must be noted, however, that the court did not hold that actual knowledge of a prohibition of lien clause is the only manner in which it can be established that the charterer lacked authority to bind the vessel. The court in *TTT Stevedores of Texas Inc. v. M/V JAGAT VIJETA, supra*, merely held that a lien would be barred if the supplier had actual knowledge of a prohibition of lien clause in a charter party prior to furnishing necessaries to the vessel.

A careful reading of the cases cited by Belcher on this issue reveals that in no case were the suppliers presented with the question as to the authority of the one ordering the supplies. In each of those cases the supplies were ordered either by one having authority, or presumed authority (§ 972) which was never questioned. Thus, the courts in each of those cases did not address the issue herein.

We therefore hold that a maritime lien, created pursuant to 46 U.S.C. § 971, may be defeated when the vessel and/or her owners establish that the supplier of necessaries either had actual knowledge that the person ordering the supplies lacked the authority to bind the vessel or had knowledge of a prohibition of lien clause in the charter.

Our holding is not, in any way, to be construed so as to either limit the supplier's ability to rely on the presumptions afforded him or to impose a duty of inquiry. However, a supplier should not be allowed to rely on such beneficial presumptions when he has actual knowledge to the contrary. Suppliers of necessaries are afforded the protection of a lien when they have no knowledge of a prohibition of lien clause and no knowledge that the person ordering the supplies has no authority to do so. These concerns are, of course, moot when a supplier has actual knowledge of the buyer's lack of authority to bind the vessel—be it by knowledge of a prohibition of lien clause or otherwise. The supplier who has such knowledge is then in a position to make an informed business decision and may refuse to supply the vessel, make other arrangements for payment, or assume the risk.

In the instant case, the record clearly supports a finding that Belcher had sufficient knowledge that Pan Atlantic Lines and CB & R lacked the authority to bind the vessel. In any event, were we to accept Belcher's contention that only actual knowledge of the prohibition of lien clause would defeat the lien, we find that the record sufficiently supports the district court's finding that Belcher had actual knowledge of the prohibition of lien clause contained in Pan Atlantic Lines charter agreement.

In light of our disposition of the above issue we do not reach Belcher's remaining contentions. Based on the foregoing, WE AFFIRM.

MARINE FUEL SUPPLY & TOWING, INC. v. M/V KEN LUCKY

859 F.2d 1405, 1989 AMC 390 (9th Cir. 1988) opinion amended and superseded by 869 F.2d 473 (9th Cir. 1988)

NELSON, Circuit Judge

Marine Fuel Supply & Towing, Inc. ("Marine Fuel") appeals the district court's refusal to grant Marine Fuel a maritime lien on the M/V KEN LUCKY ("Ken Lucky") pursuant to 46 U.S.C. §§ 971-75 (1982). The district court exercised jurisdiction pursuant to 28 U.S.C. § 1333 and we have jurisdiction pursuant to 28 U.S.C. § 1291. We reverse and remand.

Background

Ken Hieng Navigation Company S.A. ("Ken Hieng") owns the Ken Lucky. During the time Marine Fuel alleges the lien arose, Ken Hieng had time chartered the vessel to Compaigne Continental Paris ("Continental Grain"). A time charter entails a division of responsibilities between the owner and charterer. *Dampskibssel-skabet Dannebrog v. Signal Oil & Gas Co.*, 310 U.S. 268, 278, 84 L. Ed. 1197, 60 S. Ct. 937 (1940) ("*Signal Oil*"). Continental Grain in turn subchartered the vessel to Bulkferts, Inc. ("Bulkferts"). Both charter agreements contained "no lien" clauses, which prohibited maritime liens asserted by suppliers against the vessel.

When the Ken Lucky reached Tampa, Florida, in September 1984, it needed bunker fuel. To arrange for the supplies, Bulkferts' managing agent, Eurostem Maritime Limited ("Eurostem"), contacted Brook Oil Ltd. ("Brook"). Brook then instructed Gray Bunkering Services ("Gray") to place the order for the Ken Lucky's supplies with Marine Fuel. Marine Fuel asked Gray for assurances about payment before delivery of the bunkers. In response, Gray sent a telex on

September 3, 1984 notifying Marine Fuel that it had been "nominated by the owner" of the Ken Lucky to supply the vessel. Ken Lucky's local (husbanding) agent arranged for delivery of the supplies. On September 6, 1984, Marine Fuel supplied the Ken Lucky with bunkers worth $223,480.10. The master of the Ken Lucky, appointed by the owner, approved the acceptance of the supplies by the vessel's chief engineer. Marine Fuel billed Gray for the bunkers, referencing Brook's account. Marine Fuel unsuccessfully sought payment from Brook, which was forced into receivership in October of 1984.

Marine Fuel arrested the Ken Lucky in Portland, Oregon. Ken Lucky posted cash as security for Marine Fuel's claim, which counsel for the parties deposited in a Portland bank. The district court refused to grant Marine Fuel a maritime lien. The cross appeal has been dismissed. Marine Fuel timely appealed.

* * *

Discussion

I. Authorization of the Supply Order

Marine Fuel contends that Brook, the bunker broker, had presumed authority under the Federal Maritime Lien Act (the Act) from Bulkferts and Eurostem, the subcharterer and its managing agent, to incur a lien on behalf of the Ken Lucky. The district court found that because no agency relationship existed between Bulkferts and Brook, no presumed authority under the Act was established. Marine Fuel contends that Brook had implied authority from Bulkferts or the ship's owner to incur the lien. Alternatively, Marine Fuel argues that Bulkferts, as a person authorized under section 971 or 972 had presumed authority under the Act to order fuel and to incur a lien against the vessel. The district court concluded that the charter agreements' no lien clauses prevented Brook from acting pursuant to implied authority to incur a lien.

* * *

A. The Federal Maritime Lien Act

"The federal Maritime Lien Act grants a maritime lien to any person 1) furnishing repairs, supplies, or other necessaries 2) to any vessel 3) 'upon the order of the owner of such vessel, or of a person authorized by the owner.' " *Farwest I*, 769 F.2d at 623 (*quoting* 46 U.S.C. § 971). The parties agree that Marine Fuel furnished necessaries to the Ken Lucky. Ken Lucky admits that Bulkferts was in possession and control of the vessel during the time it docked in Tampa. Thus, Bulkferts qualifies as an authorized person under section 972 because it was the "person to whom the management of the vessel at the port of supply [was] intrusted."[3]

---

[3] Ken Lucky does not contest that Bulkferts, the subcharterer, is treated as a charterer for purposes of the Act. A charterer is authorized by law to 'bind the vessel. *The ASTORIAN*, 57 F.2d 85, 89-90 (9th Cir. 1932); *The Golden Gate*, 52 F.2d 397, 399 (9th Cir. 1931), *cert. denied*, 284 U.S. 682, 52 S. Ct. 199, 76 L. Ed. 2d 576 (1932). A time charterer is presumed to have the authority to bind the vessel under the Act. *Foss Launch & Tug Co. v. Char Ching Shipping U.S.A., Ltd.*, 808 F.2d 697, 700 (9th Cir.), *cert. denied*, 108 S. Ct. 96, 98 L. Ed. 2d 57 (1987); *Belcher Oil Co. v. M/V GARDENIA*, 766 F.2d 1508, 1512 (11 Cir. 1985).

The district court based its refusal to find an agency relationship between Bulkferts and Brook on two propositions: 1) that Brook was an independent corporation; and 2) that Brook was a back-to-back trader. Marine Fuel argues that Brook can be an independent corporation and still have acted as Bulkferts' agent in the disputed transaction. *See Protective Ins. Co. v. Coleman*, 144 Ill. App. 3d 682, 494 N.E.2d 1241, 1250, 98 Ill. Dec. 914 (1986); RESTATEMENT (SECOND) AGENCY § 14 (1958). We look to principles of agency to interpret the Act's references to agents. *Cactus Pipe & Supply Co. v. M/V Montmartre*, 756 F.2d 1103, 1111 (5th Cir. 1985). We examine the roles of the parties in the transactions at issue to determine if a person has presumed authority under the Act. *See, e.g.*, *Farwest I*, 769 F.2d at 623-24; *Farwest Steel Corp. v. Barge Sea-Span*, 828 F.2d 522, 525-26 (9th Cir. 1987), *cert. denied*, 485 U.S. 1034, 108 S. Ct. 1594, 99 L. Ed. 2d 909 (1988) ("*Farwest II*").

The parties agree that the order originated from Bulkferts. Thus, we need not reach the question whether the district court's conclusion that Brook was not *Bulkfert's* agent is erroneous because appellees have already admitted that the fuel and bunkers were sold to *Bulkferts*. We conclude that Marine Fuel need not establish agency between Brook and Bulkferts to fall within the scope of one entitled to a maritime lien under the Act.

Ken Lucky concedes that Bulkferts was authorized to bind the vessel. It is clear that Eurostem, as managing agent for Bulkferts, did order the fuel and it is also clear that Marine Fuel delivered the fuel *to the vessel*. Section 971 states that any person furnishing supplies or other necessaries *to a vessel* "upon" the order of a person authorized to bind the vessel shall be entitled to lien. It is clear that Eurostem, as managing agent for Bulkferts, ordered the fuel, and it is also clear that Marine Fuel delivered the fuel *to the vessel*. Bulkferts had statutory authority to order the fuel under section 972 and it did so. Marine Fuel delivered the fuel to the vessel after Bulkferts ordered it. Thus, this case can be easily distinguished from the situation present in *Farwest II*.

In *Farwest II*, we affirmed the district court's finding that the general contractor did not qualify as an "authorized person" to bind the vessel under § 972. *Id.* at 525-26. We distinguished between the general contractor's responsibility for vessel repairs and one who has broad management powers to qualify as a person "intrusted" with management of the vessel under § 972, relying on a line of cases in which courts "have uniformly held that the general repair contractor was not endowed with sufficient 'management' authority to support a section 971 lien." *Id.* at 526. However, no restrictive repair contract line of cases governs the issue here. Further, no specific instruction was given in *Farwest*, as Bulkferts gave here, authorizing Eurostem to order the bunkers through Brook.

In *Farwest*, the steel was ordered by a contractor repairing the vessel. No one with authority to lien the vessel originated the order. Here Bulkferts, which clearly possessed the statutory authority to bind the vessel, ordered and received the bunkers and fuel. Thus, we are not confronted with a *Farwest II* situation, where a person who never had authority originated the order.

B. Statutory Authority to Bind the Vessel Under Section 972

Ken Lucky also concedes that the master of the Ken Lucky, appointed by the owner, accepted the supplies. Ken Lucky contends that the master had no authority to accept the supplies and incur a lien against the vessel because of the no lien clauses in the charter agreements. However, such reasoning contradicts the language of § 972, which states that a ship's master has presumed authority to incur a lien. *See Atlantic & Gulf Stevedores, Inc. v. M/V Grand Loyalty*, 608 F.2d 197, 200 (5th Cir. 1979) (chief officer who ordered services possessed management powers envisioned by Act and thus had presumed authority as well as actual authority to incur lien).

A claimant's dealings with an intermediary at the port rather than a charterer or owner does not preclude the existence of a lien. *Reinholm Crane & Rigging Co., Inc. v. M/V Ocean Crown*, 484 F. Supp. 935, 936 (W.D. Wash. 1979). The parties agree that the order originated from Bulkferts. Eurostem, Bulkferts' managing agent, placed the order with Brook. Marine Fuel received a telex from Gray confirming that the owner authorized the order, identifying Fillette as Ken Lucky's local (husbanding) agent. Before delivering the bunkers, Marine Fuel notified Fillette of the order and Fillette arranged for delivery of the bunkers. Fillette received a telex from Bulkferts' domestic agent, WKM Ship Management Services, stating that WKM was arranging for a purchase of bunkers in the same amount for the ship. Ken Lucky's chief engineer accepted the bunkers, acknowledging receipt, with the approval of the master. The ship's master also had presumed authority to incur a lien under the Act. The vessel certainly benefited from the bunker supply.

We conclude that this sequence of events is sufficient to establish implied authority to incur a lien against the vessel for fuel. *See Yacht, MARY JANE v. Broward Marine, Inc.*, 313 F.2d 516, 517 (5th Cir. 1963) (implied authority existed because the "real" captain failed to object although he was aware of work being done for vessel); *Reinholm*, 484 F. Supp. at 936 (no objections from vessel's master, owner or charterer to obvious and prolonged services precluded summary judgment because material issue of fact remained as to the existence of implied authority); *Jan C. Uiterwyk Co. v. M/V MARE ARABICO*, 459 F. Supp. 1325, 1330-31 (D. Md. 1978) (subcharterer was held to have had implied authority from the time charterer to procure the services because masters of the vessels who ordered the services were held to be agents of persons with apparent authority to bind the vessels, the time charterer and owner).

Moreover, the district court's reliance on the no lien clause to deny the lien thwarts the purpose of the statute by charging Marine Fuel with the onerous duty of resolving the ambiguities in the Sipra-Bulkferts-Eurostem-Brook relationship. *Cf. Signal Oil*, 310 U.S. at 280 (purpose of lien act thwarted if courts compel the "material-man furnishing supplies to the vessel to resolve the ambiguities which may be found in [the charter agreements]"). We recently noted, construing a lien under the Preferred Ship Mortgage Act, that "one of the purposes of the Maritime Liens Act, 46 U.S.C. §§ 971-75 ... is to create liens in favor of those who furnish necessaries for the vessel's operation. Permitting [a] contrived financial scheme to prevail effectively destroys the liens of suppliers and subverts the purposes of the Maritime Liens Act." *Wardley Int'l Bank, Inc. v. Nasipit Bay Vessel*, 841 F.2d 259, 264 (9th Cir. 1988) (citation omitted).

* * *

C. Effect of the No Lien Clauses

Ken Lucky admits that the purpose of the Act is to help suppliers determine who has authority to incur a lien. The Act's presumption in favor of granting liens to suppliers "was enhanced in 1971 when Congress deleted the requirement that materialmen inquire about the existence of any no-lien clauses before furnishing supplies." *Farwest I*, 769 F.2d at 623; *see Foss Launch*, 808 F.2d at 700 (one purpose of amendment was "to ensure that any party to whom the management of the vessel is entrusted will be presumed to have authority to procure necessaries and supplies which may give rise to maritime liens"); *Gulf Trading & Transp. Co. v. M/V Tento*, 694 F.2d 1191, 1194 (9th Cir. 1982), *cert. denied*, 461 U.S. 929, 77 L. Ed. 2d 301, 103 S. Ct. 2091 (1983). Congress was concerned that the duty of inquiry had become a "substantial obstacle" for persons furnishing supplies. H. Rep. No. 340, 92d Cong., 1st Sess., *reprinted in* 1971 U.S. Code Cong. & Admin. News 1363, 1364-65. *See Belcher Oil*, 766 F.2d at 1511; *Lake Union Drydock Co. v. M/V Polar Viking*, 446 F. Supp. 1286, 1289-91 (W.D. Wash. 1978); *Ryan-Walsh Stevedoring Co., Inc. v. M/V Khalij Star*, 507 F. Supp. 36, 38 (W.D. Wash. 1980).

> [The] duty of inquiry became quite impractical in light of the various chartering and sub-chartering practices of foreign and domestic vessels. Furthermore, vessel owners and charterers engaged in sub-chartering activities began to insert "prohibition of lien" or "no lien" provisions in charter parties. This practice effectively shifted the risk of loss to the supplier....

Belcher Oil, 766 F.2d at 1511; *see Atlantic*, 608 F.2d at 201 & n.7 (no lien provisions a primary concern of the amendments).

The 1971 amendment obviously was directed at reducing the force of owners' and charterers' prohibition of lien clauses. Gilmore & Black, The Law of Admiralty § 9-39, at 669-70 (2d ed. 1975). However, Congress did not explicitly prohibit no lien clauses and the effectiveness of prohibition of lien clauses after the amendment has not been settled. *See id.* § 9-46a, at 685-86. This presents an issue of first impression in this circuit. Several courts have held that a no lien clause is not effective to rebut a statutory presumption of authority without proof of the supplier's actual knowledge of the clause. *See, e.g., Ramsay Scarlett & Co., Inc. v. S.S. Koh Eun*, 462 F. Supp. 277, 284-85 (E.D. Va. 1978); *Lake Union Drydock*, 446 F. Supp. at 1291. We agree. Even though a no lien clause is present, we conclude that the purposes of the Act, in light of the 1971 amendment, would be thwarted if the actual knowledge inquiry were not undertaken.

The record below reveals that the issue of notice was before the trial court. The defendant Ken Lucky had an opportunity to present evidence that Marine Fuel had knowledge of the no lien clause, but defendant offered no such evidence. Therefore, the no lien clause is not effective to rebut a statutory presumption of authority. *Belcher Oil*, 766 F.2d at 1512 (*quoting Jan C. Uiterwyk Co.*, 459 F. Supp. at 1331). "[T]he Act now requires that the owner take affirmative action to notify the supplier of necessaries that the master of a vessel or the charterer is *not* authorized to order services, the performance of which will result in the creation of liens."

Jan C. Uiterwyk, 459 F. Supp. at 1331. Knowledge that the charterer is mere "time charterer" does not amount to actual knowledge of the time charterer's lack of authority to incur a lien for necessaries. *Ramsay Scarlett*, 462 F. Supp. at 284-85. II.

* * *

REVERSED.

Notes

1. Compare the *Ken Lucky* case with *Galehead, Inc. v. M/V Anglia*, 183 F.3d 1242, 1999 AMC 2952 (11th Cir. 1999). In *Anglia*, Genesis, the charterer of the vessel, contacted Polygon to obtain bunkers for the ANGLIA. Polygon contacted Assamar to supply the fuel. Assamar, in turn, contracted with Coastal, which actually supplied the fuel. The bunker confirmation prepared by Polygon listed Coastal as the supplier and Assamar as the seller. Assamar paid Coastal and, when Genesis failed to pay Assamar, the vessel was arrested. The court held that, although Assamar provided necessaries to the ANGLIA, it did not do so "on the order of the owner or agent," and, thus, had no maritime lien. In other words, the bunkers were not supplied "on the order of the owner or a person authorized by the owner." Assamar provided the bunkers on the order of Polygon and Polygon was not a "person presumed to have authority to procure necessaries." The court observed that there was no evidence that Polygon acted as Genesis' agent as opposed to one merely under a contract to supply Genesis with fuel.
2. In *Lake Charles Stevedores, Inc. v. M/V Professor Vladimir Popov*, 199 F.3d 220, 2000 AMC 2273 (5th Cir. 1999), a stevedore that had been hired by the shipper of a cargo of rice claimed to have a maritime lien over the ship for the cost of its stevedoring services. The U.S. Court of Appeals for the Fifth Circuit rejected the stevedore's claim, holding that a stevedore hired by a shipper would not have a maritime lien absent evidence that the shipper had actual or apparent authority to employ stevedores on behalf of the vessel, rather than on its own behalf.

Note: Subcontractors

Where a general contractor which has entered into a contract with a person authorized to procure necessaries, subcontracts some of the work, does the subcontractor have a maritime lien? *Compare Turecamo of Savannah, Inc. v. U.S.*, 36 F.3d 1083, 1996 AMC 2003 (11th Cir. 1994), *cert. denied*, 516 U.S. 1028, 116 S. Ct. 673, 133 L. Ed. 2d 522 and *Marine Coatings of Alabama, Inc. v. U.S.*, 932 F.2d 1370, 1991 AMC 2487 (11th Cir. 1991) with *Crescent City Marine, Inc. v. M/V NUNKI*, 20 F.3d 665, 1994 AMC 2195 (5th Cir. 1994) and *Bonanni Ship Supply, Inc. v. U.S.*, 959 F.2d 1558, 1992 AMC 2165 (11th Cir. 1992).

Note: Additional Persons to Whom the Vessel is "Entrusted"

Is a watchman a person to whom the vessel is "entrusted"? In *The F.S. Loop*, 63 F. Supp. 105, 1946 AMC 467 (S.D. Cal. 1945), the court found the following:

> Under the allegations of the libel, the gasoline and supplies, for which claim is made, were allegedly furnished at the request of the owner. When one who claims to be the agent of the owner furnishes such supplies, no maritime lien arises. Furthermore, I do not think that a watchman can be called a "person to whom the management of the vessel at the port of supply is entrusted." These words imply a broader direction and control of the vessel than is implied in the mere act of watching a vessel out of commission.

A part owner and prospective purchaser of a vessel is a person entrusted with the vessel under 46 U.S.C. § 31341 and presumed to have the authority of the owner. *Hercules Co. v. The Brigadier General Absolom Baird*, 214 F.2d 66, 1954 AMC 1201 (3d Cir. 1954). What would be the effect of an anti-lien clause in a conditional sale agreement? *See Kane v. M/V Leda*, 355 F. Supp. 796, 1972 AMC 2094 (E.D. La. 1972). In this case, the court held that the purchaser of a vessel under a conditional sale was not a person authorized by the owner to create liens for necessaries under 46 U.S.C. § 972. Provisions of state law according to which the purchaser was "owner" were held to be immaterial. At any rate, the conditional sale agreement contained an anti-lien clause of which the repairman had notice.

Is a person who assumes the position of a master "entrusted with the vessel?" In *Findley v. Red Top Super Markets*, 188 F.2d 834, 1951 AMC 1113 (5th Cir. 1951), supplies were ordered by a person who purported to be the master of the vessel. The court dismissed a libel on the ground that ordinary care would have shown that the impostor did not have the authority of the owner. Should the solution be the same after the 1971 amendment? Under the current provisions of Chapter 313—Commercial Instruments and Maritime Liens?

Is a time charterer presumed to have authority from the owner under 46 U.S.C. § 972? *See Clubb Oil Tools, Inc. v. M/V George Vergottis*, 460 F. Supp. 835, 1980 AMC 556 (S.D. Tex. 1978). The court held that the time charterer was liable for breach of contract (rental of pipeline equipment for the loading of the vessel) and that the liability of the shipowner on the maritime lien was joint and several with the liability of the time charterer on the breach of contract claim. There was no anti-lien clause in the charter party.

Note: Authority of "an Agreed Buyer"

Under 46 U.S.C. § 973 "an agreed purchaser in possession of the vessel" was presumed to have authority to lien a vessel. In *First National Bank & Trust Co. of Vicksburg, Mississippi v. The Towboat Seneca*, 179 F. Supp. 847, 1960 AMC 766 (E.D. La. 1960), repairs were ordered by one Flowers who had exercised an option to purchase the vessel and was in possession of it in his capacity as master. At the time, the vessel was under a charter that contained an anti-lien clause. After the repairs were done, the contract of sale was executed and preferred ship mortgage was granted and recorded. Upon default of payment, the mortgage creditor sought foreclosure and the repairman claimed a preferred maritime lien for repairs. The court denied the lien. It reasoned:

> It is true that Flowers was the master of the Seneca and that ordinarily a shipyard may rely on that officer's presumed authority to lien the vessel. But such presumption does not relieve the shipyard of its statutory duty to use reasonable diligence to determine whether or not such authority does in fact exist. Where it is shown that the shipyard, by reasonable diligence, could have ascertained the truth, the presumption of authority in the master of the vessel disappears. Here, admittedly, a simple request to see the ship's papers, after Flowers' representation that that was acting for her owner, would have disclosed the true facts. It would have disclosed (a) that Flowers was neither the owner nor its representative, (b) that the charterer was prohibited from liening the vessel, and (c) that a maritime mortgage to the Merchants Bank existed, which mortgage, incidentally, was retired with the money raised through the mortgage in suit.
>
> Further inquiry would also have disclosed that DeSoto had exercised its option of purchase the vessel. But such disclosure would not justify the shipyard in accepting Flowers' interpretation of the legal effect of that exercise. True such disclosure would have advised the shipyard that DeSoto was "an agreed purchaser in possession of the vessel." However, as the statute specifically provides, the duty of the shipyard to use reasonable diligence to determine whether such "agreed purchaser" has authority to bind the vessel still persists. Actually, as the record demonstrates, shipyard intervenor was not concerned with binding the vessel. Flowers, as master of the Seneca, had a course of dealings with intervenor for many months. The shipyard's bills were always addressed to and paid by the charterer. The disclosure that the charterer might not be the owner of the vessel would have been of little interest to intervenor, at least insofar as payment of its bills was concerned, particularly in view of the then outstanding maritime mortgage.

The history of the Ship Mortgage Act shows that Congress was interested in encouraging the investment of capital in the American Merchant Marine. Before the passage of the Act, because a mortgage on a vessel was not a maritime contract, such mortgage was primed by all maritime liens, whenever attached. Under the Act, the maritime ship mortgage, with certain exceptions, protects the investor against all maritime liens subsequently attached. The Act goes further, however. It protects the maritime ship mortgage against prior obligations resulting from repairs or supplies to the vessel unless those repairs or supplies were authorized by her owner. The Act provides the means by which an owner may charter his vessel and prohibit the attachment of liens by the charterer. In this way an investor requiring a ship mortgage may accept with assurance the owner's certificate that no prior maritime liens have attached, at least during the pendency of the charter. Consequently, if an investor is to be given the protection intended by Congress, he should be allowed to proceed with confidence on the recorded ship's documents. He should not be required to guess who the equitable owner of the vessel may be. He should be able to rely, as to ownership at least, on the title which is recorded with the Collector of Customs as required by law.

Here, the bank did just that. It had the title to the Seneca examined in the proper offices. It received the certificate of her recorded owner that no prior maritime liens existed. It studied the charter party prohibiting the charterer from liening the vessel. Under the circumstances, its investment should be protected against putative owners of the vessel who, having had the vessel repaired prior to the execution of the warranty deed and ship mortgage, failed to disclose to the title owner and the bank that the bill for such repairs remained unpaid, or even that it had ever been incurred. It is true that the shipyard here may also have been victimized by these putative owners. But if the shipyard had used the reasonable diligence required by the Act, it would have learned, in advance of the repairs, that the vessel would not be bound therefor.

Decree accordingly.

Would the court have reached the same conclusion even in the absence of a preferred ship mortgage? How would this case be decided after the 1971 amendment to 46 U.S.C § 973? After the enactment of 46 U.S.C. § 31341 ("an agreed buyer in possession of the vessel" is presumed to have authority to procure necessaries)?

E. Persons Who May Acquire Maritime Liens

MEDINA v. MARVIRAZON COMPANIA NAVIERA, S.A.

533 F. Supp. 1279, 1983 AMC 2116 (D. Mass. 1982)
aff'd, 709 F.2d 124, 1983 AMC 2113 (1st Cir. 1983)

* * *

Dr. Elias Tsavaris claims a seaman's wage lien for money he advanced to satisfy obligations of Saint Constantinos Shipping Company (hereinafter, Saint Constantinos), the crew's employer, to the crew.

* * *

IV. Objection of Dr. Tsavaris

Mr. Elias J. Tsavaris, who advanced $51,884.40 to pay wage claims of the crew, objects to the finding of the special master that he is not entitled to a seaman's wage lien for that amount as assignee of those his funds paid. A seaman's wage lien is assignable. *The Kongo*, 6 Cir. 1946, 155 F. 2d 492, 494, *cert. denied*, 329 U.S. 735, 67 S. Ct. 99, 91 L. Ed. 635 (1946), and a person who, acting on the order of one with authority for the ship, advances money to the ship to satisfy wage or other lien claims is entitled to a lien equal in dignity to that met. *See Payne v. SS Tropic Breeze*, *supra* at 240 n. 12. But the assignee must be a stranger to the title and not someone who is an owner or part owner. 2 BENEDICT ON ADMIRALTY, *supra* at § 26. Although the special master found that Tsavaris did not own the M/V Constantinos, he denied Tsavaris a maritime lien on three independent grounds: that he occupied a fiduciary relationship with the vessel or its owners, that he did not prove that he relied on the credit of the owners rather than on that of the vessel, and that he controlled totally the vessel's destiny at the time his claim arose. Dr. Tsavaris objects to each rationale.

Dr. Tsavaris' second objection has some merit. The Federal Maritime Lien Act provides that "(a)ny person furnishing ... other necessaries ... to any vessel ... shall have a maritime lien on the vessel ... and it shall not be necessary to allege or prove that credit was given to the vessel." 46 U.S.C. § 971. Some authority includes seamen's wages as within the term "other necessaries," *In re SS Norberto Capay and SS Galicia Defender*, N.D.Cal. 1970, 330 F. Supp. 825; *The Lakeport*, W.D.N.Y. 1926, 15 F. 2d 575, and thus would exempt those making such advances from the requirement of alleging and proving reliance on the vessel. Moreover, Dr. Tsavaris correctly argues that control of a vessel's destiny at the moment an advance is made can not alone be sufficient to deny the advancer a lien. For, in a sense, any party who advances funds crucial to furnish a vessel with goods or services essential to its operations which would not otherwise be obtainable controls the vessel's destiny.

We do find, however, that the first ground upon which the special master relied-the nature of the relationship Tsavaris had with the vessel and its owners-suffices to deny Tsavaris a seaman's wage lien. In *The Gloucester*, D. Mass., 1923, 285 F. 579, 582, the court observed:

> where a party who would otherwise have a maritime lien has been held not entitled to it because of the relation in which he stood to the vessel, he was either (1) a real part owner of her, or (2) occupied a fiduciary relation towards her and her owners, or (3) dealt with himself on her account. Even within these classes the lien has under peculiar circumstances occasionally been allowed. In other words, the lien is really denied because of insuperable legal difficulties in the enforcement of it, or because-on grounds similar to estoppel-to recognize it would be inequitable to other claimants.

The precise nature of Tsavaris' relationship to the vessel is unclear. The ship's log described him as "owner"; he signed documents which identified him as president; he submitted an affidavit stating that he was formerly a vice president of Saint Constantinos Shipping Company; an acquaintance and associate of Tsavaris in some investments offered an affidavit calling Tsavaris a vice president. Moreover, the special master was not clearly erroneous, and we believe not erroneous at all, in concluding that Dr. Tsavaris' cavalier attitude towards an investment of $50,000 to $60,000-he advanced the funds without receiving any security or promissory note in return-coupled with his willingness to sign documents for the company when corporate officers were present suggest a fiduciary relationship sufficient to deny him a lien. In view of Tsavaris' close relationship to the operating company, it would be inequitable to allow him to assert a lien that would exclude parties whose claims arose from arm's-length transactions with the vessel from recovering *in rem*. We, therefore, sustain the special master's finding that Dr. Tsavaris has an *in personam* claim for $51,884.40 against Saint Constantinos, but no maritime lien.

* * *

Note: Owners, Stockholders, and Agents

Owners, part-owners, and general agents may not acquire maritime liens. This may seem an application of the civil law principle of confusion of rights: one may not have a partial right in a thing owned because ownership is an all-inclusive right. However, the rule is better explained in the light of policy considerations. Since most maritime liens are secret, an owner should not be allowed to establish such equities for his benefit to the prejudice of creditors.

The question whether one is "owner" of a vessel is not always easy to determine. *Cf. Diaz v. The Steamship Seathunder*, 191 F. Supp. 807, 1961 AMC 561 (D. Md. 1961); *The Josephine Lanasa (Findley v. Lanasa)*, 276 F.2d 907, 1960 AMC 1444 (5th Cir. 1960).

A part owner occupies the same position as a full owner; he may not assert a maritime lien on the ship she owns in indivision. *See The Lena Mowbray*, 71 F. 720 (S.D. Ala. 1895); *The Morning Star*, 1 F.2d 410, 1924 AMC 1571 (W.D. Wash. 1924). However, a joint venturer for the purchase of a vessel who incurs expenses for outfitting may have a lien for necessaries. *See Compagnia Maritima La Empresa v. Pickard*, 320 F.2d 829, 1964 AMC 109 (5th Cir. 1963); *The Odysseus III*, 77 F. Supp. 297, 1948 AMC 608 (S.D. Fla. 1948).

When advances are made by a stockholder, a lien may or may not arise depending on the circumstances. A stockholder has to overcome the presumption that the advances were made on general credit. *See The Cimbria*, 214 F. 131 (D.N.J. 1914). If he overcomes this presumption, a lien may arise if other creditors are not unfairly prejudiced. *See The Puritan*, 258 F. 271 (D. Mass. 1919); *The Murphy Tugs*, 28 F. 429 (E.D. Mich. 1886).

A "general agent" represents the owner and occupies the same position as a part owner. He is presumed to rely on the credit of the owner for any advances he makes. *See Savas v. Maria Trading Co.*, 285 F.2d 336, 1961 AMC 260 (4th Cir. 1960). For rebuttal of the presumption, *see Compagnia Maritime La Empresa S.A. v. Pickard, supra.*

Note: Advances and Assignment of Liens

A maritime lien may be assigned, and the assignee is subrogated to the rights of the assignor, unless, of course, the assignee is a person who may not acquire a maritime lien. One who advances sums for the discharge of a maritime lien occupies the position of an assignee. He acquires a lien of the same class and rank as the lien that has been discharged. *Sasportes v. M/V Sol de Copacabana*, 581 F.2d 1204, 1980 AMC 791 (5th Cir. 1978).

The lien discharged by an advance of money need not be in existence at the time of the advance. Thus one who advances money for necessaries acquires a lien under 46 U.S.C. § 31342 (formerly codified as 46 U.S.C. 971). *See Crustacean Transportation Corp. v. Atlanta Trading Corp.*, 1967 AMC 362 (5th Cir. 1966).

F. Priorities of Liens

Introductory Note

The sale of a vessel in an *in rem* proceeding generates a fund in the registry of an admiralty court. When this fund, or comparable security posted by the shipowner to secure the vessel's release, is insufficient to satisfy all valid liens and claims, the priority of the different catagories of claims becomes of paramount importance.

There is no authoritative scheme of priorities among maritime liens. No statute has created it and, although a number of judicial decisions give an order of ranking, in each case it is incomplete. Consequently, the issue of ranking competing maritime liens and claims has been left to legal scholars and to the federal courts. *See* W. TETLEY, MARITIME LIENS AND CLAIMS, 392-304 (2d ed. 1989); George L. Varian, *Rank and Priority of Maritime Liens*, 47 TUL. L. REV. 751 (1973); G. GILMORE & C. BLACK, THE LAW OF ADMIRALTY §§ 9-58-76 (2d ed. 1975); *Rayon Y Celanese Peruano, S.A. v. M/V PHGH*, 471 F. Supp. 1363 (S.D. Ala. 1979). However, the ranking of maritime lien claims by the district and circuit courts in conjunction with the priority rules codified in 46 U.S.C. §§ 31301(5)-(6), 31326(b)(1)-(2) has resulted in allowing the following rules of ranking to be generally observed:

1. expenses of justice during *custodia legis* (*see* 46 U.S.C. § 31326(b)(1));
2. the following preferred maritime liens (*see* 46 U.S.C. § 31301(5)(A)-(F)):
   (a) wages of the crew; maintenance and cure; as to masters'wages, *see* 46 U.S.C. § 11112; wages of stevedore when directly employed by the shipowner or his agent (*see* 46 U.S.C. § 31341);
   (b) salvage, including contract salvage, and general average;
   (c) maritime torts, including personal injury, property damage and cargo tort liens;
3. All maritime contract liens *which arise before the filing of a preferred ship mortgage* (U.S. flag vessel) (*see* 46 U.S.C. § 31301(5)(A)). These include liens for "necessaries", such as repairs, supplies, towage, and the use of a dry dock or marine railway (*see* 46 U.S.C. § 31301(4)), as well as cargo contract damage liens and contract charterer's liens;
4. preferred ship mortgages (U.S. flag vessels);
5. other maritime contract liens which accrue *after* the filing of a preferred ship mortgage (U.S. flag vessels) and *prior* to a foreign preferred ship mortgage. *However*: all necessaries provided in the United States have priority over foreign preferred ship mortgages irrespective of the time they arose. (*See* 46 U.S.C. § 31326(b)(2));
6. foreign preferred ship mortgages;
7. maritime contract liens, excluding those for necessaries provided in the U.S., accruing *after* foreign preferred ship mortgages such as contract cargo damage liens and contract charterer's liens;
8. state-created liens of a maritime nature;
9. maritime liens for penalties and forfeitures for violation of federal statutes;
10. perfected non-maritime claims, including tax liens;
11. attaching liens in causes of action within the admiralty and maritime jurisdiction (foreign attachment);
12. maritime liens in bankruptcy;
13. all other general creditors/claimants.

According to the above ranking scheme, competing liens are initially ranked as to superiority by class. The top priority liens will of course be paid first. If, however, the funds in the registry of the admiralty court are insufficient to fully pay all of the claims within a particular class, the issue of priority of claims within the class itself must be resolved. There are various rules of ranking claims within the same class which are generally agreed upon. "The basic general rule is the *inverse order* rule that claims of the same class are given priority amongst themselves according to the inverse order of their accrual. In other words 'the last lien given will supercede the preceeding'." TETLEY, *supra*, at 399 (*citing The St. Jago de Cuba*, 22 U.S. (9 Wheat) 409, 416, 6 L. Ed. 122 (1824); *The John G. Stevens*, 170 U.S. 113, 119, 18 S. Ct. 544, 42 L. Ed. 969 (1898)). Though the inverse order rule is the basic general rule for the ranking of claims within a class, for practical reasons the rule has been "subjected to a series of special rules which in effect have largely displaced it." GILMORE & BLACK, *supra*, § 9-62 at 744.

1. *Priority of Wage Claims*

In *The C.J. Saxe*, 145 F. 749 (S.D.N.Y. 1906), the court held that a claim for wages ranks higher than a claim for damages for collision. This holding remains unchallenged. In *Fredelos v. Merritt-Chapman & Scott (The Padre Island)*, 447 F.2d 435, 1971 AMC 2192 (5th Cir. 1971), the court held that a claim for maintenance and cure has the same priority as a wage claim and ranks higher than a claim for salvage. One court has stated that 46 U.S.C. § 10313 affords seamen a "super priority" for unpaid wages. *Isbrandtsen Marine Services, Inc. v. M/V Inagua Tania*, 93 F.3d 728, 1997 AMC 912 (11th Cir. 1996).

2. *Tort vs. Contract Liens*

A maritime tort lien takes priority over a maritime contract lien. In *The John G. Stevens*, 170 U.S. 113, 122, 18 S. Ct. 544, 548, 42 L. Ed. 969 (1898), the Court said:

> That the maritime lien upon a vessel, for damages caused by her fault to another vessel, takes precedence of a maritime lien for supplies previously furnished to the offending vessel, is a reasonable inference, if not a necessary conclusion, from the decisions of this court, above referred to, the effect of which may be summed up as follows:
>
> The collision, as soon as it takes place, creates, as security for the damages, a maritime lien or privilege, *jus in re*, a proprietary interest in the offending ship, and which, when enforced by admiralty process *in rem*, relates back to the time of the collision. The offending ship is considered as herself the wrongdoer and as herself bound to make compensation for the wrong done. The owner of the injured vessel is entitled to proceed *in rem* against the offender, without regard to the question who may be her owners, or to the division, the nature or the extent of their interests in her. With the relations of the owners of those interests, as among themselves, the owner of the injured vessel has no concern. All the interests, existing at the time of the collision, in the offending vessel, whether by way of part-ownership, of mortgage, of bottomry bond or of other maritime lien for repairs or supplies, arising out of contract with the owners or agents of the vessel, are parts of the vessel herself, and as such are bound by and responsible for her wrongful acts...

The Court went on to conclude that "a suit by the owner of a tow against her tug, to recover for an injury to the tow by the negligence on the part of the tug, is a suit *ex delicto* and not *ex contractu*". 170 U.S. 113, 125, 18 S. Ct. 544, 549.

3. *Claims for Negligent Towage*

In *The Interstate No. 1*, 290 F. 926, 1923 AMC 1118 (2d Cir.), *cert. denied*, 262 U.S. 753, 43 S. Ct. 701, 67 L. Ed. 1216 (1923), liens for negligent towage were subordinated to liens for supplies furnished in the same voyage, apparently on the theory that such claims arise out of contract rather than tort.

When a tug with a flotilla of barges collides with a third vessel due to the fault of the tug, the owner of the third vessel has a lien against the tug only. *See Sturgis v. Boyer*, 65 U.S. (24 How.) 110, 16 L. Ed. 591 (1860); *Walker v. Tug Diane*, 350 F. Supp. 1388, 1974 AMC 1567 (D.V.I. 1972). In the last case, the court held that the tow is not liable *in rem* when it is not manned at the time of the collision. *But see The Sif*, 266 F. 166 (2d Cir. 1920); *S.C. Loveland Co. v. United States*, 207 F. Supp. 450, 1963 AMC 260 (E.D. Pa. 1962) [barges liable for general average contribution]. The tow has a lien against the tug. *See The Steamer Webb*, 81 U.S. (14 Wall.) 406, 20 L. Ed. 774 (1872).

1. Ranking of Liens of the Same Class: the "Inverse Order" Rule

Introductory Note: The Inverse Order Rule

In *The William Leishear*, 21 F.2d 862, 863 (D. Md. 1927), the court described the "inverse order" rule in the following way:

> There is the general rule that maritime liens rank in an order inverse to the order of their creation (*The St. Jago de Cuba*, 9 Wheaton, 409, 6 L. Ed. 122), a principle contrary to what is common in other branches of the law. Without going at any length into the ancient historical reasons for this anomaly, suffice it to say that in this country two theories exist as the basis of this admiralty doctrine. They are, first, that each person acquires a *jus in re*, and becomes a sort of coproprietor in the *res*, and therefore subjects his claim to the next similar lien which attaches; and, second, that the last beneficial service is the one that continues the activity of the ship as long as possible, and therefore should be preferred, provided that what is produced or contributed to by the service is a voyage. *The Glen Island* (D.C.) 194 F. 744. Under the second theory, there is the consideration that beneficial additions subsequent to earlier liens add to the value of the ship, and that, therefore, to prefer such additions will not deprive the earlier lienors of any interest which they would have had, if no such services had been rendered.
>
> Generally speaking, the law of maritime liens may be said to be made up of exceptions to the above doctrine, which gives priority to the lien latest in point of time, so that to-day it is possible to deduce, from the decisions, the following order of priority, existing irrespective of time, which represents the weight of authority: (1) Seamen's wages; (2) salvage; (3) tort and collision liens; (4) repairs, supplies, towage, wharfage, pilotage, and other necessaries; (5) bottomry bonds in inverse order of application; (6) nonmaritime claims. This, however, is no more than a very general statement, since any summary is subject to further exceptions of more or less narrow application.

In *The Frank G. Fowler*, 17 F. 653 (S.D.N.Y. 1883), the court reasoned that the inverse order rule applies to successive service liens because each incumbrance "is actually benefited by reason of the successive incumbrance." Since this rationale is inapplicable to successive tort liens, the court held that the sufferer of the first tort of collision "ought not to lose the benefit of his lien arising out of the first tort or collision." This decision was criticized in *The America*, 168 F. 424 (D.N.J. 1909) as follows:

> Judge Blatchford's reasoning was in effect that, since the second collision did not benefit the vessel, it was not entitled to priority over the lien created by the first collision, thereby seemingly adopting the rule that a subsequent lien is entitled to priority only when it has benefited or increased the value of the vessel out of which all liens are to be satisfied. It is manifest, however, that priorities between collision liens cannot be determined on the theory of benefit to the offending vessel. No collision, be it the first, the second, or the third, can or does benefit the vessel. *The John G. Stevens*, *supra*, moreover, expressly held that a tort lien, although it did not benefit the vessel, nevertheless had priority over an earlier lien for supplies, which presumably did. There is no apparent reason why the rule in cases of collision should be different than it is in the matter of successive liens for repairs or supplies, which are ordinarily paid in their inverse order. The proprietary interest created in the vessel in favor of the party injured by the first collision is subject, like all other proprietary interests in her, to subsequent marine perils, including collisions. That a maritime lien created by collision gives a proprietary interest in the *res* to the injured party is laid down in many cases, among them *The John G. Steven*, *supra*.

The "proprietary interest" rationale may adequately explain the inverse order rule; however, it fails to explain the postponement of contract liens to tort liens or the postponement of salvage and tort liens to liens for wages. What is the rationale for these rules?

---

1. *Maritime Contract Liens*

> The inverse order rule has the benefit of forcing the claimant to act quickly but it could also incite a supplier of necessaries to arrest the vessel on the same day as the necessaries were supplied in order to remain ahead of future suppliers. Such a practice would contradict the basic purpose of the maritime lien which is to provide security for a claim whilst permiting the ship to proceed on her way in order to earn the freight or hire necessary to pay of the claim. In consequence, various special time rules—voyage, season and calendar year—have been devised, whereby liens of a class accruing during a specific period are ranked *pari passu* [without preference]. TETLEY, *supra* at 399-400.

The oldest special time rule, the voyage rule, results in all contract and service liens from the same voyage having an equal priority and sharing *pro rata*. However, these liens will be primed by all contract and service liens "which accrue in connection with the next voyage." George L. Varian, *Rank and Priority of Maritime Liens*, 47 TUL. L. REV. 751, 760 (1973). For a discussion of additional special time rules *see Todd Shipyards Corp. v. The City of Athens, infra.*

2. *Other Maritime Liens*

> Outside the service lien field the inverse order rule is simple, easy to apply and causes no great difficulty or discussion. With respect to wage claims, the issue never arises: these claims have an over-riding priority and are paid in full, without regard to when they were earned, before any other liens share in the distribution. If the proceeds were not enough even to pay all wages, the decision whether all wage claimants should prorate or whether the claims for more recent wages should have priority would undoubtedly lie within the discretion of the trial judge. In the salvage field, it is rare that more than one set of salvage liens is in issue: if two or more salvage operations had been performed on distinct occasions, the more recent liens would have priority as a matter of course. The same is true for collision tort liens: successive collisions are rare but they do happen; when they happen, the inverse order rule applies, even as to collisions that take place on the same voyage. The problem of successive personal injury liens is seldom raised. If several such liens arise on a single occasion—collision or fire, and the ship lost—they share equally, both in the value of the ship and in the [$420] per ton set up for their benefit by the Limitation of Liability Act. If the liens arise on "distinct occasions" the Limitation Act requires the setting up of separate [$420] per ton funds for each occasion, so that the question of priorities between the groups of liens arising on each "occasion" could arise only if the [$420] per ton funds were insufficient.

GILMORE & BLACK, *supra*, § 9-62 at 743.

3. *Maritime Contract Liens —Time of Attachment*

Barge owner exercised its option to extend a charter of a towboat for an additional year. Thereafter the owner sold the towboat. The purchaser (new owner) obtained a preferred ship mortgage to finance the transaction. After the mortgage had been obtained, the new owner breached the charter party by failing to deliver the vessel or an equivalent vessel to the charterer. A question arose as to when lien for the breach of the charter party arose, at the time that the contract was entered into or at the time of the breach. The Court of Appeals for the Fifth Circuit relying on venerable authorities held that a "maritime lien attaches at the commencement of the undertaking and any subsequent breach perfecting the lien relates back to that time." The court found that the executory contract doctrine was not applicable inasmuch as this was time charter party and not a contract of affreightment. Pursuant to the charter party, prior to extension of its term, the vessel had been delivered to the charterer and had made several voyages. *Bank One, Louisiana N.A., v. Mr. Dean M/V*, 293 F.3d 830, 2002 AMC 1617 (5th Cir. 2002).

4. ***No Inverse Order Rule for Attachments***

The inverse order rule applies only to maritime liens, which can be enforced by an action *in rem* under Rule C. It does not apply to successive attachments under Rule B, where the usual "first in time, first in right" rule applies. In *A. Coker & Co. Ltd v. National Shipping Agency Corp.*, 2000 AMC 489 (E.D. La. 1999), the court said:

> Bisso argues that the theory behind the inverse-order rule applies equally to Rule B attachment liens as to Rule C maritime liens. The Court disagrees. The rationale underlying this rule is that "the vessel must get on" and that the most recent lienholders perform services that keep the vessel in operation so that revenue can be generated to satisfy the earlier claims. *See* GILMORE & BLACK, *supra,* 9-62, at 742-43 (*citing The St. Jago de Cuba,* 22 U.S. 409, 416 (1824)). As stated above, this case does not involve a seized vessel but simply cash held in an agent's account. That Bisso may have provided necessary services to a vessel owned by NSAC does not benefit Coker. Accordingly, the Court finds no exception to the rule set forth in *Triton,* that competing attachment lien claims have priority according to the first-in-time rule.

---

2. Special Time Rules

TODD SHIPYARDS CORPORATION v. THE CITY OF ATHENS

83 F. Supp. 67 (D. Md. 1949)

CHESNUT, District Judge

The SS "City of Athens", a trans-Atlantic passenger-cargo ship, was libelled in the Port of Baltimore on July 12, 1947 by the Todd Shipyards Corporation of New York, for the balance due for repairs and reconstruction of the ship in the total amount of $491,077. Many intervening libels and other claims against the ship were filed; and in due course the ship was sold by the Marshal of the court on August 13, 1947 to the Panamanian Lines, Inc., for $400,000, which sum (together with the sum of $1837.71 representing earned freight) less certain expenses of administration, represents the total sum available for lien claims in the amount of $775,457.82. On August 14, 1947 the case was referred to Mr. L. Vernon Miller, a member of the Baltimore Bar thoroughly experienced in admiralty matters, as Commissioner, "to take evidence therein and to report to the Court his findings of law and fact therein with all convenient speed", and the clerk was directed to give notice by publication that all claims against the proceeds of the ship should be filed within a specified time. The Commissioner's report was filed October 7, 1948.

* * *

Schedule X (the last page of the report) lists in summary all claims allowed as liens. They embrace basic wages of the crew in the amount of $24,733.74; additional wages for the crew at $15,141.54; one extra month's pay for certain members of the crew $2,033; repatriation claims $945; additional wages to skeleton crew July 12 to July 22, 1947, $1,375.66; maintenance and cure $236.25; personal injury claims $4,000, and unclassified crew claims in the amount of $8,422.25; head tax claims of $1,624, and cargo claims $1,074.57. The total of such claims was $59,586.01. Other claims for supplies or "necessaries" to the ship on various voyages allowed as liens aggregated $715,871.81. Of this latter amount those accruing in the calendar year 1947 amounting to $291,921.68 were determined to be paid in full as having priority, and the remainder, $423,950.13, a large amount of which was allowed to the Todd Shipyards Corporation arising in 1946, was to be deferred to the prior payment claims. The estimated net fund available for distribution after deducting certain expenses of administration including the Commissioner's fee, will be about $380,000. The total claims allowed priority in payment and thus to be paid in full, aggregate $351,507.69. As the deferred claims aggregate $423,950.13, and the remainder of the fund available for distribution is only about $30,000 it appears that the claims deferred in payment by the Commissioner's report will receive a dividend of less than 10%.

* * *

The ship was built in 1920 at Hog Island, Pennsylvania, and named "The American Banker". She was of 7430 gross tonnage, 436.9 feet in length and 58.2 foot beam. Later she was renamed the "Ville D'Anviers" and under that name acquired in 1946 by the Sociedad Naviera Trans-Atlantica S.A. a Panamanian corporation, and registered under the Honduras flag. The corporation seems to have had little or no assets other than the ownership of the ship, but the stock of the corporation was owned by Basil Hanioti, of Greek extraction but a citizen of the United States. He also owned directly or indirectly at the time one or more other ships. It is said that Hanioti paid $430,000 for the ship which he purchased for the special purpose of passenger and cargo transportation between New York and Mediterranean ports. The ship had previously been used as troop transport. To adapt her to the new and anticipated large passenger traffic, it was deemed essential to make extensive repairs and for that purpose the Todd Shipyards, a New York corporation, was employed. Todd began work on the ship in October 1946. It was evidently a rush job because Hanioti was insistent upon early completion to take advantage of anticipated large passenger business. It appears that the work was done night and day with much overtime and possibly without adequate detailed supervision in the interests of the owner. But the Commissioner found no satisfactory evidence to contradict the reasonableness of the itemized invoices and accounts rendered by Todd in support of its claim. By November 12, 1946 Todd had done work as per invoices in the amount of $646,105. The ship made her first voyage to Europe leaving New York in November 1946. In due course she returned to New York about January 1, 1947 and thereafter during 1947 made three additional round-trips, the last one terminating at Baltimore in early July 1947. During 1947 Todd performed additional repair and construction work on the ship making its aggegate charges $758,010, with total cash and credits paid or allowed in the amount of $266,933, with balance now claimed to be due in the amount of $491,077, of which amount the Commissioner by schedule D (page 157) has allowed $104,972 as ranking in 1947; and allowed a balance of $386,105 ranked in 1946 for deferred payment.

It appears from the report that the cost of repair of the ship by Todd was very greatly in excess of what Hanioti had anticipated, and that his insufficient capital resources finally resulted in the libelling of the ship. After the ship was libelled in Baltimore Hanioti was unable to pay the wages due to the crew not only for the last voyage but for some preceding voyages. During each of the ship's voyages it became necessary to obtain for her, frequently in foreign ports, supplies and "other necessaries". Claims for these have been filed in these proceedings and practically all have been allowed by the Commissioner as maritime liens, all those arising from the last three voyages of the ship in 1947 to be paid in full and those incidental to the first voyage in 1946 were also allowed but defered as to payment.

* * *

The second question of general importance arising on the exceptions relates to the *marshalling of maritime liens.* The applicable law is to be found in judicial decisions, and is not controlled by any federal statute. With respect to the ranking of liens of different classes, the judicial decisions, while not entirely uniform, are substantially in accord. The law was conveniently summarized in this court by Judge Coleman twenty years ago in the case of *The William Leishear*, D.C., 21 F. 2d 862, 863.... In the instant case there are several classes of liens including seamen's wages, a tort claim, and liens for repairs, supplies and other necessaries; but as the case presents no controversy with respect to the preferred payment of seamen's wages and the tort claim, the only question of priority of payment arising with respect to the claims for repairs, supplies and other necessaries, all of which are claims of the same class and rank. But, as the fund for distribution is insufficient to pay all of them in full, there is necessarily involved here the question where the line is to be drawn between those claims of this latter class.

On this point it has sometimes been said that the judicial decisions are in confusion; but an examination of very many cases leads to the conclusion that this statement is correct only insofar as it is applicable to other than ocean voyages of ships. The rule originally developed in admiralty law and still the basic rule is that maritime liens of the same class are entitled to priority of payment in the inverse order of the time of accrual and that therefore liens arising in connection with the last voyage of the ship have priority of payment over liens accruing on a prior voyage. The rule was thus expressed by Judge Brown in the well-known case of *The Proceeds of the Gratitude*, D.C.N.Y. 1890, 42 F. 299, at page 300—

> The general maritime law adjusts all liens by the voyage.... By the general rule ... the priority of liens continues only till the next voyage. The liens connected with every new voyage start with a priority over all former ones after the ship has sailed, if there has previously been opportunity to enforce them.

* * *

Cases which have departed from the "voyage" rule will be found, without exception I think, to have related to ships engaged in other than ocean voyages, as for instance, harbor tugs, coastwise vessels, transportation on the Great Lakes, and comparatively small craft plying local waters. The voyage rule contemplates that at the end of each voyage liens that have arisen during its course should be promptly enforced before the ship departs on another voyage, if there is opportunity to the claimant to so enforce it by libel. As indicated in the opinion of Judge Smith for the Court of Appeals for the Fourth Circuit in the case above cited, the application of the voyage rule presupposes that the voyages are separated "by an appreciable length of time". While this is necessarily still true with respect to transatlantic or other similar ocean voyages, it is obviously not so with respect to the much shorter and more frequent voyages of harbor craft and merely coastwise vessels or other comparatively local transportation. To meet the necessities of such particular local conditions and to accord with the customary business practice locally prevailing it has been found necessary to substitute a rule of priorities other than the voyage rule, and the tendency seems to have been to adopt, as the period allowed prior to the filing of the libel for preferential claims arising therein, a period which can be regarded as a reasonable time for the extension of credit. Thus for New York harbor craft, that period has been fixed at 40 days, and in Puget Sound at 90 days; while on the Great Lakes, where the rigor of winter generally interrupts navigation, the period has been fixed as the navigating season, and thus claims arising during such a particular season are preferred over those of a prior season. More recently, apparently by analogy to this so-called season rule, a rule of priority has been applied by which liens arising in a particular calendar year are given priority over those arising in a prior year; and in a number of cases this latter rule, the so-called "calendar" year rule, has been applied to vessels engaged in coastwise commerce. *The Interstate No. 1, supra*, 290 F. at page 934. About twenty years ago, in a series of three cases in this court, Judge Coleman applied this latter calendar year rule to small craft locally engaged. While there seems to be no case in the Supreme Court dealing with this particular subject, it seems clearly established in the First Circuit (*The Interstate No. 1, supra*, 290 F. at page 934) that the voyage rule still applies with respect to "vessels engaged in commerce on the ocean." And it is, I think, likewise, the rule announced in this Fourth Circuit in the case of the *Steam Dredge A*, 204 F. 262, 264, although on what appears to have been a factually unsatisfactory record, the rule actually applied in the case of a ship apparently engaged in coastwise trade was the socalled calendar year rule.

In the instant case the Commissioner's report expresses his preference for the *voyage* rule but actually applied the *calendar year* rule. It is important, however, to note that in doing so he found that in effect both the voyage rule and the calendar year rule would produce the same actual result with respect to payment of the liens. This was true because the ship made four voyages, one in the latter months of 1946 and the remaining three in 1947; and the fund for distribution was sufficient to pay in full all the allowed lien claims arising in 1947, leaving a balance for a percentage distribution of less than 10% to the lien claims arising in connection with the first voyage in 1946. It was, therefore, unnecessary in applying the voyage rule, to distinguish between claims arising on the second, third and fourth voyages as to respective priority. In particular figures the Commissioner thus allowed for prior payment claims for supplies and other necessaries arising on the last three voyages in the aggregate amount of $291,921.68, all to be paid in full from the fund, while those arising in 1946 and to be deferred to the former amounted to $423,950.13, of which the balance due Todd Shipyards represents nearly 90%.

Counsel for Todd and the few other claimants whose liens arose in connection with the first voyage, vigorously protest the correctness of the classification made by the Commissioner. In the first place they point out that in the cases applying the so-called calendar year rule the expression sometimes used by the court is the "year" rule and that, therefore, the period of time referred to should be considered a twelve-month period preceding the date of the libel; but as to this an examination of most if not all of the cases referred to shows from the facts involved that claims allowed (with only trivial exceptions, if any) were those which arose during the calendar year in which the libel was filed; and I have found no case which establishes a twelve month period for the classification of preferred and deferred lien claims.

The next argument advanced is that by reason of changed conditions with respect to ocean voyages which are now generally of much shorter duration than when the voyage rule was established, and since means of communication between the owner and the master of the ship, possibly in a foreign port, are more rapid because of the facilities of cable and radio, the voyage rule should be regarded as obsolete and a different new rule substituted therefor.

In support of this contention particular reference is made to the view expressed by Robinson on Admiralty p. 427, in which that generally excellent author, after referring to the season rule prevailing with regard to shipping on the Great Lakes, and the 90-day rule for credit in navigation in Puget Sound said:

> It is questionable how much further the application of this principle can be carried and to what jurisdictions it extends. But it is sufficient here to point out that for short trips the voyage rule is no longer a test and has given place to rules in which there are local variances. Even where the longer voyages of ocean steamers are concerned, the courts have ceased to apply a technical interpretation of the term 'voyage' and talk in terms of years.
>
> The year is considered representative of the voyage. This shows a tendency, even in the case of larger vessels, to apply a time measured by *a reasonable period of credit* rather than voyage. Passenger liners today make the transatlantic run in less than a week so that the larger steamship companies in a certain measure are beset with the same problem which faced harbor craft at an earlier date. Judge Brown in *The Gratitude ante*, note 181, remarked of the 40 day rule: 'It accords in some degree with the period of modern (1890) voyages.' (Italics supplied)

However, an examination of the four cases mentioned in the note documenting this view fails to show that any of them related to transatlantic or other ocean voyages. Two of the cases were among those decided some twenty years ago by Judge Coleman and which have been above referred to. They related to small craft locally navigating the Chesapeake Bay.

While counsel for the particular exceptants concede that there is no definite judicial authority in support of their contention they urge that, as the decided cases present such variable rules for determining priorities, some new and definite rule should now be established, and further urge that the new rule to be adopted should be the year rule as they contend it should be understood, that is, that all liens arising in a period of one year prior to the libel should rank *pari passu*; or, in other words, that the period of a year as "a reasonable period of credit" should be established as the test rather than that of the voyage.

My conclusion of law is that the voyage rule still prevails despite greater rapidity of transportation and communication. The reasons which originally gave rise to the voyage rule still exist even though their importance in some respects may have been lessened. Many ocean voyages are still of several months' duration and there is still at times the most imperative need that a ship in a port far distant from the owner should have the ability to obtain repairs and supplies on the credit of the ship itself. This ability to obtain such credit would obviously be much impaired if a long prior claim originating in connection with a previous voyage, as in this case, and amounting to a sum much larger than the sale value of the ship, were to rate equally with the supplies or repairs on the last voyage, imperatively needed to keep the ship a "going concern", and to enable it to return to its home.

* * *

With regard to the argument that the court should establish a new rule with respect to priorities and lien claimants, it is sufficient to say that I would not feel warranted in doing so where, as I find, the voyage rule is still the established one for ocean voyages. Nor do I think this case presents in its factual situation a proper one for the establishment of the new twelve-months rule which is advocated. I will add that while I have concluded that the voyage rule must be observed here, I do not think, apart from it, the facts of the case would justify the application of the calendar year rule. If we were to disregard the voyage rule and accept in lieu thereof as a test, a reasonable period of credit, the facts of the particular case do not furnish an adequate basis for determining what this period should be. Should it be forty days as a possible inference from what Judge Brown said in the case of *The Gratitude* above quoted, or two months for a transatlantic liner, or six months as the calendar year rule has in effect been applied by the Commissioner's report, or a year or at least eight months as contended for by the exceptants? While the calendar year rule, analogized to the season rule, may be fairly applicable to the smaller craft navigating locally only, the court is not in possession of sufficient information in this case with respect to conditions in general affecting transatlantic or ocean voyages to say what period of time should be regarded as reasonable. Change in the law in this respect and in the establishment of such a definite period, if to be made at all, should be made only after the fullest possible information of all relevant conditions which ordinarily could be brought to the attention of a legislative body with full powers of investigation. While it may be entirely appropriate and desirable for a court dealing with a particular local situation, as for instance affecting the New York harbor or Puget Sound or the Great Lakes or the Chesapeake Bay, to lay down a general rule that is locally applicable, it is a far more difficult and wider question to determine such a rule for ocean voyages which, in many cases, may involve navigation extending around the globe.

* * *

Note: Periods of Priority: Service Liens

For another application of the voyage rule, *see Rayon y Celanese Peruana, S.A. v. M/V Phgh*, 471 F. Supp. 1363, 1974 AMC 2682 (S.D. Ala. 1979). A "season rule" applies in the Great Lakes. *See The City of Tawas*, 3 F. 170 (E.D.

Mich. 1880). There is a forty-day priority period in the New York harbor. *See Proceeds of the Gratitude*, 42 F. 299 (S.D.N.Y. 1890); *The Samuel Little*, 221 F. 308 (2d Cir. 1915). In *The Interstate No. 1*, 290 F. 926, 1923 AMC 1118 (2d Cir.), *cert. denied*, 262 U.S. 753, 43 S. Ct. 701, 67 L. Ed. 1216 (1923), the Second Circuit held that the forty-day period in the New York harbor is a single priority period. All other liens of the same rank dating more than forty days share in the proceeds *pro rata*. A ninety-day rule applies in Seattle Harbor and the Puget Sound. *See The Edith*, 217 F. 300 (W.D. Wash. 1914). In certain parts of the United States a calendar year rule applies.

---

3. *"Preferred" Maritime Liens*

Note: Ship Mortgage Foreclosures

Prior to the enactment of the Ship Mortgage Act in 1920, ship mortgages were subordinate to maritime liens. However, as a result of the Act, common law rules regulating competing maritime liens were altered with the statutory creation of "preferred" maritime liens. This term was defined in 46 U.S.C. § 953.

THE SHIP MORTGAGE ACT

46 U.S.C. § 953

(superseded version)

§ 953. Preferred Maritime Lien; Priorities; Other Liens

(a) When used hereinafter in this chapter, the term "preferred maritime lien" means (1) a lien arising prior in time to the recording and indorsement of a preferred mortgage in accordance with the provisions of this chapter; or (2) a lien for damages arising out of tort, for wages of a stevedore when employed directly by the owner, operator, master, ship's husband, or agent of the vessel, for wages of the crew of the vessel, for general average, and for salvage, including contract salvage.

(b) Upon the sale of any mortgaged vessel by order of a district court of the United States in any suit *in rem* in admiralty for the enforcement of a preferred mortgage lien thereon, all preexisting claims in the vessel, including any possessory common-law lien of which a lienor is deprived under the provisions of section 952 of this title, shall be held terminated and shall thereafter attach, in like amount and in accordance with their respective priorities, to the proceeds of the sale; except that the preferred mortgage lien shall have priority over all claims against the vessel, except (1) preferred maritime liens, and (2) expenses and fees allowed and costs taxed, by the court.

Unless a lien met the requirements set forth in section 953, it did not have preferred status and was therefore primed by a preferred ship mortgage (U.S. flag vessel). The Ship Mortgage Act has been amended and recodified at 46 U.S.C. § 31301, *et seq.* The current statutory provisions relating to preferred maritime liens and their ranking, which make no substantive change in the law, are as follows:

Commercial Instruments and Maritime Liens

46 U.S.C. §§ 31301, et seq.

§ 31301

(5) "preferred maritime lien" means a maritime lien on a vessel—
 (A) arising before a preferred mortgage was filed under section 31321 of this title;
 (B) for damage arising out of maritime tort;
 (C) for wages of a stevedore when employed directly by a person listed in section 31341 of this title;
 (D) for wages of the crew of the vessel;
(E) for general average; or
(F) for salvage, including contract salvage; and

§ 31326. Court sales to enforce preferred mortgage liens and maritime liens and priority of claims

(a) When a vessel is sold by order of a district court in a civil action *in rem* brought to enforce a preferred mortgage lien or a maritime lien, any claim in the vessel existing on the date of sale is terminated, including a possessory common law lien of which a person is deprived under section 31325(e)(2) of this title, and the vessel is sold free of all those claims.

(b) Each of the claims terminated under subsection (a) of this section attaches, in the same amount and in accordance with their priorities to the proceeds of the sale, except that—

(1) the preferred mortgage lien has priority over all claims against the vessel (except for expenses and fees allowed by the court, costs imposed by the court, and preferred maritime liens); and

(2) for a foreign vessel, the preferred mortgage lien is subordinate to a maritime lien for necessaries provided in the United States.

(Added Pub. L. 100-710, Title I, § 102(c), Nov. 23, 1988, 102 Stat. 4746.)

---

a. Liens for Cargo Damage: Contract or Tort?

ALL ALASKAN SEAFOODS, INC. v. M/V SEA PRODUCER

882 F.2d 425, 1989 AMC 2935 (9th Cir. 1989)

DAVID R. THOMPSON, Circuit Judge

All Alaskan Seafoods Inc. ("All Alaskan"), a shipper and the plaintiff in this admiralty case, appeals the district court's partial summary judgment. The district court held that All Alaskan's maritime lien on a vessel was subordinate to a mortgagee's ship's mortgage. The district court determined that under the Ship Mortgage Act, All Alaskan's claim for cargo damage could only arise under contract law, not under tort law; therefore the claim was not entitled to priority as a maritime lien under 46 U.S.C. § 953(a)(2). We reverse and remand.

Facts

In October 1986, All Alaskan commenced an action for cargo damage against the vessel M/V Sea Producer and against Express Marine Transportation Co. ("Express Marine"), the vessel's operator. In its complaint, All Alaskan alleged that it suffered losses of approximately $1.5 million when its shipment of frozen king crab thawed while in transit from Molar, Alaska to Seattle, Washington, and was contaminated by a refrigerant leakage in the hold of the Sea Producer. All Alaskan further alleged that the losses it suffered were caused by the negligence of Express Marine.

In April 1987, People's National Bank of Washington ("People's") intervened in the action to foreclose a preferred maritime mortgage on the Sea Producer.

Before discovery commenced, All Alaskan and People's filed cross-motions for partial summary judgment on the issue of the priority of their respective liens against the Sea Producer. The district court denied All Alaskan's motion and granted partial summary judgment for People's Bank, holding that All Alaskan's claim sounded only in contract, not in tort, and thus was inferior to the lien created by People's preferred mortgage. All Alaskan appeals that judgment.

* * *

B. Merits

All Alaskan contends that the district court erred in ruling that, under the Ship Mortgage Act, a claim for cargo damage could sound only in contract, not in tort, and thus that All Alaskan's lien was subordinate to People's mortgage. We review de novo the district court's grant of partial summary judgment. *See Ashton v. Cory*, 780 F. 2d 816, 818 (9th Cir. 1986).

The Ship Mortgage Act (the "Act"), gives lien status and relatively high priority to a mortgage which complies with the Act. 46 U.S.C. § 953. The statutory mortgage, sometimes referred to as a preferred ship mortgage, was created to encourage investment in the shipping industry. *See Seattle First Nat'l Bank v. Bluewater Partnership*, 772 F. 2d 565, 569 (9th Cir. 1985). Under the Act, a preferred ship mortgage lien has priority over most claims against a vessel, including contract claims, but is subordinate to preferred maritime liens. Subsection 953(a)(2) defines "preferred maritime liens" to include "a lien for damages arising out of tort...."

In its motion for summary judgment on the issue of lien priority, All Alaskan alleged that damage to its shipment of king crab resulted from the negligent operation of the vessel Sea Producer as a common carrier. Thus, All Alaskan argued, its cargo damage claim gave rise to a tort lien which was superior, under the Ship Mortgage Act, to People's Mortgage. The district court acknowledged that liens against a ship for cargo damage are "hard to rank with precision," and have been viewed by courts as both "breaches of the contract of affreightment or as breaches of a duty imposed by law and, therefore tort." The district court was concerned however, that allowing All Alaskan to plead its cargo damage claim in tort, and thus secure priority over the bank's preferred ship mortgage, would undercut the purpose of the Ship Mortgage

Act, that of encouraging investment in shipping. Thus, without determining what duty of care Express Marine owed to All Alaskan under common law or maritime statutory law, the district court ruled that All Alaskan's claim for cargo damage could sound only in contract. As a result, it was not entitled to priority under 46 U.S.C. 953(a)(2).

In ruling as it did, the district court considered the contractual relationship between All Alaskan and Express Marine to preclude a maritime lien for damages premised on tort liability. We disagree with this premise. In *The John G. Stevens*, 170 U.S. 113 , 42 L. Ed. 969, 18 S. Ct. 544 (1898), the Supreme Court held that a claim for damage to a tow sounded in tort independent of any contract made, and was thus superior as a maritime lien to other purely contractual liens. In the course of its opinion, the Court rejected the argument that the tug's liability was analogous to that of a common carrier for loss of goods carried and thus could sound only in contract. The Court stated:

> But even an action by a passenger, or by an owner of goods against a carrier, for neglect to carry and deliver in safety, is an action for the breach of a duty imposed by the law, independently of contract or of consideration, and is therefore founded in tort.

Id. at 124-25. Although this statement may be read as dictum, it has served as a basis for classifying claims for cargo damage as torts and for giving such claims tort priority. *See, e.g.*, *Oriente Com'l v. American Flag Vessel M/V Floridian*, 529 F. 2d 221, 222 (4th Cir. 1975); *The Henry Breyer*, 17 F. 2d 423, 429 (D.Md. 1927); *Morrisey v. S.S.A. & J. Faith*, 252 F. Supp. 54, 59 (N.D.Ohio 1965).

The proposition that the existence of a contractual relationship between the parties does not limit claims between them to contract actions was reaffirmed by the Supreme Court in *Stevens v. The White City*, 285 U.S. 195, 201 , 76 L. Ed. 699 , 52 S. Ct. 347 (1932), and in *Cortes v. Baltimore Insular Line*, 387 U.S. 367, 372 (1932). In *Cortes*, the Court held that a seaman who fell ill aboard a ship and died ashore after his ship reached home port had a remedy in tort against the owner of the vessel for breach of the Jones Act duty of maintenance and cure. Judge Cardozo, writing for the Court, rejected the argument that the only duty owed the seaman was a contract duty incident to the seaman's contract of employment:

> We think the origin of the duty is consistent with the remedy in tort, since the wrong if a violation of the contract, is also something more. The duty, as already pointed out, is one annexed by law to a relation, annexed as an inseparable incident without heed, to any expression of the will of the contracting parties. For breach of a duty thus imposed, the remedy upon the contract does not exclude an alternative remedy built upon the tort.

Cortes, 287 U.S. at 372 (emphasis added).

Applying these principles, the Fourth Circuit in a case similar to the one now before us held that a claim for cargo damage against a ship as a common carrier was a claim for damages arising out of tort and thus a preferred maritime lien under 46 U.S.C. § 953(a). *Oriente Com'l v. American Flag Vessel, M/V Floridian*, 529 F. 2d 221, 223 (4th Cir. 1975). In *Oriente*, the shipper, Oriente Commercial, Inc. ("Oriente") was one of many *in rem* claimants against the M/V Floridian which was arrested and sold. The United States held two valid preferred ship mortgages on the vessel. Oriente took a default judgment on its claim that a shipment of meat had been negligently damaged in transit. The various liens asserted against the vessel exceeded the proceeds from its sale. Litigation over priority of the liens ensued.

The district court in *Oriente*, guided by the same policy concerns that informed the district court decision at issue here, reasoned that because cargo claims should be subordinated to preferred mortgages such claims should sound only in contract as a matter of law. The Fourth Circuit reversed. After reviewing the Supreme Court's decision in *John Stevens* as well as a number of lower court decisions which recognized that cargo damage claims may give rise to tort liability, the Fourth Circuit observed that the:

> [Ship Mortgage Act] draws no distinction between cargo claims that sound in tort, the so-called hybrid liens, and any other type of claim for damages arising out of tort. While Congress might have been well advised to subordinate cargo claims, it flatly granted priority to all claims arising out of tort. The result reached by the district court and pressed by the United States would carve out an exception to the statute unwarranted by its language. Whatever Congress meant, it stated that all tort liens are prior to preferred mortgage liens. In light of cases decided both before and after enactment of the Ship Mortgage Act, holding that cargo claims such as those in the instant case sound in tort, we cannot say that Congress intended something else.

Id. at 223.

We find the Fourth Circuit's analysis cogent and follow it in this case. Although the district court here was guided by important policy considerations, neither the weight of authority nor the language of the Ship Mortgage Act justifies the district court's decision. If Express Marine breached its duty of care with respect to All Alaskan then that breach of duty can give rise to tort liability irrespective of contract obligations between the parties. *See Oriente*, 529 F. 2d at 222-23. Accordingly, we hold it was error for the district court to rule, as a matter of law, that All Alaskan's cargo claims could not sound in tort.

* * *

Conclusion

The district court's partial summary judgment is reversed. This case is remanded to the district court. On remand the district court should determine the merits of All Alaskan's claim, and resolve the dispute as to whether the Sea Producer was a common carrier in its carriage of All Alaskan's goods, or whether the parties contracted that the duties of a common carrier would be owed to All Alaskan regardless of whether the Sea Producer was a common carrier.

REVERSED AND REMANDED.

Note: Priority of Preferred Liens: Expiration

Liens for supplies and repairs attaching after the creation of a maritime mortgage (U.S. flag vessels) are maritime liens, though subordinated to the mortgage. *Morse Dry Dock & Repair Co. v. Steamship Northern Star*, 271 U.S. 552, 46 S. Ct. 589, 70 L. Ed. 1082, 1926 AMC 977 (1926). However, the priority of the lien of a preferred ship mortgage does not expire on the date of the maturity of the mortgage; thus, supplies furnished after the date of maturity are subordinated to the preferred mortgage. *The Favorite*, 120 F.2d 899 (2d Cir. 1941). The court left open the question whether the priority of the lien of a preferred mortgage may be lost by laches by a finding that the mortgage creditor was not guilty of a delay in the pursuit of his claim.

The priority of a preferred lien for necessaries may be lost when the conduct of the lienor is tainted by deception and concealment. *See Florida Bahamas Lines, Ltd. v. Steel Barge Star 800 of Nassau*, 433 F.2d 1243, 1970 AMC 2189 (5th Cir. 1970).

Note: Conflicts of Law

According to choice of law rules developed by federal courts, a maritime lien may arise under the law of a foreign country in which a contract was made or in which services or supplies were furnished. Parties may thus plead and prove foreign law. In the absence of proof, foreign law may be presumed to be the same as United States law. *See Symonette Shipyards, Ltd. v. Clark*, 365 F.2d 464, 1966 AMC 2383 (5th Cir. 1966), *cert. denied*, 387 U.S. 908, 87 S. Ct. 1690, 18 L. Ed. 2d 625 (1967); *Rayon y Celanese Peruana, S.A. v. M/V Phgh*, 471 F. Supp. 1363, 1979 AMC 2682 (S.D. Ala. 1979).

U.S. courts will apply American law to protect an American supplier of fuel to a foreign vessel in a U.S. port even if the supply contract was made in a foreign jurisdiction. *See Gulf Trading & Transportation Co. v. Vessel Hoegh Shield*, 658 F.2d 363, 1982 AMC 1138 (5th Cir. 1981). In *Gulf Trading & Transportation Co. v. M/V Tento*, 694 F.2d 1191, 1983 AMC 872 (9th Cir. 1982), the Ninth Circuit addressed the issue of choice of law in maritime lien cases.

In the *M/V Tento*, liens were filed against the vessel when it docked in California. The underlying claims arose from two separate transactions. The Norwegian owner of the vessel placed it under a time charter to a U.S. company, which subchartered the vessel to another U.S. company. The owner's charter provided that U.S. law would govern certain aspects of the agreement and that the charterer was responsible for obtaining the vessel's fuel oil. On the voyage giving rise to these claims, the vessel embarked from the U.S. for the Suez Canal.

While en route the subcharterer decided to refuel in Italy, where the transaction with Gulf occurred. Gulf, a Delaware corporation, used an Italian company to deliver the fuel oil in Italy. Gulf paid the Italian company and charged the vessel. Neither the subcharterer nor the owner had paid the invoice.

The second transaction was with Permal, a New York corporation. Permal advanced approximately $40,000 for the vessel's Suez Canal transit. Permal's invoice has not been paid. The court stated:

> Gulf and Permal initiated these *in rem* actions against the vessel. The owner contends that Italian and Egyptian law govern the transactions, and that under those laws the owner's vessel is not subject to liens for expenses incurred by a subcharterer. It argues that the correct choice of law is determined by a single point of contact for the separate transactions—namely, the country where supplies were obtained.
>
> In *Lauritzen v. Larsen*, 345 U.S. 571 (1953), the U.S. Supreme Court resolved a choice of law question in a maritime tort suit under the Jones Act. It adopted an approach similar to the RESTATEMENT (SECOND) OF CONFLICT OF LAWS, setting forth the points of contact between the transaction and various jurisdictions and weighing them. Its review included the place of the wrongful act, the flag of the ship, allegiance or domicile of the injured seaman allegiance of the shipowner, place of signing the employment contract accessibility of a foreign court, and the law of the forum.
>
> The Second Circuit has already discredited the notion that choice of law in maritime lien cases should be made by looking solely to the law of the place of supply. *Rainbow Line, Inc. v. M/V Tequila*, 480 F.2d 1024 (1973). Instead, the court required consideration of all points of contact with the various nations.

To hold that the choice of law in maritime lien cases is controlled by the significance of multiple contacts is consistent with this court's previous holdings, both in maritime cases involving other types of disputes and in non-maritime contract choice of law cases. A single contact approach would run counter to an important principle—the desirability, even the necessity, of accommodating the legitimate interests of separate sovereigns in vindicating their own legal policies. This court concludes that all relevant contacts must be considered in maritime lien cases.

* * *

A shipowner can protect itself by bonding the charterer or by dealing only with reliable charterers. It is not, moreover, inequitable to require shipowners whose charters make orders on a multinational level to know the law of the nation in which their charterers have extensive contacts.

A test giving dominance to the location where supplies were delivered does not even have the advantage of simplicity to recommend it. Where the place of furnishing supplies to provide the law for resolving each contractual dispute involving a ship that stops at many ports, courts would be required to embark upon an odyssey in foreign law that both they and the law would soon regret. Judicial efficiency is a relevant factor in choice of law analysis, and it is not served by the place of supply rule advocated here.

In short, choice of law questions involving maritime liens are to be resolved by weighing and evaluating the points of contact between the transaction and the sovereign legal systems touched and affected by it. The substantial contacts between the U.S. and the Gulf and Permal transactions point towards U.S. law as the most appropriate for resolving this litigation.

In *Ocean Ship Supply Ltd v. M/V Leah*, 729 F.2d 971, 1984 AMC 2089 (4th Cir. 1984), the court undertook a "points of contact" choice of law inquiry before holding that Canadian law governed the question whether a necessaries supplier acquired a maritime lien for the supply of necessaries in Canada. The supplier's claim to have a maritime lien failed, because Canadian law gave no maritime lien.

In *Liverpool and London S.S. Protection and Indemnity Ass'n v. M/V Queen of Leman*, 296 F.3d 350, 2002 AMC 1521 (5th Cir. 2002), the court held that U.S. law governed the question whether a U.K.-based P. & I. Club had a maritime lien for unpaid calls (i.e., insurance premiums). The court did not apply U.S. law as the law of the forum (*lex fori*) but because the contract in question (the P. & I. Club Rules) provided that it was to be governed by English law but enforcement was to be "in accordance with local law". Although English law would not give the Club a maritime lien for its unpaid calls, U.S. law did, and it was applicable for enforcement purposes as the relevant "local law".

Note: Ranking of Liens: Law of the Forum

The ranking of all liens is determined under the law of the forum. Thus, a lien created under the law of a foreign country will be given the priority of a corresponding lien under the laws of the United States. *See Potash Co. of Canada, Limited v. M/V Raleigh*, 361 F. Supp. 120, 1973 AMC 2658 (D.D.C. Zone 1973); *Rayon y Celanese Peruana S.A. v. M/V Phgh, supra. See also Rainbow Line, Inc. v. M/V Tequila*, 341 F. Supp. 459, 1972 AMC 1540 (S.D.N.Y. 1972), *aff'd*, 480 F.2d 1024, 1973 AMC 1431 (2d Cir. 1973).

G. Extinction of Maritime Liens

1. Laches

BERMUDA EXP., N.V. v. M/V LITSA (Ex. LAURIE U)

872 F.2d 554, 1989 AMC 1537 (3d Cir. 1989)

Opinion of the Court

SLOVITER, Circuit Judge

I.

Issues

The appellant vessel in an *in rem* action appeals from the district court's final adjudication and judgment awarding three stevedoring companies the full amount of their claims based on maritime liens for unpaid invoices for stevedoring services provided to the vessel before it was sold to its present owner. The principal issue on appeal is whether the claims of the stevedore lienors were barred by the equitable doctrine of laches. The conflicting interests involve, on one hand, those of maritime lienors whose services are essential for the smooth functioning of maritime commerce and, on the other hand, those of bona fide purchasers in good faith of vessels which may be subject to such liens....

* * *

II.

Facts

Most of the facts relevant to this appeal are not in dispute. Appellees, Port Stevedoring, Inc. (Port), Ryan-Walsh Stevedoring Company (Ryan-Walsh), and Southeastern Maritime Company (Semco), are in the business of supplying stevedoring services to vessels at various ports in the southern portion of the United States. In 1982, Uiterwyk Corporation (Uiterwyk), the general agent for Uiterwyk Lines, Ltd. which owned the vessel, contracted with appellees to provide stevedoring services for vessels nominated by Uiterwyk. This contract covered the vessel involved in this litigation, then known as the M/V LAURIE U, which sailed under Liberian registry. The contracts all called for payment of 80% of the amount due for services rendered upon completion of such services for each vessel and presentation of an invoice. Under the Port and Semco contracts, the balance became due a reasonable time after presentation of duly documented bills, while under the Ryan-Walsh contract final payment was due within sixty days after the presentation of such bills.

Semco provided services to the M/V LAURIE U on May 27 and 28, 1982 in Charleston, giving rise to a claim of $22,184.87. Ryan-Walsh provided services to the M/V LAURIE U on July 26-August 6, 1982 in New Orleans, giving rise to a claim for $25,404.21. Port provided services to the M/V LAURIE U in Houston on three occasions in 1982, May 13-

23, August 11-14, and October 14-20, giving rise to claims for $112,994.71, $46,692.26, and $71,873.97 respectively.

On October 21, the M/V LAURIE U left United States waters and did not return until April 2, 1983. In the interim, two significant events took place. On December 8, 1982, Uiterwyk Lines, Ltd. sold the M/V LAURIE U to Star Warrant Shipping Corp. (Star), a shipping company operating out of Piraeus, Greece. In the contract of sale, Uiterwyk Lines, Ltd. warranted to Star that there were no maritime liens against the vessel, and Star's search of the Liberian registry in New York revealed that no claims had been filed against the ship. Star renamed the vessel M/V LITSA. Shortly after the sale, on January 27, 1983, Uiterwyk, the general agent, filed a petition in bankruptcy in the Middle District of Florida.

Upon learning of the bankruptcy, appellees filed individual claims in the bankruptcy court and contacted Lloyds Watch of London to determine the status of Uiterwyk vessels which they had serviced. Lloyds informed appellees of the purchase of the M/V LAURIE U and the name change, and continued to track the vessel's movements until it returned to United States waters on April 2, 1983. Bermuda Express, another claimant who has since settled with Star, arrested the M/V LITSA in the Port of Philadelphia on April 6, 1983. The district court had jurisdiction over this suit in admiralty under 28 U.S.C. § 1333 (1982).

Appellees intervened as plaintiffs and proceeded to trial against the M/V LITSA on their claims. After a bench trial, the district court determined that all three appellees had acted with the extraordinary degree of diligence required to preserve their maritime liens, and that neither their participation in the bankruptcy proceedings nor their failure to file notice of their maritime liens waived their right to assert those liens....

* * *

III.

Legal Principles

A.

* * *

In *The Bold Buccleugh*, 7 MOORE, P.C. 267 (1852), the English Privy Council case which serves as the original authority on the issue, G. Gilmore & C. Black at 595, the court enforced a maritime lien against the ship although it had since been sold; the court, however, noted that the lien may be lost "by negligence or delay where the rights of third parties may be compromised." *Id.* at 285.

Shortly thereafter, the United States Supreme Court enunciated a similar principle. In *The Key City*, 81 U.S. (14 Wall.) 653, 660, 20 L. Ed. 896 (1872), the Court stated that "laches or delay in the judicial enforcement of maritime liens will, under proper circumstances, constitute a valid defence;" that there is no "arbitrary or fixed period of time" for its operation but that the determination that a lienor was guilty of laches would "depend on the peculiar equitable circumstances of that case;" and that "where the lien is to be enforced to the detriment of a purchaser for value, without notice of the lien, the defence will be held valid under shorter time, and a more rigid scrutiny of the circumstances of the delay, than when the [party claiming laches] is the owner at the time the lien accrued."

The parties dispute whether a maritime lienor must exercise "extraordinary diligence" in order to preserve a claim against a bona fide purchaser ... or whether "reasonable diligence" is sufficient ... we believe that the lienor should be held to a "reasonable diligence" standard. *See Merchants & Marine Bank v. The T.E. Welles*, 289 F.2d 188, 190 (5th Cir. 1961) (applying a reasonable diligence test). The lienor must take such steps as are appropriate under the circumstances. The district court used the standard most favorable to the vessel and found nonetheless that the lienors exercised the "extraordinary high degree of diligence" required to preserve and enforce the liens.... If we conclude that there is the requisite support for a conclusion of reasonable diligence, we are bound to affirm.

B.

Appellant argues that in considering the diligence of the lienors in this case, we need look no further than the analysis used by the courts in the two *Everosa* cases decided half a century ago. In the first *Everosa* case, *The Everosa (Southern Coal & Coke Co. v. Kugniecibas)*, 93 F.2d 732 (1st Cir. 1937), the libelant, Southern Coal & Coke Company, had provided coal to the vessel at issue on November 22, 1933 and May 8, 1934 for which it had received only partial payment. Shortly after the second coaling, the ship sailed for foreign waters and did not return until November 1934, at which time Southern libeled the ship. *Id.* at 733-35. While it had been in foreign waters, it was sold to a bona fide purchaser.

* * *

The appellate court ... considered the ship's laches defense, apparently as a matter of first impression, and held that laches did not bar enforcement of the lien for the second coaling because the ship left the United States nine days after the coaling and "[a]bsence of the vessel from the country operates to relieve the lienor to some extent from the imputation of laches." *Id.* at 735. Although the court noted that there was evidence that the ship had returned to this country before the voyage on which she was libeled, *id.*, it nonetheless held "there was clearly no laches." *Id.*

The question of the enforceability of the lien for the first coaling was, the court noted, "very close." *Id.* It concluded that that lien was barred by laches because the ship had "called at various gulf ports of this country half a dozen times between the first coaling and the second," and thus the lienor "unquestionably" had "a reasonable opportunity to enforce the lien." *Id.* The court also noted that the lienor "knew or could easily have discovered" that the vessel at the time of the coalings was held by the party receiving the coal under charter and not as owner, "and that rights of third persons might be affected." *Id.* at 735-36.

The second *Everosa* case, *The Everosa (Swan & Sons v. Kugniecibas)*, 20 F. Supp. 8 (E.D.N.Y. 1937), involved claims filed by companies which had supplied the vessel in Norfolk, Virginia, in February 1934 and in New Orleans in April 1934 before it sailed for foreign waters in May 1934. In this case, however, the lienors did not file their libels until 1937, although the ship had returned to United States waters twice in the interim. The court held that inasmuch as the company supplying the vessel at Norfolk had an opportunity to enforce its lien when the vessel returned to Norfolk in May 1934 before it sailed abroad, and that the creditors (including the libelant) were notified of the bankruptcy proceeding of the operator which was initiated in June 1934, *see id.* at 11, both of which events were prior to the transfer of title of the ship in August 1934, the balance of equities required dismissal of the libel. On the other hand, the court held that the second lienor was not barred by laches because the ship sailed abroad within a month of its supply services, and, although the ship returned to the United States at various times, it did not return to New Orleans during those visits. It held that failure to take advantage of those opportunities for affirmative action "does not fatally portray lack of diligence." *Id.* at 13.

Appellant urges that the *Everosa* cases mandate a finding that Semco, Ryan-Walsh, and Port did not exercise the requisite diligence in enforcing their liens. Although some of the facts in the *Everosa* cases are analogous to the M/V LAURIE U situation, all of the cases stress that the question of due diligence is one peculiar to the facts of each case. For this reason, it is not particularly useful to review the facts of the many other cases referred to by appellant and the distinguishing factors pointed out by appellees. We accept the legal principles from the *Everosa* cases that lienors are not required to attempt to enforce their liens in foreign waters and that the existence of a reasonable opportunity for the lienor to arrest the vessel before the purchase is an important factor in the laches analysis.

However, the fact that it would have been possible or even feasible to locate and arrest the vessel at a port in the United States is not dispositive of the question of whether or when the appellees in this case should have done so. The custom of the shipping industry, for example, must also inform the analysis of what constitutes diligence under the circumstances of a given case.

The arrest of a vessel is a remedy of last resort, and one which has the potential to seriously disrupt the flow of maritime commerce. Therefore, we decline to establish a firm rule which would require a maritime lienor to arrest a vessel, particularly if there are available other reasonable methods, consistent with industry custom, to secure payment. The relevant consideration instead is what would have been the commercially reasonable practice. Components of diligence thus include industry custom, the amount of the lien, the pattern of dealing between the parties, and whether the lienor had information that the interests of a third party would likely be adversely affected by its failure to act.

Appellant argues that we should also consider whether the lienors filed their claims on the ship's register. It claims that the lienors' failure to file claims of their liens on the Liberian Registry in New York, a relatively simple and inexpensive means of giving notice, evinces a failure of the lienors to exercise the requisite degree of diligence.

Several cases have treated failure to record a claim of lien as a relevant factor in assessing the equities of a laches defense. *See, e.g., Tagaropulos, S.A. v. S.S. Santa Paula*, 502 F.2d 1171, 1172 (9th Cir. 1974); *John W. Stone Oil Distributor, Inc. v. M/V Miss Bern*, 663 F. Supp. 773, 780 (S.D. Ala. 1987); *Dixie Machine Welding and Metal Works, Inc. v. M/V Andino*, 1983 A.M.C. 1166, 1168 (S.D. Fla. 1982); *Waterways Marine, Inc. v. Brooks Liquid Transport, Inc.*, 291 F. Supp. 703 (N.D. Ill. 1968). Each case, however, has its own set of facts and no situation directly parallels the one before us.

All parties agree that there is no statutory requirement that a maritime lien be filed in order to be valid. At the time Congress enacted the Maritime Liens Act, it could have but failed to require filing. It has made no attempt to change the statute in this respect since then. The district court thus concluded that the lienors here did not lack diligence "merely because the claims were not filed with the Liberian Ship Registry in New York." App. at 376 (emphasis added). Obviously, however, the ability to have filed the lien is a consideration that cannot be completely ignored in the relevant balancing. It is significant whether it was a custom of the industry to record liens for necessaries.

Poised against the diligence or lack thereof of the lienor is the action of the purchaser of the vessel. A balancing of the equities requires consideration not only of the bona fides of the purchaser, *i.e.*, its lack of actual knowledge of unpaid liens and its search of the ship's registry, but also of its efforts to ascertain whether, in light of the absence of any legal requirement of filing liens, there are in fact liens outstanding. *See Tagaropulos S.A. v. S.S. Santa Paula*, 502 F.2d 1171, 1172 (9th Cir. 1974) (Purchaser "made every effort to unearth all claims against the ship." It checked both the home port and ship's log for liens; although no liens were entered in the log, purchaser discovered entries for repairs, contacted shipyards and learned of outstanding unpaid bills).

Finally, we note that it is for the district court in the first instance to perform the equitable balancing of all the relevant factors. Our review will be facilitated if the district courts fully discuss the factors considered on the issue of diligence and make explicit their balancing of the equities in reaching a decision on laches. We thus proceed to examine the record to discern the factors which explicitly or implicitly informed the district court's judgment in this case.

C.

* * *

The initial inquiry relevant to appellees' diligence is thus whether they had a reasonable opportunity to enforce their liens between the time each lien arose and October 21, 1982, when the ship left United States waters.

Patently, Port could not have taken any action in United States waters to enforce its third lien, that based on the services it provided between October 14-20, 1982, because the vessel left the United States immediately thereafter. Semco and Ryan-Walsh, on the other hand, had provided their services earlier. However, throughout the entire period following the services provided by Semco in Charleston (May 27 and 28) and by Ryan-Walsh in New Orleans (July 26—August 6), the vessel was out of the country except for two Houston stops (August 9-14 and October 14-21) and one stop at Port Arthur, Texas (October 9-14). If we look to the vessel's return to the particular port where the stevedoring company provided the services, which was the dispositive factor leading the court to determine that laches did not bar one of the claims in the second *Everosa* case, 20 F. Supp. at 13, we note that the vessel did not return to Charleston or New Orleans following the provision of services by Semco and Ryan-Walsh at these ports.

We are aware, as appellant argues, that modern technology associated with the shipping industry has made it easier than in the *Everosa* period for lienors to track ships, thus increasing opportunities to arrest vessels and enforce liens. Nonetheless, we cannot rule on the record developed by the appellant here that the stevedore companies had the obligation to track the vessel, which primarily served foreign ports throughout this entire period, to the Texas ports and arrest the ship on one of the three occasions when it would have been possible to do so.

It is true, as appellant argues, that these companies could have easily filed their liens on the ship's registry and thereby given notice to a prospective purchaser. However, we have pointed out that there is no legal requirement for such an action and, significantly, there was no evidence of an industry custom to do so.

* * *

Appellees' failure to enforce the liens was consistent with their past practice in dealing with Uiterwyk, which was a slow payer. Previously, their demands for payment and threats to arrest vessels were sufficient to procure payment, albeit belatedly. Appellant has not shown it was commercially unreasonable of appellees to wait for payment. In light of these circumstances, we find no basis to question the district court's conclusion that these lienors exercised the requisite diligence with respect to their liens and that Port exercised such diligence with respect to its October lien.

It is more difficult to evaluate Port's diligence in the case of its two earlier liens, that arising from its May services and that arising from its August services. Port clearly had the opportunity to take action against the ship because it returned to Houston where Port provided additional services notwithstanding the unpaid bills. In both instances Port extended further credit for new services.

However, Port's liens were only five months and two months old at the time the ship left United States waters. In many of the relevant cases the liens had been outstanding for substantially over a year before the lienor sought enforcement. *See Tagaropulos, S.A. v. S.S. Santa Paula*, 502 F.2d 1171, 1172 (9th Cir. 1974) (two years); *Phelps v. The Cecelia Ann*, 199 F.2d 627, 628 (4th Cir. 1952) (more than two years); *The John Cadwalader*, 99 F.2d 678, 679 (3d Cir. 1938) (five to nine years); *Dixie Machine Welding and Metal Works, Inc. v. M/V Andino*, 1983 A.M.C. 1166 (S.D. Fla. 1982) (two and one-half years).

Appellant has shown little that Port could have done short of the draconian measure of arresting the ship, with the exception of filing the lien which we have noted is not required as a matter of law. Appellant introduced no evidence of other commercially reasonable practice available to Port. Port's Vice-President testified that it was not customary for Port or any other stevedoring company to require advance payment before it rendered services.... Moreover, Port was receiving payments from Uiterwyk through 1982. While it did not receive any payment which was applied to the invoices for this particular vessel, it did receive $100,000 from Uiterwyk on November 10, 1982 which was applied to older bills ... thus giving it reason to believe that it would eventually be paid. Therefore, we cannot conclude that Port was guilty of a lack of diligence that would deprive it of its maritime lien.

Under these circumstances, we need not consider whether there were some steps that Star, a sophisticated shipowner which purchased over 70 vessels, could have taken to protect itself which it failed to take, such as the inquiry of the general agent or of the port agents and suppliers in the ports that the vessel had visited. *See Tagaropulos*, 502 F.2d at 1172.

* * *

VI.

Conclusion

We recognize that it may appear inequitable to permit enforcement of maritime liens against a purchaser without notice of those liens, particularly when giving notice through registration of the liens is a simple matter. However, whether such registration should be imposed as a requirement for the ability to satisfy liens against a ship when it has been acquired by a subsequent purchaser is a policy decision that is more appropriately made by Congress than by the courts. The judicial decision on a laches defense must be made without interposition of our view as to what the law should be. In this case, we cannot say that the outstanding liens were so long overdue that, in the circumstances here, the district court was obliged to hold that they could not be enforced.

Note: Private Sale and Laches

The private sale of a vessel to a bona fide purchaser without notice or knowledge of pre-existing liens does not result in the extinction of the liens. However, in appropriate circumstances, a court may conclude that the lien sought to be enforced against the purchaser has been extinguished by laches. *See The Dredge Gloucester (McLaughlin v. The Dredge Gloucester)*, 230 F. Supp. 623, 1964 AMC 2123 (D.N.J. 1964):

> Where a maritime lien is to be enforced to the detriment of a bona fide purchaser without notice, the libellant must act with extraordinary diligence. As against such a purchaser such lien will be lost in equity after the lapse of a much shorter period of time under the doctrine of laches, than under analogous limitation statutes.
>
> * * *
>
> In *Robert Gaskin*, 9 F. 62 (E.D. Mich. 1881), where the libellant let 6 years elapse before filing his libel, the vessel having been within the jurisdiction several times and further, the vessel having been sold to a bona fide purchaser having no knowledge of the claim, it was held that libellant could not recover even though the libel had been filed before the sale, but process not effected until 3 months thereafter. In *The Lauretta*, 9 F. 622 (D. N.J. 1881), at page 624, the following is aptly stated:
>
> There is no explanation of the delay in the present case. The alleged liability of the vessel was incurred in August 1876. Nearly two years elapsed before the libel was filed. In the meantime the vessel was transferred to the claimant, without notice of the lien. She was within reach of the process of the courts (Philadelphia oyster rader in Delaware River and Bay), if the libellant had made nay effort to hold her. I am clearly of the opinion that he ought no now be allowed to collect his claim out of the property of an innocent purchaser, and that the libel must be dismissed.' (Parenthesis supplied.)

---

2. Comparison: Foreign Attachment and Actions in Rem

BELCHER CO. OF ALABAMA, INC. v. M/V MARATHA MARINER

724 F.2d 1161, 1984 AMC 1679 (5th Cir. 1984)

Alvin B. RUBIN, Circuit Judge
[The facts are stated *supra.*]

* * *

The Fourth Circuit has held that the judicial sale of a vessel in a Mexican bankruptcy action was sufficiently similar in substance to an American *in rem* action to remove an *in rem* lien on the vessel. *Gulf and Southern Terminal Corp. v. The SS President Roxas*, 701 F.2d 1110 (4th Cir.), *cert. denied*, 462 U.S. 1133, 103 S. Ct. 3115, 77 L. Ed. 2d 1369 (1983). In that case, the Mexican bankruptcy court had possession of the vessel, and sold it "free of encumbrances." The sale erased the lien despite the fact that Mexican law does not provide explicitly for an *in rem* proceeding both because the procedures employed were "virtually identical to those which are denominated as an *in rem* proceeding under American law" and because "the vessel was an asset of the bankrupt, under the control and proper jurisdiction of the Mexican court." *Id.* 701 F.2d at 112. A bankruptcy court that has possession of any property has the power to sell the property free and clear of liens.[7]

Attachment does in many respects resemble arrest. In each proceeding the vessel is seized and it may later be sold to satisfy a judgment. In each, the vessel itself may be released and other security substituted. Nevertheless, not only do the issues in the two actions differ; the basic theory on which each is brought is different. In the *in rem* proceeding the owner bears no personal liability. The vessel is sold solely to satisfy the lien. If the proceeds of the sale are inadequate, there is no liability on the owner's part for the residue. Indeed the admiralty court will not render a personal judgment against the owner in excess of the amount of the release bond.[8] Only a personal action against the owner can establish such liability. In the attachment action, the object of the action is a personal judgment for the full sum due. The vessel is seized only to compel the owner's appearance by subjecting to the court's control property within its territorial jurisdiction. If the proceeds of sale of the vessel do not satisfy the judgment, the owner remains liable for the balance of the debt.

Chowgule asserts that, when it provided security to release the vessel from attachment, this discharged the lien. With respect to the lien sought to be enforced, the release does transfer the lien from the vessel to the fund represented by the bond or letter of undertaking.[9] This does not imply that release from an attachment likewise clears the lien. An

---

[7] *Matter of Buchman*, 600 F.2d 160, 165 (8th Cir. 1979).

[8] *The Susana*, 2 F.2d 410, 412-13 (4th Cir. 1924); *Red Star Towing & Transp. Co.*, 5 F. Supp. 502 (E.D.N.Y. 1933); G. Gilmore & C. Black, *supra*, at 802.

In a few cases, however, owners appearing in an *in rem* action to contest the libelants' claims have been "treated as if they had been brought into court by personal process" and held personally liable for judgment in excess of the security. *The Fairisle*, 76 F. Supp. 27, 34 (D. Md. 1947), *aff'd sub nom. Waterman S.S. Corp. v. Dean*, 171 F.2d 408 (4th Cir. 1948) (*quoted in Treasure Salvors v. The Unidentified Wrecked and Abandoned Sailing Vessel*, 569 F.2d 330, 335 (5th Cir.1978)); *see also Mosher v. Tate*, 182 F.2d 475, 479-80 (9th Cir. 1950); G. Gilmore & C. Black, *supra*, at 802-02.

[9] *Gray v. Hopkins-Carter Hardware Co. (The Lois)*, 32 F.2d 876, 878 (5th Cir. 1929); G. Gilmore & C. Black, *supra*, at 799.

execution sale in an *in rem* proceeding clears the vessel of all liens.[10] An execution sale pursuant to a writ of attachment is not, however, the equivalent of a judicial sale in admiralty. The ship is not sold free of all liens; instead only the owner's interest, whatever it may be, is adjudicated.[11] Indeed, it could not do so, for the attachment bond does not substitute for a lien but only for the owner's personal liability.

In its analysis of the *lis alibis pendens* argument, the district court correctly stated the applicable rule: a court having jurisdiction should exercise it unless a compelling reason not to do so is demonstrated. It found compelling reason, however, in the supposed hardship on Chowgule of defending two actions and in the possibility of double recovery. Both of these can readily be averted without the damage to Belcher that dismissal occasions. The Netherlands action has been tried and is awaiting decision. Staying proceedings in this action would avoid repetitive litigation of the issues there involved. If Belcher prevails, its judgment will be satisfied out of the security posted in that court. Thus both the expense of the second litigation and the possibility of double liability will be averted. If Chowgule prevails in the Netherlands action, its undertaking will be released and only those issues unique to the *in rem* action need be determined in the United States court. If, on the other hand, this action is dismissed and Belcher fails to prevail in the Netherlands action, it will be deprived of an opportunity to prove its claim *in rem*. No hardship is imposed on Chowgule by continuing the action, for the same undertaking posted in the Netherlands stands as security for the *in rem* action.[12]

For these reasons the judgment is REVERSED and the case is REMANDED for further proceedings consistent with this opinion.

Note: Judicial Sale

Ever since the decision in *The Trenton*, 4 F. 657 (E.D. Mich. 1880), it has been assumed that the judicial sale of a ship by a foreign court of competent jurisdiction discharges all maritime liens. In this case, the court declared that a foreign judgment may be impeached by the owner or other person interested by showing:

> (1) that the court or officer making the sale had no jurisdiction of the subject-matter by actual seizure and custody of the thing sold. Whether it be not also essential that there should have been proper judicial proceedings upon which to found the decree, and personal or public notice of the pendency of such proceedings, it is unnecessary here to determine, since it appears that sworn petitions were filed, and notice of the pendency of the proceedings given through the newspapers, pursuant to the practice of the maritime court. (2) That the sale was made by fraudulent collusion, to which the purchaser at such sale was a party. (3) That the sale was contrary to natural justice. In case of sale by a master, the court will inquire into the circumstances and see whether it was necessary and for the interest of all concerned; but the effect of such sale to discharge liens is the same. *The Amelie*, 73 U.S. (6 Wall.) 18, 18 L. Ed. 806 (1867).

---

10 *The Trenton*, 4 F. 657 (E.D. Mich. 1880); *Zimmern Coal Co. v. Coal Trading Association of Rotterdam* (*The Totila x Harold*), 30 F.2d 933 (5th Cir. 1929); G. Gilmore & C. Black, *supra*, at 787, *et seq.*

11 G. Gilmore & C. Black, *supra*, at 802.

12 *See Gulf Oil Corp. v. Gilbert*, 330 U.S. 501, 67 S. Ct. 839, 91 L. Ed. 1055 (1947); *The Belgenland*, 114 U.S. 355, 5 S. Ct. 860, 29 L. Ed. 152 (1885); *Chiazor v. Transworld Drilling Co. Ltd.*, 648 F.2d 1015, 1019 (5th Cir. 1981); *Poseidon Schiffahrt, G.M.B.H. v. The M/S Netuno*, 474 F.2d 203, 204 (5th Cir. 1973); *Perusahaan Umum Listrik Negara Pusat v. M/V Tel Aviv*, 711 F.2d 1231 (5th Cir. 1983) (upholding conditional dismissal on *forum non conveniens* grounds because only connection with U.S. forum was *in rem* action and adequate alternative forum was substantially more convenient; conditional dismissal preserved plaintiff's rights and remedies).

Should constitutional limitations of due process, applicable to arrests and attachments of vessels in the United States, be also applicable to proceedings before foreign courts? *See* Chapter on Admiralty Jurisdiction and Procedure.

A vessel may be attached and sold by a state court in the same way as any other things that belong to a debtor. Such a sale, however, does not extinguish maritime liens. *See The Winnebago*, 205 U.S. 354, 27 S. Ct. 509, 51 L. Ed. 836 (1907); *The Gazelle*, 10 Fed. Cas. 127, No. 5, 289 (D. Mass. 1858). Likewise, a sale under a state forfeiture statute does not extinguish maritime liens. *See Bard v. The Silver Wave*, 98 F. Supp. 271, 1951 AMC 1079 (D. Md. 1951).

---

3. Effect of Sale by Foreign Court of Competent Jurisdiction

ATLANTIC SHIP SUPPLY, INC. v. M/V LUCY

392 F. Supp. 179 (M.D. Fla. 1975)

KRENTZMAN, District Judge

* * *

The primary issue which this Court was called upon to resolve was the effect of the sale of a Costa Rican flag vessel by a Costa Rican Court with respect to maritime liens (46 USCA § 941) existing in favor of American suppliers which antedated such sale. For the reasons hereinafter stated, this Court holds that the maritime liens asserted by plaintiff and intervening plaintiffs were extinguished by the sale of the vessel by the Second Civil Court of San Jose, Costa Rica. Having heard the evidence without a jury, the Court makes the following findings of fact:

The plaintiff, Atlantic Ship Supply, Inc., is a Florida corporation and brings this action to foreclose its maritime lien against the M/V LUCY (formerly the M/V EL CENTROAMERICANO) for supplies and necessaries furnished to that vessel in the Port of Tampa, Florida, between January 16 and January 24, 1973 in the total amount of $8,242.63.

Intervening plaintiff, Metro Stevedores, Inc., is a Florida corporation and brings this action to foreclose its maritime lien against the M/V LUCY for stevedoring services supplied to that vessel at the Port of Tampa, Florida, between January 17 and January 24, 1973, in the total amount of $8,886.00.

Intervening plaintiff, Central Oil Company, Inc., is a Florida corporation and brings this action to foreclose its maritime lien against the M/V LUCY for diesel oil and intermediate fuel oil supplied to that vessel at the Port of Tampa, Florida, on or about January 1, 1973, in the total amount of $6,348.03.

Claimant, Hercules Trading Company, S.A. Panama, is a Panamanian corporation and is the present owner of the M/V LUCY and derives its title to such vessel from a Mr. George Lymberopoulos, who was the successful bidder at a public auction of that vessel which was held in Costa Rica on July 27, 1973, pursuant to Court order.

On or about the 27th day of March, 1974, the M/V LUCY (formerly the EL CENTROAMERICANO) was arrested in Tampa, Florida, by the United States Marshal pursuant to process issued out of this Court pursuant to Supplemental Admiralty and Maritime Rule C, and was at all times relevant to this lawsuit properly within the jurisdiction of this Court.

Claimant, Hercules Trading Co., S.A. Panama, after the arrest of said vessel in Tampa, Florida, made claim to that vessel and appeared in this action to defend its interests, and upon the consent of all the parties to this action, said vessel was released from arrest by order of this Court, it appearing that satisfactory security had been posted to secure the liens of the plaintiff and the intervening plaintiffs herein.

* * *

The M/V LUCY (formerly the EL CENTROAMERICANO) was at the time of the services provided by the plaintiff and intervening plaintiffs, a vessel of Costa Rican Registry engaged in general commerce.

On the 5th day of March, 1973, an action was commenced in the Second Civil Court of San Jose, Costa Rica, by Citizens & Southern International Bank, an American banking corporation, to foreclose a first preferred ship's mortgage on the M/V LUCY which was duly recorded in accordance with Costa Rican law.

Pursuant to said action, the Second Civil Court of San Jose, Costa Rica, ordered that the M/V LUCY be "embargoed" which in our parlance is equivalent to arrest. On March 10, 1973, the M/V LUCY was duly arrested while she lay in territorial waters of Costa Rica at the Port of Puerto Limon, Costa Rica.

Plaintiff and intervening plaintiffs argue that:

1. The sale of the vessel did not comply with the formalities of Costa Rican law in that notice of the proceedings was never published in the Judicial Bulletin in conformity with Article 579 of the Commercial Code of 1964 and that therefore, such proceedings were void;
2. Even if such proceedings were not void under Costa Rican law by reason of failure to publish notice thereof in the Judicial Bulletin, the failure to publish offends our traditional Constitutional protections of notice and an opportunity to be heard, and therefore, this Court should not give its judgment full faith and credit or comity; and,
3. The proceedings in Costa Rica were analogous to our common law mortgage foreclosure proceedings and are therefore only binding on the parties before the Court and not strangers to such proceedings who were neither present and who did not have actual notice thereof.

Costa Rican Law

Article 579 of the Costa Rican Commercial Code of 1964, upon which plaintiffs rely to support their contention that Costa Rican law requires publication of notice of proceedings, only requires such publication when a known person cannot be located by the Court. It does not require publication of notice of the proceedings to the world at large. (*Compare*

Supplemental Admiralty and Maritime Rule C(4)). This interpretation is supported by a reading of the relevant Article an the testimony of claimant's expert witness, Fernando Fournier, who fully explained the relevant Article and its interpretation in Costa Rica.

Notice and an Opportunity to be Heard

Plaintiffs' argument that they were denied our Constitutional protection of notice and an opportunity to be heard has been decided by the Fifth Circuit Court of Appeals in *Zimmern Coal v. Coal Trading Association of Rotterdam*, 30 F.2d 933 (5th Cir. 1929).

In that case a supplier of coal arrested a vessel to enforce a maritime lien after the vessel had been sold at a judicial sale in Holland. Its lien, like the ones at bar, *ante*-dated the sale. Dutch law, like Costa Rican law, did not require publication of notice of the proceedings, and the Court held that the failure to publish did not affect the validity of the sale.

It is not publication of notice of the proceedings which is the notice required by law. Seizure of the thing itself is the constructive notice which makes the decree of an admiralty court in an *in rem* proceeding binding on the entire world. A person having an interest in the *res* has constructive notice of its seizure. 2 BENEDICT ON ADMIRALTY § 231 (6th Ed.)

The evidence at trial was clear that the plaintiffs could have intervened in Costa Rica to protect their lien interests. Others did so. The fact that they may not have had actual notice of the proceedings is not controlling because they did have constructive notice.

The Nature of the Costa Rican Proceedings

Plaintiffs argue that the Costa Rican proceedings were not *in rem* but were *in personam* and were analogous to our common law mortgage foreclosure proceedings.

It must first be stated that it is a recognized principle of admiralty that the sale of a vessel by a court with admiralty jurisdiction gives title to the purchaser good against the entire world:

> That the sale of a vessel made pursuant to the decree of a foreign court of admiralty will be held valid in every other country, and will vest a clear and indefeasible title in the purchaser, is entirely settled, both in England and America.... (cites omitted) *The Trenton*, 4 Fed. 657, 659 (E.D. Mich. 1880)

* * *

This Court is of the ... opinion that the Costa Rican proceedings were truly *in rem*: The *res* was in the jurisdiction and under the control of a Court having the power to adjudicate its disposition. The Court's decree or Edict specified that the vessel was sold "free of encumbrances". And the proceedings were directed at the *res* because under Costa Rican law the litigants had to first exhaust their remedies against the property before they could look to any satisfaction *in personam*.

For the foregoing reasons the Court makes the following additional findings of fact:

The Second Civil Court of San Jose does have admiralty and maritime jurisdiction, and this jurisdiction derives from Book III of the Costa Rican Commercial Code of 1853.

The Commercial Code of 1853 provides in pertinent part that if a vessel is sold through judicial intervention that the purchaser at the sale of that vessel receives title to it free and clear of all liens and encumbrances.

Under Costa Rican law a first preferred mortgage on a vessel such as the one in favor of the Citizens & Southern International Bank creates a maritime lien on that vessel, and foreclosure of such lien, under Costa Rican law, renders to the purchaser at a public auction title free and clear of all liens and encumbrances.

The Second Civil Court of San Jose exercised its maritime jurisdiction with respect to the M/V LUCY.

All the procedural requirements of Costa Rican law were complied with in this instance, and the M/V LUCY was duly sold by Court order at public auction on July 27, 1973, and the purchaser at that sale, Mr. George Lymberopoulos, received title to the M/V LUCY free and clear of all maritime liens and encumbrances, including those of the plaintiff and intervening plaintiffs in this cause.

The Court further finds that under Costa Rican law a foreign judgment or decree is entitled to full faith and credit and that this Court should give equal treatment to the judgment and decree of the Court of Costa Rica which had subject matter jurisdiction and properly exercised that jurisdiction in this instance.

---

4. Admiralty and Bankruptcy

Notes

1. *Jurisdiction*

A petition in bankruptcy does not extinguish maritime liens. The automatic stay of all other proceedings mandated by the Bankruptcy Code, 11 U.S.C. § 362(a), applies to admiralty proceedings *in rem. In re Louisiana Ship Management, Inc.*, 761 F.2d 1025, 1985 AMC 2667 (5th Cir. 1985). Upon filing of a bankruptcy petition, the bankruptcy court has exclusive jurisdiction over the debtor's property, including any vessels that have been subject to arrest pursuant to *in rem* proceedings. *U.S. v. LeBouf Bros. Towing Co., Inc.*, 45 B.R. 887, 1985 AMC 1956 (E.D. La. 1985). It is possible for concurrent jurisdiction in admiralty and bankruptcy to exist if *in rem* proceedings in admiralty are brought while the vessel is subject to the exclusive jurisdiction of the bankruptcy court. *Peter Pan Seafoods, Inc. v. M/V Polar Viking*, 446 F. Supp. 1283, 1978 AMC 2606 (W.D. Wash. 1977). *See generally* Frank R. Kennedy, *Jurisdictional Problems Between Admiralty and Bankruptcy Courts*, 59 TUL. L. REV. 1182, 1182-1211 (1985).

2. *Bankruptcy and Reorganization*

Neither bankruptcy nor reorganization results in extinction of maritime liens. *See In re Sterling Navigation Co. Ltd. (The Regal Sword)*, 31 B.R. 619, 1983 AMC 2240 (S.D.N.Y. 1983). A maritime lien on subfreights for breach of charter party is not subject to Article 9 of the Uniform Commercial Code and has priority over the trustee without need to file.

One bankruptcy court has held that the automatic stay bars a lienholder from seizing a vessel in which the debtor has any legal or equitable interest, including a vessel under time charter to the debtor. *In re American Trading & Shipping, Inc.*, 24 B.R. 32 (Bankr. S.D. Fla. 1982).

Is the "pragmatic" approach to the conflict of bankruptcy and admiralty workable? In the 1978 legislation Congress apparently intended that bankruptcy courts consider not only matters directly related to the debtor's reorganization and bankruptcy but also any litigation to which the debtor is a party. 28 U.S.C. §§ 1471 and 1481. This means that splintered jurisdiction between admiralty and bankruptcy was eliminated and that *in rem* actions to enforce maritime liens must either be halted or continued in the bankruptcy court upon the filing of the debtor's bankruptcy petition. However, this broadening of jurisdiction of the bankruptcy courts was thrown into doubt by *Northern Pipeline Construction Co. v. Marathon Pipeline Co.*, 458 U.S. 50, 102 S. Ct. 2858, 73 L. Ed. 2d 598 (1982), which held that the bankruptcy courts could not constitutionally entertain Article III litigation because the judges were not granted life tenure. It is expected that curative legislation will remove this problem and that bankruptcy courts will in the future be able to assume complete jurisdiction over a vessel and will be able to enjoin proceedings against a vessel in any other forum.

---

5. Waiver

THE FEDERAL MARITIME LIEN ACT

46 U.S.C. § 971, et seq.

(Superseded Version)

§ 974. Waiver of Right to Lien

Nothing in this chapter shall be construed to prevent the furnisher of repairs, supplies, towage, use of dry dock or marine railway, or other necessaries, or the mortgagee, from waiving his right to a lien, or in the case of a preferred mortgage lien, to the preferred status of such lien, at any time by agreement or otherwise; and this chapter shall not be construed to affect the rules of law existing on June 5, 1920, in regard to (1) the right to proceed against the vessel for advances, (2) laches in the enforcement of liens upon vessels, (3) the right to proceed *in personam*, (4) the rank of preferred maritime liens among themselves, or (5) priorities between maritime liens and mortgages, other than preferred mortgage, upon vessels of the United States.

a. Current Statutory Provisions Relating to Maritime Liens

Commercial Instruments and Maritime Liens

46 U.S.C. § 31301, et seq.

§ 31305. Waiver of Lien Rights

This chapter does not prevent a mortgagee or other lien holder from waiving or subordinating at any time by agreement or otherwise the lien holder's right to a lien, the priority or, if a preferred mortgage lien, the preferred status of the lien.

MARITREND, INC. v. SERAC & CO. (SHIPPING) LTD

348 F.3d 469, 2003 AMC 2743 (5th Cir. 2003)

DENNIS, Circuit Judge

Maritrend, Inc., appeals the district court's ruling that it waived its maritime lien on a vessel to which it had provided stevedoring services. We reverse and remand this case for the entry of judgment in favor of Maritrend on its *in rem* claim against the vessel.

I. BACKGROUND

In July 2000, Maritrend contracted with Serac & Company (Shipping) Ltd. ("Serac"), the agent for an undisclosed charterer, to provide stevedoring services to the M/V SEVILLA WAVE in the Port of New Orleans. After providing those services, Maritrend sent invoices to Serac but never received payment.

Seeking to recover the value of its services, Maritrend filed an *in personam* action against Serac in the United States District Court for the Eastern District of Louisiana. Maritrend later amended its complaint to add an *in rem* claim against the SEVILLA WAVE, which it simultaneously seized. Pimpernel Shipping Company, Ltd. ("Pimpernel"), claimed ownership of the vessel and filed an answer to the amended complaint.

After a full bench trial, the district court found Serac liable *in personam* to Maritrend for the claimed amount, $73,104.80, plus interest. But the court rejected Maritrend's *in rem* claim against the SEVILLA WAVE, concluding that Maritrend had relied solely on Serac's credit for payment for its stevedoring services and had therefore waived its maritime lien against the vessel. Maritrend timely appealed.

II. ANALYSIS

* * *

B. Creation and Waiver of Federal Maritime Liens

Congress enacted the Federal Maritime Lien Act ("FMLA") in 1910 to bring uniformity to the law governing maritime liens. Although Congress recodified the FMLA in 1988 as part of the Commercial Instruments and Maritime Liens Act ("CIMLA"), it did not make any substantive changes to the law. Section 31342(a) of the current codification provides that a person providing necessaries to a vessel on the order of the owner or a person authorized by the owner—(1) has a maritime lien on the vessel; (2) may bring a civil action in rem to enforce the lien; and (3) is not required to allege or prove in the action that credit was given to the vessel.

"Necessaries" include stevedoring services, and there is no dispute here that Maritrend provided such services to the SEVILLA WAVE. It is likewise undisputed that Serac had the authority to procure necessaries, including stevedoring services, for the SEVILLA WAVE. The only question before us is whether Maritrend relied on the credit of the SEVILLA WAVE for payment for its services.

* * *

Because the statutory presumption in favor of a maritime lien is a strong one, we are usually reluctant to conclude that a supplier has waived its lien. We have held that the supplier's primary reliance on the personal credit of a charterer is insufficient to rebut the statutory presumption. For example, in *Gulf Trading & Transportation Co. v. The Vessel HOEGH SHIELD ("HOEGH SHIELD")*658 F.2d 363, 364-65 (5th Cir. Unit A Oct.1981), the plaintiff brought an *in rem* action against a vessel to which it had supplied fuel within the territorial jurisdiction of the United States pursuant to a contract with the vessel's English charterer. After delivering the fuel, the plaintiff sent an invoice to the charterer in London, but the charterer never made payment. In the action against the vessel, the vessel's owner argued that the plaintiff had waived its maritime lien because: (1) according to the deposition testimony of the plaintiff's credit agent, the fuel was supplied on the charterer's credit; (2) there had been no conversations between the plaintiff and the vessel's owner; (3) the plaintiff never sent an invoice to the vessel's owner; and (4) the plaintiff took no action against the vessel until the charterer became insolvent. Although these facts clearly indicated that the plaintiff was relying on the charterer's credit when it supplied the fuel, we held that they were insufficient to establish sole reliance on that credit or to permit an inference that the plaintiff purposefully intended to forgo its lien on the vessel.

Similarly, we concluded in *Gulf Oil Trading Co. v. M/V CARIBE MAR* 658 F.2d 363, 364-65 (5th Cir. Unit A Oct.1981), that sole reliance on personal credit, as opposed to the credit of the vessel, was not established even though the creditor had a long-term business relationship with the charterer, had extended large amounts of credit to the charterer in the past, and was aware of the prohibition of lien clause in the contract. Thus, "the simple existence of a business relationship and credit arrangements could hardly be realistically construed as an intent or purpose by [the creditor] to waive its lien on the vessel." *Id.*

Despite our prior caselaw reiterating the difficulty of proving that a creditor has waived its lien, two cases subsequent to *Hoegh Shield* and *Gulf Oil Trading Co.* identify the circumstances that support a finding of waiver. In *Equilease Corp. v. M/V SAMPSON,* this court determined that sufficient evidence exists to find that a creditor waives its right to a federal maritime lien when a creditor's testimony that he relied solely on entities besides the vessel for credit is combined with unambiguous statements in the creditor's original brief indicating the credit relied on was not the vessel's. The fact that the creditor also testified that "[t]here was no intent for us to give up anything" did not disturb the district court's finding that any federal maritime lien that existed was waived because the bulk of the evidence and testimony showed that creditor did not rely on the credit of the vessel.

In *Racal Survey U.S.A., Inc. v. M/V COUNT FLEET,* 231 F.3d 183, 189 this court found that a creditor had clearly indicated its intent to forgo a federal maritime lien based on the testimony of the creditor company's president. When asked whether the creditor was relying on the credit of the ship, the creditor's president testified that there was no reliance because the customer was a stevedoring company, not the vessel or the vessels' owner, and thus he had no contract or dealings with the ship. In finding waiver, this court stated that "[a]lmost nothing is more conclusive than such testimony" on the critical issue of the reliance necessary to preserve the lien. *Id.* at 190.

Taken together, *Equilease* and *Racal Survey* stand for the proposition that testimony regarding which party a creditor relied on can be determinative of whether the maritime lien was waived. But those decisions did not weaken the heavy burden placed on the party attacking the presumption. If the evidence shows that the claimant relied on the credit of the vessel *to some extent,* we will not find a waiver of the maritime lien.

C. The Evidence at Trial and Review of the District Court's Decision

A bench trial in this case was held on January 14, 2002. At trial, the district court heard testimony and was presented exhibits on behalf of both parties. Maritrend president William Bergeron ("Bergeron") testified that Maritrend "initially rel[ies] upon the contract that we have with the party, but we always rely on a maritime lien right," as a "fallback position." Indeed, in his testimony, Bergeron attests to this belief at least five times. Bergeron also indicated that he thought Serac owned the vessel to which Maritrend was providing stevedoring services. Similarly, Donald Broussard, an employee at Maritrend, testified that "the first course of action" was always to recover payment from Serac, but if it failed to pay, the company "implemented vessel seizure procedures." Finally, Petra Smith, Maritrend's vice president, testified that it was her responsibility to collect delinquent and overdue invoices for stevedoring services and that she only contacted Serac, as opposed to the owners or managers of the SEVILLA WAVE, for payment.

Among the exhibits offered at trial were the tariff document and copies of invoices. The tariff document, which was part of the stevedoring services contract, was prepared by Maritrend and placed on file with the Board of Commissioners of the Port of New Orleans. The tariff document does not explicitly state that the SEVILLA WAVE was responsible for stevedoring services, however, as the district court noted, there was no indication in the tariff document or any of the record evidence that Maritrend intended to waive its federal maritime lien. While the invoices were not sent directly to the SEVILLA WAVE, they indicated on their face that the charges contained therein were made "FOR THE ACCOUNT OF THE OWNER(S)/AGENT(S) AND/OR CHARTERER(S) OF THE M/V SEVILLA WAVE." There is no language on the invoices that indicates any intent to waive a maritime lien.

In holding for Pimpernel, the district court found that the trial testimony established that "Maritrend relied solely on the credit of Serac, its customer, for payment of [the stevedoring] services." It rested its decision on the both testimonial and documentary evidence. The principal testimony that the district court relied on was the testimony that Maritrend failed to seek payment from the vessel until several months after non-payment by Serac and that Maritrend expected its customer, Serac, to pay the invoices. The district court also noted that the documentary evidence supported its conclusion because Maritrend's invoices were only addressed and sent to Serac and the tariff document was silent as to whether the vessel was responsible for stevedoring charges.

The district court also stated that in light of our decisions in *Racal Survey* and *Equilease,* it was bound to rule against Maritrend. It decided this despite the fact that it found Bergeron's testimony that Maritrend always relied on the credit of the vessel as a fallback position when providing stevedoring services was "completely credible," and "the record evidence did not suggest any reason that Maritrend would relinquish its right to a lien."

After reviewing the record and applicable case law, we find that there was insufficient evidence adduced at trial to overcome the presumption that Maritrend relied on the credit of the SEVILLA WAVE with respect to the stevedoring services it provided in order to preserve a federal maritime lien. This court has repeatedly indicated the strength of the maritime lien presumption, especially in traditional areas such as stevedoring. *See Atlantic & Gulf Stevedores, Inc. v. M/V GRAND LOYALTY,* 608 F.2d 197, 201 (5th Cir.1979). Such a strong presumption in favor of a lien places a "heavy burden" on parties seeking to show a waiver of the lien, forcing them to show that a creditor "*deliberately intended* to forego the valuable privilege which the law accords and look solely to the owner's personal credit." *Gulf Oil Trading Co.,* 757 F.2d at 750 (emphasis in original) (citations and internal quotation marks omitted). Neither *Equilease Corp.* nor *Racal Survey* weakens this presumption or the burden placed on the party attacking the presumption.

In applying this standard, this court has found testimonial evidence sufficient to defeat this presumption only in cases where testimony "*clearly indicate[d]* that [the creditor] did not rely on the credit of the vessels," *Racal Survey,* 231 F.3d at 190 (emphasis added) and there was no other evidence, testimonial or otherwise, supporting the creditor's reliance on the vessel. Furthermore, this court has found evidence such as only invoicing the charterer or a long-standing business relationship with the charterer to be inadequate to show that a creditor relied solely on such charterer. *Gulf Oil Trading Co.,* 757 F.2d at 750.

Here, neither testimonial nor documentary evidence supports the conclusion that Maritrend "solely relied" on the credit of Serac. First, although the testimony as a whole shows that Maritrend relied on Serac for payment, it also shows that Maritrend did not rely solely on Serac because it was aware of and generally relied upon its maritime lien rights against the SEVILLA WAVE. Bergeron, who the district court found "completely credible," testified that Maritrend always intended to rely on the credit of the vessel as a "fallback" position. This testimony was further supported by Broussard's statement that Maritrend's practice was to implement ship seizure procedures when invoices for stevedoring services were not timely paid. Therefore, this situation is unlike the cases in *Equilease* and *Racal Survey,* where there was clear testimonial evidence by the party seeking to impose a federal maritime lien that it did not rely on the credit of the vessel

Second, the documents presented to the district court provide no evidence that Maritrend did not rely on the credit of the vessel. As discussed above, invoicing only the charterer is not dispositive because it only shows that a party attempted to receive the payment from the charterer first, not that it never intended to rely on the credit of the vessel. It is true that the tariff document expressly identifies certain charges to be applied to the vessel and that this list does not include stevedoring services. Again, this only shows that Serac, the charterer, was initially responsible for the stevedoring payments. Nothing in the tariff document shows that Maritrend did not intend to seek payment from the vessel in the event that Serac failed to pay. Therefore, these documents are insufficient to overcome the strong presumption that a federal maritime lien exists when necessaries, such as stevedoring services, are provided to a vessel.

In sum, we disagree that our decisions in *Equilease* and *Racal Survey* compelled the district court to rule against Maritrend based on these case facts. As the district court observed, Maritrend's resorting to its lien only after Serac defaulted is "typical of what is done in the normal course of business." If a supplier of necessaries forfeits his lien on the vessel by conducting his business in accordance with this prevailing practice, then the lien would be available only to suppliers who do not need it. Neither the CIMLA nor our cases interpreting its provisions supports such a result. The implied maritime lien is a security device, and its purpose is "to enable a vessel to obtain supplies or repairs necessary to her continued operation by giving a temporary underlying pledge of the vessel which will hold until payment can be made or more formal security given." *PROFESSOR VLADIMIR POPOV,* 199 F.3d at 223 (quoting *S. Coal & Coke Co. v. F. Grauds Kugniecibas ("The Everosa"),* 93 F.2d 732, 735 (1st Cir.1937)). We would frustrate this purpose if we prohibited enforcement of the lien whenever the supplier's efforts to collect from the person who ordered the necessaries were unsuccessful.

Although Maritrend expected Serac to pay for the stevedoring services, and its conduct reflected that reasonable expectation, Bergeron's trial testimony established that Maritrend relied on the credit of the SEVILLA WAVE as a "fallback position," which is exactly what the law contemplates. Because Pimpernel offered no evidence to rebut that testimony, and the district court did not find that testimony incredible, it could not meet its burden of proving that Maritrend relied solely on Serac's credit. We therefore hold that the district court's finding that Maritrend waived its lien on the SEVILLA WAVE was erroneous as a matter of law.

III. CONCLUSION

For the foregoing reasons, we reverse the district court's ruling that Maritrend waived its maritime lien on the SEVILLA WAVE and remand this case for the entry of judgment in favor of Maritrend on its *in rem* claim against the vessel for the value of the stevedoring services it provided.

REVERSED AND REMANDED WITH INSTRUCTIONS.

Note: Destruction and Release of the Res

A maritime lien may be extinguished by the permanent and total destruction of the *res* or by the release of the *res* on bond which is a substitute for the *res*.

For extinction of liens as a result of the destruction of the *res, see Walsh v. Tadlock*, 104 F.2d 131, 1939 AMC 1278 (9th Cir. 1939):

> With the total destruction of the vessel the liens thereon were of necessity extinguished. 38 C.J.S. 1247. These liens did not attach to the proceeds of the insurance, nor did appellants' lien on the boat per se entitle them to participate in the division of the insurance money.... Their right to do that was dependent on the contract of insurance.

When the destruction of the *res* is only partial, maritime liens continue to burden the part that remains. *See Chapman v. Engines of Greenpoint*, 38 F. 671 (S.D.N.Y. 1889). Likewise, when a vessel is dismantled and reassembled, maritime liens persist. *See Dann v. Dredge Sandpiper*, 222 F. Supp. 838 (D. Del. 1963). In such a case, the destruction of the *res* is not permanent.

For release of a vessel on bond, *see Hawgood & Avery Transit Co. v. Dingman*, 94 F. 1011 (8th Cir. 1899):

> When a ship which has been arrested under a libel is released upon an appraisal and a deposit, or a bond, or a stipulation, not given under the limited liability act, the deposit or bond or stipulation is substituted for the vessel as to all those who have then filed their libels and become parties to the proceedings but as to no other parties. The proceeds of the deposit, bond, or stipulation inure to the benefit of those who were parties to the proceeding when the release was made. But they inure to the benefit of no others. The vessel is discharged from the liens of these parties, and upon their liens only. Lienholders who have not filed their libels, and have not become parties to the proceeding when the ship is discharged, may not be permitted to share in the proceeds of the deposit or bond or stipulation, and their liens are neither detached nor affected by the release. The vessel returns to the claimant subject to the maritime liens of all who were not parties to the proceeding before the discharge was made, and they may libel and arrest her to enforce their liens to the same extent and with the same effect as though she had never been seized before.

For the effect that a judgment *in personam* may have on maritime liens, *see Pratt v. United States*, 340 F.2d 174, 1967 AMC 1302 (4th Cir. 1964).

Chapter 9

LIMITATION OF LIABILITY

Introductory Note

Shipowners have long been granted the privilege of being able to obtain from a court a decree granting limitation of liability with respect to marine casualties. Although the origin of this practice has been traced to the medieval sea laws, the modern law dates from 1734 in England and from 1851 in the United States. Despite increased criticism in recent years, limitation of liability remains an important part of maritime law. This section covers the process and standards contained in the basic law in the United States, The Limitation of Shipowner's Liability Act. Limitation with regard to liability for cargo damage claims and fire damage is considered in the chapter on Carriage of Goods. For limitation of liability in the context of pollution, *see* the chapter on Environmental law.

A review of the law in this area can be found in the *Admiralty Law Institute Symposium on Limitation of Liability*, 53 TUL. L. REV. 999 (1979).

A. Practice and Procedure

1. The Federal Limitation of Shipowner's Liability Act

Federal Limitation of Shipowner's Liability Act

46 U.S.C.A. §§ 30501-30512

§ 30501. Definition

In this chapter, the term "owner" includes a charterer that mans, supplies, and navigates a vessel at the charter's own expense or by the charterer's own procurement.

§ 30502. Application

Except as otherwise provided, this chapter (except section 30503) applies to seagoing vessels and vessels used on lakes or rivers or in inland navigation, including canal boats, barges, and lighters.

§ 30503. Declaration of nature and value of goods

(a) In General—If a shipper of an item named in subsection (b), contained in a parcel, package, or trunk, loads the item as freight or baggage on a vessel, without at the time of loading giving to the person receiving the item a written notice of the true character and value of the item and having that information entered on the bill of lading, the owner and master of the vessel are not liable as carriers. The owner and master are not liable beyond the value entered on the bill of lading.

(b) Items—The items referred to in subsection (a) are precious metals, gold or silver plated articles, precious stones, jewelry, trinkets, watches, clocks, glass, china, coins, bills, securities, printings, engravings, pictures, stamps, maps, paper, silks, furs, lace, and similar items of high value and small size.

§ 30504. Loss by fire

The owner of a vessel is not liable for loss or damage to merchandise on the vessel caused by a fire on the vessel unless the fire resulted from the design or neglect of the owner.

§ 30505. General limit of liability

(a) In General—Except as provided in section 30506 of this title, the liability of the owner of a vessel for any claim, debt, or liability described in subsection (b) shall not exceed the value of the vessel and pending freight. If the vessel has more than one owner, the proportionate share of the liability of any one owner shall not exceed that owner's proportionate interest in the vessel and pending freight.

(b) Claims Subject to Limitation—Unless otherwise excluded by law, claims, debts, and liabilities subject to limitation under subsection (a) are those arising from any embezzlement, loss, or destruction of any property, goods, or merchandise shipped or put on board the vessel, any loss, damage, or injury by collision, or any act, matter, or thing, loss, damage, or forfeiture, done occasioned, or incurred, without the privity or knowledge of the owner.

(c) Wages—Subsection (a) does not apply to a claim for wages.

§ 30506. Limit of liability for personal injury or death

(a) Application—This section applies only to seagoing vessels, but does not apply to pleasure yachts, tugs, towboats, towing vessels, tank vessels, fishing vessels, fish tender vessels, canal boats, scows, car floats, barges, lighters, or nondescript vessels.

(b) Minimum liability—If the amount of the vessel owner's liability determined under section 30505 of this title is insufficient to pay all losses in full, and the portion available to pay claims for personal injury or death is less than $420 time the tonnage of the vessel, that portion shall be increased to $420 times the tonnage of the vessel. That portion may be used only to pay claims for personal injury or death.

(c) Calculation of tonnage—Under subsection (b), the tonnage of a self-propelled vessel is the gross tonnage without the deduction for engine room, and the tonnage of a sailing vessel is the tonnage for documentation. However, space for the use of seamen is excluded.

(d) Claims arising on distinct occasions—Separate limits of liability apply to claims for personal injury or death arising on distinct occasions.

(e) Privity or knowledge—In a claim for personal injury or death, the privity or knowledge of the master or the owner's superintendent or managing agent, at or before the beginning of each voyage, is imputed to the owner.

§ 30507. Apportionment of losses

If the amounts determined under sections 30505 and 30506 of this title are insufficient to pay all claims—

(1) all claimants shall be pain in proportion to their respective losses out of the amount determined under section 30505 of this title; and
(2) personal injury and death claimants, if any, shall be paid an additional amount in proportion to their respective losses out of the additional amount determined under section 30506(b) of this title.

§ 30508. Provisions requiring notice of claim or limiting time for bringing action

(a) Application—This section applies only to seagoing vessels, but does not apply to pleasure yachts, tugs, towboats, towing vessels, tank vessels, fishing vessels, fish tender vessels, canal boats, scows, car floats, barges, lighters, or nondescript vessels.

(b) Minimum time limits—The owner, master, manager, or agent of a vessel transporting passengers or property between ports in the United States, or between a port in the United States and a port in a foreign country, may not limit by regulation, contract, or otherwise the period for—

(1) giving notice of, or filing a claim for, personal injury or death to less than 6 months after the date of the injury or death; or
(2) bringing a civil action for personal injury or death to less than one year after the date of the injury or death.

(c) Effect of failure to give notice—When notice of a claim for personal injury or death is required by a contract, the failure to give the notice is not a bar to recovery if—

(1) the court finds that the owner, master, or agent of the vessel had knowledge of the injury or death and the owner has not been prejudiced by the failure;
(2) the court finds there was a satisfactory reason why the notice could not have been given; or
(3) the owner of the vessel fails to object to the failure to give the notice.

(d) Tolling of period to give notice—If a claimant is a minor or mental incompetent, or if a claim is for wrongful death, any period provided by a contract for giving notice of the claim is tolled until the earlier of—

(1) the date a legal representative is appointed for the minor, incompetent, or decedent's estate; or
(2) 3 years after the injury or death.

§ 30509. Provisions limiting liability for personal injury or death

(a) Prohibition—

(1) In general—The owner, master, manager, or agent of a vessel transporting passengers between ports in the United States, or between a port in the United States and

a port in a foreign country, may not include in a regulation or contract a provision limiting—

(A) the liability of the owner, master, or agent for personal injury or death caused by the negligence or fault of the owner or the owner's employees or agents; or
(B) the right of a claimant for personal injury or death to a trial by court of competent jurisdiction.

(2) Voidness—A provision described in paragraph (1) is void.

(b) Emotional distress, mental suffering, and psychological injury—

(1) In general—Subsection (a) does not prohibit a provision in a contract or in ticket conditions of carriage with a passenger that relieves an owner, master, manager, agent, operator, or crewmember of a vessel from liability for infliction of emotional distress, mental suffering, or psychological injury so long as the provision does not limit such liability when the emotional distress, mental suffering, or psychological injury is—

(A) the result of physical injury to the claimant caused by the negligence or fault of a crewmember or the owner, master, manager, agent, or operator;
(B) the result of the claimant having been at actual risk of physical injury, and the risk was caused by the negligence or fault of a crewmember or the owner, master, manager, agent, or operator; or

(C) intentionally inflicted by a crewmember or the owner, master, manager, agent or operator.

(2) Sexual offenses—This subsection does not limit the liability of a crewmember or the owner, master, manager, agent, or operator of a vessel in a case involving sexual harassment, sexual assault, or rape.

§ 30510. Vicarious liability for medical malpractice with regard to crew
In a civil action by any person in which the owner or operator of a vessel or employer of a crewmember is claimed to have vicarious liability for medical malpractice with regard to a crewmember occurring at a shoreside facility, and to the extent the damages resulted from the conduct of any shoreside doctor, hospital, medical facility, or other health care provider, the owner, operator, or employer is entitled to rely on any statutory limitations of liability applicable to the doctor, hospital, medical facility, or other health care provider in the State of the United States in which the shoreside medical care was provided.

§ 30511. Action by owner for limitation

(a) In general—The owner of a vessel may bring a civil action in a district court of the United States for limitation of liability under this chapter. The action must be brought within 6 months after a claimant gives the owner written notice of a claim.

(b) Creation of Fund—When the action is brought, the owner (at the owner's option) shall—

(1) deposit with the court, for the benefit of claimants—

(A) an amount equal to the value of the owner's interest in the vessel and pending freight, or approved security; and

(B) an amount, or approved security, that the court may fix from time to time as necessary to carry out this chapter; or

(2) transfer to a trustee appointed by the court, for the benefit of claimants—

(A) the owner's interest in the vessel and pending freight; and

(B) an amount, or approved security, that the court may fix from time to time as necessary to carry out this chapter.

(c) Cessation of other actions—When an action has been brought under this section and the owner has complied with subsection (b), all claims and proceedings against the owner related to the matter in question shall cease.

§ 30512. Liability as master, officer, or seaman not affected

This chapter does not affect the liability of an individual as a master, officer, or seaman, even though the individual is also an owner of the vessel.

Federal Limitation of Shipowner's Liability Act

(Superseded Version)

46 app. U.S.C. §§ 181-189

§ 181. Liability of masters as carriers

If any shipper of platina, gold, gold dust, silver, bullion, or other precious metals, coins, jewelry, bills of any bank or public body, diamonds or other precious stones, or any gold or silver in a manufactured or unmanufactured state, watches, clocks, or timepieces of any description, trinkets, orders, notes, or securities for payment of money, stamps, maps, writings, title deeds, printings, engravings, pictures, gold or silver plate or plated articles, glass, china, silks in a manufactured or unmanufactured state, and whether wrought up or not wrought up with any other material, furs, or lace, or any of them, contained in any parcel, or package, or trunk, shall lade the same as freight or baggage, on any vessel, without at the time of such lading giving to the master, clerk, agent, or owner of such vessel receiving the same a written notice of the true character and value thereof, and having the same entered on the bill of lading therefor, the master and owner of such vessel shall not be liable as carriers thereof in any form or manner; nor shall any such master or owner be liable for any such goods beyond the value and according to the character thereof so notified and entered.

* * *

[§ **182**, which deals with loss by fire, is considered in the chapter on Carriage of Goods.]

§ 183. Amount of liability: loss of life or bodily injury; privity imputed to owner; "seagoing vessel"

(a) The liability of the owner of any vessel, whether American or foreign, for any embezzlement, loss, or destruction by any person of any property, goods, or merchandise shipped or put on board of such vessel, or for any loss, damage, or injury by collision, or for any act, matter, or thing, loss, damage, or forfeiture, done, occasioned, or incurred, without the privity or knowledge of such owner or owners, shall not, except in the cases provided for in subsection (b) of this section, exceed the amount or value of the interest of such owner in such vessel, and her freight then pending.

(b) In the case of any seagoing vessel, if the amount of the owner's liability as limited under subsection (a) of this section is insufficient to pay all losses in full, and the portion of such amount applicable to the payment of losses in respect of loss of life or bodily injury is less than $420 per ton of such vessel's tonnage, such portion shall be increased to an amount equal to $420 per ton, to be available only for the payment of losses in respect of loss of life or bodily injury. If such portion so increased is insufficient to pay such losses in full, they shall be paid therefrom in proportion to their respective amounts.

(c) For the purposes of this section the tonnage of a seagoing steam or motor vessel shall be her gross tonnage without deduction on account of engine room, and the tonnage of a seagoing sailing vessel shall be her registered tonnage: *Provided*, That there shall not be included in such tonnage any space occupied by seamen or apprentices and appropriated to their use.

(d) The owner of any such seagoing vessel shall be liable in respect of loss of life or bodily injury arising on distinct occasions to the same extent as if no other loss of life or bodily injury had arisen.

(e) In respect of loss of life or bodily injury the privity or knowledge of the master of a seagoing vessel or of the superintendent or managing agent of the owner thereof, at or prior to the commencement of each voyage, shall be deemed conclusively the privity or knowledge of the owner of such vessel.

(f) As used in subsections (b), (c), (d) and (e) of this section and in section 183b of this title, the term "seagoing vessel" shall not include pleasure yachts, tugs, towboats, towing vessels, tank vessels, fishing vessels or their tenders, self-propelled lighters, nondescript self-propelled vessels, canal boats, scows, car floats, barges, lighters, or nondescript non-self-propelled vessels, even though the same may be seagoing vessels within the meaning of such term as used in section 188 of this title.

[Former § 183a was repealed in 1936—Eds.]

§ 183b. Stipulations limiting time for filing claims and commencing suit

(a) It shall be unlawful for the manager, agent, master, or owner of any sea-going vessel (other than tugs, barges, fishing vessels and their tenders) transporting passengers or merchandise or property from or between ports of the United States and foreign ports to provide by rule, contract, regulation, or otherwise a shorter period for giving notice of, or filing claims for loss of life, or bodily injury, than six months, and for the institution of suits on such claims, than one year, such period for institution of suits to be computed from the day when the death or injury occurred.

(b) Failure to give such notice, where lawfully prescribed in such contract, shall not bar any such claim—

(1) If the owner or master of the vessel or his agent had knowledge of the injury, damage, or loss and the court determines that the owner has not been prejudiced by the failure to give such notice; nor

(2) If the court excuses such failure on the ground that for some satisfactory reason such notice could not be given; nor

(3) Unless objection to such failure is raised by the owner.

(c) If a person who is entitled to recover on any such claim is mentally incompetent or a minor, or if the action is one for wrongful death, any lawful limitation of time prescribed in such contract shall not be applicable so long as no legal representative has been appointed for such incompetent, minor, or decedent's estate, but shall be applicable form the date of the appointment of such legal representative: *Provided, however*, That such appointment be made within three years after the date of such death or injury.

§ 183c. Stipulations limiting liability for negligence invalid

(a) Negligence

It shall be unlawful for the manager, agent, master, or owner of any vessel transporting passengers between ports of the United States or between any such port and a foreign port to insert in any rule, regulation, contract, or agreement any provision or limitation (1) purporting, in the event of loss of life or bodily injury arising from the negligence or fault of such owner or his servants, to relieve such owner, master, or agent from liability, or from liability beyond any stipulated amount, for such loss or injury, or (2) purporting in such event to lessen, weaken, or avoid the right of any claimant to a trial by court of competent jurisdiction on the question of liability for such loss or injury, or the measure of damages therefor. All such provisions or limitations contained in any such rule, regulation, contract, or agreement are declared to be against public policy and shall be null and void and of no effect.

(b) Infliction of emotional distress, mental suffering, or psychological injury

(1) Subsection (a) of this section shall not prohibit provisions or limitations in contracts, agreements, or ticket conditions of carriage with passengers which relieve a crewmember, manager, agent, master, owner, or operator of a vessel from liability for infliction of emotional distress, mental suffering, or psychological injury so long as such provisions or limi-

tations do not limit such liability if the emotional distress, mental suffering, or psychological injury was—

(A) the result of physical injury to the claimant caused by the negligence or fault of a crewmember or the manager, agent, master, owner, or operator;

(B) the result of the claimant having been at actual risk of physical injury, and such risk was caused by the negligence or fault of a crewmember or the manager, agent, master, owner, or operator; or

(C) intentionally inflicted by a crewmember or the manager, agent, master, owner, or operator.

(2) Nothing in this subsection is intended to limit the liability of a crewmember or the manager, agent, master, owner, or operator of a vessel in a case involving sexual harassment, sexual assault, or rape.

§ 184. Apportionment of compensation

Whenever any such embezzlement, loss, or destruction is suffered by several freighters or owners of goods, wares, merchandise, or any property whatever, on the same voyage, and the whole value of the vessel, and her freight for the voyage, is not sufficient to make compensation to each of them, they shall receive compensation from the owner of the vessel in proportion to their respective losses; and for that purpose the freighters and owners of the property, and the owner of the vessel, or any of them, may take the appropriate proceedings in any court, for the purpose of apportioning the sum for which the owner of the vessel may be liable among the parties entitled thereto.

§ 185. Petition for limitation of liability; deposit of value of interest in court; transfer of interest to trustee

The vessel owner, within six months after a claimant shall have given to or filed with such owner written notice of claim, may petition a district court of the United States of competent jurisdiction for limitation of liability within the provisions of this chapter and the owner (a) shall deposit with the court, for the benefit of claimants, a sum equal to the amount or value of the interest of such owner in the vessel and freight, or approved security therefor, and in addition such sums, or approved security therefor, as the court may from time to time fix as necessary to carry out the provisions of section 183 of this title, or (b) at his option shall transfer, for the benefit of claimants, to a trustee to be appointed by the court his interest in the vessel and freight, together with such sums, or approved security therefor, as the court may from time to time fix as necessary to carry out the provisions of section 183 of this title. Upon compliance with the requirements of this section all claims and proceedings against the owner with respect to the matter in question shall cease.

§ 186. Charterer may be deemed owner

The charterer of any vessel, in case he shall man, victual, and navigate such vessel at his own expense, or by his own procurement, shall be deemed the owner of such vessel within the meaning of the provisions of this chapter relating to the limitation of the liability of the owners of vessels; and such vessel, when so chartered, shall be liable in the same manner as if navigated by the owner thereof.

§ 187. Remedies reserved

Nothing in sections 182, 183, 184, 185 and 186 of this title shall be construed to take away or affect the remedy to which any party may be entitled, against the master, officers, or seamen, for or on account of any embezzlement, injury, loss, or destruction of merchandise, or property, put on board any vessel, or on account of any negligence, fraud, or other malversation of such master, officers, or seamen, respectively, nor to lessen or take away any responsibility to which any master or seaman of any vessel may by law be liable, notwithstanding such master or seaman may be an owner or part owner of the vessel.

§ 188. Limitation of liability of owners applied to all vessels

Except as otherwise specifically provided therein, the provisions of sections 182, 183, 183b-187, and 189 of this title shall apply to all seagoing vessels, and also to all vessels used on lakes or rivers or in inland navigation, including canal boats, barges, and lighters.

§ 189. Limitation of liability of owners of vessels for debts

The individual liability of a shipowner shall be limited to the proportion of any or all debts and liabilities that his individual share of the vessel bears to the whole; and the aggregate liabilities of all the owners of a vessel on account of the same shall not exceed the value of such vessels and freight pending: *Provided*, That this provision shall not prevent any claimant from joining all the owners in one action; nor shall the same apply to wages due to persons employed by said shipowners.

---

2. Federal Rules of Civil Procedure, Supplemental Rule F

Supplemental Admiralty Rule F of the Federal Rules of Civil Procedure, which follows, should be studied carefully to determine the procedure and content of the pleadings in a limitation action.

Rule F—Limitation of Liability

(1) *Time for Filing Complaint: Security.* Not later than six months after his receipt of a claim in writing, any vessel owner may file a complaint in the appropriate district court, as provided in subdivision (9) of this rule, for limitation of liability pursuant to statute. The owner (a) shall deposit with the court, for the benefit of claimants, a sum equal to the amount or value of his interest in the vessel and pending freight, or approved security therefor, and in addition such sums, or approved security therefor, as the court may from time to time fix as necessary to carry out the provisions of the statutes as amended; or (b) at his option shall transfer to a trustee to be appointed by the court, for the benefit of claimants, his interest in the vessel and pending freight, together with such sums, or approved security therefor, as the court may from time to time fix as necessary to carry out the provisions of the statutes as amended. The plaintiff shall also give security for costs and, if he elects to give security, for interest at the rate of 6 per cent annum from the date of the security.

(2) *Complaint.* The complaint shall set forth the facts on the basis of which the right to limit liability is asserted, and all facts necessary to enable the court to determine the amount

to which the owner's liability shall be limited. The complaint my demand exoneration from as well as limitation of liability. It shall state the voyage, if any, on which the demands sought to be limited arose, with the date and place of its termination; the amount of all demands including all unsatisfied liens or claims of lien, in contract or in tort or otherwise, arising on that voyage, so far as known to the plaintiff, and what actions and proceedings, if any, are pending thereon; whether the vessel was damaged, lost, or abandoned, and, if so, when and where; the value of the vessel at the close of the voyage or, in case of wreck, the value of her wreckage, strippings, or proceeds, if any, and where and in whose possession they are; and the amount of any pending freight recovered or recoverable. If the plaintiff elects to transfer his interest in the vessel to a trustee, the complaint must further show any prior paramount liens thereon, and what voyages or trips, if any, she has made since the voyage or trip on which the claims sought to be limited arose, and any existing liens arising upon any such subsequent voyage or trip, with the amounts and causes thereof, and the names and addresses of the lienors, so far as known; and whether the vessel sustained any injury upon or by reason of such subsequent voyage or trip.

(3) *Claims Against Owner: Injunction.* Upon compliance by the owner with the requirements of subdivision (1) of this rule all claims and proceedings against the owner or his property with respect to the matter in question shall cease. On application of the plaintiff the court shall enjoin the further prosecution of any action or proceeding against the plaintiff or his property with respect to any claim subject to limitation in the action.

(4) *Notice to Claimants.* Upon the owner's compliance with subdivision (1) of this rule the court shall issue a notice to all persons asserting claims with respect to which the complaint seeks limitation, admonishing them to file their respective claims with the clerk of the court and to serve on the attorneys for the plaintiff a copy thereof on or before a date to be named in the notice. For cause shown, the court may enlarge the time within which claims may be filed. The notice shall be published in such newspaper or newspapers as the court may direct once a week for four successive weeks prior to the date fixed for the filing of claims. The plaintiff not later than the day of second publication shall also mail a copy of the notice to every person known to have made any claim against the vessel or the plaintiff arising out of the voyage or trip on which the claims sought to be limited arose. In cases involving death a copy of such notice shall be mailed to the decedent at his last known address, and also to any person who shall be known to have made any claim on account of such death.

(5) *Claims and Answer.* Claims shall be filed and served on or before the date specified in the notice provided for in subdivision (4) of this rule. Each claim shall specify the facts upon which the claimant relies in support of his claim, the items thereof, and the dates on which the same accrued. If a claimant desires to contest either the right to exoneration from or the right to limitation of liability he shall file and serve an answer to the complaint unless his claim has included an answer.

(6) *Information to be Given Claimants.* Within 30 days after the date specified in the notice for filing claims, or within such time as the court thereafter may allow, the plaintiff shall mail to the attorney for each claimant (or if the claimant has no attorney to the claimant

himself) a list setting forth (a) the name of each claimant, (b) the name and address of his attorney (if he is known to have one), (c) the nature of his claim, *i.e.*, whether property loss, property damage, death, personal injury, etc., and (d) the amount thereof.
(7) *Insufficiency of Fund or Security*. Any claimant may by motion demand that the funds deposited in court or the security given by the plaintiff be increased on the ground that they are less than the value of the plaintiff's interest in the vessel and pending freight. Thereupon the court shall cause due appraisement to be made of the value of the plaintiff's interest in the vessel and pending freight; and if the court finds that the deposit or security is either insufficient or excessive it shall order its increase or reduction. In like manner any claimant may demand that the deposit or security be increased on the ground that it is insufficient to carry out the provisions of the statutes relating to claims in respect of loss of life or bodily injury; and, after notice and hearing, the court may similarly order that the deposit or security be increased or reduced.
(8) *Objections to Claims: Distribution of Fund*. Any interested party may question or controvert any claim without filing an objection thereto. Upon determination of liability the fund deposited or secured, or the proceeds of the vessel and pending freight, shall be divided pro rata, subject to all relevant provisions of law, among the several claimants in proportion to the amounts of their respective claims, duly proved, saving, however, to all parties any priority to which they may be legally entitled.
(9) *Venue; Transfer*. The complaint shall be filed in any district in which the vessel has been attached or arrested to answer for any claim with respect to which the plaintiff seeks to limit liability; or, if the vessel has not been attached or arrested, then in any district in which the owner has been sued with respect to any such claim. When the vessel has not been attached or arrested to answer the matters aforesaid, and suit has not been commenced against the owner, the proceedings may be had in the district in which the vessel may be, but if the vessel is not within any district and no siut has been commenced in any district, then the complaint may be filed in any district. For the convenience of parties and witnesses, in the interest of justice, the court may transfer the action to any district; if venue is wrongly laid the court shall dismiss or, if it be in the interest of justice, transfer the action to any district in which it could have been brought. If the vessel shall have been sold, the proceeds shall represent the vessel for the purposes of these rules.

COMPLAINT OF CARIBBEAN SEA TRANSPORT, LTD.

748 F.2d 622, 1985 AMC 1995 (11th Cir. 1984)

James C. HILL, Circuit Judge

This admiralty appeal challenges the district court's order requiring the plaintiff/appellant shipowner to post security pursuant to sections 183(a) and 183(b) of the Limitation of Liability Act, 46 U.S.C. § 183 *et seq.* We affirm in part, but remand for a more complete hearing as to whether security need be posted pursuant to section 183(b).

This admiralty case arises from a collision between the M/V ANTILLES SUN (ANTILLES), a steel cargo carrier, and the CORAIN II (CORAIN). After leaving Miami on February 11, 1982, and discharging cargo at several Caribbean ports, the ANTILLES was on its way back to Miami from Kingston, Jamaica, when the collision occurred in waters off Cuba on February 24, 1982. The ANTILLES sank in deep waters where salvage was impossible. Appellee-claimant Francisco Russo, the second mate on the CORAIN, apparently suffered a back injury as a result of the collision.

On July 27, 1982, plaintiff-appellant Caribbean Sea Transport, Ltd, the owner of the ANTILLES, filed a petition for exoneration from or limitation of liability in the district court, pursuant to 46 U.S.C. § 183 *et seq.* and Rule F of the Supplemental Rules for Certain Admiralty and Maritime Claims (Admiralty Rules). Claims against the ANTILLES were then filed by cargo shippers, the owners of the CORAIN, and Russo.

On October 6, 1983, claimant Russo brought a motion pursuant to Admiralty Rule F(7) to require appellant to post security required by 46 U.S.C. § 183 and Admiralty Rule F(1). Following a non-evidentiary hearing on November 4, 1983, the district court ordered that the appellant post security in the amount of $112,000 plus interest: $82,000 pursuant to section 183(a) and $30,000 pursuant to section 183(b). Appellants, who still have not posted the amount, appealed.

Discussion

A. Background on Limitation of Liability in Admiralty

The Limitation of Liability Act (Limitation Act), 46 U.S.C. § 183 *et seq.*, is intended to limit the liability of shipowners following maritime accidents. The Limitation Act provides that the liability of the shipowner for any maritime injury or loss shall be limited (to all but personal injury claimants, who may be entitled to a greater, but still limited, amount) to the extent of the shipowner's investment in and earnings from the voyage, provided that the injury or loss involves no privity or knowledge on the owner's part. Admiralty Rule F sets up the procedural provisions for limitation of liability actions.

* * *

The Limitation Act's protection is typically triggered when the shipowner files a complaint seeking limitation of liability pursuant to section 185 and Admiralty Rule F(1). Rule F(1) also provides that as a condition to filing the complaint, the shipowner

> shall deposit with the court, for the benefit of claimants, a sum equal to the amount or value of his interest in the vessel and pending freight, or approved security therefor, and in addition such sums, or approved security therefor, as the court may from time to time fix as necessary to carry out the provisions of the statutes as amended;

or, in the alternative, shall transfer his interest in the vessel and pending freight to a trustee. Admiralty Rule F(1). The posting of security must include six percent yearly interest. *Id.* If a claimant is at any time concerned that the amount of security posted is insufficient, Admiralty Rule F(7) provides that

> [a]ny claimant may by motion demand that the funds deposited in court or the security given by the plaintiff be increased on the ground that they are less than the value of the plaintiff's interest in the vessel and pending freight. Thereupon the court shall cause due appraisement to be made of the value of the plaintiff's interest in the vessel and pending freight; and if the court finds that the deposit or security is either insufficient or excessive it shall order its increase or reduction. In like manner any claimant may demand that the deposit or security be increased on the ground that it is insufficient to carry out the provisions of the statutes relating to claims in respect of loss of life or bodily injury; and, after notice and hearing, the court may similarly order that the deposit or security be increased or reduced.

Once an action is filed and security posted, the court proceeds to determine if the owner should be exonerated from liability or if he is entitled to limitation of liability. An owner will be exonerated from liability when he, his vessel, and crew are found to be completely free from fault. *Tittle v. Aldacosta*, 544 F.2d 752, 755 (5th Cir. 1977). To limit his liability to the amounts calculated under section 183, the shipowner must merely show that he had no privity to or knowledge of the negligence or unseaworthiness which caused injuries. *Id.* at 756. If the owner is not exonerated but prevails in his plea for limitation, the section 183 security fund is distributed on a pro rata basis to claimants and the owner's liability is at an end. Admiralty Rule F(8). Therefore, a determination of the amount of security that need be posted under section 183 constitutes a determination of the maximum amount of liability that the shipowner will be subject to under the Limitation Act.

* * *

[The remainder of the court's opinion deals with issues relating to the Limitation Fund and is discussed *infra*. Eds.]

---

3. Concursus of Claims

LEWIS v. LEWIS & CLARK MARINE, INC.

531 U.S. 438, 121 S. Ct. 993, 148 L. Ed. 2d 931, 2001 AMC 913 (2001)

Justice O'CONNOR delivered the opinion of the Court.

This case concerns a seaman's ability to sue a vessel owner in state court for personal injuries sustained aboard a vessel. Federal courts have exclusive jurisdiction over admiralty and maritime claims, but the jurisdictional statute "sav[es] to suitors in all cases all other remedies to which they are otherwise entitled." 28 U.S.C. § 1333(1). Another statute grants vessel owners the right to seek limited liability in federal court for claims of damage aboard their vessels. 46 U.S.C.App. § 181 *et seq.* In this case, the District Court, after conducting proceedings to preserve the vessel owner's right to seek limited liability, dissolved the injunction that prevented the seaman from litigating his personal injury claims in state court. The Eighth Circuit Court of Appeals reversed, concluding that the vessel owner had a right to contest liability in federal court, and that the seaman did not have a saved remedy in state court. The question presented is whether the District Court abused its discretion in dissolving the injunction.

I

Petitioner, James F. Lewis, worked as a deckhand aboard the M/V *Karen Michelle,* owned by respondent, Lewis & Clark Marine, Inc. Petitioner claims that on March 17, 1998, he was injured aboard the M/V *Karen Michelle* when he tripped over a wire and hurt his back. App. 12. In April 1998, petitioner sued respondent in the Circuit Court of Madison County, Illinois.... Petitioner did not demand a jury trial in state court.

In anticipation of petitioner's suit, respondent had filed a complaint for exoneration from, or limitation of, liability in the United States District Court for the Eastern District of Missouri pursuant to the Limitation of Liability Act (Limitation Act or Act), 46 U.S.C.App. § 181 *et seq.* The District Court followed the procedure for a limitation action provided in Supplemental Admiralty and Maritime Claims Rule F. The court entered an order approving a surety bond of $450,000, representing respondent's interest in the vessel. The court ordered that any person with a claim for the events of March 17, 1998, file a claim with the court within a specified period. The court then enjoined the filing or prosecution of any suits against respondent related to the incident on March 17, 1998. App. 30-33.

Petitioner filed an answer to respondent's complaint, a claim for damages for injury, and a motion to dissolve the restraining order. Petitioner averred that he was the sole claimant concerning the events of March 17, 1998. He waived any claim of res judicata concerning limited liability based on a state court judgment; he stipulated that respondent could relitigate issues relating to the limitation of liability in District Court. *Id.,* at 72. Petitioner later stipulated that the value of his claim was less than the value of the limitation fund, *id.,* at 102, recanting his earlier allegation that his claim exceeded the vessel's value.

The District Court dissolved the restraining order that prevented petitioner from proceeding with his cause of action in state court. *In re Complaint of Lewis & Clark Marine, Inc.,* 31 F. Supp. 2d 1164 (E.D. Mo. 1998). The court recognized that federal courts have exclusive jurisdiction to determine whether a vessel owner is entitled to limited liability. The court also noted, however, that the statute that confers exclusive jurisdiction over admiralty and maritime claims to federal courts contains a clause that saves to suitors "all other remedies to which they are otherwise entitled." 28 U.S.C. § 1333(1). The court reasoned that "a tension exists between the exclusive jurisdiction vested in the admiralty courts to determine a vessel owner's right to limited liability and the savings to suitors clause." 31 F. Supp. 2d, at 1168.

The District Court found two exceptions to exclusive federal jurisdiction under which a claimant is allowed to litigate his claim in state court. The first is where the value of the limitation fund exceeds the total value of all claims asserted against the vessel owner. The second is where a single claimant brings an action against the vessel owner seeking damages in excess of the value of the vessel. The court concluded that it should dissolve the injunction in this case because petitioner met the limited fund exception and probably met the single claimant exception as well. *Id.,* at 1169, and n. 3. The court decided to retain jurisdiction over the limitation action to protect the vessel owner's right to limitation in the event that the state proceedings necessitated further proceedings in federal court.

The Eighth Circuit Court of Appeals held that the District Court abused its discretion in dissolving the injunction. 196 F.3d 900 (1999). The Court of Appeals, like the District Court, recognized potential tension between the saving to suitors clause in the jurisdictional statute and the Limitation Act. The Court of Appeals, however, perceived no conflict between those provisions in the instant case. The Court of Appeals explained that a court must consider whether the vessel owner has the right to remain in federal court and whether the claimant is seeking a saved remedy in another forum. The court concluded that respondent had a right to seek exoneration from liability, not merely limitation of liability, in federal court. The court also concluded that because petitioner did not request a trial by jury, he had not sought a saved remedy in state court. The court determined that there was no substantive difference between the remedies afforded petitioner in state court and federal court. For these reasons, the court held that there was no basis for dissolving the injunction.

* * *

II

A

* * *

Thus, the saving to suitors clause preserves remedies and the concurrent jurisdiction of state courts over some admiralty and maritime claims. *See also Madruga v. Superior Court of Cal., County of San Diego,* 346 U.S. 556, 560-561, 74 S.Ct. 298, 98 L.Ed. 290 (1954); *American_Steamboat Co. v. Chase,* 83 U.S. [16 Wall.] 522, 533-534, 21 L.Ed. 369 (1872).

B

Admiralty and maritime law includes a host of special rights, duties, rules, and procedures. *See, e.g.,* 46 U.S.C. App. § 721 *et seq.* (wrecks and salvage); § 741 *et seq.* (suits in admiralty by or against vessels or cargoes of the United States); 46 U.S.C. § 10101 *et seq.* (merchant seamen protection and relief). Among these provisions is the Limitation Act, 46 U.S.C. App. § 181 *et seq.* The Act allows a vessel owner to limit liability for damage or injury, occasioned without the owner's privity or knowledge, to the value of the vessel or the owner's interest in the vessel. The central provision of the Act provides:

> The liability of the owner of any vessel, whether American or foreign, for any embezzlement, loss, or destruction by any person of any property, goods, or merchandise shipped or put on board of such vessel, or for any loss, damage, or injury by collision, or for any act, matter, or thing, loss, damage, or forfeiture, done, occasioned, or incurred, without the privity or knowledge of such owner or owners, shall not, except in the cases provided for in subsection (b) of this section, exceed the amount or value of the interest of such owner in such vessel, and her freight then pending. § 183(a).

See also § 183(b) (requiring supplemental fund for some vessels for personal injury and death claimants).

Congress passed the Limitation Act in 1851 "to encourage ship-building and to induce capitalists to invest money in this branch of industry." *Norwich & N.Y. Transp. Co. v. Wright,* 13 Wall. 104, 121, 20 L.Ed. 585 (1871). *See also British Transport Comm'n v. United States,* 354 U.S. 129, 133-135, 77 S.Ct. 1103, 1 L.Ed.2d 1234 (1957); *Just v. Chambers,* 312 U.S. 383, 385, 61 S.Ct. 687, 85 L.Ed. 903 (1941). The Act also had the purpose of "putting American shipping upon an equality with that of other maritime nations" that had their own limitation acts. *The Main v. Williams,* 152 U.S. 122, 128, 14 S.Ct. 486, 38 L.Ed. 381 (1894). *See also Norwich Co., supra,* at 116-119 (discussing history of limitation acts in England, France, and the States that led to the passage of the Limitation Act).

The Act is not a model of clarity. *See* 2 T. Schoenbaum, Admiralty and Maritime Law 299 (2d ed. 1994) ("Th[e] 1851 Act, badly drafted even by the standards of the time, continues in effect today"). Having created a right to seek limited liability, Congress did not provide procedures for determining the entitlement. This Court did not have an opportunity to review the Act in detail until 20 years after its enactment. *See Norwich Co., supra.* Deeming the Act "incapable of execution" without further instructions to courts, *id.,* at 123, we designed the procedures that govern a limitation action, and promulgated them the same Term, *see* Supplementary Rules of Practice in Admiralty, 13 Wall. xii-xiv. We later explained that the scheme "was sketched in outline" by the Act, and "the regulation of details as to the form and modes of proceeding was left to be prescribed by judicial authority." *Providence & New York S.S. Co. v. Hill Mfg. Co.,* 109 U.S. 578, 590, 3 S.Ct. 379, 27 L.Ed. 1038 (1883).

The 1872 rules were "intended to facilitate the proceedings of the owners of vessels for claiming the limitation of liability secured by the statute." *The Benefactor,* 103 U.S. 239, 244, 26 L.Ed. 351 (1880). Under the rules, a vessel owner seeking limitation of liability had to file a petition. The district court would obtain an appraisal of the vessel's value or the owner's interest in the vessel, and ensure that payment or some guarantee of payment was deposited with the court. The court would then order all claimants to appear. Supplemental Rule of Practice in Admiralty 54, 13 Wall. at xii-xiii. In the process of seeking limited liability, the owner was permitted to contest the fact of liability. Rule 56, 13 Wall., at xiii. The ability to contest liability relieved vessel owners of the "very onerous" English rule, which required vessel owners to confess liability in order to seek the benefit of limitation. *The "Benefactor," supra,* at 243 ("[T]his court, in preparing the rules of procedure for a limitation of liability, deemed it proper to allow a party seeking such limitation to contest any liability whatever"). The claimants would then contest the vessel owner's claims for exoneration and limitation of liability. Rule 56, 13 Wall., at xiii. If the owner succeeded in its effort to limit liability, but was not exonerated, the court was responsible for distributing the fund deposited in the court among the claimants. Rule 55, 13 Wall., at xiii.

The procedure for a limitation action is now found in Supplemental Admiralty and Maritime Claims Rule F. Much like its predecessor provisions, Rule F sets forth the process for filing a complaint seeking exoneration from, or limitation of, liability. The district court secures the value of the vessel or owner's interest, marshals claims, and enjoins the prosecution of other actions with respect to the claims. In these proceedings, the court, sitting without a jury, adjudicates the claims. The court determines whether the vessel owner is liable and whether the owner may limit liability. The court then determines the validity of the claims, and if liability is limited, distributes the limited fund among the claimants.

C

Some tension exists between the saving to suitors clause and the Limitation Act. One statute gives suitors the right to a choice of remedies, and the other statute gives vessel owners the right to seek limitation of liability in federal court. We confronted this tension in *Langnes v. Green,* 282 U.S. 531, 51 S.Ct. 243, 75 L.Ed. 520 (1931). The respondent in *Langnes* was employed on the petitioner's vessel. The employee sued the vessel owner in state court for $25,000 for personal injuries suffered aboard the vessel. The vessel owner later filed a petition for limitation of liability in Federal District Court. The District Court enjoined any further proceedings in state court and issued a notice that all claimants appear. The employee filed his claim in District Court. The parties stipulated that the vessel was worth no more than $5,000.

The employee sought dissolution of the injunction. He argued that the state court had jurisdiction over his claim, that he was the only possible claimant, that there was only one vessel owner, and therefore the vessel owner could claim the benefit of the Limitation Act by proper pleading in state court. The District Court denied the motion and proceeded to decide the merits, concluding that the vessel owner was not liable. The Court of Appeals reversed on the issue of limitation.

On review, this Court concluded that both courts erred in failing to recognize that the state court was competent to hear the employee's personal injury claim and the vessel owner's claim for limitation. In our view, the choice before the District Court was whether it should retain the limitation action and preserve the right of the vessel owner but destroy the right of the employee in state court to a common law remedy, or allow the action in state court to proceed and preserve the rights of both parties. We concluded that the latter course was just. We decided that the District Court should have dissolved the injunction and allowed the employee to proceed with his claim in state court, and retained jurisdiction over the petition for limitation of liability in the event that the state proceedings necessitated further proceedings in federal court. We explained that the District Court's decision is "one of discretion in every case," and remanded for further proceedings. *Id.,* at 544, 51 S.Ct. 243.

After our decision, the employee was permitted to pursue his claim in state court. *See Ex parte Green,* 286 U.S. 437, 52 S.Ct. 602, 76 L.Ed. 1212 (1932). In those proceedings, notwithstanding this Court's recognition of the vessel owner's right to seek limitation of liability in federal court, the employee sought to litigate that issue in state court. We approved of the District Court's decision to enjoin any further proceedings in state court until the employee agreed to withdraw his submission on the issue of limited liability. *Id.,* at 440, 52 S.Ct. 602.

We have also considered the conflict between the saving to suitors clause and the Limitation Act in a case where several claimants attempted to sue a vessel owner in state court. *Lake Tankers Corp. v. Henn,* 354 U.S. 147, 77 S.Ct. 1269, 1 L.Ed.2d 1246 (1957). A pleasure yacht, the *Blackstone,* capsized after a collision with a tug that was push-towing a barge, injuring several persons and killing one. Claimants sued the owner of the tug and barge in state court actions. The owner filed a petition for exoneration from, or limitation of, liability in federal court. The owner also filed a bond for the tug in the amount of approximately $119,000 and a bond for the barge in the amount of $165,000. The District Court enjoined other proceedings concerning the collision. Thereafter, the claimants made their demands for damages; the total claims were less than the amount of the two bonds. All claimants relinquished any right to damages in excess of that set forth in their claims. They further waived any claim of res judicata relating to the issue of the vessel owner's ability to limit liability. The District Court decided to dissolve the injunction because the total limitation fund exceeded the amount of the claims. The Court of Appeals affirmed.

We affirmed the Court of Appeals' decision. In examining the Limitation Act and its history, we found it "crystal clear that the operation of the Act is directed at misfortunes at sea where the losses incurred exceed the value of the vessel and the pending freight." *Id.,* at 151, 77 S.Ct. 1269. Where the value of the vessel and the pending freight exceed the claims, however, there is no necessity for the maintenance of the action in federal court. *Id.,* at 152, 77 S.Ct. 1269. The stipulations, in addition to other restrictions on the state court proceedings, ensured "beyond doubt that [the owner's] right of limitation under the Act was fully protected." *Ibid.* We explained that to expand the scope of exclusive jurisdiction to prevent the state court actions

> would transform the Act from a protective instrument to an offensive weapon by which the shipowner could deprive suitors of their common-law rights, even where the limitation fund is known to be more than adequate to satisfy all demands upon it. The shipowner's right to limit liability is not so boundless. The Act is not one of immunity from liability but of limitation of it and we read no other privilege for the shipowner into its language over and above that granting him limited liability. In fact, the Congress not only created the limitation procedure for the primary purpose of apportion-

ing the limitation fund among the claimants where that fund was inadequate to pay the claims in full, but it reserved to such suitors their common-law remedies. *Id.,* at 152-153, 77 S.Ct. 1269.

Since these decisions, the Courts of Appeals have generally permitted claimants to proceed with their claims in state court where there is only a single claimant, as in *Langnes,* or where the total claims do not exceed the value of the limitation fund, as in *Lake Tankers.* See, *e.g., Beiswenger Enterprises Corp. v. Carletta,* 86 F.3d 1032 (C.A.11 1996); *Linton v. Great Lakes Dredge & Dock Co.,* 964 F.2d 1480 (C.A.5 1992). *See also Kreta Shipping S.A. v. Preussag International Steel Corp.,* 192 F.3d 41 (C.A.2 1999) (foreign forum).

III

In the instant case, we believe that the District Court properly exercised its discretion in dissolving the injunction that prevented petitioner from pursuing his claims in state court. The District Court, guided by our prior cases, attempted to reconcile petitioner's right to his remedy under the saving to suitors clause with respondent's right to seek limited liability under the Limitation Act. The court dissolved the injunction against the state court proceedings after it concluded that respondent's right to seek limitation of liability would be adequately protected. Respondent's rights were protected by petitioner's stipulation that his claim did not exceed the limitation fund, petitioner's waiver of any defense of res judicata with respect to limitation of liability, and the District Court's decision to stay the Limitation Act proceedings pending state court proceedings.

The Eighth Circuit held that the District Court should not have dissolved the injunction without first "finding ... actual statutory conflict between the Limitation Act and the 'saving to suitors' clause in the case at bar." 196 F.3d, at 906. The Court of Appeals concluded that there was no conflict here because respondent had a right to seek exoneration from liability in federal court, and petitioner did not have a saved remedy under the saving to suitors clause. That reasoning misapprehends this Court's prior decisions.

In this case, there was a conflict between the saving to suitors clause and the Limitation Act. Petitioner sued respondent in state court; under the saving to suitors clause, that court had jurisdiction to hear his claims. Respondent sought limited liability for petitioner's claims in federal court; the Limitation Act granted the federal court jurisdiction over that action. Both parties selected legitimate forums for their claims, and therein lies the conflict. Had petitioner sought to institute *in rem* proceedings against respondent in state court, that court would have lacked jurisdiction because the saving to suitors clause does not reach actions *in rem.* Similarly, had respondent sought limited liability for payment of wages in federal court, that court would not have had jurisdiction under the Limitation Act because claims for wages due employees are not covered. 46 U.S.C.App. § 189. *See also In re East River Towing Co.,* 266 U.S. 355, 367, 45 S.Ct. 114, 69 L.Ed. 324 (1924). Here, however, there appears to have been no obstacle to each party pursuing its claim in the forum of its choice, except the competing action.

In deciding that the case should proceed in federal court, the Court of Appeals relied on two flawed premises: that the Limitation Act grants vessel owners a right to obtain exoneration from liability in federal court where limitation of liability is not at issue, and that the saving to suitors clause reserves to claimants only the right to receive a jury trial.

By its own terms, the Limitation Act protects the right of vessel owners to limit their liability to the value of the vessel, provided that the events or circumstances giving rise to the damage occurred without the vessel owner's privity or knowledge. The Act was designed to encourage investment and protect vessel owners from unlimited exposure to liability. We have also made clear, however, that the scope of exclusive federal jurisdiction is proportional to the federal interest in protecting the vessel owner's right to seek limitation of liability. *See Lake Tankers,* 354 U.S., at 153, 77 S.Ct. 1269. We have explained that "[t]he Act is not one of immunity from liability but of limitation of it." *Id.,* at 152, 77 S.Ct. 1269. We see no reason to revisit that conclusion and decline respondent's invitation to expand the scope of the Act.

In construing the Limitation Act, this Court long ago determined that vessel owners may contest liability in the process of seeking limited liability, and we promulgated rules to that effect pursuant to our "power to regulate ... proceedings." *The Benefactor,* 103 U.S., at 244; Supplemental Rule of Practice in Admiralty 56, 13 Wall., at xiii; Supplemental Admiralty and Maritime Claims Rule F(2). Thus, we agree with respondent that a vessel owner need not confess liability in order to seek limitation under the Act. The Act and the rules of practice, however, do not create a freestanding right to exoneration from liability in circumstances where limitation of liability is not at issue. In this case, petitioner stipulated that his claim for damages would not exceed the value of the vessel and waived any claim of res judicata from the state court action concerning issues bearing on the limitation of liability. The District Court concluded that these stipulations would protect the vessel owner's right to seek limited liability in federal court. Then, out of an "abundance of caution," the court stayed the limitation proceedings so that it could act if the state court proceedings jeopardized the vessel owner's rights under the Limitation Act. 31 F.Supp.2d, at 1170-1171. We believe nothing more was required to protect respondent's right to seek a limitation of liability.

The district courts have jurisdiction over actions arising under the Limitation Act, and they have discretion to stay or dismiss Limitation Act proceedings to allow a suitor to pursue his claims in state court. If the district court concludes that the vessel owner's right to limitation will not be adequately protected—where for example a group of claimants cannot agree on appropriate stipulations or there is uncertainty concerning the adequacy of the fund or the number of claims—the court may proceed to adjudicate the merits, deciding the issues of liability and limitation. *See, e.g., Lake Tankers, supra,* at 152, 77 S. Ct. 1269; *Port Arthur Towing Co. v. John W. Towing, Inc.,* 42 F.3d 312, 314 (C.A.5 1995). But where, as here, the District Court satisfies itself that a vessel owner's right to seek limitation will be protected, the decision to dissolve the injunction is well within the court's discretion.

The Court of Appeals reasoned that the District Court also erred in dissolving the injunction because petitioner had no saved remedy in state court. The Court of Appeals apparently treated as dispositive petitioner's failure to demand a jury trial in state court. The jurisdictional statute, however, reserves to suitors "all other remedies to which they are otherwise entitled." 28 U.S.C. § 1333(1). Tracing the development of the clause since the Judiciary Act of 1789, it appears that the clause was designed to protect remedies available at common law. *See, e.g., The Hine v. Trevor,* 4 Wall. 555, 18 L.Ed. 451 (1866). We later explained that the clause extends to "all means other than proceedings in admiralty which may be employed to enforce the right or to redress the injury involved." *Red Cross Line,* 264 U.S., at 124, 44 S. Ct. 274. Trial by jury is an obvious, but not exclusive, example of the remedies available to suitors. *See Lake Tankers, supra,* at 153, 77 S. Ct. 1269; *Red Cross Line, supra,* at 123-125, 44 S. Ct. 274.

The Court of Appeals concluded that forum choice could not be a saved remedy under the saving to suitors clause because a claimant does not have the ability to control the forum in which his claim will be heard. 192 F.3d, at 909. The prospect that a vessel owner may remove a state court action to federal court, however, does not limit a claimant's forum choice under the saving to suitors clause any more than other litigants' forum choices may be limited. We have previously refused to hold that admiralty claims, such as a limitation claim, fall within the scope of federal question jurisdiction out of concern that saving to suitors actions in state court would be removed to federal court and undermine the claimant's choice of forum. *Romero v. International Terminal Operating Co.,* 358 U.S. 354, 371-372, 79 S.Ct. 468, 3 L.Ed.2d 368 (1959). We explained that to define admiralty jurisdiction as federal question jurisdiction would be a "destructive oversimplification of the highly intricate interplay of the States and the National Government in their regulation of maritime commerce." *Id.,* at 373, 79 S.Ct. 468. Moreover, in this case respondent raised a Jones Act claim, which is not subject to removal to federal court even in the event of diversity of the parties. *See* 28 U.S.C. § 1445(a) (incorporated by reference into the Jones Act, 46 U.S.C.App. § 688(a)). Respondent's arguments to limit and enumerate the saved remedies under the saving to suitors clause must fail in view of the consistent recognition by Congress and this Court that both state and federal courts may be proper forums for adjudicating claims such as petitioner's.

In sum, this Court's case law makes clear that state courts, with all of their remedies, may adjudicate claims like petitioner's against vessel owners so long as the vessel owner's right to seek limitation of liability is protected. Respondent seeks to invert that rule, making run of the mill personal injury actions involving vessels a matter of exclusive federal jurisdiction except where the claimant happens to seek a jury trial. We reject that proposal and hold that the Court of Appeals erred in reversing the District Court's decision to dissolve the injunction.

The judgment of the United States Court of Appeals for the Eighth Circuit is therefore reversed, and the case is remanded for further proceedings consistent with this opinion.

It is so ordered.

Notes

1. *Sufficiency of Stipulations*

Stipulations are required to cover claims for contributions, indemnity, cost and attorney's fees. *Odeco Oil & Gas Co. v. Bonnette*, 74 F.3d 671, 1996 AMC 913 (5th Cir. 1996).

2. *The Six-Month Rule*

The six-month rule of 46 U.S.C.A. § 30511 (formerly 46 app. U.S.C. § 185) is a time bar with respect to a vessel owner's filing of a petition for limitation of liability. But suppose a plaintiff asserts a claim that is substantially less than the value of the ship and, four years later, amends his complaint to assert additional damages. When does the six-month period begin? *See Complaint of Morania Barge No. 190, Inc.*, 690 F.2d 32, 1982 AMC 2679 (2d Cir. 1982).

3. *Trial by Jury*

There is no right to a jury trial in limitation proceeding. If, however, a party is entitled to a jury determination as to a liability issue, the court may impanel a jury for this purpose. *See McKeithen v. Steamship Frosta*, 75 F.R.D. 7, 1978 AMC 12 (E.D. La. 1977). Where the exceptions to the concursus rule are not applicable and plaintiffs are enjoined from bringing their common law claims in state court, should their request for a jury trial on the merits of their claims be granted. *See Complaint Poling Transp. Corp.*, 776 F. Supp. 779, 1992 AMC 1075 (S.D.N.Y. 1991).

4. *Joinder of Parties and Claims*

Liberal rules of joinder are applied in a limitation proceeding, allowing the court to adjudicate the claims and cross-claims of all vessel interests. *See British Transport Commission v. United States*, 354 U.S. 129, 77 S. Ct. 1103, 1 L. Ed. 2d 1234, 1957 AMC 1151 (1957).

What is the procedure if limitation is denied? *Compare Hartford Accident & Indemnity Co. v. Southern Pacific Co.*, 273 U.S. 207, 47 S. Ct. 357, 71 L. Ed. 612, 1927 AMC 402 (1927) and *In re Petition of Wood*, 230 F.2d 197, 1956 AMC 547 (2d Cir. 1956).

---

4. Interplay of State and Federal Proceedings: Raising Limitation Defensively

Notes

1. *Raising Limitation Defensively*

A shipowner has two procedural methods for limiting its liability under the Act. It may file a limitation petition in federal district court within six months of receiving "written notice of claim". 46 U.S.C.A. § 30511 (formerly 46 app. U.S.C. § 185). Alternatively, the shipowner may plead limitation as a defense in an answer filed in any court, including a state court. 46 U.S.C.A. §§ 30505-30506 (formerly 46 app. U.S.C. § 183). However, if the shipowner's right to limit liability is contested, only a federal court may exercise jurisdiction of the matter. Langnes v. Green, 282 U.S. 531, 51 S. Ct. 243, 75 L. Ed. 2d 520 (1931).

In Vatican Shrimp Co. Inc. v. Solis, 820 F.2d 674, 1987 AMC 2426 (5th Cir. 1987), the court held that a shipowner sued in state court forfeits its right to limit liability if it does not file a §185 petition in federal court within six months. The court said:

> [W]e recognize that shipowners may choose to set up the defense of limitation of liability under either method: by pleading the substantive provisions of section 183 in a properly filed answer in any court, or by filing a section 185 petition in a federal district court. However, if a shipowner is sued in state court, the owner's

failure to file a section 185 petition in a federal district court within six months after receiving written notice of the claim will result in forfeiture of the right to limit liability should the claimant contest the limitation defense. This is so because solely filing in the state court an answer in which limitation is pled obviously does not provide a federal court with jurisdiction to act. In contrast, defensive pleading under section 183 in a federal district court answer does not present the same jurisdictional problems. The district court, having jurisdiction to hear the entire case initially filed with it, can adjudicate and rule on a limited liability issue that is raised in a properly filed answer.

In sum, once written notice of a claim is received, unless that notice is a complaint filed in federal court, the prudent shipowner would file a timely section 185 petition in district court and move to stay the federal proceedings on the limitation petition until such time as limited liability is contested. This practice will ensure that a federal court may exercise its exclusive jurisdiction to hear the limitation issue even if the claimant eventually files suit in a state court and contests limitation more than six months after giving written notice of the claim.

Vatican Shrimp Co. Inc. v. Solis, 820 F.2d 674, 678-79 (5th Cir. 1987).

2. *State Court Proceedings*

Notwithstanding *Vatican Shrimp, supra,* several courts have held that the limitation of liability statute may be raised in a state court even though no concursus limitation proceeding had been filed in federal court. *Mapco Petroleum, Inc. v. Memphis Barge Line, Inc.*, 849 S.W.2d 312, 1993 AMC 2113 (Tenn.), *cert. denied,* 510 U.S. 815, 114 S. Ct. 64, 126 L. Ed. 2d 33 (1993); *Howell v. American Casualty Co.*, 691 So. 2d 715, 1997 AMC 1739 (La. App. 4 Cir. 1997).

3. *Federal Court Proceedings in Diversity*

In *Hellweg v. Baja Boats, Inc.*, 818 F. Supp. 1022, 1993 AMC 2122 (E.D. Mich. 1992), the court disagreed with the *obiter* view expressed by the *Vatican Shrimp* court that:

[D]efensive pleading under section 183 in a federal district court answer does not present the same jurisdictional problems. The district court, having jurisdiction to hear the entire case initially filed with it, can adjudicate and rule on a limited liability issue that is raised in a properly filed answer.

The *Hellweg* court held that this might be true if the federal district court had jurisdiction over the filed claim in admiralty, but it was not true if the basis of the district court's jurisdiction was diversity. The court said:

> As previously stated, a case present before the district court as a civil action over which the court has jurisdiction solely due to the diversity of the parties, must be treated as would the same action filed in state court. This treatment includes the realization that the court in diversity cannot adjudicate matters only cognizable before a court exercising its admiralty jurisdiction. This disposition does not deny shipowners their admiralty rights to limit their liability pursuant to 46 U.S.C.App. §§ 183 and 185. Section 183 can be raised as a defense to an *in personam* action filed in any court. If contested, however, the issue can only be adjudicated by a district court presiding over the case as filed in admiralty. This is so because § 183 provides a defense to admiralty actions that are not filed *in rem* and, therefore, are not otherwise limited to the value of the vessel. The relief provided by the procedures of § 185 is available to any shipowner sued in any court so long as the procedures are followed. Defendants did not comply with the procedures of § 185, and this Court will not allow them to circumvent these procedures and now petition the Court to exercise its admiralty jurisdiction through § 183. Defendants can raise the defense, but that does not confer jurisdiction where it does not already lie. Defendants failed to petition the Court under § 185 at their own peril, and now they must accept the consequences.

Hellweg, 818 F. Supp. at 1028-29.

B. The Limitation Fund

COMPLAINT OF CARIBBEAN SEA TRANSPORT, LTD.

748 F.2d 622, 1985 AMC 1995 (11th Cir. 1984)

[The facts and first part of the court's opinion are provided *supra*, Eds.]

* * *

B. Section 183(a) and Pending Freight

As mentioned above, a condition to bringing a limitation action is that the shipowner deposit with the court as security a sum equal to the value of the vessel and pending freight, unless the owner transfers his interest in the vessel and freight to a trustee. The law is well established that the valuation of the vessel is its value at the termination of the voyage. *Norwich Co. v. Wright*, 13 Wall. (80 U.S.) 104, 20 L. Ed. 585 (1872). "Freight," as used in the Limitation Act, refers to the compensation received for carriage of goods, and not the goods themselves. "Pending freight" is the total earnings for the voyage, both prepaid and uncollected. *The Main v. Williams*, 152 U.S. 122, 131, 14 S. Ct. 486, 488, 38 L. Ed. 381 (1894); *The William J. Riddle*, 111 F. Supp. 657, 658 (S.D.N.Y. 1953).

[On Petition for rehearing, *Complaint of Caribbean Sea Transport, Ltd.*, 753 F.2d 948, 949 (11th Cir. 1985) the following paragraph was substituted for deleted language:]

> Freight is generally not "earned," and thus is not pending," until the cargo is carried to and delivered at the place of destination. *Pacific Coast Co. v. Reynolds*, 114 F. 877, 881-82 (9th Cir.), *cert. denied*, 187 U.S. 640, 23 S. Ct. 841, 47 L. Ed. 345 (1902); *see* G. GILMORE & C. BLACK, JR., THE LAW OF ADMIRALTY § 10-32 (2d Ed. 1975). However, pending freight includes "prepaid freight which under the terms of [the shipowner's] agreement with his shippers is not to be returned in case the voyage is not completed." 3 BENEDICT ON ADMIRALTY § 65 (7th Ed. 1983); *see In re LaBourgogne*, 210 U.S. 95, 136, 28 S. Ct. 664, 679, 52 L. Ed. 973 (1908).

In our present case it is undisputed that the vessel is lying at the bottom of the sea and has no value whatsoever. However, appellant raises a number of attacks on the court's $82,000 valuation of "freight pending on the voyage." Peeling away the appellant's various arguments, the bone of contention on this issue boils down to the factual question of what constitutes "the voyage" in this case. Appellant asserts that "the voyage" was merely the ship's return trip from Kingston to Miami. The appellee contends that "the voyage" encompasses the entire round trip of the ship from Miami back to Miami.

What constitutes a voyage is a question of fact, which depends on the circumstances of the situation. *The William J. Riddle*, 111 F. Supp. at 658. Where an accident occurs on the return of a round-trip voyage, it may be that only the freight on the return voyage is "pending." For instance, in *In re La Bourgogne*, 210 U.S. 95, 28 S. Ct. 664, 52 L. Ed. 973 (1908), a vessel made trips between France and New York without any intermediate stops, discharging freight and picking up new freight at each end of the journey. The vessel collided with another ship on one of its trips from New York to France. The court held that each of these trips between France and New York or vice-versa was a separate voyage, so that the owner did not need to surrender freight earned in the ship's prior sailing from France to New York. *Id.*

However, if a round-trip voyage is equivalent to a "single adventure," earned freight *for the round trip* must be surrendered even if the collision occurs on the return leg of the trip after delivery of all cargo to various points. For example, in *The San Simeon*, 63 F.2d 798 (2d Cir.), *cert. denied*, 290 U.S. 643, 54 S. Ct. 61, 78 L. Ed. 558 (1933), the ship was on a voyage from the Pacific Coast to New York and Philadelphia. She had delivered cargo in New York, thus necessarily earning freight on it, and she was sailing up the Delaware River with the remainder of her cargo when she collided. The Second Circuit determined that "the voyage" encompassed the entire trip from the West Coast to Philadelphia; and that "pending freight" thus included freight already earned on cargo that was delivered in New York. Likewise, in *The William J. Riddle*, 111 F. Supp. 657, the court held that the round trip constituted the voyage. There, a steamship carrying a cargo of animals to foreign ports delivered the animals to the ports and returned to the United States empty except for the animal handlers. The following evidence indicated that "the voyage" encompassed the round trip: there was no expectation of return cargo; the ship's accountant carried the round trip on his logs as a single voyage; and the bill of lading and manifest of the ship provided for the round trip of the animal handlers. *Id.* at 658. *La Bourgogne* was distinguished as a situation where each east or west-bound trip had no connection whatsoever in purpose with the preceding trip in the other direction. *Id.*

The facts of this case fall under the holdings of *The William J. Riddle* and *The San Simeon*. Evidence indicated that the ANTILLES was running a typical "liner" service in which it would pick up cargo in Miami, make a circle of deliveries, and come back to the originating port in Miami, normally with an empty cargo hold. The cargo manifests of the ANTILLES, kept in the ordinary course of business, classified as a single voyage the entire trip leaving from Miami on February 11th to deliver cargo in Aruba, Curacao, and Antigua. From this evidence in the record, the district judge properly determined that the entire trip constituted "the voyage."[2] Thus, all freight earned on the deliveries of cargo prior to the collision should be posted as security pursuant to section 183.

[On Petition for rehearing, *Complaint of Caribbean Sea Transport, Ltd.* 753 F.2d 948, 949-50 (11th Cir. 1985) the following language was substituted for deleted language:]

> The cargo manifests of the ANTILLES indicate that the appellant earned freight on the voyage in the amount of $74,558.71 by the completed delivery of cargo prior to the collision. This is pending freight that must be posted as security pursuant to sec-

[2] Appellant distorts the *Le Bourgogne* holding, arguing that the concept of "voyage" in admiralty practice is equivalent to each trip from one port to another. However, under our present facts each trip from one port to another was merely a leg of the voyage. As the district judge realized, appellant's interpretation would mean that a ship would never have "pending freight" in the situation of an open sea collision, because the ship could not have earned any freight between the time it left its last port and the time of the collision. The only time there would then be "pending freight" is when the ship arrives at a port, delivers its cargo, and right after delivery sinks before it can leave port.

tion 183(a). However, it appears that when the ship sank it still contained cargo which was to have been delivered to Antigua, for which freight was prepaid in the amount of $7,900. The record on appeal does not indicate whether the shipping agreement underlying this carriage of goods permits the shipper to recover the amount of prepaid freight in the event the goods are not delivered because the voyage cannot be completed. Therefore, we affirm the district court's order as far as it requires the posting of $74,558.71 as security pursuant to section 183(a). This amount, plus 6% interest running from July 27, 1982 (the date this limitation proceeding was commenced), must be immediately posted to enable appellant to continue these limitation proceedings. We vacate the portion of the district court's order requiring the posting of security under section 183(a) over the amount of $74,558.71, and remand for further proceedings to determine whether an additional $7,900 should be posted under that section. If, under the terms of the shipping agreement, the prepaid freight can and will be recovered by the shipper because the goods were not delivered, then the appellant need not post the $7,900 amount. *Pacific Coast*, 114 F. at 882. If the shipping agreement does not permit the shipper to recover this prepaid freight, the $7,900 is completely earned, constitutes "pending freight," and must be posted as security. *LaBourgone*, 210 U.S. at 136, 28 S. Ct. at 679; *The Steel Inventor*, 36 F.2d 399, 400 (S.D.N.Y. 1929).

C. Section 183(b) and the Personal Injury Claim

Section 183(b) was passed to protect claimants who have suffered bodily injury or loss of life, and provides that when the section 183(a) limitation fund "is insufficient to pay all losses in full," then the shipowner will be required to meet the claims for personal injuries up to an amount equal to $60* per ton of the vessel's tonnage. Appellant contends that the district court improperly granted the $30,000 of additional security under this subsection, arguing that additional security should be required only when the section 183(a) limitation fund is rendered insufficient to meet all the claims: that is, only once the limitation proceeding is concluded and the personal injury claims are liquidated; or in the alternative, only upon a clear showing that the section 183(a) fund will be insufficient to cover all the personal injury claims.

The law is not clear as to when, how, and under what conditions the court can order additional security posted under section 183(b). As Gilmore states;

> [a]ssume that death and injury claims have been filed against a shipowner who petitions for limitation, alleging that the value of the ship (which has been lost) is zero. Could the court with which the limitation petition is filed require the owner, as a condition of limitation, to post bond in an amount sufficient (up to the statutory ceiling) to satisfy his maximum liability under the claims (which are still unliquidated); or should the court first determine the basic questions of liability and right to limitation before requiring the owner to provide funds or sureties to satisfy the judgments? The first alternative would be more satisfactory to claimants who would be

* [Subsequently increased to $420 per ton. Eds.]

> protected against supervening insolvency of the shipowner or dissipation of assets during possible protracted judicial proceedings; the second alternative would be more to the shipowner's liking. The statute offers no sure guide to solution, although, on a purely verbal level of statutory construction, the statement that the $60 per ton fund comes into operation only "if the amount of the owner's liability as limited under subsection (a) is insufficient" might be read to suggest that the questions of liability and limitation under section 183(a) must be first settled before the additional fund is set up. However in two recent cases where the aggregate of the death and injury claims was many times in excess of the section 183(a) fund, the trial judges sensibly ordered that section 183(b) funds be set up at the outset of the proceedings.

G. Gilmore & C. Black, Jr., The Law of Admiralty, § 10-34 (2d Ed. 1975). Gilmore also notes that the provision in Admiralty Rule F(7), that "any claimant may demand that the deposit or security be increased on the ground that it is insufficient to carry out the provision of the statutes relating to claims in respect of loss of life or bodily injury," should presumably be taken to increase the limitation court's discretion in granting such "demands." *Id.* at n.138a.

The two recent cases cited by Gilmore are *In Re Pan Oceanic Tankers Corp.*, 332 F. Supp. 313 (S.D.N.Y. 1971), and *In Re Alva Steamship Company*, 262 F. Supp. 328 (S.D.N.Y. 1966), which were both mass disaster cases where the district courts required the posting of additional security pursuant to section 183(b) when the dollar amount of personal injury and loss of life claims was much greater than the section 183(a) limitation fund.[4] These cases indicate that a district judge does have discretion to augment the security fund pursuant to section 183(b) prior to the conclusion of the limitation proceedings and the liquidation of personal injury claims.

However, section 183(b) does provide that the owner's liabiity to personal injury claimants will be increased only if the section 183(a) fund "is insufficient to pay all losses in full." Thus we think that personal injury claimants must make a clear, preliminary showing that the section 183(a) fund will be insufficient to cover all personal injury claims before a court should augment that fund under section 183(b). We hold that in order to augment the security fund pursuant to section 183(b), the district court must make preliminary determinations of the nature and extent of personal injury claims and the likelihood of recovery based on those claims, concluding that there is a likelihood that the section 183(a) fund will be insufficient to pay those claims in full. This will usually require some sort of evidentiary hearing. We emphasize that the product of such a hearing does not represent a final adjudication of liability and damages, but merely represents a preliminary appraisal of the shipowner's exposure to damages.

---

[4] In *Pan Oceanic*, the section 183(a) fund was $100.00, compared to unliquidated claims for loss of life or bodily injury totalling $28,500,000.00. Thus the court considered it appropriate to increase the fund pursuant to section 183(b). 332 F. Supp. at 314-15. In *Alva Steamship*, the shipowner was faced with approximately $30,000,000.00 in personal injury claims. Although he had already posted section 183(a) security, the court required the owner to post bond under section 183(b) equivalent to $60.00 per ton of his vessel. 262 F. Supp. at 330.

In our present case, the district court required the posting of section 183(b) security after a cursory hearing in which no evidence was taken. It does appear that evidence as to Russo's injury was available in the form of medical reports and Russo's deposition; but none of this evidence is present in the record of this case. At the hearing, Russo's counsel alleged that as a result of the collision Russo was knocked unconscious and hospitalized with a fractured vertebra; but there is no indication of the seriousness of this injury. Russo is the only claimant alleging personal injury in this case, so this is certainly not a mass disaster situation with huge potential liability. A remand would be unnecessary if Russo's counsel had presented any evidence regarding the nature and extent of injury; but under the circumstances of this case, we must vacate that portion of the district court's order requiring the posting of $30,000 security pursuant to section 183(b), and remand to the district court for a hearing and preliminary factual determination under the aforementioned standards.[5]

Therefore, the district court's opinion is AFFIRMED in part, and VACATED and REMANDED in part for further proceedings not inconsistent with this opinion.

Note: Prior Encumbrances

Supplemental Rule F does not require a shipowner to pay or secure all pre-existing encumbrances against the vessel before filing a limitation proceeding. The pleader must simply "show in his complaint the prior paramount liens and any existing liens that arose upon subsequent voyages." *In the Matter of Rodco Marine Services v. Migliaccio*, 651 F.2d 1101, 1985 AMC 605 (5th Cir. 1981). In *Rodco Marine Services*, the court held that a ship mortgage affecting the vessel is not a prior encumbrance that bars the owner from filing a proceeding to limit his liability and that "salvage claims are not prior encumbrances but instead are part of the claims arising from the voyage during which the casualty occurred and probably become a part of the limitation proceeding." The court stated that:

> [T]here is no condition precedent to an owner of a vessel filing a petition for limitation of his liability. The petitioner must offer to surrender title of the vessel to a trustee to be appointed by the court or alternatively offer to pay into court a sum equal to the value of the vessel. If a trustee is appointed the vessel must be sold and the proceeds paid into the registry of the court. The court then determines the priority of the liens against the fund. If the entire fund is not available to voyage claimants, distribution should be made to the proper lienors and the owner denied exoneration.

Note: Computation of the Limitation Fund

Under American law the fund is equal to the value of the vessel after the casualty plus the pending freight. *Norwich & New York Transportation Co. v. Wright*, 80 U.S. (13 Wall.) 104, 20 L. Ed. 585 (1871). Compare the following provisions of the 1976 Convention on the Limitation of Maritime Claims, as amended by the 1996 Protocol:

---

[5] At this hearing, the appellant shipowner may also present evidence as to the space occupied by seamen on the ANTILLES, which is excluded from the gross tonnage of the ship to reach the "tonnage" figure which is multiplied by $60 to obtain the amount of the section 183(b) fund. *See* 46 U.S.C. § 183(b), (c). We think that the shipowner properly has the burden of proof on the calculation of "tonnage" under section 183(c).

Article 6 - The General Limits

1. The limits of liability for claims other than those mentioned in Article 7, arising on any distinct occasion, shall be calculated as follows:

(a) in respect of claims for loss of life or personal injury,

(i) 2 million Units of Account for a ship with a tonnage not exceeding 2,000 tons,
(ii) for a ship with a tonnage in excess thereof, the following amount in addition to that mentioned in (i): for each ton from 2,001 to 30,000 tons, 800 Units of Account; for each ton from 30,001 to 70,000 tons, 600 Units of Account; and for each ton in excess of 70,000 tons, 400 Units of Account,

(b) in respect of any other claims,

(i) 1 million Units of Account for a ship with a tonnage not exceeding 2,000 tons,
(ii) for a ship with a tonnage in excess thereof, the following amount in addition to that mentioned in (i): for each ton from 2,001 to 30,000 tons, 400 Units of Account; for each ton from 30,001 to 70,000 tons, 300 Units of Account; and for each ton in excess of 70,000 tons, 200 Units of Account.

2. Where the amount calculated in accordance with paragraph 1(a) is insufficient to pay the claims mentioned therein in full, the amount calculated in accordance with paragraph 1(b) shall be available for payment of the unpaid balance of claims under paragraph 1(a) and such unpaid balance shall rank ratably with claims mentioned under paragraph 1(b).
3. However, without prejudice to the right of claims for loss of life or personal injury according to paragraph 2, a State Party may provide in its national law that claims in respect of damage to harbor works, basins and waterways and aids to navigation shall have such priority over other claims under paragraph 1(b) as is provided by that law.
4. The limits of liability for any salvor not operating from any ship or for any salvor operating solely on the ship to, or in respect of which he is rendering salvage services, shall be calculated according to a tonnage of 1,500 tons.
5. For the purpose of this Convention the ship's tonnage shall be the gross tonnage calculated in accordance with the tonnage measurement rules contained in Annex I of the International Convention on Tonnage Measurement of Ships, 1969.

Article 7—The Limits for Passenger Claims

1. In respect of claims arising on any distinct occasion for loss of life or personal injury to passengers of a ship, the limit of liability of the shipowner thereof shall be an amount of 175,000 Units of Account multiplied by the number of passengers which the ship is authorized to carry according to the ship's certificate.
2. For the purpose of this Article "claims for loss of life or personal injury to passengers of a ship" shall mean any such claims brought by or on behalf of any person carried in that ship:

(a) under a contract of passenger carriage, or
(b) who, with the consent of the carrier, is accompanying a vehicle or live animals which are covered by a contract for the carriage of goods.

Article 8 - Unit of Account

1. The Unit of Account referred to in Articles 6 and 7 is the Special Drawing Right as defined by the International Monetary Fund. The amounts mentioned in Articles 6 and 7 shall be converted into the

> national currency of the State in which limitation is sought, according to the value of that currency at the date the limitation fund shall have been constituted, payment is made, or security is given which under the law of that State is equivalent to such payment. The value of a national currency in terms of the Special Drawing Right, of a State Party which is a member of the International Monetary Fund, shall be calculated in accordance with the method of valuation applied by the International Monetary Fund in effect at the date in question of its operations and transactions. The value of a national currency in terms of the Special Drawing Right, of a State Party which is not a member of the International Monetary Fund, shall be calculated in a manner determined by that State Party.

[**NB:** The International Monetary Fund publishes exchange rates for the Special Drawing Right to various international currencies. They can be found at http://www.imf.org/external/np/tre/sdr/db/rms_five.cfm. On December 21st, 2004, the exchange rate of the S.D.R. to the U.S. dollar was 1 to 1.539620. At that exchange rate, the 2 million S.D.R. limit in the first step of the scale for loss of life or personal injury would be worth US$3,079,240. The limit for subsequent steps would be correspondingly higher. Eds.]

Note: The "Flotilla" Rule

In *Liverpool, Brazil and River Plate Steam Navigation Co. v. Brooklyn Eastern District Terminal*, 251 U.S. 48, 40 S. Ct. 66, 64 L. Ed. 130 (1919), the court held that where two or more vessels under common ownership are involved in the same accident, only the vessel actively at fault (the tug) must be valued or surrendered for purposes of the limitation fund. In *Sacramento Navigation Co. v. Salz*, 273 U.S. 326, 47 S. Ct. 368, 71 L. Ed. 663, 1927 AMC 397 (1927), the court, in a Harter Act case not involving the limitation act, stated that a tug and barge were considered one vessel. In dicta, the court distinguished *Liverpool* as involving "pure tort, not a contract of affreightment". This spawned the "flotilla" rule based on a contractual obligation theory that all vessels engaged in a marine venture must be included in the limitation fund. *Standard Dredging Co. v. Kristiansen*, 67 F.2d 548, 1933 AMC 1621 (2d Cir. 1933).

In *South Carolina State Highway Department v. Jacksonville Shipyards, Inc.*, 1976 AMC 456 (S.D. Ga. 1975), the court, in a case in which the master of a tug negligently allowed a barge to hit a bridge, included only the value of the tug and her freight in the limitation proceeding. The court explained:

> Lower courts have reluctantly followed *Liverpool* in pure tort situations.... In [one] case the district court said that it is "at least doubtful whether the *Liverpool* doctrine is responsive to the realities of the situation."
>
> The rigidity of the "pure tort" concept has been relaxed by distinct courts able to find that the barge itself was an "offending vessel" independently of the propelling tug to which it was attached or temporarily detached. A distinction has been drawn where a tow breaks away from a tug and "the independent act of the barge breaking its mooring ... resulted in damage to the pier." A similar result was reached [in another case where] barges had been moored by a tug that temporarily detached itself and in the interim they had broken loose from their mooring damaging a lock an dam on the Ohio River.
>
> * * *
>
> The doctrinal treatment by federal courts of limitation of liability in flotilla type situations is illogical when the result is (a) that a tug and attached barge are considered as two separate vessels if the damage to a third party amounts to a *tort* and the tug is the offending instrumentality, but (b) where a *contractual* element is involved, the same tug and barge constitute a single vessel when damage to a contracting party occurs through fault of the tow.
>
> The collision with the Hilton Head bridge was by the barge and not the tug. It would not have occurred except for the presence of the former alongside *Jax I* which considerably increased the total beam of the flotilla. The barge was pushed into the fenders by the tug which was the offending vessel. The barge was merely a

passive, well-less component of the rig. In short, the instant case simply cannot be distinguished from the fact background that underlay the 56-year old decision in *Liverpool.*

The able, always interesting and occasionally crusading authors of THE LAW OF ADMIRALTY [GILMORE AND BLACK] (who predict it to be most unlikely that the Supreme Court "will ever agree to hear another flotilla case") challenge "some daring federal judge" to come forward and give the *Liverpool* decision that "cavalier treatment" which the federal courts have accorded to it in the case of the exception where a flotilla is used in performance of a contract. The worst that can happen to such a judge is that he will be reversed....

Several comments are appropriate in respect to this ringing call to district court judges. First, the Congress enacted the legislation out of which grew the controversial interpretation thereof in Liverpool. The legislative branch can change the law when it desires. Secondly (and relatedly), the question of flotilla liability is subsumed by the imperious issue of continued existence of the limitation theory. Should it be scuttled as an archaic vestige of the days of merchant sailing ships and coal-burning steamships? Finally, district courts are bound by decisions of the Supreme Court and the law is settled by *Liverpool....*

All that can be hoped of in this case, assuming an appeal and affirmance, is that the Supreme Court will see fit to grant certiorari and agree to reappraise its 1919 decision which so effectively and regrettably forecloses a contrary ruling below.

Some courts have been more adventurous. Notwithstanding the *Liverpool, Brazil and River Plate* decision by the Supreme Court, several lower courts have required that the limitation fund equal the value of several vessels engaged in a common project, even when the claims are made in tort. *In re United States Dredging Corp.*, 264 F.2d 339 (2d Cir. 1959); *Brown & Root Marine Operators, Inc. v. Zapata Off-Shore Co.*, 377 F.2d 724, 727 (5th Cir. 1967), *Cenac Towing Co. v. Terra Resources, Inc.*, 734 F.2d 251 (5th Cir. 1984), *Complaint of Tom-Mac, Inc.*, 76 F.3d 678, 684, 1996 AMC 1244 (5th Cir. 1996), *In re Offshore Specialty Fabricators, Inc.*, 2002 AMC 2055 (E.D. La. 2002).

Note: Distribution of the Fund

Rule F (8) governs the distribution of the limitation fund. In distributing the fund, courts apply lien priority rules as principles of equitable subordination to give preference to personal injury and cargo claimants over a negligent vessel's claim for collision damages. *The CATSKILL*, 95 F. 700 (S.D.N.Y. 1899).

In collision cases the balance of damages must be struck before limitation. *The North Star*, 106 U.S. 17, 26-29, 1 S. Ct. 41, 27 L. Ed. 91 (1882).

Are personal injury claimants restricted to the 46 U.S.C.A. § 30506(b) (formerly section 183 (b)) tonnage fund? *See Oliver J. Olsen & Co. v. American Steamship Marine Leopard,* 356 F.2d 728, 1966 AMC 1064 (9th Cir. 1966).

C. Parties and Vessels Entitled to Limit

1. Demise vs. Time Charterer

Note

In Complaint of Cook Transportation System, Inc., 431 F. Supp. 437, 442-43 (W.D. Tenn. 1976), the court said:

A demise or bareboat charterer may, then, also rely upon the limitation act in the same fashion as the owner. Spooner & Son v. Conn. Fire Ins. Co., 206 F. Supp. 495, 507 (S.D.N.Y., 1962); the limitation act, Sec.

186, "unamended since 1851, provides that a charterer who shall 'man, victual and navigate' the vessel, 'at his own expense, or by his own procurement' shall be deemed an 'owner' within the meaning of the act." GILMORE & BLACK, THE LAW OF ADMIRALTY, (1957) Chapter X, Page 673. The authors proceed to point out that "this means that so-called bareboat or demise charterers may limit but that time charters under the usual arrangement may not." (Sec. 10-10). This is further explained by the same authors in Sec. 10-28: 'The time charterer or the voyage charterer, where the owner continues to man, victual and navigate the vessel, may not limit.'

---

2. *Shipowner's Insurer*

Notes

1. *Insurance*

In Louisiana and Puerto Rico, by statute, direct actions against the insurer are allowed, but insurance carriers are denied the benefit of limitation of liability because this privilege is personal to the shipowner. In *Maryland Casualty Co. v. Cushing*, 347 U.S. 409, 74 S. Ct. 608, 98 L. Ed. 806, 1954 AMC 837 (1954), in a 4-1-4 split opinion, a majority of the justices nevertheless agreed that any conflict between a direct action statute and the Limitation Act could be resolved by staying the direct action suit until completion of the limitation proceeding. Thus, in these jurisdictions, if insurance policy amounts are sufficient to cover all claims, the limitation proceeding is moot. If, however, the insurance is insufficient, the shipowner who is granted limitation will receive credit for the insurance recovery. The maximum sum available to pay claims is then the greater of either the insurance fund or the limitation fund. *See in re Independent Towing Co.*, 242 F. Supp. 950, 1965 AMC 818 (E.D. La. 1965).

How does this differ from jurisdictions with no direct action statute?

2. *Direct Actions Against Insurers: The Limitation of Liability Defense*

In *Olympic Towing Corp. v. Nebel Towing Co.*, 419 F.2d 230, 1969 AMC 1571 (5th Cir. 1969), the court held that a shipowner's limitation of liability defense was personal and consequently not available to the shipowner's insurer when the latter was sued under the Louisiana direct action statute. In *Crown Zellerbach Corporation v. Ingram Enterprises, Inc.*, 783 F.2d 1296, 1986 AMC 1471 (5th Cir. 1986) (*en banc*), the insurer, who, sued under the Louisiana direct action statute, did not seek limitation of his liability on grounds of the owner's statutory right to limit under the Limitation of Liability Act. Instead, the insurer relied on a provision in the policy of insurance that limited his liability under the policy to the amount of the shipowner's liability after limitation. In an en banc decision, the court distinguished Nebel Towing and upheld the validity of the insurance policy clause that limited the insurer's exposure to the amount of the shipowner's liability after limitation. For discussion, *see* Gordon P. Gates, *Crown Zellerbach Dethrones Nobel Towing: Shipowner's Limitation of Liability Is Available To Insurers*, 62 Tul. L. Rev. 615, 615-23 (1988).

A limiting term in a marine insurance policy thus gives rise to a valid defense, and a direct-action plaintiff may not successfully challenge such a policy term on the grounds that the term contravenes either the Louisiana law or federal maritime law. *In the Matter of Magnolia Marine Transportation Co. v. Laplace Towing Corporation*, 964 F. 2d 1571, 1994 AMC 303 (5th Cir. 1992). The interpretation of a limiting term in a marine insurance policy does not fall within the exclusive jurisdiction of the limitation forum; state courts have concurrent jurisdiction under the "saving to suitors" clause. Id.

3. *Persons Entitled to Limit Liability*

Who is the "owner" of a vessel for purposes of asserting limitation? *See Caulkins v. Graham*, 667 F.2d 1292, 1982 AMC 2433 (9th Cir. 1982). Does limitation apply in favor of the United States? *See Dick v. United States*, 671 F.2d 724, 1982 AMC 913 (2d Cir. 1982).

Should the right to limit be extended to include time charterers and insurers? What about the master, the crew, salvors, or an independent contractor like a shipyard? Consider the following provision of the Convention on the Limitation of Maritime Claims, 1976:

Article 1. Persons Entitled to Limit Liability

1. Shipowners and salvors, as hereinafter defined, may limit their liability in accordance with the rules of this Convention for claims set out in Article 2. [claims subject to limitation].
2. The term shipowner shall mean the owner, charterer, manager and operator of a seagoing ship.
3. Salvor shall mean any person rendering services in direct connection with salvage operations. Salvage operations shall also include operations referred to in Article 2, paragraph 1 (d), (e) and (f) [raising, removal or destruction of the ship or cargo].
4. If any claims set out in Article 2 are made against any person or whose act, neglect or default the shipowner or salvor is responsible, such person shall be entitled to avail himself of the limitation of liability provided for in this Convention.
5. In this Convention the liability of a shipowner shall include liability in an action brought against the vessel herself.
6. An insurer of liability for claims subject to limitation in accordance with the rules of this Convention shall be entitled to the benefits of this Convention to the same extent as the assured himself.
7. The act of invoking limitation of liability shall not constitute an admission of liability.

4. ***Vessels Subject to Limitation***

Pleasure boats are, generally, vessels for purposes of admiralty jurisdiction. *See Sisson v. Ruby*, 497 U.S. 358, 110 S. Ct. 2892, 111 L. Ed. 2d 292, 1990 AMC 1801 (1990). Are pleasure boats also vessels for purposes of the Limitation of Liability Act? *See* Rodriguez and Jaffe, *An Overview of U.S. Law of Shipowners Limitation of Liability*, MLA Report 9621, 9625-9628 (October 31, 1991):

> The application of the Act to pleasure vessels has been more problematic, and this issue has generated considerable litigation in the last several years. Since 1975, eight federal courts of appeal have taken up the question. Seven of these courts have concluded that the Act is applicable to pleasure craft. However, in 1989, the Seventh Circuit decided to "go it alone" in the *Sisson* case by holding that limitation was unavailable to a private pleasure craft. This holding was reversed by the U.S. Supreme Court, but the Court did not specifically address the issue of the Act's general applicability to pleasure craft.
>
> Those courts which have held that the Act applies to pleasure craft have noted that, as originally enacted, the Limitation Act expressly stated that it did not apply to "any canal boat, barge, or lighter, or to any vessel of any description whatsoever, used in rivers or inland navigation." In 1886, Congress amended that Act to extend it to include "... all vessels used on lakes or rivers or in inland navigation." Thereafter, the Act was applied to pleasure craft as early as 1927; yet when the Act was amended in 1935, 1936, and 1984, no attempt was made to exclude pleasure craft from its ambit. Therefore, these courts have determined that, although application of the Act to pleasure craft might be illogical, the working of the Act and its legislative history dictate such a result.
>
> The circuit court in *Sisson* and those district courts which have refused to permit application of the Act to pleasure craft have adopted a quite different approach, relying on jurisdictional arguments to deny limitation. In particular, these courts have held that where there is no admiralty jurisdiction over the underlying tort, the Limitation Act does not provide a separate basis for admiralty jurisdiction. Under this analysis, the court would be without subject matter jurisdiction to decide limitation. It also has been held that the Limitation Act does not confer upon the federal court either Federal Question jurisdiction or Commerce Clause jurisdiction.
>
> In *Sisson*, a pleasure yacht docked at a marina on Lake Michigan caught fire. The fire destroyed the yacht and caused extensive damage to the marina and several other boats. The Seventh Circuit held that, although the fire at the marina satisfied the locality test of admiralty jurisdiction, it did not meet the Nexus test as the tort did not bear a significant relationship to "traditional maritime activity." The circuit court, therefore, held that there was no admiralty jurisdiction. Additionally, the court rejected the argument that the Limitation Act

provides a separate basis of admiralty jurisdiction notwithstanding a 1911 Supreme Court decision which held the Act to be applicable both to non-maritime and maritime torts. The court of appeals refuse to follow the 1911 decision because 1) the need that inspired that decision no longer exists and 2) the decision predated the new, more restrictive tests for admiralty jurisdiction.

The Supreme Court decision in the *Sisson* case reversed that of the Seventh Circuit and remanded the case for further proceedings. The court held that a fire in a marina does meet the admiralty nexus test and therefore that admiralty jurisdiction existed. Additionally, the Supreme Court left open the question of whether the Limitation Act itself provides an independent basis for admiralty jurisdiction where the facts of a case do not meet the "nexus" test of admiralty jurisdiction. Interestingly, even though the Supreme Court had requested the parties to brief the continuing validity of that case even though it has been strongly questioned and expressly not followed by the Seventh Circuit.

By limiting its ruling solely to the admiralty tort jurisdiction test, and by expressing this test in broad terms, the Supreme Court has left open many potential challenges to application of the Limitation Act to pleasure craft. Therefore, it is likely that, notwithstanding the appellate decisions holding that the Act does apply to pleasure craft, the considerable amount of litigation on this point will continue.

One of the most dramatic examples of the application of the Limitation Act to pleasure craft is a decision holding that the Act applies to limit the liability of the owner of a jet-ski. *Keys Jet Ski Inc. v. Kays,* 893 F.2d 1225, 1990 AMC 609 (11th Cir. 1990).

Are airplanes, seaplanes, and helicopters "vessels" for purposes of limitation of liability? *See Hubschman v. Antilles Airboats*, 440 F. Supp. 828 (D. V. I. 1977); *Noakes v. Imperial Airways*, 29 F. Supp. 412 (S.D.N.Y. 1939).

Is a wharfboat a vessel for purposes of limitation of liability? *See Evansville & Bowling Green Packet Co. v. Chero Cola Bottling Co.*, 271 U.S. 19, 46 S. Ct. 379, 70 L. Ed. 805 (1926).

Are offshore structures "vessels"? *See Texas Co. v. Savoie*, 240 F.2d 674, 1957 AMC 747 (5th Cir. 1957) and *In re United States Air Force Texas Tower No. 4*, 203 F. Supp. 215 (S.D.N.Y. 1962).

D. Grounds for Denying Limitation: Privity or Knowledge

WATERMAN STEAMSHIP CORPORATION v. GAY COTTONS

414 F.2d 724 (9th Cir. 1969)

DUNIWAY, Circuit Judge

On February 7, 1962, the S.S. CHICKASAW ran aground on Santa Rosa Island, off the coast of Southern California. The island is 40 miles long and 400 feet high. The ship had left Yokohama for Los Angeles on January 27, 1962. No celestial fixes had been obtained after noon on February 5, because of stormy weather. The crew took several fixes with the radio direction finder, which had no recent compensation card, but obtained "wildly divergent" results. The vessel's mechanical sounding device had been pried off the deck in Japan and sold for scrap. The fathometer was not used because Third Mate Jensen thought it was inoperative. He had last tried to use it while the ship was on Japan's Inland Sea on December 25, 1961, when he obtained red flashes all around the dial. He had told the master, Capt. Patronas, that the fathometer was inoperable, but the master did not have it checked at the next port. And the radar was broken, having stopped operating just before the ship's arrival in Japan. It had not been fixed because the repair company in Yokohama could not obtain the necessary part in Japan.

The stranding resulted in total loss of the vessel and substantial loss of cargo. Waterman Steamship Corp., her owner, petitioned for complete exoneration of liability under the Carriage of Goods by Sea Act (COGSA), 46 U.S.C. § 1300 *et seq.* or alternatively, for limitation of liability to the amount of its limitation fund, about $250,000, under the Limitation of Liability Act, 46 U.S.C. § 183(a). The cargo is claimed to be worth about two million dollars. Determination of the actual damages has been deferred until the question of liability has been resolved.

* * *

The District Court entered findings of fact and conclusions of law denying both exoneration and limitation. The court also filed a memorandum opinion which is reported at 265 F. Supp. 595, 1966 A.M.C. 2219. Waterman has appealed pursuant to 28 U.S.C. § 1292(a) (3). *See Republic of France v. United States*, 5 Cir., 1961, 290 F.2d 395, 397. We affirm.

Although there was substantial evidence that the vessel was unseaworthy because much of its navigational equipment was in poor shape and had not been inspected recently, the District Court rested its denial of exoneration and limitation solely on the ground that Capt. Patronas was negligent in failing to check the fathometer after Jensen had told him it was inoperative, and that Capt. Patronas' negligence was imputed to Waterman because he had been delegated entire managerial responsibility over repairs to the vessel in the Far East. The court specifically rejected findings proposed by appellees[3] which would have found "direct fault" by Waterman because of its failure to inspect and maintain the equipment, on the ground that such findings were beyond the scope of its memorandum decision.

Limitation of Liability—Negligence of the Captain

Under COGSA, 46 U.S.C. § 1304, the lack of due diligence of any employee which occurs before or at the beginning of a voyage and results in unseaworthiness is sufficient to preclude complete exoneration of liability. Under the Limitation of Liability Act, 46 U.S.C. § 183 (a), however, a shipowner is permitted to limit its liability to the value of its ship, plus freight charges, if it can prove that the lack of due diligence to make seaworthy was not within its "privity or knowledge."

But appellees contend that, because the owner's duty to make a vessel seaworthy is nondelegable, any negligence which results in unseaworthiness is presumed as a matter of law to be within the privity and knowledge of the owner. They rely on statements to that effect in *Federazione Italiana Dei Corsorzi Agrari v. Mandask Compania de Vapores, S.A. (THE PERAMA)*, 2 Cir., 1968, 388 F.2d 434, 439-440, in *States S.S. Co. v. United States (THE PENNSYLVANIA)*, 9 Cir., 1958, 259 F.2d 458, 474, and in GILMORE & BLACK, ADMIRALTY 696, 701-02 (2d ed. 1957). The *Perama* language, however, is dictum. The court had found that the lack of due diligence was attributable to employees who were "sufficiently high in the managerial hierarchy of the appellant so that their general and

[3] Appellees are claimants whose cargo was lost or damaged in the standing: Gay Cottons, Inc., Shalom Baby Wear, and the United States.

detailed knowledge and their close privity to the repair project was imputed to the corporation." 388 F.2d at 439 n.6. The *Perama* court cited GILMORE & BLACK, *States S.S. Co., supra,* and *W.R. Grace & Co. v. Charleston Lighterage & Transfer Co. (THE ONE LIGHTER),* 4 Cir., 1952, 193 F.2d 539. The latter case involved an old rotting barge which had not been repaired or properly inspected for a number of years. The court in *Perama* ignored several of its own recent cases which recognize that COGSA has different standards from those applicable under the Limitation Act.[12]

The *States Steamship* language was also dictum. The court had found that the negligence was attributable to one Vallet, a "port engineer" who was in charge of maintenance and repair of all the owner's vessels. On a petition for rehearing, we emphasized that we were denying limitation because the lack of due diligence was charged to managing officers of the corporation. We said that we were not holding that "in any case where the Steamship Company fails to use due diligence to make the vessel seaworthy at the inception of her voyage, limitation must be denied." 259 F.2d at 471-472. *See Avera v. Florida Towing Co. (THE EILEEN ROSS),* 5 Cir., 1963, 322 F.2d 155, 163 n.13, where the court, in discussing this circuit's opinion in *Admiral Towing Co. v. Woolen (THE COMPANION),* 9 Cir., 1961, 290 F.2d 641, 646-649, said "The 9th Circuit was especially careful not to adopt the broad view suggested in GILMORE & BLACK, ADMIRALTY, § 10-24, pp. 701-704 (1957), that privity and knowledge for a corporate shipowner is equated with nondelegable duties. *See* 290 F.2d 641 at 648, and note 6, p. 649."

Notwithstanding the conclusion of Gilmore & Black, we have found no case which has denied limitation of liability because of the negligence of a non-managerial employee. On the contrary, all cases denying limitation of liability to a corporate shipowner have emphasized that the negligence or lack of due diligence to make seaworthy was attributable to managerial personnel. Many cases have granted limitation of liability because the corporate owner proved that none of its managerial personnel were negligent or had notice of any negligence.

We conclude that standards under the Limitation Act are different from those under COGSA. The Shipowner is entitled to limitation of liability if it can show that the lack of due diligence is not within its "privity or knowledge." As to corporate owners, this has been interpreted to mean that the negligence must be that of a "managing officer" or, more properly, a "supervisory employee."

> While the cases generally speak of the knowledge of managing officers as being the knowledge of the corporation, the real test is not as to their being officers in a strict sense but as to the largeness of their authority. *In re P. Sanford Ross, Inc.*, 2 Cir., 1913, 204 F. 248, 251.

---

[12] In *Petition of Kinsman Transit Co.* (*THE MacGILVRAY SHIRAS*), 2 Cir., 1964, 338 F.2d 708, 714-716, limitation was granted where a non-managerial employee negligently moored a steamer in Buffalo. The company was headquartered in Cleveland, but at that time had four of its five vessels moored in Buffalo. In *Moore-McCormack Lines, Inc. v. Armco Steel Co.* (*THE MORMACKITE*), 2 Cir., 1959, 272 F.2d 873, 876-877, limitation was granted where the corporate owner's managing officers had no notice of the improper stowage of ore in South American ports in violation of the company's own rules. "As was obviously necessary in foreign ports, it was left to those in charge to follow these directions, and if they failed, their failure did not charge the owners with 'privity or knowledge.'"

> [A managing officer is] any one to whom the corporation has committed the general management or general superintendence of the whole or a particular part of its business. *The Marguerite*, 7 Cir., 1944, 140 F.2d 491, 494. *Petition of United States (THE EDMUND FANNING), supra*, 105 F. Supp. at 371. *See also Coryell v. Phipps (THE SEMINOLE)*, 1943, 317 U.S. 406, 410-411, 63 S. Ct. 291, 87 L. Ed. 363.

The District Court recognized that the negligence of a master is normally not imputed to the owner, but concluded that, because "entire managerial responsibility" had been delegated to Capt. Patronas to oversee repairs in the Far East, he was a "managing officer" with respect to decisions made within that delegation of authority. Consequently, his failure to check the fathometer after Jensen had said it was inoperative was within the "privity and knowledge" of Waterman.[17] Waterman does not contest the finding that its "entire managerial responsibility as respects repairs" had been delegated to Patronas. Instead, it only contests the conclusion that such delegation is sufficient to deny limitation of liability.

Although Capt. Patronas was the master of the S.S. CHICKASAW, his negligence, as found by the court, did not arise out of his authority over the vessel on the high seas. Instead, the finding rests on his failure to have the fathometer checked in the next port after Jensen had told him that it was inoperative. Certainly there is language in some of the cases which would indicate that limitation might be denied under such circumstances. Thus, in *Spencer Kellogg & Sons, Inc. v. Hicks (THE LINSEED KING)*, 1932, 285 U.S. 502, 511-512, 52 S. Ct. 450, 453, 76 L. Ed. 903, the Supreme Court distinguished *La Bourgogne*, 1908, 210 U.S. 95, 28 S. Ct. 664, 52 L. Ed. 973, as involving the master's failure to obey rules on the high seas, and said:

> There is no analogy between such a situation and that presented in the cited cases where the emergency must be met by the master alone. In these there is no opportunity of consultation or cooperation or of bringing the proposed action of the master to the owner's knowledge. The latter must rely upon the master's obeying rules and using reasonable judgment.

In *Admiral Towing Co. v. Woolen (THE COMPANION)*, 9 Cir., 1961, 290 F.2d 641, 648, limitation was denied where the individual owner of a tugboat knew that the master was going to hire a crewman, but made no attempt to insure that the crewman was competent. In dictum, we said that limitation would be granted even where the master has been given unlimited authority but his negligence was "instantaneous negligence ... over which

---

[17] *See* Finding of Fact 6:

> It was the Waterman Steamship Corporation's obligation to exercise due diligence to make the S.S. CHICKASAW seaworthy at the commencement of the voyage from the Far East. This included an obligation that the ship's navigational equipment be put in a suitable state of repair before going to sea.... As to repairs, Waterman placed all authority, including authority to decide whether repairs should be made at all, with the master, and had in the Far East no supervisory or managerial personnel to carry out its obligation to exercise due diligence to make the vessel seaworthy. Waterman therefore had delegated to the master its entire managerial responsibility as respects such repairs at the commencement

the shipowner could not possibly exercise control." In *The Argent,* S.D.N.Y., 1915, 1940 A.M.C. 508, 509, Judge Hough said:

> The philosophy of shipowners' limitation seems to me this: There are so many things which shipowners must do by deputy, and must have done at great distances and under circumstances where human fallibility is peculiarly prone to produce error, that they long have been saved by statute from the consequences of their agents' acts.

Yet it is clear that an owner cannot close its eyes to what prudent inspections would disclose. An owner must avail itself of whatever means of knowledge are reasonably necessary to prevent conditions likely to cause losses. "If lack of actual knowledge were enough, imbecility, real or assumed, on the part of owners would be at a premium." *The Argent, supra,* 1940 A.M.C. at 509.

However, we must be careful to avoid indiscriminately transferring to the case at bar the broad language of other cases with vastly different fact situations. The great majority of the cases denying limitation of liability have involved old barges, tugs, and other vessels obviously more capable of control by the home office than a freighter thousands of miles away. And most of these cases involved either a long-standing practice of failing adequately to inspect the vessel, or otherwise to exercise control over activities in the home port.

In contrast, limitation of liability has been granted much more often where the vessel involved was a large ship and the negligence did not occur in the home port or in a drydock. Limitation has been denied in large ship cases under a variety of circumstances, but we have found no case which has attributed the negligence of the master to the corporate owner.

> [The] more restricted the operation in which a vessel is engaged, the greater will be the degree of control which the corporate owner will be required to exercise over master, crew and subordinate shoreside employees.... [The] duty to control increases along with the possibility of control.... GILMORE & BLACK, ADMIRALTY (2d ed. 1957) 704, *quoted in Avera v. Florida Towing Co. (THE EILEEN ROSS),* 5 Cir., 1963, 322 F.2d 155, 165.

The District Court's conclusion that Waterman had privity and knowledge of Capt. Patronas' failure to have the fathometer checked in Japan because he had sole authority over repairs in the Far East would be a substantial extension from prior cases. Indeed, it would be inconsistent with the recent cases of *Petition of Kinsman Transit Co. (THE MacGILVRAY SHIRAS)* and *Moore-McCormack Lines, Ltd. v. Armco Steel Co. (THE MORMACKITE), supra* note 12. We do not believe that such an extension is warranted. Although modern communication and transportation facilities make all acts performed in any foreign port within the potential control of the shipowner, we believe that an extension of the requirement of privity or knowledge to cover all such acts should only come from Congress. We are unwilling to impose on all shipowners the burden of maintaining at every port of call an agent with authority over maintenance and repair. We are equally unwilling to transmute the master into such an agent whenever the ship calls at a foreign port in which the owner does not have such an agent. The statute applies to both small and large carriers; many small ones may be unable to meet the burden of such requirements.

We conclude that Capt. Patronas' failure to have the fathometer checked at the next port after Jensen told him that it was inoperative does not support the denial of limitation of liability.

Limitation of Liability—Defective equipment

Appellees contend that the denial of limitation of liability can be affirmed on other grounds. Although they filed no cross-appeals, they argue that certain of the District Court's findings of fact were clearly erroneous.

* * *

The District Court found that:

> The S.S. CHICKASAW was equipped with a radio direction finder, which instruments often have deviational errors which vary depending upon the bearing of the stations and which may change from time to time. It is normal and good practice for a vessel to have available for use with a radio direction finder a card or chart so that its readings may be corrected and that such a card be checked for accuracy at least once a year. No such card had been prepared for the S.S. CHICKASAW in recent years, and while this stranding took place in 1962, the card posted dated back to 1957....

This finding is fully supported by the record.

Failure to have on board an up-to-date correction card or chart was not merely contrary to good practice; it was a violation of a statutory duty.

Under 47 U.S.C. § 351(a) (2), (1964), it was unlawful for the CHICKASAW

> to be navigated ... in the open sea, or ... to leave any harbor or port of the United States for a voyage in the open sea, unless ... equipped with an efficient radio direction finding apparatus (radio compass) properly adjusted in operating condition as hereinafter provided, which apparatus is approved by the [Federal Communications] Commission....

* * *

The District Court, however, found that the condition of the radio direction finder did not cause or contribute to the stranding.

The court did not specifically consider the burden of proof. But because there was a statutory violation, the Pennsylvania Rule (*The Pennsylvania*, 1873, 86 U.S. (19 Wall.) 125, 136, 22 L. Ed. 148) places a very heavy burden of proof on Waterman:

> But when, as in this case, a ship at the time of a collision is in actual violation of a statutory rule intended to prevent collisions, it is no more than a reasonable presumption that the fault, if not the sole cause, was at least a contributory cause of the disaster. In such a case the burden rests upon the ship of showing not merely that her fault might not have been one of the causes, or that it probably was not, but that it could not have been. Such a rule is necessary to enforce obedience to the mandate of the statute.

* * *

We hold that the court's finding that the stranding was not caused by the ship's failure to have an efficient radio direction finder, is, in the light of the Pennsylvania Rule, clearly erroneous.

Finally, it is urged that the court did not find that the defective condition of the R.D.F. that we have described was with the privity and knowledge of Waterman, and that, absent such privity and knowledge, limitation cannot be denied. It is true that the court made no such finding; it was unnecessary for it to do so, because as we have seen, it found lack of causation. Because we hold that that finding was clearly erroneous, we must consider the privity and knowledge of Waterman.

* * *

The question then is, would the record support a finding that the defect was without the privity or knowledge of Waterman? If the evidence is such that a finding either way would be supported, we should remand for a finding on this question. On the other hand, if the record requires a finding of privity and knowledge, so that a contrary finding would be clearly erroneous, such a remand would be futile, particularly in this case. This action was filed on July 30, 1962. The question was fully explored. If the action can be properly terminated now, that is what should be done. We think that it can properly be done.

Waterman's Port Captain, Frank Murdock, testified that Waterman had no program for insuring that a recent table of corrections is kept on board. It relied on the annual check by the FCC and on RCA, which it hired to check the R.D.F. According to Murdock, the last time a cam was cut to adjust the functioning of the R.D.F. was in 1952. He had no knowledge of the last time that the ship was swung to test the accuracy of the R.D.F. He knew of no entry in the CHICKASAW's log showing that this had been done, as company rules require, within 90 days before the annual FCC check. Waterman had no program for finding out whether the R.D.F. needed repairs; it relied solely on the Master, the chief mate of the deck department or the FCC to recommend that repairs be made. He knew of no piece of paper handed to the FCC or RCA men showing that the R.D.F. had been checked. Waterman left it to the master to check and to furnish a certificate to the FCC; it considered that the FCC provided an automatic check. He knew that the FCC would accept up to 5 degrees error in R.D.F. bearings, and that there should be a table that the crew could use to correct R.D.F. readings. He never had any check made on board ship to see that there was such a table on board. The company had no system or program for doing so. The second mate and the captain have the most to do with the navigational equipment.

The chief mate may be bucking for master and therefore also be extremely interested in that equipment. He could recall no conversation with any of those officers about the R.D.F. before the ship was grounded. He was on board the CHICKASAW several times, but could not remember noting the tables of radio direction finder error that the captain had posted in the ship.

Captain Patronas was given no instruction to check the R.D.F. against visual bearings. The second mate, Filippone, knew of no time that this had been done since 1958. Jensen, the third mate gave similar testimony, as did English, the first mate. And neither Patronas nor Filippone knew whether the 1957 table, the only one on board, was accurate. As Waterman's expert, Capt. Slack said: "Q. ... it really isn't possible, sir, to use this instrument for accurate navigation unless you know what this error is, is it? A. That is correct."

* * *

As we have previously pointed out, an owner cannot close its eyes to what prudent inspection would disclose. *See also States Steamship Co. v. United States, (THE PENNSYLVANIA), supra*, 259 F.2d at 466. That is just what Waterman did in this case. We conclude that a finding of lack of privity or knowledge on Waterman's part would be clearly erroneous.

AFFIRMED.

Note: Privity or Knowledge of Corporate Shipowners

When the shipowner is a corporation (as is often the case), it is necessary to determine whether "privity or knowledge" of an employee should be attributed to the corporation. Generally speaking, the employee must be relatively senior in the corporate hierarchy before her or his "privity or knowledge" is regarded as being that of the corporation. See *American Dredging Co. v. Lambert*, 81 F.3d 127, 130, 1996 AMC 2929 (11th Cir. 1996) ("[W]hen the shipowner is a corporation, privity or knowledge means the privity or knowledge of a managing agent, officer, or supervisory employee"). See, however, *McNeil v. Lehigh Valley R. Co.*, 387 F.2d 623, 624 (2d Cir. 1967) ("The evidence showed that appellant's General Marine Inspector inspected the barge at least once every three weeks. Adequate inspection would have disclosed the hole in the planking. Negligent failure to discover constitutes privity and knowledge within the meaning of the statute").

Note: Breaking the Assertion of Limitation

The Convention of Limitation of Liability for Maritime Claims, 1976 provides as follows:

> Article 4 - Conduct Barring Limitation
>
> A person liable shall not be entitled to limit his liability if it is proved that the loss resulted from his personal act or omission, committed with the intent to cause such loss, or recklessly and with knowledge that such loss would probably result.

How would this change the present American rule?

For a more recent case applying the American rule, *see Complaint of Bankers Trust Co.*, 651 F.2d 160, 1981 AMC 1497 (3d Cir. 1981).

E. Claims Subject to Limitation

SIGNAL OIL & GAS CO. v. BARGE W-701

654 F.2d 1164, 1982 AMC 2603 (5th Cir. 1981)

GEE, Circuit Judge

* * *

Signal Oil & Gas Company, Louisiana Land & Exploration Company, Amerada Hess Corporation, and Marathon Oil Company ("SLAM") jointly operated an oil production rig in the Gulf of Mexico off the coast of Louisiana. The SLAM pipeline was the conduit for production from the SLAM platform to shore. Sun Oil Company ("Sun") operated a platform nearby but did not enjoy a similar access to shore. SLAM and Sun negotiated an agreement allowing Sun to hook up to the SLAM pipeline. Sun agreed to indemnify SLAM for any losses it might suffer thereby. Sun contracted with J. Ray McDermott ("McDermott") to handle this construction. McDermott, in turn agreed to indemnify Sun for any losses incident to the construction. McDermott contracted with Williams-McWilliams ("Williams"), the vessel owner, for the use of a barge and crew in aid of its construction activities. McDermott and Williams did not enter into any indemnity agreement.

While operating near the SLAM platform, the Williams barge fouled anchor on an obstruction—the SLAM pipeline, as was shortly seen. Meeting resistance in his efforts to retrieve the anchor and change positions, the barge superintendent, Southon, ordered a "dogging" technique to free it. In "dogging," the anchor line is drawn tight and secured while the barge is in a trough; when the barge is lifted by the next swell, the power of the sea itself is used to dislodge the anchor. Unfortunately for all concerned, this retrieval also "dislodged" a chunk of SLAM pipeline. SLAM production operations were interrupted and substantial repairs required.

A roundrobin of claims were consolidated for trial. In the liability phase of this bifurcated trial, the judge arrived at the following conclusions: (1) the negligence of the barge superintendent, for which Williams bore full responsibility, was the sole proximate cause of the accident; (2) Williams was consequently liable to SLAM in tort; (3) Sun was liable to SLAM on its contract of indemnity; (4) McDermott was liable on its indemnity agreement to Sun; and (5) Williams was liable for tort indemnity to Sun and McDermott. These findings were affirmed on appeal in an opinion of this court dated November 29, 1976, and are not before us on this appeal.

The tidy circle above, in which the negligent party was to bear the loss, was broken by the judge's more recent decision on damages that prompts this appeal. The district court found SLAM entitled to full recovery of its loss—$1,116,234.62. The tortfeasor Williams, however, pursuant to 46 U.S.C. § 181 *et seq.*, was entitled to limit its legal liability to the value of the barge, subsequently found by the district judge to be $450,000. The insurance carried by Williams in excess of its first $500,000 of coverage was held not subject to the Louisiana direct action statute. [This conclusion was based on the fact that the excess insurance, which was taken out by Williams's parent corporation, Zapata Norness, was not written or delivered within Louisiana and the accident took place outside the boundaries of the state.—Eds.] The combined effect of Williams' resort to the limitations statute and the inaccessibility to suit of its excess insurance coverage produced a maximum recovery, extractable from Williams and its insurers, of $500,000. Plaintiff SLAM consequently turned to indemnitor Sun for relief and Sun to McDermott. McDermott, left holding the bag with instructions to fill it, is the chief appellant here. It maintains that the district court erred ... in allowing Williams to limit its liability for the results of this accident.

* * *

McDermott does not dispute that the nature of the accident and the parties makes this incident generally the kind in which the vessel owner may move to limit its liability. Rather, the argument that this limitation defense should have been denied Williams relies on McDermott's allegations that by its actions Williams has incurred liability that traditionally escapes the statute's protective sweep. McDermott argues that Williams' actual liability should exceed the limitation amount under the "Personal Contract Doctrine."

* * *

Before further considering its application to this case, we examine briefly the nature of the Personal Contract Doctrine. ... As noted by G. GILMORE & C. BLACK, THE LAW OF ADMIRALTY § 10-26, at 899 (2d ed. 1975) (hereinafter GILMORE & BLACK), subsequent cases have rendered such a reading of the doctrine improper. "It is by no means clear exactly what a 'personal contract' is, but it is clear that not all contracts are 'personal', even though entered into personally by the shipowner." *Id.* Analysis of the cases delineating the types of contracts that fall within the designation "personal" is of scant assistance to our inquiry. For example, bills of lading have been held not to be personal contracts, *Earle & Stoddart, Inc. v. Ellerman's Wilson Line, Ltd.*, 287 U.S. 420, 53 S. Ct. 200, 77 L. Ed. 403 (1932); GILMORE & BLACK, § 10-26 at 899. Charter parties, on the other hand, have been four times treated as personal contracts by the Supreme Court in denying limitation to vessel owners. GILMORE & BLACK, *id.* The parties have not directed our attention to, nor have we found, any case discussing the proper characterization of this contract for the services of a workover barge in offshore oil production.

The initial characterization, moreover, does not necessarily dispose of the question whether liability resulting from a vessel owner's contractual relationships is properly subject to limitation under the statute: "To call a given type of contract 'personal' does not automatically lead to the conclusion that the shipowner will under all circumstances be denied the right to limit against the claims of his promisee." GILMORE & BLACK, § 10-27 at 904. Learned Hand, sitting as a district judge in *The Soerstad*, 257 F. 130 (S.D.N.Y. 1919), suggested a narrow reading of the personal contract doctrine, restricting its application to situations in which the breach, as well as the execution, of the contract could be said to be "personal" to the vessel owner. His approach in *The Soerstad* has gathered support in subsequent cases, including dicta considered supportive by GILMORE AND BLACK, *see* § 10-27 at 904-05, in *Cullen Fuel Co. v. W.E. Hedger, Inc.*, 290 U.S. 82, 88-89, 54 S. Ct. 10, 11, 78 L. Ed. 189 (1933). There is no more recent or more certain authority. This case, however, does not require us to fill that gap. Whether *The Soerstad's* narrowing of the personal contract doctrine is correct or appropriate need not concern us here; McDermott, the party seeking application of the doctrine, presents its grounds for Williams' liability in post-*Soerstad* terms: breaches of warranties of seaworthiness, performance in a workmanlike manner, and provision of "effectual" insurance coverage. McDermott makes no claim that Williams should be denied limitation simply because it personally agreed to provide the vessel in aid of the construction operation. We leave, then, further consideration of the scope of the personal contract doctrine to scholarly commentators and to judges directly confronting the issue.

* * *

Even if the first two warranties were made and could theoretically form the basis of a recovery beyond the limitation fund, they were not here breached. McDermott's seaworthiness and workmanlike performance arguments would impose on Williams a responsibility more direct than *respondeat superior* for the barge superintendent's negligent act. In loosing on an unsuspecting world an inadequately trained and poorly schooled master of the vessel, the argument runs, Williams has incurred a liability that should penetrate the statute's protective cover; it must answer for its "own fault, neglect, and contracts." Whether the law might support McDermott's contentions need not concern us, since the facts clearly do not. The trial judge found that "the on-the-job training which was provided to him [Southon, the barge superintendent] created an obviously capable man with an excellent reputation...." 468 F. Supp. at 815. In ten years as a barge superintendent Southon had suffered only one similar incident. He was an experienced, able captain with a good safety record. As the district court found, "it is clear that Captain Southon was not incompetent but merely negligent." 468 F. Supp. at 814. Furthermore, despite McDermott's vigorous argument to the contrary, we find that Williams violated no duty in failing to promulgate formal written procedures for freeing anchors and unfouling lines. Its reliance on the skill and judgment of its superintendents does not become negligently misplaced merely because of this accident. The attempt to bootstrap the negligence of Southon into a breach of warranties of seaworthiness and workmanlike performance is insupportable in fact. From the results of its employees' negligence, Williams is entitled to the full benefit of the limitation statute.

The third claim of breach of warranty, that Williams failed to secure its promised insurance coverage, ... was simply not breached here. Williams purchased all the coverage indicated in its notices of insurance to McDermott. That insurance was in effect and available to satisfy appropriate claims. Unfortunately for McDermott, a statute embodying the congressional policy of encouraging the mid-nineteenth century American shipping industry allowed Williams and its insurers to cut the losses they otherwise would have suffered. Under these circumstances, the trial court's decision that the umbrella insurance policy held by Williams' parent corporation could not be reached directly ... does make this coverage in some sense "ineffectual," as leaving McDermott liable for an unanticipated loss. McDermott's quarrel, however, is with Congress and the Louisiana legislature, not with

Williams. In this instance, McDermott stands exactly where it would in any one of the 48 states that allow no direct action against insurers. Insurance in those states is clearly not "ineffectual" merely because tortfeasors alone, and not their carriers, may be sued.

* * *

After review of the arguments raised to avoid application of the limitation statute here, we arrive at the same conclusion reached by the district judge: Williams is entitled to limit its liability to the value of the barge W-701 at the time of the accident.

* * *

Note: Excluded Claims

The personal contract doctrine was applied in the leading case of *Cullen Fuel Oil v. W.E. Hedger, Inc.*, 290 U.S. 82, 54 S. Ct. 10, 78 L. Ed. 189 (1933) [charter parties]. 46 U.S.C.A. § 30505 (formerly 46 app. U.S.C. § 189) specifically excludes wages of seamen from limitation, and claims for maintenance and cure are said to be rights arising form a seaman's employment contract and therefore not subject to limitation. *See Hugney v. Consolidation Coal Co.*, 345 F. Supp. 1079, 1973 AMC 534 (W.D. Pa. 1971). Contracts for supplies and repairs have also been excluded. *Richardson v. Harmon*, 222 U.S. 96, 32 S. Ct. 27, 56 L. Ed. 110 (1911).

Is liability for wreck removal under the Wreck Act [33 U.S.C. § 409] subject to limitation? *See Wyandotte Transportation Co. v. United States*, 389 U.S. 191, 88 S. Ct. 379, 19 L. Ed. 2d 407 (1967) and *In re Pacific Far East Line*, 314 F. Supp. 1339, 1970 AMC 1592 (N.D. Cal. 1970), *aff'd*, 472 F.2d 1382 (9th Cir. 1973).

Is liability for pollution under state law subject to limitation? *See Askew v. American Waterways, Inc.*, 411 U.S. 325, 93 S. Ct. 1590, 36 L. Ed. 2d 280, 1973 AMC 811 (1973) and the discussion in the section regarding state legislation in the Chapter on Environmental Law. Liability for pollution damages under federal law is generally not subject to limitation under 46 app. U.S.C. § 183; other concepts of limitation of liability apply. *See* the Chapter on Environmental Law.

In contrast to the American law, the 1976 Convention on Limitation of Maritime Claims provides as follows:

Article 2 - Claims Subject to Limitation

1. Subject to Articles 3 and 4 the following claims, whatever the basis of liability may be, shall be subject to limitation of liability:
   (a) claims in respect of loss of life or personal injury or loss of or damage to property (including damage to harbour works, basins and waterways and aids to navigation), occurring on board or in direct connection with the operation of the ship or with salvage operations, an consequential loss resulting therefrom;
   (b) claims in respect of loss resulting from delay in the carriage by sea of cargo, passengers or their luggage;
   (c) claims in respect of other loss resulting from infringement of rights other than contractual rights, occurring in direct connection with the operation of the ship or salvage operations;
   (d) claims in respect of the raising, removal, destruction or the rendering harmless of a ship which is sunk, wrecked, stranded or abandoned, including anything that is or has been on board such ship;
   (e) claims in respect of the removal, destruction or the rendering harmless of the cargo of the ship;
   (f) claims of a person other than the person liable in respect of measures taken in order to avert or minimize loss for which the person liable may limit his liability in accordance with this Convention, and further loss caused by such measures.

2. Claims set out in paragraph 1 shall be subject to limitation of liability even if brought by way of recour or for indemnity under a contract or otherwise. However, claims set out under paragraphs 1(d), (e) an (f) shall not be subject to limitation of liability to the extent that they relate to remuneration under contract with the person liable.

Article 3 - Claims Excepted From Limitation
The rules of this Convention shall not apply to:

(a) claims for salvage or contribution in general average;
(b) claims for oil pollution damage within the meaning of the International Convention on Civil Liabil ity for Oil Pollution Damage, dated 29 November 1969 or of any amendment or Protocol theret which is in force;
(c) claims subject to any international convention or national legislation governing or prohibitin limitation of liability for nuclear damage;
(d) claims against the shipowner of a nuclear ship or nuclear damage;
(e) claims by servants of the shipowner or salvor whose duties are connected with the ship or the salvag operations, including claims of their heirs, dependents or other persons entitled to make such claims if under the law governing the contract of service between the shipowner or salvor and such servant the shipowner or salvor is not entitled to limit his liability in respect of such claims, or if he is by such law only permitted to limit his liability to an amount greater than that provided for in Article 6.

F. Choice of Law

1. The Nature of Limitation Law: Substantive or Procedural

Note

In Matter of Bethlehem Steel Corp., 631 F.2d 441, 1980 AMC 2122 (6th Cir. 1980), the ship Steelton allided with a highway bridge in Canada. The owner of the ship instituted limitation proceedings in federal district court in the United States. The district court held that the Canadian limitation of liability provisions were procedural in nature. Because the law of the forum determines procedural matters, the district court thus refused to apply the Canadian limitation provisions and held that 46 app. U.S.C. § 183 (recodified as 46 U.S.C.A. §§ 30505-30506) determined the maximum limitation fund, as the law of the forum. The U.S. Court of Appeals for the Sixth Circuit affirmed, saying:

> [A]n American court may not assume that a foreign limitation of liability act is procedural. It must make a determination whether an independent basis of liability exists or whether under that nation's law "the wrong creates no greater liability than that recognized ..." by the limitation act. If the right to recover is coextensive with the limitation on amount of recovery, then a limitation act is substantive and must be enforced by the forum.
>
> * * *
>
> This court accepts the district court's conclusion that the Canadian limitation statute is procedural. This conclusion is supported by competent testimony. Furthermore, it represents a desirable choice-of-laws decision. The Steelton is an American ship. The parties who will be affected by this limitation decision chose to sue the Steelton's owner in a court of the United States rather than a court of Canada. Though the collision occurred in Canadian waters, insofar as the limitation between the present parties is concerned, the interest of

the United States in applying its own legislatively determined concept of limitation is stronger than that of Canada. This appears to be a proper case for application of the law of the forum.

Matter of Bethlehem Steel Corp., 631 F.2d 441, 445-46 (6th Cir. 1980).

---

2. The Brussels Convention: Procedural in Nature

COMPLAINT OF COMPANIA GIJONESA DE NAVEGACION, S.A.

590 F. Supp. 241, 1985 AMC 1469 (S.D.N.Y. 1984)

CANNELLA, District Judge

Wah Yuen Shipping, Inc.'s ["Wah Yuen"] motion to increase the security fund is granted. FED. R. CIV. P., Supp. R. F(7) for Admiralty & Maritime Claims ["Rule F(7)"].

Background

On July 6, 1983, Compania Gijonesa De Navegacion, S.A. ["Gijonesa"] commenced this action claiming exoneration from liability from a vessel collision and seeking the application of liability limitations pursuant to the Limitation of the Liability of Owners of Sea-Going Ships (1957) ["Brussels Convention"] and 46 U.S.C. § 183. This action arises out of a collision in Spain on January 11, 1983 of its Spanish vessel, the M/V Cimadevilla ["Cimadevilla"] with the M/V Crusader, a Panamanian vessel owned by the claimant Wah Yuen. As a result of the collision, Wah Yuen presented its damages claim of $607,644.10 to Gijonesa and thereafter, Gijonesa instituted this action and asserted that its interest in the Cimadevilla was $98,110.77. It then deposited that amount as security with the court for the benefit of claimants, permitting them to challenge the amount.

As a claimant Wah Yuen objected to the amount of security and challenges the law employed by Gijonesa in calculating the limited fund. Wah Yuen asserts that the security should be increased to total $1,784,800, representing Gujonesa's $1,715,000 interest in the Cimadevilla at the end of the voyage plus $34,800, the value of the freight. In addition, Wah Yuen timely filed a claim in this Court for $607,644.10.

Wah Yuen argues that the Brussels Convention is a matter of procedural rather than substantive law and that a Spanish court would not apply the official rate of exchange of gold for conversion of pesatas into poincare francs. Wah Yuen's expert on Spanish law opines that a Spanish court would apply Article 837 of Spain's Commercial Code which provides that the limitation fund equals the value of the vessel plus the value of pending freight. This is also the valuation specified in Rule F(7) and 46 U.S.C. § 183(a). With respect to the instant dispute, Wah Yuen argues that the court, as the forum court should apply the federal liability limitation.

Gijonesa alleges that generally 46 U.S.C. § 183 and the Federal Rules of Civil Procedure limit liability *unless* the foreign substantive law which limits the right provides a different and lower limitation, as Spanish law does in the instant action. Thus, Gijonesa argues that the Brussels Convention is substantive and applies to the limitation of liability issue because it attaches to a right and limits it. Gijonesa argues that Spanish law mandate the limitation value used herein because of its domestic enactment of the Brussels Convention.

With respect to the valuation of the poincare franc, Gijonesa argues that Spanish court would use the official rate for the value of gold in converting poincare francs, based on the opinion of its expert. The official rate of gold was the only rate at the time of the formulation of the Brussels Convention.

Discussion

Generally, "in the absence of some overriding domestic policy translated into law, the right to recover for a tort depends upon and is measured by the law of the place where the tort occurred." *Black Diamond S.S. Corporation v. Robert Stewart & Sons (Norway Victory)*, 336 U.S. 386, 396 (1949) ["Black Diamond"] (citations omitted). Because the collision occurred in the territorial waters of Spain, the rights and liabilities of the parties are governed by Spanish substantive law.

With respect to procedural rules, it is well-settled that the law of the forum controls. *See Bournias v. Atlantic Maritime Co.*, 220 F.2d 152, 154 (2d Cir. 1955). Gijonesa, when it deposited the $98,110.77 with the court, claimed that Spanish law provides that this is the monetary limit pursuant to the Brussels Convention. Gijonesa contends that the Brussels Convention is a substantive rather than procedural part of the laws of Spain. Wah Yuen contends that while the substantive rights involved are governed by Spanish law, it claims that the calculation of the liability limitation is a matter of procedure governed by the forum's laws.

Wah Yuen further argues, in the alternative, that if Spanish substantive laws were to apply, its Commercial Code would control rather than the Brussels Convention. The Spanish Commercial Code provides that the limitation of liability is the value of the vessel plus pending freight. This valuation is identical to that of the laws of the United States. Calculating liability is further complicated by the fact that the "official" rate has been eliminated in Spain and no other rate has been adopted.

Wah Yuen also argues that even if the Brussels Convention applied, Article 4 directs:

> Without prejudice to the provisions of Article 3, § 2, of this Convention, the rules relating to the constitution and distribution of the limitation fund, if any, and the rules of procedure shall be governed by the national law of the State in which the fund is constituted.

Thus, Wah Yuen argues that even the Brussels Convention's laws mandate that limiting the fund is a matter of procedural law governed by United States law.

The Supreme Court determined that the procedural rules of the forum would control the amount of the security to be posted in limitation proceedings. *Oceanic Steam Navigation Co. v. Mellor (Titanic)*, 233 U.S. 718 (1914) ["The Titanic"]. Thereafter, the Supreme Court although not overruling *The Titanic*, determined that if the substantive rights of the arties are controlled by foreign law and if the foreign limitation "attaches" to such rights, ıen the foreign limitation governs rather than the forum state's limitation laws. *See Black Diamond, supra*, 336 U.S. at 395-396; *See also Matter of Bowoon Sangsa Co.*, 720 F.2d 595, 99 & n.5 (9th Cir. 1983). In *Black Diamond, supra*, the Supreme Court further stated in icta that if foreign law merely provides "procedural machinery" to already existing claims, ıe forum's procedural laws would apply. 336 U.S. at 396. Thus, pursuant to the Supreme Court's directive, the Court must determine whether Spain's limitation of liability is a ıatter of substantive or procedural law. *See Matter of Bethlehem Steel Corp.*, 435 F. Supp. 44, 947 (N.D. Ohio 1976), *aff'd*, 631 F.2d 441 (3d Cir. 1980), *cert. denied*, 450 U.S. 21 (1981).

The parties have submitted affidavits of Spanish lawyers, knowledgeable in Spanish ιw, which indicate disagreement on the issue of whether the Brussels Convention is a ıatter of substantive or procedural law. Wah Yuen's witness, Manuel Gonzalez Rodriguez, ontends that the Brussels Convention is considered procedural in Spain. He further states ıat a Spanish Court would apply its Commercial Code to the instant dispute. He contends that the right to recover monetary damages caused by a collision was created statutoily by Article 826 of the commercial Code of 1885. The Brussels Convention was not nacted until much later. Thus, he concludes that the limitation of liability provision of ıe Brussels Convention merely modifies a pre-existing right and, therefore, is procedural. Recognizing that the official rate of gold was eliminated as the basis of the international ıonetary system by the International Monetary Fund ["IMF"] in 1975, *see Trans World Airlines v. Franklin Mint Corp.*, 466 U.S. 243, 104 S. Ct. 1776, 80 L. Ed. 2d 273 (1984), vhich Gijonesa's witness José Maria Alcántara concedes, Mr. Rodriguez contends that the fficial conversion rate is not used in Spain.

Mr. Alcantara contends that the Brussels Convention is a matter of substantive law in pain, claiming that it "qualifies the right of limitation itself in a substantive manner." He urther opines that the Commercial Code was substantively amended by the Brussels Convention and that a Spanish Court would apply the Brussels Convention and the official onversion rate when calculating the limitation fund.

Initially, the Court notes that there is no Spanish or Second Circuit case that is dispositive on the issues involved in this action. Following the analysis of *Black Diamond*, it appears that the foreign limitation of liability is procedural. *First*, the limitation of liability provision of the Brussels Convention does not attach to the right of recovery resulting from collision because it is a pre-existing right by virtue of the Spanish Commercial Code. *See Matter of Bethlehem Steel Corp., supra*, 435 F. Supp. at 948. The right to recovery existed as arly as 1810 and continues to exist pursuant to the Commercial Code. The subsequent nactment of the Brussels Convention in Spain, does not alter this fact. *Second*, limitation of liability which determines the amount to be posted for claimants, defines the remedy, nd is a matter of procedure. *See Kloeckner, Reederei und Kohlenhandel v. A/S Hakedal, (The Western Farmer)*, 210 F.2d 754, 756 (2d Cir. 1954), *appeal dismissed*, 348 U.S. 801 (1955). The limitation of liability simply measures damages and does not attach to a pre-existing right. It merely provides a limited fund for all claimants. *See Black Diamond, supra,* 3 U.S. at 395-96.

Because the limitation of liability provision at issue is procedural, the Court applies t laws of the forum—United States law. Mindful that such a determination could result forum shopping, the facts and circumstances of this action support a finding that t Brussels Convention, if applicable, is procedural in nature. United States law directs th Gijonesa deposit security that equals the value of the vessel plus pending freight. *See* Ru F(7); 46 U.S.C. § 183. The Court notes that this valuation is similarly defined by sectic 837 of the Commercial Code.

Furthermore, the Court notes that the parties agree that the official rate of gold h been eliminated by the IMF and Spain. Thus, even assuming *arguendo* that the substanti law of Spain is to be applied, it is disputed what calculation would govern. There is lack proof in this area. Furthermore, the formula of the Brussels Convention has not been a plied in Spain. The Commercial Code uses the same valuation as the federal rules. Whi Gijonesa seeks to employ the official rate of gold and values a poincare franc in Spain 4.6434 pesetas, the Court declines to do so for the reasons asserted above. Because the ra of conversion employed in Spain has not been adequately established, the Court woul have to assume that Spanish law is the same as United States law and would apply the san valuation for calculating the limitation of liability.

In conclusion, Gijonesa is directed to increase the security posted with the Court that it equals $1,784,800.00.

Conclusion

Wah Yuen's motion to increase the security fund from $98,110.77 to $1,784,800.0 is granted. FED. R. CIV. P., Supp. R. F(7).

Gijonesa is directed to post, within fourteen (14) days of this Memorandum and O der, additional security with the Court so that the total sum will equal $1,784,800.00.

The parties have sixty (60) days from the date of this Memorandum and Order t complete discovery.

SO ORDERED.

www.ingramcontent.com/pod-product-compliance
Lightning Source LLC
LaVergne TN
LVHW082001200926
848481LV00010B/2782
* 9 7 8 1 5 8 7 9 8 2 9 6 5 *